Issues Regarding Items in Financial Statements (under various GAAPs) *(continued)*	Chapters
• Fair value and cash flow hedges	16
• Foreign currency translation	16
• Business combination	12
• Consolidated statements on date of acquisition	NA
• Consolidated financial statements subsequent to acquisition date	NA
• Joint ventures: proportionate consolidation or equity method	NA
• Complex financial instruments (e.g., perpetual debt, convertible debt, derivatives)	16
Financial Statement Analysis	
• Vertical and horizontal analysis	5A, 23, and all chapters
• Ratios and benchmarking	5A, 23, and all chapters
• Financial statement results for various users	5A, 23, and all chapters
• Pro forma statements	NA
• Impact of financial results on the whole organization	5A, 23, and all chapters

Meeting Financial Reporting Technical Competencies in the CPA Competency Map—The following table maps the Financial Reporting technical competencies from the CPA Competency Map to *Intermediate Accounting, Eleventh Canadian Edition* (Volume 2). The textbook covers the Financial Reporting competencies as noted below (see also Volume 1 for coverage of Chapters 1–12). Detailed mapping of specific CPA Financial Reporting competencies to specific textbook Learning Objectives is provided in the charts at the beginning of each chapter.

FINANCIAL REPORTING

1.1 Financial Reporting Needs and Systems	Chapters
1.1.1 Evaluates financial reporting needs	13, 14, 15, 16, 17, 18, 19, 20, 21, 22, 23
1.1.2 Evaluates the appropriateness of the basis of financial reporting	13, 14, 15, 16, 18, 19, 20, 22, 23
1.1.3 Evaluates reporting processes to support reliable financial reporting	19, 20, 22, 23
1.1.4 Explains implications of current trends and emerging issues in financial reporting	13, 14, 15, 16, 17, 18, 19, 20, 21, 22, 23
1.1.5 Identifies financial reporting needs for the public sector	NA
1.1.6 Identifies specialized financial reporting requirements for specified regulatory and other filing requirements	NA
1.2 Accounting Policies and Transactions	
1.2.1 Develops or evaluates appropriate accounting policies and procedures	13, 14, 15, 16, 17, 18, 19, 20, 21, 22, 23
1.2.2 Evaluates treatment for routine transactions	13, 14, 15, 16, 17, 18, 19, 20, 21, 22, 23
1.2.3 Evaluates treatment for non-routine transactions	13, 14, 15, 16, 18, 19, 20, 22, 23
1.2.4 Analyzes treatment for complex events or transactions	14, 15, 16, 17, 18, 19
1.3 Financial Report Preparation	
1.3.1 Prepares financial statements	13, 14, 15, 16, 17, 18, 19, 20, 21, 22, 23
1.3.2 Prepares routine financial statement note disclosure	13, 14, 15, 16, 17, 18, 19, 20, 21, 22, 23
1.4 Financial Statement Analysis	
1.4.1 Analyzes complex financial statement note disclosure	14, 15, 16, 18, 19, 20, 21, 23
1.4.2 Evaluates financial statements including note disclosures	13, 14, 15, 16, 17, 18, 19, 20, 21, 22, 23
1.4.3 Analyzes and provides input in the preparation of the management communication (e.g., management discussion and analysis (MD&A))	15, 21, 23
1.4.4 Interprets financial reporting results for stakeholders (external or internal)	13, 14, 15, 16, 17, 18, 19, 21, 22, 23
1.4.5 Analyzes and predicts the impact of strategic and operational decisions on financial results	14, 15, 17, 22, 23

Other Technical Competencies—Coverage of other technical competencies (that is, Strategy and Governance, Management Accounting, Audit and Assurance, Finance, and Taxation competencies) is indicated here and has also been identified in the charts at the beginning of each chapter and in the end-of-chapter material. Selected enabling competencies have also been identified throughout.

2. Strategy and Governance	Chapters
2.1 Governance	16
2.3 Strategy Development	2, 4, 5, 9, 10, 15, 16, 20
2.4 Strategy Implementation	7
3. Management Accounting	
3.1 Management Reporting Needs and Systems	2, 7
3.2 Planning, Budgeting, and Forecasting	22
3.3 Cost Management	8, 16, 21
4. Audit and Assurance	
4.1 Internal Control	3, 7
4.3 Internal Audit Projects and External Assurance Engagements	2, 4, 8, 23
5. Finance	
5.1 Financial Analysis and Planning	4, 5, 7, 8, 9, 11, 12, 13, 14, 15, 16, 17, 18, 19, 20, 22, 23
5.2 Treasury Management	1, 5, 7, 9, 13, 14, 15, 16, 17, 19, 20, 21, 22, 23
5.4 Valuation	3, 4, 11, 12, 16
5.5 Financial Risk Management	4, 16
5.6 Corporate Finance Transactions	14
6. Taxation	
6.1 Corporate Tax	2, 11, 18, 19, 20, 21
6.2 Personal Tax	2, 13, 15, 16

WileyPLUS with ORION

Quickly identify areas of strength and weakness before the first exam, and use the information to build a learning path to success.

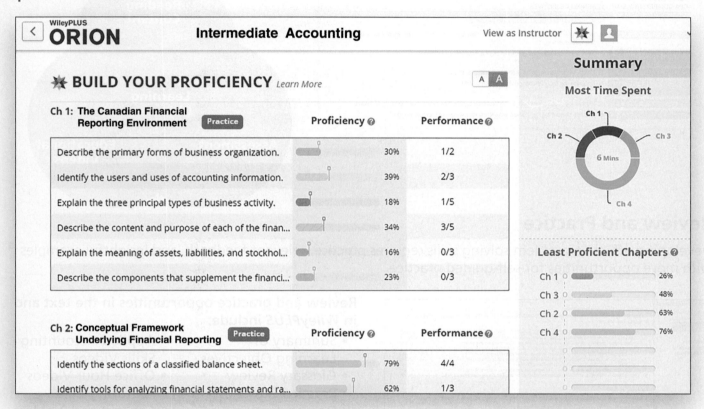

A little time with ORION goes a long way.

Based on usage data, students who engage in ORION adaptive practice—just a few minutes per week—get better outcomes. In fact, students who used ORION five or more times over the course of a semester reported the following results:

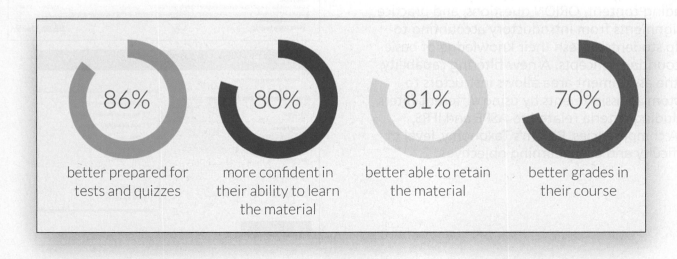

Streamlined Learning Objectives

Easy to follow learning objectives help students make the best use of their time outside of class. Each learning objective is addressed by reading content, watching educational videos, and answering a variety of practice questions, so that no matter where students begin their work, the relevant resources and practice are readily accessible. Learning objectives include references to the CPA competency map. This lets students know which of the CPA competencies they are mastering when they study a particular topic.

Review and Practice

Developing effective problem-solving skills requires practice, relevant feedback, and insightful examples with more opportunities for self-guided practice.

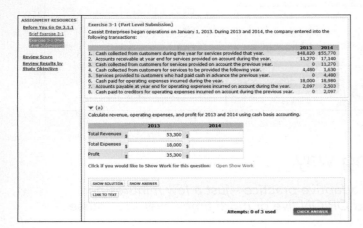

A new bridge course in *WileyPLUS* includes reading content, ORION questions, and practice assignments from introductory accounting to help students refresh their knowledge of basic accounting concepts. A new filtering capability in the assignment area allows instructors to customize assignments by using different filters including criteria related to ASPE and IFRS, CPA competencies, Bloom's Taxonomy, level of difficulty and even learning objectives.

Review and practice opportunities in the text and in *WileyPLUS* include:

- Summary of Learning Objectives
- Glossary Review
- Practice Exercises
- Demonstration Problems
- Applied Accounting Skills Videos
- Office Hour Videos Featuring Core Concept and Problem Walkthroughs

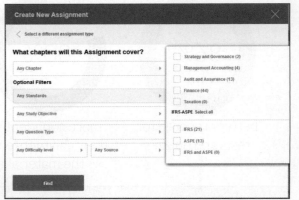

INTERMEDIATE ACCOUNTING

ELEVENTH CANADIAN EDITION

INTERMEDIATE ACCOUNTING

Donald E. Kieso, Ph.D., CPA
KPMG Peat Marwick Emeritus Professor of Accounting
Northern Illinois University
DeKalb, Illinois

Jerry J. Weygandt, Ph.D., CPA
Arthur Andersen Alumni Professor of Accounting
University of Wisconsin
Madison, Wisconsin

Terry D. Warfield, Ph.D.
PWC Professor in Accounting
University of Wisconsin
Madison, Wisconsin

Nicola M. Young, M.B.A., FCPA, FCA
Saint Mary's University
Halifax, Nova Scotia

Irene M. Wiecek, FCPA, FCA
University of Toronto
Toronto, Ontario

Bruce J. McConomy, Ph.D., CPA, CA
Wilfrid Laurier University
Waterloo, Ontario

Library and Archives Canada Cataloguing in Publication

Kieso, Donald E., author
  Intermediate accounting / Donald E. Kieso, PhD, CPA (KPMG Peat Marwick Emeritus Professor of Accounting, Northern Illinois University, DeKalb, Illinois), Jerry J. Weygandt, PhD, CPA (Arthur Andersen Alumni Professor of Accounting, University of Wisconsin-Madison, Wisconsin), Terry D. Warfield, PhD (Associate Professor, University of Wisconsin-Madison, Wisconsin), Nicola M. Young, MBA, FCA (Saint Mary's University, Halifax, Nova Scotia), Irene M. Wiecek, FCPA, FCA (University of Toronto, Toronto, Ontario), Bruce J. McConomy, PhD, CPA, CA (Wilfrid Laurier University, Waterloo, Ontario). — Eleventh Canadian edition.

Includes bibliographical references and indexes.
ISBN 978-1-119-04853-4 (volume 1: bound).—ISBN 978-1-119-04854-1 (volume 2: bound)

  1. Accounting—Textbooks.   I. Weygandt, Jerry J., author   II. Warfield, Terry D., author   III. Young, Nicola M., author   IV. Wiecek, Irene M., author   V. McConomy, Bruce J. (Bruce Joseph), 1958-, author   VI. Title.

HF5636.K54 2015   657'.044   C2015-906298-5

Production Credits
Executive Editors: Zoë Craig and Emily McGee
Vice President and Director, Market Solutions: Veronica Visentin
Senior Marketing Manager: Anita Osborne
Editorial Manager: Karen Staudinger
Developmental Editor: Daleara Jamasji Hirjikaka
Media Editor: Luisa Begani
Assistant Editor: Ashley Patterson
Production and Media Specialist: Meaghan MacDonald
Typesetting: Aptara
Cover and Interior Design: Joanna Vierra
Cover Photo: Rolf Hicker/All Canada Photos/Getty
Printing and Binding: Quad Graphics

Printed and bound in the United States of America

2 3 4 5 QVS 20 19 18 17

Dedicated to accounting educators in Canada
who, as mentors, are helping the next generation of accountants
develop ethical and integrative frameworks for decision-making.

About the Authors

Canadian Edition

Nicola (Nickie) M. Young, M.B.A., FCPA, FCA, is a Professor of Accounting in the Sobey School of Business at Saint Mary's University, with teaching responsibilities varying from introductory to advanced financial accounting courses to the survey course in the Executive M.B.A. program. She has received teaching awards, and has contributed to the life of the university through membership on the Board of Governors, and the Pension and other committees. Nickie was associated with the Atlantic School of Chartered Accountancy for over 25 years in roles varying from teaching to program development and reform. She has been active in the provincial and national accounting profession, including having served on boards of the CICA (now CPA Canada) dealing with licensure, education, and governance; and has been associated with the Canadian Public Sector Accounting Board and many of its related task forces for almost 25 years. She and Irene Wiecek co-authored the *IFRS Primer: International GAAP Basics* (Canadian and U.S. editions). Nickie is currently working on a phased retirement.

Irene M. Wiecek, FCPA, FCA, is an Associate Professor, Teaching Stream at the University of Toronto, where she is cross-appointed to the Joseph L. Rotman School of Management. She teaches financial reporting in various programs, including the Commerce Program (Accounting Specialist) and the CPA-accredited Master of Management & Professional Accounting Program (MMPA). Currently the Director and previously the Associate Director of the MMPA Program for many years, she co-founded and is Director of the CPA/Rotman Centre for Innovation in Accounting Education, which supports and facilitates innovation in accounting education. Irene has been involved in professional accounting education for over 25 years, sitting on various provincial and national professional accounting organization committees as well as developing and directing the CICA IFRS Immersion Programs for practising accountants. She was appointed a member of the E&Y Academic Resource Center, where she helped to author a new IFRS curriculum for the Americas. In the area of standard setting, she has chaired the CAAA Financial Reporting Exposure Draft Response Committee and is currently a member of the IFRS Discussion Group (IDG). Irene co-authored the *IFRS Primer: International GAAP Basics* (Canadian and U.S. editions) and was the co-editor and contributor for the books *Leveraging Change— The New Pillars of Accounting Education* and *Educating Professionals: Ethics and Judgment in a Changing Learning Environment.* Currently, she co-authors the *Guide to IFRS in Canada* series, which is published by CPA Canada.

Bruce J. McConomy, Ph.D., CPA, CA, is a Professor of Accounting at Wilfrid Laurier University in Waterloo, Ontario. He was a Senior Audit Manager with Deloitte and Touche before returning to Queen's University to obtain his Ph.D. in accounting. Bruce has been the Director of the CPA/Laurier Centre for the Advancement of Accounting Research and Education since it was created in 2005, and is the CPA Ontario Professor of Accounting at Laurier. He has been teaching intermediate financial accounting since the mid-1990s to undergraduates, and since the start of Laurier's CPA Accredited CPA/M.B.A. program (and its predecessor the CMA/M.B.A.) to graduate students. He also teaches in Laurier's Ph.D. in Management program. Bruce has published articles in *Contemporary Accounting Research, Journal of Accounting, Auditing and Finance, Journal of Business, Finance and Accounting,* and *Accounting, Auditing & Accountability Journal.* He has also published cases in *Accounting Perspectives, Issues in Accounting Education,* and *Journal of Accounting Case Research.* Bruce was elected to and served on Council at the Institute of Chartered Accountants of Ontario from 2006 to 2010. Bruce is an Associate Editor of *Accounting Perspectives.*

U.S. Edition

Donald E. Kieso, Ph.D., CPA, received his bachelor's degree from Aurora University and his doctorate in accounting from the University of Illinois. He has served as chair of the Department of Accountancy and is currently the KPMG Emeritus Professor of Accountancy at Northern Illinois University. He has public accounting experience with Price Waterhouse & Co. (San Francisco and Chicago) and Arthur Andersen & Co. (Chicago) and research experience with the Research Division of the American Institute of Certified Public Accountants (New York). He has done post-doctorate work as a Visiting Scholar at the University of California at Berkeley and is a recipient of NIU's Teaching Excellence Award and four Golden Apple Teaching Awards. Professor Kieso is the author of other accounting and business books and is a member of the American Accounting Association, the American Institute of Certified Public Accountants, and the Illinois CPA Society. He is the recipient of the Outstanding Accounting Educator Award from the Illinois CPA Society, the FSA's Joseph A. Silvoso Award of Merit, the NIU Foundation's Humanitarian Award for Service to Higher Education, the Distinguished Service Award from the Illinois CPA Society, and in 2003 received an honorary doctorate from Aurora University.

Jerry J. Weygandt, Ph.D., CPA, is Arthur Andersen Alumni Professor of Accounting at the University of Wisconsin-Madison. He holds a Ph.D. in accounting from the University of Illinois. His articles have appeared in *Accounting Review, Journal of Accounting Research, Accounting Horizons, Journal of Accountancy,* and other academic and professional journals. Professor Weygandt is the author of other accounting and financial reporting books and is a member of the American Accounting Association, the American Institute of Certified Public Accountants, and the Wisconsin Society of Certified Public Accountants. He has been actively involved with the American Institute of Certified Public Accountants and has been a member of the Accounting Standards Executive Committee (AcSEC) of that organization. He also served on the FASB task force that examined the reporting issues related to accounting for income taxes. He is the recipient of the Wisconsin Institute of CPAs' Outstanding Educator's Award and the Lifetime Achievement Award. In 2001, he received the American Accounting Association's Outstanding Accounting Educator Award.

Terry D. Warfield, Ph.D., is the PWC Professor in Accounting at the University of Wisconsin-Madison. He received a B.S. and M.B.A. from Indiana University and a Ph.D. in accounting from the University of Iowa. Professor Warfield's area of expertise is financial reporting, and prior to his academic career, he worked for five years in the banking industry. He served as the Academic Accounting Fellow in the Office of the Chief Accountant at the U.S. Securities and Exchange Commission in Washington, D.C., from 1995–1996. Professor Warfield's primary research interests concern financial accounting standards and disclosure policies. He has published scholarly articles in *The Accounting Review, Journal of Accounting and Economics, Research in Accounting Regulation,* and *Accounting Horizons,* and he has served on the editorial boards of *The Accounting Review, Accounting Horizons,* and *Issues in Accounting Education.* Professor Warfield has served on the Financial Accounting Standards Committee of the American Accounting Association (Chair 1995–1996) and the AAA-FASB Research Conference Committee. He currently serves on the Financial Accounting Standards Advisory Council of the Financial Accounting Standards Board. Professor Warfield has received teaching awards at both the University of Iowa and the University of Wisconsin, and he was named to the Teaching Academy at the University of Wisconsin in 1995. Professor Warfield has developed and published several case studies based on his research for use in accounting classes. These cases have been selected for the AICPA Professor-Practitioner Case Development Program and have been published in *Issues in Accounting Education.*

Preface

In the last decade, we have come through a period of unprecedented change in accounting standards. More recently, in Canada, we have witnessed the evolution of the accounting profession from three main accounting bodies (representing Chartered Accountants, Certified Management Accountants, and Certified General Accountants) into one unified group: Chartered Professional Accountants Canada (CPA Canada). We now have a freshly minted CPA education program, a new CPA Competency Map (CM), a new CPA Knowledge Supplement (KS), and new CPA Common Final Examinations. Many of us have remapped our curricula to the CPA CM and created new courses and programs (some of which have been accredited by the CPA profession). The pace of change for standard setting and related educational requirements for professional accountants sometimes seems staggering! Change has become the new norm for us and things don't seem to be slowing down.

This state of flux has made many of us rethink our learning environments. Some fundamental questions are being revisited. How can we and our students keep up with the changing standards? What does it mean to be a competent accountant? How much do we emphasize the use of technology as a learning platform? And finally, how does what we do fit with the changing professional landscape?

From our perspective, we see the need for

- increased emphasis on helping faculty and students understand how to cope with changes in standards,

- a broadened perspective on what it means to be competent,

- increased use of a variety of technologies to promote learning, and

- renewed acknowledgement that what we do in our classrooms is only part of the journey that students embark on to become professional accountants.

In our roles as educators, many of us increasingly see ourselves as facilitators as opposed to purveyors of knowledge. At the heart of things, we still want to produce good, ethical decision-makers as well as to encourage thoughtfulness and reflection. We also want our graduates to be competent and skilled. Our students have to at least begin to master our complex body of knowledge and also to be competent in applying it. This is a lot to ask, especially when things keep shifting.

This edition is about learning to live with a constantly changing body of knowledge. To this end, we have incorporated new accounting standards where the standards have already been issued (even if they are not yet mandatory). In addition, we have included the "Looking Ahead" section again at the end of each chapter, which signals changes in accounting standards coming down the pipe. We are committed to helping our accounting faculty and students steer their way through standards changes that are issued between editions of this text. To this end, we will continue to issue supplements and updates between editions as we have done for the past few years.

This edition is also about integration along the following dimensions:

- integration of financial reporting with other areas (such as assurance and finance);

- integration of our learning environments and frameworks with those of the accounting profession, including a competency-based framework; and

- increased integration with a learning environment that features technology, including *WileyPLUS* and our new Office Hour Videos.

We have also included charts showing how the textbook integrates with the CPA Competency Map and Knowledge Supplement throughout the text and within *WileyPLUS*. This is discussed in the New Features section that follows. We encourage you to have a quick look. Below is a brief overview that highlights the new features of this edition.

New Features

As noted above, several new features have been added to this edition.

Emphasis on Integration with Related Areas

We have included integration icons in each chapter to help identify key areas of integration (in addition to our existing finance and law icons). Many of our end-of-chapter questions have an integration aspect. For those problems that most directly focus on integration, we also include integration icons so that they are easily identified. We have added an Office Hour Video feature, which provides a short video discussion of selected end-of-chapter questions per chapter, and an additional integration-related topic in most chapters.

Augmented End-of-Chapter Material

End-of-chapter material has been expanded to include questions that provide students with Excel spreadsheets to help them prepare solutions. We also continued our emphasis on having students evaluate the differences in solutions prepared using IFRS versus ASPE. Our new Office Hour Video feature provides a short walkthrough of select questions and solutions.

CPA Competency Map Integration

At the start of each chapter, we now provide a chart linking that chapter's Learning Objectives with the related requirements of the CPA Competency Map. This information will help students planning to obtain their Advanced Certificate in Accounting and Finance (ACAF) or write the Common Final Evaluation (CFE) to link the coverage of intermediate accounting topics to the CPA educational requirements. We have also mapped the content of the book against the Competency Map and Knowledge Supplement. These appear on the inside front cover of the text. In addition, the material in *WileyPLUS* has been more comprehensively mapped.

Task-Based Simulations

We have added a new type of question to our end-of-chapter material that is in a format similar to questions used in the CPA Professional Education program. Task-Based Simulations after Chapters 5, 9, 12, 15, 17, and 23 combine material from the current chapter with previous chapters and present it in this new hands-on format. This allows students to become familiar with the new exam format while getting a sense of how the various concepts fit together.

Continuing Features

Many features have contributed to the success of this textbook over the years. The following points outline just a few.

Emphasis on Business

The focus of the feature story that starts each chapter in this edition is on the business models of various companies and industries, along with accounting issues that affect them. The first section of most chapters focuses on **Understanding the Business**, which introduces the accounting topic in the context of everyday business. Many chapters have a **business transactions example box**. In most business transactions, you give something up and receive something. These boxes are meant to help you understand what has been given up and what has been received in the transaction. This is tremendously helpful when you are trying to decide how to account for a transaction or economic event.

Emphasis on IFRS and ASPE

Icons: Individual IFRS and ASPE icons call attention to items treated differently by the two sets of standards. The joint IFRS-ASPE icon indicates a direct comparison between the two approaches.

Side-by-side journal entries: These journal entries illustrate differences in treatment between IFRS and ASPE.

Enhanced comparison charts: The end-of-chapter charts that identify the major differences between IFRS and ASPE include a column with cross-references to relevant illustrations and brief exercises that describe the differences outlined in the comparison chart. As before, where there is a new standard being proposed, we have added a column to the end-of-chapter charts so that you understand what may be in store in the near future, or provided a discussion within the chapter's Looking Ahead feature to alert you to upcoming changes expected.

Emphasis on Professional and Ethical Behaviour

ETHICS

Rather than featuring ethics coverage and problem material in isolation, we use an ethics icon to highlight ethical issues as they are discussed within each chapter. This icon also appears beside exercises, problems, or cases where ethical issues must be dealt with in relation to all kinds of accounting situations.

Emphasis on Readability

The readability of the text has been improved by using fewer abbreviations, plainer language, shorter sentences, numbered lists, and clearer headings. An **end-of-book glossary** provides definitions of key terms highlighted in the text. **Alternative Terminology** notes within the chapter familiarize students with other commonly used terms.

Grounding in Accounting Research and Theory

THEORY

We have always emphasized concepts and principles, including those that span other disciplines, such as law and finance. In addition to this, the **Accounting Theory** icon calls attention to accounting theory that underpins much of the accounting body of knowledge, introducing students to an accounting research perspective.

Real World Emphasis

REAL WORLD EMPHASIS

Because intermediate accounting is a course in which students must understand the application of accounting principles and techniques in practice, we strive to include as many real-world examples as possible.

Reinforcement of the Concepts

WHAT DO THE NUMBERS MEAN?

UNDERLYING CONCEPT

Throughout each chapter, you are asked What Do the Numbers Mean? and are presented with discussions applying accounting concepts to business contexts. This feature builds on the opening feature stories in making the accounting concepts relevant to you. Through current examples of how accounting is applied, you will be better able to relate to and understand the material. The underlying concepts icons in each chapter alert you to remember that the issue under discussion draws on concepts identified in Chapter 2 as part of the conceptual framework. More emphasis has been placed on measuring fair values using the new IFRS 13 standard. In addition, an Analysis section is present in most chapters. This section discusses the effect on the financial statements of many of the accounting choices made by corporate management, alerting you to look behind the numbers. Finally, the accounting equation appears in the margin next to key journal entries to help you understand the impact of each transaction on the company's financial position and cash flows.

Helping Students Practise

The end-of-chapter material is comprehensive. Brief exercises, exercises, and problems focus on quantitative material. Case material allows you to analyze business transactions and apply both IFRS and ASPE, with particular attention to integration being provided by Integrated Case questions. Research and Analysis questions allow you to explore the nature of GAAP differences and understand how different accounting standard setters can arrive at different solutions in terms of standards.

A summary of the Case Primer guiding you through the case study method appears inside the back cover of this text. This is in addition to the full Case Study Primer available on *WileyPLUS* and the Student Website.

Analysis doesn't have to be just part of the cases. Our Digging Deeper feature asks you to look more closely at the results you obtain in the problems and exercises. For instance, you might be asked to comment on results or determine how things might be different if one of the original variables were to change. Digging Deeper questions are identified using the icon shown here.

WileyPLUS is an innovative, research-based on-line environment for effective teaching and learning. *WileyPLUS* builds students' confidence because it takes the guesswork out of studying by providing students with a clear roadmap: **what to do, how to do it, and if they did it right**. Students will take more initiative so you'll have a greater impact on their achievement in the classroom and beyond.

Among its many features, this on-line learning interface allows students to study and practise using the digital textbook, quizzes, and algorithmic exercises. The immediate feedback helps students understand where they need to focus their study efforts. We have standardized the chart of accounts to reduce complexity and to facilitate on-line practice.

Based on cognitive science, **WileyPLUS with Orion** is a personalized adaptive learning experience that gives students the practice they need to build proficiency on topics while using their study time more effectively. The adaptive engine is powered by hundreds of unique questions per chapter, giving students endless opportunities for practice throughout the course. Orion is available with this text.

Currency and Accuracy

As in past editions, we have endeavoured to make this edition the most current and accurate text available. Where there has been a significant change in the accounting standard or how it is applied, it has been highlighted with a significant change icon. Where change is on the horizon, we have noted this at the end of each chapter under the Looking Ahead section. We are also committed to issuing brief update supplements on *WileyPLUS* when new standards are issued.

The following list outlines the revisions and improvements made to the chapters in Volume Two of this text.

Chapter 13   Non-Financial and Current Liabilities

- The impact of IFRS 15 (*Revenue from Contracts with Customers*) on items such as accounting for assurance-type and service-type warranties is discussed.
- An overview of the impact of the new IASB Exposure Draft entitled "Conceptual Framework for Financial Reporting" that was issued in May 2015, and a new IASB Staff Paper on Research—provisions, contingent liabilities, and contingent assets (IAS 37) issued in June 2015 is provided.

Chapter 14   Long-Term Financial Liabilities

- The chapter has been updated for IFRS 9 requirements relating to impairments as they relate to troubled debt situations.
- The discussion relating to off–balance-sheet financing has been updated for changes in IFRS relating to leases.
- The Looking Ahead section provides an update on where the IASB stands with respect to how to present liabilities and also the different characteristics of debt and equity.

- A note disclosure example has been added.
- The end-of-chapter material has been linked to Chapter 3 methods for calculating present values.

Chapter 15   Shareholders' Equity

- Excerpts have been updated emphasizing statement of changes in shareholders' equity and capital disclosures under IFRS.

Chapter 16   Complex Financial Instruments

- A section has been added to Appendix 16C on fair value disclosures.
- The IFRS versus ASPE difference in accounting for induced early conversions has been highlighted.
- A five-step approach to hedge accounting has been added.
- More side-by-side IFRS and ASPE journal entries have been added for hedge accounting.
- The discussion on hedge accounting and ASPE has been streamlined.
- A brief update on the IASB's macro hedging project has been provided.

Chapter 17   Earnings per Share

- The chapter has been updated and streamlined.
- A learning objective relating to analysis has been added.

Chapter 18   Income Taxes

- A discussion of the impact of the trend to lower international and Canadian corporate tax rates is provided.
- Real World Emphasis illustrations have been added that focus on the impact of IFRS on Canadian-based companies.
- The Looking Ahead section discusses proposed amendments to IAS 12 being considered by the IASB with a proposed January 1, 2017 effective date. A related research project launched by the IASB in July 2015 and a draft IFRIC interpretation titled "Uncertainty over Income Tax Treatments" are also discussed.

Chapter 19   Pensions and Other Post-Employment Benefits

- Changes to ASPE requirements to eliminate the deferral and amortization approach and to require only one approach (consistent with what used to be called the immediate recognition approach) have now been integrated throughout the chapter.
- The worksheet approach has been updated to take into account changes to ASPE requirements.
- Extensive new end-of-chapter material comparing and contrasting the IFRS and ASPE requirements has been included in the chapter and in *WileyPLUS*.
- The defer and amortize approach that had been provided in the former Appendix 19B has been eliminated.

Chapter 20   Leases

- The chapter has been updated to incorporate the impact of IFRS 16, the new accounting standard for lease accounting introduced by the IASB in January 2016.
- The ASPE requirements are retained, pending any updates from the Accounting Standards Board. If a new ASPE standard is issued, an update will be provided on the companion website and in *WileyPLUS*.
- Extensive new end-of-chapter material has been included providing examples using the new IFRS 16 requirements.

- IAS 17 *Leases* accounting requirements are provided in a new Appendix 20B, as the IASB intends to eliminate IAS 17 effective January 1, 2019. Related end-of-chapter material has been retained for those who choose to cover both IAS 17 and IFRS 16 requirements.

Chapter 21   Accounting Changes and Error Analysis

- The chapter has been refreshed and updated.
- Material has been added on estimation uncertainty and required disclosures including sensitivity analysis.

Chapter 22   Statement of Cash Flows

- The chapter builds on Chapter 5 and provides more comprehensive examples of the preparation of the statement of cash flows under the indirect method, followed by the direct method.
- Examples comparing and contrasting the direct and indirect approach for the statement of cash flows are provided based on Stantec Inc.'s 2014 and 2013 financial statements, including a detailed discussion and analysis of the company's 2014 operating, investing, and financing activities.

Chapter 23   Other Measurement and Disclosure Issues

- The new section on financial statement analysis incorporated into the tenth edition has been updated and tied in to CPA Competency Map requirements.
- The chapter also addresses a wide variety of smaller topics, such as segmented reporting and interim reporting requirements. These have been updated to the extent that standards have evolved over the past few years (for example, to incorporate new terminology being used for auditor's reports and changes to IAS 1.31 regarding materiality within note disclosures).
- A new learning objective identifying the major considerations relating to bankruptcy and receivership has been provided, including a discussion of the use of the Companies' Creditors Arrangement Act by insolvent companies.

Special Student Supplements

The *Study Guide to Accompany Intermediate Accounting*, Eleventh Canadian Edition, provides a solid review of the concepts presented in the intermediate accounting course, and gives students strategies for dealing with the complexities of applying those concepts. The following are included in this guide to help you make your way through each chapter.

To Help Gain a Solid Understanding of the Concepts

- A chapter **Overview** introduces the reader to the topics covered and their importance.
- **Study Steps** review the business transaction under discussion; show how to recognize, measure, and disclose issues related to that transaction; and demonstrate how to then make the appropriate calculations and apply the appropriate accounting methods.
- **Tips** alert learners to common pitfalls and misconceptions and to remind students of important terminology, concepts, and relationships.
- A **Toolkit** printed on cards can be detached from the guide and referred to throughout the course. These cards present material such as a review of the conceptual triangle from the book, a glossary of definitions, and summary of key ratios.

To Aid in Applying Concepts Successfully

- **Exercises and Multiple-Choice Questions** allow students to practise using material that is representative of homework assignments and exam questions they are likely to encounter.
- **Purposes** identify the essence of each exercise or question and link it to the text material.

- **Solutions** show students the appropriate worked-out solutions for each exercise and multiple-choice question.

- **Explanations** give users the details of how selected solutions were derived and explain why things are done as shown.

- **Approaches** coach students on the particular model, computational format, or other strategy to be used to solve particular problems.

The Intermediate Accounting Simulation Practice Set by Fred Pries will help students see how the individual topics they study in intermediate accounting are related to the accounting systems of an organization and to the financial statements as a whole. Students play the role of a newly hired accountant for Woodlawn Engineering, an owner-managed company, and prepare a full set of financial statements starting from an unadjusted trial balance. Each module of the simulation is linked to a particular topic covered in the intermediate accounting course and introduces new information. Students analyze this information, recommend what adjustments are needed to the books and financial statements of the company, and write reports to the chief financial officer explaining the basis for their recommendations.

Canadian Financial Accounting Cases by Camillo Lento and Jo-Anne Ryan provides additional cases at the intermediate level that may be used either for assignment purposes or for in-class discussion. The cases are keyed to various topics covered by the two volumes of *Intermediate Accounting* and have been developed using IFRS and ASPE.

Acknowledgements

We thank the users of our tenth edition, including the many instructors, faculty, and students who contributed to this revision through their comments and instructive criticism.

Appreciation is also extended to colleagues at the University of Toronto and the Lazaridis School of Business and Economics, Wilfrid Laurier University, who provided input, suggestions, and support, especially Peter Thomas, for his professionalism and wisdom.

It takes many people and coordinated efforts to get an edition off the ground. Many thanks to the team at John Wiley & Sons Canada, Ltd., who are superb: Zoë Craig, Executive Editor; Daleara Hirjikaka, Developmental Editor; Veronica Visentin, V.P. and Director, Market Solutions; Karen Staudinger, Editorial Manager, who has been an integral part of the last six editions; Luisa Begani, Media Editor, for managing this increasingly important aspect of the text; Deanna Durnford, Supplements Coordinator; Anita Osborne, Senior Marketing Manager; Kaitlyn Sykes, Editorial Intern; and Sara Veltkamp, Kristen Vanderkooy, and Duncan Moore, Digital Solutions Managers. Their enthusiasm and support have been invaluable. The editorial contributions of Laurel Hyatt, Zofia Laubitz, Merrie-Ellen Wilcox, and Belle Wong are also very much appreciated.

We are grateful to Peter Alpaugh, Robert Collier, Catherine Duffy, Peter Martin, Carrie McMillan, Ross Meacher, and Don Smith for reviewing selected chapters of the text.

We are particularly grateful to Kareen Brown, Sandra Daga, Jessica Di Rito, Cécile Laurin, Camillo Lento, Marisa Moriello, Michelle Lum, Sandra Scott, Laura Simeoni, Heather Sceles, and Ruth Ann Strickland for all their help with the end-of-chapter material and solutions. Thanks also go to Darrin Ambrose, Ann-Marie Cederholm, Laura Cumming, Angela Davis, Amy Hoggard, Debra Lee Hue, Mark Magee, Ross Meacher, Lisa Ricci, Ouafa Sakka, Joel Shapiro, Marie Sinnot, Ruth Ann Strickland, and Ralph Tassone, who contributed so much to the related supplements.

We thank CPA Canada and the IFRS Foundation for allowing us to quote from their materials and Brookfield Asset Management for permitting us to use its 2014 financial statements for our specimen financial statements.

We appreciate the opportunity to reach out to so many colleagues and students through this book. Your conversations and input have greatly helped shape the book and make it all it can be. We are thankful to be part of a group of such dedicated educators! Let's keep the conversation going.

Suggestions and comments are always appreciated. We have striven to produce an error-free text, but if anything has slipped through the variety of checks undertaken, please let us know so that corrections can be made to subsequent printings.

Irene M. Wiecek
TORONTO, ONTARIO
wiecek@rotman.utoronto.ca

Bruce McConomy
WATERLOO, ONTARIO
bmcconomy@wlu.ca

March 2016

Brief Contents

Contents

REFERENCE TO THE CPA COMPETENCY MAP

LEARNING OBJECTIVES

After studying this chapter, you shculd be able to:

1.1.1, 1.1.2, 1.1.4, 5.2.1	**1.** Understand the importance of non-financial and current liabilities from a business perspective.
1.2.1, 1.2.2	**2.** Define liabilities, distinguish financial liabilities from other liabilities, and identify how they are measured.
1.2.1, 1.2.2, 5.2.1, 6.2.1	**3.** Define current liabilities and idertify and account for common types of current liabilities.
1.2.1, 1.2.2	**4.** Identify and account for the major types of employee-related liabilities.
1.2.1, 1.2.2, 1.2.3	**5.** Explain the recognition, measurement, and disclosure requirements for decommissioning and restoration obligations.
1.2.1, 1.2.2	**6.** Explain the issues and account for unearned revenues.
1.2.1, 1.2.2	**7.** Explain the issues and account for product guarantees and other customer program obligations.
1.1.1, 1.2.1, 1.2.2, 1.3.1, 1.3.2	**8.** Explain and account for contingencies and uncertain commitments, and identify the accounting and reporting requirements for guarantees and commitments.
1.4.2, 1.4.4, 5.1.1	**9.** Indicate how non-financial and current liabilities are presented and analyzed.
1.1.4	**10.** Identify differences in accounting between IFRS and ASPE and what changes are expected in the near future.

GETTING A CHARGE OUT OF WARRANTY ACCOUNTING

THE CAR BUSINESS is cutthroat, and one way that auto manufacturers compete is by offering better warranties than their competitors. That's one reason why Tesla Motors, makers of luxury electric vehicles, decided to extend the warranty on its Model S sedan, which sells for an average of around U.S. $113,000. In late 2014, Tesla announced that it was extending the warranty on the Model S drive unit from four to eight years, and on the vehicle's battery from four to eight years or 125,000 miles (about 200,000 kilometres) or unlimited miles, depending on the battery size.

Including a warranty on products sold represents a liability to companies because eventually they will have to honour the warranty on some of their products. A warranty is a guarantee by the company that a product will be free of defects for a certain period. Tesla records a warranty reserve—money it sets aside as an estimate of the costs it will incur to honour the warranty by repairing or replacing any defective items. Extending the warranty on its Model S vehicle caused Tesla to increase its warranty reserve by U.S. $14.0 million in 2014.

The estimated cost that Tesla will incur in honouring its warranties is recorded as warranty expense, which is included as part of its cost of automotive sales. "Warranty

Teddy Leung/Shutterstock

expense is recorded as a component of cost of revenues in the consolidated statements of operations. The portion of the warranty provision which is expected to be incurred within 12 months from the balance sheet date is classified as current, while the remaining amount is classified as long-term," the company said in its 2014 annual report. In 2014, Tesla's warranty expense was U.S. $6.9 million.

If car buyers want to extend their warranties, they can usually pay an extra fee. Tesla offers extended warranties, known as service plans, on its vehicles. For example, it had been charging U.S. $4,000 to extend the warranty on its Model S by an additional four years or 50,000 miles (about 80,000 kilometres). When customers buy service plans, Tesla records the money it receives for these plans as deferred revenues, which it then allocates over the service coverage periods. For the year ended December 31, 2014, Tesla had deferred revenues of $24.9 million from the sale of service plans. Tesla recognized U.S. $3.0 million of revenue related to these service plans in 2014.

While Tesla can calculate how much it earns from service plans and spends on honouring warranties, it can't know for certain how much its warranties influence car buyers. One thing is for sure: demand for its Model S was so strong that the company had to ramp up production in 2014.

Sources: Maria Armental, "Tesla Motors Extends Model S Warranty Retroactively," *The Wall Street Journal*, August 15, 2014; Chuck Jones, "How Much Could Tesla's 'Infinite Mile Warranty' Cost the Company?," Forbes.com, August 18, 2014; Tesla Motors, Inc. 2014 annual report; Tesla Motors, Inc. corporate website, www.teslamotors.com/.

PREVIEW OF CHAPTER 13

This chapter explains the basic principles underlying the accounting and reporting for many common current liabilities and for a variety of non-financial liabilities, such as unearned revenues, product warranty and other customer obligations, and asset retirement obligations. It also addresses contingencies, commitments, and guarantees. We explain issues related to long-term financial liabilities in Chapter 14.

The chapter is organized as follows:

NON-FINANCIAL AND CURRENT LIABILITIES						
Understanding Non-Financial and Current Liabilities	**Recognition and Measurement**	**Common Current Liabilities**	**Employee-Related Liabilities**	**Non-Financial Liabilities**	**Presentation, Disclosure, and Analysis**	**IFRS/ASPE Comparison**
	▪ Liability definition and characteristics ▪ Financial liabilities and non-financial liabilities ▪ Measurement	▪ What is a current liability? ▪ Bank indebtedness and credit facilities ▪ Accounts payable ▪ Notes payable ▪ Current maturities of long-term debt ▪ Short-term debt expected to be refinanced ▪ Dividends payable ▪ Rents and royalties payable ▪ Customer advances and deposits ▪ Taxes payable	▪ Payroll deductions ▪ Short-term compensated absences ▪ Profit-sharing and bonus agreements	▪ Decommissioning and restoration obligations ▪ Unearned revenues ▪ Product guarantees and customer programs ▪ Contingencies, uncertain commitments, and requirements for guarantees and other commitments	▪ Presentation and disclosure of current liabilities ▪ Presentation and disclosure of contingencies, guarantees, and commitments ▪ Analysis	▪ A comparison of IFRS and ASPE ▪ Looking ahead

UNDERSTANDING NON-FINANCIAL AND CURRENT LIABILITIES

Objective 1
Understand the importance of non-financial and current liabilities from a business perspective.

The asset and liability approach to accounting, as summarized in the conceptual framework, includes asset and liability definitions that relate to the statement of financial position, but that also affect the statement of comprehensive income. For example, the recognition of an expense often occurs at the same time as the recognition of an increase in a liability or a decrease in an asset. Volume 1 of this text concentrated on the recognition and measurement of a variety of assets. Volume 2 continues by beginning with a closer look at liabilities in general and then several specific types of common liabilities.

The explanations in this chapter about non-financial liabilities under international standards are based on current IAS 37 *Provisions, Contingent Liabilities and Contingent Assets.* We provide an overview of potential future revisions to this standard in the Looking Ahead section at the end of the chapter.[1]

There are many kinds of liabilities. As a consumer, a common one you're familiar with is a warranty. When you purchase a new automobile or computer, one major consideration is the length of the warranty provided by the manufacturer or retailer, and whether you should pay an additional amount to extend the warranty. As shown in our feature story about Tesla Motors, from the seller's perspective, the warranty provided to customers represents a liability to be reported on the statement of financial position. It's considered a liability because the manufacturer or retailer has an obligation to repair or replace any defects that are covered in the warranty, usually for no additional charge. A typical warranty on a new automobile is three years or 60,000 kilometres. As a consumer, you might choose to extend the warranty to five or six years. As a manufacturer or retailer, the warranty you offer will affect your competitive advantage relative to other vendors, and will complicate your accounting over the life of the warranty. We will explore several alternatives for accounting for warranty transactions in this chapter.

TREASURY MANAGEMENT 5.2.1

It is important for businesses to properly account for their liabilities so they can keep an eye on their cash flow. Cash flow management is a key control factor for most businesses. Taking advantage of supplier discounts for prompt payment is one step companies can take to control their cash flows. Control of expenses and related accounts payable can improve the efficiency of a business, and can be particularly important during economic downturns.

In this chapter, we focus on current liabilities and non-financial liabilities. As we will see, companies need to account for typical items such as trade accounts payable and less obvious liabilities including constructive obligations that arise based on past practice. We will look at the related definitions under IFRS and ASPE next before examining the detailed accounting requirements.

RECOGNITION AND MEASUREMENT

Liability Definition and Characteristics

Objective 2
Define liabilities, distinguish financial liabilities from other liabilities, and identify how they are measured.

Chapter 2 of this text presented the elements of financial statements and their definitions. It explained that the IASB is developing revised definitions of terms such as assets and **liabilities** as part of its conceptual framework project. For example, proposed new definitions are included as part of a May 2015 Exposure Draft entitled *Conceptual Framework for Financial Reporting.* In this text, we apply the definitions as they were being used when the text went to press. In the Looking Ahead section of the chapter, we briefly discuss the changes under consideration by the IASB as it moves toward updated standards. Illustration 13-1 provides the definition of liabilities in the existing IFRS, and under ASPE in the *CPA Canada Handbook*, Part II.[2]

Illustration 13-1

Definition of Liabilities

Definition in Existing IFRS and *CPA Canada Handbook*, Part II (a summary)

A **liability** is an obligation that arises from past transactions or events, which may result in a transfer of assets or provision of services.

Liabilities have three essential characteristics:

1. They embody a **duty or responsibility to others**.

2. The entity has **little or no discretion to avoid the duty**.

3. The **transaction** or event that obliges the entity **has occurred**.

The three characteristics of a liability are essential to the current definition. First, a liability must represent a duty or responsibility; for example, to pay a supplier for goods that it has purchased. The entity has little (or no) discretion to avoid the obligation; otherwise, there could be negative consequences such as the supplier suing for breach of contract. And the liability relates to a transaction that has occurred (the goods were purchased, they have been delivered, and title has passed). So an economic obligation exists **at the date of the statement of financial position**. The existence of a present obligation is not always clear, as we will see later in this chapter. For example, there may be uncertainty about whether an event that has occurred results in a present obligation, or how a law or regulation applies to that event. Judgement is needed in many circumstances, with management drawing on evidence such as the entity's past experience, other entities' experience with similar items, and opinions of experts and others.[3]

LAW

The idea that an entity must have a duty or responsibility to perform in a particular way suggests it is required to bear the economic obligation, and this requirement can be **enforced by legal or equivalent means**. This means that a law, a contract enforceable by law, or a constructive obligation exists. A **constructive obligation** arises when past or present company practice shows that the entity acknowledges a potential economic burden. This comes about because the entity has indicated to others that it will accept a specific responsibility and other parties can reasonably expect the entity to meet its responsibility. For example, a company may be required by provincial legislation to provide 4% vacation pay to its employees, but it may have paid 6% over the past number of years. Therefore, even though the company may not be required by law or contract to pay the extra 2%, the expectation is that it will continue to provide it. Therefore a constructive obligation exists, and amounts owing at the date of the statement of financial position are recognized as a liability, based on the 6%.

All entities must also comply with the statutes, laws, and regulations in the legal jurisdiction in which they operate; however, these result in liabilities only if the entity violates their provisions. A liability does not result if the transaction or event obliging the company has not yet taken place.

Under current **recognition** requirements, non-financial liabilities are recognized only if it is probable (that is, more likely than not) that the obligation would result in an outflow of cash or other economic resources from the entity. That is, the uncertainty of the amount is an issue as to whether the obligation is recognized as a liability.

Financial Liabilities and Non-Financial Liabilities

Because a number of accounting standards refer to the recognition, measurement, and reporting of **financial instruments** specifically, it is important to be able to identify those that are financial **liabilities**. Under both accounting standards for private enterprises (ASPE) and IFRS, a **financial liability** is any liability that is a **contractual obligation**:

1. to deliver cash or other financial assets to another entity, or

2. to exchange financial assets or financial liabilities with another entity under conditions that are potentially unfavourable to the entity.[4]

UNDERLYING CONCEPT

To be able to properly classify specific financial instruments, proper definitions are needed for assets, liabilities, and equities. The conceptual framework definitions are used as the basis for settling difficult classification issues.

Note that this definition requires the liability to be based on an obligation that is created by a contract. Liabilities that are created by legislation, such as income taxes payable, do not qualify as financial liabilities and therefore are not covered by the same accounting standards as financial liabilities. In this chapter, most current liabilities are financial in nature, but if the obligation will be met by the delivery of goods or services, such as in the case of unearned revenue and warranty obligations, it is not considered a financial liability.

The classification of liabilities into financial and non-financial liabilities is important because the accounting standard that applies depends on how the liability is classified.

Measurement

Financial Liabilities

Financial liabilities are recognized initially at their fair value. After acquisition, though, most of the financial liabilities that are discussed in this and later chapters are accounted for **at their amortized cost**.[5] Consistent with cost-based measurement, the original fair value of a financial liability is generally adjusted for transaction costs that are directly attributable to the issue of the financial liability (to defer the difference between fair value and the transaction price). However, transaction costs associated with the issue of financial liabilities that are accounted for after acquisition at fair value through profit or loss are recognized in net income as incurred.

When liabilities are short-term in nature, such as regular trade payables with 30- or 60-day payment terms, they are usually accounted for, on practical grounds, at their maturity value. This is appropriate because the difference between the liability's fair value and its maturity value is not significant. The slight overstatement of liabilities that results from carrying many current liabilities at their maturity value is accepted if it is immaterial.

Non-Financial Liabilities

Non-financial liabilities, on the other hand, are usually not payable in cash. Therefore, they are measured in a different way. **ASPE** does not separately address the issue of non-financial liabilities, so these are measured in a variety of ways, depending on the specific liability. For example, unearned revenue is usually measured at the fair value of the goods or services to be delivered in the future.

Under IFRS, non-financial liabilities are measured initially and at each subsequent reporting date at the best estimate of the amount the entity would rationally pay at the date of the statement of financial position to settle the present obligation. This is usually the present value of the resources needed to fulfill the obligation, measured at the expected value or probability-weighted average of the range of possible outcomes.[6]

With this introduction to liabilities, we now take a closer look at specific current liabilities found on most companies' statements of financial position.

COMMON CURRENT LIABILITIES

What Is a Current Liability?

Objective 3
Define current liabilities and identify and account for common types of current liabilities.

Because liabilities result in a future disbursement (payment) of assets or services, one of their most important features is the timing of when they are due. Obligations that mature in the short term place a demand on the entity's current assets. They are demands that must be satisfied on time and in the ordinary course of business if operations are to continue. Liabilities with a distant due date generally do not result in a claim on the company's current assets and are therefore classified differently. This difference in timing and the effect on current assets is a major reason for the division of liabilities into (1) current liabilities and (2) non-current liabilities.

Another reason for classifying current assets and liabilities separately from long-term assets and liabilities is to provide information about the working capital used by the entity in its normal operating cycle. The normal **operating cycle** is the period of time between acquiring the goods and services for processing in operations and receiving cash from the eventual sale of the processed goods and services. Industries that manufacture products that go through an aging process and certain capital-intensive industries may have an operating cycle of much longer than one year. On the other hand, most retail and service establishments have several operating cycles in a single year. The operating cycle is sometimes referred to as the cash-to-cash cycle. If the length of the cycle is not obvious, accounting standards typically assume it is 12 months.

The definition of a **current liability** and of the length of the operating cycle is directly related to that of a current asset. A liability is classified as current under IFRS when one of the following conditions is met:

1. It is expected to be settled in the entity's normal operating cycle.

2. It is held primarily for trading.

3. It is due within 12 months from the end of the reporting period.

4. The entity does not have an unconditional right to defer its settlement for at least 12 months after the date of the statement of financial position.[7]

ASPE provides a similar definition, suggesting that current liabilities include amounts payable within one year from the date of the balance sheet or within the normal operating cycle, when that is longer than a year.[8] There may be minor differences in application.

We will now illustrate a variety of current liabilities commonly found in companies' financial statements.

Bank Indebtedness and Credit Facilities

TREASURY MANAGEMENT 5.2.1

A major element of a company's liquidity position is its bank indebtedness for current operating purposes and its **line of credit** or **revolving debt** arrangements related to this debt. Instead of having to negotiate a new loan every time it needs funds, a company generally enters into an agreement with its bank that allows it to make multiple borrowings up to a negotiated limit. As previous borrowings are partly repaid, the company is permitted to borrow again under the same contract. Because the financial institution commits itself to making money available to the entity, the bank often charges an additional fee for this service over and above the interest that it charges on the funds that are actually advanced. Under such agreements, the financial institution usually requires collateral and often sets restrictions on the company's activities or financial statement ratios that must be maintained.

The amount of actual bank indebtedness is reported on the statement of financial position, while the total funds that the credit arrangement allows the company to borrow and any restrictions that are imposed by the financial institution are disclosed in the notes.

WHAT DO THE NUMBERS MEAN?

REAL WORLD EMPHASIS

Borrowings and growth must be carefully managed! Maintaining close working relationships with customers, banks, suppliers, and other creditors is central to getting through a cash crunch. Based in British Columbia, **Pacific Safety Products Inc.** (PSP) enjoyed a 69% increase in sales in one year several years ago and suffered the liquidity problems that often come with such success. The company's annual report indicated that one of PSP's major challenges during the year had been to manage its cash flow so that it could pay suppliers. This was necessary to ensure a continuous flow of raw materials needed in the manufacturing process in order to meet customer orders on a timely basis.

PSP reported bank indebtedness of almost $3 million in its current liabilities at the company's year end. Providing details on the indebtedness, a note to the financial statements indicated a maximum operating line of credit of $3 million with the Bank of Nova Scotia, which was secured by accounts receivable, inventory, and an assignment of insurance. The note also reported that the company was not in compliance with the covenants imposed by the bank for its current ratio and tangible net worth, but that the bank was allowing PSP to operate outside its covenants.

One year later, PSP reported sales that were only 75% of those reported for the preceding fiscal year, but its cash flow from operating activities was almost twice as high as in the earlier period! The uncollected receivables from one year earlier had been collected and this allowed the company to get over its cash crunch. Bank indebtedness was reduced to only $102,417, the operating line was reduced to $2 million, and the company was once again in compliance with the bank's covenants.

Accounts Payable

Accounts payable, or **trade accounts payable**, are balances owed to others for goods, supplies, or services related to the entity's ordinary business activities that are purchased on open account. This means that evidence of the obligations' existence comes from regular invoices rather than from separate contracts for each transaction. Accounts payable arise because of the time lag between the receipt of goods and services and the payment for them. This period of extended credit is usually stated in the terms of sale and purchase; for example, 2/10, n/30 or 1/10, E.O.M., net 30. The period is commonly 30 to 60 days long.[9]

Most accounting systems are designed to record liabilities for purchases of goods when the goods are received. Sometimes there is a delay in recording the goods and the related liability on the books, such as when waiting for an invoice. If title has passed to the purchaser before the goods are received, the transaction should be recorded when the title passes. Attention must be paid to transactions that occur near the end of one accounting period and the beginning of the next so that the goods and services received (the inventory or expense) are recorded in the same accounting period as the liability (accounts payable) and both are recorded in the proper period. Chapter 8 discussed this cut-off issue in greater detail and illustrated the entries for accounts payable and purchase discounts.

Notes Payable

LAW

Notes payable are written promises to pay a certain sum of money on a specified future date and may arise from purchases, financing, or other transactions. In some industries, instead of the normal procedure of extending credit on an open account, notes (often referred to as **trade notes payable**) are required as part of the sale or purchase transaction. Notes payable to banks or loan companies are generally created by cash loans. Notes may be classified as current (short-term) or long-term (non-current), depending on the payment due date. Notes may also be interest-bearing or non–interest-bearing (that is, zero-interest-bearing). Accounting for them is the mirror image of accounting for notes receivable illustrated in Chapter 7.

Interest-Bearing Note Issued

Assume that Provincial Bank agrees to lend $100,000 on March 1, 2017 to Landscape Corp. and the company signs a $100,000, four-month, 12% note. The entry to record the cash received by Landscape Corp. on March 1 is:

A   =   L   +   SE
+100,000   +100,000

Cash flows: ↑ 100,000 inflow

| March 1 | Cash | 100,000 | |
| | Notes Payable | | 100,000 |

If Landscape Corp. has a December 31 year end, but prepares financial statements semi-annually, an adjusting entry is required to recognize the four months of interest expense and interest payable of $4,000 ($100,000 × 12% × $^4/_{12}$) on June 30. The adjusting entry is:

A   =   L   +   SE
+4,000   −4,000

Cash flows: No effect

| June 30 | Interest Expense | 4,000 | |
| | Interest Payable | | 4,000 |

At maturity on July 1, Landscape Corp. pays the note's face value of $100,000 plus the $4,000 of interest. The entry to record payment of the note and accrued interest is as follows:

	A = L + SE		
−104,000 −104,000			

Cash flows: ↓ 104,000 outflow

July 1	Notes Payable	100,000	
	Interest Payable	4,000	
	Cash		104,000

Zero-Interest-Bearing Note Issued

A zero-interest-bearing note may be issued instead of an interest-bearing note. Despite its name, a **zero-interest-bearing note does have an interest component**. The interest is just not added on top of the note's face or maturity value; instead, it is included in the face amount. The interest is the difference between the amount of cash received when the note is signed and the higher face amount that is payable at maturity. The borrower receives the note's present value in cash and pays back the larger maturity value.

To illustrate, assume that Landscape Corp. issues a $100,000, four-month, zero-interest-bearing note payable to the Provincial Bank on March 1. The note's present value is $96,154, based on the bank's discount rate of 12%. Landscape's entry to record this transaction is as follows:

	A = L + SE		
+96,154 +96,154			

Cash flows: ↑ 96,154 inflow

| March 1 | Cash | 96,154 | |
| | Notes Payable[10] | | 96,154 |

Notes Payable is credited for the note's fair value, which is less than the cash due at maturity. In effect, this is the amount borrowed. If Landscape Corp. prepares financial statements at June 30, the interest expense for the four-month period to June 30 must be recognized along with the increase in the Note Payable, $96,154 \times 12\% \times {}^{4}/_{12} = \$3,846$, as follows:

	A = L + SE		
+3,846 −3,846			

Cash flows: No effect

| June 30 | Interest Expense | 3,846 | |
| | Notes Payable | | 3,846 |

The Notes Payable account now has a balance of $96,154 + $3,846 = $100,000. This is the amount borrowed plus interest to June 30 at 12%. On July 1 the note is repaid:

	A = L + SE		
−100,000 −100,000			

Cash flows: ↓ 100,000 outflow

| July 1 | Notes Payable | 100,000 | |
| | Cash | | 100,000 |

We discuss the accounting issues related to long-term notes payable in Chapter 14.

Current Maturities of Long-Term Debt

Bonds, mortgage notes, and other long-term indebtedness that mature within 12 months from the date of the statement of financial position—**current maturities of long-term debt**—are reported as current liabilities. What if only part of a long-term obligation is to be paid within the next 12 months, as in the case of a mortgage or of serial bonds that are to be retired through a series of annual instalments? In that case, **only the maturing portion of the principal of the long-term debt is reported as a current liability**. The balance of the principal is reported as a long-term liability.

Portions of long-term obligations that will mature in the next 12 months should not be included as current liabilities if, by contract, they are to be retired by assets accumulated for this purpose that properly have not been reported as current assets. In this situation, no current assets are used and no other current liabilities are created in order to repay the maturing liability. Therefore, it is correct to classify the liability as long-term.

A liability that is **due on demand** (that is, callable by the creditor), or that will be due on demand within a year, is also classified as a current liability. Often companies have debt agreements that, while due on demand, have payment schedules set up to pay the obligation over a number of years. The management of these entities may argue that only the

LAW

portion due to be paid within 12 months should be classified as current. Managers may further argue that financial statement readers will be misled if the whole of the debt is reported as a current liability, because the company's liquidity position is misrepresented. The standard setters, on the other hand, indicate that all of such **callable debt** meets the definition of a current liability, and that additional information about the callable debt can be explained in the notes to the financial statements.

Liabilities often become callable by the creditor if there is a violation of a debt agreement. For example, most debt agreements require the borrower to maintain a minimum ratio of equity to debt or, as illustrated in the Pacific Safety Products situation above, specify minimum current ratio requirements.

If a long-term debt agreement is violated and the liability becomes payable on demand, the debt is reclassified as current. Under IFRS, this position holds, even if the lender agrees between the date of the statement of financial position and the date the financial statements are released that it will not demand repayment because of the violation. This position is consistent with the fact that, at the date of the statement of financial position, the entity did not have an unconditional right to defer the payment beyond 12 months from the reporting date. That right could only be exercised by the lender.

Under ASPE, the liability is reclassified to the current category unless:

1. the creditor waives in writing the covenant (agreement) requirements, **or**

2. the violation has been cured or rectified within the grace period that is usually given in these agreements

and it is not likely that the company will violate the covenant requirements within a year from the date of the statement of financial position.[11]

Short-Term Debt Expected to Be Refinanced

Short-term debt obligations are amounts scheduled to mature within one year from the date of the statement of financial position. However, a classification issue arises when such a liability is expected to be refinanced on a long-term basis, and therefore current assets are not expected to be needed for it. Where should these **short-term obligations expected to be refinanced** on a long-term basis be reported?[12]

At one time, the accounting profession generally agreed with not including short-term obligations in current liabilities if they were "expected to be refinanced" on a long-term basis. Because the profession gave no specific guidelines, however, determining whether a short-term obligation was expected to be refinanced was usually based solely on management's **intent**. Classification was not clear-cut and the proper accounting was therefore uncertain. For example, a company might want a five-year bank loan but handle the actual financing with 90-day notes that it keeps renewing. In this case, is the loan long-term debt or a current liability?

Consistent with the international standard for callable debt, under IFRS, if the debt is due within 12 months from the reporting date, it is classified as a current liability. This classification holds even if a long-term refinancing has been completed before the financial statements are released. The only exception accepted for continuing long-term classification is if, at the date of the statement of financial position, the entity expects to refinance it or roll it over **under an existing agreement** for at least 12 months and the decision is **solely at its discretion**.

Also consistent with the ASPE standard for callable debt, the short-term liability expected to be refinanced is classified as a current liability unless either the liability has been refinanced on a long-term basis or there is a non-cancellable agreement to do so before the financial statements are completed and nothing stands in the way of completing the refinancing. That is, if there is irrefutable evidence by the time the financial statements are completed that the debt has been or will be converted into a long-term obligation, ASPE allows currently maturing debt to be classified as long-term on the balance sheet.

If an actual refinancing occurs, the amount of the short-term obligation that is excluded from current liabilities cannot be higher than the proceeds from the new obligation or equity securities that are used to retire it. For example, assume that Montavon Winery has $3 million of short-term debt at the reporting date. The company then issues $2 million of long-term debt after the balance sheet date but before the financial statements are issued. It uses the proceeds from the issue to partially liquidate the short-term liability. If the net proceeds from the issue of the new long-term debt total $2 million, only $2 million of the short-term debt can be excluded from current liabilities.

Under IFRS, the whole $3 million of maturing debt would still be classified as a current obligation. That is, the international standard has a more stringent requirement: the agreement must be in place **at the date of the statement of financial position**.

Another issue is whether a short-term obligation can be excluded from current liabilities if it is paid off after the date of the statement of financial position and then replaced by long-term debt before the financial statements are issued. To illustrate, assume that Marquardt Limited pays off short-term debt of $40,000 on January 17, 2018 and issues long-term debt of $100,000 on February 3, 2018. Marquardt's financial statements dated December 31, 2017 are issued on March 1, 2018. Because the refinancing does not appear to be linked to the short-term debt, ASPE requires the debt to be classified as current. In addition, because its repayment occurred **before** funds were obtained through long-term financing, the repayment **used existing** current assets. Illustration 13-2 shows this situation.

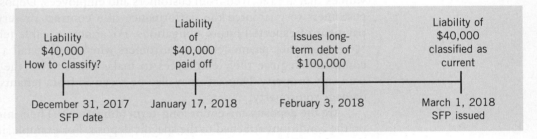

Illustration 13-2

Short-Term Debt Paid Off after Date of Statement of Financial Position and Later Replaced by Long-Term Debt under Both IFRS and ASPE

Dividends Payable

UNDERLYING CONCEPT

Preferred dividends in arrears are economic obligations for which the entity is the obligor, but they are not present obligations until declared. Using a note to disclose the preferred dividends in arrears improves the predictive value of the financial statements.

A cash **dividend payable** is an amount that a corporation owes to its shareholders because the board of directors has authorized a dividend payment. At the dividend declaration date, the corporation incurs a liability that places the shareholders in the position of creditors for the amount of dividend declared. Because cash dividends are normally paid within one year of the declaration (generally within three months in actual practice), they are classified as current liabilities.

Accumulated but undeclared dividends on cumulative preferred shares **are not recognized as a liability**, because **preferred dividends in arrears** are not an obligation until formal action is taken by the board of directors to authorize the distribution. Nevertheless, the company is required to disclose the existence of cumulative dividends in arrears that are undeclared in a note to the financial statements.

Dividends that are payable in the form of additional shares **are not recognized as a liability**. Such share or stock dividends (discussed further in Chapter 15) do not meet the definition of a liability because they do not require future outlays of economic resources. In addition, they are not enforceable in that the board of directors can revoke them at any time before they are issued. On declaration, an entry is prepared that reduces (debits) Retained Earnings and credits a contributed capital account such as Stock Dividends Distributable. This latter account is reported in the shareholders' equity section because it represents a transfer of equity from retained earnings to contributed capital.

Rents and Royalties Payable

LAW

Rents and royalties payable is another common type of current liability. This obligation may be created by a **contractual agreement in which payments are conditional on the amount of revenue that is earned or the quantity of product that is produced or extracted**. For example, franchisees are usually required to pay franchise fees to the franchisor that are calculated as a percentage of sales. Tenants in shopping centres may be obligated to pay additional rents on sales that are above a predetermined amount. Manufacturers may have licensing agreements that require them to pay the holder of a patent a royalty for each unit that the manufacturer produces.

Liabilities for expenses that are based on revenues earned or units produced are usually easy to measure. For example, if a lease calls for a fixed rent payment of $500 per month and 1% of all sales over $300,000 per year, the annual rent obligation amounts to $6,000 plus $0.01 for each dollar of revenue over $300,000. Or a royalty agreement may require the accrual of $1 per unit that is produced under a patented process, or the accrual of $0.50 on every barrel of oil that is extracted, with the accrued amount then paid to the owner of the mineral rights. As each additional unit of product is produced or extracted, an additional obligation, usually a current liability, is created.

Customer Advances and Deposits

A company's current liabilities may include **returnable cash deposits** or **customer advances** that are received from customers and employees. Deposits may be received from customers to guarantee the performance of a contract or service or to guarantee the payment of expected future obligations. For example, cable television companies often require advance payments from customers when they install a cable connection. Some companies require their employees to make deposits for the return of keys or other company property. Deposits may also be received from tenants to cover possible future damage to property.

Are the deposits current or long-term obligations? Their initial classification depends on the conditions attached to the specific deposit. For example, if the entity does not have the right to defer the settlement of the deposit for a period of at least 12 months from the date of the statement of financial position, the deposit is reported as a current liability.

Taxes Payable

Sales Tax

Provincial sales taxes on transfers of tangible property and on certain services must be collected from customers and remitted to the tax authority, usually a provincial or territorial government.[13] The balance in the Sales Tax Payable account is the liability for sales taxes that have been collected from customers but not yet remitted to the appropriate government. The following entry shows the accounting for a sale on account of $3,000 when a 7% sales tax is in effect:

A   =   L   +   SE
+3,210   +210   +3,000

Cash flows: No effect

Accounts Receivable	3,210	
Sales Revenue		3,000
Sales Tax Payable		210

Goods and Services Tax

Most businesses in Canada are subject to the Goods and Services Tax (GST). The GST, a **value-added tax** of 5% (since July 1, 2008), is a tax on the value added to the goods and services provided by each taxable entity. The net amount that an entity pays to the Canada

CORPORATE TAX
6.1.1

Revenue Agency (CRA), which administers this tax, is determined as follows. The entity deducts its **input tax credit** (the GST the company paid on goods and services it purchased from suppliers) from the amount of GST the company collected, on behalf of the government, on sales to its customers. The Harmonized Sales Tax (HST) is accounted for **in the same way** as the GST in those provinces that have agreed on the combined provincial tax and GST.[14]

Accounting for the GST involves setting up a liability account—GST Payable—that is credited with GST charged on sales, and an asset account—GST Receivable—that is debited for GST paid to suppliers. Normally, the amount that is collected on sales is higher than the amount paid on purchases, and a net remittance is therefore made to the Canada Revenue Agency. Since GST is also paid on purchases of capital assets, it is possible for the GST Receivable account to have a larger balance. In these instances, a claim for reimbursement is made to the CRA.

Let's look at the accounting for the GST. Purchases of taxable goods and services are recorded by debiting the GST Receivable account for the amount of GST to be paid and debiting the appropriate asset or expense account(s) for the purchase price. Since the GST paid is recoverable from the federal government, the GST is not included in the cost of the item(s) acquired. As an example, assume that Bateman Limited purchases merchandise for $150,000 plus GST of 5% ($7,500). The entry to record this transaction is as follows, assuming a perpetual inventory system is used:

A = L + SE
+157,500 +157,500

Cash flows: No effect

Inventory	150,000	
GST Receivable	7,500	
Accounts Payable		157,500

If these goods are sold for $210,000 plus GST of 5% ($10,500), the sale entry is:

A = L + SE
+220,500 +10,500 +210,000

Cash flows: No effect

Accounts Receivable	220,500	
Sales Revenue		210,000
GST Payable		10,500

In many cases, GST and provincial sales taxes are levied on the same sale and purchase. Assume, for example, that Smith Ltd. sells supplies to Jones Corp. for $1,000 and both a 7% provincial sales tax and 5% GST are charged on this amount. The entry made by each company follows:

A = L + SE
+1,120 +120 +1,000

Cash flows: No effect (for vendor)

A = L + SE
+50 +1,120 −1,070

Cash flows: No effect (for purchaser)

Smith Ltd. (vendor company)		Jones Corp. (purchaser company)	
Accounts Receivable	1,120	Supplies Expense	1,070
Sales Revenue	1,000	GST Receivable	50
Sales Tax Payable	70	Accounts Payable	1,120
GST Payable	50	(To record purchase from Smith Ltd.)	
(To record sale to Jones Corp.)			

Notice that the purchaser includes the provincial sales tax **in the cost** of the goods or services purchased. The provincial sales tax, unlike the GST, is not recoverable by the purchaser.[15] In the provinces with a Harmonized Sales Tax, the full HST amount is treated as shown for the GST.

Because companies are permitted under the legislation to offset the GST receivable and payable amounts, only the net balance of the two accounts is reported on the statement of financial position. Until a net credit balance is remitted to the Receiver General for Canada, it is reported as a current liability. A net debit balance, on the other hand, is reported as a current asset.

LAW

Income Tax

CORPORATE TAX 6.1.1

In Canada, federal and provincial income taxes are levied on a company's taxable income. Most businesses consider the amount of income tax payable as an estimate because corporate tax returns are often finalized after the financial statements have been issued. In addition, the meaning and application of numerous tax rules, especially new ones, are debatable and often depend on a court's interpretation. Using the best information and advice available, a business prepares its income tax return at the end of its fiscal year and calculates its best estimate of the income tax payable for the period.

Assume that Forest Ltd. determines, based on its taxable income for the year, that an income tax liability of $21,000 is payable, and further assume that no accruals or instalments have been made during the year. Forest makes the following entry at year end:

A   =   L   +   SE
    +21,000 −21,000

Cash flows: No effect

Current Tax Expense	21,000	
Income Tax Payable		21,000

Most corporations are required to make periodic tax instalments (payments) throughout the year based on the previous year's income tax or estimates of the current year's income tax. If Forest Ltd. made a $20,000 tax instalment at the end of the year, the following entry would also have been made:

A   =   L   +   SE
−20,000 −20,000

Cash flows: ↓ 20,000 outflow

Income Tax Payable	20,000	
Cash		20,000

Taking into account the $21,000 tax liability from above, Forest Ltd. would report an Income Tax Payable balance of $1,000 in the current liabilities section of its year-end statement of financial position ($21,000 − $20,000). Alternatively, if the company had made instalments of $23,000, there would be a $2,000 debit balance in the Income Tax Payable account ($23,000 − $21,000). This would be reported as Income Tax Receivable, a current asset.

An alternative approach that is often used charges (debits) the instalment payments to expense. When the tax return is completed at year end and the actual amount of tax for the year is calculated, the expense is then adjusted. This series of entries is as follows:

Instalment payments of $20,000			Instalment payments of $23,000		
Current Tax Expense	20,000		Current Tax Expense	23,000	
Cash		20,000	Cash		23,000
Income taxes per tax return: $21,000			**Income taxes per tax return: $21,000**		
Current Tax Expense	1,000		Income Tax Receivable	2,000	
Income Tax Payable		1,000	Current Tax Expense		2,000

Regardless of the approach used, the resulting financial statements are identical.

If the CRA assesses an additional tax on an earlier year's income, Income Tax Payable is credited and the income tax expense is usually charged to current operations as a change in estimate. However, if, for example, the additional tax was caused by an obvious arithmetic error that occurred when the tax was originally calculated, the error would be corrected through retained earnings.

It is common for there to be differences between taxable income **under the tax laws** and accounting income **under generally accepted accounting principles**. Because of these differences, the total income tax payable to the government in any specific year may differ substantially from the total income tax expense reported on the financial statements. Chapter 18 focuses on the problems of accounting for income tax and presents an extensive discussion of related issues that are both complex and interesting.

Unlike corporations, proprietorships and partnerships are not taxable entities. It is the individual proprietor and the members of a partnership, not the business itself, that are subject to personal income taxes on their share of the business's taxable income. Therefore, income tax liabilities do not appear on the financial statements of proprietorships and partnerships.

PERSONAL TAX
6.2.1

EMPLOYEE-RELATED LIABILITIES

Objective 4
Identify and account for the major types of employee-related liabilities.

Amounts that are owed to employees for salaries or wages at the end of an accounting period are a common current liability, often referred to as Salaries and Wages Payable. The following additional items related to employee compensation are also usually reported as current liabilities:

1. Payroll deductions

2. Short-term compensated absences

3. Profit-sharing and bonuses

Payroll Deductions

The most common types of **payroll deductions** are employee income taxes, Canada (or Quebec) Pension Plan contributions, Employment Insurance premiums, and miscellaneous items such as other insurance premiums, employee savings, and union dues. Any amounts that have been deducted but not yet remitted to the proper authority by the end of the accounting period are recognized as current liabilities. This is also true for any matching amounts that the employer is required to pay.

Canada (Quebec) Pension Plan (CPP/QPP) and the Ontario Retirement Pension Plan (ORPP)

LAW

The Canada and Quebec pension plans are financed by the governments through a tax on both the employer and the employee. All employers are required to collect the employee's share of this tax. They deduct it from the employee's gross pay and remit it regularly to the government along with the employer's share. Both the employer and the employee are taxed at the same rate (which was 4.95% each in 2015) based on the employee's gross pay up to maximum contributory earnings of $50,100. This maximum amount is determined by subtracting the basic yearly exemption of $3,500 from the maximum amount of pensionable earnings of $53,600. The maximum annual contribution for each of the employee and employer was therefore 4.95% of $50,100, or $2,479.95 in 2015. In 2015, the Ontario government announced a new Ontario Retirement Pension Plan, which would give employees in that province additional benefits beyond the CPP. The ORPP was scheduled to be introduced in 2017, with employee and employer rates capped at 1.9% each.

Employment Insurance

Another payroll tax that the federal government levies on both employees and employers is used for the system of Employment Insurance (EI). Employees must pay a premium of 1.88% (2015) of insurable earnings to an annual maximum contribution of $930.60 while the employer is required to contribute 2.632% or 1.4 times the amount of employee premiums.[16] Insurable earnings are gross wages above a preset minimum and below a maximum amount of $49,500. Both the premium rates and insurable earnings are adjusted periodically.

Income Tax Withholding

Income tax laws require employers to withhold from each employee's pay the approximate amount of income tax that will be due on those wages. The amount of income tax that is withheld is calculated by the employer according to a government-prescribed formula or a government-provided income tax deduction table. The amount depends on the length of the pay period and each employee's wages, marital status, claimed dependants, and other permitted deductions.

Illustration of Payroll Deductions

Assume a weekly payroll of $10,000 that is entirely subject to CPP (4.95%), Employment Insurance (1.88%), income tax withholdings of $1,320, and union dues of $88. The entry to record the salaries and wages paid and the employee payroll deductions is:

A   =   L   +   SE
−7,909   +2,091   −10,000

Cash flows: ↓ 7,909 outflow

Salaries and Wages Expense	10,000	
Employee Income Tax Deductions Payable		1,320
CPP Contributions Payable		495
EI Premiums Payable		188
Union Dues Payable		88
Cash		7,909

The required employer payroll taxes are recognized as compensation-related expenses in the same accounting period as the payroll is recorded. The entry for the required employer contributions (rounded) is as follows:

A   =   L   +   SE
        +758   −758

Cash flows: No effect

Payroll Tax Expense	758	
CPP Contributions Payable ($495 × 1.0)		495
EI Premiums Payable ($188 × 1.4)		263

The employer then sends to the Receiver General for Canada the amount of income tax, CPP, and EI deductions withheld from the employees, along with the employer's required contributions for CPP and EI. The entry to record the payment to the CRA for the payroll described above is:

A   =   L   +   SE
−2,761   −2,761

Cash flows: ↓ 2,761 outflow

Employee Income Tax Deductions Payable	1,320	
CPP Contributions Payable ($495 + $495)	990	
EI Premiums Payable ($188 + $263)	451	
Cash		2,761

Until they are remitted to the government and the union, these amounts are all reported as current liabilities. In a manufacturing enterprise, all payroll costs (wages, payroll taxes, and fringe benefits) are allocated to appropriate cost accounts, such as Direct Labour, Indirect Labour, Sales Salaries, or Administrative Salaries.

This abbreviated and somewhat simplified discussion of payroll costs and deductions does not give a clear sense of the large volume of records and clerical work that is involved in maintaining a sound and accurate payroll system.

UNDERLYING CONCEPT

Accounting for obligations for compensated absences is based on liability definition, recognition, and measurement concepts.

Short-Term Compensated Absences

Compensated absences are periods of time taken off from active employment for which employees are paid, such as statutory holidays and vacation. The entitlement to such benefits is one of two types:

1. accumulating or

2. non-accumulating.

Accumulating Rights to Benefits

LAW

Employers are required under provincial law to give each employee vacation equal to a specified number of days, or to pay them in lieu of the vacation. As a result, employers have an **unconditional obligation** for vacation pay that accrues (or accumulates) as the employees work. This obligation (or liability) is usually satisfied by paying employees their regular salaries when they are absent from work while taking vacation.

Employees may have **vested rights** to some of their benefits that accumulate with service. This means that the employer is legally required to pay the benefits even if the employee no longer works for the organization; thus, vested rights do not depend on an employee's continued service. For example, assume that you have earned 10 days of vacation as at December 31, the end of your employer's fiscal year. Because vacation pay is prescribed by law, your employer will have to pay you for these 10 days even if you resign from your job before taking those days off. In this case, the 10 days of vacation pay is a vested right and the costs are accrued by the company as expense **in the period in which the benefit is earned by the employee**.

Now assume that a company offers its employees an entitlement to vacation days above the legal requirement. Further assume that this entitlement **is not vested**, but that the right to any unused additional vacation can be carried forward to future periods. If you continue to work for the company, you are entitled to the additional unused vacation days, but if you leave the company, you lose the right to them. Although the rights are not vested, they are accumulated rights and the company will have to honour the majority of those benefits that have been earned. **Accumulated rights**, therefore, are rights that accrue with employee service. They are not necessarily vested but can still be carried forward to future periods if they are not used in the period in which they are earned. In accounting for accumulated rights, the employer recognizes an expense and a liability for the cost of these compensated absences as they are earned by employees. However, the estimated cost and obligation take into account the fact that, because of employee turnover, some of these benefits will never be paid.

Entitlement to **sick pay** varies greatly among employers. In some companies, sick pay vests and employees are allowed to accumulate unused sick time. They can take time off from work with pay even though they are not ill, or they will be paid for the unused sick days when they leave the company. In this case, an obligation exists to pay future amounts; therefore, **the liability and expense are accrued** as the employees earn the benefit. We discuss this type of longer-term liability in Chapter 19.

When sick days accumulate with time, but do not vest (that is, they are paid only when an employee is absent due to illness), it may be very difficult to estimate the expense that is associated with the benefits earned by the employees. In estimating the obligation, management takes into account the likelihood that many of the accumulated benefits will never be paid. Usually if the estimate is an immaterial amount, no accrual is made and the entity accounts for such non-vesting sick pay on a pay-as-you-go basis. This means that the expense is recognized in the accounts as the sick days are taken.

What rate should be used to accrue the compensated absence expense and liability: the current rate or an estimated future rate? The **best measure is the additional amount the entity expects to pay in the future** as a result of the benefits accumulated to the reporting date.[17] Many companies use the current rate of pay as the best estimate of the future amount, but other companies use future amounts that are likely to be paid, or that have already been agreed on under collective agreements, for example.

To illustrate, assume the following information for Amutron Limited, which began operations on January 1, 2017.

- The company employs 10 individuals who are paid $880 per week, and this is the best estimate of the following year's wages as well.

- A total of 20 weeks of vacation is earned by all employees in 2017, but none is taken during the year.

- In 2018, the vacation weeks earned in 2017 are used when the current rate of pay has increased to $900 per week.

The entry at December 31, 2017 to accrue the vacation pay entitlement earned by the employees is as follows:

A   =   L   +   SE
        +17,600   −17,600
Cash flows: No effect

Salaries and Wages Expense	17,600	
Vacation Wages Payable ($880 × 20)		17,600

At December 31, 2017, the company reports a current liability of 20 weeks × $880 or $17,600 on its statement of financial position, and an expense of $17,600 for the benefits earned by employees in 2017. In 2018, the vacation time that is paid for (and that was earned in 2017) is recorded as follows:

A   =   L   +   SE
−18,000   −17,600   −400
Cash flows: ↓ 18,000 outflow

Vacation Wages Payable	17,600	
Salaries and Wages Expense	400	
Cash ($900 × 20)		18,000

In 2018, the vacation weeks are used and the liability is eliminated. Note that the difference between the cash paid and the reduction in the liability account is recorded as an adjustment to Wages Expense in the period when it is paid. This difference occurs because the liability account was accrued at the lower rate of $880 per week. The cash paid, however, is based on the rate of pay in effect when the benefit is taken. If the future pay rates had been estimated accurately and used to calculate the accrual in 2017, then the cash paid in 2018 would have been the same as the liability.

Non-Accumulating Rights to Benefits

Non-accumulating compensated absences, on the other hand, are benefits that employees are entitled to by virtue of their employment and the occurrence of an obligating event. The rights to these benefits do not vest and are accounted for differently than those that accumulate with service. A good example is the additional compensation and time off for parental (maternity, paternity, and adoption) leave beyond what the government provides, and some short-term disability benefits. Employees' rights to such benefits do not accrue as they work. The rights accrue only when the requirements of the parental leave or short-term disability plan have been met.[18]

Because the employer has no basis on which to accrue the costs of these benefits and the associated liability, no entry is made until the obligating event occurs. When the parental leave is taken or the employee becomes disabled, the **total** estimated liability and expense associated with the event is recognized at that time. This **event accrual method** of accounting is applied as follows. Assume that Resource Corp. provides a parental leave benefit plan that promises to pay a qualifying employee, for a period of up to one year, an amount equal to the difference between the employee's current salary and the amount paid by Employment Insurance during the leave. Sue Kim, an employee, applies for and is granted a one-year parental leave to begin on April 18. Resource Corp. calculates that the benefit payable to Sue Kim will be $200 per week. The company makes the following entry when she begins her leave on April 18:

A   =   L   +   SE
        +10,400   −10,400
Cash flows: No effect

Employee Benefit Expense	10,400	
Parental Leave Benefits Payable		10,400
($200 × 52 weeks = $10,400)		

As the compensated absence (the parental leave) is taken and Sue Kim is paid, the liability is reduced. Assuming Resource Corp. has a biweekly payroll, the following entry is made each pay period (disregarding other payroll deductions):

A   =   L   +   SE
−400   −400
Cash flows: ↓ 400 outflow

Parental Leave Benefits Payable	400	
Cash		400

The compensated absences discussed in this section of the chapter are all relatively short-term in nature. When the associated obligations will be met within 12 months from the date of the statement of financial position, there is no need to discount the future cash outflows when measuring the outstanding liability.[19]

Profit-Sharing and Bonus Agreements

UNDERLYING CONCEPT

Accounting for bonuses or profit-sharing plans follows underlying concepts. For example, in Japan, traditionally bonuses to members of boards of directors were considered distributions of profits and therefore were charged against retained earnings.

Many companies have a **bonus** or a **profit-sharing** plan for their employees. These plans may be open to all employees or be restricted to those in managerial positions or perhaps only to key company officers. Payments under such plans are in addition to the regular salary or wage and may be a percentage of the employees' regular rates of pay, or they may depend on productivity increases or the amount of the company's annual profit. From the entity's viewpoint, **bonus and profit-sharing payments to employees** are considered additional compensation and are therefore a type of wage or salary expense in determining the net income for the year. Obligations for amounts outstanding are usually reported as current liabilities at the reporting date because they relate to and are based on the results of the period just ended, and are usually payable in the near term.

To illustrate, assume that a company has income before bonuses of $400,000 for 2017. The company has an annual bonus plan and determines in January 2018 that it will pay out bonuses of $40,700 related to the prior year. An adjusting entry dated December 31, 2017 is made to record the bonus as follows:

A = L + SE
    +40,700   −40,700

Cash flows: No effect

| Bonus Expense | 40,700 | |
| Bonus Payable | | 40,700 |

In January 2018, when the bonus is paid, the entry is:

A = L + SE
−40,700   −40,700

Cash flows: ↓ 40,700 outflow

| Bonus Payable | 40,700 | |
| Cash | | 40,700 |

It is important to be careful when calculating bonus and profit-sharing amounts, especially if the formula specifies that the bonus is based on **after-tax** income. Because the additional amount to be paid is itself a tax-deductible expense, simultaneous equations may have to be set up and solved to determine both the expense and tax amounts. Keep in mind that under IFRS, bonus and profit-sharing payments are accrued for constructive obligations where a reasonable estimate of the obligation can be made; that is, where the "entity has no realistic alternative but to make the payments" as a result of past practice (IAS 19.19).

NON-FINANCIAL LIABILITIES

Most liabilities that companies incur can be measured fairly accurately by the amount of cash (or the cash equivalent value of other financial assets) that the company must give up to discharge the obligation. In addition, the timing of the payment is usually clear. However, some liabilities are more difficult to measure because the obligations will be met with goods and services (that is, non-financial resources), and the timing of meeting the obligation and its amount are not fixed. Examples include unearned revenues, product guarantees and warranties, and obligations under customer loyalty programs. Other examples include obligations related to the dismantling and retirement of assets. These are referred to under IFRS as **provisions**: liabilities of uncertain timing or amount.

Even though the exact amount and timing of these obligations may not be known, whenever they involve unconditional obligations that are enforceable and that exist at the date of the statement of financial position, they are liabilities. We start by reviewing two such obligations where there is little or no uncertainty about the existence of the liability, although there may be uncertainty about its measurement.

Decommissioning and Restoration Obligations

Objective 5

Explain the recognition, measurement, and disclosure requirements for decommissioning and restoration obligations.

In many industries, the construction and operation of long-lived assets means taking on obligations associated with the eventual retirement of those assets. For example, when a mining company opens up a strip mine, it likely also makes a commitment to restore the land on which the mine is located once the mining activity is completed. Similarly, when an oil company erects an offshore drilling platform, it may be obligated to dismantle and remove the platform at the end of its useful life. Such obligations occur in a variety of ways. For example, they may arise from acquisition of an asset with an existing asset retirement obligation (such as an oil rig), or they may increase over time through normal operations (such as a mine site that expands over time). Further examples of restorative activities include the following:

LAW

1. Decommissioning nuclear facilities

2. Dismantling, restoring, and reclaiming oil and gas properties

3. Certain closure, reclamation, and removal costs of mining facilities

4. Closure and post-closure costs of landfills

In general, the obligation associated with the retirement of a long-lived asset that results from acquiring, constructing, developing, or operating it must be recognized by the company **in the period when the obligation is incurred.**[20] This liability is known as an **asset retirement obligation (ARO)** or **site restoration obligation.**

While this general principle underlies both the IFRS and ASPE standards, there is a difference in the type of obligation that is recognized and which activities' costs are capitalized as part of the capital asset's cost. A table indicating the differences was presented in Chapter 10, and it is reproduced here as Illustration 13-3.

	IFRS	**ASPE**
Category of obligations	Recognizes costs of **both legal** and **constructive obligations**, such as when an entity creates an expectation in others, through its own actions, that it will meet this obligation.	Recognizes costs associated with **legal obligations** only.
Category of activities	Costs included as capital assets are only those related to the acquisition of the asset, not those related to the subsequent production of goods or services (product costs).	Costs included as capital assets are both ARO-related costs resulting from the acquisition of the asset and its subsequent use in producing inventory, such as coal.

The first difference relates to the fact that IFRS recognizes a broader group of non-financial obligations as liabilities: both legal and constructive obligations. The position on the second difference is consistent with the concept that costs incurred in the production of goods and services are inventory or product costs. ASPE recognizes all such costs as part of the capital asset. Because the costs capitalized to property, plant, and equipment under ASPE are often amortized subsequently as product costs, this GAAP difference may not have a significant effect on financial results.

Measurement

The liability is initially measured at "the best estimate of the expenditure required to settle the present obligation" at the reporting date.[21] Under the proposed revisions to the international standard set out in the 2015 Exposure Draft, *Conceptual Framework for Financial Reporting*, a liability is defined as a present obligation to transfer an economic resource as a result of past events. Because the obligation will often be met many years in the future, discounting the future costs is one requirement in determining the present amount required. Significant application guidance is provided on how this measurement should be approached.

Recognition and Allocation

As explained in Chapter 10, the estimated ARO costs associated with the asset's acquisition are added to the carrying amount of the related asset and a liability is recognized for the same amount. An asset retirement cost is recorded as part of the cost of the related asset because it is considered necessary in order to acquire and operate the asset, and to receive its economic benefits. Because no future economic benefit is associated with capitalized asset retirement costs as a stand-alone asset, these costs are not recorded separately from the asset account.

Later, the ARO cost is amortized to expense over the related asset's useful life. While the straight-line method is acceptable, other systematic and rational allocations are also allowed. As the expected retirement obligation and costs increase due to further damage to the site from production activities, ASPE adds these both to the recognized liability and to the capital asset account, increasing the future depreciation amount. Under IFRS, the obligation amount is increased; however, the incremental costs caused by production are added to inventory as production overhead costs.

Note that environmental cleanup costs that are required after such events as a major oil spill or accidental runoff of chemicals into a water table **do not result in an asset retirement obligation and addition to the cost base** of the underlying asset. These catastrophes do not result in future benefits, and therefore do not justify an increase in the asset's cost.

Illustration of Accounting for Initial Recognition

To illustrate the accounting for the obligation, assume that on January 1, 2017, Wildcat Oil Corp. erects an oil platform off the Newfoundland coast. Wildcat is legally required to dismantle and remove the platform at the end of its five-year useful life. The total cost of dismantling and removal is estimated to be $1 million. Based on a 10% discount rate, the present value of the asset retirement obligation is $620,920 ($1,000,000 × 0.62092). Wildcat makes the following entry to recognize this liability under both ASPE and IFRS:

A = L + SE
+620,920 +620,920
Cash flows: No effect

| Jan. 1, 2017 | Drilling Platform | 620,920 | |
| | Asset Retirement Obligation | | 620,920 |

If only 80% of the $1-million estimate is caused by the asset acquisition itself, with the other 20% caused by the use of the platform in production, only 80% of the $620,920 is recognized at January 1, 2017. This is the only part that is a present obligation at that date. As the platform is used and the retirement costs increase due to production, the present value of the estimated increase in the obligation is added to the production overhead costs (IFRS) or to the Drilling Platform asset (ASPE). To keep our example relatively simple, let's assume that 80% of the $1-million estimate is caused by acquisition of the asset and the remaining 20% relates to production in the first year that the asset is used. Wildcat would initially recognize 80% of this liability under both ASPE and IFRS:

A = L + SE
+496,736 +496,736
Cash flows: No effect

| Jan. 1, 2017 | Drilling Platform | 496,736 | |
| | Asset Retirement Obligation | | 496,736 |

Over the asset's life, the retirement cost is depreciated. Using the straight-line method, Wildcat makes the following entry in 2017 and similar entries in 2018, 2019, 2020, and 2021 to record this expense:

A   =   L   +   SE
−99,347   −99,347

Cash flows: No effect

| Dec. 31, 2017 | Depreciation Expense ($496,736 ÷ 5) | 99,347 | |
| | Accumulated Depreciation—Drilling Platform | | 99,347 |

In addition, because the liability is measured on a discounted basis, interest on the liability is accrued each period. An entry is made at December 31, 2017 to record the expense and the related increase or **accretion** in the liability's carrying amount. Under IFRS, the interest adjustment to the liability account **due to the passage of time** is recognized as a borrowing cost. Under ASPE, it is recognized as an operating expense on the income statement—accretion expense—but not as interest or a borrowing cost. Illustration 13-4A shows the difference in treatment between ASPE and IFRS.

Illustration 13-4A

Accretion/Interest Expense on ARO

A   =   L   +   SE
       +49,674   −49,674

Cash flows: No effect

IFRS		ASPE	
Dec. 31, 2017		Dec. 31, 2017	
Interest Expense	49,674	Accretion Expense	49,674
Asset Retirement Obligation	49,674	Asset Retirement Obligation	49,674
($496,736 × 10%)		($496,736 × 10%)	

On December 31, 2017, Wildcat estimates that the increase in the ARO in 2017 incurred related to the production of oil in 2017 was $136,602. Under ASPE, the increase in cost would be added to the cost of the drilling platform. Under IFRS, the added cost would be charged to production (that is, inventory, assuming the oil was not yet sold). The related journal entries are shown in Illustration 13-4B.

Illustration 13-4B

Accounting for Increases in ARO Relating to Production

A   =   L   +   SE
+136,602   +136,602

Cash flows: No effect

IFRS		ASPE	
Dec. 31, 2017		Dec. 31, 2017	
Inventory	136,602	Drilling Platform	136,602
Asset Retirement Obligation	136,602	Asset Retirement Obligation	136,602

In 2018 and subsequent years, under ASPE, the depreciation expense for the drilling platform would be increased to reflect the additional amount capitalized on December 31, 2017. Under IFRS, cost of goods sold would be increased as the inventory is sold. As mentioned above, because the drilling costs capitalized to property, plant, and equipment under ASPE are often amortized subsequently as product costs, this ASPE/IFRS difference may not have a significant effect on financial results.

On January 10, 2022, Wildcat pays Rig Reclaimers, Inc. for dismantling the platform at the contract price of $995,000. Wildcat then makes the following entry to record the settlement of the liability:

A   =   L   +   SE
−995,000   −1,000,000   +5,000

Cash flows: ↓ 995,000 outflow

Jan. 10, 2022	Asset Retirement Obligation	1,000,000*	
	Gain on Settlement of ARO		5,000
	Cash		995,000

*ARO on Dec. 31, 2017 = (496,736 × 1.10) + 136,602 = 683,012. Taking into account the time value of money, this would increase as follows (to December 31, 2021): 683,012 × 1.1 × 1.1 × 1.1 × 1.1 = 683,012 × (1.1)^4 = 1,000,000 (rounded).

Subsequent Recognition and Measurement of AROs: Summary

To summarize, under ASPE, the expense for the interest element (accretion) is calculated first. This is followed by an adjustment to the carrying amount of the Asset Retirement Obligation account for any increase or decrease in the cost estimates. This adjustment is also made to the carrying amount of the long-lived asset to which it relates and, of course, to the amount of annual depreciation.[22] IFRIC 1 indicates that IFRS is applied in a similar way, except that the change in obligation due to production would be inventoried instead of added to the capital asset's cost.

Unearned Revenues

Objective 6
Explain the issues and account for unearned revenues.

REAL WORLD EMPHASIS

When a company receives cash or other assets in advance for specific goods or services to be delivered or performed in the future, the entity recognizes the obligation as a liability. For example, a magazine publisher such as **Rogers Media Inc.** receives payments from customers when subscriptions to magazines such as *Maclean's* are ordered, and an airline such as **Air Canada** usually sells tickets in advance for flights. For their part, retail stores increasingly issue gift certificates that can be redeemed for merchandise. In all these situations, the assets received in advance require the entity to perform in the future. This obligation is a liability that is generally referred to as **unearned revenue**. The company's liability is measured at the fair value of the outstanding obligation and this revenue is then recognized as the goods are delivered or the services are provided.

To illustrate, assume that the Rambeau Football Club sells 5,000 season tickets at $50 each for its five-game home schedule. The entry for the sale of the season tickets is:

A = L + SE
+250,000 +250,000
Cash flows: ↑ 250,000 inflow

| Cash | 250,000 | |
| Unearned Revenue | | 250,000 |

As each game is completed, the following entry is made to recognize the revenue earned:

A = L + SE
−50,000 +50,000
Cash flows: No effect

| Unearned Revenue | 50,000 | |
| Revenue | | 50,000 |

The balance in the Unearned Revenue account is reported as a current liability in the statement of financial position. As the Rambeau Football Club plays each game, part of the obligation is met, revenue is earned, and a transfer is made from Unearned Revenue to a revenue account on the income statement. The costs associated with that revenue are deducted as expenses in the same period to determine the period's net income.

Unearned revenue is material for some companies. In the airline industry, for example, tickets sold for future flights represent a significant portion of total current liabilities. **WestJet**'s advance ticket sales represented 43.0% of its current liabilities at December 31, 2014, up from 39.2% at December 31, 2013. At the same dates, Air Canada reported advance ticket sales equal to 50.7% and 52.9% of current liabilities, respectively. The following table shows specific unearned revenue (statement of financial position) accounts and earned revenue (income statement) accounts that might be used in different industries.

REAL WORLD EMPHASIS

Alternative Terminology
Unearned Revenue and Earned Revenue account names often vary by industry.

| | Account Title | |
Industry Type	Unearned Revenue	Earned Revenue
Airline	Advance Ticket Sales	Passenger Revenue
Magazine publisher	Deferred Subscription Revenue	Subscription Revenue
Hotel	Advance Room Deposits	Room Revenue
Equipment maintenance	Unearned Maintenance Contract Fees	Maintenance Contract Revenue

Objective 7
Explain the issues and account for product guarantees and other customer program obligations.

Product Guarantees and Customer Programs

Businesses often offer continuing care or other customer programs that require them to provide goods and services after they have delivered the initial product or service. This is an area where the accounting for the entity's continuing obligations has been evolving. Historically, an expense approach has been used to account for the outstanding liability, and this type of approach is still used for assurance-type warranties, as initially discussed in Chapter 6. More recent standards have moved to a revenue approach for warranties that are not included in the sales price of the product (that is, for service-type warranties). Let us start with an overview of warranties and then see how the two approaches are applied in specific situations.

Product Guarantees and Warranty Obligations

A **warranty** (product guarantee) is a promise made by a seller to a buyer to correct problems experienced with a product's quantity, quality, or performance. Warranties are commonly used by manufacturers to promote sales. Automakers such as Tesla in our feature story, for example, may attract additional business by extending the length of their new-car warranty. For a specified period of time following the date of sale to the consumer, a manufacturer may promise to be responsible for all or part of the cost of replacing defective parts, to perform any necessary repairs or servicing without charge, to refund the purchase price, or even to double your money back. Warranties and product guarantees are **stand-ready obligations** at the reporting date that result in future costs that are often significant.

Accounting for warranties is in a state of transition. In the past and still applied in some circumstances, as a holdover from times when the matching principle predominated, the expense approach was widely used. Increasingly today, the asset and liability view and faithful representation drive the accounting model, resulting in the **bifurcation** or separation of the proceeds received into two or more revenue amounts for the various deliverables promised.

Assurance-Type Warranty

Under IFRS 15, when the warranty is part of the sales price, the outstanding liability is measured at the cost of the economic resources needed to meet the obligation. This **assurance-type warranty** (expense-based approach) assumes that, along with the liability that is required to be recognized at the reporting date, the associated expense needs to be measured and matched with the revenues of the period. In fact, the need to match expenses has driven this approach over the years. As the actual costs are incurred in subsequent periods, the liability is reduced. This type of approach has historically been used under ASPE.

Service-Type Warranty

SIGNIFICANT
CHANGE

Under IFRS 15, when the warranty is sold as an additional service beyond the assurance-type warranty, the outstanding liability is measured at the value of the obligation. It is an output price rather than an input price or cost measure. This is the situation when assets are received in advance for a variety of performance obligations to be delivered in the future. Under a **service-type warranty** (revenue-based approach), the proceeds received for any goods or services yet to be delivered or performed are unearned at the point of sale. Until the revenue is earned, the obligation—the unearned revenue—is reported at its sales or fair value. The liability is then reduced as the revenue is earned. Revenue recognition concerns are at the base of this approach. This parallels the contract-based approach to revenue recognition explained in Chapter 6 where the liability represents a performance obligation for insurance type warranties that are sold separately. Revenue is recognized when the service is provided and the performance obligation is satisfied. Under ASPE, this approach has been used increasingly with bundled sales to bifurcate them (or separate them).

There are two major differences between the two approaches:

1. Under the expense approach for assurance-type warranties, the liability is **measured at the estimated cost** of meeting the obligation. Under the revenue approach for service-type warranties, the liability recognized is **measured at the value of the service** to be provided, not at its cost.

2. Under the expense approach, and assuming the estimate of the cost of the obligation to be met in the future is close to the actual future cost, there is **no effect on future income**.[23] Under the revenue approach, **future income is affected**. Some amount of unearned revenue is recognized as a liability, and this is recognized as revenue in future

periods when it is earned or the performance obligation is met. Any expenses associated with that revenue are also recognized in the future. Therefore, **future income amounts are affected** by the profit or loss earned on the delivery of the goods or services provided in subsequent periods.

Two examples are provided to illustrate how these approaches are applied.

Assurance-Type Warranty Illustrated

In this situation, the warranty is **provided with** an associated product or service, with no additional fee being charged for it. All of the revenue from the sale of the product or service is considered earned on delivery of the product or service, but matching requires that all costs associated with that revenue be recognized as an expense in the same accounting period as the sale. Therefore, the future costs to be incurred to make good on the outstanding warranty are estimated and recognized in the same period as the sale, along with the associated obligation (liability) to provide the warranty service in the future. As the actual costs are incurred in subsequent periods, the warranty liability is reduced.

Assume that Denson Corporation begins production of a new machine in July 2017 and sells 100 units for $5,000 each by its year end, December 31, 2017. Denson provides a one-year warranty promising to fix any inherent manufacturing problems. The company has estimated, from experience with a similar machine, that the warranty cost will average $200 per unit. Under IFRS, the estimate is measured using a probability-weighted expected value, while ASPE will probably use the value of the most likely estimate.[24] Denson incurs $4,000 in actual warranty costs in 2017 to replace parts on machines that were sold before December 31, 2017. It estimates further costs of $16,000 in 2018. Illustration 13-5 shows how the expense approach recognizes these events.

Illustration 13-5
Assurance-Type Warranty and Warranty Liability Entries

Sale of 100 machines at $5,000 each, July to December 2017:

Accounts Receivable	500,000	
Sales Revenue		500,000

Actual warranty costs incurred, July to December 2017:

Warranty Expense	4,000	
Materials, Cash, Payables, etc.		4,000

Year-end adjusting entry to accrue outstanding warranty obligations at December 31, 2017:

Warranty Expense	16,000	
Warranty Liability		16,000

December 31, 2017 financial statement amounts reported:

Income Statement	
Sales Revenue	$500,000
Warranty Expense	$20,000
Statement of Financial Position	
Warranty Liability	$16,000

Actual warranty costs incurred, 2018:

Warranty Expense	16,000	
Materials, Cash, Payables, etc.		16,000

Adjusting entry, December 31, 2018, to adjust liability account to correct balance of $0:

Warranty Liability	16,000	
Warranty Expense		16,000

(continued)

Illustration 13-5

Assurance-Type Warranty and Warranty Liability Entries (continued)

December 31, 2018 financial statement amounts reported:	
Income Statement	
Sales Revenue	$0
Warranty Expense	$0
Statement of Financial Position	
Warranty Liability	$0

The entries illustrate the fact that the actual warranty costs are initially charged to expense as they are incurred. At the end of the accounting period, the remaining estimated expense associated with the 2017 sales is recognized and the liability account is adjusted for the same amount. At December 31, 2017, the liability was increased to $16,000 as this additional expense was recognized, and at December 31, 2018, it was adjusted to the correct balance at that time of $0, because the warranty period had expired for the machines sold in 2017.

In situations where the warranty costs are very immaterial or when the warranty period is relatively short, the product guarantee is sometimes accounted for on a cash basis. Under the **cash basis**, warranty costs are charged to expense as incurred; that is, they are recognized in expense **in the period when the seller or manufacturer honours the warranty**. No liability is recognized for future costs arising from warranties, and the expense is not necessarily recognized in the period of the related sale. If the cash basis is applied to the facts in the Denson example, $4,000 is recorded as warranty expense in 2017 and $16,000 as warranty expense in 2018, with the total sales being recorded as revenue in 2017. This method is used for income tax purposes, but not generally for financial reporting.

UNDERLYING CONCEPT

Using the cash method when the costs are immaterial or the warranty period is short is an application of the materiality concept.

Service-Type Warranty Illustrated

Under the revenue approach used for service-type warranties, the warranty service is considered to be a separate deliverable from the underlying product or service sold. It is either sold as a **separate** service or (in addition to being sold separately) the warranty is sold as part of a **bundle** with the associated goods. In the latter case, the amount of revenue attributable to the warranty has to be broken out and recognized separately. Under this method, the proceeds received for (or allocated to) the separate service to maintain the product in good order are unearned at the point of sale. The revenue is earned as the warranty service is provided.

To illustrate, assume that Hamlin Corp. sells an equipment/warranty package for $20,000 on January 2, 2017. Included in the equipment package is a warranty agreement for two years, during which time Hamlin agrees to repair and maintain the equipment. Warranty agreements similar to this are available separately and are estimated to have a stand-alone value of $1,200. Therefore, Hamlin allocates $1,200 of the proceeds of the bundled sale to the warranty contract. The entry to record the sale on January 2, 2017 is:

```
A    =    L    +   SE
+20,000  +1,200  +18,800
Cash flows: ↑ 20,000 inflow
```

Cash	20,000	
Sales Revenue		18,800
Unearned Warranty Revenue		1,200

This approach recognizes revenue as Hamlin performs under the warranty contract. Assuming the revenue is earned evenly over the two-year contract term, the entry to remeasure the Unearned Warranty Revenue account to its correct balance at December 31, 2017 is as follows:

```
A    =    L    +   SE
         -600      +600
Cash flows: No effect
```

Unearned Warranty Revenue	600	
Warranty Revenue		600

If costs of $423 were incurred in 2017 as a result of servicing this contract, Hamlin's entry is:

A = L + SE
−423   −423

Cash flows: ↓ by cash paid

Warranty Expense	423	
Materials, Cash, Payables, etc.		423

In 2018, the remainder of the unearned warranty revenue is recognized and any warranty costs incurred under the contract are recognized in 2018 expense. If the costs of performing services under the extended warranty contract are not expected to be incurred in a straight-line pattern (as historical evidence might indicate), revenue is recognized over the contract period in the same pattern as the costs are expected to be incurred. In addition, if the costs of providing services under the contract are expected to be more than the remaining unearned revenue (in other words, it is an **onerous contract**), a loss and related liability are recognized for any expected shortfall.

Which approach is considered GAAP? IFRS 15 is clear about when the expense approach should be used (for assurance-type warranties) and when the revenue approach should be used (service-type warranties). Similarly, under ASPE the principle is that revenue that covers a variety of deliverables (bundled sales) should be unbundled and the revenue allocated to the various goods or services that are required to be performed. This method has been used increasingly over the past few years, while the expense approach tends to be used when the warranty is not a separate choice for the purchaser, but is included as part of the sales price.

Customer Loyalty Programs

Customer **loyalty programs**, such as those offered by Hilton, Hudson's Bay, and Shoppers Drug Mart, are very popular, with all of them promising future benefits to the customer in exchange for current sales. Canadians' participation in such loyalty programs is high, with the average Canadian household being members of more than eight loyalty programs.[25] Other programs that have been adopted widely include the frequent flyer programs that are used by all major airlines. On the basis of mileage or the number of trips accumulated, frequent flyer members are awarded discounted or free airline tickets. Airline customers can earn points or "miles" toward free travel by making long-distance phone calls, staying in hotels, and charging items such as groceries and gasoline on a related credit card.

How should companies account for such programs? Standard setters now interpret programs where customer loyalty credits are awarded to be revenue arrangements with multiple deliverables. IFRS initially addressed this via IFRIC Interpretation 13 *Customer Loyalty Programmes*, which is being superseded by IFRS 15. The revenue from the original transaction should be allocated between the award credits and the other components of the sale. The fair value of the award credits is recognized as unearned revenue, a liability. This is later recognized in revenue when the credits are exchanged for the promised awards. ASPE does not explicitly address the issue of accounting for loyalty programs; however, it does reflect the general principle that the revenue recognition criteria should be applied "to the separately identifiable components of a single transaction in order to reflect the substance of the transaction."[26]

REAL WORLD EMPHASIS

VIA Rail Canada Inc. has a wide variety of deferred revenue items, including gift cards, advance ticket sales, and its VIA Préférence customer loyalty program, in which members earn award points as they travel on trains. Members can then exchange a certain number of award points for free train travel. The company notes in its financial statements that it takes into account the probability of awards being converted into tickets when determining the fair value of award points. Illustration 13-6 presents VIA's deferred revenue note disclosure showing that total deferred revenue under IFRS increased by $3.7 million (12%) in 2014.

Illustration 13-6

Note Disclosure of Deferred Revenue—VIA Rail Canada Inc.

Note 17. Deferred Revenue

Deferred revenue is comprised of the following:

(In millions of dollars)	2014	2013
Advanced ticket sales	**12.8**	11.1
Gift cards	**3.0**	2.7
Non-monetary transactions	**2.7**	2.3
VIA Préférence[1]	**16.0**	14.0
Other	**–**	0.7
Total deferred revenue	**34.5**	30.8

[1] The deferred revenue related to the loyalty program points is measured at fair value on a recurring basis and is evaluated based on train ticket price (level 2 of fair value hierarchy i.e. on significant input other than quoted prices included in active markets that are observable for asset or liability, either directly or indirectly).

Premiums and Rebates

Many companies offer premiums or other benefits to customers in return for box tops, coupons, labels, wrappers, or other evidence of having purchased a particular product. The **premiums** may be such items as silverware, dishes, small appliances, toys, or cash values against future purchases.

UNDERLYING CONCEPT

Similar to warranties, obligations for most premiums and coupons meet the definition of a liability. Under ASPE the liability is the Estimated Liability for Premiums, while under IFRS the liability is for the separate performance obligation represented by Unearned Revenue.

Printed coupons that can be redeemed for a cash discount on items purchased are extremely popular marketing tools, as is the cash rebate, which the buyer can obtain by returning the store receipt, a rebate coupon, and the Universal Product Code (UPC label or bar code) to the manufacturer. **Contests** have also been widely used to get consumers' attention and their sales dollars, with the **Tim Hortons** "Roll up the Rim to Win" promotion being one of the most successful contests in Canadian history. A wide variety of prizes are offered, including automobiles, vacations, major sporting events tickets, and free coffee!

With the life of many contests running a few months and the average coupon being valid for approximately six months, many companies have the practical problem of accounting for these marketing costs, because they often affect more than one fiscal period. Historically, such programs have been accounted for under the expense approach. The accounting issue is that, while these promotions **increase current sales revenue**, the associated costs are often incurred **in future periods**. The matching concept requires companies to deduct the total estimated costs against the current period's revenue and the cost is charged to an expense account such as Premium or Promotion Expense. In addition, the obligations existing at the date of the statement of financial position must also be recognized and reported in a liability account such as Estimated Liability for Premiums or Estimated Liability for Coupons Outstanding.

The following hypothetical example illustrates alternate accounting treatments commonly used for premium offers. In 2017, Fluffy Cakemix Corporation offers its customers a large non-breakable mixing bowl in exchange for $1.00 and 10 box tops. The mixing bowl costs Fluffy Cakemix Corporation $2.30, and the company estimates that 60% of the box tops will be redeemed. Illustration 13-7 shows journal entries to account for the premium offer.

Illustration 13-7

Premium Offers—ASPE vs. IFRS

A = L + SE
0

Cash flows: ↓ 46,000 outflow

1. Purchase of 20,000 mixing bowls at $2.30 each:

Inventory of Premiums	46,000	
Cash		46,000

2. Sales of 300,000 boxes of cake mix at $2.10. We consider two alternative scenarios below: (a) Fluffy Cakemix is a small Canadian company following ASPE and prefers to use the expense approach, and (b) Fluffy Cakemix is a public company following IFRS and prefers the revenue approach. Assume that 5% of the amount received from customers for cake mix relates to the separate performance obligation relating to the premiums to be awarded.

(continued)

ASPE—Expense Approach		IFRS—Revenue Approach	
Cash	630,000	Cash	630,000
Sales Revenue	630,000	Sales Revenue	598,500
		Unearned Revenue	31,500

Illustration 13-7

Premium Offers—ASPE vs.
IFRS (continued)

ASPE
A = L + SE
+630,000   +630,000

IFRS
A = L + SE
+630,000 +31,500 +598,500

Cash flows: ↑ 630,000 inflow

3. Redemption of 60,000 box tops, receiving $1.00 with every 10 box tops, and the delivery of 6,000 mixing bowls (60,000 ÷ 10). (Note: this represents one third of the total of the premiums expected to be awarded. See part 4 below for the calculation.)

ASPE—Expense Approach			IFRS—Revenue Approach		
Cash	6,000		Cash	6,000	
[(60,000 ÷ 10) × $1.00]			[(60,000 ÷ 10) × $1.00]		
Premium Expense	7,800		Premium Expense	7,800	
Inventory of Premiums (60,000/10) × 2.30 = $13,800		13,800	Inventory of Premiums (60,000/10) × $2.30 = $13,800		13,800
			Unearned Revenue ($31,500 × 1/3) = $10,500	10,500	
			Sales Revenue		10,500

ASPE
A = L + SE
−7,800   −7,800

IFRS
A = L + SE
−7,800 −10,500 +2,700

Cash flows: ↑ 6,000 inflow

4. Under ASPE, assuming Fluffy Cakemix uses the expense approach, it would also require the following adjusting entry to recognize the remaining expense and estimated liability for outstanding premiums at the end of the period. This journal entry would not be required under IFRS under the revenue approach.

	ASPE—Expense Approach	IFRS—Revenue Approach
Premium Expense	15,600	
Estimated Liability for Premiums	15,600	N/A
Calculation:		
Total boxes sold in 2017	300,000	
Total estimated redemptions (60%)	180,000	
Box tops redeemed in 2017	60,000	
Estimated future redemptions	120,000	
Cost per premium: $2.30 − $1.00 =	$1.30	
Cost of estimated claims outstanding: (120,000 ÷ 10) × $1.30 =	$15,600	

ASPE
A = L + SE
  +15,600 −15,600

Cash flows: No effect

Under the expense approach, the December 31, 2017 statement of financial position of Fluffy Cakemix Corporation reports an inventory of premium mixing bowls of $32,200 as a current asset and an estimated liability for premiums of $15,600 as a current liability. The 2017 income statement reports a $23,400 premium expense among the selling expenses. Under the revenue approach, the December 31, 2017 statement of financial position of Fluffy Cakemix Corporation reports an inventory of premium mixing bowls of $32,200 as a current asset and an estimated liability for unearned sales revenue of $21,000 as a current liability. The 2017 income statement reports a $7,800 premium expense among the selling expenses and sales revenue related to the premiums of $10,500.

If the costs associated with premiums and rebates are really **marketing expenses**, the expense approach applied in the illustration is a reasonable way to account for them. On the other hand, IFRS 15 (and previously IAS 18.13 and IFRIC 13) suggest that it may be more appropriate to use the revenue approach, and allocate some of the consideration received from the sales transaction to unearned revenue for the performance obligation associated with the premium or rebate.

Contingencies, Uncertain Commitments, and Requirements for Guarantees and Other Commitments

Contingencies and Uncertain Commitments

Objective 8

Explain and account for contingencies and uncertain commitments, and identify the accounting and reporting requirements for guarantees and commitments.

REAL WORLD EMPHASIS

Companies are often involved in situations where it is uncertain whether an obligation to transfer cash or other assets actually exists at the statement of financial position date or what amount will be required to settle the obligation. For example, **BlackBerry Limited** provided information about litigation and legal proceedings in the Management Discussion and Analysis (MD&A) section of its annual report and further discussion in the notes to its financial statements for its year ended February 28, 2015. BlackBerry follows U.S. GAAP, which has rules similar to the ASPE requirements below. The litigation mostly involved alleged patent infringements and class action lawsuits. BlackBerry noted that there were no claims where the potential loss was both probable to result and reasonably estimable; therefore, it made no accruals. **Thomson Reuters Corporation** also discussed lawsuits and legal claims in notes to its December 31, 2014 financial statements, including matters such as property infringement claims, employment-related items, and commercial matters. In addition, the company stated that the outcome of the proceedings was subject to future resolution and the uncertainties of litigation. The company stated that, when the claims are resolved, they are not expected to have a material adverse effect.

Broadly speaking, these situations are referred to as contingencies. A **contingency** is "an existing condition or situation involving uncertainty as to possible gain or loss to an enterprise that will ultimately be resolved when one or more future events occur or fail to occur. Resolution of the uncertainty may confirm the acquisition of an asset or the reduction of a liability."[27] As indicated in Chapter 5, **gain contingencies** and **contingent assets** are not recorded in the accounts, so our discussion is limited to uncertainty and the recognition of liabilities. How the uncertainty is dealt with currently in accounting is explained below for both ASPE and IFRS. Another approach that reflects the ongoing thinking about contingencies and provisions under IFRS, based on an IAS 37 Exposure Draft, is described briefly in the Looking Ahead section of the chapter.

Under current ASPE, the term **contingent liability** includes the **whole population** of existing or possible obligations that depend on the occurrence of one or more future events to confirm either their existence or the amount payable, or both. As we'll see below, some of these contingent liabilities are recognized in the accounts, some require only note disclosure, and others are not referred to at all in the financial statements. In contrast, under IFRS, the term "contingent liability" is used **only** for those existing or possible obligations that are **not** recognized.

The approach taken by current standards to deal with whether a liability should be recognized when there is a contingency is to determine the probability of a future event occurring (or not occurring) that would establish whether the outcome is a loss. How likely it is that a future event will confirm the incurrence of a loss and a liability can range from highly probable to remote or unknown.

Under ASPE, the following range is used:

Term	Interpretation
Likely	High
Unlikely	Slight
Not determinable	Cannot be determined

A contingent loss is recognized in income and as a liability **only if both the following conditions** are met:[28]

ASPE

1. It is **likely** that a future event will confirm that an asset has been impaired or a liability has been incurred at the date of the financial statements.

2. The loss amount can be **reasonably estimated**.

Aside from the "likely" probability, the first condition requires that the liability relate to events that occurred on or before the date of the statement of financial position. The second criterion indicates that it has to be possible to make a reasonable and reliable estimate of the liability; otherwise, it cannot be accrued as a liability. The evidence that is used to estimate the liability may be the company's own experience, the experience of other companies in the industry, engineering or research studies, legal advice, or educated guesses by personnel who are in the best position to know. Often, **a range of possible amounts** may be determined. If a specific amount within the range is a better estimate than others, this is the amount that is accrued. If no particular amount is better than another, the bottom of the range is recognized, and the amount of the remaining exposure to possible loss is disclosed in the notes.

When the liability recognition criteria are not met because a reasonable estimate of the loss amount cannot be determined, or the likelihood of a confirming future event cannot be determined, or when the entity is exposed to loss above the amount accrued, additional information is disclosed in the notes to the statements. Information is disclosed about:

1. the nature of the contingency,

2. the estimated amount of the contingent loss or a statement that an estimate cannot be made, and

3. the extent of exposure to losses in excess of the amount that has been recognized.

Under current IFRS requirements, provisions are required for situations such as lawsuits where it is more likely than not that a present obligation exists. Because it is more likely than not that the company will lose, these are considered liabilities (not "contingent liabilities") under IFRS. Provisions are not required for contingent liabilities under IFRS because these are defined as "possible obligations" whose existence will only be confirmed by uncertain future events that may or may not occur. So, for example, for a lawsuit where it is not probable that an outflow of resources will be required to settle an obligation, the obligation would be considered a contingent liability. To summarize, the recognition criterion used to determine if a provision should be recognized is based on whether it is **"probable"** that there will be an outflow of resources. Probable is interpreted to mean "more likely than not." This is a somewhat lower hurdle than the "likely" required under ASPE. If the amount cannot be measured reliably, the item would be considered a contingent liability and no liability is recognized under IFRS either; however, the standard indicates that it is only in very rare circumstances that this would be the case.

If recognized, IAS 37 requires the best estimate and an "expected value" method to be used to measure the liability. This approach assigns weights to the possible outcomes according to their associated probabilities if a range of possible amounts is available. Unless the likelihood of needing future resources to settle a contingent liability is **remote**, disclosures are required about the nature of these uncertain amounts and, if practicable:

1. an estimate of the financial effect,

2. information about the uncertainties related to the amount or timing of any outflows, and

3. whether any reimbursements are possible.

As you might expect, using the terms "likely" or "probable" to determine the accounting for contingencies and provisions involves considerable judgement and subjectivity. So does the requirement that the amounts be "reliably measurable." Practising accountants often express concern over the variety of interpretations of these terms. Current accounting practice for these situations relies heavily on the exact language that is used in responses from lawyers. However, the language of lawyers may be necessarily biased and protective rather than predictive of the outcome. As a result, the recognition of losses and liabilities varies considerably in practice. There is agreement, however, that general risks that are inherent in business operations, such as the possibility of war, strike, uninsurable catastrophes, or an economic recession, are not accounting "contingencies" and are neither recognized nor reported in the financial statements.

The table below identifies some common examples of potential losses and how they are generally accounted for now.

	Not Accrued	May Be Accrued[a]
Loss Related to		
1. Risk of damage of enterprise property by fire, explosion, or other hazards	X	
2. General or unspecified business risks	X	
3. Risk of damage from catastrophes assumed by property and casualty insurance companies including reinsurance companies	X	
4. Threat of expropriation of assets		X
5. Pending or threatened litigation		X
6. Actual or possible claims and assessments		X
7. Guarantees of indebtedness of others[b]		X
8. Agreements to repurchase receivables (or the related property) that have been sold		X

[a] Will be accrued when all recognition criteria are met regarding likelihood and measurability.
[b] See chapter section on Financial Guarantees.

The most common types of loss contingencies and provisions have to do with litigation, claims by others, and assessments.[29] To recognize a loss and a liability in the accounts, **the cause for litigation must have occurred on or before the date of the financial statements**. It does not matter if the company did not become aware of the existence or possibility of the lawsuit or claims until after the date of the financial statements.

To evaluate the **likelihood of an unfavourable outcome**, management considers the nature of the litigation, the progress of the case, the opinion of legal counsel, the experience of the company and others in similar cases, and any company response to the lawsuit.[30] **Estimating the amount of loss** from pending litigation, however, can rarely be done with any certainty. And, even if the evidence that is available at the date of the statement of financial position does not favour the defendant, it is not reasonable to expect the company to publish in its financial statements a dollar estimate of the likely negative outcome. Such specific disclosures could weaken the company's position in the dispute and encourage the plaintiff to step up its efforts for more compensation. There is a fine line between a shareholder's right to know about potential losses and information that could hurt the company's interests.

REAL WORLD EMPHASIS

Note 38 of the December 31, 2014 year-end financial statements of **adidas AG**, shown in Illustration 13-8, provides an example of disclosures related to contingencies.

Illustration 13-8

Note Disclosure of Contingencies and Commitments—adidas AG

Note 38. Commitments and contingencies (extracts):
Other financial commitments
The Group has other financial commitments for promotion and advertising contracts, which mature as follows:
Financial commitments for promotion and advertising (€ in millions)

	Dec. 31, 2014	Dec. 31, 2013
Within 1 year	836	724
Between 1 and 5 years	2,590	2,054
After 5 years	1,766	1,013
Total	5,193*	3,791

Commitments with respect to advertising and promotion maturing after five years have remaining terms of up to 16 years from December 31, 2014.

(continued)

Illustration 13-8

*Note Disclosure of
Contingencies and
Commitments—adidas AG
(continued)*

Commitments for promotion and advertising contracts increased by €1.4 billion compared to December 31, 2013 due to the conclusion of new contracts and the prolongation of existing partnerships. The increase mainly resulted from the long-term promotion contract concluded with Manchester United F.C.

Litigation and other legal risks

The Group is currently engaged in various lawsuits resulting from the normal course of business, mainly in connection with distribution agreements as well as intellectual property rights. The risks regarding these lawsuits are covered by provisions when a reliable estimate of the amount of the obligation can be made. In the opinion of Management, the ultimate liabilities resulting from such claims will not materially affect the assets, liabilities, financial position and profit or loss of the Group.

*as rounded in the original annual report

Financial Guarantees

Closely related to the topic of contingencies are the requirements for companies to account for and provide information about a variety of types of **financial guarantees** that they have provided. One of the most common types is a financial guarantee contract. In this situation, one party (the guarantor) contracts to reimburse a second party for a loss incurred if a third party (the debtor) does not make required payments when due.[31] Such a guarantee qualifies as a financial liability because the guarantor has an unconditional obligation to transfer cash in the future if the debtor fails to meet its obligations. How is such a guarantee reported in the financial statements?

Under ASPE, such guarantees fall under the loss contingency standards discussed earlier in this section of the chapter, as well as the disclosure provisions for guarantees set out in an accounting guideline.[32] Specific disclosures are required even if the probability of having to make payments under the guarantee is remote. Users are interested in knowing what types of guarantees the company has made, the maximum potential obligation the company is exposed to, how much has been recognized in the accounts as a liability, the prospects for recovery from third parties, and details of guarantees issued to benefit related parties.

Under IFRS, the guarantee is recognized initially at fair value, usually equal to the premium charged by the guarantor. After this, it is measured at the higher of:

1. the best estimate of the payment that would be needed to settle the obligation at the reporting date, and

2. any unamortized premium received as a fee for the guarantee (unearned revenue).[33]

Similar to warranties, if this is a single obligation, the best estimate would be the "most likely" amount. However, if there are many similar obligations, the expected value of the possible outcomes is determined. The time value of money is taken into consideration if the effects are significant. In addition to reconciling the opening to the closing balance for this type of obligation, the other disclosures are similar to those under ASPE. The objective under both sets of standards is to give readers better information about the entity's obligations and **particularly about the risks that are assumed as a result of issuing guarantees**.

Illustration 13-9 presents **RONA inc.**'s disclosure on guarantees from Note 22 of the company's financial statements for its year ended December 28, 2014 (in thousands).

Illustration 13-9

*Disclosure of Guarantees and
Commitments—RONA inc.*

22. Guarantees And Commitments

GUARANTEES

In the ordinary course of business, the Corporation reaches agreements that could meet the definition of "guarantees".

Pursuant to the terms of inventory repurchase agreements, the Corporation is committed towards financial institutions to buy back the inventory of certain customers at an average of 65% of the cost of the inventories to a maximum of $48,661. In the event of recourse, this inventory would be sold in the ordinary course of the Corporation's operations. These agreements have undetermined periods. In the opinion of management, the likelihood that significant payments would be incurred as a result of these commitments is low.

(continued)

Illustration 13-9

Disclosure of Guarantees and Commitments—RONA inc. (continued)

COMMITMENTS

The Corporation has entered into operating lease agreements expiring until 2022 which call for lease payments of $40,456 for the rental of automotive equipment, computer hardware, distribution equipment, a warehouse and the building housing the head office and the distribution centre in Québec. The Corporation has also entered into operating lease agreements expiring until 2030 for corporate store space for minimum lease payments of $530,691, the majority of which are noncancellable.

As part of the operation of RONA's banners with dealer-owners, the Corporation is initially involved as a primary tenant and then signs a subleasing agreement with the dealer-owners. In this respect, the Corporation is committed under agreements expiring until 2031 which call for minimum lease payments of $106,237 for the rental of premises and land on which the Corporation erected a building. In consideration thereof, the Corporation has signed subleasing agreements for an equivalent amount.

As at December 28, 2014, the minimum lease payments and minimum amounts receivable under operating lease agreements and other commitments for the next years are as follows:

	Minimum Lease Payments	Minimum Lease Receivables
Less than 1 year	$111,554	$ 16,391
Between 1 – 5 years	357,567	55,130
Over than 5 years	208,661	34,716
	$677,782	$106,237

Following the disposal of assets and the store closures, the Corporation has assigned its rights in certain non-cancellable operating leases for which the Company remains liable for obligations associated with these leases until their expiry dates including renewal periods in the amount of $24,723. The remaining terms to maturity of these leases range from one to six years.

Commitments

Companies conduct business by entering into agreements with customers, suppliers, employees, and other parties. These agreements are known as **executory contracts**—contracts where neither party has yet performed. Executory contracts are not recognized as liabilities in the accounts. Although they are not recognized as liabilities at the date of the statement of financial position, unrecognized **contractual commitments** or **contractual obligations** commit the company and its assets into the future. While it would not be reasonable or desirable to require companies to disclose all of their outstanding contractual obligations, it is useful to have them highlight commitments that have certain characteristics. As discussed in Chapter 8, if there are unavoidable costs associated with completing a contract that exceed the benefits to be received, it would be considered an onerous contract. This concept also applies to commitments. For example, onerous contracts include instances where a company is committed to executing a contract at a loss or paying the other party a penalty for failing to fulfill the contract.

REAL WORLD EMPHASIS

Disclosures are therefore required of commitments to make expenditures that are abnormal relative to the company's financial position and usual operations and for commitments that involve significant risk. Examples include major property, plant, and equipment and intangible asset expenditure commitments, and commitments to make lease payments.[34] Illustration 13-9 includes RONA inc.'s commitments disclosure from Note 22 to its 2014 financial statements.

PRESENTATION, DISCLOSURE, AND ANALYSIS

Presentation and Disclosure of Current Liabilities

Objective 9

Indicate how non-financial and current liabilities are presented and analyzed.

The current liability accounts are commonly presented in Canada as the first classification in the statement of financial position's liabilities and shareholders' equity section. IFRS illustrates an "upside-down" presentation in IAS 1 *Presentation of Financial Statements*, with the long-term assets and liabilities at the top and the current assets and liabilities at the bottom of the statement of financial position. However, the standard does not require this form of presentation. In some instances, current liabilities are presented as a group immediately below current assets, with the total of the current liabilities deducted from the current assets total. Although this presentation is not seen often, it is an informative one that focuses on the company's investment in **working capital**.

REAL WORLD EMPHASIS

Within the current liabilities section, the accounts may be listed in the order of either their maturity or liquidation preference, whichever provides more useful information to readers of the financial statements. Many companies list bank indebtedness first (sometimes called "commercial paper," "bank loans," or "short-term debt"), regardless of their relative amounts, then follow with accounts payable, notes payable, and then end the section with the current portion of long-term debt. An excerpt from the May 3, 2014 balance sheet of **Empire Company Limited** is presented in Illustration 13-10. Empire Company has considerable real estate holdings in addition to its activities in the food and grocery industry, and is best known for its Sobeys chain of stores. The company first adopted IFRS in its May 2012 financial statements.

Illustration 13-10

Balance Sheet Presentation of Current Liabilities—Empire Company Limited

(in millions)	May 3, 2014	May 4, 2013
LIABILITIES		
Current		
Bank indebtedness (Note 14)	$ —	$ 6.0
Accounts payable and accrued liabilities	**2,246.0**	1,765.8
Income taxes payable	**21.0**	75.2
Provisions (Note 15)	**82.4**	30.6
Long-term debt due within one year (Note 11)	**218.0**	47.6
	2,567.4	1,925.2

As indicated earlier in the chapter, IAS 37 uses the term "provisions" to refer to liabilities where there is uncertainty about their timing or the amount of the future expenditure. It requires that companies report provisions separately and provide a reconciliation of the opening and closing balances of each class of provisions. A 2010 IFRS Exposure Draft proposed amendments to IAS 37 that would replace the term "provision" and use the general term "liability" instead. However, as discussed in the Looking Ahead section below, research remains ongoing regarding this and other possible changes to IAS 37.

Entities should disclose enough supplementary information about their current liabilities so that readers can understand and identify the entity's current needs for cash. Such information usually includes identifying the major classes of current liabilities, such as bank loans, trade credit and accrued liabilities, income taxes, dividends, and unearned revenue. Also, amounts owing to officers, directors, shareholders, and associated companies are reported separately from amounts that are owed to enterprises that the reporting entity deals with at arm's length. Secured liabilities and any assets that have been pledged as collateral should be identified clearly.

Presentation and Disclosure of Contingencies, Guarantees, and Commitments

Under ASPE, companies are required to disclose their contingent liabilities when any of the following is true:

1. It is likely that a future event will confirm the existence of a loss but the loss cannot be reasonably estimated.

2. A loss has been recognized, but there is an exposure to loss that is higher than the amount that was recorded.

3. It is not possible to determine the likelihood of the future confirming event.

Companies reporting under ASPE are also required to report any contractual obligations that are significant relative to their current financial position or future operations. In addition, guarantors must report information about any guarantees they have made, even if the likelihood of having to make any payments is slight. This includes information about the nature of the guarantees, maximum potential payments, potential recoveries, and the existence of any collateral. Under IFRS, companies are required to disclose a brief description for each class of contingent liability, unless the probability of outflow is remote. They are also encouraged to disclose an estimate of the financial effect of the liability.

RONA inc., as shown in Illustration 13-9, provides information in Note 22 to its 2014 financial statements regarding guarantees and commitments. **Marks & Spencer Group plc's** Note 25, from its 2015 financial statements, reports on the following commitments:

REAL WORLD EMPHASIS

- Capital commitments related to properties in the course of construction and computer software under development

- Commitment to purchase property, plant, and equipment if there is a change in trading arrangements with certain warehouse operators

- Commitments for payments under non-cancellable operating leases totalling £4,671.3 million

Analysis

Because the ability to pay current obligations as they come due is critical to a company's short-term financial health and continued existence, analysts pay particular attention to the current liabilities section of the statement of financial position. As with most financial statement items, it is not the absolute dollar amount of the current liabilities that is important, but rather its relationship to other aspects of the company's position and results.

Current liabilities result from **both operating and financing activities**. Trade liabilities, provisions, and other liabilities that **arise from operations**—such as payroll, rent, insurance, and taxes payable—are the most common. In addition, advances from customers are a source of operating credit, and it is important to distinguish them from other operating sources. Why? This liability requires the company to provide a service or product in the future rather than make cash payments, and will therefore result in the recognition of revenue in the future. An increase in this category of liability predicts future revenues, not cash outflows.

FINANCIAL ANALYSIS AND PLANNING
5.1.1

Short-term notes and the current portion of long-term debt result **from financing activities**. The company must either generate operating cash flows to repay these liabilities or arrange for their refinancing. Refinancing, however, may not always be possible or may come at a higher cost to the borrower than the original note or debt.

Identifying current liabilities separately from long-term obligations is important because it provides information about the company's liquidity. **Liquidity** is a company's ability to convert assets into cash to pay off its current liabilities in the ordinary course of business. The higher the proportion of assets expected to be converted to cash over liabilities currently due, the more liquid the company. A company with higher liquidity is better able to survive financial downturns and has a better chance of taking advantage of investment opportunities that arise.

As indicated in earlier chapters of the text, basic ratios such as net cash flow provided by operating activities to current liabilities and the turnover ratios for receivables and inventory **are useful in assessing liquidity**. Three other key ratios are the current ratio, the acid-test ratio, and the days payables outstanding.

The **current ratio** is the ratio of total current assets to total current liabilities. The formula is shown in Illustration 13-11.

Illustration 13-11	
Current Ratio Formula	$$\text{Current ratio} = \frac{\text{Current assets}}{\text{Current liabilities}}$$

The current ratio shows how many dollars of current assets are available for each dollar of current liabilities. Sometimes it is called the **working capital ratio** because working capital is the excess of current assets over current liabilities. The higher the ratio, the more likely it is that the company can generate cash to pay its currently maturing liabilities.

A company with a large amount of current assets that is made up almost entirely of inventory may have a satisfactory current ratio, but it may not be very liquid. The current ratio does not show whether a portion of the current assets is tied up in slow-moving inventories. With inventories—especially raw materials and work in process—there is a question of how long it will take to transform them into finished goods, to convert the finished product into accounts receivable by selling it, and then to collect the amounts that customers owe. Better information may be provided to assess liquidity by eliminating inventories and other non-liquid current assets such as prepaid expenses from the current asset ratio numerator. Many analysts prefer to use the resulting **acid-test** or **quick ratio**, shown in Illustration 13-12. This ratio relates quick assets—such as cash, investments held for trading purposes, and receivables, which are all easily convertible to cash—to total current liabilities.

Illustration 13-12	
Acid-Test Ratio Formula	$$\text{Acid-test ratio} = \frac{\text{Cash + Marketable securities + Net receivables}}{\text{Current liabilities}}$$

The current ratio and acid-test ratio are especially useful when analyzing a company over time and when comparing it with other companies in the same industry.

The third ratio, the **days payables outstanding**, zeroes in on how long it takes a company to pay its trade payables. In other words, it determines the average age of the payables. **Trade payables** are amounts that the entity owes to suppliers for providing goods and services related to normal business operations. In other words, they are amounts that result from operating transactions. When cash is managed well, the payment of payables is delayed as long as possible, but is done in time to meet the due date. If there is a trend where the age of the payables outstanding is increasing, particularly if it is above the normal credit period for the industry, it may indicate that the company is having liquidity problems. Illustration 13-13 shows the formula for this ratio.

Illustration 13-13	
Days Payables Outstanding Formula	$$\text{Days payables outstanding} = \frac{\text{Average trade accounts payable}}{\substack{\text{Average daily cost of goods sold} \\ \text{or average daily cost of total} \\ \text{operating expenses}}}$$

The formula provides a more consistent result if all the suppliers that are represented in the payables amount (the numerator) provide the goods and services that are captured in the cost of goods sold amount (the denominator). If the trade accounts payable include the suppliers for most of the company's operating goods and services in addition to the inventory purchases, analysts prefer to use the "average daily cost of total operating expenses" as the denominator.

To illustrate the calculation of these ratios, partial balance sheet and income statement information is provided in Illustration 13-14 for the year ended January 31, 2015 for **Reitmans (Canada) Limited**, a women's clothing retailer. The amounts are reported in thousands of Canadian dollars.

REAL WORLD EMPHASIS

Balance Sheet (extracts)
As at January 31, 2015, and February 1, 2014
(in thousands)

	2015	2014
ASSETS		
CURRENT ASSETS		
Cash and cash equivalents (note 5)	**$139,913**	$122,355
Marketable securities (note 6)	**57,364**	55,062
Trade and other receivables	**4,599**	6,422
Derivative financial asset (note 6)	**20,635**	11,775
Income taxes recoverable	**1,977**	5,656
Inventories (note 7)	**106,440**	109,601
Prepaid expenses	**12,148**	12,512
Total Current Assets	**343,076**	323,383
CURRENT LIABILITIES		
Trade and other payables (note 12)	**$ 91,719**	$90,734
Derivative financial liability (note 6)	**96**	3,065
Deferred revenue (note 13)	**21,073**	19,998
Current portion of long-term debt (note 14)	**1,780**	1,672
Total Current Liabilities	**114,668**	115,469
Statements of Earnings (extract)		
Sales	**$939,376**	$960,397
Cost of goods sold (note 7)	**372,033**	365,458
Gross profit	**567,343**	594,939
Selling and distribution expenses	**507,244**	544,448
Administrative expenses	**47,603**	47,385
Results from operating activities	**12,496**	3,106

The calculation of the current, acid-test, and days payables outstanding ratios for Reitmans is as follows:

$$\text{Current ratio} = \frac{\text{Current assets}}{\text{Current liabilities}} = \frac{\$343,076}{\$114,668} = 3.0$$

$$\text{Acid-test ratio} = \frac{\text{Quick assets}}{\text{Current liabilities}} = \frac{\$139,913 + \$57,364 + \$4,599 + \$20,635 + \$1,977}{\$114,668} = 2.0$$

$$\text{Days payables outstanding} = \frac{\text{Average trade accounts payable}}{\text{Average daily total operating expenses}}$$

$$= \frac{\dfrac{\$91,719 + \$90,734}{2}}{\dfrac{\$372,033 + \$507,244 + \$47,603}{365}} = \frac{\$91,226.5}{\$2,539.4} = 35.9 \text{ days}$$

While a 3.0-to-1 current ratio and a 2.0-to-1 acid-test ratio appear in the higher-than-necessary range, it is often difficult to make a definite statement about a company's liquidity from these ratios alone. What amounts to an acceptable ratio depends on the industry and how it operates. In some industries, companies need significant amounts of current and quick assets compared with their current liabilities. In other industries, such as those that generate cash from cash sales or whose receivables and inventory turn over quickly, companies may be very liquid, with low current and quick ratios. Too high a ratio may indicate poor use of assets in cash, near-cash, receivables, and inventory, because there are carrying costs associated with maintaining these balances. Reitmans probably converts a significant portion of its inventory to cash daily as customers pay cash or use debit or credit cards such as Visa and MasterCard. (Credit card receipts from retail companies are deposited daily as if they were cash.) The length of its cash cycle is reduced because it does not have to carry large receivable balances. For these reasons, Reitmans' working capital ratios could be lower and still indicate ample liquidity. An analyst might question why this company's ratios are so high.

Reitmans' accounts payable are, on average, 35.9 days old. It appears that the company is not experiencing problems keeping up with payments, especially since cash and cash equivalents exceed current liabilities! It may be that supplier credit terms are in the 30- to 40-day range. It is difficult to draw any definite conclusions about these numbers by themselves. They need to be compared with results from previous years, with credit policies, and with the ratios of other companies in the same industry.

IFRS/ASPE COMPARISON

Objective 10

Identify differences in accounting between IFRS and ASPE and what changes are expected in the near future.

A Comparison of IFRS and ASPE

Illustration 13-15 indicates the differences between ASPE and IFRS as this text went to print, and an indication of what is expected in a revised standard on liabilities, a replacement of IAS 37 *Provisions, Contingent Liabilities and Contingent Assets*.

Illustration 13-15

IFRS and ASPE Comparison Chart

	ASPE—*CPA Canada Handbook*, Part II, Sections 1510, 1540, 3110, 3280, 3290, 3400, 3856, and Accounting Guideline 14	IFRS—IAS 1, 7, 19, 37, and 39; IFRS 15; IFRIC 1 and 13	IAS 19, IASB Exposure Draft of Conceptual Framework for Financial Reporting; Proposed Amendments to IAS 37, January 2010, which are subject to further changes if the IASB decides to make amendments to IAS 37 an active project	References to Related Illustrations and Select Brief Exercises
Scope and definitions — Terminology	A liability is an obligation arising from past transactions and events, the settlement of which may result in the transfer or use of assets, provision of services, or other yielding of economic benefits in the future.	A liability is a present obligation arising from past events in which the settlement is expected to result in an outflow of resources that embody economic benefits.	A liability is defined in the conceptual framework Exposure Draft in a manner similar to the current framework. (The ED defines a liability as a present obligation to transfer an economic resource as a result of past events.)	Illustration 13-1
	Contingent liability refers to uncertain situations, some of which may be recognized as a liability and others not.	A contingent liability refers only to those that do not meet the recognition criteria.	The contingent liability term was being considered for elimination under the 2010 ED for IAS 37. The IASB is considering whether to start a new active project to amend IAS 37.	BE 13-30

(continued)

	ASPE—*CPA Canada Handbook*, Part II, Sections 1510, 1540, 3110, 3280, 3290, 3400, 3856, and Accounting Guideline 14	IFRS—IAS 1, 7, 19, 37, and 39; IFRS 15; IFRIC 1 and 13	IAS 19, IASB Exposure Draft of Conceptual Framework for Financial Reporting; Proposed Amendments to IAS 37, January 2010, which are subject to further changes if the IASB decides to make amendments to IAS 37 an active project	References to Related Illustrations and Select Brief Exercises
	The term "provision" is not defined. ASPE requires companies to apply recognition criteria separately when the selling price includes an identifiable amount for subsequent servicing.	A provision is defined as "a liability of uncertain timing or amount." Under IFRS 15, warranties are considered either assurance-type or service-type.	The term "liability" would replace the term "provision" under the 2010 ED for IAS 37.	BE 13-31
—Scope	No specific accounting standard addresses non-financial liabilities.	IAS 37 basically addresses non-financial liability issues, including guarantees and onerous contracts.	A revised standard would likely apply to all liabilities unless covered by another standard.	
	Accounting for financial guarantees is addressed by the loss contingency standards.	Financial guarantees may be covered by insurance standards.	No change.	Illustration 13-9
	Customer loyalty programs are not explicitly addressed in the standards.	Customer loyalty programs are addressed by IFRIC 13 and IFRS 15, which require the current proceeds to be split between the original transaction and the award credits (as unearned revenue).	IFRIC 13 will be withdrawn when IFRS 15 becomes mandatory. Customer loyalty programs will be subject to the requirements of IFRS 15.	Illustration 13-7
Recognition —Restoration and decommissioning obligations	Recognize costs associated with legal obligations only.	Recognize costs of both legal and constructive obligations.	Recognize a liability if it meets the definition of a liability and can be reliably measured; management considers all available evidence to determine the existence of an obligation.	Illustration 13-3
	Costs recognized are capitalized to property, plant, and equipment.	Costs capitalized associated with the asset are recognized as property, plant, and equipment. Those that accrue as a result of production are considered product costs and are charged to inventory	No changes were expected for decommissioning obligations.	Illustration 13-3 BE 13-22
—Contingencies and uncertain commitments	Recognize if occurrence of a future confirming event is "likely," meaning a high probability and measurable.	Recognize if occurrence of a future confirming event is "probable," meaning more likely than not and measurable—a lower threshold than under ASPE.	Recognize a liability if it meets the definition of a liability (see above) and can be reliably measured; management considers all available evidence to determine the existence of an obligation.	BE 13-30
—Contingent gains	Contingent gains are not recognized.	A potential reimbursement is recognized only when virtually certain of recovery.	The right to reimbursement would be recognized if it can be reliably measured.	

Illustration 13-15

IFRS and ASPE Comparison Chart (continued)

(continued)

Measurement — Non-financial liabilities	An asset retirement obligation is measured at the best estimate of the expenditure required to settle the present obligation at the date of the statement of financial position or transfer it to a third party.	A provision is measured at the best estimate of the expenditure required to settle the present obligation at the balance date or to transfer it to a third party.	A liability would be measured at the amount an entity would rationally pay to be relieved of the present obligation: the lowest of the present value of the resources needed to fulfill the obligation, the amount needed to cancel the obligation, and the amount needed to transfer it to a third party under the 2010 ED.	Illustration 13-4A, 13-4B and related example
	The most likely value is used.	A probability-weighted expected value is required where a large population of items is being measured.	Probability-weighted measures would continue to be used.	N/A
	The interest adjustment recognized to the Asset Retirement Obligation account due to the passage of time is recognized as Accretion Expense.	The interest adjustment to the Asset Retirement Obligation account due to the passage of time is recognized as a borrowing cost (interest expense).	There is no proposed change from existing IFRS.	Illustration 13-4A BE13-20 and BE13-21
— Contingencies and uncertain commitments	Measure the amount of the liability at the best estimate in the range of possible outcomes; if none, use lowest point in the range and disclose the remaining exposure to loss.	Measure the amount at the probability-weighted expected value of the loss.	The same measurement as described above applies to all obligations within the scope of IAS 37.	BE 13-31
Presentation — Current/non-current classification	If long-term debt becomes callable due to a violation of a debt agreement, it can be reported as long-term under certain conditions.	If long-term debt becomes callable due to a violation of a debt agreement, it cannot be reported as long-term even if the creditor agrees not to call the debt before the date the statements are released.	There is no proposed change from the existing IFRS.	BE 13-13
	Short-term debt expected to be refinanced is reported as long-term if refinanced on a long-term basis before the statements are completed.	Short-term debt expected to be refinanced is reported as a current liability even if refinanced on a long-term basis before the statements are released, unless refinanced under an existing agreement at the reporting date and solely at the entity's discretion.	There is no change from existing IFRS.	BE 13-14
	No guidance is provided for onerous contractual obligations such as may occur with purchase commitments.	A liability and loss are required to be recognized for onerous contracts if the unavoidable costs exceed the benefits from receiving the contracted goods or services.	There is no proposed change from the existing IFRS.	
Disclosure	There are no general disclosure requirements for liabilities similar to the provisions. Disclosures are less extensive than required under international standards.	IAS 37 identifies specific disclosures for "provisions" including descriptions and a reconciliation of balances between beginning and ending balances.	Disclosures in the 2010 ED were similar to those in IAS 37 with increased requirements in situations where liabilities are not recognized due to lack of reliability of measurement and situations of uncertainty of existence.	

Illustration 13-15

IFRS and ASPE Comparison Chart (continued)

Looking Ahead

The IASB issued an Exposure Draft in May 2015 entitled *Conceptual Framework for Financial Reporting* that, among other things, provides clearer definitions of assets and liabilities, including more detailed guidance for interpreting the definitions.

Accounting for a variety of liabilities, including contingencies, continues to be under review by the IASB. Exposure Drafts (EDs) were issued in 2005 and 2010, proposing amendments to the measurement requirements of IAS 37. However, due to the significant opposition expressed to the EDs, the project was suspended. In June 2015 a Staff Paper on *Research—provisions, contingent liabilities, and contingent assets* (IAS 37) was published. The objective of the research was to decide if the IASB should take on an active project to amend IAS 37. The IASB was expected to wait until revisions to the conceptual framework were finalized (expected in 2016) before publishing possible amendments to IAS 37.

The 2010 Exposure Draft of Proposed Amendments to IAS 37 *Provisions, Contingent Liabilities and Contingent Assets* suggested that the term "contingent liabilities" be eliminated. Under the proposed changes to IFRS, liabilities would arise only from **unconditional** (or **non-contingent**) obligations. This is a more conceptually defensible approach to determining what is recognized as a non-financial liability. Uncertainty about the amounts that might be payable would be taken into account in the **measurement** of the liability, not its **existence**. However, the June 2015 Staff Paper has made it clear that the current research project is looking at all the issues afresh.

SUMMARY OF LEARNING OBJECTIVES

1 Understand the importance of non-financial and current liabilities from a business perspective.

Cash flow management is a key control factor for most businesses. Taking advantage of supplier discounts for prompt payment is one step companies can take. Control of expenses and related accounts payable can improve the efficiency of a business, and can be particularly important during economic downturns.

2 Define liabilities, distinguish financial liabilities from other liabilities, and identify how they are measured.

Liabilities are defined as present obligations of an entity arising from past transactions or events that are settled through a transfer of economic resources in the future. They must be enforceable on the entity. Financial liabilities are a subset of liabilities. They are contractual obligations to deliver cash or other financial assets to another party, or to exchange financial assets or liabilities with another party under conditions that are potentially unfavourable. Financial liabilities are initially recognized at fair value, and subsequently either at amortized cost or fair value. ASPE does not specify how non-financial liabilities are measured. However, unearned revenues are generally measured at the fair value of the goods or services to be delivered in the future, while others are measured at the best estimate of the resources needed to settle the obligation. Under IFRS, non-financial liabilities other than unearned revenues are measured at the best estimate of the amount the entity would rationally pay at the date of the statement of financial position to settle the present obligation.

3 Define current liabilities and identify and account for common types of current liabilities.

Current liabilities are obligations that are payable within one year from the date of the statement of financial position or within the operating cycle if the cycle is longer than a year. IFRS also includes liabilities held for trading and any obligation where the entity does not have an unconditional right to defer settlement beyond 12 months after the date of the statement of financial position. There are several types of current liabilities. The most common are accounts and notes payable, and payroll-related obligations.

4 Identify and account for the major types of employee-related liabilities.

Employee-related liabilities include (1) payroll deductions, (2) compensated absences, and (3) profit-sharing and bonus agreements. Payroll deductions are amounts that are withheld from employees and result in an obligation to the government or another party. The employer's matching contributions are also included in this obligation. Compensated absences earned by employees are company obligations that are recognized as employees earn an entitlement to them, as long as they can be reasonably measured. Bonuses based on income are accrued as an expense and liability as the income is earned.

5 Explain the recognition, measurement, and disclosure requirements for decommissioning and restoration obligations.

A decommissioning, restoration, or asset retirement obligation (ARO) is an estimate of the costs a company is obliged to incur when it retires certain assets. It is recorded as a liability and is usually long-term in nature. Under ASPE, only legal obligations are recognized. They are measured at the best estimate of the cost to settle them at the date of the statement of financial position, and the associated cost is included as part of the cost of property, plant, and equipment. Under IFRS, both legal and constructive obligations are recognized. They are measured at the amount the entity would rationally pay to be relieved of the obligation, and are capitalized as part of property, plant, and equipment or to inventory, if due to production activities. Over time, the liability is increased for the time value of money and the asset costs are amortized to expense. Entities disclose information about the nature of the obligation and how it is measured, with more disclosures required under IFRS than ASPE.

6 Explain the issues and account for unearned revenues.

When an entity receives proceeds in advance or for multiple deliverables, unearned revenue is recognized to the extent the entity has not yet performed. This is measured at the fair value of the remaining goods or services that will be delivered. When costs remain to be incurred in revenue transactions where the revenue is considered earned and has been recognized, estimated liabilities and expenses are recognized at the best estimate of the expenditures that will be incurred. This is an application of the matching concept.

7 Explain the issues and account for product guarantees and other customer program obligations.

Historically, an expense approach has been used to account for the outstanding liability, and this type of approach is still used for assurance-type warranties as initially discussed in Chapter 6. More recently, standards such as IFRS 15 have moved to a revenue approach for warranties that are not included in the sales price of the product (that is, for service-type warranties). Under the expense approach, the outstanding liability is measured at the cost of the economic resources needed to meet the obligation. The assumption is that, along with the liability that is required to be recognized at the reporting date, the associated expense needs to be measured and matched with the revenues of the period. Under the revenue approach, the outstanding liability is measured at the value of the obligation. The proceeds received for any goods or services yet to be delivered or performed are considered to be unearned at the point of sale. Until the revenue is earned, the obligation—the liability—is reported at its sales or fair value. The liability is then reduced as the revenue is earned.

8 Explain and account for contingencies and uncertain commitments, and identify the accounting and reporting requirements for guarantees and commitments.

Under existing standards, a loss is accrued and a liability recognized if (1) information that is available before the issuance of the financial statements shows that it is likely (or more likely than not under IFRS) that a liability has been incurred at the date of the financial statements, and (2) the loss amount can be reasonably estimated (under IFRS, it would be a rare situation where this could not be done). An alternative approach that may be required in new standards being considered by the IASB is described in the Looking Ahead section of the chapter.

Guarantees in general are accounted for similarly to contingencies. Commitments, or contractual obligations, do not usually result in a liability at the date of the statement of financial position. Information about specific types of outstanding commitments is reported at the date of the statement of financial position.

9 Indicate how non-financial and current liabilities are presented and analyzed.

Current liability accounts are commonly presented as the first classification in the liability section of the statement of financial position, although under IFRS, an alternate presentation is to present current assets and liabilities at the bottom of the statement. Within the current liability section, the accounts may be listed in order of their maturity or in order of their liquidation preference. IFRS requires information about and reconciliations of any provisions. Additional information is provided so that there is enough to meet the requirement of full disclosure. Information about unrecognized loss contingencies is reported in notes to the financial statements, including their nature and estimates of possible losses. Commitments at year end that are significant in size, risk, or time are disclosed in the notes to the financial statements, with significantly more information required under IFRS. Three common ratios used to analyze liquidity are the current, acid-test, and days payables outstanding ratios.

10 Identify differences in accounting between IFRS and ASPE and what changes are expected in the near future.

The IASB issued an Exposure Draft in May 2015 entitled *Conceptual Framework for Financial Reporting* that, among other things, provides clearer definitions of assets and liabilities, including more detailed guidance for interpreting the definitions. Accounting for a variety of liabilities, including contingencies, continues to be under review by the IASB. An Exposure Draft (ED) was issued in 2010 proposing amendments to the measurement requirements of IAS 37. However, due to the significant opposition expressed to the EDs, the project was suspended. In June 2015, a Staff Paper entitled *Research— provisions, contingent liabilities, and contingent assets* (IAS 37)—was published. Based on the research in the Staff Paper, the IASB was expected to decide whether to start an active project to amend IAS 37 after revisions to the conceptual framework are finalized.

KEY TERMS

accretion, p. 810	customer advances, p. 800	premiums, p. 816
accumulated rights, p. 805	days payables outstanding, p. 825	profit-sharing, p. 807
acid-test ratio, p. 825	dividend payable, p. 799	provisions, p. 807
asset retirement obligation (ARO), p. 808	event accrual method, p. 806	quick ratio, p. 825
assurance-type warranty, p. 812	executory contracts, p. 822	returnable cash deposits, p. 800
bifurcation, p. 812	financial guarantees, p. 821	revolving debt, p. 795
bonus, p. 807	financial liability, p. 793	service-type warranty, p. 812
callable debt, p. 798	input tax credit, p. 801	short-term obligations expected to be
compensated absences, p. 804	liabilities, p. 792	refinanced, p. 798
constructive obligation, p. 793	line of credit, p. 795	site restoration obligation, p. 808
contingency, p. 818	liquidity, p. 824	stand-ready obligation, p. 812
contingent liability, p. 818	loyalty programs, p. 815	trade accounts payable, p. 796
contractual commitments, p. 822	non-accumulating compensated	trade notes payable, p. 796
contractual obligation, p. 793	absences, p. 806	trade payables, p. 825
current liability, p. 795	notes payable, p. 796	unconditional obligation, p. 805
current maturities of long-term	operating cycle, p. 795	unearned revenue, p. 811
debt, p. 797	payroll deductions, p. 803	vested rights, p. 805
current ratio, p. 824	preferred dividends in arrears, p. 799	warranty, p. 812

Note: Completion of this end-of-chapter material will help develop CPA-enabling competencies (such as ethics and professionalism, problem-solving and decision-making and communication) and technical competencies. We have highlighted selected items with an integration icon and material in *WileyPLUS* has been linked to the competencies. All cases emphasize integration, especially of the enabling competencies. The brief exercises, exercises, and problems generally emphasize problem-solving and decision-making.

Brief Exercises

(LO 1) BE13-1   Wellson Ltd. has current assets, including cash, accounts receivable, and inventory, and current liabilities, including accounts payable and short-term notes payable. Wellson manages its working capital by focusing on management of current assets. Wellson has effective systems in place for granting credit to customers, collecting overdue accounts, and managing inventory. (a) Discuss why management of working capital is important for effective business operations. (b) Discuss how Wellson can improve its management of working capital.

(LO 3) BE13-2   Roley Corporation uses a periodic inventory system and the gross method of accounting for purchase discounts. On July 1, Roley purchased $60,000 of inventory, terms 2/10, n/30, f.o.b. shipping point. Roley paid freight costs of $1,200. On July 3, Roley returned damaged goods and received a credit of $6,000. On July 10, Roley paid for the goods. Prepare all necessary journal entries for Roley.

(LO 3) BE13-3   Refer to the information for Roley Corporation in BE13-2. Assume instead that Roley uses a perpetual inventory system and the net method of accounting for purchase discounts. (a) Prepare all necessary journal entries for Roley. (b) Prepare the payment on account assuming the payment was made on July 30.

(LO 3) BE13-4   Upland Limited borrowed $40,000 on November 1, 2017 by signing a $40,000, three-month, 9% note. Prepare Upland's November 1, 2017 entry; the December 31, 2017 annual adjusting entry; and the February 1, 2018 entry.

(LO 3) BE13-5   Refer to the information for Upland Limited in BE13-4. Assume that Upland uses reversing entries. Prepare the 2018 journal entry(ies) for Upland.

(LO 2, 3) BE13-6   Takemoto Inc. borrowed $60,000 on November 1, 2017 by signing a $61,350, three-month, zero-interest-bearing note. (a) Using a financial calculator or Excel, calculate the effective interest charged on the note. (b) Prepare Takemoto's November 1, 2017 entry; the December 31, 2017 annual adjusting entry; and the February 1, 2018 entry. (*Hint:* For a review of present value concepts, see Appendix 3B of Volume 1.)

(LO 3) BE13-7 Cartwright Springs Brewery Ltd. (CSB) operates a microbrewery and sells beer directly to customers, bars, and restaurants. CSB uses one-litre blue glass refillable bottles featuring a swing-top ceramic lid. The bottles cost CSB $4.90 each. CSB charges customers a refundable deposit of $5 for each bottle at the point of sale of their beer and records amounts received to the account Returnable Deposits. The $5 deposit amount is standard for this specialized segment of the micro beer industry and is close to the cost of the bottles. In addition, since the bottle returns must be made at the brewery location, CSB is using this relatively high deposit amount as a marketing strategy because it provides an incentive for customers to return to the brewery to have their bottles refilled. Based on past experience, CSB estimates that 60% of the bottles do not get returned for refund. CSB makes an adjustment at the end of the fiscal year for unreturned deposits to the account Container Sales Revenue. (a) Using the periodic system, prepare a summary journal entry for the cash sale of 1,000 bottles of beer with a selling price of $8, plus bottle deposit. (b) Prepare the year-end adjusting entry for unreturned bottles using the information provided and your entry in part (a).

(LO 3) BE13-8 DeGroot Limited conducts all of its business in a province with HST of 13%. Prepare the summary journal entry to record DeGroot's sales for the month of July, during which customers purchased $37,500 of goods on account and a journal entry for the cash purchase of furniture with a selling price of $2,860, before tax, for use in the office. Round amounts to the nearest cent.

(LO 3) BE13-9 Refer to the information for DeGroot Limited in BE13-8. Assume that the amounts include tax. Prepare the entries for DeGroot. Round amounts to the nearest cent.

(LO 3) BE13-10 Louise Inc. operates in Alberta, where it is subject to GST of 5%. In August, Louise purchased $29,400 of merchandise inventory, and had sales of $45,000 on account. Louise uses a periodic inventory system. Prepare (a) the summary entry to record the purchases for August, (b) the summary entry to record sales for August, and (c) the subsequent entry to record the payment of any GST owing to the Receiver General.

(LO 3) BE13-11 Clausius Ltd. made four quarterly payments of $3,200 each to the CRA during 2017 as instalment payments on its estimated 2017 corporate tax liability. At year end, Clausius's controller completed the company's 2017 tax return, which showed income tax of $20,000 on its 2017 income. (a) Prepare the summary entry for the quarterly tax instalments and the year-end adjusting entry to recognize the 2017 income tax. (b) Identify any year-end statement of financial position amount that is related to corporate income tax and indicate how it should be classified.

(LO 3) BE13-12 Refer to the information about Clausius Ltd. in BE13-11. Assume instead that the tax return indicated 2017 income tax of $10,200. (a) Prepare the adjusting year-end entry to recognize the 2017 income tax. (b) Identify any year-end statement of financial position amount that is related to income tax and indicate how it should be classified.

(LO 3, 10) BE13-13 At December 31, 2017, Parew Corporation has a long-term debt of $700,000 owing to its bank. The existing debt agreement imposes several covenants related to Parew's liquidity and solvency. At December 31, 2017, Parew was not in compliance with the covenants related to its current ratio and debt to total assets ratio; however, the bank was allowing Parew to operate outside of its covenants. Parew prepares financial statements in accordance with IFRS. (a) Should the debt be reported as a current liability at December 31, 2017? (b) How would your answer to part (a) be different if Parew prepared financial statements in accordance with ASPE?

(LO 3, 10) BE13-14 At December 31, 2017, Burr Corporation owes $500,000 on a note payable due February 15, 2018. Assume that Burr follows IFRS and that the financial statements are completed and released on February 20, 2018. (a) If Burr refinances the obligation by issuing a long-term note on February 14 and by using the proceeds to pay off the note due February 15, how much of the $500,000 should be reported as a current liability at December 31, 2017? (b) If Burr pays off the note on February 15, 2018, and then borrows $1 million on a long-term basis on March 1, how much of the $500,000 should be reported as a current liability at December 31, 2017? (c) How would the answers to parts (a) and (b) be different if Burr prepared financial statements in accordance with ASPE?

(LO 4) BE13-15 Whirled Inc.'s weekly payroll of $23,000 included employee income taxes withheld of $3,426, CPP withheld of $990, EI withheld of $420, and health insurance premiums withheld of $250. Prepare the journal entry to record Whirled's weekly payroll.

(LO 4) BE13-16 Refer to the information for Whirled Inc. in BE13-15. Assume now that the employer is required to match every dollar of the CPP contributions of its employees and to contribute 1.4 times the EI withholdings. (a) Prepare the journal entry to record Whirled's payroll-related expenses. (b) Prepare Whirled's entry to record its payroll-related payment to the Receiver General.

(LO 4) BE13-17 At December 31, 2017, 30 employees of Kasten Inc. have each earned one week of vacation time. The employees' average salary is $1,000 per week. Prepare Kasten's December 31, 2017 adjusting entry.

(LO 4) BE13-18 Laurin Corporation offers parental benefits to its staff as a top-up on Employment Insurance benefits so that employees end up receiving 100% of their salary for 12 months of parental leave. Ruzbeh Awad, who earns $74,000 per year, announced that he will be taking parental leave for a period of 17 weeks starting on December 1, 2017. Assume that the Employment Insurance program pays him a maximum of $720 per week for the 17 weeks. Prepare all entries that Laurin Corporation must make during its 2017 fiscal year related to the parental benefits plan as it applies to Ruzbeh Awad. For the payment entry, ignore withholding taxes, CPP, and EI and round amounts to the nearest cent.

(LO 4) BE13-19 Primeau Inc. pays its officers bonuses based on income. For 2017, the bonuses total $350,000 and are paid on February 15, 2018. Prepare Primeau's December 31, 2017 adjusting entry and the February 15, 2018 entry. For the payment entry, ignore withholding taxes, CPP, and EI.

(LO 2, 5) BE13-20 Lu Corp. erected and placed into service an offshore oil platform on January 1, 2017 at a cost of $10 million. Lu is legally required to dismantle and remove the platform at the end of its nine-year useful life. Lu estimates that it will cost $1 million to dismantle and remove the platform at the end of its useful life and that the discount rate to use should be 8%. Prepare the entry to record the asset retirement obligation. Assume that none of the $1 million cost relates to production.

(LO 5, 10) BE13-21 Refer to the information for Lu Corp. in BE13-20. Prepare any necessary adjusting entries that are associated with the asset retirement obligation and related expenses at December 31, 2017, assuming that Lu follows (a) IFRS, and (b) ASPE. Ignore production-related costs for this question.

(LO 5, 10) BE13-22 Refer to the information for Lu Corp. in BE13-20 and BE13-21. Assume that the increase in the asset retirement obligation in 2017 related to the production of oil in 2017 was $61,942. Prepare any necessary entries to record the increase in the asset retirement obligation at December 31, 2017, assuming that Lu follows (a) IFRS, and (b) ASPE.

(LO 6) BE13-23 Sport Pro Magazine sold 12,000 annual subscriptions on August 1, 2017 for $18 each. Prepare Sport Pro's August 1, 2017 journal entry and the December 31, 2017 annual adjusting entry, assuming the magazines are published and delivered monthly.

(LO 6) BE13-24 Cozy Home Inc. offers its customers two furnace maintenance services. One service is for a one-time cleaning and servicing of a home furnace at a cost of $100. Customers can earn a 5% discount from this price if they pay before Cozy's calendar fiscal year end for maintenance services to be performed in the following year. The second service offered by Cozy is a three-year maintenance plan that sells for $250. The first year's maintenance service for this three-year plan will be delivered before Cozy's fiscal year end. No discount for early payment is offered for the second plan. (a) Prepare the summary journal entry for the cash sale of 200 one-time plans for the current year, 100 discounted one-time plans for the following year, and 300 three-year maintenance plans. (b) Determine the balance sheet classification of the unearned portion of the revenue collected.

(LO 7) BE13-25 Jupiter Corp. provides at no extra charge a two-year warranty with one of its products, which was first sold in 2017. In that year, Jupiter sold products for $2.5 million and spent $68,000 servicing warranty claims. At year end, Jupiter estimates that an additional $420,000 will be spent in the future to service warranty claims related to the 2017 sales. Prepare Jupiter's journal entry(ies) to record the sale of the products, the $68,000 expenditure, and the December 31 adjusting entry under the assurance-type warranty approach.

(LO 7) BE13-26 Refer to the information for Jupiter Corp. in BE13-25. (a) Prepare entries for the warranty that recognize the sale as a multiple deliverable with the warranty as a separate service that Jupiter bundled with the selling price of the product. Sales in 2017 occurred evenly throughout the year. Warranty agreements similar to this are available separately, are estimated to have a stand-alone value of $600,000, and are earned over the warranty period as follows: 2017, 25%; 2018, 50%; and 2019, 25%. (b) Also prepare the entry(ies) to record the $68,000 expenditure for servicing the warranty during 2017, and the adjusting entry required at year end, if any, under the revenue approach used for service-type warranties.

(LO 7) BE13-27 Henry Corporation sells home entertainment systems. The corporation also offers to sell its customers a two-year warranty contract as a separate service. During 2017, Henry sold 20,000 warranty contracts at $99 each. The corporation spent $180,000 servicing warranties during 2017, and it estimates that an additional $900,000 will be spent in the future to service the warranties. Henry recognizes warranty revenue based on the proportion of costs incurred out of total estimated costs. Prepare Henry's journal entries for (a) the sale of warranty contracts, (b) the cost of servicing the warranties, and (c) the recognition of warranty revenue under the revenue approach used for service-type warranties.

(LO 7) BE13-28 In July 10, 2017, Nguyen Ltd. sold $1.7 million worth of compressors to retailers on account. Nguyen had paid $960,000 for these compressors. Nguyen grants the right to return compressors that do not sell in three months following delivery. Past experience indicates that the normal return rate is 15%. By October 11, 2017, retailers returned compressors to Nguyen and were granted credits totalling $248,000. Prepare Nguyen's journal entries to record (a) the sale on July 10, 2017, and (b) $248,000 of returns on October 11, 2017. Nguyen uses a perpetual inventory system and follows IFRS.

(LO 7, 10) BE13-29 Wynn Corp. offers a set of building blocks to customers who send in three codes from Wynn cereal, along with $1. Wynn purchased 100,000 building block sets in 2017 for $2.50 each, and paid for them by cash. During 2017, Wynn sold one million boxes of cereal for $4 per box. Wynn estimates that 10% of the sales amount received from customers relates to the building block sets to be awarded. Wynn expects 30% of the codes to be sent in, and in 2017, 240,000 codes were redeemed. Prepare all necessary journal entries for 2017 if (a) Wynn follows IFRS and prefers to use the revenue approach, and (b) Wynn follows ASPE and prefers to use the expense approach.

(LO 8, 10) BE13-30 At December 31, 2017, Lawton & Border Inc. (L&B) is involved in a lawsuit. Under existing standards in IAS 37, (a) prepare the December 31 entry assuming it is probable (and very likely) that L&B will be liable for $700,000 as a result of this suit. (b) Prepare the December 31 entry, if any, assuming it is probable (although not likely) that L&B will be liable for a payment as a result of this suit. (c) Would your answer change if it was not probable that L&B would be liable? (d) Repeat parts (a) and (b) assuming that L&B follows ASPE.

(LO 8) BE13-31 Siddle Corp. was recently sued by a competitor for patent infringement. Lawyers have determined that it is probable (and very likely) that Siddle will lose the case, and that Siddle will have to pay between $100,000 and $250,000 in damages. Siddle follows IFRS. (a) What entry(ies), if any, should Siddle record in respect of this lawsuit? (b) Repeat part (a) assuming that Siddle follows ASPE.

(LO 9) BE13-32 Yuen Corporation shows the following financial position and results for the three years ended December 31, 2017, 2018, and 2019 (in thousands):

	2019	2018	2017
Cash	$ 650	$ 700	$ 600
FV-NI investments	500	500	500
Accounts receivable	900	1,000	1,300
Inventory	4,900	4,600	4,000
Prepaid expenses	1,300	1,000	900
Total current assets	$ 8,250	$ 7,800	$ 7,300
Accounts payable	$ 1,550	$ 1,700	$ 1,750
Accrued liabilities	2,250	2,000	1,900
Total current liabilities	$ 3,800	$ 3,700	$ 3,650
Cost of goods sold	$15,000	$18,000	$17,000

For each year, calculate the current ratio, quick ratio, and days payables outstanding ratio, and comment on your results.

Exercises

(LO 2, 10) E13-1 (Balance Sheet Classification of Various Liabilities) The following items are to be reported on a balance sheet.

1. Accrued vacation pay

2. Income tax instalments paid in excess of the income tax liability on the year's income

3. Service-type warranties issued on appliances sold

4. A bank overdraft, with no other accounts at the same financial institution

5. Employee payroll deductions unremitted

6. Accrued but unpaid bonus to officer

7. A deposit received from a customer to guarantee performance of a contract

8. Sales tax payable

9. Gift certificates sold to customers but not yet redeemed

10. Premium offers outstanding

11. A royalty fee owing on units produced

12. Travel advances given to sales employees for future business trips

13. Current maturities of long-term debts to be paid from current assets

14. Cash dividends declared but unpaid

15. Dividends in arrears on preferred shares

16. Loans from officers

17. HST collected on sales, in excess of HST paid on purchases

18. An asset retirement obligation

19. The portion of a credit facility that has been used

Instructions

(a) How would each of the above items be reported on the balance sheet according to ASPE? If you identify an item as a liability, indicate whether or not it is a financial liability.

(b) Would your classification of any of the above items change if they were reported on a statement of financial position prepared according to IFRS?

(LO 3) E13-2 **(Accounts and Notes Payable)** The following are selected 2017 transactions of Darby Corporation.

Sept. 1	Purchased inventory from Orion Ltd. on account for $50,000. Darby uses a periodic inventory system and records purchases using the gross method of accounting for purchase discounts.
Oct. 1	Issued a $50,000, 12-month, 8% note to Orion in payment of Darby's account.
1	Borrowed $75,000 from the bank by signing a 12-month, non–interest-bearing $81,000 note.

Instructions

(a) Prepare journal entries for the selected transactions above.

(b) Prepare adjusting entries at December 31, 2017.

(c) Calculate the net liability, in total, to be reported on the December 31, 2017 statement of financial position for (1) the interest-bearing note, and (2) the non–interest-bearing note.

(LO 3) E13-3 **(Notes Payable and Reversing Entry)** Refer to the information for Darby Corporation in E13-2.

Instructions

(a) Prepare the journal entries for the payment of the notes at maturity.

(b) Repeat part (a) assuming Darby uses reversing entries. (Show the reversing entries at January 1, 2018.) Would the use of reversing entries be efficient for both types of notes?

(LO 3, 10) E13-4 **(Liability for Returnable Containers)** Diagnostics Corp. follows IFRS and sells its products in expensive, reusable containers that can be tracked. The customer is charged a deposit for each container that is delivered and receives a refund for each container that is returned within two years after the year of delivery. When a container is not returned within the time limit, Diagnostics accounts for the container as being sold at the deposit amount and credits the account Container Sales Revenue. Information for 2017 is as follows:

Containers held by customers at December 31, 2016 from deliveries in:	2015	$170,000	
	2016	480,000	$650,000
Containers delivered in 2017			894,000
Containers returned in 2017 from deliveries in:	2015	$115,000	
	2016	280,000	
	2017	310,400	705,400

Instructions

(a) Prepare all journal entries required for Diagnostics Corp. for the returnable deposits during 2017.

(b) Calculate the total amount that Diagnostics should report as a liability for returnable deposits at December 31, 2017.

(c) Should the liability calculated in part (b) be reported as current or long-term? Explain

(d) Had Diagnostics followed ASPE, would any of your answers in parts (a) to (c) be different?

(AICPA adapted)

(LO 3) E13-5 **(Entries for Sales Taxes)** Sararas Ltd. is a merchant and operates in the province of Ontario, where the HST rate is 13%. Sararas uses a perpetual inventory system. Transactions for the business for the months of March and April are as follows:

Mar. 1 Paid March rent to the landlord for the rental of a warehouse. The lease calls for monthly payments of $5,500 plus 13% HST.

3 Sold merchandise on account and shipped merchandise to Marcus Ltd. for $20,000, terms n/30, f.o.b. shipping point. This merchandise cost Sararas $11,000.

5 Granted Marcus a sales allowance of $500 (exclusive of taxes) for defective merchandise purchased on March 3. No merchandise was returned.

7 Purchased merchandise for resale on account from Tinney Ltd. at a list price of $4,000, plus applicable tax.

12 Purchased a desk for the shipping clerk, and paid by cash. The price of the desk was $600 before applicable tax.

Apr. 15 Paid the monthly remittance of HST to the Receiver General.

30 Paid the monthly PST remittance to the Treasurer of the province (where applicable).

Instructions

(a) Prepare the journal entries to record these transactions on the books of Sararas Ltd.

(b) Assume instead that Sararas operates in the province of Alberta, where PST is not applicable. GST is charged at the rate of 5%. Prepare the journal entries to record these transactions on the books of Sararas.

(c) Assume instead that Sararas operates in a province where 10% PST is also charged on the 5% GST. Prepare the journal entries to record these transactions on the books of Sararas. Rental payments and inventory purchased for resale are PST-exempt.

(LO 3, 10) E13-6 (Income Tax) Shaddick Corp., a public company following IFRS, began its 2017 fiscal year with a debit balance of $11,250 in its Income Tax Receivable account. During the year, Shaddick made quarterly income tax instalment payments of $8,100 each. In early June, a cheque was received from the Canada Revenue Agency for Shaddick's overpayment of 2016 taxes. The refunded amount was exactly as Shaddick had calculated it would be on its 2016 income tax return. On completion of the 2017 income tax return, it was determined that Shaddick's income tax based on 2017 income was $37,800.

Instructions

(a) Prepare all journal entries that are necessary to record the 2017 transactions and events.

(b) Indicate how the income tax will be reported on Shaddick's December 31, 2017 statement of financial position.

 (c) Assume that the cheque from the CRA in early June is for $2,750, instead of $11,250. The difference arose because of calculation errors on Shaddick's 2016 tax return. How would you account for the difference of $8,500? Where would it be shown on Shaddick's financial statements?

DIGGING DEEPER (d) Would any of your answers for parts (a) to (c) be different if ASPE had been followed?

(LO 3, 4, 6, 7, 8, 10) E13-7 (Financial Statement Impact of Liability Transactions) The following is a list of possible transactions.

1. Purchased inventory for $80,000 on account. (Assume a perpetual system is used.)

2. Issued an $80,000 note payable in payment of an account (see item 1 above).

3. Recorded accrued interest on the note from item 2 above.

4. Borrowed $100,000 from the bank by signing a $104,000, six-month, non–interest-bearing note.

5. Recognized four months of interest expense on the note from item 4 above.

6. Recorded cash sales of $81,900, which includes 5% provincial sales tax.

7. Recorded salaries and wages expense of $35,000. The cash paid was $25,000; the difference was due to various amounts withheld.

8. Recorded employer's payroll taxes.

9. Accrued accumulated vacation pay.

10. Signed a $2-million contract with Construction Corp. to build a new plant.

11. Recorded bonuses due to employees.

12. Recorded a provision on a lawsuit that the company will probably lose.

13. Accrued assurance-type warranty expense.

14. Paid warranty costs that were accrued in item 13 above.

15. Recorded sales of product and separately sold service-type warranties.

16. Paid warranty costs under contracts from item 15 above.

17. Recognized warranty revenue (see item 15 above).

18. Recorded estimated liability for premium claims outstanding.

19. Recorded the receipt of a cash down payment on services to be performed in the next accounting period.

20. Received the remainder of the contracted amount and performed the services related to item 19 above.

Instructions

(a) Set up a table using the format that follows and, using ASPE, analyze the effects of the 20 transactions on the financial statement categories in the table. Use the following codes: increase (I), decrease (D), or no net effect (NE).

Transaction	Assets	Liabilities	Shareholders' Equity	Net Income
1				

(b) Determine if any of the transactions would have different criteria applied for recognition had IFRS been followed.

(LO 3, 9, 10) **E13-8** **(Refinancing of Short-Term Debt)** On December 31, 2017, Hornsby Corporation had $1.2 million of short-term debt in the form of notes payable due on February 2, 2018. On January 21, 2018, in order to ensure that it had sufficient funds to pay for the short-term debt when it matured, Hornsby issued 25,000 common shares for $38 per share, receiving $950,000 in proceeds after brokerage fees and other costs of issuance. On February 2, 2018, the proceeds from the sale of the shares, along with an additional $250,000 cash, were used to liquidate the $1.2-million debt. The December 31, 2017 balance sheet is issued on February 23, 2018.

Instructions

(a) Assuming that Hornsby follows ASPE, show how the $1.2 million of short-term debt should be presented on the December 31, 2017 balance sheet, including the note disclosure.

(b) Assuming that Hornsby follows IFRS, explain how the $1.2 million of short-term debt should be presented on the December 31, 2017 statement of financial position.

DIGGING DEEPER (c) Considering only the effect of the $1.2-million short-term notes payable, would Hornsby's current ratio appear higher if Hornsby followed ASPE, or if Hornsby followed IFRS? Discuss your answer from the perspective of a creditor.

(LO 3, 9, 10) **E13-9** **(Refinancing of Short-Term Debt)** On December 31, 2017, Zimmer Corporation has $7.9 million of short-term debt in the form of notes payable that will be due periodically in 2018 to Provincial Bank. On January 28, 2018, Zimmer enters into a refinancing agreement with the bank that will permit it to borrow up to 60% of the gross amount of its accounts receivable. Receivables are expected to range between a low of $5.7 million in May and a high of $7.0 million in October during 2018. The interest cost of the maturing short-term debt is 15%, and the new agreement calls for a fluctuating interest rate at 1 percentage point above the prime rate on notes due in 2019. Zimmer's December 31, 2017 balance sheet is issued on February 15, 2018.

Instructions

(a) Assuming that Zimmer follows ASPE, prepare a partial balance sheet for Zimmer Corporation at December 31, 2017 that shows how its $7.9 million of short-term debt should be presented, including any necessary note disclosures.

(b) Assuming that Zimmer follows IFRS, explain how the $7.9 million of short-term debt should be presented on the December 31, 2017 statement of financial position.

(LO 4) **E13-10** **(Payroll Tax Entries)** The payroll of Sumerlus Corp. for September 2017 is as follows. Total payroll was $485,000. Pensionable (CPP) and insurable (EI) earnings were $365,000. Income taxes in the amount of $85,000 were withheld, as were $8,000 in union dues. The EI tax rate was 1.88% for employees and 2.632% for employers, and the CPP rate was 4.95% for employees and 4.95% for employers.

Instructions

(a) Prepare the necessary journal entries to record the payroll if the salaries and wages paid and the employer payroll taxes are recorded separately.

(b) Prepare the entries to record the payment of all required amounts to the Receiver General and to the employees' union.

DIGGING DEEPER (c) For every dollar of salaries and wages that Sumerlus commits to pay, what is the actual payroll cost to the company?

(d) Discuss any other costs, direct or indirect, that you think would add to the company's costs of having employees.

(LO 4) **E13-11** **(Compensated Absences—Vacation and Sick Pay)** Mustafa Limited began operations on January 2, 2016. Mustafa employs nine individuals who work eight-hour days and are paid hourly. Each employee earns 10 paid vacation days and 6 paid sick days annually. Vacation days may be taken after January 15 of the year following the year in which they are earned. Sick days may be taken as soon as they are earned; unused sick days accumulate. Additional information is as follows:

	Actual Hourly Wage Rate		Vacation Days Used by Each Employee		Sick Days Used by Each Employee	
	2016	2017	2016	2017	2016	2017
	$20	$21	0	9	4	5

Mustafa Limited has chosen to accrue the cost of compensated absences at rates of pay in effect during the period when they are earned and to accrue sick pay when it is earned. For the purpose of this question, ignore any tax, CPP, and EI deductions when making payments to the employees.

Instructions

(a) Prepare the journal entry(ies) to record the transactions related to vacation entitlement during 2016 and 2017.

(b) Prepare the journal entry(ies) to record the transactions related to sick days during 2016 and 2017.

DIGGING DEEPER

(c) Calculate the amounts of any liability for vacation pay and sick days that should be reported on the statement of financial position at December 31, 2016 and 2017.

(d) How would your answers to parts (b) and (c) change if the entitlement to sick days did not accumulate?

(LO 4) E13-12 (Compensated Absences—Vacation and Sick Pay) Refer to the data in E13-11 and assume instead that Mustafa Limited has chosen not to recognize paid sick leave until it is used, and has chosen to accrue vacation time at expected future rates of pay without discounting. Mustafa uses the following projected rates to accrue vacation time:

Year in Which Vacation Time Was Earned	Projected Future Pay Rates Used to Accrue Vacation Pay
2016	$20.75 per hour
2017	$21.60 per hour

Instructions

(a) Prepare the journal entry(ies) to record the transactions related to vacation entitlement during 2016 and 2017.

(b) Prepare the journal entry(ies) to record the transactions related to sick days during 2016 and 2017.

(c) Calculate the amounts of any liability for vacation pay and sick days that should be reported on the statement of financial position at December 31, 2016 and 2017.

(LO 4) E13-13 (Compensated Absences—Parental Benefits) Goldwing Corporation offers enriched parental benefits to its staff. While the government provides compensation based on Employment Insurance legislation for a period of 12 months, Goldwing increases the amounts received and extends the period of compensation. The benefit program tops up the amount received to 100% of the employee's salary for the first 12 months, and pays the employee 75% of his or her full salary for another six months after the Employment Insurance payments have ceased.

Zeinab Jolan, who earns $54,000 per year, announced to her manager in early June 2017 that she was expecting a baby in mid-November. On October 29, 2017, nine weeks before the end of the calendar year and Goldwing's fiscal year, Zeinab applied for and began her 18-month maternity leave. Assume that the Employment Insurance program pays her a maximum of $720 per week for 52 weeks.

For the purpose of this question, ignore any tax, CPP, and EI deductions when making payments to Zeinab.

Instructions
Round all answers to the nearest dollar.

(a) Prepare all entries that Goldwing Corporation must make during its 2017 fiscal year related to the maternity benefits plan in regard to Zeinab Jolan. Include the date of each entry.

(b) Prepare one entry to summarize all entries that Goldwing will make in 2018 relative to Zeinab Jolan's leave.

(c) Calculate the amount of maternity benefits payable at December 31, 2017 and 2018. Explain how these amounts will be shown on Goldwing's statement of financial position.

(LO 4, 10) E13-14 (Bonus Calculation and Income Statement Preparation) The incomplete income statement of Justin Corp. follows.

Sales revenue		$10,000,000
Cost of goods sold		7,000,000
Gross profit		3,000,000
Administrative and selling expenses	$1,000,000	
Profit-sharing bonus to employees	?	?
Income before income taxes		?
Income taxes		?
Net income		$?

The employee profit-sharing plan requires that 20% of all profits remaining after the deduction of the bonus and income tax be distributed to the employees by the first day of the fourth month following each year end. Justin follows ASPE, the income tax rate is 30%, and the bonus is tax-deductible.

Instructions

(a) Complete the condensed income statement of Justin Corp. for the year ended December 31, 2017. You will need to develop two simultaneous equations to solve for the bonus amount: one for the bonus and one for the tax.

(b) Prepare the journal entry to record the bonus at December 31, 2017.

(c) Would the calculation of the bonus have changed if Justin were following IFRS?

(LO 5, 10) E13-15   (Asset Retirement Obligation) On January 1, 2017, Offshore Corporation erected a drilling platform at a cost of $5,460,000. Offshore is legally required to dismantle and remove the platform at the end of its six-year useful life, at an estimated cost of $950,000. Offshore estimates that 70% of the cost of dismantling and removing the platform is caused by acquiring the asset itself, and that the remaining 30% of the cost is caused by using the platform in production. The present value of the increase in asset retirement obligation related to the production of oil in 2017 and 2018 was $32,328 and $34,914, respectively. The estimated residual value of the drilling platform is zero, and Offshore uses straight-line depreciation. Offshore prepares financial statements in accordance with IFRS.

Instructions

(a) Prepare the journal entries to record the acquisition of the drilling platform, and the asset retirement obligation for the platform, on January 1, 2017. An appropriate interest or discount rate is 8%. (*Hint:* For a review of present value concepts, see Appendix 3B of Volume 1.)

(b) Prepare any journal entries required for the platform and the asset retirement obligation at December 31, 2017.

(c) Prepare any journal entries required for the platform and the asset retirement obligation at December 31, 2018.

(d) Assume that on December 31, 2022, Offshore dismantles and removes the platform for a cost of $922,000. Prepare the journal entry to record the settlement of the asset retirement obligation. Also assume its carrying amount at that time is $950,000.

(e) Repeat parts (a) through (d) assuming that Offshore prepares financial statements in accordance with ASPE.

(LO 5, 10) E13-16   (Asset Retirement Obligation) Crude Oil Limited purchased an oil tanker depot on July 2, 2017 at a cost of $600,000 and expects to operate the depot for 10 years. After the 10 years, Crude Oil is legally required to dismantle the depot and remove the underground storage tanks. It is estimated that it will cost $75,000 to do this at the end of the depot's useful life. Crude Oil follows ASPE.

Instructions

(a) Calculate the present value of the asset retirement obligation (that is, its fair value) on the date of acquisition, based on an effective interest rate of 6%. Prepare the journal entries to record the acquisition of the depot and the accrual for the asset retirement obligation for the depot on July 2, 2017. (*Hint*: For a review of present value concepts, see Appendix 3B of Volume 1.)

(b) Prepare any journal entries required for the depot and the asset retirement obligation at December 31, 2017. Crude Oil uses straight-line depreciation. The estimated residual value of the depot is zero.

(c) Show how all relevant amounts will be reported on Crude Oil Limited's financial statements at December 31, 2017.

(d) Prepare the schedule to calculate the balance in the Asset Retirement Obligation account for all years from 2017 to 2027, assuming there is no change in the estimated cost of dismantling the depot.

(e) On June 30, 2027, Crude Oil pays a demolition firm to dismantle the depot and remove the tanks at a cost of $80,000. Prepare the journal entry for the settlement of the asset retirement obligation.

DIGGING DEEPER

(f) How would the accretion expense be reported on the statement of cash flows?

(g) Discuss how Crude Oil would account for the asset retirement costs and obligation if the company reported under IFRS. Be specific.

(LO 6) E13-17 (Unearned Revenue) On May 1, 2017, Green Machine Inc. entered into a contract to deliver one of its specialty mowers to Schroeter Landscaping Co. The contract requires Schroeter to pay the contract price of $3,200 in advance on May 15, 2017. Schroeter pays Green Machine on May 15, 2017, and Green Machine delivers the mower (with cost of $2,150) on May 31, 2017. Green Machine has a perpetual inventory system.

Instructions

(a) Prepare the journal entry on May 1, 2017 for Green Machine.

(b) Prepare the journal entry on May 15, 2017 for Green Machine.

(c) Prepare the journal entry on May 31, 2017 for Green Machine.

(LO 7) E13-18 (Deposits, HST, and ARO) Listed below are selected transactions of Schultz Department Store for the current year ending December 31.

1. On December 5, the store received $500 from the Selig Players as a deposit to be returned after certain furniture to be used in a stage production was returned on January 15.

2. During December, cash sales totalled $797,780, which includes 13% HST.

3. On December 10, the store purchased for cash three delivery trucks for a total of $125,995. The purchase price includes 13% HST.

4. The store determined it will cost $100,000 to restore the area (considered a land improvement) surrounding one of its store parking lots, when the store is closed in two years. Schultz estimates the present value of the obligation at December 31 is $84,000.

Instructions

Prepare all the journal entries necessary to record the transactions noted above as they occurred and any adjusting journal entries relative to the transactions that would be required at December 31. Assume that adjusting entries are recorded only once a year on December 31.

(LO 7, 10) E13-19 (Warranties—Assurance-Type and Cash Basis) Cléroux Corporation sold 150 colour laser copiers in 2017 for $4,000 each, including a one-year warranty. Maintenance on each machine during the warranty period averages $300.

Instructions

(a) Prepare entries to record the machine sales and the related warranty costs under the expense approach. Actual warranty costs incurred in 2017 were $17,000.

(b) Based on the information above and assuming that the cash basis is used, prepare the appropriate entries.

(c) Is the method in part (b) ever acceptable under GAAP? Explain.

(d) Are assurance-type warranties recorded differently in IFRS and ASPE?

(LO 7, 10) E13-20 (Warranties—Assurance-Type) Cool Sound Ltd. manufactures a line of amplifiers that carry a three-year warranty against defects. Based on experience, the estimated warranty costs related to dollar sales are as follows: first year after sale—2% of sales; second year after sale—3% of sales; and third year after sale—4% of sales. Sales and actual warranty expenditures for the first three years of business were:

	Sales	Warranty Expenditures
2015	$ 810,000	$16,500
2016	1,070,000	47,200
2017	1,036,000	83,000

Instructions

(a) Calculate the amount that Cool Sound Ltd. should report as warranty expense on its 2017 income statement and as a warranty liability on its December 31, 2017 statement of financial position using the assurance-type warranty (expense-based approach). Assume that all sales are made evenly throughout each year and that warranty expenditures are also evenly spaced according to the rates above.

(b) Are assurance-type warranties recorded differently in IFRS and ASPE?

(c) Assume that Cool Sound's warranty expenditures in the first year after sale end up being 4% of sales, which is twice as much as was forecast. How would management account for this change?

(LO 7, 10) E13-21   (Warranties—Assurance-Type and Service-Type) Selzer Equipment Limited sold 500 Rollomatics on account during 2017 for $6,000 each. During 2017, Selzer spent $30,000 servicing the two-year warranties that are included in each sale of the Rollomatic. All servicing transactions were paid in cash.

Instructions

(a) Prepare the 2017 entries for Selzer using the assurance-type (expense-based) approach for warranties. Assume that Selzer estimates that the total cost of servicing the warranties will be $120,000 for two years.

(b) Prepare the 2017 entries for Selzer assuming that the warranties are not an integral part of the sale, but rather a separate service that is considered to be bundled with the selling price. Use the service-type (revenue-based) approach for warranties. Assume that of the sales total, $160,000 is identified as relating specifically to sales of warranty contracts. Selzer estimates the total cost of servicing the warranties will be $120,000 for two years. Because the repair costs are not incurred evenly, warranty revenues are recognized based on the proportion of costs incurred out of the total estimated costs.

(c) What amounts would be shown on Selzer's income statement under parts (a) and (b)? Explain the resulting difference in the Selzer's net income.

(d) Are assurance-type and service-type warranties recorded differently in IFRS and ASPE?

(e) Assume that the equipment sold by Selzer undergoes technological improvements and management now has no past experience on which to estimate the extent of the warranty costs. The chief engineer believes that product warranty costs are likely to be incurred, but they cannot be reasonably estimated. What advice would you give on how to account for and report the warranties?

(LO 7, 10) E13-22   (Warranties—Assurance-Type and Service-Type) Novack Machinery Co. manufactures equipment to a very high standard of quality; however, it must still provide a warranty for each unit sold, and there are instances where the machines do require repair after they have been put into use. Novack started in business in 2017, and as the controller, you are trying to determine whether to use the assurance-type or service-type warranty approach to measure the warranty obligation. You would like to show the company president how this choice would affect the financial statements for 2017, and advise him of the better choice, keeping in mind that the service-type approach is consistent with IFRS, and there are plans to take Novack public in a few years.

You have determined that sales on account for the year were 1,000 units, with a selling price of $3,000 each. The warranty is for two years, and the estimated warranty cost averages $200 per machine. Actual costs of servicing warranties for the year were $105,000. You have done some research and determined that if the service-type approach were to be used, the portion of revenue allocated to the warranty portion of the sale would be $350. Because the costs of servicing warranties are not incurred evenly, warranty revenues are recognized based on the proportion of costs incurred out of the total estimated costs.

Instructions

(a) For both the assurance-type and the service-type approach, prepare the necessary journal entries to record all of the transactions described, and determine the warranty liability and expense amounts for 2017.

(b) Are assurance-type and service-type warranties recorded differently in IFRS and ASPE?

(c) What are the advantages and disadvantages of the two choices? What do you think is the best choice in this situation? Why?

(LO 7, 10) E13-23   (Customer Loyalty Programs) To increase sales, Bélanger Inc., a public company following IFRS, implemented a customer loyalty program that rewards a customer with 1 loyalty point for every $10 of purchases on a select group of products. Each point is redeemable for a $1 discount on any purchases of Bélanger merchandise in the next two years. Following the implementation of the program, during 2017, customers purchased select group products for $100,000 and earned 10,000 points redeemable for future purchases. (All products are sold to provide a 45% gross profit.) The stand-alone selling price of the purchased products is $100,000. Based on prior experience with incentive programs like this, Bélanger expects 9,500 points to be redeemed related to these sales. (Bélanger appropriately uses this experience to estimate the value of future consideration related to bonus points.)

Instructions

(a) Identify the separate performance obligation in the Bélanger bonus point programs, and briefly explain when the performance obligations are satisfied.

(b) Prepare the journal entries for cash sales including the issuance of bonus points for Bélanger in 2017.

(c) Would the accounting of the customer loyalty program be different if Bélanger had been following ASPE?

(LO 7, 10) E13-24 (Premium Entries) Moleski Limited, a private company following ASPE, includes one coupon in each box of soap powder that it produces, and 10 coupons are redeemable for a premium (a kitchen utensil). In 2017, Moleski purchased 8,800 premiums at $0.90 each and sold 120,000 boxes of soap powder at $3.30 per box. In total, 44,000 coupons were presented for redemption in 2017. It is estimated that 60% of the coupons will eventually be presented for redemption. Moleski uses the expense approach to account for premiums.

Instructions

(a) Prepare all the entries that would be made for sales of soap powder and for the premium plan in 2017.

(b) What amounts relative to soap powder sales and premiums would be shown on Moleski's financial statements for 2017?

(c) What method did Moleski follow? Would the same method apply if Moleski had followed IFRS?

(LO 7) E13-25 (Premiums) Three independent situations follow.

Situation 1: Marquart Stamp Corporation records stamp service revenue and provides for the cost of redemptions in the year stamps are sold to licensees. The stamps can be collected and then redeemed for discounts on future purchases from Marquart as an incentive for repeat business. Marquart's past experience indicates that only 80% of the stamps sold to licensees will be redeemed. Marquart's liability for stamp redemptions was $13 million at December 31, 2016. The cost of redemptions for stamps sold prior to January 1, 2017 was $6 million. If all the stamps sold in 2017 were presented for redemption in 2018, the redemption cost would be $5.2 million.

Instructions

What amount should Marquart report as a liability for stamp redemptions at December 31, 2017?

Situation 2: In packages of its products, ITSS Inc. includes coupons that may be presented at retail stores to obtain discounts on other ITSS products. Retailers are reimbursed for the face amount of coupons redeemed plus 10% of that amount for handling costs. ITSS honours requests for coupon redemption by retailers up to three months after the consumer expiration date printed on the coupon. ITSS estimates that 60% of all coupons issued will eventually be redeemed. Information relating to coupons issued by ITSS during 2017 (the first year of the promotion) is as follows:

Consumer expiration date	12/31/17
Total face amount of coupons issued	$800,000
Total payments to retailers as at 12/31/17	$330,000

Instructions

(a) What amount should ITSS report as a liability for unredeemed coupons at December 31, 2017?

(b) What amount of premium expense should ITSS report on its 2017 income statement?

Situation 3: Baylor Corp. sold 700,000 boxes of pie mix under a new sales promotion program. Each box contains one coupon that entitles the customer to a baking pan when the coupon is submitted with an additional $4.75 from the customer. Baylor pays $5.00 per pan and $1.25 for shipping and handling. Baylor estimates that 60% of the coupons will be redeemed even though only 105,000 coupons had been processed during 2017. Each box of pie mix is sold for $4.50, and Baylor estimates that $1.00 of the sale price relates to the baking pan to be awarded. Baylor follows IFRS and accounts for its promotional programs in accordance with the revenue approach and IFRIC 13.

Instructions

(a) What amount related to the promotional program should Baylor report as a liability at December 31, 2017?

(b) What amount of premium expense will Baylor report on its 2017 income statement as a result of the promotional program?

(c) Prepare any necessary 2017 journal entries to record revenue, the liability, and coupon redemptions.

DIGGING
DEEPER

(d) Discuss the conceptual merit of recording the sales revenue related to unredeemed coupons as unearned revenue.

(AICPA adapted)

(LO 7, 10) E13-26 (Premiums) Timo van Leeuwen operates a very busy roadside fruit and vegetable stand from May to October every year as part of his farming operation, which has a December 31 year end and uses ASPE. Each time a customer purchases over $10 of produce, Timo gives the customer a special fruit-shaped sticker that can't be copied. If a customer collects 10 of these stickers, they can have $10 worth of produce for no charge. The stickers must be redeemed by June 30 of the following year. During the current year, 25,000 stickers were given out to customers. Timo knows from experience that some stickers will never be cashed in, because the customer may not shop at his stand frequently enough to collect 10 stickers, or they get lost or forgotten. In previous years, 10% of stickers have been redeemed. During the current year, 6% of the stickers given out were redeemed. Timo uses the expense approach to account for premiums and estimates that product costs are 60% of their selling prices.

Instructions

(a) Determine the amount that should be reported as premium expense on the December 31 income statement and the amount of any liability at December 31.

(b) Prepare all the necessary journal entries to record the premium expense associated with the stickers and the related liability at year end.

(c) Would the accounting of the premiums have been different if Timo had followed IFRS?

(LO 7) **E13-27   (Coupons and Rebates)** St. Thomas Auto Repairs is preparing the financial statements for the year ended November 30, 2017. As the accountant, you are looking over the information regarding short-term liabilities, and determining the amounts that should be reported on the balance sheet. St. Thomas Auto Repairs reports under ASPE. The following information regarding new corporate initiatives has been brought to your attention.

1. St. Thomas printed a coupon in the local newspaper in November 2017. The coupon permits customers to take 10% off the cost of any service between November 1, 2017 and January 30, 2018. The newspaper has a circulation of 10,000 customers. In November, 30 coupons were used by customers, resulting in sales reductions of $250. It is expected that 50 more coupons will be used before January 30, and the average sales transaction for St. Thomas is $75.

2. In order to reduce the costs associated with production downtime due to sick days taken, St. Thomas developed a new plan in 2017. Employees are permitted up to six sick days per year with pay. If these days are not all used, then 50% of the unused time will be accumulated and can be used as paid vacation within the next year; otherwise, the rights will expire at the end of the next fiscal year. During 2017, two employees were eligible for the plan and each used two of their six days. The daily rate of pay for each employee is $200. These two individuals are long-term employees of the company who are unlikely to resign in the near future and who have been relatively healthy in the past.

3. St. Thomas is considering starting a customer loyalty program. The program would involve tracking the purchases of each customer on a small card that is retained by the customer. Each time a customer reaches $250 in total purchases, a $10 discount would be offered on the next purchase.

Instructions

(a) For items that affect the 2017 financial statements, determine the amount of any liability that should be reported and the related expense.

(b) Discuss the accounting issues that the proposed customer loyalty program raises. Explain how the program should be accounted for.

(LO 7) E13-28   (Customer Returns) Islim Limited manufactures faux fur coats of all types and sizes that are sold to specialty stores throughout Canada. Sales to retailers provide for payment within 60 days of delivery and the retailer may return a maximum of 25% of an order at the retailer's expense for the freight. Past experience indicates that the normal return rate is 12%, although Islim only offers the return special once per year (for its Canada Day Sale on July 1). Islim has a perpetual inventory system and follows IFRS.

Instructions

(a) On July 1, 2017, Islim shipped faux furs invoiced at $3 million (cost $1.7 million). Prepare the journal entry to record this transaction.

(b) On October 3, 2017, $340,000 of the invoiced July sales were returned according to the return policy, and the remaining balances on account were paid. Prepare the journal entries for the return and collection.

(LO 8, 10) E13-29   (Contingencies and Commitments) Four independent situations follow.

Situation 1:   During 2017, Sugarpost Inc. became involved in a tax dispute with the CRA. Sugarpost's tax lawyers have informed management that Sugarpost will likely lose this dispute. They also believe that Sugarpost will have to pay the

CRA between $900,000 and $1.4 million. After the 2017 financial statements were issued, the case was settled with the CRA for $1.2 million.

Instructions

What amount, if any, should be reported as a liability for this contingency as at December 31, 2017, assuming that Sugarpost follows ASPE?

Situation 2: Toward the end of Su Li Corp.'s 2017 fiscal year, employer–union talks broke off, with the wage rates for the upcoming two years still unresolved. Just before the new year, however, a contract was signed that gave employees a 5% increase in their hourly wage effective January 1, 2018. Su Li had spent $1.2 million in wages on this group of workers in 2017.

Instructions

Prepare the entry, if any, that Su Li Corp. should make at December 31, 2017. Briefly explain your answer.

Situation 3: On October 1, 2017, the provincial environment ministry identified Jackhammer Chemical Inc. as a potentially responsible party in a chemical spill. Jackhammer's management, along with its legal counsel, have concluded that it is likely that Jackhammer will be found responsible for damages, and a reasonable estimate of these damages is $5 million. Jackhammer's insurance policy of $9 million has a clause requiring a deductible of $500,000.

Instructions

(a) Assuming ASPE is followed, how should Jackhammer Chemical report this information in its financial statements at December 31, 2017?

(b) Briefly identify any differences if Jackhammer followed IFRS.

Situation 4: Etheridge Inc. had a manufacturing plant in a foreign country that was destroyed in a civil war. It is not certain who will compensate Etheridge for this destruction, but Etheridge has been assured by that country's government officials that it will receive a definite amount for this plant. The compensation amount will be less than the plant's fair value, but more than its carrying amount.

Instructions

How should the contingency be reported in the financial statements of Etheridge Inc. under ASPE?

(LO 9) E13-30 (Ratio Calculations and Discussion) Kawani Corporation has been operating for several years. On December 31, 2017, it presented the following statement of financial position.

KAWANI CORPORATION
Statement of Financial Position
December 31, 2017

Cash	$ 40,000	Accounts payable	$ 70,000
Accounts receivable (net)	75,000	Mortgage payable	140,000
Inventory	95,000	Common shares	160,000
Equipment (net)	220,000	Retained earnings	60,000
	$430,000		$430,000

Cost of goods sold in 2017 was $420,000, operating expenses were $51,000, and net income was $27,000. Accounts payable suppliers provided operating goods and services. Assume that total assets are the same in 2016 and 2017.

FINANCE

Instructions

Calculate each of the following ratios:

(a) Current ratio

(b) Acid-test ratio

(c) Debt to total assets ratio

(d) Rate of return on assets

(e) Days payables outstanding

For each ratio, also indicate how it is calculated and what its significance is as a tool for analyzing Kawani's financial position, profitability, and liquidity.

(LO 9) E13-31   (Ratio Calculations and Analysis) Harold Limited's condensed financial statements provide the following information:

HAROLD LIMITED
Statement of Financial Position

	Dec. 31, 2017	Dec. 31, 2016
Cash	$ 52,000	$ 60,000
Accounts receivable (net)	198,000	80,000
FV-NI investments (short-term)	80,000	40,000
Inventory	440,000	360,000
Prepaid expenses	3,000	7,000
Total current assets	773,000	547,000
Property, plant, and equipment (net)	857,000	853,000
Total assets	$1,630,000	$1,400,000
Accounts payable	$ 220,000	$ 145,000
Other current liabilities	20,000	15,000
Bonds payable	400,000	400,000
Common shareholders' equity	990,000	840,000
Total liabilities and shareholders' equity	$1,630,000	$1,400,000

Income Statement
For the Year Ended December 31, 2017

Sales		$1,640,000
Cost of goods sold		(800,000)
Gross profit		840,000
Selling and administrative expenses	$360,000	
Interest expense	20,000	
Income tax expense	100,000	480,000
Net income		$ 360,000

FINANCE

Instructions

(a) Determine the following:

1. Current ratio at December 31, 2017
2. Acid-test ratio at December 31, 2017
3. Accounts receivable turnover for 2017
4. Inventory turnover for 2017

5. Days payables outstanding for 2017
6. Rate of return on assets for 2017
7. Profit margin on sales

(b) Prepare a brief evaluation of the financial condition of Harold Limited and of the adequacy of its profits.

DIGGING DEEPER

(c) In examining the other current liabilities on Harold Limited's statement of financial position, you notice that unearned revenues have declined in the current year compared with the previous year. Is this a positive indicator about the client's liquidity? Explain.

(LO 9) E13-32   (Ratio Calculations and Effect of Transactions) Financial information for Cao Inc. follows.

CAO INC.
Statement of Financial Position
December 31, 2017

Cash		$ 45,000	Notes payable (short-term)	$ 50,000
Receivables	$110,000		Accounts payable	32,000
Less: Allowance	15,000	95,000	Accrued liabilities	5,000
Inventory		170,000	Share capital (52,000 shares)	260,000
Prepaid insurance		8,000	Retained earnings	241,000
Land		20,000		
Building (net)		250,000		
		$588,000		$588,000

Income Statement
For the Year Ended December 31, 2017

Sales		$1,400,000
Cost of goods sold		
Inventory, Jan. 1, 2017	$200,000	
Purchases	790,000	
Cost of goods available for sale	990,000	
Inventory, Dec. 31, 2017	170,000	
Cost of goods sold		820,000
Gross profit on sales		580,000
Operating expenses		170,000
Income before income taxes		410,000
Income tax expense		125,000
Net income		$ 285,000

FINANCE

Instructions

(a) Calculate the following ratios or relationships of Cao Inc. Assume that the ending account balances are representative unless the information provided indicates differently.

1. Current ratio
2. Inventory turnover
3. Receivables turnover
4. Average age of receivables (days sales outstanding)
5. Average age of payables (days payables outstanding)
6. Earnings per share
7. Profit margin on sales
8. Rate of return on assets

(b) For each of the following transactions, indicate whether the transaction would improve, weaken, or have no effect on the current ratio of Cao Inc. at December 31, 2017.

1. Writing off an uncollectible account receivable for $2,200
2. Receiving a $20,000 down payment on services to be performed in 2017
3. Paying $40,000 on notes payable (short-term)
4. Collecting $23,000 on accounts receivable
5. Purchasing equipment on account
6. Giving an existing creditor a short-term note in settlement of an open account payable
7. Recording an impairment loss on land

Problems

P13-1   The following are selected transactions of Pendlebury Department Store Ltd. (PDSL) for the current year ending December 31. PDSL is a private company operating in the province of Manitoba.

1. On February 2, PDSL purchased goods having cash discount terms of 2/10, n/30 from Hashmani Limited for $46,000. Purchases and accounts payable are recorded using the periodic system at net amounts after cash discounts. The invoice was paid on February 26.

2. On April 1, PDSL purchased a truck for $50,000 from Schuler Motors Limited, paying $5,000 cash and signing a one-year, 8% note for the balance of the purchase price.

3. On May 1, PDSL borrowed $83,000 from First Provincial Bank by signing a $92,000 non–interest-bearing note due one year from May 1.

4. On June 30 and December 31, PDSL remitted cheques for $19,000 each as instalments on its current year tax liability.

5. On August 14, PDSL's board of directors declared a $13,000 cash dividend that was payable on September 10 to shareholders of record on August 31.

6. On December 5, PDSL received $750 from Jefferson Ltd. as a deposit on a trailer that Jefferson is using for an office move. The deposit is to be returned to Jefferson after it returns the trailer in good condition on January 15.

7. On December 10, PDSL purchased new furniture and fixtures for $8,000 on account. Provincial sales tax of 8% and GST of 5% were charged by the supplier on the purchase price.

8. During December, cash sales of $79,000 were recorded, plus 8% provincial sales tax and 5% GST that must be remitted by the 15th day of the following month. Both taxes are levied on the sale amount to the customer.

9. PDSL's lease for its store premises calls for a $2,500 monthly rental payment plus 3% of net sales. The payment is due one week after month end.

10. PDSL was advised during the month of December that it is legally required to restore the area (considered a land improvement) surrounding one of its new store parking lots, when the store is closed in 12 years. PDSL estimates that the fair value of this obligation at December 31 is $46,000.

11. The corporate tax return indicated taxable income of $205,000. PDSL's income tax rate is 20%.

Instructions

(a) Prepare all the journal entries that are necessary to record the above transactions when they occurred and any adjusting journal entries (except for depreciation expense) relative to the transactions that would be required to present financial statements at December 31 in accordance with GAAP. Date each entry.

(b) Identify the current liabilities that will be reported on PDSL's December 31 statement of financial position, and indicate the amount of each one.

(c) Prepare the journal entries for transactions 7 and 8 above if the 8% sales tax was applied on the purchase or sale amount plus the GST.

(d) Why is the liabilities section of the statement of financial position of primary significance to bankers?

(e) How are current liabilities related to current assets?

(f) Comment on any differences that would apply in your accounting treatment for parts (a) though (c) if Pendlebury had followed IFRS.

DIGGING DEEPER

P13-2 Bian Inc. financed the purchase of equipment costing $85,000 on January 1, 2017 using a note payable. The note requires Bian to make annual $23,971 payments of blended interest and principal on January 1 of the following four years, beginning January 1, 2018. The note bears interest at the rate of 5%.

Instructions

(a) Prepare the debt amortization schedule for the note over its term. Using a financial calculator or Excel, prove that the blended payment will cost Bian Inc. 5%.

(b) Prepare the journal entry(ies) that are required for the year ended December 31, 2017 and the first instalment payment on January 1, 2018.

FINANCE

(c) Prepare the statement of financial position presentation of the note at December 31, 2017 (include both the current and long-term portions) and any interest outstanding.

(d) Prepare the statement of financial position presentation of the note at December 31, 2018 and any interest outstanding.

(e) Redo part (c) assuming that the equipment was purchased on July 1, 2017 and the payments are due beginning July 1, 2018.

(f) If the repayments in the note had been a fixed principal repayment each year, what would have been the amount of the annual principal payment? Prepare the debt amortization schedule for the note over its term.

(g) Compare the interest costs for the term of the note with fixed payments in part (a) and with fixed principal repayment in part (f). Which has the highest interest costs?

DIGGING DEEPER

(h) You are the lender. Would you rather negotiate a note with fixed principal payments or fixed payments? Why?

P13-3 Hrudka Corp. has manufactured a broad range of quality products since 1988. The operating cycle of the business is less than one year. The following information is available for the company's fiscal year ended February 28, 2017. Hrudka follows ASPE.

1. Hrudka has $4 million of bonds payable outstanding at February 28, 2017, which were issued at par in 2006 and are due in 2026. The bonds carry an interest rate of 7%, payable semi-annually each June 1 and December 1.

2. Hrudka has several notes payable outstanding with its primary banking institution at February 28, 2017. In each case, the annual interest is due on the anniversary date of the note each year (same as the due dates listed). The notes are as follows:

Due Date	Amount Due	Interest Rate
Apr. 1, 2017	$150,000	8%
Jan. 31, 2018	200,000	9%
Mar. 15, 2018	500,000	7%
Oct. 30, 2019	250,000	8%

3. Hrudka uses the expense approach to account for assurance-type warranties. The company has a two-year warranty on selected products, with an estimated cost of 1% of sales being returned in the 12 months following the sale, and a cost of 1.5% of sales being returned in months 13 to 24 following the sale. The warranty liability outstanding at February 28, 2016 was $5,700. Sales of warrantied products in the year ended February 28, 2017 were $154,000. Actual warranty costs incurred during the current fiscal year are as follows:

Warranty claims honoured on 2015–2016 sales	$4,900
Warranty claims honoured on 2016–2017 sales	1,100
	$6,000

4. The accounts payable subsidiary ledger shows balances of regular trade payables for supplies and purchases of goods and services on open account. Included in the net balance of $394,000 are accounts with credit balances totalling $414,000 and accounts with debit balances totalling $20,000 at February 28, 2017. Included in trade payables is a loan of $23,000 owing to an affiliated company.

5. The following information relates to Hrudka's payroll for the month of February 2017. Hrudka's required contribution for EI is 1.4 times the employee contribution; for CPP, it is 1.0 times the employee contribution.

Salaries and wages outstanding at February 28, 2017	$220,000
For the last payroll of the year, the following balances apply:	
EI withheld from employees	9,500
CPP withheld from employees	16,900
Income taxes withheld from employees	48,700
Union dues withheld from employees	21,500

6. Hrudka regularly pays GST owing to the Receiver General of Canada on the 15th of the month. Hrudka's GST transactions include the GST that it charges to customers and the GST that it is charged by suppliers of goods and services. During February 2017, purchases attracted $28,000 of GST, while the GST charged on invoices to customers totalled $39,900. At January 31, 2017, the balances in the GST Receivable and GST Payable accounts were $34,000 and $60,000, respectively.

7. Other miscellaneous liabilities included $50,000 of dividends payable on March 15, 2017; $25,000 of bonuses payable to company executives (75% payable in September 2017 and 25% payable in March 2018); and $75,000 in accrued audit fees covering the year ended February 28, 2017.

8. Hrudka sells gift cards to its customers. The company does not set a redemption date and customers can use their cards at any time. At March 1, 2016, Hrudka had a balance outstanding of $95,000 in its Unearned Revenue account. Hrudka received $22,500 in cash for gift cards purchased during the current year and $37,500 in redemptions took place during the year. Based on past experience, 15% of customer gift card balances never get redeemed. At the end of each year, Hrudka recognizes 15% of the opening balance of Unearned Revenue as earned during the year.

Instructions

(a) Prepare the current liability section of the February 28, 2017 balance sheet of Hrudka Corp. Identify any amounts that require separate presentation or disclosure under ASPE.

(b) For each item included as a current liability, identify whether the item is a financial liability. Explain.

(c) If you have excluded any items from the category of current liabilities, explain why you left them out.

(d) Assume that Hrudka Corp. is not in compliance with the debt covenants in the note payable due October 30, 2019 in item 2 above. How would this affect the classification of the note on the balance sheet?

DIGGING
DEEPER

(e) For a manufacturer such as Hrudka, how should the revenue from unredeemed gift cards be shown on the income statement, as opposed to revenue from redeemed gift cards?

(f) Comment on any differences that would apply in your accounting treatment for parts (a) though (e) if Hrudka had followed IFRS.

P13-4   Healy Corp., a leader in the commercial cleaning industry, acquired and installed, at a total cost of $110,000 plus 15% HST, three underground tanks to store hazardous liquid solutions needed in the cleaning process. The tanks were ready for use on February 28, 2017.

The provincial ministry of the environment regulates the use of such tanks and requires them to be disposed of after 10 years of use. Healy estimates that the cost of digging up and removing the tanks in 2027 will be $28,000. An appropriate interest or discount rate is 6%.

Healy also manufactures commercial cleaning machines that it sells to dry cleaning establishments throughout Nova Scotia. During 2017, Healy sold 20 machines at a price of $12,000 each plus 15% HST. The machines were sold with a two-year warranty for parts and labour. Similar warranty agreements are available separately and are estimated to have a stand-alone value of $970. Sales in 2017 occurred evenly throughout the year. Any revenue related to the warranty agreements is assumed to be earned evenly over the two-year contract term as follows: 2017, 25%; 2018, 50%; and 2019, 25%. Healy estimates the total cost of servicing the warranties will be $10,800 over the two-year contract term. Healy incurred actual warranty expenditures of $2,700 in 2017.

Instructions

Answer the following, assuming Healy follows IFRS and has a December 31 fiscal year end.

(a) Assuming straight-line depreciation and no residual value for the tanks at the end of their 10-year useful life, what is the balance in the asset Storage Tanks account, net of accumulated depreciation, at December 31, 2017?

(b) What is the balance of the asset retirement obligation liability at December 31, 2019, assuming there has been no change to the estimate of the final cost of disposal?

(c) Determine the balance of the warranty-related liability that would be reported on the December 31, 2017 statement of financial position. Ignore HST and assume that Healy uses the service-type approach to account for warranties.

(d) Determine the Warranty Expense that would be reported on Healy's 2017 income statement.

(e) Healy has been permitted to file its HST return on December 31 each year and either send a cheque or request a refund on this date. Assuming there are no other HST transactions during the year, will Healy be sending a cheque or requesting a refund on December 31, 2017? What will be the amount of the cheque paid or refund claimed?

DIGGING DEEPER

(f) From the perspective of a potential investor, comment on Healy's assumption that revenue related to the warranty agreements is earned evenly over the three-year contract term.

P13-5   Sultanaly Limited, a private company following ASPE, pays its office employees each week. A partial list follows of employees and their payroll data for August. Because August is the vacation period, vacation pay is also listed.

Employee	Weekly Pay	Vacation Pay to Be Received in August
Mark Olly	$ 450	$ 900
Bill Ganton	610	1,220
Laurie Evans	550	
Louise Bérubé	1,250	2,500
Jeff Huziak	780	

Assume that the income tax withheld is 10% of salaries and that union dues withheld are 1% of gross salary. Vacations are taken in the second and third weeks of August by Olly, Ganton, and Bérubé. The Employment Insurance rate is 1.88% for employees and 1.4 times that for employers. The CPP rate is 4.95% each for employee and employer.

Instructions

(a) Prepare the journal entries that are necessary for each of the four August payrolls. The entries for the payroll and for Sultanaly's payroll tax are made separately.

(b) Prepare the entry to record the monthly payment of accrued payroll liabilities.

(c) Prepare the entry to accrue the 4% vacation entitlement that was earned by employees in August. (No entitlement is earned on vacation pay.)

DIGGING DEEPER

(d) When Sultanaly prepares its income statement, it groups salaries and wages expense with payroll tax expense and labels the amount "Salaries and related expenses." Therefore, the bank cannot figure out exactly how much is being paid to employees. Any outstanding vacation wages payable is grouped with other accruals of expenses and shown as accrued liabilities in the current liability section of Sultanaly's balance sheet. You are Sultanaly's banker. Do you feel that you require more detail concerning the combined expense on the income statement or combined accrued liabilities on the balance sheet?

P13-6 The following is a payroll sheet for Bayview Golf Corporation for the first week of November 2017. The Employment Insurance rate is 1.88% and the maximum annual deduction per employee is $930.60. The employer's obligation for Employment Insurance is 1.4 times the amount of the employee deduction. Assume a 15% income tax rate for all employees, and a 4.95% CPP premium charged to both the employee and employer, up to an annual maximum of $2,479.95 per employee. Union dues are 1% of earnings. Bayview is a private corporation following ASPE.

Name	Earnings to Oct. 31	1st Week Nov. Earnings	Income Tax Deducted	CPP	EI	Union Dues
L. Meloche	$36,120	$ 840				
P. Groot	33,540	780				
D. Beaux	54,180	1,260				
C. Regier	6,000	1,000				

Instructions

FINANCE

(a) Complete the payroll sheet and prepare the necessary entry to record the payment of the payroll.

(b) Prepare the entry to record the employer's payroll tax expense.

(c) Prepare the entries to record the payments of the payroll liabilities (1) to the Receiver General and (2) to the employees' union. Assume that Bayview pays all payroll liabilities at the end of each month.

(d) What is the total expense that Bayview will report for the first week of November 2017 relative to employee compensation? (Ignore any vacation pay accrual.) What percentage of gross pay is the payroll tax expense? Will this percentage be a constant for all pay periods?

DIGGING DEEPER

(e) Bayview's management is considering laying off all of its employees and immediately thereafter entering into contracts with each employee, creating a contractor relationship with the business. Bayview reasons that severance packages do not need to be paid because immediate reinstatement with the company will be made available to all employees. This way all payroll tax expenses are avoided and the total labour expense would not only be reduced but be characterized as contract service expense on the income statement. Assume the plan is put into place for the current year. As a potential investor who is looking at the current year's comparative income statement, how will your decisions be affected by the reclassification of labour costs?

P13-7 Huang Inc., a private business following ASPE, has a contract with its president, Ms. Shen, to pay her a bonus during each of the years 2017, 2018, and 2019. Huang has the practice of paying Ms. Shen her bonus in quarterly payments at the end of March, June, September, and December of the following fiscal year. Statutory deductions are applied through the payroll system when the quarterly bonus payments are made. Assume a corporate income tax rate of 30% during the three years. The profit before deductions for bonus and income tax was $250,000 in 2017, $308,000 in 2018, and $350,000 in 2019. The president's bonus of 12% is deductible for corporate income tax purposes in each year and is to be calculated as follows:

1. In 2017, the bonus is to be based on profit before deductions for bonus and income tax.

2. In 2018, the bonus is to be based on profit after deduction of bonus but before deduction of income tax.

3. In 2019, the bonus is to be based on profit before deduction of bonus but after deduction of income tax.

Instructions

(a) Calculate the amounts of the annual bonus and the corporate income tax for each of the three years.

(b) Determine the classification of any balances owing to Ms. Shen at the year end of December 31, 2017 under each of the formulas.

(c) Assume now that Huang issues quarterly financial statements. How would Huang record the bonus expense in each quarter of 2017?

(d) What difference, if any, would apply in parts (a) through (c) above if Huang had followed IFRS?

DIGGING DEEPER

(e) Because Huang has a calendar year end, the final calculation of the annual bonus due to Ms. Shen is made following the completion of the year end. Year-end procedures and final adjustments to the accounts include the accrual of Ms. Shen's bonus. Ms. Shen would like to receive advances on her bonus during the year, similar to commission payments made by Huang to its sales force. Under this proposal, Huang would continue to make quarterly payments as was done in past years and for amounts based on the total previous year's bonus for the first three quarters. Ms. Shen does not want any of the advances received toward the annual bonus to go through the payroll system when received. She wishes to postpone the income tax payment until the following calendar taxation year. The fourth and final quarterly payment in March of the following year would constitute the payment of the full annual bonus. For this final payment, the full amount of the annual bonus would be recorded through payroll, personal income tax deductions would be withheld, and the advances to date would be repaid from the net amount. If the balance owing after deductions does not cover the advances, Ms. Shen is to repay Huang by the end of April of that year.

TAXATION

1. Taking the perspective of the Canada Revenue Agency, do you believe that what is being proposed is acceptable for tax purposes? In your opinion, should the accounting and tax treatment be the same? Should the advances be recorded as salaries and wages expense when paid and therefore taxed when paid, or treated as a reduction of an accrued liability?

2. Do you believe the proposal from Ms. Shen is ethical? Why or why not?

ETHICS   **P13-8**   In preparing Sahoto Corporation's December 31, 2017 financial statements under ASPE, the vice-president, finance, is trying to determine the proper accounting treatment for each of the following situations.

1. As a result of uninsured accidents during the year, personal injury suits for $350,000 and $60,000 have been filed against Sahoto. It is the judgement of Sahoto's lawyers that an unfavourable outcome is unlikely in the $60,000 case but that an unfavourable verdict for approximately $225,000 is likely in the $350,000 case.

2. In early 2017, Sahoto received notice from the provincial environment ministry that a site Sahoto had been using to dispose of waste was considered toxic, and that Sahoto would be held responsible for its cleanup under provincial legislation. The vice-president, finance, discussed the situation over coffee with the vice-president, engineering. The engineer stated that it would take up to three years to determine the best way to remediate the site and that the cost would be considerable, perhaps as much as $500,000 to $2 million or more. The engineering vice-president advocates recognizing at least the minimum estimate of $500,000 in the current year's financial statements. The financial vice-president advocates just disclosing the situation and the inability to estimate the cost in a note to the financial statements.

3. Sahoto Corporation has a foreign division that has a net carrying amount of $5,725,000 and an estimated fair value of $8.7 million. The foreign government has told Sahoto that it intends to expropriate the assets and business of all foreign investors. Based on settlements that other firms have received from this same country, Sahoto expects to receive 40% of the fair value of its properties as compensation.

4. Sahoto's chemical products division consists of five plants and is uninsurable because of the special risk of injury to employees and losses due to fire and explosion. Consequently, Sahoto must self-insure for these risks. The year 2017 is considered one of the safest in the division's history because there were no losses due to injury or casualty. Having suffered an average of three casualties a year during the rest of the past decade (ranging from $60,000 to $700,000), management is certain that next year Sahoto will not be so fortunate.

Instructions

(a) Prepare the journal entries that should be recorded as at December 31, 2017 to recognize each of the situations above.

(b) Indicate what should be reported relative to each situation in the financial statements and accompanying notes. Explain why.

ETHICS

(c) Are there any ethical issues involved in accounting for contingencies?

(d) You are a potential investor. Do you view Sahoto's investment in the expropriated division as being negligent on the part of the board of directors (because the company would have known or should have known of the political difficulties when making the initial investment)?

DIGGING DEEPER

P13-9   Ramirez Inc., a publishing company, is preparing its December 31, 2017 financial statements and must determine the proper accounting treatment for the following situations. Ramirez has retained your firm to help with this task.

1. Ramirez sells subscriptions to several magazines for a one-year, two-year, or three-year period. Cash receipts from subscribers are credited to Unearned Subscriptions Revenue, and this account had a balance of $2.3 million at December 31, 2017. Outstanding subscriptions at December 31, 2017, expire as follows:

During 2018	$600,000
During 2019	500,000
During 2020	800,000

2. On January 2, 2017, Ramirez discontinued collision, fire, and theft coverage on its delivery vehicles and became self-insured for these risks. Actual losses of $50,000 during 2017 were charged to Delivery Expense. The 2016 premium for the discontinued coverage amounted to $80,000 and the controller wants to accrue a reserve for self-insurance by a debit to Delivery Expense of $30,000 and a credit to the Reserve for Self-Insurance of $30,000.

3. A suit for breach of contract seeking damages of $1 million was filed by an author against Ramirez on July 1, 2017. Ramirez's legal counsel believes that an unfavourable outcome is likely. A reasonable estimate of the court's award to the plaintiff is between $300,000 and $700,000. No amount within this range is a better estimate of potential damages than any other amount.

4. Ramirez's main supplier, Bartlett Ltd., has been experiencing liquidity problems over the last three quarters. In order for Bartlett's bank to continue to extend credit, Bartlett has asked and Ramirez has guaranteed its indebtedness. The bank loan stands at $500,000 at December 31, 2017, but the guarantee extends to the full credit facility of $900,000. There is currently no indication that Bartlett will default on any of its bank loans.

5. Ramirez's landlord has informed the company that its warehouse lease will not be renewed when it expires in six months. Ramirez entered into a $2-million contract on December 15, 2017 with Complete Construction Company Ltd., committing Ramirez to building an office and warehouse facility.

6. During December 2017, a competitor company filed suit against Ramirez for industrial espionage, claiming $1.5 million in damages. In the opinion of management and company counsel, it is reasonably possible that damages will be awarded to the plaintiff. However, the amount of potential damages awarded to the plaintiff cannot be reasonably estimated.

FINANCE

Instructions

(a) For each of the above situations, provide the journal entry that should be recorded as at December 31, 2017 under ASPE, or explain why an entry should not be recorded. For each situation, identify what disclosures are required, if any.

(b) Would your answer to any of the above situations change if Ramirez followed current IFRS standards?

(c) You are a potential investor. Do you view Ramirez's decision for self-insurance as negligent on the part of the board of directors? Why or why not?

DIGGING DEEPER

P13-10 Brooks Inc. sells portable computer equipment with a two-year warranty contract that requires the corporation to replace defective parts and provide the necessary repair labour. During 2017, the corporation sells for cash 400 computers at a unit price of $2,500. Based on experience, the two-year warranty costs are estimated to be $155 for parts and $185 for labour per unit. (For simplicity, assume that all sales occurred on December 31, 2017.) The warranty is not sold separately from the equipment, and no portion of the sales price is allocated to warranty sales. Brooks follows ASPE.

Instructions

Answer parts (a) to (d) based on the information above.

(a) Record the 2017 journal entry, assuming the cash basis is used to account for the warranties.

(b) Record the 2017 journal entries, assuming the accrual basis under the assurance-type approach is used to account for the warranties.

(c) What liability relative to these transactions would appear on the December 31, 2017 balance sheet? How would it be classified if the cash basis is used?

(d) What liability relative to these transactions would appear on the December 31, 2017 balance sheet? How would it be classified if the accrual basis assurance-type approach is used?

Answer parts (e) to (h) assuming that in 2018 the actual warranty costs incurred by Brooks were $21,400 for parts and $39,900 for labour.

(e) Record the necessary entry in 2018, applying the cash basis.

(f) Record the necessary entry in 2018, applying the accrual basis assurance-type approach.

DIGGING DEEPER

(g) Which method of accounting for warranties would you recommend to Brooks? Why?

(h) Assume that the warranty costs incurred by Brooks in 2019 were substantially higher than estimated. How would Brooks deal with the discrepancy between the estimated warranty liability and the actual warranty expense?

P13-11 Smythe Corporation sells televisions at an average price of $850 and they come with a standard one-year warranty. Smythe also offers each customer a separate three-year extended warranty contract for $90 that requires the company to perform periodic services and replace defective parts. The extended warranty begins one year after the purchase date. During 2017, Smythe sold 300 televisions and 270 extended warranty contracts for cash. Company records indicate that warranty costs in the first year after purchase average $25 per set: $15 for parts and $10 for labour. Smythe estimates the average three-year extended warranty costs as $20 for parts and $40 for labour. Assume that all sales occurred on December 31, 2017, and that all warranty costs are expected to be incurred evenly over the warranty period. Smythe uses the assurance-type approach for the one-year warranty and the service-type approach for the extended warranty contracts.

Instructions

Answer parts (a) and (b) based on the information above.

(a) Record any necessary journal entries in 2017.

(b) What liabilities relative to these transactions would appear on the December 31, 2017 statement of financial position? How would they be classified?

Answer parts (c) and (d) assuming that in 2018 Smythe Corporation incurred actual costs relative to 2017 television warranty sales of $4,410 for parts and $2,940 for labour.

(c) Record any necessary journal entries in 2018 relative to the 2017 television warranties.

(d) What amounts relative to the 2017 television warranties would appear on the December 31, 2018 statement of financial position? How would they be classified?

Answer parts (e) and (f) assuming that in 2019 Smythe Corporation incurred the following costs relative to the extended warranties sold in 2017: $2,000 for parts and $3,000 for labour.

(e) Record any necessary journal entries in 2019 relative to the 2017 television warranties.

(f) What amounts relative to the 2017 television warranties would appear on the December 31, 2019 statement of financial position? How would they be classified?

DIGGING
DEEPER

(g) You are a potential investor and see warranty liability accruals on the statement of financial position of the business you are interested in. The business includes warranties in the selling prices of its products and it accounts for these warranties using the assurance-type method. You have heard of numerous product recalls by competitors of the company you have selected. Are the costs of these product recalls included in the amount accrued for product warranties?

P13-12   Renew Energy Ltd. (REL) manufactures and sells directly to customers a special long-lasting rechargeable battery for use in digital electronic equipment. Each battery sold comes with a guarantee that the company will replace free of charge any battery that is found to be defective within six months from the end of the month in which the battery was sold. On June 30, 2017, the Warranty Liability account had a balance of $45,000, but by December 31, 2017, this amount had been reduced to $5,000 by charges for batteries returned.

REL has been in business for many years and has consistently experienced an 8% return rate. However, effective October 1, 2017, because of a change in the manufacturing process, the rate increased to a total of 10%. Each battery is stamped with a date at the time of sale so that REL has developed information on the likely pattern of returns during the six-month period, starting with the month following the sale. (Assume no batteries are returned in the month of sale.)

Month Following Sale	% of Total Returns Expected in the Month
1st	20%
2nd	30%
3rd	20%
4th	10%
5th	10%
6th	10%
	100%

For example, for January sales, 20% of the returns are expected in February, 30% in March, and so on. Sales of these batteries for the second half of 2017 were:

Month	Sales Amount
July	$1,800,000
August	1,650,000
September	2,050,000
October	1,425,000
November	1,000,000
December	900,000

REL's warranty also covers the payment of the freight cost on defective batteries returned and on new batteries sent as replacements. This freight cost is 10% of the sales price of the batteries returned. The manufacturing cost of a battery is roughly 60% of its sales price, and the salvage value of the returned batteries averages 14% of the sales price. Assume that REL follows IFRS and that it uses the expense approach to account for warranties.

Instructions

(a) Calculate the warranty expense that will be reported for the July 1 to December 31, 2017 period.

(b) Calculate the amount of the accrual that you would expect in the Warranty Liability account as at December 31, 2017, based on the above likely pattern of returns.

(c) Would your answer to any of the above situations change if REL followed ASPE?

DIGGING DEEPER

FINANCE

(d) You are a potential investor reading REL's December 31, 2017 annual report, which was released on March 20, 2018. While reading the CEO's report, you find a description of plans to be implemented beginning April 1, 2018 that address REL's warranty policy and declining sales, which began October 1, 2017. An advertising agency has been hired that will help REL launch a new warranty policy. The new policy will extend the return period to 12 months and change the conditions of return to: "if for any reason the customer is dissatisfied with the product." Consequently, customers will no longer need to prove any product defect, allowing for faster returns and more satisfied customers. This change is expected to not only restore sales to the levels prior to the change in the product's manufacturing process, but also take sales away from REL's competitors. What additional disclosure, if any, are you expecting in the December 31, 2017 financial statements for this change in warranty policy taking effect on April 1, 2018?

P13-13 To increase the sales of its Sugar Kids breakfast cereal, KW Foods Limited (KW) places one coupon in each cereal box. Five coupons are redeemable for a premium consisting of a child's hand puppet. In 2017, KW purchases 40,000 puppets at $1.50 each and sells 480,000 boxes of Sugar Kids at $3.75 a box. KW estimates that $0.20 of the sale price relates to the hand puppet to be awarded. From its experience with other similar premium offers, KW estimates that 40% of the coupons issued will be mailed back for redemption. During 2017, 115,000 coupons are presented for redemption. KW is a private company following ASPE.

Instructions

(a) Prepare the journal entries that should be recorded in 2017 relative to the premium plan, assuming that KW follows a policy of charging the cost of coupons to expense as they are redeemed and adjusting the liability account at year end.

(b) Prepare the journal entries that should be recorded in 2017 relative to the premium plan, assuming that KW follows a policy of charging the full estimated cost of the premium plan to expense when the sales are recognized.

(c) How would the accounts resulting from the entries in parts (a) and (b) above be presented on the 2017 financial statements?

(d) Prepare the journal entries that should be recorded in 2017 relative to the premium plan, assuming that KW follows IFRS and accounts for its promotional programs in accordance with the revenue approach and IFRIC 13.

(e) How would the accounts resulting from the entries in part (d) above be presented on the 2017 financial statements?

DIGGING DEEPER

(f) Compare your answer to part (c) with your answer to part (e). Which approach to accounting for premiums would you recommend to KW? Why?

P13-14 The Hwang Candy Corporation (HCC) offers a mini piggy bank as a premium for every five chocolate bar wrappers that customers send in along with $2.00. The chocolate bars are sold by HCC to distributors for $0.30 each. The purchase price of each piggy bank to HCC is $1.80; in addition, it costs $0.50 to mail each bank. The results of the premium plan for the years 2017 and 2018 are as follows (all purchases and sales are for cash):

	2017	2018
Mini piggy banks purchased	250,000	330,000
Chocolate bars sold	2,895,400	2,743,600
Wrappers redeemed	1,200,000	1,500,000
2017 wrappers expected to be redeemed in 2018	290,000	
2018 wrappers expected to be redeemed in 2019		350,000

Instructions

(a) Prepare the journal entries that should be made in 2017 and 2018 to record the transactions related to HCC's premium plan using the expense approach under ASPE.

(b) Indicate the account names, amounts, and classifications of the items related to the premium plan that would appear on HCC's statement of financial position and the income statement at the end of 2017 and 2018.

(c) For each liability that you identified in part (b), indicate whether it is a financial liability and, if so, why.

(d) What additional information would you need to record the transactions of HCC's premium promotional plan, assuming the revenue approach had been followed in accordance with IFRS?

P13-15   Mullen Music Limited (MML) carries a wide variety of musical instruments, sound reproduction equipment, recorded music, and sheet music. MML uses two sales promotion techniques—warranties and premiums—to attract customers.

Musical instruments and sound equipment are sold with a one-year warranty for replacement of parts and labour. The estimated warranty cost, based on experience, is 2% of net sales.

A premium is offered on the recorded and sheet music. Customers receive one point for each dollar spent on recorded music or sheet music. Customers may exchange 200 points plus $20 for a set of speakers. MML pays $34 for each set of speakers and estimates that 60% of the points given to customers will be redeemed.

MML's net sales for 2017 were $7.2 million: $5.4 million from musical instruments and sound reproduction equipment, and $1.8 million from recorded music and sheet music. Replacement parts and labour for warranty work totalled $164,000 during 2017. A total of 6,500 sets of speakers used in the premium program were purchased during the year and there were 1.2 million points redeemed in 2017.

The expense approach is used by MML to account for the warranty and premium costs for financial reporting purposes. The balances in the accounts related to warranties and premiums on January 1, 2017, were:

Inventory of premiums	$ 39,950
Estimated liability for premiums	44,800
Warranty liability	136,000

Instructions

(a) MML is preparing its financial statements for the year ended December 31, 2017 in accordance with ASPE. Determine the amounts that will be shown on the 2017 financial statements for the following:

1. Warranty expense
2. Warranty liability
3. Premium expense
4. Inventory of premiums
5. Estimated liability for premiums

AUDIT AND ASSURANCE

(b) Assume that MML's auditor determined that both the one-year warranty and the points for the sets of speakers were, in fact, revenue arrangements with multiple deliverables that should be accounted for under the revenue approach because MML is following IFRS. Explain how this would change the way in which these two programs were accounted for in part (a).

(CMA adapted)

P13-16   Dungannon Enterprises Ltd. sells a specialty part that is used in widescreen televisions and provides the ultimate in screen clarity. To promote sales of its product, Dungannon launched a program with some of its smaller customers. In exchange for making Dungannon their exclusive supplier, Dungannon guarantees these customers to their creditors so that Dungannon will assume the customers' long-term debt in the event of non-payment to the creditors. In addition to charging for parts, Dungannon also charges a fee to customers who take the guarantee program. It bases the fee on the time frame that the guarantee covers, which is typically three years. In the current fiscal year, these fees amounted to $30,000 for the three-year coverage period.

Six months before Dungannon's fiscal year end, one of its customers, Hutter Corp., began to experience financial difficulties and missed two months of mortgage payments. Hutter's lender then called on Dungannon to make the mortgage payments. At its fiscal year end on December 31, 2017, Dungannon had recorded a receivable of $15,000 related to the payments made by Dungannon on Hutter's behalf. Hutter owes the lender an additional $30,000 at this point. The lender is thinking of putting a lien on Hutter's assets that were pledged as collateral for the loans. However, the collateral involves rights to the development of new state-of-the-art three-dimensional television technology that is still unproven. Dungannon follows ASPE.

Instructions

(a) Prepare all required journal entries and adjusting entries on Dungannon's books to recognize the transactions and events described above.

(b) Identify any disclosures that must be made as a result of this information and prepare the note disclosure for Dungannon for the period ended December 31, 2017.

P13-17   Hamilton Airlines is faced with two situations that need to be resolved before the financial statements for the company's year ended December 31, 2017 can be issued.

1. The airline is being sued for $4 million for an injury caused to a child as a result of alleged negligence while the child was visiting the airline maintenance hangar in March 2017. The suit was filed in July 2017. Hamilton's lawyer states that it is likely that the airline will lose the suit and be found liable for a judgement costing anywhere from $400,000 to $2 million. However, the lawyer states that the most probable judgement is $800,000.

2. On November 24, 2017, 26 passengers on Flight No. 901 were injured upon landing when the plane skidded off the runway. On January 11, 2018, personal injury suits for damages totalling $5 million were filed against the airline by 18 injured passengers. The airline carries no insurance. Legal counsel has studied each suit and advised that it can reasonably expect to pay 60% of the damages claimed.

Instructions

(a) Prepare any disclosures and journal entries for the airline required by (1) ASPE, and (2) IFRS in the preparation of the December 31, 2017 financial statements.

(b) Ignoring the 2017 accidents, what liability due to the risk of loss from lack of insurance coverage should Hamilton Airlines record or disclose? During the past decade, Hamilton Airlines has experienced at least one accident per year and incurred average damages of $3.2 million. Discuss fully.

DIGGING DEEPER

(c) Your are the manager at Hamilton Airlines who is assessing the two lawsuit cases for financial reporting purposes. Describe how you (1) arrived at the assessment of the likelihood of the outcome in each case, and (2) measured the amount of the probable judgement.

Case

ENABLING COMPETENCIES

Refer to the Case Primer on the Student Website and in *WileyPLUS* to help you answer this case.

CA13-1 ABC Airlines carried more than 11.9 million passengers to over 160 destinations in 17 countries in 2017. ABC is the descendant of several predecessor companies, including AB Air and BC Airlines. The amalgamated company was created in 1999. In the years that followed, the world air travel industry slumped and caused many airlines to go bankrupt or suffer severe financial hardship. ABC weathered the storm by going through a significant restructuring. One of the changes as a result of the restructuring was to have ABC employees take share options as part of their remuneration. This resulted in employees investing $200 million in the company. The company is privately owned.

In 2017, ABC was still suffering losses, now partly due to increased competition and falling seat prices. Losses were $187 million in 2015 and $194 million in 2016. The CEO announced a new restructuring plan that would hopefully put an end to the continuing losses. The plan focused on three areas: improved network profitability, decreased overhead costs, and decreased labour costs. For the latter, employees were asked to accept reduced wages over a four-year period.

Just like most companies, ABC is now concerned with increasing market share and maintaining customer loyalty. On the company's website, the following advertisement appears:

"Fly 5, Fly Free—Fly five times with ABC Airlines and its worldwide partners and earn a free trip. The more you fly, the more the world is within reach."

Free flights are also offered by ABC through its well-publicized frequent flyer program. Under the program, customers earn points for flying with ABC and, once they accumulate enough points, they can then use them to take free flights. In the notes to its financial statements, ABC notes that the incremental costs of frequent flyer points are accrued as the entitlements to free flights are earned. The accrual is included as part of accrued liabilities.

Excerpts from the 2017 financial statements follow (in millions):	
Total assets (including current assets of $456.5)	$1,866
Current liabilities	765
Long-term debt	841
Preferred shares	289
Common shares	407
Deficit	(436)
Total liabilities and equity	$1,866

Instructions

Adopt the role of company management and discuss the treatment of the "Fly 5, Fly Free" program for financial reporting purposes. The company is interested in understanding how the program would be accounted for under both IFRS and ASPE.

Integrated Cases

ENABLING COMPETENCIES

IC13-1 Envirocompany Limited (EL) is a pulp and paper company that has been in operation for 50 years. Its shares trade on a major stock exchange. It is located in a small town in Northern Ontario and employs thousands of people. In fact, the town exists mainly because of the jobs created by EL. Its equipment is fairly outdated and pollutes the surrounding water and air with chemicals that have been shown to be possible carcinogens. The old equipment is part of the reason for the company's "success" since it is all paid for and requires little maintenance. The employees tolerate the pollution because EL gives them good jobs and keeps the local economy going.

Last year, a new chairman of the board of directors was appointed to EL, Charles Champion. He first became aware of the size of the pollution problem before being appointed to the board and he felt that he would like to do something about it. He took this mission as a personal challenge. In the first year of his appointment, he commissioned several in-depth studies on how EL might reduce or eliminate the pollution. He wanted to be careful to protect himself and the other members of the board because directors were increasingly being held personally liable for the actions of companies. EL has begun cultivating an image implying that it would like to become more environmentally conscious while at the same time preserving jobs.

Most studies pointed to the old machinery and recommended that it be replaced by new state-of-the-art equipment. Cost estimates ran into the millions of dollars and the board of directors felt that the company would not be able to survive that type of expenditure. One study proved that the company would not even be in business any more, given the cost of new environmentally friendly equipment, declining demand for unrecycled newsprint, and increasing competition from abroad. That study was quickly put away on a shelf.

Recent environmental studies have shown that the pollutants from the area near EL and neighbouring manufacturers were seeping into the water table and finding their way into neighbouring communities. The studies showed that there were increasing incidences of birth defects in animals and humans in the affected areas, including increases in sterility for certain aquatic and marine life. This caused several politicians to start grandstanding and calling for tighter pollution controls and steeper fines.

In the past year, there have been reports of people living downstream getting sick, possibly from the chemical pollutants from EL. One individual threatened to sue, and EL's lawyers were privately acknowledging the potential for a class action suit. EL has insurance that would cover up to $5 million in damages.

Meanwhile, the accountants were struggling with how to account for the problem in the year-end financial statements.

Instructions

Adopt the role of the company controller and discuss the financial reporting issues under both IFRS and ASPE.

IC13-2 Landfill Limited (LL) is a private company that collects and disposes of household garbage. Waste is collected and trucked to local disposal sites, where it is dumped and then covered with topsoil. The disposal sites are owned by LL and were financed by debt from Nova Bank at an average interest rate of 5%.

LL has several disposal sites that will be filled with garbage and later sold as industrial land. LL estimates that the sites will take 20 years on average to fill up. Varying amounts of garbage will be dumped each year. Salvage values are not known at the time, although land normally holds its value unless toxic chemicals are found.

AUDIT AND ASSURANCE

Government regulations require that the company perform capping, closure, and post-closure activities. Capping involves covering the land with topsoil and planting vegetation. Closure activities include drainage, engineering, and demolition. Post-closure activities include maintaining the landfill once the government has given final certification. They also include monitoring the ground and surface water, gas emissions, and air quality. If the land is sold, the purchaser reduces the acquisition cost by an estimate of this cost. LL must also guarantee that the land is toxin-free, and if it is later found to contain toxins, LL will pay for cleanup.

In the past year, one of these landfill sites was sold. However, the company recently received notification from the purchaser's lawyers that high levels of toxins had been found leaking into the water table.

Obtaining new waste removal contracts, as well as keeping old ones, depends on many factors. These include competitive bidding, the company's profile in the community, its past work performance, its financial stability, and having a history of adhering strictly to environmental standards. Financial statements are therefore relevant in the process of obtaining new contracts as they are examined by those who award them.

Instructions

Adopt the role of the company auditor and discuss the financial reporting issues. Landfill Limited is one of your new audit clients this year. The client is interested in how these issues would be accounted for under both ASPE and IFRS.

IC13-3 Candelabra Limited (CL) is a manufacturing company that is privately owned. The company's production facilities produce a significant amount of carbon dioxide, and currently the town is suing CL for polluting the surrounding area. The company is enjoying a period of significant prosperity and earnings have been steadily increasing. CL plans to double in size within the next 10 years. The production facility was financed by a 100-year bond that pays 5% interest annually. The bond includes a covenant that stipulates that the debt to equity ratio must not exceed 2:1. The debt to equity ratio is currently just below this threshold.

The government has recently introduced a system to control pollution whereby each company is allocated a certain number of "carbon credits." The carbon credits allow the company to produce a certain amount of carbon dioxide as a by-product from its production facilities. CL has been allocated a fixed number of these credits by the government at no cost. If CL produces more carbon dioxide than allowed, it will have to pay a fine. CL is pretty sure that it will exceed the amount allowed under the government-allotted carbon credits. Many companies in the surrounding area have extra carbon credits and, as a result, the government has established an informal marketplace whereby companies can trade their extra credits. The value of the contracts changes depending on supply and demand.

AUDIT AND ASSURANCE

CL has purchased several carbon credit contracts in the marketplace just in case. At the time it acquired the contracts, there was an oversupply and so CL was able to acquire them at very little cost. Currently, demand for the credits has increased significantly.

As another backup plan, CL is investigating diverting excess carbon dioxide to an underground cave that is situated on company-owned property. Currently, CL has spent a significant amount of funds to investigate the feasibility of diverting and storing the extra carbon dioxide it produces. The engineers working on the project are still not convinced of the feasibility of this type of storage on a larger scale. At present, they have started to store some excess carbon dioxide there on a test basis.

In order to fund the work on the cave, the company has issued shares. The shares are redeemable in cash at the company's option if its carbon dioxide levels (excluding any amounts that will be stored in the cave) reach a certain point. The shares are currently held by a large pension company.

Instructions

Assume the role of CL's auditors and analyze the financial reporting issues. Note where there are differences between IFRS and ASPE.

RESEARCH AND ANALYSIS

REAL WORLD EMPHASIS

RA13-1 Empire Company Limited

Access the annual financial statements of **Empire Company Limited** for its year ended May 2, 2015 at www.sedar.com or the company's website.

Instructions

Review Empire Company Limited's consolidated financial statements and provide answers to the following questions.

(a) What key business(es) does the company operate in?

(b) Review the accounting policy note related to Empire's customer loyalty programs. Describe the company's customer loyalty program in effect until the fourth quarter of its year ended May 2, 2015, and explain how it was accounted for. Describe the company's customer loyalty program that is now in effect. How will this new program be accounted for?

(c) What is the total amount of "provisions" reported by Empire on its statement of financial position at May 2, 2015? Identify Empire's accounting policies for provisions and what these provisions relate to. Explain why these are considered provisions.

(d) One of the reasons provided for the change in the balance of the provisions account over the fiscal year is "change due to discounting." Briefly explain this change.

REAL WORLD EMPHASIS

RA13-2 Canadian Tire Corporation, Limited

The 2014 financial statements (for its 53-week period ended January 3, 2015) and 10-year financial review of **Canadian Tire Corporation, Limited** can be found at www.sedar.com or on the company's website.

Instructions

(a) What makes up Canadian Tire's current liabilities? Suggest at least five different types of liabilities that are likely included in "trade and other payables." What is included in deposits?

(b) What were Canadian Tire's working capital, acid-test ratio, and current ratio for the two most recent years of data that are provided? How do these results compare with the measures over the last five years? Comment on the company's current liquidity in general, and compared with its liquidity five years ago. What is the 2014 inventory turnover and what role does this ratio play in assessing liquidity in general, and for Canadian Tire specifically? What is in the accounts receivable and what role does it play in assessing liquidity for Canadian Tire? Can a turnover ratio be calculated for these accounts receivable?

(c) What is the current portion of long-term debt? Explain clearly what makes up this amount. If the company does not borrow any additional long-term funds during 2015, how much would you expect to see on the 2015 end-of-year balance sheet as the current portion of long-term debt? Explain clearly what would make up this amount. Are there any concerns arising from this amount?

(d) What types of commitments and contingencies has Canadian Tire reported in its financial statements? Identify which items are commitments and which are contingencies. What is management's reaction to the contingencies?

(e) What covenants does the company have to maintain under its existing debt agreements? Was it in compliance at the year end? (*Hint*: See the Capital Management Disclosures note.)

RA13-3   Deutsche Lufthansa AG

REAL WORLD EMPHASIS

The consolidated financial statements of **Deutsche Lufthansa AG** for the year ended December 31, 2014 are available in the company's 2014 Annual Report on the www.lufthansagroup.com website.

Instructions

(a) What is included in the current liabilities for Lufthansa? How have the percentages of each item to total current liabilities changed from 2013 to 2014?

(b) What specific items are included in Other Provisions; Trade Payables and Other Financial Liabilities; and Advance Payments Received, Deferred Income and Other Non-Financial Liabilities? What is included in Liabilities from Unused Flight Documents?

(c) What types of employee benefit liabilities are included in Other Provisions? How does the company estimate environmental obligations?

(d) What changes have occurred in Other Provisions between December 31, 2013 and December 31, 2014? Prepare a reconciliation of the opening and closing balances for 2014.

(e) How does the company currently account for the bonus miles program, Lufthansa's customer loyalty program? What is the amount in liabilities that represents this obligation? How many miles have been accumulated? (See Note 2 to the 2014 financial statements.)

(f) What contingencies does the company have? Have any of these been recognized?

(g) What makes up the current portion of borrowings for Lufthansa at December 31, 2014? Be specific.

RA13-4   Memo to CFO

ETHICS

You, the ethical accountant, are the new controller at ProVision Corporation. It is January 2018 and you are currently preparing the December 31, 2017 financial statements. ProVision manufactures household appliances. It is a private company and has been considering a move to IFRS, effective for the 2017 financial statements. During your review of the accounts and discussion with the lawyer, you discover the following possible liabilities.

1. ProVision began production of a new dishwasher in June 2017, and by December 31, 2017, had sold 100,000 units to various retailers for $500 each. Each dishwasher is sold with a one-year warranty included. The company estimates that its warranty expense per dishwasher will amount to $25. By year end, the company had already paid out $1 million in warranty expenditures on 35,000 units. ProVision's records currently show a warranty expense of $1 million for 2017. Warranties similar to these are available for sale for $75. (Assume both the assurance-type and service-type approaches are alternatives.)

2. ProVision's retail division rents space from Meadow Malls. ProVision pays a rental fee of $6,000 per month plus 5% of the amount of yearly retail profits over $500,000. ProVision's CEO, Burt Wilson, tells you that he had instructed the previous accountant to increase the estimate of bad debt expense and warranty costs in order to keep the retail division's profits at $475,000.

3. ProVision's lawyer, Robert Dowski, informed you that ProVision has a legal obligation to dismantle and remove the equipment used to produce the dishwashers and clean up the rental premises as part of the lease agreement. The equipment, costing $10 million, was put into production on June 1, 2017, and has a useful life of 120 months. The dismantling and removal costs are estimated to be $3 million. In addition, as a result of the production process, there are clean-up costs incurred, estimated to be $5,000 per month during production, which will be totally paid (estimated in total to be $600,000) when the equipment is removed. (The appropriate discount rate to be used for determining the present value of the cash flows is 0.5% per month.)

4. ProVision is the defendant in a patent infringement lawsuit filed by Heidi Golder over ProVision's use of a hydraulic compressor in several of its products. Robert Dowski claims that, if the suit goes against ProVision, the loss may be as much as $5 million. It is more likely than not that ProVision will have to pay some amount on settlement. Although the exact amount is not known, the lawyer has been able to assign probabilities and expected payment amounts as follows: 20% probability that the settlement will be $5 million, 35% probability that the settlement will be $3 million, and 45% that no settlement will be required.

Instructions

(a) In the form of a memorandum to the CFO, address each of the above issues. Explain what the problem is and what choices the company has to report these liabilities under ASPE and IFRS. Prepare the journal entries that would be required under adoption of either standard. Explain any differences in the reported income under the various approaches.

(b) Identify and explain any issues where you consider an ethical perspective is particularly important. Suggest what should be done.

RA13-5   Differing Accounting for Two Issues under ASPE and IFRS

City Goods Limited (CG) is a sports clothing and equipment retailer that has a chain of 10 stores across Canada. You have just been hired as the new controller for the company. You are currently meeting with the CFO to discuss some accounting-related topics that have arisen in the preparation of the company's January 31, 2018 financial statements. City Goods is a private company. The following is a summary of your notes from this meeting.

1. Customer loyalty program: In this fiscal year, the company implemented a new customer loyalty program that grants "CG points" to members based on the amount they spend in the store. The points have no expiry date and can be redeemed against future purchases in the store. The company has already determined that the fair value of each point is $0.50. During the year, 700,000 points were awarded to members, of which 80,000 were subsequently redeemed for purchases in the stores. The company anticipates that 90% of the points will be redeemed at some point in time.

2. The company entered into an agreement on April 1, 2014 to lease a retail location for five years. In December 2017, City Goods decided to close that retail location due to very poor sales. The company has not been able to sublet the premises and is not able to terminate the lease agreement. The monthly lease payment, which includes all operating costs, is $2,300 per month.

Instructions

For each of the two issues above, explain the situation and the appropriate accounting treatment under ASPE and IFRS. Show any required journal entries. Where necessary, use a discount rate of 0.5% per month.

RA13-6   Employee Benefits

Conduit Corporation has 45 current employees: 5 managers and 40 non-managers. The average wage paid is $250 per day for non-managers. The company has just finished negotiating a new employee contract with the non-managers that would see this increase by 3% effective January 1, 2018. The company's fiscal year end is December 31, 2017.

You are the controller for Conduit and are completing the year-end adjusting journal entries. The company has the following employee benefit plans.

1. Non-manager employees are entitled to two sick leave days per month. If any days are not taken, they may accumulate and be taken as vacation or paid in cash. The sick days may be carried forward to the end of the next year. At the end of the year, there were 60 accumulated sick leave days that had not yet been taken.

2. Any employee is entitled to one year's parental leave. The company will pay the amount to top up the employment insurance benefits received to make up the employee's annual salary at the time the leave is taken. Currently, there is one employee on parental leave, who started her maternity leave on December 15, 2017. It is expected that the top-up required will be $1,000 per month for 12 months and the employee was paid $500 on December 31, 2017. There is another employee who is trying to adopt a child and has also said that he will want paternity leave at the time the adoption occurs. The top-up is also estimated to be $1,000 per month for this employee.

3. A profit-sharing plan provides for employees to receive a bonus of 3% of net profit before the bonus and taxes for all employees who worked for the company during the year. The net profit before the bonus and taxes is estimated to be $2 million. The bonus is allocated 30% to the five managers and 70% to the remaining employees. However, the bonus is not paid until October 31 of the following year, and only to employees who remain with the company. The company expects a 5% turnover by October 31, 2018 for the non-manager group.

4. The company pays on average three weeks' vacation pay, even though Conduit's legal obligation is only for two weeks. This vacation pay accumulates and can be carried over for up to one year. However, if the employee leaves before the vacation is taken, then they are only legally entitled to the two-week rate. At the end of the year, there were 10 non-manager employees who had only taken one week of their annual entitlement during 2017. There is a probability of 15% that one of these employees will leave before the full vacation accrual is taken.

5. The company is being sued by a former employee. The non-manager employee contends that not enough severance was paid when he was let go in June 2017. The ex-employee's lawyers are asking for a severance payment of two weeks' pay for each year worked, which in this case was 25 years. The company agreed to pay the employee severance of $30,000 when he was asked to leave the company. This $30,000 has already been accrued in the accounting records. The case is still being disputed and will go to arbitration early in March 2018. Conduit's lawyers believe that the probabilities of settlements for additional amounts (over and above the $30,000) are as follows: 25% probability of settling at $20,000, 60% probability of settling at $28,000, and 15% probability of settling at $30,000.

Instructions

You are the controller for Conduit and are completing the year-end adjusting journal entries. Discuss each of the above issues and determine the journal entries that would be required under IFRS and ASPE.

RA13-7   Research Topics

There are many interesting company programs and circumstances that relate to the definition, recognition, and measurement of liabilities. Examples include customer loyalty programs, retail gift cards, corporate restructuring obligations, air miles programs, product liability lawsuits, liability accruals on interim financial statements, environmental liabilities, onerous contracts, and many employee benefit programs.

Instructions

Choose one of the programs or circumstances listed above. Research your choice using international and Canadian sources, and prepare a one-page summary of the liability recognition and measurement issues that are involved. If possible, identify any accounting standards that may help resolve the issues.

ENDNOTES

[1] The underlying materials are the 2005 Exposure Draft of Proposed Amendments to IAS 37 *Provisions, Contingent Liabilities and Contingent Assets*, the related January 2010 Exposure Draft *Measurement of Liabilities in IAS 37*, and a May 2015 Staff Paper providing research relating to possible changes to IAS 37.

[2] *CPA Canada Handbook*, Part II, Section 1000.29 and IFRS *Conceptual Framework* 4.15–4.19.

[3] This continues to be an issue. See IASB Staff Paper, *Summary of Decisions Reached Since Publishing Exposure Draft: Liabilities—Amendments to IAS 37*, September 30, 2009, p. 5.

[4] IAS 32 *Financial Instruments: Presentation*, para. 11. Copyright © International Financial Reporting Standards Foundation. All rights reserved. Reproduced by John Wiley & Sons Canada, Ltd. with the permission of the International Financial Reporting Standards Foundation.® Reproduction and use rights are strictly limited. No permission granted to third parties to reproduce or distribute. IAS 32.11 also discusses instances where a financial liability is a contract that may be settled in the entity's own equity instruments. See also *CPA Canada Handbook*, Part II, Section 3856.05 for similar ASPE requirements.

[5] For purposes of intermediate financial accounting, financial liabilities at fair value through profit or loss accounted for at fair value include derivatives, and other financial liabilities accounted for using the fair value option. These financial liabilities are discussed further in Chapters 14, 15, and 16.

[6] The standard also addresses the issue of possible reimbursements that apply when an entity settles a provision. In this case, a reimbursement must be virtually certain of being received, so there may be timing differences between when a non-financial liability is recognized and when the corresponding recovery is recognized. See IAS 37.53 for further details. Copyright © International Financial Reporting Standards Foundation. All rights reserved. Reproduced by John Wiley & Sons Canada, Ltd with the permission of the International Financial Reporting Standards Foundation®. Reproduction and use rights are strictly limited. No permission granted to third parties to reproduce or distribute.

[7] IAS 1 *Presentation of Financial Statements*, para. 69. The IASB has made a tentative decision in its Financial Statement Presentation project (December 2009) that the current (short-term) and non-current (long-term) classifications should be based only on a fixed period of one year. In June 2010, the IASB decided to do more outreach before finalizing and publishing a revised exposure draft on financial statement presentation. In July 2010, a Staff Draft of an exposure draft was published suggesting that the term "current" would be replaced by "short-term" and would be based on a fixed period of one year from the reporting date. Copyright © International Financial Reporting Standards Foundation. All rights reserved. Reproduced by John Wiley & Sons Canada, Ltd with the permission of the International Financial Reporting Standards Foundation®. Reproduction and use rights are strictly limited. No permission granted to third parties to reproduce or distribute.

[8] *CPA Canada Handbook*, Part II, Section 1510.08 to 1510.11.

[9] As explained in Chapter 7, 2/10, n/30 means there is a 2% discount if the invoice is paid within 10 days with the full amount due in 30 days; and 1/10, E.O.M., net 30 means that there is a 1% discount if the invoice is paid before the 10th day of the following month with full payment due by the 30th day of the following month (where E.O.M. is "end of month").

[10] Alternatively, the note payable could have been recorded at its face value of $100,000, with the $3,846 difference between the cash received and the face value debited to Discount on Notes Payable. Discount on Notes Payable is a contra account to Notes Payable and therefore is subtracted from Notes Payable on the statement of financial position.

[11] *CPA Canada Handbook*, Part II, Section 1510.14.

[12] Refinancing a short-term obligation on a long-term basis means either replacing it with a long-term obligation or with equity securities or renewing, extending, or replacing it with short-term obligations for an uninterrupted period that is more than one year from the date of the company's balance sheet.

[13] The rate of provincial sales tax (PST) varies from province to province. When this text went to print, Alberta and the territories had no sales tax, while Quebec's rate was 9.975%, Manitoba's rate was 8%, British Columbia's was 7%, and Saskatchewan charged 5%. The tax is usually applied to the sale amount. As discussed below, in Ontario and the Maritime provinces, the PST and GST have been combined into a harmonized sales tax (HST).

[14] In Ontario, New Brunswick, Newfoundland and Labrador, Prince Edward Island (PEI), and Nova Scotia, the provincial retail sales tax has been combined with the federal Goods and Services Tax (5%) to form the HST. The 13% HST (14% in PEI and 15% in Nova Scotia) is administered for the most part by the Canada Revenue Agency and is accounted for on the same basis as the GST for the other provinces and territories. In Quebec, both the Quebec Sales Tax and the GST are administered by the province.

[15] One exception is in the province of Quebec, where for the Quebec Sales Tax and the GST, all amounts paid are recoverable by the entity through a system of input tax refunds, similar to the input tax credits for the GST.

[16] The Quebec rates are somewhat lower than in the rest of Canada because Quebec provides parental benefits separately under a different plan.

[17] IAS 19.16 *Employee Benefits* specifies that the "expected cost of accumulating paid absences" should be measured as "the additional amount that the entity expects to pay as a result of the unused entitlement that has accumulated at the end of the reporting period." ASPE does not specifically address this issue. Copyright © International Financial Reporting Standards Foundation. All rights reserved. Reproduced by John Wiley & Sons Canada, Ltd with the permission of the International Financial Reporting Standards Foundation®. Reproduction and use rights are strictly limited. No permission granted to third parties to reproduce or distribute.

[18] In Canada, statutory parental leave comes under the Employment Insurance program. Many companies, however, offer additional paid parental leave benefits to their employees above the regulated absence from the workplace, usually once they are considered permanent employees.

[19] Longer-term employee benefit obligations associated with compensated absences, including post-retirement benefits, are the subject of Chapter 19.

[20] ASPE recognizes this type of liability only when a reasonable estimate can be made of the amount.

[21] *CPA Canada Handbook*, Part II, Section 3110.09 (*Asset Retirement Obligations*) and IAS 37.36 (*Provisions, Contingent Liabilities and Contingent Assets*). Copyright © International Financial Reporting Standards Foundation. All rights reserved. Reproduced by John Wiley & Sons Canada, Ltd. with the permission of the International Financial Reporting Standards Foundation.® Reproduction and use rights are strictly limited. No permission granted to third parties to reproduce or distribute.

[22] *CPA Canada Handbook*, Part II, Section 3110.19 to 3110.21 (*Asset Retirement Obligations*).

[23] To the extent that the estimates are not exact, future income will be affected by the difference between the estimated expense/liability and the actual costs incurred. These differences are usually minor.

[24] For this example, the authors are assuming the result is the same under both methods. These measurements are explained in Chapters 3 and 6. In summary, IFRS requires that all possible outcomes be weighted by the probability of their occurrence, and that the sum of these weighted amounts is the expected value to be used as the cost estimate. ASPE does not dictate any particular method, so the outcome that is most probable could be chosen as the cost estimate.

[25] Based on research by Colloquy, a service provider for the global loyalty-marketing industry, as reported by abacusinsider.com (accessed August 8, 2015).

[26] IFRIC 13, paragraphs 5 to 8 and *CPA Canada Handbook*, Part II, Section 3400.11.

[27] *CPA Canada Handbook*, Part II, Section 3290.05.

[28] Loss contingencies that result in the incurrence of a liability (under ASPE) are the most relevant ones for the discussion in this chapter. IFRS defines a "provision" as "a liability of uncertain timing or amount." Provisions under IFRS capture items, such as lawsuits, that are considered loss contingencies under ASPE.

In short, the terminology is different between ASPE and current IFRS, but the underlying accounting decisions of whether to accrue or disclose items such as lawsuits are quite similar. Copyright © International Financial Reporting Standards Foundation. All rights reserved. Reproduced by John Wiley & Sons Canada, Ltd with the permission of the International Financial Reporting Standards Foundation®. Reproduction and use rights are strictly limited. No permission granted to third parties to reproduce or distribute.

[29] CPA Canada's *Financial Reporting in Canada, 2008 Edition* reports that the four most common types of contingent losses disclosed by its sample of 200 Canadian companies were lawsuits, environmental matters, contingent consideration, and possible tax reassessments.

[30] For some companies, litigation presents significant costs in employee time and legal fees, even if the outcomes are positive. For example, in 2003, giant **Walmart Stores Inc.** reported that it was the target of 6,649 active lawsuits of all sorts.

[31] IASB, IAS 39.9 and IFRS 9. This chapter does not discuss the revenue recognition issues for insurance contracts.

[32] *CPA Canada Handbook*, Part II, Disclosure of Guarantees, AcG-14.

[33] For further details, see IFRS 9, IAS 37 and IAS 39.47.

[34] *CPA Canada Handbook*, Part II, Contractual Obligations, Section 3280.

REFERENCE TO THE CPA COMPETENCY MAP	LEARNING OBJECTIVES
	After studying this chapter, you should be able to:
1.1.1, 1.1.2, 1.2.1, 1.2.2, 1.2.3, 1.2.4, 1.4.5, 5.1.1, 5.2.3	**1.** Understand the nature of long-term debt financing arrangements.
1.2.1, 1.2.2, 1.2.3, 1.4.5, 5.2.3	**2.** Understand how long-term debt is measured and accounted for.
1.2.1, 1.2.2, 1.2.3, 1.2.4, 5.6.2	**3.** Understand when long-term debt is recognized and derecognized, including how to account for troubled debt restructurings.
1.2.1, 1.2.2, 1.2.3, 1.2.4, 1.3.1	**4.** Explain how long-term debt is presented on the statement of financial position.
1.3.2, 1.4.1	**5.** Identify disclosure requirements.
1.4.1, 1.4.2, 1.4.4, 5.1.1	**6.** Calculate and interpret key ratios related to solvency and liquidity.
1.1.4	**7.** Identify major differences in accounting standards between IFRS and ASPE, and what changes are expected in the near future.

HOW MUCH DEBT IS TOO MUCH?

IN CAPITAL-INTENSIVE INDUSTRIES SUCH as manufacturing, companies usually have high debt to equity ratios. Banks and other lenders are keen to lend money to such companies because their assets are valuable collateral. A certain amount of debt is good. But how much debt is too much?

Companies carry debt because debt payments are tax-deductible, whereas issuing more shares is not. For instance, by using debt to increase operating capacity, such as buying new equipment to increase production, companies can earn more revenues, and anything earned beyond the interest paid to the bank on a loan goes to shareholders.

Long-term debt financing for companies in capital-intensive industries is crucial because they typically do not have enough free cash flow for big capital investments, which can cost billions of dollars and take years to pay off. But too much debt can be bad for many reasons.

Take Bombardier Inc. as an example. The Montreal-based company, which calls itself "the world's leading manufacturer of both planes and trains," had U.S. $7.6 billion in long-term debt as of December 31, 2014. Three years earlier, it had U.S. $4.7 billion in long-term debt.

Bombardier recognized that it "currently has, and will continue to have, a substantial amount of debt and significant

© Busa Photography/Getty Images

interest payment requirements." Its level of indebtedness "could have significant consequences," the company said in its 2014 annual report. Too much debt could make it harder to satisfy its obligations to pay back the debt. It could increase Bombardier's vulnerability to an economic downturn. It could require the company "to dedicate a substantial portion of its cash flows from operations to making interest and principal payments on its indebtedness, reducing the availability of its cash flows to fund capital expenditures, working capital, acquisitions, new business initiatives and other general corporate purposes." Too much debt could also limit Bombardier's ability to borrow more money "on commercially reasonable terms" and lenders may make their covenants more restrictive. The company may be forced to sell assets on unfavourable terms in order to pay back its loans.

Bombardier's debt levels had risen over several years as the company burned through cash on its delayed launch of the C Series of commercial jets. When companies carry high debt levels, their ratings can be downgraded by bond-rating services. In mid-2015, for example, Moody's Investors Service downgraded Bombardier's debt and increased its assessment of probability of default. Such downgrades can also affect

a company's share price. After the Fitch ratings agency downgraded Bombardier's debt in mid-2015, its share price fell 4% to $1.45.

Analysts suggested that if Bombardier sold some assets, such as its train-building business, it could help pay off some of its debt. The company had also signalled it could launch an initial public offering for its train division to raise cash.

Sources: Frederic Tomesco, "Bombardier Considers Selling Rail Stake or Offering IPO to Raise Cash," *Montreal Gazette*, October 30, 2015; "Bombardier Stock Falls after Fitch Gives It a Negative Outlook," CBC News online, August 13, 2015; Kristine Owram, "Bombardier Inc. Downgraded by Moody's Over 'Very High' Debt Levels," *Financial Post*, August 7, 2015; Bombardier Inc. 2014 annual report; Bombardier corporate website, www.bombardier.com.

PREVIEW OF CHAPTER 14

Long-term debt and financial liabilities continue to play an important role in our capital markets because companies and governments need large amounts of capital to finance their growth. In many cases, the most effective way to obtain capital is by issuing long-term debt. This chapter explains the accounting issues that are related to long-term debt and financial liabilities. We will cover the more basic issues regarding bonds and notes in this chapter, and discuss the more complex instruments in Chapter 16. As you might expect, the accounting for long-term notes payable mirrors the accounting for long-term notes receivable, which we presented in Chapter 7. We will discuss special topics such as pensions and leases in Chapters 19 and 20.

The chapter is organized as follows:

LONG-TERM FINANCIAL LIABILITIES				
Understanding Debt Instruments	**Measurement**	**Recognition and Derecognition**	**Presentation, Disclosure, and Analysis**	**IFRS/ASPE Comparison**
▪ Bonds and notes payable ▪ Credit ratings ▪ Defeasance ▪ Types of companies that have significant debt financing ▪ Information for decision-making	▪ Bonds and notes issued at par ▪ Discounts and premiums ▪ Special situations	▪ Repayment before maturity date ▪ Exchange of debt instruments ▪ Troubled debt restructurings ▪ Defeasance revisited ▪ Off-balance sheet financing	▪ Presentation ▪ Disclosures ▪ Analysis	▪ A comparison of IFRS and ASPE ▪ Looking ahead

UNDERSTANDING DEBT INSTRUMENTS

Objective 1
Understand the nature of long-term debt financing arrangements.

Long-term debt consists of obligations that are not payable within a year or the operating cycle of the business, whichever is longer, and will therefore require probable sacrifices of economic benefits in the future. Bonds payable, long-term notes payable, mortgages payable, pension liabilities, and lease liabilities are examples of long-term debt or liabilities.[1]

The process that leads to incurring long-term debt is often very formal. For example, the bylaws of corporations usually require that the board of directors and the shareholders give their approval before bonds can be issued or other long-term debt arrangements can be contracted. When companies arrange for financing, the details of the arrangements are generally documented in legal contracts. The contracts determine the rights and obligations of the lender and borrower and state the terms of the arrangement, including the interest

Cash

Promise to repay

Company   Creditor

rate, the due date or dates, call provisions, property pledged as security, and sinking fund requirements.

The contracts may also include **restrictive covenants** (terms or conditions) that are meant to limit activities and protect both lenders and borrowers. Examples of these types of covenants include working capital and dividend restrictions, and limitations on incurring additional debt. Covenants to restrict the amount of additional debt are common. Additional debt increases the risk of insolvency and there is a limit to the amount of risk that creditors are willing to accept even though some lenders can tolerate more risk than others.

LAW

Bonds and Notes Payable

Bonds are the most common type of long-term debt that companies report on their statements of financial position.

Characteristics

The main purpose of bonds is to borrow for the long term when the amount of capital that is needed is too large for one lender to supply. When bonds are issued in $100, $1,000, or $10,000 denominations, a large amount of long-term indebtedness can be divided into many small investing units, which makes it possible for more than one lender to participate in the loan.

A bond is created by a contract known as a **bond indenture** and represents a promise to pay both of the following: (1) a sum of money at a designated maturity date, and (2) periodic interest at a specified rate on the maturity amount (face value). Individual bonds are evidenced or supported by a paper certificate and they typically have a $1,000 face value. Bond interest payments are usually made semi-annually, but the interest rate is generally expressed as an annual rate.

TREASURY MANAGEMENT
5.2.3

An entire bond issue may be sold to an investment banker who acts as a selling agent and markets the bonds. In such arrangements, investment bankers may do one of two things. They may underwrite the entire issue by guaranteeing a certain sum to the corporation, thus taking the risk of selling the bonds for whatever price the agent can get (which is known as **firm underwriting**). They may instead sell the bond issue for a commission that will be deducted from the proceeds of the sale (which is known as **best efforts underwriting**). Alternatively, the issuing company may choose to place a bond issue privately by selling the bonds directly to a large institution—which may or may not be a financial institution—without the aid of an underwriter. This situation is known as **private placement**.

UNDERLYING CONCEPT

Even though the legal form of a note is different from a bond, the economic substance is the same because they both represent liabilities. They therefore receive substantially the same treatment from an accounting perspective, depending on the features that the specific note or bond carries.

The difference between current notes payable and long-term notes payable is the maturity date. As discussed in Chapter 13, short-term notes payable are expected to be paid within a year or the operating cycle, whichever is longer. Long-term notes are similar in substance to bonds in that both have fixed maturity dates and carry either a stated or implicit interest rate. However, notes do not trade as easily as bonds in the organized public securities markets, and sometimes do not trade at all.

Types

TREASURY MANAGEMENT
5.2.3

The following are some of the more common types of long-term debt that are found in practice. Each type of instrument has specific contractual features that manage risk for the company and/or the holder. For instance, a secured bond is less risky and therefore often has a lower rate of interest. Any feature that gives the holder more choice or options is generally more desirable to the investor, who may be willing to pay a premium for the flexibility. Where the company has choices and options, such as an option to convert the bond into shares, this may be seen as less desirable by the investors because the choices and options are beyond their control. Each feature noted below changes the riskiness and desirability of the instruments and therefore affects the pricing of the instrument. Note that debt may be denominated in a foreign currency. This means that the interest and principal repayments must be paid using foreign currency.

Registered and Bearer (Coupon) Bonds

Bonds that are issued in the owner's name are called **registered bonds**. To sell a registered bond, the current certificate has to be surrendered and a new certificate is then issued. A **bearer** or **coupon bond**, however, is not recorded in the owner's name and may therefore be transferred from one owner to another by simply delivering it to the new owner.

Because the various features of debt instruments alter the risk profile, the full disclosure principle would support disclosing specific information about these features.

Secured and Unsecured Debt

Secured debt is backed by a pledge of some sort of collateral. **Mortgage bonds or notes** are secured by a claim on real estate. **Collateral trust bonds or notes** are secured by shares and bonds of other corporations. Debt instruments that are not backed by collateral are **unsecured**; for example, **debenture bonds**. **Junk bonds** are unsecured and also very risky, and therefore pay a high interest rate. These bonds are often used to finance leveraged buyouts.

Term, Serial, and Perpetual Bonds or Notes

Debt issues that mature on a single date are called **term bonds or notes**, and issues that mature in instalments are called **serial bonds or notes**. Serial bonds are frequently used by schools, municipalities, and provincial or federal governments. **Perpetual bonds or notes** have unusually long terms; that is, 100 years or more, or no maturity date. These are often referred to as century or millennium bonds, depending on the length of the term.

Income, Revenue, and Deep Discount Bonds

Income bonds pay no interest unless the issuing company is profitable. **Revenue bonds** have this name because the interest on them is paid from a specified revenue source. **Deep discount bonds or notes**—which are also referred to as **zero-interest debentures, bonds, or notes**—have very little or no interest each year and therefore are sold at a large discount that basically provides the buyer with a total interest payoff (at market rates) at maturity.

Commodity-Backed Bonds

Commodity-backed debt, also called **asset-linked debt**, is redeemable in amounts of a commodity, such as barrels of oil, tonnes of coal, or ounces of rare metal.

Callable Bonds and Notes and Convertible Debt with Various Settlement and Other Options

Callable bonds and notes give the issuer the right to call and retire the debt before maturity. (These are sometimes referred to as demand loans.) **Convertible debt** allows the holder or the issuer to convert the debt into other securities such as common shares. Certain bonds or other financial instruments give the issuer the option to repay or settle the principal in either cash or common shares, or give the right to decide to the holder.

One of the more interesting innovations in the bond market is bonds whose interest or principal payments are tied to changes in the weather. The incidence of unusual and extreme weather events has been increasing, along with potential losses from these often unexpected events. Many insurers are feeling the impact of this in terms of profits. The Office of the Superintendent of Financial Institutions, the regulatory body in Canada for financial institutions including insurance companies, has signalled that it is open to allowing insurance companies to issue these weather bonds to help manage risk.

Holders of the bonds would lose their rights to some or all of the interest and/or principal payments if a "triggering event" occurred. A triggering event could be anything from an excess amount of rainfall to a hailstorm or drought. Why would an investor buy this type of security? The instrument would have to be priced to compensate for the riskiness of the instrument by offering a higher interest return or being sold at a discount.

These instruments are part of a larger group of instruments sometimes referred to as catastrophe bonds ("cat" bonds), which are used globally. The bonds are often sold in private placement offerings, meaning that they are sold to large institutional investors. Because many bonds do not repay the principal if the triggering event occurs, they are referred to as "principal-at-risk variable-rate notes."

Credit Ratings

FINANCIAL ANALYSIS AND PLANNING
5.1.1

A credit rating is assigned to each new public bond issue by independent credit rating agencies. This rating reflects a current assessment of the company's ability to pay the amounts that will be due on that specific borrowing. The rating may be changed up or down during the issue's outstanding life because the quality is constantly monitored. Note that institutional investors, such as insurance companies and pension funds, invest heavily in **investment grade securities**. Investment grade securities are high-quality securities (not speculative) and therefore only certain securities qualify. There is pressure on a company to ensure that its debt instruments are rated investment grade so that it can have greater access to capital. Credit rating analysts review many business models and industry factors when they make their determinations. Trends in costs and revenues are especially important.

WHAT DO THE NUMBERS MEAN?

Two major companies, **Moody's Investors Service** and **Standard & Poor's Corporation**, issue quality ratings on every public debt issue. The following graph shows the categories of ratings issued by Standard & Poor's, along with historical default rates on bonds receiv-

ing these ratings.[2] As expected, bonds receiving the highest quality rating of AAA have the lowest historical default rates. Bonds rated below BBB, which are considered below investment grade ("junk bonds"), experience very high default rates.

Source: Diane Vazza, Nick W. Kraemer. *2013 Annual Global Corporate Default Study and Rating Transitions.* Standard & Poor's Financial Services LLC. March 2014.

The next chart shows default rates by industry.

High tech – High technology/computers/office equipment.   E&NR – Energy and natural resources.
Health – Health care/chemicals.   AACGM – Aerospace/automotive/capital goods/metal.
Frst. prods. – Forest and building products/home builders.

Source: Diane Vazza, Nick W. Kraemer. *2013 Annual Global Corporate Default Study and Rating Transitions.* Standard & Poor's Financial Services LLC. March 2014.

Debt ratings reflect credit quality. The market closely monitors these ratings when determining the required yield and pricing of bonds at issuance and in periods after issuance, especially if a bond's rating is upgraded or downgraded. It is not surprising, then, that bond investors and companies that issue bonds keep a close watch on debt ratings, both when bonds are issued and while the bonds are outstanding.

Defeasance

LAW

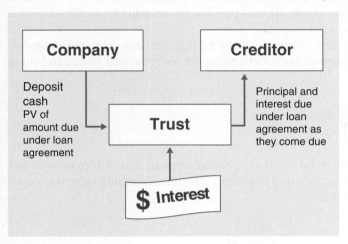

Occasionally, a company may want to extinguish or pay off debt before its due date, but economic factors, such as early repayment penalties, may stop it from doing so. One option is to set aside the money in a trust or other arrangement and allow the trust to repay the original debt (principal and interest) as it becomes due according to the original agreement. To do this, the company must set aside sufficient funds so that the investment and any return will be enough to pay the principal and interest directly to the creditor. This is known as **defeasance**. If the creditor of the original debt agrees to look to the trust for repayment and give up its claim on the company, this is known as **legal defeasance**.

In this case, the trust becomes the debtor and the creditor looks to the trust for payment because the company no longer has a contractual obligation under the original loan agreement. A new legal agreement would be agreed to by all parties stating that the principal and interest payments would be made by the trust. Accounting for defeasance is discussed further below.

Types of Companies that Have Significant Debt Financing

TREASURY MANAGEMENT 5.2.3

As noted in earlier chapters, the business model involves obtaining financing to invest in assets that are then used to produce income. Financing is generally obtained through three sources:

1. Borrowing
2. Issuing equity (shares)
3. Using internally generated funds

There are advantages and disadvantages to using each of the above-noted sources of financing. Borrowed funds must be repaid and therefore increase liquidity and solvency risk. However, on the positive side, borrowed funds (if invested properly) can increase profits. This is known as **leverage**: the practice of using other people's money to maximize returns to shareholders. As long as the interest paid on debt financing is less than the return earned when the funds are invested, the excess is profit.

Issuing shares does not affect liquidity or solvency because share capital does not need to be repaid and dividends are not mandatory (unless specified by the terms of the share). However, issuing shares may result in dilution of ownership. Using internally generated funds is fine as long as the company's business model is producing excess funds and as long as the company makes an assessment regarding other potential uses for the funds. In other words, the company must ask itself whether this is the best use of funds or whether they should be used for other things, such as to pay down debt or pay dividends to shareholders.

WHAT DO THE NUMBERS MEAN?

Certain industries have a greater ability to borrow funds. These include capital-intensive industries (those with significant tangible assets), such as transportation and hotel companies. Lenders are able to structure the lending agreements in such a way as to secure the loans with the underlying tangible assets. For instance, **Canadian Pacific Railway**

Limited, a hotel and railway transportation company, has a long-term debt to equity ratio of 1.71:1 based on its 2014 financial statements. **Trimac Transportation Ltd.**, a trucking company, has a long-term debt to equity ratio of 2.47:1 based on its 2014 financial statements.

Information for Decision-Making

Companies must manage their cash flows and borrowings to ensure that there are enough funds to continue to operate and to maximize profits and benefit from opportunities. Continued access to low-cost funds is important. For this reason, the amount of long-term debt financing is an important ratio. Too little long-term debt financing means the company is not taking advantage of leverage. Too much means the company may be over extended. This could result in higher costs of capital, and possibly the inability to access additional debt financing should the need arise.

For all these reasons, financial ratios that focus on liquidity and debt are monitored. These include ratios such as current ratio, debt to equity, debt to total assets, and times interest earned.

MEASUREMENT

Objective 2

Understand how long-term debt is measured and accounted for.

When issued, bonds and notes are valued at the present value of their future interest and principal cash flows (generally representing fair value). The initial carrying value is adjusted by any directly attributable issue costs.[3]

UNDERLYING CONCEPT

Refer back to Chapters 2 and 3 for a discussion of fair values.

Bonds and Notes Issued at Par

When bonds are issued on an interest payment date at par (that is, at face value), no interest has accrued and there is no premium or discount. The accounting entry is made simply for the cash proceeds and the bonds' face value. To illustrate, assume that a company plans to issue 10-year term bonds with a par value of $800,000, dated January 1, 2017, and bearing interest at an annual rate of 10% payable semi-annually on January 1 and July 1. If the company decides to issue the bonds on January 1 at par, the entry on its books would be as follows:

A   =   L   +   SE
+800,000   +800,000

Cash flows: ↑ 800,000 inflow

Cash	800,000	
Bonds Payable		800,000

The entry to record the first semi-annual interest payment of $40,000 ($800,000 × 0.10 × ¹/₂) on July 1, 2017, would be:

A   =   L   +   SE
−40,000   −40,000

Cash flows: ↓ 40,000 outflow

Interest Expense	40,000	
Cash		40,000

The entry to record accrued interest expense at December 31, 2017 (the year end), would be:

A   =   L   +   SE
+40,000 −40,000

Cash flows: No effect

Interest Expense	40,000	
Interest Payable		40,000

Similarly, in Chapter 7, we discussed the recognition of a $10,000, three-year note issued at face value by Scandinavian Imports to Bigelow Corp. In this transaction, the stated rate and the effective rate were both 10%. The time diagram and present value calculation in Chapter 7 for Bigelow Corp. would be the same for the issuer of the note, Scandinavian Imports, in recognizing the note payable. Because the note's present value and its face value are the same ($10,000), no premium or discount is recognized. The issuance of the note is recorded by Scandinavian Imports as follows:

A = L + SE
+10,000   +10,000
Cash flows: ↑ 10,000 inflow

Cash	10,000	
Notes Payable		10,000

Discounts and Premiums

TREASURY MANAGEMENT
5.2.3

The issuance and marketing of bonds to the public does not happen overnight. It usually takes weeks or even months. Underwriters must be arranged, the approval of the relevant securities commission must be obtained, audits and the issuance of a prospectus may be required, and certificates must be printed. Frequently, the terms in a bond indenture are decided well in advance of the bond sale. Between the time the terms are set and the time the bonds are issued, the market conditions and the issuing corporation's financial position may change significantly. Such changes affect the bonds' marketability and, thus, their selling price.

A bond's selling price is set by the supply and demand of buyers and sellers, relative risk, market conditions, and the state of the economy. The investment community values a bond at the present value of its future cash flows, which consist of (1) interest and (2) principal. The rate that is used to calculate the present value of these cash flows is the interest rate that would give an acceptable return on an investment that matches the issuer's risk characteristics.

The interest rate that is written in the terms of the bond indenture (and is ordinarily printed on the bond certificate) is known as the **stated, coupon,** or **nominal rate.** This rate, which is set by the bond issuer, is expressed as a percentage of the bond's **face value,** also called the **par value, principal amount,** or **maturity value.** If the rate that is required by the investment community (the buyers) is different from the stated rate, when buyers calculate the bond's present value, the result will be different from the bond's face value, and its purchase price will therefore also differ. The difference between the bond's face value and its present value is either a **discount** or **premium.**[4] If the bonds sell for less than their face value, they are being sold at a discount. If the bonds sell for more than their face value, they are being sold at a premium.

The interest rate that is actually earned by the bondholders is called the **effective yield** or **market rate.** If bonds sell at a **discount,** the effective yield is **higher** than the stated rate. Conversely, if bonds sell at a **premium,** the effective yield is **lower** than the stated rate. While the bond is outstanding, its price is affected by several variables, but especially by the market rate of interest. There is an inverse relationship between the market interest rate and the bond price. That is, when interest rates increase, the bond's price decreases, and vice versa.

To illustrate the calculation of the present value of a bond issue, assume that Discount Limited issues $100,000 in bonds that are due in five years and pay 9% interest annually at year end. At the time of issue, the market rate for such bonds is 11%. Illustration 14-1 shows both the interest and the principal cash flows.

Illustration 14-1

Present Value Calculation of Bond Selling at a Discount

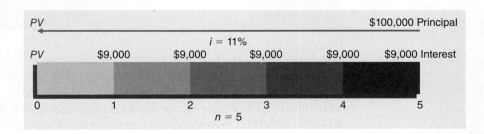

The actual principal and interest cash flows are discounted at an 11% rate for five periods as follows:

Present value of the principal: $100,000 × 0.59345	$59,345
Present value of the interest payments: $9,000 × 3.69590	33,263
Present value (selling price) of the bonds	$92,608

By paying $92,608 at the date of issue, the investors will realize an effective rate or yield of 11% over the five-year term of the bonds. These bonds would therefore sell at a discount of $7,392 ($100,000 − $92,608). Note that the price at which the bonds sell is typically stated as a percentage of their face or par value. For example, we would say that the Discount Limited bonds sold for 92.6 (92.6% of par). If Discount Limited had received $102,000, we would say the bonds sold for 102 (102% of par).

When bonds sell below their face value, it means that investors are demanding a rate of interest that is higher than the stated rate. The investors are not satisfied with the stated rate because they can earn a greater rate on alternative investments of equal risk. Because they cannot change the stated rate, they therefore refuse to pay face value for the bonds and instead achieve the effective rate of interest that they require by lowering the amount invested in the bonds. The result is that the investors receive interest at the stated rate calculated on the face value, but they are essentially earning an effective rate that is higher than the stated rate because they paid less than face value for the bonds. Although notes do not trade as readily as bonds in stock markets, the same issues arise where the stated rate on the notes is different from the market rate at the date of issuance.

Most long-term debt is subsequently measured at amortized cost. Under this method, the interest is adjusted for any premium or discount over the life of the bond.

Straight-Line Method

The **straight-line method** is valued for its simplicity. It might be used by companies whose financial statements are not constrained by GAAP or by companies following ASPE that choose the straight-line method as part of their accounting policy.[5]

If the $800,000 of bonds illustrated earlier were issued on January 1, 2017, at 97 (97% of par), the issuance would be recorded as follows:

A = L + SE
+776,000 +776,000

Cash flows: ↑ 776,000 inflow

Cash ($800,000 × 0.97)	776,000	
Bonds Payable		776,000

Because of its relationship to interest, discussed above, the discount is amortized and charged to interest expense over the period of time that the bonds are outstanding.

Under the straight-line method, the amount that is amortized each year is constant. For example, using the bond discount above of $24,000, the amount amortized to interest expense each year for 10 years is $2,400 ($24,000 ÷ 10 years) and, if amortization is recorded annually, it is recorded as follows:

A = L + SE
+2,400 −2,400

Cash flows: No effect

Interest Expense	2,400	
Bonds Payable		2,400

At the end of the first year, 2017, as a result of the amortization entry above, the unamortized balance of the discount is $21,600 ($24,000 − $2,400).

If the bonds were dated and sold on October 1, 2017, and if the corporation's fiscal year ended on December 31, the discount amortized during 2017 would be only $3/12$ of $1/10$ of $24,000, or $600. Three months of accrued interest must also be recorded on December 31.

A premium on bonds payable is accounted for in much the same way as a discount on bonds payable. If the $800,000 of par value, 10-year bonds are dated and sold on January 1, 2017, at 103, the following entry is made to record the issuance:

A = L + SE
+824,000 +824,000

Cash flows: ↑ 824,000 inflow

Cash ($800,000 × 1.03)	824,000	
Bonds Payable		824,000

At the end of 2017 and for each year that the bonds are outstanding, the entry to amortize the premium on a straight-line basis is:

A = L + SE
    -2,400 +2,400

Cash flows: No effect

Bonds Payable	2,400	
Interest Expense		2,400

Bond interest expense is increased by amortizing a discount and decreased by amortizing a premium. Amortization of a discount or premium under the effective interest method is discussed later in this chapter.

Some bonds are **callable** by the issuer after a certain date and at a stated price so that the issuing corporation may have the opportunity to reduce its debt or take advantage of lower interest rates. Whether or not the bond is callable, any premium or discount must be amortized over the bond's life up to the maturity date because it is not certain that the issuer will call the bond and redeem it early.

Bond interest payments are usually made semi-annually on dates that are specified in the bond indenture. When bonds are issued between interest payment dates, bond buyers will pay the seller the interest that has accrued from the last interest payment date to the date of issue. By paying the accrued interest, the purchasers of the bonds are, in effect, paying the bond issuer in advance for the portion of the full six-month interest payment that the purchasers are not entitled to (but will receive) because they have not held the bonds during the entire six-month period. The purchasers will receive the full six-month interest payment on the next semi-annual interest payment date.

To illustrate, assume that $800,000 of par value, 10-year bonds, dated January 1, 2017 and bearing interest at an annual rate of 10% payable semi-annually on January 1 and July 1, are issued on March 1, 2017 at par plus accrued interest. The entry on the books of the issuing corporation is:

A = L + SE
+813,333 +800,000 +13,333

Cash flows: ↑ 813,333 inflow

Cash	813,333	
Bonds Payable		800,000
Interest Expense ($800,000 × 0.10 × ²/₁₂)		13,333*
*Interest Payable might be credited instead.		

The purchaser is thus advancing two months of interest because on July 1, 2017, four months after the date of purchase, the purchaser will receive six months of interest from the issuing company. The issuing company makes the following entry on July 1, 2017:

A = L + SE
-40,000   -40,000

Cash flows: ↓ 40,000 outflow

Interest Expense	40,000	
Cash		40,000

The expense account now contains a debit balance of $26,667, which represents the proper amount of interest expense: four months at 10% on $800,000.

The above illustration was simplified by having the January 1, 2017 bonds issued on March 1, 2017 at par. If, however, the 10% bonds were issued at 102, the entry on March 1 on the issuing corporation's books would be:

A   =   L   +   SE
+829,333   +816,000   +13,333

Cash flows: ↑ 829,333 inflow

Cash [($800,000 × 1.02) + ($800,000 × 0.10 × ²/₁₂)]	829,333	
Bonds Payable		816,000
Interest Expense		13,333

The premium would be amortized from the date of sale, March 1, 2017, not from the date of the bonds, January 1, 2017.

Effective Interest Method

A common method for amortizing a discount or premium is the **effective interest method**. This method is required under IFRS and allowed as an accounting policy choice under ASPE. Under the effective interest method, the steps are as follows:

1. Interest expense is calculated first by multiplying the **carrying value**[6] of the bonds or notes at the beginning of the period by the effective interest rate.

2. The discount or premium amortization is then determined by comparing the interest expense with the interest to be paid.

Illustration 14-2 shows the formula for calculating the amortization under this method.

Illustration 14-2

Bond Discount and Premium Amortization Calculation

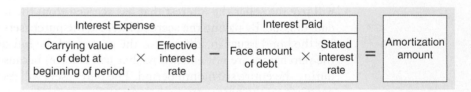

The effective interest method produces a periodic interest expense that is equal to a constant percentage of the bonds' or notes' carrying value.

Both the effective interest and straight-line methods result in the same total amount of interest expense over the term of the bonds.

Example: Bonds Issued at a Discount

To illustrate the amortization of a discount using the effective interest method, assume that Master Corporation issued $100,000 of 8% term bonds on January 1, 2017 that are due on January 1, 2022, with interest payable each July 1 and January 1. Because the investors required an effective interest rate of 10%, they paid $92,278 for the $100,000 of bonds, creating a $7,722 discount. The $7,722 discount is calculated as in Illustration 14-3.[7]

Illustration 14-3

Calculation of Discount on Bonds Payable

Maturity of bonds payable		$100,000
Present value of $100,000 due in 5 years at 10%, interest payable semi-annually ($100,000 × 0.61391)	$61,391	
Present value of $4,000 interest payable semi-annually for 5 years at 10% annually ($4,000 × 7.72173)	30,887	
Proceeds from sale of bonds		92,278
Discount on bonds payable		$ 7,722

The five-year amortization schedule appears in Illustration 14-4.

Illustration 14-4

*Bond Discount
Amortization Schedule*

		SCHEDULE OF BOND DISCOUNT AMORTIZATION		
		Effective Interest Method—Semi-Annual Interest Payments		
		5-Year, 8% Bonds Sold to Yield 10%		
Date	Cash Paid	Interest Expense	Discount Amortized	Carrying Amount of Bonds
1/1/17				$ 92,278
7/1/17	$ 4,000[a]	$ 4,614[b]	$ 614[c]	92,892[d]
1/1/18	4,000	4,645	645	93,537
7/1/18	4,000	4,677	677	94,214
1/1/19	4,000	4,711	711	94,925
7/1/19	4,000	4,746	746	95,671
1/1/20	4,000	4,783	783	96,454
7/1/20	4,000	4,823	823	97,277
1/1/21	4,000	4,864	864	98,141
7/1/21	4,000	4,907	907	99,048
1/1/22	4,000	4,952	952	100,000
	$40,000	$47,722	$7,722	

[a]$4,000 = $100,000 × 0.08 × 6/12 [c]$614 = $4,614 − $4,000
[b]$4,614 = $92,278 × 0.10 × 6/12 [d]$92,892 = $92,278 + $614

The entry to record the issuance of Master Corporation's bonds at a discount on January 1, 2017, is:

A = L + SE
+92,278 +92,278

Cash flows: ↑ 92,278 inflow

Cash	92,278	
Bonds Payable		92,278

The journal entry to record the first interest payment on July 1, 2017 and amortization of the discount is:

A = L + SE
−4,000 +614 −4,614

Cash flows: ↓ 4,000 outflow

Interest Expense	4,614	
Bonds Payable		614
Cash		4,000

The journal entry to record the interest expense accrued at December 31, 2017 (the year end) and amortization of the discount is:

A = L + SE
+4,645 −4,645

Cash flows: No effect

Interest Expense	4,645	
Interest Payable		4,000
Bonds Payable		645

Example: Bonds Issued at Premium

If instead it had been a market where the investors were willing to accept an effective interest rate of 6% on the bond issue described above, they would have paid $108,530 or a premium of $8,530, calculated as in Illustration 14-5.

Illustration 14-5

*Calculation of Premium
on Bonds Payable*

Maturity value of bonds payable		$100,000
Present value of $100,000 due in 5 years at 6%, interest payable semi-annually ($100,000 × 0.74409)	$74,409	
Present value of $4,000, interest payable semi-annually for 5 years at 6% annually ($4,000 × 8.53020)	34,121	
Proceeds from sale of bonds		108,530
Premium on bonds payable		$ 8,530

The five-year amortization schedule appears in Illustration 14-6.

Illustration 14-6

Bond Premium Amortization Schedule

SCHEDULE OF BOND PREMIUM AMORTIZATION				
Effective Interest Method—Semi-Annual Interest Payments				
5-Year, 8% Bonds Sold to Yield 6%				
Date	**Cash Paid**	**Interest Expense**	**Premium Amortized**	**Carrying Amount of Bonds**
1/1/17				$108,530
7/1/17	$ 4,000[a]	$ 3,256[b]	$ 744[c]	107,786[d]
1/1/18	4,000	3,234	766	107,020
7/1/18	4,000	3,211	789	106,231
1/1/19	4,000	3,187	813	105,418
7/1/19	4,000	3,162	838	104,580
1/1/20	4,000	3,137	863	103,717
7/1/20	4,000	3,112	888	102,829
1/1/21	4,000	3,085	915	101,914
7/1/21	4,000	3,057	943	100,971
1/1/22	4,000	3,029	971	100,000
	$40,000	$31,470	$8,530	

[a]$4,000 = $100,000 \times 0.08 \times {}^{6}/_{12}$ [c]$744 = $4,000 - $3,256$
[b]$3,256 = $108,530 \times 0.06 \times {}^{6}/_{12}$ [d]$107,786 = $108,530 - 744

The entry to record the issuance of the Master Corporation bonds at a premium on January 1, 2017 is:

A = L + SE
+108,530 +108,530

Cash flows: ↑ 108,530 inflow

Cash	108,530	
Bonds Payable		108,530

The journal entry to record the first interest payment on July 1, 2017, and amortization of the premium is:

A = L + SE
−4,000 −744 −3,256

Cash flows: ↓ 4,000 outflow

Interest Expense	3,256	
Bonds Payable	744	
Cash		4,000

Because the discount or premium should be amortized as an adjustment to interest expense over the life of the bond, it results in a **constant interest rate** when it is applied to the carrying amount of debt that is outstanding at the beginning of any specific period.

Accruing Interest

In our examples for Master Corporation up to now, the dates on the amortization tables coincide with the dates of the interest payments (that is January 1 and July 1). However, what happens if Master wishes to report financial statements at the end of February 2017? In this case, as Illustration 14-7 shows, the premium is prorated by the appropriate number of months to arrive at the proper interest expense. Note that if a financial calculator or Excel were used, the number would be slightly different due to compounding.

Illustration 14-7

Calculation of Interest Expense

Interest accrual ($4,000 \times {}^{2}/_{6}$)	$1,333.33
Premium amortized ($744 \times {}^{2}/_{6}$)	(248.00)
Interest expense (Jan. to Feb.)	$1,085.33

The journal entry to record this accrual is:

A = L + SE
+1,085 −1,085

Cash flows: No effect

Bonds Payable	248	
Interest Expense	1,085	
Interest Payable		1,333

If the company prepares financial statements six months later, the same procedure is followed to amortize the premium, as Illustration 14-8 shows.

Illustration 14-8

Calculation of Premium Amortization

Premium amortized (Mar.–June) ($744 × ⁴/₆)	$496.00
Premium amortized (July–Aug.) ($766 × ²/₆)	255.33
Premium amortized (Mar.–Aug. 2017)	$751.33

The calculation is much simpler if the straight-line method is used. In the Master situation, for example, the total premium is $8,530 and this amount needs to be allocated evenly over the five-year period. The premium amortization per month is therefore $142 ($8,530 ÷ 60 months).

Special Situations

Non-Market Rates of Interest—Marketable Securities

Financial liabilities should initially be recognized at fair value, which is generally the exchange value that exists when two arm's-length parties are involved in a transaction. If a zero-interest-bearing (non–interest-bearing) **marketable** security is issued for cash only, its fair value is the cash received by the security's issuer. The implicit or **imputed interest rate** is the rate that makes the cash that is received now equal to the present value of the amounts that will be received in the future. This rate should also equal the market rate of interest. The difference between the security's face amount and the present value is a discount and is amortized to interest expense over the life of the note.

To illustrate the entries and the amortization schedule, assume that your company is the one that issued the $10,000, three-year, zero-interest-bearing note to Jeremiah Company that was illustrated in Chapter 7. Let's assume further that the note is marketable. The implicit rate that equated the total cash to be paid ($10,000 at maturity) to the present value of the future cash flows ($7,721.80 cash proceeds at the date of issuance) was 9%. Assume that the market rate of interest for a similar note would also be 9%. (The present value of $1 for three periods at 9% is $0.77218.) The time diagram that shows the one cash flow is as follows:

The entry to record issuance of the note would be:

A = L + SE
+7,722   +7,722

Cash flows: ↑ 7,722 inflow

Cash	7,722	
Notes Payable		7,722

The discount is amortized and interest expense is recognized annually. The three-year discount amortization and interest expense schedule is shown in Illustration 14-9 using the effective interest method.

Illustration 14-9

*Schedule of Note Discount
Amortization*

		Interest	Discount	Carrying
	Cash Paid	Expense	Amortized	Amount of Note
SCHEDULE OF NOTE DISCOUNT AMORTIZATION				
Effective Interest Method				
0% Note Discounted at 9%				
Date of issue				$ 7,721.80
End of year 1	$–0–	$ 694.96[a]	$ 694.96[b]	8,416.76[c]
End of year 2	–0–	757.51	757.51	9,174.27
End of year 3	–0–	825.73[d]	825.73	10,000.00
	$–0–	$2,278.20	$2,278.20	

[a]$7,721.80 × 0.09 = $694.96
[b]$694.96 – 0 = $694.96
[c]$7,721.80 + $694.96 = $8,416.76
[d]Adjustment to compensate for rounding

Interest expense at the end of the first year using the effective interest method is recorded as follows:

A = L + SE
      +695 –695

Cash flows: No effect

Interest Expense ($7,722 × 9%)	695	
Notes Payable		695

The total amount of the discount, $2,278 in this case, represents the interest expense to be incurred and recognized on the note over the three years.

Non-Market Rates of Interest—Non-Marketable Instruments

If the loans or notes do not trade on a market (that is, they are not securities) and the interest rate is a non-market interest rate, the situation must be analyzed carefully. The cash consideration that is given may not be equal to the fair value of the loan or note.

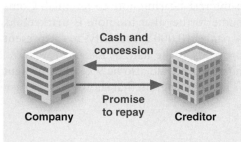

Normally, in an arm's-length reciprocal transaction, the loan would be issued with an interest rate approximating the market rate and therefore the consideration would approximate fair value. If the loan is issued with an interest rate that is less than the market rate, this concession should be accounted for separately.

In these cases, the entity must measure the value of the loan by discounting the cash flows using the market rate of interest, which is done by considering similar loans with similar terms. Any difference between the cash consideration and the discounted amount (the fair value of the loan) would be booked to net income unless it qualified as some other asset or liability.[8]

For example, assume that a government entity issues at face value a zero-interest-bearing loan that is to be repaid over five years with no stated interest. In doing this, the government is giving an additional benefit to the company beyond the debt financing. It is forgiving the interest that the company would normally be charged. Thus, the company is getting a double benefit—the loan and a grant for the interest that would otherwise be paid. The extra benefit would be accounted for separately as a government grant.

To illustrate, assume that to help a company finance the construction of a building, the government provides $100,000 cash, in exchange for a $100,000, five-year, zero-interest-bearing note at face value when the market rate of interest is 10%. To record the loan, the company records a discount of $37,908, which is the difference between the loan's $100,000 face amount and its fair value of $62,092 ($100,000 × the present value factor for five years at 10% = $100,000 × 0.62092). The rest may be booked to the related building account under government grant accounting because it relates to the construction of an asset. The issuer's journal entry is:

A = L + SE
+62,092 +62,092

Cash flows: ↑ 100,000 inflow

Cash	100,000	
Notes Payable		62,092
Buildings		37,908

The discount is subsequently amortized to interest expense. The net value of the building (that is, net of the government grant) is depreciated, thus spreading the grant over the life of the asset.[9] In this situation, the write-off of the discount and the amortization of the government grant are at different rates.

Notes Issued for Property, Goods, and Services

When a non-marketable debt instrument is exchanged for property, goods, or services in a bargained, arm's-length transaction, there are additional measurement issues. As with other transactions, it should be booked at fair value. But what is the fair value? If the issued debt is a marketable security, the value of the transaction would be easy to determine. If it is not, we must try to estimate the fair value. Normally, for monetary transactions, when measuring the transaction's price, we first try to measure the value of the monetary asset or liability and, if this is not possible, we then attempt to value the nonmonetary assets in the transaction. In this case, the note is a monetary liability and so we would try to value this first. The note could be valued using a valuation technique such as discounting. Similar to the previous example, the cash flows from the debt instrument could be discounted using a market rate of interest for similar debt with similar terms. If this is not possible, and if the fair value of the property, goods, or services is readily determinable, this fair value of the property, goods, or services could then be used to measure the transaction.

For example, assume that Scenic Development sold land having a cash sale price of $200,000 to Health Spa Inc. in exchange for Health Spa's five-year, $293,860, zero-interest-bearing note. The $200,000 cash sale price represents the present value of the $293,860 note discounted at 8% for five years. The 8% interest rate is the market rate for a similar loan with similar terms. If both parties were to record the transaction on the sale date at the $293,860 face amount of the note, Health Spa's Land account and Scenic's sales would be overstated by $93,860. This is because the $93,860 is the interest for five years at an effective rate of 8%. Interest revenue to Scenic and interest expense to Health Spa for the five-year period would also then be correspondingly understated by $93,860.

The transaction could be measured by using a valuation technique to measure the value of the debt or alternatively by using the fair value of the land ($200,000) if it is not possible to measure the debt. In this case, we know the fair value of the land and we also know that the market rate is 8%. Because the present value of the note is equal to the land value, we use $200,000. The difference between the cash sale price of $200,000 and the face amount of the note, $293,860, represents interest at an effective rate of 8%. The transaction is recorded at the exchange date as follows:

A = L + SE
+200,000 +200,000

Cash flows: No effect

A = L + SE
+200,000 +200,000

Cash flows: No effect

Health Spa Inc.			Scenic Development Company		
Land	200,000		Notes Receivable	200,000	
Notes Payable		200,000	Sales Revenue		200,000

During the five-year life of the note, Health Spa annually amortizes a portion of the discount of $93,860 as a charge to interest expense. Scenic Development records interest revenue totalling $93,860 over the five-year period by also amortizing the discount.

If a higher interest rate were determined to be the market rate of interest, the land and selling price would be measured at a lower amount because there is an inverse relationship between the discount rate and the present value of the cash flows. This might cause us to question whether the land's so-called cash sales price has been overstated because the vendor would want to receive consideration equal to the land's fair value. At some point, a judgement call is required to determine which is more reliable: the imputed interest rate or the asset's stated fair value.

SIGNIFICANT CHANGE

Fair Value Option

Generally, long-term debt is measured at amortized cost; however, as discussed earlier in the text, there is an option to value financial instruments at fair value (referred to as the

fair value option). Although ASPE allows the fair value option for all financial instruments, IFRS explicitly requires that the option be used only where fair value results in more relevant information. This would be the case where the use of fair value eliminates or reduces measurement and/or recognition inconsistencies or where the financial instruments are managed or performance is evaluated on a fair value basis.

One significant issue arises when the fair value option is used for measuring the entity's own debt instruments. As a general rule, fair value should always incorporate information about the riskiness of the cash flows associated with a particular instrument (including information about the entity's own liquidity and solvency). However, this gives some peculiar and counterintuitive results; that is, if the debt increases in risk, it would have a lower fair value, thus resulting in recognition of a gain for the company that issued it. Therefore, even though the company is worse off, it recognizes a gain.

IFRS 13, which deals with fair value measurement, requires that non-performance risk (which includes credit risk) be included in the fair value measurement.[10] IFRS 9 requires that subsequent changes in fair value due to changes in credit risk that arise on remeasurement of the fair value of financial liabilities under the fair value option be presented in other comprehensive income.[11] Under ASPE, all changes in fair value are recognized in net income where the fair value option is selected.

As an example, assume that Friction Limited has bonds outstanding in the amount of $100,000. The company has chosen to apply the fair value option in accounting for this liability. At the end of the current year, the company's credit risk has increased and therefore the fair value of its debt is $95,000. Assume that the change in fair value is due solely to the change in credit risk.

Illustration 14-10 shows how the gain would be accounted for.

Illustration 14-10

Use of the Fair Value Option in Valuing a Long-Term Liability (IFRS versus ASPE)

A = L + SE
       −5,000 +5,000

Cash flows: No effect

	IFRS: IFRS 9	ASPE
To record the change in fair value of debt that is accounted for under the fair value option		
Bonds Payable	5,000	5,000
Unrealized Gain or Loss		5,000
Unrealized Gain or Loss—OCI	5,000	

RECOGNITION AND DERECOGNITION

Objective 3
Understand when long-term debt is recognized and derecognized, including how to account for troubled debt restructurings.

Like all financial instruments, long-term debt is recognized in the financial statements when the company becomes party to the contractual provisions (when the financing deal is finalized or bonds are issued). The debt remains on the books until it is extinguished. When debt is extinguished, it is **derecognized** from the financial statements. If the instrument is held to maturity, no gain or loss is calculated. This is because any premium or discount and any issue costs will be fully amortized at the date the instrument matures. As a result, the carrying amount will be equal to the instrument's maturity (face) value. And as the maturity or face value is also equal to the instrument's market value at that time, there is no gain or loss.

From a financial reporting perspective, the **extinguishment of debt** is recorded when either of the following occurs:

1. The debtor discharges the liability by paying the creditor.

2. The debtor is legally released from primary responsibility for the liability by law or by the creditor (for example, due to cancellation or expiry).[12]

Repayment before Maturity Date

In some cases, debt is extinguished before its maturity date. The amount paid on extinguishment before maturity, including any call premium and expenses of reacquisition or early repayment, is called the **reacquisition price**. On any specified date, the bond's net carrying amount is the amount that is payable at maturity, adjusted for any unamortized premium or discount and cost of issuance. If the net carrying amount is more than the reacquisition price, the excess amount is a gain from extinguishment. Conversely, if the reacquisition price exceeds the net carrying amount, the excess is a loss from extinguishment. At the time of reacquisition, the unamortized premium or discount and any costs of issue that apply to the bonds must be amortized up to the reacquisition date.

To illustrate, assume that on January 1, 2017, General Bell Corp. issued bonds with a par value of $800,000 at 97 (which is net of issue costs), due in 20 years. Eight years after the issue date, the entire issue is called at 101 and cancelled. The loss on redemption (extinguishment) is calculated as in Illustration 14-11, which uses straight-line amortization for simplicity.

	Illustration 14-11
	Calculation of Loss on Redemption of Bonds

Reacquisition price ($800,000 × 1.01)		$808,000
Net carrying amount of bonds redeemed:		
Face value	$800,000	
Unamortized discount ($24,000ª × $^{12}/_{20}$)		
(amortized using straight-line basis)	(14,400)	785,600
Loss on redemption		$ 22,400

ª[$800,000 × (1 − 0.97)]

The entry to record the reacquisition and cancellation of the bonds is:

A	=	L	+	SE
−808,000		−785,600		−22,400

Cash flows: ↓ 808,000 outflow

Bonds Payable	785,600	
Loss on Redemption of Bonds	22,400	
Cash		808,000

Exchange of Debt Instruments

The replacement of an existing issuance with a new one is sometimes called **refunding**. Generally, an exchange of debt instruments that have **substantially different terms** between a borrower and lender is viewed as an extinguishment of the old debt and the issuance of a new one.[13]

UNDERLYING CONCEPT

If the new debt is substantially the same as the old debt, the economic substance is that it is a continuation of the old debt, even though, legally, the old debt may have been settled.

Companies may refund or replace debt to get more favourable terms. These early extinguishments would generally be bound by the initial debt agreement. (For example, there are provisions that allow early repayment.) The debtor may experience a loss and sometimes a gain depending on the prepayment options in the original agreement. If the bonds are marketable securities, the company can simply buy them back in the marketplace.

Sometimes, however, companies are forced to repay or restructure their debt because they cannot make interest and principal payments. This is sometimes referred to as troubled debt restructuring. An example of the accounting for a settlement through an exchange of debt instruments is noted in the next section.

Troubled Debt Restructurings

LAW

A **troubled debt restructuring** occurs when, for economic or legal reasons that are related to the debtor's financial difficulties, a creditor grants a concession to the debtor that it would not offer in ordinary circumstances. This is what separates a troubled debt restructuring from an ordinary early repayment or exchange.

A troubled debt restructuring can be either one of these two basic types of transactions:

1. **Settlement** of the debt at less than its carrying amount

2. **Continuation** of the debt, but with a **modification** of its terms

Settlement of Debt

**CORPORATE
FINANCE
TRANSACTIONS
5.6.2**

When the debt is settled, meaning there is early repayment or refunding, this is referred to as **debt settlement**. In this case, the old debt and all related discount, premium, and issuance costs will be removed from the debtor's books. (That is, they will be derecognized.) Unlike with a normal early repayment or refunding, a gain will usually be recognized in most cases because the creditor generally makes favourable concessions to the debtor in troubled debt situations. The creditor removes the loan receivable from its books and may recognize a further loss.

In order to settle the debt, the debtor may do one of the following:

1. Transfer non-cash assets (real estate, receivables, or other assets).

2. Issue shares.

3. Issue new debt to another creditor and use the cash to repay the existing debt.

If non-cash assets are used to settle the debt, the debtor will recognize a gain or loss on the disposal of the asset for the amount of the difference between the fair value of those assets and their carrying amount (book value). The creditor may force the debtor to transfer the asset if there is a legal charge on the asset (such as in the case of collateral or a mortgage). This is referred to as a **loan foreclosure**. The creditor takes the underlying security (the asset) as a replacement for payment of the loan.

To illustrate a transfer of assets, assume that Halifax City Bank has loaned $20 million to Union Trust. Union Trust in turn has invested these monies in residential apartment buildings, but because of low occupancy rates it cannot meet its loan obligations. Halifax City Bank agrees to accept from Union Trust a building with a fair value of $16 million in full settlement of the $20-million loan obligation. The building has a recorded value of $21 million on the books of Union Trust, net of accumulated depreciation of $5 million. For simplicity, assume that no prior allowance for doubtful accounts has been set up on the note and no impairment has been recognized on the building.[14] The entry to record this transaction on the books of Halifax City Bank (the creditor) is as follows:

A = L + SE
−4,000,000   −4,000,000

Cash flows: No effect

Buildings	16,000,000	
Loss on Loan Settlement	4,000,000	
Notes Receivable		20,000,000

The building is recorded at its fair value, and a charge is made to the income statement to reflect the loss.[15]

The entry to record this transaction on the books of Union Trust (the debtor) is as follows:

A = L + SE
−21,000,000 −20,000,000 −1,000,000

Cash flows: No effect

Accumulated Depreciation—Buildings	5,000,000	
Notes Payable	20,000,000	
Loss on Sale of Buildings (NBV − FV = 21,000,000 − 16,000,000)	5,000,000	
Buildings		26,000,000
Gain on Restructuring of Debt (FV of loan − FV of payment = 20,000,000 − 16,000,000)		4,000,000

Union Trust has a loss on the disposal of the building in the amount of $5 million, which is the difference between the $21-million book value and the $16-million fair value. In addition, it has a gain on restructuring of debt of $4 million, which is the difference between the $20-million carrying amount of the note payable and the $16-million fair market value of the real estate.

To illustrate the granting of an equity interest (that is, shares), assume that Halifax City Bank had agreed to accept from Union Trust 320,000 of Union's common shares, with a market value of $16 million, in full settlement of the $20-million loan obligation. Assume also that the bank had previously recognized a loss on impairment of $4 million. Halifax decides to treat the investments as FV-NI. The entry to record this transaction on the books of Halifax City Bank (the creditor) is as follows:

A   =   L   +   SE
0
Cash flows: No effect

FV-NI Investments	16,000,000	
Allowance for Doubtful Accounts	4,000,000	
Notes Receivable		20,000,000

The shares that are received by Halifax City Bank are recorded as an investment and at their fair value (equal to market value) on the date of the restructuring.

The entry to record this transaction on the books of Union Trust (the debtor) is as follows:[16]

A   =   L   +   SE
   −20,000,000 +20,000,000
Cash flows: No effect

Notes Payable	20,000,000	
Common Shares		16,000,000
Gain on Restructuring of Debt		4,000,000

In some cases, a debtor will have serious short-term cash flow problems that lead it to request one or a combination of the following modifications:

1. Reduction of the stated interest rate

2. Extension of the maturity date of the debt's face amount

3. Reduction of the debt's face amount

4. Reduction or deferral of any accrued interest

5. Change in currency

If there are substantial modifications, the transaction is treated like a settlement. The modifications would be considered substantial in either of these two situations:

1. The discounted present value under the new terms (discounted using the original effective interest rate) is at least 10% different from the discounted present value of the remaining cash flows under the old debt.

2. There is a change in creditor and the original debt is legally discharged.[17]

If one of these conditions is met, the transaction is considered a settlement. Otherwise, it is treated as a modification.

When the economic substance is a **settlement**, the old liability is eliminated and a new liability is assumed. The new liability is measured at the present value of the revised future cash flows discounted at the current prevailing market interest rate, as is done for the initial recording of a bond. The gain is measured as the difference between the current present value of the revised cash flows and the carrying value of the old debt.

Assume that on December 31, 2017, Manitoba National Bank enters into a debt restructuring agreement with Resorts Development Corp., which is experiencing financial difficulties. The bank restructures a $10.5-million loan receivable issued at par (interest paid up to date) by doing all of the following:

1. It reduces the principal obligation from $10.5 million to $9 million.

2. It extends the maturity date from December 31, 2017 to December 31, 2021.

3. It reduces the interest rate from 12% to 8%. (The market rate is currently 9%.)

Is this a settlement or a modification? Has a substantial modification in the debt occurred? The test to establish whether this is a settlement or not involves the cash flows. The present value of both cash flow streams is calculated as follows, using the historic rate as the discount rate for consistency and comparability:

Old debt: PV = $10,500,000 (because the debt is currently due)

New debt: PV = $9,000,000 $(PVF_{4,12\%})$ + $720,000 $(PVFOA_{4,12\%})$ (see Tables A-2 and A-4)

New debt: PV = $9,000,000 (0.63552) + $720,000 (3.03735) = $7,906,572

The new debt's value differs by more than 10% of the old debt's value, so the renegotiated debt would therefore be considered a settlement, and a gain would be recorded through the following journal entry:

A = L + SE
−1,791,532 +1,791,532
Cash flows: No effect

Notes Payable	10,500,000	
Notes Payable		8,708,468
Gain on Restructuring of Debt		1,791,532

Because it is new debt, it would be recorded at the present value of the new cash flows at the market interest rate as follows: $PVF_{4,9\%} + PVFOA_{4,9\%} = \$9,000,000 (0.70843) + \$720,000 (3.23972) = \$8,708,468$.

Manitoba National Bank would record a modification gain or loss. The recorded amount of the loan receivable would be reduced to the amount of the net cash flows receivable (but under the modified terms) discounted at the historical effective interest rate that is inherent in the loan. Because it is a restructuring, the uncollectible amount would be written off (as opposed to setting up an allowance). At the date of restructuring, Manitoba National Bank would record a loss of $2,193,428 (assuming it had previously recognized an impairment of $400,000) through the following journal entry:

A = L + SE
−2,193,428   −2,193,428
Cash flows: No effect

Modification Gain or Loss	2,193,428	
Notes Receivable	7,906,572	
Allowance For Doubtful Accounts	400,000	
Notes Receivable		10,500,000

Non-Substantial Modification of Terms

Where debt is exchanged but the terms of the new debt are not substantially different (modified) from the old debt, the accounting is different. The old debt is seen to continue to exist but with new terms. A new effective interest rate is imputed by equating the carrying amount of the original debt with the present value of the revised cash flows.

Looking back to our example above for Manitoba National Bank and Resorts Development Corp., if the substantial modification test was not met, the debt would remain on the books at $10.5 million and no gain or loss would be recognized. As a result, no entry would be made by Resorts Development Corp. (debtor) at the date of restructuring. The debtor would calculate a new effective interest rate, however, in order to record interest expense in future periods. In this case, the new rate is calculated by relating the pre-restructure carrying amount ($10.5 million) to the total future cash flows ($9,000,000 + [4 × $720,000]). Using a financial calculator or spreadsheet formula, we can determine that the rate to discount the total future cash flows ($11,880,000) to the present value that is equal to the remaining balance ($10.5 million) is 3.46613%.

Based on the effective rate of 3.46613%, the schedule in Illustration 14-12 is prepared.

Illustration 14-12

Schedule Showing Reduction of Carrying Amount of Note

RESORTS DEVELOPMENT CORP. (DEBTOR)				
Date	Interest Paid (8%)	Interest Expense (3.46613%)	Reduction of Carrying Amount	Carrying Amount of Note
12/31/17				$10,500,000
12/31/18	$ 720,000[a]	$ 363,944[b]	$ 356,056[c]	10,143,944
12/31/19	720,000	351,602	368,398	9,775,546
12/31/20	720,000	338,833	381,167	9,394,379
12/31/21	720,000	325,621	394,379	9,000,000
	$2,880,000	$1,380,000	$1,500,000	

[a]$720,000 = $9,000,000 × 0.08
[b]$363,944 = $10,500,000 × 3.46613%
[c]$356,056 = $720,000 − $363,944

Thus, on December 31, 2018 (the date of the first interest payment after the restructuring), the debtor makes the following entry:

A = L + SE
−720,000 −356,056 −363,944

Cash flows: ↓ 720,000 outflow

December 31, 2018		
Notes Payable	356,056	
Interest Expense	363,944	
Cash		720,000

A similar entry (except for different amounts for debits to Notes Payable and Interest Expense) is made each year until maturity. At maturity, the following entry is made:

A = L + SE
−9,000,000 −9,000,000

Cash flows: ↓ 9,000,000 outflow

December 31, 2021		
Notes Payable	9,000,000	
Cash		9,000,000

In this case also, Manitoba National Bank would account for the restructuring in the same way as if there had been a substantial modification.

The decision tree in Illustration 14-13 summarizes the process for deciding how to account for early retirements and modifications of debt.

Illustration 14-13

Accounting for Early Retirements and Modifications of Debt

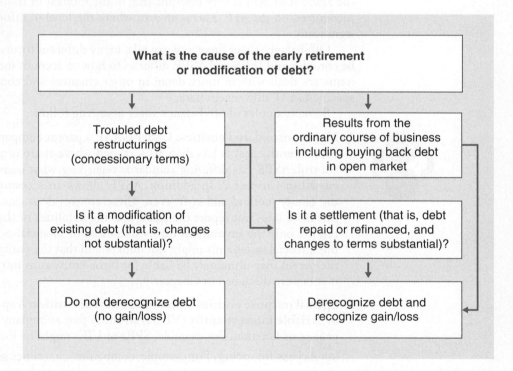

Note that in other than troubled debt situations, companies would generally not exchange debt because there is little economic incentive to do so. They would either buy back the debt in the open market or exercise an early prepayment option, if one existed in the original debt agreement. Thus the accounting would take the form of settlement accounting and the debt would be derecognized.

Defeasance Revisited

Earlier in the chapter, we discussed defeasance. Let's revisit defeasance and look at the accounting. Where **legal defeasance** occurs, the debt is extinguished and the creditor looks to the trust for repayment. The creditor no longer has any claim on the company and therefore the company treats the transaction as an extinguishment and thus derecognizes the liability.

In some cases, however, the company does not inform the creditor of the arrangement or the creditor does not release the company from the primary obligation to settle the debt. Thus the original loan agreement is still in force. This version of the arrangement is often called **in-substance defeasance**. Does in-substance defeasance result in extinguishment of the debt on the company's books? In essence, if the trust is properly set up—for example, the money is invested in low-risk or risk-free investments in an irrevocable trust—it can be argued that the debt has been prepaid and there is little risk to the company. On the other hand, the company still has the primary obligation according to the original loan agreement. IFRS and ASPE do not allow derecognition of debt under in-substance defeasance arrangements because the company still owes the money.

Off–Balance Sheet Financing

THEORY

Off–balance sheet financing occurs when a company structures a financing deal that results in the obligations not being recorded as debt on the statement of financial position. It is an issue of extreme importance to accountants as well as to general management. Because increased debt signals increased solvency risk, there is a reporting bias to keep low debt levels on the statement of financial position (SFP). From a user perspective, however, the amount of debt is very relevant and, in the interest of transparency, all debt should be recognized on the SFP. This is an area where the level of information asymmetry may be significant.

Off–balance sheet financing can take many different forms. The accounting issues can be complex and IFRS and ASPE differ as to how to account for these items. Because these items are dealt with in more detail in other chapters and courses, we will not cover the specific GAAP differences here.

Some examples of off–balance sheet financing follow.

1. **Non-consolidated entities:** Under GAAP, a parent company does not have to consolidate an entity that is less than 50% owned where there is no control. IFRS 10 defines control. ASPE has differing standards regarding what constitutes control, as was discussed in Chapter 2. In addition, ASPE allows an accounting policy choice between the equity method and cost, even where control does exist. In such cases, the parent therefore does not report the assets and the liabilities of the entity. Instead, the parent reports only the investment on its statement of financial position. As a result, users of the financial statements might not understand that the entity has considerable debt that the parent may ultimately be liable for if the entity runs into financial difficulty. Investments were discussed in Chapter 9.

2. **Special purpose entities or variable interest entities:** A special purpose entity (SPE) or **variable interest entity** (VIE) is an entity that a company creates to perform a special project or function. For example, SPEs or VIEs might be formed to do the following:

    (a) **Access financing.** For example, companies sometimes set up SPEs and VIEs to buy assets, such as accounts receivable or investments, from the company. The company then sells the assets to the SPE/VIE in return for cash, thus obtaining financing. Investors invest in the SPE/VIE to benefit from the return on the assets and certain tax advantages. This process is known as a **securitization** of assets. In this way, the company essentially takes a pool of assets and turns it into securities. Whether the company treats this as a sale or financing was discussed in Chapter 7.

    (b) **Take on risk from the company.** As in the example above, the sale of the receivables or investments eliminates price and cash flow risks for the company because it now holds cash instead of the riskier receivables or investments. The SPEs/VIEs provide a ready market for buying the assets.

    (c) **Isolate certain assets from other company assets.** For example, the pension assets of company employees are often segregated in a trust fund or SPE. This arrangement allows greater security for the employees and the company gets certain tax advantages when it contributes money to the plan. Chapter 19 discusses recognition of unfunded pension obligations.

SPEs and VIEs thus serve valid business functions. They only become a problem when they are used primarily to make a company's statement of financial position look better by disguising risk. As a general rule, these entities should be consolidated when the company is the main beneficiary of the SPE/VIE. Except for the overview we just presented, the accounting for SPEs and VIEs is beyond the scope of this book.

ETHICS

3. **Operating leases:** Another way that companies keep debt off the SFP is by leasing. Instead of owning the assets, companies lease them. By meeting certain conditions, the company has to report only rent expense each period and provide note disclosure of the transaction. Chapter 20 discusses accounting for leases. IFRS now requires most leases to be fully recognized.

The accounting profession's response to these off–balance sheet financing arrangements has been to tighten up the accounting guidance for guarantees, SPEs, leases, and pensions and also to mandate increased note disclosure requirements. This response follows an efficient markets philosophy. The important question has not been whether the presentation is off–balance sheet, but whether the items are disclosed at all.[18]

As part of the conceptual framework project, the IASB has been working on this issue of what constitutes the economic entity.

PRESENTATION, DISCLOSURE, AND ANALYSIS

The reporting of long-term debt is one of the most controversial areas in financial reporting. Because long-term debt has a significant impact on a company's cash flow, reporting requirements must be substantive and informative. One problem is that the definition of a liability and the recognition criteria in the conceptual framework are not precise enough to prevent the argument from being made that certain obligations do not need to be reported as debt.

Presentation

Current versus Long-Term Debt

Objective 4
Explain how long-term debt is presented on the statement of financial position.

Companies that have large amounts and many issues of long-term debt often report only one amount in the statement of financial position and give details about the amount through comments and schedules in the accompanying notes. Long-term debt that **matures within one year** should generally be reported as a **current liability**, unless it will be retired using something other than current assets. If the debt is to be refinanced, the company must treat it as current unless the refinancing has occurred before the release of the financial statements or a refinancing agreement is in place.[19] IFRS requires that the financing be in place by the date of the statement of financial position.[20]

Where it is more relevant to present information according to liquidity, the entity should present assets and liabilities in order of liquidity. If this is the case, the amounts to be recovered or paid within the next 12 months should be disclosed.[21]

Debt versus Equity

As financial instruments become more complex, the line between what is debt and what is equity is becoming more blurred. As noted above, there is significant pressure on companies to watch their debt levels. We will discuss the debt-versus-equity issue in Chapter 16, which examines more-complex financial instruments.

Disclosures

Note disclosures generally indicate the following:

- the nature of the liabilities,
- maturity dates,
- interest rates,
- call provisions,
- conversion privileges,
- restrictions imposed by the creditors, and
- assets designated or pledged as security.

Any assets that have been pledged as security for the debt should be shown as such in the assets section of the statement of financial position. The fair value of the long-term debt should also be disclosed. Disclosure is required of future payments for sinking fund requirements and maturity amounts of long-term debt during each of the next five years. Disclosures are also required regarding risks related to the debt (such as solvency and liquidity). The purpose of these disclosures is to help financial statement users evaluate the amounts and timing of future cash flows.

Disclosure requirements are significant. The paragraph above is just a very high-level summary. IFRS 7 details the disclosure requirements for IFRS whereas Section 3856 covers this under ASPE. There are fewer disclosure requirements under ASPE than under IFRS.

Illustration14-14 is from **Enbridge Pipelines Inc.** and shows required disclosures for long-term debt.

17. Debt
December 31,

(millions of Canadian dollars)	Weighted Average Interest Rate	Maturity	**2014**	2013
Liquids Pipelines				
Debentures	8.2%	2024	**200**	200
Medium-term notes[1]	4.8%	2015–2043	**2,986**	2,985
Southern Lights project financing[2,3]	4.0%	2040	**1,571**	1,480
Commercial paper and credit facility draws			**163**	266
Other[4]			**9**	11
Sponsored Investments				
Junior subordinated notes[5]	8.1%	2067	**464**	425
Senior notes[6]	6.1%	2016–2040	**4,815**	4,201
Commercial paper and credit facility draws[7]			**2,474**	676
Corporate				
Promissory Notes[8]		2015	**103**	—
Other[9]			**(10)**	(9)
Total debt			**12,775**	10,235
Current maturities			**(304)**	(1,695)
Short-term borrowings			**(103)**	—
Long-term debt			**12,368**	8,540

[1] Included in medium-term notes is $100 million with a maturity date of 2112.
[2] 2014—$348 million and US$1,054 million (2013—$352 million and US$1,061 million).
[3] On August 18, 2014, long-term private debt was issued with the proceeds utilized to repay the construction credit facilities on a dollar-for-dollar basis.
[4] Primarily capital lease obligations.
[5] 2014—US$400 million (2013—US$400 million).
[6] 2014—US$4,150 million (2013—US$3,950 million).
[7] 2014—US$2,132 million (2013—US$635 million).
[8] A non-interest bearing demand promissory note that was subsequently paid on January 9, 2015.
[9] Primarily debt discount.

For the years ending December 31, 2015 through 2019, debenture and term note maturities are $302 million, $397 million, $58 million, $948 million, $1,041 million, respectively, and $7,290 million

(continued)

Illustration 14-14

*Enbridge Pipelines Inc. 2014
Financial Statements—Note 17
(continued)*

thereafter. The Company's debentures and term notes bear interest at fixed rates and the interest obligations for the year ending December 31, 2015 through 2019 are $553 million, $544 million, $515 million, $472 million and $392 million, respectively. At December 31, 2014, all debt was unsecured and at December 31, 2013, all debt was unsecured except for the Southern Lights project financing, which was collateralized by the Southern Lights project assets of approximately $2,680 million.

Interest Expense

Year ended December 31,	**2014**	2013	2012
(millions of Canadian dollars)			
Debenture and term notes	**630**	514	506
Commercial paper and credit facility draws	**19**	5	3
Southern Lights project financing	**49**	40	38
Interest on loans from affiliated companies (*Note 29*)	**500**	322	143
Capitalized	**(285)**	(152)	(101)
	913	729	589

Credit Facilities

		December 31, 2014			December 31, 2013
	Maturity Dates	Total Facilities	Draws[1]	Available	Total Facilities
(millions of Canadian dollars)	2016				
Liquids Pipelines	2016–2019				
Sponsored Investments		300	163	137	300
		4,031	2,601	1,430	4,281
Total committed credit facilities[2]		**4,331**	**2,764**	**1,567**	4,581

[1] Includes facility draws, letters of credit and commercial paper issuances that are back-stopped by the credit facility.
[2] On August 18, 2014, long-term private debt was issued for $352 million and US$1,061 million related to Southern Lights project financing. The proceeds were utilized to repay the construction credit facilities on a dollar-for-dollar basis. Excluded from December 31, 2014 total facilities above was Southern Lights project financing facilities of $28 million (2013—$1,570 million). Included in the 2013 facilities for Southern Lights were $63 million for debt service reserve letters of credit.

In addition to the committed credit facilities noted above, as at December 31, 2014, the Company has utilized $255 million (2013—nil) of uncommitted demand credit facilities.

Credit facilities carry a weighted average standby fee of 0.2% per annum on the unused portion and draws bear interest at market rates. Certain credit facilities serve as a back-stop to the commercial paper programs and the Company has the option to extend the facilities, which are currently set to mature from 2016 to 2019.

Commercial paper and credit facility draws, net of short-term borrowings, of $2,534 million (2013—$942 million) are supported by the availability of long-term committed credit facilities and therefore have been classified as long-term debt.

Analysis

Objective 6
Calculate and interpret key ratios related to solvency and liquidity.

FINANCIAL ANALYSIS AND PLANNING
5.1.1

ETHICS

A company's level of debt is of great interest to key stakeholders, as we saw in the chapter-opening story. Many investors and creditors focus on this number for resource allocation decisions. How much debt is the right amount? It depends. The higher the debt, the greater the risk that the company may not be able to repay it. Capital markets respond to this additional solvency risk by increasing the cost of capital and making it more difficult for companies with high debt levels to access additional capital.

As mentioned earlier in the chapter, lenders put covenants in lending agreements stating the amount of debt that a company is allowed to have. Covenants normally state certain financial tests and ratios that the borrower must meet or the debt will become payable. Because of this, restrictive covenants can encourage reporting bias. The company may feel forced to meet the test even if it means using aggressive accounting to do so. Although debt holders assume that the covenants will protect them, covenants are often written in a way that can be interpreted (or misinterpreted) in different ways. Therefore, covenants may provide little or no protection.

UNDERLYING CONCEPT

Users of financial statements must be aware when covenants exist so that they understand the potential for misstating the financial statements. Whenever these conditions are important for users to have a complete understanding of the company's financial position and results of operations, they should be described in the body of the financial statements or the accompanying notes.

Long-term creditors and shareholders are interested in a company's long-term **solvency**, particularly its ability to pay interest as it comes due and to repay the face value of debt at maturity. **Debt to total assets** and **times interest earned** are two of several ratios that provide information about debt-paying ability and long-term solvency. Companies have a vested interest in making sure that they manage their debt levels in a way that does not weaken their solvency position. The **debt to total assets ratio** measures the percentage of the total assets that is provided by creditors. It is calculated by dividing total debt (both current and long-term liabilities) by total assets, as shown in the following formula:

$$\text{Debt to total assets} = \frac{\text{Total debt}}{\text{Total assets}}$$

The **higher the percentage** of debt to total assets, the **greater the risk** that the company may be unable to meet its maturing obligations.

The **times interest earned ratio** indicates the company's ability to meet interest payments as they come due. The higher the ratio, the better the company's ability to ensure that its interest payments are made. It is calculated by dividing income before interest expense and income taxes by interest expense:

$$\text{Times interest earned} = \frac{\text{Income before income taxes and interest expense}}{\text{Interest expense}}$$

WHAT DO THE NUMBERS MEAN?

To illustrate these ratios, we will use data from the **Canadian Tire Corporation** (CTC) 2014 financial statements, which disclosed total liabilities of $8,922 million, total assets of $14,553 million, interest expense of $139 million, income tax expense of $239 million, and net income of $639 million. CTC's debt to total assets ratio is calculated as follows:

$$
\begin{aligned}
\text{Debt to total assets} &= \text{total debt} \div \text{total assets} \\
&= \$8{,}922 \div \$14{,}553 \\
&= 61.3\%
\end{aligned}
$$

CTC has a moderate debt to total assets percentage of 61.3%. The company is capitalized by debt, shares, and retained earnings.

The interest coverage ratio is calculated as follows:

$$
\begin{aligned}
\text{Interest coverage ratio} &= \text{Income before income taxes and interest expense} \div \text{interest expense} \\
&= (\$639 + \$239 + \$139) \div \$139 \\
&= 7.32 \ \text{(which is a good coverage ratio)}
\end{aligned}
$$

This is due to the fact that debt levels are reasonable and the company is profitable.

Objective 7

Identify major differences in accounting standards between IFRS and ASPE, and what changes are expected in the near future.

IFRS/ASPE COMPARISON

A Comparison of IFRS and ASPE

Illustration 14-15 summarizes the differences in accounting for long-term financial liabilities between IFRS and ASPE.

	IFRS—IAS 1 and 32; IFRS 7 and 9	ASPE—*CPA Canada Handbook*, Part II, Sections 1510, 1521, and 3856	References to Related Illustrations and Select Brief Exercises
Measurement	There is no specific guidance on related party transactions.	There is specific guidance on measuring related party transactions (which we will cover in Chapter 23).	See Chapter 23—BE23-12, 13, and 15.
	Subsequent to initial recognition, liabilities are generally measured at amortized cost using the effective interest method (unless measured at fair value under the fair value option or because it is a derivative).	Subsequent to initial recognition, liabilities are generally measured at amortized cost using the effective interest or other method (unless measured at fair value under the fair value option or because it is a derivative).	See Chapter 9—Illustrations 9-4 and 9-6 and subsequent journal entries. (Note that Chapter 9 deals with the amortization issue from the asset side but the calculations are similar on the liability side.)
	Where the fair value option is used, credit risk is incorporated into the measurement and resulting gains/losses are booked through net income. However, if IFRS 9 is adopted early, gains/losses related to changes in credit risk are booked though other comprehensive income.	Where the fair value option is used, credit risk is incorporated into the measurement and resulting gains/losses are booked through net income.	Illustration 14-10 and BE14-18
Presentation	Normally the SFP is segregated into current/non-current except where presentation on the basis of liquidity is more relevant (then debt is presented in order of liquidity).	Normally the balance sheet is segregated into current/non-current; however, this may not be appropriate for certain industries.	BE14-24
	Refinanced long-term debt may be classified as long-term where refinanced by SFP date.	Refinanced long-term debt may be classified as long-term where refinanced by date of issue of financial statements.	BE14-20

Illustration 14-15

IFRS and ASPE Comparison Chart

Looking Ahead

The IASB has been working on several projects related to long-term debt as follows:

1. **Financial instruments with the characteristics of equity:** This project will affect how debt and equity instruments are classified and presented on the statement of financial position. At the time of writing, the IASB was in discussions and the next step was expected to be a Discussion Paper. The AcSB was doing a post-implementation review of Section 3856.

2. **Conceptual framework project:** As part of this project, the standard setters have been trying to identify the economic entity for financial reporting purposes. They were also looking at revising the definitions for financial statement elements as well as guidance on measurement and recognition. An Exposure Draft was released, with the comment period ending in November 2015. We discussed this briefly in Chapter 2.

SUMMARY OF LEARNING OBJECTIVES

1 Understand the nature of long-term debt financing arrangements.

Incurring long-term debt is often a formal procedure. Corporation bylaws usually require the approval of the board of directors and the shareholders before bonds can be issued or other long-term debt arrangements can be contracted. Generally, long-term debt has various covenants or restrictions. The covenants and other terms of the agreement between the borrower and the lender are stated in the bond indenture or note agreement. Notes are similar in substance to bonds but do not trade as readily in capital markets, if at all.

The variety of types of bonds and notes is a result of attempts to attract capital from different investors and risk takers and to satisfy the issuers' cash flow needs.

External credit rating agencies rate bonds and assign a credit rating based on the riskiness. The credit rating helps investors decide whether to invest in a particular bond. Companies sometimes extinguish debt early using a defeasance arrangement. In a defeasance arrangement, funds are deposited into a trust and the trust continues to make the regularly scheduled payments until maturity.

By using debt financing, companies can maximize income through the use of leverage. Capital-intensive industries often have higher levels of debt. Continued access to low-cost debt is important for maximizing shareholder value.

2   Understand how long-term debt is measured and accounted for.

The investment community values a bond at the present value of its future cash flows, which consist of interest and principal. The rate that is used to calculate the present value of these cash flows is the interest rate that provides an acceptable return on an investment that matches the issuer's risk characteristics. The interest rate written in the terms of the bond indenture and ordinarily appearing on the bond certificate is the stated, coupon, or nominal rate. This rate, which is set by the issuer of the bonds, is expressed as a percentage of the bond's face value, which is also called the par value, principal amount, or maturity value. If the rate used by the buyers differs from the stated rate, the bond's present value calculated by the buyers will differ from the bond's face value. The difference between the bond's face value and the present value is either a discount or a premium. Long-term debt is measured at fair value on initial recognition, including transaction costs where the instruments will be valued at amortized cost. Subsequently, the instruments are measured at amortized cost or, in certain limited situations, fair value, under the fair value option.

The discount (premium) is amortized and charged (credited) to interest expense over the period of time that the bonds are outstanding. IFRS requires the effective interest method; however, ASPE allows a choice and often, smaller private entities use the straight-line method.

Bonds and notes may be issued with zero interest or for a nonmonetary consideration. Measurement of the bonds and the consideration must reflect the underlying substance of the transaction. In particular, reasonable interest rates must be imputed. The fair value of the debt and of the nonmonetary consideration should be used to value the transaction.

3   Understand when long-term debt is recognized and derecognized, including how to account for troubled debt restructurings.

At the time of reacquisition, the unamortized premium or discount and any costs of issue that apply to the debt must be amortized up to the reacquisition date. The amount that is paid on extinguishment or redemption before maturity, including any call premium and expense of reacquisition, is the reacquisition price. On any specified date, the debt's net carrying amount is the amount that is payable at maturity, adjusted for unamortized premium or discount and the cost of issuance. Any excess of the net carrying amount over the reacquisition price is a gain from extinguishment, whereas the excess of the reacquisition price over the net carrying amount is a loss from extinguishment. Legal defeasance results in derecognition of the liability. In-substance defeasance does not.

Where debt is settled by exchanging the old debt with new debt (generally in troubled debt situations), it is treated as a settlement where the terms of the agreements are substantially different, including a size test, and where the new debt is with a new lender. If not treated as a settlement, it is treated as a modification of the old debt and a new interest rate is imputed.

Off–balance sheet financing is an attempt to borrow funds in such a way that the obligations are not recorded. One type of off–balance sheet financing involves the use of certain variable interest entities. Accounting standard setters have been studying this area with the objective of coming up with a new definition of what constitutes the reporting entity.

4   Explain how long-term debt is presented on the statement of financial position.

Companies that have large amounts and many issues of long-term debt often report only one amount in the SFP and support this with comments and schedules in the accompanying notes. Long-term debt that matures within one year should be reported as a current liability, unless it will be retired without using current assets. If the debt is to be refinanced, converted into shares, or retired from a bond retirement fund, it should continue to be reported as non-current and accompanied by a note explaining the method to be used in its liquidation unless certain conditions are met.

5   Identify disclosure requirements.

Note disclosures are significant and generally indicate the nature of the liabilities, maturity dates, interest rates, call provisions, conversion privileges, restrictions imposed by the creditors, and assets designated or pledged as security as well as other details.

6   Calculate and interpret key ratios related to solvency and liquidity.

Debt to total assets and times interest earned are two ratios that provide information about debt-paying ability and long-term solvency.

7   Identify major differences in accounting standards between IFRS and ASPE, and what changes are expected in the near future.

IFRS and ASPE are largely converged as they relate to long-term debt. Small differences relate to whether the debt is presented as current or non-current and in measurement. For example, ASPE has measurement standards for related party transactions. The standard setters have been working on several large projects, including the conceptual framework and financial instruments with the characteristics of equity.

KEY TERMS

Note: Completion of this end-of-chapter material will help develop CPA enabling competencies (such as ethics and professionalism, problem-solving and decision-making, and communication) and technical competencies. We have highlighted selected items with an integration icon and material in *WileyPLUS* has been linked to the competencies. All cases emphasize integration, especially of the enabling competencies. The brief exercises, exercises, and problems generally emphasize problem-solving and decision-making.

Unless otherwise indicated, depreciation expense should be calculated to the nearest whole month. If the question requires part-year present value calculations for journal entries (for instance between interest dates), please pro-rate the number using the number of months as shown in the chapter (see illustration 14-7) unless otherwise directed.

Brief Exercises

(LO 1) BE14-1 Lamanna Laundry Ltd. is a full-service laundry provider, focusing on high-end clientele. Lamanna Laundry has recently invested in new technology to improve efficiency. In order to finance the new technology, the company issued a 10-year bond on January 1, 2017. On issuance, the bonds were assigned a BBB–credit rating by Standard & Poor's, and the market rate for the bonds was 9%. During the year, competition heightened in the industry, and Lamanna Laundry experienced four consecutive quarters of increasing losses and deteriorating financial position in 2017. (a) Discuss the potential impact on the bonds' credit rating, if any. (b) Discuss the potential impact on investors' required yield on the bonds, if any.

(LO 1) BE14-2 Jensen & Jensen Incorporated, a telecommunications equipment manufacturer, has a debt to total assets ratio of 55%, while competing companies of similar size operating in the same industry have an average debt to total assets ratio of 62%. Jensen & Jensen is planning to expand its operations by adding two new plants next year. Jensen & Jensen currently is privately owned by the Jensen brothers, and they would like to keep the company closely held, but will issue shares if necessary. (a) Discuss three sources for financing the expansion. (b) Recommend the most suitable source of financing for Jensen & Jensen, based on the information provided.

(LO 2) BE14-3 Buchanan Corporation issues $500,000 of 11% bonds that are due in 10 years and pay interest semi-annually. At the time of issue, the market rate for such bonds is 10%. Using time value of money tables, a financial calculator, and computer spreadsheet functions, calculate the bonds' issue price. (*Hint*: Refer to Appendix 3B for tips on calculating.)

(LO 2) BE14-4 Samwall Ltd. needed funding to bridge the gap between paying its suppliers and collecting its receivables. As such, Samwall issued a $300,000, four-year, 8% note at face value to Easy Loan Bank on January 1, 2017 and received $300,000 cash. The note requires annual interest payments each December 31. Prepare Samwall's journal entries to record (a) the note issuance and (b) the December 31, 2017 interest payment.

FINANCE

(LO 2) **BE14-5**   On May 1, 2017, Jadeja Corporation, a publicly listed corporation, issued $200,000 of five-year, 8% bonds, with interest payable semi-annually on November 1 and May 1. The bonds were issued to yield a market interest rate of 6%. Jadeja uses the effective interest method. (a) Calculate the present value (issue price) of the bonds on May 1 using time value of money tables, a financial calculator, and computer spreadsheet functions. (*Hint*: Refer to Appendix 3B for tips on calculating.) (b) Record the issue of the bonds on May 1. (c) Prepare the journal entry to record the first and second interest payments on November 1, 2017 and May 1, 2018.

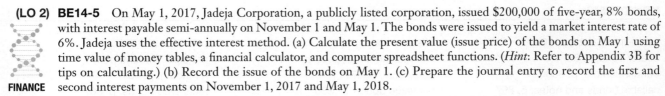

FINANCE

(LO 2) **BE14-6**   Sophia Incorporated issued a $105,000, five-year, zero-interest-bearing note to Angelica Corp. on January 1, 2017 and received $52,000 cash. Sophia uses the effective interest method. (a) Using a financial calculator and computer spreadsheet functions, calculate the implicit interest rate. (b) Prepare Sophia's journal entry for the January 1 issuance. (c) Prepare Sophia's journal entry for the December 31 recognition of interest. (d) Prepare an effective-interest amortization table for the note.

FINANCE

(LO 2) **BE14-7**   Brestovacki Corporation issued a $50,000, five-year, 5% note to Jernigan Corp. on January 1, 2017 and received a piece of equipment that normally sells for $38,912. The note requires annual interest payments each December 31. The market interest rate for a note of similar risk is 11%. (a) Prepare Brestovacki's journal entry for the January 1, 2017 issuance. (*Hint*: Refer to Appendix 3B for tips on calculating.) (b) Prepare the entry for the December 31, 2017 interest payment using the effective interest method.

(LO 2) **BE14-8**   Big Country Corporation is in the business of selling cattle. Due to recent diseases plaguing cattle, Big Country is experiencing a cash shortage. Big Country issued a $280,000, six-year, zero-interest-bearing note to Little Town Corp. on January 1, 2017 and received $200,000 cash. In addition, to conserve cash, Big Country agreed to sell cattle to Little Town for an amount less than the regular selling price over the six-year period. The market interest rate for similar notes is 8%. Big Country uses the effective interest method. Prepare Big Country's January 1 journal entry.

(LO 2) **BE14-9**   Pflug Ltd. signed an instalment note on January 1, 2017 in settlement of an account payable of $40,000 owed to Mott Ltd. Pflug is able to borrow funds from its bank at 11%, whereas Mott can borrow at the rate of 10%. The note calls for two equal payments of blended principal and interest to be made at December 31, 2017 and 2018. Using time value of money tables, a financial calculator, and computer spreadsheet functions, calculate the amount of the equal instalment payments that will be made to Mott Ltd. (*Hint*: Refer to Appendix 3B for tips on calculating.)

(LO 2) **BE14-10**   Watson Corporation issued $500,000 of 8%, 10-year bonds on January 1, 2017 at face value. The bonds require annual interest payments each December 31. Costs associated with the bond issuance were $25,000. Watson follows ASPE and uses the straight-line method to amortize bond issue costs. Prepare the journal entry for (a) the January 1, 2017 issuance and (b) the December 31, 2017 interest payment and bond issuance cost amortization. (c) What are the general principles surrounding accounting for transaction costs associated with the issue of notes or bonds? (d) What are the implications if the bonds were trading on the market for more than their face value?

(LO 2) **BE14-11**   Grenier Limited issued $300,000 of 10% bonds on January 1, 2017. The bonds are due on January 1, 2022, with interest payable each July 1 and January 1. The bonds are issued at face value. Grenier uses the effective interest method. Prepare the company's journal entries for (a) the January issuance, (b) the July 1, 2017 interest payment, and (c) the December 31, 2017 adjusting entry.

(LO 2) **BE14-12**   Assume that the bonds in BE14-11 were issued at 98. Assume also that Grenier Limited records the amortization using the straight-line method. Prepare the journal entries related to the bonds for (a) January 1, (b) July 1, and (c) December 31.

(LO 2) **BE14-13**   Assume that the bonds in BE14-11 were issued at 103. Assume also that Grenier Limited records the amortization using the straight-line method. Prepare the journal entries related to the bonds for (a) January 1, (b) July 1, and (c) December 31.

(LO 2) **BE14-14**   The City of Fram issued 100 bonds at their face value of $6,000 each plus accrued interest on June 1, 2017. The term of the bonds was January 1, 2017 to January 1, 2023, with interest payable semi-annually each January 1 and July 1 at 6%. Fram uses the effective interest method. Prepare the company's journal entries for (a) the date of issuance, (b) the July 1 interest payment, and (c) the December 31 adjusting entry.

(LO 2) **BE14-15**   On January 1, 2017, Quinton Corporation issued $600,000 of 7% bonds that are due in 10 years. The bonds were issued for $559,229 and pay interest each July 1 and January 1. The company uses the effective interest method. Assume an effective rate of 8%. (a) Prepare the company's journal entry for the January 1 issuance. (b) Prepare the company's journal entry for the July 1 interest payment. (c) Prepare the company's December 31 adjusting entry. (d) Assume that the effective interest of 8% was not given in the data. Prove the effective interest rate of 8% using a financial calculator and computer spreadsheet functions. (e) Prepare the first three payments of an effective-interest amortization table for the bonds.

FINANCE

(LO 2) **BE14-16**   Assume that the bonds in BE14-15 were issued for $644,632 and the effective interest rate was 6%. (a) Prepare the company's journal entry for the January 1 issuance. (b) Prepare the company's journal entry for the July 1 interest payment. (c) Prepare the company's December 31 adjusting entry. (d) Assume that the effective interest of 6% was not given in the data. Prove the effective interest rate of 6% using a financial calculator and computer spreadsheet functions. (e) Prepare the first three payments of an effective-interest amortization table for the bonds.

FINANCE

(LO 2) BE14-17 Travel In Style Limited issued $1,000,000 of 9% bonds on September 1, 2017 for $1,058,671. The term of the bonds is September 1, 2017 to September 1, 2025, with interest payable quarterly each December 1, March 1, June 1, and September 1. The company uses the effective interest method with an effective rate of 8%. (a) Prepare the company's journal entry for the September 1 issuance. (b) Prepare the company's journal entry for the December 1 interest payment.

(LO 2) BE14-18 Hanson Incorporated issued $1 million of 7%, 10-year bonds on July 1, 2016 at face value. Interest is payable each December 31. The company has chosen to apply the fair value option in accounting for the bonds. A risk assessment at December 31, 2017 shows that Hanson's credit risk has increased, and as a result of the increased credit risk, the fair value of the bonds is $900,000 on that date. Prepare the company's journal entries on December 31, 2017 if Hanson follows (a) ASPE, and (b) IFRS 9.

(LO 3) BE14-19 On January 1, 2017, Jamil Incorporated redeemed bonds prior to their maturity date of January 1, 2018. The face value of the bonds was $800,000, and the redemption was performed at 97. As at the redemption date, the unamortized premium was $6,500. Prepare the corporation's journal entry to record the redemption of the bonds.

(LO 3) BE14-20 Assume that Theo Limited has a loan that is currently due at year end. The debt is being refinanced with a five-year loan and the deal to refinance the debt is signed two days after year end. How would the original loan be classified in the year-end statements under IFRS and ASPE? Theo presents a classified statement of financial position.

(LO 3) BE14-21 Lawrence Incorporated owes $100,000 to Ontario Bank Inc. on a two-year, 10% note due on December 31, 2017. The note was issued at par. Because Lawrence is in financial trouble, Ontario Bank agrees to extend the maturity date of the note to December 31, 2019, reduce the principal to $75,000, and reduce the interest rate to 8%, payable annually on December 31. Present value of the new debt is calculated as $72,397. Lawrence prepares financial statements in accordance with IFRS. Prepare the journal entry on Lawrence's books on each of December 31, 2017, 2018, and 2019.

(LO 3) BE14-22 On January 1, 2017, Steinem Corporation established a special purpose entity to buy $1 million of accounts receivable from Steinem. Investors have invested in the special purpose entity to benefit from the return on assets and certain tax advantages. The special purpose entity has used the cash invested by the investors to buy the $1 million of accounts receivable from Steinem. (a) Has Steinem's liquidity improved as a result of this transaction? (b) Will Steinem's statement of financial position show increased debt or equity as a result of this transaction? (c) What type of transaction is this? (d) From the perspective of an investor, what is the related risk?

FINANCE

(LO 4) BE14-23 At December 31, 2017, Jelena Incorporated has a bond payable with a carrying value of $1,200,000 (based on amortized cost) due September 1, 2018 and a current value of $1,250,000. The interest payable as at December 31, 2017 is $25,000. Show how the above amounts should be presented on the December 31, 2017 statement of financial position, and with the proper classifications. The company uses amortized cost.

(LO 4) BE14-24 Ambrosia Limited has the following balances as at December 31, 2017: accounts payable and accrued liabilities $20,000, wages payable $15,000, severance payable (due September 30, 2019) $15,000, and bonds payable of $140,000 due September 30, 2020 (current portion of $30,000). Prepare the liabilities section of the statement of financial position if Ambrosia presents liabilities (a) in order of liquidity, and (b) segregated into current and non-current.

(LO 6) BE14-25 Sports International had total debt of $500,000 and $750,000 as at December 31, 2017 and December 31, 2016, respectively, of which $100,000 and $150,000 was current. In addition, the company had total assets of $900,000 and $700,000 as at December 31, 2017 and December 31, 2016, respectively, of which $120,000 and $140,000 was current. Evaluate the company's debt-paying ability in 2017 and 2016.

FINANCE

Exercises

(LO 1) E14-1 (Features of Long-Term Debt) The following examples describe possible features or characteristics of long-term debt:

1. The debt agreement includes a covenant that requires the debtor to maintain a minimum amount of working capital.

2. The stated rate of a bond issue is less than the market rate.

3. The debt is backed by a claim on the debtor's real estate.

4. The debt agreement includes a covenant that limits the amount of additional debt that the debtor can incur.

5. The debt matures on a single date in 20 years.

6. The bond gives the holder the right to call the debt before maturity.

7. The debtor arranges for defeasance of the debt.

8. The debt is a debenture bond.

Instructions

(a) Match each example in the preceding list to the number below that best describes it:

    i. Increases the riskiness of the long-term debt

    ii. Decreases the riskiness of the long-term debt

    iii. Does not affect the riskiness of the long-term debt

FINANCE

(b) For a feature or characteristic that increases the riskiness of the long-term debt, discuss the effect of the feature or characteristic on investors' required yield on the long-term debt.

(LO 1, 2) E14-2   (Information Related to Various Bond Issues) Anaconda Inc. has issued three types of debt on January 1, 2017, the start of the company's fiscal year:

    1. $10 million, 10-year, 13% unsecured bonds, with interest payable quarterly, priced to yield 12%

    2. $2.5 million par of 10-year, zero-coupon bonds at a price to yield 12% per year

    3. $15 million, 10-year, 10% mortgage bonds, with interest payable annually to yield 12%

Instructions

Prepare a schedule that identifies the following items for each bond:

(a) The maturity value

(b) The number of interest periods over the life of the bond

(c) The stated rate for each interest period

(d) The effective interest rate for each interest period

(e) The payment amount per period

FINANCE

(f) Using time value of money tables, a financial calculator, and computer spreadsheet functions, calculate the present value of the bonds at the date of issue. (*Hint*: Refer to Appendix 3B for tips on calculating.)

(g) Each instrument has different features. Comment on how the instruments are different, discussing the underlying nature of the debt. Which bonds are riskiest and why?

(LO 2) E14-3   (Entries for Bond Transactions) Two independent situations follow:

    1. On January 1, 2017, Divac Limited issued $300,000 of 10-year, 9% bonds at par. Interest is payable quarterly on April 1, July 1, October 1, and January 1.

    2. On June 1, 2017, Verbitsky Inc. issued at par, plus accrued interest, $200,000 of 10-year, 12% bonds dated January 1. Interest is payable semi-annually on July 1 and January 1.

Instructions

For each of these two independent situations, prepare journal entries to record:

(a) The issuance of the bonds

(b) The payment of interest on July 1

(c) The accrual of interest on December 31

(LO 2) E14-4   (Entries for Bond Transactions—Effective Interest) Foreman Inc. issued $800,000 of 10%, 20-year bonds on January 1, 2017 at 102. Interest is payable semi-annually on July 1 and January 1. Foreman Inc. uses the effective interest method of amortization for any bond premium or discount. Assume an effective yield of 9.75%. (With a market rate of 9.75%, the issue price would be slightly higher. For simplicity, ignore this.)

Instructions

Prepare the journal entries to record the following (round to the nearest dollar):

(a) The issuance of the bonds

(b) The payment of interest and the related amortization on July 1, 2017

(c) The accrual of interest and the related amortization on December 31, 2017

(LO 2) E14-5   (Entries for Bond Transactions—Straight-Line) Foreman Inc. issued $800,000 of 20-year, 10% bonds on January 1, 2017 at 102. Interest is payable semi-annually on July 1 and January 1. The company uses the straight-line method of amortization for any bond premium or discount.

Instructions

(a) Prepare the journal entries to record the following:

    1. The issuance of the bonds

    2. The payment of interest and the related amortization on July 1, 2017

3. The accrual of interest and the related amortization on December 31, 2017

(b) Briefly explain how the entries would change depending on whether Foreman follows IFRS or ASPE.

(LO 2) E14-6 (Entries for Non–Interest-Bearing Debt) On January 1, 2017, Landlord Corporation acquired the following properties:

1. Land and an apartment building in Toronto for $1.5 million. To finance this transaction, Landlord Corporation issued a five-year interest-free promissory note to repay $2,307,941 on January 1, 2022.

2. Vacant land in Rome, Italy for $2 million. To finance this transaction, Landlord Corporation obtained a 7% mortgage secured by the land, with a maturity date of January 1, 2027. Interest is payable annually. If Landlord Corporation borrowed this money from the bank, the company would need to pay 9% interest.

Instructions

(a) Using time value of money tables, a financial calculator, and computer spreadsheet functions, calculate the value of the mortgage. Using the calculation from the tables record Landlord Corporation's journal entries on January 1, 2017 for each of the purchases. (*Hint*: Refer to Appendix 3B for tips on calculating.)

(b) Record the interest at the end of the first year on both instruments using the effective interest method.

(LO 2) E14-7 (Imputation of Interest) Two independent situations follow.

1. On January 1, 2017, Spartan Inc. bought land that had an assessed value of $390,000 at the time of purchase. A $600,000, non–interest-bearing note due on January 1, 2020 was given in exchange. There was no established exchange price for the land, and no ready market value for the note. The interest rate that is normally charged on a note of this type is 12%.

2. On January 1, 2017, Geimer Furniture Ltd. borrowed $4 million (face value) from Aurora Inc., a major customer, through a non–interest-bearing note due in four years. Because the note was non–interest-bearing, Geimer Furniture agreed to sell furniture to this customer at lower than market price. A 10% rate of interest is normally charged on this type of loan.

Instructions

(a) For situation 1, using time value of money tables, a financial calculator, and computer spreadsheet functions, determine at what amount the land should be recorded at January 1, 2017. (*Hint*: Refer to Appendix 3B for tips on calculating.) Determine the interest expense to be reported in 2017 related to this transaction. Discuss how the assessed value of the land could be used in this situation.

(b) For situation 2, using time value of money tables, a financial calculator, and computer spreadsheet functions, calculate the amount that the note would be recorded at on January 1, 2017. (*Hint*: Refer to Appendix 3B for tips on calculating.)

(LO 2) E14-8 (Purchase of Land with Instalment Note) Desrocher Ltd. issued an instalment note on January 1, 2017 (with a required yield of 9%) in exchange for land that it purchased from Safayeni Ltd. Safayeni's real estate agent had listed the land on the market for $120,000. The note calls for three equal blended payments of $43,456 that are to be made at December 31, 2017, 2018, and 2019.

Instructions

(a) Discuss how the purchase price of the land will be established.

DIGGING DEEPER

(b) Using time value of money tables, a financial calculator, and computer spreadsheet functions, prove that the note will cost Desrocher Ltd. 9% interest over the note's full term. (*Hint*: Refer to Appendix 3B for tips on calculating.)

(c) Prepare an effective-interest amortization table for the instalment note for the three-year period.

(d) Prepare Desrocher's journal entry for the purchase of the land.

(e) Prepare Desrocher's journal entry for the first instalment payment on the note on December 31, 2017.

FINANCE

(f) From Safayeni Ltd.'s perspective, what are the advantages of an instalment note compared with a regular interest-bearing note?

(LO 2) E14-9 (Purchase of Equipment with Non–Interest-Bearing Debt) Buon Appetito Limited has been experiencing increased customer demand for its specialty food products. In order to meet this demand, the company has bought additional refrigeration units to hold more inventory. To finance this purchase, Buon Appetito issued a four-year non–interest-bearing note, with a face value of $400,000. The prevailing interest rate for similar instruments is 10%. The company agreed to repay the note in four equal instalments. Buon Appetito used the effective interest method to amortize any premium or discount.

Instructions

(Round to the nearest dollar in all calculations.)

(a) Using time value of money tables, a financial calculator, and computer spreadsheet functions, prepare the journal entry(ies) at the date of purchase. (*Hint*: Refer to Appendix 3B for tips on calculating.)

(b) Prepare the journal entry(ies) at the end of the first year to record the payment and interest.

(c) Prepare the journal entry(ies) at the end of the second year to record the payment and interest.

(LO 2) E14-10   (Purchase of Computer with Non–Interest-Bearing Debt) Collins Corporation bought a computer on December 31, 2017, paying $30,000 down with a further $75,000 payment due on December 31, 2020. An interest rate of 10% is implicit in the purchase price. Collins uses the effective interest method and has a December 31 year end. Collins prepares financial statements in accordance with ASPE.

Instructions

(a) Using time value of money tables, a financial calculator, and computer spreadsheet functions, prepare the journal entry(ies) at the purchase date. (Round to two decimal places.) (*Hint*: Refer to Appendix 3B for tips on calculating.)

(b) Prepare any journal entry(ies) required at December 31, 2018, 2019, and 2020.

(c) Can Collins choose a different method of amortizing any premium or discount on its notes payable? Explain your answer.

(LO 2) E14-11   (Entries for Bond Transactions) On January 1, 2017, Osborn Inc. sold 12% bonds having a maturity value of $800,000 for $860,652, which provides the bondholders with a 10% yield. The bonds are dated January 1, 2017 and mature on January 1, 2022, with interest payable on January 1 of each year. The company follows IFRS and uses the effective interest method. Round calculations to the nearest dollar.

Instructions

(a) Prepare the journal entry at the date of issue.

(b) Prepare a schedule of interest expense and bond amortization for 2017 through 2020.

(c) Prepare the journal entry to record the interest payment and the amortization for 2017.

(d) Prepare the journal entry to record the interest payment and the amortization for 2019.

(e) If Osborn prepares financial statements in accordance with ASPE, can Osborn choose a different method of amortizing any premium or discount on its bonds payable? Explain your answer.

(LO 2) E14-12   (Amortization Schedules—Straight-Line) Cinderella Shoes Inc. is having difficulty meeting its working capital requirements. As a result, on January 1, 2017, the company sold bonds with a face value of $1 million, receiving $800,000 in cash. The bonds have an interest rate of 8% and mature on January 1, 2019. Interest is payable semi-annually on January 1 and July 1.

Instructions

Set up a schedule of interest expense and discount amortization under the straight-line method.

(LO 2) E14-13   (Amortization Schedule—Effective Interest) Minor Inc. sells 10% bonds having a maturity value of $3 million for $2,783,713. The bonds are dated January 1, 2017 and mature on January 1, 2022. Interest is payable annually on January 1.

Instructions

DIGGING
DEEPER

(a) Set up a schedule of interest expense and discount amortization under the effective interest method. Round calculations to the nearest dollar. (*Hint*: The effective interest rate must be calculated using a financial calculator and computer spreadsheet functions.) (*Hint*: Refer to Appendix 3B for tips on calculating.)

(b) Which method of discount amortization results in higher interest expense for the year ended December 31, 2017? Which method of discount amortization results in higher interest expense for the year ended December 31, 2021? Explain the results. From the perspective of a user of Minor's financial statements, which method would you prefer the company to use, if you would like the company's income statement to reflect the most faithfully representative measure of net income?

(LO 2) E14-14   (Determine Proper Amounts in Account Balances) Four independent situations follow.

1. Wen Corporation incurred the following costs when it issued bonds: printing and engraving costs, $25,000; legal fees, $69,000; and commissions paid to underwriter, $70,000.

2. Griffith Inc. sold $3 million of 10-year, 10% bonds at 104 on January 1, 2017. The bonds were dated January 1, 2017 and pay interest on July 1 and January 1.

3. Kennedy Inc. issued $600,000 of 10-year, 9% bonds on June 30, 2017 for $562,613. This price provided a yield of 10% on the bonds. Interest is payable semi-annually on December 31 and June 30.

4. Bergevin Corporation issued $800,000 of bonds on January 1, 2017 with interest payable each January 1. The bonds' carrying amount on December 31, 2017 is $850,716.97. Bergevin has chosen to apply the fair value option in accounting for the bonds. An assessment of the company's credit risk at December 31, 2017 shows that it has increased. As a result, the bonds' fair value is $838,000 on that date. Bergevin prepares financial statements in accordance with IFRS.

Instructions

(a) In situation 1, what accounting treatment could be given to these costs?

(b) In situation 2, if Griffith follows ASPE and uses the straight-line method to amortize bond premium or discount, determine the amount of interest expense to be reported on July 1, 2017 and December 31, 2017.

(c) In situation 3, if Kennedy uses the effective interest method, determine the amount of interest expense to record if financial statements are issued on October 31, 2017.

(d) In situation 4, what accounting treatment should be given to the bonds at December 31, 2017?

(LO 2) E14-15 (Interest-Free Government Loans) Sunshine Incorporated provides solar energy services to Toronto. Sunshine needed to buy additional solar energy panels to meet the demand for its energy product. The government of Ontario offered an interest-free forgivable loan to Sunshine in the amount of $500,000. The loan will be forgiven if Sunshine is able to produce a stated number of kilowatts of energy per year for the next five years. If these conditions are not met, the amount is due to the government in full in five years. Sunshine believes it will be able to meet the conditions. Sunshine recently obtained a similar loan from the bank with an annual interest rate of 12%.

Instructions

(a) Discuss the financial reporting issues related to obtaining the interest-free loan from the government of Ontario.

(b) Using time value of money tables, a financial calculator, and computer spreadsheet functions, calculate the value of the loan and prepare an amortization table for the loan using the effective interest method. Present the first three years of the loan. (*Hint*: Refer to Appendix 3B for tips on calculating and for the amortization table, use the amount arrived at using the time value of money tables.)

(c) Prepare the entry on December 31, 2017 to record the interest-free loan.

(d) Prepare any adjusting journal entry that is necessary at December 31, 2018, the company's fiscal year end.

(LO 2, 4) E14-16 (Entries and Questions for Bond Transactions) On June 30, 2017, Mosca Limited issued $4 million of 20-year, 13% bonds for $4,300,920, which provides a yield of 12%. The company uses the effective interest method to amortize any bond premium or discount. The bonds pay semi-annual interest on June 30 and December 31.

Instructions

(a) Prepare the journal entries to record the following transactions:

1. The issuance of the bonds on June 30, 2017
2. The payment of interest and the amortization of the premium on December 31, 2017
3. The payment of interest and the amortization of the premium on June 30, 2018
4. The payment of interest and the amortization of the premium on December 31, 2018

(b) Show the proper statement of financial position presentation for the liability for bonds payable on the December 31, 2017 statement of financial position.

(c) Answer the following questions.

1. What amount of interest expense is reported for 2017?
2. Will the bond interest expense that is reported in 2017 be the same as, greater than, or less than the amount that would be reported if the straight-line method of amortization were used?
3. What is the total cost of borrowing over the life of the bond?
4. Will the total bond interest expense for the life of the bond be greater than, the same as, or less than the total interest expense if the straight-line method of amortization were used?

(LO 3) E14-17 (Entries for Retirement and Issuance of Bonds) Friedman Corporation had bonds outstanding with a maturity value of $500,000. On April 30, 2017, when these bonds had an unamortized discount of $10,000, they were called in at 104. To pay for these bonds, Friedman had issued other bonds a month earlier bearing a lower interest rate. The newly issued bonds had a life of 10 years. The new bonds were issued at 103 (face value $500,000). Issue costs related to the new bonds were $3,000. All issue costs were capitalized. Friedman prepares financial statements in accordance with IFRS.

Instructions

Ignoring interest, calculate the gain or loss and record this refunding transaction.

(LO 2, 4) E14-18   (Entries for Retirement and Issuance of Bonds—Straight-Line) On June 30, 2010, Auburn Limited issued 12% bonds with a par value of $800,000 due in 20 years. They were issued at 98 and were callable at 104 at any date after June 30, 2017.

Because of lower interest rates and a significant change in the company's credit rating, it was decided to call the entire issue on June 30, 2017 and to issue new bonds. New 10% bonds were sold in the amount of $1 million at 102; they mature in 20 years. The company follows ASPE and uses straight-line amortization. The interest payment dates are December 31 and June 30 of each year.

Instructions

(a) Prepare journal entries to record the retirement of the old issue and the sale of the new issue on June 30, 2017.

(b) Prepare the entry required on December 31, 2017 to record the payment of the first six months of interest and the amortization of the bond premium.

(LO 3) E14-19   (Entries for Retirement and Issuance of Bonds—Effective Interest) Refer to E14-18 and Auburn Limited.

Instructions

Repeat the instructions of E14-18 assuming that Auburn Limited follows IFRS and uses the effective interest method. Provide an effective-interest table for the bonds from the inception of the bond to the date of the redemption. (*Hint*: Using a financial calculator and computer spreadsheet functions, you need to first calculate the effective interest rate on the 2010 and 2017 bonds. Round the semi-annual interest percentage to three decimal places.) (*Hint*: Refer to Appendix 3B for tips on calculating.)

(LO 3) E14-20   (Entry for Retirement of Bond; Costs for Bond Issuance) On January 2, 2012, Kowalchuk Corporation, a small company that follows ASPE, issued $1.5 million of 10% bonds at 97 due on December 31, 2021. Legal and other costs of $110,000 were incurred in connection with the issue. Kowalchuk Corporation has a policy of capitalizing and amortizing the legal and other costs incurred by including them with the bond recorded at the date of issuance. Interest on the bonds is payable each December 31. The $110,000 in issuance costs are being deferred and amortized on a straight-line basis over the 10-year term of the bonds. The discount on the bonds is also being amortized on a straight-line basis over the 10 years. (The straight-line method is not materially different in its effect compared with the effective interest method.)

The bonds are callable at 102 (that is, at 102% of their face amount), and on January 2, 2017, the company called a face amount of $850,000 of the bonds and retired them.

Instructions

DIGGING DEEPER

(a) Ignoring income taxes, calculate the amount of loss, if any, that the company needs to recognize as a result of retiring $850,000 of bonds in 2017. Prepare the journal entry to record the retirement.

(b) How would the amount of the loss calculated in part (a) differ if Kowalchuk's policy had been to carry the bonds at fair value and thus expense the costs of issuing the bonds at January 2, 2012? Assuming that Kowalchuk Corporation had followed this policy, prepare the journal entry to record the retirement. Assume the redemption price approximates fair value.

(c) How would your answers to parts (a) and (b) change if Kowalchuk were to follow IFRS?

(LO 3) E14-21   (Entries for Retirement and Issuance of Bonds) Jyoti Inc. had outstanding $10 million of 8% bonds (interest payable March 31 and October 31) due in 12 years. Jyoti was able to reduce its risk rating through investing in more real estate. As a result, on September 1, it issued $5 million of 10-year, 6% bonds (interest payable July 1 and January 1) at 97. A portion of the proceeds was used to call the 8% bonds at 105 on October 1. The unamortized bond discount for the 8% bonds was $1.1 million on October 1. Jyoti prepares financial statements in accordance with IFRS.

Instructions

Prepare the necessary journal entries to record the issue of the new bonds and the retirement of the old bonds.

(LO 3) E14-22   (Impairments) On December 31, 2016, Mohr Inc. borrowed $81,241 from Par Bank, signing a $125,000, five-year, non–interest-bearing note. The note was issued to yield 9% interest. Unfortunately, during 2017 Mohr began to experience financial difficulty. As a result, this was determined to be a significant increase in risk, and at December 31, 2017, Par Bank estimated that it was probable that it would receive only $93,750 at maturity. For simplicity, assume that this reflects the probability weighted amount. The market rate of interest on loans of this nature is now 11%. Both companies prepare financial statements in accordance with IFRS 9.

Instructions

(a) Prepare the entry to record the issuance of the loan by Par Bank on December 31, 2016.

(b) Using time value of money tables, a financial calculator, and computer spreadsheet functions, prepare the entry (if any) to record the impairment of the loan on December 31, 2017 by Par Bank. (*Hint*: Refer to Appendix 3B for tips on calculating.)

(c) Prepare the entry (if any) to record the existence of financial difficulty on December 31, 2017 by Mohr.

(LO 3) E14-23 (Settlement of Debt) Strickland Inc. owes Heartland Bank $200,000 plus $18,000 of accrued interest. The debt is a 10-year, 10% note. During 2017, Strickland's business declined due to a slowing regional economy. On December 31, 2017, the bank agrees to accept an old machine and cancel the entire debt. The machine has a cost of $390,000, accumulated depreciation of $221,000, and a fair value of $180,000. The bank plans to dispose of the machine at a cost of $6,500. Both Strickland and Heartland Bank prepare financial statements in accordance with IFRS 9.

Instructions

(a) Prepare the journal entries for Strickland Inc. and Heartland Bank to record this debt settlement. Assume Heartland had previously recognized an allowance for doubtful accounts for the impairment prior to the settlement.

(b) How should Strickland report the gain or loss on disposal of the machinery and on the restructuring of debt in its 2017 income statement?

(c) Assume that instead of transferring the machine, Strickland decides to grant the bank 15,000 of its common shares, which have a fair value of $190,000. This is in full settlement of the loan obligation. Assuming that Heartland Bank treats Strickland's shares as FV-NI investments, prepare the entries to record the transaction for both parties. Assume Heartland had previously recognized an allowance for doubtful accounts for the impairment prior to the settlement.

(LO 3) E14-24 (Term Modification—Debtor's Entries) On December 31, 2017, Green Bank enters into a debt restructuring agreement with Troubled Inc., which is now experiencing financial trouble. The bank agrees to restructure a $2-million, 12% note receivable issued at par by the following modifications:

1. Reducing the principal obligation from $2 million to $1.9 million

2. Extending the maturity date from December 31, 2017 to December 31, 2020

3. Reducing the interest rate from 12% to 10%

Troubled pays interest at the end of each year. On January 1, 2021, Troubled Inc. pays $1.9 million in cash to Green Bank. Troubled prepares financial statements in accordance with IFRS 9.

Instructions

(a) Using time value of money tables, a financial calculator, and computer spreadsheet functions, discuss whether or not Troubled should record a gain. (*Hint*: Refer to Appendix 3B for tips on calculating.)

(b) Using a financial calculator and computer spreadsheet functions, calculate the rate of interest that Troubled should use to calculate its interest expense in future periods. (*Hint*: Refer to Appendix 3B for tips on calculating.)

(c) Prepare the interest payment entry for Troubled on December 31, 2019.

(d) What entry should Troubled make on January 1, 2021?

(LO 3) E14-25 (Term Modification—Creditor's Entries) Assume the same information as in E14-24 and answer the following questions related to Green Bank (the creditor). Green Bank prepares financial statements in accordance with IFRS 9. There is no evidence of a significant increase in credit risk and 12-month expected credited losses are calculated at zero. For simplicity, assume that Green Bank had not recognized any impairment prior to this (although it likely would have done so under the expected loss model).

Instructions

(a) What interest rate should Green Bank use to calculate the loss on the debt restructuring?

(b) Using time value of money tables, a financial calculator, and computer spreadsheet functions, calculate the loss that Green Bank will accrue based on the debt restructuring. (*Hint*: Refer to Appendix 3B for tips on calculating.) Prepare the journal entry to record the loss.

(c) Prepare the amortization schedule for Green Bank after the debt restructuring.

(d) Prepare the interest receipt entry for Green Bank on December 31, 2019.

(e) What entry should Green Bank make on January 1, 2021?

(LO 3) E14-26 (Settlement—Debtor's Entries) Use the same information as in E14-24 but assume now that Green Bank reduced the principal to $1.6 million rather than $1.9 million. On January 1, 2021, Troubled Inc. pays $1.6 million in cash to Green Bank for the principal. The market rate is currently 10%.

Instructions

(a) Using time value of money tables, a financial calculator, and computer spreadsheet functions, determine if Troubled can record a gain under this term modification. If yes, calculate the gain. (*Hint*: Refer to Appendix 3B for tips on calculating.)

(b) Prepare the journal entries to record the gain on Troubled's books.

(c) What interest rate should Troubled use to calculate its interest expense in future periods? Will your answer be the same as in E14-24? Why or why not?

(d) Prepare the amortization schedule of the note for Troubled after the debt restructuring.

(e) Prepare the interest payment entries for Troubled on December 31, 2018, 2019, and 2020.

(f) What entry should Troubled make on January 1, 2021?

(LO 3) E14-27   (Settlement—Creditor's Entries) Use the information in E14-24 and the assumptions in E14-26 and answer the following questions related to Green Bank (the creditor).

Instructions

(a) What interest rate should Green Bank use to calculate the loss on the debt restructuring?

(b) Using time value of money tables, a financial calculator, and computer spreadsheet functions, calculate the loss that Green Bank will accrue under this new term modification. (*Hint*: Refer to Appendix 3B for tips on calculating.) Prepare the journal entry to record the loss on Green Bank's books.

(LO 3) E14-28   (Debtor Entries for Settlement of Troubled Debt) Vargo Limited owes $270,000 to First Trust Inc. on a 10-year, 12% note due on December 31, 2017. The note was issued at par. Because Vargo is in financial trouble, First Trust Inc. agrees to extend the maturity date to December 31, 2019, reduce the principal to $220,000, and reduce the interest rate to 5%, payable annually on December 31. The market rate is currently 5%. Vargo prepares financial statements in accordance with IFRS.

Instructions

Using time value of money tables, a financial calculator, and computer spreadsheet functions, prepare the journal entry on Vargo's books on December 31, 2017, 2018, and 2019. (*Hint*: Refer to Appendix 3B for tips on calculating.)

(LO 4) E14-29   (Classification of Liabilities) The following are various accounts:

1. Bank loans payable of a winery, due March 10, 2021 (the product requires aging for five years before it can be sold)

2. $10 million of serial bonds payable, of which $2 million is due each July 31

3. Amounts withheld from employees' wages for income tax

4. Notes payable that are due January 15, 2020

5. Interest payable on a note payable (the note is due January 15, 2020 and the interest is due June 30, 2018)

6. Credit balance in a customer's account arising from returns and allowances after collection in full of the account

7. Bonds payable of $2 million maturing June 30, 2021

8. An overdraft of $1,000 in a bank account (no other balances are carried at this bank)

9. An overdraft of $1,000 in a bank account (other accounts are carried at this bank and have positive account balances)

10. Deposits made by customers who have ordered goods

Instructions

(a) Indicate whether each of the items above should be classified under IFRS on December 31, 2017 as a current or long-term liability or under some other classification. Consider each item independently from all others; that is, do not assume that all of them relate to one particular business. If the classification of some of the items is doubtful, explain why in each case.

(b) Assume instead that the company follows ASPE. Repeat part (a) for the items that would be classified differently.

(LO 4) E14-30   (Classification) The following items are found in Bogdan Limited's financial statements:

1. Interest expense (debit balance)

2. Loss on restructuring of debt

3. Mortgage payable (payable in full in five years)

4. Debenture bonds payable (maturing in two years). The company breached the covenant during the year, which makes the amount payable immediately. After year end, the company obtained a waiver from the lender indicating they will not demand early repayment.

5. Promissory notes payable (due in equal instalments over 10 years)

6. Income bonds payable (due in one year)

Instructions

(a) Indicate how each of these items should be classified in the financial statements under IFRS.

(b) Assume instead that the company follows ASPE. Repeat part (a) for the items that would be classified differently.

(LO 5) E14-31 (Long-Term Debt Disclosure) At December 31, 2017, Reddy Inc. has three long-term debt issues outstanding. The first is a $2.2-million note payable that matures on June 30, 2020. The second is a $4-million bond issue that matures on September 30, 2021. The third is a $17.5-million sinking fund debenture with annual sinking fund payments of $3.5 million in each of the years 2019 through 2023.

Instructions

Prepare the note disclosure that is required for the long-term debt at December 31, 2017.

Problems

P14-1 Adventureland Incorporated purchased metal to build a new roller coaster on December 31, 2017. Adventureland provided a $500,000 down payment and agreed to pay the balance in equal instalments of $200,000 every December 31 for five years. Adventureland could have received a loan from the bank for this amount at 9% interest. Adventureland prepares financial statements in accordance with IFRS.

Instructions

(a) Using time value of money tables, a financial calculator, and computer spreadsheet functions, prepare the journal entries that would be recorded for the purchase and for the payments and interest on December 31, 2017, 2018, 2019, 2020, 2021, and 2022. (*Hint:* Refer to Appendix 3B for tips on calculating.)

DIGGING DEEPER **(b)** From the lender's perspective, what are the advantages of an instalment note compared with an interest-bearing note?

P14-2 On June 1, 2017, MacDougall Corporation approached Silverman Corporation about buying a parcel of undeveloped land. Silverman was asking $240,000 for the land and MacDougall saw that there was some flexibility in the asking price. MacDougall did not have enough money to make a cash offer to Silverman and proposed to give, in return for the land, a $300,000, five-year promissory note that bears interest at the rate of 4%. The interest is to be paid annually to Silverman Corporation on June 1 of each of the next five years. Silverman insisted that the note taken in return become a mortgage note. Silverman accepted the amended offer, and MacDougall signed a mortgage note for $300,000 due June 1, 2022. MacDougall would have had to pay 10% at its local bank if it were to borrow the cash for the land purchase. Silverman, on the other hand, could borrow the funds at 9%. Both MacDougall and Silverman have calendar year ends.

Instructions

(a) Discuss how MacDougall Corporation would determine a value for the land in recording the purchase from Silverman Corporation.

DIGGING DEEPER **(b)** What is the difference between a promissory note payable and a mortgage note payable? Why would Silverman Corporation insist on obtaining a mortgage note payable from MacDougall Corporation?

(c) Using time value of money tables, a financial calculator, and computer spreadsheet functions, calculate the purchase price of the land and prepare an effective-interest amortization table for the term of the mortgage note payable that is given in the exchange. (*Hint:* Refer to Appendix 3B for tips on calculating.)

(d) Prepare the journal entry for the purchase of the land.

(e) Prepare any adjusting journal entry that is required at the end of the fiscal year and the first payment made on June 1, 2018, assuming no reversing entries are used.

(f) Assume that Silverman had insisted on obtaining an instalment note from MacDougall instead of a mortgage note. Then do the following:

1. Using time value of money tables, a financial calculator, and computer spreadsheet functions, calculate the amount of the instalment payments that would be required for a five-year instalment note. (*Hint:* Refer to Appendix 3B for tips on calculating.) Use the same cost of the land to MacDougall Corporation that you determined for the mortgage note in part (a).

2. Prepare an effective-interest amortization table for the five-year term of the instalment note.

3. Prepare the journal entry for the purchase of the land and the issuance of the instalment note.

4. Prepare any adjusting journal entry that is required at the end of the fiscal year and the first payment made on June 1, 2018, assuming no reversing entries are used.

5. Compare the balances of the two different notes payable and related accounts at December 31, 2017. Be specific about the classifications on the statement of financial position.

6. Why would Silverman insist on an instalment note in this case?

P14-3   The following amortization and interest schedule is for the issuance of 10-year bonds by Capulet Corporation on January 1, 2017 and the subsequent interest payments and charges. The company's year end is December 31 and it prepares its financial statements yearly.

Amortization Schedule

Year	Cash	Interest	Amount Unamortized	Carrying Amount
Jan. 1, 2017			$5,651	$ 94,349
Dec. 31, 2017	$11,000	$11,322	5,329	94,671
2018	11,000	11,361	4,968	95,032
2019	11,000	11,404	4,564	95,436
2020	11,000	11,452	4,112	95,888
2021	11,000	11,507	3,605	96,395
2022	11,000	11,567	3,038	96,962
2023	11,000	11,635	2,403	97,597
2024	11,000	11,712	1,691	98,309
2025	11,000	11,797	894	99,106
2026	11,000	11,894	–0–	$100,000

Instructions

(a) Indicate whether the bonds were issued at a premium or a discount and explain how you can determine this fact from the schedule.

(b) Indicate whether the amortization schedule is based on the straight-line method or the effective interest method and explain how you can determine which method is used. Are both amortization methods accepted for financial reporting purposes?

(c) Determine the stated interest rate and the effective interest rate.

FINANCE

(d) Based on the schedule above, prepare the journal entry to record the issuance of the bonds on January 1, 2017.

(e) Based on the schedule above, prepare the journal entry(ies) to reflect the bond transactions and accruals for 2017. (Interest is paid January 1.)

(f) Based on the schedule above, prepare the journal entry(ies) to reflect the bond transactions and accruals for 2025. Capulet Corporation does not use reversing entries.

P14-4   Venezuela Inc. is building a new hockey arena at a cost of $2.5 million. It received a down payment of $500,000 from local businesses to support the project, and now needs to borrow $2 million to complete the project. It therefore decides to issue $2 million of 10-year, 10.5% bonds. These bonds were issued on January 1, 2017 and pay interest annually on each January 1. The bonds yield 10% to the investor and have an effective interest rate to the issuer of 10.4053%. (There is an increased effective interest rate due to the capitalization of the bond issue costs.) Any additional funds that are needed to complete the project will be obtained from local businesses. Venezuela Inc. paid and capitalized $50,000 in bond issuance costs related to the bond issue. Venezuela prepares financial statements in accordance with IFRS.

Instructions

(a) Using time value of money tables, a financial calculator, and computer spreadsheet functions, calculate the value of the bonds and prepare the journal entry to record the issuance of the bonds on January 1, 2017. (*Hint*: Refer to Appendix 3B for tips on calculating. For the journal entry, use the amount arrived at using the time value of money tables.)

(b) Prepare a bond amortization schedule up to and including January 1, 2022 using the effective interest method.

(c) Assume that on July 1, 2020, the company retires half of the bonds at a cost of $1,065,000 plus accrued interest. Prepare the journal entry to record this retirement.

DIGGING DEEPER

(d) Assume that the costs incurred by Venezuela Inc. to issue the bonds totalled $50,000 as above. If Venezuela Inc. chose to apply the fair value option and thus expense these costs, how would this affect the amount of interest expense that it recognized each year and over the 10-year term of the bonds in total, compared with its current accounting practice of capitalizing the bond issue costs? Assume that Venezuela would apply the fair value option under IFRS 9.

P14-5   In the following two independent cases, the company closes its books on December 31:

1. Armstrong Inc. sells $2 million of 10% bonds on March 1, 2017. The bonds pay interest on September 1 and March 1. The bonds' due date is September 1, 2020. The bonds yield 12%.

2. Ouelette Ltd. sells $6 million of 11% bonds on June 1, 2017. The bonds pay interest on December 1 and June 1. The bonds' due date is June 1, 2021. The bonds yield 10%. On October 1, 2018, Ouelette buys back $1.2 million worth of bonds for $1.4 million, including accrued interest.

Instructions

For the two cases above, prepare all of the relevant journal entries using time value of money tables, a financial calculator, and computer spreadsheet functions from the time of sale until the date indicated. (*Hint*: Refer to Appendix 3B for tips on calculating.) For situation 1, prepare the journal entries through December 31, 2018; for situation 2, prepare the journal entries through December 1, 2019. Use the effective interest method for discount and premium amortization, and prepare any necessary amortization tables. Amortize any premium or discount on the interest dates and at year end. Assume that no reversing entries were made. Use the amounts arrived at from using the financial calculator.

P14-6   Selected transactions on the books of Pfaff Corporation follow:

May 1, 2017	Bonds payable with a par value of $700,000, which are dated January 1, 2017, are sold at 105 plus accrued interest. They are coupon bonds, bear interest at 12% (payable annually at January 1), and mature on January 1, 2027. (Use an interest expense account for accrued interest.)
Dec. 31	Adjusting entries are made to record the accrued interest on the bonds and the amortization of the proper amount of premium. (Use straight-line amortization.)
Jan. 1, 2018	Interest on the bonds is paid.
April 1	Par value bonds of $420,000 are repurchased at 103 plus accrued interest and are retired. (Bond premium is to be amortized only at the end of each year.)
Dec. 31	Adjusting entries are made to record the accrued interest on the bonds, and the proper amount of premium amortized.

Instructions

(a) Assume that Pfaff follows ASPE. Prepare the journal entries for the transactions above.

(b) How would your answers to the above change if Pfaff were to follow IFRS?

P14-7   On December 31, 2017, Faital Limited acquired a machine from Plato Corporation by issuing a $600,000, non–interest-bearing note that is payable in full on December 31, 2021. The company's credit rating permits it to borrow funds from its several lines of credit at 10%. The machine is expected to have a five-year life and a $70,000 residual value.

Instructions

(a) Using time value of money tables, a financial calculator, and computer spreadsheet functions, calculate the value of the note and prepare the journal entry for the purchase on December 31, 2017. (*Hint*: Refer to Appendix 3B for tips on calculating and use the amount arrived at by using the time value of money tables for the journal entry.)

(b) Prepare any necessary adjusting entries related to depreciation of the asset (use straight-line) and amortization of the note (use the effective interest method) on December 31, 2018.

DIGGING DEEPER

(c) Prepare any necessary adjusting entries related to depreciation of the asset and amortization of the note on December 31, 2019.

(d) Assume that on December 31, 2017, before buying the machine, Faital had total debt of $432,000 and total assets of $896,000. From the perspective of a creditor, discuss the effect of the purchase on Faital's debt-paying ability.

P14-8   Thompson Limited, a private company with no published credit rating, completed several transactions during 2017. In January, the company bought under contract a machine at a total price of $1.2 million. It is payable over five years with instalments of $240,000 per year, with the first payment due January 1, 2017. The seller considered the transaction to be an instalment sale with the title transferring to Thompson at the time of the final payment. If the company had paid cash for the machine at the time of the sale, the machine would have cost $1,050,000. The company could have borrowed from the bank to buy the machine at an interest rate of 7%. It is expected that the machine will last 10 years.

On July 1, 2017, Thompson issued $10 million of bonds priced at 99 with a coupon of 10% payable July 1 and January 1 of each of the next 10 years to a small group of large institutional investors. As a result, the bonds are closely held. The July 1 interest was paid and on December 30 the company transferred $500,000 to the trustee, Holly Trust Limited, for payment of the January 1, 2018 interest.

Thompson purchased $500,000 (face value) of its 6% convertible bonds for $455,000. It expects to resell the bonds at a later date to a small group of private investors.

Finally, due to economic conditions, Thompson obtained some government financing to help buy some updated technology to be used in the plant. The government provided a $500,000 loan with an interest rate of 1% on December 31, 2017. The company must repay $500,000 in five years: December 31, 2022. Interest payments of $5,000 are due for the next five years, starting on December 31, 2018. The company could have borrowed a similar amount of funds for an interest rate of 6% on December 31, 2017.

Instructions

(a) As Thompson's accountant, using time value of money tables, a financial calculator, and computer spreadsheet functions, calculate the value of the note and prepare journal entries for the machine purchase and the government loan transactions described above. (*Hint*: Refer to Appendix 3B for tips on calculating and use the calculations arrived at from the time value of money tables for the journal entry.) Because Thompson is a private company, indicate any differences in treatment that might arise under ASPE and IFRS. For any fair value discussions, outline the level of fair value hierarchy that has been used.

DIGGING DEEPER

(b) Having prepared the statement of financial position as at December 31, 2017, you have presented it to the company president. She asks you the following questions about it. Answer these questions by writing a brief paragraph that justifies your treatment of the items in the statement of financial position.

1. Why is the new machine being valued at $1,050,000 on the books, when we are paying $1.2 million in total? Why has depreciation been charged on equipment being purchased under contract? Title has not yet passed to the company and, therefore, the equipment is not yet our asset. Would it not be more correct for the company to show on the left side of the statement of financial position only the amount that has been paid to date instead of showing the full contract price on the left side and the unpaid portion on the right side? After all, the seller considers the transaction an instalment sale.

2. Bond interest is shown as a current liability. Did we not pay our trustee, Holly Trust Limited, the full amount of interest that is due this period?

3. The repurchased bonds (sometimes referred to as treasury bonds) are shown as a deduction from bonds payable issued. Why are they not shown as an asset, since they can be sold again? Are they the same as bonds of other companies that we hold as investments?

4. What is this government grant showing on the statement of financial position? We received a loan, not a grant, since we have to pay it back. Why is the government loan showing substantially less than the $500,000 that we will have to repay?

P14-9 Jeremiah Limited issued 10-year, 7% debentures with a face value of $2 million on January 1, 2010. The proceeds received were $1.7 million. The discount was amortized on the straight-line basis over the 10-year term. The terms of the debenture stated that the debentures could be redeemed in full at any point before the maturity date, at a price of 105 of the principal. There was no requirement for a sinking fund.

On January 1, 2017, Jeremiah issued a mortgage at 101 with a principal of $3 million secured by land and building. The mortgage had a 25-year amortization period, with interest payable at 8%. Upon issuance of the mortgage, Jeremiah used the proceeds to redeem the 7% debentures. Jeremiah prepares financial statements in accordance with ASPE.

Instructions

(a) Prepare journal entries to record the issuance of the 8% mortgage and the retirement of the 7% debentures.

(b) Indicate the income statement treatment of the gain or loss on redemption of debentures and prepare the note disclosure that is required. Assume that 2017 income before taxes and before any gain or loss on redemption of debentures is $1.7 million, the income tax rate is 19%, and the weighted average number of common shares outstanding is 1.2 million.

P14-10 Four independent situations follow:

1. On March 1, 2017, Wilkie Inc. issued $4 million of 9% bonds at 103 plus accrued interest. The bonds are dated January 1, 2017 and pay interest semi-annually on July 1 and January 1. In addition, Wilkie incurred $27,000 of bond issuance costs.

2. On January 1, 2017, Langley Ltd. issued 9% bonds with a face value of $500,000 for $469,280 to yield 10%. The bonds are dated January 1, 2017 and pay interest annually. Langley prepares financial statements in accordance with ASPE.

3. Chico Building Inc., a private company that prepares financial statements in accordance with ASPE, has several long-term bonds outstanding at December 31, 2017. These long-term bonds have the following sinking fund requirements and maturities for the next six years:

	Sinking Fund	Maturities
2018	$300,000	$100,000
2019	$100,000	$250,000
2020	$100,000	$100,000
2021	$200,000	–0–
2022	$200,000	$150,000
2023	$200,000	$100,000

4. In the long-term debt structure of Czeslaw Inc., the following three bonds were reported: mortgage bonds payable, $10 million; collateral trust bonds, $5 million; and bonds maturing in instalments, secured by plant equipment, $4 million.

Instructions

(a) For situation 1, calculate the net amount of cash received by Wilkie as a result of the issuance of these bonds.

(b) For situation 2, what amount should Langley report for interest expense in 2017 related to these bonds, assuming that it uses the effective interest method for amortizing any bond premium or discount? Could Langley choose to use the straight-line method for amortizing any bond premium or discount?

(c) For situation 3, indicate how this information should be reported in Chico's financial statements at December 31, 2017.

(d) For situation 4, determine the total amount of debenture bonds that is outstanding, if any.

P14-11 On April 1, 2017, Taylor Corp. sold 12,000 of its $1,000 face value, 15-year, 11% bonds at 97. Interest payment dates are April 1 and October 1, and the company uses the straight-line method of bond discount amortization. On March 1, 2018, Taylor extinguished 3,000 of the bonds by issuing 100,000 shares. At this time, the accrued interest was paid in cash to the bondholders whose bonds were being extinguished. In a separate transaction on March 1, 2018, 120,000 of the company's shares sold for $31 per share.

Instructions

Prepare Taylor Corp.'s journal entries to record the following:

(a) April 1, 2017: issuance of the bonds

(b) October 1, 2017: payment of the semi-annual interest

(c) December 31, 2017: accrual of the interest expense

(d) March 1, 2018: extinguishment of 3,000 bonds by the issuance of common shares (no reversing entries are made)

P14-12 Refer to P14-11 and Taylor Corp.

Instructions

Repeat the instructions of P14-11 assuming that Taylor Corp. uses the effective interest method. Provide an effective interest table for the bonds for two interest payment periods. (*Hint*: Using a financial calculator and computer spreadsheet functions, you need to first calculate the effective interest rate on the bonds.) (*Hint*: Refer to Appendix 3B for tips on calculating. Round the semi-annual interest percentage to four decimal places.)

 P14-13 In each of the following independent cases, the company closes its books on December 31.

1. Sanford Co. sells $500,000 of 10% bonds on March 1, 2017. The bonds pay interest on September 1 and March 1. The due date of the bonds is September 1, 2020. The bonds yield 12%. Give entries through December 31, 2018.

2. Titania Co. sells $400,000 of 12% bonds on June 1, 2017. The bonds pay interest on December 1 and June 1. The due date of the bonds is June 1, 2021. The bonds yield 10%. On October 1, 2018, Titania buys back $120,000 worth of bonds for $126,000 (includes accrued interest). Give entries through December 1, 2019.

Instructions

For the two cases, prepare all of the relevant journal entries from the time of sale using time value of money tables, a financial calculator, and computer spreadsheet functions, until the date indicated. (*Hint*: Refer to Appendix 3B for tips on calculating and use the calculations from the financial calculator for the journal entries.) Use the effective-interest method for discount and premium amortization. Construct amortization tables where applicable. Amortize premium or discount on interest dates and at year end. Assume that no reversing entries were made.

P14-14 On January 1, 2017, Batonica Limited issued a $1.2-million, five-year, zero-interest-bearing note to Northern Savings Bank. The note was issued to yield 8% annual interest. Unfortunately, during 2017 Batonica fell into financial trouble due to increased competition. After reviewing all available evidence on December 31, 2017, Northern Savings Bank decided that the loan was impaired and that there was a significant change in credit risk. Batonica will probably pay back only $800,000 of the principal at maturity. For simplicity, assume that this reflects the probability weighted amount. Both Batonica and Northern Savings Bank prepare financial statements in accordance with IFRS 9.

Instructions

(a) Using time value of money tables, a financial calculator, and computer spreadsheet functions, prepare journal entries for both Batonica and Northern Savings Bank to record the issuance of the note on January 1, 2017. (Round to the nearest $10.) (*Hint*: Refer to Appendix 3B for tips on calculating.)

(b) Assuming that both Batonica and Northern Savings Bank use the effective interest method to amortize the discount, prepare the amortization schedule for the note.

(c) How would Northern Savings Bank determine the impairment loss for Batonica's note?

(d) Using time value of money tables, a financial calculator, and computer spreadsheet functions, estimate the loss that Northern Savings Bank will suffer from Batonica's financial distress on December 31, 2017. (*Hint*: Refer to Appendix 3B for tips on calculating.) What journal entries should be made to record this loss?

P14-15 Daniel Perkins is the sole shareholder of Perkins Inc., which is currently under bankruptcy court protection. As a debtor in possession, he has negotiated a revised loan agreement with United Bank. Perkins Inc.'s $600,000, 10-year, 12% note issued at par was refinanced with a $600,000, 10-year, 5% note. Assume the market rate of interest is 12% at the refinancing date. Both Perkins and United Bank prepare financial statements in accordance with IFRS 9.

Instructions

(a) Using time value of money tables, a financial calculator, and computer spreadsheet functions, assess the accounting nature of this transaction. (*Hint*: Refer to Appendix 3B for tips on calculating and use the amounts arrived at from using the time value of money tables for the journal entries.)

(b) Prepare the journal entry to record this refinancing (1) on the books of Perkins Inc. and (2) on the books of United Bank. Assume for simplicity that United Bank had not previously recognized any impairment, although under the expected loss method, it is likely that they would have recognized some loss.

(c) Discuss whether the financial statements provide the information that would be useful to managers and potential investors in this situation.

FINANCE

P14-16   Rocky Mountain Corp. currently has an issued debenture outstanding with Abbra Bank. The note has a principal of $2 million, was issued at face value, and interest is payable at 7%. The term of the debenture was 10 years, and was issued on December 31, 2010. The current market rate for this debenture is 9%. Rocky Mountain Corp. has been experiencing financial difficulties and has asked Abbra Bank to restructure the note. Both Rocky Mountain and Abbra Bank prepare financial statements in accordance with IFRS. It is currently December 31, 2017.

Instructions

For each of the following independent situations related to the above scenario, prepare the journal entry that Rocky Mountain Corp. and Abbra Bank would make for the restructuring that is described. Use PV tables to calculate the amounts for the journal entries.

(a) Abbra Bank has agreed to accept common shares with a market value of $1.5 million in exchange for relinquishing this note. Assume that the bank had previously recognized a loss on impairment.

(b) Abbra Bank has agreed to accept a building in exchange for relinquishing this debenture. The building has a carrying amount of $500,000 (original cost was $1,900,000) and a fair value of $1.5 million. Assume that the bank had already recognized a loss on impairment.

(c) Abbra Bank agrees to modify the note by allowing Rocky Mountain to not pay the interest on the note for the remaining period. (*Hint*: Refer to Appendix 3B for tips on calculating and use the time value of money tables.) Assume that the bank had not previously recognized any loss on impairment.

(d) Abbra Bank agrees to reduce the principal to $1.7 million and require interest only in the third year at 4%, waiving the first two years' worth of interest. (*Hint*: Refer to Appendix 3B for tips on calculating and use the time value of money tables.) Assume that the bank had not previously recognized any loss on impairment.

P14-17   Gaming Inc. issued a debenture bond to Karamoutz Bank to finance new technology it developed. The debenture was for $500,000, issued at face value, with a 10-year term and interest payable at 10%. Gaming Inc.'s new technology proved not to be technically feasible, and caused it to go into financial distress. The debenture is due today, December 31, 2017, and Gaming does not have the funds to repay the debenture nor the interest. As a result, Karamoutz agreed to extend the debenture due date for five more years and reduce the principal amount to $300,000 in exchange for receiving 20,000 common shares of Gaming, currently trading at $5 per share. Interest will still be payable at 10% and will continue to be due annually on December 31 of each year. Gaming Inc. could get a similar debenture at 12%. Gaming prepares financial statements in accordance with IFRS.

Instructions

Using time value of money tables prepare all the necessary journal entries on the books of Gaming Inc. from the time of restructuring the debenture through maturity.

P14-18   At December 31, 2016, Shutdown Manufacturing Limited had outstanding a $300,000, 12% note payable to Thornton National Bank. Dated January 1, 2014, the note was issued at par and due on December 31, 2017, with interest payable each December 31. During 2017, Shutdown notified Thornton that it might be unable to meet the scheduled December 31, 2017 payment of principal and interest because of financial difficulties. On September 30, 2017, Thornton sold the note, including interest accrued since December 31, 2016, for $280,000 to Orsini Foundry, one of Shutdown's oldest and largest customers. On December 31, 2017, Orsini agreed to accept inventory that cost $240,000 but was worth $315,000 from Shutdown in full settlement of the note. Thornton, Shutdown, and Orsini prepare financial statements in accordance with IFRS.

Instructions

(a) Prepare the journal entry to record the September 30, 2017 transaction on the books of Thornton, Shutdown, and Orsini. For each company, indicate whether the transaction is a restructuring of troubled debt.

(b) Prepare the journal entries to record the December 31, 2017 transaction on the books of Shutdown and Orsini. For each company, indicate whether this transaction is a restructuring of troubled debt.

P14-19   Mazza Corp. owes Tsang Corp. a $110,000, 10-year, 10% note issued at par plus $11,000 of accrued interest. The note is due today, December 31, 2017. Because Mazza Corp. is in financial trouble, Tsang Corp. agrees to forgive the accrued interest and $10,000 of the principal, and to extend the maturity date to December 31, 2020. Interest at

10% of the revised principal will continue to be due on December 31 of each year. Assume the market rate of interest is 10% at the date of refinancing. Mazza and Tsang prepare financial statements in accordance with IFRS.

Instructions

(a) Using time value of money tables, a financial calculator, and computer spreadsheet functions, determine if this is a settlement or a modification. (*Hint*: Refer to Appendix 3B for tips on calculating.)

(b) Prepare a schedule of the debt reduction and interest expense for the years 2017 through 2020.

(c) Calculate the gain or loss for Tsang Corp. and prepare a schedule of the receivable reduction and interest income for the years 2017 through 2020.

(d) Prepare all the necessary journal entries on the books of Mazza Corp. for the years 2017, 2018, and 2019.

(e) Prepare all the necessary journal entries on the books of Tsang Corp. for the years 2017, 2018, and 2019. Assume that Tsang had not previously recognized any impairment.

P14-20 Lindall Limited (LL) has a 10-year loan issued by the bank that is due in five years. The VP Finance feels that the company is carrying too much debt on its statement of financial position and would like to repay the loan early. Unfortunately, the early repayment penalty is significant and therefore LL is looking for other options to reduce the amount of debt on the statement of financial position. The company is looking at the following transactions:

1. Set up a trust that will be used to repay the principal and interest on the original loan as these payments come due.

2. Transfer funds to the trust in the amount equal to the present value of the principal and interest payments.

3. Invest the funds in low-risk investments such that the investments will be able to generate sufficient return to make the principal and interest payments.

The VP Finance is not sure whether they need the bank to discharge the original loan and agree to look to the trust for repayment (legal defeasance). She would like to derecognize the debt on the LL statement of financial position once the deal is in place. LL follows IFRS.

Instructions

Adopt the role of the ethical accountant and discuss the financial reporting issues.

(a) What is the difference between legal defeasance and in-substance defeasance? How does this affect the accounting?

(b) Are there arguments for removing the debt under both legal and in-substance defeasance?

FINANCE AND LAW

(c) How should the company account for the defeasance arrangement?

Case

ENABLING COMPETENCIES

Refer to the Case Primer on the Student Website and in *WileyPLUS* to help you answer this case.

CA14-1 Kitchener Mechanical Incorporated is looking to expand its manufacturing facilities and buy more equipment to meet raised customer demand. The company's strategy is to build an add-on to the current facility, and bring in new equipment that will increase the efficiency of the production line, and subsequently phase out the old, less-efficient equipment in the current facility. While the new facility and equipment is being constructed, the current facility will continue to manufacture product to meet current demand. However, the company has experienced some cash flow difficulties, due to delayed and non-payments from its largest customer. The company also has a debt to equity ratio stipulated by Nexis Bank for its current line of credit of 1:2. As a result, Kitchener Mechanical has been reluctant to expand, because it would require additional debt financing, worsening the debt to equity ratio and increasing its cash flow demands.

The president of Kitchener Mechanical, Jayden Besker, approached the president of Magmum Production, its major customer, and asked for prompt payment of all outstanding debts. Jayden indicated that Kitchener cannot continue to fund Magmum's cash flow, and it would not sell any more product until all amounts are paid. Magmum's president apologized for the delayed payment, saying it was not intentional. Magmum had issues with its controller, who was recently fired, and Magmum would make all payments the next day. Jayden also mentioned the company's cash flow issues, and Magmum's president said he may be able to help. After some discussion, a two-part plan was worked out. First, Magmum would build the additional facility next to Kitchener's current facility, and the plant would initially belong to Magmum. Second, Kitchener would sign a 20-year lease agreement to lease the facility from Magmum. The lease payment would be based on a flat amount plus a percentage of the additional revenue earned through the new facility. After 20 years, Kitchener would buy the facility from Magmum for 1.2 times market price at that time.

Instructions

Adopt the role of the controller and discuss the financial reporting issues. The company is a private company. (*Hint*: Use first principles.) Because the company is considering going public in the future, where IFRS and ASPE differ, these differences should be highlighted to the controller.

Integrated Cases

**ENABLING
COMPETENCIES**

IC14-1   Big Bath Emporium (BBE), a private company based in Toronto, is the city's largest manufacturer and vendor of bathtubs, showers, and sinks. The company sells products direct to consumers, and also sells wholesale to other retailers.

BBE is owned by Bob Bresher, who runs the operations side of the business. His brother, Thomas Bresher, manages all of the accounting functions. Bob performed market research and determined that the next step for BBE is to expand sales to Quebec. BBE has slowly reduced its debt load over the years, but still relies on creditors and bankers to finance its operations. BBE went to the bank to obtain additional financing to expand to Quebec. The bank agreed to provide $1.5 million in financing at face value, at a rate of 9%, interest payable annually. The bank indicated that audited financial statements would be required this year, and BBE would need to maintain a debt to equity ratio of 1:1, where debt is defined as all liabilities.

Brayden LLP is a local audit firm engaged to perform the December 31, 2017 year-end audit to satisfy the bank requirements. You are the senior accountant assigned to this audit engagement. It is January 2018, and Thomas Bresher has asked that the work be performed as soon as possible. You meet with Bob and Thomas and note the following transactions that occurred during the year.

1. During 2017, BBE sold 100 warranties for $5,000 each on its bathtubs. The warranty period is five years. Historically, the warranties have resulted in a cost of approximately $500 per year. BBE uses the cash basis to recognize the warranty expense and revenue. During 2017, no warranty costs were incurred.

2. On December 31, 2017, BBE was notified that its plant will need to perform a cleanup every 10 years of the area surrounding the plant. BBE estimated that the costs of the cleanup will be approximately $500,000 in 10 years. Thomas indicated that because the amount is not due for years, there is no need to recognize anything at this point.

3. BBE bought inventory on January 1, 2017. The purchase was financed through an interest-free vendor take-back loan, with a promise to repay $200,000 in two years. Thomas recorded the loan on the balance sheet at $200,000. As at December 31, 2017, the inventory's net realizable value was $100,000.

4. On June 30, 2017, an employee launched a wrongful dismissal suit against BBE for $150,000. BBE's lawyers have indicated that they expect a payment of $100,000 to $120,000, but the lawsuit is still in court proceedings. Thomas didn't recognize any amount for this because he believes that BBE will be able to successfully defend the suit.

5. On December 31, 2017, BBE issued 10,000 redeemable and retractable preferred shares at $50 per share, for tax planning purposes. The shares are redeemable and retractable at any date up to December 31, 2022, at which point the redeemable and retractable feature expires. The preferred shares pay a mandatory dividend of $10 per share per year until the end of the redeemable and retractable period, after which the dividends are not cumulative and not mandatory. Thomas recorded these shares as equity, and the first dividend payment on December 1, 2017 was recorded through equity.

BBE's balance sheet shows that the company has $1.3 million in debt and $2.4 million in equity. Because the equity is so much higher than the debt and the debt to equity ratio is easily met, Bob indicated that a dividend will be declared this year for $800,000.

Instructions

**AUDIT AND
ASSURANCE**

Provide a report to your manager indicating the accounting issues you anticipate facing once the audit begins. Note where there are differences between ASPE and IFRS.

IC14-2   RTL is a family-owned and operated business that prints flyers and banners. It has been in operation for over 20 years and is being passed on to the next generation. Profits from the past two years have been significantly declining. This is a direct result of the changing landscape of the industry, which has been moving toward digital printing. RTL management has an aggressive plan to change the revenue mix from traditional to digital printing.

To finance this transition, RTL borrowed money from the bank at the end of 2015 to buy digital printing equipment. Some changes were made to the original equipment to accommodate for the printing of banners.

Despite an increase in digital sales, RTL did not achieve its revenue target for 2016 or 2017. In addition to the slow digital revenue growth, RTL has recently lost its top two traditional print clients, who accounted for 50% of overall revenues. Management is concerned with RTL's ability to continue making payments on the outstanding loan under the current conditions.

Management is actively communicating with the bank regarding potential alternatives. Given RTL's history with the bank, the bank will make concessions, including a reduction of the interest rate from 10% to 8%, a three-year extension of the current maturity, and a reduction of principal from $2 million to $1.5 million. The restructuring agreement was signed just before year end. Management is confident that the old debt would be eliminated from the balance sheet. The current market discount rate is 9%.

RTL also has a new sales plan that it is offering to digital customers. Revenue contracts include an upfront non-refundable fee and a term of two to three years. Customers are charged a per-unit fee for each digital print and a flat fee for any change in concept or design. Each contract has a minimum value so RTL earns a flat rate even if digital printing jobs are never performed. The catch to the lucrative contracts is that RTL must be available to print on-demand 24 hours a day, 7 days a week. All of RTL's current digital print customers are small businesses, two of which have recently filed for bankruptcy.

RTL plans to use the digital printing equipment only for five years. At the end of this period, RTL is expecting to pay $100,000 for any modifications needed to update and prepare the equipment for sale to another vendor. A liability of $100,000 has already been recorded in the books in 2015. The accountant who prepared the journal entry has asked the controller to review this past transaction for accuracy.

Instructions

It is the end of 2017. The financial controller is preparing notes for the upcoming meeting with the auditors. Adopt the role of the controller and discuss any financial reporting issues that should be addressed before the meeting. Identify the necessary journal entries. RTL would like to use more simplified GAAP if possible.

RESEARCH AND ANALYSIS

REAL WORLD EMPHASIS

FINANCE

RA14-1 Brookfield Asset Management Inc.

Refer to the year-end financial statements and accompanying notes of **Brookfield Asset Management Inc.** in the Appendix at the end of Volume 2 of this text.

Instructions

(a) Using ratio analysis, prepare an assessment of Brookfield Asset Management Inc.'s solvency and financial flexibility for the fiscal years ended December 31, 2014 and December 31, 2013.

(b) What types of interest-bearing debt have Brookfield and its subsidiaries issued? Provide a summary of the extent to which the total interest-bearing debt reported is due within the following 12 months, 2 to 5 years, 6 to 10 years, and more than 10 years from the reporting date of December 31, 2014. Is any of this debt secured? Explain briefly.

(c) Provide a summary of the currency in which the interest-bearing debt is repayable. How are these amounts reported on Brookfield's balance sheet?

(d) Briefly explain why the subsidiary borrowings are included in Brookfield's liabilities.

REAL WORLD EMPHASIS

FINANCE

RA14-2 Loblaw Companies Limited and Empire Company Limited

Instructions

Access the financial statements for **Loblaw Companies Limited** for the year ended January 3, 2015 and **Empire Company Limited** for the year ended May 2, 2015, through SEDAR (www.sedar.com) and then answer the following questions.

(a) Calculate the debt to total assets ratio and the times interest earned ratio for these two companies. Comment on the quality of these two ratios for both companies.

(b) What financial ratios do both companies use in the annual reports to monitor and present their debt financial condition? Do both companies use the same ratios? Are the ratios calculated in the same way?

(c) Review the type of debt that each company has issued and provide a brief description of the nature of debt issued. What credit rating does each company have? (This may be found in the Management Discussion and Analysis section.) Compare the debt ratings of the two companies and comment on whether this is what would be expected given the analysis done in part (a).

(d) Review each company's capital management disclosure note. For each company, explain its objectives in managing the capital, what is included in capital and the total of managed capital, the key ratios that are monitored, and any covenants that are imposed on the company.

(e) Do the companies have any variable interest or structured entities? If so, explain the nature of these entities and how they have been reported by the companies.

REAL WORLD EMPHASIS

FINANCE

RA14-3 DBRS

DBRS is a large bond-rating agency in Canada that develops credit ratings for companies as a whole and also for its specific securities.

Instructions

Access the agency's website at www.dbrs.com and, under the "About Ratings" heading, locate and investigate information for any specific non-financial industry on how DBRS approaches credit rating analysis within that industry. Also search and find the document: "DBRS Criteria:

Financial Ratio Definitions and Accounting Adjustments—Non-Financial Companies."

(a) Briefly explain the role that the financial risk rating plays in the overall DBRS rating analysis process.

(b) Identify the particular industry you have chosen. List the factors considered in assessing the specific industry, a company's general business risk profile, and the general financial risk profile, including any primary financial risk assessment metrics determined (specific ratios considered).

(c) For the financial ratios identified in part (b) above, provide definitions that DBRS uses for all terms used in calculating the specific ratios. Is ratio analysis an art or a science? Explain.

RA14-4   Air Canada and WestJet Airlines Ltd.

REAL WORLD EMPHASIS

Instructions

Access the financial statements of **Air Canada** and **WestJet Airlines Ltd.** for their years ended December 31, 2014 through SEDAR (www.sedar.com) or the companies' websites. Review the financial statements, including the notes, and then answer the following questions.

(a) Calculate the debt to equity ratio and the times interest earned ratio for these two companies based on numbers provided on their statements of financial position and their income statements. Comment on the comparative results of these two ratios for both companies.

(b) Refer to the companies' capital disclosure notes. Using the "adjusted debt" amounts reported in these notes, recalculate the debt to equity ratios. Comment on the results relative to those in part (a) above. Did both Air Canada and WestJet adjust their debt numbers in the same way? How did each company define and measure "equity" for determining its debt to equity ratio used internally? Comment briefly.

(c) How can Air Canada and WestJet adjust their capital structures to meet their capital management objectives?

ENDNOTES

[1] "Long-term debt" and "long-term liabilities" meet the definition of a financial liability in the *CPA Canada Handbook*, Part II, Section 3856 and Part I, IAS 32 because they represent contractual obligations to deliver cash. These terms have the same meaning and are used interchangeably throughout the text.

[2] Data source: Standard & Poor's Corp. Standard & Poor's Financial Services LLC (S&P) does not guarantee the accuracy, completeness, timeliness or availability of any information, including ratings, and is not responsible for any errors or omissions (negligent or otherwise), regardless of the cause, or for the results obtained from the use of ratings. S&P gives no express or implied warranties, including, but not limited to, any warranties of merchantability or fitness for a particular purpose or use. S&P shall not be liable for any direct, indirect, incidental, exemplary, compensatory, punitive, special or consequential damages, costs, expenses, legal fees, or losses (including lost income or profits and opportunity costs) in connection with any use of ratings. S&P's ratings are statements of opinions and are not statements of fact or recommendations to purchase, hold or sell securities. They do not address the market value of securities or the suitability of securities for investment purposes, and should not be relied on as investment advice.

[3] *CPA Canada Handbook*, Part II, Section 3856.07, IAS 39.43 and IFRS 9.5.1.1. Note that where the liabilities will subsequently be measured at fair value (for example, under the fair value option), the transaction costs should not be included in the initial measurement. Instead, the costs would be expensed.

[4] Until the 1950s, it was common for corporations to issue bonds with low, even-percent coupons (such as 4%) to demonstrate their financial soundness. Frequently, the result was larger discounts. More recently, it has become acceptable to set the stated rate of interest on bonds in more precise terms (such as 6⅞%). Companies usually try to match the stated rate as closely as possible to the market or effective rate at the time of issue. While discounts and premiums continue to occur, their absolute size tends to be much smaller, and often it is immaterial. A study conducted in the mid-1980s documented that out of 685 new debt offerings, none were issued at a premium. Approximately 95% were issued either with no discount or at a price above 98. Now, however, zero-interest (deep-discount) bonds are more popular, which causes substantial discounts.

[5] Although the effective interest method is required under IFRS, ASPE does not specify that this method must be used and therefore the straight-line method is also an option.

[6] The carrying value, also called the book value, equals the face amount minus any unamortized discount, or plus any unamortized premium. As previously noted, issue costs are deducted as long as the instrument is not subsequently measured using fair value. For simplicity's sake, these costs are assumed to be zero in most of the examples.

[7] Because interest is paid semi-annually, the interest rate that is used is 5% (10% $\times$ $^6/_{12}$) and the number of periods is 10 (5 years $\times$ 2).

[8] *CPA Canada Handbook*, Part II, Section 3856.A8, IAS 39.AG64 and IFRS 9B5.1.1.

[9] Note that a deferred credit/revenue account could be used to record the government grant or alternatively a contra asset account. Government grants were discussed in Chapter 10.

[10] IFRS 13.42.

[11] IFRS 9.5.7.7. Note that IFRS 9 is not mandatorily adoptable until 2018 (although it may be adopted early). Until that time, IAS 39 would be followed. IAS 39 does not prescribe any special treatment for gains and losses arising from remeasurement of financial liabilities under the fair value option. Therefore, if a financial liability were accounted for under the fair value option, all gains and losses would be recognized in net income, similar to ASPE.

[12] *CPA Canada Handbook*, Part II, Section 3856.26, IAS 39.39 and IFRS 9.3.3.1.

[13] *CPA Canada Handbook*, Part II, Section 3856.27, IAS 39.40, IAS 39.AG57 and IFRS 9.3.3.2. Copyright © International Financial Reporting Standards Foundation. All rights reserved. Reproduced by John Wiley & Sons Canada, Ltd with the permission of the International Financial Reporting Standards Foundation®. Reproduction and use rights are strictly limited. No permission granted to third parties to reproduce or distribute.

[14] In reality, a loss should likely have been recognized when the bank first determined that the loan was impaired. This would usually be done before a loan is restructured or settled.

[15] The creditor must decide whether the asset meets the criteria to be classified as held for sale. If it does, the asset will subsequently be valued at its fair value less the costs to sell it.

[16] This type of transaction is sometimes referred to as a debt for equity swap. IFRIC Interpretation 19 deals with the accounting by the debtor (only) and supports the measurement of the common shares issued at fair value. For the debtor, general accounting principles would require the investment in the shares to be initially recognized at fair value. This is supported by *CPA Canada Handbook*, Part II, Section 3856.28.

[17] *CPA Canada Handbook*, Part II, Section 3856.A52, IAS 39.40/AG62 and IFRS 9.B3.3.6. Copyright © International Financial Reporting Standards Foundation. All rights reserved. Reproduced by John Wiley & Sons Canada, Ltd with the permission of the International Financial Reporting Standards Foundation®. Reproduction and use rights are strictly limited. No permission granted to third parties to reproduce or distribute.

[18] It is unlikely that the accounting profession will be able to stop all types of off–balance sheet transactions. Developing new financial instruments and arrangements to sell to customers is profitable for investment banking firms, especially where there is a demand for them. Many banks are discontinuing these types of products, however, due to the highly publicized negative connotations surrounding SPEs, the abuse of which was one reason for the downfall of **Enron Corporation**.

[19] *CPA Canada Handbook*, Part II, Section 1510.10.

[20] IAS 1.72.

[21] *CPA Canada Handbook*, Part II, Section 1510.02 and IAS 1.61.

15 | SHAREHOLDERS' EQUITY

REFERENCE TO THE CPA COMPETENCY MAP | LEARNING OBJECTIVES

After studying this chapter, you should be able to:

1.1.1, 1.1.2, 5.1.1, 5.2.3, 5.2.4, 5.2.6, 6.2.3	**1.** Discuss the characteristics of the corporate form of organization, rights of shareholders, and different types of shares.
1.2.1, 1.2.2, 1.4.5, 2.3.3, 5.2.3	**2.** Explain how to account for the issuance, reacquisition, and retirement of shares, stock splits, and dividend distribution.
1.2.1, 1.2.2, 1.3.1	**3.** Understand the components of shareholders' equity and how they are presented.
1.2.1, 1.2.2, 1.3.1, 1.3.2, 1.4.1, 1.4.2, 1.4.3	**4.** Understand capital disclosure requirements.
1.4.4, 1.4.5, 5.1.1	**5.** Calculate and interpret key ratios relating to equity.
1.1.4	**6.** Identify the major differences in accounting between IFRS and ASPE, and what changes are expected in the near future.

After studying the appendices to this chapter, you should be able to:

1.2.1, 1.2.3	**7.** Explain how to account for par value and treasury shares.
1.2.1, 1.2.3, 1.2.4	**8.** Explain how to account for a financial reorganization.

SOMETHING VENTURED, SOMETHING GAINED

A PUBLICLY TRADED COMPANY can raise additional capital by issuing more shares to sell to the public. But how does a private company get extra money to expand? One way is through venture capitalists, individuals or organizations that give money to private companies, especially start-ups, in return for equity in the business, becoming private shareholders.

The popular CBC television show *Dragons' Den* is one way that Canadian private companies can get venture capital. Entrepreneurs pitch an idea for a product or service they want to launch or expand, in the hopes that one or more of the venture capitalist panellists will invest in their business. In exchange, the panellists (all successful entrepreneurs) receive a certain percentage of the business's equity or shares, and will share in an equivalent percentage of the earnings. The panellists will also often ask for a say in how the business is run to help increase its success and get a good return on their investment. The recipient businesses benefit not just from the cash, but from the panellists' advice and the television publicity.

Companies that get venture capital from *Dragons' Den* can use that to fuel sometimes exponential growth. For example, Whistler, British Columbia–based Love Child Organics, which makes organic baby food, nabbed a $750,000 equity deal from

CBC Licensing

former "Dragons" David Chilton and Arlene Dickinson. After the show was taped, the company founders received an additional $1 million in venture capital from Mr. Chilton and Ms. Dickinson and another investor. A year later, Love Child Organics doubled its revenues to $5 million and then it was sold to a Toronto public company for $6 million (including debt)—not a bad return on investment.

In 2014, a Nanaimo, B.C. business landed the largest investment in the Canadian *Dragons' Den* show history: $2 million from panellists Jim Treliving and Michael Wekerle in exchange for a 5% share of the company. The business, Real Estate Webmasters, creates on-line marketing campaigns for real estate agents.

Real Estate Webmasters' founder Morgan Carey walked away from the Dragons' deal after the show aired, landing a deal instead with a venture capitalist on a similar U.S. show, *Shark Tank*, on NBC. The next year, Real Estate Webmasters doubled its revenues from $10 million to $20 million. Mr. Carey appreciates that the $2 million that the Dragons were prepared to hand over represented a huge commitment. "That's not something that's going to skyrocket our business into the stratosphere," says Mr. Carey. "But for anyone who's investing, to consider a $2 million investment is huge because that's all money that you've already earned that you have to put on the table."

Venture capital doesn't always pay off for investors. Former panellist Kevin O'Leary says that only about 2 of 10 venture capital deals in the wider market make money for investors.

Sources: Brenda Bouw, "Does Dragons' Den Reflect Real Life?," *The Globe and Mail*, October 7, 2015; Mary Teresa Bitti, "Real Estate Webmasters Walked Away from a Dragons' Den Deal—And Captured a Shark Tank Investor," *Financial Post*, June 26, 2015; Murad Hemmadi, "How to Win the Biggest Investment in Dragons' Den History," PROFITguide.com, December 19, 2014.

PREVIEW OF CHAPTER 15

Capital markets are highly important in any economy that functions based on private ownership rather than government ownership. The markets provide a forum where prices are established, and these prices then become signals and incentives that guide the allocation of the economy's financial resources. This chapter explains the various accounting issues for different types of shares or equity instruments[1] that corporations issue to raise funds in capital markets. The chapter also examines the accounting issues for retained earnings and other components of shareholders' equity.

The chapter is organized as follows:

SHAREHOLDERS' EQUITY					
Understanding the Corporate Form, Share Capital, and Profit Distribution	**Recognition, Derecognition, and Measurement**	**Presentation, Disclosure, and Analysis**	**IFRS/ASPE Comparison**	**Appendix 15A—Par Value and Treasury Shares**	**Appendix 15B—Financial Reorganization**
▪ Corporate law and the share capital system ▪ Types of shares ▪ Limited liability of shareholders ▪ Formality of profit distribution	▪ Issuance of shares ▪ Reacquisition, retirement, and conversion of shares ▪ Dividends	▪ Components of shareholders' equity ▪ Capital disclosures ▪ Analysis	▪ A comparison of IFRS and ASPE ▪ Looking ahead	▪ Par value shares ▪ Treasury shares	▪ Comprehensive revaluation

LAW

Many different meanings are attached to the word **capital** because the word is often used differently by various user groups. In corporate **finance**, for example, capital commonly refers to **sources of financing**. In **law**, capital is considered that portion of shareholders' equity that is required by statute to **be retained in the business for the protection of creditors**. Accountants use the word "capital" when referring not only to shareholders' equity but also to long-term assets (capital assets) or to whether an expenditure should be treated as an asset (capitalized) or expensed. It is therefore important to pay careful attention to **the context** in which the term is being used.

UNDERSTANDING THE CORPORATE FORM, SHARE CAPITAL, AND PROFIT DISTRIBUTION

Objective 1

Discuss the characteristics of the corporate form of organization, rights of shareholders, and different types of shares.

Of the three **primary forms of business organization—the proprietorship, the partnership, and the corporation—**the most common form of business for mid-size and larger companies is the corporate form. Although the corporate form has several advantages (as well as disadvantages) over the other two forms, its main advantage is that a corporation is a **separate legal entity** and, therefore, the entity's owners have **greater legal protection** against lawsuits. An additional important advantage is that incorporation involves the issue of shares, which gives **access to capital markets** for companies that choose to raise funds in this way.

Corporations may be classified by the nature of their ownership as follows:

1. **Public sector corporations**

    (a) Government units such as municipalities, cities, and so on. No shares issued.

    (b) Government business enterprises such as Canada Post and provincial liquor control boards (that is, companies owned by the government and sometimes referred to as Crown corporations). Shares issued.

2. **Private sector corporations**

    (a) Not-for-profit: entities whose main objective is something other than profit (such as churches, charities, and colleges). No shares issued.

    (b) For-profit: companies whose main objective is to increase shareholder value and maximize profit. Shares issued.

    Private companies: companies whose shares are held by a few shareholders and are not available for public purchase. These entities are governed by shareholder agreements, which dictate who may hold the shares and how shareholder interests may or may not be transferred or disposed of. There are many private companies in Canada, from small businesses to large corporate entities such as McCain Foods and Maple Lodge Farms.

    Public companies: companies whose shares are available for purchase by the general public, normally through a stock market or exchange, such as the Toronto Stock Exchange (TSX).[2] Public companies must follow securities laws that have been established by provincial securities commissions, corporations law, and finally rules established by the exchanges and markets that the companies trade on.

PERSONAL
TAX
6.2.3

This text focuses on the for-profit type of corporation operating in the private sector. Public sector entities and not-for-profit entities are generally covered in advanced accounting courses.

**WHAT
DO THE
NUMBERS
MEAN?**

**REAL WORLD
EMPHASIS**

Real estate income or investment trusts (REITs) have created a lot of interest in the past couple of decades. Legally, these funds are often set up as limited purpose **trust funds**. Their activities are restricted and they may be fairly passive. Under the Income Tax Act, as long as the trust pays out its income to investors, the trust itself pays no income tax. The investors then pay tax on the cash that they receive from the trust. Investors are referred to as "unitholders" and their liability is normally limited, but not as limited as the liability of a shareholder. It is important for the trustees of the trust (essentially the fund management) to ensure that the trust's insurance and other legal actions protect the unitholders adequately.

REITs are special purpose entities, otherwise known as variable interest entities. Their special purpose is to invest in real estate. **Canadian Real Estate Investment Trust** is the oldest REIT in the Canadian marketplace, having listed on the TSX in 1993. The trust was started in 1984. In Canada, many other industries followed the REIT model in order to take advantage of the tax structure, including trusts for Yellow Pages, Swiss Water Decaffeinated, Enbridge, Gateway Casino, Boston Pizza, and A&W. In 2007, the Canadian government passed a law to revoke the tax-free status of these non–real estate trusts. The change in law was phased in gradually by 2011 and these non–real estate trusts are no longer exempt from taxes.

Corporate Law and the Share Capital System

LAW

Anyone who wants to establish a corporation must submit articles of incorporation to the provincial or federal government, depending on whether the person wants to do business in a specific province or across Canada. Once the requirements are properly fulfilled, the corporation charter is issued, and the corporation is recognized as a legal entity under the relevant business corporations act. While the provisions of most provincial business corporations acts are reasonably similar, there are some differences. Consequently, when we discuss legal aspects in this chapter, we will consider only the Canada Business Corporations Act (CBCA).

The articles of incorporation specify such things as the company name,[3] place of registered office, classes and maximum numbers of shares authorized, restrictions of rights to transfer shares, number of directors, and any restrictions on the corporation's business. Once it has been incorporated, the corporation prepares share certificates and issues them to shareholders.

A corporation's share capital is generally made up of a large number of units or shares. These shares may be organized into groups or **classes**, such as Class A shares versus Class B shares. Within a class, each share is exactly equal to every other share. The number of shares that are possessed determines each owner's interest. If a company has only one class of shares and it is divided into 1,000 shares, a person owning 500 shares has one half of the corporation's ownership interest, and a person holding 10 shares would have a one-hundredth interest.

Each share has certain rights and privileges that can be restricted only by provisions in the articles of incorporation. If there are no restrictive provisions, each share gives the following **basic or inherent rights**:

1. To share proportionately in profits and losses

2. To share proportionately in management (that is, the share gives the right to vote for directors)

3. To share proportionately in the corporate assets upon liquidation of the corporation

The CBCA allows a corporation to assign a fourth right: the right to share proportionately in any new issues of shares of the same class. This right is known as a **pre-emptive right**.

The first three rights are expected in the ownership of any business; the last right may be used in a corporation to protect each shareholder's proportional interest in the enterprise. The preemptive right protects an existing shareholder from the involuntary dilution of the shareholder's ownership interest. Without this right, the corporation would be able to issue additional shares without notifying the shareholders and at prices that are not favourable to the shareholders. This could result in the shareholders' specific percentage interest (the proportional ownership of the corporation) being reduced. Because the preemptive right that attaches to existing shares makes it inconvenient for corporations to make large issuances of additional shares, as they frequently do in acquiring other companies, many corporations have eliminated it.

The great advantage of the share system is that it makes it very easy to transfer an interest in a business from one individual to another. Individuals who own shares in a corporation may sell them to others at any time and at any price without obtaining the consent of the company or other shareholders. Each share is the personal property of the owner and may be disposed of at will.[4] For its part, the corporation is only required to maintain a list or subsidiary ledger of shareholders, which it needs as a guide to dividend payments, issuance of share rights, voting proxies, and similar elements. Because shares of public companies are so easily and frequently transferred, the corporation must update the subsidiary ledger of shareholders periodically, generally before every dividend payment or shareholders' meeting. Major stock exchanges require controls over record keeping that are costly for the typical corporation. As a result, public companies generally outsource this task to registrars and transfer agents that specialize in providing services for recording and transferring shares.

Types of Shares

Common Shares

In every corporation, there is one class of shares that represents the basic ownership interest. That class is called common shares. **Common shares** represent the residual ownership interest in the company. Common shares suffer the ultimate risks of loss and receive the benefits of success. A common shareholder is not guaranteed annual dividends and is not guaranteed assets upon dissolution of the corporation. However, common shareholders generally control the corporation management through the voting rights attached to these shares.[5] They also tend to profit the most if the company is successful. If a corporation has only one authorized issue of capital shares, that issue is, by definition, common shares, and this is true even if the corporation's charter does not designate the shares as common.

Shares may be **in-substance common shares**. These are shares that, even though they have the same characteristics as common shares, cannot be or are not called common shares for legal purposes. The following should be considered when deciding whether to treat financial instruments as common shares for financial statement purposes.

Common shares carry the residual risks and rewards of ownership.

- Subordination: The shares do not have a preferred rank over other shares for dividend distributions or for the distribution of company assets upon windup of the company.

- Risks and rewards of ownership: The shares participate in the earnings/losses of the company and the appreciation/depreciation in value of the company.

- Obligation to transfer value: These shares have no obligation to transfer value. Given that they represent a residual interest in the company, they have value only if the company's net assets have value.

- No other common shares: All shares in the class in question have the same features.

- Redemption: The shares are retractable/redeemable only upon windup of the company.[6]

Preferred Shares

Nature of Preferred Shares

In an effort to attract all types of investors, corporations may offer two or more classes of shares, with each class having different rights or privileges. The preceding section pointed out that each share of a particular issue has the same rights as other shares of the same issue and that there are three inherent rights in every share. By special contracts between the corporation and its shareholders, some of these rights may be sacrificed by the shareholder in return for other special rights or privileges. This creates special classes of shares, and because they have certain preferential rights, such shares are usually called **preferred shares**. In return for any special preference, the preferred shareholder is always required to sacrifice some of the basic rights of common share interests.

A typical type of preference is to give the preferred shareholders a priority claim on earnings and on assets (upon dissolution or windup of the company), compared with the claims of the common shareholders. This means that preferred shareholders are assured a dividend, usually at a stated rate, before any amount may be distributed to the common shareholders. They are also assured that if the company goes bankrupt, they rank before the common shareholders in terms of getting their money back. In return for this preference, the preferred shareholders may sacrifice the right to a voice in management or the right to share in profits beyond the stated rate.

Instead of issuing both common and preferred shares, a company may accomplish much the same thing by issuing two classes of shares, Class A shares and Class B shares. In this case, one of the issues is the common share and the other issue has some preference or restriction of basic shareholder rights. Preferred shares may be issued with a dividend preference that is expressed as a **percentage of the issue price**. Thus, holders of 8% preferred shares issued at $100 are entitled to an annual dividend of $8 per share, if a preferred dividend is declared. This share is commonly referred to as an 8% preferred share. The dividend may also be expressed as a **specific dollar amount** per share; for example, $8 per share. A preference as to dividends does not assure shareholders that dividends will be paid; it only means that the stated dividend rate or amount that applies to the preferred share must be paid before any dividends can be paid on the common shares.

Features of Preferred Shares

A corporation may attach whatever preferences or restrictions it desires to a preferred share issue, and in whatever combination (as long as it does not specifically violate its incorporation law), and it may issue more than one class of preferred share. Some preferred share features include the following:

1. **Cumulative.** Dividends on cumulative shares that are not paid in any given year are known as dividends in arrears. These dividends must be made up in a later year before any profits can be distributed to common shareholders. There is no liability, however, until the board of directors **declares** a dividend. According to common law, if the corporate charter is silent about the cumulative feature, the preferred share is considered cumulative.

2. **Convertible.** This feature allows the company or holder to exchange the shares for common shares at a predetermined ratio. Thus, the shareholder has the relative security of the preferred share yet may gain from the appreciation of the company by converting preferred shares to common shares.

TREASURY MANAGEMENT 5.2.3 and 5.2.4

3. **Callable/redeemable.** The issuing corporation can call or redeem at its option (through its own choice) the outstanding preferred shares at specified future dates and at specified prices. The callable feature permits the corporation to use the capital that it has obtained through the issuance of such shares until the need has passed or having the issued shares is no longer an advantage. The existence of a call price or prices tends to set a ceiling on the market value of the preferred shares unless they are convertible into common shares. When a preferred share is called for redemption, any dividends in arrears must be paid.

4. **Retractable.** The holders of the shares can put or sell their shares to the company, normally after having given adequate notice, and the company must then pay the holders for the shares. The retraction option makes this instrument more attractive to the holders because it gives them more choice, that is. They can sell their shares in the open market if it's a public company or sell them back to the company itself at a more favourable price.

5. **Participating.** Participating preferred shareholders share (at the same rate as common shareholders) in any profit distributions that are higher than the prescribed rate of the preferred share. That is, a 5% preferred share, if it is fully participating, will receive not only its 5% return, but also dividends at the same rate that is paid to common shareholders if the common shareholders are paid amounts higher than 5% of stated value. Note that participating preferred shares are not always fully participating. That is, they can also be partially participating. For example, provision may be made that a 5% preferred share will be participating up to a maximum total rate of 10%, after which it ceases to participate in additional profit distributions, or a 5% preferred share may participate only in additional profit distributions that exceed a 9% dividend rate on the common share.

ETHICS

Preferred shares are often issued instead of debt because a company's debt to equity ratio has become too high. The issuing company may structure the instrument such that its legal form represents shares in hopes of avoiding treating the instruments as debt on the financial statements. Accounting for preferred shares can be complex because of their many and varied features and because accountants must account for the instruments in accordance with their economic substance as opposed to their legal form. Chapter 16 discusses the more complex aspects of these financial instruments.

Finally, issuances of common, preferred, or other shares may be made through **private placements**[7] as opposed to through stock markets and exchanges. The difference between the two is that the company remains private if it has no shares that trade on a stock market or exchange and it is therefore not subject to the same regulations as a public company.

Limited Liability of Shareholders

LAW

Those who own a corporation—the shareholders—contribute cash, property, or services to the enterprise in return for ownership shares. The property or service that has been invested in the enterprise is the limit on a shareholder's possible loss. That is, if the corporation has losses that are so large that the remaining assets are not enough to pay creditors, the creditors have no recourse against the personal assets of the individual shareholders. This is unlike in a partnership or proprietorship, where the owners' personal assets can be accessed to satisfy unpaid claims against the enterprise. Ownership interests in a corporation are legally protected against such a contingency. The shareholders are thus said to have **limited liability**: they may lose their investment but they cannot lose more than their investment.

While the corporate form of organization gives the protective feature of limited liability to the shareholders, it also stipulates that the amount of the shareholders' investment that is represented in share capital accounts cannot be withdrawn unless all prior claims on corporate assets have been paid. This means that the corporation must maintain this capital until dissolution of the corporation. Upon dissolution, it must then satisfy all prior claims before distributing any amounts to the shareholders. In a proprietorship or partnership, the owners or partners may withdraw amounts whenever and in whatever amount they choose because all their personal assets can be accessed to protect creditors from loss.

Shares issued by corporations must be without a nominal or par value (according to the CBCA). This simply means that all proceeds from the issuance of the shares must be credited to the appropriate share capital account and become part of the shareholders' investment referred to above. In some provinces and in the United States, shares that have a fixed per-share amount printed on each share certificate are called **par value shares**.

Par value has only one real significance: in jurisdictions where the concept of par value is legally allowed, it establishes the maximum responsibility of a shareholder in the event of insolvency or other involuntary dissolution. Par value is thus not value in the ordinary sense of the word. It is merely an amount per share that has been determined by the incorporators of the company and stated in the corporation charter or certificate of incorporation. Appendix 15A discusses par value shares in greater detail.

Formality of Profit Distribution

Legality of Dividend Distribution

LAW

An enterprise's owners decide what to do with profits that are realized through operations. Profits may be left in the business for a future expansion or simply to have a margin of safety, or they may be withdrawn and divided among the owners. In a proprietorship or partnership, this decision is made by the owner or owners informally and requires no specific action. In a partnership, the partnership agreement would usually specify how profits or losses are to be shared. In a corporation, however, profit distribution (referred to as **dividends**) is controlled by certain legal restrictions. Not all shares carry the right to receive dividends.

First, no amounts may be distributed among the owners unless the corporate capital is kept intact. This restriction is based on the presumption that there have to be sufficient net assets or security left in the corporation to satisfy the liability holders after any assets have been distributed to shareholders as dividends. Various tests of corporate solvency have been used over the years. Under the CBCA, dividends may not be declared or paid if there are reasonable grounds for believing that (1) the corporation is, or would be after the dividend, unable to pay its liabilities as they become due; or (2) the realizable value of the corporation's assets would, as a result of the dividend, be less than the total of its liabilities and stated or **legal capital** for all classes of shares.

Second, distributions to shareholders must be formally approved by the board of directors and recorded in the minutes of the board's meetings. As the top executive body in the corporation, the board of directors must make certain that no distributions are made to shareholders that are not justified and directors are generally held personally liable to creditors if liabilities cannot be paid because company assets have been illegally paid out to shareholders.

Third, dividends must fully agree with stipulations in the share capital contracts. Once the corporation has entered into contracts with various classes of shareholders, the stipulations of such contracts must be followed.

Financial Condition and Dividend Distribution

Determining the proper amount of dividends to pay is a difficult financial management decision. Companies that are paying dividends are extremely reluctant to reduce or eliminate their dividends, because they believe that the securities market could negatively view this action. As a consequence, companies that have been paying cash dividends will make every effort to continue to do so.

Very few companies pay dividends in amounts equal to their legally available retained earnings. The major reasons that companies have for limiting the dividend amount are as follows:

FINANCIAL ANALYSIS AND PLANNING 5.1.1 and 5.2.6

1. There are agreements (bond covenants) with specific creditors that require all or a portion of the earnings to be retained in the form of assets in order to build up additional protection against possible loss.

2. The company wants to retain assets that would otherwise be paid out as dividends, in order to finance growth or expansion. This is sometimes called internal financing, reinvesting earnings, or plowing the profits back into the business.

3. The company wants to smooth out dividend payments from year to year by accumulating earnings in good years and using such accumulated earnings as a basis for dividends in bad years.

4. The company wants to build up a cushion or buffer against possible losses or errors in the calculation of profits.

Dividend policies vary among corporations. Some older, well-established firms take pride in a long, unbroken string of quarterly dividend payments.[8] They would lower or not declare the dividend only if they were forced to do so by a sustained decline in earnings or a critical shortage of cash. Growth companies, on the other hand, pay few or no cash dividends because their policy is to expand as rapidly as internal and external financing permit. Investors in these companies hope that their share price will appreciate in value and that they will realize a profit when they sell their shares. In other words, they hope to benefit from capital appreciation.

Good business management means paying attention to more than just the legality of dividend distribution. **Economic conditions** also need to be considered and, most importantly, liquidity. Assume the following extreme situation:

Statement of Financial Position			
Plant assets	$500,000	Share capital	$400,000
		Retained earnings	100,000
	$500,000		$500,000

The company has a retained earnings credit balance, and generally, unless the balance is restricted, the company can therefore declare a dividend of $100,000. But because all its assets are plant assets and are used in operations, paying a cash dividend of $100,000 would require selling plant assets or borrowing.

Even if we assume a statement of financial position that shows current assets, the question remains whether those assets are needed for other purposes.

Statement of Financial Position				
Cash	$100,000	Current liabilities		$ 60,000
Plant assets	460,000	Share capital	$400,000	
		Retained earnings	100,000	500,000
	$560,000			$560,000

The existence of current liabilities implies very strongly that some of the cash is needed to meet current debts as they mature. In addition, day-to-day cash requirements for payrolls and other expenditures that are not included in current liabilities also require cash.

Thus, before a dividend is declared, management must consider the availability of funds to pay the dividend. Other demands for cash should also be investigated by preparing a cash forecast. A dividend should not be paid unless both the present and future financial position appear to justify the distribution. Directors must also consider the effect of inflation and replacement costs before making a dividend commitment. During a period of significant inflation, some costs that are charged to expense under historical cost accounting are understated in terms of comparative purchasing power. This is because the amounts represent older dollars since the asset was purchased earlier when the dollars were likely worth more than today. Because these costs are not adjusted for inflation, income is therefore overstated.

WHAT DO THE NUMBERS MEAN?

The non-payment of dividends can also significantly affect a company. For instance, **Torstar Corporation** has Class B shares that are normally non-voting, but if the company does not pay dividends for eight consecutive quarters, the shares then have voting rights. An excerpt from the 2014 financial statements follows:

20. SHARE CAPITAL

(a) Rights attaching to the Company's share capital:

   (i) Class A (voting) and Class B (non-voting) shares, no par value

   Class A and Class B shareholders may elect to receive dividends in cash or stock dividends in the form of Class B shares. Class A shares are convertible at any time at the option of the holder into Class B shares.

(ii) Voting provisions

   Class B shares are non-voting unless the Company has failed to pay the full quarterly preferential dividend (7.5 cents per annum) on the Class B non-voting shares in each of eight consecutive quarters.

(iii) Restrictions on transfer

   Registration of the transfer of any of the Company's shares may be refused if such transfer could jeopardize either the ability of the Company to engage in broadcasting or its status as a Canadian newspaper or periodical publisher.

RECOGNITION, DERECOGNITION, AND MEASUREMENT

Issuance of Shares

Objective 2

Explain how to account for the issuance, reacquisition, and retirement of shares, stock splits, and dividend distribution.

In issuing shares, companies undertake the following procedures.

1. The shares are **authorized**.

2. Shares are **offered for sale** and contracts to sell shares are entered into.

3. Amounts to be received for the shares are **collected** and the **shares are issued**.

**TREASURY
MANAGEMENT
5.2.3**

Share Issue—Basic

Shares are sold for the price that they will bring in the marketplace. Normally the company will hire specialists (such as investment banking firms and underwriters) to value the shares[9] and help **promote and sell them**. As payment for their services, the underwriters take as commission a percentage of the total share consideration that is received from investors. The **net** amount that is received by the company becomes the credit to common or preferred shares. For example, assume that Video Electronics Corporation is organized with 10,000 authorized common shares. The only entry that is made for this authorization is a memorandum entry. There is no journal entry because there is no monetary amount involved in the authorization. If 500 shares are then issued for cash at $10 per share, the entry should be:

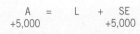

A = L + SE
+5,000   +5,000

Cash flows: ↑ 5,000 inflow

Cash	5,000	
Common Shares		5,000

Entries for preferred shares are the same as for common shares as long as the preferred shares are classified as equity.[10] Because par value shares are relatively uncommon in Canada, we briefly cover the issues that are unique to them in Appendix 15A.

Sometimes companies issue shares but do not require the purchaser to pay right away. This may be the case for instances where the company lends its employees money to buy new shares. There is controversy in such cases about how this receivable should be presented on the statement of financial position (SFP). Some argue that the receivable should be recorded as an asset like other receivables. Others argue that the receivable should be reported as a reduction of shareholders' equity.

The U.S. Securities and Exchange Commission (SEC) requires companies to report the receivable for issued but unpaid-for shares as a reduction of shareholders' equity (similar to the accounting for shares sold on a subscription basis) because the risk of collection on these types of transactions is often very high. IFRS is not definitive on this issue but the conceptual framework would support presenting the receivables as a reduction of shareholders' equity unless there is substantial evidence that the company is not at risk for declines in the value of the shares and there is reasonable assurance that the company will collect the amount in cash. ASPE specifically supports this approach.[11]

Shares Sold on a Subscription Basis

Shares may also be sold on a subscription basis. Sales of **subscribed shares** generally occur when new, small companies go public or when corporations offer shares to employees so they can participate in the business ownership. When a share is sold on a subscription basis, its full price is not received immediately. Normally, only a **partial payment** is made, and the share is not issued until the full subscription price is received.

The journal entries for handling shares that are sold on a subscription basis are illustrated by the following example. Assume that Lubradite Corp. offers shares on a subscription basis to selected individuals, giving them the right to purchase 10 common shares at a price of $20 per share. Fifty individuals accept the company's offer and agree to pay 50% down and the remaining 50% at the end of six months. Lubradite's entries would be as follows:

**UNDERLYING
CONCEPT**

Subscriptions receivable appear to meet the definition of an asset because they represent a future benefit to the company in terms of incoming cash. However, treating them as an asset results in the share capital increasing even though the shares are not yet issued. This does not provide transparent financial reporting.

A = L + SE
         0

Cash flows: No effect

A = L + SE
+5,000   +5,000

Cash flows: ↑ 5,000 inflow

At date of receipt of subscriptions		
Share Subscriptions Receivable (10 × $20 × 50)	10,000	
Common Shares Subscribed		10,000
(To record receipt of subscriptions for 500 shares)		
Cash	5,000	
Share Subscriptions Receivable		5,000
(To record receipt of first instalment representing 50% of total due on subscribed shares)		

ETHICS

Whether the Subscriptions Receivable account should be presented as an asset or a contra equity account is a matter of professional judgement, although conceptually, it makes sense to record it as a reduction of equity. In the United States, the SEC requires the account to be treated as a reduction of equity. ASPE provides guidance for share purchase loan receivables, as discussed earlier in the chapter.

When the final payment is received and the shares are issued, the entries are:

A = L + SE
+5,000   +5,000

Cash flows: ↑ 5,000 inflow

Six months later		
Cash	5,000	
Share Subscriptions Receivable		5,000
(To record receipt of final instalment on subscribed shares)		

A = L + SE
0

Cash flows: No effect

Common Shares Subscribed	10,000	
Common Shares		10,000
(To record issuance of 500 shares upon receipt of final instalment from subscribers)		

Defaulted Subscription Accounts

Sometimes a subscriber is unable to pay all instalments and therefore defaults on the agreement. The question is what to do with the balance of the subscription account and the amount that has already been paid in. The answer is determined by the subscription contract, corporate policy, and any applicable law of the jurisdiction of incorporation. There are several possible courses of action a company could take, including the following.

1. Return the amount already paid by the subscriber (possibly after deducting some expenses).

2. Treat the amount paid as forfeited and therefore transfer it to the Contributed Surplus account.

3. Issue fewer shares to the subscriber so that the number of shares issued is equivalent to what the subscription payments already received would have paid for fully.

For example, assume that a subscriber to 50 Lubradite common shares defaults on the final payment. If the subscription contract stated that amounts paid by the defaulting subscriber would be refunded, Lubradite would make the following entry when the default occurs, assuming that the refund was to be paid at a later date:

A = L + SE
+500 -500

Cash flows: No effect

Common Shares Subscribed	1,000	
Share Subscriptions Receivable		500
Accounts Payable		500
(To record default on 50 shares subscribed for $20 each and on which 50% had been paid)		

If the amount paid by the subscriber were forfeited, there would be a $500 credit to Contributed Surplus because this is a **capital transaction**.

Shares Issued with Other Securities (Lump-Sum Sales)

Generally, corporations sell each class of shares separately so that they can determine the proceeds for each class and, ordinarily, even for each lot of shares in the class. Occasionally, however, two or more classes of securities are issued for a single payment or lump sum. It is not uncommon, for example, for more than one type or class of security to be issued in the acquisition of another company. The accounting problem in such **lump-sum sales** is how to allocate the proceeds among the several classes of securities, or how to measure the separate classes of shares.

Two alternative measurement techniques are used: (1) the **relative fair value method** and (2) the **residual value method**.[12] These measurement techniques are often used in accounting, for example to allocate the cost of a joint acquisition of land and a building. The first method values each instrument according to its fair value and then proportionally allocates the lump-sum value to each instrument. The second method values one instrument (often the one that is easier to measure) and then allocates the rest of the amount to the other instrument. Examples of these methods are presented in other chapters. These same techniques are used to bifurcate bundled sales for revenue recognition purposes (Chapter 6), allocate the costs of inventory and/or property, plant, and equipment in basket or lump-sum purchases (Chapters 8 and 10), and measure the respective parts of compound financial instruments (Chapter 16).

Costs of Issuing Shares

Direct incremental costs that are incurred to sell shares, such as underwriting costs, accounting and legal fees, printing costs, and taxes, should be reported as a reduction of the amounts paid in. Issue costs are therefore debited to Common Shares because they are capital transactions rather than operating transactions.

Management salaries and other indirect costs related to the share issue should be expensed as they are incurred because it is difficult to establish a relationship between these costs and the proceeds that are received from the sale. In addition, corporations annually incur costs for maintaining the shareholders' records and handling ownership transfers. These recurring costs, which are mainly registrar and transfer agents' fees, are normally charged to expense in the period in which they are incurred.

Reacquisition, Retirement, and Conversion of Shares

It is not unusual for companies to buy back their own shares. In fact, share buybacks now exceed dividends as a form of distribution to shareholders.[13]

While corporations have varied reasons for purchasing their outstanding shares, some of the major ones are as follows:

1. **To increase earnings per share and return on equity.** By reducing shares outstanding and reducing shareholders' equity, corporations often improve certain performance ratios, such as earnings per share and return on equity. In 2011, **CGI Group** (Canada's largest information technology outsourcing firm) spent $287 million to buy back its own shares. This pushed the share price up 11.6%.

2. **To provide shares for employee share compensation contracts or to meet potential merger needs. Honeywell Inc.** reported that part of its purchase of 1 million common shares was to be used for employee share option contracts. Other companies acquire shares to have them available for business acquisitions.

3. **To stop takeover attempts or to reduce the number of shareholders.** By reducing the number of shares that are held by the public, the current owners and management may find it easier to keep outsiders from gaining control or significant influence. When American media mogul Ted Turner tried to acquire **CBS**, CBS started a substantial buyback of its shares.

4. **To make a market in the share.** By purchasing shares in the marketplace, management creates a demand that may stabilize the share price or, in fact, increase it. Over a period of four years, **Nexfor Inc.**, a large North American producer of building materials, repurchased and cancelled 15.5 million shares for $122 million (representing 10% of the company's shares). The company felt that the shares were undervalued and represented a good deal.

5. **To return cash to shareholders.** In 2015, **Apple Inc.** announced that it was increasing its share repurchase program to U.S. $140 billion as part of a larger capital return program.

Some publicly held corporations have chosen to go private; that is, they decided to eliminate public (outside) ownership by purchasing their entire float of outstanding shares. This is often done through a **leveraged buyout**, which occurs when management or another employee group purchases the company shares and finances the purchase by using the company assets as collateral.

Once shares are reacquired, they may either be retired or held in the treasury for re-issue. If they are not retired, such shares are referred to as **treasury shares**. Technically, a treasury share is a corporation's own share that has been reacquired after having been issued and fully paid. In Canada, the CBCA, with minor exceptions, requires that repurchased shares be cancelled and, if a company's articles of incorporation limit the number of authorized shares, that the shares be restored to the status of authorized but unissued shares. While some provincial jurisdictions do allow treasury shares to exist, such shares remain relatively uncommon in Canada. This is unlike the United States, where many companies hold treasury shares. Appendix 15A briefly reviews the accounting for these shares.

ASPE

When shares are purchased or redeemed by the issuing corporation, it is likely that the price paid will differ from the amount that was received for the shares when they were issued. Because this is a capital transaction, any gains or losses are booked through equity[14] (rather than through the income statement).

If the acquisition cost **is greater than** the original cost, then the acquisition cost should be allocated as follows:

1. First, to Share Capital, in an amount equal to the par, stated, or assigned value of the shares

2. Second, for any excess after the first allocation, to Contributed Surplus, to the extent that the contributed surplus was created by a net excess of proceeds over cost on a cancellation or resale of shares of the same class

3. Third, for any excess after the second allocation, to Contributed Surplus in an amount equal to the proportional share of the portion of contributed surplus that arose from transactions, other than those above, in the same class of shares

4. Last, for any excess after the third allocation, to Retained Earnings

If the acquisition cost **is less than** the original cost, then the acquisition cost should be allocated as follows:

1. First, to Share Capital, in an amount equal to the par, stated, or assigned value of the shares

2. Second, for the difference after the first allocation, to Contributed Surplus

For shares with no par value (which means most shares in Canada), the assigned value is equal to the average per share amount in the account for that class of shares at the transaction date. The difference between the stated or assigned value and the lower cost of acquisition is credited to Contributed Surplus and is seen as a contribution by the original shareholders that now accrues to the remaining shareholders.

Applying the formulas noted above, in cases where the acquisition cost is greater than the assigned cost, this would normally result in debiting Share Capital (step 1) and Retained Earnings (step 4). Contributed Surplus would be adjusted only if there were a prior balance in the Contributed Surplus account that related to the shares that are being acquired.

To illustrate, assume that Cooke Corporation has the following in its shareholders' equity accounts:

Share capital:	
Class A, 10,500 shares issued and outstanding	$ 63,000
Class B, 50,000 shares issued and outstanding	100,000
Total share capital	163,000
Retained earnings	300,000
Total shareholders' equity	$463,000

On January 30, 2017, Cooke purchased and cancelled 500 Class A shares at a cost of $4 per share. The required entry is:

A = L + SE
−2,000   −2,000
Cash flows: ↓ 2,000 outflow
	Class A Shares [500 × ($63,000 ÷ 10,500)] 3,000
	     Cash
	     Contributed Surplus*
		
		2,000
		1,000

*Average per share amount (assigned value) = $63,000 ÷ 10,500 = $6. Excess of assigned value over reacquisition cost = $6 − 4 = $2 per share for 500 shares.

On September 10, 2017, the company purchased and cancelled an additional 1,000 Class A shares. The purchase cost was $8 per share. The transaction is recorded as follows:

A = L + SE −8,000 −8,000 Cash flows: ↓ 8,000 outflow	**Class A shares [1,000 × ($60,000 ÷ 10,000)]** 6,000 Contributed Surplus* 1,000 Retained Earnings 1,000 Cash	 8,000

*Equals the whole amount of the excess from the above

IFRS gives no specific guidance for the reacquisition and retirement of shares. However, the accounting may end up being similar to ASPE if basic principles are followed.

As noted earlier, some preferred shares may have a conversion feature allowing the shareholders to convert the preferred shares to common shares at a predetermined ratio. Assume that Arcon Inc. has 1,000 convertible shares outstanding with a carrying value of $100,000. The shares are convertible to common shares based on 10 preferred shares for every common share. On conversion, the following journal entry would be made:

A = L + SE
         0
Cash flows: No effect
	Preferred Shares 100,000
	     Common Shares
		
		100,000

Dividends

UNDERLYING CONCEPT

A declared dividend is a liability because once the dividend has been declared, the company cannot avoid paying it.

There are basically two classes of dividends:

1. Those that are a return on capital (a share of the earnings)
2. Those that are a return of capital, referred to as **liquidating dividends**

The natural expectation of any shareholder who receives a dividend is that the corporation has operated successfully and that he or she is receiving a share of its earnings. A liquidating dividend should therefore be adequately described in the financial statements. We will discuss this type of dividend in greater depth later in the chapter.

Dividends are commonly paid in cash but occasionally they are paid in shares or other assets. **Dividends generally reduce the total shareholders' equity in the corporation**, because the equity is reduced through an immediate or promised future distribution of assets. Stock dividends are different, however. When a stock dividend is declared, the corporation does not pay out assets or incur a liability. It issues additional shares to each shareholder and nothing more. Both types of dividends are discussed below.

Cash Dividends

The board of directors votes on the declaration of dividends and if the resolution is properly approved, the dividend is declared. Before the dividend is paid, a current list of shareholders must be prepared. For this reason, there is usually a time lag between the declaration and payment. A resolution approved at the January 10 (**date of declaration**) meeting of the board of directors might be declared payable on February 5 (**date of payment**) to all shareholders of record on January 25 (**date of record**).[15]

The period from January 10 to January 25 gives time for any transfers in process to be completed and registered with the transfer agent. The time from January 25 to February 5 provides an opportunity for the transfer agent or accounting department, depending on who does this work, to prepare a list of shareholders as at January 25 and to prepare and distribute dividend payments (via cheque or direct deposit).

To illustrate the declaration and payment of an ordinary dividend that is payable in cash, assume that on June 10 Rajah Corp. declared a cash dividend of 50 cents a share on 1.8 million shares and payable on July 16 to all shareholders of record on June 24. The following entries are required:

A = L + SE
+900,000 –900,000

Cash flows: No effect

A = L + SE
–900,000 –900,000

Cash flows: ↓ 900,000 outflow

At date of declaration (June 10)		
Dividends	900,000	
Dividends Payable		900,000
At date of record (June 24)		
No entry		
At date of payment (July 16)		
Dividends Payable	900,000	
Cash		900,000

To have a ledger account that shows the amount of dividends declared during the year, the company can debit Dividends instead of debiting Retained Earnings at the time of declaration. This account is then closed to Retained Earnings at year end. Dividends may be declared either as a certain percentage of par or stated value, such as a 6% dividend, or as an amount per share, such as 60 cents per share. In the first case, the rate is multiplied by the par or stated value of outstanding shares to get the total dividend; in the second, the amount per share is multiplied by the number of shares outstanding. **Cash dividends are not declared and paid on treasury shares because the shares are owned by the company itself.**

Dividends in Kind

Dividends that are payable in corporation assets other than cash are called property dividends or **dividends in kind**. Property dividends may be merchandise, real estate, or investments, or whatever form the board of directors designates. Because of the obvious difficulties of dividing units and delivering them to shareholders, the usual property dividend is in the form of securities of other companies that the distributing corporation holds as an investment.

A property dividend is a non-reciprocal transfer of nonmonetary assets between an enterprise and its owners. These dividends should generally be measured at the fair value of the asset that is given up unless they are considered to represent a spinoff or other form of restructuring or liquidation, in which case they should be recorded at the carrying value of the nonmonetary assets or liabilities transferred.[16] No gain or loss would be recorded in the second instance.

WHAT DO THE NUMBERS MEAN?

When the U.S. Supreme Court decided that **DuPont's** 23% investment in **General Motors** violated antitrust laws, DuPont was ordered to divest itself of the GM shares within 10 years. The shares represented 63 million of GM's 281 million shares then outstanding. DuPont could not sell the shares in one block of 63 million, nor could it sell 6 million shares annually for the next 10 years without severely depressing the value of the GM shares. At that time, the entire yearly trading volume in GM shares was not even 6 million shares. DuPont solved its problem by declaring a property dividend and distributing the GM shares as a dividend to its own shareholders.

Stock Dividends

Management may want to "capitalize" part of the earnings (that is, reclassify amounts from earned to contributed capital) so that earnings are permanently retained in the business. In this case, the corporation may issue a **stock dividend**. No assets are distributed and each shareholder has exactly the same proportionate interest in the corporation, and the same total book value, after the issue of the stock dividend as before the declaration. The book value per share is lower, however, because there are now more shares being held.

There is no clear guidance on how to account for stock dividends. The major issue is whether or not they should be treated in the same way as other dividends.[17] If they are treated like other dividends, they should be recorded by debiting Retained Earnings and crediting Share Capital. In terms of measuring the transaction, fair value would be used. (It would be measured by looking at the market value of the shares issued, at the declaration date.)

Where the stock dividends give the option to the holder to receive them in cash or shares, the stock dividend is considered a nonmonetary transaction under GAAP and must be treated as a regular dividend, valued at fair value.[18] Where there is no option to receive the dividend in cash, GAAP is silent; however, the CBCA states that for stock dividends, the declared amount of the dividend must be added to the stated capital account. The CBCA does not allow shares to be issued until they are fully paid for, at an amount not less than the fair equivalent of money that the corporation would have received had the shares been issued for cash. Therefore, if the company is incorporated under the CBCA, all stock dividends should be recorded as dividends and measured at fair value.

To illustrate a stock dividend, assume that a corporation has 1,000 common shares outstanding and retained earnings of $50,000. If the corporation declares a 10% stock dividend, it issues 100 additional shares to current shareholders. If it is assumed that the shares' fair value at the time of the stock dividend is $130 per share and that the shareholders had the option to take the dividend in cash but chose not to, the entry is:

$A = L + SE$
$ 0$

Cash flows: No effect

At date of declaration and distribution		
Dividends	13,000	
Common Shares		13,000

If the dividend is declared before it is distributed, then the journal entry would be a debit to Dividends or Retained Earnings and a credit to Stock Dividends Distributable. Upon share issue, the journal entry would be a debit to Stock Dividends Distributable and a credit to Common Shares. Note that no asset or liability has been affected. The entry merely reflects a reclassification of shareholders' equity. No matter what the fair value is at the time of the stock dividend, each shareholder retains the same proportionate interest in the corporation. Illustration 15-1 proves this point.

Illustration 15-1

Effects of a Stock Dividend

Before dividend:	
Common shares, 1,000 shares	$100,000
Retained earnings	50,000
Total shareholders' equity	$150,000

Shareholders' interests:	
A—400 shares, 40% interest, book value	$ 60,000
B—500 shares, 50% interest, book value	75,000
C—100 shares, 10% interest, book value	15,000
	$150,000

After declaration and distribution of 10% stock dividend:	
If fair value ($130) is used as basis for entry	
Shareholders' common shares, 1,100 shares	$113,000
Retained earnings ($50,000 – $13,000)	37,000
Total shareholders' equity	$150,000

Shareholders' interests:	
A—440 shares, 40% interest, book value	$ 60,000
B—550 shares, 50% interest, book value	75,000
C—110 shares, 10% interest, book value	15,000
	$150,000

Note, in Illustration 15-1, that the total shareholders' equity has not changed as a result of the stock dividend. Also note that the proportion of the total shares outstanding that is held by each shareholder is unchanged.

Liquidating Dividends

Some corporations use contributed surplus as a basis for dividends. Without proper disclosure of this fact, shareholders may wrongly believe that the corporation has been paying dividends out of profits. We mentioned in Chapter 11 that companies in the extractive industries may pay dividends equal to the total of accumulated income and depletion. The portion of these dividends that is in excess of accumulated income represents a return of part of the shareholders' investment.

For example, assume that McChesney Mines Inc. issued a dividend to its common shareholders of $1.2 million. The cash dividend announcement noted that $900,000 should be considered income and the remainder a return of capital. The entry is:

$$A = L + SE$$
$$+1,200,000 - 1,200,000$$

Cash flows: No effect

At date of declaration		
Retained Earnings (or Dividends)	900,000	
Contributed Surplus	300,000	
Dividends Payable		1,200,000

In some cases, management may simply decide to cease business and declare a liquidating dividend. In these cases, liquidation may take place over several years to ensure an orderly and fair sale of all assets.

Dividend Preferences

The examples that now follow illustrate the effects of various dividend preferences on dividend distribution to common and preferred shareholders. Assume that in a given year, $50,000 is to be distributed as cash dividends, outstanding common shares have a book value of $400,000, and 1,000 $6-preferred shares are outstanding (issued for $100,000). Dividends would be distributed to each class as follows, under the particular assumptions:

1. If the preferred shares are non-cumulative and non-participating, the effects are shown in Illustration 15-2.

Illustration 15-2

Dividend Distribution, Non-Cumulative and Non-Participating Preferred Shares

	Preferred	Common	Total
$6 × 1,000	$6,000	$ –0–	$ 6,000
The remainder to common	–0–	44,000	44,000
Totals	$6,000	$44,000	$50,000

2. If the preferred shares are cumulative and non-participating, and dividends were not paid on the preferred shares in the preceding two years, the effects are shown in Illustration 15-3.

Illustration 15-3

Dividend Distribution, Cumulative and Non-Participating Preferred, Shares with Dividends in Arrears

	Preferred	Common	Total
Dividends in arrears,			
$6 × 1,000 for 2 years	$12,000	$ –0–	$12,000
Current year's dividend, $6 × 1,000	6,000	–0–	6,000
The remainder to common	–0–	32,000	32,000
Totals	$18,000	$32,000	$50,000

3. If the preferred shares are non-cumulative and fully participating, the effects are shown in Illustration 15-4.[19]

Illustration 15-4		Preferred	Common	Total
Dividend Distribution,	Current year's dividend, $6	$ 6,000	$24,000	$30,000
Non-Cumulative and Fully	Participating dividend—pro rata (proportional)	4,000	16,000	20,000
Participating Preferred Shares	Totals	$10,000	$40,000	$50,000

The participating dividend was determined as follows:

Current year's dividend:
Preferred, $6 × 1,000 = $6,000
Common, 6% of $400,000 = $24,000 (= a like amount) $ 30,000
The 6% represents $6,000 on preferred shares ÷ $100,000
Amount available for participation ($50,000 − $30,000) $ 20,000
Carrying value of shares that are to participate ($100,000 + $400,000) $500,000
Rate of participation ($20,000 ÷ $500,000)   4%
Participating dividend:
Preferred (4% of $100,000) $ 4,000
Common (4% of $400,000)   16,000
                                                                    $ 20,000

4. If the preferred shares are cumulative and fully participating, and if dividends were not paid on the preferred shares in the preceding two years, the effects are shown in Illustration 15-5. (The same procedure that was used in example 3 is used again here to carry out the participation feature.)

Illustration 15-5		Preferred	Common	Total
Dividend Distribution,	Dividends in arrears,			
Cumulative and Fully	$6 × 1,000 for 2 years	$12,000	$ –0–	$12,000
Participating Preferred Shares,				
with Dividends in Arrears	Current year's dividend, $6	6,000	24,000	30,000
	Participating dividend, 1.6%			
	($8,000 ÷ $500,000)	1,600	6,400	8,000
	Totals	$19,600	$30,400	$50,000

Stock Splits

If a company has undistributed earnings over several successive years and has thus accumulated a sizable balance in retained earnings, the market value of its outstanding shares is likely to increase. Shares that were issued at prices of less than $50 a share can easily reach a market value of more than $200 a share. The higher the share's market price, the harder it is for some investors to purchase it. The managements of many corporations believe that, for better public relations, the corporation's shares should be widely owned. They wish, therefore, to have a market price that is low enough to be affordable to the majority of potential investors.

To reduce the market value of shares, the common device that is used is the stock split.[20] From an accounting standpoint, no entry is recorded for a stock split; a memorandum note, however, is made to indicate that the number of shares has increased.

LAW

Differences between a Stock Split and Stock Dividend

From a legal standpoint, a **stock split** is distinguished from a stock dividend, because a stock split results in an increase in the number of shares outstanding with no change in the share capital or the retained earnings amounts. As noted earlier, legally, the stock dividend may result in an increase in both the number of shares outstanding and the share capital while reducing the retained earnings (depending on the legal jurisdiction).

A stock dividend, like a stock split, may also be used to increase the share's marketability. If the stock dividend is large, it has the same effect on market price as a stock split. In the United States, the accounting profession has taken the position that, whenever additional shares are issued to reduce the unit market price, then the distribution more closely resembles a stock split than a stock dividend. **This effect usually results only if the number of shares issued is more than 20% to 25% of the number of shares that were previously outstanding.** A stock dividend of more than 20% to 25% of the number of shares previously outstanding is called a **large stock dividend**.

In principle, it must be determined whether the large stock dividend is more like a stock split or a dividend (from an economic perspective). Professional judgement must be used in determining this because there is no specific guidance under ASPE or IFRS.

Legal requirements must be considered as a constraint. As noted earlier, for instance, companies that are incorporated under the CBCA must measure any newly issued shares at market (including those issued as stock dividends). This means, therefore, that all stock dividends for such companies are to be treated as dividends and measured at market. On the other hand, in jurisdictions where legal requirements for stated share capital values are not a constraint, the following options would be available for stock dividends:

1. Treat as a dividend (debit Retained Earnings and credit Common Shares) and measure at either the market value of the shares or their par or stated value.

2. Treat as a stock split (memo entry only).

The SEC supports the second approach for large stock dividends of more than 25%. Illustration 15-6 summarizes and compares the effects of dividends and stock splits.

Illustration 15-6

Effects of Dividends and Stock Splits

Declaration and Distribution of Dividends and Stock Splits					
Effect on:	Declaration of Cash Dividend	Payment of Cash Dividend	(Small) Stock Dividend	(Large) Stock Dividend	Stock Split
Retained earnings	Decrease	—	Decrease[a]	Decrease[b]	—
Common shares	—	—	Increase	Increase	—
Contributed surplus	—	—	—	—	—
Total shareholders' equity	Decrease	—	—	—	—
Working capital	Decrease	—	—	—	—
Total assets	—	Decrease	—	—	—
Number of shares outstanding	—	—	Increase	Increase	Increase

[a] Generally equal to market value of shares.
[b] May be equal to par, stated value of shares, or market value. Note that some companies may choose to interpret GAAP such that the dividend is treated as a stock split. In Canada, this is a matter of judgement and is governed by legal requirements regarding the value of stated capital and economic substance.

PRESENTATION, DISCLOSURE, AND ANALYSIS

Objective 3
Understand the components of shareholders' equity and how they are presented.

Components of Shareholders' Equity

Owners' equity in a corporation is defined as **shareholders' equity** or corporate capital. The following four categories normally appear as part of shareholders' equity:

1. Common and/or preferred shares

2. Contributed surplus

3. Retained earnings (deficit)

4. Accumulated other comprehensive income[21]

The first two categories, shares and contributed surplus, form the contributed capital. The third and fourth categories, retained earnings and accumulated other comprehensive income, represent the enterprise's earned capital.

Illustration 15-7 shows a partial statement of financial position for **Cameco Corporation**.

Shareholders' equity		
Share capital	1,862,646	1,854,671
Contributed surplus	196,815	186,382
Retained earnings	3,333,099	3,314,049
Other components of equity	51,084	(6,837)
Total shareholders' equity attributable to equity holders	5,443,644	5,348,265
Non-controlling interest	160	1,129
Total shareholders' equity	5,443,804	5,349,394

**WHAT
DO THE
NUMBERS
MEAN?**

Note that Cameco describes accumulated other comprehensive income as "other components of equity" in its SFP. This is acceptable under IFRS. Further details as to changes in this account will be provided in Illustration 15-8.

The company has a considerable balance in its Retained Earnings account, implying that on a cumulative basis, it has been quite profitable. Note 19 provides more detail regarding share capital, including the fact that the company has common shares and one Class B share outstanding. The province of Saskatchewan owns this Class B share, which gives the holder the right to vote as a class on any proposal to relocate the Cameco head office outside of Saskatchewan.

Contributed (paid-in) capital is the total amount that shareholders provide to the corporation for it to use in the business. **Earned capital** is the capital that is created by the business operating profitably. It consists of all undistributed income that remains invested in the enterprise. The distinction between paid-in capital and earned capital is important from both legal and economic points of view. Legally, there are restrictions on dividend payouts. These were discussed earlier in the chapter. Economically, management, shareholders, and others want to see earnings for the **corporation's** continued existence and growth. Maintaining the level of contributed capital is also a goal.[22]

**REAL WORLD
EMPHASIS**

Illustration 15-8 shows an example of a consolidated statement of changes in shareholders' equity for Cameco. Note that under ASPE, given that other comprehensive income and accumulated other comprehensive income do not exist, companies provide a statement of changes in retained earnings only. Changes in share capital and contributed surplus are generally shown in the notes.

Note that the "other components of equity" as noted in the prior illustration on the SFP (Illustration 15-7) are presented here in significant detail. There are three items included in other components of equity: foreign currency translation, cash flow hedges, and available-for-sale assets. Foreign currency translation will be discussed in your advanced accounting course, cash flow hedges will be discussed in Chapter 16, and available-for-sale investments were referred to in Chapter 9. As of 2014, Cameco had not yet switched over to IFRS 9 and so was using the IAS 39 classifications for investments. Amounts relating to remeasurement of pension plans are reclassified to Retained Earnings as allowed under IAS 19.

**REAL WORLD
EMPHASIS**

Consolidated statements of changes in equity

($Cdn thousands)	Share capital	Contributed surplus	Retained earnings	Foreign currency translation	Cash flow hedges	Available-for-sale assets	Total	Non-controlling interest	Total equity
Balance at January 1, 2014	$1,854,671	$186,382	$3,314,049	$(7,165)	$300	$28	$5,348,265	$1,129	$5,349,394
Net earnings	—	—	185,234	—	—	—	185,234	(1,821)	183,413
Other comprehensive income	—	—	(7,952)	58,832	(300)	(611)	49,969	58	50,027
Total comprehensive income for the year	—	—	177,282	58,832	(300)	(611)	235,203	(1,763)	233,440
Share-based compensation	—	15,808	—	—	—	—	15,808	—	15,808
Share options exercised	7,975	(5,375)	—	—	—	—	2,600	—	2,600
Dividends	—	—	(158,232)	—	—	—	(158,232)	—	(158,232)
Transactions with owners contributed equity	—	—	—	—	—	—	—	794	794
Balance at December 31, 2014	$1,862,646	$196,815	$3,333,099	$51,667	$ —	$(583)	$5,443,644	$160	$5,443,804
Balance at January 1, 2013	$1,851,507	$168,952	$2,913,134	$3,699	$4,092	$ —	$4,941,384	$580	$4,941,964
Net earnings	—	—	318,495	—	—	—	318,495	(808)	317,687
Other comprehensive loss	—	—	241,785	(10,864)	(3,792)	28	227,157	72	227,229
Total comprehensive income for the year	—	—	560,280	(10,864)	(3,792)	28	545,652	(736)	544,916
Share-based compensation	—	19,008	—	—	—	—	19,008	—	19,008
Share options exercised	3,164	(1,578)	—	—	—	—	1,586	—	1,586
Dividends	—	—	(158,177)	—	—	—	(158,177)	—	(158,177)
Acquisition of non-controlling interest in subsidiary	—	—	—	—	—	—	—	97	97
Change in ownership interest in subsidiary	—	—	(1,188)	—	—	—	(1,188)	1,188	—
Balance at December 31, 2013	$1,854,671	$186,382	$3,314,049	$(7,165)	$300	$28	$5,348,265	$1,129	$5,349,394

Illustration 15-8

Example of Disclosures of Changes in Shareholders' Equity—Cameco Corporation

Contributed Surplus

The term "surplus" is used in an accounting sense to designate the excess of net assets over the total paid-in, par, or stated value of a corporation's shares. As previously mentioned, this surplus is further divided between earned surplus (retained earnings) and contributed surplus. Contributed surplus may be affected by a variety of transactions or events, as Illustration 15-9 shows.

Illustration 15-9

Transactions that May Affect Contributed Surplus

- Par value share issue and/or retirement (see Appendix 15A)
- Treasury share transactions (see Appendix 15A)
- Liquidating dividends
- Financial reorganizations (see Appendix 15B)
- Stock options and warrants (see Chapter 16)
- Issue of convertible debt (see Chapter 16)
- Forfeited share subscriptions
- Donated assets by a shareholder
- Redemption or conversion of shares

Retained Earnings (Deficit)

The basic source of **retained earnings**—earnings retained for use in the business—is income from operations. Shareholders assume the greatest risk in enterprise operations because shareholders' equity declines with any losses. In return, they also reap the rewards, sharing in any profits resulting from enterprise activities. Any income that is not distributed among the shareholders becomes additional shareholders' equity. Net income includes a considerable variety of income sources. These include the enterprise's main operation (such as manufacturing and selling a product), plus any secondary activities (such as disposing of scrap or renting out unused space), plus the results of unusual items. All these items lead to net income that increases retained earnings. The more common items that either increase or decrease retained earnings are summarized in Illustration 15-10.

RETAINED EARNINGS	
Debits	Credits
1. Net loss	1. Net income
2. Prior period error corrections and certain changes in accounting principle	2. Prior period error corrections and certain changes in accounting principle
3. Cash, property, and most stock dividends	3. Adjustments due to financial reorganization
4. Some treasury share transactions	

Accumulated Other Comprehensive Income

Accumulated other comprehensive income is the cumulative change in equity that is due to the revenues and expenses, and gains and losses that stem from non-shareholder transactions that are excluded from the calculation of net income. It is considered to represent earned income as well. Comprehensive income was previously discussed in Chapters 4, 5, 9, and 10 and will be referred to in Chapter 16. Recall that the concept of comprehensive income is not applicable under ASPE.

Capital Disclosures

Objective 4
Understand capital disclosure requirements.

Numerous disclosures are required under GAAP regarding capital.[23] For example, basic disclosures include the amounts of authorized share capital, issued share capital, and changes in capital since the last SFP date.[24] Under IFRS, the company is required to disclose the changes in all equity accounts—including Retained Earnings, Accumulated Other Comprehensive Income, and Share Capital—since the last SFP date in the statement of changes in equity (instead of the statement of retained earnings). In many corporations, there are restrictions on retained earnings or dividends and these should be disclosed. The note disclosure should reveal the source of the restriction, pertinent provisions, and the amount of retained earnings that is restricted, or the amount that is unrestricted. Restrictions may be based on maintaining a certain retained earnings balance, the corporation's ability to observe certain working capital requirements, additional borrowing, and other considerations.

The following details would normally be disclosed on the face of the statement of financial position, in the statement of changes in shareholders' equity, or in the notes:[25]

1. The authorized number of shares or a statement noting that this is unlimited

2. The existence of unique rights (such as dividend preferences and the amounts of such dividends, redemption and/or retraction privileges, conversion rights, and whether or not the dividends are cumulative)

3. The number of shares issued and amount received including those held by the entity or its subsidiaries or associates

4. Whether the shares are par value or no par value

5. The amount of any dividends in arrears for cumulative preferred shares

6. Details of changes during the year (presented in the statement of changes in equity under IFRS)

7. Restrictions on retained earnings

8. Any shares reserved for future issue including terms and amounts

Under IFRS, companies must also disclose information about their objectives, policies, and processes for managing capital. They must include summary quantitative data about what the company manages as capital and about any changes in capital.[26] The reason for requiring this disclosure is to give users of financial statements better insight into the way the company's capital is managed. Additional detailed disclosures are required under IFRS.[27] Illustration 15-11 shows a sample of these types of disclosures for Cameco Corporation.

Illustration 5-11

Excerpt from the Financial Statements of Cameco Corporation—Example of Required Capital Disclosures

REAL WORLD EMPHASIS

29. Capital management

Cameco's capital structure reflects our vision and the environment in which we operate. We seek growth through development and expansion of existing assets by acquisition. Our capital resources are managed to support achievement of our goals. The overall objectives for managing capital in 2014 remained unchanged from the prior comparative period.

Cameco's management considers its capital structure to consist of bank overdrafts, long-term debt, short-term debt (net of cash and cash equivalents and short-term investments), non-controlling interest and shareholders' equity.

The capital structure at December 31 was as follows:

	2014	2013
Bank overdraft	$ —	$ 41,226
Long-term debt [note 16]	1,491,198	1,293,383
Short-term debt [note 15]	—	50,230
Cash and cash equivalents	(566,583)	(229,135)
Net debt	924,615	1,155,704
Non-controlling interest	160	1,129
Shareholders' equity	5,443,644	5,348,265
Total equity	5,443,804	5,349,394
Total capital	$6,368,419	$6,505,098

Cameco is bound by certain covenants in its general credit facilities. These covenants place restrictions on total debt, including guarantees and set minimum levels for net worth. As of December 31, 2014, Cameco met these requirements.

The terms of NUKEM's revolving loan facility contain a financial covenant that places restrictions on total debt and working capital balances. The facility also requires Cameco, as guarantor, to maintain a minimum credit rating. As of December 31, 2014, the Company is in compliance with all requirements under this facility.

Analysis

Objective 5

Calculate and interpret key ratios relating to equity.

Several ratios use amounts related to shareholders' equity to evaluate a company's **profitability** and **long-term solvency**. The following four ratios are discussed and illustrated next: (1) rate of return on common shareholders' equity, (2) payout ratio, (3) price earnings ratio, and (4) book value per share.

Rate of Return on Common Shareholders' Equity

FINANCIAL ANALYSIS AND PLANNING

5.1.1

A widely used ratio that measures profitability from the common shareholders' viewpoint is **rate of return on common shareholders' equity**. This ratio shows how many dollars of net income were earned for each dollar invested by the owners. It is calculated by dividing net income less preferred dividends by average common shareholders' equity. For example, assume that Garber Inc. had net income of $360,000, declared and paid preferred dividends of $54,000, and had average common shareholders' equity of $2,550,000. Garber's ratio is calculated as follows:

$$\text{Rate of return on common shareholders' equity} = \frac{\text{Net income} - \text{Preferred dividends}}{\text{Average common shareholders' equity}}$$

$$= \frac{\$360,000 - \$54,000}{\$2,550,000}$$

$$= 12\%$$

As the calculation shows, because preferred shares are present, preferred dividends are deducted from net income to calculate the income available to common shareholders. Similarly, the carrying value of preferred shares is deducted from total shareholders' equity to arrive at the amount of common shareholders' equity used in this ratio.

WHAT DO THE NUMBERS MEAN?

When the rate of return on total assets is lower than the rate of return on the common shareholders' investment, the company is said to be trading on the equity at a gain. **Trading on the equity** is the practice of using borrowed money at fixed interest rates or issuing preferred shares with constant dividend rates in hopes of obtaining a higher rate of return on the money used. (This is sometimes also referred to as **leverage.**) Because these debt issues must be given a prior claim on some or all of the corporate assets, the advantage to common shareholders of trading on the equity must come from borrowing at a lower rate of interest than the rate of return that is obtained on the assets that have been borrowed. If this can be done, the capital obtained from bondholders or preferred shareholders earns enough to pay the interest or preferred dividends and to leave a margin for the common shareholders. When this occurs, trading on the equity is profitable.

Payout Ratio

Another measure of profitability is the **payout ratio**, which is the ratio of cash dividends to net income. If preferred shares are outstanding, this ratio is calculated for common shareholders by dividing cash dividends paid to common shareholders by net income available to common shareholders. Assuming that Troy Corp. has cash dividends of $100,000, net income of $500,000, and no preferred shares outstanding, the payout ratio is calculated as follows:

$$\text{Payout ratio} = \frac{\text{Cash dividends to common shareholders}}{\text{Net income} - \text{Preferred dividends}}$$

$$= \frac{\$100,000}{\$500,000}$$

$$= 20\%$$

For some investors, it is important that the payout be high enough to provide a good yield on the shares.[28] However, payout ratios have declined for many companies because many investors now view appreciation in the share value as more important than the dividend amount.

Price Earnings Ratio

The **price earnings** (P/E) **ratio** is an oft-quoted statistic that analysts use in discussing the investment potential of an enterprise. It is calculated by dividing the share's market price by the earnings per share. For example, assuming that Soreson Corp. has a market price of $50 and earnings per share of $4, its price earnings ratio would be calculated as follows:

$$\text{Price earnings ratio} = \frac{\text{Market price of share}}{\text{Earnings per share}}$$

$$= \$50 \div \$4$$

$$= 12.5$$

Book Value per Share

A much-used basis for evaluating net worth is the book or equity value per share. Book value per share is the amount that each share would receive if the company were liquidated, based on the amounts reported on the SFP. However, the figure loses much of its relevance if the valuations on the statement of financial position do not approximate the fair market value of the assets. **Book value per share** is calculated by dividing common shareholders' equity by the number of common shares outstanding. To illustrate, assuming that Chen Corporation's common shareholders' equity is $1 million and it has 100,000 shares outstanding, its book value per share is calculated as follows:

$$\text{Book value per share} = \frac{\text{Common shareholders' equity}}{\text{Number of shares outstanding}}$$

$$= \frac{\$1,000,000}{100,000}$$

$$= \$10 \text{ per share}$$

When preferred shares are present, an analysis of the covenants involving the preferred shares should be conducted. If preferred dividends are in arrears, the preferred shares are participating, or the preferred shares have a redemption or liquidating value higher than their carrying amount, then retained earnings must be allocated between the preferred and common shareholders in calculating book value.

To illustrate, assume the following information for Pelletier Corporation.

Shareholders' equity	Preferred	Common
Preferred shares, 5%	$300,000	
Common shares		$400,000
Contributed surplus		37,500
Retained earnings	–0–	162,582
Totals	$300,000	$600,082
Shares outstanding		4,000
Book value per share		$150.02

In the preceding calculation, it is assumed that no preferred dividends are in arrears and that the preferred shares are not participating. Now assume the same facts for Pelletier Corporation except that the 5% preferred shares are cumulative and participating up to 8%, and that dividends for three years before the current year are in arrears. The common shares' book value is then calculated as follows, assuming that no action has yet been taken concerning dividends for the current year.

Shareholders' equity	Preferred	Common
Preferred shares, 5%	$300,000	
Common shares		$400,000
Contributed surplus		37,500
Retained earnings:		
Dividends in arrears (3 years at 5% a year)	45,000	
Current year requirement at 5%	15,000	20,000
Participating additional 3%	9,000	12,000
Remainder to common	–0–	61,582
Totals	$369,000	$531,082
Shares outstanding		4,000
Book value per share		$132.77

In connection with the book value calculation, the analyst should also consider the following items: the number of authorized and unissued shares, the number of treasury shares on hand, any commitments with respect to the issuance of unissued shares or the reissuance of treasury shares, and the relative rights and privileges of the various types of shares authorized.

Objective 6

Identify the major differences in accounting between IFRS and ASPE, and what changes are expected in the near future.

IFRS/ASPE COMPARISON

A Comparison of IFRS and ASPE

Illustration 15-12 summarizes the major differences in accounting for equity between ASPE and IFRS.

	IFRS—IAS 1, 7, and 32	ASPE—*CPA Canada Handbook*, Part II, Sections 3240, 3251, and 3856	References to Related Illustrations and Select Brief Exercises
Recognition/derecognition	No explicit guidance is given, although the accounting may end up the same using basic principles.	Specific guidance is given for reacquisition of shares. The cost should be allocated first to share capital, then to contributed surplus, and then to retained earnings.	N/A
	No explicit guidance is given, although the accounting may end up the same due to basic principles.	Receivables for loans issued to buy shares are recognized as assets if the shareholder is at risk for changes in value of the shares and there is reasonable assurance that the company will be able to collect in cash. Otherwise, they are not recognized or if recognized, are presented as contra equity.	N/A
Measurement	No explicit guidance is given for accounting for financial reorganizations. Note that IFRS allows revaluation of property, plant, and equipment and intangibles (using the revaluation method); and investment properties (under the fair value method). This is covered in Chapter 10.	Specific guidance is given for comprehensive revaluation of assets where a financial reorganization of the company occurs. Assets are revalued, the debt and equity accounts are adjusted to reflect the new capital structure, and any deficit or retained earnings are reclassified to other equity accounts.	Comprehensive revaluation accounting is covered in Appendix 15B.
	No explicit guidance is given; however, related-party transactions are not remeasured.	Dividends in kind that represent a spinoff of assets to shareholders are measured at carrying value unless it is a transaction with controlling shareholders, in which case the transaction is treated as a related-party transaction and may be remeasured.	Related-party transactions are covered in Chapter 23.
Presentation	Changes in all equity accounts are presented in a separate statement of changes in equity.	Changes in retained earnings are presented in a retained earnings statement. Changes in capital accounts are presented in the notes. The concept of comprehensive income is not discussed.	Illustration 15-8 gives an example of the statement of changes in shareholders' equity. Examples of this statement as well as statements of changes in retained earnings are given throughout the text.
Disclosures	Specific disclosures are required regarding how a company manages its capital.	Specific disclosures about how a company manages its capital are not explicitly mandated.	Illustration 15-11

Illustration 15-12

IFRS and ASPE Comparison Chart

Looking Ahead

The IASB is working on several projects, including the Presentation of Financial Statements project (formerly referred to as the performance reporting project), the Disclosure Initiative, and the project entitled Financial Instruments with Characteristics of Equity.

Because the Presentation of Financial Statements project is closely related to the Disclosure Initiative, the IASB is waiting to see how the disclosure project unfolds before deciding how to move forward with the Presentation of Financial Statements project.

Discussions have now begun again on the Financial Instruments with Characteristics of Equity project and the IASB plans to issue a Discussion Paper. No dates have yet been announced.

SUMMARY OF LEARNING OBJECTIVES

1 Discuss the characteristics of the corporate form of organization, rights of shareholders, and different types of shares.

The three main forms of organization are the proprietorship, partnership, and corporation. Incorporation gives shareholders protection against claims on their personal assets and allows greater access to capital markets.

If there are no restrictive provisions, each share carries the following rights: (1) to share proportionately in profits and losses, (2) to share proportionately in management (the right to vote for directors), and (3) to share proportionately in corporate assets upon liquidation. An additional right to share proportionately in any new issues of shares of the same class (called the preemptive right) may also be attached to the share.

Preferred shares are a special class of share that possess certain preferences or features that common shares do not have. Most often, these features are a preference over dividends and a preference over assets in the event of liquidation. Many other preferences may be attached to specific shares. Preferred shareholders give up some or all of the rights normally attached to common shares.

2 Explain how to account for the issuance, reacquisition, and retirement of shares, stock splits, and dividend distribution.

Shares are recognized and measured at net cost when issued. Shares may be issued on a subscription basis, in which case they are not considered legally issued until they are paid up. Shares may also be issued as a bundle with other securities, in which case the cost must be allocated between the securities. The residual or relative fair value methods (sometimes called the incremental or proportional methods) may be used to allocate the cost.

If the reacquisition cost of the shares is greater than the original cost, the acquisition cost is allocated to share capital, then contributed surplus, and then retained earnings. If the cost is less, the cost is allocated to share capital (to stated or assigned cost) and to contributed surplus.

Dividends paid to shareholders are affected by the dividend preferences of the preferred shares. Preferred shares can be cumulative or non-cumulative, and fully participating, partially participating, or non-participating.

A stock dividend is a capitalization of retained earnings that generally results in a reduction in retained earnings and a corresponding increase in certain contributed capital accounts. The total shareholders' equity remains unchanged with a stock dividend. A stock split results in an increase or decrease in the number of shares outstanding. However, no accounting entry is required.

3 Understand the components of shareholders' equity and how they are presented.

Contributed surplus is additional surplus coming from shareholder transactions. Accumulated other comprehensive income is accumulated non-shareholder income that has not been booked through net income. ASPE does not discuss this concept. The shareholders' equity section of a balance sheet includes share capital, contributed surplus, retained earnings, and accumulated other comprehensive income. A statement of changes in shareholders' equity is required under IFRS.

4 Understand capital disclosure requirements.

Basic disclosure requirements include authorized and issued share capital and changes during the period. Rights attached to shares should be presented, and where dividends are in arrears, this should also be disclosed. Where there are restrictions on retained earnings or dividends, this should be disclosed. Under IFRS, companies must also disclose information about their objectives, policies, and processes for managing capital and show summary quantitative information regarding what the company considers its capital.

5 Calculate and interpret key ratios relating to equity.

Common ratios used in this area are the rate of return on common shareholders' equity, payout ratio, price earnings ratio, and book value per share.

6 Identify the major differences in accounting between IFRS and ASPE, and what changes are expected in the near future.

In several cases, ASPE provides more guidance, as noted in the comparison chart in Illustration 15-12. IFRS requires a statement of changes in shareholders' equity, whereas ASPE requires a statement of changes in retained earnings (with additional note disclosure regarding the changes in equity). The IASB is continuing to work on a financial statements project as well as a liability and equity project.

KEY TERMS

APPENDIX 15A

PAR VALUE AND TREASURY SHARES

Objective 7
Explain how to account for par value and treasury shares.

Neither par value shares nor treasury shares are allowed under the Canada Business Corporations Act. As mentioned in the chapter, however, these types of shares are allowed under certain provincial business corporations acts and are common in the United States. For this reason, we will now discuss them in greater detail in this appendix.

Par Value Shares

The par value of a share has no relationship to its fair market value. At present, the par value that is associated with most capital share issuances is very low ($1, $5, or $10). To show the required information for the issuance of par value shares, accounts must be kept for each class of share as follows:

1. **Preferred or common shares.** These accounts reflect the par value of the corporation's issued shares. They are credited when the shares are originally issued. No additional entries are made in these accounts unless additional shares are issued or shares are retired.

2. **Contributed surplus (paid-in capital in excess of par or, in the United States, additional paid-in capital).** This account indicates any excess over par value that was paid in by shareholders in return for the shares issued to them. Once it has been paid in, the excess over par becomes a part of the corporation's paid-in capital, and the individual shareholder has no greater claim on the excess paid in than all other holders of the same class of shares.

To illustrate how these accounts are used, assume that Colonial Corporation sold 100 shares for $1,100 with a par value of $5 per share. The entry to record the issuance is:

A = L + SE
+1,100   +1,100

Cash flows: ↑ 1,100 inflow

Cash	1,100	
Common Shares		500
Contributed Surplus		600

When the shares are repurchased and cancelled, the same procedure is followed as was described in the chapter.

Treasury Shares

Treasury shares are created when a company repurchases its own shares but does not cancel them. Generally, the repurchase and resale are treated as a single transaction. The repurchase of treasury shares is the first part of a transaction that is completed when the shares are later resold. Consequently, the holding of treasury shares is viewed as a transitional phase between the beginning and end of a single activity.

When shares are purchased, the total cost is debited to Treasury Shares on the statement of financial position. This account is shown as a deduction from the total of the components of shareholders' equity in the SFP. An example of such disclosure follows:

Shareholders' equity:	
Common shares, no par value; authorized 24,000,000 shares;	
issued 19,045,870 shares, of which 209,750 are in treasury	$ 27,686,000
Retained earnings	253,265,000
	280,951,000
Less: Cost of treasury shares	(7,527,000)
Total shareholders' equity	$273,424,000

When the shares are sold, the Treasury Shares account is credited for their cost. If they are sold at more than their cost, the excess is credited to Contributed Surplus. If they are sold at less, the difference is debited to Contributed Surplus (if it is related to the same class of shares) and then to Retained Earnings. If the shares are subsequently retired, the journal entries shown in the chapter would be followed.

Note also that dividends on treasury shares should be reversed because a company cannot receive dividend income on its own shares (dr. Dividends Payable, cr. Retained Earnings).

SUMMARY OF LEARNING OBJECTIVE FOR APPENDIX 15A

7 Explain how to account for par value and treasury shares.

These shares may only be valued at par value in the common or preferred share accounts. The excess goes to contributed surplus. On a repurchase or cancellation, the par value is removed from the common or preferred share accounts and any excess or deficit is booked to contributed surplus or retained earnings, as was discussed for no par shares.

Treasury shares are created when a company repurchases its own shares and does not cancel or retire them at the same time; that is, they remain outstanding. The single-transaction method is used when treasury shares are purchased. This method treats the purchase and subsequent resale or cancellation as part of the same transaction.

APPENDIX 15B

FINANCIAL REORGANIZATION

Objective 8
Explain how to account for a financial reorganization.

A corporation that consistently suffers net losses accumulates negative retained earnings, or a deficit. Shareholders generally presume that dividends are paid out of profits and retained earnings and, therefore, a deficit sends a very negative signal about the company's ability to pay dividends. In addition, certain laws in some jurisdictions specify that no dividends may be declared and paid as long as a corporation's paid-in capital has been reduced by a deficit. In these cases, a corporation with a debit balance of retained earnings must accumulate enough profits to offset the deficit before it can pay any dividends.

This situation may be a real hardship on a corporation and its shareholders. A company that has operated unsuccessfully for several years and accumulated a deficit may have finally turned the corner. The development of new products and new markets, the arrival of a new management group, or improved economic conditions may point to much improved operating results in the future. However, if the law prohibits dividends until the deficit has been replaced by earnings, the shareholders must wait until such profits have been earned, which can take quite a long time. Furthermore, future success may depend on obtaining additional funds through the sale of shares, but if no dividends can be paid for some time, the market price of any new share issue is likely to be low, assuming the shares can be marketed at all.

Thus, a company with excellent prospects may not be able to carry out its plans because of a deficit, although present management may have had nothing at all to do with the years during which the deficit was built up. To allow the corporation to go ahead with its plans might well be in everyone's best interest; to require it to eliminate the deficit through profits might force it to liquidate.

One way that a company that has gone through financial difficulty can proceed with its plans without having to recover from a deficit is a **financial reorganization**. A financial reorganization is defined as:

LAW

> a substantial realignment of an enterprise's equity and non-equity interests such that the holders of one or more of the significant classes of non-equity interests and the holders of all of the significant classes of equity interests give up some (or all) of their rights and claims on the enterprise.[29]

In other words, in a financial reorganization, creditors often give up their claim on the company and take back ownership rights (shares).

A financial reorganization is the outcome of negotiation and results in an eventual agreement between non-equity and equity holders in the corporation. These negotiations may take place under a legal act (such as the Companies' Creditors Arrangement Act) or a less formal process.[30] The result gives the company a fresh start and the accounting is often referred to as **fresh start accounting**.

Comprehensive Revaluation

ASPE

When a financial reorganization occurs, where the same party does not control the company both before and after the reorganization, and where new costs are reasonably determinable, the company's assets and liabilities should undergo a **comprehensive revaluation**.[31]

Under ASPE, this requires three steps:[32]

1. The deficit balance (retained earnings) is brought to zero. Any asset writedowns or impairments that existed before the reorganization should be recorded first. The deficit is reclassified to Share Capital, Contributed Surplus, or a separately identified account within Shareholders' Equity.

2. The changes in debt and equity that have been negotiated are recorded. Often, debt is exchanged for equity, reflecting a change in control.

3. The assets and liabilities are comprehensively revalued. This step assigns appropriate going concern values to all assets and liabilities based on the negotiations. The difference between the carrying values before the reorganization and the new values after is known as a **revaluation adjustment**. The revaluation adjustment and any costs incurred to carry out the financial reorganization are accounted for as capital transactions and are closed to Share Capital, Contributed Surplus, or a separately identified account within Shareholders' Equity. Note that the new costs of the identifiable assets and liabilities must not be greater than the entity's fair value if this is known.[33]

Entries Illustrated

The series of entries that follows illustrates the accounting procedures that are applied in a financial reorganization. Assume that New Horizons Inc. shows a deficit of $1 million before the reorganization comes into effect on June 30, 2017. Under the terms of the negotiation, the creditors are giving up rights to payment of the $150,000 debt in return for 100% of the common shares. The original shareholders agree to give up their shares. Assume the other numbers as given.

1. **Restate impairments of assets that existed before the reorganization:**

A = L + SE			
−750,000 −750,000	Deficit	750,000	
Cash flows: No effect	Inventory (loss on writedown)		225,000
	Intangible Assets—Patents (loss on writedown)		525,000

Elimination of deficit against contributed capital:

A = L + SE			
0	Common Shares	1,750,000	
Cash flows: No effect	Deficit		1,750,000

2. and 3. **Restate assets and liabilities to recognize unrecorded gains and losses and to record the negotiated change in control:**

A = L + SE			
+400,000 −150,000 +550,000	Buildings (gain on write-up)	400,000	
Cash flows: No effect	Notes Payable (gain on writedown)	150,000	
	Common Shares		550,000

Note that, if there is no change in control, ASPE does not allow a comprehensive revaluation.

When a financial reorganization occurs and is accounted for as such, the following requirements must be fulfilled:

1. The proposed reorganization should receive the **approval** of the corporation's shareholders before it is put into effect.

2. The new asset and liability valuations should be **fair** and not deliberately understate or overstate assets, liabilities, and earnings.

3. After the reorganization, the corporation must have a zero balance of retained earnings, although it may have contributed surplus arising from the reorganization.

Disclosure

In the period of the reorganization, the following must be disclosed:

1. The date of the reorganization

2. A description of the reorganization

3. The amount of the change in each major class of assets, liabilities, and shareholders' equity resulting from the reorganization

In the following fiscal period, in subsequent reports, the following must be disclosed:

1. The date of the reorganization

2. The revaluation adjustment amount and the shareholders' equity account in which it was recorded

3. The amount of the deficit that was reclassified and the account to which it was reclassified

SUMMARY OF LEARNING OBJECTIVE FOR APPENDIX 15B

8 Explain how to account for a financial reorganization.

A corporation that has accumulated a large debit balance (deficit) in retained earnings may enter into a process known as a financial reorganization. During a reorganization, creditors and shareholders negotiate a deal to put the company on a new footing. This generally involves a change in control and a comprehensive revaluation of assets and liabilities. The procedure consists of the following steps: (1) The deficit is reclassified so that the ending balance in Retained Earnings is zero. (2) The change in control is recorded. (3) All assets and liabilities are comprehensively revalued at current values so that the company will not be burdened with having to complete inventory or fixed asset valuations in following years.

KEY TERMS

comprehensive revaluation, p. 943

financial reorganization, p. 943

fresh start accounting, p. 943

revaluation adjustment, p. 944

Note: Completion of this end-of-chapter material will help develop CPA enabling competencies (such as ethics and professionalism, problem-solving and decision-making, and communication) and technical competencies. We have highlighted selected items with an integration icon and material in *WileyPLUS* has been linked to the competencies. All cases emphasize integration, especially of the enabling competencies. The brief exercises, exercises, and problems generally emphasize problem-solving and decision-making.

LAW

FINANCE

Brief Exercises

Note: All assignment material with an asterisk (*) relates to the appendices to the chapter.

(LO 1) BE15-1 Explain the pros and cons of incorporating.

(LO 1) BE15-2 List the types of dividends. Why do companies or investors have a preference for one or the other?

(LO 1) BE15-3 Walter Corporation has three classes of shares: Series A, Series B, and Class A. How should Walter classify and present the different classes if the characteristics of each class are as follows?

Series A shares	The shares are mandatorily redeemable and carry a dividend rate of 4%.
Series B shares	The shares are cumulative, non-voting, and carry a dividend rate of $2 per share. They are subordinated to the Series A shares for dividend distribution.
Class A shares	The shares are subordinated to both Series A and Series B shares for dividend distribution and participate in the earnings and losses of the company above a non-cumulative dividend of $0.50 per share. The shares have a voting right of one vote per share.

(LO 2) BE15-4 Bonata Inc. sells 1,400 common shares on a subscription basis at $65 per share on June 1 and accepts a 45% down payment. On December 1, Bonata collects the remaining 55% and issues the shares. Prepare the company's journal entries.

(LO 2) BE15-5 On March 1, Kramers Inc. sells 1,000 common shares to its employees at $25 per share and lends the money to the employees to buy the new shares. The employees pay 50% of the price on the transaction date and pay the balance in one year. (a) Prepare the company's necessary journal entries. (b) Assuming a December 31 fiscal year end, how should the receivable for the uncollected amount on the share issue be presented on the statement of financial position (1) under ASPE and (2) under IFRS?

(LO 2) BE15-6 Platinum Corporation issued 4,000 of its common shares for $66,000. The company also incurred $1,700 of costs associated with issuing the shares. Prepare a single combined journal entry to record the issuance of the company's shares.

(LO 2) BE15-7 Higgins Inc. has 52,000 common shares outstanding. The shares have an average cost of $21 per share. On July 1, 2017, Higgins reacquired 800 shares at $56 per share and retired them. Assume no contributed surplus balances exist from previous share repurchases. (a) Prepare the journal entry to record this transaction if Higgins prepares financial statements in accordance with ASPE. (b) Discuss how the answer to part (a) may be different if Higgins prepared financial statements in accordance with IFRS.

(LO 2) BE15-8 Spencer Limited has 50,000 common shares outstanding, with an average issue price per share of $8. On August 1, 2017, the company reacquired and cancelled 600 shares at $40 per share. There was contributed surplus of $0.25 per share at the time of the reacquisition (total $12,500), which arose from net excess of proceeds over cost on a previous cancellation of common shares. (a) Prepare the journal entry to record this transaction if Spencer prepares financial statements in accordance with ASPE. (b) Discuss how the answer to part (a) may be different if Spencer prepared financial statements in accordance with IFRS.

(LO 2) BE15-9 Abourawes Services Inc. issued 1,000 $2 convertible preferred shares at $75 and 5,000 common shares at $25 each in 2016. Each preferred share is convertible into three common shares. On March 15, 2017, preferred shareholders converted 200 preferred shares into common shares. Record the conversion.

(LO 2) BE15-10 Hamza Inc. declared a cash dividend of $0.60 per share on its 1.5 million outstanding shares. The dividend was declared on August 1 and is payable on September 9 to all shareholders of record on August 15. Prepare all necessary journal entries for those three dates.

(LO 2) BE15-11 Martinez Ltd. has the following equity accounts at January 1, 2017.

Preferred shares outstanding: 2,500 shares	$ 62,500
Common shares outstanding: 4,000 shares	400,000

(a) What was the average issue price of the preferred shares? (b) Of the common shares? (c) If the preferred shares pay a dividend of $1 per share and are participating, what is the per share dividend that would be allocated to the common shares before any additional dividend would be paid to preferred shareholders for participation?

(LO 2) BE15-12 Mallard Inc. owns shares of Oakwood Corporation that are classified as Mallard's fair value through net income (FV-NI) investment portfolio and accounted for using the FV-NI model. At December 31, 2016, the securities were carried in Mallard's accounting records at their cost of $850,000, which equalled their fair value. On September 21, 2017, when the securities' fair value was $1.3 million, Mallard declared a property dividend that will result in the Oakwood securities being distributed on October 23, 2017 to shareholders of record on October 8, 2017. Prepare all necessary journal entries for the three dates.

(LO 2) BE15-13 On April 20, Raule Mining Corp. declared a dividend of $400,000 that is payable on June 1. Of this amount, $150,000 is a return of capital. Raule had no contributed surplus on April 20. Prepare the April 20 and June 1 journal entries for Raule.

(LO 2) BE15-14 Chadwick Corporation has 450,000 common shares outstanding. The corporation declares a 6% stock dividend when the common shares' fair value is $30 per share. (Their carrying value is $18 per share.) Prepare the journal entries for the company for both the date of declaration and the date of distribution.

(LO 2) BE15-15 Kindey Corporation has 185,000 common shares outstanding with a carrying value of $20 per share. Kindey declares a 4-for-1 stock split. (a) How many shares are outstanding after the split? (b) What is the carrying value per share after the split? (c) What is the total carrying value after the split? (d) What journal entry is necessary to record the split?

(LO 2) BE15-16 Use the information for Kindey Corporation from BE15-15. Assume instead that Kindey declared a 1-for-5 reverse stock split, and answer the same questions.

(LO 3) BE15-17 Lu Corporation has the following account balances at December 31, 2017:

Common Shares Subscribed	$ 250,000
Common Shares	310,000
Subscriptions Receivable	80,000
Retained Earnings	1,340,000
Contributed Surplus	320,000
Accumulated Other Comprehensive Income	560,000

Prepare the December 31, 2017 shareholders' equity section of the statement of financial position.

(LO 3) BE15-18 The Sawgrass Corporation, a public company, reported the following balances at January 1, 2017:

Common Shares (32,000 shares issued, unlimited authorized)	$ 800,000
Retained Earnings	1,500,000
Contributed Surplus	145,000
Accumulated Other Comprehensive Income	40,000

During the year ended December 31, 2017, the following summary transactions occurred:

Net income earned during the year	$400,000
Unrealized gain on fair value through other comprehensive income (FV-OCI) investments	25,000
Reduction of contributed surplus during the year due to repurchase of common shares	17,500
Reduction of common shares account balance during the year due to repurchase of 1,000 common shares	25,000
Dividends declared during the year on common shares	70,000
Issued 2,000 common shares during the year	100,000

(a) Prepare a statement of changes in shareholders' equity for the year as required under IFRS.

(b) Prepare the shareholders' equity section of the statement of financial position at December 31.

(c) How would the answer to parts (a) and (b) be different if Sawgrass prepared financial statements in accordance with ASPE?

(LO 5) BE15-19 Khalid Inc. has the following selected financial data:

	2017	2016
Net income	$ 720,000	$ 680,000
Total assets	5,136,000	4,525,000
Preferred shares, 4%, cumulative	600,000	600,000
Common shares	350,000	350,000
Retained earnings	2,786,000	2,190,000
Accumulated other comprehensive income	145,000	130,000
Total shareholders' equity	3,881,000	3,270,000
Cash dividends paid in the year	124,000	170,000
Market price of common shares	$97.46	$64.33
Weighted average number of common shares	80,000	80,000

There were no preferred dividends in arrears. (a) Calculate the following ratios for 2017: (1) rate of return on common shareholders' equity, (2) payout ratio, (3) price earnings ratio, (4) book value, and (5) rate of return on total assets. (b) Is **FINANCE** Khalid Inc. trading on the equity?

(LO 7) *BE15-20 Sullivan Limited issued 2,000 shares of no par value common shares for $79,000. Prepare Sullivan's journal entry if (a) the shares have no par value, and (b) the shares have a par value of $11 per share.

*BE15-21 Hanover Corporation has 750,000 shares outstanding. The shares have an average cost of $45 per share. **(LO 7)** On September 5, 2017, the company repurchases 1,500 of its own shares at $75 per share and does not cancel them. The shares are classified as treasury shares. On November 20, 2017, the company resells 1,000 of the treasury shares at $80 per share. Prepare the journal entries for the repurchase and subsequent sale of the treasury shares.

(LO 7) ***BE15-22**   Use the information for Hanover Corporation in BE15-21. Assume now that the company resells the 1,000 treasury shares at $55 per share. Prepare the journal entries for the repurchase and subsequent sale of the treasury shares.

(LO 8) ***BE15-23**   Tsui Corporation went through a financial reorganization by writing down its buildings by $107,000 and eliminating its deficit, which was $182,000 before the reorganization. As part of the reorganization, the creditors agreed to take back 55% of the common shares in lieu of payment of the debt of $1.8 million (notes payable). Prepare the entries to record the financial reorganization assuming that Tsui follows ASPE.

Exercises

(LO 2) **E15-1**   **(Recording Issuance of Common and Preferred Shares)** Yang Inc. was organized on January 1, 2017. It is authorized to issue an unlimited number of common shares and 100,000 preferred shares with a $4 dividend. The following share transactions were completed during the first year:

Jan. 10   Issued 200,000 common shares for cash at $23 per share.
Mar. 1   Issued 17,000 preferred shares for cash at $119 per share.
Apr. 1   Issued 3,000 common shares for land. The asking price for the land was $67,000; its fair value was $60,000.
May   1   Issued 20,000 common shares for cash at $18 per share.
Aug. 1   Issued 1,000 common shares to lawyers in payment of their bill of $19,000 for services rendered in helping the company incorporate.
Sept. 1   Issued 32,500 common shares for cash at $16 per share.
Nov. 1   Issued 1,500 preferred shares for cash at $125 per share.

Instructions

Prepare the journal entries to record the above transactions.

(LO 2) **E15-2**   **(Subscribed Shares)** Callaghan Inc. decided to sell shares to raise additional capital so that it could expand into the rapidly growing service industry. The corporation chose to sell these shares through a subscription basis and publicly notified the investment world. The offering was 40,000 shares at $22 a share. The terms of the subscription were 35% down and the balance was due at the end of six months. All shares were subscribed for during the offering period.

Instructions

(a) Prepare the journal entries for the original subscription, the collection of the down payments, the collection of the balance of the subscription price, and the issuance of the shares.

(b) Discuss how the Share Subscriptions Receivable account should be presented on the statement of financial position if it is still outstanding at the end of the reporting period.

(c) Discuss how Callaghan should account for the balance in the subscription account and the amounts already collected if the subscriber defaults before making the final payment.

(LO 2) **E15-3**   **(Share Issuances and Repurchase)** As of December 31, 2016, Cayenne Ltd., a public company, has 40,000 common shares outstanding. During 2017, Cayenne had the following transactions.

1. Issued 6,000 common shares at $29 per share, less $2,000 in costs related to the issuance of the shares.

2. Issued 3,750 common shares for land appraised at $130,000. The closing price for the shares traded on the TSX was $32 per share on the date of issuance.

3. Purchased and retired 500 of the company's shares at $28 per share. The repurchased shares have an average issue price per share of $30.

Instructions

(a) Prepare the journal entries to record the three transactions listed.

DIGGING DEEPER   (b) When shares are repurchased, is the original issue price of those individual shares relevant? Explain.

(LO 2) **E15-4**   **(Correcting Entries for Equity Transactions)** Stankovic Inc. recently hired a new accountant with extensive experience in accounting for partnerships. Because of the pressure of the new job, the accountant was unable to review what he had learned earlier about corporation accounting. During the first month, he made the following entries for the corporation's common shares:

May 12	Cash	221,000	
	Common Shares		221,000
	(Issued 13,000 common shares at $17 per share)		
10	Cash	400,000	
	Common Shares		400,000
	(Issued 8,000 preferred shares at $50 per share)		
15	Common Shares	15,000	
	Cash		15,000
	(Purchased and retired 1,000 common shares at $15 per share)		
31	Cash	9,000	
	Common Shares		7,500
	Gain on Sale of Shares		1,500
	(Issued 500 shares at $18 per share)		

Instructions

Assume that no other common share transactions had been recorded earlier. Based on the explanation for each entry, prepare the entries that should have been made for the common share transactions. Explain your reasoning.

(LO 2) E15-5 (Preferred Dividends) The outstanding share capital of Meadowcrest Corporation consists of 3,000 shares of preferred and 7,000 common shares for which $280,000 was received. The preferred shares carry a dividend of $7 per share and have a $100 stated value.

Instructions

FINANCE

DIGGING DEEPER

Assuming that the company has retained earnings of $95,000 that is to be entirely paid out in dividends and that preferred dividends were not paid during the two years preceding the current year, state how much each class of shares should receive under each of the following conditions.

(a) The preferred shares are non-cumulative and non-participating.

(b) The preferred shares are cumulative and non-participating.

(c) The preferred shares are cumulative and participating.

(d) Assume that Meadowcrest's current year net income was $90,000. Calculate the current year payout ratio under each of the conditions above. Comment on the results of your analysis from the perspective of a potential investor.

(LO 2) E15-6 (Preferred Dividends) McNamara Limited's ledger shows the following balances on December 31, 2017:

Preferred shares outstanding: 25,000 shares	$ 625,000
Common shares outstanding: 40,000 shares	3,000,000
Retained earnings	890,000

Instructions

Assuming that the directors decide to declare total dividends in the amount of $445,000, determine how much each class of shares should receive under each of the conditions that follow. Note that one year's dividends are in arrears on the preferred shares, which pay a dividend of $1.50 per share.

(a) The preferred shares are cumulative and fully participating.

(b) The preferred shares are non-cumulative and non-participating.

(c) The preferred shares are non-cumulative and are participating in distributions in excess of a 10% dividend rate on the common shares.

(LO 2) E15-7 (Participating Preferred and Stock Dividend) The following is the shareholders' equity section of Suozzi Corp. at December 31, 2017:

Preferred shares,[a] authorized 100,000 shares; issued 25,000 shares	$ 750,000
Common shares (unlimited authorized, 60,000 issued)	1,800,000
Contributed surplus	150,000
Total paid-in capital	2,700,000
Retained earnings	2,470,500
Total shareholders' equity	$5,170,500

[a] The preferred shares have a $2 dividend rate, are cumulative, and participate in distributions in excess of a $3 dividend on the common shares.

Instructions

(a) No dividends were paid in 2015 or 2016. On December 31, 2017, Suozzi wants to pay a cash dividend of $4 per share to common shareholders. How much cash would be needed for the total amount to be paid to preferred and common shareholders? (*Hint:* When calculating the participating preferred share dividend, round any percent calculations to 2 significant digits).

(b) The company decides instead that it will declare a 15% stock dividend on the outstanding common shares. The common shares' fair value on the date of declaration is $45 per share. Prepare the entry on the date of declaration.

(c) The company decides instead to acquire and cancel 10,500 common shares at the current fair value of $45 per share. Prepare the entry to record the retirement, assuming the contributed surplus balance arose from previous cancellations of common shares.

(LO 2) E15-8   (Dividend Entries) The following data were taken from the statement of financial position accounts of Bedard Corporation on December 31, 2017:

Current assets	$1,040,000
FV-NI investments	824,000
Common shares (unlimited authorized, 600,000 shares issued and outstanding)	6,000,000
Contributed surplus	350,000
Retained earnings	1,840,000

Instructions

Prepare the required journal entries for the following unrelated events in January 2018.

(a) A 6% stock dividend is declared and distributed at a time when the shares' fair value is $48 per share.

(b) A 4-for-1 stock split is effected.

(c) A dividend in kind is declared on January 8, 2018 and paid on January 28, 2018 in fair value-net income investments. The investments have a carrying amount of $160,000 (fair value at December 31, 2017) and a January 8 fair value of $165,000.

(LO 2) E15-9   (Stock Split and Stock Dividend) The common shares of Hoover Inc. are currently selling at $143 per share. The directors want to reduce the share price and increase the share volume before making a new issue. The per share carrying value is $34. There are currently 1 million shares issued and outstanding.

Instructions

(a) Prepare the necessary journal entries assuming that:
   1. The board votes a 2-for-1 stock split.
   2. The board votes a 100% stock dividend.

(b) Briefly discuss the accounting and securities market differences between these two methods of increasing the number of shares outstanding.

(LO 2) E15-10   (Reverse Stock Split and Convertible Preferred Shares) Singh Inc., a public company, has been experiencing financial difficulty in the past few years. As a result, the common shares have been trading at a per share price of just over $1. If the stock trades at below $1 in the future, the stock exchange would delist Singh. To avoid delisting, the Singh board of directors declares a reverse stock split of 1 for 10 shares.

FINANCE

Instructions

(a) Following the reverse stock split, at what market price are the common shares likely to be trading?

(b) From the perspective of a current shareholder, will the board of directors' decision be well received?

(c) Assume that Singh Inc. also has issued and outstanding $4 preferred shares that are convertible into common shares. The conversion rate is 1 preferred share for 5 common shares. Will the reverse stock split affect the $4 per share per year dividend rate? Will the conversion ratio automatically change when the reverse stock split is executed? If so, what would be the new ratio?

(LO 2) E15-11   (Entries for Stock Dividends and Stock Splits) The shareholders' equity accounts of Abbasi Inc. have the following balances on December 31, 2017:

Common shares, 400,000 shares issued and outstanding	$10,000,000
Contributed surplus	300,000
Retained earnings	42,400,000

Common shares are currently selling on the Toronto Stock Exchange at $59.

Instructions

Prepare the appropriate journal entries for each of the following cases.

(a) A stock dividend of 10% is declared and issued.

(b) A stock dividend of 100% is declared and issued.

(c) A 2-for-1 stock split is declared and issued.

(LO 2, 3) E15-12 (Dividends and Shareholders' Equity Section) Falkon Corp. reported the following amounts in the shareholders' equity section of its December 31, 2016 statement of financial position:

Preferred shares, $8 dividend (10,000 shares authorized, 2,000 shares issued)	$ 200,000
Common shares (unlimited authorized, 25,000 issued)	600,000
Contributed surplus	55,000
Retained earnings	250,000
Accumulated other comprehensive income	75,000
Total	$1,180,000

During 2017, the company had the following transactions that affect shareholders' equity.

1. Paid the annual 2016 $8 per share dividend on preferred shares and a $3 per share dividend on common shares. These dividends had been declared on December 31, 2016.

2. Purchased 3,700 shares of its own outstanding common shares for $35 per share and cancelled them.

3. Issued 1,000 shares of preferred shares at $105 per share (at the beginning of the year).

4. Declared a 10% stock dividend on the outstanding common shares when the shares were selling for $45 per share.

5. Issued the stock dividend.

6. Declared the annual 2017 $8 per share dividend on preferred shares and a $2 per share dividend on common shares. These dividends are payable in 2018.

The contributed surplus arose from net excess of proceeds over cost on a previous cancellation of common shares. Total assets at December 31, 2016 were $2,140,000, and total assets at December 31, 2017 were $2,616,000. The company follows IFRS.

DIGGING DEEPER

Instructions

(a) Prepare journal entries to record the transactions above.

(b) Prepare the statement of changes in shareholders' equity for the year ended December 31, 2017.

(c) Prepare the December 31, 2017 shareholders' equity section. Assume 2017 net income was $450,000 and comprehensive income was $455,000.

(d) Calculate the rate of return on common shareholders' equity and the rate of return on total assets for 2017. Is Falkon trading on the equity? Evaluate the results from the perspective of a common shareholder.

FINANCE

(LO 2, 3) E15-13 (Statement of Changes in Shareholders' Equity) Miss M's Dance Studios Ltd. is a public company, and accordingly uses IFRS for financial reporting. The corporate charter authorizes the issuance of an unlimited number of common shares and 50,000 preferred shares with a $2 dividend. At the beginning of the December 31, 2017 year, the opening account balances indicated that 25,000 common shares had been issued for $4 per share, and no preferred shares had been issued. Opening retained earnings were $365,000. The transactions during the year were as follows:

Jan.	15	Issued 10,000 common shares at $6 per share.
Feb.	12	Issued 2,000 preferred shares at $60 per share.
Sept.	2	Issued 5,000 common shares in exchange for land valued at $25,000.
Oct.	31	Declared and paid a dividend on preferred shares of $2 per share.
Nov.	1	Declared and paid a dividend on common shares of $1.50 per share.
	15	Purchased and retired 500 preferred shares at $62 per share.
Dec.	31	After preliminary closing entries, the Income Summary account had a credit balance of $232,000.

Instructions

(a) Prepare journal entries to record the transactions above.

(b) Prepare the statement of changes in shareholders' equity.

(c) Prepare the closing entries for the income summary and dividends at December 31, 2017.

(LO 2, 3) **E15-14** **(Equity Transactions and Statement of Changes in Shareholders' Equity)** On January 1, 2017, Copeland Ltd. (a public company) had the following shareholders' equity accounts:

Preferred shares, $5 non-cumulative, unlimited number authorized, none issued	–0–
Common shares, unlimited number authorized, 800,000 issued	$5,600,000
Retained earnings	1,323,000
Accumulated other comprehensive income	142,000

The following selected transactions occurred during 2017:

Jan.	2	Issued 100,000 preferred shares at $100 per share.
Mar.	5	Declared the quarterly cash dividend to preferred shareholders of record on March 20, payable April 1.
Apr.	18	Issued 130,000 common shares at $11 per share.
June	5	Declared the quarterly cash dividend to preferred shareholders of record on June 20, payable July 1.
Sept.	5	Declared the quarterly cash dividend to preferred shareholders of record on September 20, payable October 1.
Dec.	5	Declared the quarterly cash dividend to preferred shareholders of record on December 20, payable January 1.
	31	Net income for the year was $374,000.

Instructions

(a) Prepare journal entries to record the transactions above, as well as the closing entries for Income Summary and Dividends.

(b) Post the entries to the shareholders' equity and dividends T accounts.

(c) Prepare the statement of changes in shareholders' equity for the year.

(d) Prepare the shareholders' equity section of the statement of financial position at December 31.

(e) Prepare the financing activities section of the statement of cash flows for the year ended December 31.

(LO 2, 3, 5) ***E15-15** **(Shareholders' Equity Section)** Radford Corporation's charter authorized 1 million shares of $11 par value common shares, and 300,000 shares of 6% cumulative and non-participating preferred shares, with a par value of $100 per share. The corporation made the following share transactions through December 31, 2017: 300,000 common shares were issued for $3.6 million and 10,000 preferred shares were issued for machinery valued at $1,475,000. Subscriptions for 10,500 common shares have been taken, and 30% of the subscription price of $16 per share has been collected. The shares will be issued upon collection of the subscription price in full. In addition, 10,000 common shares have been repurchased for $15 and retired. The Retained Earnings balance is $180,000 before considering the transactions above.

DIGGING DEEPER

Instructions

(a) Prepare the shareholders' equity section of the statement of financial position in good form.

(b) Repeat part (a) assuming the common shares and preferred shares are no par.

FINANCE

(c) Discuss the alternative presentations of the Share Subscriptions Receivable account. Would the presentation of the receivable affect the book value or the rate of return on shareholders' equity?

(LO 2, 6) **E15-16** **(Equity Items on Statement of Financial Position)** The following are selected transactions that may affect shareholders' equity.

1. Converted bonds to common shares.

2. Declared a cash dividend.

3. Effected a stock split.

4. Recorded the expiration of insurance coverage that was previously recorded as prepaid insurance.

5. Paid the cash dividend declared in item 2 above.

6. Recorded accrued interest expense on a note payable.

7. Recorded an increase in the fair value of an FV-OCI investment that will be distributed as a property dividend. The carrying amount of the FV-OCI investment was greater than its cost. The shares are traded in an active market.

8. Declared a property dividend (see item 7 above).

9. Distributed the investment to shareholders (see items 7 and 8 above).

10. Declared a stock dividend.

11. Distributed the stock dividend declared in item 10.

12. Repurchased common shares for less than their initial issue price.

13. Converted preferred shares into common shares.

Instructions

(a) In the table below, assuming the company follows IFRS (including IAS 39), indicate the effect that each of the 13 transactions has on the financial statement elements that are listed. Use the following codes: increase (I), decrease (D), and no effect (NE). Indicate I/D where there is both an increase and a decrease to the same element.

Item	Assets	Liabilities	Shareholders' Equity	Share Capital	Cont. Surplus	Retained Earnings	Acc. Other Compr. Income	Net Income

(b) Would the effect of any of the above items change if the company were to follow ASPE?

(LO 3) E15-17 (Shareholders' Equity Section) Brubacher Corporation's post-closing trial balance at December 31, 2017 was as follows:

BRUBACHER LIMITED
Post-Closing Trial Balance
December 31, 2017

	Dr.	Cr.
Accounts payable		$ 310,000
Accounts receivable	$ 480,000	
Accumulated depreciation—buildings		185,000
Accumulated other comprehensive income		100,000
Allowance for doubtful accounts		30,000
Bonds payable		300,000
Buildings	1,450,000	
Cash	190,000	
Common shares		200,000
Contributed surplus—common		1,460,000
Dividends payable on preferred shares		4,000
Inventories	360,000	
FV-NI investments	200,000	
Land	400,000	
Preferred shares		500,000
Prepaid expenses	40,000	
Retained earnings		201,000
Treasury shares (10,000 common shares)	170,000	
Totals	$3,290,000	$3,290,000

At December 31, 2017, Brubacher had the following numbers for its common and preferred shares:

	Common	Preferred
Authorized	600,000	60,000
Issued	200,000	10,000
Outstanding	190,000	10,000

The dividends on preferred shares are $5 cumulative. In addition, the preferred shares have a preference in liquidation of $50 per share.

Instructions

Prepare the shareholders' equity section of Brubacher's statement of financial position at December 31, 2017. The company follows IFRS.

(AICPA adapted)

(LO 5) E15-18 (Comparison of Alternative Forms of Financing) What follows are the liabilities and shareholders' equity sections of the statements of financial position for Kao Corp. and Bennington Corp. Each has assets totalling $4.2 million.

Kao Corp.		Bennington Corp.	
Current liabilities	$ 300,000	Current liabilities	$ 600,000
Long-term debt, 10%	1,200,000	Common shares	
Common shares		(145,000 shares issued)	2,900,000
(100,000 shares issued)	2,000,000	Retained earnings	
Retained earnings		(Cash dividends, $328,000)	700,000
(Cash dividends, $220,000)	700,000		
	$4,200,000		$4,200,000

For the year, each company has earned the same income before interest and tax.

	Kao Corp.	Bennington Corp.
Income before interest and taxes	$1,200,000	$1,200,000
Interest expense	120,000	–0–
	1,080,000	1,200,000
Income taxes (30%)	324,000	360,000
Net income	$ 756,000	$ 840,000

At year end, the market price of Kao's shares was $101 per share; it was $63.50 for Bennington's.

Instructions

(a) Which company is more profitable in terms of return on total assets?

(b) Which company is more profitable in terms of return on shareholders' equity?

(c) Which company has the greater net income per share? Neither company issued or reacquired shares during the year.

(d) From the point of view of income, is it advantageous to Kao's shareholders to have the long-term debt outstanding? Why or why not?

(e) What is each company's price earnings ratio?

(f) What is the book value per share for each company?

(LO 8) *E15-19 (Financial Reorganization) The following account balances are available from the ledger of Yutao Shui Corporation on December 31, 2016:

Common Shares (20,000 shares authorized and outstanding)	$1,000,000
Retained Earnings (Deficit)	(190,000)

On January 2, 2017, the corporation put into effect a shareholder-approved reorganization by agreeing to pass the common shares over to the creditors in full payment of the $260,000 Notes Payable, writing up Buildings by $135,600, and eliminating the deficit. Assume that Yutao Shui follows ASPE.

Instructions

Prepare the required journal entries for the financial reorganization of Yutao Shui Corporation.

(LO 8) *E15-20 (Financial Reorganization) The condensed balance sheets of Rockford Limited, a small private company that follows ASPE, follow for the periods immediately before, and one year after, it had completed a financial reorganization:

	Before Reorganization	One Year After		Before Reorganization	One Year After
Current assets	$ 300,000	$ 420,000	Common shares	$2,400,000	$1,550,000
Buildings (net)	1,700,000	1,290,000	Contributed surplus	220,000	
	$2,000,000	$1,710,000	Retained earnings	(620,000)	160,000
				$2,000,000	$1,710,000

For the year following the financial reorganization, the company reported net income of $190,000 and depreciation expense of $80,000, and paid a cash dividend of $30,000. As part of the reorganization, the company wrote down inventories by $120,000 in order to reflect circumstances that existed before the reorganization. Also, the deficit, and any revaluation adjustment, was accounted for by charging amounts against contributed surplus until it was eliminated, with any remaining amount being charged against common shares. The common shares are widely held and there is no controlling interest. No purchases or sales of plant assets and no share transactions occurred in the year following the reorganization.

Instructions

Prepare all the journal entries made at the time of the reorganization.

Problems

P15-1   Transactions of Kent Corporation are as follows.

1. The company is granted a charter that authorizes the issuance of 150,000 preferred shares and an unlimited number of common shares.

2. The founders of the corporation are issued 10,000 common shares for land valued by the board of directors at $210,000 (based on an independent valuation).

3. Sold 15,200 preferred shares for cash at $110 per share.

4. Repurchased and cancelled 3,000 shares of outstanding preferred shares for cash at $100 per share.

5. Paid $85,000 in dividends that were declared in the previous period.

6. Repurchased for cash and cancelled 500 shares of the outstanding common shares issued in item 2 above at $49 per share.

7. Issued 2,000 preferred shares at $99 per share.

Instructions

**DIGGING
DEEPER**

FINANCE

(a) Prepare entries in journal form to record the transactions listed above. No other transactions affecting the capital share accounts have occurred.

(b) Assuming that the company has retained earnings from operations of $1,032,000, prepare the shareholders' equity section of its statement of financial position after considering all the transactions above.

(c) Why is the distinction between paid-in capital and retained earnings important?

(d) Describe the features of callable/redeemable preferred shares. Outline how the corporation can make use of these features to the benefit of the corporation.

(e) Describe the features of retractable preferred shares. Outline how this feature gives an advantage to the shareholder.

P15-2   Oregano Inc. was formed on July 1, 2014. It was authorized to issue an unlimited number of common shares and 100,000 shares of cumulative and non-participating preferred shares carrying a $2 dividend. The company has a July 1 to June 30 fiscal year. The following information relates to the company's shareholders' equity account.

Common Shares

Before the 2016–17 fiscal year, the company had 110,000 outstanding common shares issued as follows:

1. 95,000 shares issued for cash on July 1, 2014, at $31 per share

2. 5,000 shares exchanged on July 24, 2014 for a plot of land that cost the seller $70,000 in 2004 and had an estimated fair value of $220,000 on July 24, 2014

3. 10,000 shares issued on March 1, 2015; the shares had been subscribed for $42 per share on October 31, 2014

Oct. 1, 2016	Subscriptions were received for 10,000 shares at $46 per share. Cash of $92,000 was received in full payment for 2,000 shares and share certificates were issued. The remaining subscription for 8,000 shares was to be paid in full by September 30, 2017 and the certificates would then be issued on that date.
Nov. 30, 2016	The company purchased 2,000 of its own common shares on the open market at $39 per share. These shares were restored to the status of authorized but unissued shares.
Dec. 15, 2016	The company declared a 5% stock dividend for shareholders of record on January 15, 2017 to be issued on January 31, 2017. The company's common shares were selling at $52 per share on December 15, 2016.
June 20, 2017	The company sold 500 of its own common shares for $21,000.

Preferred Shares

The company issued 50,000 preferred shares at $44 per share on July 1, 2014.

Cash Dividends

The company has followed a schedule of declaring cash dividends each year in December and June and making the payment to shareholders of record in the following month. The cash dividend declarations have been as follows since the company's first year and up until June 30, 2017:

Declaration Date	Common Shares	Preferred Shares
Dec. 15, 2015	$0.30 per share	$3.00 per share*
June 6, 2016	$0.30 per share	$1.00 per share
Dec. 15, 2016	—	$1.00 per share

*Includes dividend arrears of $2 from the 2014–15 fiscal year

No cash dividends were declared to common shareholders during June 2017 due to the company's liquidity problems.

Retained Earnings

DIGGING DEEPER

As at June 30, 2016, the company's Retained Earnings account had a balance of $690,000. For the fiscal year ended June 30, 2017, the company reported net income of $40,000.

Instructions

FINANCE

(a) Prepare the shareholders' equity section of the company's statement of financial position as at June 30, 2017, as it should appear in its annual report to the shareholders.

(b) Prepare the journal entries for the 2016–17 fiscal year.

(c) Discuss why the common shareholders might be willing to accept a stock dividend during the year rather than a cash dividend.

(CMA adapted)

P15-3   Parker Corporation's charter authorizes the issuance of 1 million common shares and 500,000 preferred shares that have a dividend rate of $6 per share per year. The following transactions involving share issues were completed. Assume that Parker follows IFRS and that each transaction is independent of the others.

1. Issued 4,200 common shares for machinery. The machinery had been appraised at $74,500, and the seller's carrying amount was $58,600. The common shares' most recent market price is $18 a share.

2. The board of directors declared a $6 dividend on both the 17,000 shares of outstanding common and the 40,000 shares of outstanding preferred.

3. Issued 2,500 common shares and 1,200 preferred shares for a lump sum of $125,000. The common shares had been selling at $13 and the preferred at $80.

4. Issued 2,200 common shares and 135 preferred shares for furniture. The common shares had a fair value of $14 per share and the furniture was appraised at $36,000.

Instructions

Prepare the journal entries to record the transactions.

†P15-4   Manitoba Deck System Corporation (MDSC) is a public company whose shares are actively traded on the Toronto Stock Exchange. The following transactions occurred in 2017:

Jan.	1	The company was granted a charter that authorizes the issuance of an unlimited number of common shares, and 250,000 preferred shares that entitle the holder to a $4 per share annual dividend.
	10	Issued 10,000 common shares to the founders of the corporation for land that has a fair value of $450,000.
Mar.	10	Issued 4,000 preferred shares for cash for $100 per share.
Apr.	15	Issued 110 common shares to a car dealer in exchange for a used vehicle. The asking price for the car is $6,400. The asking price is negotiable. At the time of the exchange, the common shares are selling at $55 per share.
Aug.	20	Decided to issue shares on a subscription basis to select individuals, giving each person the right to purchase 250 common shares at $60 per share. Forty individuals accepted the company's offer and agreed to pay 10% down and the remainder in three equal monthly instalments starting in February 2018.
Oct.	11	Issued 3,000 common shares and 600 preferred shares for a lump sum of $230,000 cash. At the time of sale, both the common and preferred shares were actively traded. The common shares were trading at $58 each; the preferred shares at $105 each.
Dec.	31	Declared cash dividends totalling $26,000, payable on January 31, 2018, to holders of record on January 15, 2018.

Instructions

(a) Prepare the general journal entries to record the transactions.

(b) Provide support for the exchange value of the April 15, 2017 transaction, referring to the conceptual framework.

DIGGING DEEPER

†This item was originally published by *Certified General Accountants Association of Canada* (CGA Canada) as an examination question. Adapted with permission of the Chartered Professional Accountants of Canada, Toronto, Canada. Any changes to the original material are the sole responsibility of the publisher and have not been reviewed or endorsed by the Chartered Professional Accountants of Canada.

P15-5 Kanish Corporation's general ledger includes the following account balances:

Contributed Surplus	Common Shares	Retained Earnings
$8,000	$270,000	$85,000

The Contributed Surplus account arose from net excess of proceeds over cost on a previous cancellation of common shares. The average cost of the common shares bought and cancelled in the first two transactions is $30 per share.

Instructions

Assuming that the above balances existed before any of the transactions that follow, record the journal entries for each transaction.

(a) Bought and cancelled 430 shares at $38 per share.

(b) Bought and cancelled 200 shares at $44 per share.

(c) Sold 3,200 shares at $41 per share.

(d) Sold 1,500 shares at $47 per share.

(e) Bought and cancelled 1,000 shares at $50 per share.

P15-6 Stellar Corp. had the following shareholders' equity on January 1, 2017:

Common shares, unlimited number authorized, 100,000 shares issued and outstanding	$ 270,000
Contributed surplus	310,000
Retained earnings	2,300,000
Total shareholders' equity	$2,880,000

The contributed surplus arose from net excess of proceeds over cost on a previous cancellation of common shares. Stellar prepares financial statements in accordance with ASPE.

The following transactions occurred, in the order given, during 2017.

1. Subscriptions were sold for 12,000 common shares at $26 per share. The first payment was for $10 per share.

2. The second payment for the sale in item 1 above was for $16 per share. All payments were received on the second payment except for 2,000 shares.

3. In accordance with the subscription contract, which requires that defaulting subscribers have all their payments refunded, a refund cheque was sent to the defaulting subscribers. At this point, common shares were issued to subscribers who had fully paid on the contract.

4. Repurchased 22,000 common shares at $29 per share. They were then retired.

5. Sold 5,000 preferred shares and 3,000 common shares together for $300,000. The common shares had a fair value of $31 per share.

Instructions

(a) Prepare the journal entries to record the transactions for the company for 2017.

(b) Assume that the subscription contract states that defaulting subscribers forfeit their first payment. Prepare the journal entries for items 2 to 4 above.

DIGGING DEEPER

(c) Discuss how Stellar may have determined the fair value of its common shares, given that the company prepares financial statements in accordance with ASPE and is a private company.

FINANCE

P15-7 Original Octave Inc. (OOI) is a widely held, publicly traded company that designs equipment for tuning musical instruments. Information about its shareholders' equity is as follows.

ORIGINAL OCTAVE INC.
Shareholders' Equity
December 31, 2016

Share capital	
Preferred shares, no par value, $8, cumulative, and participating	
(20,000 authorized; 1,000 issued and outstanding)	$100,000
Common shares, unlimited number authorized, 40,000 issued and outstanding	500,000
Contributed capital, preferred share retirement	20,000
	620,000
Retained earnings	280,000
Shareholders' equity	$900,000

The preferred share dividend was not paid in 2016.

Several transactions affecting shareholders' equity took place during the fiscal year ended December 31, 2017 and are summarized in chronological order as follows.

1. Exchanged 10,000 common shares for prototype piano tuning equipment. The equipment was valued at $100,000 by an independent appraiser. On the transaction date, OOI's shares were actively trading at $10 per share.

2. Purchased and retired 10,000 common shares at $12.50 per share.

3. Paid the annual dividend on the preferred shares. The common shares were then paid a $2 per share dividend.

Original Octave's net income for 2017 was $65,000.

Instructions

(a) Prepare journal entries for each of the three transactions.

(b) Calculate the company's payout ratio for 2017. Would the payout ratio for 2017 be different if the preferred share dividend was paid in 2016?

(c) Comment on the results of your analysis from the perspective of a potential investor.

*P15-8 Laurentian Mills Ltd. had the following shareholders' equity at January 1, 2017.

Preferred shares, 8%, $100 par value, 10,000 shares authorized, 4,000 shares issued	$ 400,000
Common shares, $2 par value, 200,000 shares authorized, 80,000 shares issued	160,000
Common shares subscribed, 10,000 shares	20,000
Contributed surplus—preferred	20,000
Contributed surplus—common	940,000
Retained earnings	780,000
	2,320,000
Less: Common share subscriptions receivable	40,000
Total shareholders' equity	$2,280,000

The contributed surplus accounts arose from amounts received in excess of the par value of the shares when issued. During 2017, the following transactions occurred:

1. Equipment was purchased in exchange for 100 common shares. The shares' fair value on the exchange date was $12 per share.

2. Sold 1,000 common shares and 100 preferred shares for the lump-sum price of $24,500. The common shares had a market price of $14 at the time of the sale.

3. Sold 2,000 preferred shares for cash at $102 per share.

4. All of the subscribers paid their subscription prices into the firm.

5. The common shares subscribed were issued.

6. Repurchased and retired 1,000 common shares at $15 per share.

7. Net income for 2017 was $246,000.

Instructions
Prepare the shareholders' equity section for the company as at December 31, 2017. (The use of T accounts may help you organize the material.)

P15-9 The books of Binkerton Corporation carried the following account balances as at December 1, 2017:

Cash	$1,300,000
Preferred shares, $2 cumulative dividend, non-participating, 25,000 shares issued	750,000
Common shares, 300,000 shares issued	4,500,000
Contributed surplus (preferred)	150,000
Retained earnings	327,000

The preferred shares have dividends in arrears for the past year (2016). On December 21, 2017, the board of directors declared the following: The current year dividends shall be $2 per share on the preferred and $0.70 per share on the common; the dividends in arrears shall be paid first by issuing one share of common shares for each 10 shares of preferred held.

The preferred shares are currently selling at $35 per share and the common shares at $20 per share. Net income for the year ending December 31, 2017 is estimated at $56,000.

Instructions

DIGGING DEEPER

(a) Prepare the journal entries that are required for the dividend declaration, distribution, and payment, assuming that they occur at the same time.

(b) Could the company give the preferred shareholders two years of cash dividends and common shareholders a $0.70 per share dividend, all in cash? Explain your reasoning.

P15-10 Lasson Corp. has 5,000 preferred shares outstanding ($2 dividend), which were issued for $150,000, and 30,000 common shares, which were issued for $550,000.

Instructions

The following schedule shows the amount of dividends paid out over the past four years. Allocate the dividends to each type of share under assumptions (a) and (b). Express your answers in per share amounts and using the format that is shown. Round amounts to the nearest cent.

		Assumptions			
		(a)		(b)	
		Preferred, non-cumulative, and non-participating		Preferred, cumulative, and fully participating	
Year	Paid-out	Preferred	Common	Preferred	Common
2014	$ 8,000				
2015	$ 24,000				
2016	$ 60,000				
2017	$126,000				

P15-11 Guoping Limited provides you with the following condensed statement of financial position information:

Assets		Liabilities and Shareholders' Equity		
Current assets	$ 40,000	Current and long-term liabilities		$100,000
Investments in Geneva Inc.—		Shareholders' equity		
fair value through net income		Common shares		
(10,000 shares)	60,000	10,000 shares issued	$130,000	
Equipment (net)	250,000	Retained earnings	180,000	310,000
Intangibles	60,000	Total liabilities and		
Total assets	$410,000	shareholders' equity		$410,000

Instructions

(a) For each transaction below, indicate the dollar impact (if any) on the following four items: (1) total assets, (2) common shares, (3) retained earnings, and (4) shareholders' equity. (Each situation is independent.)

1. The company declares and pays a $0.50 per share dividend.

2. The company declares and issues a 10% stock dividend when the shares' market price is $12 per share.

3. The company declares and issues a 40% stock dividend when the shares' market price is $17 per share.

4. The company declares and distributes a property dividend. The company gives one Geneva share for every two company shares held. Geneva is selling for $8 per share on the date when the property dividend is declared.

5. The company declares a 3-for-1 stock split and issues new shares.

DIGGING DEEPER

(b) What are the differences between a stock dividend and a cash or property dividend?

P15-12 Some of the account balances of Vos Limited at December 31, 2016 are as follows:

$6 Preferred shares (2,000 shares authorized, 2,000 shares issued and outstanding)	$520,000
Common shares (unlimited authorized, 50,000 shares issued and outstanding)	500,000
Contributed surplus	103,000
Retained earnings	774,000
Accumulated other comprehensive income	22,350

The price of the company's common shares has been increasing steadily on the market; it was $21 on January 1, 2017 and advanced to $24 by July 1 and to $27 at the end of 2017. The preferred shares are not openly traded but were appraised at $120 per share during 2017. Vos follows IFRS and had net income of $154,000 during 2017.

Instructions

(a) Prepare the journal entries for each of the following.

1. The company declared a property dividend on April 1. Each common shareholder was to receive one share of Waterloo Corp. for every 10 shares outstanding. Vos had 8,000 shares of Waterloo (2% of the outstanding shares), and had purchased them in 2012 for $68,400. The shares are accounted for using the FV-OCI model. The accumulated other comprehensive income relates only to these shares. The fair value of the Waterloo shares was $16 per share on April 1. The property dividend was distributed on April 21 when the fair value of the Waterloo shares was $18.50. The Waterloo shares remained at a fair value of $18.50 until year end.

2. On July 1, the company declared a 5% stock dividend to the remaining common shareholders. The stock dividend was distributed July 22.

3. A shareholder, in an effort to persuade Vos to expand into her city, donated to the company a plot of land with an appraised value of $42,000.

(b) Prepare the shareholders' equity section of Vos's statement of financial position at December 31, 2017.

DIGGING DEEPER

(c) How should Vos account for the difference in fair value of the Waterloo shares between the date of declaration and date of distribution? Does the declaration of a property dividend create a financial liability?

P15-13   Perfect Ponds Inc. (PPI) is a backyard pond design and installation company. PPI was incorporated during 2017, with an unlimited number of common shares, and 50,000 preferred shares with a $3 dividend rate authorized. PPI follows ASPE. The following transactions took place during the first year of operations with respect to these shares:

Jan.	1	The articles of incorporation were filed and state that an unlimited number of common shares and 50,000 preferred shares are authorized.
	15	30,000 common shares were sold by subscription to three individuals, who each purchased 10,000 shares for $50 per share. The terms require 10% of the balance to be paid in cash immediately. The balance was to be paid by December 31, 2018, at which time the shares will be issued.
Feb.	20	70,000 common shares were sold by subscription to seven individuals, who each purchased 10,000 shares for $50 per share. The terms require that 10% of the balance be paid in cash immediately, with the balance to be paid by December 31, 2017. Shares are to be issued once the full payment is received.
Mar.	3	50,000 common shares were sold by an underwriter for $52 per share. The underwriter charged PPI a 5% commission on the sale.
May	10	PPI paid $2,000 to a printing company for costs involved in printing common share certificates. As well, an invoice for legal fees related to the issue of common shares was received for $15,000.
Sept.	23	PPI issued a combination of 2,000 common and 1,000 preferred shares to a new shareholder for a total price of $200,000. PPI was unable to estimate a fair value of the preferred shares, and the most recent sale of common shares was used to estimate the value of the common share portion of the transaction.
Nov.	28	PPI wanted to recognize the efforts of a key employee and offered him the opportunity to purchase 500 common shares for $52, to be paid by December 31, 2018. The employee accepted the offer. No interest was to be charged on the outstanding balance; however, the shares were issued immediately.
Dec.	31	Of the seven subscriptions issued on February 20, five subscriptions were paid in full and two subscribers defaulted. According to the subscription contract, the defaulting subscribers would not be issued shares for any amount that had been paid and no cash would be refunded.
	31	PPI declared a dividend of $200,000 for 2017. Net income for the year was $800,000.

Instructions

(a) Prepare the journal entries to record the transactions for the year.

(b) What was amount of the dividend per share declared on December 31? Round to the nearest cent.

DIGGING DEEPER

(c) Prepare the shareholders' equity section of the balance sheet as of December 31, 2017.

(d) Provide support for the statement of financial position presentation of the November 28 transaction, referring to the conceptual framework.

P15-14   Secord Limited has two classes of shares outstanding: preferred ($6 dividend) and common. At December 31, 2016, the following accounts and balances were included in shareholders' equity:

Preferred shares, 300,000 shares issued (authorized, 1,000,000 shares)	$ 3,000,000
Common shares, 1,000,000 shares (authorized, unlimited)	25,000,000
Contributed surplus—preferred	200,000
Contributed surplus—common	2,000,000
Retained earnings	5,500,000
Accumulated other comprehensive income	250,000

The contributed surplus accounts arose from net excess of proceeds over cost on previous cancellations of shares of each respective class. The following transactions affected shareholders' equity during 2017:

Jan.	1	Issued 25,000 preferred shares at $25 per share.
Feb.	1	Issued 50,000 common shares at $20 per share.
June	1	Declared a 2-for-1 stock split (common shares).
July	1	Purchased and retired 30,000 common shares at $15 per share. Round average cost of shares to the nearest cent.
Dec.	31	Net income is $2.1 million; comprehensive income is $2,050,000.
	31	The preferred dividend is declared, and a common dividend of $0.50 per share is declared.

Assume that Secord follows IFRS.

Instructions

(a) Prepare the statement of changes in shareholders' equity and the shareholders' equity section of the statement of financial position for the company at December 31, 2017. Show all supporting calculations using T accounts.

(b) Prepare the journal entry for the repurchase of 30,000 common shares on July 1, 2017.

(c) Prepare the journal entry for the repurchase of 30,000 common shares assuming instead that the repurchase took place on May 31 at the same repurchase price of $15. Round average cost of shares to the nearest cent. What effect will the change in the date have on total shareholders' equity?

(d) How would the answer to part (a) be different if Secord followed ASPE?

P15-15 Gateway Corporation has outstanding 200,000 common shares that were issued at $10 per share. The balances at January 1, 2017 were $21 million in its Retained Earnings account; $4.3 million in its Contributed Surplus account; and $1.1 million in its Accumulated Other Comprehensive Income account. During 2017, Gateway's net income was $3.2 million and comprehensive income was $3,350,000. A cash dividend of $0.70 per share was declared and paid on June 30, 2017, and a 5% stock dividend was declared and distributed to shareholders of record at the close of business on December 31, 2017. You have been asked to give advice on how to properly account for the stock dividend. The existing company shares are traded on a national stock exchange. The shares' market price per share has been as follows:

Oct. 31, 2017	$31
Nov. 30, 2017	33
Dec. 31, 2017	38
Average price over the two-month period	35

Instructions

(a) Prepare a journal entry to record the cash dividend.

(b) Prepare a journal entry to record the stock dividend.

(c) Prepare Gateway's shareholders' equity section (of the statement of financial position) for the year 2017 based on the information given. Prepare a schedule outlining the activity to the Retained Earnings account for the year. Write a note to the financial statements that states the accounting basis for the stock dividend.

(d) Prepare a statement of changes in shareholders' equity for 2017.

Case

ENABLING COMPETENCIES

Refer to the Case Primer on the Student Website and in *WileyPLUS* to help you answer this case.

*CA15-1 "You can't write up assets," said Nick Toby, internal audit director of Nadir International Inc., to his boss, Jim Majewski, vice-president and chief financial officer. "Nonsense," said Jim, "I can do this as part of a quasi-reorganization of our company." For the past three years, Nadir International, a farm equipment manufacturing firm, has experienced a downturn in its profits as a result of stiff competition with overseas firms and a general downturn in the North American economy. The company is hoping to turn a profit by modernizing its property, plant, and equipment. This will require Nadir

International to raise a lot of money. Management is very optimistic as to the future of the company, as the economy is entering a significant growth period.

Over the past few months, Jim has tried to raise funds from various financial institutions, but they are unwilling to lend capital. The reason they give is that the company's net book value of fixed assets on the balance sheet, based on historic cost, is not large enough to sustain major funding. Jim attempted to explain to bankers and investors that these assets are more valuable than their recorded amounts, especially since the company used accelerated amortization methods and tended to underestimate the useful lives of assets. Jim also believes that the company's land and buildings are substantially undervalued because of rising real estate prices over the past several years.

Jim's proposed solution to raise funds is a simple one: First, declare a large dividend to company share-holders that results in Retained Earnings having a large debit balance. Then, write up the fixed assets of Nadir International to an amount that is equal to the deficit in the Retained Earnings account.

AUDIT AND ASSURANCE

Instructions

Adopt the role of the internal auditor and discuss the financial reporting issues. Nadir is thinking of going public.

Integrated Cases

ENABLING COMPETENCIES

IC15-1   Sandolin Incorporated (SI) is a global, diversified firm whose shares trade on the major Canadian and U.S. stock markets. It owns numerous toll highways, several companies in the energy business, and an engineering consulting firm. Currently, its shares are trading at a 52-week high and its credit rating on all debt issues is AA. This is partly due to its revenues, which have doubled, and is also due to a recent restructuring. The restructuring is in the energy business and allows the company to position itself as a low-cost competitor in the industry. The restructuring involved laying off 5,000 employees and mothballing several oil and gas wells. The cost to extract oil and gas from the wells is currently too high. The company plans to retain the wells and work on new technology to reduce the extraction costs.

SI is putting together its annual financial statements and the VP Finance, Santos Suarez, is planning to meet with the company's auditors next week for a preliminary audit planning meeting. Santos is concerned about a phone call that he recently received from the government, as it was threatening legal action relating to the transportation part of the business. Among other things, SI owns a toll highway that stretches approximately 100 km across a major urban centre. The road is very profitable because non-toll roads in the area are congested and people use the toll road to commute. SI recently raised toll rates on the road and the government is claiming it is prohibited from doing this without government consent, which the government does not plan to give. Santos is concerned that if this news gets out, the credit rating and

share price will suffer. SI believes that its contract allows it to change toll rates whenever it wants. SI's lawyers have reviewed the contracts and feel that SI's position is justifiable. The value of the toll road as a business is substantially less if the company loses the right to change the tolls.

While reviewing the company's dramatic increase in revenues, Santos became aware of a new type of transaction that the company has been entering into with increasing frequency in the past two months. As part of the energy business, SI employs a group of traders who make deals that reduce the company's exposure to fluctuating commodity prices. According to several e-mails between the traders, the deals are known as "round trip" trades. Several large trades involved purchases and sales with the same party for the same volume at substantially the same price. They have been treated as sales and account for 40% of the increase in revenues. The trader's position is that the company does make a commission on these deals, which adds up depending on the volume. The company never takes possession of the commodity that is being bought and sold.

Just before year end, the company acquired a mid-sized engineering firm. As part of the deal, the company issued shares to the vendor. The value of the issued shares was higher than the fair value of the engineering firm and the vendor gave SI a one-year note receivable for the difference. If profits from the engineering firm exceed a certain threshold—in other words, if the firm outperforms expectations—the note will not be paid. Currently, SI has recorded the note receivable as an asset.

AUDIT AND ASSURANCE

Instructions

Adopt the role of Santos Suarez and analyze the financial reporting issues.

IC15-2   Wind and Solar Inc. (WSI) is in the business of providing electricity. The company started up in 2016. Currently, it is owned by Winifred Wind and Winston Chang. Both Winston and Winifred own 50% of the WSI common shares. Under the terms of the shareholder agreement, either party may buy the other out at a price of 10 times the current net income. This buyout clause becomes effective immediately. WSI plans to go public within five years if all goes well.

During the year, the company obtained financing from the local bank and purchased land on which it has built large wind turbines (windmills) and solar panels. The company will be generating electrical energy through wind power and solar power. The loan was also

used to finance the construction of the windmills and solar panels. Under the terms of the loan, the company must maintain a debt to equity ratio of 1:1.

The cost of building windmills and wind turbines is very expensive and as a result, half way through the year, the company had used up all of the bank financing. The bank declined to advance more funds. Winston and Winifred entered into an agreement with Windy Developments (WD) to help them build more windmills. Under the terms of the agreement, WD will advance the funds needed to build the windmills upfront. In return, WSI has agreed to pay WD a percentage of the revenues generated from the additional windmills once they become operational. The additional windmills are 50% complete.

WSI has several engineers working on the projects who are currently not being paid a salary for their services. Instead, they have been given shares in the company. WSI has set aside 10% of the total shares outstanding in order to remunerate the engineers. Under the terms of this agreement, the engineers may convert their shares to cash at the end of 2017. WSI plans to have a valuation done of the company at the end of 2017 and 10% of the value will be attributable to the engineers' shares. The valuation will be based on the average income from 2016 and 2017.

During 2016, some of the windmills and solar panels were up and running and had started to generate revenues. The company's largest customer was the local government, which had signed a contract with WSI to purchase half of the output of electricity for 2016 and 2017. At a minimum, the government was locked in to pay $1 million. The price per KW hour was fixed upfront and the government had already paid half of the money in advance. The contract was non-cancellable, and even if WSI was unable to deliver the minimum amount of electricity, the government would still be committed to pay the full $1 million. The government noted that it considered the $1 million as a type of grant to support the development of clean energy and was happy to pay the funds in order to support the clean energy movement.

By the end of 2016, Winston had decided that he wanted Winifred to buy out his shares according to the shareholder agreement. The first year of operations had been so stressful for him that he had developed several health problems.

AUDIT AND ASSURANCE

Instructions

Adopt the role of the company's auditors and discuss the financial reporting issues.

RESEARCH AND ANALYSIS

REAL WORLD EMPHASIS

RA15-1 Bombardier Inc.

Access the **Bombardier Inc.** financial statements for the year ended December 31, 2014, which can be found on SEDAR (www.sedar.com).

FINANCE

Instructions

(a) The company has many different types of shares authorized, issued, and/or outstanding at the end of 2014. Prepare a chart that shows the following: name of share class, number of authorized shares, number of issued and outstanding shares, number of votes per share, and rights in terms of dividends.

(b) Why would a company structure its capital in this way? Is there a need for the various classes of shares?

(c) Calculate the book value per common share at December 31, 2014 and 2013. Compare these values with the closing share price at each year end. (*Hint:* Look at the Annual Information Form.) Comment briefly.

(d) For the common (Class A and B) shares, indicate whether the number of shares is increasing or decreasing and what caused the changes in them over the two-year period ended December 31, 2014.

(e) Indicate the amount of dividends declared in 2014. What amount of dividends were paid?

(f) For 2014 and 2013, calculate the rate of return on the common shareholders' equity of Bombardier's shareholders, the payout ratio, and the price earnings ratio based on the year-end closing share price. Comment on the amounts calculated.

(g) Examine the Capital Management note. What are the company's strategy and objectives in managing its capital? How does it manage its capital, and what does it include in its definition of capital?

REAL WORLD EMPHASIS

RA15-2 Bank of Montreal and Royal Bank of Canada

The **Bank of Montreal** and **Royal Bank of Canada** financial statements for their years ended October 31, 2015 can be found on SEDAR (www.sedar.com).

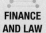

FINANCE AND LAW

Instructions

(a) What is the average carrying amount of each company's common shares? Compare these values with market prices. What stock exchanges do these banks trade on?

(b) What is the authorized share capital of each company?

(c) Comment on how each company presents its shareholders' equity.

(d) Describe the changes (number of shares and price) in each company's common share accounts over the past three years. What types of activities are contributing to the changes?

(e) What amounts of cash dividends per share were declared by each company during the fiscal 2015 year? What was the total dollar effect of the cash dividends on each company's shareholders' equity?

(f) What is each company's rate of return on common shareholders' equity for the 2015 fiscal year? Which company has the higher return on its common shareholders' equity?

RA15-3   Canadian Tire Corporation Limited

REAL WORLD
EMPHASIS

Refer to the financial statements and accompanying notes of **Canadian Tire Corporation Limited** for its year ended January 3, 2015. The financial statements are available on SEDAR (www.sedar.com).

Instructions

FINANCE
AND LAW

(a) What are the issued and authorized shares for both classes of shares of the company? What percentages of the authorized shares have been issued?

(b) Identify the rights that are attached to each type of share. Are the Class A shares more like preferred shares or common shares?

(c) How did the company account for the excess of the amount paid on reacquisition over the carrying amount of the shares it repurchased in 2014? Recreate the journal entry.

(d) What was the average per share carrying amount of the Class A shares at the beginning of the year? At the end of the year? At what average price were the shares repurchased during 2014? Compare these prices with the year-end market price of the shares.

(e) Review the capital disclosure note. What are the company's objectives in managing its capital? What is included in capital for the company? How does it monitor its capital?

RA15-4   Toronto-Dominion Bank

REAL WORLD
EMPHASIS

On December 5, 2013, the **Toronto-Dominion Bank** (TD) announced, and on January 31, 2014 the bank paid, a stock dividend of one common share for each common share issued and outstanding. Access TD's December 5, 2013 news release and its financial statements for the fiscal years ended October 31, 2013 and 2014 on SEDAR (www.sedar.com) or the company's website.

FINANCE

Instructions

(a) Why might TD have paid a stock dividend? Was this a stock dividend in substance, or was it a stock split? Explain briefly.

(b) What effect did this share transaction have on (1) total shareholders' equity, (2) total book value of the common shares' contributed capital reported, (3) number of outstanding shares, and (4) book value per share? Examine the 2013 numbers as originally filed and the restated 2013 comparison numbers in the 2014 year-end annual financial statements to reflect this change for number of shares outstanding, the total dollar value of common shares outstanding, and earnings per share data.

(c) What effect did the transaction have on the dividends declared and paid per common share and on the share's market value? What has since happened to its price on the Toronto Stock Exchange?

RA15-5   Brookfield Asset Management Inc.

REAL WORLD
EMPHASIS

Locate and review **Brookfield Asset Management**'s statement of changes in shareholders' equity in its financial statements for the fiscal years ended December 31, 2014 and 2013, at the end of Volume 2 of this text.

Instructions

FINANCE

(a) Identify the shareholders' equity components that are reported on the face of Brookfield Asset Management's consolidated balance sheet. Identify the more detailed components whose changes are reconciled in the statement of changes in shareholders' equity.

(b) IFRS requires a full statement of changes in shareholders' equity, while ASPE requires only a statement of retained earnings. Comment on why users might find a full statement of changes in equity more useful than a statement of retained earnings, referring to your findings in part (a) above. Which of the components found on Brookfield's statement of changes in equity would be similar to those of a private enterprise? Which components are unlikely to be found in the equity of a private enterprise? Explain the source of these equity items.

(c) Review the Capital Management note provided by Brookfield. What does the company include in its definition of "capital," and what are its capital management objectives? How does it determine whether its objectives are being met?

RA15-6   Impact of Different Legal Systems on IFRS

REAL WORLD
EMPHASIS

LAW

Companies around the globe have moved to, or are in the process of moving to, IFRS. Evidence has shown that it is preferable to adopt IFRS in its entirety, with no deviations from the standards. This chapter shows how much the legal environment affects the accounting for shares. Different countries will have differing legal systems and environments, which may affect the accounting on a country-by-country basis.

Instructions

Discuss the issues raised in the paragraph above in terms of adopting IFRS.

RA15-7   Goldcorp Inc.

REAL WORLD
EMPHASIS

Access the audited annual financial statements of **Goldcorp Inc.** for its year ended December 31, 2014 from SEDAR (www.sedar.com) or the company's website.

Instructions

FINANCE

(a) Describe the business that Goldcorp Inc. operates in.

(b) Identify the components making up the total equity of Goldcorp Inc. as set out in the statement of changes in equity, indicating the amount of each at December 31, 2014. Prepare a short explanation of the source of each of the components.

(c) Reconcile the beginning and ending balances in each of the components of equity in 2014, briefly explaining how each of the components changed during the company's 2014 fiscal year.

(d) Did Goldcorp Inc. declare and pay dividends on its common shares during 2014? If so, how much was declared, and how much was paid in total and per share? Given the company's net accumulated losses, explain how it was able to distribute dividends to shareholders.

(e) What amount of dividends per share has been paid in the periods since the end of its 2014 fiscal year end? (*Hint:* Check the "Investor Resources – Investor FAQ" pages on the company's website.) Suggest what key variables management might consider in determining the amount of dividends to declare and pay each year, referring to the note to the financial statements on the management of capital.

RA15-8   Rogers Sugar Inc.

REAL WORLD EMPHASIS

Access the audited annual financial statements of **Rogers Sugar Inc.** for the year ended October 3, 2015 from SEDAR (www.sedar.com) or the company's website.

FINANCE

Instructions

(a) Identify the components of the company's shareholders' equity, including the reasons for any current and prior year changes to the amounts reported. Comment on any accounting treatment that appears unusual. Prepare the journal entries that were made to record the purchase and cancellation of shares in each year.

(b) Review the company's capital management objectives. Briefly describe these and explain how the company works to achieve these objectives.

(c) What amount of dividends were declared per share and in total in the year ended October 3, 2015? What total amount of dividends were paid in this period? Determine the company's payout ratios for 2015 and 2014 and explain how the company managed to pay this percentage.

ENDNOTES

[1] An equity instrument is "any contract that evidences a residual interest in the assets of an entity after deducting its liabilities," according to the *CPA Canada Handbook*, Part II, Section 3856.05(e) and IAS 32.11. Most shares (including common and preferred shares) may be considered equity instruments; however, some preferred shares with debt-like features are classified as financial liabilities. These will be discussed in Chapter 16. Copyright © International Financial Reporting Standards Foundation. All rights reserved. Reproduced by John Wiley & Sons Canada, Ltd with the permission of the International Financial Reporting Standards Foundation®. Reproduction and use rights are strictly limited. No permission granted to third parties to reproduce or distribute.

[2] An exchange is a more formal marketplace that is more heavily regulated and uses a specific mechanism for pricing shares. Companies must meet certain requirements to be initially listed on the exchange, and then must continue to meet these ongoing requirements to remain listed. These requirements include numerous financial tests, such as asset and revenue levels. Stock markets use a different share pricing mechanism and may be less heavily regulated. There is a wide range of types of stock markets. At the more formal end of the range is NASDAQ and at the less formal end are alternate trading systems, which are unstructured, Internet-based marketplaces where interested buyers and sellers may meet and trade shares. The TSX is the senior exchange in Canada, whereas the TSX Venture Exchange deals with smaller, start-up companies.

[3] Under the CBCA, the name must include the words "Incorporated," "Limited," or "Corporation," or their respective short forms, in either English or French.

[4] The company issuing the shares records a journal entry only when it first issues and sells the shares and when it buys them back. When shareholders buy and sell shares from each other, this is not recorded by the company.

[5] Shareholders who have voting rights elect the board of directors to make major decisions for them.

[6] *CPA Canada Handbook*, Part II, Section 3856. A27 and A28 and IAS 32.16A to D. Copyright © International Financial Reporting Standards Foundation. All rights reserved. Reproduced by John Wiley & Sons Canada, Ltd with the permission of the International Financial Reporting Standards Foundation®. Reproduction and use rights are strictly limited. No permission granted to third parties to reproduce or distribute.

[7] The term "private placement" refers to a situation where the shares are only offered privately to a select group of interested investors. In other words, they are not floated for sale on the stock exchange or market. Private placements are often directed at large institutional or individual investors.

[8] **Bank of Montreal** and **Bank of Nova Scotia** have been paying dividends consistently since 1829 and 1833, respectively. The Bank of Montreal notes on its website that it is the "longest-running dividend-paying" company in Canada. It seeks to pay out 40% to 50% of its earnings over time.

[9] The shares may be valued using valuation models that include expected future cash flow or operating income from the company. This often results in pressure on the income numbers because a higher income results in a higher share price.

[10] Some of the more complex features of preferred shares that were noted earlier can result in their being accounted for as debt.

[11] *CPA Canada Handbook*, Part II, Section 3251.10.

[12] These methods are sometimes called the proportional method (relative fair value method) and the incremental method (residual value method). Conceptually, the relative fair value method is preferable where fair values are available. However, sometimes the method is mandated by GAAP. For example, for convertible

debt under IFRS, the debt is valued first and the remaining balance is allocated to the equity portion.

[13] At the beginning of the 1990s, the situation was just the opposite; that is, share buybacks were less than half the level of dividends. As previously discussed, companies are extremely reluctant to reduce or eliminate their dividends. On the other hand, many companies are no longer raising their dividend per share at the same percentage rate as increases in earnings per share, which effectively reduces the dividend payout over time.

[14] IAS 32.33 requires any consideration paid or received to be recognized directly in equity but does not specify how to allocate between the various equity accounts. ASPE 3240 specifies the treatment. Legal and tax requirements of the specific jurisdiction must be taken into account.

[15] Determining the date of record is not always straightforward. It is generally the date prior to what is known as the ex-dividend date. Theoretically, the ex-dividend date is the day after the date of record. However, to allow time for the transfer of shares, stock exchanges generally advance the ex-dividend date by two to four days. Therefore, a party who owns the shares on the day prior to the expressed ex-dividend date receives the dividend, and a party who buys the stock on or after the ex-dividend date does not receive the dividend. Between the declaration date and the ex-dividend date, the market price of the shares includes the dividend.

[16] *CPA Canada Handbook*, Part II, Section 3831.14. Note that if the transaction is with a controlling shareholder, then *CPA Canada Handbook*, Part II, Section 3840 dealing with related parties applies. IFRS does not remeasure related-party transactions.

[17] From a tax perspective, the Canada Revenue Agency treats stock dividends received in the same way as other dividends.

[18] *CPA Canada Handbook*, Part II, Section 3831, paras. .05 (f)(ii) and .06.

[19] When preferred shares are participating, there may be different agreements on how the participation feature is executed. However, if there is no specific agreement, the following procedure is recommended:

(a) After the preferred shares are assigned their current year's dividend, the common shares will receive a "like" percentage. In example 3, this amounts to 6% of $400,000.

(b) If there is a remainder of declared dividends for participation by the preferred and common shares, this remainder will be shared in proportion to the carrying value in each share class. In example 3, the proportion is:

Preferred $100,000 ÷ 500,000 × $20,000 = $4,000

Common $400,000 ÷ 500,000 × $20,000 = $16,000

[20] Some companies use reverse stock splits. A reverse stock split reduces the number of shares outstanding and increases the price per share. This technique is used when the share price is unusually low. Note that a company's debt covenants or listing requirements might require that the company's shares trade at a certain level. A reverse stock split might help get the price up to where the company needs it to be.

[21] Accumulated other comprehensive income is used under IFRS to represent the cumulative balance of other comprehensive income. ASPE does not mention either other comprehensive income or accumulated other comprehensive income.

[22] Chapter 4 discussed the concept of **capital maintenance**. The idea of creating shareholder value is based on at least retaining contributed capital and, ideally, causing it to grow through earnings. Note that the IASB is moving away from the earned versus contributed distinction, since it is felt that income that is included as other comprehensive income is not really earned by the company, nor is it contributed. It might be argued, however, that the income is indeed earned because management made decisions that resulted in these gains/losses.

[23] *CPA Canada Handbook*, Part II, Sections 3240, 3251, and 3856 and IFRS 7.

[24] *CPA Canada Handbook*, Part II, Section 3240.20 – .22 and IAS 1.79.

[25] *CPA Canada Handbook*, Part II, Section 3240.20 – .22 and IAS 1.79. Copyright © International Financial Reporting Standards Foundation. All rights reserved. Reproduced by John Wiley & Sons Canada, Ltd with the permission of the International Financial Reporting Standards Foundation®. Reproduction and use rights are strictly limited. No permission granted to third parties to reproduce or distribute.

[26] IAS 1.134 – .138.

[27] ASPE does not explicitly require these disclosures. This is because many private companies have shares that are closely held and therefore this type of information is not necessarily required in the statements.

[28] Another closely watched ratio is the dividend yield: the cash dividend per share divided by the market price. This ratio gives investors some idea of the rate of return that will be received in the form of cash dividends.

[29] *CPA Canada Handbook*, Part II, Section 1625.03.

[30] *CPA Canada Handbook*, Part II, Section 1625.15.

[31] *CPA Canada Handbook*, Part II, Section 1625.04.

[32] IFRS does not explicitly cover accounting for financial reorganizations, although the same accounting principles and procedures may be applied as noted under ASPE where legally permissible. IFRS already allows revaluation of investment properties; property, plant, and equipment; as well as intangibles. In addition, financial instruments are allowed to be valued at fair value if certain conditions are met.

[33] *CPA Canada Handbook*, Part II, Section 1625.35 – 42.

Cumulative Coverage and Task-Based Simulation: Chapters 13 to 15

FINANCE

Templates to complete this task-based simulation are available in WileyPLUS and on the instructor website.

Cinefilm (CF) is an entertainment and media company established in 1976 by two brothers in Toronto. Originally, the company started with a single movie theatre in Toronto. CF has now grown into a large, nationally recognized company that is publicly traded on the TSX with the symbol CF. CF has three operating segments: movie theatres, streaming content, and advertising.

- The movie theatre segment generates revenues from theatre attendance, including box office, food service, and gaming revenues. CF operates 100 theatres from coast to coast.

- The streaming content segment offers pay-per-view movies, specialy programming, and on-line games. The services are provided through the Internet or large cable providers.

- The advertising segment consists of all in-theatre advertising revenues and costs (such as pre-show, show-time, magazine, and lobby advertising) and streaming-content advertising (such as commercials and banner ads).

CF's shares are widely held and have a strong following of analysts. CF's share price has experienced significant growth in recent years due to strong growth in all three operating segments.

The management team is preparing the company's financial statements for the December 31, 2017 year end. Analysts' expectations for fiscal 2017 can be summarized as follows:

	Expectation
Earnings per share	$1.45 (diluted)
Revenue	$145 million
Debt to equity ratio	1.5:1
Return on assets	10% (net income/total assets)

The CFO and accounting department are currently analyzing the following issues in preparing the year-end financial statements.

1. During the year, CF launched a new loyalty program called the Movie Points Program (MPP). Individuals can sign up for a loyalty card and earn 1 MP for every movie ticket purchased. Seven MPs are required for a free movie.

   The program has been a big success, and 345,548 MPs were issued during 2017, with 25,152 free movies being awarded. Management expects that 14% of the points will never be redeemed (that is, 1 of 7 points).

   No journal entries have been recorded in the financial statements related to the MPP. On average, a movie ticket has a retail value of $10 and a total cost of $3.

2. On January 1, 2015, the company issued a $1-million, five-year bond with a coupon rate of 5% when the market rate was 6%. The bond pays interest annually and has no conversion features. The bond was issued for $957,876.

   On December 31, 2017, the company reacquired the bond for $950,000. The bond discount is amortized with the effective interest method.

3. On December 1, 2017, the company reacquired 210,000 common shares from the public market for $60 per share. Management reacquired the common shares as a means to signal to shareholders that they believe the shares are undervalued.

   Prior to the acquisition, the shareholders' equity section of the statement of financial position was as follows:

Preferred shares (250,000 authorized, 250,000 issued)	
Cumulative dividend of $1 per share	$ 2,500,000
Common shares (unlimited authorized, 9,500,000 issued)	228,000,000
Contributed surplus, common share retirement	545,000
Retained earnings	125,575,000

4. On December 31, 2017, the board of directors declared a total dividend of $714,500 to be paid out to the preferred and common shareholders.

Instructions

Part A: Movie Points

Note that the revenue approach is the only option under IFRS. The expense approach is adopted in this question for illustration purposes only.

(a) Record the year-end journal entry to recognize the loyalty program under both the revenue and the expense approach.

(b) Place only one "X" in each row in the table below in assessing whether the revenue or expense approach will have the most negative impact on the metric identified for 2017.

	Revenue Approach	Expense Approach	Both Approaches Have the Same Impact	Not determinable
Earnings per share				
Warranty Expense				
Revenue				
Debt to equity ratio				
Return on assets				

Part B: Bond Derecognition

(a) Complete the amortization table below up to December 31, 2017.

	Beginning Value	Cash Interest	Interest Expense	Amortization	Ending Value
December 31, 2015	$957,876				
December 31, 2016					
December 31, 2017					

(b) Record the journal entry to reflect the derecognition of the bond.

(c) Determine the impact of the bond reacquisition journal entry on the financial statement key metrics. Use the following words to describe the impact for each metric: positive, negative, no impact, or not determinable.

	Earnings Per Share	Revenue	Debt to Equity	Return on Assets
Reacquisition of bond				

Part C: Share Reacquisition

(a) Prepare the journal entry to record the reacquisition of the common shares.

(b) Determine the impact of the share reacquisition journal entry on the financial statement key metrics. Use the following words to describe the impact for each metric: positive, negative, no impact, or not determinable.

	Earnings Per Share	Revenue	Debt to Equity	Return on Assets
Reacquisition of common shares				

Part D: Dividend Payment

Calculate the dividend per share for the common shareholders.

REFERENCE TO THE CPA COMPETENCY MAP | LEARNING OBJECTIVES

After studying this chapter, you should be able to:

| **1.1.1, 2.3.1, 3.3.1, 5.1.1, 5.1.2, 5.5.1, 5.5.2** | **1.** Understand what derivatives are and how they are used to manage risks. |

| **1.1.2, 1.2.1, 1.2.2, 1.2.3, 1.2.4, 1.3.1, 5.5.2** | **2.** Understand how to account for derivatives. |

| **1.2.1, 1.2.2, 1.2.3, 1.2.4, 1.3.1, 5.2.3** | **3.** Analyze whether a hybrid/compound instrument issued for financing purposes represents a liability, equity, or both. |

| **1.2.1, 1.2.2, 1.2.3, 1.2.4, 1.3.1, 1.4.4, 5.1.1, 5.2.3, 6.2.4** | **4.** Explain the accounting for hybrid/compound instruments. |

| **1.2.1, 1.2.2, 1.2.3, 1.2.4, 2.1.1** | **5.** Describe the various types of stock compensation plans. |

| **1.2.1, 1.2.2, 1.2.3, 1.2.4, 1.3.2** | **6.** Describe the accounting for share-based compensation. |

| **1.1.4** | **7.** Identify the major differences in accounting between IFRS and ASPE, and what changes are expected in the near future. |

After studying Appendix 16A, you should be able to:

| **1.2.1, 1.2.2, 1.2.3, 1.2.4, 1.4.4, 2.3.2, 5.5.2** | **8.** Understand how derivatives are used in hedging and explain the need for hedge accounting standards. |

| **1.2.1, 1.2.2, 1.2.3, 1.2.4, 1.3.1, 5.5.2** | **9.** Understand how to apply hedge accounting standards. |

After studying Appendix 16B, you should be able to:

| **1.2.1, 1.2.2, 1.2.3, 1.2.4** | **10.** Account for share appreciation rights plans. |

After studying Appendix 16C, you should be able to:

| **1.2.1, 1.2.2, 1.2.3, 1.2.4, 5.4.1** | **11.** Understand how options pricing models are used to measure financial instruments. |

| **1.3.2, 1.4.1, 1.4.2** | **12.** Describe and analyze required fair value disclosures for financial instruments. |

WEATHERING RISK WITH FINANCIAL INSTRUMENTS

EVERY BUSINESS TRIES to mitigate risk. One way to do that is by buying and selling some complex financial instruments—those that are complex to administer, complex to account for, and sometimes complex for investors to understand—to spread the risk of losses among several parties.

One risk faced by many Canadian entities is the weather. Insurance companies can face billion-dollar payouts to policyholders after a flood, tornado, or ice storm. Farmers can lose an entire harvest with a hailstorm or drought.

To help mitigate the risk of weather events causing large losses, weather derivatives were created. They derive their value from an entity betting on a triggering weather event, such as a certain amount of rainfall or a certain amount of damage

© Don Farrall/Getty Images

caused by a storm. For example, an insurance company selling a weather derivative to an investor such as a pension fund pays the investor an agreed-upon amount of interest over a certain amount of time. If the triggering event happens in that period, then the investor loses its principal. The insurance company would use the investors' principal to help pay out claims to policyholders for any damage caused by the weather. If the triggering event does not happen within the specified period of the weather derivative, the investor gets its principal back and keeps the interest earned. Both the derivative seller and buyer assume some risk in return for the possibility of a reward. In this case, the insurance company assumes the risk of having to pay out interest, in return for the possibility of keeping the investor's principal if a weather event happens. The investor takes on the risk of losing its principal if there's bad weather in return for the possibility of earning interest. In other words, the weather derivative seller is betting that a weather event will happen while the investor is betting that it won't.

It's believed the first weather derivative was developed by the ill-fated energy company Enron Corporation in 1997,

to hedge against the risk that unseasonal temperatures would affect the sales of gas. By 2005–06, just before the global financial crisis hit, trading in weather derivatives peaked at U.S. $45 billion worldwide. Energy companies continue to be the biggest traders in weather derivatives, with the triggering event most commonly being unusual temperatures.

Weather derivatives are less common in Canada. The federal Office of the Superintendent of Financial Institutions has been considering allowing their use for insurance companies. Canadian farmers have started using weather derivatives to hedge against the effects of abnormal temperatures and precipitation, although a survey of Saskatchewan farmers in 2014 found that only 10% used them, mainly because they weren't familiar with how such instruments work.

Sources: Maggie Van Camp, "Weather Derivatives to Mitigate Weather Risk to Crops," CountryGuide.com, November 23, 2015; "Come Rain or Shine: The Outlook for the Business of Hedging Against the Elements," *The Economist*, February 4, 2012; Tara Perkins, "Ready to Bet on the Weather?", *Globe and Mail*, October 6, 2009.

PREVIEW OF CHAPTER 16

Complex financial instruments are used by companies in many different industries. These instruments are used in an effort to manage risk, gain access to pools of financing, and minimize the cost of capital and taxes. In response to this trend, the accounting profession has developed guidance for dealing with these instruments in the financial statements. Earlier in the text, we discussed the accounting for basic financial instruments, including accounts and notes receivable/payable, investments, loans, and shares. This chapter focuses on complex financial instruments, such as hybrid and compound debt and equity instruments as well as derivatives.[1] Since employee compensation plans often include derivatives such as stock options, these plans will also be discussed in this chapter.

The chapter is organized as follows:

COMPLEX FINANCIAL INSTRUMENTS

Derivatives	Debt versus Equity: Issuer Perspective	Share-Based Compensation	IFRS/ASPE Comparison	Appendix 16A—Hedging	Appendix 16B—Stock Compensation Plans—Additional Complications	Appendix 16C—Advanced Models for Measuring Fair Value and Disclosure of Fair Value Information
▪ Managing risks ▪ Accounting for derivatives	▪ Economics of complex financial instruments ▪ Presentation and measurement of hybrid/compound instruments	▪ Types of plans ▪ Recognition, measurement, and disclosure of share-based compensation	▪ A comparison of IFRS and ASPE ▪ Looking ahead	▪ Derivatives used for hedging and the need for hedge accounting standards ▪ Hedge accounting	▪ Share appreciation rights plans ▪ Performance-type plans	▪ Options pricing models ▪ Fair value disclosure for financial instruments

DERIVATIVES

If you recall from previous chapters, **financial instruments** are contracts that create both a financial asset for one party and a financial liability or equity instrument for the other party.[2] Financial instruments can be primary or derivative. **Primary financial instruments** include most basic financial assets and financial liabilities, such as receivables and payables, as well as **equity instruments**, such as shares. The accounting issues for primary financial instruments were covered in earlier chapters. **Derivative instruments**, on the other hand, are more complex. They are called derivatives because they derive (get) their value from an **underlying** primary instrument, index, or non-financial item, such as a commodity (called the "underlying"). Derivatives may trade on exchanges such as the Canadian Derivatives Exchange and "over-the-counter" markets. "Over-the-counter" markets are less formal markets and often involve financial institutions as the financial intermediary (meaning that the instruments are purchased or negotiated through financial institutions such as banks). Weather derivatives, as mentioned in our feature story, trade on the Chicago Mercantile Exchange. Where there is a market for the derivative, it is easier to value. Certain derivatives do not trade on any exchange or market. For instance, certain executive stock options are tailor-made, as opposed to standardized, foreign exchange forward contracts to buy or sell foreign currency at a future date.

Accounting standards define derivatives as financial instruments that "create rights and obligations that have the effect of transferring, between parties to the instrument, one or more of the financial risks that are inherent in an underlying primary instrument." They transfer risks that are inherent in the underlying primary instrument without either party having to hold any investment in the underlying.[3]

Derivatives have three characteristics.

1. Their value changes in response to the **underlying instrument (the "underlying")**.

2. They require **little or no initial investment**.

3. They are settled at a **future** date.[4]

Options, forwards, and futures are common types of derivative instruments. As a basic rule, derivatives are measured at fair value with gains and losses booked through net income. Derivatives may be embedded in contracts. This means that the contract has more than one part: a host (non-derivative) part and one or more derivatives.

We will discuss the accounting for the common types of derivative instruments further in this chapter. Special accounting exists for derivatives that are part of a hedging relationship and this is discussed in Appendix 16A. We will illustrate the notion of an **underlying** with examples throughout the chapter. The accounting for **embedded derivatives** is complex and is generally beyond the scope of this text. Having said that, the chapter will discuss this area briefly in the context of compound instruments issued by companies.

Managing Risks

Objective 1
Understand what derivatives are and how they are used to manage risks.

FINANCIAL RISK MANAGEMENT
5.5.2

Why do derivatives exist? In short, they exist to help companies manage risks. Companies operate in an environment of constant change caused by volatile markets, new technology, and deregulation, among other things. This increases overall business risk as well as financial risk. The response from the financial community has been to develop products to manage some of these risks, with one result being the rise of derivatives. Recall from Appendix 5A the differing types of risk that a company faces. Managers of successful companies have always and will continue to manage risks to minimize unfavourable financial consequences and to maximize shareholder value. While managing risk helps keep uncertainty at an acceptable level (which may differ depending on the stakeholders), it also has its costs.

There are many layers of costs relating to the use of derivatives. Three categories of costs are as follows:

1. Direct costs

2. Indirect costs

3. Other costs, such as opportunity costs

UNDERLYING CONCEPT

As always, the benefits of entering into certain transactions, especially complex ones, should exceed the costs; otherwise, the company will be reducing shareholder value rather than creating it.

COST MANAGEMENT
3.3.1

In order to enter into contracts that manage risk, such as insurance and derivative contracts, transaction costs are normally incurred, including bank service charges, brokerage fees, and insurance premiums. These are the **direct**, visible costs that are charged by an intermediary or the other party to the transaction. Then there are **indirect**, less visible costs. For example, the activity of researching, analyzing, and executing these transactions uses a significant amount of employee time. Finally, there are **other costs,** which may not be so visible. For example, the use of too many complicated financial instruments increases the complexity of financial statements and therefore reduces their transparency and understandability. Capital markets may penalize such companies by increasing costs of capital and/or limiting or denying access to capital. Another type of hidden cost is the **opportunity cost,** because managing risk sometimes results in limiting the potential or opportunity for gain. Companies must consider all of the costs that are associated with derivatives and weigh them against the benefits.

The growth in the use of derivatives has been aided by the development of powerful calculation and communication technology, which provides new ways to analyze information about markets as well as the power to process high volumes of payments. Thanks to these developments, many corporations are now using derivatives extensively and successfully.

WHAT DO THE NUMBERS MEAN?

The Bank of Canada performed research in 2014 to see which Canadian firms use financial derivatives. According to its report, financial institutions were the most significant users of financial derivatives, but many non-financial corporations also use these financial instruments. The Bank looked at 1,522 non-financial companies over the period 2005 to 2013 and found that 33% used financial derivatives.

The following chart illustrates derivative usage by sector and notes the different types of derivatives being used in each sector.

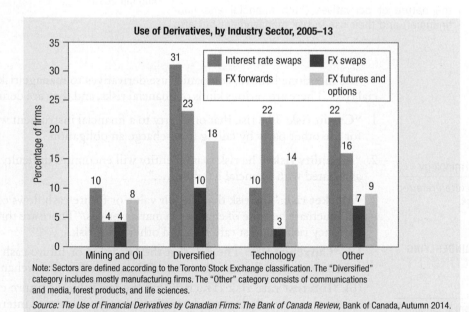

Note: Sectors are defined according to the Toronto Stock Exchange classification. The "Diversified" category includes mostly manufacturing firms. The "Other" category consists of communications and media, forest products, and life sciences.

Source: *The Use of Financial Derivatives by Canadian Firms: The Bank of Canada Review,* Bank of Canada, Autumn 2014.

The largest derivatives users in the survey were diversified corporations (which consist mostly of manufacturing firms). In addition, as the chart above shows, interest rate swaps and foreign exchange forwards were most commonly used across all sectors. Larger firms were the main users (defined as those with a market value of higher than $250 million). The following chart illustrates the types of derivatives used by small and large firms.

When we look at these data and combine them with the derivatives usage by financial institutions, which as

Use of Derivatives, by Firm Size, 2005–13

Note "Small firms" are defined as firms with market values that are lower than the sample median.

Source: The Use of Financial Derivatives by Canadian Firms: The Bank of Canada Review, Bank of Canada, Autumn 2014.

noted above, are the most significant users of derivatives in Canada, we see that use of these instruments is widespread. In addition, this research deals only with the use of financial derivatives. Many Canadian companies use non-financial derivatives (those relating to commodities such as wheat, oil, and pork bellies), and thus the use of all derivatives in Canada is extremely pervasive.

It is therefore very important that preparers and users of financial statements understand not only the nature of derivatives (both financial and non-financial) and their use in risk management but also

how to account for them. The IASB issued its revised standard on financial instruments, IFRS 9, in 2014, effective 2018. This standard includes guidance on accounting for derivatives as well as updated guidance on how to account for hedges (which generally include the use of derivatives).

Sources: The Use of Financial Derivatives by Canadian Firms: The Bank of Canada Review, Bank of Canada, Autumn 2014.

As mentioned above, companies use derivatives to manage risks, and especially financial risks. There are various kinds of financial risks, and they are defined in IFRS as follows.[5]

1. **"Credit risk**: The risk that one party to a financial instrument will cause a financial loss for the other party by failing to discharge an obligation."

2. **"Liquidity risk**: The risk that an entity will encounter difficulty in meeting obligations associated with financial liabilities...."

3. **"Market risk**: The risk that the fair value or future cash flows of a financial instrument will fluctuate because of changes in market prices." There are three types of market risk: currency risk, interest rate risk, and other price risk.

   (a) **"Currency risk**: The risk that the fair value or future cash flows of a financial instrument will fluctuate because of changes in foreign exchange rates."

   (b) **"Interest rate risk**: The risk that the fair value or future cash flows of a financial instrument will fluctuate because of changes in market interest rates."

   (c) **"Other price risk**: The risk that the fair value or future cash flows of a financial instrument will fluctuate because of changes in market prices (other than price changes arising from **interest rate risk** or **currency risk**), whether those changes are caused by factors that are specific to the individual financial instrument or its issuer, or factors that affect all similar financial instruments being traded in the market."

It is important for companies and users of financial statements to identify and understand which risks a company currently has and how it plans to manage these risks. Keep in

Alternative Terminology

Market risk is often referred to as *price risk*.

UNDERLYING CONCEPT

Remember from finance courses that increased risk may bring the opportunity for increased rewards. Thus, some companies expose themselves to increased risks in order to maximize shareholder value. This is often referred to as the risk/return trade-off.

FINANCIAL ANALYSIS AND PLANNING 5.1.1 AND 5.1.2 AND FINANCIAL RISK MANAGEMENT 5.5.1 AND 5.5.2

mind that derivatives often expose the company to additional risks. As long as the company identifies and manages these risks, this is not a problem. There is a problem, however, when stakeholders do not understand the risk profile of derivative instruments. The use of derivatives can be dangerous, and it is critical that all the parties involved understand the risks and rewards involved with these contracts.[6]

An entity might use derivatives to reduce or offset various risks (normally referred to as **hedging**). It is also possible to enter into derivative contracts to create positions that are expected to be profitable.[7] Both are acceptable strategies and depend on the company's risk tolerance profile; that is, the nature of the risks that the company can comfortably undertake and the amount of exposure to each risk that it is willing to accept. There are special optional accounting rules that a company can use when a derivative is used to hedge certain risk. Although hedging will be discussed in the body of the chapter, **hedge accounting** will be discussed in Appendix 16A due to its added complexity.

What types of business models and processes generate financial risk? Virtually all business models generate financial (and indeed other) risks. The following are some examples:

market and currency risk

- Any business that purchases commodities such as fuel, agricultural products, or renewable resources as inputs has a **market risk** associated with these inputs. These companies know that commodity prices vary significantly depending on supply and demand. This affects the company's profitability and may lead to volatile net income. Often, the commodities are priced in different currencies, which creates a **currency risk**.

market risk

- Likewise, any company that sells commodities has a **market risk**. Depending on the commodity pricing when the commodity is sold, the company might make more or less profit, which again can lead to volatile or unpredictable net income.[8]

- Companies that sell on credit have **credit risks**: the risk that the customer or other party (**counterparty**) may fail to make a payment.

credit risk

- Companies that borrow money or incur liabilities increase **liquidity risk**: the risk that they will not be able to pay their obligations. Debt also creates **interest rate risk**.

- Companies that buy goods, finance purchases, create inventory, sell goods, and collect receivables have **market risks**: the risk that the value of the assets will change while the company is holding them.

liquidity risk and interest rate risk

Remember that derivative transactions may be the most efficient way of managing these risks. Alternatively, or in addition, the company may rely on other tools to manage the risks, including internal controls (such as credit checks on customers to reduce or eliminate credit risk).

A company may try to structure its business model such that it is not exposed to certain financial risks and thus does not need to manage them. For instance, by having a policy of selling only for cash, the company is not exposed to credit risk. By using "just-in-time" inventory ordering, a company gets rid of the market risk associated with stockpiling or holding inventory.

Producers and Consumers as Derivative Users

McCain Foods Limited is a large producer of potatoes for the consumer market. Assume that McCain believes that the present price for potatoes is excellent, but that McCain will need two months to harvest its potatoes and deliver them to market. The company has **market risk** related to its inventory. Because the company is concerned that the price of potatoes will drop, it signs a contract in which it agrees to sell its potatoes today at the current market price, but for delivery in two months.

This locks in the market price. Known as a **forward contract**, this type of contract reduces the **market risk** related to the potatoes (both in terms of price and cash flows).

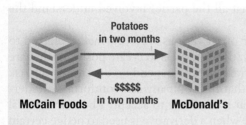

Potatoes
in two months

$$$$$
in two months

McCain Foods   **McDonald's**

Who would buy this contract? Suppose **McDonald's Corporation** is on the other side of the contract and it wants to have potatoes (for french fries) in two months and is worried that prices will increase.[9] McDonald's also has **market risk**. It therefore agrees to delivery in two months at the current fixed price because it knows that it will need potatoes in two months and that it can make an acceptable profit at the current price level. McDonald's is also managing its **market risk**.

In this situation, if the price of potatoes increases before delivery, you might conclude that McCain loses and McDonald's wins. Conversely, if prices decrease, McCain wins and McDonald's loses. However, the objective is not to gamble on the outcome. In other words, regardless of which way the price moves, both companies should be pleased because both have received a price at which they can make an acceptable profit. In summary:

**STRATEGY
DEVELOPMENT**
2.3.1
**FINANCIAL RISK
MANAGEMENT**
5.5.1

- Both companies have existing risks because of the way they do business (their business model).

- Both seek to manage these risks.

- Both are using derivatives to reduce these risks.

- Both are seen to be hedging their risks because they are reducing uncertainty.

Commodity prices are volatile and depend on factors such as weather, crop disasters, and general economic conditions. For the producer of a product and its consumer to plan effectively, it makes good sense to lock in specific future revenues or input costs in order to run their businesses successfully. This is a key way to manage cash flows to limit the risk of going bankrupt.

Speculators and Arbitrageurs as Derivative Users

In some cases, instead of a company like McDonald's buying the contract, a **speculator** may purchase the contract from McCain. The speculator is not trying to reduce risk, however. Instead the objective is to maximize potential returns by being exposed to greater risks. The speculator is betting that the price of potatoes will increase and that the value of the forward contract will therefore also increase. The speculator, who may be in the market for only a few hours, will then sell the forward contract to another speculator or to a company like McDonald's. The speculator will never take delivery of the potatoes because this was never their intention. The goal was to generate a cash profit from trading in the derivative instrument itself. The difference between this transaction and the earlier hedging transaction is that in the earlier transaction the company was entering into a derivative to reduce a pre-existing risk. In the case of the speculator, there is no pre-existing risk, just a desire to take on additional risk in the hope of increasing profits.

Another user of derivatives is an **arbitrageur**. These market players try to take advantage of inefficiencies in different markets. They try to lock in profits by simultaneously entering into transactions in two or more markets. For example, an arbitrageur might trade in a futures contract and at the same time in the commodity that underlies the futures contract, hoping to achieve small price gains on the difference between the two. Arbitrageurs exist because there is information asymmetry in different markets. This occurs when the same information is not available to all market participants in the different markets. Some markets are more efficient than others. The arbitrageurs force the prices in the different markets to move toward each other because they create demand and supply where previously there might not have been any, thus driving the prices either up or down.

Speculators and arbitrageurs are very important to markets because they keep the market liquid on a daily basis.

Accounting for Derivatives

Objective 2

Understand how to account for derivatives.

The basic principles regarding accounting for derivatives are as follows:

1. Financial instruments (including financial derivatives) and certain non-financial derivatives represent rights or obligations that meet the definitions of assets or liabilities and should be recognized in financial statements when the entity becomes party to the contract.

2. Fair value is the most relevant measure.

3. Gains and losses should be booked through net income.

Special optional hedge accounting exists for derivatives and other items that have been designated as being part of a hedging relationship for accounting purposes. These are described in Appendix 16A.

Recall the discussion regarding fair value measurement from Chapters 2 and 3. Appendix 16C discusses more advanced measurement techniques and models.

Non-Financial Derivatives and Executory Contracts

LAW

Derivatives may be financial or non-financial. An example of a financial derivative is a forward contract to buy U.S. dollars. An example of a non-financial derivative is a contract to buy pork bellies or potatoes as in the earlier example. GAAP provides accounting guidance for financial instruments (including financial derivatives), as well as certain non-financial derivatives. Thus many commodities futures are accounted for in the same manner as financial derivatives.

What about purchase commitments? Are they derivatives? For instance, many companies enter into contracts intending to take delivery of raw materials in the future in order to lock in a supply. These contracts may be structured as commodities futures or forward contracts in legal form and therefore are derivatives from a finance perspective. However, they may also be structured as regular purchase commitments. Under both types of contracts, the company is agreeing to take delivery of the raw materials at an agreed-upon price in the future. What separates the two types of contracts from an accounting perspective? What makes the forwards and futures derivatives from a finance perspective but not the purchase commitments? Should they both be accounted for as derivatives?[10]

Purchase commitments are generally labelled as **executory contracts**: contracts to do something in the future (where no cash or product changes hands up front). Note that derivatives are similarly contracts to do something in the future and could arguably also be referred to as executory contracts. In this regard, the two are similar. Purchase commitments are not structured as derivatives contracts from a legal perspective, however, and they do not trade on commodities exchanges (as do futures and options, for instance).[11] Historically, these contracts have not been recognized in the financial statements. An issue exists, however, because technically, purchase commitments meet the accounting definition of derivatives. This is because their value changes with the value of the underlying (in this case, the raw material); there is no investment up front and the contract will be settled in the future.

Under ASPE, purchase commitments and similar commodities contracts are generally not accounted for as derivatives unless they are exchange traded futures. This is partly due to the fact that they may be difficult to measure. They are not recognized in the financial statements until the goods are received. Contracts dealing with purchase or sale of commodities are otherwise not covered by Handbook Section 3856.

IFRS considers whether contracts have net settlement features, meaning that they can be settled on a net basis by paying cash or other assets as opposed to taking delivery of the underlying product.[12] For contracts with net settlement features, as long as the company intends to take delivery of the raw materials, the contracts are designated as "expected use," and are not accounted for as derivatives. Purchase contracts that must be settled by taking delivery or delivering the underlying products are not accounted for as derivatives. As such, they are not recognized until delivery of the underlying non-financial asset takes place (for example, the inventory is delivered or received).

Illustration 16-1 analyzes the nature of purchase commitments and forward/futures/ options contracts that relate to non-financial assets such as commodities.

	Purchase commitments for non-financial assets (such as inventory)	Forward/futures/options to buy/sell non-financial assets (such as inventory)
Legal form	Purchase contract/commitment. Generally does not include net settlement clause.	Forward/futures/option contract
Does it trade on a market (thus establishing liquidity and fair value)?	No	Yes and generally net settleable
Does it meet the definition of an executory contract (that is, it promises to do something in the future where neither party has yet performed)?	Yes. A contract is signed up front but no money or goods change hands until later.	Yes. A contract is signed up front but no money or goods change hands until later.
Does it meet the definition of a derivative (that is, its value depends on the underlying, there is little or no upfront investment, and it will be settled in the future)?	Yes. The value of the contract depends upon the value of the underlying (for example, inventory), there is no upfront investment, and it will be settled in the future.	Yes. The value of the contract depends upon the value of the underlying (for example, inventory), there is no upfront investment, and it will be settled in the future.
Perspective for accounting purposes	Generally accounted for as an unexecuted contract and not recognized until the underlying non-financial item is delivered. (Derivative accounting does not apply to these contracts either because they are not exchange traded [ASPE] or because they are not settleable on a net basis [IFRS].)	Generally accounted for as a derivative (recognized and measured at FV-NI). Under ASPE, these contracts are accounted for as derivatives only if they are exchange-traded futures. Accounted for as an executory contract under IFRS, where there is no net settlement feature or where one exists but the company expects to take delivery or deliver the underlying asset.

Illustration 16-1

Accounting for Contracts Involving Non-Financial Assets

We will now discuss three basic types of derivatives: options and warrants, forwards, and futures.

Options and Warrants

LAW

Options and warrants are derivative instruments. An option or warrant gives the holder the contractual right to acquire or sell an underlying instrument at a specific price within a specific term. The specific price is called the **exercise** or **strike price**—the agreed-upon price at which the option may be settled. The specific term is called the **exercise period**. A good example is an option to purchase shares of a company for a fixed price, on a specified date. The **underlying** is the shares; that is, this option derives its value from the share price of the underlying shares. If the share price goes up, the option is worth more. If it goes down, the option may become worthless.

The option allows the holder to protect himself or herself against declines in the market value of the underlying shares but also allows the holder to participate in increases in the share value without having to hold the actual shares. Derivative instruments do not result in the transfer of the underlying (the shares in our example) at the contract's inception and perhaps not even when it matures. They also require a relatively low upfront investment (which is the cost of the option premium). The cost of the option is a fraction of the cost of the actual share itself. Before the end of the option period, the holder may sell the option to capture the value. The holder has the right to exercise the option but is not obliged to buy the shares at the exercise price.

A Framework for Options

**FINANCIAL
RISK
MANAGEMENT
5.5.2**

Options may be purchased (**purchased options**) or written (**written options**) by a company. If a company **purchases** an option, it will pay a fee or premium and gain a right to do something. If a company **writes** an option, it charges a fee or premium and gives the holder/purchaser the right to do something. The "right" in question may be either of the following:

1. A right to **buy** the underlying (a **call option**)
2. A right to **sell** the underlying (a **put option**)

A framework for categorizing options is shown in Illustration 16-2.

Illustration 16-2

A Framework for Options

	Call—right to buy	**Put**—right to sell
Written	**Sell option for** Transfer right to buy shares/underlying	**Sell option for** Transfer right to sell shares/underlying
Purchased	**Pay $ for option** Obtain right to buy shares/underlying	**Pay $ for option** Obtain right to sell shares/underlying

A written option is riskier for the company because the writer has no control over whether it will be required to deliver something. The company is obligated to perform under the option. This is different from a purchased option, which gives the company the right but not the obligation to do something. Assume that a company writes or sells an option for $5 cash. Because this creates an obligation for the company that has written the option, the option is generally accounted for as a liability.

An example of a purchased call option follows.

Illustration of a Purchased Call Option

Assume that Abalone Inc. purchases a **call option** contract on January 2, 2017 from Baird Investment Corp.[13] The option gives Abalone the right to purchase 1,000 Laredo Corp. shares (the underlying) at $100 per share (the exercise/strike price), and it expires April 30, 2017. For the right to buy the shares at this fixed price, Abalone pays a premium of $400. This is a financial derivative because the underlying is a financial asset (the Laredo shares).

$400

Call option
(right to buy 1,000
Laredo shares
for $100 each)

Abalone   Baird

At the time of the transaction, Laredo shares are trading at $100. If the price of Laredo shares increases above $100, Abalone can exercise the option and purchase the shares for $100 per share. Alternatively, Abalone may sell the option to someone else. Here, Baird has the market risk associated with the shares. Abalone has **market risk** associated with the option itself, or the $400. At worst, the option becomes worthless and Abalone loses the $400. If Baird has written the option without holding an investment in Laredo (a "naked" position), it will suffer a loss if the price of Laredo increases. If Baird holds shares in Laredo offsetting the option sold (a "covered call"), its profit on the investment will be limited to the difference between $100 and the price it paid for the shares plus the $400 premium received from Abalone. If Laredo's share price never increases above $100 per share, the call option is worthless and Abalone recognizes a loss equal to the initial price of the call option.

The option is accounted for as a derivative because it meets all three criteria in our definition as follows:

1. The value of the option depends upon the value of the Laredo shares (the underlying).

2. The option costs $400, which is small compared with the value of the shares of $100,000 (1,000 × $100).

3. The option is settleable in future (April 30, 2017).

Abalone would make the following journal entry at the acquisition date of January 2, 2017:

A = L + SE
0

Cash flows: ↓ 400 outflow

Derivatives—Financial Assets/Liabilities	400	
Cash		400

The option premium is composed of two amounts: (1) the intrinsic value and (2) the time value. Illustration 16-3 shows the formula to calculate the option premium.

Illustration 16-3

Option Premium Formula

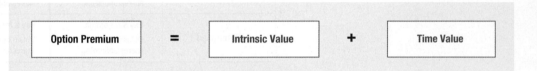

Intrinsic value is the difference between the market price of the underlying and the strike or exercise price at any point in time. It represents the amount that would be realized by the option holder if the option were exercised immediately. On January 2, 2017, the intrinsic value of the option related to the Laredo shares is zero because the market price is equal to the strike price of $100. **Time value** refers to the option's value over and above its intrinsic value. Time value reflects the **possibility that the option will have a fair value greater than zero because there is some expectation that the price of Laredo shares will increase above the strike price during the option term**. As indicated, the option's time value is $400.[14]

On March 31, 2017, the price of Laredo shares has increased to $120 per share and the intrinsic value of the call option contract is now $20,000. That is, Abalone could exercise the call option and purchase 1,000 shares from Baird for $100 per share and then sell the shares in the market for $120 per share. This gives Abalone a potential gain of $20,000 ($120,000 – $100,000) on the option contract.

The options may be worth more than this due to the time value component; that is, the possibility that the shares may increase in value over the remaining month. Assume the options are trading at $20,100. In addition, we must consider the original cost of the option. The entry to record this change in value of the option at March 31, 2017 is as follows:[15]

A = L + SE
+19,700   +19,700

Cash flows: No effect

Derivatives—Financial Assets/Liabilities	19,700	
Gain		19,700[a]

[a]$20,100 – $400

At March 31, 2017, the call option is reported on the statement of financial position (SFP) at its fair value of $20,100 and the net gain increases net income for the period. The options are "in-the-money"; that is, they have value.

On April 1, 2017, assuming the shares are still worth $120 and that Abalone settles the option in cash rather than by taking delivery of the shares of Laredo (net settlement), the entry to record the settlement of the call option contract with Baird is as follows:

A = L + SE	
-100 -100	
Cash flows: ↑ 20,000 inflow	

Cash	20,000	
Loss	100[16]	
Derivatives—Financial Assets/Liabilities		20,100

Illustration 16-4 summarizes the effects of the call option contract on net income.

Illustration 16-4

Effect on Income—Option

Date	Transaction	Income (Loss) Effect
March 31, 2017	Net increase in value of call option ($20,100 − $400)	$19,700
April 1, 2017	Settle call option	(100)
	Total net income	$19,600[a]

[a]This amount is net of $400 cost for the right to participate in the increase in the value of the shares.

On April 1, 2017, Abalone could have taken delivery of the shares under the option contract. Assuming that the company decides to present the investment in the shares as FV-NI, the entry to record this is as follows:

A = L + SE	
-100 -100	
Cash flows: ↓ 100,000 outflow	

FV-NI Investments	120,000	
Loss	100	
Cash		100,000
Derivatives—Financial Assets/Liabilities		20,100

FINANCIAL RISK MANAGEMENT 5.5.2

Abalone could have purchased the Laredo shares directly on January 2 instead of buying an option. To make the initial investment in Laredo shares, Abalone would have had to pay the full cost of the shares up front and would therefore have had to pay more cash than it did for the option. If the price of the Laredo shares then increased, Abalone would realize a gain; however, Abalone would also be at risk for a loss if the Laredo shares declined in value. The option allowed the company to participate in potential gains (the upside "risk"). By spending the $400, the company eliminated its downside risk.

We will return to the discussion of options in Appendix 16A. Chapter 17 will also revisit the option framework when looking at the potentially dilutive impact of options in calculating earnings per share.

Forwards

LAW

A **forward contract** is another type of derivative. Under a forward contract, the parties to the contract each commit up front to do something in the future. For example, one party commits to buy an item (referred to as the underlying) and the other to sell the item at a specified price on a specified date. The price and time period are locked in under the contract. The contracts are specific to the transacting parties based on their needs. These instruments generally do not trade on exchanges because the terms are unique to the parties involved. That is, the terms are not standardized, as most exchange-traded contracts are.

Usually banks buy and sell these contracts or act as intermediaries between the parties to the contract. Forwards are measured at the present value of any future cash flows under the contract—discounted at a rate that reflects risk.

Illustration of a Forward Contract

To illustrate, assume that on January 2, 2017, Abalone Inc. agrees to buy $1,000 in U.S. currency for $1,150 in Canadian currency in 30 days from Bowen Bank. The forward contract not only transfers to the holder the right to increases in value of the underlying (in this case, U.S. dollars), it also creates an obligation to pay a fixed amount at a specified date (in this case, $1,150). This is different than the purchased option, which creates a right but not an obligation: with a purchased option, the holder may choose to exercise the option but does not have to. The forward contract transfers the **currency risk** inherent in the Canada-U.S. exchange rate. In addition, the contract creates **credit risk** and **liquidity risk**. The credit risk is the risk that at the end of the contract, the counterparty (Bowen in this case) will not deliver the underlying (U.S. $1,000). The liquidity risk is the risk that Abalone will not be able to honour its commitment to deliver Canadian $1,150 at the end of the contract. This is a financial derivative because the underlying is a financial asset: foreign currency.

FINANCIAL RISK MANAGEMENT 5.5.2

Upon inception, the contract is priced such that the value of the forward contract is zero. Assume in the example above that on the date on which the transaction is entered into, U.S. $1 = Canadian $1.10. No journal entry would be recorded at this point because we must consider the fair value of the contract—not just the difference between the spot rate[17] and the forward rate. Like the option, the value of the forward considers both the intrinsic value and the time value component. It is generally valued at the present value of the future net cash flows under the contract.

Under derivatives accounting, subsequently, the forward is remeasured at fair value. The value will vary depending on interest rates as well as on what is happening with the spot prices (the current value) and forward prices (future value as quoted today) for the U.S. dollar. If the U.S. dollar appreciates in value, in general, the contract will have value because Abalone has locked in to pay only $1,150 for the U.S. $1,000.

The forward is accounted for as a derivative because it meets the three criteria in our definition as follows:

1. The value of the contract will vary based on the value of the U.S. dollar (the underlying).

2. There is no payment up front.

3. The contract will be settled in 30 days.

Assuming that the fair value of the contract is $50, on January 5, 2017, Abalone would record the following:

A = L + SE			
+50 +50	Derivatives—Financial Assets/Liabilities	50	
Cash flows: No effect	Gain		50

The derivative would be presented as an asset on the statement of financial position and measured at fair value with gains and losses, both unrealized and realized, being booked through net income.

Suppose on January 31, the contract moves into a loss position; that is, if the contract were settled today, the company would suffer an overall loss of $30. This might occur for instance if the value of the U.S. currency declines. In this case, Abalone is locked in to pay $1,150 for something that is worth less than that amount. The following journal entry would be booked:

A = L + SE			
−80 −80	Loss	80	
Cash flows: No effect	Derivatives—Financial Assets/Liabilities		80

The original gain is reversed and the additional loss must be booked.

Because the derivative contract can sometimes be an asset while at other times it can be a liability, it can be presented as either an asset or a liability on the SFP. In our example, the Derivatives—Financial Assets/Liabilities account would now be presented as a liability on the SFP.

Assume that on February 1, the settlement date, the U.S. dollar is worth $1.05 Canadian. The following entry would be booked to settle the contract if it was settled on a net basis:

A = L + SE
-100 -30 -70

Cash flows: ↓ 100 outflow

Loss	70	
Derivatives—Financial Assets/Liabilities	30 (to eliminate carrying value)	
Cash		100[a]

[a] U.S. $1,000 × (1.15 − 1.05)

If instead Abalone actually took delivery of the U.S. dollars, the following journal entry would be booked:

A = L + SE
-100 -30 -70

Cash flows: ↓ 100 outflow

Cash	1,050 (U.S. $ at the spot/current exchange rate)	
Derivatives—Financial Assets/Liabilities	30 (to eliminate carrying value)	
Loss	70	
Cash		1,150

Futures

Futures contracts, another popular type of derivative, are the same as forwards except for the following:

1. They are standardized as to amounts and dates.

2. They are exchange traded and therefore have ready market values.

3. They are settled through clearing houses, which generally removes the credit risk.

4. There is a requirement to put up collateral in the form of a "margin" account. The margin account represents a percentage of the contract's value. Daily changes in the value of the contract are settled daily against the margin account by the clearing house (known as marking to market) and resulting deficiencies in the margin account must be made up daily.

The initial margin is treated as a deposit account similar to a bank account, and is increased or decreased as the margin amount changes. The gain or loss on the contract, reflected in the daily change in the account, is recognized in income.

$100 and promise to sell grain for $1,000

Promise to buy grain for $1,000

Fairway Inc.   Broker

Illustration of a Futures Contract

For example, assume Fairway Inc. entered into a futures contract to sell grain for $1,000 in 30 days. This contract helps the company manage its **market risk** by locking in the amount it will get when it sells the grain. The broker requires a $100 initial margin (normally a percentage of the market value of the contract or a fixed amount multiplied by the number of contracts). This amount is deposited in cash with the broker. Like the forward, the futures contract would have a zero value up front. This is a non-financial derivative because the underlying is a non-financial commodity (grain).

The futures contract is accounted for as a derivative because it meets our definition as follows:

1. Its value will vary with the price of grain (the underlying).

2. The initial amount paid ($100) is small compared with the value of the underlying (the grain).

3. The contract will be settled in 30 days.

At the date when the contract is entered into, the following journal entry would be booked to show the margin that has been deposited with the broker. The contract is otherwise valued at $0 on inception.

A = L + SE
0

Cash flows: ↓ 100 outflow

Deposits	100	
Cash		100

FINANCIAL RISK MANAGEMENT
5.5.2

Assume that the value of the grain increases after the contract has been entered into. The contract is marked to market by the broker. Assume that the market value of the contract decreases by $50. This is because Fairway has agreed to sell the grain for a fixed amount that is lower than the current market value. The clearing house then requires Fairway to deposit an additional $50. The entries to record the loss and the additional deposit would be:

A = L + SE
     +50   −50

Cash flows: ↓ 50 outflow

Loss	50	
Derivatives—Financial Assets/Liabilities		50
Deposits	50	
Cash		50

If the contract is closed out (settled net without delivering the grain) with no further changes in value, the following entry would be booked.

A = L + SE
−50 −50

Cash flows: ↑ 100 inflow

Cash	100	
Derivatives—Financial Assets/Liabilities	50	
Deposits		150

Fairway suffered a loss of $50, which was booked to net income already through the journal entries above. This is because it had agreed to sell the grain for $1,000 when it was worth more. Instead of delivering the grain, Fairway paid the difference in cash—thus locking in the loss. Note that the net impact is a loss of $50 on the contract. On the income statement, a decision would be made about how to present the loss because it is now realized.

Derivatives Involving the Entity's Own Shares

Sometimes companies enter into derivative contracts that deal with their own shares. For instance, a company might buy or write options dealing with its own shares or enter into forward contracts to buy or sell its own shares at a future date. Examples of "own equity" derivative instruments include:

1. Options
    (a) Purchased call or put options to buy or sell the entity's own shares
    (b) Written call or put options to buy or sell the entity's own shares

2. Forwards
    (a) To buy the entity's own shares
    (b) To sell the entity's own shares

Assume Abalone Inc. paid $400 to Baker Corp. for the right to buy 1,000 of Abalone's own common shares for $30 each. Assume further that the contract may only be settled by exercising the option and buying the shares. Why would Abalone do this? Perhaps Abalone is looking to buy back its own shares to boost share values.

Should the cost of the option be treated as an investment as in the earlier example where the underlying is a share from another company as opposed to the entity's own shares?

$400

Right to buy
1,000 Abalone
shares for $30 each

Abalone   Baker

IFRS states that this transaction would be presented as a reduction in shareholders' equity and not as an investment.[18] Contracts where the entity agrees **to issue a fixed number of its own shares for a fixed amount of consideration** are also generally presented as equity (for example, written call options and forwards to sell shares). This is sometimes referred to as the "fixed for fixed" principle when discussing how to account for derivatives that are settleable with own equity instruments. ASPE is silent on this matter but general principles would support presenting the financial instrument as contra equity because it does not meet the definition of an asset.

Not all contracts involving own equity instruments are treated as equity, however. Some end up being treated as financial liabilities or financial assets. This area of accounting is very complex. As a general rule, any analysis should go back to basic principles and definitions. The following two points are worthy of note.

1. **Fixed for fixed override:** What happens when a derivative contract is entered into that creates an obligation to pay cash or other assets, even if it is for a fixed number of the entity's shares—for example, a written put option or forward contract to buy shares? In this case, it overrides the "fixed for fixed" principle noted earlier and the contract should generally be treated as a financial liability. As always, any time there is an obligation to pay cash, a financial liability is recognized.

2. **Settlement options:** What happens when the derivative contract allows choice in how the instruments will be settled—for example, one party can choose to settle net in cash or by exchanging shares? In this case, the instrument is a financial asset/liability by default under IFRS unless all possible settlement options result in it being an equity instrument.[19] Under ASPE, the instrument would likely be treated as equity if the entity can avoid settling with cash or other assets (that is, where the entity has the option to choose the way the contract is settled and can avoid paying cash or other assets).

UNDERLYING CONCEPT

Often, complex transactions are best analyzed by looking at basic definitions. This helps by focusing on the substance of the transaction.

Illustration 16-5 summarizes IFRS requirements for own equity instruments. As mentioned above, ASPE is not as explicit in this area and generally the analysis defaults to whether the definition of a liability is met or not.

Illustration 16-5

Summary of Accounting for Own Equity Instruments under IFRS

	Presentation under IFRS	Analysis
Written call options	Equity	Holder has the right to buy a **fixed** number of the company's shares for a **fixed** amount of cash and no contractual obligation to pay cash. This is therefore equity on the company's SFP.
Written put options	Financial liabilities	Holder has the right to sell a **fixed** number of the company's shares to the company for a **fixed** amount of cash. Even though this is a fixed for fixed contract, the obligation to pay cash creates a liability.
Purchased call/put options	Contra equity	The company has the right to buy or sell a **fixed** amount of its own shares for a **fixed** amount of cash. There is no contractual obligation to pay cash. This is therefore equity.
Forward contract to buy shares	Financial liabilities	The company has committed to buy a **fixed** number of its own shares for a **fixed** amount of cash. Even though this is a fixed for fixed contract, the obligation to pay cash creates a liability.
Forward contract to sell shares	Equity	The company has committed to sell a **fixed** number of its own shares for a **fixed** amount of cash. There is no contractual obligation to pay cash. This is therefore equity.
Contracts that may or will be settled net (settlement option)	Financial assets/liabilities	These are not fixed for fixed contracts because they will be settled either in cash (net) or for a variable number of shares that equal the net cash settlement value.

DEBT VERSUS EQUITY: ISSUER PERSPECTIVE

Economics of Complex Financial Instruments

Objective 3
Analyze whether a hybrid/compound instrument issued for financing purposes represents a liability, equity, or both.

In companies with very simple capital structures, financing is obtained through debt instruments (loans, bonds, and debentures) and common shares. Both these simple financing vehicles have very different legal and economic characteristics. Debt instruments are generally repaid, pay interest, and rank in preference to common shares upon windup or liquidation. Common shares, on the other hand, are seen as permanent capital, pay dividends, and are residual in nature, meaning that upon windup or liquidation, the shareholders get whatever is left after paying off all debts. These characteristics are summarized in Illustration 16-6.

Illustration 16-6

Characteristics of Simple Financing Instruments—Debt and Common Shares

	Loan or Bonds Payable	Common Shares
Term	Maturity date/repayment schedule.	Permanent capital.
Return to investor/lender	Interest, which is a function of the principal amount, time, and risk.	Dividends, which are a function of profits, cash flows, value of shares, and company policy.
Seniority in terms of liquidation, windup, or bankruptcy	Often secured by company assets. Generally ranks in preference upon liquidation, windup, or bankruptcy.	Unsecured residual interest. Shareholders get whatever is left after other capital providers such as creditors are paid out.[20]
Advantages to entity	Interest is tax deductible.	Does not increase solvency or liquidity risk.
	Company does not have to give up ownership.	Company does not have to pay out dividends.
	Leverage (maximize profits to shareholders by using creditors' money).	Unsecured and so assets are not at risk except in bankruptcy.
Disadvantages to entity	Too much debt increases liquidity and solvency risk and may result in higher cost of capital and/or lack of access to capital.	Issuance of more shares dilutes existing shareholder base. Missed leverage opportunity.

TREASURY MANAGEMENT
5.2.3

Over the years, the capital markets have sought to profit from the best attributes of both these types of instruments and have created many hybrid-type instruments that are neither straight debt (sometimes referred to as "plain vanilla" debt) nor straight common shares. **Hybrid/compound instruments** have more than one component, including debt and equity (such as debt with detachable warrants), or may have the dual attributes of both debt and equity. Preferred shares were probably the first hybrid or compound instrument. They are not quite common shares because they rank in preference to common shares regarding dividend payout and payout upon liquidation, windup, or bankruptcy. They often pay dividends annually, similar to debt. Other examples of hybrid or compound instruments are certain convertible debt instruments, term preferred shares, and mandatorily redeemable shares.

From an economic perspective, every time a new instrument is issued, it is priced or benchmarked against the standard instruments of debt and common shares, keeping in mind tax treatments that may be more or less favourable depending on whether the instrument is seen as debt or equity. So companies may, for instance, be able to pay less interest if the instrument also gives the holder some equity-like features (for instance, a conversion option). These designer-type financial instruments allow companies to create a specific type of instrument, keeping in mind the amount of capital required, desired risk profile, and acceptable cost of capital. Unfortunately, sometimes one of the design criteria is a desire to show less debt on the statement of financial position.

ETHICS

Presentation and Measurement of Hybrid/Compound Instruments

Objective 4
Explain the accounting for hybrid/compound instruments.

Why is there so much fuss about hybrid/compound instruments? The capital marketplace focuses on liquidity and solvency and these are calculated using financial statement numbers. Excessive debt on an SFP signals increased riskiness and will affect the cost of capital and ultimately access to capital. Given that demand exists by both companies and investors for these types of instruments, and given the current accounting model that requires separate presentation of debt and equity, accountants must figure out a way to systematically and consistently classify these instruments such that the financial statements provide useful information to users including investors and creditors.

For this reason, these hybrid/compound instruments must be analyzed carefully for accounting purposes. They may be classified as debt, equity, or part debt and part equity. The economic substance must be reviewed as well as the contractual terms. Does the contract obligate the entity to pay out cash or other assets? If so, some or all of the instrument is a liability.

FINANCIAL ANALYSIS AND PLANNING
5.1.1

Presentation of Hybrid/Compound Instruments

LAW

When analyzing whether the contract is debt, equity, or both, consider the following:

1. Contractual terms
   (a) Does the instrument explicitly obligate the entity to pay out cash or other assets?
   (b) Does the instrument give the holder the choice to force the company to pay out cash (in which case, it may create an obligation for the entity)?
   (c) Are there settlement options (in which case, it may create an obligation for the entity)?

2. Economic substance

   Does the instrument contain any equity-like features that may need to be separated out? Keep in mind that generally when the instrument gives the holder increased flexibility or choice, the instrument is worth more. For instance, a convertible bond (explained below) is worth more because it allows the holder to have the security of debt but also exposes the investors to the risks and rewards of share ownership. Thus, part of the instrument is equity-like.

3. Definitions of financial statement elements

   A **financial liability** is defined under both IFRS and ASPE as a contractual obligation to do either of the following:
   (a) deliver cash or another financial asset to another party, or
   (b) exchange financial instruments with another party under conditions that are potentially unfavourable.[21]

   In addition, under IFRS, the definition of a financial liability includes guidance where the instrument is settleable using the entity's shares instead of cash. Essentially, where the company settles the instrument using a variable number of shares (instead of cash), it is still a financial liability. This is supported by ASPE as well, although it is not part of the definition.

   An **equity instrument** under both IFRS and ASPE is any contract that represents a residual interest in the assets of an entity after deducting all of its liabilities.[22]

In addition, under IFRS, the guidance includes the following with respect to instruments settleable in the entity's own equity instruments. The instrument is equity only if it will be settled by exchanging a **fixed number** of the issuer's own equity instruments for a **fixed amount** of cash or other assets (and it is not a liability).[23]

These definitions are critical in determining how to present the instruments.

Illustration 16-7 shows some examples of hybrid/compound instruments indicating SFP presentation.

Illustration 16-7

Examples of Hybrid/Compound Instruments

Contract	Presentation
Convertible debt (convertible at the option of the holder into a fixed number of common shares of the company).	*Liability and equity.* The conversion option is essentially an embedded written call option and this part is equity because a fixed number of shares will be issued. The debt carries with it a contractual obligation to pay interest and principal.*
Puttable shares (holder has the option to require the company to take the instruments back and pay cash).	*Liability.* This instrument contains a written put option that requires the entity to pay a fixed amount of cash for a fixed number of financial instruments if the option is exercised. The holder has the right to exercise the option and therefore this is beyond the entity's control. The exception to this is noted in the next example below.
Shares that give the holder the option to require the company to surrender a pro rata share of net assets upon windup.	*Equity.* Although these are technically liabilities because of the put option, they may be presented as equity as long as they are "in-substance common shares." (Recall these criteria from Chapter 15 under the discussion "Types of Shares".)
Mandatorily redeemable preferred shares.	*Liability.* The mandatory redemption imposes a contractual obligation to deliver cash or other assets. As an exception, high/low preferred shares are presented as equity under ASPE (see the chapter text below this illustration).
Debt with detachable warrants. The warrants are for a fixed number of shares.	*Liability and equity.* Since the warrants are detachable, they are separate financial instruments and are treated as written call options. The instruments allow for a fixed number of shares to be exchanged for a fixed amount of cash. The debt carries with it a contractual obligation to pay interest and principal.*
Preferred shares that must be repaid if certain conditions are met (for example, if the market price of the common shares exceeds a certain threshold).	*Liability.* Under IFRS, a liability exists because the contingent settlement provision is based on an event outside the company's control. Under ASPE, the instrument would be accounted for as a liability only where the contingency is highly likely to occur.[24]
Debt that will be settled by issuing a variable number of common shares equal to the face value of the debt (or where the holder has the option to require settlement in cash or a variable number of shares).	*Liability.* The common shares are used as currency to settle the obligation, which is equal to the face value of the debt regardless of who has the option to choose.
Perpetual debt.	*Liability.* The economic value of this instrument is determined by discounting the interest payments (which represent a contractual obligation to pay cash).

*Note that ASPE allows the entity to measure the equity portion at $0 as an accounting policy choice. We will discuss this later in the chapter.

Redeemable shares are often used in tax and succession planning. Many small businesses are created and run by individuals who at some point decide that they would like to hand the company over to their children. One orderly way of doing this that minimizes taxes is through the use of redeemable preferred shares, sometimes referred to as **high/low preferred shares**. The business assets can be transferred to a new company, which makes it possible to take advantage of special tax provisions that minimize taxes, and the owner takes redeemable preferred shares as part of the consideration. The children then buy the common shares in the new company for a nominal amount, which allows them to benefit from subsequent increases in the company's value. This also gives them some or all of the voting control because the common shares would normally be voting shares.

PERSONAL TAX 6.2.4

WHAT DO THE NUMBERS MEAN?

ASPE

The redemption amount of the preferred shares is set at the company's fair value at the time of the transaction. This means that the fair value is frozen for the individual at a point in time (which is why the label "estate freeze" is sometimes given to this type of transaction). All subsequent increases in value will go to the children through ownership of the common shares. The owner of the former company will eventually get his or her money (which represents the fair value of the assets that he or she put in) out of the new company at a future point by redeeming the preferred shares.

This is a good example of yet another business reason to use complex financial instruments. Note

that the redemption feature causes this instrument to be recorded as a (huge) liability since the company has an obligation to deliver cash upon redemption. Many small business owners are not happy with this accounting since it makes the company look highly leveraged when, in fact, the shares will normally not be redeemed in the short or medium term. Treating the shares as liabilities on the balance sheet may also cause the company to violate pre-existing debt covenants. As a result of this, ASPE requires these particular instruments to be treated as equity.[25]

One last presentation issue is whether the financial instruments should be offset against other financial instruments when presented on the SFP. When a company offsets one or more financial instruments, such as financial assets and liabilities, the instruments are generally shown as a net number. For instance, if the company has a receivable of $100 and a payable of $75, and they are presented on a net basis, only net assets of $25 would be presented. The potential problem with this is that it tends to obscure the fact that the $25 asset is really made up of the two components. Therefore there are some restrictions on offsetting.

When can a company show these amounts on a net basis? Only when certain criteria are met, as follows:

1. The company has a legally enforceable right[26] to net the amounts (in other words, if the instruments were to be settled, then they could legally be settled on a net basis).

2. The company intends to settle the instruments on a net basis or simultaneously (that is, collect the receivable and immediately pay out the payable).[27]

Measurement of Hybrid/Compound Instruments

UNDERLYING CONCEPT

Well-defined measurement tools help cope with measurement uncertainty. These tools ultimately help in preparing financial information that is more reliable. Recall the guidance discussed in Chapters 2 and 3.

Upon initial recognition, financial instruments are measured at fair value, which is generally the exchange value. If they have components of both debt and equity, they may require bifurcation (splitting into debt and equity). This is therefore a measurement issue. Whatever the classification that is chosen upon inception, this classification continues to be used until the instrument is removed from the SFP.

The **measurement** of hybrid/compound instruments is complicated by the fact that the economic value of these instruments can be attributed to **both** the debt and equity components. That is, the instrument is neither 100% debt nor 100% equity, and instead is part debt and part equity. How should these two components be measured?

As noted in previous chapters, there are two approaches to allocating the value of a transaction to its respective parts: the **residual value method** (sometimes referred to as the **incremental method**) and the **relative fair value method** (sometimes referred to as the **proportional method**). We have referred to these tools in earlier chapters and used them for instance to help bifurcate bundled sales and purchases. The mechanics are the same.

1. Relative fair value method: Determine the market values of similar individual instruments.

2. Residual value method: Value only one component (the one that is easier to value, which is often the debt component). The other component is valued at whatever is left.

IFRS requires the use of the residual value method, with any debt components being valued first and the residual being allocated to the equity components. ASPE allows the equity component to be valued at zero or the residual value method to be used, with the more easily measurable component being valued first.[28] Subsequently, debt is measured at amortized cost unless the fair value option is selected (or it is a derivative).

Let's look at a very common financial instrument—convertible debt—and how it is accounted for.

Convertible Debt

A **convertible bond** is a bond that may be converted into common shares of the company. It combines the benefits of a bond with the privilege of exchanging it for common shares **at the holder's option**. It is purchased by investors who want the security of a bond holding—guaranteed interest—plus the added option of conversion if the value of the common shares increases significantly.

TREASURY MANAGEMENT 5.2.3

Corporations issue convertible debt for two main reasons. One is the desire to raise equity capital without giving up more ownership control than necessary. To illustrate, assume that a company wants to raise $1 million at a time when its common shares are selling at $45 per share. Such an issue would require selling 22,222 shares (ignoring issue costs). By selling 1,000 bonds at $1,000 par, and with each bond being convertible into 20 common shares, the enterprise may raise $1 million by committing only 20,000 common shares.[29] Investors may be willing to take the bonds because they give the investors greater security (especially if the bonds are secured by company assets) yet allow them to participate in the company's growth through the option to convert the bonds to common shares.

REAL WORLD EMPHASIS

A second, more common reason that companies have for issuing convertible securities is to obtain debt financing at cheaper rates. Many enterprises would have to issue debt at higher interest rates unless a convertible feature was attached. The conversion privilege entices the investor to accept a lower interest rate than would normally be the case on a straight debt issue. For example, **Amazon.com** at one time issued convertible bonds that paid interest at an effective yield of 4.75%, which was much lower than Amazon.com would have had to pay if it had issued straight debt. For this lower interest rate, the investor received the right to buy Amazon.com's common shares at a fixed price until the bonds' maturity.

There are reporting issues in the accounting for convertible debt at all of the following times:

1. Issuance

2. Conversion

3. Retirement

Convertible Debt at Time of Issuance

As previously mentioned, the conversion feature on a convertible bond makes the instrument more valuable to an investor, and, therefore, the option feature itself has value. The obligation to deliver cash under the bond represents a financial liability and the right to acquire the company's common shares represents an equity instrument. Compound instruments must be split into their components and presented separately in the financial statements. Since the embedded option to convert to common shares is an equity instrument, that part of the instrument is presented as equity. The remaining component is presented as a liability. Recall that ASPE allows an accounting policy choice to measure the equity portion at $0.

For example, assume that Bond Corp. offers three-year, 6% convertible bonds (par $1,000). Each $1,000 bond may be converted into 250 common shares, which are currently trading at $3 per share. Similar straight bonds carry an interest rate of 9%. One thousand bonds are issued at par.

Allocating the proceeds to the liability and equity components under the residual value or incremental method involves valuing one component first and then allocating the rest of the value to the other component. Assume that the company decides to use the residual method and measure the debt first. The bond may be measured at the PV of the stream of interest payments ($1 million × 6% for three years) plus the PV of the bond itself ($1 million) all discounted at 9%, which is the market rate of interest. The remainder of the proceeds is then allocated to the option. This allocation is shown in Illustration 16-8.

Illustration 16-8

Incremental Allocation of Proceeds between Liability and Equity Components

Total proceeds (at par in this case)	$1,000,000
Less:	
Value of bonds (PV annuity 3 years, 9%, $60,000 + PV $1,000,000, in 3 years, 9%)	(924,061)
Incremental value of option	$ 75,939

The journal entry to record the issuance would be as follows:

IFRS
A = L + SE
+1,000,000 +924,061 +75,939

ASPE
A = L + SE
+1,000,000 +1,000,000

Cash flows: ↑ 1,000,000 inflow

	IFRS	ASPE, valuing the equity component at zero as an accounting policy choice*
Cash	1,000,000	1,000,000
Bonds Payable	924,061	1,000,000
Contributed Surplus—		
Conversion Rights	75,939	0

*ASPE also allows the residual method to be used with the more easily measurable component being measured first. Normally the debt component is more easily measurable so this option is consistent with IFRS.

Convertible Debt at Time of Conversion

If bonds are converted into other securities, the main accounting issue is to determine the amount at which to record the securities that have been exchanged for the bond. Assume that holders of the convertible debt of Bond Corp. decide to convert their convertible bonds before the bonds mature. The bond discount will be partially amortized at this point. Assume that the unamortized portion is $14,058. The entry to record the conversion would be as follows:

A = L + SE
 −985,942 +985,942

Cash flows: No effect

Bonds Payable ($1,000,000 − $14,058)	985,942	
Contributed Surplus—Conversion Rights	75,939	
Common Shares		1,061,881

This method, referred to as the **book value method** of recording the bond conversion, is the method that is required under IFRS and ASPE.[30] Support for the book value approach is based on the argument that an agreement was established at the date when the bond was issued either to pay a stated amount of cash at maturity or to issue a stated number of shares of equity securities. Therefore, when the debt is converted to equity in accordance with the pre-existing contract terms, no gain or loss would be recognized upon conversion.[31] Any accrued interest that was forfeited would be treated as part of the new book value of the shares (and credited to Common Shares).

UNDERLYING CONCEPT

Note that the convertible debt in the example above is treated the same as the debt with detachable warrants. This is because the economic substance of the instruments is the same: they both have debt and give the holder the option to hold shares.

Sometimes the issuer wants to induce (cause) a prompt conversion of its convertible debt to equity securities in order to reduce interest costs or to improve its debt to equity ratio. As a result, the issuer may offer some form of additional consideration—known commonly as a sweetener—such as cash. This situation is referred to as an **induced conversion**. The additional premium paid should be allocated between the debt and equity components at the time of the transaction. The approach that is used should be consistent with the method that was used when the debt was originally recorded (for example, the incremental or residual value method).

Assume that Bond Corp. wants to reduce interest costs at some point during the life of the debt. It therefore offers an additional cash premium of $15,000 to the bondholders to convert, at a time when the carrying amount of the debt was $972,476. Assume further that the **residual value method** was used to allocate the issue price originally between debt and equity components, with the debt being measured at its discounted cash flows and the equity being valued as the residual amount. The bond's fair value at the conversion time is $981,462 (ignoring the conversion feature) due to lower market interest rates. Under ASPE, the first step in the allocation of the inducement premium is to determine the difference between the bonds' fair value and carrying value:

$$\$981,462 - \$972,476 = \$8,986$$

Then the residual method would be used to allocate the inducement premium between the debt and equity components (because this method was originally used):

$$\$15,000 - \$8,986 = \$6,014$$

Thus, under ASPE, $8,986 would be treated as a debt retirement cost and $6,014 as a capital transaction similar to a share redemption cost. Under IFRS, the whole amount would be recognized as a loss.[32] The journal entry would be as follows:

A = L + SE
−15,000 −972,476 +957,476

Cash flows: ↓ 15,000 outflow

	ASPE		IFRS	
Bonds Payable	972,476		972,476	
Loss on Redemption of Bonds	8,986	(above)	15,000	
Contributed Surplus—Stock		(previously	75,939	
Options	75,939	calculated)		
Retained Earnings	6,014	(above)		
Common Shares			1,048,415	1,048,415
Cash			15,000	15,000

The shares are now valued at the total carrying amount of the bonds, plus the option, as follows:

$$\$972,476 + \$75,939 = \$1,048,415$$

Retirement of Convertible Debt

The normal retirement of the liability component of convertible debt at maturity (its repayment) is treated the same way as non-convertible bonds, as explained in Chapter 14. The equity component remains in Contributed Surplus. What happens, however, if the instrument is retired early and the company pays off the debt with cash? Assume that Bond Corp. decides to retire the convertible debt early and offers the bondholders $1,070,000 cash, which is the fair value of the instrument at the time of early retirement. The following journal entry would be booked:

A = L + SE
−1,070,000 −972,476 −97,524

Cash flows: ↓ 1,070,000 outflow

Bonds Payable	972,476	
Loss on Redemption of Bond	8,986	
Contributed Surplus—Conversion Rights	75,939	
Retained Earnings	12,599	
Cash		1,070,000

The amounts related to the instrument (including the bonds payable, any remaining discount, and the contributed surplus) are zeroed out and the loss is allocated between the debt portion and the equity portion. The portion allocated to the debt is the same as the amount in the previous example (that is, the difference between the debt's carrying value and its fair value). If the residual method is used, the rest is allocated to the equity portion. Note that the fair value of $1,070,000 includes the fair value of the bond and the embedded option. The option is also removed from the books because it is seen as settled.

Interest, Dividends, Gains, and Losses

Once the determination is made to classify something on the SFP as debt, equity, or part debt and part equity, the related interest, dividends, gains, and losses must be consistently treated. For instance, a term preferred share would be presented as a liability and, therefore, related dividends would be booked as interest or dividend expense and charged to the income statement (not to Retained Earnings).

SHARE-BASED COMPENSATION

Objective 5
Describe the various types of stock compensation plans.

Thus far, we have covered off several instances in previous chapters where shares and other equity instruments are used as compensation (instead of cash); for instance, when purchasing inventory and fixed assets. This section focuses on stock compensation plans that remunerate or compensate employees for services provided.

It is generally agreed that effective compensation programs:

1. Motivate employees to high levels of performance

2. Help retain executives and recruit new talent

3. Base compensation on employee and company performance

4. Maximize the employee's after-tax benefit and minimize the employer's after-tax cost

5. Use performance criteria that the employee can control

GOVERNANCE 2.1.1

Although straightforward cash compensation plans (salary and, perhaps, a bonus) are an important part of any compensation program, they are oriented to the short term. Many companies recognize that a more long-term compensation plan is often needed in addition to cash.

Long-term compensation plans aim to develop a strong loyalty toward the company. An effective way to do this is to give the employees an equity interest based on changes in their company's long-term measures, such as increases in earnings per share, revenues, share price, or market share. These plans come in many different forms. Essentially, they provide the executive or employee with the opportunity to receive shares or cash in the future if the company's performance is satisfactory. Stock-based compensation plans also help companies conserve cash. When they are used, the company does not expend any cash. In fact, if options are used to compensate employees, the employees actually pay cash into the company when they exercise the option. Start-up companies find this very useful since they are often cash-poor in that early phase.

Types of Plans

Many different types of plans are used to compensate employees and especially management. In all these plans, the reward amount depends on future events. Consequently, continued employment is a necessary element in almost all types of plans. The popularity of a particular plan usually depends on prospects in the stock market and tax considerations. For example, if it appears that appreciation will occur in a company's shares, a plan that offers the option to purchase shares is attractive to an executive.

Conversely, if it appears that price appreciation is unlikely, then compensation might be tied to some performance measure such as an increase in book value or earnings per share.

Four common compensation plans that illustrate different objectives are:

1. Compensatory stock option plans (CSOPs)

2. Direct awards of stock

3. Stock appreciation rights plans (SARs)

4. Performance-type plans

The main accounting issues relate to recognition of the plan (determining when the cost of the plan should be recognized) and measurement (determining how the cost should be measured). We will discuss SARs and performance-type plans in Appendix 16B.

Stock Options Revisited

Before looking at the accounting for employee stock option plans, it is useful to revisit the earlier discussion about options in this chapter. So far, options have been discussed in the following contexts:

1. as derivatives, used to manage risk (hedge or speculation), and

2. as debt with detachable warrants (options), used as sweeteners with bonds to access pools of capital and reduce the cost of capital.

The above instruments are sometimes **exchange-traded options**; that is, they trade on an options or stock exchange.

Companies also use stock options for the following reasons:

1. To **give employees an opportunity to own part of the company**, with the issue being made to a wide group of people (such as all employees). Another benefit of these plans if they are widely subscribed to is that the company raises cash. These are generally called **employee stock option or purchase plans (ESOPs)**.

2. To **remunerate management or employees**. These are called **compensatory stock option plans (CSOPs)**.

3. As **compensation in a particular purchase or acquisition transaction**, with the stock options being provided instead of paying cash or another asset, or incurring a liability. For instance, a company might buy another company and pay for the investment with stock options. These are valued at fair value. The accounting is similar to the accounting covered in Chapter 10 under acquisition of assets upon issuance of shares.

Illustration 16-9 reviews the different types of options and option plans. Note that ESOPs and CSOPs are generally not traded on an exchange. As a result, the fair value cannot be measured as readily.

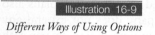

Illustration 16-9

Different Ways of Using Options

What is the difference between ESOPs and CSOPs in terms of accounting? The answer has to do with the underlying nature of the transaction. The main difference between the two plans is that, with ESOPs, the employee usually pays for the options (either fully or partially). Thus these transactions are seen as **capital** transactions (charged to equity accounts). The employee is investing in the company. CSOPs, on the other hand, are primarily seen as an **alternative way to compensate** the employees for their services, like a barter transaction. The services are rendered by the employee in the act of producing revenues. This information must be recognized on the income statement as an operating transaction (expensed).

Illustration 16-10 summarizes the difference between CSOPs and non-compensatory plans, or ESOPs.

Illustration 16-10

Compensatory versus Non-Compensatory Plans

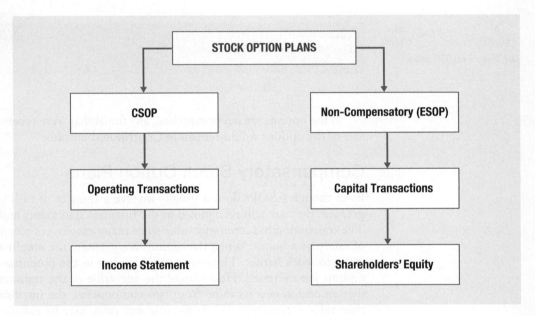

The following factors indicate whether or not a plan is compensatory:

1. **Option terms** (such as dealing with enrolment and cancellation): Non-standard terms that give the employees a longer time to enrol and the ability to cancel the option imply that the options are compensatory.

2. **Discount from market price**: A large discount implies that the plan is compensatory.[33]

3. **Eligibility**: Making options available only to certain restricted groups of employees, often management, implies that a plan is compensatory. Plans that are available to all employees are seen as non-compensatory.[34]

Recognition, Measurement, and Disclosure of Share-Based Compensation

Objective 6
Describe the accounting for share-based compensation.

Under an ESOP, when an option or share right is sold to an employee, the Cash account is debited and the Contributed Surplus or other equity account is credited for the amount of the premium (that is, the cost of the option). When the right or option is exercised, the Cash account is again debited for the exercise price, along with the Contributed Surplus account (to reverse the earlier entry) and the Common Shares account is credited to show the issuance of the shares.

To illustrate, assume that Fanco Limited set up an ESOP that gives employees the option to purchase company shares for $10 per share. The option premium cost is $1 per share and Fanco has set aside 10,000 shares. On January 1, 2017, employees purchase 6,000 options for $6,000. The journal entry is as follows:

A = L + SE
+6,000   +6,000

Cash flows: ↑ 6,000 inflow

| Cash | 6,000 | |
| Contributed Surplus—Stock Options | | 6,000 |

Subsequently, all 6,000 options are exercised, resulting in 6,000 shares being issued. The journal entry is as follows:

A = L + SE
+60,000   +60,000

Cash flows: ↑ 60,000 inflow

Cash	60,000	
Contributed Surplus—Stock Options	6,000	
Common Shares		66,000

If the options are never exercised, any funds that were received by the company on the sale of the options would remain in Contributed Surplus.

Compensatory Stock Option Plans

Even though CSOPs do not usually involve a transfer of cash when the options are first granted, they are still recognized in the financial statements and measured at fair value.[35] The transaction has economic value since many employees accept the stock options in lieu of salary or a bonus. When the options are granted, the employees presumably are motivated to work harder. The economic value lies in the potential for future gain when the options are exercised. How should the fair value of the transaction be measured? Recall that an option gets its value from two components: the intrinsic value component and a time value component. While the intrinsic value may be easy to measure (the shares' fair value less the exercise price), the time value component is more difficult to measure. Even though it is difficult to value the stock options themselves, it is even more difficult to value the services rendered by the employees.

The compensation cost that arises from employee stock options should be recognized as the services are being provided.[36]

Determining Expense

The total compensation expense is calculated on the date when the options are granted to the employee (the **grant date**) and is based on the fair value of the options that are expected to **vest**.[37] The grant date is the date when the employee and company agree on the value of what is to be exchanged. **The grant date is therefore the measurement date.** Fair value for public companies is estimated using market prices, and if not available, using a valuation technique (for example, an options pricing model). No adjustments are made after the grant date for any subsequent changes in the share price, either up or down. The options pricing model incorporates several input measures:

1. The exercise price

2. The expected life of the option

3. The current market price of the underlying stock

4. The volatility of the underlying stock

5. The expected dividend during the option life

6. The risk-free rate of interest for the option life

The **measurement date** may be later for plans that have variable terms (that is, if the number of shares and/or option price are not known) that depend on events after the date of grant. For such variable plans, the compensation expense may have to be estimated based on assumptions about the final number of shares and the option price (usually at the exercise date).

Allocating Compensation Expense

In general, compensation expense is recognized in the periods in which the employee performs the service (the **service period**). Unless something different is specified, the service period is the **vesting period**: the time between the grant date and the vesting date. Thus, the total compensation cost is determined at the grant date and allocated to the periods that benefit from the employee services. Illustration 16-11 presents the relevant dates and time frames.

Illustration 16-11

Key Dates in Accounting for Stock Option Plans

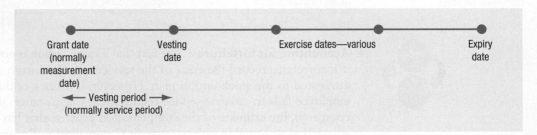

To illustrate the accounting for a stock option plan, assume that on November 1, 2017, the shareholders of Chen Corp. approve a plan that grants options to the company's five executives to purchase 2,000 of the company's common shares each. The options are granted on January 1, 2018, and may be exercised at any time after December 31, 2019. The exercise price per share is $60.

To keep this illustration simple, we will assume that the fair value, as determined using an options pricing model, results in a total compensation expense of $220,000. The following section discusses the recognition of compensation expense at various dates.

1. **Grant date:** Recall that the option's value is recognized as an expense in the periods in which the employee performs services. In the case of Chen Corp., assume that the documents that are associated with the issuance of the options indicate that the expected period of benefit/service is two years, starting on the grant date. The journal entries to record the transactions related to this option are as follows:

January 1, 2018		
No entry		
December 31, 2018		
Compensation Expense	110,000	
Contributed Surplus—Stock Options ($220,000 ÷ 2)		110,000
December 31, 2019		
Compensation Expense	110,000	
Contributed Surplus—Stock Options		110,000

A = L + SE
      0
Cash flows: No effect

A = L + SE
      0
Cash flows: No effect

The compensation expense is allocated evenly over the two-year service period, assuming that equal service is provided during the entire period.

2. **Exercise date:** If 20% or 2,000 of the 10,000 options were exercised on June 1, 2021 (three years and five months after date of grant), the following journal entry would be recorded:

A   =   L   +   SE
+120,000   +120,000

Cash flows: ↑ 120,000 inflow

June 1, 2021		
Cash (2,000 × $60)	120,000	
Contributed Surplus—Stock Options (20% × $220,000)	44,000	
Common Shares		164,000

3. **Expiration:** If the remaining stock options are not exercised before their expiration date, the balance in the Contributed Surplus account would remain. If the company kept several Contributed Surplus accounts, the balance would be shifted to a specific Contributed Surplus account that is used for options that have expired. The entry to record this transaction at the date of expiration is:

A   =   L   +   SE
                    0

Cash flows: No effect

Contributed Surplus—Stock Options	176,000	
Contributed Surplus—Expired Stock Options (80% × $220,000)		176,000

4. **Accounting for forfeitures:** The fact that a stock option is not exercised does not make it incorrect to record the costs of the services received from executives that have been attributed to the stock option plan. However, if a stock option is forfeited because an employee fails to satisfy a service requirement (for instance, if the employee leaves the company), the estimate of the compensation expense that has been recorded should be adjusted as a change in estimate (credit Compensation Expense and debit Contributed Surplus). ASPE allows a choice: either estimate forfeitures up front or account for them as they occur. IFRS requires the former treatment. If estimated up front, the entity will likely have to adjust subsequently to reflect the actual number of options forfeited.[38]

Direct Awards of Stock

Stock may be awarded directly as compensation for services provided by an employee. This type of transaction is more broadly known as a **nonmonetary reciprocal transaction**. The transaction is nonmonetary because it involves little or no cash, and it is reciprocal because it is a two-way transaction. The company gives something up (shares) and gets something in return (the employee's services).

Almost all business transactions are reciprocal. As a **nonmonetary** transaction, direct awards of stock are recorded at the fair value of the item that is given up (the stock).[39] For instance, instead of paying a cash salary, the company may offer company shares as remuneration. This would be recorded as salary expense at the shares' fair value. The value of the shares is used because it is difficult to value the services provided.

Companies whose shares are traded on stock exchanges are able to measure the value of the options more readily since they can measure volatility. Private companies, however, do not have volatility measures yet must nonetheless attempt to measure it.

Private companies have another issue. If they issue CSOPs to their employees, how do the employees realize the value? If an employee exercises the option and buys the shares, there is no ready market in which to sell the shares and the value is therefore locked in. Often private companies will offer to buy back the shares from the employee. If the company has a policy and past practice of repurchasing the shares, does this create a liability? This requires professional judgement but a good argument may be made for recognizing a liability instead of equity. In other words, the past practice of repurchasing the shares and the probability that this will be done again (since the employees cannot sell the shares elsewhere) support the recognition of a liability. The company in substance has an obligation to the employee.[40] The liability would have to be remeasured on an ongoing basis with the difference being charged to income as compensation expense.

Most CSOPs are equity settled; that is, they will be settled by issuing shares to the employee. Sometimes, the CSOPs are cash settled or there is a choice between cash and equity. This will be addressed in Appendix 16B.

Disclosure of Compensation Plans

Full disclosure should be made of the following:

* The accounting policy that is being used

* A description of the plans and modifications

* Details of the numbers and values of the options issued, exercised, forfeited, and expired

* A description of the assumptions and methods being used to determine fair values

* The total compensation cost included in net income and contributed surplus

* Other[41]

IFRS/ASPE COMPARISON

Objective 7
Identify the major differences in accounting between IFRS and ASPE and what changes are expected in the near future.

Many complex financial instruments exist and must be accounted for in the company's financial statements. It is important to understand the nature of the instruments from an economic perspective: why would the company issue this type of instrument and why would an investor invest in it? It is also important to understand what creates the instrument's value. This will help in understanding the economic substance of the instrument. The accounting issues relate to presentation (determining if it is debt or equity or both) and measurement.

Derivatives have been the focus of some very negative publicity in the past few years, with companies suffering significant losses and perhaps even going bankrupt due to derivative instruments. This is partially due to the complexity of these contracts and the fact that they are not well understood by many who use them.

Do complex accounting standards add any value in the capital marketplace? They certainly add to the costs of preparing financial statements. Accountants in industry must stay up to date on these standards, as must auditors. There is a very real risk that investors and creditors do not understand the standards and perhaps may not even have the educational background that is required to be able to work through the complexities.

A Comparison of IFRS and ASPE

Illustration 16-12 compares IFRS with ASPE for complex financial instruments, providing additional information to that included in the comparison illustrations in Chapters 14 and 15.

Illustration 16-12

IFRS and ASPE Comparison Chart

	IFRS—IAS 32, 39, and IFRS 2, 9	Accounting Standards for Private Enterprises (ASPE)—*CPA Canada Handbook*, Part II, Sections 3856 and 3870	References to Related Illustrations and Select Brief Exercises
Presentation —Purchase commitments	Accounted for as executory contracts unless the contracts allow for net settlement and the entity does not expect to take delivery of the inventory (in which case they are treated as derivatives).	Accounted for as executory contracts since not exchange traded.	BE16-3 and Illustration 16-1
—Own equity instruments	The definitions of financial liabilities and equity instruments include references to instruments settled in the entity's own instruments. As a general rule, the instrument is equity only if it will be settled by issuing a fixed amount of cash for a fixed number of shares and there is no contractual obligation.	Less detailed guidance is provided under ASPE. Consider the basic definitions of financial liability and equity. If the definition of a liability is not met, then the instrument is presented as equity. For most instruments, this will be the same treatment. More complex scenarios are beyond the scope of the text.	

(continued)

	IFRS—IAS 32, 39, and IFRS 2, 9	Accounting Standards for Private Enterprises (ASPE)—*CPA Canada Handbook*, Part II, Sections 3856 and 3870	References to Related Illustrations and Select Brief Exercises
—Certain puttable shares	Treated as equity if certain criteria are met. No special treatment for certain tax planning arrangements. The criteria establish whether the instruments are "in-substance" equity instruments. This was also discussed in Chapter 15.	Treated as equity if certain criteria are met including under certain tax planning arrangements. The criteria establish whether the instruments are "in-substance" equity instruments. This was also discussed in Chapter 15.	BE16-18
Recognition —Hybrid/compound instruments with contingent settlement provisions	Instruments with contingent settlement provisions represent liabilities where the contingency is outside the control of the issuer.	Instruments with contingent settlement provisions are financial liabilities if the contingency is highly likely to occur.	BE16-19
Measurement —Components of compound instruments	Always measure the debt component first (generally at the present value of the cash flows). The rest of the value is assigned to equity since it is a residual item.	May measure the equity component at $0. Alternatively, measure the component that is most easily measurable and apply the residual to the other component.	Illustration 16-8 BE16-11 and BE16-12
	A financial liability that is indexed to the entity's financial performance or changes in equity would be analyzed to determine if an embedded derivative exists. Embedded derivatives are beyond the scope of the text.	Where a financial liability is indexed to the entity's financial performance or changes in equity, it is measured at the higher of the amortized cost and the amount owing at the balance sheet date given the index feature.	
	Allowed to value the entire financial instrument at fair value under the fair value option as long as certain conditions are met. Gains/losses due to changes in the entity's own credit risks are booked through other comprehensive income (OCI).	Allowed to value the entire financial instrument at fair value under the fair value option.	Illustration 14-10
	Where induced early conversion, gains/losses booked to income.	Where induced early conversion, gains/losses split between income and equity.	See discussion following Illustration 16-8
—CSOP when using an options pricing model	Volatility generally measurable. Must estimate forfeitures up front.	Volatility is not readily available for private entities but an attempt must be made to measure. May choose whether to recognize forfeitures up front or later. No difference as long as recognize forfeitures up front under ASPE.	
Presentation —Equity-settled CSOP for private entities	N/A	Generally presented as equity although history of repurchasing the shares after the employee has exercised the CSOP may indicate that the CSOP is a liability.	N/A
Recognition and measurement —Hedge accounting (Appendix 16A)	Specifies fair value hedges and cash flow hedges. Under fair value hedge accounting, the hedged item is valued at fair value with gains and losses booked through income. Under cash flow hedge accounting, the gains and losses on the hedging item are booked through OCI and may be recycled to income when the hedged item is booked to net income.	Does not specify accounting for fair value hedges or cash flow hedges. Instead, the standard lists certain types of specific hedging transactions that may qualify for hedge accounting including hedges of anticipated transactions and hedges of interest-bearing assets and liabilities. Hedge accounting generally stipulates that the hedging item is not recognized until it is settled (using accrual accounting).	Illustrations 16A-1, 2, 3, 7, 8, 9, and 11
—Accounting for cash-settled and other stock compensation plans (Appendix 16B)	Cash-settled plans are measured at fair value (using valuation methods such as options pricing models, which incorporate both intrinsic value and time value). All equity-settled instruments are measured at fair value.	Cash-settled plans such as SARs are measured at intrinsic value. Entities have a choice as to how to measure equity-settled SARs.	BE16-23 and BE16-24

Illustration 16-12

IFRS and ASPE Comparison Chart (continued)

Looking Ahead

The IASB hedge accounting project has been split into two phases: a general hedge accounting phase and a macro hedging phase. Macro hedging refers to hedging based on a portfolio of financial instruments such as investments. The guidance relating to general hedge accounting has already been issued and is incorporated into IFRS 9 and also into this chapter (Appendix 16A). The IASB issued a Discussion Paper on macro hedging in 2014 entitled *Accounting for Dynamic Risk Management: A Portfolio Revaluation Approach to Macro Hedging.* The board was discussing next steps at the time of writing. Most of the issues being discussed are beyond the scope of this text.

The AcSB issued an Exposure Draft in 2014 entitled *Redeemable Preferred Shares Issued in a Tax Planning Arrangement.* The AcSB was deliberating the issues relating to this type of preferred share when this text went to press.

SUMMARY OF LEARNING OBJECTIVES

1 Understand what derivatives are and how they are used to manage risks.

Derivatives are financial instruments that derive (get) their value from an underlying instrument. They are attractive because they transfer risks and rewards without having to necessarily invest directly in the underlying instrument. They are used for both speculative purposes (to expose a company to increased risks in the hope of increased returns) and for hedging purposes (to reduce existing risk).

Financial risks include credit, currency, interest rate, liquidity, market, and other price risks. Credit risk is the risk that the other party to a financial instrument contract will fail to deliver. Currency and interest rate risk are the risk of a change in value and cash flows due to currency or interest rate changes. Liquidity risk is the risk that the company itself will not be able to honour a contract due to cash problems. Finally, market risk is the risk of a change in value and/or cash flows related to market forces.

2 Understand how to account for derivatives.

Derivatives are recognized on the SFP on the date that the contract is initiated. They are remeasured, on each SFP date, to their fair value. The related gains and losses are recorded through net income. Written options create liabilities. Futures contracts require the company to deposit a portion of the contracts' value with the broker/ exchange. The contracts are marked to market by the broker/exchange daily and the company may have to deposit additional funds to cover deficiencies in the margin account. Purchase commitments that are net settleable and are not "expected use" contracts are accounted for as derivatives under IFRS. Under ASPE, purchase commitments are never accounted for as derivatives because they are not exchange-traded futures contracts. Exchange-traded derivatives relating to commodities are generally accounted for as derivatives under ASPE. Special hedge accounting may affect how derivatives are accounted for.

Under IFRS, derivatives that are settleable in the entity's own equity instruments are accounted for as equity (or contra equity) if they will be settled by exchanging a fixed number of equity instruments for a fixed amount of cash or other assets and they do not create an obligation to deliver cash or other assets. Otherwise, they are financial assets/liabilities. In general, if the instruments are net settleable or have settlement options, they most often do not meet the criteria for equity presentation and are therefore financial assets/liabilities. IFRS provides significantly more guidance with respect to the accounting for these instruments.

3 Analyze whether a hybrid/compound instrument issued for financing purposes represents a liability, equity, or both.

Complex instruments include compound and hybrid instruments where the legal form may differ from the economic substance. The economic substance dictates the accounting. The main issue is that of presentation: should the instrument be presented as debt or equity? The definitions of debt and equity are useful in analyzing this. It is also important to understand what gives the instruments their value from a finance or economic perspective. If an instrument has both debt and equity components, use of the proportional and incremental methods will help in allocating the carrying value between the two components. There are differences in measuring compound financial instruments under IFRS versus ASPE. Related interest, dividends, gains, and losses are treated in a way that is consistent with the SFP presentation.

4 Explain the accounting for hybrid/compound instruments.

The method for recording convertible bonds at the date of issuance is different from the method that is used to record straight debt issues. As the instrument is a compound instrument and contains both debt and equity components, these must be measured separately and presented as debt and equity, respectively. Any discount or premium that results from the issuance of convertible bonds is amortized, assuming the bonds will be held to maturity. If bonds are converted into other securities, the principal accounting problem is to determine the amount at which to record the securities that have been exchanged for the bond. The book value method is often used in practice. ASPE allows an entity to value the equity portion of compound instruments at $0.

5   Describe the various types of stock compensation plans.

Stock compensation includes direct awards of stock (when a company gives the shares to an employee as compensation), compensatory stock option plans whereby an employee is given stock options in lieu of salary, share appreciation rights (SARs), and performance-type plans. SARs and performance-type plans are discussed in Appendix 16B.

Employee stock option plans are meant to motivate employees and raise capital for the company. They are therefore capital transactions. Compensatory stock

option plans are operating transactions since they are meant to compensate the employee for service provided.

6   Describe the accounting for share-based compensation.

CSOPs and direct awards of stock are measured at fair value (using an options pricing model) at the grant date. The cost is then allocated to expense over the period that the employee provides service. As noted above, SARs and performance-type plans are discussed in Appendix 16B.

7   Identify the major differences in accounting between IFRS and ASPE and what changes are expected in the near future.

The differences are noted in the comparison chart in Illustration 16-12. The stock-based compensation standards are largely converged and stable; however, the IASB is currently working on several projects relating to financial instruments, including macro hedging.

KEY TERMS

book value method, p. 991
call option, p. 979
compensatory stock option plans (CSOPs), p. 994
convertible bond, p. 990
counterparty, p. 975
credit risk, p. 974
currency risk, p. 974
derivative instruments, p. 972
embedded derivatives, p. 972
employee stock option or purchase plans (ESOPs), p. 994
equity instruments, p. 972
executory contracts, p. 977
exercise period, p. 978

exercise price, p. 978
financial instruments, p. 971
financial liability, p. 987
forward contract, p. 976
grant date, p. 996
hedging, p. 975
hybrid/compound instruments, p. 986
incremental method, p. 989
induced conversion, p. 991
interest rate risk, p. 974
intrinsic value, p. 980
liquidity risk, p. 974
market risk, p. 974
nonmonetary reciprocal transaction, p. 998

other price risk, p. 974
primary financial instruments, p. 971
proportional method, p. 989
purchased options, p. 979
put option, p. 979
relative fair value method, p. 989
residual value method, p. 989
service period, p. 997
speculator, p. 976
strike price, p. 978
time value, p. 980
vest, p. 996
vesting period, p. 997
written options, p. 979

APPENDIX 16A

Objective 8
Understand how derivatives are used in hedging and explain the need for hedge accounting standards.

HEDGING

Derivatives Used for Hedging and the Need for Hedge Accounting Standards

In the body of the chapter, we discussed basic issues related to derivatives. This appendix will focus on the **accounting for hedging**. How does hedging actually reduce risk from an economic perspective and what are the accounting implications?

Companies that are already exposed to financial risks because of existing business transactions that arise from their business models may choose to protect themselves by managing and reducing those risks. For example, most public companies borrow and lend

**FINANCIAL RISK
MANAGEMENT**
5.5.2
**STRATEGY
DEVELOPMENT**
2.3.2

substantial amounts in credit markets and are therefore exposed to significant financial risks. They face substantial risk that the fair values or cash flows of interest-sensitive assets or liabilities will change if interest rates increase or decrease (known as **interest rate risk**). These same companies often also have cross-border transactions or international operations that expose them to **exchange rate risk**. The borrowing activity creates **liquidity risk** for the company and the lending activity creates **credit risk**.

Because the value and/or cash flows of derivative financial instruments can vary according to changes in interest rates, foreign currency exchange rates, or other external factors, derivatives may be used to offset the associated risks. Using derivatives or other instruments to offset risks is called **hedging**. In a hedging relationship, there is a **hedged item** (the risk or exposure) and a **hedging item** (often a derivative contract entered into to reduce risk). A properly hedged position should result in no economic loss to the company. It may result in no gain, and there may be costs involved to effect the transactions, but it should limit or eliminate any potential losses. It reduces uncertainty and risk, and therefore volatility, and that is what gives hedging its value.

It is important to separate the **act of hedging** to reduce economic and financial risks from the **accounting** for these hedges. Hedge accounting is optional and in some cases not even necessary. A company may choose to apply it or not. It is an accounting policy choice.

Why do we need special accounting rules for hedges? They exist in part due to the following:

1. The mixed measurement model under IFRS and ASPE (for example, choices include fair value, amortized cost, and cost)

2. The treatment of the related gains and losses where fair value is used (under IFRS sometimes the resulting gains and losses are booked to income and sometimes to OCI)

3. The existing practice of hedging future transactions that are not yet recognized on the SFP (as part of the company's risk management strategy)

As noted earlier, when a position is properly hedged, no further gains or losses from the hedged position should arise on a net basis. Another way to think of it is this: while gains and losses may arise on the hedged and hedging items separately, they should offset each other. If the way we are otherwise accounting for the hedged and hedging items results in something other than this, then hedge accounting is available as an option to "fix" the problem.

Let's look at a few concrete examples that illustrate this. It may be helpful to follow a few steps to analyze whether hedge accounting is necessary. There are five steps, as noted below:

1. Identify the hedged item. Which risk is being hedged?

2. Identify the hedging item. This is usually a derivative instrument that the company has purchased or signed a contract for (such as a forward, future, option, or swap). If a risk is properly hedged, the hedging item reduces the risk noted in step 1 above.[42]

3. Identify how the hedged item is being accounted for without hedge accounting. Note that it might not even be recognized on the SFP yet if it is an anticipated transaction such as a future purchase. Is it accounted for at FV-NI or FV-OCI or some sort of cost basis?

4. Note that the hedging item, which is normally a derivative, will be accounted for using FV-NI unless hedge accounting is applied. Therefore, if the hedged item is accounted for in any other way, we may need to consider using hedge accounting if IFRS and/or ASPE allow it.

5. Locate where the recognized gains and losses for the hedged and hedging items are recognized (net income, OCI, or perhaps not at all). Do the gains and losses from the hedged item and hedging items offset? If they do, then we would say that there is symmetry in the accounting. The gains and losses are treated similarly in terms of measuring net income or OCI. If they do not offset, then we may need to consider hedge accounting if IFRS and/or ASPE allow it. In this case, we would argue that there is no symmetry in accounting unless we apply hedge accounting.

Symmetry in Accounting—No Need for Special Hedge Accounting

ECONOMICS

Consider the situation where a company has a U.S. $100 receivable that is due in 30 days. The company is exposed to a **foreign currency risk**. Each time the currency rate changes, the economic value of the asset changes. Under existing IFRS and ASPE, at each SFP date, we revalue the asset to reflect the current spot rate for the U.S. dollar. If the U.S. dollar depreciates against the Canadian dollar, the receivable is worth less and the resulting loss gets booked to the income statement. Now let's assume that the company does not want this foreign currency exposure (the hedged item) and it enters into a forward contract (the hedging item) to sell U.S. $100 for $102 Canadian in 30 days. This provides an **effective (economic) hedge** against changes in the value of the asset. If the U.S. dollar subsequently depreciates in value, then the forward contract increases in value because, under the contract, we can still sell the U.S. $100 for $102 Canadian no matter what happens to the exchange rate. From an **economic perspective**, the gains on the forward offset the losses on the receivable.

From an **accounting perspective**, let's analyze the above situation using the five steps.

1. The hedged item is the foreign currency risk associated with the receivable.

2. The hedging item is the forward contract.

3. The account receivable is revalued each period, with gains and losses booked to net income.

4. The forward contract is accounted for using FV-NI, so gains and losses are also being booked through net income.

5. Since the gains and losses from both the hedged position and the hedging item are being booked through net income, they already offset and hedge accounting is unnecessary.

No Symmetry in Accounting—Potential Need for Special Hedge Accounting

UNDERLYING CONCEPT

Using hedge accounting increases transparency—reflecting the decrease in income volatility where the company has hedged its positions.

If instead, the company had an investment in a security classified as fair value through other comprehensive income (using IFRS), losses due to decreases in the value of the security would be booked to other comprehensive income. Suppose the company decided to purchase an option (the hedging item) to sell the security at a fixed price. This would protect it against future declines in value of the shares (the hedged item) and would therefore be an effective (economic) hedge against future losses. If the value of the shares declined, the value of the option to sell at a set price would increase, resulting in a gain.

From an **accounting perspective**, let's analyze the above situation using the five steps.

1. The hedged item is the risk that the shares will decline in value (market risk).

2. The hedging item is the option to sell the shares at a fixed price.

3. The investment is accounted for using FV-OCI so gains/losses are booked through OCI.

4. The option is a derivative and is accounted for using FV-NI.

5. The gains and losses do not offset (one goes to OCI and the other to net income); therefore, hedge accounting may be considered if allowed under IFRS.

We will look at the journal entries for this example later in this appendix.

Hedge Accounting

Objective 9
Understand how to apply hedge accounting standards.

As we mentioned, hedge accounting is optional and modifies the normal accounting. It is designed to ensure that the timing of the recognition of gains/losses in net income is the same for both the hedged item and the hedging item. It will result in recognition and measurement that are different than under pre-hedge accounting GAAP. Thus, it is important to ensure that the hedge is effective and properly identified and documented in order to allow it to qualify for this "special" treatment.

Hedges may qualify for optional hedge accounting when the following criteria are met.[43]

1. At the inception of the hedge, the entity must do the following:

   (a) **Identify** the exposure (such as exposure to foreign exchange fluctuations).

   (b) **Designate** that hedge accounting will be applied.

   (c) **Document** the risk management objectives and strategies, the hedging relationship, the items being hedged and used to hedge, the methods of assessing the effectiveness of the hedge, and the method of accounting for the hedge.

2. At the inception and throughout the term, the entity should have reasonable assurance that the relationship is **effective and consistent with the risk management policy.** As a result, all of the following must be respected:

   (a) The **effectiveness** of the hedge should be reliably measurable.[44]

   (b) The **hedging** relationship should be reassessed regularly.

   (c) Where the hedge involves forecast transactions, it should be probable that these transactions will occur.

Under ASPE, hedge accounting is greatly simplified, with only certain pre-specified transactions qualifying for optional hedge accounting treatment. These include the following:

1. Anticipated purchase/sale of a commodity hedged with a forward contract where either or both are denominated in a foreign currency

2. Anticipated foreign exchange–denominated transactions hedged with a forward contract

3. Interest-bearing assets/liabilities hedged with interest rate or cross-currency swaps

4. Net investments in a foreign subsidiary[45]

As a general rule under ASPE, hedge accounting greatly simplifies how we account for the hedged position. It allows the company to not recognize the hedging item (normally a derivative) until the derivative contract is settled or cash is paid/payable or received/receivable under the derivative contract.

Under IFRS, hedge accounting divides hedges into two basic groups: fair value hedges and cash flow hedges. **Fair value hedge** accounting is used to account for hedges of exposures relating to recognized assets/liabilities and unrecognized purchase commitments.[46] **Cash flow hedge** accounting is used to account for hedges of exposures relating to future cash flows such as future interest payments on variable rate debt. We will discuss each below. Let's take a closer look at the way hedge accounting is applied under both IFRS and ASPE.

Fair Value Hedges

A derivative may be used to hedge or offset the exposure to changes in the fair value of a recognized asset or liability (or of a previously unrecognized firm commitment), and thus reduce market risk. In a perfectly hedged position, the economic gain/loss on the fair value of the derivative (the hedging item) and that of the hedged asset or liability (the hedged item) should be equal and offsetting. Under IFRS fair value hedge accounting, the hedged item must be recognized on the SFP and measured (or remeasured) at fair value and the related gains/losses must be booked through net income. So for instance, if the asset was normally measured at cost, it would have to be remeasured to fair value under hedge accounting. In addition, if the gains/losses were normally booked through OCI, a journal entry would be booked to reclassify them to net income under hedge accounting.

Let's look at a specific example.

Using Hedge Accounting—Recognized Assets as Hedged Items

To illustrate, assume that Pathay Inc. purchases an investment for $1,000. This exposes the company to a market risk—the risk that the shares will decline in value. The shares trade on a local stock exchange. Assume further that the investment is designated as fair value through other comprehensive income (FV-OCI) under IFRS. Under ASPE, the shares are accounted for as FV-NI investments because there is an active market. Illustration 16A-1 shows the journal entries to record the initial investment at January 1, 2018.

<table>
<tr><td></td><td>IFRS</td><td></td><td>ASPE</td><td></td></tr>
<tr><td>FV-OCI Investments</td><td>1,000</td><td></td><td></td><td></td></tr>
<tr><td>FV-NI Investments</td><td></td><td></td><td>1,000</td><td></td></tr>
<tr><td>   Cash</td><td></td><td>1,000</td><td></td><td>1,000</td></tr>
</table>

Illustration 16A-1

Acquisition of Investment

A = L + SE
0

Cash flows: ↓ 1,000 outflow

Assume that on the same date, the company also enters into a derivative contract in which it purchases an option to sell the shares at $1,000 to protect itself against losses in value of the security. The cost of the option is $10. If the value of the shares declines, the company can sell the shares under the option for $1,000—thus limiting any loss. As a derivative, the option will be measured at fair value, with subsequent gains and losses booked to net income. Illustration 16A-2 shows the journal entry.

<table>
<tr><td></td><td>IFRS</td><td></td><td>ASPE</td><td></td></tr>
<tr><td>Derivatives—Financial
  Assets/Liabilities</td><td>10</td><td></td><td>10</td><td></td></tr>
<tr><td>   Cash</td><td></td><td>10</td><td></td><td>10</td></tr>
</table>

Illustration 16A-2

Acquisition of Derivative Contract to Hedge Market Risk

A = L + SE
0

Cash flows: ↓ 10 outflow

If at December 31, 2018, the investment's fair value increased by $7, the derivative would decrease in value by $7. This is because the option is now less valuable given that it allows the holder to sell the shares for (only) an amount that is less than the current market value. (In fact, the loss on the option would not exactly offset the gains on the investment because the value of the option incorporates other variables.)

The journal entries to record this are in Illustration 16A-3.

Illustration 16A-3

Recognition of Change in Value of Derivative and Hedge Accounting

A = L + SE
0   0

Cash flows: No effect

<table>
<tr><td>December 31, 2018</td><td colspan="2">IFRS: optional hedge accounting</td><td colspan="2">ASPE: not eligible for hedge accounting</td></tr>
<tr><td>FV-OCI Investments</td><td>7</td><td></td><td></td><td></td></tr>
<tr><td>FV-NI Investments</td><td></td><td></td><td>7</td><td></td></tr>
<tr><td>   Unrealized Gain or Loss—OCI</td><td></td><td>7</td><td></td><td></td></tr>
<tr><td>   Unrealized Gain or Loss</td><td></td><td></td><td></td><td>7</td></tr>
<tr><td>Unrealized Gain or Loss</td><td>7</td><td></td><td>7</td><td></td></tr>
<tr><td>   Derivatives—Financial
      Assets/Liabilities</td><td></td><td>7</td><td></td><td>7</td></tr>
<tr><td>Unrealized Gain or Loss—OCI</td><td>7</td><td></td><td>N/A</td><td></td></tr>
<tr><td>   Unrealized Gain or Loss</td><td></td><td>7</td><td></td><td>N/A</td></tr>
</table>

As previously mentioned, the derivative is always valued at fair value, with the gains/losses being booked to net income. However, normally the gain on the FV-OCI investment would be booked to other comprehensive income under IFRS. There is therefore a mismatch. This is a fair value hedge under IFRS, since the hedged item is the risk that the value of the investment, which is a recognized asset, will decline. Fair value hedge accounting under IFRS allows the gain on the hedged item to be booked through net income so it may be offset by the loss on the derivative, as noted in the last journal entry above. Hedge accounting allows us to modify the way we would normally account for the FV-OCI investment.

As noted in Illustration 16A-3, this transaction is not eligible for hedge accounting under ASPE (since it is not on the list of allowable transactions noted earlier). In the end, the impact on net income is the same when we compare the accounting for this transaction under ASPE (without using hedge accounting) and IFRS (using hedge accounting). This is because under ASPE, where OCI does not exist, the accounting for the investment and the derivative is already symmetrical and the gains and losses offset without having to apply hedge accounting.

Using Hedge Accounting—Purchase Commitments as Hedged Items

Assume the company has committed to purchase a certain amount of raw materials at a fixed price denominated in U.S. dollars in order to secure a stable supply of the raw materials. This would create a foreign currency risk because the price is fixed in U.S. dollars, the value of which will vary over time. Normally, a company would not recognize purchase commitments for which it intends to take delivery of the raw materials unless there was a contingent loss that was measurable and probable.[47]

Assume further that the company chooses to hedge the foreign currency risk by entering into a forward contract to purchase U.S. dollars at a future date at a fixed exchange rate. This would lock in the rate and therefore remove the foreign currency risk. The forward would be recognized on the SFP and measured at FV-NI. If the purchase commitment were not recognized on the SFP, there would be a mismatch.

Therefore, under IFRS fair value hedge accounting, the purchase commitment would also need to be recognized on the SFP and measured at fair value (with gains/losses booked through net income). Since the purchase commitment might be difficult to measure, the entity also has the option under IFRS hedge accounting to account for this as a cash flow hedge. This would result in leaving the purchase commitment off–balance sheet and booking any unrealized gains or losses on the forward contract through OCI. We will look at an example of cash flow hedge accounting later in the appendix.

This transaction qualifies for hedge accounting under ASPE since it is on the list of transactions where hedge accounting is allowed. It is an anticipated purchase that is hedged with a foreign currency forward contract. Without hedge accounting, the purchase commitment would not be recorded but the forward contract would be, because it is a U.S.-dollar derivative. If hedge accounting is applied, neither the purchase commitment nor the derivative would be recognized until the goods were delivered and the contracts settled. The raw materials would be measured using the locked-in forward exchange rate for the U.S. dollars.

Cash Flow Hedges

A cash flow hedge deals with transactions that offset the effects of future variable cash flows, such as future interest payments on variable rate debt. Because the debt has a variable rate, the interest to be paid out will fluctuate, and this therefore makes future cash flows uncertain. Since the hedged position (that is, the potential change in future interest payments) is not yet recognized on the SFP, the gains/losses related to changes in value (and hence the cash flows) are not captured. Thus, under hedge accounting per IFRS, any gains/losses on the hedging item should not be included in net income either. They are therefore recognized in other comprehensive income.

Recall that under ASPE, the term "other comprehensive income" is not used. Therefore, hedge accounting under ASPE for these types of transactions essentially requires that the hedging item not be recognized until the transaction is settled. (In other words, it remains off–balance sheet.) The purchase commitment example above illustrates this.

In a cash flow hedge, the company is trying to protect itself against variations in future cash flows. Different derivative instruments may be used to effect this. Let's look at an example.

Using Hedge Accounting—Interest Rate Swaps as Hedging Items

When a company has a series of similar transactions that it wants to hedge, a **swap contract** may be used. A swap is a transaction between two parties in which the first party promises to make a series of payments to the second party. Similarly, the second party promises to make simultaneous payments to the first party. The parties swap payments. A swap is a series of forward contracts. The most common type of swap is the **interest rate swap**, in which one party makes payments based on a fixed or floating rate and the second party does just the opposite. In most cases, financial institutions and other intermediaries find the two parties, bring them together, and handle the flow of payments between the two parties, as shown in Illustration 16A-4.

Illustration 16A-4

Swap Transaction

FINANCIAL RISK MANAGEMENT
5.5.2

To illustrate the accounting for a cash flow hedge, assume that Jones Corporation issues $1 million of five-year, floating-rate bonds on January 2, 2018. The entry to record this transaction is as follows:

A = L + SE
+1,000,000   +1,000,000

Cash flows: ↑ 1,000,000 inflow

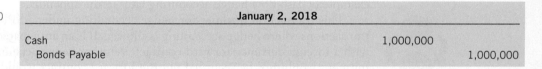

January 2, 2018		
Cash	1,000,000	
Bonds Payable		1,000,000

A floating interest rate was offered to appeal to investors, but Jones is concerned about the cash flow uncertainty associated with the variable rate interest. To protect against the **cash flow uncertainty**, Jones decides to hedge the risk by entering into a five-year interest rate swap. Under the terms of the swap contract, the following will occur:

1. Jones will pay fixed payments at 8% (based on the $1-million amount) to a counterparty.

2. Jones will receive, from the counterparty, variable or floating rates that are based on the market rate in effect throughout the life of the swap contract.

As Illustration 16A-5 shows, by using this swap, Jones can change the interest on the bonds payable from a floating rate to a fixed rate. Jones thus swaps the floating rate, assumed to be 9% in the example, for a fixed rate.

Illustration 16A-5

Interest Rate Swap

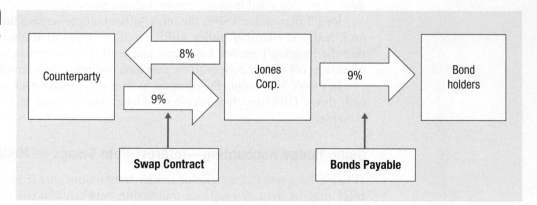

The settlement dates for the swap correspond to the interest payment dates on the debt (December 31). On each interest payment date (**settlement date**), Jones and the counterparty will calculate the difference between current market interest rates (9% in the example) and the fixed rate of 8%, and settle the difference.[48] Both parties will also need to value the swap contract on each SFP date using a discounted cash flow model. If interest rates rise, the value of the swap contract to Jones increases; in other words, Jones has a gain. At the same time, Jones's floating-rate debt obligation becomes larger; in other words, Jones has an economic loss. The swap is an effective risk management tool in this setting because its value is related to the same underlying (interest rates) that will affect the value of the floating-rate bond payable. Thus, if the swap's value goes up, it offsets the loss related to the debt obligation.

Assuming that the swap was entered into on January 2, 2018 (the same date as the issuance of the debt), the swap at this time has no value and there is therefore no need for a journal entry.

January 2, 2018
No entry required. Memorandum to indicate that the swap contract is signed.

At the end of 2018, the interest payment on the bonds is made to the bondholders. Assume the floating rate is 9%. The journal entry to record this transaction is as follows:

A = L + SE
−90,000   −90,000
Cash flows: ↓ 90,000 outflow

December 31, 2018		
Interest Expense	90,000	
Cash (9% × $1,000,000)		90,000

At the end of 2018, market interest rates have increased to 9%, and the value of the swap contract has therefore increased. Recall (see Illustration 16A-5) that in the swap Jones is to receive a floating rate of 9%, or $90,000 ($1,000,000 × 9%), and pay a fixed rate of 8%, or $80,000. Jones therefore receives $10,000 ($90,000 − $80,000) as a settlement payment on the swap contract on the first interest payment date. The entry to record this transaction is booked as an interest rate adjustment as follows:

A = L + SE
+10,000   +10,000
Cash flows: ↑ 10,000 inflow

December 31, 2018		
Cash	10,000	
Interest Expense		10,000

So far, the journal entries would be the same under IFRS and ASPE before any hedge accounting is applied.

Now, let's assume that the fair value of the interest rate swap has increased by $40,000. As a derivative, as previously noted, this swap contract is recognized on the SFP, and the gain in fair value is normally reported in net income. Under IFRS hedge accounting, this is a cash flow hedge because it relates to the anticipated changes in interest rates related to the variable rate loan. Using IFRS cash flow hedge accounting, the gain on the hedging item (the swap) is reported in other comprehensive income (as opposed to net income). Note that we could have prepared two journal entries: the first to book the gain to Unrealized Gain or Loss and the second to transfer the gain to Unrealized Gain or Loss—OCI. This increase in value is recorded as follows:[49]

A = L + SE
+40,000   +40,000
Cash flows: No effect

December 31, 2018	IFRS: optional hedge accounting		ASPE: optional hedge accounting	
Derivatives—Financial Assets/Liabilities	40,000		N/A	
Unrealized Gain or Loss—OCI		40,000		N/A

Without the hedge accounting, there is asymmetry in the accounting. The losses on the bond payable (due to the fact that it is a variable rate loan and interest rates keep rising) do not get recognized because they are opportunity costs.

Under IFRS cash flow hedge accounting, the unrealized gain will gradually be reflected in net income when the benefit of the locked-in (lower) interest rate is realized as reduced interest expense, as the earlier entries showed. Under ASPE, the transaction qualifies for hedge accounting because it is on the list of allowed transactions and under hedge accounting, the swap contract is not recognized on the balance sheet. Instead only the payments/receipts of interest are accrued as interest expense/income adjustments as shown in the earlier journal entries.

By the end of the swap contract, the market value of the contract will be nil and the company will have recorded net interest expense that reflects the fixed rate. This will be the case whether hedge accounting was used or not.

Illustration 16A-6 shows the presentation of a cash flow hedge on the SFP assuming IFRS cash flow hedge accounting is used.

Illustration 16A-6	
Statement of Financial Position Presentation of Cash Flow Hedge	

JONES CORPORATION
Statement of Financial Position (partial)
December 31, 2018

Non-current assets:	
Swap contract	$ 40,000
Long-term liabilities	
Bonds payable	$1,000,000
Equity	
Other comprehensive income	$ 40,000

On the income statement, interest expense of $80,000 is reported. Jones has effectively changed the debt's interest rate from variable to fixed. That is, by receiving a floating rate and paying a fixed rate on the swap, the floating rate on the bond payable is converted to variable, which results in an effective interest rate of 8% in 2018. The economic gain on the swap offsets the economic loss related to the debt obligation (since interest rates are higher), and therefore the net gain or loss on the hedging activity is zero.

One last point on interest rate swaps. As noted above, they may be used as cash flow hedges but they may also be used as fair value hedges and be eligible for hedge accounting under both IFRS and ASPE. Interest rate swaps would protect against changes in fair value of a recorded asset or liability that would occur when market interest rates change and where the asset or liability has a fixed interest rate. They can be used to offset the increase in the (fair) value of a fixed rate bond obligation when interest rates are declining or to offset a decline in the value of a bond investment when market interest rates are increasing.

In the previous example, assume instead that the $1-million debt had a fixed interest rate of 8% and that the company was concerned that they were locked into paying a higher rate of interest when interest rates were declining. The company decides to enter into a swap contract to protect itself against the risk of further potential increases in the fair value of the liability.

Under the swap agreement, the company will receive 8% and pay variable rates. As a derivative (before any hedge accounting), the swap would be recognized on the SFP and remeasured at reporting dates, and gains/losses would be recognized in income. If IFRS hedge accounting were used, this would be a fair value hedge because it relates to the risk that the fair value of the fixed-rate liability is increasing due to declining interest rates. Under IFRS fair value hedge accounting, the liability would be revalued to fair value with gains/losses being booked through income so that they offset the gains/losses on the swap. Therefore, if the fair value of the debt increased by $40,000 (due to decreases in interest rates only) and the fair value of the swap increased by a corresponding $40,000, the following entries would be booked:

A = L + SE
+40,000 +40,000

Cash flows: No effect

December 31, 2018	IFRS: optional hedge accounting		ASPE: optional hedge accounting	
Unrealized Gain or Loss	40,000		N/A	
Bonds Payable		40,000		N/A
Derivatives—Financial Assets/Liabilities	40,000			
Unrealized Gain or Loss		40,000		

This transaction qualifies for hedge accounting under ASPE. Under ASPE hedge accounting, these journal entries would not be booked. As noted earlier, only the payments/receipts of interest would be booked.

Using Hedge Accounting—Anticipated Purchases as Hedged Items

Another example of a cash flow hedge is a hedge of an anticipated future transaction, such as a raw material purchase.

Let's illustrate the accounting for this type of cash flow hedge under IFRS. Assume that in September 2018, Allied Can Co. anticipates purchasing 1,000 metric tonnes of aluminum in January 2019. Allied is concerned that prices for aluminum will increase in the next few months, and it wants to protect against possible price increases for aluminum inventory. To hedge the risk that it might have to pay higher prices for inventory in January 2019, Allied enters into a cash-settled aluminum forward contract. Assume that the contract is an exchange-traded futures contract.

The contract requires Allied to pay any difference between $1,550 per tonne and the spot price for aluminum, if lower, to the counterparty. If the price of aluminum increases, the counterparty will make a payment for the difference to Allied.[50] In other words, this contract is net settled. The contract matures on the expected purchase date in January 2019. The underlying for this derivative is the price of aluminum. If the price of aluminum rises above $1,550, the value of the contract to Allied increases because Allied will be able to purchase the aluminum at the lower price of $1,550 per tonne.

Assume that the contract was entered into on September 1, 2018, and that the price to be paid today for inventory to be delivered in January, the forward price, was equal to the current spot price adjusted for the time between September and January. On a net present value basis, the fair value of this contract will be zero. Therefore, no entry is necessary.

September 1, 2018
No entry required. Memorandum to indicate that the contract is signed.

Assume that at December 31, 2018, the price for January delivery of aluminum has increased. The fair value of the contract has therefore also increased, with its value now assumed to be $25,000. Under IFRS, because the contract is a net-settled commodities contract where the company does not intend to take delivery of the actual aluminum, it is accounted for as a derivative contract (FV-NI). Under ASPE, because it is an exchange-traded futures contract relating to a commodity, it is also accounted for as a derivative.

Allied would make the entry as shown in Illustration 16A-7 to record this increase in the value of the forward contract.

Illustration 16A-7

Change in Value of Derivative Contract

A = L + SE
+25,000 +25,000

Cash flows: No effect

	IFRS: optional hedge accounting		ASPE: optional hedge accounting	
Derivatives—Financial Assets/Liabilities	25,000		N/A	
Unrealized Gain or Loss—OCI		25,000		N/A

The derivative contract is reported on the SFP as an asset. The gain on the contract would normally be recorded through net income under both IFRS and ASPE. However, under IFRS hedge accounting, it is reported as part of other comprehensive income. Since Allied has not yet purchased and sold the inventory, this is an anticipated transaction. In this type of transaction, gains or losses on the futures contract are accumulated in other comprehensive income until the period in which the inventory is sold and earnings is affected.

Under ASPE hedge accounting, the derivative contract would not be recognized at all until it is settled (when the inventory is recognized). The gain/loss would be recorded in future as an adjustment to inventory. Note further that, if the forward contract was not exchange traded, it would normally not be accounted for as a derivative because non–exchange-traded commodities contracts are not covered under Section 3856. Therefore, hedge accounting under ASPE would not be needed.

Assume now that in January 2019, Allied purchases (separately) 1,000 metric tonnes of aluminum for $1,575. It would make the entry shown in Illustration 16A-8.

Illustration 16A-8

Acquisition of Inventory

A   =   L   +   SE
0

Cash flows: ↓ 1,575,000 outflow

	IFRS: optional hedge accounting	ASPE: optional hedge accounting
Inventory ($1,575 × 1,000 tonnes)	1,575,000	1,575,000
Cash	1,575,000	1,575,000

At the same time, Allied makes final settlement on the derivative contract and makes the entry shown in Illustration 16A-9.

Illustration 16A-9

Settlement of Derivative Contract

A   =   L   +   SE
0

Cash flows: ↑ 25,000 inflow

	IFRS: optional hedge accounting	ASPE: optional hedge accounting
Cash	25,000	25,000
Derivatives—Financial Assets/Liabilities ($1,575,000 – $1,550,000)	25,000	
Inventory		25,000

Through use of the derivative contract, Allied has been able to fix the cost of its inventory. The $25,000 contract settlement payment offsets the amount paid to purchase the inventory at the prevailing market price of $1,575,000. The result is that the net cash outflow is at $1,550 per metric tonne, as desired. In this way, Allied has hedged the cash flow for the purchase of inventory, as shown in Illustration 16A-10.

Illustration 16A-10

Effect of Hedge on Cash Flows

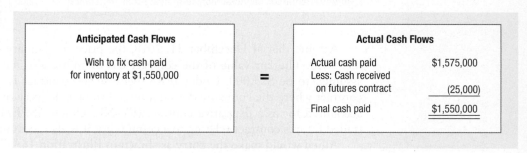

There are no income effects at this point. The gain on the futures contract is accumulated in equity as part of accumulated other comprehensive income under IFRS until the period when the inventory is sold and earnings is affected through cost of goods sold.

For example, assume that the aluminum is processed into cans, the finished goods. The total cost of the cans (including the aluminum purchases in January 2019) is $1.7 million. Allied sells the cans in July 2019 for $2 million. The entry to record the sale is as shown in Illustration 16A-11.

			IFRS: optional hedge accounting		ASPE: optional hedge accounting	
Cash			2,000,000		2,000,000	
	Sales Revenue			2,000,000		2,000,000
Cost of Goods Sold			1,700,000		1,675,000	
	Inventory			1,700,000		1,675,000
Unrealized Gain or Loss—OCI			25,000		N/A	
	Cost of Goods Sold			25,000		N/A

Illustration 16A-11

Recognition of Sale of Finished Goods

IFRS
A	=	L	+	SE
+300,000				+300,000

Cash flows: ↑ 2,000,000 inflow

ASPE
A	=	L	+	SE
+325,000				+325,000

Cash flows: ↑ 2,000,000 inflow

The gain on the futures contract, which was reported as part of other comprehensive income, now reduces the cost of goods sold. As a result, the cost of aluminum included in the overall cost of goods sold is $1,550,000. The derivative contract has worked as planned to manage the cash paid for aluminum inventory and the amount of cost of goods sold. Note that under IFRS, this entry could also be made at the date when the inventory was acquired, except that the credit would be booked to Inventory. Thus, the cost of goods sold in July 2019 would be $1,675,000 (versus $1,700,000).

SUMMARY OF LEARNING OBJECTIVES FOR APPENDIX 16A

8 Understand how derivatives are used in hedging and explain the need for hedge accounting standards.

Any company or individual that wants to protect itself against different types of business risk often uses derivative contracts to achieve this objective. In general, where the intent is to manage and reduce risk, these transactions involve some type of hedge. Derivatives are useful tools for this since they have the effect of transferring risks and rewards between the parties to the contract. Derivatives can be used to hedge a company's exposure to fluctuations in interest rates, foreign currency exchange rates, equity, or commodity prices.

Hedge accounting is optional accounting that ensures that properly hedged positions will reduce volatility in net income created by hedging with derivatives. It seeks to match gains and losses from hedged positions with those of the hedging items so that they may be offset.

9 Understand how to apply hedge accounting standards.

Since this is special accounting, companies must ensure that there is in fact a real hedge (that the contract insulates the company from economic loss or undesirable consequences) and that the hedge remains effective. Proper documentation of the risks and risk management strategy is important. Under IFRS, there are fair value hedges and cash flow hedges. A fair value hedge reduces risks relating to fair value changes of recorded assets and liabilities as well as purchase commitments. Cash flow hedges protect against future losses due to future cash flow changes relating to exposures that are not captured on the SFP. ASPE does not discuss fair value or cash flow hedges but rather stipulates the accounting for certain types of specific hedge transactions.

Properly hedged positions reduce income fluctuations because gains and losses are offset. Under IFRS, for cash flow hedges, the gains and losses on the hedging items are booked through other comprehensive income and are brought into net income in the same (future) period that the hedged items are booked to net income. For fair value hedges, hedge accounting adjusts the hedged asset to ensure that it is recognized and measured at fair value and that related gains/losses are booked through net income. Both types of hedges ensure that the gains/losses of the hedged and hedging positions offset. Under ASPE hedge accounting, the hedging item (which is generally a derivative) is not recognized on the balance sheet until the hedging item is settled. Thus both the hedged item (usually a future transaction) and the hedging item (the derivative) are off–balance sheet and there is no mismatch.

KEY TERMS

cash flow hedge, p. 1005

fair value hedge, p. 1005

hedged item, p. 1003

hedging item, p. 1003

interest rate swap, p. 1008

settlement date, p. 1009

swap contract, p. 1007

APPENDIX 16B

STOCK COMPENSATION PLANS— ADDITIONAL COMPLICATIONS

Two common stock compensation plans (beyond the stock option plans discussed in the chapter) that illustrate different accounting issues are:

1. Share appreciation rights plans

2. Performance-type plans

We will discuss these below. In addition, this appendix will discuss briefly accounting where settlement options exist.

Share Appreciation Rights Plans

Objective 10
Account for share appreciation rights plans.

One of the main drawbacks of compensatory stock option plans is that, in order to realize the stock options' benefit, the employees must exercise the options and then sell the shares. This is a somewhat complex process and usually involves incurring transaction costs. One solution to this problem was the creation of **share appreciation rights (SARs)**. In this type of plan, the executive or employee is given the right to receive compensation equal to the share appreciation, which is defined as the excess of the shares' fair value at the date of exercise over a pre-established price. This share appreciation may be paid in cash, shares, or a combination of both.

The major advantage of SARs is that the employee often does not have to make a cash outlay at the date of exercise, and instead receives a payment for the share appreciation. Unlike shares that are acquired under a stock option plan, the shares that constitute the basis for calculating the appreciation in a SARs plan are not issued. The executive is awarded only cash or shares having a fair value equivalent to the appreciation.

As indicated earlier, the usual date for measuring compensation related to stock compensation plans is the date of grant. However, with SARs, the final amount of the cash (or shares, or combination of the two) to be distributed is not known until the date of exercise—the measurement date. Therefore, total compensation expense cannot be measured until this date.

How then should compensation expense be recorded during the interim periods from the date of grant to the date of exercise? This determination is not easy because it is impossible to know what the total compensation cost will be until the date of exercise, and the service period will probably not coincide with the exercise date.

For cash-settled SARs, ASPE and IFRS differ in how to measure the value of the SAR and hence the compensation between the date of grant and date of exercise. Under ASPE, the value of the SAR is estimated using what is known as the **intrinsic value method**. The intrinsic value method measures the value of the SAR by starting with the market or fair value of the share, deducting the pre-established price noted in the SAR, and multiplying by the number of SARs outstanding. IFRS requires use of an options pricing model to estimate fair value of the SAR.[51] Both are attempts to measure the value of the SAR but the options pricing model is a more complex and sophisticated valuation technique.

Regardless of how fair value is estimated for the compensation and liability, this total estimated compensation expense is then allocated over the service period, to record an expense (or decrease expense if the market price falls) in each period. At the end of each interim period, the total compensation expense reported to date should equal the percentage of the total service period that has elapsed, multiplied by the estimated compensation cost.

For example, assume that at the end of an interim period, the service period is 40% complete and the total estimated compensation is $100,000. At this time, the cumulative compensation expense reported to date should equal $40,000 ($100,000 × 0.40). As a second example, assume the following: In the first year of a four-year plan, the company charges one fourth of the appreciation to date. In the second year, it charges off two fourths or 50% of the appreciation to date, less the amount that was already recognized in the first year. In the third year, it charges off three fourths of the appreciation to date, less the amount recognized previously, and in the fourth year it charges off the remaining compensation expense.

A special problem arises when the exercise date is later than the service period. In the previous example, if the SARs were not exercised at the end of four years, it would be necessary to account for the subsequent change in value of the SAR and compensation in the fifth year. In this case, the compensation expense is adjusted whenever a change in value of the SAR occurs in subsequent reporting periods until the rights expire or are exercised, whichever comes first.

Increases or decreases in the fair value of the SARs between the date of grant and the exercise date, therefore, result in a change in the measure of compensation. Some periods will have credits to compensation expense if the fair value falls from one period to the next; the credit to Compensation Expense, however, cannot exceed previously recognized compensation expense. In other words, cumulative compensation expense cannot be negative.

To illustrate, assume that Hotels Inc. establishes a SARs program on January 1, 2018, which entitles executives to receive cash at the date of exercise (any time after the service period) for the difference between the shares' fair value and the pre-established or stated price of $10 on 10,000 SARs. The SARs' fair value on December 31, 2018 is $30,000 and the service period runs for two years (2018 to 2019). Illustration 16B-1 shows the amount of compensation expense to be recorded each period, assuming that the executives exercise their rights after holding the SARs for three years.

Illustration 16B-1							
Compensation Expense, Share Appreciation Rights	**SHARE APPRECIATION RIGHTS** **Schedule of Compensation Expense**						
	(1)	(2)	(3)	(4)			
	Date	Fair Value of SARs[a]	Percentage Accrued[b]	Cumulative Compensation Accrued to Date	Expense 2018	Expense 2019	Expense 2020
	12/31/18	$30,000	50%	$15,000	$15,000		
				55,000		$55,000	
	12/31/19	$70,000	100%	70,000			
				(20,000)			$(20,000)
	12/31/20	$50,000	100%	$50,000			

[a]Cumulative compensation for unexercised SARs to be allocated to periods of service.
[b]The percentage accrued is based on a two-year service period (2018 to 2019).

In 2018, Hotels would record compensation expense of $15,000 because 50% of the $30,000 total compensation cost estimated at December 31, 2018 is allocable to 2018.

In 2019, the fair value increased to $70,000; therefore, the additional compensation expense of $55,000 ($70,000 – $15,000) was recorded. The SARs were held through 2020, during which time the fair value decreased to $50,000. The decrease is recognized by recording a $20,000 credit to Compensation Expense and a debit to Liability Under Share Appreciation Rights Plans. Note that, after the service period ends, since the rights are still outstanding, the rights are adjusted to fair value at December 31, 2020. Any such credit to Compensation Expense cannot exceed previous charges to expense that can be attributed to that plan.

As the compensation expense is recorded each period, the corresponding credit should be to a liability account if the stock appreciation is to be paid in cash. According to GAAP, SARs that call for settlement in cash are indexed liabilities and the measurement date is therefore the settlement date.[52]

The entry to record compensation expense in the first year, assuming that the SARs ultimately will be paid in cash, is as follows:

A   =   L   +   SE
     +15,000   −15,000

Cash flows: No effect

Compensation Expense	15,000	
Liability Under Share Appreciation Rights Plans		15,000

The liability account would be credited again in 2019 for $55,000 and debited for $20,000 in 2020, when the negative compensation expense is recorded. The entry to record the negative compensation expense is as follows:

A   =   L   +   SE
     +20,000   +20,000

Cash flows: No effect

Liability Under Share Appreciation Rights Plans	20,000	
Compensation Expense		20,000

At December 31, 2020, the executives receive $50,000. The entry removing the liability is as follows:

A   =   L   +   SE
−50,000   −50,000

Cash flows: ↓ 50,000 outflow

Liability Under Share Appreciation Rights Plans	50,000	
Cash		50,000

There are some complexities involved with SARs. Sometimes there are choices as to how the instrument will be settled (in cash or shares). Judgement should be used to determine whether the instrument should be accounted for as an equity-settled instrument (like the CSOP) or a cash-settled instrument (like the SAR above). Under ASPE, SARs that require equity settlement are presented as equity. The issuer can choose to estimate the SAR's fair value using the intrinsic value method or other valuation technique, such as the options pricing model.[53] Under IFRS, equity-settled SARs are presented as contributed surplus and measured at fair value using an options pricing model.

SARs are often issued in combination with compensatory stock options (referred to as **tandem** or **combination plans**). The executive must then select which of the two sets of terms to exercise and which one to cancel. The existence of alternative plans running concurrently poses additional problems. Based on the facts available each period, it must be determined which of the two plans is more likely to be exercised and that plan is then accounted for and the other is ignored.

Performance-Type Plans

Some executives have become disenchanted with stock compensation plans in which payment depends ultimately on an increase in the common shares' market price. They do not like having their compensation and judgement of performance at the mercy of the stock market's erratic behaviour. As a result, there has been a large increase in the use of **performance-type plans** that award the executives common shares (or cash) if specified performance criteria are attained during the performance period (generally three to five years). Many large companies now have some type of plan that does not rely on share price appreciation. The performance criteria usually include increases in return on assets or equity, growth in sales, growth in earnings per share (EPS), or a combination of these factors.

A performance-type plan's measurement date is the date of exercise because the number of shares that will be issued or the cash that will be paid out when performance is achieved is not known at the date of grant. The company must use its best estimates to measure the compensation cost before the date of exercise. The compensation cost is allocated to the periods involved in the same way as is done with stock appreciation rights; that is, the percentage approach is used.

Tandem or combination awards are popular with these plans. The executive has the choice of selecting between a performance or stock option award. Companies such as **General Electric** and **Xerox** have adopted plans of this nature. In these cases, the executive has the best of both worlds: if either the share price increases or the performance goal is achieved, the executive gains. Sometimes, the executive receives both types of plans, so that the monies received from the performance plan can finance the exercise price on the stock option plan.

SUMMARY OF LEARNING OBJECTIVE FOR APPENDIX 16B

10 Account for share appreciation rights plans.

SARs are popular because the employee can share in increases in value of the company's shares without having to purchase them. The increases in value over a certain amount are paid to the employee as cash or shares. Obligations to pay cash represent a liability that must be remeasured. The cost is therefore continually adjusted, with the measurement date being the exercise date. The related expense is spread over the service period. If the SARs are not exercised at the end of the service period,

the liability must continue to be remeasured. Cash-settled SARs are measured using intrinsic values under ASPE and fair value (using options pricing models) under IFRS. Some SARs are settled using equity instruments. These are treated as equity and measured at fair value. ASPE allows an accounting policy choice as to how to measure equity-settled SARs.

Performance-type plans are tied to performance (of the entity, the individual, or a group of individuals). There is therefore more measurement uncertainty.

KEY TERMS

combination plans, p. 1016

intrinsic value method, p. 1014

share appreciation rights (SARs), p. 1014

tandem plans, p. 1016

APPENDIX 16C

ADVANCED MODELS FOR MEASURING FAIR VALUE AND DISCLOSURE OF FAIR VALUE INFORMATION

Options Pricing Models

Objective 11
Understand how options pricing models are used to measure financial instruments.

Chapter 2 introduced the use of a framework for determining fair values. Basic models for calculating fair value include discounted cash flow models, which were reviewed in that chapter. This appendix goes one step further and looks briefly at more advanced models for measuring fair value.

VALUATION
5.4.1

There are numerous **options pricing models** and they are usually covered in more advanced finance texts and courses. The Black-Scholes and binomial tree options pricing models are two of these models.

Options pricing models incorporate the following information (at a minimum) as inputs to the model:

1. The exercise price. This is the price at which the option may be settled. It is agreed upon by both parties to the contract.

2. The expected life of the option. This is the term of the option. It is agreed upon by both parties to the contract. Some options may only be settled at the end of the term (known as European options) while others may be settled at points during the term (known as American options).

3. The current market price of the underlying stock. This is readily available from the stock market.

4. The volatility of the underlying stock. This is the magnitude of future changes in the market price. Volatility looks at how the specific stock price moves relative to the market.

5. The expected dividend during the option life.

6. The risk-free rate of interest for the option life. In general, government bonds carry a return that is felt to be the risk-free return.

Where possible, the fair value is more robust if the inputs make use of external and objective market information. For items such as volatility and dividends, judgement is required in arriving at the input value. Entities look to historical data to help determine these amounts, but care should be taken because historical data are not necessarily indicative of the future. In addition, for some entities, such as newly listed companies, there will be no history. In this case, the entity may look to similar entities in the same industry. The same problem exists for private entities. For these entities, the company also benchmarks against other similar companies and industries in an attempt to calculate the volatility measure.

Any other inputs that a knowledgeable market participant would consider in valuing the option would also be taken into account. These include the employees' ability to exercise the option (whether it is restricted or not and whether the option may be exercised early or not).

Recall further that financial instrument values have two components: an **intrinsic value** component and a **time value** component. These two components are used in the Black-Scholes model, which requires the following two amounts to be calculated. Note that this model can be used with published tables.

1. *The standard deviation of proportionate changes in the fair value of the asset underlying the options, multiplied by the square root of the time to expiry of the option.* This amount relates to the time value portion and the potential for the value of the asset underlying the option to change over time. The volatility of the shares as compared with the volatility of the market in general is an important factor here. The more volatile the shares, the greater the fair value of the options. This is because volatility introduces more risk and the higher the risk, the higher the return.

2. *The ratio of the fair value of the asset underlying the option to the present value of the option exercise price.* This relates to the intrinsic value.

The calculations of fair value using options pricing models are beyond the scope of this text.

Fair Value Disclosure for Financial Instruments

Objective 12

Describe and analyze required fair value disclosures for financial instruments.

Throughout the textbook we have discussed disclosure requirements for financial instruments (Chapters 7, 9, 14, and 15). We have also discussed fair value disclosures (Chapter 3) and disclosures relating to risks and uncertainty (Chapter 21). This appendix goes into a bit more detail regarding fair value disclosures for financial instruments.

One requirement related to fair value disclosure is that both the cost and the fair value of all financial instruments must be reported in the notes to the financial statements. This enables financial statement users to understand the fair value of the company's financial instruments and the potential gains and losses that might occur in the future as a result of these instruments.

The IASB also decided that companies should disclose information that enables users to determine the extent of usage of fair value and the inputs used to implement fair value measurement. Two reasons for additional disclosure beyond the simple itemization of fair values are:

1. Differing levels of reliability exist in the measurement of fair value information. It therefore is important to understand the varying risks involved in measurement. It is difficult to incorporate these levels of uncertainty into the financial statements. Disclosure provides a framework for addressing the qualitative aspects related to risk and measurement.

2. Changes in the fair value of financial instruments are reported differently in the financial statements, depending on the type of financial instrument involved and whether the fair value option is used. Note disclosure provides an opportunity to explain more precisely the impact that changes in the value of financial instruments have on financial results. In assessing the inputs, the IASB recognizes that the reliability of the fair value measurement is of extreme importance. Many financial instruments are traded in active markets, and their valuation is not difficult. Other instruments are complex and/or illiquid, and their valuation is difficult.

To highlight these levels of reliability in valuation, the IASB established a fair value hierarchy. As discussed in Chapters 2 and 3, this hierarchy identifies three broad levels—1, 2, and 3—related to the measurement of fair values. Level 1 is the most reliable measurement because fair value is based on quoted prices in active markets for identical assets or liabilities. Level 2 is less reliable; it is not based on quoted market prices for identical assets and liabilities but instead may be based on similar assets or liabilities. Level 3 is least reliable; it uses unobservable inputs that reflect the company's assumption as to the value of the financial instrument.

Illustration 16C-1 is an example of a fair value note disclosure for Sabathia Company. It includes both the fair value amounts and the reliability level. (A similar disclosure would be presented for liabilities.)

Illustration 16C-1

Example of Fair Value Hierarchy

SABATHIA COMPANY
Notes to the Financial Statements

($ in 000s)

Fair Value Measurements at Reporting Data Using

Description	Fair Value 12/31/17	Quoted Prices in Active Markets for Identical Assets (Level 1)	Significant Other Observable Inputs (Level 2)	Significant Unobservable Inputs (Level 3)
Trading securities	$115	$105	$10	
Available-for-sale securities	75	75		
Derivatives	60	25	15	$20
Venture capital investments	10			10
Total	$260	$205	$25	$30

For assets and liabilities measured at fair value and classified as Level 3, a reconciliation of Level 3 changes for the period is required. In addition, companies should report an analysis of how Level 3 changes in fair value affect total gains and losses and their impact on net income. Illustration 16C-2 is an example of this disclosure.

($ in 000s)	Fair Value Measurements Using Significant Unobservable Inputs (Level 3)		
	Derivatives	Venture Capital Investments	Total
Beginning balance	$14	$11	$25
Total gains or losses (realized/unrealized)			
Included in earnings (or changes in net assets)	11	(3)	8
Included in other comprehensive income	4		4
Purchases, issuances, and settlements	(7)	2	(5)
Transfers in and/or out of Level 3	(2)		(2)
Ending balance	$20	$10	$30
The amount of total gains or losses for the period included in earnings (or changes in net assets) attributable to the change in unrealized gains or losses relating to assets still held at the reporting date	$ 7	$ 2	$ 9

Gains and losses (realized and unrealized) included in earnings (or changes in net assets) for the period (above) are reported in trading revenues and in other revenues as follows.

	Trading Revenues	Other Revenues
Total gains or losses included in earnings (or changes in net assets) for the period (as shown in the table above)	$11	$(3)
Change in unrealized gains or losses relating to assets still held at reporting date	$7	$2

Sabathia Company's disclosure gives the user of the financial statements an understanding of the following:

1. The carrying amount and the fair value of the company's financial instruments segregated by level of reliability. Thus, the reader of the financial statements has a basis for judging what credence should be given to the fair value amounts.

2. For Level 3 financial instruments, a reconciliation of the balance from the beginning to the end of the period. This reconciliation enables the reader to understand the composition of the change. It is important because these calculations are most affected by subjective estimates and could be subject to manipulation.

3. The impact of changes in fair value on the net assets of the company from one period to the next.

For companies that choose to use the fair value option for some or all of their financial instruments, they are permitted to incorporate the entire guidelines related to fair value measurement into one master schedule, or they can provide in a separate schedule information related solely to the fair value option.

Finally, companies must provide the following (with special emphasis on Level 3 measurements):

1. Quantitative information about significant unobservable inputs used for all Level 3 measurements.

2. A qualitative discussion about the sensitivity of recurring Level 3 measurements to changes in the unobservable inputs disclosed, including interrelationships between inputs.

3. A description of the company's valuation process.

4. Any transfers between Levels 1 and 2 of the fair value hierarchy.

5. Information about non-financial assets measured at fair value at amounts that differ from the assets' highest and best use.

6. The proper hierarchy classification for items that are not recognized on the statement of financial position but are disclosed in the notes to the financial statements.

A typical disclosure related to Level 3 fair value measurements is presented in Illustration 16C-3.

Illustration 16C-3

Quantitative Information about Level 3 Fair Value Measurements

($ in millions)	Fair Value at 12/31/2017	Valuation Technique(s)	Unobservable Input	Range (Weighted Average)
Residential mortgage-backed securities	125	Discounted cash flow	Constant prepayment rate Probability of default Loss severity	3.5%–5.5% (4.5%) 5%–50% (10%) 40%–100% (60%)
Collateralized debt obligations	35	Consensus pricing	Offered quotes Comparability adjustments (%)	20–45 –10%– +15% (+5%)
Direct venture capital investments: Health care	53	Discounted cash flow	Weighted average cost of capital Long-term revenue growth rate Long-term pre-tax operating margin Discount for lack of marketability[a] Control premium[a]	7%–16% (12.1%) 2%–5% (4.2%) 3%–20% (10.3%) 5%–20% (17%) 10%–30% (20%)
		Market-comparable companies	EBITDA multiple[b] Revenue multiple[b] Discount for lack of marketability[a] Control premium[a]	6.5–12 (9.5) 1.0–3.0 (2.0) 5%–20% (10%) 10%–20% (12%)
Credit contracts	38	Option model	Annualized volatility of credit[c] Counterparty credit risk[d] Own credit risk[d]	10%–20% 0.5%–3.5% 0.3%–2.0%

[a]Represents amounts used when the reporting entity has determined that market participants would take into account these premiums and discounts when pricing the investments.
[b]Represents amounts used when the reporting entity has determined that market participants would use such multiples when pricing the investments.
[c]Represents the range of the volatility curves used in the valuation analysis that the reporting entity has determined that market participants would use when pricing the contracts.
[d]Represents the range of the credit default swap spread curves used in the valuation analysis that the reporting entity has determined that market participants would use when pricing the contracts.

(*Note*: For liabilities, a similar table should be presented.)

SUMMARY OF LEARNING OBJECTIVES FOR APPENDIX 16C

11 Understand how options pricing models are used to measure financial instruments.

Fair value is most readily determined where there is an active market with published prices. Where this is not the case, a valuation technique is used. More basic techniques include discounted cash flows. More complex techniques include options pricing models such as the Black-Scholes and binomial tree models. Where possible, valuation techniques should use available external inputs to ensure that they are more objective. Having said this, significant judgement goes into determining fair values using options pricing models.

12 Describe and analyze required fair value disclosures for financial instruments.

Additional disclosures relating to fair values of financial instruments provide useful information about the reliability of fair value estimates. As discussed in earlier chapters, including Chapters 2 and 3, the IASB has established a fair value hierarchy that ranks the reliability of the fair value measures. Note disclosures under IFRS require information about which financial instruments are classified as levels 1, 2, or 3 in the fair value hierarchy. Additional information is required to be disclosed where the financial instruments are Level 3 instruments because Level 3 measurements are less reliable.

Note: Completion of this end-of-chapter material will help develop CPA-enabling competencies (such as ethics and professionalism, problem-solving and decision-making, and communication) and technical competencies. We have highlighted selected items with an integration icon and material in *WileyPLUS* has been linked to the competencies. All cases emphasize integration, especially of the enabling competencies. The brief exercises, exercises, and problems generally emphasize problem-solving and decision-making.

Note: All assignment material with an asterisk (*) relates to an appendix to the chapter.

Brief Exercises

(LO 1, 2, 7) **BE16-1** Sometimes an entity issues financial instruments that require settlement using its own shares. Examples of these include purchased or written options to buy or sell its own shares, or forward contracts to buy or sell its own shares. Explain the accounting issues that result from the existence of these instruments. How does IFRS tend to treat these types of instruments? Give examples to support the different treatments that are available under IFRS. Note any differences under ASPE.

FINANCE

(LO 1, 2) **BE16-2** Saver Rio Ltd. purchased options to acquire 1,000 common shares of Spender Limited for $20 per share within the next six months. The premium (cost) related to the options was $500. How should this be accounted for in the financial statements of Saver Rio? Explain which financial risks the transaction exposes the entity to.

FINANCE

(LO 1, 2, 7) **BE16-3** On February 1, 2017, Daily Produce Ltd. entered into a purchase commitment contract to buy apples from Farmers Corporation. According to the contract, Daily Produce could settle the contact on a net basis; however, Daily Produce intends to take delivery of the apples so that they can be sold in its grocery stores. On April 1, 2017, Daily Produce takes delivery of the apples for a cost of $1,500, and charges the amount on account. (a) How should this be accounted for in Daily Produce's financial statements if it applies IFRS? (b) How should this be accounted for in Daily Produce's financial statements if it applies ASPE? (c) Explain which financial risks the transaction exposes the entity to.

FINANCE

(LO 1, 2) **BE16-4** On January 1, 2017, Ginseng Inc. entered into a forward contract to purchase U.S. $6,000 for $6,336 Canadian in 30 days. On January 15, the fair value of the contract was $40 (reflecting the present value of the future cash flows under the contract). Assume that the company would like to update its records on January 15. (a) Prepare only the necessary journal entries on January 1 and 15, 2017. (b) Explain which financial risks the transaction exposes the entity to.

FINANCE

(LO 2) **BE16-5** Refer to BE16-4. Assume the same facts except that the forward contract is a futures contract that trades on the Futures Exchange. Ginseng Inc. was required to deposit $30 with the stockbroker as a margin. Prepare the journal entries to update the books on January 1 and 15.

(LO 2) **BE16-6** On January 1, 2017, Wolfgang Ltd. paid $1,000 for the option to buy 5,000 of its common shares for $25 each. The contract stipulates that it may only be settled by exercising the option and buying the shares. How should this be accounted for in the financial statements of Wolfgang Ltd.? Assume that Wolfgang Ltd. complies with IFRS.

(LO 3, 4) **BE16-7** Jamieson Limited, a publicly accountable enterprise, issued bonds that will not be due until 2114. The bonds carry interest at 5%. Explain how this instrument should be presented on the statement of financial position.

(LO 3, 4) **BE16-8** Verhage Limited, a private company that complies with accounting standards for private enterprises (ASPE), has redeemable preferred shares outstanding that carry a dividend of 5%. If the shares are not redeemed within five years, the dividend will double every five years from then on. How should Verhage account for this instrument? How should Verhage treat the dividends associated with the redeemable preferred shares?

(LO 3, 4, 7) **BE16-9** Milano Ltd. issued 1,000 preferred shares for $10 per share. The preferred shares pay an annual, cumulative dividend of $0.50 per share, and become mandatorily redeemable if net income drops below $500,000 in any fiscal year. Discuss how Milano Ltd. should account for the preferred shares under IFRS. Would the accounting for the preferred shares differ if Milano Ltd. adopted ASPE?

(LO 3, 4, 7) **BE16-10** During 2017, Genoa Limited issued retractable preferred shares. The shares may be presented to the company by the holder for redemption after 2020. Explain how these should be presented in the financial statements under IFRS and ASPE.

(LO 3, 4, 7) **BE16-11** On January 1, 2017, MacGregor Ltd. issued 1,000 five-year, 10% convertible bonds at par of $1,000, with interest payable each December 31. Each bond is convertible into 100 common shares, and the current fair value of each common share is $6 per share. Similar straight bonds carry an interest rate of 12%. (a) Calculate the PV of the debt component by itself. (b) How should MacGregor record the issuance if it follows IFRS? (c) How should MacGregor record the issuance if it follows ASPE?

(LO 4, 7) **BE16-12** Bantry Capital Ltd. issued 500 $1,000 bonds at 103. Each bond was issued with 10 detachable stock warrants. After issuance, similar bonds were sold at 97, and the warrants had a fair value of $2.50. (a) Record the issuance of the bonds and warrants assuming that Bantry Capital follows IFRS. (b) Assuming that Bantry Capital follows ASPE, discuss the two options available to record the issuance of the bonds and warrants, and prepare the journal entry for each option.

(LO 4) **BE16-13** Refer to BE16-12 but assume that the instruments are convertible bonds and that they have now been converted. Assume that Bantry Capital Ltd. follows ASPE, and that all of the proceeds were allocated to the debt component upon initial recognition. At the time of conversion, the unamortized bond premium was $10,000, and the common shares had a fair value of $50 per share. Record the conversion using the book value method.

(LO 4) **BE16-14** Refer to BE16-12. Assume that Bantry Capital Ltd. follows IFRS and recorded the issuance of the bonds and warrants accordingly. On a date when the bonds had a carrying value of $489,100, Bantry paid $14,000 to the bond-holders to induce early conversion. Record the conversion using the book value method.

(LO 4) **BE16-15** Refer to BE16-12. Assume that Bantry Capital Ltd. follows ASPE and valued the debt component of the instruments first, applying the residual to the equity component. On a date when the bonds had a carrying value of $489,100 and fair value of $492,370, Bantry paid $530,000 in cash to the bondholders to retire the bonds early. Record the retirement using the book value method.

(LO 4) **BE16-16** Trelawny Ltd. issued 13,000 common shares upon conversion of 10,000 preferred shares. The preferred shares were originally issued at $9 per share and the Contributed Surplus—Conversion Rights account for the pre-ferred shares had a balance of $9,000. The common shares were trading at $14 per share at the time of conversion. Record the conversion of the preferred shares.

(LO 4, 7) **BE16-17** Davison Corporation has puttable common shares outstanding. These shares give the holder the option to require Davison to repurchase the shares for cash. In the event of liquidation, the holders of these shares are also entitled to a pro rata share of Davison's net assets (where net assets are those assets that remain after all other claims on the company's assets are satisfied). The shares do not have a preferred rank over other shares for dividend distributions, and there are no other common shares. (a) How should the shares be classified on the statement of financial position if Davison applies IFRS? (b) Would the answer to part (a) be different if Davison applies ASPE?

(LO 4, 7) **BE16-18** Next Generation Corporation (a private company) has preferred shares outstanding, which require Next Generation to redeem the shares for cash at an amount equal to the fair value of the company's business assets at the time of issuance of the preferred shares. The preferred shares are held by Richard Parent (the founder and former pres-ident of Parent Corporation), who intends to redeem the preferred shares at some point in the future. At the time of issuance of the preferred shares, Parent had transferred the business assets of Parent Corp. to Next Generation (a newly established corporation at the time) as part of an estate freeze transaction, and received these preferred shares as con-sideration. (a) How should the preferred shares be classified on the statement of financial position if Next Generation follows IFRS? (b) Would the answer to part (a) be different if Next Generation follows ASPE? (c) Discuss why this type **TAXATION** of transaction involving preferred shares is called an "estate freeze."

(LO 4, 7) **BE16-19** In January 2017, Parker Inc. issued preferred shares that must be redeemed by Parker if the fair value of the company's common shares exceeds $100 per share. At time of issuance of the preferred shares, Parker's common shares had a fair value of $60 per share. At December 31, 2017, Parker's common shares have a fair value of $50 per share, and it is considered unlikely that Parker's common shares will exceed a fair value of $100 per share. (a) How should the preferred shares be classified on the statement of financial position as at December 31, 2017 if Parker follows IFRS? (b) Would the answer to part (a) be different if Parker follows ASPE?

(LO 5) **BE16-20** List the types of stock compensation plans and discuss the objectives of effective stock compensation plans.

(LO 5) **BE16-21** Explain the differences between employee and compensatory option plans and other options.

(LO 6) **BE16-22** On January 1, 2017, Blaine Corporation granted 6,000 options to executives. Each option entitles the holder to purchase one share of Blaine's common shares at $35 per share at any time after January 1, 2019. The shares' market price is $50 per share on the date of grant, and the required service period is two years. Prepare Blaine's journal entries for January 1, 2017 and December 31, 2017 and 2018. Assume that the options' fair value as calculated using an options pricing model is $126,000. Ignore forfeitures for simplification purposes.

(LO 7, 10) ***BE16-23** Applegate Inc. established a share appreciation rights (SARs) program on January 1, 2017, which entitles executives to receive cash at the date of exercise for the difference between the shares' fair value and the pre-established price of $16 on 3,700 SARs. The required service period is two years. The shares' fair value is $18 per share on December 31, 2017 and $28 per share on December 31, 2018. The SARs are exercised on January 1, 2019. (a) Calculate Applegate's compensation expense for 2017 and 2018 assuming it follows ASPE. (b) Would the accounting for the SARs program differ if Applegate adopted IFRS?

(LO 7, 10) *BE16-24 Spencer Ltd. established a share appreciation rights (SARs) program on January 1, 2017, which entitles executives to receive cash at the date of exercise (anytime in the next three years) for the difference between the shares' fair value and the pre-established price of $20 on 10,000 SARs. As at December 31, 2017, the shares' fair value is $30 per share, the SARs' fair value is $150,000, and the executives have not exercised their rights yet. The service period runs for two years (2017 to 2018), and at December 31, 2017, the service period is considered 50% complete. (a) Record compensation expense for 2017 assuming that Spencer follows IFRS. (b) Record compensation expense for 2017 assuming that Spencer follows ASPE.

(LO 10) *BE16-25 Explain what performance-type plans are and how they differ from other types of compensatory plans.

(LO 11) *BE16-26 Explain how options pricing models are useful in determining fair value. What are the inputs to such models?

(LO 12) *BE16-27 Discuss whether and how financial instruments are disclosed under IFRS, and the reason for the disclosure requirement.

Exercises

(LO 1, 2) E16-1   (Derivative Transaction) RIT Co. has an investment of 5,000 shares in a public company, SIT Ltd. In October 2017, RIT Co. purchased 5,000 put options for SIT Ltd. shares at a price of $2 per put option. The strike price associated with the put options is $100 per share, which is equal to the current trading price of the shares.

FINANCE

Instructions

(a) What is the purpose of the put options purchased by RIT Co.?

(b) How would RIT account for the purchase of the put options? Assume that the value of the shares of SIT subsequently declines. How would this be accounted for?

(c) Is this accounting treatment transparent?

(LO 1, 2) E16-2   (Derivative Transaction) On January 1, 2017, Roper Inc. agrees to buy 3 kilos of gold at $40,000 per kilo from Golden Corp on April 1, 2017, but does not intend to take delivery of the gold. On the day that the contract was entered into, the fair value of this forward contract was zero. The fair value of the forward subsequently fluctuated as follows:

Date	Fair Value of Forward Contract
January 20, 2017	$450
February 6, 2017	$125
February 28, 2017	$360
March 14, 2017	$700

On the settlement date, the spot price of gold is $41,000 per kilo. Assume that Roper complies with IFRS.

Instructions

(a) Prepare the journal entries for the day the forward contract was signed.

(b) Prepare the journal entries to recognize the changes in the fair value of the forward contract.

(c) Prepare the journal entries that would be required if Roper settled the contract on a net basis on April 1, 2017.

(LO 1, 2) E16-3   (Derivative Transaction) Refer to E16-2. Assume the same facts except that the forward contract is a futures contract that trades on the Futures Exchange. On January 1, 2017, Roper is required to deposit $65 with the stockbroker as a margin.

Instructions

(a) Prepare the journal entries for the day the futures contract was signed.

(b) Prepare the journal entries to recognize the changes in the fair value of the futures contract.

(c) Prepare the journal entries that would be required if Roper settled the contract on a net basis on April 1, 2017.

(LO 1, 2) E16-4   (Derivative Transaction) On January 2, 2017, Jackson Corporation purchased a call option for $500 on Walter's common shares. The call option gives Jackson the option to buy 1,000 shares of Walter at a strike price of $30 per share any time during the next six months. The market price of a Walter share was $30 on January 2, 2017 (the intrinsic value was therefore $0). On March 31, 2017, the market price for Walter stock was $42 per share, and the fair value of the option was $17,500.

Instructions

(a) Prepare the journal entry to record the purchase of the call option on January 2, 2017.

(b) Prepare the journal entry(ies) to recognize the change in the call option's fair value as at March 31, 2017.

(c) What was the effect on net income of entering into the derivative transaction for the period January 2 to March 31, 2017?

(d) Based on the available facts, explain whether the company is using the option as a hedge or for speculative purposes.

FINANCE

(e) Explain which financial risks the transaction exposes the entity to.

(LO 1, 2) E16-5 (Derivative Transaction) On April 1, 2017, Petey Ltd. paid $175 for a call to buy 700 shares of NorthernTel at a strike price of $27 per share any time during the next six months. The market price of NorthernTel's shares was $27 per share on April 1, 2017. On June 30, 2017, the market price for NorthernTel's stock was $38 per share, and the fair value of the option was $10,000.

Instructions

(a) Prepare the journal entry to record the purchase of the call option on April 1, 2017.

(b) Prepare the journal entry(ies) to recognize the change in the call option's fair value as at June 30, 2017.

(c) Prepare the journal entry that would be required if Petey Ltd. exercised the call option and took delivery of the shares as soon as the market opened on July 1, 2017.

DIGGING DEEPER

(d) Why is there a gain or loss when the option is exercised?

(LO 2, 7) E16-6 (Purchase Commitment) On January 1, 2017, Fresh Juice Ltd. entered into a purchase commitment contract to buy 10,000 oranges from a local company at a price of $0.50 per orange anytime during the next year. The contract provides Fresh Juice with the option either to take delivery of the oranges at any time over the next year, or to settle the contract on a net basis for the difference between the agreed-upon price of $0.50 per orange and the market price per orange for any oranges that have not been delivered. As at January 31, 2017, Fresh Juice Ltd. did not take delivery of any oranges, and the market price for an orange was $0.49.

Instructions

(a) Assuming that Fresh Juice Ltd. follows IFRS, how should Fresh Juice Ltd. account for this purchase agreement if it fully intends to take delivery of all 10,000 oranges over the next year? Provide any required journal entries at January 1 and January 31.

(b) How would your answer to part (a) change if Fresh Juice Ltd. did not intend to take delivery of the oranges? Provide any required journal entries at January 1 and January 31.

(c) Assuming that Fresh Juice Ltd. follows ASPE, how would Fresh Juice Ltd. account for this purchase agreement if it fully intends to take delivery of all 10,000 oranges over the next year?

(LO 2) E16-7 (Derivatives Involving the Entity's Own Shares) Cambridge Ltd. paid $250 for the option to buy 1,000 of its common shares for $15 each. The contract stipulates that it may only be settled by exercising the option and buying the shares. Cambridge Ltd. follows IFRS.

Instructions

(a) Provide the journal entry required to account for the purchase of the call option.

(b) Assume that the contract allows both parties a choice to settle the option by either exchanging the shares or settling on a net basis. Would this change your conclusion in part (a)?

(LO 2, 3, 4, 7) E16-8 (Various Complex Financial Instruments) The following situations occur independently.

1. A company knows that it will require a large quantity of euros to pay for some imports in three months. The current exchange rate is satisfactory, and as a result, the company purchases a forward contract committing it to acquire 10 million euros at the current exchange rate in three months' time.

2. A shipping company uses large quantities of fuel to power its ships. Shipping rates are set well in advance of when the actual transportation of goods will take place. The company purchases forward contracts for fuel to ensure that it knows the price it will have to pay for fuel in the future. The contracts are exchange-traded futures.

3. An exporting company exports a significant amount of wheat to China. In order to protect itself against the risk that prices will drop significantly, it uses a just-in-time inventory management system to keep stock at the lowest possible levels.

4. A manufacturing company uses a large quantity of steel in its products. In order to ensure the cost of this steel is known, the company enters into executory contracts where it agrees to take delivery of predetermined quantities of steel at predetermined prices in the future.

5. A company pays a shareholder $5,000 for the right to buy 500 of its own common shares for $25 per share at a future date. The contract is not net settleable.

6. A company enters into a futures contract with a margin account to sell its grain for $2,500.

7. A company issues preferred shares on January 1, 2017, with the following terms and conditions: the shares are redeemable by the company for $50/share on January 1, 2020, and the redemption price doubles every 12 months after January 1, 2020.

8. A company issues debt with detachable warrants. The warrants can be sold separately, and entitle the holder to purchase one share at a future date for a predetermined price.

9. A company issues debt that, at the option of the holder, can be converted into 100,000 common shares of the company.

10. A company issues shares that can be redeemed for a fixed amount at the request of the shareholder at any time.

Assume the companies above are not using hedge accounting.

Instructions

For each of the above situations:

(a) Describe the type of financial instrument involved.

(b) Indicate when the financial instrument should be recognized in the financial statements.

(c) Indicate the measurement that should be used for accounting purposes.

(d) Describe how gains or losses should be recorded.

(e) Note if there are differences between ASPE and IFRS for any items.

(LO 4, 7) E16-9   (Issuance and Conversion of Bonds) The following are unrelated transactions.

1. On March 1, 2017, Loma Corporation issued $300,000 of 8% non-convertible bonds at 104, which are due on February 28, 2037. In addition, each $1,000 bond was issued with 25 detachable stock warrants, each of which entitled the bondholder to purchase one of Loma's no par value common shares for $50. The bonds without the warrants would normally sell at 95. On March 1, 2017, the fair value of Loma's common shares was $40 per share and the fair value of each warrant was $2. Loma prepares its financial statements in accordance with IFRS.

2. Grand Corp. issued $10 million of par value, 9% convertible bonds at 97. If the bonds had not been convertible, the company's investment banker estimates they would have been sold at 93. Grand Corp. has adopted ASPE, and would like to explore all options available to report the convertible bond.

3. Hussein Limited issued $20 million of par value, 7% bonds at 98. One detachable stock purchase warrant was issued with each $100 par value bond. At the time of issuance, the warrants were selling for $6. Hussein Limited has adopted ASPE.

4. On July 1, 2017, Tien Limited called its 9% convertible bonds for conversion. The $10 million of par value bonds were converted into 1 million common shares. On July 1, there was $75,000 of unamortized discount applicable to the bonds, and the company paid an additional $65,000 to the bondholders to induce conversion of all the bonds. At the time of conversion, the balance in the account Contributed Surplus—Conversion Rights was $270,000, and the bond's fair value (ignoring the conversion feature) was $9,955,000. The company records conversion using the book value method.

5. On December 1, 2017, Horton Company issued 500 of its $1,000, 9% bonds at 103. Attached to each bond was one detachable stock warrant entitling the holder to purchase 10 of Horton's common shares. On December 1, 2017, the fair value of the bonds, without the stock warrants, was 95, and the fair value of each stock warrant was $50. Horton Company prepares its financial statements in accordance with IFRS.

Instructions

Present the required entry(ies) to record each of the above transactions. For transaction 4, prepare the journal entries if Tien Limited prepares its financial statements using IFRS and if it uses ASPE.

(LO 4, 7) E16-10   (Conversion of Bonds) Daisy Inc. issued $6 million of 10-year, 9% convertible bonds on June 1, 2017 at 98 plus accrued interest. The bonds were dated April 1, 2017, with interest payable April 1 and October 1. Bond discount is amortized semi-annually. Bonds without conversion privileges would have sold at 97 plus accrued interest.

On April 1, 2018, $1.5 million of these bonds were converted into 30,000 common shares. Accrued interest was paid in cash at the time of conversion but only to the bondholders whose bonds were being converted. Assume that the company follows IFRS.

Instructions

(a) Prepare the entry to record the issuance of the convertible bonds on June 1, 2017.

(b) Prepare the entry to record the interest expense at October 1, 2017 by pro-rating the number of months. Assume that interest payable was credited when the bonds were issued. (Round to nearest dollar.)

(c) Prepare the entry(ies) to record the conversion on April 1, 2018. (The book value method is used.) Assume that the entry to record amortization of the bond discount and interest payment has been made.

(d) Repeat part (c) by using a computer spreadsheet to calculate the bond discount.

(e) Assume that Daisy follows ASPE. Discuss how the issuance of convertible bonds is recorded, and prepare the entry(ies) to record the issuance of the convertible bonds on June 1, 2017.

(f) What do you believe was the likely fair value of the common shares as at April 1, 2018 (the date of conversion)?

DIGGING DEEPER

(LO 4) E16-11 (Conversion of Bonds) Vargo Limited had $2.4 million of bonds payable outstanding and the unamortized premium for these bonds amounted to $44,500. Each $1,000 bond was convertible into 20 preferred shares. All bonds were then converted into preferred shares. The Contributed Surplus—Conversion Rights account had a balance of $22,200. Assume that the company follows IFRS.

FINANCE

Instructions

(a) Assuming that the book value method was used, what entry would be made?

(b) Assume that Vargo Ltd. offers $9,000 to induce early conversion. What journal entry would be made?

(c) From the perspective of the bondholders, what is the likely motive for the conversion of bonds into preferred shares? What are the advantages of each investment that are given up or obtained by the bondholders who chose to convert their investment?

DIGGING DEEPER

(LO 4) E16-12 (Conversion of Bonds and Expired Rights) Dadayeva Inc. has $5 million of 6% convertible bonds outstanding. Each $1,000 bond is convertible into 50 no par value common shares. The bonds pay interest on January 31 and July 31. On July 31, 2017, the holders of $1,250,000 of these bonds exercised the conversion privilege. On that date, the market price of the bonds was 110, the market price of the common shares was $40, the carrying value of the common shares was $20, and the Contributed Surplus—Conversion Rights account balance was $700,000. The total unamortized bond premium at the date of conversion was $362,990. The remaining bonds were never converted and were retired when they reached the maturity date. Assume that the company follows IFRS.

Instructions

(a) Assuming that the book value method was used, record the conversion of the $1,250,000 of bonds on July 31, 2017.

(b) Prepare the journal entry that would be required for the remaining amount in Contributed Surplus—Conversion Rights when the maturity of the remaining bonds is recorded.

(LO 4) E16-13 (Conversion of Bonds) On January 1, 2017, when the fair value of its common shares was $80 per share, Hammond Corp. issued $10 million of 8% convertible debentures due in 20 years. The conversion option allowed the holder of each $1,000 bond to convert the bond into five common shares. The debentures were issued for $10.8 million. The bond payment's present value at the time of issuance was $8.5 million and the corporation believes the difference between the present value and the amount paid is attributable to the conversion feature. On January 1, 2018, the corporation's common shares were split 2 for 1, and the conversion rate for the bonds was adjusted accordingly. On January 1, 2019, when the fair value of the corporation's common shares was $135 per share, holders of 30% of the convertible debentures exercised their conversion option. Hammond Corp. applies ASPE, and uses the straight-line method for amortizing any bond discounts or premiums.

Instructions

(a) Prepare the entry to record the original issuance of the convertible debentures.

(b) Using the book value method, prepare the entry to record the exercise of the conversion option. Show supporting calculations in good form.

(c) How many shares were issued as a result of the conversion?

FINANCE

(d) From the perspective of Hammond Corp., what are the advantages and disadvantages of the conversion of the bonds into common shares?

(e) Assume, instead, that Hammond Corp. decides to retire the bonds early, on January 1, 2019, by paying cash of $3,306,000 to the bondholders. On that date, the fair value of a similar bond without the conversion feature is $870 per bond. Prepare the journal entry using the book value method.

DIGGING DEEPER

(LO 4) E16-14 (Conversion of Bonds) Somerton Corporation had two issues of securities outstanding: common shares and a 6% convertible bond issue in the face amount of $6 million. Interest payment dates of the bond issue are June 30 and December 31. The conversion clause in the bond indenture entitles the bondholders to receive 50 no par value common shares in exchange for each $1,000 bond. The value of the equity portion of the bond issue is $90,000. On June 30, 2017, the holders of $1.8 million of the face value bonds exercised the conversion privilege. The market price of the bonds on that date was $1,200 per bond and the market price of the common shares was $36. The total unamortized bond discount at the date of conversion was $500,000.

Instructions

Prepare the entry to record the exercise of the conversion option, using the book value method. Assume the company follows IFRS.

(LO 4) **E16-15** **(Conversion of Bonds)** On January 1, 2017, Olson Corporation issued $6 million of 10-year, 7% convertible debentures at 104. Investment bankers believe that the debenture would have sold at 102 without the conversion privilege. Interest is to be paid semi-annually on June 30 and December 31. Each $1,000 debenture can be converted into five common shares of Olson after December 31, 2018. On January 1, 2019, $400,000 of debentures is converted into common shares, and on March 31, 2019, an additional $400,000 of debentures is converted into common shares. Fair value of Olson's common shares is $110 and $115 per share on January 1, 2019 and March 31, 2019, respectively. Accrued interest at March 31 will be paid on the next interest date. Bond premium is amortized on a straight-line basis. Olson follows ASPE.

Instructions

(a) Make the necessary journal entries for
  1. December 31, 2018
  2. January 1, 2019
  3. March 31, 2019
  4. June 30, 2019

FINANCE

Record the conversions using the book value method.

(b) From the perspective of the debenture holders, why would they be motivated to wait for the conversion of the bonds into common shares? What are the risks involved in waiting and what could the bondholders ultimately give up by waiting too long?

**DIGGING
DEEPER**

(LO 4) **E16-16** **(Issuance of Bonds with Detachable Warrants)** On September 1, 2017, Oxford Corp. sold at 102 (plus accrued interest) 5,200 of its $1,000 face value, 10-year, 9% non-convertible bonds with detachable stock warrants. Each bond carried two detachable warrants; each warrant was for one common share at a specified option price of $10 per share. Shortly after issuance, the warrants were selling for $5 each. Assume that no fair value is available for the bonds. Interest is payable on December 1 and June 1. Oxford Corp. prepares its financial statements in accordance with ASPE.

FINANCE

Instructions

(a) Prepare in general journal format the entry to record the issuance of the bonds under both options available under ASPE.

**DIGGING
DEEPER**

(b) From the perspective of a creditor, discuss the effect of each option on Oxford Corp.'s debt to total assets ratio.

(AICPA adapted)

(LO 4) **E16-17** **(Issuance of Bonds with Redemption Feature)** On January 1, 2017, Tiamund Corp. sold at 103, 100 of its $1,000 face value, five-year, 9% non-convertible, retractable bonds. The retraction feature allows the holder to redeem the bonds at an amount equal to three times net income, to a maximum of $1,200 per bond. Tiamund has net income of $250, $350, and $450 for the fiscal years of December 31, 2017, 2018, and 2019, respectively. Tiamund Corp. prepares its financial statements in accordance with ASPE.

Instructions

(a) Prepare the entry to record the issuance of the bonds.

(b) Using straight-line amortization, how much would the bond be carried at on the statement of financial position for the 2017, 2018, and 2019 year ends?

(LO 6) **E16-18** **(Issuance and Exercise of Stock Options)** On November 1, 2016, Aymar Corp. adopted a stock option plan that granted options to key executives to purchase 45,000 common shares. The options were granted on January 2, 2017, and were exercisable two years after the date of grant if the grantee was still a company employee; the options expire six years from the date of grant. The option price was set at $42, and total compensation expense was estimated to be $550,000. Note that the calculation did not take forfeitures into account.

On April 1, 2018, 3,500 options were terminated when some employees resigned from the company. The fair value of the shares at that date was $28. All of the remaining options were exercised during the year 2019: 31,500 on January 3 when the fair value was $52, and 10,000 on May 1 when the fair value was $58 a share. Assume that the entity follows ASPE and has chosen not to reflect forfeitures in its upfront estimate of compensation expense.

Instructions

(a) Prepare journal entries relating to the stock option plan for the years 2017, 2018, and 2019. Assume that the employees perform services equally in 2017 and 2018, and that the year end is December 31.

FINANCE

(b) What is the significance of the fact that the pricing model did not take forfeitures into account? Would taking expected forfeitures into account make the estimate of the total compensation expense higher or lower?

(c) What are the main differences between an employee stock option plan and a compensatory stock option plan?

(LO 6) E16-19 (Issuance, Exercise, and Termination of Stock Options) On January 1, 2017, Waldorf Corporation granted 40,000 options to key executives. Each option allows the executive to purchase one share of Waldorf's common shares at a price of $30 per share. The options were exercisable within a two-year period beginning January 1, 2019, if the grantee was still employed by the company at the time of the exercise. On the grant date, Waldorf's shares were trading at $25 per share, and a fair value options pricing model determined total compensation to be $1,680,000. Management has assumed that there will be no forfeitures because they do not expect any of the key executives to leave.

On May 1, 2019, 12,000 options were exercised when the market price of Waldorf's shares was $34 per share. The remaining options lapsed in 2020 because executives decided not to exercise their options. Management was indeed correct in their assumption regarding forfeitures in that all executives remained with the company. Assume that Waldorf follows IFRS.

Instructions

(a) Prepare the necessary journal entries related to the stock option plan for the years ended December 31, 2017 through 2020.

FINANCE

(b) What is the significance of the $25 market price of the Waldorf shares at the date of grant? Would the exercise price normally be higher or lower than the market price of the shares on the date of grant?

(c) What is the significance of the $34 market price of the Waldorf shares at May 1, 2019, the date of the exercise of the stock options?

(d) What likely happened to the market price of the shares in 2020?

DIGGING DEEPER

(e) What motive might an employee have for delaying the exercise of the stock option? What are the risks involved?

(LO 6) E16-20 (Issuance, Exercise, and Termination of Stock Options) On January 1, 2017, Kasan Corp. granted stock options to its chief executive officer. This is the only stock option that Kasan offers and the details are as follows:

Option to purchase:	2,500 common shares
Option price per share:	$36.00
Fair value per common share on date of grant:	$28.50
Stock option expiration:	The earlier of eight years after issuance or the employee's cessation of employment with Kasan for any reason other than retirement
Date when options are first exercisable:	The earlier of four years after issuance or the date on which the employee reaches the retirement age of 65
Fair value of options on date of grant:	$8.00

On January 1, 2022, 2,000 of the options were exercised when the fair value of the common shares was $39. The remaining stock options were allowed to expire. The CEO remained with the company throughout the period.

Instructions

Record the journal entries at the following dates. Assume that the entity follows ASPE and has decided not to include an estimate of forfeitures upon initial recognition of the compensation expense.

(a) January 1, 2017

(b) December 31, 2017, the fiscal year end of Kasan Corp.

(c) January 1, 2022, the exercise date

(d) December 31, 2024, the expiry date of the options

(LO 9) *E16-21 (Cash Flow Hedge) On January 2, 2017, Thompson Corp. issued a $100,000, four-year note at prime plus 1% variable interest, with interest payable semi-annually. On the same date, Thompson entered into an interest rate swap where it agreed to pay 6% fixed and receive prime plus 1% for the first six months on $100,000. At each six-month period, the variable rate will be reset. The prime interest rate is 5.7% on January 2, 2017, and is reset to 6.7% on June 30, 2017. On December 31, 2017, the fair value of the swap has increased by $25,000. Thompson follows ASPE and uses hedge accounting. Assume that the swap qualifies for hedge accounting under ASPE.

FINANCE

Instructions

(a) For this transaction:

1. Identify the hedged item.
2. Identify the hedging item.
3. Identify how the hedged item is being accounted for without hedge accounting.
4. Identify how the hedging item is accounted for.
5. Indicate how the gains and losses for the hedged and hedging items are recognized.

(b) Calculate the net interest expense to be reported for this note and the related swap transaction as at June 30 and December 31, 2017.

(c) Prepare the journal entries relating to the interest for the year ended December 31, 2017.

(d) Explain why this is a cash flow hedge.

(e) Assume, instead, that Thompson follows IFRS. Prepare the journal entries for this cash flow hedge.

(LO 9) ***E16-22** **(Cash Flow Hedge)** On January 2, 2017, Yellowknife Corp. issues a $10-million, five-year note at LIBOR, with interest paid annually. To protect against the cash flow uncertainty related to interest payments that are based on LIBOR, Yellowknife entered into an interest rate swap to pay 6% fixed and receive LIBOR based on $10 million for the term of the note. The LIBOR rate for the first year is 5.8%. The LIBOR rate is reset to 6.6% on January 2, 2018. Yellowknife follows ASPE and uses hedge accounting. On December 31, 2017, the fair value of the swap decreased by $13,500: it increased by $4,000 on December 31, 2018. Assume that the criteria for hedge accounting under ASPE are met.

Instructions

FINANCE

(a) For this transaction:

1. Identify the hedged item.
2. Identify the hedging item.
3. Identify how the hedged item would be accounted for without hedge accounting.
4. Identify how the hedging item is accounted for.
5. Indicate how the gains and losses for the hedged and hedging items are recognized.

(b) Calculate the net interest expense to be reported for this note and related swap transactions as at December 31, 2017 and 2018.

(c) Prepare the journal entries relating to the interest for the years ended December 31, 2017 and 2018.

(d) Explain why this is a cash flow hedge.

(e) Explain how the accounting would change if the company were to use hedge accounting under IFRS.

(f) Prepare the journal entries to recognize the swap, assuming the company follows hedge accounting under IFRS.

(LO 9) ***E16-23** **(Fair Value Hedge)** Anchovy Corp. issued a $1-million, four-year, 7.5% fixed-rate interest only, non-prepayable bond on December 31, 2016. Anchovy later decided to hedge the interest rate and change from a fixed rate to variable rate, so it entered into a swap agreement with M&S Corp. The swap agreement specified that Anchovy will receive a fixed rate of 7.5% and pay variable rate interest with settlement dates that match the interest payments on the instrument. Assume that interest rates declined during 2017 and that Anchovy received $13,000 as a net settlement on the swap for the settlement at December 31, 2017. The loss related to the debt (due to interest rate changes) was $48,000. The value of the swap contract increased by $48,000. The company follows IFRS. Assume criteria for hedge accounting are met and that the company has chosen to use hedge accounting.

Instructions

(a) For this transaction:

1. Identify the hedged item.
2. Identify the hedging item.
3. Identify how the hedged item would be accounted for without hedge accounting.
4. Identify how the hedging item is accounted for.
5. Indicate how the gains and losses for the hedged and hedging items are recognized.

(b) Prepare the journal entry to record the payment of interest on December 31, 2017.

(c) Prepare the journal entry to record the receipt of the swap settlement on December 31, 2017.

(d) Prepare the journal entry to record the change in the fair value of the swap contract on December 31, 2017.

(e) Prepare the journal entry to record the change in the fair value of the bond on December 31, 2017 (under hedge accounting).

(f) Explain why fair value hedge accounting can be applied to this hedge.

(g) Assume that the company applies hedge accounting under ASPE. How would the journal entries change?

(LO 10) ***E16-24** **(Share Appreciation Rights)** Barrett Limited established a share appreciation rights program that entitled its new president, Angela Murfitt, to receive cash for the difference between the Barrett Limited common shares' fair value and a pre-established price of $32 (also fair value on December 31, 2016), on 40,000 SARs. The date of grant is December 31, 2016, and the required employment (service) period is four years. The common shares' fair value fluctuated as follows: December 31, 2017, $36; December 31, 2018, $40; December 31, 2019, $45; December 31, 2020, $36; and December 31, 2021, $48. Barrett Limited recognizes the SARs in its financial statements. Angela Murfitt exercised half of the SARs on June 1, 2022 when the share price was $46. Assume that Barrett follows ASPE.

Instructions

(a) Prepare a five-year (2017 to 2021) schedule of compensation expense pertaining to the 40,000 SARs granted to Murfitt.

(b) Prepare the journal entries for compensation expense in 2017, 2020, and 2021 pertaining to the 40,000 SARs.

(c) Prepare the entry at June 1, 2022 for the exercise of the SARs.

(d) If Barrett Limited was a publicly accountable entity, would your answer to part (a) differ? Explain.

(e) From the perspective of an investor, comment on the effect of Barrett's SARs program on the company's reported profit, for the years 2017 to 2021.

DIGGING DEEPER

(LO 10) ***E16-25** **(Share Appreciation Rights)** At the end of its fiscal year, December 31, 2017, Javan Limited issued 200,000 share appreciation rights to its officers that entitled them to receive cash for the difference between the fair value of its shares and a pre-established price of $12. The fair value fluctuated as follows: December 31, 2018, $15; December 31, 2019, $11; December 31, 2020, $21; and December 31, 2021, $19. An options pricing model determined that the fair value of all 200,000 share appreciation rights fluctuated as follows: December 31, 2018, $780,000; December 31, 2019, $0; December 31, 2020, $1,850,000; and December 31, 2021, $1,400,000. The required service period is four years, and the exercise period is three years from the end of the service period. The company recognizes the SARs in its financial statements. Assume that Javan follows IFRS.

Instructions

(a) Prepare a schedule that shows the amount of compensation expense that is allocable to each year that is affected by the share appreciation rights plan.

(b) Prepare the entry at December 31, 2021 to record compensation expense, if any, in 2021.

(c) Prepare the entry at January 1, 2022, assuming that all 200,000 SARs are exercised on that date, and that fair value of the shares on that date is $19.

(d) If the firm accounted for SARs using ASPE, would the calculation of compensation expense for 2019 reflect the drop in fair value of the shares to below the pre-established price of $12 per share? Why or why not?

DIGGING DEEPER

(LO 10) ***E16-26** **(Share Appreciation Rights)** Parsons Limited established a share appreciation rights program that entitled its new president, Brandon Sutton, to receive cash for the difference between the shares' fair value and a pre-established price of $32 (also fair value on December 31, 2016), on 50,000 SARs. The date of grant is December 31, 2016, and the required employment (service) period is four years. The president exercised all of the SARs on December 31, 2021. The shares' fair value fluctuated as follows: December 31, 2017, $36; December 31, 2018, $39; December 31, 2019, $45; December 31, 2020, $36; and December 31, 2021, $48. The company recognizes the SARs in its financial statements. Assume that Parsons follows ASPE.

Instructions

(a) Prepare a five-year (2017 to 2021) schedule of compensation expense pertaining to the 50,000 SARs granted to Brandon Sutton.

(b) Prepare the journal entry for compensation expense in 2017, 2020, and 2021 relative to the 50,000 SARs.

(c) From the perspective of the employee, contrast the features of a share appreciation right to the features of a compensatory stock option.

DIGGING DEEPER

(d) Discuss what a performance-type compensation plan is, giving examples.

Problems

P16-1 The treasurer of Hing Wa Corp. has read on the Internet that the stock price of Ewing Inc. is about to take off. In order to profit from this potential development, Hing Wa purchased a call option on Ewing common shares on July 7, 2017 for $480. The call option is for 240 shares (notional value), and the strike price is $80. The option expires on January 31, 2018. The following data are available with respect to the call option:

Date	Fair Value of Option	Market Price of Ewing Shares
Sept. 30, 2017	$1,780	$86 per share
Dec. 31, 2017	$ 965	$83 per share
Jan. 4, 2018	$1,550	$85 per shar

Instructions

Prepare the journal entries for Hing Wa for the following dates:

(a) July 7, 2017: Invests in call option on Ewing shares.

(b) September 30, 2017: Hing Wa prepares financial statements.

(c) December 31, 2017: Hing Wa prepares financial statements.

(d) January 4, 2018: Hing Wa settles the call option net on the Ewing shares (that is, without buying the shares).

P16-2   Refer to P16-1, but assume that Hing Wa wrote (sold) the call option for a premium of $480 (instead of buying it). Assume that the market price of the shares and the fair value of the option are otherwise the same.

Instructions

Prepare the journal entries for Hing Wa for the following dates:

(a) July 7, 2017: Sale of the call option on Ewing shares.

(b) September 30, 2017: Hing Wa prepares financial statements.

(c) December 31, 2017: Hing Wa prepares financial statements.

(d) January 4, 2018: Hing Wa settles the call option net on the Ewing shares (that is, without selling the shares).

P16-3   Brondon Corp. purchased a put option on Mykia common shares on July 7, 2017 for $480. The put option is for 350 shares, and the strike price is $50. The option expires on January 31, 2018. The following data are available with respect to the put option:

Date	Fair Value of Option	Market Price of Mykia Shares
Sept. 30, 2017	$250	$56 per share
Dec. 31, 2017	$100	$58 per share
Jan. 31, 2018	$ 0	$62 per share

Instructions

Prepare the journal entries for Brondon Corp. for the following dates:

(a) July 7, 2017: Invests in put option on Mykia shares.

(b) September 30, 2017: Brondon prepares financial statements.

(c) December 31, 2017: Brondon prepares financial statements.

(d) January 31, 2018: Put option expires.

P16-4   Chatham Inc. purchased an option to buy 10,000 of its common shares for $35 each. The option cost $750, and explicitly stipulates that it may only be settled by exercising the option and buying the shares.

Instructions

(a) Provide the journal entry required to account for the purchase of the call option assuming Chatham Inc. complies with IFRS.

(b) Assume that the contract allows both parties a choice to settle the option by either exchanging the shares or settling on a net basis. Would this change your conclusion in part (a)?

(c) Assume that Chatham Inc. complies with ASPE. Would this change your conclusion in part (a)?

P16-5   The shareholders' equity section of Finley Inc. at the beginning of the current year is as follows:

Common shares, 1,000,000 shares authorized, 300,000 shares issued and outstanding	$3,600,000
Retained earnings	570,000

During the current year, the following transactions occurred.

1. The company issued 100,000 rights to the shareholders. Ten rights are needed to buy one share at $32 and the rights are void after 30 days. The shares' market price at this time was $34 per share.

2. The company sold the public a $200,000, 10% bond issue at par. The company also issued with each $100 bond one detachable stock purchase warrant, which provided for the purchase of common shares at $30 per share. Shortly after issuance, similar bonds without warrants were selling at 96 and the warrants at $8.

3. All but 10,000 of the rights issued in item 1 were exercised in 30 days.

4. At the end of the year, 80% of the warrants in item 2 had been exercised, and the remaining were outstanding and in good standing.

5. During the current year, the company granted stock options for 5,000 common shares to company executives. The company, using an options pricing model, determined that each option is worth $10. The exercise or strike price is $30. The options were to expire at year end and were considered compensation for the current year.

6. All but 1,000 shares related to the stock option plan were exercised by year end. The expiration resulted because one of the executives failed to fulfill an obligation related to the employment contract.

Instructions

(a) Prepare general journal entries for the current year to record each of the transactions. Assume the company follows IFRS.

(b) Prepare the shareholders' equity section of the statement of financial position at the end of the current year. Assume that retained earnings at the end of the current year is $750,000.

(c) Assume instead that the executives in items 5 and 6 had fulfilled the employment contract, and that the stock options expired because the share price was lower than the exercise or strike price. Would it be incorrect to have recorded compensation expense related to the expired stock options, during the service period? Why or why not? Would the journal entry to record the expiration be any different than the journal entry for item 6 recorded in part(a)? If so, prepare the journal entry.

DIGGING
DEEPER

P16-6 Floral Gardens Incorporated is a nationwide chain of garden centres that operates as a private company. In 2017, it issued three new financial instruments. All three of these instruments are new to you (in your role as controller), and you are working on determining how they are to be accounted for under both ASPE and IFRS.

The first financial instrument was a loan. On January 1, 2017, the company borrowed $5 million from a key shareholder at a rate of 3%, at a time when the market rate of interest was 5%. In order to convince the shareholder to lend the money to the company at a rate lower than the market rate of interest, the company agreed that, in five years, the shareholder would have the option of either accepting full repayment of the debt, or receiving 500,000 shares in the company.

The second financial instrument was one that you benefited from. The company gave its 10 key management employees a compensatory stock option plan for the first time. The purpose was to provide additional remuneration for key employees at a time when financial constraints were making it difficult for the company to increase salaries. The plan allowed the key employees to purchase 5,000 options (each) to purchase shares for $50 each when they were generally considered to be worth $100. The options were granted on January 1, 2017, and could be exercised at the end of the year or anytime in the next two years. Total compensation expense was estimated to be $550,000, and the expected period of benefit was one year beginning on the grant date. No other management employees exercised their options during the year, but you exercised all of your options on December 31, 2017.

The final new transaction that you have to determine how to account for is a forward contract. The company had not used these before, but as the Canada/U.S. exchange rate had been very good toward the end of the year, the company decided to enter into a forward contract to purchase U.S. currency (on December 15, 2017). The company agreed to buy $7 million in U.S. currency for $7,070,000 (U.S. $1 = Canadian $1.01) from Foreign Currency Inc. using a 90-day forward contract. Any changes in value of the Canadian dollar would be transferred to Floral Gardens. On December 31, 2017, the U.S. dollar strengthened in relation to the Canadian dollar, and the new value was U.S. $1 = Canadian $1.02. Assume that the fair value of the contract was $50,000 at December 31, 2017.

Instructions

(a) Prepare all the 2017 journal entries to account for the three financial instruments under both ASPE (assuming that the company chooses to value the equity component of compound instruments at $0) and IFRS.

(b) Determine the carrying amount of each statement of financial position item at year end, December 31, 2017, under both ASPE and IFRS.

P16-7 Cornwall Inc., a publicly accountable enterprise that reports in accordance with IFRS, issued convertible bonds for the first time on January 1, 2017. The $1 million of six-year, 10% (payable annually on December 31, starting December 31, 2017), convertible bonds were issued at 107, yielding 7%. The bonds would have been issued at 97 without a conversion feature, and yielded a higher rate of return. The bonds are convertible at the investor's option.

The company's bookkeeper recorded the bonds at 107 and, based on the $1,070,000 bond carrying value, recorded interest expense using the effective interest method for 2017. He prepared the following amortization table:

Date	Cash Interest (10%)	Effective Interest (7%)	Premium Amortization	Carrying Amount of Bonds
Jan. 1, 2017				$1,070,000
Dec. 31, 2017	$100,000	$74,900	$25,100	1,044,900

You were hired as an accountant to replace the bookkeeper in November 2018. It is now December 31, 2018, the company's year end, and the CEO is concerned that the company's debt covenant may be breached. The debt covenant requires Cornwall to maintain a maximum debt to equity ratio of 2.3. Based on the current financial statements, the debt to equity ratio would be 2.6. The CEO recalls hearing that convertible bonds should be reported by separating out the liability and equity components, yet he does not see any equity amounts related to the bonds on the current financial statements. He has asked you to look into the bond transactions recorded and make any necessary adjustments. He would also like you to explain how any adjustments that you make affect the debt to equity ratio.

Instructions

(a) Determine the amount that should have been reported in the equity section of the statement of financial position at January 1, 2017 for the conversion right, considering that the company must comply with IFRS. Prepare the journal entry that should have been recorded on January 1, 2017.

(b) Explain whether ASPE offers any alternatives that are not available under IFRS.

(c) Using a financial calculator or computer spreadsheet functions, calculate the effective rate (yield rate) for the bonds. Leave at least four decimal places in your calculation.

(d) Prepare a bond amortization schedule from January 1, 2017 to December 31, 2021, using the effective interest method and the corrected value for the bonds.

FINANCE

(e) Prepare the journal entry(ies) dated January 1, 2018 to correct the bookkeeper's recording errors in 2017. Ignore income tax effects.

(f) Prepare the journal entry at December 31, 2018 for the interest payment on the bonds.

DIGGING DEEPER

(g) Explain the effect that the error correction prepared in part (e) has on the debt to equity ratio.

P16-8 On January 1, 2017, Salem Corp. issued $1.1 million of five-year, zero-interest-bearing notes along with warrants to buy 1 million common shares at $22 per share. On January 1, 2017, Salem had 9.3 million common shares outstanding and the market price was $21 per share. Salem Corp. received $1 million for the notes and warrants. If offered alone, on January 1, 2017, the notes would have been issued to yield 11% to the creditor. Assume that the company follows IFRS.

Instructions

(a) Prepare the journal entry(ies) to record the issuance of the zero-interest-bearing notes and warrants for the cash consideration that was received.

(b) Prepare an amortization table for the notes using the effective interest method.

(c) Prepare adjusting journal entries for Salem Corp. at the end of its fiscal year of December 31, 2017.

(d) Prepare the journal entry required for Salem Corp. if a quarter of the warrants are exercised on January 1, 2020.

P16-9 On September 30, 2017, Gargiola Inc. issued $4 million of 10-year, 8% convertible bonds for $4.6 million. The bonds pay interest on March 31 and September 30 and mature on September 30, 2027. Each $1,000 bond can be converted into 80 no par value common shares. In addition, each bond included 20 detachable warrants. Each warrant can be used to purchase one common share at an exercise price of $15. Immediately after the bond issuance, the warrants traded at $3 each. Without the warrants and the conversion rights, the bonds would have been expected to sell for $4.2 million.

On March 23, 2020, half of the warrants were exercised. The common shares of Gargiola Inc. were trading at $20 each on this day.

Immediately after the payment of interest on the bonds, on September 30, 2022, all bonds outstanding were converted into common shares. Assume the entity follows IFRS.

Instructions

(a) Prepare the journal entry to record the issuance of the bonds on September 30, 2017.

FINANCE

(b) Using a financial calculator or computer spreadsheet functions, calculate the effective rate (yield rate) for the bonds. Leave at least four decimal places in your calculation.

(c) Prepare a bond amortization schedule from September 30, 2017 to September 30, 2022, using the effective interest rate.

(d) Prepare the December 31, 2017 year-end adjusting journal entries and the payment of interest on March 31, 2018. Assume that Gargiola Inc. does not use reversing entries. For amortization of premium, pro-rate using number of months.

(e) Prepare the journal entry to account for the exercise of the warrants on March 23, 2020. How many common shares were issued in this transaction?

(f) Prepare the journal entry to account for the bond redemption on September 30, 2022.

DIGGING
DEEPER

(g) How many shares were issued on September 30, 2022? What do you believe was the likely market value of the common shares as at the date of the conversion, September 30, 2022?

P16-10 Vanstone Corp., a public company, adopted a stock option plan on November 30, 2017 that designated 70,000 common shares as available for the granting of options to officers of the corporation at an exercise price of $8 a share. The market value was $12 a share on November 30, 2017.

On January 2, 2018, options to purchase 28,000 shares were granted to President Don Pedro: 15,000 for services to be rendered in 2018, and 13,000 for services to be rendered in 2019. Also on that date, options to purchase 14,000 shares were granted to Vice-President Beatrice Leonato: 7,000 for services to be rendered in 2018, and 7,000 for services to be rendered in 2019. The shares' market value was $14 a share on January 2, 2018. The options were exercisable for a period of one year following the year in which the services were rendered. On January 2, 2018, the value of the options was estimated at $400,000.

In 2019, neither the president nor the vice-president exercised their options because the shares' market price was below the exercise price. The shares' market value was $7 a share on December 31, 2019, when the options for 2018 services lapsed.

On December 31, 2020, both the president and vice-president exercised their options for 13,000 and 7,000 shares, respectively, when the market price was $16 a share. The company's year end is December 31.

Instructions

Prepare the necessary journal entries in 2017 when the stock option plan was adopted, in 2018 when the options were granted, in 2019 when the options lapsed, and in 2020 when the options were exercised.

*P16-11 On December 31, 2017, Master Corp. had a $10-million, 8% fixed-rate note outstanding that was payable in two years. It decided to enter into a two-year swap with First Bank to convert the fixed-rate debt to floating-rate debt. The terms of the swap specified that Master will receive interest at a fixed rate of 8% and will pay a variable rate equal to the six-month LIBOR rate, based on the $10-million amount. The LIBOR rate on December 31, 2017 was 7%. The LIBOR rate will be reset every six months and will be used to determine the variable rate to be paid for the following six-month period. Master Corp. designated the swap as a fair value hedge. Assume that the hedging relationship meets all the conditions necessary for hedge accounting and that IFRS is a constraint. The six-month LIBOR rate and the swap and debt fair values were as follows:

Date	6-Month LIBOR Rate	Swap Fair Value	Debt Fair Value
Dec. 31, 2017	7.0%		$10,000,000
June 30, 2018	7.5%	$(200,000)	9,800,000
Dec. 31, 2019	6.0%	60,000	10,060,000

FINANCE

Instructions

(a) For this transaction:

1. Identify the hedged item.

2. Identify the hedging item.

3. Identify how the hedged item would be accounted for without hedge accounting.

4. Identify how the hedging item is accounted for.

5. Indicate how the gains and losses for the hedged and hedging items are recognized.

(b) Present the journal entries to record the following transactions:

1. The entry, if any, to record the swap on December 31, 2017

2. The entry to record the semi-annual debt interest payment on June 30, 2018

3. The entry to record the settlement of the semi-annual swap amount receivable at 8%, less the amount payable at LIBOR, 7%

4. The entry, if any, to record the change in the debt's fair value at June 30, 2018

5. The entry, if any, to record the change in the swap's fair value at June 30, 2018

(c) Indicate the amount(s) reported on the statement of financial position and income statement related to the debt and swap for the year ended December 31, 2017.

(d) Indicate the amount(s) reported on the statement of financial position and income statement related to the debt and swap for the six months ended June 30, 2018.

(e) Indicate the amount(s) reported on the statement of financial position and income statement related to the debt and swap for the year ended December 31, 2018.

(f) Assume that the company applies hedge accounting under ASPE. How would the journal entries change?

*P16-12   LEW Jewellery Corp. uses gold in the manufacture of its products. LEW anticipates that it will need to purchase 500 ounces of gold in October 2017 for jewellery that will be shipped for the holiday shopping season. However, if the price of gold increases, LEW's cost to produce its jewellery will increase, which could reduce its profit margins.

FINANCE

To hedge the risk of increased gold prices, on April 1, 2017, LEW enters into a gold futures contract and designates this contract as a cash flow hedge of the anticipated gold purchase (under IFRS). The notional amount of the contract is 500 ounces, and the terms of the contract require LEW to purchase gold at a price of $300 per ounce on October 31, 2017 or to settle the contract net on the basis of the difference between the $300 and the gold price at October 31. LEW expects to settle the contract on a net basis. Assume the following data with respect to the price of the futures contract. Assume no margin deposits were paid.

Date	Fair Value of Futures Contract
Apr. 1, 2017	$ –0–
June 30, 2017	$5,000
Sept. 30, 2017	$7,500
Oct. 31, 2017	$7,500

Instructions

(a) For this transaction:

1. Identify the hedged item.

2. Identify the hedging item.

3. Identify how the hedging item is accounted for.

4. Indicate how the gains and losses for the hedged and hedging items are recognized.

Prepare the journal entries for items (b) through (f):

(b) April 1, 2017: Inception of the forward contract.

(c) June 30, 2017: LEW prepares financial statements.

(d) September 30, 2017: LEW prepares financial statements.

(e) October 31, 2017: LEW purchases 500 ounces of gold at the market price of $315 per ounce, and settles the futures contract on a net basis.

(f) December 20, 2017: LEW sells for $350,000 jewellery containing the gold purchased in October 2017. The cost of the finished goods inventory is $200,000.

(g) Indicate the amount(s) reported on the statement of financial position and statement of comprehensive income related to the futures contract for the six months ended June 30, 2017.

(h) Indicate the amount(s) reported on the statement of comprehensive income related to the futures contract and the inventory transactions for the year ended December 31, 2017.

(i) Explain how the accounting would be different using hedge accounting under ASPE.

*P16-13   Some complex financial instruments require that the Black-Scholes formula be used to measure their fair value. Examples of these complex instruments include derivatives that are options, bonds issued by the entity that are convertible into shares of the entity, and compensatory stock option plans.

Instructions

(a) For each example provided, explain why it requires the use of the Black-Scholes model in measuring fair value. Discuss how these instruments are initially recorded and subsequently measured under IFRS and ASPE.

(b) Discuss the inputs required in using the Black-Scholes formula for compensatory stock option plans and where this information comes from. Discuss the implications in determining the inputs under IFRS and ASPE.

FINANCE

(c) State the impact on the year-over-year compensation expense for newly granted compensatory stock option plans of making the following changes to the inputs used for the Black-Scholes formula, assuming all other inputs remain unchanged:

1. The risk-free rate has increased from 3% to 5%.

2. The volatility has decreased from 45% to 30%.

3. The expected life has increased from four years to six years.

(d) The Black-Scholes formula was originally designed to determine the fair value of options that are exchange traded. As a result, there has been some disagreement as to whether or not the Black-Scholes formula is the appropriate method to be used for measuring compensatory stock options. What are some of the arguments put forth to support this view? (Consider differences between exchange-traded options on shares and compensatory stock options provided to employees.)

Cases

ENABLING COMPETENCIES

Refer to the *Case Primer* on the Student Website and in *WileyPLUS* to help you answer these cases.

REAL WORLD EMPHASIS

*CA16-1   Air Canada is Canada's largest domestic and international airline, providing scheduled and charter air transportation for passengers and cargo. The airline industry has suffered many difficulties and financial setbacks in the past decade. The high costs associated with operating an airline have claimed many "victims," including Canadian Airlines, which was purchased by Air Canada in 2000 in a highly publicized takeover battle. One of the largest cost components on Air Canada's income statement is aircraft fuel.

Since aircraft fuel is a commodity good, its price is subject to significant fluctuations. The cost of a barrel of aircraft fuel is determined by supply and demand relationships and other global economic conditions that affect production. As a result, Air Canada, like all other airlines, faces a high amount of uncertainty about the cost that it will be required to pay for aircraft fuel. In order to reduce the uncertainty and attempt to limit exposure, Air Canada uses a fuel hedging strategy to manage the risk. The notes to the company's 2014 financial statements describe the airline's strategy for its fuel hedging and provide additional disclosure as follows:

Fuel Price Risk Management

Fuel price risk is the risk that future cash flows will fluctuate because of changes in jet fuel prices. In order to manage its exposure to jet fuel prices and to help mitigate volatility in operating cash flows, Air Canada enters into derivative contracts with financial intermediaries. Air Canada uses derivative contracts based on jet fuel, heating oil and crude oil based contracts. Air Canada's policy permits hedging of up to 75% of the projected jet fuel purchases for the next 12 months, 50% for the next 13 to 24 months and 25% for the next 25 to 36 months. These are maximum (but not mandated) limits. There is no minimum monthly hedging requirement. There are regular reviews to adjust the strategy in light of market conditions.

In 2014:

• Air Canada recorded a loss of $36 million in Fuel and other derivatives on Air Canada's consolidated statement of operations related to fuel derivatives (loss of $6 million in 2013).

• Air Canada purchased crude-oil and refined products-based call options covering a portion of 2014 and 2015 fuel exposure. The cash premium related to these contracts was $44 million ($39 million in 2013 for 2013 and 2014 exposures).

• Fuel derivative contracts cash settled with a fair value of $24 million in favour of Air Canada ($29 million in favour of Air Canada in 2013).

As of December 31, 2014, approximately 22% of Air Canada's anticipated purchases of jet fuel for 2015 was hedged at an average West Texas Intermediate ("WTI") equivalent capped price of US$97 per barrel. Air Canada's contracts to hedge anticipated jet fuel purchases over the 2015 period are comprised of call options with notional volumes of 6,267,000 barrels. The fair value of the fuel derivatives portfolio at December 31, 2014 was $4 million in favour of Air Canada ($20 million in favour of Air Canada in 2013) and is recorded within Prepaid expenses and other current assets.

Instructions

Discuss the various accounting issues that arise as a result of Air Canada's aircraft fuel hedging strategy. Specifically, discuss whether or not it makes sense for the company to use hedge accounting (which is optional) and, from an accounting perspective, what type of hedge this is.

FINANCE

ETHICS

CA16-2   The executive officers of Coach Corporation have a performance-based compensation plan that links performance criteria to growth in earnings per share. When annual earnings per share (EPS) growth is 12%, the Coach executives earn 100% of a predetermined bonus amount; if growth is 16%, they earn 125%. If EPS growth is lower than 8%, the executives receive no additional compensation.

In 2017, Joanna Tse, the controller of Coach, reviews year-end estimates of bad debt expense and warranty expense. She calculates the EPS growth at 15%. Peter Reiser, a member of the executive group, remarks over lunch one day that the estimate of bad debt expense might be decreased, increasing EPS growth to 16.1%. Tse is not sure she should do this, because she believes that the current estimate of bad debts is sound. On the other hand, she recognizes that a great deal of subjectivity is involved in the calculation.

Instructions

Discuss the financial reporting issues. Assume this is a public company.

CA16-3   CopMin Inc. is a private enterprise that is involved in copper mining operations. The company currently owns two operating mines. It is January 1, 2017, and CopMin has recently entered into two types of contracts. For its Papula Mine, it has entered into a sales contract with one of its major customers. As part of this contract, it has agreed to sell 75% of its annual production at a fixed price that increases 1% each year for inflation. The contract is for five years (until December 31, 2021) and cash will be received on delivery of the copper, which will be made on a monthly basis. For its second mine, Minera Mine, the company has purchased a variety of option contracts to sell copper that are exchange traded. The company has options on 60% of the mine's production for 2017 and 40% of the production for 2018. The company has the option to sell copper at a fixed price and all of the contracts can be settled on a net cash basis any time before expiry. The company paid a fee to buy these option contracts at the time they were purchased.

Instructions

(a) Explain how CopMin would record these two different contracts under IFRS and ASPE. Assume no hedge accounting.

(b) How would your answer in part (a) change if the contract for the Papula Mine could be settled net in cash?

*CA16-4   Soron Limited is a private company that uses derivatives to mitigate a variety of risks. The ethical accountant, Leon Price, has just been hired as the new controller and has recently met with the CEO. The CEO has just explained to him the following derivatives that the company is currently party to. The CEO has further explained that he would like to avoid showing the losses on the financial statements. Assume any requirements for hedge accounting are met.

1. The company recently purchased 10,000 shares in a company. These shares are publicly traded. At the same time, the company purchased exchange-traded options to sell these shares at a future date.
2. The company recently sold goods to a customer in the United States and the invoice was priced in U.S. dollars, which should be collected in six months. At the same time, to mitigate the loss on the exchange value of this receivable, Soron entered into a forward contract to sell the same amount of U.S. dollars in six months.
3. Soron has a division that operates in Australia. All of the transactions in this division are translated into Canadian dollars for reporting purposes. In order to mitigate the risk of the exchange rate fluctuation between the Australian dollar and the Canadian dollar, the company has entered into forward contracts to buy Australian dollars in the future at varying amounts over the next year. These forward contracts have experienced a foreign exchange loss in the current year as the Canadian dollar appreciated relative to the Australian dollar.

Instructions

Discuss how these derivatives should be accounted for.

ENABLING COMPETENCIES

Integrated Cases

IC16-1   On-line Deals Inc. (ODI) is in the business of selling things on-line. The company is currently owned by two founding partners, Jay and Wen. Due to the rise in Internet commerce, Jay and Wen are thinking about taking the company public. Revenues have increased steadily over the past few years and demand for this type of service appears to be growing.

ODI sells airline tickets as well as hotel rooms. Sometimes it will buy a block of rooms or airline flights from a company and sell them on-line to interested individuals. Other times airline and hotel companies advise ODI when they have excess capacity and ODI passes this information on to its customers, hoping that they will buy. All transactions are booked as revenues when the customer pays for them. The amount of revenues is generally equal to the fair value of the flight or hotel room (which is equal to what the customer pays).

During the year, in response to increased competition from other on-line businesses, ODI has spent a significant amount of money on revamping its website. It unveiled the "new look" just before year end and customers appear to really like the new features built into the website. In this business, it is very important to have a fresh and current look to the website to keep customers coming back. ODI has a large staff of dedicated information technology and service staff who deal with this. Like Jay and Wen, the senior management team do not yet draw salaries from the company but are paid with stock options. It is very difficult to determine the value of these options because the company is not yet public.

In the past year, the company's website and customer database were attacked by computer hackers. This was very embarrassing for ODI and many customers were very angry. Jay and Wen made a public announcement that they would spend whatever it took to increase security so it would never happen again. Several customers are suing the company in a class action lawsuit. The case goes to trial early next year. ODI's lawyers are a bit worried since similar lawsuits for other companies have ended up with the company paying out a fairly large settlement. Part of the problem in this case was that ODI relies on an outside company (Store All Inc., or SAI) that stores all of its data. The breach occurred at SAI although Jay and Wen also know that part of the problem was their own computer system, which they had spent significant funds to develop. ODI has since terminated its dealings with SAI and is building a new company-owned technology facility that will be up and running by next year. The new facility is state of the art and is very expensive. Jay and Wen have been heavily involved in the design of the new facility. They have been discussing with their lawyers their intention to sue SAI for the problems caused.

In order to finance the new facility, ODI issued financial instruments to a large institutional investor. The terms of the financial instruments are below:

- The face value is $100 million.
- They are repayable when revenues exceed two times the historic revenue levels.
- Each year, the financial instruments pay out a dividend of 3%.
- An annual audit must be performed.

AUDIT AND ASSURANCE

Instructions

Adopt the role of the auditors and discuss the financial reporting issues.

IC16-2 Saltworks Inc. (SI) produces salt. Its main assets are two properties that have two salt mines in them (mine 1 and mine 2). Both mines are currently in production. The salt exists in a crystalline layer of rock that rests about 50 metres below ground level. In order to mine the salt, tunnels are created by drilling through the rock. When the salt layer is reached, several holes are drilled to the bottom of the layer. Spring water is then fed through the holes. The water dissolves the salt and a cave is gradually created over time that is filled with salty water. The salt water is siphoned out of the hole, concentrated, and dried. It is then ground up and packaged. The life of a salt mine is about 30 years. Mine 1 is almost fully mined, so there is very little salt left. Mine 2 is a new mine and the tunnels are currently being dug. So far, $500,000 of costs have been incurred this year to drill and build tunnels for mine 2.

Mine 1 is completely depreciated and has a zero carrying value (net book value). Recently, SI discovered a new vein of salt in the mountain where mine 1 previously existed. The company's engineers feel that this new mine (mine 3) will produce at least as much salt as mine 1. Costs of $300,000 have been incurred to date to locate and test the salt. The salt from mine 3 is of a different quality and SI is not sure that a market currently exists for this salt or that the costs of mining will be recoverable from future revenues. Nonetheless, the company plans to continue developing the mine in the meantime to confirm this.

The mountain that houses mine 2 is covered with pine trees. An unrelated company (Logging Co. or LC) has approached SI for the rights to cut the trees down.

SI has agreed to sell these rights for $400,000, which has been paid up front. The contract gives LC the right to cut down a certain number of trees over the next three years. In order to gain access to the trees, logging roads must be built. LC has approached SI about sharing the costs (equally) of building the roads. SI has agreed as it feels it can use the roads later to transport salt. Already, costs of $1 million have been incurred to build the roads. Unfortunately, the work done to date on the roads has to be redone due to excessive rainfall, which led to a huge flood. The flood washed out parts of the new road.

During the year (before the flood), SI had purchased a weather derivative contract. SI paid a premium of $100,000 for the contract. Under the terms of the contract, the counterparty will pay SI $500,000 if more than 250 mm of rain falls within a certain period (causing flooding). Since this has happened, SI has approached the counterparty for payout.

A local environmental group has discovered that LC will be cutting down trees and is currently in discussions with SI. The group's members are demanding that SI replant the mountain with small seedlings that will grow into trees and eventually replace the trees that will be cut down. Although no contracts have been signed and SI has not specifically agreed to any course of action, SI has assured the group that it is company policy to be environmentally conscientious.

SI's president recently had a meeting with the CEO of a public company that is looking to purchase SI in the next year. The CEO is anxious to have a look at SI's financial statements and has asked that they be prepared in accordance with IFRS.

Instructions

Assume the role of the accountant for SI and discuss the financial reporting issues relating to the above. SI is a private company. (*Hint*: Use the conceptual framework to analyze any issues that are more complex.)

RESEARCH AND ANALYSIS

REAL WORLD EMPHASIS

VALUATION

RA16-1 Potash Corporation of Saskatchewan Inc.

Access the financial statements of Saskatoon-based **Potash Corporation of Saskatchewan Inc.** for its year ended December 31, 2014 from the company's website or SEDAR (www.sedar.com). PotashCorp is a well-known Canadian global fertilizer and related industrial and feed producer.

Instructions

(a) The company has several share-based compensation plans. Compare these plans, noting such things as who is eligible, whether they have to buy shares to access any benefit, what the benefit or compensation is based on (profits or share price), vesting periods, expiry periods, how the compensation cost is determined, where the offsetting amounts are reported (equity or liabilities), when the compensation expense is recorded, and whether the amount is subsequently adjusted. Prepare a chart to present your findings. (*Note:* Summarize the same types of plans together.)

(b) Discuss the effects of the share-based plans on the financial statements for the year. How much was reported in compensation expense, contributed surplus, and common shares during the year, and what related liability balance exists at December 31, 2014?

(c) Comment on any professional judgement that is required in accounting for PotashCorp's stock option plans. Have these estimates changed over the 2010 to 2014 period? Comment on what the effect on the compensation expense would be as a result of changes in each of these inputs, if all other inputs remained unchanged.

REAL WORLD EMPHASIS

FINANCIAL RISK MANAGEMENT, DERIVATIVES, AND STRATEGY DEVELOPMENT

RA16-2 Canadian Tire Corporation

Access the annual report of **Canadian Tire Corporation** for its year ended January 2, 2016 from the company's website or SEDAR (www.sedar.com). According to Note 1 to the financial statements, the company operates in three main segments: retail, a real estate investment trust, and financial services. Note 6 to the financial statements, as well as the Management Discussion and Analysis report, provides additional details about each of these segments.

Instructions

(a) From the Management Discussion and Analysis sections that deal with risk management and from Note 6 to the financial statements, identify and summarize the various business and financial risks that the company is exposed to. Explain how these risks stem from the underlying nature of the business (that is, the business model).

(b) How does the company manage its foreign currency and interest rate risks?

(c) What derivatives are used by the company? What does the company use hedge accounting for?

(d) From various notes to the financial statements, identify the fair values of the derivatives at the year end and where they were reported. Indicate how these fair values were determined by the company, and what level in the fair value hierarchy their measurement was attributed to. Explain briefly what this level represents.

REAL WORLD EMPHASIS

RA16-3 Loblaw Companies Limited

Access the financial statements of **Loblaw Companies Limited** for its year ended January 3, 2015. The statements are available on the company's website or SEDAR (www.sedar.com).

Instructions

(a) Loblaw's balance sheet reports an item entitled "Capital Securities." How are these securities classified on the balance sheet? How would they be classified legally? Describe the features of these securities, indicate how much the shares were originally issued for, how the company measures and reports them, and what their balances are at January 3, 2015 and December 28, 2013. Explain why the company measured and presented them as it did, and why there is a difference in the amount reported from one year to the next.

(b) How much was paid in dividends on these shares during 2014? How was the cost of these dividends reported?

(c) Identify the measurement methods used by Loblaw in preparing its financial statements, indicating what is measured under each method identified.

(d) Identify what financial instruments are accounted for at fair value, and the type of information that is provided about them. Are financial instruments significant to an interpretation of Loblaw's financial position and results? Explain.

REAL WORLD EMPHASIS

FINANCE: FINANCIAL RISK MANAGEMENT, VALUATION

RA16-4 Brookfield Asset Management Inc.

Locate and review **Brookfield Asset Management's** financial statements, including selected notes to its financial statements for the year ended December 31, 2014, located at the end of Volume 2 of this text. Alternatively, the full set of its annual financial statements can be found on SEDAR at www.sedar.com.

Paragraph 1 of IFRS 7 *Financial Instruments: Disclosures* indicates that the objective of this IFRS is to provide information to enable users to evaluate:

(i) The significance of financial instruments to an entity's financial position and financial performance, and

(ii) The nature and extent of the financial risks the entity is exposed to that are associated with its financial instruments, both during the fiscal period and at the end of the period; and how these risks are managed.

Instructions

(a) Review and identify the major disclosures provided by Brookfield about the fair values of its financial instruments.

(b) Using the information reported in the sources identified in part (a), comment on the reliability (of measurement) and significance of Brookfield's financial instruments to its financial position.

(c) Using the information provided in the notes to the financial statements, comment on the reliability and significance of financial instruments to the company's financial performance.

(d) Identify the disclosures provided by Brookfield about the financial risks to which the company is exposed that are associated with its financial instruments, and explain how the company manages these risks.

(e) Identify which derivatives are designated as cash flow hedges and which are designated as fair value hedges for 2014. Explain why the hedges have been designated as cash flow or fair value.

(f) Related to the derivatives and hedging activities, what amount was recognized in other comprehensive income in 2014, and what amount remains in accumulated other comprehensive income at the end of the fiscal year? Can you determine the related amount that was transferred from accumulated other comprehensive income to earnings during the year? Explain your answer.

ENDNOTES

1 Many derivatives are self-standing but some are embedded in other contracts. Compound and hybrid instruments often contain embedded derivatives.

2 *CPA Canada Handbook—Accounting*, Part II, Section 3856.05 and IAS 32.11. Copyright © International Financial Reporting Standards Foundation. All rights reserved. Reproduced by John Wiley & Sons Canada, Ltd with the permission of the International Financial Reporting Standards Foundation®. Reproduction and use rights are strictly limited. No permission granted to third parties to reproduce or distribute.

3 *CPA Canada Handbook—Accounting*, Part II, Section 3856.05 and IAS 32.AG16. Copyright © International Financial Reporting Standards Foundation. All rights reserved. Reproduced by John Wiley & Sons Canada, Ltd with the permission of the International Financial Reporting Standards Foundation®. Reproduction and use rights are strictly limited. No permission granted to third parties to reproduce or distribute.

4 IFRS 9 Appendix A and *CPA Canada Handbook—Accounting*, Part II, Section 3856.05. Copyright © International Financial Reporting Standards Foundation. All rights reserved. Reproduced by John Wiley & Sons Canada, Ltd with the permission of the International Financial Reporting Standards Foundation®. Reproduction and use rights are strictly limited. No permission granted to third parties to reproduce or distribute.

5 IFRS 7 Appendix A and *CPA Canada Handbook—Accounting*, Part II, Section 3856.A66. Copyright © International Financial Reporting Standards Foundation. All rights reserved. Reproduced by John Wiley & Sons Canada, Ltd with the permission of the International Financial Reporting Standards Foundation®. Reproduction and use rights are strictly limited. No permission granted to third parties to reproduce or distribute.

6 There are some well-publicized examples of companies that have suffered sizable losses as a result of using derivatives. For example, companies such as **Showa Shell Sekiyu** (Japan), **Metallgesellschaft** (Germany), **Procter & Gamble** (United States), and **Air Products & Chemicals** (United States) have incurred significant losses from investments in derivative instruments. Companies sometimes suffer losses because they take too much risk, they do not understand the markets or positions taken, or they suffer from the timing of closing out the contracts and positions.

7 When companies create positions that are expected to be profitable, there is often a risk of loss as well. Some refer to this as **speculating**.

8 All business inputs have price risks associated with them. There is always a risk that prices to acquire the inputs will vary over time.

9 Why would one party think that prices will rise and the other that they will fall? The same information is rarely available to all parties. In most contract negotiations, there is information asymmetry, which leads to the parties sometimes expecting different outcomes.

10 Recall that derivatives are contracts themselves, just like the purchase commitment, and it is the terms of the contract that give rise to contractual rights and obligations that accountants must then account for. Sometimes, accounting is complicated by the fact that accountants like to put labels like "derivatives" on things. This labelling complicates the accounting since standard setters must determine whether it is appropriate to apply the label (and the designated accounting) or not.

11 Commodities contracts generally trade in liquid markets and by virtue of the fact that they trade on an exchange, they have a net cash settlement feature. This means that the option exists to close out the position and take cash instead of delivery of the underlying product itself.

12 Under IFRS 9.2.6, there are various ways in which contracts can be settled net in cash or other financial instruments, including:

– where explicitly allowed by contract,

– where there is a history of settling net in cash or taking delivery and immediately selling the item for profit, or

– where the item is readily convertible to cash. (Items are readily convertible to cash where there is a ready market to buy and sell the items.)

The ability to settle net is an important differentiating feature since, where it does not exist, the contract will have to settle by delivering or taking delivery of the underlying item. There is no choice. Where net settlement is an option, then an additional hurdle must be cleared to prove that the contract was entered into for expected use. Copyright © International Financial Reporting Standards Foundation. All rights reserved. Reproduced by John Wiley & Sons Canada, Ltd with the permission of the International Financial Reporting Standards Foundation®. Reproduction and use rights are strictly limited. No permission granted to third parties to reproduce or distribute.

[13] Baird Investment Corp. is referred to as the **counterparty**. Recall that derivatives are financial instruments. Recall also that financial instruments are a contract between two parties. Counterparties frequently are investment bankers or other entities that hold inventories of financial instruments.

[14] The value is estimated using options pricing models, such as the Black-Scholes model. The fair value estimate is affected by the volatility of the underlying stock, the expected life of the option, the risk-free rate of interest, and expected dividends on the underlying shares during the option term. This model is further explained in Appendix 16C.

[15] The decline in value of the time value portion of the options from $400 to $100 reflects both the decreased likelihood that the Laredo shares will continue to increase in value over the option period and the shorter time to maturity of the option contract.

[16] A loss exists due to the decrease in the time value component of the option. As time passes, the time value component declines and is zero at the end of the contract.

[17] Spot rate is the current market rate.

[18] IAS 32 *Financial Instruments: Presentation*, Illustrative Examples. Quite a comprehensive group of examples is presented in IAS 32. This area is currently being studied by the IASB.

[19] IAS 32.26. The IASB made this decision to prevent entities from designing financial instruments so as to achieve a certain accounting outcome per the basis for the Conclusions document for IAS 32. Note that ASPE looks to the basic definitions of financial liabilities and equity to resolve the presentation issue. Whether a contract can or may be settled net is an interesting question. If the contract is a non-traded contract between two parties (as opposed to involving instruments that trade in the marketplace), then this would presumably be determined by the terms of the contract. However, when the derivatives are purchased in the capital marketplace (such as a stock market or exchange), the entity may trade out of the position (settle net) by selling the contract in the open market. Thus, derivatives that trade in the marketplace involving settlement in own equity instruments are most likely accounted for as financial assets/liabilities and not equity instruments because they effectively allow for net settlement.

[20] This actually depends upon the laws in the respective legal jurisdiction.

[21] IAS 32.11 and *CPA Canada Handbook—Accounting*, Part II, Section 3856.05. Copyright © International Financial Reporting Standards Foundation. All rights reserved. Reproduced by John Wiley & Sons Canada, Ltd with the permission of the International Financial Reporting Standards Foundation®.

Reproduction and use rights are strictly limited. No permission granted to third parties to reproduce or distribute.

[22] Ibid. Copyright © International Financial Reporting Standards Foundation. All rights reserved. Reproduced by John Wiley & Sons Canada, Ltd with the permission of the International Financial Reporting Standards Foundation®. Reproduction and use rights are strictly limited. No permission granted to third parties to reproduce or distribute.

[23] This was mentioned earlier in this chapter when discussing derivatives. Recall also that Chapter 15 provided a discussion about "in-substance shares," which are treated as equity as long as certain conditions are met even though the holder has the option to require the entity to pay cash.

[24] *CPA Canada Handbook—Accounting*, Part II, Section 3856.A26.

[25] *CPA Canada Handbook—Accounting*, Part II, Section 3856.23. This treatment is currently under discussion and may change. These types of transactions generally relate more to private entities and not public entities and therefore are not mentioned in IFRS.

[26] The legally enforceable right could exist, for instance, due to the contracts governing the instruments, laws in certain jurisdictions, or rules governing the operation of stock exchanges (if the instruments are traded on a particular exchange).

[27] *CPA Canada Handbook—Accounting*, Part II, Section 3856.24 and IAS 32.42. Copyright © International Financial Reporting Standards Foundation. All rights reserved. Reproduced by John Wiley & Sons Canada, Ltd with the permission of the International Financial Reporting Standards Foundation®. Reproduction and use rights are strictly limited. No permission granted to third parties to reproduce or distribute.

[28] *CPA Canada Handbook—Accounting*, Part II, Section 3856.22 and IAS.32.31.

[29] In fact, the bonds would sell at a premium due to the embedded stock option.

[30] *CPA Canada Handbook—Accounting*, Part II, Section 3856.A34 and IAS 32.AG32.

[31] An alternative approach that has some conceptual merit uses the market value to record the conversion. Under this method, the common shares would be recorded at market value (their market value or the market value of the bonds); the contributed surplus, bonds payable, and discount amounts would be zeroed out; and a gain/credit or loss/debit would result. Since the Canada Business Corporations Act requires shares to be recorded at their cash equivalent value, legal requirements would tend to partially support this approach.

[32] *CPA Canada Handbook—Accounting*, Part II, Section 3856.A37 and IAS 32.AG35.

[33] Note that a company might offer an option under an ESOP at less than the fair value of the option. As long as this discount is small and effectively represents the issue costs that a company might otherwise have incurred had it done a public offering, this is not seen as compensatory.

[34] IFRS 2.4 and *CPA Canada Handbook—Accounting*, Part II, Section 3870.28. Note that the wording of the respective standards is different although the substance of the content is the same. IFRS approaches the analysis differently, looking at whether the employee is acting in the role of shareholder or employee.

[35] *CPA Canada Handbook—Accounting*, Part II, Section 3870.24 and IFRS 2.10 and .11.

[36] Stock options that are issued to non-employees in exchange for other goods or services must be measured according to their fair value as nonmonetary transactions.

[37] To "vest" means to earn the rights to something. An employee's award becomes vested at the date that the employee's right to receive or retain shares of stock or cash under the award no longer depends on the employee remaining in the employer's service or fulfilling some other prescribed condition.

[38] *CPA Canada Handbook—Accounting*, Part II, Section 3870.43-.46 and IFRS 2.19 and .20.

[39] *CPA Canada Handbook—Accounting*, Part II, Section 3870.24 and IFRS 2.11.

[40] *CPA Canada Handbook—Accounting*, Part II, Section 3870.03.

[41] *CPA Canada Handbook—Accounting*, Part II, Section 3870.65-.68 and IFRS 2.44-.52. Copyright © International Financial Reporting Standards Foundation. All rights reserved. Reproduced by John Wiley & Sons Canada, Ltd with the permission of the International Financial Reporting Standards Foundation®. Reproduction and use rights are strictly limited. No permission granted to third parties to reproduce or distribute.

[42] Note that the trade-off to reducing market risk with a derivative is an increase in credit, liquidity, and operational risks (the risk related to designing and monitoring the hedge position).

[43] *CPA Canada Handbook—Accounting*, Part II, Section 3856.31, IFRS 9.6.4, and IFRS 9.6.3.3.

[44] Under IFRS, effectiveness is proven by showing that the changes in the hedged item are highly correlated with the changes in the hedging item. Although no method is specified in the standard, regression analysis is often used. Under ASPE, the entity must prove that the critical terms of the contracts for the hedged and hedging items are essentially the same (thus indirectly proving that the hedge will be effective). This is known as the "critical terms match" test.

[45] *CPA Canada Handbook—Accounting*, Part II, Section 3856.32 and A62-A65.

[46] If a firm commitment such as a purchase commitment is hedged, then the commitment itself must be recognized on the SFP so that resulting gains and losses offset the gains and losses generated by the hedging item.

[47] If the terms of the contract allowed the contract to also be settled net in cash, it may meet the definition of a derivative and have to be recognized as being such, as noted earlier in the chapter (under IFRS), unless the company intended to take delivery of the underlying.

[48] The decision to make an interest rate swap is based on a recognized index of market interest rates. The most commonly used index is the London Interbank Offer Rate, or LIBOR. The prime lending rate is another rate that is commonly referenced in loan agreements and other financial instruments. This rate is set periodically by the Bank of Canada. The interest rates that are attached to various instruments are normally above prime (such as P + 1% or P + 2%).

[49] Theoretically, this fair value change reflects the present value of expected future differences in variable and fixed interest rates and any changes in the counterparty's credit risk.

[50] Under the net settlement feature, the actual aluminum does not have to be exchanged. Rather, the parties to the contract may settle by paying the cash difference between the forward price and the price of aluminum on the settlement date.

[51] IFRS 2.30-.33. Note that IFRS 2 is scoped out of IFRS 13 *Fair Value Measurements*. ASPE refers to the shares' market price or value. Since the shares of private entities do not trade on exchanges by definition, the standard assumes internal markets for the shares.

[52] *CPA Canada Handbook—Accounting*, Part II, Section 3870.39.

[53] *CPA Canada Handbook—Accounting*, Part II, Section 3870.64.

EARNINGS PER SHARE

REFERENCE TO THE CPA COMPETENCY MAP	LEARNING OBJECTIVES
	After studying this chapter, you should be able to:
1.1.1	**1.** Understand why earnings per share (EPS) is an important number.
1.2.1, 1.2.2, 1.3.1, 1.3.2, 1.4.5	**2.** Understand when and how earnings per share must be presented, including related disclosures.
1.2.1, 1.2.2, 1.3.1, 1.3.2, 5.2.3	**3.** Calculate earnings per share for companies with a simple capital structure.
1.2.4, 1.3.1, 1.3.2, 5.2.3	**4.** Calculate earnings per share for companies with a complex capital structure.
1.4.2, 1.4.4, 5.1.1	**5.** Understand how analysis helps users of financial statements assess performance.
1.1.4	**6.** Identify the major differences in accounting between IFRS and ASPE, and what changes are expected in the near future.

CATCHING THE MARKET BY SURPRISE

WHEN A PUBLIC COMPANY announces its quarterly or annual financial results, the amount of earnings is usually not a surprise. Often, the company will signal ahead of time to the market what it thinks its earnings will be, such as by holding a conference call with investors and analysts to provide earnings guidance. Analysts who closely monitor the company's financial statements will issue predictions about upcoming results based on earnings guidance, past numbers, the company's announcements about sales and revenues during the period, and economic conditions in general and for the industry.

But sometimes, announced earnings will be above or below what the market expected, which is called an earnings surprise. One reason this occurs is that there is information asymmetry in the market; that is, the companies know more about their performance than the analysts do, until the results are announced. Earnings surprises are published daily by the NASDAQ stock exchange for the benefit of investors, though the Toronto Stock Exchange does not do this. Investors want to know a company's earnings per share: how much each share contributes to income.

What are the implications for a company after an earnings surprise? It has no legal or financial obligation to meet anyone's expectations, but the market will react. A negative earnings surprise—when a company's earnings are lower than expected—usually results in its share price falling, while

© istockphoto.com/H-Agall

a positive earnings surprise—when a company's earnings are higher than expected—usually results in its share price rising. For example, the American retail giant Wal-Mart Stores Inc. had a negative earnings surprise in the quarter ending in July 2015. It had earnings per share of $1.08, which was lower than the $1.12 that analysts were expecting. The day the results were announced, Wal-Mart's share price fell from $71.91 to $69.48. Calgary-based WestJet Airlines Ltd. had a positive earnings surprise in the third quarter of 2015. It posted earnings per share of $0.82, surpassing analysts' predictions of $0.75. While WestJet's share price was virtually unchanged the day its results were released, the volume of stock trading more than quadrupled.

Research has found that most companies tend to share good news with investors right away. But some companies may understate their expected earnings in advance of releasing results in order to get a positive earnings surprise and therefore an increase in share price. If positive earnings surprises happen too often, the market eventually catches on and revises a company's earnings expectations upwards, closer to its actual expected earnings.

Sources: The Canadian Press, "WestJet Airlines Ltd Profit Soars to Record High Despite Economic Downturn," *Financial Post*, November 3, 2015; "Westjet Airlines Ltd (WJA.TO) Historical Prices," Yahoo! Canada Finance, November 3, 2015, https://ca.finance.yahoo.com/q/hp?s=WJA.TO&a=10&b=1&c=2015&d=10&e=15&f=2015&g=d; "Wal-Mart Stores, Inc. Earnings Surprise," Nasdaq, August 18, 2015, www.nasdaq.com/symbol/wmt/earnings-surprise; David Milstead "Investors Eye Guidance as Earnings Season Begins," *Globe and Mail*, January 6, 2013; Jonathan Ratner, "Positive Earnings Surprises Not That Surprising," *Financial Post*, July 25, 2012; Allison Koester, Russell Lundholm, and Mark Soliman, "Attracting Attention in a Limited Attention World: An Exploration of the Forces Behind Positive Extreme Earnings Surprises," unpublished paper, September 2010.

PREVIEW OF CHAPTER 17

Earnings per share data are frequently reported in the financial press and are widely used by shareholders and potential investors in evaluating a company's profitability and value. This chapter examines how basic and diluted earnings per share figures are calculated and what information they contain.

The chapter is organized as follows:

EARNINGS PER SHARE			
Overview	**Basic EPS**	**Diluted EPS**	**Analysis and IFRS/ASPE Comparison**
■ Objective of EPS ■ Presentation and disclosure	■ Capital structure ■ Income available to common/ordinary shareholders ■ Weighted average common/ordinary shares ■ Comprehensive illustration	■ Complex capital structure ■ Convertible securities ■ Options and warrants ■ Contingently issuable shares ■ Antidilution revisited ■ Additional disclosures ■ Comprehensive earnings per share exercise	■ Analysis ■ A comparison of IFRS and ASPE and looking ahead

OVERVIEW

Objective of EPS

Objective 1
Understand why earnings per share (EPS) is an important number.

Common[1] shareholders need to know how much of a company's available income can be attributed to the shares that they own. This helps them assess future dividend payouts and the value of each share. As noted in Chapters 15 and 16, common shares are different from other forms of financing, such as debt and preferred shares. Common shareholders have a residual interest in the company. The return on investment is not based on a predetermined interest rate, the passage of time, or a face value (as it is for debt). If the company does well, common shareholders are the ones who gain the most. Similarly, if a company does not do well, common shareholders stand to lose the most. This is because there may not be anything left after a company covers its costs and obligations. How big is the common shareholders' part of the profit pie? How is it affected by financial instruments such as convertible debt and options? Earnings per share disclosures help investors (both existing shareholders and potential investors) by indicating the amount of income that is earned by each common share: in other words, the common shareholders' piece of the earnings pie. Common shares are sometimes referred to as ordinary shares. The basic calculation is shown in Illustration 17-1.

Illustration 17-1

The EPS Formula

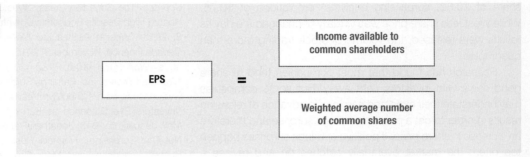

Note that EPS is normally calculated only for common shares. The calculation is done for both basic EPS and diluted EPS. **Basic EPS** looks at actual earnings and the actual number of common shares outstanding (with this number prorated for the amount of time that the shares have been outstanding). **Diluted EPS** is a **"what if"** calculation that takes into account the possibility that financial instruments such as convertible debt and options (and others) might have a negative impact on existing shareholder returns and, therefore, the shares' value. This chapter will deal first with the calculations for basic EPS and then the calculations for diluted EPS.

Presentation and Disclosure

Objective 2
Understand when and how earnings per share must be presented, including related disclosures.

Because of the importance of earnings per share information, companies whose shares trade on a stock exchange or market or companies that are in the process of listing on a stock exchange or market are required to report this information on the face of the income statement.[2] ASPE does not require EPS calculations or disclosures in the financial statements. This is because of cost-benefit considerations as well as the fact that these entities may be closely held. Generally, earnings per share information is reported below income in the income statement.

When the income statement presents discontinued operations, earnings per share should be disclosed for income from continuing operations, discontinued operations, and net income.[3] The EPS numbers related to discontinued operations may be disclosed on the face of the statement or in the notes. The EPS data in Illustration 17-2 are representative of this disclosure, and assume that the EPS numbers for discontinued operations are presented on the face of the income statement.

Illustration 17-2

Income Statement Presentation of EPS Components

Earnings per share:	
Income from continuing operations	$4.00
Loss from discontinued operations, net of tax	(0.60)
Net income	$3.40

These disclosures make it possible for users of the financial statements to know the specific impact of income from continuing operations on EPS. This is the opposite of a single EPS number, which also includes the impact of gains and losses on operations that will not continue in the future. If a corporation's capital structure is complex, the earnings per share presentation would include both basic and diluted EPS, as shown in Illustration 17-3.

Illustration 17-3

EPS Presentation—Complex Capital Structure

Earnings per common share:	
Basic earnings per share	$3.80
Diluted earnings per share	$3.35

When a period's earnings include discontinued operations, per share amounts (where applicable) should be shown for both diluted and basic EPS. Illustration 17-4 gives an example of a presentation format that reports a discontinued operation.

Illustration 17-4

EPS Presentation, with Discontinued Operations

Basic earnings per share:	
Income before discontinued operations	$3.80
Discontinued operations	(0.80)
Net income	$3.00
Diluted earnings per share:	
Income before discontinued operations	$3.35
Discontinued operations	(0.65)
Net income	$2.70

IFRS requires the following:

1. Earnings per share amounts must be shown for all periods that are presented.

2. If there has been a stock dividend or stock split, all per share amounts of prior period earnings should be restated using the new number of outstanding shares.

3. If diluted EPS data are reported for at least one period, they should be reported for all periods that are presented, even if they are the same as basic EPS.

4. When the results of operations of a prior period have been restated—for instance, as a result of an error correction—the corresponding earnings per share data should also be restated. The restatement's effect should then be disclosed in the year of the restatement.

BASIC EPS

Capital Structure

Objective 3
Calculate earnings per share for companies with a simple capital structure.

When a corporation's capital structure consists only of common shares and preferred shares and/or debt without conversion rights, the company is said to have a **simple capital structure**. In contrast, a company is said to have a **complex capital structure** if the structure includes securities that could have a dilutive or negative effect (that is, a lowering effect) on earnings per common share. In the EPS formula given in Illustration 17-1, any increase in the denominator will result in a decrease in EPS. These other, potentially dilutive securities are called potential common shares. A **potential common/ordinary share** is a security or other contract that may give its holder the right to obtain a common/ordinary share during or after the end of the reporting period. Examples are debt and equity instruments (such as preferred shares) that are convertible into common shares, warrants, options, and contingently issuable shares.[4] **Contingently issuable shares** are shares that are issuable for little or no consideration once a condition involving uncertainty has been resolved.[5] For instance, in an acquisition of another company, the acquirer may promise to issue some additional shares (at a later date) as part of the purchase consideration if the acquired company performs well.

Companies with simple capital structures only need to calculate and present basic EPS. Those with complex capital structures must calculate and present both basic and diluted EPS. The table in Illustration 17-5 summarizes the reporting requirements.

Illustration 17-5

EPS Reporting Requirements for Different Capital Structures

Capital Structure	Major Types of Equity Instruments	Impact on EPS Calculations
Simple	— Common (residual, voting) shares — Preferred shares	— Need only calculate basic EPS

Complex	— Common shares
	— Potential common shares
	  • Convertible preferred shares
	  • Convertible debt
	  • Options/warrants
	  • Contingently issuable shares
	  • Other
		— Must calculate basic and
		  diluted EPS

**TREASURY
MANAGEMENT
5.2.3**

The calculation of earnings per share for a simple capital structure involves two items: income available to common/ordinary shareholders and the weighted average number of common shares outstanding. We examine these separately in the next sections.

Income Available to Common/Ordinary Shareholders

As noted earlier, basic EPS looks at **actual** earnings that are left or available after paying operating costs (including interest) and after paying or setting aside funds for dividends on shares that rank in preference (most often preferred shares) over the common shares.

Illustration 17-6 shows the concept of income available to common shareholders as a residual component of income.

Illustration 17-6

Income Available to Common Shareholders (CSH)

Income available to common shareholders is equal to net income less amounts that have been set aside to cover obligations of other instruments, such as preferred shares that rank in preference over common shares. Because these instruments are senior, they rank in preference in terms of return on investment and these funds must be set aside before looking at how much is available for the common or residual shareholders.

When a company has both common and preferred shares outstanding, the dividends for the current year on these preferred shares are subtracted from net income to arrive at income available to common shareholders.

In reporting earnings per share information, dividends declared on preferred shares should be subtracted from income from continuing operations **and** from net income to arrive at income available to common shareholders. If dividends on preferred shares are declared and a net loss occurs, the preferred dividend increases the loss in calculating the loss per share. If the preferred shares are cumulative and the dividend is not declared in the current year, an amount equal to the dividend that should have been declared for the current year only should be subtracted from net income or added to the net loss. Dividends in arrears for previous years would have been included in the previous years' calculations.

Assume, for example, that Michael Limited has net income of $3 million and two classes of preferred shares, in addition to common shares. Class A preferred shares are cumulative and carry a dividend of $4 per share. There are 100,000 shares outstanding throughout the year. No dividend declaration has been made and no dividends have been paid during the year. Class B preferred shares are non-cumulative and carry a dividend of $3 per share. There are 100,000 shares outstanding throughout the year and the dividends have not been declared or paid in the current year. The income available for common shareholders would be calculated as follows:

Net income	$3,000,000
Less:	
Preferred dividends—Class A	(400,000)
Income available to common shareholders	$2,600,000

Note that the Class A share dividends are deducted even though they have not been declared or paid. This is because they are cumulative and will eventually have to be paid. No dividends are set aside for the Class B shares because they are non-cumulative and have not been declared. Because they are non-cumulative, the company never has to make up a lost dividend to the Class B shareholders.

Weighted Average Common/Ordinary Shares

In all calculations of earnings per share, the **weighted average number of shares** outstanding (WACS) during the period is the basis for the per share amounts that are reported. Shares that are issued or purchased during the period affect the amount outstanding and must be weighted by the fraction of the period that they have been outstanding. The rationale for this approach is that the income was generated on the issue proceeds for only part of the year. Accordingly, the number of shares outstanding should be weighted by the same factor. To illustrate, assume that Salomski Inc. has the data in Illustration 17-7 for the changes in its common shares outstanding for the period.

Illustration 17-7

Common Shares Outstanding, Ending Balance—Salomski Inc.

Date	Share Changes	Shares Outstanding
Jan. 1	Beginning balance	90,000
Apr. 1	Issued 30,000 shares for cash	30,000
		120,000
July 1	Repurchased 39,000 shares	(39,000)
		81,000
Nov. 1	Issued 60,000 shares for cash	60,000
Dec. 31	Ending balance	141,000

To calculate the weighted average number of shares outstanding, the calculation is done as in Illustration 17-8.

Dates Outstanding	(A) Shares Outstanding	(B) Fraction of Year	(C) Weighted Shares (A × B)
Jan. 1–Mar. 31	90,000	3/12	22,500
Apr. 1–June 30	120,000	3/12	30,000
July 1–Oct. 31	81,000	4/12	27,000
Nov. 1–Dec. 31	141,000	2/12	23,500
Weighted average number of shares outstanding			103,000

As illustrated, 90,000 shares were outstanding for three months, which translates to 22,500 whole shares for the entire year. Because additional shares were issued on April 1, the number of shares outstanding changes and these shares must be weighted for the time that they have been outstanding. When 39,000 shares were repurchased on July 1, this reduced the number of shares outstanding and a new calculation again has to be made to determine the proper weighted number of shares outstanding.

Stock Dividends, Splits, and Reverse Splits

When stock dividends or stock splits occur, calculation of the weighted average number of shares requires a restatement of the shares outstanding before the stock dividend or split.[6] For example, assume that a corporation had 100,000 shares outstanding on January 1 and issued a 25% stock dividend on June 30. For purposes of calculating a weighted average for the current year, the additional 25,000 shares outstanding as a result of the stock dividend are assumed to have been outstanding since the beginning of the year. Thus, the weighted average for the year would be 125,000 shares.

The issuance of a stock dividend or stock split requires a restatement (which is applied retroactively), but the issuance or repurchase of shares for cash does not. Why? Stock splits and stock dividends do not increase or decrease the net enterprise's assets; only additional shares are issued. Therefore, the weighted average number of shares must be restated. By restating the number, valid comparisons of earnings per share can be made between periods before and after the stock split or stock dividend. Conversely, the issuance or purchase of shares for cash changes the amount of net assets. The company earns either more or less in the future as a result of this change in net assets. Stated another way, a stock dividend or split does not change the shareholders' total investment; it only increases (or decreases if it is a reverse stock split) the **number** of common shares.

To illustrate how a stock dividend affects the calculation of the weighted average number of shares outstanding, assume that Baiye Limited has the data in Illustration 17-9 for the changes in its common shares during the year.

Date	Share Changes	Shares Outstanding
Jan. 1	Beginning balance	100,000
Mar. 1	Issued 20,000 shares for cash	20,000
		120,000
June 1	60,000 additional shares (50% stock dividend)	60,000
		180,000
Nov. 1	Issued 30,000 shares for cash	30,000
Dec. 31	Ending balance	210,000

Illustration 17-10 shows the calculation of the weighted average number of shares outstanding.

		(A)	(B)	(C)	(D)
	Dates Outstanding	Shares Outstanding	Restatement	Fraction of Year	Shares Weighted (A × B × C)
	Jan. 1–Feb. 28	100,000	1.50	2/12	25,000
	Mar. 1–May 31	120,000	1.50	3/12	45,000
	June 1–Oct. 31	180,000		5/12	75,000
	Nov. 1–Dec. 31	210,000		2/12	35,000
	Weighted average number of shares outstanding				180,000

Illustration 17-10

Weighted Average Number of Shares Outstanding—Share Issue and Stock Dividend

UNDERLYING CONCEPT

Restating the number of shares allows users to better predict the impact of the stock dividend or split on future EPS calculations.

The shares outstanding before the stock dividend must be restated. The shares outstanding from January 1 to June 1 are adjusted for the stock dividend so that these shares are stated on the same basis as shares issued after the stock dividend. Shares issued after the stock dividend do not have to be restated because they are already on the new basis. The stock dividend simply restates existing shares. A stock split is treated in the same way.

If a stock dividend or stock split occurs after the end of the year, but before the financial statements are issued, the weighted average number of shares outstanding for the year (and any other years presented in comparative form) must be restated. For example, assume that Hendricks Corp. calculates its weighted average number of shares to be 100,000 for the year ended December 31, 2017. On January 15, 2018, before the financial statements are issued, the company splits its shares 3 for 1. In this case, the weighted average number of shares used in calculating earnings per share for 2017 would be 300,000 shares. If earnings per share information for 2016 is provided as comparative information, it also must be adjusted for the stock split.

Mandatorily Convertible Instruments

Where common shares will be issued in future due to mandatory conversion of a financial instrument that is already outstanding, it is assumed that the conversion has already taken place for EPS calculation purposes. For these instruments, the denominator of the basic EPS calculation would be adjusted as though the instruments had already been converted to common shares and the common shares were outstanding. An adjustment may be needed for the numerator depending on how the instruments were presented in the financial statements (that is, as debt, common shares, or preferred shares). Note that if the instruments were presented as common share equity already, there would be no need to adjust the numerator. The concern would only be to ensure the number of common shares was adjusted for these shares that were not yet outstanding.

Contingently Issuable Shares

Contingently issuable shares are potential common shares, as mentioned earlier. If these shares are issuable simply with the passage of time (as with the mandatorily convertible instruments noted above), they are not considered contingently issuable because it is certain that time will pass. Where they are issuable based on something else (for example, profit levels or performance targets), they are included in the calculation of basic EPS when the conditions are satisfied.

Comprehensive Illustration

Leung Corporation has income of $580,000 before income from discontinued operations (net of tax) of $240,000. In addition, it has declared preferred dividends of $1 per share on 100,000 preferred shares outstanding. Leung Corporation also has the data shown in Illustration 17-11 for changes in its common shares outstanding during 2017.

Illustration 17-11

Shares Outstanding, Ending Balance—Leung Corp.

Dates	Share Changes	Shares Outstanding
Jan. 1	Beginning balance	180,000
May 1	Purchased 30,000 shares	30,000
		150,000
July 1	300,000 additional shares issued (3-for-1 stock split)	300,000
		450,000
Dec. 31	Issued 50,000 shares for cash	50,000
Dec. 31	Ending balance	500,000

To calculate the earnings per share information, the weighted average number of shares outstanding is first determined as in Illustration 17-12.

Illustration 17-12

Weighted Average Number of Shares Outstanding

	(A) Shares Outstanding	(B) Restatement	(C) Fraction of Year	(D) Shares Weighted (A × B × C)
Dates Outstanding				
Jan. 1–Apr. 30	180,000	3	4/12	180,000
May 1–Dec. 31	150,000	3	8/12	300,000
Weighted average number of shares outstanding				480,000

In calculating the weighted average number of shares, the shares sold on December 31, 2017 are ignored because they have not been outstanding during the year. Income before discontinued operations and net income are then divided by the weighted average number of shares to determine the earnings per share. Leung Corporation's preferred dividends of $100,000 are subtracted from income before discontinued operations ($580,000) to arrive at income from continuing operations available to common shareholders of $480,000 ($580,000 – $100,000). Deducting the preferred dividends from the income from continuing operations has the effect of also reducing net income without affecting the amount of the discontinued operations. The final amount is referred to as income available to common shareholders. Illustration 17-13 shows the calculation of income available to common shareholders.

Illustration 17-13

Calculation of Income Available to Common Shareholders

	(A) Income Information	(B) Weighted Shares	(C) Earnings per Share (A ÷ B)
Income from continuing operations available to common shareholders	$480,000	480,000	$1.00
Income from discontinued operations (net of tax)	240,000	480,000	0.50
Income available to common shareholders	$720,000	480,000	$1.50

Disclosure of the per share amount for the discontinued operations (net of tax) must be reported either on the face of the income statement or in the notes to the financial statements. Income and per share information would be reported as in Illustration 17-14.

Illustration 17-14

Earnings per Share, with Discontinued Operations

Income from continuing operations	$580,000
Income from discontinued operations, net of tax	240,000
Net income	$820,000

(continued)

Illustration 17-14

Earnings per Share, with Discontinued Operations (continued)

Earnings per share:	
Income from continuing operations	$1.00
Income from discontinued operations, net of tax	0.50
Net income	$1.50

DILUTED EPS

Complex Capital Structure

Objective 4
Calculate earnings per share for companies with a complex capital structure.

TREASURY
MANAGEMENT
5.2.3

One problem with a basic EPS calculation is that it fails to recognize the potentially dilutive impact on outstanding shares when a corporation has dilutive securities in its capital structure. **Dilutive securities must be considered because their conversion or exercise often decreases earnings per share.** This adverse effect can be significant and, more important, unexpected, unless financial statements call attention to the potentially dilutive effect.

A complex capital structure exists when a corporation has potential common shares such as convertible securities, options, warrants, or other rights that could dilute earnings per share if they are converted or exercised. **Therefore, as noted earlier, when a company has a complex capital structure, both basic and diluted earnings per share are generally reported.** The calculation of diluted EPS is similar to the calculation of basic EPS. The difference is that diluted EPS includes the effect of all dilutive potential common shares that were outstanding during the period, on both income and shares. The formula in Illustration 17-15 shows the relationship between basic EPS and diluted EPS.

Illustration 17-15

Relationship between Basic and Diluted EPS

Note that companies with complex capital structures will not report diluted EPS if the securities in their capital structure are antidilutive. **Antidilutive securities** are securities that, upon conversion or exercise, would increase earnings per share (or reduce the loss per share). The purpose of presenting both EPS numbers is to inform financial statement users of situations that may occur and to provide worst-case dilutive situations. If the securities are antidilutive, the likelihood of conversion or exercise is considered remote. **Thus, companies that have only antidilutive securities report only the basic EPS number.**[7]

We showed the calculation of basic EPS in the previous section. The discussion in the following sections addresses the effects of convertible and other dilutive securities on EPS calculations.

Convertible Securities

At conversion, convertible securities are exchanged for common shares. Convertible securities are therefore potential common shares and may be dilutive. The method that is used to measure the dilutive effects of a potential conversion on EPS is sometimes called the **if-converted method.**[8]

If-Converted Method

The if-converted method for convertible debt or preferred shares assumes both of the following:

1. It assumes that the convertible securities are converted at the **beginning of the period** (or at the time of the security issuance, if they are issued during the period).[9]

2. It assumes **the elimination of related interest, net of tax** and the elimination of preferred share dividends. If the debt/equity had been converted at the beginning of the period, there would be no bond interest expense/preferred dividend. No tax effect is calculated for preferred share dividends, because preferred dividends generally are not tax-deductible.

Thus the denominator—the weighted average number of shares outstanding—is increased by the additional shares that are assumed to be issued. The numerator—net income—is increased by the amount of interest expense, net of tax and any preferred share dividends, that are associated with those convertible securities.

As an example, assume that Field Corporation has net income for the year of $410,000 and a weighted average number of common shares outstanding during the period of 100,000 shares. The basic earnings per share is therefore $4.10 ($410,000 ÷ 100,000).

The company has two convertible debenture bond issues outstanding.[10] One is a 6% issue sold at 100 (total $1 million) in a prior year and convertible into 20,000 common shares. The other is a 10% issue sold at 100 (total $500,000) on April 1 of the current year and convertible into 32,000 common shares. The tax rate is 30%.

As shown in Illustration 17-16, to determine the numerator, we add back the interest on the if-converted securities less the related tax effect. Because the if-converted method assumes that conversion occurs at the beginning of the year, no interest on the convertible securities is assumed to be paid during the year. The interest on the 6% convertible bonds is $60,000 for the year ($1,000,000 × 6%). The increased tax expense is $18,000 ($60,000 × 0.30), and the interest added back net of taxes is $42,000 [$60,000 − $18,000, or simply $60,000 × (1 − 0.30)].

Because the 10% convertible bonds are issued after the beginning of the year, the shares that are assumed to have been issued on that date, April 1, are weighted as outstanding from April 1 to the end of the year. In addition, the interest adjustment to the numerator for these bonds would reflect the interest for only nine months. Thus, the interest added back on the 10% convertible security would be $26,250 [$500,000 × 10% × 9/12 year × (1 − 0.30)]. The calculation of earnings (the numerator) for diluted earnings per share is shown in Illustration 17-16. Note that both debentures are individually dilutive.

Net income for the year	$410,000
Add: Adjustment for interest (net of tax)	
6% debentures ($60,000 × [1 − 0.30])	42,000
10% debentures ($50,000 × 9/12 × [1 − 0.30])	26,250
Adjusted net income	$478,250

Illustration 17-16
Calculation of Adjusted Net Income

The calculation of the weighted average number of shares adjusted for dilutive securities—the denominator in a diluted earnings per share calculation—is shown in Illustration 17-17.

Weighted average number of shares outstanding	100,000
Add: Shares assumed to be issued:	
6% debentures (as of beginning of year)	20,000
10% debentures (as of date of issue, April 1; 9/12 × 32,000)	24,000
Weighted average number of shares adjusted for dilutive securities	144,000

Illustration 17-17
Calculation of Weighted Average Number of Shares—Dilutive Securities

Field Corporation would then report earnings per share based on a dual presentation on the face of the income statement; that is, it would present both basic and diluted earnings per share.[11] The presentation is shown in Illustration 17-18.

Net income for the year	$410,000
Earnings per share:	
Basic earnings per share ($410,000 ÷ 100,000)	$4.10
Diluted earnings per share ($478,250 ÷ 144,000)	$3.32

Other Factors

UNDERLYING CONCEPT

Showing both basic and diluted EPS reflects the full disclosure principle. The diluted EPS calculation shows the maximum possible negative impact of conversions.

The example above assumed that Field Corporation's debentures were sold at their face amount. If the bonds were instead sold at a premium or discount, interest expense would have to be adjusted each period to account for related amortization. Therefore, the amount of interest expense added back, net of tax, to net income is the interest expense reported on the income statement, not the interest paid in cash during the period. Likewise, because the convertible debentures are compound instruments, a portion of the proceeds would actually be allocated to the equity component, and the discount rate on the debt would be the market interest rate on straight debt. Finally, if the company had the option to settle the debentures using shares or cash, we would assume shares were used. (Further discussion of these factors is beyond the scope of this text.)

The conversion rate on a dilutive security may change over the period that the dilutive security is outstanding. In this situation, for the diluted EPS calculation, the most advantageous conversion rate available to the security holder is used.[12] For example, assume that a convertible bond was issued January 1, 2015, with a conversion rate of 10 common shares for each bond starting January 1, 2017; beginning January 1, 2020, the conversion rate is 12 common shares for each bond; and beginning January 1, 2025, it is 15 common shares for each bond. In calculating diluted EPS in 2015, the conversion rate of 15 shares to one bond would be used.

Options and Warrants

Recall from Chapter 16 that stock options allow the holder to buy or sell shares at a pre-set price (the **exercise price**). The company may either **write** the options or **purchase** them. The options may also allow the holder to buy the shares (**call options**) or sell the shares (**put options**).[13]

Written Options

When the company writes or sells the options, it gives the holder or purchaser the right to either buy (call) or sell (put) the shares. **Thus, if the holder or purchaser decides to exercise the options, the company will have to deliver (either buy or sell the shares).** Generally speaking, the holder of the options will exercise the right if the options are **in the money**. They are in the money if the holder of the options will benefit from exercising them. If the option is a call option—giving the holder the right to buy the shares at a preset price—the holder will exercise it if the pre-set or exercise price is lower than the current market price. **Written options and their equivalents must be included in the diluted EPS calculations if they are dilutive.** Generally speaking, they are **dilutive when they are written options that are in the money.**

Assume, for example, that Gaddy Limited sold (or wrote) **call options** for $2 that allow the purchaser to buy shares of Gaddy at $10 (the exercise price). At the time, Gaddy shares were trading at $9. Assume further that the market price of Gaddy shares subsequently increases to $15. The options are now in the money because they have value to the

**TREASURY
MANAGEMENT**
5.2.3

holder. If the holder exercises the options, Gaddy will have to issue its own shares for the exercise price ($10). This will result in dilution for Gaddy and so must be considered in the diluted EPS calculation. Note that if the shares of Gaddy never go above $10, the holder will not exercise them and the options will expire. Expired options as well as options that are not in the money are excluded from the diluted EPS calculation.

If Gaddy had instead sold **put options** that allow the purchaser to sell shares of Gaddy to Gaddy at an exercise price of $8, these might also be dilutive. Assume that when the put options were issued, Gaddy shares were $9, and that the shares subsequently went down to $6. If the put option is exercised, Gaddy will have to buy the shares from the option holder and will have to pay $8—the exercise price. Again, this must be incorporated in the diluted EPS calculation because it is in the money for the holder. The holder can sell the shares for more than their market value. Once again, if the options expire or are not in the money, they are not included in the diluted EPS calculation (because it is assumed that they will not be exercised).

Written put options, where the company may be forced to buy the shares at an unfavourable price, have the same impact on the calculation as **forward purchase contracts**. Forward purchase contracts are included in the calculations if they represent a liability; that is, if the forward purchase price is higher than the average market price. Similarly, written call options have the same impact on the calculation as **forward sales contracts**. Forward sales contracts are included in the calculations if they represent a liability; that is, if the forward selling price is lower than the market price. In both cases, the instruments are in the money to the other party and are therefore dilutive.

Purchased Options

Purchased options, on the other hand, do not result in the company having an obligation (as opposed to written options, which potentially result in an obligation). When the company buys options, it obtains the right but not the obligation to buy (call) or sell (put) its own shares. When will it exercise these options? Like any option holder, it is assumed that the company will exercise the options when they are in the money. Thus, when the underlying shares in a purchased call option have a market value that is greater than the exercise price, they are in the money. Alternatively, when the underlying shares in a purchased put option have a market value that is less than the exercise price, the options are in the money and it is assumed that they will be exercised. Illustration 17-19 summarizes this.

Illustration 17-19

In-the-Money Options

	Call	Put
Written	In the money when market price is greater than exercise price	In the money when market price is less than exercise price
Purchased	In the money when market price is greater than exercise price	In the money when market price is less than exercise price

Purchased options will always be antidilutive because they will only be exercised when they are in the money and this will always be favourable to the company. They are therefore not considered in the calculation.[14]

Treasury Stock Method

Written options and warrants, and their equivalents, are included in earnings per share calculations through what is sometimes referred to as the treasury stock and/or reverse treasury stock method.

The **treasury stock method** applies to **written call options and equivalents** and assumes that:

1. the options and warrants or equivalents are exercised **at the beginning of the year** (or on the date of issue if it is later), and

2. the proceeds are used to purchase common shares for the treasury at the **average market price** during the year.

If the exercise price is lower than the average market price, then the proceeds from exercise are not sufficient to buy back all the shares. This would result in more shares being issued than purchased and the effect will therefore be dilutive. **The excess number of the shares to be issued over the number of shares that would be purchased is added to the weighted average number of shares outstanding in calculating the diluted earnings per share. Note that no adjustment is made to the numerator.**

Assume, for example, that 1,500 (written) call options are outstanding at an exercise price of $30 for a common share. The average common share market price per share is $50. Because the market price is greater than the exercise price, the options are considered in the money and the holder is assumed to exercise them. The holder can buy the shares for a price that is less than market price—a bargain. By applying the treasury stock method, there would be 600 incremental shares outstanding, calculated as in Illustration 17-20.[15]

Illustration 17-20

Calculation of Incremental Shares

Proceeds from exercise of 1,500 options (1,500 × $30)	$45,000
Shares issued upon exercise of options	1,500
Treasury shares purchasable with proceeds ($45,000 ÷ $50)	900
Incremental shares outstanding (additional potential common shares)	600

Thus, if the exercise price of the call option or warrant is lower than the shares' market price, dilution occurs because, on a net basis, more common shares are assumed to be outstanding after the exercise. If the exercise price of the call option or warrant is higher than the shares' market price, the options would not be exercised and would therefore be irrelevant to the EPS calculation.[16] As a practical matter, a simple average of the weekly or monthly prices is adequate, as long as the prices do not fluctuate significantly.

To illustrate the application of the treasury stock method, assume that Kubitz Industries, Inc. has net income for the period of $220,000. The average number of shares outstanding for the period was 100,000 shares. Hence, basic EPS, ignoring all dilutive securities, is $2.20. The average number of shares that are issuable under written call options at an option price of $20 per share is 5,000 shares (although the options are not exercisable at this time). The average market price of the common shares during the year was $28. Illustration 17-21 shows the calculation.

Illustration 17-21

Calculation of Earnings per Share—Treasury Stock Method

	Basic Earnings per Share	Diluted Earnings per Share
Average number of shares issuable under options:		5,000
Option price per share		× $20
Proceeds upon exercise of options		$100,000
Average market price of common shares		$28
Treasury shares that could be repurchased with proceeds ($100,000 ÷ $28)		3,571
Excess of shares under option over the treasury shares that could be repurchased (5,000 − 3,571)—potential incremental common shares		1,429
Average number of common shares outstanding	100,000	100,000
Total average number of common shares outstanding and potential common shares	100,000 (A)	101,429 (C)
Net income for the year	$220,000 (B)	$220,000 (D)
Earnings per share	$2.20 (B ÷ A)	$2.17 (D ÷ C)

Reverse Treasury Stock Method

The **reverse treasury stock method** is used for (written) put options and forward purchase contracts. It assumes both of the following:

1. The company would issue enough common shares **at the beginning of the year** in the marketplace (at the average market price) to generate sufficient funds to buy the shares under the option/forward.

2. The proceeds from the above would be used to buy back the shares under the option/forward at the beginning of the year.

If the options are in the money, the company would have to buy the shares back under the options/forward at a higher price than the market price. Thus, it would have to issue more shares at the beginning of the year to generate sufficient funds to meet the obligation under the option/forward.

Assume, for example, that 1,500 (written) put options are outstanding at an exercise price of $30 for a common share. The average market price per common share is $20. Because the market price is less than the exercise price, the options are considered in the money and the holder is assumed to exercise them. The holder can sell the shares for a price that is higher than market price—again, a bargain. By applying the reverse treasury stock method, there would be 750 additional (incremental) shares outstanding, calculated as in Illustration 17-22.

<table>
<tr><td>Illustration 17-22
Calculation of
Incremental Shares</td><td>Amount needed to buy 1,500 shares under put option (1,500 × $30)</td><td>$45,000</td></tr>
<tr><td></td><td>Shares issued in market to obtain $45,000 ($45,000 ÷ $20)</td><td>2,250</td></tr>
<tr><td></td><td>Number of shares purchased under the put options</td><td>1,500</td></tr>
<tr><td></td><td>Incremental shares outstanding (potential common shares)</td><td>750</td></tr>
</table>

This is dilutive because there would be 750 more shares outstanding. If the market price were higher than the exercise price, the options would never be exercised. (This is because the holder could sell the shares in the marketplace for a higher amount.) Thus, options that are not in the money are ignored in the diluted EPS calculation. Likewise, when the forward purchase price of a forward purchase contract is lower than the market price, the forward contract is antidilutive because the company would theoretically have to issue fewer shares in the marketplace in order to generate sufficient money to honour the forward contract. In other words, it would issue fewer shares than it would buy back, resulting in fewer common shares outstanding (not more).

Contingently Issuable Shares

Contingently issuable shares are potential common shares, as mentioned earlier. If the shares are issuable upon attaining a certain earnings or market price level, for instance, and this level is met at the end of the year, they should be considered as outstanding from the beginning of the year for the calculation of diluted earnings per share. If the conditions have not been met, however, the diluted EPS may still be affected. The number of contingently issuable shares included in the diluted EPS calculation would be based on the number of shares (if any) that would be issuable if the end of the reporting period were the end of the contingency period and if the impact were dilutive.

For example, assume that Walz Corporation purchased Cardella Limited in 2017 and agreed to give the shareholders of Cardella 20,000 additional shares in 2019 if Cardella's net income in 2018 is $90,000. Assume also that in 2017 Cardella's net income is $100,000, which is higher than the $90,000 target for 2018. Because the contingency of stipulated earnings of $90,000 is already being attained in 2017, and because 2017 is treated as though it were the end of the contingency period, Walz's diluted earnings per share for 2017 would include the 20,000 contingent shares in the calculation of the number of shares outstanding.

Antidilution Revisited

In calculating diluted EPS, the combined impact of all dilutive securities must be considered. However, it is necessary to first determine which potentially dilutive securities are in fact individually dilutive and which are antidilutive. As was stated earlier, securities that are antidilutive have to be excluded from EPS calculations; they therefore cannot be used to offset dilutive securities.

Recall that antidilutive securities are securities whose inclusion in earnings per share calculations **would increase earnings per share (or reduce net loss per share)**. Convertible debt is antidilutive if the addition to income of the interest (net of tax) would cause a greater percentage increase in income (the numerator) than a conversion of the bonds would cause a percentage increase in common and potentially dilutive shares (the denominator). In other words, convertible debt is antidilutive if conversion of the security would cause common share earnings to increase by a greater amount per additional common share than the earnings per share amount before the conversion.

To illustrate, assume that Kohl Corporation has a $1-million, 6% debt issue that is convertible into 10,000 common shares. Net income for the year is $210,000, the weighted average number of common shares outstanding is 100,000 shares, and the tax rate is 30%. In this case, assume also that conversion of the debt into common shares at the beginning of the year requires the adjustments to net income and the weighted average number of shares outstanding that are shown in Illustration 17-23.

Illustration 17-23

Test for Antidilution

Net income for year	$210,000	Average number of shares outstanding	100,000
Add: Adjustment for interest (net of tax)		Add: Shares issued upon assumed	
on 6% debentures $60,000 × (1 − 0.30)	42,000	conversion of debt	10,000
Adjusted net income	$252,000	Average number of common and	
		potential common shares	110,000

Basic EPS = $210,000 ÷ 100,000 = $2.10
Diluted EPS = $252,000 ÷ 110,000 = $2.29 (Antidilutive)

As a shortcut, the convertible debt can also be identified as antidilutive by comparing the incremental EPS resulting from conversion, $4.20 ($42,000 additional earnings ÷ 10,000 additional shares), with EPS before inclusion of the convertible debt, $2.10.

With options or warrants, whenever the option or warrant is not in the money, it is irrelevant to the calculations because the holder would not exercise it.

Additional Disclosures

Complex capital structures and a dual presentation of earnings require the following additional disclosures in note form:

1. The amounts used in the numerator and denominator in calculating basic and diluted EPS

2. A reconciliation of the numerators and denominators of basic and diluted per share calculations for income before discontinued operations (including the individual income and share amounts of each class of securities that affects EPS)

3. Securities that could dilute basic EPS in the future but were not included in the calculations because they have antidilutive features

4. A description of common share transactions that occur after the reporting period that would have significantly changed the EPS numbers

Illustration 17-24 presents an example of the reconciliation and related disclosure that is needed to meet the standard's disclosure requirements. Assume that stock options to purchase 1 million common shares at $85 per share were outstanding during the second half of 2017 but that the options are antidilutive.

Illustration 17-24

Reconciliation for Basic and Diluted EPS

	For the Year Ended December 31, 2017		
	Income (Numerator)	Shares (Denominator)	Per Share Amount
Net Income	$7,500,000		
Less: Preferred stock dividends	(45,000)		
Basic EPS			
Income available to common shareholders	7,455,000	3,991,666	$1.87
Warrants		30,768	
Convertible preferred shares	45,000	308,333	
4% convertible bonds (net of tax)	60,000	50,000	
Diluted EPS			
Income available to common shareholders after assumed conversions	$7,560,000	4,380,767	$1.73

Related disclosure: Stock options to purchase 1 million common shares at $85 per share were outstanding during the second half of 2017 but were not included in the calculation of diluted EPS because the options' exercise price was greater than the average market price of the common shares. The options were still outstanding at the end of 2017 and expire on June 30, 2024.

One final note on additional disclosures: an entity may choose to report additional per share calculations based on other reported components of comprehensive income. If this is done, the weighted average number of shares would be the same and the basic and diluted EPS numbers must be presented with equal prominence. This is illustrated below.

WHAT DO THE NUMBERS MEAN?

REAL WORLD EMPHASIS

Air Canada included the following note disclosure in its 2014 financial statements.

15. EARNINGS PER SHARE

The following table outlines the calculation of basic and diluted EPS:

IN MILLIONS, EXCEPT PER SHARE AMOUNTS	2014	2013
NUMERATOR:		
NUMERATOR FOR BASIC AND DILUTED EARNINGS PER SHARE:		
Net income attributable to shareholders of Air Canada	$100	$6
DENOMINATOR:		
WEIGHTED-AVERAGE SHARES	286	277
Effect of potential dilutive securities:		
Stock options	7	4
Warrants	–	2
Shares held in Trust for employee share-based compensation award	–	1
Total potential dilutive securities	7	7
ADJUSTED DENOMINATOR FOR DILUTED EARNINGS PER SHARE	293	284
BASIC EPS	$0.35	$0.02
DILUTED EPS	$0.34	$0.02

The calculation of EPS is based on whole dollars and not on rounded millions. As a result, the above amounts may not be recalculated to the per share amount disclosed above.

Basic EPS is calculated based on the weighted average number of common shares outstanding after deducting shares held in trust for the purposes of the Employee Recognition Award. All of the remaining shares held in trust for the Employee Recognition Award vested in 2014.

Excluded from the 2014 calculation of diluted EPS were 2,680,000 (2013–7,027,000) outstanding options where the options' exercise prices were greater than the average market price of the common shares for the year.

In addition, the company included in its Management Discussion and Analysis the following non-GAAP calculations:

ADJUSTED NET INCOME AND ADJUSTED NET INCOME PER SHARE—DILUTED

Air Canada uses adjusted net income and adjusted net income per share—diluted to assess the performance of its business without the effects of foreign exchange, net financing income (expense) relating to employee benefits, mark-to-market adjustments on fuel and other derivatives and unusual items. These measures are not recognized measures for financial statement presentation under GAAP, do not have a standardized meaning and may not be comparable to similar measures presented by other public companies.

CANADIAN DOLLARS IN MILLIONS, EXCEPT PER SHARE VALUES	FOURTH QUARTER			FULL YEAR		
	2014	2013	$ Change	2014	2013	$ Change
NET INCOME (LOSS) FOR THE PERIOD ATTRIBUTABLE TO SHAREHOLDERS	$(101)	$ (7)	$ (94)	$100	$ 6	$ 94
Adjusted for:						
One-time payments – ACPA[1]	30	–	30	30	–	30
Benefit plan amendments[2]	–	(82)	82	–	(82)	82
Tax-related provision adjustments[3]	–	–	–	(41)	–	(41)
Impairment charge[4]	–	6	(6)	–	30	(30)
Foreign exchange loss	115	55	60	307	120	187
Interest charge[5]	–	–	–	–	95	(95)
Net financing expense relating to employee benefits	32	53	(21)	134	208	(74)
(Gain) loss on fuel and other derivatives	(9)	(22)	13	1	(37)	38
ADJUSTED NET INCOME	$ 67	$ 3	$ 64	$ 531	$ 340	$ 191
Weighted average number of outstanding shares used in computing diluted income per share (in millions)	294	291	3	293	284	9
ADJUSTED NET INCOME PER SHARE – DILUTED	$ 0.23	$0.01	$ 0.22	$1.81	$1.20	$ 0.61

[1]In 2014, one-time payments totaling $30 million were made to ACPA members under a collective agreement concluded in October 2014.
[2]In 2013, Air Canada recorded an operating expense reduction of $82 million related to amendments to defined benefit pension plans.
[3]In 2014, Air Canada recorded favourable tax-related provision adjustments of $41 million.
[4]In 2013, Air Canada recorded impairment charges amounting to $30 million.
[5]In 2013, Air Canada recorded an interest charge of $95 million related to the purchase of its senior secured notes due in 2015 and 2016.

There are a few things to note:

1. The adjusted net income per share is higher than the GAAP-based calculation.

2. In calculating the adjusted income per share, the main items that increase the number are foreign exchange losses and net financing expenses relating to employee benefits.

3. As previously discussed in the text, care should be taken when presenting these non-GAAP numbers because the calculations are not standardized. How does the company decide which items to adjust for? This is a good question. Ideally as noted above—they are trying to remove any unusual or one-time items so they can show ongoing results from operations.

Comprehensive Earnings per Share Exercise

The purpose of the following exercise is to show the method of calculating dilution when many securities are involved. Illustration 17-25 presents a section of the statement of financial position of Andrews Corporation, our assumed company; assumptions about the company's capital structure follow the illustration.

Long-term debt:	
Notes payable, 14%	$ 1,000,000
7% convertible bonds payable	2,000,000
9% convertible bonds payable	3,000,000
Total long-term debt	**$ 6,000,000**
Shareholders' equity:	
$10 cumulative dividend, convertible preferred shares, no par value; 100,000 shares authorized, 20,000 shares issued and outstanding	$ 2,000,000
Common shares, no par value; 5,000,000 shares authorized, 400,000 shares issued and outstanding	400,000
Contributed surplus	2,100,000
Retained earnings	9,000,000
Total shareholders' equity	**$ 13,500,000**

Notes and Assumptions

December 31, 2017

1. Options were granted or written in July 2015 to purchase 30,000 common shares at $15 per share. The average market price of Andrews' common shares during 2017 was $25 per common share. The options expire in 2025 and no options were exercised during 2017.

2. The 7% bonds were issued in 2016 at face value. The 9% convertible bonds were issued on July 1, 2017 at face value. Each convertible bond is convertible into 50 common shares. (Each bond has a face value of $1,000.)

3. The $10 cumulative, convertible preferred shares were issued at the beginning of 2014. Each preferred share is convertible into four common shares.

4. The average income tax rate is 30%.

5. The 400,000 common shares were issued at $1 per share and were outstanding during the entire year.

6. Preferred dividends were not declared in 2017.

7. Net income was $1.2 million in 2017.

8. No bonds or preferred shares were converted during 2017.

Instructions

(a) Calculate basic earnings per share for Andrews Corporation for 2017.

(b) Calculate diluted earnings per share for Andrews for 2017, following these steps:

1. Determine, for each dilutive security, the incremental per share effect if the security is exercised or converted. Where there are multiple dilutive securities, rank the results from the lowest earnings effect per share to the largest; that is, rank the results from the most dilutive to least dilutive. The instruments with the lowest incremental EPS calculation will drag the EPS number down the most and are therefore most dilutive.

2. Beginning with the basic earnings per share based upon the weighted average number of common shares outstanding, recalculate the earnings per share by adding the most dilutive per share effects from the first step. If the results from this recalculation are less than EPS in the prior step, go to the next most dilutive per share effect and recalculate the earnings per share. This process is continued as long

as each recalculated earnings per share amount is smaller than the previous amount. The process will end either because there are no more securities to test or because a particular security maintains or increases the earnings per share (that is, it is antidilutive).

(c) Show the presentation of earnings per share for Andrews for 2017.

Solution to Comprehensive EPS Exercise

(a) Basic earnings per share

The calculation of basic earnings per share for 2017 starts with the amount based upon the weighted average number of common shares outstanding, as shown below.

Net income	$1,200,000
Less: $10 cumulative, convertible preferred share dividend requirements	200,000
Income applicable to common shareholders	$1,000,000
Weighted average number of common shares outstanding	400,000
Earnings per common share	$2.50

Note the following points about the above calculation:

1. When preferred shares are cumulative, the preferred dividend is subtracted to arrive at the income that is applicable to common shares, whether or not the dividend is declared.

2. The earnings per share of $2.50 is calculated as a starting point because the per share amount is not reduced by the existence of convertible securities and options.

(b) Diluted earnings per share

The steps in calculating diluted EPS are now applied to Andrews Corporation. (Note that net income and income available to common shareholders are not the same because the preferred dividends are cumulative.) Andrews Corporation has four items that could reduce EPS: options, 7% convertible bonds, 9% convertible bonds, and the convertible preferred shares.

The first step in calculating diluted earnings per share is to determine an incremental per share effect for each potentially dilutive security. Illustrations 17-26 through 17-29 show these calculations. Anything that is less than basic EPS is potentially dilutive.

Illustration 17-26

Incremental Impact of Options

Number of shares under option	30,000
Option price per share	× $15
Proceeds upon assumed exercise of options	$450,000
Average 2017 market price of common shares	$ 25
Treasury shares that could be acquired with proceeds ($450,000 ÷ $25)	18,000
Excess shares under option over treasury shares that could be repurchased (30,000 − 18,000)	12,000
Per share effect:	
Incremental numerator effect: None	
Incremental denominator effect: 12,000 shares	$ 0
Therefore potentially dilutive	

Illustration 17-27

*Incremental Impact of
7% Bonds*

Interest expense for year ($2,000,000 × 7%)	$140,000
Income tax reduction due to interest (30% × $140,000)	42,000
Interest expense avoided (net of tax)	$ 98,000
Number of common shares issued, assuming conversion of bonds (2,000 bonds × 50 shares)	100,000
Per share effect:	
Incremental numerator effect: $98,000	
Incremental denominator effect: 100,000 shares	$ 0.98
Therefore potentially dilutive	

Illustration 17-28

*Incremental Impact of
9% Bonds*

Interest expense for year ($3,000,000 × 9%)	$270,000
Income tax reduction due to interest (30% × $270,000)	81,000
Interest expense avoided (net of tax)	$189,000
Number of common shares issued, assuming conversion of bonds (3,000 bonds × 50 shares)	150,000
Per share effect (outstanding 1/2 year):	
Incremental numerator effect: $189,000 × 0.5 = $94,500	
Incremental denominator effect: 150,000 shares × 0.5 = 75,000	$ 1.26
Therefore potentially dilutive	

Illustration 17-29

*Incremental Impact of
Preferred Shares*

Dividend requirement on cumulative preferred (20,000 shares × $10)	$200,000
Income tax effect (dividends not a tax deduction): None	–0–
Dividend requirement avoided	$200,000
Number of common shares issued, assuming conversion of preferred (4 × 20,000 shares)	80,000
Per share effect:	
Incremental numerator effect: $200,000	
Incremental denominator effect: 80,000 shares	$ 2.50
Therefore neutral	

Illustration 17-30 shows the ranking of all four potentially dilutive securities.

Illustration 17-30

*Ranking of Potential Common
Shares (Most Dilutive First)*

	$ Effect Per Share
Options	–0–
7% convertible bonds	0.98
9% convertible bonds	1.26
$10 convertible preferred	2.50

The next step is to determine earnings per share and, through this determination, to give effect to the ranking in Illustration 17-30. Starting with the basic earnings per share of $2.50 calculated previously, add the incremental effects of the options to the original calculation, as shown in Illustrations 17-31 to 17-34.

Illustration 17-31

*Step-by-Step Calculation of
Diluted EPS, Adding Options
First (Most Dilutive)*

Options	
Income applicable to common shareholders	$1,000,000
Add: Incremental numerator effect of options: None	–0–
Total	$1,000,000

(continued)

Illustration 17-31

Step-by-Step Calculation of Diluted EPS, Adding Options First (Most Dilutive) (continued)

Weighted average number of common shares outstanding	400,000
Add: Incremental denominator effect of options—Illustration 17-26	12,000
Total	412,000
Recalculated earnings per share ($1,000,000 ÷ 412,000 shares)	$ 2.43

Since the recalculated earnings per share is reduced (from $2.50 to $2.43), the effect of the options is dilutive. Again, this effect could have been anticipated because the average market price exceeded the option price ($15).

Illustration 17-32 shows the recalculated earnings per share assuming the 7% bonds are converted.

Illustration 17-32

Step-by-Step Calculation of Diluted EPS, Adding 7% Bonds Next (Next Most Dilutive)

7% Bonds	
Numerator from previous calculation	$1,000,000
Add: Interest expense avoided (net of tax)—Illustration 17-27	98,000
Total	$1,098,000
Denominator from previous calculation (shares)	412,000
Add: Number of common shares assumed issued upon conversion of bonds—Illustration 17-27	100,000
Total	512,000
Recalculated earnings per share ($1,098,000 ÷ 512,000 shares)	$ 2.14

Since the recalculated earnings per share is reduced (from $2.43 to $2.14), the effect of the 7% bonds is dilutive.

Next, in Illustration 17-33, earnings per share is recalculated assuming the conversion of the 9% bonds.

Illustration 17-33

Step-by-Step Calculation of Diluted EPS, Adding 9% Bonds Next (Next Most Dilutive)

9% Bonds	
Numerator from previous calculation	$1,098,000
Add: Interest expense avoided (net of tax)—Illustration 17-28	94,500
Total	$1,192,500
Denominator from previous calculation (shares)	512,000
Add: Number of common shares assumed issued upon conversion of bonds—Illustration 17-28	75,000
Total	587,000
Recalculated earnings per share ($1,192,500 ÷ 587,000 shares)	$ 2.03

Since the recalculated earnings per share is reduced (from $2.14 to $2.03), the effect of the 9% convertible bonds is dilutive.

The final step (Illustration 17-34) is the recalculation that includes the 10% preferred shares.

Illustration 17-34

Step-by-Step Calculation of Diluted EPS, Adding Preferred Shares Next (Least Dilutive)

Preferred Shares	
Numerator from previous calculation	$1,192,500
Add: Dividend requirement avoided—Illustration 17-29	200,000
Total	$1,392,500
Denominator from previous calculation (shares)	587,000

(continued)

Illustration 17-34

Step-by-Step Calculation of Diluted EPS, Adding Preferred Shares Next (Least Dilutive) (continued)

Add: Number of common shares assumed issued upon conversion of preferred—Illustration 17-29	80,000
Total	667,000
Recalculated earnings per share ($1,392,500 ÷ 667,000 shares)	$ 2.09

The effect of the $10 convertible preferred shares is antidilutive, because the per share effects result in a higher EPS of $2.09. Since the recalculated earnings per share is not reduced, the effects of the convertible preferred shares are not used in the calculation. Diluted earnings per share to be reported is therefore $2.03.

(c) Presentation of EPS

The disclosure of earnings per share on the income statement for Andrews Corporation is shown in Illustration 17-35.

Illustration 17-35

Presentation of EPS

Net Income	$1,200,000
Basic earnings per common share	$ 2.50
Diluted earnings per common share	$ 2.03

Illustration 17-36 summarizes the calculations for the comprehensive EPS exercise. In summary, when calculating EPS, follow the steps noted below:

Illustration 17-36

Summary of Calculations for the Comprehensive EPS Exercise

	Income	Shares	Per share amounts
Net Income	$1,200,000		
Less: Preferred stock dividends (20,000 × $10)	(200,000)		
Basic EPS	$1,000,000	400,000	$2.50
Options		12,000	
	1,000,000	412,000	2.43
7% Bonds	98,000	100,000	
	1,098,000	512,000	2.14
9% Bonds	94,500	75,000	
Diluted earnings per share	1,192,500	587,000	2.03
Preferred shares	200,000	80,000	
	$1,392,500	667,000	$2.09

1. For basic EPS: calculate income available to common shareholders and weighted average number of common shares. Divide.

2. For diluted EPS:

   (a) Obtain income available to common shareholders and weighted average number of common shares from the basic EPS calculation. This is your starting point before you adjust for the dilutive securities.

   (b) Identify potential dilutive securities (potential common shares).

   (c) Calculate the incremental impact on EPS for each potential dilutive security. In other words, if the security was converted, what would be the impact on the numerator and denominator of the EPS calculation?

   (d) Rank the potentially dilutive security from most dilutive to least.

   (e) Recalculate EPS by starting with the most dilutive security. If the recalculated EPS number is lower, add in the next most dilutive security. Stop when the recalculated EPS is lowest. This is the diluted EPS.

ANALYSIS AND IFRS/ASPE COMPARISON

Analysis

EPS is one of the most highly visible standards of measurement for assessing management stewardship and predicting a company's future value. It is therefore a very important number and, because of this importance, IFRS is very specific regarding its calculation.

Recall Illustration 17-6, which showed the common shareholders' claim on only residual income. Earnings per share provides shareholders with information that helps them predict the value of their shareholdings. The diluted EPS calculation is especially useful because there are many potential common shares outstanding through convertible securities, options and warrants, and other financial instruments, and shareholders need to understand how these instruments can affect their holdings. From an economic perspective, it is therefore important to carefully analyze the potential dilutive impact of the various securities instruments, and the IASB is helping make it possible to do such analyses by continually striving to ensure greater transparency in EPS calculations. Sometimes this is not so easy due to the complexity of the financial statements.

Earnings per share is also useful in valuing companies. When companies or their shares are valued, "earnings" are often discounted to arrive at an estimated value. While there are many different ways of doing this, discounted cash flow calculations (with earnings often used as a substitute for the calculation) or net present value calculations are commonly used to estimate company or share value. Ideally, a **normalized or sustainable cash flow or earnings** number should be used in the valuation calculation because earnings or net income may be of higher or lower quality (as noted in Chapter 4). However, since calculating normalized or sustainable cash flows and earnings requires significant judgement, when valuing common shares, the EPS number is sometimes used instead because it is felt to be more reliable and all-inclusive.

As noted in Chapter 15, the price earnings ratio provides useful information by relating earnings to the price that the shares are trading at. It is sometimes used to generate a quick estimate of the value of the shares, and therefore the company. It allows an easy comparison with other companies and the information is often readily available. The price earnings ratio divides the price of the share by the earnings per share number. The result is often called the **multiplier**. The multiplier shows the per share value that each dollar of earnings generates. For example, if the share value is $10 and EPS is $1, the multiplier is 10 (10 ÷ 1). **Therefore, each additional dollar of earnings is felt to generate an additional $10 in share price.** This is a very rough calculation only, especially when you think of the judgement that went into calculating that EPS number in the first place. Consider the hundreds of financial reporting choices, such as accounting methods, measurement uncertainty, bias, and other judgements. This is one of the major reasons why preparers of financial statements must be aware of the impact of all financial reporting decisions on the bottom line.

A Comparison of IFRS and ASPE and Looking Ahead

The main difference between the standards is that ASPE does not prescribe standards for calculating EPS at all. The EPS standards therefore only apply to publicly accountable entities in Canada and private enterprises that choose to apply IFRS.

Where do we go from here? As the accounting for derivatives and financial instruments continues to evolve, standard setters are gradually revisiting other areas to determine the impact of the standards for financial instruments on these other areas. Earnings per share is one such area.

Conversion features included in instruments, such as convertible debt and convertible preferred shares, are in substance embedded options. For instance, in many convertible debt instruments, the conversion feature represents a written call option. Why, then, would we not treat these embedded options as we treat stand-alone options? Why not use the treasury stock or reverse treasury stock method instead of the if-converted method?

Some derivative instruments, such as written put options and forwards to purchase the entity's own shares, are in fact liabilities. How should they be treated for EPS purposes?

With respect to financial instruments that are carried at fair value with gains/losses being booked through net income, many feel that the potentially dilutive impact is already captured when the instruments are revalued to their fair value. This category includes some derivatives that are settleable in the entity's own equity instruments, which are treated as financial assets/liabilities.

At the time of writing, the IASB and FASB had paused work in this area.

SUMMARY OF LEARNING OBJECTIVES

1 Understand why earnings per share (EPS) is an important number.

Earnings per share numbers give common shareholders an idea of the amount of earnings that can be attributed to each common share. This information is often used to predict future cash flows from the shares and to value companies.

2 Understand when and how earnings per share must be presented, including related disclosures.

Under IFRS, EPS must be presented for all public companies or companies that are intending to go public. The calculations must be presented on the face of the income statement for net income from continuing operations and net income (for both basic EPS and diluted EPS in the case of complex capital structures). When there are discontinued operations, the per share impact of these items must also be shown, but it can be shown either on the face of the income statement or in the notes to the financial statements. Comparative calculations must also be shown.

3 Calculate earnings per share for companies with a simple capital structure.

Basic earnings per share is an actual calculation that takes income available to common shareholders and divides it by the weighted average number of common shares outstanding during the period.

4 Calculate earnings per share for companies with a complex capital structure.

Diluted earnings per share is a "what if" calculation that considers the impact of potential common shares. Potential common shares include convertible debt and preferred shares, options and warrants, contingently issuable shares, and other instruments that may result in additional common shares being issued by the company. They are relevant because they may cause the present interests of the common shareholders to become diluted.

The if-converted method considers the impact of convertible securities such as convertible debt and preferred shares. It assumes that the instruments are converted at the beginning of the year (or issue date, if later) and that any related interest or dividend is thus avoided.

The treasury stock method looks at the impact of written call options on EPS numbers. It assumes that the options are exercised at the beginning of the year and that the money from the exercise is used to buy back shares in the open market at the average common share price.

The reverse treasury stock method looks at the impact of written put options. It assumes that the options are exercised at the beginning of the year and that the company first issues shares in the market (at the average share price) to obtain sufficient funds to buy the shares under the option.

Antidilutive potential common shares are irrelevant because they would result in diluted EPS calculations that are higher than the basic EPS. Diluted EPS must show the worst possible EPS number. Note that purchased options and written options that are not in the money are ignored for purposes of calculating diluted EPS because they are either antidilutive or will not be exercised.

5 Understand how analysis helps users of financial statements assess performance.

EPS is one of the most commonly used metrics for assessing performance. Diluted EPS is especially important because it allows for the effects of potential dilution. The price earnings ratio is often used to value companies.

6 Identify the major differences in accounting between IFRS and ASPE, and what changes are expected in the near future.

ASPE does not prescribe accounting standards for EPS. The IASB was working on a revised plan of action to study the issues. At the time of writing, work on the project was paused.

KEY TERMS

antidilutive securities, p. 1053	exercise price, p. 1055	put options, p. 1055
basic EPS, p. 1046	if-converted method, p. 1053	reverse treasury stock method, p. 1058
call options, p. 1055	income available to common	simple capital structure, p. 1047
complex capital structure, p. 1047	shareholders, p. 1048	treasury stock method, p. 1057
contingently issuable shares, p. 1047	in the money, p. 1055	weighted average number of
diluted EPS, p. 1046	potential common/ordinary share, p. 1047	shares, p. 1049

Note: Completion of this end-of-chapter material will help develop CPA enabling competencies (such as ethics and professionalism, problem-solving and decision-making and communication) and technical competencies. We have highlighted selected items with an integration icon and material in *WileyPLUS* has been linked to the competencies. All cases emphasize integration, especially of the enabling competencies. The brief exercises, exercises, and problems generally emphasize problem-solving and decision-making.

Brief Exercises

(LO 1, 2, 5) **BE17-1** The 2017 income statement of Tanel Corporation showed net income of $860,000, which included a loss from discontinued operations of $140,000. Tanel had 25,000 common shares outstanding all year. (a) Calculate earnings per share for 2017 as it should be reported to shareholders. (b) Discuss why Tanel Corporation's reporting of earnings per share is useful to financial statement users.

(LO 3) **BE17-2** Hedley Corporation had 2017 net income of $1.4 million. During 2017, Hedley paid a dividend of $5 per share on 100,000 preferred shares. Hedley also had 220,000 common shares outstanding during the year. Calculate Hedley's 2017 earnings per share.

(LO 3) **BE17-3** Assume the same information for Hedley Corporation as in BE17-2 except that the preferred shares are non-cumulative and the dividend has not been declared or paid.

(LO 3) **BE17-4** Assume the same information for Hedley Corporation as in BE17-2 except that the preferred shares are cumulative and the dividends have not yet been declared or paid.

(LO 3) **BE17-5** Dencil Corporation had 600,000 common shares outstanding on January 1, 2017. On March 1, 2017, Dencil issued 150,000 shares. On September 1, Dencil repurchased and cancelled 50,000 shares. Calculate Dencil's weighted average number of shares outstanding for the year ended December 31, 2017.

(LO 3) **BE17-6** Laurin Limited had 42,000 common shares outstanding on January 1, 2017. On March 1, 2017, Laurin issued 20,000 shares in exchange for equipment. On July 1, Laurin repurchased and cancelled 10,000 shares. On October 1, 2017, Laurin declared and issued a 10% stock dividend. Calculate the weighted average number of shares outstanding for Laurin for the year ended December 31, 2017.

(LO 3) **BE17-7** Assume the same information as in BE17-6 except that on October 1, 2017, Laurin declared a 3-for-1 stock split instead of a 10% stock dividend.

(LO 3) **BE17-8** Assume the same information as in BE17-6 except that on October 1, 2017, Laurin declared a 1-for-2 reverse stock split instead of a 10% stock dividend.

(LO 3) **BE17-9** Bantec Corporation had 500,000 common shares outstanding on January 1, 2017. On May 1, Bantec issued 50,000 shares. (a) Calculate the weighted average number of shares outstanding for the year ended December 31, 2017 if the 50,000 shares were issued for cash. (b) Calculate the weighted average number of shares outstanding for the year ended December 31, 2017 if the 50,000 shares were issued in a stock dividend.

(LO 3) **BE17-10** Ethan Corporation had 100,000 common shares outstanding on December 31, 2016. During 2017, the company issued 12,000 shares on March 1, retired 5,000 shares on July 1, issued a 20% stock dividend on October 1, and issued 18,000 shares on December 1. For 2017, the company reported net income of $400,000 after a loss from discontinued operations of $50,000 (net of tax). The company issued a 2-for-1 stock split on February 1, 2018, and the company's financial statements for the year ended December 31, 2017 were issued on February 28, 2018. Calculate earnings per share for 2017 as it should be reported to shareholders.

(LO 4) **BE17-11** Francine Limited was incorporated with share capital consisting of 100,000 common shares. In January 2017, it issued 20,000 mandatorily convertible preferred shares. The terms of the prospectus for the issuance of the preferred shares require the convertible preferred shares to be converted into common shares, at the rate of one preferred share for one common share, during the fourth quarter of 2018. The preferred shares pay an annual dividend of $4 per share. Assume that for the fiscal year ended December 31, 2017, the company made an after-tax profit of $140,000. Calculate the 2017 earnings per share.

(LO 4) BE17-12   Milliken Corporation reported net income of $700,000 in 2017 and had 115,000 common shares outstanding throughout the year. Also outstanding all year were 9,500 of cumulative preferred shares, with each being convertible into two common shares. The preferred shares pay an annual dividend of $5 per share. Milliken's tax rate is 30%. Calculate Milliken's 2017 diluted earnings per share.

(LO 4) BE17-13   Thiessen Corporation earned net income of $300,000 in 2017 and had 100,000 common shares outstanding throughout the year. Also outstanding all year was $800,000 of 10% bonds that are convertible into 26,000 common shares. Thiessen's tax rate is 25%. Calculate Thiessen's 2017 diluted earnings per share. For simplicity, ignore the IFRS requirement to record the debt and equity components of the bonds separately.

(LO 4) BE17-14   Assume the same information as in BE17-13 except that the 10% bonds are convertible into 10,000 common shares. Calculate Thiessen's 2017 diluted earnings per share.

(LO 4) BE17-15   Melanie Corporation reported net income of $550,000 in 2017 and had 900,000 common shares outstanding throughout the year. On May 1, 2017, Melanie issued 5% convertible bonds. Each $1,000 bond is convertible into 120 common shares. Total proceeds at par amounted to $1 million, and was allocated to the liability and equity components under the residual value method. The liability component was measured first, at present value of the stream of interest payments plus present value of the bond maturity value, all discounted at 8% (the interest rate that applies to similar straight bonds). At the time of issuance, the liability component was recorded at $922,685. Melanie's tax rate is 30%. Calculate Melanie's 2017 diluted earnings per share.

(LO 4) BE17-16   Assume the same information as in BE17-15 except that Melanie reported net income of $350,000 in 2017. Calculate Melanie's 2017 diluted earnings per share.

(LO 4, 5) BE17-17   Strait Inc. has 300,000 common shares outstanding throughout the year. On June 30, Strait issued 10,000 convertible preferred shares that are convertible into two common shares each. Calculate the weighted average number of common shares to use in calculating the diluted EPS. Assume that the preferred shares are dilutive.

(LO 4) BE17-18   Bedard Corporation reported net income of $300,000 in 2017 and had 200,000 common shares outstanding throughout the year. Also outstanding all year were 45,000 (written) options to purchase common shares at $10 per share. The average market price for the common shares during the year was $15 per share. Calculate the diluted earnings per share.

(LO 4) BE17-19   Redpath Limited purchased 25,000 call options during the year. The options give the company the right to buy its own common shares for $4 each. The average market price during the year was $7 per share. Calculate the incremental shares outstanding for Redpath Limited.

(LO 4) BE17-20   Use the same information as in BE17-19 and assume that Redpath also wrote put options that allow the holder to sell 25,000 of Redpath's shares to Redpath at $8 per share. Calculate the incremental shares outstanding for Redpath Limited.

(LO 4) BE17-21   Assume the same information as in BE17-19 except that Redpath purchased put options to give it the option of selling 25,000 of its own common shares for $5 each. How should the options be treated when calculating the diluted EPS?

(LO 4) BE17-22   Assume the same information as in BE17-20 except that the put options allow the holder to sell Redpath's shares to Redpath at $6 each. How should these options be treated when calculating the diluted EPS?

(LO 5) BE17-23   Rhonda is considering investing in the shares of either East Corporation or West Ltd. Both companies are publicly traded. How would an analysis of each company's EPS help Rhonda decide which company to add to her investment portfolio?

(LO 6) BE17-24   Flory Corporation is a rapidly growing privately owned company that is considering changing from ASPE to IFRS in order to prepare for a future public offering of shares. As Flory's financial advisor, what advice would you give to management regarding EPS reporting requirements?

Exercises

(LO 3) E17-1   **(Weighted Average Number of Shares)** On January 1, 2017, Manfred Manufacturers had 300,000 common shares outstanding. On April 1, the corporation issued 30,000 new common shares to raise additional capital. On July 1, the corporation declared and distributed a 10% stock dividend on its common shares. On November 1, the corporation repurchased on the market 10,000 of its own outstanding common shares to make them available for issuances related to its key executives' outstanding stock options.

Instructions

(a) Calculate the weighted average number of shares outstanding as at December 31, 2017.

(b) Assume that Manfred Manufacturers had a 1-for-10 reverse stock split instead of a 10% stock dividend on July 1, 2017. Calculate the weighted average number of shares outstanding as at December 31, 2017.

(LO 1, 3, 5, 6) **E17-2** **(Weighted Average Number of Shares)** Gogeon Inc. is publicly traded and uses a calendar year for financial reporting. The company is authorized to issue 50 million common shares. At no time has Gogeon issued any potentially dilutive securities. The following list is a summary of Gogeon's common share activities:

Number of common shares issued and outstanding at December 31, 2015	6,500,000
Shares issued as a result of a 10% stock dividend on September 30, 2016	650,000
Shares issued for cash on March 31, 2017	2,500,000
Number of common shares issued and outstanding at December 31, 2017	9,650,000

Gogeon issued its 2017 financial statements on February 28, 2018. A 3-for-1 stock split of Gogeon's common shares occurred on March 31, 2018.

Instructions

(a) Calculate the weighted average number of common shares to use in calculating earnings per common share for 2016 on the 2016 comparative income statement.

(b) Calculate the weighted average number of common shares to use in calculating earnings per common share for 2016 on the 2017 comparative income statement.

(c) Calculate the weighted average number of common shares to use in calculating earnings per common share for 2017 on the 2017 comparative income statement.

(d) Calculate the weighted average number of common shares to use in calculating earnings per common share for 2017 on the 2018 comparative income statement.

(e) Calculate the weighted average number of common shares to use in calculating earnings per common share for 2018 on the 2018 comparative income statement.

(f) Referring to how EPS is used and applied, discuss why the weighted average number of common shares must be adjusted for stock dividends and stock splits. How is this information helpful for analysis by financial statement users?

(g) Assume Gogeon Inc. was privately owned and used ASPE. How would the EPS requirements differ from the requirements using IFRS?

(CMA adapted)

(LO 2, 3, 5, 6) **E17-3** **(EPS—Simple Capital Structure)** Koala Inc., a publicly traded company, had 210,000 common shares outstanding on December 31, 2016. During 2017, the company issued 8,000 shares on May 1 and retired 14,000 shares on October 31. For 2017, the company reported net income of $229,690 after a loss from discontinued operations of $40,600 (net of tax).

Instructions

(a) Calculate earnings per share for 2017 as it should be reported to shareholders.

(b) Assume that Koala Inc. issued a 3-for-1 stock split on January 31, 2018, and that the company's financial statements for the year ended December 31, 2017 were issued on February 15, 2018. Calculate earnings per share for 2017 as it should be reported to shareholders.

(c) Discuss why Koala Inc.'s reporting of earnings per share is useful for financial statement analysis.

(d) Is it possible for a corporation to have a simple capital structure one fiscal year and a complex capital structure in another fiscal year? If yes, how could this happen?

(e) How would Koala's EPS reporting requirements differ if the company was a privately owned company using ASPE?

(LO 2, 3) **E17-4** **(EPS—Simple Capital Structure)** On January 1, 2017, Logan Limited had shares outstanding as follows:

6% cumulative preferred shares, $100 par value, 10,000 shares issued and outstanding	$1,000,000
Common shares, 200,000 shares issued and outstanding	2,000,000

To acquire the net assets of three smaller companies, the company authorized the issuance of an additional 330,000 common shares. The acquisitions were as follows:

Date of Acquisition	Shares Issued
Company A: April 1, 2017	190,000
Company B: July 1, 2017	100,000
Company C: October 1, 2017	40,000

On May 14, 2017, Logan realized a $97,000 gain (before tax) on a discontinued operation from a business segment that had originally been purchased in 1997.

On December 31, 2017, the company recorded income of $680,000 before tax, not including the discontinued operation gain. Logan has a 30% tax rate.

Instructions

(a) Calculate earnings per share for 2017 as it should be reported to shareholders.

(b) Assume that Logan declared a 1-for-2 reverse stock split on February 10, 2018, and that the company's financial statements for the year ended December 31, 2017 were issued on February 28, 2018. Calculate earnings per share for 2017 as it should be reported to shareholders.

(c) What determines that Logan has a simple capital structure?

(LO 3) E17-5 (EPS—Simple Capital Structure) On January 1, 2017, Trigson Ltd. had 580,000 common shares outstanding. During 2017, it had the following transactions that affected the common share account:

Feb. 1	Issued 180,000 shares.
Mar. 1	Issued a 10% stock dividend.
May 1	Acquired 200,000 common shares and retired them.
June 1	Issued a 3-for-1 stock split.
Oct. 1	Issued 60,000 shares.

The company's year end is December 31.

Instructions

(a) Determine the weighted average number of shares outstanding as at December 31, 2017.

(b) Assume that Trigson earned net income of $2.5 million during 2017. In addition, it had 100,000 of 8%, $100 par, non-convertible, non-cumulative preferred shares outstanding for the entire year. Because of liquidity limitations, however, the company did not declare and pay a preferred dividend in 2017. Calculate earnings per share for 2017, using the weighted average number of shares determined in part (a).

(c) Assume the same facts as in part (b), except that the preferred shares were cumulative. Calculate earnings per share for 2017.

DIGGING DEEPER

(d) Assume the same facts as in part (b), except that net income included a loss from discontinued operations of $200,000, net of applicable income tax. Calculate earnings per share for 2017.

(e) What is the reasoning behind using a weighted average calculation for the number of shares outstanding in the EPS ratio?

(LO 3) E17-6 (EPS—Simple Capital Structure) Esau Inc. presented the following data:

FINANCE

Net income	$5,500,000
Preferred shares: 50,000 shares outstanding, $100 par, 8%	
cumulative, not convertible	$5,000,000
Common shares: Shares outstanding, Jan. 1, 2017	650,000
Issued for cash, May 1, 2017	100,000
Acquired treasury shares for cash, Sept. 1, 2017 (shares cancelled)	150,000
2-for-1 stock split, Oct. 1, 2017	

As of January 1, 2017, there were no dividends in arrears. On December 31, 2017, Esau declared and paid the preferred dividend for 2017.

Instructions

(a) Calculate earnings per share for the year ended December 31, 2017.

(b) Discuss what the effect would be on your calculation in part (a) if the stock split had been declared on January 30, 2018 instead of on October 1, 2017, assuming the financial statements of Esau Inc. for the year ending December 31, 2017 were issued after January 30, 2018.

(c) Assume that Esau did not declare or pay a preferred dividend in 2017. Calculate earnings per share for the year ended December 31, 2017.

(d) Assume that as of January 1, 2017, Esau had two years of dividends in arrears, and that on December 31, 2017, Esau declared and paid the dividends in arrears and the preferred dividend for 2017. Calculate earnings per share for the year ended December 31, 2017.

DIGGING DEEPER

(e) Assume that the preferred shares are non-cumulative, and that the preferred dividend was paid in 2017. Calculate earnings per share for the year ended December 31, 2017.

(f) Assume that the preferred shares are non-cumulative, and that Esau did not declare or pay a preferred dividend in 2017. Calculate earnings per share for the year ended December 31, 2017.

(g) Discuss the effect of a stock split on Esau Inc.'s market price per share. Would a current shareholder favour Esau Inc.'s declaration of a stock split?

(LO 3) E17-7 (EPS—Simple Capital Structure) A portion of the combined statement of income and retained earnings of Snap Ltd. for the current year ended December 31, 2017 follows:

Income before discontinued operations		$ 5,000,000
Loss from discontinued operations, net of applicable income tax (Note 1)		400,000
Net income		4,600,000
Retained earnings at beginning of year		25,400,000
		30,000,000
Dividends declared:		
On preferred shares, $4.00 per share	$ 200,000	
On common shares, $2.00 per share	3,000,000	3,200,000
Retained earnings at end of year		$26,800,000

Note 1. During the year, Snap Inc. suffered a loss from discontinued operations of $400,000 after the applicable income tax reduction of $100,000.

At the end of 2017, Snap Inc. has outstanding 1.5 million common shares and 50,000 shares of preferred. On April 1, 2017, Snap Inc. issued 1 million common shares for $6 per share to help finance the loss.

Instructions

(a) Calculate the earnings per share on common shares for 2017 as it should be reported to shareholders.

(b) Assume that Snap Inc. issued a 10% stock dividend on September 1, 2017. Calculate the earnings per share on common shares for 2017 as it should be reported to shareholders.

(LO 3) E17-8 (EPS—Simple Capital Structure) At January 1, 2017, Ming Limited's outstanding shares included the following:

> 280,000 $50 par value, 7%, cumulative preferred shares
> 900,000 common shares

Net income for 2017 was $2,130,000. No cash dividends were declared or paid during 2017. On February 15, 2018, however, all preferred dividends in arrears were paid, together with a 5% stock dividend on common shares. There were no dividends in arrears before 2017.

On April 1, 2017, 550,000 common shares were sold for $10 per share and on October 1, 2017, 310,000 common shares were purchased for $20 per share.

The financial statements for 2017 were issued in March 2018.

Instructions

(a) Calculate earnings per share for the year ended December 31, 2017.

(b) What is the significance of the declaration and payment date of February 15, 2018 for the dividend on preferred shares? What effect, if any, will this transaction have on the December 31, 2017 financial statements?

(c) Would your answer in part (b) change if the dividend arrears on preferred shares were for two years as at December 31, 2017?

DIGGING
DEEPER

(LO 4) E17-9 (EPS with Convertible Bonds, Various Situations) In 2016, Capstone Ltd. issued $50,000 of 8% bonds at par, with each $1,000 bond being convertible into 100 common shares. The company had revenues of $75,000 and expenses of $40,000 for 2017, not including interest and tax. (Assume a tax rate of 25%.) Throughout 2017, 1,000 common shares were outstanding, and none of the bonds were converted or redeemed. (For simplicity, assume that the convertible bonds' equity element is not recorded.)

Instructions

(a) Calculate diluted earnings per share for the year ended December 31, 2017.

(b) Repeat the calculation in part (a), but assume that the 50 bonds were issued on October 1, 2017 (rather than in 2016), and that none have been converted or redeemed.

(c) Repeat the calculation in part (a), but assume that 10 of the 50 bonds were converted on July 1, 2017.

(LO 4) E17-10 (EPS with Convertible Bonds) On June 1, 2015, Gustav Corp. and Gabby Limited merged to form Fallon Inc. A total of 800,000 shares were issued to complete the merger. The new corporation uses the calendar year as its fiscal year.

On April 1, 2017, the company issued an additional 400,000 shares for cash. All 1.2 million shares were outstanding on December 31, 2017. Fallon Inc. also issued $600,000 of 20-year, 8% convertible bonds at par on July 1, 2017. Each $1,000 bond converts to 40 common shares at any interest date. None of the bonds have been converted to date. If the bonds had been issued without the conversion feature, the annual interest rate would have been 10%.

Fallon Inc. is preparing its annual report for the fiscal year ended December 31, 2017. The annual report will show earnings per share figures based on a reported after-tax net income of $1,540,000. (The tax rate is 30%.)

Instructions

(a) Determine for 2017 the number of shares to be used in calculating:

1. Basic earnings per share
2. Diluted earnings per share

(b) Determine for 2017 the earnings figures to be used in calculating:

1. Basic earnings per share
2. Diluted earnings per share

(CMA adapted)

(LO 4) E17-11   (EPS with Convertible Bonds and Preferred Shares) Ottey Corporation issued $4 million of 10-year, 7% callable convertible subordinated debentures on January 2, 2017. The debentures have a face value of $1,000, with interest payable annually. The current conversion ratio is 14:1, and in two years it will increase to 18:1. At the date of issue, the bonds were sold at 98 to yield a 7.2886% effective interest rate. Bond discount is amortized using the effective interest method. Ottey's effective tax was 25%. Net income in 2017 was $7.5 million, and the company had 2 million shares outstanding during the entire year. For simplicity, ignore the requirement to record the debentures' debt and equity components separately.

Instructions

(a) Prepare a schedule to calculate both basic and diluted earnings per share for the year ended December 31, 2017.

(b) Discuss how the schedule would differ if the security were convertible preferred shares.

(c) Assume that Ottey Corporation experienced a substantial loss instead of income for the fiscal year ended December 31, 2017. How would you respond to the argument made by a friend who states: "The interest expense from the conversion of the debentures is not actually saved, and there is no income tax to be paid on the additional income that is assumed to have been created from the conversion of the debentures."

DIGGING DEEPER

(LO 4) E17-12   (EPS with Convertible Bonds and Preferred Shares) On January 1, 2017, Draper Inc. issued $4 million of face value, five-year, 6% bonds at par. Each $1,000 bond is convertible into 20 common shares. Draper's net income in 2017 was $200,000, and its tax rate was 25%. The company had 100,000 common shares outstanding throughout 2017. None of the bonds were exercised in 2017. For simplicity, ignore the requirement to record the bonds' debt and equity components separately.

Instructions

(a) Calculate diluted earnings per share for the year ended December 31, 2017.

(b) Calculate diluted earnings per share for 2017, assuming the same facts as above, except that $2 million of 6% cumulative convertible preferred shares was issued instead of the bonds. Each $100 preferred share is convertible into five common shares.

(LO 4) E17-13   (EPS with Convertible Bonds and Preferred Shares) Mininova Corporation is preparing earnings per share data for 2017. The net income for the year ended December 31, 2017 was $400,000 and there were 60,000 common shares outstanding during the entire year. Mininova has the following two convertible securities outstanding:

10% convertible bonds (each $1,000 bond is convertible into 25 common shares)	$100,000
5% convertible $100 par value preferred shares (each share is convertible into two common shares)	$50,000

Both convertible securities were issued at face value in 2014. There were no conversions during 2017, and Mininova's income tax rate is 24%. The preferred shares are cumulative. For simplicity, ignore the requirement to record the debt and equity components of the bonds separately.

Instructions

(a) Calculate Mininova's basic earnings per share for 2017.

(b) Calculate Mininova's diluted earnings per share for 2017.

(c) Recalculate Mininova's basic and diluted earnings per share for 2017, assuming instead that the preferred shares pay a 14% dividend.

(LO 4) E17-14   (EPS with Convertible Bonds with Conversion and Preferred Shares) Use the same information as in E17-13, except for the changes in part (c). Assume instead that 40% of the convertible bonds were converted to common shares on April 1, 2017.

Instructions

(a) Calculate Mininova's weighted average common shares outstanding.

DIGGING DEEPER

(b) Calculate Mininova's basic earnings per share for 2017.

(c) Calculate Mininova's diluted earnings per share for 2017.

(d) What do you notice about the results of the diluted earnings per share calculation when conversions occur during the year and when they do not occur?

(LO 4) E17-15 (EPS with Convertible Bonds and Preferred Shares) Hayward Corporation had net income of $50,000 for the year ended December 31, 2017, and weighted average number of common shares outstanding of 10,000. The following information is provided regarding the capital structure:

1. 7% convertible debt, 200 bonds each convertible into 40 common shares. The bonds were outstanding for the entire year. The income tax rate is 25%. The bonds were issued at par ($1,000 per bond). No bonds were converted during the year.

2. 4% convertible, cumulative $100 preferred shares, 1,000 shares issued and outstanding. Each preferred share is convertible into two common shares. The preferred shares were issued at par and were outstanding the entire year. No shares were converted during the year.

Instructions

DIGGING DEEPER

(a) Calculate the basic earnings per share for 2017.

(b) Briefly explain the if-converted method.

(c) Calculate the diluted earnings per share for 2017, using the if-converted method. For simplicity, ignore the requirement to record the debt and equity components of the bonds separately.

(d) When Hayward Corporation issued the 7% convertible debt, would the company's interest rate on straight debt have been higher or lower than 7%? Explain your answer.

(LO 4) E17-16 (EPS with Options, Various Situations) Standard Corp's net income for 2017 is $150,000. The only potentially dilutive securities outstanding were 1,000 call options issued during 2016, with each option being exercisable for one share at $20. None have been exercised, and 30,000 common shares were outstanding during 2017. The average market price of the company's shares during 2017 was $25.

Instructions

(a) Calculate diluted earnings per share for the year ended December 31, 2017. (Round to nearest cent.)

(b) Assuming that the 1,000 call options were instead issued on November 1, 2017 (rather than in 2016), calculate diluted earnings per share for the year ended December 31, 2017. (Round to nearest cent.) The average market price during the last two months of 2017 was $25.

(c) How would your answers for parts (a) and (b) change if, in addition to the information for parts (a) and (b), the company issued (wrote) 1,000 put options with an exercise price of $15?

(LO 4) E17-17 (EPS with Warrants) Howard Corporation earned $480,000 during a period when it had an average of 100,000 common shares outstanding. The common shares sold at an average market price of $23 per share during the period. Also outstanding were 18,000 warrants that could each be exercised to purchase one common share for $10.

Instructions

(a) Are the warrants dilutive?

(b) Calculate basic earnings per share.

(c) Calculate diluted earnings per share.

(LO 4) E17-18 (EPS with Contingent Issuance Agreement) Brush Inc. recently purchased Paint Pro, a large home-painting corporation. One of the terms of the merger was that if Paint Pro's net income for 2018 was $110,000 or more, 10,000 additional shares would be issued to Paint's shareholders in 2019. Paint Pro's net income for 2017 was $120,000.

Instructions

DIGGING DEEPER

(a) Would the contingent shares have to be considered in Brush's 2017 earnings per share calculations?

(b) Assume the same facts, except that the 10,000 shares are contingent on Paint Pro achieving a net income of $130,000 in 2018. Would the contingent shares have to be considered in Brush's earnings per share calculations for 2017?

(c) Provide support for the accounting treatment of the contingent shares discussed in part (a), referring to the conceptual framework.

Problems

P17-1   Mavis Corporation is a new audit client of yours and has not reported earnings per share data in its annual reports to shareholders in the past. The treasurer, Andrew Benninger, has asked you to provide information about the reporting of earnings per share data in the current year's annual report in accordance with generally accepted accounting principles according to IFRS.

Instructions

(a) Define the term "earnings per share" as it applies to a corporation with a capitalization structure that is composed of only one class of common shares. Explain how earnings per share should be calculated and how the information should be disclosed in the corporation's financial statements.

(b) Discuss the treatment, if any, that should be given to each of the following items in calculating the earnings per common share for financial statement reporting:

AUDIT AND ASSURANCE

1. Outstanding preferred shares issued at a premium with a par value liquidation right

2. The exercise at a price below market value but above carrying amount of a call option on common shares that was issued during the current fiscal year to officers of the corporation

3. The replacement of a machine immediately before the close of the current fiscal year at a cost that is 20% above the original cost of the replaced machine. The new machine will perform the same function as the old machine, which was sold for its carrying amount.

4. The declaration of current dividends on cumulative preferred shares

5. The existence of purchased call options that allow the company to purchase shares of its own common shares at a price that is lower than the average market price

6. The acquisition of some of the corporation's outstanding common shares during the current fiscal year. The shares were classified as treasury shares.

7. A 2-for-1 stock split of common shares during the current fiscal year

P17-2   Loretta Corporation, a publicly traded company, is preparing the comparative financial statements to be included in the annual report to shareholders. Loretta's fiscal year ends May 31. The following information is available.

1. Income from operations before income tax for Loretta was $800,000 and $1.2 million, respectively, for the fiscal years ended May 31, 2018 and 2017.

2. Loretta experienced a loss from discontinued operations of $100,000 from a business segment disposed of on March 3, 2018.

3. A 20% combined income tax rate applies to all of Loretta Corporation's profits, gains, and losses.

4. Loretta's capital structure consists of preferred shares and common shares. The company has not issued any convertible securities or warrants and there are no outstanding stock options.

5. Loretta issued 200,000 of $10 par value, 5% cumulative preferred shares in 2010. All of these shares are outstanding, and no preferred dividends are in arrears.

6. There were 1 million common shares outstanding on June 1, 2016. On September 1, 2016, Loretta sold an additional 500,000 common shares at $20 per share. Loretta distributed a 20% stock dividend on the common shares outstanding on December 1, 2017.

7. These were the only common share transactions during the past two fiscal years.

Instructions

(a) Determine the weighted average number of common shares that would be used in calculating earnings per share on the current comparative income statement for:
   1. The year ended May 31, 2018
   2. The year ended May 31, 2017

(b) Starting with income from operations before income tax, prepare a comparative income statement for the years ended May 31, 2018 and 2017. Assume that Loretta discloses all applicable earnings per share data on the face of the income statement.

FINANCE

(c) A corporation's capital structure is the result of its past financing decisions. Furthermore, the earnings per share data that are presented on a corporation's financial statements depend on the corporation's capital structure.
   1. Explain why Loretta Corporation is considered to have a simple capital structure.
   2. Describe how earnings per share data would be presented for a corporation that had a complex capital structure.

3. Describe the usefulness of EPS disclosure for financial statement analysis.

4. Explain the difference in reporting requirements between IFRS and ASPE.

(CMA adapted)

P17-3   Audrey Inc. has 1 million common shares outstanding as at January 1, 2017. On June 30, 2017, 4% convertible bonds were converted into 100,000 additional shares. Up to that point, the bonds had paid interest of $250,000 after tax. Net income for the year was $1,298,678. During the year, the company issued the following:

1. June 30: 10,000 call options giving holders the right to purchase shares of the company for $30

2. September 30: 15,000 put options allowing holders to sell shares of the company for $25

On February 1, Audrey also purchased in the open market 10,000 call options on its own shares, allowing it to purchase its own shares for $27. Assume the average market price for the shares during the year was $35.

Instructions

(a) Calculate the required EPS numbers under IFRS. For simplicity, ignore the impact that would result from the convertible debt being a hybrid security.

(b) Show the required presentations on the face of the income statement.

P17-4   Use the same information for Audrey Inc. as in P17-3, but also assume the following.

1. On September 30, 200,000 convertible preferred shares were redeemed. If they had been converted, these shares would have resulted in an additional 100,000 common shares being issued. The shares carried a dividend rate of $3 per share to be paid on September 30. No conversions have ever occurred.

2. There are 10,000 of $1,000, 5% convertible bonds outstanding with a conversion rate of three common shares for each bond starting January 1, 2018. Beginning January 1, 2021, the conversion rate is six common shares for each bond; and beginning January 1, 2025, it is nine common shares for each bond. The tax rate is 30%.

Instructions

(a) Calculate the required EPS numbers under IFRS. For simplicity, ignore the impact that would result from the convertible debt being a hybrid security.

(b) Show the required presentations on the face of the income statement.

P17-5   Tseng Corporation Ltd. has the following capital structure at the following fiscal years ended December 31:

	2017	2016
Number of common shares	600,000	450,000
Number of non-convertible, non-cumulative preferred A shares	20,000	20,000
Amount of 4% convertible bonds	$1,000,000	$1,000,000

The following additional information is available.

1. On July 31, 2017, Tseng Corporation exchanged common shares for a large piece of equipment. This was the only transaction that resulted in issuance of common shares in 2017.

2. Income before discontinued operations for 2017 was $1.3 million, and a loss from discontinued operations of $200,000 was recorded, net of applicable tax recovery.

3. During 2017, dividends in the amount of $3.00 per share were paid on the preferred A shares.

4. Each $1,000 bond can be converted into 25 common shares.

5. There were unexercised stock options, outstanding since 2014, that allow holders to purchase 20,000 common shares at $3.00 per share.

6. Written warrants to purchase 10,000 common shares at $7.00 per share were outstanding at the end of 2016, and no warrants were exercised in 2017.

7. The average market value of the common shares in 2017 was $5.00.

8. Tseng's tax rate is 20%.

9. Tseng declared and paid a $5,000 dividend to common shareholders on June 1, 2017.

Instructions

(a) Determine the weighted average number of common shares that would be used in calculating earnings per share for the year ended December 31, 2017.

(b) Starting with the heading "Income before discontinued operations," prepare the bottom portion of the income statement for the year ended December 31, 2017. Assume that Tseng Corporation discloses all applicable earnings per share data on the face of the income statement.

(AICPA adapted)

P17-6 Bryce Corporation is preparing the comparative financial statements for the annual report to its shareholders for the fiscal years ended May 31, 2017 and May 31, 2018. The income from operations was $1.8 million and $2.5 million, respectively, for each year. In both years, the company incurred a 10% interest expense on $2.4 million of debt for an obligation that requires interest-only payments for five years. The company experienced a loss of $600,000 from the discontinued operation of its Scotland facility in February 2018. The company uses a 30% effective tax rate for income tax.

The capital structure of Bryce Corporation on June 1, 2016 consisted of 1 million common shares outstanding and 20,000 of $50, par value, 6% cumulative preferred shares. There were no preferred dividends in arrears, and the company had not issued any convertible securities, options, or warrants.

On October 1, 2016, Bryce sold an additional 500,000 common shares at $20 per share. Bryce distributed a 20% stock dividend on the common shares outstanding on January 1, 2017. On December 1, 2017, Bryce was able to sell an additional 800,000 common shares at $22 per share. These were the only common share transactions that occurred during the two fiscal years.

Instructions

(a) Identify whether the capital structure at Bryce Corporation is a simple or complex capital structure, and explain why.

(b) Determine the weighted average number of shares that Bryce Corporation would use in calculating earnings per share for the fiscal year ended:

1. May 31, 2017

2. May 31, 2018

(c) Prepare, in good form, a comparative income statement that begins with income from operations for Bryce Corporation for the fiscal years ended May 31, 2017 and May 31, 2018. Assume that Bryce Corporation discloses all applicable earnings per share data on the face of the income statement.

(CMA adapted)

P17-7 Shari Patel of the controller's office of Diamond Corporation was given the assignment of determining the basic and diluted earnings per share values for the year ended December 31, 2017. Patel has gathered the following information.

1. The company is authorized to issue 8 million common shares. As at December 31, 2016, 2 million shares had been issued and were outstanding.

2. The per share market prices of the common shares on selected dates were as follows:

	Price per Share
July 1, 2016	$20.00
Jan. 1, 2017	21.00
Apr. 1, 2017	25.00
July 1, 2017	11.00
Aug. 1, 2017	10.50
Nov. 1, 2017	9.00
Dec. 31, 2017	10.00

3. A total of 700,000 shares of an authorized 1.2 million convertible preferred shares had been issued on July 1, 2016. The shares were issued at $25, and have a cumulative dividend of $3 per share. The shares are convertible into common shares at the rate of one convertible preferred share for one common share. The rate of conversion is to be automatically adjusted for stock splits and stock dividends. Dividends are paid quarterly on September 30, December 31, March 31, and June 30.

4. Diamond Corporation is subject to a 30% income tax rate.

5. The after-tax net income for the year ended December 31, 2017 was $11,550,000.

The following specific activities took place during 2017:

1. January 1: A 5% common stock dividend was issued. The dividend had been declared on December 1, 2016 to all shareholders of record on December 29, 2016.

2. April 1: A total of 400,000 shares of the $3 convertible preferred shares were converted into common shares. The company issued new common shares and retired the preferred shares. This was the only conversion of the preferred shares during 2017.

3. July 1: A 2-for-1 split of the common shares became effective on this date. The board of directors had authorized the split on June 1.

4. August 1: A total of 300,000 common shares were issued to acquire a factory building.

5. November 1: A total of 24,000 common shares were purchased on the open market at $9 per share and cancelled.

6. Cash dividends to common shareholders were declared and paid as follows:

April 15: $0.30 per share
October 15: $0.20 per share

7. Cash dividends to preferred shareholders were declared and paid as scheduled.

Instructions

(a) Determine the number of shares to use in calculating basic earnings per share for the year ended December 31, 2017.

(b) Determine the number of shares to use in calculating diluted earnings per share for the year ended December 31, 2017.

(c) Calculate the adjusted net income amount to use as the numerator in the basic earnings per share calculation for the year ended December 31, 2017.

P17-8   Isabelle Leclerc is the controller at Camden Pharmaceutical Industries, a public company. She is currently preparing the calculation for basic and diluted earnings per share and the related disclosure for Camden's external financial statements. The following is selected financial information for the fiscal year ended June 30, 2017:

CAMDEN PHARMACEUTICAL INDUSTRIES
Selected Statement of Financial Position Information
June 30, 2017

Long-term debt	
Notes payable, 10%	$ 1,000,000
7% convertible bonds payable	5,000,000
10% bonds payable	6,000,000
Total long-term debt	$12,000,000
Shareholders' equity	
Preferred shares, $4.25 cumulative, 100,000 shares authorized,	
25,000 shares issued and outstanding	$ 1,250,000
Common shares, unlimited number of shares authorized,	
1,000,000 shares issued and outstanding	4,500,000
Contributed surplus—conversion rights	500,000
Retained earnings	6,000,000
Total shareholders' equity	$12,250,000

The following transactions have occurred at Camden:

1. Options were granted by the company in 2015 to purchase 100,000 shares at $15 per share. Although no options were exercised during 2017, the average price per common share during fiscal year 2017 was $20.

2. Each bond was issued at face value. The 7% convertible debenture will convert into common shares at 50 shares per $1,000 bond. It is exercisable after five years and was issued in 2016. Ignore any requirement to record the bonds' debt and equity components separately.

3. The $4.25 preferred shares were issued in 2015.

4. There are no preferred dividends in arrears, and preferred dividends were not declared in fiscal year 2017.

5. The 1 million common shares were outstanding for the entire 2017 fiscal year.

6. Net income for fiscal year 2017 was $1.5 million, and the average income tax rate was 30%.

Instructions

(a) For the fiscal year ended June 30, 2017, calculate the following for Camden Pharmaceutical Industries:

   1. Basic earnings per share

   2. Diluted earnings per share

DIGGING DEEPER

(b) Explain how premiums and discounts on outstanding convertible bonds affect the calculation of diluted earnings per share.

(c) From the perspective of a common shareholder, provide support for the treatment of the preferred dividends in calculating Camden Pharmaceutical Industries' basic and diluted earnings per share.

P17-9 An excerpt from the statement of financial position of Twilight Limited follows:

FINANCE

TWILIGHT LIMITED
Selected Statement of Financial Position Information
At December 31, 2017

Long-term debt	
Notes payable, 10%	$ 5,000,000
4% convertible bonds payable	2,000,000
6% convertible bonds payable	3,000,000
Total long-term debt	$10,000,000
Shareholders' equity	
$0.68 cumulative, no par value, convertible preferred shares (unlimited number of shares authorized, 600,000 shares issued and outstanding)	$ 3,000,000
Common shares, no par value (8,000,000 shares authorized, 3,000,000 shares issued and outstanding)	25,000,000
Contributed surplus	200,000
Retained earnings	7,000,000
Total shareholders' equity	$35,200,000

Notes and Assumptions
December 31, 2017

1. Options were granted/written in 2016 that give the holder the right to purchase 100,000 common shares at $8 per share. The average market price of the company's common shares during 2017 was $14 per share. The options expire in 2025 and no options were exercised in 2017.

2. The 4% bonds were issued in 2016 at face value. The 6% bonds were issued on June 1, 2017 at face value. Each bond has a face value of $1,000 and is convertible into 100 common shares.

3. The convertible preferred shares were issued at the beginning of 2017. Each share of preferred is convertible into one common share.

4. The average income tax rate is 25%.

5. The common shares were outstanding during the entire year.

6. Preferred dividends were not declared in 2017.

7. Net income was $2.5 million in 2017.

8. No bonds or preferred shares were converted during 2017.

Instructions

(a) Calculate basic earnings per share for 2017.

(b) Calculate diluted earnings per share for 2017. For simplicity, ignore the requirement to record the debt and equity components of the bonds separately.

(c) From the perspective of a common shareholder, provide support for the treatment of the preferred dividends in calculating Twilight Limited's basic and diluted earnings per share.

DIGGING DEEPER

(d) Discuss how a potential shareholder's investment decision may be affected if diluted earnings per share was not reported.

P17-10 Treeton Inc. had net income for the fiscal year ended June 30, 2017 of $5 million. There were 500,000 common shares outstanding throughout 2017. The average market price of the common shares for the entire fiscal year was $50. Treeton's tax rate was 25% for 2017.

Treeton had the following potential common shares outstanding during 2017:

1. Options to buy 100,000 common shares at $45 per share.

2. 100,000 convertible preferred shares entitled to a cumulative dividend of $10 per share. Each preferred share is convertible into 1.5 common shares.

3. 4% convertible bonds with a principal amount of $30 million, issued at par. Each $1,000 bond is convertible into 25 common shares.

Instructions

For the fiscal year ended June 30, 2017, calculate the following for Treeton Inc. For simplicity, ignore the requirement to record the debt and equity components separately.

(a) Basic earnings per share

(b) Diluted earnings per share

P17-11 As auditor for Checkem & Associates, you have been assigned to review Tao Corporation's calculation of earnings per share for the current year. The controller, Mac Taylor, has supplied you with the following calculations:

Net income	$3,374,960
Common shares issued and outstanding:	
Beginning of year	1,285,000
End of year	1,200,000
Average	1,242,500
Earnings per share:	

$$\frac{\$3,374,960}{1,242,500} = \$2.72 \text{ per share}$$

You have gathered the following additional information:

1. The only equity securities are the common shares.

2. There are no options or warrants outstanding to purchase common shares.

AUDIT AND ASSURANCE

3. There are no convertible debt securities.

4. Activity in common shares during the year was as follows:

Outstanding, Jan. 1	1,285,000
Shares acquired, Oct. 1	(250,000)
	1,035,000
Shares issued, Dec. 1	165,000
Outstanding, Dec. 31	1,200,000

Instructions

(a) Based on the information, do you agree with the controller's calculation of earnings per share for the year? If you disagree, prepare a revised calculation.

(b) Assume the same facts except that call options had also been issued for 140,000 common shares at $10 per share. These options were outstanding at the beginning of the year and none had been exercised or cancelled during the year. The average market price of the common shares during the year was $20 and the ending market price was $25. Prepare a calculation of earnings per share.

P17-12 The following information is for Polo Limited for 2017:

Net income for the year	$2,300,000
8% convertible bonds issued at par ($1,000 per bond), with each bond convertible into	
30 common shares	2,000,000
6% convertible, cumulative preferred shares, $100 par value, with each share convertible into	
three common shares	4,000,000
Common shares (600,000 shares outstanding)	6,000,000
Stock options (granted in a prior year) to purchase 75,000 common shares at $20 per share	750,000
Tax rate for 2017	30%
Average market price of common shares	$25 per share

There were no changes during 2017 in the number of common shares, preferred shares, or convertible bonds outstanding. For simplicity, ignore the requirement to book the convertible bonds' equity portion separately.

Instructions

(a) Calculate basic earnings per share for 2017.

(b) Calculate diluted earnings per share for 2017.

(c) Discuss how a potential shareholder's investment decision may be affected if diluted earnings per share was not reported.

P17-13 Jackie Enterprises Ltd. has a tax rate of 30% and reported net income of $8.5 million in 2017. The following details are from Jackie's statement of financial position as at December 31, 2017, the end of its fiscal year:

Long-term debt:

Bonds payable due Dec. 31, 2023, 10% (issued at par)	$ 5,000,000
Bonds payable, face value $9,000,000, due Dec. 31, 2024, 7.25%, convertible into common shares at the investor's option at the rate of two shares per $100 of bonds	8,600,000

Shareholders' equity:

Preferred shares, $4.50 cumulative, convertible into common shares at the rate of two common shares for each preferred share, 120,000 shares outstanding	$ 5,500,000
Preferred shares, $3.00 cumulative, convertible into common shares at the rate of one common share for each preferred share, 400,000 shares outstanding	10,000,000
Common shares, 1,700,000 shares outstanding	$ 6,000,000
Contributed surplus—conversion rights for bonds	750,000
Retained earnings	9,500,000

Other information:

1. Quarterly dividends were declared on March 1, June 1, September 1, and December 1 for the preferred shares and paid 10 days after the date of declaration.

2. Dividends paid on common shares amounted to $980,000 during the year and were paid on December 20, 2017.

3. Interest expense on bonds payable totalled $1,178,200, including bond discount amortization, which is recorded using the effective interest amortization method.

4. There were no issuances of common shares during the 2017 fiscal year, and no conversions.

Instructions

(a) Determine the amount of interest expense incurred in 2017 for each of the bonds outstanding at December 31, 2017.

(b) Calculate basic earnings per share for 2017.

(c) Determine the potential for dilution for each security that is convertible into common shares.

(d) Calculate diluted earnings per share for 2017.

(e) What is the significance of the preferred share dividends being paid quarterly? What impact, if any, does this frequency in payment have on the calculation of diluted earnings per share?

DIGGING
DEEPER

P17-14 The following information is available for Dylan Inc., a company whose shares are traded on the Toronto Stock Exchange:

Net income for 2017	$150,000
Average market price of common shares during 2017 (adjusted for stock dividend)	$20
December 31, 2017 (fiscal year end) market price of common shares	$20
Income tax rate for fiscal year 2017	30%

Transactions in common shares during 2017:	Change	Cumulative shares
Jan. 1, 2017, common shares outstanding		90,000
Mar. 1, 2017, issuance of common shares	30,000	120,000
June 1, 2017, 10% stock dividend	12,000	132,000
Nov. 1, 2017, repurchase of common shares	(30,000)	102,000

Other information:

1. For all of the fiscal year 2017, $100,000 of 6% cumulative convertible bonds have been outstanding. The bonds were issued at par and are convertible into a total of 10,000 common shares (adjusted for the stock dividend) at the option of the holder, and at any time after issuance.

2. Stock options for 20,000 common shares have been outstanding for the entire 2017 fiscal year, and are exercisable at the option price of $25 per share (adjusted for the stock dividend).

3. For all of the fiscal year 2017, $100,000 of 4% cumulative convertible preferred shares have been outstanding. The preferred shares are convertible into a total of 15,000 common shares (adjusted for the stock dividend) at the option of the holder at any time after January 2022.

Instructions

(a) Determine the weighted average number of common shares that would be used in calculating earnings per share for the year ended December 31, 2017.

(b) Calculate basic earnings per share for 2017.

(c) Determine the potential for dilution for each security that is convertible into common shares.

(d) Calculate diluted earnings per share for 2017. For simplicity, ignore the requirement to record the debt and equity components of the bonds separately.

Case

ENABLING COMPETENCIES

Refer to the Case Primer on the Student Website and in *WileyPLUS* to help you answer this case.

CA17-1 Canton Products Inc. has been in business for quite a while. Its shares trade on a public exchange and it is thinking of expanding onto the New York and London Stock Exchanges. Recently, however, the company has run into cash flow difficulties. The CEO is confident that the company can overcome this problem in the longer term because it has a solid business model; however, in the shorter term, Canton needs to be very careful in managing its cash flows. Of particular concern is the fact that it has multiple potential common shares outstanding that cause the diluted earnings per share numbers to be significantly lower than the company's basic EPS. This in turn has recently caused Canton's stock price to decline and is affecting the company's ability to get the best interest rates on its bank loans.

At a recent meeting with the CFO, the CEO decided to exchange the company's convertible senior subordinated notes (the old notes) for new senior subordinated notes (the new notes). The notes were held by a large institutional investor that agreed to the exchange. The old notes were convertible into 25 shares for each $1,000 note. The new notes have a net share settlement provision that requires that, upon conversion, the company will pay the holders up to $1,000 in cash for each note, plus an excess amount that would be settled in shares at a fixed conversion price (30 shares for each $1,000 note in the total consideration). The notes may be turned in only if the share price exceeds 20% of the fixed conversion price.

It is now year end and the share price is trading above the fixed conversion price but well below the 20% premium level. The note therefore cannot be turned in (converted). The CEO feels that the share price will not exceed the 20% premium for a couple of years.

AUDIT AND ASSURANCE

Instructions

Adopt the role of the auditors and discuss the issues related to the new notes.

Integrated Case

ENABLING COMPETENCIES

IC17-1 Tiziana's Foods Limited (TFL) is in the supermarket business. It is a public company and is thinking of going private (that is, buying up all of its shares that are available). The funds will come from a private consortium. The consortium has offered to buy all the shares if the share price hits a certain level. Although the company has come through some tough times, things have been looking up recently. This is partially due to a new strategy to upgrade the stores and increase square footage.

TFL obtains revenues from two sources: in-store sales to customers and fees from sales of new franchises and continuing franchise fees. This year was a banner year for sales of new franchises. The company sold and booked revenues for 10 new franchised stores. Most of these new stores have not yet opened but locations have been found and deposits have been taken from each of the franchisees.

Under the terms of the franchise contracts, TFL has agreed to absorb any losses that the stores suffer for the first five years. Based on market research, however, and the location of the new stores, it is highly unlikely that losses will occur. Just in case, TFL has requested that franchisees deposit a certain amount of money in a trust fund. In addition, TFL has agreed to issue shares of TFL to the franchisees if the stores are profitable in the first two years.

During the year, TFL issued long-term debt that is convertible into common shares of the company. The number of common shares varies depending on the share price. Because of the potential for taking the company private, TFL agreed to certain concessions. If the company goes private, TFL must pay back 120% of the face value of the debt.

Instructions

Assume the role of the controller and discuss the financial reporting issues.

RESEARCH AND FINANCIAL ANALYSIS

RA17-1   Sky plc

REAL WORLD EMPHASIS

FINANCE

Sky plc, formerly British Sky Broadcasting Group plc, is a pan-European pay television giant and multimedia content company whose common shares trade on the London Stock Exchange. The company produces financial statements in accordance with IFRS. Access the company's annual report for the year ended June 30, 2015 from its website (http://corporate.sky.com). We know from the annual report (page 119) that the company's shares traded at £8.93 per share at the beginning of its 2015 fiscal year and at £10.66 per share at June 30, 2015.

Instructions

FINANCE

REAL WORLD EMPHASIS

(a) Determine how the company has calculated the 2015 basic and diluted earnings per share and verify the calculations, where possible. That is, verify (by examining the relevant notes) the number of shares outstanding, adjustments made to the ordinary shares, and the dilutive shares added. Note any information that is missing in order for you to make this determination. Using the share prices disclosed in the question, determine why the company has concluded that there are no items that are antidilutive.

(b) Assume that all conditions have been met for share option awards. Determine the number of shares that would be added for the dilution using the treasury stock method for 2015. (Note any assumptions you make.)

(c) Sky has also disclosed other information on a per share basis. Explain this other per share data. Why has the company provided this information? If you were an investor, would you find it useful?

RA17-2   Molson Coors Brewing Company

REAL WORLD EMPHASIS

FINANCE

Molson Coors Brewing Company has a December 31 year end. Access the company's 2014 annual report from the company website (www.molsoncoors.com).

Instructions

(a) What types of earnings per share information does the company provide?

(b) Does the company have a complex or simple capital structure? List the types of shares that the company has

outstanding. How has the number of shares been determined for the basic EPS? Does the number of shares look reasonable?

(c) Identify the types of share-based compensation plans the company has, and any potential common shares that would be included in the diluted earnings per share calculation.

FINANCE

(d) What share-based compensation plans increased the number of shares to be used in the diluted EPS? Explain any assumptions that the company made. Explain the items that were found to be antidilutive and the reasons provided.

RA17-3   Non-GAAP Financial Measures

ETHICS

IFRS allows per share amounts to be reported on items other than earnings.

Instructions

(a) Adopt the role of the ethical accountant and write a short essay on the pros and cons of allowing companies to include alternate per share amounts in their annual reports. What other types of per share data might be helpful for investors?

(b) Currently, per share data is only required based on the profit or loss results for the year. What would be the arguments to support the disclosure of comprehensive income per share also? What would be some arguments to discourage this disclosure?

(c) In January 2016, the Canadian Securities Administrators issued CSA Staff Notice 52-306 (Revised) setting out their position on the disclosure of non-GAAP financial measures by issuers applying IFRS or other accounting principles. Briefly summarize the position taken by this Canadian regulator on such measures as alternative EPS measures.

(d) Identify an example of a company that discloses per share data for other than GAAP earnings per share, also indicating any other non-GAAP measures reported.

RA17-4   Brookfield Asset Management Inc.

REAL WORLD EMPHASIS

Refer to the financial statements of **Brookfield Asset Management Inc.** for its year ended December 31, 2014, which are reproduced at the end of Volume 2 of this text, and for its year ended December 31, 2013 found at www.sedar.com or on the company's website.

Instructions

(a) What amount of net income was earned on the consolidated net assets of Brookfield Asset Management for the year ended December 31, 2014? Determine the percentage of this income that accrues to Brookfield's common shareholders. What does this tell you about its subsidiary companies?

(b) Identify the basic and diluted earnings per share reported for 2014 and 2013. Explain each dilutive factor that contributed to the lower diluted EPS amounts.

(c) What were the U.S. dollar basic earnings per share and weighted average share prices of the Brookfield shares in each of the years 2011 to 2014? Based on your findings, what do you think a reasonable estimate of the company's price-earnings ratio would be? Explain what this means.

(d) Have the number of outstanding common shares of Brookfield Asset Management been increasing or decreasing over the four-year period ended December 31, 2014? Comment on any trends you notice.

RA17-5 BCE Inc.

BCE Inc., a well-known Canadian telecommunications and media company, has a December 31 year end. Access the company's 2014 annual report from the company website or from www.sedar.com.

REAL WORLD EMPHASIS

Instructions

(a) What per share information has the company provided each year?

(b) What types of shares does the company have outstanding? What are the dividend rates required on these shares? Indicate the amount of dividends declared and the amount of cash required for dividend payments in 2014. Why might there be differences between the amount declared and the amount paid in the year?

(c) How were the net earnings needed for basic EPS determined and described for 2014 and 2013? Explain any adjustments.

(d) Reconcile the number of shares issued and outstanding in 2014 and 2013 to the number of weighted average shares used in the basic EPS calculations for each year in the financial statements. Explain what might cause any discrepancies found.

(e) Review the calculation of the diluted earnings per share for 2014 and 2013. What has caused the dilution impact? What has been excluded from the calculations and why?

ENDNOTES

[1] IFRS refers to common shares as "ordinary shares." We use the terms interchangeably here.

[2] IAS 33 *Earnings per Share* stipulates this in IAS 33.66, .67, and .67A.

[3] IAS 33.68 and .68A. Copyright © International Financial Reporting Standards Foundation. All rights reserved. Reproduced by John Wiley & Sons Canada, Ltd with the permission of the International Financial Reporting Standards Foundation®. Reproduction and use rights are strictly limited. No permission granted to third parties to reproduce or distribute.

[4] IAS 33.5 and .7.

[5] IAS 33.5. Copyright © International Financial Reporting Standards Foundation. All rights reserved. Reproduced by John Wiley & Sons Canada, Ltd with the permission of the International Financial Reporting Standards Foundation®. Reproduction and use rights are strictly limited. No permission granted to third parties to reproduce or distribute.

[6] IAS 33.28.

[7] IAS 33.41.

[8] This terminology is used in the United States and was used in pre-2011 Canadian GAAP. IAS 33 does not label the calculations although the calculations themselves are essentially the same.

[9] IAS 33.36.

[10] To simplify, the consequences of measuring and presenting the debt and equity components of the convertible debentures separately have been ignored for this example. When initially recognized, convertible debentures would have been recognized as part debt and part equity under IFRS. The interest expense would be calculated using the market interest rate for straight debt; that is, without the conversion feature. This assumption has been made throughout the chapter and the end-of-chapter material unless otherwise noted.

[11] The conversion of bonds is dilutive because EPS with conversion ($3.32) is less than basic EPS ($4.10).

[12] IAS 33.39.

[13] Note that IAS 33 was not updated when IAS 32 was revised to provide guidance on accounting for instruments that are settled using the entity's own equity instruments (including options and forwards). IAS 33 therefore is not conceptually consistent with IAS 32 as it relates to these types of instruments, and the IASB had plans to revise the standard, having issued an exposure draft in 2008. The project has been paused.

[14] IAS 33.62.

[15] The incremental number of shares can be calculated in a simpler way: (Market price − Option price) ÷ Market price × Number of options = Number of shares ($50 − $30) ÷ $50 × 1,500 options = 600 shares.

[16] Note that options and warrants have basically the same assumptions and problems regarding calculation, although the warrants may allow or require the tendering of some other security, such as debt, in lieu of cash upon exercise. In such situations, the accounting becomes quite complex and is beyond the scope of this book.

Task-Based Simulation and Cumulative Coverage: Chapters 16 and 17

FINANCE

Templates to complete this task-based simulation are available in WileyPLUS and on the instructor website.

Nova Gold Miners (NGM) is a gold mining company. NGM currently has two mines operating in Northwestern Ontario, and many exploration claims throughout Ontario and Quebec.

The company is publicly listed on the Toronto Venture Exchange. NGM is hoping to attract new capital in the coming months, and would like to show strong financial performance for its most recent fiscal year end (December 31, 2017). Analysts are focusing on the current year's earnings per share (EPS) in assessing future growth prospects. The company's shares are currently trading at $30 per share.

You work in NGM's accounting department, and have been assigned to help the CFO prepare preliminary estimates of EPS. You are given the following summarized financial information.

The company's summarized statement of financial position for non-current liabilities and shareholders' equity:

Non-current liabilities	
Bond payable, $150,000, 5%, 5-year, 6% market yield	$ 147,250
Convertible bond, $150,000, 5%, 5-year, 5% market yield,	
convertible into 2,000 common shares	145,990
Shareholders' equity	
Class A preferred shares, 150,000 issued, $1 cumulative dividend per share	1,500,000
Class B preferred shares, 50,000 issued, $1 non-cumulative dividend per share,	
convertible on a 10:1 basis for common shares	1,000,000
Contributed surplus: 10,000 options issued with $20 exercise price, 2-year term	55,000
Contributed surplus: convertible bond option	6,319
Common shares, 1,000,000 issued	1,000,000

The company has the following summarized statement of operations:

Revenue	$1,250,000
Operating costs	589,150
Interest expense	
Non-convertible bond	8,759
Convertible bond	8,688
Pre-tax profit	643,403
Income tax (25%)	160,851
After-tax profit	$ 482,552

The company has the following summarized statement of changes in equity:

	Preferred Shares	Convertible Preferred Shares	Contributed Surplus— Options	Contributed Surplus— Convertible Bond	Common Shares	Retained Earnings
Beginning value	$1,500,000	0	$55,000	$6,319	$ 750,000	$ 750,000
Shares issued	0	$ 1,000,000	0	0	350,000	0
Shares reacquired	0	0	0	0	100,000	0
Net income	0	0	0	0	0	482,552
Dividends	0	0	0	0	0	150,000
Ending value	$1,500,000	$ 1,000,000	$55,000	$6,319	$1,000,000	$1,082,552

Notes:
1. Convertible preferred shares were issued on January 1.
2. Additional common shares were issued on September 1.
3. Common shares were reacquired on April 1.

Instructions

(a) Calculate the basic earnings per share.

(b) Calculate the diluted earnings per share. Record your calculations in the following table:

Net Income Available to Common Shareholders	Weighted Average Number of Shares Outstanding
Earnings per Share:	

(c) Assess the implications of changes in stock option terms for the fair value of the options.

	Increase	Decrease	No Impact	Not Determinable
Change the term to four years				
Change the exercise price to $30				
Change the risk-free rate to 5%				
Increase the assumed volatility of the company's share price				
Issue Class C preferred shares, with non-cumulative dividends				

(d) Assess the implications of changing the terms of Class A preferred shares for the current year's basic EPS. Complete the table below.

	Increase	Decrease	No Impact	Not Determinable
Change dividend to non-cumulative dividend assuming that dividend is regularly paid				
Make shares convertible into 200,000 common shares				
Change the dividend per share to $3 per share				

(e) Management is contemplating retiring the convertible bond for $161,000, which represents the current fair value of the bond ($152,500 for the fair value of the bond and $8,500 for the fair value of the conversion feature).

1. Prepare the journal entry to retire the bond. (Assume the retirement is at the year end.)

2. Assess the impact of management retiring the bond at December 31 on the Future EPS calculations by completing the following table.

	Increase	Decrease	No Impact	Not Determinable
Basic EPS				
Net income available to common shareholders				
Weighted average shares outstanding				
Diluted EPS				
Net income available to common shareholders				
Weighted average shares outstanding				

CHAPTER 18

INCOME TAXES

WHAT IS THE IDEAL CORPORATE TAX RATE?

THE GOAL OF ANY corporation is to maximize returns for shareholders. After a corporation has earned revenues, managed expenses, and reported profit, it then needs to pay taxes on it. Minimizing taxes paid while complying with tax laws is a major concern for corporations. Likewise, the goal of any government is to maximize the efficiency and effectiveness of its services to citizens using the money it raises in taxes. But governments know that minimizing corporate taxes to stimulate the economy is also in the public interest. Where is the "sweet spot" where the corporate tax rate is just enough? There is no easy answer.

Corporate taxes in Canada have been falling in recent years, as governments try to lessen the tax burden on businesses so they can invest in new equipment, ramp up production, and hire more people. The overall average corporate tax rate in Canada was 26.50% in 2015, compared with the global average of 23.68%, according to an international study by consultants KPMG. Governments around the world continue to deal with the fragile

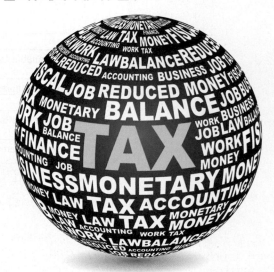

recovery after the global financial crisis of 2008, by balancing the need for revenue with the need to stimulate business activity, KPMG said. The study predicted that corporate tax rates would continue to fall around the world as countries compete for business investment. A 2012 global report by consultants PwC found that over half of the countries in the study had reduced corporate taxes over the previous seven years.

While governments are lowering their statutory (or legal) tax rate, some are tinkering a bit with the deductions that corporations can use to reduce their tax bill. For example, some European countries are considering reducing or eliminating deductions for interest payments that corporations make on loans. This won't alter corporations' statutory tax rate, but it would increase their effective tax rate and their tax bill, adding more money to government coffers to make up for maintaining or lowering the statutory tax rate.

One phenomenon under the microscope of late is the practice of some corporations to locate their head offices where tax rates are lower. A recent Canadian example is Tim

Hortons (which is now part of the Burger King chain). When it reorganized as a Canadian-based public company in 2009, its move back home was partly due to recently lowered corporate taxes in Canada. In an attempt to stem some of this corporate tax migration, the Organisation for Economic Co-operation and Development (OECD) launched an action plan to reform international tax rules. If adopted by member countries, it would limit the ability of multinational corporations to move to low or no-tax jurisdictions where little or no economic activity takes place. The OECD estimated that such "profit-shifting" represents between 4% and 10% of global corporate income tax revenues, amounting to about U.S. $100 to $240 billion a year.

Sources: "OECD Presents Outputs of OECD/G20 BEPS Project for Discussion at G20 Finance Ministers Meeting," OECD news release, October 5, 2015; KPMG, "2015 Global Tax Rate Survey," 2015; "World's Third Largest Quick Service Restaurant Company Launched with Two Iconic and Independent Brands: Tim Hortons and Burger King," Tim Hortons and Burger King joint news release, August 26, 2014; PwC, "Corporate Income Tax—A Global Analysis," 2012.

PREVIEW OF CHAPTER 18

As our opening story indicates, companies spend a considerable amount of time and effort trying to minimize their income tax payments. This is important because income taxes are a major cost of doing business for most corporations. At the same time, companies must present financial information to the investment community that provides a clear picture of present and potential tax obligations and tax benefits. In this chapter, we discuss the basic standards that both publicly accountable and private enterprises must follow in reporting income taxes. The content and organization of the chapter are as follows.

INCOME TAXES						
Income Taxes from a Business Perspective	**Current Income Taxes**	**Deferred/Future Income Taxes**	**Income Tax Loss Carryover Benefits**	**Presentation, Disclosure, and Analysis**	**IFRS/ASPE Comparison**	**Appendix 18A— Comprehensive Illustration**
	■ Accounting income and taxable income ■ Calculation of taxable income ■ Calculation of current income taxes	■ Deferred tax liabilities ■ Deferred tax assets ■ Income tax accounting objectives and analyses of temporary deductible differences ■ Tax rate considerations	■ Loss carryback illustrated ■ Loss carryforward illustrated ■ Review of deferred tax asset account	■ Statement of financial position presentation ■ Income and other statement presentation ■ Disclosure requirements ■ Analysis ■ Outstanding conceptual questions	■ A comparison of IFRS and ASPE ■ Looking ahead	■ First year of operations–2017 ■ Second year of operations–2018

INCOME TAXES FROM A BUSINESS PERSPECTIVE

Objective 1
Understand the importance of income taxes from a business perspective.

When a company decides where to set up its operations, a major consideration is the tax rate that it will face on its profits. The link between taxes and economic growth has been recognized in studies by organizations such as the Organisation for Economic Co-operation and Development (OECD). An OECD study looked at the impact on economic growth of a variety of taxes, including property taxes, consumption taxes (such as the GST), personal income taxes, and corporate income taxes. The results suggest that, of the various taxation options available to OECD countries, corporate income taxes had the most negative effect on gross domestic product per capita.[1]

**CORPORATE
TAX**
6.1.1

The fact that corporate taxes can slow growth may help to explain why governments in Canada have steadily reduced corporate tax rates for more than 20 years. For example, the combined federal and provincial tax rate for general corporations in Canada declined from an average of approximately 43% in 2000 to approximately 27% in 2015. The combined federal and provincial tax rates ranged from 26% to 31% for most provinces and territories in late 2015.[2]

Accounting for income taxes is important for businesses, individuals, and governments. In this chapter we focus on accounting for taxes by businesses in Canada. We leave the details of how to prepare corporate tax returns for courses that specialize in that subject. Our main focus is on financial reporting by companies once they have determined the amount of taxes that they owe.

Up to this point, you have learned the basic principles that corporations use to report information to investors and creditors. Corporations file income tax returns following the Income Tax Act (and related provincial legislation), which is administered by the Canada Revenue Agency (CRA).[3] Because GAAP methods differ in several ways from tax regulations, adjustments usually need to be made to the income reported on the financial statements when determining the income that is taxable under tax legislation. That is, the current year's pre-tax income on the **income statement** (the income amount as determined by applying IFRS or ASPE) and the company's taxable income usually differ. The differences are highlighted in Illustration 18-1.

Income Statement Differences between IFRS and Tax Reporting

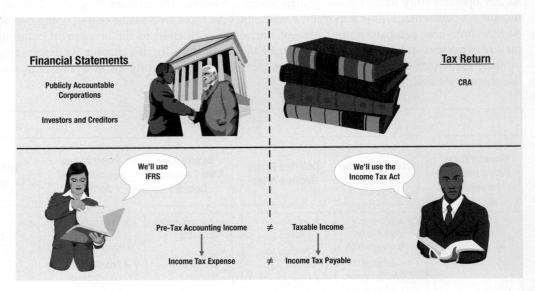

Under ASPE, adjustments also generally need to be made to pre-tax accounting income to determine taxable income. However, under ASPE, companies have the option of using the taxes payable approach where (if no tax instalments have been made) income tax expense would typically equal income taxes payable. We will discuss the taxes payable approach later in this chapter. But let's first take a closer look at the differences between accounting income and taxable income.

CURRENT INCOME TAXES

Objective 2

Explain the difference between accounting income and taxable income, and calculate taxable income and current income taxes.

Accounting Income and Taxable Income

Accounting income is a financial reporting term that is also known as "income before taxes," "income for financial reporting purposes," or **accounting profit**, as it is called in IAS 12 *Income Taxes*. In this chapter, it is a pre-tax concept, and we will use the terms "income" and "profit" interchangeably. Accounting income is determined according to IFRS (or ASPE) and is measured with the objective of providing useful information to investors and creditors. **Taxable income**, on the other hand, is a tax accounting term and indicates the amount on which income tax payable is calculated. Taxable income is determined according to the Income Tax Act and Regulations, which are designed to raise money to support government operations. It is also referred to as "income for tax purposes," or, under IAS 12, as **taxable profit**.

To illustrate how differences in IFRS and tax rules affect financial reporting and taxable income, assume that Chelsea Inc. reported revenues of $130,000 and expenses of $60,000 on its income statement in each of its first three years of operations. Illustration 18-2 shows the (partial) income statements over these three years.

Illustration 18-2				
Accounting Income		**CHELSEA INC.**		
		IFRS Reporting		
	2017	2018	2019	Total
Revenues	$130,000	$130,000	$130,000	
Expenses	60,000	60,000	60,000	
Accounting income	**$ 70,000**	**$ 70,000**	**$ 70,000**	**$210,000**

Assume that, following tax regulations, Chelsea reports the same expenses to the CRA in each of the three years. However, the $130,000 of revenue that was reported each year was taxable in different accounting periods: taxable revenues were $100,000 in 2017, $150,000 in 2018, and $140,000 in 2019, as shown in Illustration 18-3.

Illustration 18-3				
Taxable Income		**CHELSEA INC.**		
		Tax Reporting		
	2017	2018	2019	Total
Revenues	$100,000	$150,000	$140,000	
Expenses	60,000	60,000	60,000	
Taxable income	**$ 40,000**	**$ 90,000**	**$ 80,000**	**$210,000**

In reality, companies do not submit revised income statements for the tax return that list only taxable revenues and deductible expenses. Instead, they prepare a schedule that begins with accounting income and they then adjust this amount for each area of difference between it and taxable income. Chelsea's schedules would appear as in Illustration 18-4.

Illustration 18-4			
Schedule to Reconcile Accounting	**CHELSEA INC.**		
Income to Taxable Income	2017	2018	2019
Accounting income	**$70,000**	**$70,000**	**$70,000**
Less revenue taxable in a future period	(30,000)		
Add revenue recognized in previous period, taxable in current period		20,000	10,000
Taxable income	**$40,000**	**$90,000**	**$80,000**
Taxes payable (25% assumed rate)	$10,000	$22,500	$20,000

Calculation of Taxable Income

Reversing and Permanent Differences

Let's take a more detailed look at the differences between accounting income and taxable income. The Chelsea Inc. example above illustrates how to calculate taxable income when there is only one such difference. In reality, many adjustments may be needed. The major reasons for differences between accounting and taxable income follow, and examples of each type are provided.[4]

1. ***Revenues or gains are taxable after they are recognized in accounting income.*** A sale may be recorded in the current accounting period with a debit to a receivable and a credit to revenue, but the revenue may not be included in taxable income until a future year when the receivable is actually collected in cash. There is a temporary difference that will reverse in the future. A similar difference may also apply to a gain on sale or to holding gains recognized on assets being held, as these amounts may not be taxable until they have been **realized**; that is, received in cash. Examples include:

   - Instalment sales that are recognized when the sale takes place for financial reporting purposes and on the cash basis for tax purposes

CORPORATE TAX
6.1.1

   - Contracts that are accounted for under the percentage-of-completion method for financial reporting purposes and the completed contract or zero-profit basis for tax purposes, resulting in some or all of the related gross profit being deferred for tax purposes

   - Unrealized holding gains that are recognized in income or in OCI on investments or other assets carried at fair value, but that are not taxable until the assets are sold and the gains realized (or become realizable as an account receivable)

   Note that in all of these examples, the IFRS (or ASPE) statement of financial position reports an asset [an account receivable, or contract asset (construction in process), or an investment account] with a carrying amount that is higher than its tax value would be on a tax statement of financial position, if one were prepared.[5] You will need to keep this in mind in order to understand the discussion of deferred (or future) income taxes later in the chapter.

2. ***Expenses or losses are deductible for tax purposes after they are recognized in accounting income.*** Some expenses or losses that are recognized for accounting purposes are not allowed to be deducted for tax purposes until a future period. For example, for financial statement purposes, an expense may have to be accrued, but for tax purposes it may not be deductible as an expense until it is paid. That is, it is only when the liability is eventually settled that the expense or loss is deductible in calculating taxable income. Examples include the following:

   - Product warranty liabilities

   - Estimated losses and liabilities related to restructuring

   - Litigation accruals

   - Accrued pension costs

   - Holding or impairment losses on investments or other assets

   In all these examples, notice that a liability (or contra asset or direct asset reduction) is recognized on the statement of financial position when the expense or loss is recognized for financial reporting purposes. For tax purposes, however, the expense is not recognized in the current period and, therefore, neither is there a reduction of the current taxes payable.

3. ***Revenues or gains are taxable before they are recognized in accounting income.*** A company may recognize cash that it received during the year as unearned revenue if it is an advance payment for goods or services to be provided in future years. For tax purposes, the advance payment may have to be included in taxable income when the cash is received. When the entity recognizes this revenue on the income statement in later years when the goods or services are provided to customers, these amounts can be deducted in calculating taxable income. This is because they were included in taxable income in the year the cash was received. They are not taxed twice! Examples include the following:

   - Subscriptions, royalties, and rentals received in advance

   - Sale and leaseback gains, including a deferral of profit on a sale for financial reporting purposes that would be reported as realized for tax purposes

Once again, the statement of financial position is also affected. There is a difference between the carrying amount of the liability account such as Unearned Revenue and its tax base.

4. ***Expenses or losses are deductible before they are recognized in accounting income.*** The cost of assets such as equipment, for example, is deducted for financial statement purposes according to whichever depreciation method the company uses for financial statement purposes. For tax purposes, the capital cost allowance (CCA) method must be used. Therefore, depending on which accounting method was chosen, the asset's cost may be deducted faster for tax purposes than it is expensed for financial reporting purposes. When this happens, taxable income in the early years of the asset's life is lower than the accounting income. Because the asset's capital cost is the total amount that can be depreciated on the books and deducted for tax purposes, this means that future taxable income will be higher than the accounting income in those future years. Other examples include the following:

- Property and resources that are depreciated/depleted faster for tax purposes than for financial reporting purposes
- Deductible pension funding that exceeds the pension expense that is recognized
- Prepaid expenses that are deducted in calculating taxable income in the period when they are paid

These, too, will result in the carrying amount of a statement of financial position account (equipment, at cost less accumulated depreciation, for example) that is different from its tax base (the equipment's undepreciated capital cost or UCC).

5. ***Permanent differences.*** Some differences between taxable income and accounting income are permanent. **Permanent differences** are caused by items that (1) are included in accounting income but never in taxable income, or (2) are included in taxable income but never in accounting income. Examples of items that are included in accounting income but never in taxable income are:

- **Non–tax-deductible expenses** such as fines and penalties, golf and social club dues, and expenses related to the earning of non-taxable revenue
- **Non-taxable revenue**, such as dividends from taxable Canadian corporations, and proceeds on life insurance policies carried by the company on key officers or employees

Examples of items that are included in taxable income but never in accounting income are depletion allowances of natural resources that exceed the resources' cost.

Because **permanent** differences affect only the period in which they occur, there are no deferred or future tax consequences associated with the related statement of financial position accounts.

The situations identified in numbers 1 to 4 above are known as temporary differences or **reversible differences**. Their accounting treatment and tax treatment are **the same**, but the **timing** of when they are included in accounting income and when they are included in taxable income **differs**. These reversible or **timing differences** result in a temporary difference between the carrying amount of the asset or liability and its tax base, which we discuss further below.

Multiple Differences Illustrated

To illustrate a situation when there are multiple differences between accounting income and taxable income, assume that BT Corporation reports accounting income of $200,000 in each of the years 2017, 2018, and 2019. Assume also that the company is subject to a 30% tax rate in each year, and has the following differences between income reported on the financial statements and taxable income:

1. Revenue of $18,000 on a sale to a customer in 2017 is recognized for financial reporting purposes in 2017. The revenue is considered taxable when the customer pays the account—in equal monthly payments over 18 months beginning January 1, 2018.

2. A premium of $5,000 is paid in each of 2018 and 2019 for life insurance that the company carries on key officers. This is not deductible for tax purposes, but is expensed for accounting purposes.

3. A warranty with an estimated cost of $30,000 was provided on sales in 2017. This amount was recognized as expense in the same year. It was expected that $20,000 of the warranty work would be performed in 2018 and $10,000 in 2019, and this is what actually happened. For tax purposes, warranty expenses are not deductible until the expenditures are actually incurred.[6]

The first and third items above are **reversible** differences. The second item is a **permanent** difference with no future tax consequences. The reconciliation of BT's accounting income to its taxable income for each year is shown in Illustration 18-5.

Illustration 18-5

Calculation of Taxable Income

	2017	2018	2019
Accounting income	$200,000	$200,000	$200,000
Adjustments:			
Revenue from 2017 sale	(18,000)	12,000	6,000
Warranty expense	30,000	(20,000)	(10,000)
Non-deductible insurance expense		5,000	5,000
Taxable income	$212,000	$197,000	$201,000

The analysis always starts with pre-tax income reported on the income statement. This is adjusted to the taxable amount as follows: revenue items that are not taxable until a future period are deducted, and expenses that are not deductible in the year are added back. This explains the $18,000 deduction of the 2017 sale amount because this was included in 2017's accounting income but is not taxable in 2017. It will be taxable in 2018 and 2019 as the difference reverses; that is, as the receivable is collected. In 2018 and 2019, the amounts collected will be added to the accounting incomes reported to calculate the taxable income for each year.

Starting with pre-tax accounting income and adjusting it to taxable income also explains why the $30,000 of warranty expense is added back to accounting income in 2017. Because BT Corporation did not make any payments under the warranty in 2017, the company cannot deduct any warranty expense for tax purposes. The full amount of $30,000 was deducted in calculating accounting income in 2017, so it is all added back in determining taxable income. The warranty costs are deducted in calculating taxable income in the years they are actually paid by the company (that is, in 2018 and 2019) even though no warranty expense was deducted in the accounting incomes of those two years.

The original difference and its reversal affect taxable income. The **original** or **originating difference** is the cause of the initial difference between accounting and taxable income amounts. An example is the $30,000 original difference related to warranty expense in 2017. The **reversal**, on the other hand, causes the opposite effect in subsequent years, such as the $20,000 and $10,000 warranty expense differences in 2018 and 2019.

The $5,000 life insurance premium is added back to 2018 and 2019's accounting income because it was deducted as an expense in calculating accounting income in each of those years. It is not a deductible expense for tax purposes in any year and the $5,000 will not affect any future year's taxable income. Its effect is **permanent**.

Calculation of Current Income Taxes

While the calculation of taxable income may sometimes be challenging, the calculation of current tax expense and income taxes payable after determining taxable income is straightforward. To calculate this amount, the current rate of tax is simply applied to the company's taxable income. Continuing with the BT Corporation example above and the taxable incomes determined in Illustration 18-5, the calculation of the company's current tax expense and income taxes payable for each of the three years is shown in Illustration 18-6.

BT Corporation's Current Tax Expense and Income Tax Payable

	2017	2018	2019
Taxable income	$212,000	$197,000	$201,000
Tax rate	30%	30%	30%
Income tax payable and current tax expense	$ 63,600	$ 59,100	$ 60,300

The year-end adjusting entries to record current income tax each year are as follows:

Dec. 31, 2017	Current Tax Expense	63,600	
	Income Tax Payable		63,600
Dec. 31, 2018	Current Tax Expense	59,100	
	Income Tax Payable		59,100
Dec. 31, 2019	Current Tax Expense	60,300	
	Income Tax Payable		60,300

Alternative Terminology

IFRS uses the terms "current tax expense (income)" and "deferred tax expense (income)," whereas ASPE suggests "current income tax expense (benefit)" and "future income tax expense (benefit)." We use the ASPE term "benefit" rather than "income" when describing tax-related income statement accounts, and we use the other terms interchangeably in this text.

This method of calculating income tax expense is straightforward and is known as the **taxes payable method**. It is one of the methods permitted under ASPE.

Notice that although BT Corporation reported identical accounting income in each year and the tax rate stayed the same, the current **tax expense differs each year**. This fluctuation is caused mainly by the reversible differences created by the 2017 sale and warranty expense. Conceptually, the income tax expense reported on the income statement **should be directly related to the accounting income that is reported**, not to the amount that is taxable in the period. Therefore, another method, based on an asset and liability approach to income taxes, is required under IFRS and is permitted as the other accounting policy choice under ASPE. This method—the **temporary difference approach**—starts with the calculation of current income taxes as described above. It then adjusts for the effects of any changes in **deferred tax assets** and **deferred tax liabilities** and recognizes these effects as **deferred tax expense**. Note that the ASPE terminology for this same method is the **future income taxes method**; the related tax assets and liabilities are called **future income tax assets** and **future income tax liabilities**, and the associated expense is referred to as **future income tax expense**. We use the terms "deferred" and "future" interchangeably. We explain the temporary difference approach (future income taxes method) next.

DEFERRED/FUTURE INCOME TAXES

As we mentioned, reversible differences that affect taxable income each year result in an effect on the amount of income taxes payable in the future as the differences reverse. The accumulated tax effects of these differences are recognized on the balance sheet as deferred tax assets and deferred tax liabilities. The adjustment of these two statement of financial position accounts to their correct amount at the reporting date dictates the amount of deferred tax expense (or future income tax expense) to be recognized. The **deferred tax expense** and the **current tax expense** are then both reported on the income statement as components of income tax expense for the period.

The basic principle that underlies deferred taxes is as follows: If the recovery of an asset or settlement of a liability that is reported on the statement of financial position will result in the company's having to pay income taxes in the future, a deferred or future tax liability is recognized on the current period's statement of financial position. Alternatively, if the recovery or settlement will result in the company having to pay less tax in the future, a deferred or future tax asset is recognized on the current statement of financial position. We explain this further in the next sections.

The **tax base** or **tax basis** of an asset or liability is similar to a measurement attribute, such as historical cost and fair value. (IFRS uses the term "base" and ASPE uses "basis.")

The **tax base of an asset** is the amount that will be deductible for tax purposes against any taxable economic benefits that will flow to the company when it recovers the carrying amount of the asset. If the economic benefit will not be taxable, the tax base is equal to the carrying amount.[7] A good example is the undepreciated capital cost (UCC) of a depreciable asset. This amount is usually different from the asset's carrying amount in the accounting records. In other words, it is the amount that is attributed for tax purposes to the statement of financial position item. Examples from IAS 12 *Income Taxes* and *CPA Canada Handbook*, Part II, Section 3465 on Income Taxes will help explain how this is applied.

Example 1. A capital asset was acquired at an original cost (and tax base) of $1,000. By the end of Year 3, capital cost allowance totalling $424 has been deducted when calculating taxable income for Years 1 to 3. Therefore, the tax base of this asset at the end of Year 3 is $1,000 − $424 = $576. This is its UCC. Going back to the definition of tax base provided above, this is the amount that will be deductible for tax purposes in the future as the asset is used to generate cash flows and its carrying amount on the statement of financial position is recovered.

Example 2. An investment in another company's shares was purchased at a cost of $1,000. Regardless of whether this investment is accounted for on the statement of financial position at fair value or at cost, when it is sold, the company has to deduct the cost of the investment from the proceeds received to determine taxable income. The tax base of the investment is therefore $1,000.

Example 3. A company has trade accounts receivable with a carrying amount of $10,000. The related revenue is taxable as it is earned and is included in taxable income as it is recognized in the accounts. When this asset's carrying amount of $10,000 is recovered (that is, when the customer pays the account), the amount received will not be taxable, so the tax base is equal to its carrying amount. Therefore, its tax base is $10,000.

Example 4. A company holds a fully paid-for life insurance policy on the company president. The policy has a cash surrender value and carrying amount on the statement of financial position of $100,000. If the company receives the $100,000 on the president's death, the proceeds are not taxable under the Income Tax Act. Based on the definition above, the tax base of this asset is the same as its carrying amount. There are no tax consequences.

The **tax base of a liability** is its carrying amount on the statement of financial position reduced by any amount that will be deductible for tax purposes in future periods. The tax base of revenue received in advance is its carrying amount, less any amount that will **not** be taxable in the future. When a liability can be settled for its carrying amount without any tax consequences, its tax base is the same as its carrying amount. Again, let's look at some examples.

Example 1. A company has an accrued liability with a carrying amount of $1,000. The related expense that was included in accounting income when the expense was accrued is deductible for tax purposes only when it is paid. According to the definition above, the tax base of the accrued liability is its carrying amount ($1,000) less the amount deductible for tax purposes in future periods ($1,000). Therefore, its tax base is $0.

Example 2. A company receives $1,000 of interest in advance and recognizes this as unearned revenue, a liability. The interest was taxed on a cash basis, when it was received. The tax base of the unearned revenue is its carrying amount ($1,000) less the amount that will not be taxable in the future ($1,000), thus, $0.

Example 3. A company reports an accrued liability of $200 and the related expenses were deducted for tax purposes in the same period the expense and liability were recognized. The company also reports a loan payable of $500. In both cases, there is no income tax consequence when the liability is paid in the future. The tax base of the accrued liability and of the loan payable is the same as the carrying amount of each liability on the books (that is, $200 and $500, respectively).

There may be situations where an item has a tax base but it is not recognized as an asset or liability on the statement of financial position. Consider the example of research and development phase costs that have been expensed in the accounts as incurred, but that are deductible for tax purposes in a future year. Although the carrying amount on the statement of financial position is $0, the tax authorities allow the company to reduce future taxable income. The tax base of these research costs would be the amount that would be permitted as a deduction in future periods.

The difference between the tax base of an asset or liability and its reported amount in the statement of financial position is called a **temporary difference**. There are two types. A **taxable temporary difference** will result in taxable amounts in future years when the carrying amount of the asset is received or the liability is settled. That is, the effect is an increase in taxable income and income taxes in the future. A **deductible temporary difference** will decrease taxable income and taxes in the future. We will first look at the effects of **taxable** temporary differences and then discuss **deductible** temporary differences.

Deferred Tax Liabilities

Taxable Temporary Differences

Objective 3

Explain what a taxable temporary difference is, determine its amount, and calculate deferred tax liabilities.

In the Chelsea Inc. example in Illustrations 18-2 to 18-4 above, the company reported revenue of $130,000 on its 2017 income statement. For tax purposes, Chelsea reported only $100,000 of taxable revenue, the amount that was collected in cash in the year. At the end of 2017, the carrying amount of accounts receivable on the statement of financial position is $30,000 (that is, $130,000 – $100,000 collected). What is the tax base of the accounts receivable? Going back to the definition of the tax base of an asset, it is the amount that can be deducted for tax purposes from the $30,000 received. In this case, the full $30,000 will be taxable as it is collected—no amount can be deducted from this. Therefore, the tax value of the accounts receivable is $0.

In the future period when Chelsea collects the $30,000 in accounts receivable, the $30,000 will be taxable and the company will have to pay income tax on it. Therefore, the difference between the carrying amount and tax value of the accounts receivable is a taxable amount—a taxable temporary difference.

What will happen to this $30,000 temporary difference that originated in 2017 for Chelsea Inc.? Assuming that Chelsea expects to collect $20,000 of the receivables in 2018 and $10,000 in 2019, this will result in taxable amounts of $20,000 in 2018 and $10,000 in 2019. These future taxable amounts will cause future taxable income to be increased, along with the amount of income taxes to be paid. Illustration 18-7 presents the original difference, the reversal or turnaround of this temporary difference, and the resulting taxable amounts in future periods.

Illustration 18-7

Reversal of Temporary Difference, Chelsea Inc.

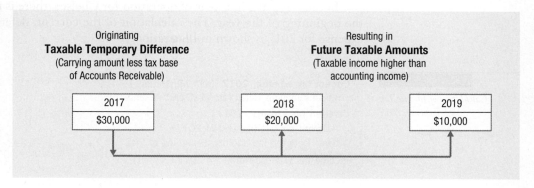

An assumption that underlies a company's IFRS or ASPE statement of financial position is that the assets and liabilities will be recovered and settled, respectively, at least at their reported amounts (carrying amounts). This assumption means that under accrual accounting we need to recognize the deferred tax consequences of temporary differences in the current year. In other words, it is necessary to recognize in the current period the amount of income taxes that will be payable, reduced, or refunded when the assets' currently reported amounts are recovered or the liabilities are settled.

In our example, we assumed that Chelsea will collect the accounts receivable and report the $30,000 collection as taxable revenue in 2018 and 2019. Based on this, additional income tax will have to be paid in those years. We therefore record the deferred tax related to the collection of the receivable in Chelsea's books **in 2017.**

Calculation of Deferred Tax Liability

A **deferred tax liability** or **future income tax liability** is the future tax consequence of a taxable temporary difference. It represents the increase in taxes payable in future years as a result of a taxable temporary difference existing at the end of the current year. Recall from the Chelsea example that income tax payable is $10,000 ($40,000 × 25%) in 2017 (Illustration 18-4). In addition, there is a deferred tax liability at the end of 2017 of $7,500, calculated as shown in Illustration 18-8.

Illustration 18-8

Calculation of Deferred Tax Liability, End of 2017

Carrying amount of accounts receivable	$30,000
Tax base of accounts receivable	–0–
Taxable temporary difference at the end of 2017	30,000
Future tax rate	25%
Deferred tax liability at the end of 2017	$ 7,500

Another way to calculate the deferred tax liability is to **prepare a schedule that shows the taxable amounts by year** as a result of existing temporary differences, as is shown in Illustration 18-9. A detailed schedule like this is needed when the tax rates in future years are different and the calculations are more complex.

Illustration 18-9

Schedule of Future Taxable Amounts

	Future Years		
	2018	2019	Total
Future taxable amounts	$20,000	$10,000	$30,000
Future tax rate	25%	25%	
Deferred tax liability at the end of 2017	$ 5,000	$ 2,500	$ 7,500

Because it is the first year of operation for Chelsea, there is no deferred tax liability at the beginning of the year. The calculation of the current, deferred, and total income tax expense for 2017 is shown in Illustration 18-10.

Illustration 18-10

Calculation of Income Tax Expense, 2017

Current tax expense, 2017 (from Illustration 18-4)		
Taxable income × tax rate ($40,000 × 25%)		$10,000
Deferred tax expense, 2017		
Deferred tax liability, end of 2017	$7,500	
Less: Deferred tax liability, beginning of 2017	–0–	7,500
Income tax expense (total) for 2017		$17,500

This calculation indicates that income tax expense has two components: current tax expense (the amount of income tax payable or refundable for the current period) and deferred tax expense. **Deferred** or **future income tax expense** is based on **the change** in the statement of financial position deferred tax asset or liability account from the beginning to the end of the accounting period.

Journal entries are needed to record both the current and deferred taxes. Taxes due and payable are credited to Income Tax Payable, while the increase in deferred taxes is credited to Deferred Tax Liability. These tax entries could be combined into one entry. However, because disclosure is required of both components, using two entries makes it easier to keep track of the current tax expense and the deferred tax expense. For Chelsea Inc., the following entries are made at the end of 2017:

A = L + SE
+10,000 −10,000

Cash flows: No effect

| Current Tax Expense | 10,000 | |
| Income Tax Payable | | 10,000 |

A = L + SE
+7,500 −7,500

Cash flows: No effect

| Deferred Tax Expense | 7,500 | |
| Deferred Tax Liability | | 7,500 |

At the end of 2018 (the second year), the taxable temporary difference—the difference between the carrying amount ($10,000) and tax base ($0) of the accounts receivable—that relates to the 2017 sales is $10,000. (Remember that $20,000 of the 2017 receivable was collected in 2018.) The $10,000 difference is multiplied by the applicable future tax rate to determine the deferred tax liability of $2,500 ($10,000 × 25%) to be reported at the end of 2018. Both the current and deferred tax expense for 2018 are calculated in Illustration 18-11.

Current tax expense, 2018 (from Illustration 18-4)		
Taxable income × tax rate ($90,000 × 25%)		$22,500
Deferred tax expense, 2018		
Deferred tax liability, end of 2018 ($10,000 × 25%)	$2,500	
Less: Deferred tax liability, beginning of 2018	7,500	(5,000)
Income tax expense (total) for 2018		$17,500

The journal entries to record income taxes for 2018 are:

A = L + SE
+22,500 −22,500

Cash flows: No effect

| Current Tax Expense | 22,500 | |
| Income Tax Payable | | 22,500 |

A = L + SE
−5,000 +5,000

Cash flows: No effect

| Deferred Tax Liability | 5,000 | |
| Deferred Tax Benefit | | 5,000 |

Notice in the second entry that an **income tax expense with a credit balance** is often referred to as an **income tax benefit**. In IAS 12, it is also known as a **tax income** account. As discussed above, we use the term "income tax benefit" in our examples.

In the entry to record deferred taxes at the end of 2019, the Deferred Tax Liability balance is reduced by another $2,500. Illustration 18-12 shows this ledger account as it appears at the end of 2019.

Deferred Tax Liability			
		7,500	2017
2018	5,000		
2019	2,500		
	−0−		Balance

As you can see, the Deferred Tax Liability account has a zero balance at the end of 2019.

Deferred Tax Assets

Deductible Temporary Differences

Objective 4
Explain what a deductible temporary difference is, determine its amount, and calculate deferred tax assets.

To help explain deductible temporary differences and deferred tax assets, assume that Cunningham Inc. sells microwave ovens on which it includes a two-year assurance-type warranty accounted for using an expense approach. In late December 2018, the company introduced a new microwave oven and estimated its warranty expense related to its 2018 sales of microwave ovens to be $500,000. Cunningham expects that $300,000 of these warranty costs will actually be incurred in 2019, and $200,000 in 2020.

Cunningham reports the $500,000 of warranty expense on its 2018 income statement and a related estimated liability for warranties of $500,000 on its December 31, 2018 statement of financial position. For tax purposes, warranty costs are deductible only when the costs are actually incurred. Therefore, no warranty expense can be deducted in determining 2018's taxable income. Because $500,000 **will be deductible in future periods** when the warranty obligation is settled, the tax base of the warranty liability at December 31, 2018 is $0. There is a temporary difference of $500,000 related to the warranty liability.

Because of this temporary difference, Cunningham Inc. recognizes **in 2018** the tax benefits (positive tax consequences) associated with the tax deductions in the future. These future deductible amounts will cause taxable income to be less than accounting income in 2019 and 2020. The deferred tax benefit is reported on the December 31, 2018 statement of financial position as a **deferred tax asset**.

Cunningham's temporary difference originates in one period (2018) and reverses over two periods (2019 and 2020). This situation is diagrammed in Illustration 18-13.

Illustration 18-13

Reversal of Temporary Difference, Cunningham Inc.

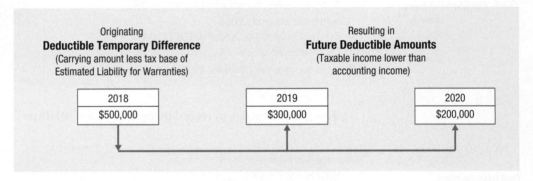

Calculation of Deferred Tax Assets

A **deferred tax asset** or **future income tax asset** is the future tax consequence of a **deductible temporary difference**. In other words, it represents the reduction in taxes payable or the increase in taxes refundable in future years as a result of a deductible temporary difference that exists at the end of the current year.[8]

To illustrate the deferred tax asset and income tax benefit, we continue with the Cunningham example. The warranty expense recognized on the income statement in 2018 is not deductible for tax purposes until the period when the actual warranty expenditures are incurred. Therefore, a deduction will be allowed for tax purposes in 2019 and again in 2020 as the liability for warranties is settled, causing taxable income in those years to be lower than accounting income. The deferred tax asset at the end of 2018 (assuming a 25% tax rate for 2019 and 2020) is calculated in Illustration 18-14.

Illustration 18-14

Calculation of Deferred Tax Asset, End of 2018

Carrying amount of warranty liability	$500,000
Tax base of warranty liability	–0–
Deductible temporary difference at the end of 2018	500,000
Future tax rate	25%
Deferred tax asset at the end of 2018	$125,000

Another way to calculate the deferred tax asset is to prepare a schedule like the one in Illustration 18-15. It shows the deductible amounts that are scheduled for the future as a result of the deductible temporary difference.

	Future Years		
	2019	2020	Total
Future deductible amounts	$300,000	$200,000	$500,000
Future tax rate	25%	25%	
Deferred tax asset at the end of 2015	$ 75,000	$ 50,000	$125,000

Assuming that 2018 is Cunningham's first year of operations and that income tax payable for this year is $600,000, income tax expense is calculated as shown in Illustration 18-16.

Current tax expense, 2018 (given)		
Taxable income × tax rate		$600,000
Deferred tax expense/benefit, 2018		
Deferred tax asset, end of 2018	$125,000	
Less: Deferred tax asset, beginning of 2018	–0–	(125,000)
Income tax expense (total) for 2018		$475,000

UNDERLYING CONCEPT

The tax benefit is only recognized if it is more likely than not that the company will be able to benefit from the deductions in the future.

The deferred tax benefit of $125,000 results from the increase in the deferred tax asset from the beginning to the end of the accounting period. The deferred tax benefit captures the fact that the warranty costs are deductible from future taxable income and recognizes this in the accounts in the current period. The total income tax expense of $475,000 on the 2018 income statement is therefore made up of two elements: a current tax expense of $600,000 and the deferred tax benefit of $125,000. The following journal entries are therefore made at the end of 2018 to recognize income taxes:

A = L + SE
    +600,000 −600,000

Cash flows: No effect

Current Tax Expense	600,000	
Income Tax Payable		600,000

A = L + SE
+125,000   +125,000

Cash flows: No effect

Deferred Tax Asset	125,000	
Deferred Tax Benefit		125,000

Assuming warranty costs are incurred in the same amounts that were expected, the liability for warranties at the end of 2019 has a carrying amount of $500,000 − $300,000 = $200,000. The tax base of this liability is still $0 and the future deductible amount is now $200,000. Therefore, the deferred tax asset at the end of 2019 is 25% of $200,000, or $50,000. Assuming the income tax payable for 2019 is $440,000, income tax expense for the year is calculated as shown in Illustration 18-17.

Current tax expense, 2019 (given)		
Taxable income × tax rate		$440,000
Deferred tax expense/benefit, 2019		
Deferred tax asset, end of 2019	$ 50,000	
Less: Deferred tax asset, beginning of 2019	(125,000)	75,000
Income tax expense (total) for 2019		$515,000

As expected, a reduction in the Deferred Tax Asset account, as with assets in general, results in an increase in the expense to be recognized. The journal entries to record income taxes in 2019 are:

A = L + SE
+440,000 −440,000
Cash flows: No effect

| Current Tax Expense | 440,000 | |
| Income Tax Payable | | 440,000 |

A = L + SE
−75,000 −75,000
Cash flows: No effect

| Deferred Tax Expense | 75,000 | |
| Deferred Tax Asset | | 75,000 |

The total income tax expense of $515,000 on the income statement for 2019 is made up of two parts: a current expense of $440,000 and a deferred tax expense of $75,000.

You may have noticed that the deferred tax expense of $75,000 that is recognized in 2019 **is not related to future events at all.** In this case, it represents the reversal of a deferred tax benefit that originated in a prior year. The deferred tax expense or benefit measures the change in the Deferred Tax Liability or Deferred Tax Asset account over the period. It is a combination of originating and reversing temporary differences, changing tax rates, and other events discussed later in this chapter.

At the end of 2020, the Deferred Tax Asset balance is further reduced by $50,000, as shown in the T account in Illustration 18-18. Deferred tax expense in 2020 is $50,000.

Illustration 18-18

Deferred Tax Asset Account after Reversals

Deferred Tax Asset			
2018	125,000		
		75,000	2019
		50,000	2020
Balance	−0−		

WHAT DO THE NUMBERS MEAN?

Some analysts dismiss deferred tax assets and deferred tax liabilities when they assess a company's financial position. However, these accounts meet the conditions set out in the conceptual framework to be recognized as assets and liabilities.

Deferred Tax Asset	Deferred Tax Liability
1. It contributes to future net cash flows.	1. It is an obligation.
2. Access to the benefit is controlled by the entity.	2. It represents a future sacrifice of economic resources.
3. It results from a past transaction or event.	3. It results from a past transaction or event.

A study by B. Ayers found that the market views deferred tax assets and liabilities in much the same way as it views other assets and liabilities, and that FASB's SFAS No. 109 increased the usefulness of future tax amounts in financial statements.

In addition, the reaction of market analysts to the write-off of deferred taxes in the past supports treating them as assets, as does management's treatment of them. When **Air Canada** ran into financial problems, it reduced its $400-million balance in its future income tax asset account at the end of one year to zero at the end of the next year. The reason? Because the airline was not sure that it would be able to generate enough taxable income in the future, its ability to realize any benefits from future deductible amounts was questionable. Like other assets with uncertain benefits, this asset was written down.

Sources: B. Ayers, "Deferred Tax Accounting Under SFAS No. 109: An Empirical Investigation of Its Incremental Value-Relevance Relative to APB No. 11," *The Accounting Review* (April 1998); "Air Canada Reports Final Year 2002 and Fourth Quarter Financial Results," company news release, May 13, 2003; John R. Graham, Jana S. Raedy, and Douglas A. Shackelford, "Research in Accounting for Income Taxes," *Journal of Accounting and Economics* (March 2011).

Income Tax Accounting Objectives and Analyses of Temporary Deductible Differences

Income Tax Accounting Objectives

Objective 5
Prepare analyses of deferred tax balances and record deferred tax expense.

One objective of accounting for income taxes is to recognize the amount of tax that is payable or refundable for the current year. In Chelsea Inc.'s case, income tax payable is $10,000 for 2017.

A second objective is **interperiod tax allocation**: to recognize the tax effects in the accounting period when the transactions and events are recognized for financial reporting purposes. We saw how this was achieved in the Cunningham example. Accounting for the effect of deferred taxes on the statement of financial position in this way is what underlies the **temporary difference approach**, also known as the **future income taxes method**. The following table illustrates how the statement of financial position amount reported for the warranty liability mirrors the net future cash outflows of Cunningham.

Deferred Tax Asset	End of 2018	End of 2019
Economic resources needed to settle the obligation:		
Future resources needed to settle the warranty liability	$500,000	$200,000
Future tax savings as liability is settled	125,000	50,000
Net future economic resources needed	$375,000	$150,000
Net liabilities reported on the statement of financial position:		
Warranty liability (in liabilities)	$500,000	$200,000
Deferred tax asset (in assets)	125,000	50,000
Net liabilities reported	$375,000	$150,000

A similar table could be constructed for Chelsea's receivables and deferred tax liability to show that the net amount of these two accounts corresponds to the net cash inflow expected as the receivables are collected.

In addition to ensuring that the statement of financial position amounts faithfully represent economic reality, deferred taxes also affect the amount of income tax expense reported in each year. With interperiod tax allocation, the expense amount is related primarily to the revenues and expenses that are reported on each year's income statement. This is shown in Illustration 18-19 for Chelsea Inc. In some years, total income tax expense is greater than taxes payable, and in others it is less. The net result is to report income tax expense that is based on the income statement amounts—in this case 25% of the accounting income, or $22,500. Deferred taxes affect the tax expense reported in all years where there are originating and reversing differences.

Illustration 18-19

Accounting Income and Total Income Tax Expense

CHELSEA INC.
Financial Reporting of Income Tax Expense

	2017	2018	2019
Revenues	$130,000	$130,000	$130,000
Expenses	60,000	60,000	60,000
Income before income tax	70,000	70,000	70,000
Less income tax expense:			
Current tax expense	10,000	22,500	20,000
Deferred tax expense	7,500	(5,000)	(2,500)
	17,500	17,500	17,500
Net income	$ 52,500	$ 52,500	$ 52,500

Analysis of Multiple Differences Illustrated

REAL WORLD EMPHASIS

As can be seen in the recent financial statements of Canadian public companies, there are a variety of causes of temporary differences that result in deferred tax assets and liabilities. These include differences between the tax base and carrying amounts of plant and equipment, tax loss carryforwards, pension assets and liabilities, share issue costs, intangible assets, site restoration and asset retirement obligations, and goodwill, among others. For example, for the 2014 fiscal year, **Loblaw Companies Limited** recorded deferred tax liabilities totalling $1.9 billion on its consolidated balance sheet. This was partially offset by deferred income tax assets of $0.2 billion. The deferred tax liabilities related primarily to goodwill, intangible assets, and fixed assets temporary differences. The deferred tax assets included amounts recorded for loss carryforwards totalling $181 million.

We will now illustrate the analysis that underlies the accounting for deferred tax accounts on the statement of financial position and deferred tax expense or benefit on the income statement when there are multiple temporary differences. We return to the BT Corporation example used earlier in the chapter to explain current income taxes. You were asked to assume that BT Corporation reports accounting income of $200,000 in each of the years 2017, 2018, and 2019; that the company is subject to a 30% tax rate in each year; and that it has the following differences between income reported on the financial statements and taxable income.

1. For tax purposes, royalty revenue of $18,000 recorded in 2017 is reported over an 18-month period at an equal amount each month as it is collected, beginning January 1, 2018. The entire revenue is recognized for financial reporting purposes in 2017.

2. A premium of $5,000 is paid in each of 2018 and 2019 for life insurance that the company carries on key officers. This is a non-deductible expense for tax purposes, but is considered a business expense for accounting purposes.

3. A warranty with an associated expense of $30,000, provided on sales in 2017, was recognized in the same year. It was expected that $20,000 of the warranty work would be performed in 2018 and $10,000 in 2019, and this is what actually happened.

The calculations of taxable income and current tax expense are shown in Illustrations 18-5 and 18-6. We now continue with the example to see how this information affects the statement of financial position and deferred tax assets and liabilities.

All differences between the accounting income and taxable income are considered in reconciling the income reported on the financial statements to taxable income. However, **only those that result in temporary differences are considered when determining deferred tax amounts for the statement of financial position.** When there are multiple differences, a schedule is prepared of the statement of financial position accounts whose carrying amounts and tax bases are different.

For BT Corporation, the royalty revenue from 2017 resulted in an $18,000 difference between the carrying amount and the tax base of its accounts receivable at the end of 2017. The sale and receivable were recognized in 2017, but no payments were received until 2018; no amounts were included in taxable income in 2017. The receivable's tax value is therefore $0. Another way to look at this is that, for tax purposes, neither the account receivable nor the royalty revenue has been recognized.

The life insurance premium expense is a permanent difference. It is not reversible and has no deferred tax consequences. Therefore, it is not considered in calculating deferred taxes.

BT Corporation ended 2017 with a warranty liability on its books of $30,000 because none of the actual warranty work had been carried out as at the end of the year. For tax purposes, however, no warranty expense or associated warranty liability has been recognized at December 31, 2017. The liability's tax value is therefore $0.

The company's analysis and calculation of the temporary differences, the net deferred tax asset or liability, and the deferred tax expense or benefit for 2017 are shown in Illustration 18-20. Because the same tax rate is assumed for all periods, calculating the deferred tax asset and liability is simplified. If the tax rate for future years has been legislated at differing rates, it would be better to use a separate schedule to calculate the deferred tax amounts as set out in Illustrations 18-9 and 18-15.

Illustration 18-20

Calculation of Deferred Tax Asset/Liability and Deferred Tax Expense—2017

Statement of Financial Position Account	Tax Base	−	Carrying Amount	=	(Taxable) Deductible Temporary Difference	×	Tax Rate	=	Deferred Tax Asset (Liability)
Accounts receivable	$-0-		$18,000		$(18,000)		.30		$(5,400)
Warranty liability	-0-		(30,000)		30,000		.30		9,000
Net deferred tax asset, December 31, 2017									3,600
Net deferred tax asset (liability) before adjustment									-0-
Increase in deferred tax asset, and deferred tax benefit, 2017									$3,600

In 2017, BT has two originating differences that result in temporary differences. One results in a deferred tax asset and the other in a deferred tax liability. While separate entries could be made to each of these accounts, the analyses and entries in this chapter work with one net account. Statement of financial position presentation is covered later in the chapter. If you find the concept of tax base confusing, it may help to focus on the related temporary difference column in Illustration 18-20 instead. For the accounts receivable, while the $18,000 has already been included in net income, it will only be taxable when the related cash is received. Therefore, in the future, BT will be required to pay tax on the $18,000 (taxable temporary difference). For the warranty, the $30,000 was expensed for accounting purposes but will only be deductible for tax purposes when the repairs are made in the future. Therefore, the $30,000 future tax deduction results in a deductible temporary difference.

The journal entries to record income taxes for 2017, based on the above analysis and the analysis for current tax expense in Illustration 18-6, are:

	A	=	L	+	SE
			+63,600		−63,600

Cash flows: No effect

Current Tax Expense	63,600	
Income Tax Payable (see Illustration 18-6)		63,600

	A	=	L	+	SE
	+3,600				+3,600

Cash flows: No effect

Deferred Tax Asset	3,600	
Deferred Tax Benefit		3,600

Illustration 18-21 sets out the analysis of the temporary differences at the end of 2018. The two differences that originated in 2017 have begun to reverse. The account receivable has been reduced to $6,000 at the end of 2018, and the warranty liability outstanding is now only $10,000. Again, as Illustration 18-21 shows, the deferred tax expense or benefit is determined **by the change** in the deferred tax asset or liability account on the statement of financial position.

Illustration 18-21

Calculation of Deferred Tax Asset/Liability and Deferred Tax Expense—2018

Statement of Financial Position Account	Tax Base	−	Carrying Amount	=	(Taxable) Deductible Temporary Difference	×	Tax Rate	=	Deferred Tax Asset (Liability)
Accounts receivable	$-0-		$ 6,000		$ (6,000)		.30		$(1,800)
Warranty liability	-0-		$(10,000)		10,000		.30		3,000
Net deferred tax asset, December 31, 2018									1,200
Less: Net deferred tax asset before adjustment									3,600
Decrease in deferred tax asset, and deferred tax expense, 2018									$2,400

The journal entries to record income taxes at December 31, 2018 are:

	A	=	L	+	SE
			+59,100		−59,100

Cash flows: No effect

Current Tax Expense	59,100	
Income Tax Payable (see Illustration 18-6)		59,100

	A	=	L	+	SE
	−2,400				−2,400

Cash flows: No effect

Deferred Tax Expense	2,400	
Deferred Tax Asset		2,400

As indicated in Illustration 18-22, by the end of 2019, all differences have reversed. This leaves no temporary differences between statement of financial position amounts and tax values.

Illustration 18-22

Calculation of Deferred Tax Asset/Liability and Deferred Tax Expense—2019

Statement of Financial Position Account	Tax Base	–	Carrying Amount	=	(Taxable) Deductible Temporary Difference	×	Tax Rate	=	Deferred Tax Asset (Liability)
Accounts receivable	$-0-		$-0-		$-0-		N/A		$-0-
Warranty liability	-0-		-0-		-0-		N/A		-0-
Net deferred tax asset, December 31, 2019									-0-
Less: Net deferred tax asset before adjustment									1,200
Decrease in deferred tax asset, and deferred tax expense, 2019									$1,200

The journal entries at December 31, 2019 reduce the Deferred Tax Asset account to zero and recognize $1,200 in deferred tax expense for 2019.

A   =   L   +   SE
     +60,300 –60,300

Cash flows: No effect

Current Tax Expense	60,300	
Income Tax Payable (see Illustration 18-6)		60,300

A   =   L   +   SE
–1,200   –1,200

Cash flows: No effect

Deferred Tax Expense	1,200	
Deferred Tax Asset		1,200

Illustration 18-23 provides a summary of the bottom portion of the income statements for BT Corporation for each of the three years.

Illustration 18-23

BT Corporation Income Statements—2017, 2018, and 2019

BT CORPORATION
Income Statements (partial) for the Years

	2017	2018	2019
Income before income tax expense	$200,000	$200,000	$200,000
Less income tax expense:			
Current expense	63,600	59,100	60,300
Deferred expense (benefit)	(3,600)	2,400	1,200
	60,000	61,500	61,500
Net income	$140,000	$138,500	$138,500

Total income tax expense reported in 2017, 2018, and 2019 is $60,000, $61,500, and $61,500, respectively. Although the statutory or enacted rate (the rate set by government legislation) of 30% applies for all three years, the effective rate is 30% for 2017 ($60,000 ÷ $200,000 = 30%) and 30.75% for 2018 and 2019 ($61,500 ÷ $200,000 = 30.75%). The **effective tax rate** is calculated by dividing total income tax expense for the period by the pre-tax income reported on the financial statements. The difference between the enacted and effective rates in 2018 and 2019 of 0.75% in this case is caused by the $5,000 non-deductible life insurance expense ([$5,000 × 0.30] ÷ $200,000).

Objective 6

Explain the effect of multiple tax rates and tax rate changes on income tax accounts, and calculate current and deferred tax amounts when there is a change in substantively enacted tax rates.

Tax Rate Considerations

In the previous illustrations, the enacted tax rate did not change from one year to the next. To calculate the deferred tax account reported on the statement of financial position, the temporary difference was simply multiplied by the current tax rate because it was expected to apply to future years as well. Tax rates do sometimes change, however.

Future Tax Rates

What happens if tax rates (or tax laws) are different for future years? Accounting standards take the position that we should use the income tax rates that are expected to apply when the tax liabilities are settled or tax assets are realized. These would normally be the future tax rates that have been enacted at the statement of financial position date. Accounting standards do recognize, however, that sometimes a **substantively enacted rate** or tax law may be more appropriate.[9]

To illustrate the use of different tax rates, we use the example of Warlen Corp. At the end of 2017, this company has a temporary difference of $300,000, as determined in Illustration 18-24.

Illustration 18-24	
Calculation of Temporary Difference	

Net carrying amount of depreciable assets	$1,000,000
Tax base of depreciable assets (UCC)	700,000
Taxable temporary difference	$ 300,000

This is a **taxable** temporary difference because, to date, Warlen has deducted $300,000 more CCA on its tax returns than it has deducted depreciation expense on its income statements. We know this because the UCC is $300,000 lower than the assets' net carrying amount in the accounts. When Warlen Corp. calculates taxable income in the future, it will have to add back its depreciation expense and deduct a lower amount of CCA. The result will be a taxable income that is higher than the accounting income.

Continuing with this example, assume that the $300,000 will reverse and that the tax rates that are expected to apply in the following years on the resulting taxable amounts are as shown in Illustration 18-25.

Illustration 18-25	
Deferred Tax Liability Based on Future Rates	

	Total	2018	2019	2020	2021	2022
Future taxable amounts	$300,000	$80,000	$70,000	$60,000	$50,000	$40,000
Tax rate		30%	30%	25%	20%	20%
Deferred tax liability	$ 78,000	$24,000	$21,000	$15,000	$10,000	$ 8,000

As indicated, the deferred tax liability is $78,000—the total deferred tax effect of the temporary difference at the end of 2017.

In this example, the income tax rates that are expected to be applied to taxable income are reducing over time. Because of this, the rates used to calculate deferred tax amounts include the tax rate reductions, if it is expected that the company will qualify for the rate reductions in the periods of reversal.[10] The general principle is to use the rates that are expected to apply to the taxable income in the periods when the temporary differences are expected to reverse, provided that the rates are enacted or substantively enacted at the statement of financial position date. The AcSB, IASB, and FASB standards all **do not permit** discounting deferred tax assets and liabilities. That is, companies should **not** take into account the timing of these payments by performing present value calculations.

Revision of Future Tax Rates

When a change in the tax rate is enacted (or substantively enacted) into law, **its effect on the existing Deferred Tax Asset and Deferred Tax Liability accounts is recorded immediately as an adjustment to income tax expense in the period of the change.**

Assume that on September 10, 2017, a new income tax rate is enacted that lowers the corporate rate from 30% to 25%, effective January 1, 2019. To illustrate this change, we use the example of Rostel Corp. If Rostel Corp. has one temporary difference at the beginning of 2017 related to $3 million of excess capital cost allowance, then it has a Deferred Tax Liability account at January 1, 2017 with a balance of $900,000 ($3,000,000 × 30%). If taxable amounts related to this difference are scheduled to increase the taxable income equally in 2018, 2019, and 2020, the deferred tax liability at September 10, 2017 is now $800,000. This is calculated as shown in Illustration 18-26.

Illustration 18-26

Schedule of Future Taxable Amounts and Related Tax Rates

	Total	2018	2019	2020
Future taxable amounts	$3,000,000	$1,000,000	$1,000,000	$1,000,000
Tax rate		30%	25%	25%
Revised deferred tax liability	$ 800,000	$ 300,000	$ 250,000	$ 250,000

An entry is made on September 10, 2017 to recognize the $100,000 decrease ($900,000 − $800,000) in the deferred tax liability:

A = L + SE
      −100,000 +100,000

Cash flows: No effect

| Deferred Tax Liability | 100,000 | |
| Deferred Tax Benefit | | 100,000 |

While ASPE does not require separate disclosure of the future tax expense or benefit due to a change in tax rates, IFRS does.

WHAT DO THE NUMBERS MEAN?

When governments change their income tax rates, the effect on corporate Canada can be a substantial hit or a tax windfall! As an example, the last time the federal, Alberta, and Saskatchewan governments significantly reduced future tax rates, it resulted in tax windfalls for many companies in the oil industry. The federal rate fell from 21% in 2007 to 16.5% in 2011 and 15% in 2012 (and remained at 15% through 2015). Companies reporting large deferred tax liabilities saw immediate reductions as they remeasured these liabilities. These companies reported a concurrent increase in earnings as they took the reduction in the deferred income tax liability into income through a deferred tax benefit. **Husky Energy Inc.**, an integrated energy and energy-related company, for example, indicated that the reduction in tax rates increased its profits for 2007 by $395 million, helping its net earnings increase by 16.8% for the year. (This amount was significantly higher than the 4.5% that it would have increased without the adjustment.) **Canadian Natural Resources Ltd.**, Canada's second-largest independent petroleum producer at the time, recognized a similar gain from the tax rate change, some $864 million, which helped to bring its reported net earnings in 2007 to more than $2.6 billion!

Sources: "Corporation Tax Rates," Canada Revenue Agency, available at www.cra-arc.gc.ca/tx/bsnss/tpcs/crprtns/rts-eng.html; Husky Energy Inc. 2007 annual report; Canadian Natural Resources Ltd. 2007 annual report.

Basic corporate tax rates do not change often, and the current rate is therefore normally used.[11] However, changes in provincial rates, the small business deduction, foreign tax rates, and surcharges on all levels of income affect the effective rate. This may require adjustments to the deferred tax accounts.

To this point in the chapter, we have covered the following topics:

• Recognition and measurement of current tax expense (benefit) and the associated income taxes that are currently payable (receivable). This describes the taxes payable approach to accounting for income taxes.

• Explanation of temporary differences and why deferred tax assets and deferred tax liabilities are required to be recognized and measured under the temporary difference approach, in addition to the current income taxes.

• Recognition and measurement of deferred tax assets and deferred tax liabilities and the associated deferred tax expense or benefit.

• Explanation of the tax rates to use and how changes in the rates are accounted for.

Appendix 18A provides a comprehensive example to help you cement your understanding of the analyses needed to support the income tax entries for the year. The example illustrates interperiod tax allocation with multiple temporary differences and a tax rate change over a two-year period.

INCOME TAX LOSS CARRYOVER BENEFITS

CORPORATE LAW AND CORPORATE TAX 6.1.1

A **loss for income tax purposes** or **tax loss** occurs when the year's tax-deductible expenses and losses exceed the company's taxable revenues and gains. The tax system would be unfair if companies were taxed during profitable periods and received no tax relief during periods of losses. Therefore, a company pays no income tax in a year in which it incurs a tax loss. In addition, the tax laws permit taxpayers to use a tax loss of one year to offset taxable income of other years. This is accomplished through the tax loss carryback and carryforward provisions of income tax legislation, which allow taxpayers to benefit from tax losses—either by recovering taxes that were previously paid or by reducing taxes that will otherwise be payable in the future.

A corporation can choose to carry a tax loss back against taxable income of the immediately preceding three years. This is a **loss carryback**. Alternatively, it can choose to carry losses forward to the 20 years that immediately follow the loss. This is a **loss carryforward**.[12] Or, it may choose to do both. Illustration 18-27 presents a diagram of the carryover periods, assuming a tax loss is incurred in 2017.

Illustration 18-27

Loss Carryback and Carryforward Procedure

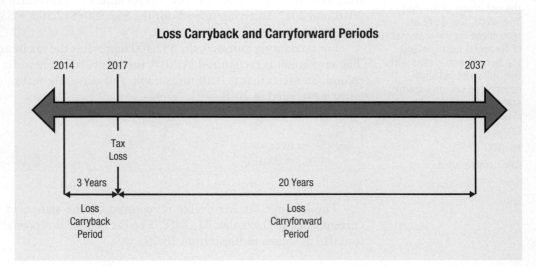

If a loss is carried back, it is usually applied against the earliest available income—2014 in the example above. The **benefit from a loss carryback is the recovery of some or all of the taxes** that were paid in those years. The tax returns for the preceding years are refiled, the current-year tax loss is deducted from the previously reported taxable income, and a revised amount of income tax payable is determined for each year. This figure is then compared with the taxes that were actually paid for each of the preceding years, and the government is asked to refund the difference.

If the full amount of the loss could not be absorbed in the carryback period, **the tax loss can be used to offset taxable income in the future so that taxes for those future years are reduced or eliminated**. The decision on how to use a tax loss depends on factors such as its size, the results of the previous years' operations, past and anticipated future tax rates, and other factors in which management sees the greatest tax advantage.[13]

Tax losses are relatively common and can be large. Companies that have suffered substantial losses are often attractive merger candidates because, in certain cases, the acquirer may use these losses to reduce its taxable income and, therefore, its income taxes. In a sense, a company that has suffered substantial losses may find itself being worth more "dead than alive," meaning that it is worth more when absorbed by another company because of the tax benefit that the acquirer may be able to use.[14]

The following sections discuss the accounting treatment of loss carrybacks and carryforwards.

Loss Carryback Illustrated

Objective 7
Account for a tax loss carryback.

To illustrate the accounting procedures for a tax loss carryback, assume that Groh Inc. has the taxable incomes and losses shown in Illustration 18-28. Assume also that there are no temporary or permanent differences in any year.

Illustration 18-28

Income and Loss Data—Groh Inc.

Year	Taxable Income or Loss	Tax Rate	Tax Paid
2014	$ 75,000	30%	$22,500
2015	50,000	25%	12,500
2016	100,000	30%	30,000
2017	200,000	20%	40,000
2018	(500,000)	—	–0–

UNDERLYING CONCEPT

The income tax receivable from the government meets the definition of an asset. Therefore, the asset is recognized on the statement of financial position and the benefit associated with this inflow of assets is recognized on the income statement.

A	=	L	+	SE
+82,500				+82,500

Cash flows: No effect

In 2018, Groh Inc. incurs a tax loss that it decides to carry back. The carryback is applied first to 2015, the third year preceding the loss year. Any unused loss is then carried back to 2016, and then to 2017. Groh files amended tax returns for each of the years 2015, 2016, and 2017, receiving refunds for the $82,500 ($12,500 + $30,000 + $40,000) of taxes paid in those years.

For accounting purposes, the $82,500 represents the **tax benefit of the loss carryback**. The tax benefit is recognized in 2018, the loss year, because the tax loss gives rise to a tax refund (an asset) that is both measurable and currently realizable. The following journal entry is prepared in 2018:

Income Tax Receivable	82,500	
Current Tax Benefit		82,500

The Income Tax Receivable is reported on the statement of financial position as a current asset at December 31, 2018. The tax benefit is reported on the income statement for 2018 as shown in Illustration 18-29.

Illustration 18-29

Recognition of the Benefit of the Loss Carryback in the Loss Year

GROH INC.	
Income Statement (partial) for 2018	
Income (loss) before income taxes	$(500,000)
Income tax benefit	
Current benefit due to loss carryback	82,500
Net income (loss)	$(417,500)

If the tax loss carried back to the three preceding years is less than the taxable incomes of those three years, the only entry needed is similar to the one above. For Groh Inc., however, the $500,000 tax loss for 2018 is more than the $350,000 in total taxable income from the three preceding years. **The remaining $150,000 loss can therefore be carried forward.** We explain next the accounting for a tax loss carryforward.

Loss Carryforward Illustrated

Objective 8
Account for a tax loss carryforward, including any note disclosures.

If a net operating loss is not fully absorbed through a carryback or if the company decides not to carry the loss back, **the loss can be carried forward for up to 20 years**. Because carryforwards are used to offset expected future taxable income, the tax benefit associated with a loss carryforward is represented by future tax savings: reductions in taxes in the future that would otherwise be payable. In order to actually benefit from this loss, the company must generate future taxable income. In some cases, the ability to do this may be highly uncertain.

The accounting issue, then, is whether the tax benefit of a loss carryforward should be recognized **in the loss year when the potential benefits arise, or in future years when the benefits are actually realized.** IFRS indicates that the potential benefit must be **probable** to recognize an asset. While this term is not defined in the income tax standard, "probable" is defined as **more likely than not** in another IFRS standard, and the IASB agreed that this was its meaning in its joint project on harmonizing tax standards with U.S. GAAP. ASPE (the future income taxes method) maintains that the potential benefit of unused tax losses meets the definition of an asset **to the extent that it is more likely than not that the benefit will be realized.** That is, it is more likely than not that there will be future taxable income against which the losses can be applied.

When it is probable that a tax loss carryforward will result in future economic benefits, it is accounted for in the same way as a deductible temporary difference: a deferred tax asset is recognized in an amount equal to the expected benefit.

Future Taxable Income Probable

To illustrate the accounting for an income tax loss carryforward, we continue with the Groh Inc. example. In 2018, after carrying back as much of the loss as possible to the three preceding years, the company has a $150,000 tax loss available to carry forward. Assuming that it is probable that the company will **generate sufficient taxable income in the future** so that the benefit of the remaining $150,000 loss will be realized, Groh records a deferred tax asset. If a tax rate of 20% applies to future years, the asset recognized is $30,000 ($150,000 × 20%). The journal entries to record the benefits of the carryback and the carryforward in 2018 are as follows:

A   =   L   +   SE
+82,500   +82,500

Cash flows: No effect

To recognize benefit of loss carryback		
Income Tax Receivable	82,500	
Current Tax Benefit		82,500

A   =   L   +   SE
+30,000   +30,000

Cash flows: No effect

To recognize benefit of loss carryback		
Deferred Tax Asset	30,000	
Deferred Tax Benefit		30,000

The Deferred Tax Asset account on the statement of financial position is a measure of the expected future tax savings from the loss, and because this asset is recognized, a $30,000 deferred tax benefit is reported on the income statement. The 2018 income statement appears as shown in Illustration 18-30.

GROH INC. Income Statement (partial) for 2018		
Income (loss) before income taxes		$(500,000)
Income tax benefit		
Current benefit due to loss carryback	$82,500	
Deferred tax benefit due to loss carryforward	30,000	112,500
Net income (loss)		$(387,500)

For 2019, assume that Groh returns to profitability and has taxable income of $200,000 from the year's operations, subject to a 20% tax rate. In this year, then, Groh can deduct the carryforward loss from the 2019 taxable income, and reduce the tax that would otherwise be payable in the year. In other words, in 2019 Groh **realizes** the benefit of the tax loss carryforward that was **recognized** for accounting purposes in 2018. The income tax payable for 2019 is determined in Illustration 18-31.

Taxable income before loss carryforward, 2019	$200,000
Tax loss carryforward deduction	(150,000)
Revised taxable income for 2019	50,000
Tax rate	20%
Income tax payable for 2019 and current tax expense	$ 10,000
Deferred tax asset, opening balance ($150,000 × 0.2)	$ 30,000
Deferred tax asset, December 31, 2019 ($0 × 0.2)	–0–
Deferred tax expense, 2019	$ 30,000

The journal entries to record income taxes for 2019 are:

A = L + SE
    +10,000 –10,000

Cash flows: No effect

Current Tax Expense	10,000	
Income Tax Payable		10,000

A = L + SE
–30,000   –30,000

Cash flows: No effect

Deferred Tax Expense	30,000	
Deferred Tax Asset		30,000

The first entry records income taxes payable for 2019 and, therefore, current tax expense. The second entry records the using up of the tax benefit that was captured as a deferred tax asset the previous year.

The 2019 income statement in Illustration 18-32 shows that the 2019 total income tax expense is based on 2019's reported income. The **benefit of the tax loss** is not reported in 2019. It was already reported in 2018.

GROH INC.
Income Statement (partial) for 2019

Income before income taxes		$200,000
Income tax expense		
Current	$10,000	
Deferred	30,000	40,000
Net income		$160,000

Future Taxable Income Not Probable

Let's return to the Groh Inc. example and 2018. A tax asset (Income Tax Receivable) was recognized in 2018 because Groh knew that the company would receive $82,500 of benefits from $350,000 of the tax loss. This left $150,000 of tax losses to carry forward. We assume now that the company's future profitability is uncertain and that at December 31, 2018 there is not enough evidence that there will be future taxable income to deduct these losses against. Therefore, we cannot recognize the potential tax benefit of the loss carryforward as an asset. In this case, the only 2018 income tax entry is:

A = L + SE
+82,500   +82,500

Cash flows: No effect

Income Tax Receivable	82,500	
Current Tax Benefit		82,500

The presentation in the 2018 income statement in Illustration 18-33 reflects the entry made—**only the benefit related to the loss carryback is recognized**. However, the unrecognized potential tax benefit associated with the remaining $150,000 of tax losses is relevant information for financial statement readers. Therefore, the amounts and expiry dates of unrecognized (unbooked) tax losses are disclosed in the notes to the financial statements. This makes readers aware of the possibility of future benefits (reduced future tax outflows) from the loss, even though the likelihood of realizing these benefits at the reporting date is too uncertain for them to be recognized in the body of the statements.

Illustration 18-33

Recognition of Benefit of Loss Carryback Only

GROH INC. Income Statement (partial) for 2018	
Income (loss) before income taxes	$(500,000)
Income tax benefit	
Current benefit due to loss carryback (see note)	82,500
Net income (loss)	$(417,500)

Note: The company has not recognized any benefits associated with $150,000 of tax losses that are available for carryforward. These will expire by 2038.

Assume now that in 2019 the company performs better than expected, generating taxable income of $200,000 from its annual operations. After applying the $150,000 loss carryforward, tax is payable on only $50,000 of income. With a tax rate of 20%, the following entry is made:

A = L + SE
+10,000 –10,000

Cash flows: No effect

Current Tax Expense	10,000	
Income Tax Payable ($50,000 × 20%)		10,000

This entry recognizes the taxes currently payable in the year. Because the potential tax benefit associated with the loss carryforward **was not recognized in 2018, it is recognized in 2019**, the year it is realized. The $10,000 of current tax expense is actually made up of two components: income taxes of $40,000 accrued on the 2019 income of $200,000, and a $30,000 tax reduction from the realization of the unrecorded loss carryforward. Separate disclosure of the benefit from the loss carried forward is not required under ASPE, but is required under IFRS if it makes up a major component of tax expense.

Illustration 18-34 shows the 2019 income statement.

Illustration 18-34

Recognition of Benefit of Loss Carryforward when Realized

GROH INC. Income Statement (partial) for 2019	
Income before income taxes	$200,000
Current tax expense (note)	10,000
Net income	$190,000

Separate disclosure (under IFRS) would also be required to indicate that current tax expense is reduced by a $30,000 benefit from deducting a previously unrecognized tax loss carryforward.

If 2019's taxable income had been less than $150,000, only a portion of the unrecorded tax loss could have been applied. The entry to record 2019 income taxes would have been similar to the entry above. In addition, a note to the financial statements is provided to disclose the amount and expiry date of the remaining unused loss.

Loss carryforwards can be sizable, even for well-known companies. For example, for its 2014 year end, Air Canada noted that "deferred income tax assets are recognized only to the extent that it is possible that future taxable profit will be available." At December 31, 2014, the airline recorded no income tax assets and disclosed non-capital loss carryforwards of $946 million, most of which only expire in 2028 and 2029!

REAL WORLD EMPHASIS

Carryforward with Valuation Allowance

In the Groh Inc. example above, we assumed that the company's future was uncertain, and that there was not enough evidence that it would be able to benefit from the remaining $150,000 of 2018 tax losses available to be carried forward. As a result, no deferred tax asset was recognized in 2018.

There is an alternative recognition approach to this situation. Under it, a deferred tax asset is recognized for the full amount of the tax effect on the $150,000 loss carryforward, **along with an offsetting valuation allowance**, a contra account to the Deferred Tax Asset account. Because the net effect on the financial statements is the same, this valuation allowance approach is also permitted under ASPE. The valuation allowance approach is not consistent with existing IAS 12 *Income Taxes*. The international standard allows recognition of a deferred tax asset only to the extent that future benefits are probable.

How does a valuation allowance work? Assuming that the entry for the loss carryback has already been made, the following entries recognize the tax effect of the full $150,000 loss carryforward and the valuation allowance to bring the Deferred Tax Asset account to its realizable value of zero at December 31, 2018:

Deferred Tax Asset ($150,000 × 20%)	30,000
Deferred Tax Benefit	30,000

A = L + SE
+30,000   +30,000
Cash flows: No effect

Deferred Tax Expense	30,000
Allowance to Reduce Deferred Tax Asset	
to Expected Realizable Value	30,000

A = L + SE
−30,000   −30,000
Cash flows: No effect

The last entry, which sets up the allowance account, indicates that there is not enough evidence that the company will benefit from the tax loss in the future. The effect on the financial statements is the same whether these two entries are made or the deferred tax asset is not recognized in the accounts at all. The income statement under the allowance approach is identical to the statement provided in Illustration 18-33.

Now assume that the company performs better than expected in 2019, generating taxable income of $200,000. After applying the $150,000 loss carryforward, tax is payable on only $50,000 of income. With a tax rate of 20%, the entry for current taxes is:

Current Tax Expense	10,000
Income Tax Payable ($50,000 × 20%)	10,000

A = L + SE
  +10,000 −10,000
Cash flows: No effect

Because the amount of tax losses available to carry forward to future years has changed, the Deferred Tax Asset account and its valuation allowance are adjusted. In this case, no tax losses remain.

Deferred Tax Expense	30,000
Deferred Tax Asset	30,000

A = L + SE
−30,000   −30,000
Cash flows: No effect

Allowance to Reduce Deferred Tax Asset	
to Expected Realizable Value	30,000
Deferred Tax Benefit	30,000

A = L + SE
+30,000   +30,000
Cash flows: No effect

The deferred tax expense of $30,000 (from adjusting the tax asset account) cancels out the $30,000 deferred tax benefit (from adjusting the allowance account). In this case, the income statement reports only the current tax expense of $10,000, as set out in Illustration 18-34, when neither the tax asset nor the allowance was recognized.

To summarize, IFRS currently requires an "affirmative judgement" approach by recognizing deferred tax assets only to the extent that it is probable that deductible temporary differences, unused tax losses, and income tax reductions will result in a deferred tax benefit. This approach differs from the "impairment approach" recommended by the FASB. The U.S. method recognizes a deferred tax asset for all deductible temporary differences, unused tax losses, and income tax reductions. It **offsets them with an impairment allowance** for the portion of the asset that does not meet the "more likely than not" threshold. ASPE permits either approach. As part of the short-term convergence project between the IASB and the FASB, the IASB had planned to move to the SFAS 109 valuation allowance approach, but this proposed change was not implemented when the IASB decided to narrow the scope of its income tax project in 2010. The IASB continues to consider possible changes to IAS 12, as discussed in the Looking Ahead section at the end of the chapter.

Review of Deferred Tax Asset Account

Objective 9

Explain why the Deferred Tax Asset account is reassessed at the statement of financial position date, and account for the deferred tax asset with and without a valuation allowance account.

Both IFRS and ASPE recommend recognizing a deferred tax asset for most deductible temporary differences and for the carryforward of unused tax losses and other income tax reductions, **to the extent that it is probable that the deferred tax asset will be realized**. In other words, this applies as long as taxable income is more likely than not to be available to apply the deductions against. Consistent with the reporting for all assets, the Deferred Tax Asset account must be reviewed at each reporting date to ensure that its carrying amount is appropriate.

To illustrate, assume that Jensen Corp. has a deductible temporary difference or loss carryforward of \$1 million at the end of its first year of operations. Its tax rate is 20% and a deferred tax asset of \$200,000 (\$1,000,000 × 20%) is recognized because it is more likely than not that enough taxable income will be generated in the future. The journal entry to record the deferred tax benefit and the change in the deferred tax asset is:

A = L + SE
+200,000   +200,000

Cash flows: No effect

Deferred Tax Asset	200,000	
Deferred Tax Benefit		200,000

Let's assume that at the end of the next period, the deductible temporary difference or loss carryforward remains at \$1 million but now only \$750,000 meets the criterion for recognition. In this case, the deferred tax asset is recalculated as 20% of \$750,000, or \$150,000. The entry to be made depends on whether the allowance approach is used or not. Both methods of adjusting the asset account are shown in Illustration 18-35.

Illustration 18-35

Revaluation of Deferred Tax Asset Account

A = L + SE
−50,000   −50,000

Cash flows: No effect

Direct Adjustment			**Allowance Method**		
Deferred Tax Expense	50,000		Deferred Tax Expense	50,000	
Deferred Tax Asset		50,000	Allowance to Reduce		
			Deferred Tax Asset to		
			Expected Realizable Value		50,000

If a valuation account is used, it is reported on the statement of financial position as a deduction from the Deferred Tax Asset account (or is explained in the notes). Regardless of approach, the net amount reported is identical. The accounts are reported within the asset section of the statement of financial position, as shown in Illustration 18-36.

Illustration 18-36

Statement of Financial Position Presentation of Remaining Deferred Tax Asset

Direct Adjustment		**Allowance Method**	
Deferred Tax Asset	\$150,000	Deferred Tax Asset	\$200,000
		Less: Allowance to Reduce	
		Deferred Tax Asset to	
		Expected Realizable Value	(50,000)
		Deferred Tax Asset (net)	\$150,000

At the end of the next period when the deferred tax asset and its realizable value are evaluated, assume it is now more likely than not that $850,000 of the original $1 million will be deductible in the future. This means the tax asset should be reported at $170,000 ($850,000 × 20%). The entry in Illustration 18-37 adjusts the accounts. Notice that a net value of $170,000 means that the allowance needs to be adjusted to $30,000. Once again, the net effect of the two approaches is identical. However, the valuation allowance method has the advantage of retaining the relationship between the Deferred Tax Asset account and the future deductible amounts.

<table>
<tr><td>**Illustration 18-37**</td><td colspan="2">**Direct Adjustment**</td><td colspan="2">**Allowance Method**</td></tr>
<tr><td>*Revaluation of Deferred Tax Asset Account*</td><td>Deferred Tax Asset</td><td>20,000</td><td>Allowance to Reduce Deferred</td><td></td></tr>
<tr><td></td><td>   Deferred Tax Benefit</td><td>   20,000</td><td> Tax Asset to Expected</td><td></td></tr>
<tr><td>A = L + SE
+20,000   +20,000</td><td></td><td></td><td> Realizable Value</td><td>20,000</td></tr>
<tr><td>Cash flows: No effect</td><td></td><td></td><td>   Deferred Tax Benefit</td><td>   20,000</td></tr>
</table>

CORPORATE TAX
6.1.1

The accounting standards offer guidance on how to determine whether it is probable that future taxable income of an appropriate nature, and relating to the same taxable entity and the same tax authority, will be available. The following possible sources of taxable income may be available **under the tax law** to realize a tax benefit for deductible temporary differences, tax loss carryovers, and other tax reductions:

1. Future reversals of existing taxable temporary differences

2. Future taxable income before taking into account reversing temporary differences, tax loss, and other tax reductions

3. Taxable income available in prior carryback years

4. Tax-planning strategies that would, if necessary, be implemented to realize a deferred tax asset. Tax strategies are actions that are prudent and feasible, and that would be applied.

When an entity has a history of recent tax losses, or circumstances are unsettled, or if the carryforward period allowed by tax law is about to expire, it must look for substantive reasons to justify recognition of a tax asset. Both favourable and unfavourable evidence is considered, with more weight attached to objectively verifiable evidence.[15] If the entity concludes that it is not probable that appropriate future taxable income will be available, a deferred tax asset is not recognized or a previously recognized tax asset is removed.

The deferred or future tax asset account is also reviewed to determine whether conditions have changed, because it may now be reasonable to recognize a deferred tax asset that was previously unrecognized. If conditions have changed, the associated tax benefit is recognized in the income statement of the same period. If the entity uses a valuation allowance account, the full deferred tax asset is already included in the account, and it is the allowance that needs to be adjusted (in this case, reduced).

PRESENTATION, DISCLOSURE, AND ANALYSIS

Statement of Financial Position Presentation

Objective 10

Identify and apply the presentation and disclosure requirements for income tax assets and liabilities, and apply intraperiod tax allocation.

Because income taxes have a unique nature, income tax assets and liabilities have to be reported separately from other assets and liabilities on the statement of financial position.

Income Taxes Receivable or Payable Currently

Income tax amounts **currently** receivable or payable are reported separately from **deferred** or **future** tax assets and liabilities. They are reported as current assets or current liabilities, and cannot be netted against one another unless there is a legal right of offset.

UNDERLYING CONCEPT

The principle about netting similar assets and liabilities only when there is a legal right of offset and the intention is to settle them on a net base is applied consistently throughout the accounting standards.

ASPE

This means that the receivable and payable usually have to belong to the same taxable entity, they have to relate to the same tax authority, and the authority has to allow a single net payment. This presentation is the same whether ASPE or IFRS is being applied.

Because corporations are required to make several instalment payments to the Canada Revenue Agency during the year, there could be a debit balance in the Income Tax Payable account. When this occurs, it is reported as a current asset called Prepaid Income Taxes or Income Tax Receivable. An income tax refund resulting from carrying a current year's tax loss back against previous years' taxable income is also reported as an income tax receivable and current asset.

Deferred Tax Assets and Liabilities

The presentation of deferred or future tax asset and liability accounts differs under IFRS and ASPE. The **IFRS requirements** are easier to apply—all deferred tax assets and liabilities are reported as **non-current** items on a classified statement of financial position.

Under ASPE requirements, however, future income tax assets and future income tax liabilities are segregated into current and non-current categories. The classification of an individual future income tax liability or asset **as current or non-current** is determined by **the classification of the asset or liability underlying the specific temporary difference**. Let's see what this means.

Step 1.
What is the classification of the asset or liability that resulted in the tax asset or liability? A tax asset or tax liability caused by a temporary difference in an asset or liability classified as non-current is identified as non-current. A tax asset or tax liability caused by a temporary difference in a current asset or liability account is classified as current. If there is no related asset or liability on the balance sheet, such as with tax losses, the future tax account is classified according to the expected reversal date of the temporary difference: if within 12 months from the reporting date, it is current; otherwise, it is non-current.

Step 2.
Determine the net current amount by netting the various future income tax asset and liability amounts that are classified as current. If the net result is an asset, report it on the balance sheet as a current **asset**; if it is a liability, report it as a current liability.

Step 3.
Determine the net non-current amount by netting the various future income tax assets and liabilities that are classified as non-current. If the net result is an asset, report it on the balance sheet as a non-current asset; if it is a liability, report it as a long-term liability.

To illustrate, assume that K. Scoffi Limited has four future income tax items at December 31, 2018. K. Scoffi reports under ASPE, has chosen to apply the future income taxes payable method of accounting for its income taxes, and operates under a single tax jurisdiction. The analysis in Illustration 18-38 shows how each temporary difference and related future income tax asset or liability is classified.

The future taxes to be classified as "current" net to a $9,000 asset ($42,000 + $12,000 − $45,000), and the future taxes to be classified as "non-current" represent a $214,000 liability. Consequently, K. Scoffi's future taxes will appear on the December 31, 2018 balance sheet as shown in Illustration 18-39.

As indicated earlier, a future income tax asset or liability **may not be related to a specific asset or liability**. One example is research costs that are recognized as expenses in the accounts when they are incurred but deferred and deducted in later years for tax purposes. Another example is a tax loss carryforward. In both cases, a future income tax asset is recognized, but there is no related, identifiable asset or liability for financial reporting purposes. In these situations, future income taxes are classified according to the date the temporary difference is expected to reverse or the tax benefit is expected to be realized.

Temporary Difference Related to:	Resulting Future Tax		Related Balance Sheet Account	Related Balance Sheet Account Classification
	Asset	Liability		
1. **Rent collected in advance:** recognized when earned for accounting purposes and when received for tax purposes	$42,000		Unearned Rent	Current
2. Use of **straight-line depreciation** for accounting purposes and accelerated depreciation for tax purposes		$214,000	Equipment	Non-current
3. Recognition of **revenue** in the period of sale for accounting purposes and during the period of collection for tax purposes		45,000	Accounts Receivable	Current
4. **Warranty liabilities:** recognized for accounting purposes at time of sale; for tax purposes at time paid	12,000		Estimated Liability under Warranties	Current
Totals	$54,000	$259,000		

If K. Scoffi has a single future tax liability account with a balance of $259,000 – $54,000 = $205,000 in it, an analysis similar to this is needed to identify each component.

Illustration 18-39

Balance Sheet Presentation of Future Income Taxes

Current Assets	
Future Income Tax Asset	$9,000
Long-Term Liabilities	
Future Income Tax Liability	$214,000

If K. Scoffi reports as a publicly accountable enterprise under IFRS, one net deferred tax liability of $205,000 is presented as a non-current liability.

Similar to taxes currently receivable or payable, **deferred** or **future** income tax assets and liabilities also cannot be netted against one another unless they relate to the same taxable entity and the same tax authority and there is a legal right to settle or realize them at the same time. This is required whether applying ASPE or international standards.

Income and Other Statement Presentation

Intraperiod tax allocation is the determination of how and where the income tax expense or benefit for the period—for both current and deferred taxes—is reported on the income and other statements that reflect transactions that attract income tax. A good place to start is to understand that the objective is to report the tax cost or benefit in the same place as **the underlying transaction or event that gave rise to the tax.** This means that the current and deferred tax expense (or benefit) of the current period related to **income before discontinued operations, discontinued operations, other comprehensive income, adjustments reported in retained earnings, and capital transactions is reported with the related item.**

To illustrate intraperiod tax allocation, assume that Copy Doctor Inc. has a tax rate of 25% and reports the following pre-tax amounts in 2018:

- A loss from continuing operations of $500,000

- Income from discontinued operations of $900,000, of which $210,000 is not taxable

- An unrealized holding gain of $25,000 on investments accounted for at fair value through other comprehensive income (FV-OCI). Assume that this will be taxable as ordinary income when it is realized.

Illustration 18-40 presents an analysis that is useful in determining how and where the current tax expense or benefit will be reported.

	Continuing Operations	Discontinued Operations	OCI	Total
Accounting income (loss)	$(500,000)	$900,000	$25,000	$425,000
Deduct non-taxable permanent difference		(210,000)		(210,000)
Deduct originating difference: gain taxable when realized			(25,000)	(25,000)
Taxable income	$(500,000)	$690,000	$ –0–	$190,000
Current tax expense expense (benefit) and tax payable at 25%	$(125,000)	$172,500	$ –0–	$ 47,500

Illustration 18-40

Analysis, Intraperiod Tax Allocation—Current Taxes, 2018

Whenever income tax is reported separately so that it appears with a particular component of comprehensive income or in another statement, prepare your analysis by setting up a separate column for each component that attracts tax, as shown in Illustration 18-40. Note that the Canada Revenue Agency is not interested in where the company reports various amounts on the IFRS or ASPE financial statements. It is interested only in the last column of the illustration; that is, in what is taxable in the year and what is not. Based on the analysis, the entry to record current income tax is:

A = L + SE
+47,500 –47,500

Cash flows: No effect

Current Tax Expense—Discontinued Operations	172,500	
Current Tax Benefit		125,000
Income Tax Payable		47,500

Deferred taxes are also allocated to the financial statement items that attract tax. In this case, we assume that the $25,000 temporary difference between the carrying amount of the FV-OCI investments and their tax base is the only temporary difference in this and previous years. Illustration 18-41 shows the calculations to determine deferred taxes.

Illustration 18-41

Analysis, Intraperiod Tax Allocation—Deferred Taxes, 2018

	Continuing Operations	Discontinued Operations	OCI	Total
Taxable temporary difference, Dec. 31, 2018	$–0–	$–0–	$25,000	$25,000
Deferred tax liability at 25% future rate, Dec. 31, 2018	$–0–	$–0–	$ 6,250	$ 6,250
Less deferred tax liability before adjustment	–0–	–0–	–0–	–0–
Deferred tax expense, 2018	$–0–	$–0–	$ 6,250	$ 6,250

The calculations are the same as those earlier in the chapter, with added columns for the different parts of the statements that attract tax. In this example, the only temporary difference is related to an item of other comprehensive income. The tax effect therefore is reported there as well. The entry to record deferred taxes is:

A = L + SE
+6,250 –6,250

Cash flows: No effect

Deferred Tax Expense—OCI	6,250	
Deferred Tax Liability		6,250

Illustration 18-42 shows how the income taxes calculated above are reported in the financial statements along with the items that attract the tax. The tax amounts are taken directly from the entries or the analysis.

Illustration 18-42

*Statement Presentation—
Intraperiod Tax Allocation*

COPY DOCTOR INC.
Income Statement
Year Ended December 31, 2018

Income (loss) from continuing operations before tax	$(500,000)	
Less: Current tax benefit	125,000	$(375,000)
Income from discontinued operations	$ 900,000	
Less: Current tax expense	(172,500)	727,500
Net income		$ 352,500

Statement of Comprehensive Income
Year Ended December 31, 2018

Net income		$352,500
Other comprehensive income:		
Unrealized gains, FV-OCI investments	$25,000	
Less: Deferred tax expense	(6,250)	18,750
Comprehensive income		$371,250

As far as the Copy Doctor example above goes, accounting under IFRS and ASPE is the same. The exception is that ASPE does not include FV-OCI investments, so there would be no separate OCI intraperiod tax allocation. However, there is a difference in how intraperiod allocation is applied when current and deferred taxes relate to transactions recognized in equity (or other comprehensive income) of a prior period. IFRS requires that, where practical, the tax effect in the current year be traced back to where the transaction was originally reported and be presented in the same statement as in the prior period. Under ASPE, income taxes are charged or credited to various equity accounts only for items recognized in the current period. Notice that this difference applies only when there is no current period event or transaction associated with the change in current or deferred taxes.[16]

Disclosure Requirements

Taxes Payable Method

If a company reporting under ASPE chooses the taxes payable accounting policy to report income taxes, a limited amount of information is required to be disclosed:

- The income tax expense or benefit included in determining income (loss) before discontinued operations and the amount related to transactions recognized in equity

- A reconciliation of the actual tax rate or expense or benefit to the statutory amount for income (loss) before discontinued operations, with information about major reconciling items

- The amount of capital gain and other reserves to be included in taxable income in each of the next five years and the amount of unused income tax credits and losses carried forward

These disclosures, while limited, still provide a financial statement reader with significant information about where there are temporary differences and potential increases in taxable income in the medium term.

Future Income Taxes Method

If a company reporting under ASPE chooses the future income taxes accounting policy, again, only limited disclosures are required:

- The amounts of current and of future income tax expense or benefit included in income before discontinued operations and the amount related to capital transactions or transactions recognized in equity

- The amount of unused income tax losses, income tax reductions, and deductible temporary differences for which no future income tax asset is recognized

  In addition, any enterprise reporting under ASPE whose income is not taxed because it is taxable directly to its owners is required to disclose this fact.

  The disclosure situation changes for publicly accountable entities reporting under IFRS. The IFRS requirements are extensive, with the following types of information identified:

- Separate disclosure of the major components of income tax expense or benefit, and the source of both current and deferred taxes

- The amount of current and deferred tax recognized in equity in the period and tax expense for each component of OCI

- A reconciliation of the effective tax rate to the statutory rates for the period and an explanation of changes in the statutory rates relative to the prior period

- Information about unrecognized deferred income tax assets and the underlying deductible temporary differences and unused tax losses, as well as supporting evidence for recognized deferred tax assets

- Information about each type of temporary difference and the deferred tax asset or liability recognized on the statement of financial position

REAL WORLD EMPHASIS

The actual standard, IAS 12 *Income Taxes*, is the best source to refer to for the specific disclosures required for public companies. Excerpts from the 2014 financial statements of **Loblaw Companies Limited** are provided in Illustration 18-43 to show what the disclosures involve. The deferred tax asset and liability accounts on the balance sheets are provided, followed by the company's complete income taxes note, Note 7. Using the bulleted list of required disclosures above, see if you can find the specific information in these excerpts.

Illustration 18-43

Disclosure of Deferred Income Taxes—Loblaw Companies Limited

Consolidated balance sheets as at January 3, 2015 and December 28, 2013

(millions of Canadian dollars)	2014	2013
Assets		
Non-current assets		
Deferred Income Tax Assets (note 7)	193	261
Liabilities and equity		
Non-current liabilities		
Deferred Income Tax Liabilities (note 7)	1,880	34

Note 7. Income Taxes

Income taxes recognized in the consolidated statements of earnings were as follows:

(millions of Canadian dollars)	2014	2013
Current income taxes:		
Current period	$297	$287
Adjustment in respect of prior periods	(18)	(1)
	$279	$286
Origination and reversal of temporary differences	(273)	(50)
Adjustment in respect of prior periods	19	(10)
	(254)	(60)
Income taxes	$ 25	$226

Income tax (recovery) expense recognized in other comprehensive income (loss) was as follows:

(millions of Canadian dollars)	2014	2013
Defined benefit plan actuarial (loss) income	$(16)	$85
Derecognized derivative instrument	—	(2)
Other comprehensive (loss) income	$(16)	$83

(continued)

Illustration 18-43

Disclosure of Deferred Income Taxes—Loblaw Companies Limited (continued)

The effective income tax rate in the consolidated statements of earnings was reported at rates different than the weighted average basic Canadian federal and provincial statutory income tax rates for the following reasons:

	2014	2013
Weighted average basic Canadian federal and provincial statutory income tax rate	26.1%	26.0%
Net increase (decrease) resulting from:		
Effect of tax rate in foreign jurisdictions	(3.2)	(0.6)
Non-deductible items	2.2	1.7
Impact of fair value adjustments of the Trust Unit Liability	5.8	0.8
Impact of statutory income tax rate changes on deferred income tax balances	—	(0.1)
Adjustments in respect of prior periods	1.2	(1.3)
Effective income tax rate applicable to earnings before income taxes	32.1%	26.5%

Unrecognized deferred tax assets Deferred income tax assets were not recognized on the consolidated balance sheet in respect of the following items:

(millions of Canadian dollars)	2014	2013
Deductible temporary differences	$19	$12
Income tax losses	57	29
Unrecognized deferred tax assets	$76	$41

The income tax losses expire in the years 2027 to 2034. The deductible temporary differences do not expire under current income tax legislation. Deferred income tax assets were not recognized in respect of these items because it is not probable that future taxable income will be available to the Company to utilize the benefits.

Recognized deferred tax assets and liabilities Deferred tax assets and liabilities were attributable to the following:

(millions of Canadian dollars)	As at January 3, 2015	As at December 28, 2013
Trade payables and other liabilities	$ 56	$ 48
Other liabilities	347	243
Fixed assets	(517)	(356)
Goodwill and intangible assets	(1,816)	(4)
Other assets	10	38
Non-capital loss carryforwards (expiring 2030 to 2034)	161	201
Capital loss carryforwards	20	1
Other	52	56
Net deferred income tax (liabilities) assets	$(1,687)	$227
Recorded on the consolidated balance sheets as follows:		
Deferred income tax assets	$ 193	$261
Deferred income tax liabilities	(1,880)	(34)
Net deferred income tax (liabilities) assets	$(1,687)	$227

Analysis

The extensive disclosures related to current and deferred taxes are required for several reasons, some of which we now discuss.

Assessment of Quality of Earnings

ETHICS

In trying to assess the quality of a company's earnings, many investors are interested in the reconciliations between accounting and tax numbers. Profits that are improved by a favourable tax effect should be examined carefully, particularly if the tax effect is non-recurring. Accounting for deferred tax assets is an area that requires considerable judgement and may, therefore, be open to abuse. To justify the recognition of deferred tax assets on the statement of financial position and tax benefits on the income statement, it takes only a small amount of optimism for management to expect flows of future taxable income against which to apply tax losses and other future deductible amounts. Valuation of deferred tax assets, either directly or through an adjustment of the valuation allowance account, usually affects bottom-line income on a dollar-for-dollar basis.

REAL WORLD EMPHASIS

A good example of management optimism is the case of **Stelco Inc.**, once a strong Canadian steel producer. In one year, the company's loss of $217 million was reduced by $81 million of deferred income tax benefits, while $139 million of deferred income tax assets were reported on its balance sheet. In the next year, the company's $9 million of income was increased by an $11-million deferred income tax benefit, and $161 million of net deferred income tax assets were reported on the statement of financial position, $74 million of which was classified as a current asset. The future deductible amounts underlying the tax asset accounts were related to the recognition of employee retirement benefit expenses in excess of amounts paid, and income tax losses carried forward.

To have classified $74 million of the deferred income tax asset as a current asset, Stelco's management must have expected the upcoming year to be an excellent one for the company! As it turned out, sales volume and prices were down, costs increased, and the cash position deteriorated, resulting in Stelco obtaining an order to launch a court-supervised restructuring under the Companies' Creditors Arrangement Act (CCAA). Stelco's operations were eventually taken over by **U.S. Steel Corporation**, and as U.S. Steel Canada Inc., it continued to suffer turmoil, including disputes with its employees and the Canadian federal government. It entered into its own CCAA restructuring in September 2014.[17]

Regardless of management's motivations in assessing the value of deferred income tax assets, financial statement readers should be aware of how big a part judgement plays in these measurements.

Better Predictions of Future Cash Flows

FINANCIAL ANALYSIS AND PLANNING
5.1.1

Examining the future portion of income tax expense provides information about whether taxes payable are likely to be higher or lower in the future. A close examination may provide insight into the company's policies on capitalization of costs and revenue recognition, and on other policies that give rise to differences between the accounting income reported and taxable income. As a result, it may be possible to predict upcoming reductions in future income tax liabilities and additional cash required for income tax payments. Such a situation may lead to a loss of liquidity.[18]

REAL WORLD EMPHASIS

From disclosures of the amounts and expiration dates of losses being carried forward, analysts can estimate income that a company may recognize in the future and on which it will pay no income tax. For example, **Versatile Systems Inc.**, a British Columbia company, focuses on software development and sales of computer software, hardware, and system integration services. Versatile reported in its 2014 consolidated financial statements that the company had almost U.S. $39.2 million of tax losses and deductions that it could use to offset future taxable income. Versatile also provided information about when the operating losses expire, the jurisdiction in which the losses are available for carryforward, and the extent to which deferred tax assets are unrecognized.

Outstanding Conceptual Questions

The IASB believes that the temporary difference approach, also known as the asset-liability method, is the most conceptually sound method of accounting for income taxes. This method's objectives are to recognize (1) the amount of taxes payable or refundable for the current year, and (2) tax liabilities and tax assets for the future tax consequences of events that have been recognized in the financial statements or tax returns.

Although this method is considered to be the most appropriate approach for publicly accountable enterprises, some conceptual questions remain.

No Discounting

FINANCIAL ANALYSIS AND PLANNING
5.1.1

Without discounting the asset or liability (that is, by not considering its present value), financial statements do not indicate the appropriate benefit of a tax deferral or the burden of a tax prepayment. This makes it more difficult to compare the financial statements, because a dollar in a short-term deferral is presented as being of the same value as a dollar in a longer-term deferral.

Recognition of Deferred Tax Assets

Some professionals believe that future deductible amounts arising from operating loss carryforwards are different than future deductible amounts arising from other causes. One rationale for this view is that a deferred tax asset arising from normal transactions results in a tax prepayment: a prepaid tax asset. In the case of losses available to carry forward, no tax prepayment has been made. Others argue that realization of a loss carryforward is less likely and thus should require a more severe test than for a net deductible amount arising from normal operations.

These controversies exist within the temporary difference approach. Others argue that a completely different type of approach should be used to report deferred taxes. In addition, some involved in the IASB conceptual framework project suggest removing the criterion of "probability" from the definition of both an asset and a liability and incorporating it in the measurement of the elements instead. Questions arise about whether deferred tax liabilities are, in fact, "present obligations." And, are deferred tax assets really "present economic resources"? If these new concepts are applied to the asset-liability approach to income taxes, it is likely that different recognition and measurement decisions will result.

IFRS/ASPE Comparison

Objective 11

Identify the major differences between IFRS and ASPE for income taxes.

A Comparison of IFRS and ASPE

While other differences exist between IFRS and ASPE than those indicated in Illustration 18-44, many relate to complexities in income tax accounting that are beyond the scope of this text.

Illustration 18-44

IFRS and ASPE Comparison Chart

	IFRS—IAS 12		Accounting Standards for Private Enterprises (ASPE)—*CPA Canada Handbook*, Part II, Section 3465		References to Related Illustrations and Select Brief Exercises
Scope, definitions, and terminology	Terminology used: • Accounting profit • Taxable profit (tax loss) • Deferred tax	• Tax expense (tax income) • Tax base • Probable	Terminology used: • Accounting income • Taxable income (taxable loss) • Future income tax	• Tax expense (tax benefit) • Tax basis • More than likely	
Recognition	No choice is permitted. All companies apply the temporary difference approach, very similar to the ASPE future income taxes approach.		A company chooses either the taxes payable method or the future income taxes method as its accounting policy. The future income taxes method is also known as the asset and liability approach and the temporary difference approach.		Illustrations 18-6, 18-20, 18-21, 18-22, 18-23 BE18-3 and BE18-24
	A deferred tax asset is permitted to be recognized only to the extent that it is probable that it will be realized in the future. A valuation account is not used.		A future income tax asset is permitted to be recognized for all deductible temporary differences, unused tax losses, and income tax reductions. For presentation purposes,		Illustrations 18-35, 18-36, and 18-37 BE18-16, BE18-17, and BE18-18

(continued)

	IFRS—IAS 12	Accounting Standards for Private Enterprises (ASPE)—*CPA Canada Handbook*, Part II, Section 3465	References to Related Illustrations and Select Brief Exercises
		a valuation allowance is permitted to be used to bring the future income tax asset to the amount that is more likely than not to be realized in the future.	
Presentation	All deferred tax asset and liability accounts are classified as non-current.	Future income tax assets and liabilities are classified as current or non-current based on the classification of the underlying asset or liability that resulted in the future income tax amount. When there is no related balance sheet account, the classification is based on when the temporary difference is expected to reverse.	Illustrations 18-38, 18-39, 18A-5, and 18A-6 BE18-23
Disclosure	Considerably more information is required to be reported under IFRS, including details that explain changes in most tax-related accounts, the reasons for temporary differences, and a breakdown of major components of deferred tax expense for the period.	Less information is required to be disclosed under both the taxes payable and future income taxes methods of accounting for income taxes than is required under the IFRS approach.	Illustration 18-43
	There is no similar disclosure requirement.	An enterprise whose income is not taxed because it is taxed directly to its owners is required to identify this situation.	N/A

Looking Ahead

In March 2009, the IASB issued an Exposure Draft (ED) of a standard to replace IAS 12 *Income Taxes*. The intent was to eliminate many of the differences between the IFRS and FASB standards. The 2009 ED also dealt with accounting for **uncertain tax positions**; that is, how to handle uncertainty in tax measurements. In December 2010, the IASB decided to narrow the scope of the income tax project, but left open the possibility that a fundamental review of the accounting for income taxes could be part of a future consultation process.

In August 2014, the IASB issued an ED that proposed amendments to IAS 12 entitled "Recognition of Deferred Tax Assets for Unrealized Losses" that clarifies the recognition of deferred tax assets that relate to debt instruments measured at fair value. In July 2015, the IASB indicated that it planned to issue the final amendments to IAS 12 related to the August 2014 ED by the end of 2015, with a January 1, 2017 effective date. In October 2015 the IASB issued a draft IFRIC interpretation titled "Uncertainty over Income Tax Treatments." The IFRIC suggests that uncertain tax treatments (that, for example, give rise to a tax reassessment by the CRA) should be based on whether or not it is probable that the CRA or other tax authority will accept the proposed tax treatment. The IASB noted in its 2015 work plan that IAS 12 has been criticized as being "difficult to understand," resulting in "many problems in practice." In addition, it launched a research project in 2015 with a goal of better understanding the needs of stakeholders regarding income taxes. This leaves the process open for further changes to accounting requirements for income taxes.

SUMMARY OF LEARNING OBJECTIVES

1 Understand the importance of income taxes from a business perspective.

When a company decides where to set up its operations, a major consideration is the tax rate that it will face on its profits. The fact that corporate taxes can slow growth may help to explain why governments in Canada have steadily reduced corporate tax rates over time. For example, the combined federal and provincial tax rate declined from an average of approximately 43% to approximately 28% between 2000 and 2015.

2   Explain the difference between accounting income and taxable income, and calculate taxable income and current income taxes.

Accounting income is calculated in accordance with generally accepted accounting principles. Taxable income is calculated in accordance with prescribed tax legislation and regulations. Because tax legislation and GAAP have different objectives, accounting income and taxable income often differ. To calculate taxable income, companies start with their accounting income and then add and deduct items to adjust the GAAP measure of income to what is actually taxable and tax deductible in the period. Current tax expense and income taxes payable are determined by applying the current tax rate to taxable income.

3   Explain what a taxable temporary difference is, determine its amount, and calculate deferred tax liabilities.

A taxable temporary difference is the difference between the carrying amount of an asset or liability and its tax base with the consequence that, when the asset is recovered or the liability is settled in the future for an amount equal to its carrying value, the taxable income of that future period will be increased. Because taxes increase in the future as a result of temporary differences that exist at the SFP date, the future tax consequences of these taxable amounts are recognized in the current period as a deferred tax liability.

4   Explain what a deductible temporary difference is, determine its amount, and calculate deferred tax assets.

A deductible temporary difference is the difference between the carrying amount of an asset or liability and its tax base with the consequence that, when the asset is recovered or the liability is settled in the future for an amount equal to its book value, the taxable income of that future period will be reduced. Because taxes are reduced in the future as a result of temporary differences that exist at the SFP date, the future tax consequences of these deductible amounts are recognized in the current period as a deferred tax asset.

5   Prepare analyses of deferred tax balances and record deferred tax expense.

The following steps are taken: (1) identify all temporary differences between the carrying amounts and tax bases of assets and liabilities at the statement of financial position date; (2) calculate the correct net deferred tax asset or liability balance at the end of the period; (3) compare the balance in the deferred tax asset or liability before the adjustment with the correct balance at the SFP date—the difference is the deferred tax expense/benefit; and (4) make the journal entry, which is based on the change in the amount of the net deferred tax asset or liability.

6   Explain the effect of multiple tax rates and tax rate changes on income tax accounts, and calculate current and deferred tax amounts when there is a change in substantively enacted tax rates.

Tax rates other than the existing rates can be used only when the future tax rates have been enacted into legislation or are substantively enacted. Deferred tax assets and liabilities are measured at the tax rate that applies to the specific future years in which the temporary difference is expected to reverse. When there is a change in the future

tax rate, its effect on the future tax accounts is recognized immediately. The effects are reported as an adjustment to deferred tax expense in the period of the change.

7   Account for a tax loss carryback.

A company may carry a taxable loss back three years and receive refunds to a maximum of the income taxes paid in those years. Because the economic benefits related to the losses carried back are certain, they are recognized in the period of the loss as a tax benefit on the income statement and as an asset (income tax receivable) on the balance sheet.

8   Account for a tax loss carryforward, including any note disclosures.

A post-2009 tax loss can be carried forward and applied against the taxable incomes of the next 20 years. If the economic benefits related to the tax loss are more likely than not to be realized during the carryforward period, they are recognized in the period of the loss as a deferred tax benefit in the income statement and as a deferred tax asset on the statement of financial position. Otherwise, they are not recognized in the financial statements. Alternatively, ASPE also allows the use of a contra valuation allowance account, but this approach is not used under IFRS. Disclosure is required of the amounts of tax loss carryforwards and their expiry dates. If previously unrecorded tax losses are subsequently used to benefit a future period, the benefit is recognized in that future period.

9   Explain why the Deferred Tax Asset account is reassessed at the statement of financial position date, and account for the deferred tax asset with and without a valuation allowance account.

Every asset must be assessed to ensure that it is not reported at an amount higher than the economic benefits that are expected to be received from the use or sale of the asset. The economic benefit to be received from the deferred tax asset is a reduction in deferred taxes payable. If it is unlikely that sufficient taxable income will be generated in the future to allow the future deductions, the income tax asset may have to be written down. If previously unrecognized amounts are now expected to be realizable, a deferred tax asset is recognized. These entries may be made directly to the Deferred Tax Asset account.

10 Identify and apply the presentation and disclosure requirements for income tax assets and liabilities, and apply intraperiod tax allocation.

Under all methods, current income taxes payable or receivable are reported separately as a current liability or current asset. Under IFRS, the deferred tax accounts are all classified as non-current. Current and deferred tax expense is reported separately with income before discontinued operations, discontinued operations, items in OCI, retained earnings, and other capital. Separate disclosure is required of the amounts and expiry dates of unused tax losses, and the amount of deductible temporary differences for which no deferred tax asset has been recognized. Under ASPE and assuming a single tax authority, future income tax assets and liabilities are classified as one net current amount and one net non-current amount based on the classification of the asset or liability to which the temporary difference relates. Other future tax accounts are classified according to when the temporary differences are expected to reverse. ASPE calls for limited disclosures, but under IFRS, additional disclosures are required about temporary differences and unused tax losses, the major components of income tax expense, and the reasons for the difference between the statutory tax rate and the effective rate indicated on the income statement.

11 Identify the major differences between IFRS and ASPE for income taxes.

ASPE allows an accounting policy choice—either the taxes payable method or the future income taxes method—while IFRS requires use of the temporary difference approach (a method consistent with the future income taxes method). The main differences relate to terminology, the statement of financial position classification of deferred/future tax assets and liabilities, use of a valuation allowance, and the extent of disclosure.

KEY TERMS

accounting income, p. 1090
accounting profit, p. 1090
deductible temporary difference, p. 1097
deferred tax assets, p. 1095
deferred tax expense, p. 1095
deferred tax liabilities, p. 1095
effective tax rate, p. 1106
future income tax assets, p. 1095
future income tax expense, p. 1095
future income tax liabilities, p. 1095
future income taxes method, p. 1095
income tax benefit, p. 1099

interperiod tax allocation, p. 1103
intraperiod tax allocation, p. 1118
loss carryback, p. 1109
loss carryforward, p. 1109
loss for income tax purposes, p. 1109
more likely than not, p. 1111
originating difference, p. 1194
permanent differences, p. 1093
probable, p. 1111
reversible differences, p. 1093
substantively enacted rate, p. 1107
tax base/basis, p. 1095

tax base of an asset, p. 1096
tax base of a liability, p. 1096
tax income, p. 1099
tax loss, p. 1109
taxable income, p. 1091
taxable profit, p. 1091
taxable temporary difference, p. 1097
taxes payable method, p. 1095
temporary difference, p. 1097
temporary difference approach, p. 1095
timing differences, p. 1093
valuation allowance, p. 1114

APPENDIX 18A

COMPREHENSIVE ILLUSTRATION

Objective 12

Apply the temporary difference approach (future income taxes method) of accounting for income taxes in a comprehensive situation.

The example below walks you through a comprehensive illustration of an income tax problem with several temporary and permanent differences. It assumes the reporting company either reports under IFRS or applies the future income taxes method under ASPE. The illustration follows one company through two complete years, 2017 and 2018. Study it carefully. It should help cement your understanding of the concepts and procedures presented in the chapter.

First Year of Operations—2017

Allteak Corporation, which began operations early in 2017, makes various products on a contract basis. The company's year end is December 31. Each contract generates a gross profit of $56,000. Some of Allteak's contracts provide for the customer to pay on an instalment basis. In such cases, the customer pays one fifth of the contract revenue in the year of the sale and one fifth in each of the following four years. Gross profit is recognized in the year when the contract is completed for financial reporting purposes (accrual basis) and in the year when cash is collected for tax purposes (cash basis). Information on Allteak's operations for 2017 is as follows:

1. In 2017, the company completed 10 contracts that allow the customer to pay on an instalment basis. The related gross profit of $560,000 on sales of $1.5 million (to be collected at a rate of $300,000 per year beginning in 2017) is recognized for financial reporting purposes, but only $112,000 of gross profit on these sales is reported on the 2017 tax return. Future collections on the related instalment receivables are expected to result in taxable amounts of $112,000 in each of the next four years.

2. At the beginning of 2017, Allteak Corporation purchased depreciable assets with a cost of $540,000. For financial reporting purposes, Allteak depreciates these assets using the straight-line method over a six-year service life with no residual value expected. For tax purposes, the assets fall into CCA Class 8, permitting a 20% rate. For the first year, the half-year rule is applied. Any UCC remaining at the end of 2022 is expected to be tax deductible in that year as a "terminal loss." (A "terminal loss" is the term used by the CRA for the balance remaining in a CCA class at the time when the taxpayer no longer owns any property in that class.) Illustration 18A-1 shows the depreciation and net asset value schedules for both financial reporting and tax purposes.

<table>
<tr><th rowspan="3">Illustration 18A-1</th></tr>
</table>

Depreciation and Net Asset Value Schedules for Financial Reporting and Tax Purposes

| Year | Accounting | | Tax | |
	Depreciation	Carrying Amount, End of Year	CCA	UCC, End of Year
2017	$ 90,000	$450,000	$ 54,000	$486,000
2018	90,000	360,000	97,200	388,800
2019	90,000	270,000	77,760	311,040
2020	90,000	180,000	62,208	248,832
2021	90,000	90,000	49,766	199,066
2022	90,000	—	199,066	—
	$540,000		$540,000	

3. The company guarantees its product for two years from the contract completion date. During 2017, the total product warranty liability accrued for financial reporting purposes was $200,000, and the 2017 expenditures for repairs under the warranty liability were $44,000. The remaining liability of $156,000 is expected to be settled by expenditures of $56,000 in 2018 and $100,000 in 2019.

4. At December 31, 2017, the company accrued non-taxable dividends receivable of $28,000, the only dividend revenue reported for the year.

5. During 2017, non-deductible fines and penalties of $26,000 were paid.

6. The 2017 accounting income before taxes is $412,000.

7. The enacted tax rate for 2017 is 30%, and for 2018 and future years it is 20%.

8. The company is expected to have taxable income in all future years.

Taxable Income, Income Tax Payable, and Current Tax Expense—2017

The first step in determining the company's income tax payable for 2017 is to calculate its taxable income. Each step in this calculation has to be thought through carefully. Remember that you are starting with what is included in the current year's revenues and expenses (the accounting income) and are adjusting this to what the net taxable income amount is. The income taxes levied on the taxable income amount are the taxes payable and also the current tax expense for the year. Illustration 18A-2 shows the results.

Illustration 18A-2

Calculation of Taxable Income and Taxes Payable—2017

Accounting income for 2017	$412,000
Permanent differences:	
Non-taxable revenue—dividends	(28,000)
Non-deductible expenses—fines and penalties	26,000
Reversible differences:	
Deferred gross profit for tax purposes ($560,000 − $112,000)	(448,000)
Depreciation per books in excess of CCA ($90,000 − $54,000)	36,000
Warranty expense per books in excess of amount deductible for tax purposes ($200,000 − $44,000)	156,000
Taxable income for 2017	$154,000
Income tax payable and current tax expense for 2017: $154,000 × 30%	$ 46,200

Deferred Tax Assets and Liabilities at December 31, 2017, and 2017 Deferred Tax Expense

Because deferred tax expense is the difference between the opening and closing balance of the deferred income tax asset or liability account, the next step is to determine the net deferred tax asset or liability at the end of 2017. (The opening balance in this case is $0 because 2017 is the first year of operations.) This represents the net tax effect of all the temporary differences between the carrying amounts and tax bases of related assets and liabilities on December 31, 2017. Illustration 18A-3 summarizes the temporary differences, the deferred tax asset and liability amounts, the correct balance of the net Deferred Tax Liability account at December 31, 2017, and the amount required for the deferred tax expense entry.

Illustration 18A-3

Determination of Deferred Tax Assets, Liabilities, and Deferred Tax Expense—2017

Statement of Financial Position Account	Tax Base	– Carrying Amount	= (Taxable) Deductible Temporary Difference	× Tax Rate	= Deferred Tax Asset (Liability)
Instalments receivable	$752,000	$1,200,000	$(448,000)	.20	$(89,600)
Plant and equipment	486,000	450,000	36,000	.20	7,200
Warranty liability	–0–	(156,000)	156,000	.20	31,200
Net deferred tax liability, December 31, 2017					(51,200)
Net deferred tax asset (liability) before adjustment					–0–
Increase in Deferred Tax Liability account, and deferred tax expense for 2017					$(51,200)

Let's review each step in this illustration. Allteak Corporation recognized all the profit on the 2017 instalment sales in its 2017 income statement. None of the $560,000 of gross profit is deferred for financial reporting purposes. However, only $112,000 of the gross profit is recognized in taxable income. Therefore, the remaining $448,000 ($560,000 – $112,000) of gross profit is deferred for tax purposes, and the taxable temporary difference will be included in taxable income in the future as the outstanding receivables on the sales are collected. The tax base of the Instalment Accounts Receivable account is $752,000. The temporary difference will result in taxable amounts in the future. At the enacted rate of 20%, this will cause an additional $89,600 of income tax to be payable in the future.

The carrying amount of the depreciable assets is $450,000 at the end of 2017, but their undepreciated capital cost, or tax value, is $486,000. Because the company has taken $36,000 **less CCA** than depreciation to the end of 2017, in the future there will be $36,000 **more CCA** deductible for tax purposes than depreciation to be taken on the books. Therefore, the $36,000 is a deductible temporary difference that will cause future taxes to be reduced by $7,200. Comparing the CCA and depreciation schedules (above) over the next few years reveals that in some years (2018, 2022) excess CCA will be claimed, while in others (2019, 2020, and 2021) less CCA than depreciation will be claimed. These net out at December 31, 2017 to $36,000 more CCA than depreciation in the future.

Allteak reports a warranty liability of $156,000 on its December 31, 2017 statement of financial position. This whole amount will be deductible when calculating taxable income in the future when the actual warranty expenditures are made and the liability settled. Because Allteak has not yet recognized the $156,000 of expenses for tax purposes, the tax base of the liability is $0. This third temporary difference, therefore, is a deductible temporary difference and, at a 20% rate, it will result in future tax savings of $31,200.

The key to the analysis is to determine whether taxable income **in a future period will be increased or decreased**. If increased, it is a **taxable** temporary difference; if decreased, it is a **deductible** temporary difference.

The tax effect of each temporary difference is calculated by using the tax rate that applies for each specific future year in which the difference reverses. In this case, because the tax rates for all future years are identical, the deferred tax amounts can be calculated by simply applying the 20% rate to the temporary differences at the end of 2017, as shown in

Illustration 18A-3. If the tax rates for each future year are not the same, a separate schedule setting out when each temporary difference is expected to reverse is needed, such as the one shown in Illustration 18A-4.

		Future Years				
(Taxable) deductible temporary differences	**Total**	**2018**	**2019**	**2020**	**2021**	**2022**
Instalments receivable	$(448,000)	$(112,000)	$(112,000)	$(112,000)	$(112,000)	
Plant and equipment	36,000	7,200	(12,240)	(27,792)	(40,234)	$109,066
Warranty liability	156,000	56,000	100,000			
Net (taxable) deductible amount	$(256,000)	$ (48,800)	$ (24,240)	$(139,792)	$(152,234)	$109,066
Tax rate enacted for year		20%	20%	20%	20%	20%
Net deferred tax asset (liability)	$ (51,200)	$ (9,760)	$ (4,848)	$ (27,958)	$ (30,447)	$ 21,813

Illustration 18A-4

Schedule of Reversals of Temporary Differences at December 31, 2017

Income Tax Accounting Entries—2017

The entries to record current taxes (Illustration 18A-2) and deferred taxes (Illustration 18A-3) for 2017 are:

A = L + SE
     +46,200 −46,200

Cash flows: No effect

Current Tax Expense	46,200	
Income Tax Payable		46,200

A = L + SE
     +51,200 −51,200

Cash flows: No effect

Deferred Tax Expense	51,200	
Deferred Tax Liability		51,200

Financial Statement Presentation—2017

Let's assume that Allteak Corporation reports under IFRS and is a single taxable entity dealing with a single taxation authority. In this case, the company is permitted to net its deferred tax asset of $38,400 ($7,200 + $31,200) and deferred tax liability of $89,600 to report one net deferred tax liability of $51,200 as a non-current liability. Otherwise, the deferred tax asset and the deferred tax liability are reported separately. IFRS does not permit any deferred tax accounts to be reported in current assets or current liabilities.

What if Allteak reports under ASPE? ASPE classifies the future income tax assets and liabilities as current and non-current on the balance sheet based on the classifications of the related assets and liabilities that underlie the temporary differences. They are then summarized into one net current and one net non-current amount (again, assuming a single taxable entity and the same taxation authority). The classification of Allteak Corporation's future tax account at the end of 2017 under ASPE is shown in Illustration 18A-5.

Illustration 18A-5

ASPE Classification of Future Income Tax Asset/Liability Accounts

Balance Sheet Account	Classification of Balance Sheet Account	Future Income Tax Asset (Liability)*	Classification of Future Income Tax Asset (Liability)	
			Current	Non-current
Instalments receivable (deferred gross profit)	Mixed: current and non-current	$(89,600)	$(22,400)	$(67,200)
Plant and equipment	Non-current	7,200		7,200
Warranty liability	Mixed: current and non-current	31,200	11,200	20,000
		$(51,200)	$(11,200)	$(40,000)

*From Illustration 18A-3

For the first temporary difference, the related account whose amount is shown on the statement of financial position is the Instalment Accounts Receivable account. The instalments receivable are classified partially as a current asset and partially as long-term. Because one fourth of the gross profit relates to the receivable due in 2018, this portion of the receivable is a current asset and the current portion of the future income tax liability is $22,400 ($89,600 × ¼). The $67,200 remainder ($89,600 − $22,400) of the future income tax liability is non-current.

The plant and equipment are classified as long-term, so the resulting future income tax asset is classified as non-current. The Warranty Liability account, like the instalment receivables, is split between the current and long-term categories. Our assumption is that $56,000 of the liability is reported as current and the remaining $100,000 as non-current. The current portion of the future income tax asset, therefore, is $11,200 ($56,000 ÷ $156,000 × $31,200). The remainder ($31,200 − $11,200 = $20,000) is non-current.

Under ASPE, using the future income taxes method of accounting for income taxes, the $51,200 net future income tax liability is reported on the balance sheet in two parts. A future income tax liability of $11,200 is reported as a **current liability**, and a future income tax liability of $40,000 is reported as a **long-term liability**. The statement of financial position presentation is shown in Illustration 18A-6 under IFRS and under ASPE. The income statement presentation is the same under both standards.

Illustration 18A-6

Financial Statement Presentation—2017

ALLTEAK CORPORATION		
Statement of Financial Position, December 31, 2017—IFRS Presentation		
Current liabilities		
Income tax payable		$ 46,200
Long-term liabilities		
Deferred tax liability		$ 51,200
Balance Sheet, December 31, 2017—ASPE Presentation		
Current liabilities		
Income tax payable		$ 46,200
Future income tax liability		$ 11,200
Long-term liabilities		
Future income tax liability		$ 40,000
Income Statement, Year Ended December 31, 2017—IFRS and ASPE		
Income before income tax		$412,000
Income tax expense		
Current	$46,200	
Deferred/Future	51,200	97,400
Net income		$314,600

Second Year of Operations—2018

1. During 2018, Allteak Corporation collected one fifth of the original sales price (or one quarter of the outstanding receivable at December 31, 2017) from customers for the receivables arising from contracts completed in 2017. Recovery of the remaining receivables is still expected to result in taxable amounts of $112,000 in each of the following three years.

2. In 2018, the company completed four new contracts with a total selling price of $1 million (to be paid in five equal instalments beginning in 2018), earning a gross profit of $320,000. For financial reporting purposes, the full $320,000 is recognized in 2018. For tax purposes, however, the gross profit is deferred and taken into taxable income as the cash is received; that is, one fifth, or $64,000, in 2018 and one fifth in each of 2019 to 2022.

3. During 2018, Allteak continued to depreciate the assets acquired in 2017 according to the depreciation and CCA schedules in Illustration 18A-1. Therefore, depreciation

expense of $90,000 is reported on the 2018 income statement and CCA of $97,200 is claimed for tax purposes.

4. Information about the product warranty liability and timing of warranty expenditures at the end of 2018 is shown in Illustration 18A-7.

Illustration 18A-7

Warranty Liability and Expenditure Information

Balance of liability at beginning of 2018	$156,000
Accrual of expense reported on the 2018 income statement	180,000
Expenditures related to contracts completed in 2017	(62,000)
Expenditures related to contracts completed in 2018	(50,000)
Balance of liability at end of 2018	$224,000

Estimated timing of warranty expenditures:
$ 94,000 in 2019 on 2017 contracts
   50,000 in 2019 on 2018 contracts
   80,000 in 2020 on 2018 contracts
$224,000

5. During 2018, non-taxable dividend revenue recognized is $24,000.

6. A loss of $172,000 is accrued for financial reporting purposes because of pending litigation. This amount is not tax deductible until the period when the loss is realized, which is estimated to be 2023.

7. Accounting income for 2018 is $504,800.

8. The tax rate in effect for 2018 is 20%; in late December, revised tax rates of 25% were enacted for 2019 and subsequent years.

Remeasurement of Deferred Tax Liability Account because of Tax Rate Change

Whenever new tax rates are substantively enacted that affect the measurement of deferred tax assets and liabilities already on the books, the balances in the deferred tax accounts are restated. This is recognized at the date the rates are changed. In the case of Allteak Corporation, the rates were increased in late December 2018; therefore, this is when the adjusting entry is made. The remeasurement is carried out on the temporary differences existing before the rate is changed, in this case those at the beginning of 2018. Illustration 18A-8 indicates how this is done.

Illustration 18A-8

Adjustment for Change in Income Tax Rates

(Taxable) deductible temporary differences	Total	Future Years				
		2018	2019	2020	2021	2022
Net (taxable) deductible amount (from Illustration 18A-4)	$(256,000)	$(48,800)	$(24,240)	$(139,792)	$(152,234)	$109,066
Revised tax rate		20%	25%	25%	25%	25%
Revised net deferred tax asset (liability)	$ (61,560)	$ (9,760)	$ (6,060)	$ (34,948)	$ (38,059)	$ 27,267
Net deferred tax liability before change in rates	(51,200)					
Adjustment: increase in deferred tax liability	$ (10,360)					

The entry to recognize the effect of the change in rates is:

A = L + SE		
+10,360 -10,360		
Cash flows: No effect		

Deferred Tax Expense	10,360	
Deferred Tax Liability		10,360

Taxable Income, Income Tax Payable, and Current Tax Expense—2018

Taxable income, income tax payable, and current tax expense for 2018 are calculated in Illustration 18A-9.

Illustration 18A-9

Calculation of Taxable Income and Taxes Payable—2018

Accounting income for 2018	$504,800
Permanent difference: Non-taxable revenue—dividends	(24,000)
Reversible differences:	
Gross profit on 2017 instalment sales, taxable in 2018	112,000
Deferred gross profit for tax—2018 contracts ($320,000 – $64,000)	(256,000)
CCA in excess of depreciation per books ($97,200 – $90,000)	(7,200)
Deductible warranty expenditures from 2017 contracts	(62,000)
Warranty expense per books—2018 contracts in excess of amount deductible for tax purposes ($180,000 – $50,000)	130,000
Litigation loss accrual per books not deductible in 2018	172,000
Taxable income for 2018	$569,600
Income tax payable and current tax expense for 2018: $569,600 × 20%	$113,920

Deferred Tax Assets and Liabilities at December 31, 2018, and 2018 Deferred Tax Expense

The next step is to determine the correct balance of the net deferred tax asset or liability account at December 31, 2018. The amount required to adjust this account to its correct balance is deferred tax expense/benefit for 2018.

Illustration 18A-10 summarizes the temporary differences at December 31, 2018, the deferred tax effects of these differences, the correct ending balance of the statement of financial position deferred tax account, and the amount required for the deferred tax benefit entry.

Illustration 18A-10

Determination of Deferred Tax Assets, Liabilities, and Deferred Tax Expense/Benefit—2018

Statement of Financial Position Account	Tax Base	–	Carrying Amount	=	(Taxable) Deductible Temporary Difference	×	Tax Rate	=	Deferred Tax Asset (Liability)
Instalments receivable									
–2017 sales	$564,000		$900,000		$(336,000)		.25		$(84,000)
–2018 sales	544,000		800,000		(256,000)		.25		(64,000)
Plant and equipment	388,800		360,000		28,800		.25		7,200
Warranty liability									
–2017 sales	–0–		(94,000)		94,000		.25		23,500
–2018 sales	–0–		(130,000)		130,000		.25		32,500
Litigation liability	–0–		(172,000)		172,000		.25		43,000

Net deferred tax liability, December 31, 2018	(41,800)
Net deferred tax asset (liability) before adjustment ($51,200) + ($10,360)	(61,560)
Decrease in deferred tax liability, and deferred tax benefit for 2018	$ 19,760

The temporary difference caused by deferring the profit on the instalment sales for tax purposes again results in a taxable temporary difference and a deferred tax liability. The company has no deferred profits in the accounts—it has all been recognized in income. For tax purposes, three fifths of the 2017 profit of $560,000 (that is, $336,000) is still deferred at December 31, 2018, while four fifths of the 2018 profit of $320,000 (that is, $256,000) is deferred. These amounts will be taxable and will increase taxable income in the future.

To the end of 2018, $28,800 less CCA has been claimed than depreciation. This can be seen by comparing the book value of the plant and equipment of $360,000 with its UCC or tax base of $388,800 at the same date. In the future, there will be $28,800 more CCA deductible for tax purposes than depreciation taken on the books. This will reduce future taxable income. The temporary difference due to warranty costs will result in deductible amounts in each of 2019 and 2020 as this difference reverses, and the $172,000 loss that is not deductible for tax this year will be deductible in the future.

Again, because the future tax rates are identical for each future year, the deferred tax liability can be calculated by applying the 25% rate to the total of the temporary differences. If instead the rates had been changed to 25% for 2019, 26% for 2020, and 27% thereafter, for example, a schedule similar to the one in Illustration 18A-4 would be prepared.

Income Tax Accounting Entries—2018

The entries to record current and deferred taxes for 2018 are:

A = L + SE
+113,920 −113,920

Cash flows: No effect

Current Tax Expense	113,920	
Current Tax Payable (Illustration 18A-9)		113,920

A = L + SE
−19,760 +19,760

Cash flows: No effect

Deferred Tax Liability (Illustration 18A-10)	19,760	
Deferred Tax Benefit		19,760

Financial Statement Presentation—2018

Continuing the assumptions about Allteak set out above Illustration 18A-5 and the related calculation in Illustration 18A-10, a net deferred tax liability of $41,800 is reported as a non-current liability under IFRS.[19] The ASPE classification of Allteak Corporation's deferred tax account at the end of 2018 is shown in Illustration 18A-11.

Illustration 18A-11	**Balance Sheet Account**	**Classification of Balance Sheet Account**	**Future Income Tax Asset (Liability)***	**Classification of Future Income Tax Asset (Liability)**	
ASPE Classification of Future Income Tax Asset/Liability Accounts				Current	Non-current
	Instalments receivable (deferred gross profit)				
	−2017 sales	Mixed: current and non-current	$(84,000)	$(28,000)	$(56,000)
	−2018 sales	Mixed: current and non-current	(64,000)	(16,000)	(48,000)
	Plant and equipment	Non-current	7,200		7,200
	Warranty liability				
	−2017 sales	Current	23,500	23,500	
	−2018 sales	Mixed: current and non-current	32,500	12,500	20,000
	Litigation liability	Non-current	43,000		43,000
			$(41,800)	$ (8,000)	$(33,800)

*From Illustration 18A-10

The future income tax accounts related to the deferred gross profit follow the statement of financial position classification of the receivables. Of the amounts owed on the 2017 sales, one third will be collected in 2019 so one third of the receivable is reported in current assets. One third of the future income tax liability ($\frac{1}{3} \times \$84,000 = \$28,000$) is also classified as a current item, with the remaining two thirds reported as non-current. The deferred gross profit on the 2018 sales is analyzed the same way—in this case, one quarter is current and three quarters non-current. The warranty liability related to 2017 sales is all expected to be paid within the next year; therefore, it is a current liability on the statement of financial position. The related future income tax asset is also designated as current. Of the $130,000 warranty liability related to the 2018 sales, $50,000 is expected to be met in 2019 and is included in current liabilities. The current portion of the future income tax asset is therefore $12,500 ($50,000 ÷ $130,000 × $32,500), and the remainder is long-term.[20] The litigation liability is reported outside current liabilities and so is its related future income tax account.

Under ASPE, using the future income taxes method of accounting for income taxes, the $41,800 net future income tax liability is reported on the balance sheet in two parts. A future income tax liability of $8,000 is reported as a **current liability**, and a future income tax liability of $33,800 is reported as a **long-term liability**. The statement of financial position presentation is shown in Illustration 18A-12 under IFRS and under ASPE. The income statement presentation is the same under both sets of standards, although there is no ASPE requirement to separately disclose the major components of tax expense other than the current income tax and future income tax expense amounts.

Illustration 18A-12

Financial Statement Presentation—2018

ALLTEAK CORPORATION
Statement of Financial Position, December 31, 2018—IFRS Presentation

Current liabilities	
Income tax payable	$113,920
Long-term liabilities	
Deferred tax liability	$ 41,800

Balance Sheet, December 31, 2018—ASPE Presentation

Current liabilities	
Income tax payable	$113,920
Future income tax liability	$ 8,000
Long-term liabilities	
Future income tax liability	$ 33,800

Income Statement, Year Ended December 31, 2018—IFRS and ASPE

Income before income tax		$504,800
Income tax expense (benefit)		
Current	$113,920	
Deferred/Future (see Note 1)	(9,400)	104,520
Net income		$400,280

Note 1. The deferred/future income tax benefit is the net result of a tax benefit of $19,760 from originating and reversing temporary differences, and a tax expense of $10,360 resulting from a change in tax rates in the year.

SUMMARY OF LEARNING OBJECTIVE FOR APPENDIX 18A

12 Apply the temporary difference approach (future income taxes method) of accounting for income taxes in a comprehensive situation.

In a comprehensive situation, take the following steps. (1) Calculate the current tax expense and payable. (2) Determine the taxable and deductible temporary differences as the difference between the carrying amounts and tax bases of the assets and liabilities; calculate the correct balance of the Deferred Tax Asset or Deferred Tax Liability account. (3) Determine the deferred tax expense as the adjustment needed to the existing statement of financial position balance. (4) Make an adjusting entry to restate the deferred tax asset or liability amounts if a change in the future tax rates has been substantively enacted. (5) Classify the net deferred/future tax asset or liability according to the accounting standards being applied.

Note: Completion of this end-of-chapter material will help develop CPA enabling competencies (such as ethics and professionalism, problem-solving and decision-making, and communication) and technical competencies. We have highlighted selected items with an integration icon and material in *WileyPLUS* has been linked to the competencies. All cases emphasize integration, especially of the enabling competencies. The brief exercises, exercises, and problems generally emphasize problem-solving and decision-making.

In the end-of-chapter material that follows, the simplifying assumption is made that unless otherwise noted all companies follow IFRS and use the term "deferred." If the end-of-chapter material specifically mentions that the company follows ASPE, then the term "future" is used for the income tax accounts related to temporary differences. It is also assumed that where warranties are used as an example of a temporary/timing difference, the company is following the expense warranty approach, and not accounting for the warranty as a separate performance obligation.

Brief Exercises

(LO 1) BE18-1 Faber Corporation is a young start-up technology company with steadily increasing sales in its first six months of operations. Faber's head office is located in a country in Eastern Europe, where the company would be subject to a corporate income tax rate of 28%. Next year, Faber plans to launch international sales of its products in a country in Asia (where the corporate income tax rate is 35%) and one in South America (where the corporate income tax rate is 38%). (a) What is the effect of income taxes on a company's profits? (b) What is the effect of income taxes on a company's cash flows? (c) Considering only the effect of income taxes, in which country should Faber register its company?

FINANCE

(LO 2) BE18-2 In 2017, Noshy Corporation had accounting income of $234,000 and taxable income of $184,000. The difference is due to the use of different depreciation methods for tax and accounting purposes. The tax rate is 25%. Calculate the amount to be reported as income tax payable at December 31, 2017.

(LO 2) BE18-3 Nilson Inc. had accounting income of $156,000 in 2017. Included in the calculation of that amount is the CEO's life insurance expense of $5,000, which is not deductible for tax purposes. In addition, the undepreciated capital cost (UCC) for tax purposes is $14,000 lower than the net carrying amount of the property, plant, and equipment, although the amounts were equal at the beginning of the year. Prepare Nilson's journal entry to record 2017 taxes, assuming IFRS and a tax rate of 25%.

(LO 2) BE18-4 The following information is available for Roginski Corporation for 2017.

1. CCA reported on the 2017 tax return exceeded depreciation reported on the income statement by $160,000. This difference is expected to reverse in equal amounts of $40,000 per year over the period 2018 to 2021.
2. Dividends received from taxable Canadian corporations were $23,000.
3. Rent collected in advance on January 1, 2017 totalled $90,000 for a three-year period. Of this amount, $60,000 was reported as unearned for book purposes at December 31, 2017.
4. The tax rates are 25% for 2017 and 30% for 2018 and subsequent years.
5. Income taxes payable are $200,000 for 2017.

Calculate (a) taxable income and (b) accounting income for 2017.

(LO 2, 3, 5) BE18-5 Mazur Corp. follows IFRS and began operations in 2017 and reported accounting income of $275,000 for the year. Mazur's CCA exceeded its book depreciation by $40,000. Mazur's tax rate for 2017 and years thereafter is 30%. In its December 31, 2017 statement of financial position, what amount of deferred tax liability should be reported?

(LO 2, 5) BE18-6 Using the information from BE18-3, calculate the effective rate of income tax for Nilson Inc. for 2017. Also make a reconciliation from the statutory rate to the effective rate, using percentages.

(LO 2, 5) BE18-7 Myers Corp. purchased depreciable assets costing $30,000 on January 2, 2017. For tax purposes, the company uses CCA in a class that has a 30% rate. For financial reporting purposes, the company uses straight-line depreciation over five years. The enacted tax rate is 25% for all years. This depreciation difference is the only reversing difference the company has. (a) Calculate the amount of capital cost allowance and depreciation expense from 2017 to 2021, as well as the corresponding balances for carrying amount and undepreciated capital cost of the depreciable assets at the end of each of the years 2017 to 2021. (b) Determine the amount of deferred taxes that should be reported in the statement of financial position for each year from 2017 to 2021.

(LO 3, 5) BE18-8 At December 31, 2017, Watzman Inc. owned equipment that had a book value of $178,000 and a tax base of $136,000 due to the use of different depreciation methods for accounting and tax purposes. The enacted tax rate is 30%. Calculate the amount that Watzman should report as a deferred tax liability at December 31, 2017.

(LO 3, 5) **BE18-9**   Using the information from BE18-5, and assuming that the $40,000 difference is the only difference between Mazur's accounting income and taxable income, prepare the journal entry(ies) to record the current tax expense, deferred tax expense, income tax payable, and the deferred tax liability.

(LO 4) **BE18-10**   At December 31, 2017, Camille Corporation had an estimated warranty liability of $256,000 for accounting purposes and $0 for tax purposes. (The warranty costs are not deductible until they are paid.) The tax rate is 25%. Calculate the amount that Camille should report as a deferred tax asset at December 31, 2017.

(LO 4, 5) **BE18-11**   At December 31, 2016, Chai Inc. had a deferred tax asset of $40,000. At December 31, 2017, the deferred tax asset is $62,000. The corporation's 2017 current tax expense is $70,000. What amount should Chai report as total 2017 income tax expense? Prepare the journal entries to record income taxes for 2017.

(LO 5) **BE18-12**   At December 31, 2016, Ambuir Corporation had a deferred tax liability of $35,000. At December 31, 2017, the deferred tax liability is $52,000. The corporation's 2017 current tax expense is $53,000. What amount should Ambuir report as total 2017 income tax expense?

(LO 5, 6) **BE18-13**   Powell Corporation has a taxable temporary difference related to net book value versus UCC of $715,000 at December 31, 2017. This difference will reverse as follows: 2018, $53,000; 2019, $310,000; and 2020, $352,000. Enacted tax rates are 25% for 2018 and 2019, and 30% for 2020. Calculate the amount that Powell should report as a deferred tax asset or liability at December 31, 2017. If the tax rate for 2020 had been 25%, and unexpectedly increased to 30% at the end of 2017, how would the increase in the tax rate for 2020 have affected the deferred tax asset or liability, and the related expense, in 2017?

(LO 4, 6) **BE18-14**   At December 31, 2016, Palden Corporation had a deferred tax asset of $800,000, resulting from future deductible amounts of $3.2 million and an enacted tax rate of 25%. In May 2017, new income tax legislation is signed into law that raises the tax rate to 30% for 2017 and future years. Prepare the journal entry for Palden to adjust the deferred tax account.

(LO 7) **BE18-15**   Roper Corporation had the following tax information:

Year	Taxable Income	Tax Rate	Taxes Paid
2014	$390,000	31%	$120,900
2015	325,000	30%	97,500
2016	400,000	30%	120,000

In 2017, Roper suffered a net operating loss of $550,000, which it decided to carry back. The 2017 enacted tax rate is 25%. Prepare Roper's entry to record the effect of the loss carryback.

(LO 7, 8) **BE18-16**   Kyle Inc. incurred a net operating loss of $580,000 in 2017. Combined income for 2014, 2015, and 2016 was $460,000. The tax rate for all years is 30%. Prepare the journal entries to record the benefits of the carryback and the carryforward, assuming it is more likely than not that the benefits of the loss carryforward will be realized.

(LO 7, 8) **BE18-17**   Use the information for Kyle Inc. given in BE18-16, but assume instead that it is more likely than not that the entire tax loss carryforward will not be realized in future years. Prepare all the journal entries that are necessary at the end of 2017 assuming (a) that Kyle does not use a valuation allowance account, and (b) that Kyle does use a valuation allowance account.

(LO 7, 8, 9) **BE18-18**   Use the information for Kyle Inc. given in BE18-16. Assume now that Kyle earns taxable income of $25,000 in 2018 and that at the end of 2018 there is still too much uncertainty to recognize a deferred tax asset. Prepare all the journal entries that are necessary at the end of 2018 assuming (a) that Kyle does not use a valuation allowance account, and (b) that Kyle does use a valuation allowance account.

(LO 7, 8, 9) **BE18-19**   At December 31, 2017, Tapper Corporation has a deferred tax asset of $420,000. After a careful review of all available evidence, it is determined that it is more likely than not that $85,000 of this deferred tax asset will not be realized. Prepare the necessary journal entry assuming (a) that Tapper does not use a valuation allowance account, and (b) that Tapper does use a valuation allowance account.

(LO 10) **BE18-20**   In 2017, Borovya Limited purchased shares of Gurvir Corp. at a cost of $52,000. This was the first time the company had ever acquired an investment to be accounted for at fair value through other comprehensive income (FV-OCI). At December 31, 2017, the Gurvir Corp. shares had a fair value of $43,000. Borovya Limited's income tax rate is 30%. Assume that any gains that are ultimately realized on the sale of the Gurvir Corp. shares will be taxable as ordinary income when the gains are realized. Prepare the necessary journal entries to record the unrealized loss and the related income taxes in 2017. Prepare the statement of comprehensive income for Borovya Limited, beginning with the line for net income of $60,000. Assume Borovya Limited reports under IFRS.

(LO 10) **BE18-21**   Sandeep Corporation had income before income tax of $230,000 in 2017. Sandeep's current tax expense is $43,000, and deferred tax expense is $27,000. (a) Prepare Sandeep's 2017 income statement, beginning with income before income tax. (b) Calculate Sandeep's effective tax rate.

(LO 10) **BE18-22** Weiss Inc. reported income from continuing operations of $87,000 and a loss from discontinued operations of $16,000 in 2017, all before income taxes. All items are fully taxable and deductible for tax purposes. Prepare the bottom of the income statement for Weiss Inc., beginning with income from continuing operations before income tax. Assume a tax rate of 25%.

(LO 10, 11) **BE18-23** Sonia Corporation has historically followed ASPE, but is considering a change to IFRS. It has temporary differences at December 31, 2017 that result in the following statement of financial position future income tax accounts:

Deferred tax liability, current	$33,000
Deferred tax asset, current	$48,000
Deferred tax liability, non-current	$91,000
Deferred tax asset, non-current	$24,000

Indicate how these balances will be presented in Sonia's December 31, 2017 statement of financial position, assuming (a) that Sonia reports under the ASPE future income taxes method, and (b) that Sonia follows IFRS for reporting purposes.

(LO 11) **BE18-24** Using the information from BE18-3, prepare Nilson's journal entry to record 2017 income tax. Assume a tax rate of 25% and that Nilson uses the taxes payable method of accounting for income taxes under ASPE.

Exercises

(LO 2, 3, 4) **E18-1** (Terminology, Relationships, Calculations, Entries)

Instructions

Complete the following statements by filling in the blanks or choosing the correct answer in parentheses.

(a) In a period in which a taxable temporary difference reverses, the reversal will cause taxable income to be (less than/greater than) accounting income.

(b) In a period in which a deductible temporary difference reverses, the reversal will cause taxable income to be (less than/greater than) accounting income.

(c) If a $76,000 balance in the Deferred Tax Asset account were calculated using a 25% rate, the underlying temporary difference would amount to $ _____.

(d) Deferred taxes (are/are not) recorded to account for permanent differences.

(e) If a taxable temporary difference originates in 2017, it causes taxable income of 2017 to be (less than/greater than) accounting income for 2017.

(f) If total income tax expense is $50,000 and deferred tax expense is $65,000, then the current portion of the total income tax expense is referred to as a current tax (expense/benefit) of $ _____.

(g) If a corporation's tax return shows taxable income of $100,000 for Year 2 and a tax rate of 25%, the amount that will appear on the December 31 Year 2 statement of financial position for "Income tax payable" if the company has made estimated tax payments of $16,500 for Year 2 will be $ _____.

(h) An increase in the Deferred Tax Liability account on the statement of financial position is recorded by a (debit/credit) to the Deferred Tax Expense account.

(i) An income statement that reports current tax expense of $82,000 and a deferred tax benefit of $23,000 will report total income tax expense of $ _____.

(j) Under ASPE, a valuation account may be used whenever it is judged to be more likely than not that a portion of a deferred tax asset (will be/will not be) realized.

(k) If the tax return shows total income taxes due for the period of $75,000 but the income statement shows total income tax expense of $55,000, the difference of $20,000 is referred to as a deferred tax (expense/benefit).

(l) If a company's income tax rate increases, the effect will be to (increase/decrease) the amount of a deferred tax liability and (increase/decrease) the amount of a deferred tax asset.

(m) The difference between the tax base of an asset or liability and its carrying amount is called a _____ difference. Differences between accounting income and taxable income that will reverse in the future are called _____ differences.

(LO 2, 3, 4) **E18-2** (Identifying Reversing and Permanent Differences) The following are independent situations for Bramwell Corp.

1. Estimated warranty costs (covering a three-year warranty) are expensed for financial reporting purposes at the time of sale but deducted for income tax purposes when they are paid.

2. Equity investments have a quoted market value that is recorded at fair value through net income and is adjusted to their fair value at the balance sheet date.

3. The depreciation on equipment is different for book and income tax purposes because of different bases of carrying the asset, which was acquired in a trade-in. The different bases are a result of different rules that are used for book and tax purposes to calculate the cost of assets acquired in a trade-in.

4. A company properly uses the equity method to account for its 30% investment in another taxable Canadian corporation. The investee pays non-taxable dividends that are about 10% of its annual earnings.

5. Management determines that the net realizable value of the inventory is below cost, causing a writedown in the current year.

6. A company reports a contingent loss (ASPE) or provision (IFRS) that it expects will result from an ongoing lawsuit. The loss is not reported on the current year's tax return. Half the loss is a penalty it expects to be charged by the courts. This portion of the loss is not a tax-deductible expenditure, even when it is paid.

7. The company uses the revaluation model for reporting its land and buildings. Due to current economic conditions, the fair value of the properties declined and the writedown was recorded against the revaluation surplus reported in equity.

8. The company settles its retirement obligation on a drilling platform that is put out of service. The actual settlement was less than the amount accrued, and the company recognizes a gain on settlement in its accounting net income.

Instructions

For each of the situations above:

(a) Indicate whether it results in a reversing (timing) difference or a permanent difference in the year. Be sure to note any differences between ASPE and IFRS.

(b) Discuss the nature of any deferred tax accounts that result from the situations in part (a), including their possible classifications in the company's balance sheet. Indicate how these accounts should be reported. Note any differences between IFRS and the asset-liability method under ASPE.

(LO 2, 3, 4) **E18-3 (Identifying Reversing and Permanent Differences; Deferred Tax Liabilities and Deferred Tax Assets)** The following are independent items.

1. The excess amount of a charge to the accounting records (allowance method) over a charge to the tax return (direct writeoff method) for uncollectible receivables.

2. The excess amount of accrued pension expense over the amount paid.

3. The receipt of dividends from a taxable Canadian corporation that are treated as income for accounting purposes but are not subject to tax.

4. Expenses incurred in obtaining tax-exempt income.

5. A trademark that is acquired directly from the government and is capitalized and amortized over subsequent periods for accounting purposes and expensed for tax purposes.

6. A prepaid advertising expense that is deferred for accounting purposes and deducted as an expense for tax purposes.

7. Premiums paid on life insurance of officers (where the corporation is the beneficiary).

8. A penalty paid for filing a late tax return.

9. Proceeds of life insurance policies on lives of officers.

10. Restructuring costs that are recognized as an unusual item on the income statement and are not deductible until actual costs are incurred.

11. Unrealized gains and losses that are recognized on investments, recorded as fair value through net income (FV-NI) or FV-OCI, and are not taxable or deductible until realized for tax purposes.

12. Excess depletion for accounting purposes over the amount taken for tax purposes.

13. The estimated gross profit on a long-term construction contract that is reported in the income statement, with some of the gross profit being deferred for tax purposes.

Instructions

Indicate for each item above if

(a) the situation is a permanent difference or a reversing difference, and

(b) the situation will usually create future taxable amounts resulting in a deferred tax liability, future deductible amounts resulting in a deferred tax asset, or whether it will have no future tax implications.

(LO 2, 4, 5) E18-4 (One Reversing Difference through Three Years, One Rate) Allen Corporation reports the following amounts in its first three years of operations.

	2017	2018	2019
Taxable income	$245,000	$121,000	$125,000
Accounting income	160,000	139,000	131,000

The difference between taxable income and accounting income is due to one reversing difference. The tax rate is 30% for all years and the company expects to continue with profitable operations in the future.

Instructions

(a) For each year, (1) identify the amount of the reversing difference originating or reversing during that year, and (2) indicate the amount of the temporary difference at the end of the year.

(b) Indicate the balance in the related deferred tax account at the end of each year and identify it as a deferred tax asset or liability.

(c) Prepare the journal entries at the end of all three years to record current and deferred taxes.

(LO 2, 3, E18-5 (Intraperiod Tax Allocation—Other Comprehensive Income) Hang Technologies Inc. held a portfolio of
4, 5, 10) shares and bonds that it accounted for using the fair value through other comprehensive income model at December 31, 2017. This was the first year that Hang had purchased investments. In part due to Hang's inexperience, by December 31, 2017, the market value of the portfolio had dropped below its original cost by $28,000. Hang recorded the necessary adjustments at December 31, 2017 and was determined to hold the securities until the unrealized loss of 2017 could be recovered. By December 31, 2018, Hang's goals of recovery had been realized and the original portfolio of shares and bonds had a fair market value $5,500 higher than the original purchase costs. Hang's income tax rate is 30% for all years. Assume that any gains that will ultimately be realized on the sale of the shares and bonds are taxable as ordinary income when they are realized. Hang applies IFRS.

Instructions

(a) Prepare the journal entries at December 31, 2017 to accrue the unrealized loss on Hang's securities and the related income tax.

(b) Prepare the journal entries at December 31, 2018 to accrue the unrealized gain on the securities and the related income tax.

(c) Prepare a comparative statement of comprehensive income for the fiscal years ended December 31, 2017 and 2018. Assume net income of $100,000 in each fiscal year.

(d) Indicate how the deferred tax accounts should be presented on the statement of financial position at December 31, 2018.

(LO 2, 3, E18-6 (Identifying Reversing or Permanent Differences and Showing Effects) The accounting for the items in
4,) the numbered list that follows is commonly different for financial reporting purposes than it is for tax purposes.

1. For financial reporting purposes, the straight-line depreciation method is used for plant assets that have a useful life of 10 years. For tax purposes, the CCA declining-balance method is used with a rate of 20%. (Ignore the half-year rule.)

2. A landlord collects rents in advance. Rents are taxable in the period when they are received.

3. Non-deductible expenses are incurred in obtaining income that is exempt from taxes.

4. Costs of guarantees and warranties are estimated and accrued for financial reporting purposes.

5. Instalment sales are accounted for by the accrual method for financial reporting purposes and the cash basis for tax purposes.

6. For some assets, straight-line depreciation is used for both financial reporting purposes and tax purposes but the assets' lives are shorter for tax purposes.

7. Pension expense is reported on the income statement before it is funded. Pension costs are deductible only when they are funded.

8. Proceeds are received from a life insurance company because of the death of a key officer. (The company carries a policy on key officers.)

9. The company reports dividends received from taxable Canadian corporations as investment income on its income statement, even though the dividends are non-taxable.

10. Estimated losses on pending lawsuits and claims are accrued for financial reporting purposes. These losses are tax deductible in the period(s) when the related liabilities are settled.

11. Security investments accounted for using the FV-NI model are adjusted at the end of the year to their fair value. This is the first year that the company has such investments and the fair value is lower than the cost.

12. An impairment loss is recorded for goodwill in the current accounting period.

Instructions

(a) Match each item in the preceding list to the number below that best describes it:

i. A reversing difference that will result in future deductible amounts and, therefore, will usually give rise to a deferred tax asset

ii. A reversing difference that will result in future taxable amounts and, therefore, will usually give rise to a deferred tax liability

iii. A permanent difference

(b) For each item in the preceding list, indicate if the amounts that are involved in the current year will be added to or deducted from accounting income to arrive at taxable income.

(LO 2, 3, 4, 5, 10) **E18-7** **(Two Reversing Differences, Future Taxable and Deductible Amounts, No Beginning Deferred Taxes, One Tax Rate)** Sayaka Tar and Gravel Ltd. operates a road construction business. In its first year of operations, the company obtained a contract to construct a road for the municipality of Cochrane West, and it is estimated that the project will be completed over a three-year period starting in June 2017. Sayaka uses the percentage-of-completion method of recognizing revenue on its long-term construction contracts. For tax purposes, and in order to postpone the tax on such revenue for as long as possible, Sayaka uses the completed-contract method allowed by the CRA. By its first fiscal year end, the accounts related to the contract had the following balances:

Accounts Receivable	$320,000
Construction in Process	500,000
Revenue from Long-Term Contracts	500,000
Construction Expenses	350,000
Billings on Construction in Process	400,000

The accounts related to the equipment that Sayaka purchased to construct the road had the following balances at the end of the first fiscal year ended December 31, 2017 for accounting and tax purposes:

Equipment	$1,100,000
Accumulated Depreciation—Equipment	170,000
Undepreciated Capital Cost	980,000

Sayaka's tax rate is 25% for 2017 and subsequent years. Income before income tax for the year ended December 31, 2017 was $195,000. Sayaka reports under IFRS.

Instructions

(a) Calculate the deferred tax asset or liability balances at December 31, 2017.

(b) Calculate taxable income and income tax payable for 2017.

(c) Prepare the journal entries to record income taxes for 2017.

(d) Prepare the income statement for 2017, beginning with the line "Income before income tax."

(e) Provide the statement of financial position presentation for any resulting deferred tax balance sheet accounts at December 31, 2017. Be specific about the classification.

(f) Repeat the balance sheet presentation in part (e) assuming Sayaka follows ASPE.

(LO 2, 3, 10, 11, 12) **E18-8** **(Two Reversing Differences, Future Taxable and Deductible Amounts, Beginning Deferred Taxes, One Tax Rate)** Refer to E18-7 for Sayaka Tar and Gravel Ltd., and assume the same facts for the fiscal year ended December 31, 2017. For the second year of operations, Sayaka made progress on the construction of the road for the municipality. The account balances at December 31, 2018 for the construction project and the accounting and tax balances of accounts related to the equipment used for construction follow. (The balances at December 31, 2017 are also listed.)

	2018	2017
Accounts Receivable	$ 105,000	$ 320,000
Construction in Process	940,000	500,000
Revenue from Long-Term Contracts	440,000	500,000
Construction Expenses	410,000	350,000
Billings on Construction in Process	390,000	400,000
Equipment	1,100,000	1,100,000
Accumulated Depreciation—Equipment	460,000	170,000
Undepreciated Capital Cost	620,000	980,000

Sayaka's tax rate continues to be 25% for 2018 and subsequent years. Income before income tax for the year ended December 31, 2018 was $120,000.

Instructions

(a) Calculate the deferred tax asset or liability balances at December 31, 2018.

(b) Calculate taxable income and income tax payable for 2018.

(c) Prepare the journal entries to record income taxes for 2018.

(d) Prepare a comparative income statement for 2017 and 2018, beginning with the line "Income before income tax."

(e) Provide the comparative balance sheet presentation for any resulting deferred tax balance sheet accounts at December 31, 2017 and 2018. Be specific about the classification.

(f) Repeat the balance sheet presentation in part (e) assuming Sayaka follows ASPE.

(LO 2, 3, 6, 10, 12) E18-9   (Two Reversing Differences, Future Taxable and Deductible Amounts, Beginning Deferred Taxes, Change in Tax Rate) Refer to E18-7 for Sayaka Tar and Gravel Ltd., and assume the same facts as in E18-8 for the fiscal year ended December 31, 2018, except that the enacted tax rate for 2019 and subsequent years was reduced to 20% on September 15, 2018.

Instructions

(a) Prepare the journal entry to record the effect of the change in the enacted tax rate.

(b) Calculate any deferred tax balances at December 31, 2018.

(c) Calculate taxable income and income tax payable for 2018.

(d) Prepare the journal entries to record income taxes for 2018.

(e) Prepare a comparative income statement for 2017 and 2018, beginning with the line "Income before income tax" and provide details about the components of income tax expense.

(f) Provide the comparative statement of financial position presentation for any resulting deferred tax balance sheet accounts at December 31, 2017 and 2018. Be specific about the classification.

(g) Repeat the balance sheet presentation in part (f) assuming Sayaka follows ASPE.

(LO 2, 3, 4, 5, 6) E18-10   (Reversing and Permanent Differences, Future Taxable Amount, No Beginning Deferred Taxes) Christina Inc. follows IFRS and accounts for financial instruments based on IFRS 9. Christina holds a variety of investments, some of which are accounted for at fair value through net income and some of which are accounted for at fair value through other comprehensive income. On January 1, 2017, the beginning of the fiscal year, Christina's accounts and records include the following information:

	Cost	Market Value
Fair value through net income investments	$60,000	$60,000
Fair value through other comprehensive income investments	71,000	71,000

Market values for the FV-NI investments and FV-OCI investments at December 31, 2017 were $58,000 and $75,000, respectively. Computers that are used to track investment performance were purchased during 2017 for $10,000. For tax purposes, assume the computers are in Class 10 with a CCA rate of 30%. Depreciation expense for the year was $2,000. Christina recorded meals and entertainment expenses of $24,000 related to "wining and dining" clients. The CRA allows 50% of these costs as a deductible business expense.

Christina's income before income tax for 2017 is $110,000. This amount does not include any entries to adjust investments to market values at December 31, 2017. Christina's tax rate for 2017 is 25%, although changes enacted in tax legislation before December 31, 2017 will result in an increase in this rate to 30% for 2018 and subsequent taxation years. Assume that these rates apply to all income that is reported. There were no deferred tax accounts at January 1, 2017.

Instructions

(a) Prepare journal entries to reflect the difference between the carrying amount and market value for the above investments at Christina's year end of December 31, 2017.

(b) Explain the tax treatment that should be given to the unrealized gains or losses reported on Christina's statement of income and statement of comprehensive income.

(c) Calculate the deferred tax asset or liability balances at December 31, 2017 and indicate their classification.

(d) Calculate taxable income and income tax payable for 2017.

(e) Prepare the journal entries to record income taxes for 2017.

(LO 2, 3,   **E18-11**   **(One Reversing Difference, Future Taxable Amounts, One Rate, No Beginning Deferred Taxes)**
5, 10, 11)   Henry Limited had investments in securities on its statement of financial position for the first time at the end of its fiscal year ended December 31, 2017. Henry reports under IFRS and its investments in securities are to be accounted for at fair value through net income. During 2017, realized losses and gains on the trading of shares and bonds resulted in investment income, which is fully taxable in the year. Henry also accrued unrealized gains at December 31, 2017, which are not taxable until the investment securities are sold. The portfolio of trading securities had an original cost of $314,450 and a fair value on December 31, 2017 of $318,200. The entry recorded by Henry on December 31, 2017 was as follows:

FV-NI Investments	3,750	
Investment Income or Loss		3,750

Income before income tax for Henry was $302,000 for the year ended December 31, 2017. There are no other permanent or reversing differences in arriving at the taxable income for Henry Limited for the fiscal year ended December 31, 2017. The enacted tax rate for 2017 and future years is 30%.

Instructions

(a) Explain the tax treatment that should be given to the unrealized gain that Henry Limited reported on its income statement.

(b) Calculate the deferred tax balance at December 31, 2017.

(c) Calculate the current income tax for the year ended December 31, 2017.

(d) Prepare the journal entries to record income taxes for 2017.

(e) Prepare the income statement for 2017, beginning with the line "Income before income tax."

(f) Provide the statement of financial position presentation for any resulting income tax statement of financial position accounts at December 31, 2017. Be clear on the classification you have chosen and explain your choice.

 (g) Repeat part (f) assuming Henry follows the ASPE future/deferred income taxes method and has chosen the fair value through net income model to account for its securities investments.

(LO 2,   **E18-12**   **(One Reversing Difference, Future Taxable Amounts, One Rate, No Beginning Deferred Taxes)**
3, 5)   Sorpon Corporation purchased equipment very late in 2017. Based on generous capital cost allowance rates provided in the Income Tax Act, Sorpon Corporation claimed CCA on its 2017 tax return but did not record any depreciation because the equipment had not yet been put into use. This temporary difference will reverse and cause taxable amounts of $25,000 in 2018, $30,000 in 2019, and $40,000 in 2020. Sorpon's accounting income for 2017 is $200,000 and the tax rate is 30% for all years. There are no deferred tax accounts at the beginning of 2017.

Instructions

(a) Calculate the deferred tax balance at December 31, 2017.

(b) Calculate taxable income and income tax payable for 2017.

(c) Prepare the journal entries to record income taxes for 2017.

 (d) Prepare the income tax expense section of the income statement for 2017, beginning with the line "Income before income tax."

(LO 2,   **E18-13**   **(One Reversing Difference, Future Taxable Amounts, One Rate, Beginning Deferred Taxes)** Use the
3, 5)   information for Sorpon Corporation in E18-12. Assume that the company reports accounting income of $180,000 in each of 2018 and 2019, and that there are no temporary differences other than the one identified in E18-12.

Instructions

 (a) Calculate the deferred tax balances at December 31, 2018 and 2019.

DIGGING
DEEPER (b) Calculate taxable income and income tax payable for 2018 and 2019.

(c) Prepare the journal entries to record income taxes for 2018 and 2019.

(d) Prepare the income tax expense section of the income statements for 2018 and 2019, beginning with the line "Income before income tax."

(e) What trend do you notice in the amount of net income reported for 2018 and 2019 in part (d)? Is this a coincidence? Explain.

(LO 2, 3,   **E18-14**   **(One Temporary Difference, Future Taxable Amounts, No Beginning Deferred Taxes, Change in**
5, 6)   **Rate)** Use the information for Sorpon Corporation in E18-12. Assume that the company reports accounting income of $180,000 in each of 2018 and 2019, and that there are no reversing differences other than the one identified in E18-12.

In addition, assume now that Sorpon Corporation was informed on December 31, 2018 that the enacted rate for 2019 and subsequent years is 25%.

Instructions

(a) Calculate the deferred tax balances at December 31, 2018 and 2019.

(b) Calculate taxable income and income tax payable for 2018 and 2019.

(c) Prepare the journal entries to record income taxes for 2018 and 2019.

(d) Prepare the income tax expense section of the income statements for 2018 and 2019, beginning with the line "Income before income tax."

(LO 4, 5, 10, 11) **E18-15** **(Permanent and Reversing Differences, Calculating Taxable Income, Entry for Taxes)** Zdon Inc. reports accounting income of $105,000 for 2017, its first year of operations. The following items cause taxable income to be different than income reported on the financial statements.

1. Capital cost allowance (on the tax return) is greater than depreciation on the income statement by $16,000.

2. Rent revenue reported on the tax return is $24,000 higher than rent revenue reported on the income statement.

3. Non-deductible fines appear as an expense of $15,000 on the income statement.

4. Zdon's tax rate is 30% for all years and the company expects to report taxable income in all future years. Zdon reports under IFRS.

Instructions

(a) Calculate taxable income and income tax payable for 2017.

(b) Calculate any deferred tax balances at December 31, 2017.

(c) Prepare the journal entries to record income taxes for 2017.

(d) Prepare the income tax expense section of the income statement for 2017, beginning with the line "Income before income tax."

(e) Reconcile the statutory and effective rates of income tax for 2017.

(f) Provide the statement of financial position presentation for any resulting deferred tax accounts at December 31, 2017. Be specific about the classification.

(g) Repeat part (f) assuming Zdon follows ASPE.

(LO 2, 4, 5) **E18-16** **(One Reversing Difference, Future Deductible Amounts, One Rate, No Beginning Deferred Taxes)** Jenny Corporation recorded warranty accruals as at December 31, 2017 in the amount of $150,000. This reversing difference will cause deductible amounts of $50,000 in 2018, $35,000 in 2019, and $65,000 in 2020. Jenny's accounting income for 2017 is $135,000 and the tax rate is 25% for all years. There are no deferred tax accounts at the beginning of 2017.

Instructions

(a) Calculate the deferred tax balance at December 31, 2017.

(b) Calculate taxable income and current income tax payable for 2017.

(c) Prepare the journal entries to record income taxes for 2017.

(d) Prepare the income tax expense section of the income statement for 2017, beginning with the line "Income before income tax."

(LO 2, 4, 5) **E18-17** **(One Reversing Difference, Future Deductible Amounts, One Rate, Beginning Deferred Taxes)** Use the information for Jenny Corporation in E18-16. Assume that the company reports accounting income of $155,000 in each of 2018 and 2019 and that the warranty expenditures occurred as expected. No reversing difference exists other than the one identified in E18-16.

Instructions

DIGGING DEEPER

(a) Calculate the deferred tax balances at December 31, 2018 and 2019.

(b) Calculate taxable income and income tax payable for 2018 and 2019.

(c) Prepare the journal entries to record income taxes for 2018 and 2019.

(d) Prepare the income tax expense section of the income statements for 2018 and 2019, beginning with the line "Income before income tax."

(e) What trend do you notice in the amount of net income reported for 2018 and 2019 in part (d)? Is this a coincidence? Explain.

(LO 2, 4, 5, 6, 10) **E18-18** **(One Temporary Difference, Future Taxable Amount Becoming Future Deductible Amount, One Rate, Change in Rate)** Refer to the information for Henry Limited in E18-11. Following the year ended December 31, 2017, Henry continued to actively trade its securities investments until the end of its 2018 fiscal year, when it was forced to sell several of them at a loss, because of the need for cash for operations. By December 31, 2018, the portfolio of investments contained a single investment in shares, which was purchased in November 2018. Henry Limited had paid $42,000 for these remaining shares. At December 31, 2018, the shares' market value was $40,000. Income before income tax for Henry was $120,000 for the year ended December 31, 2018. There are no other permanent or reversing/timing differences in arriving at the taxable income for Henry Limited for the fiscal year ended December 31, 2018. The enacted tax rate for 2018 and future years is 30%.

Instructions

(a) Prepare the necessary journal entry for Henry Limited to accrue the unrealized loss on its securities investments.

(b) Explain the tax treatment that should be given to the unrealized accrued loss that Henry Limited reported on its income statement.

(c) Calculate the deferred tax balance at December 31, 2018.

(d) Calculate the current tax expense for the year ended December 31, 2018.

(e) Prepare the journal entries to record income taxes for 2018. Assume that there have been no entries to the ending balances of deferred taxes reported at December 31, 2017.

(f) Prepare the income statement for 2018, beginning with the line "Income before income tax."

(g) Provide the presentation for the statement of financial position for any resulting deferred tax accounts at December 31, 2018. Be clear on the classification you have chosen and explain your choice.

(h) Prepare the journal entries in part (e) under the assumption that, late in 2018, the income tax rate changed to 25% for 2019 and subsequent years.

(i) Repeat the balance sheet presentation in part (g) assuming Henry reports under the ASPE future/deferred income taxes method and has chosen the fair value through net income model to account for its securities investments.

(LO 2, 4, 5, 6) **E18-19** **(One Reversing Difference, Future Deductible Amounts, No Beginning Deferred Taxes, Change in Rate)** Use the information for Jenny Corporation in E18-16. Assume that the company reports accounting income of $155,000 in each of 2018 and 2019, and that there is no reversing difference other than the one identified in E18-16. In addition, assume now that Jenny Corporation was informed on December 31, 2018 that the enacted rate for 2019 and subsequent years is 28%.

Instructions

(a) Calculate the deferred tax balances at December 31, 2018 and 2019.

(b) Calculate taxable income and income tax payable for 2018 and 2019.

(c) Prepare the journal entries to record income taxes for 2018 and 2019.

(d) Prepare the income tax expense section of the income statements for 2018 and 2019, beginning with the line "Income before income tax."

(LO 2, 5, 11) **E18-20** **(Depreciation, Reversing Difference over Five Years, Determining Taxable Income, Taxes Payable Method)** Zak Corp. purchased depreciable assets costing $600,000 on January 2, 2017. For tax purposes, the company uses CCA in a class that has a 40% rate. For financial reporting purposes, the company uses straight-line depreciation over five years. The enacted tax rate is 30% for all years. This depreciation difference is the only reversing difference the company has. Assume that Zak has income before income tax of $340,000 in each of the years 2017 to 2021.

Instructions

(a) Calculate the amount of capital cost allowance and depreciation expense from 2017 to 2021, as well as the corresponding balances for carrying amount and undepreciated capital cost of the depreciable assets at the end of each of the years 2017 to 2021.

(b) Determine the amount of taxable income in each year from 2017 to 2021.

(c) Determine the amount of deferred taxes that should be reported in the statement of financial position for each year from 2017 to 2021.

(d) Prepare the journal entries to record income taxes for each year from 2017 to 2021.

(e) Prepare the income tax entry(ies) to record income taxes for each year, assuming the management and owners have decided on the taxes payable method.

(LO 2, 3, 6, 10, 11) **E18-21** **(Deferred Tax Liability, Change in Tax Rate)** Yen Inc.'s only temporary difference at the beginning and end of 2017 is caused by a $4.8-million deferred gain for tax purposes on an instalment sale of a plant asset. The related receivable (only one half of which is classified as a current asset) is due in equal instalments in 2018 and 2019. The related deferred tax liability at the beginning of the year is $1,440,000. In the third quarter of 2017, a new tax rate of 29% is enacted into law and is scheduled to become effective for 2019. Taxable income is expected in all future years.

Instructions

(a) Determine the amount to be reported as a deferred tax liability at the end of 2017. Indicate its proper classification(s) if Yen Inc. applies ASPE.

(b) Indicate the classification of the Deferred Tax Asset or Deferred Tax Liability account if Yen Inc. applies IFRS.

(c) Prepare the journal entry (if any) that is necessary to adjust the deferred tax liability when the new tax rate is enacted into law.

(LO 2, 5, 6, 10) **E18-22** **(Two Differences, No Beginning Deferred Taxes, Multiple Rates)** Adelphi Corp. in its first year of operations has the following differences between its carrying amounts and the tax bases of its assets and liabilities at the end of 2017.

	Carrying Amount	Tax Basis
Equipment (net)	400,000	340,000
Estimated Warranty Liabilities	200,000	0

It is estimated that the warranty liability will be settled in 2018. The difference in equipment (net) will result in future taxable amounts of $20,000 in 2018, $30,000 in 2019, and $10,000 in 2020. The company has taxable income of $520,000 in 2017. As of the beginning of 2017, the enacted tax rate is 30% for 2017 to 2019 and 25% for 2020. Adelphi expects to report taxable income through 2020.

Instructions

(a) Prepare the journal entry to report current and deferred income tax expense.

(b) Indicate how deferred income taxes would be reported on the statement of financial positon/balance sheet at the end of 2017 under IFRS and ASPE.

(LO 5, 6) **E18-23** **(One Difference, Multiple Rates, Beginning Deferred Taxes, Change in Rates)** At the end of 2016, Valerie Corporation reported a deferred tax liability of $41,000. At the end of 2017, the company had $241,000 of temporary differences related to property, plant, and equipment. Depreciation expense on this property, plant, and equipment has been lower than the CCA claimed on Valerie's income tax returns. The resulting future taxable amounts are as follows:

2018	$ 78,000
2019	62,000
2020	55,000
2021	46,000
	$241,000

The tax rates enacted as of the beginning of 2016 are as follows: 31% for 2016 and 2017; 30% for 2018 and 2019; and 25% for 2020 and later. Taxable income is expected in all future years.

Instructions

(a) Calculate the deferred tax account balance at December 31, 2017.

(b) Prepare the journal entry for Valerie to record deferred taxes for 2017.

(c) Early in 2018, after the 2017 financial statements were released, new tax rates were enacted as follows: 29% for 2018 and 27% for 2019 and later. Prepare the journal entry for Valerie to recognize the change in tax rates.

(LO 6, 7, 8) **E18-24** **(Loss Carryback and Carryforward)** Alliance Inc. reports the following incomes (losses) for both book and tax purposes (assume the carryback provision is used where possible):

Year	Accounting Income (Loss)	Tax Rate
2014	$ 130,000	25%
2015	105,000	25%
2016	(305,000)	30%
2017	50,000	30%

The tax rates listed were all enacted by the beginning of 2014.

Instructions

(a) Prepare the journal entries for each of the years 2014 to 2017 to record income taxes, assuming at December 31, 2016 that it was more likely than not that the company would not be able to benefit from the remaining losses available to carry forward.

(b) Prepare the income tax section of the income statements for each of the years 2014 to 2017, beginning with the line "Income (loss) before income tax."

(LO 6, 7, 8) **E18-25** **(Carryback and Carryforward of Tax Loss)** The accounting income (loss) figures for Farah Corporation are as follows:

2012	$ 160,000
2013	250,000
2014	80,000
2015	(160,000)
2016	(380,000)
2017	130,000
2018	145,000

Accounting income (loss) and taxable income (loss) were the same for all years involved. Assume a 30% tax rate for 2012 and 2013, and a 25% tax rate for the remaining years.

Instructions

Prepare the journal entries for each of the years 2014 to 2018 to record income tax expense and the effects of the tax loss carrybacks and carryforwards, assuming Farah Corporation uses the carryback provision first. All income and losses relate to normal operations and it is more likely than not that the company will generate substantial taxable income in the future.

(LO 6, 7, 8) **E18-26** **(Loss Carryback and Carryforward)** Riley Inc. reports the following pre-tax incomes (losses) for both financial reporting purposes and tax purposes:

Year	Accounting Income (Loss)	Tax Rate
2015	$ 120,000	25%
2016	90,000	25%
2017	(280,000)	30%
2018	220,000	30%

The tax rates listed were all enacted by the beginning of 2015. Riley reports under the ASPE future/deferred income taxes method.

Instructions

(a) Prepare the journal entries for each of the years 2015 to 2018 to record income tax. Assume the tax loss is first carried back and that at the end of 2017, the loss carryforward benefits are judged more likely than not to be realized in the future.

(b) Using the assumptions in part (a), prepare the income tax section of the 2017 and 2018 income statements, beginning with the line "Income (loss) before income tax."

(c) Prepare the journal entries for 2017 and 2018. Assume that it is more likely than not that one quarter of the carryforward benefits will not be realized. This company does not use a valuation allowance.

(d) Using the assumptions in part (c), prepare the income tax section of the 2017 and 2018 income statements, beginning with the line "Income (loss) before income tax."

(e) Using the assumptions in part (c), discuss what information should be disclosed in the notes to the financial statements.

(LO 6, 7, 8, 9, 10) **E18-27** **(Loss Carryback and Carryforward Using a Valuation Allowance)** Refer to the information for Riley Inc. in E18-26.

Instructions

(a) Assume that Riley Inc. uses a valuation allowance to account for deferred tax assets, and also that it is more likely than not that 25% of the carryforward benefits will not be realized. Prepare the journal entries for 2017 and 2018.

(b) Based on your entries in part (a), prepare the income tax section of the 2017 and 2018 income statements, beginning with the line "Income (loss) before income tax."

(c) Indicate how the deferred tax asset account will be reported on the December 31, 2017 and 2018 balance sheets.

DIGGING DEEPER

(d) Assume that on June 30, 2018 the enacted tax rates changed for 2018. Should management record any adjustment to the accounts? If yes, which accounts will be involved and when should the adjustment be recorded?

(e) Repeat part (c) assuming Riley Inc. follows IFRS.

(LO 9) E18-28 **(Deferred Tax Asset—Different Amounts to Be Realized)** Roux Corp. had a Deferred Tax Asset account with a balance of $81,000 at the end of 2016 due to a single temporary difference of $270,000 related to warranty liability accruals. At the end of 2017, this same temporary difference has increased to $300,000. Taxable income for 2017 is $912,000. The tax rate is 30% for all years.

Instructions

(a) Calculate and record income taxes for 2017, assuming that it is more likely than not that the deferred tax asset will be realized.

(b) 1. Assuming it is more likely than not that $25,000 of the deferred tax asset will not be realized, prepare the journal entries to record income taxes for 2017. Roux does not use a valuation allowance account.

2. In 2018, the company's prospects improved. While there was no change in the temporary deductible differences underlying the Deferred Tax Asset account, it was now considered more likely than not that the company would be able to make full use of the temporary differences. Prepare the entry, if applicable, to adjust the Deferred Tax Asset account.

(LO 9) E18-29 **(Deferred Tax Asset—Different Amounts to Be Realized; Valuation Allowance)** Refer to the information provided about Roux Corp. in E18-28.

Instructions

(a) Assuming that it is more likely than not that $25,000 of the deferred tax asset will not be realized, prepare the journal entries to record income taxes for 2017. Roux uses a valuation allowance account.

(b) In 2018, the company's prospects improved. While there was no change in the temporary deductible differences underlying the Deferred Tax Asset account, it was now considered more likely than not that the company would be able to make full use of the temporary differences. Prepare the entry, if applicable, to adjust the Deferred Tax Asset and related account(s).

(LO 3, 4, E18-30 **(Three Differences, Classification of Deferred Taxes)** Darrell Corporation reports under IFRS. At
5, 10, 11) December 31, 2017, the company had a net deferred tax liability of $402,000. An explanation of the items that make up this balance follows:

Temporary Differences	Resulting Balances in Deferred Tax Account
1. Excess of accumulated tax depreciation over book depreciation	$275,000
2. Accrual, for book purposes, of estimated loss contingency from pending lawsuit that is expected to be settled in 2017. The loss will be deducted on the tax return when it is paid	(91,000)
3. Accrual method (account receivable) used for book purposes and instalment method used for tax purposes for an isolated instalment sale of an investment, due in 2018	218,000
	$402,000

Instructions

(a) Indicate how deferred tax should be presented on Darrell Corporation's December 31, 2017 statement of financial position.

(b) How would your response to part (a) change if Darrell Corporation followed the ASPE future/deferred income taxes method?

(LO 2, 5, E18-31 **(Intraperiod Tax Allocation—Discontinued Operations)** Geoff Corp.'s operations in 2017 had mixed
10, 11) results. One division, Vincenti Group, again failed to earn income at a rate that was high enough to justify its continued operation, and management therefore decided to close the division. Vincenti Group earned revenue of $118,000 during 2017 and recognized total expenses of $110,500. The remaining two divisions reported revenues of $273,000 and total expenses of $216,000 in 2017.

In preparing the annual income tax return, Geoff Corp.'s controller took into account the following information:

1. The CCA exceeded depreciation expense by $3,700. There were no depreciable assets in the Vincenti Group division.

2. Included in Vincenti's expenses is an accrued litigation loss of $5,100 that is not deductible for tax purposes until 2018.

3. Included in the continuing divisions' expenses are the president's golf club dues of $4,500, and included in their revenues are $1,700 of dividends from taxable Canadian corporations.

4. There were no deferred tax account balances for any of the divisions on January 1, 2017.

5. The tax rate for 2017 and future years is 30%.

6. Geoff Corp. reports under IFRS.

Instructions

(a) Calculate the taxable income and income tax payable by Geoff Corp. in 2017 and the Deferred Tax Asset or Deferred Tax Liability balances at December 31, 2017.

(b) Prepare the journal entry(ies) to record income tax for 2017.

(c) Indicate how income taxes will be reported on the income statement for 2017 by preparing the bottom portion of the statement, beginning with "Income before income tax and discontinued operations." Assume that 10,000 common shares were outstanding throughout 2017.

(d) Provide the statement of financial position presentation for any resulting deferred tax accounts at December 31, 2017. Be specific about the classification.

(e) How would your response to part (d) change if Geoff Corp. followed the ASPE future/deferred income taxes method?

(LO 2, 10, 11) **E18-32** **(Taxes Payable Method)** Refer to the information in E18-11 for Henry Limited. Assume that the company reports under ASPE and that the taxes payable method of accounting is used for income tax.

Instructions

(a) Prepare the journal entry(ies) to record income tax at December 31, 2017.

(b) Prepare the income statement for 2017, beginning with the line "Income before income tax."

(c) Provide the balance sheet presentation for any resulting income tax accounts at December 31, 2017.

(d) Prepare the disclosures that are necessary because the taxes payable method is being used.

DIGGING DEEPER

(e) Now that Henry Limited has adopted the taxes payable method, how do you think the creditors would react to this accounting policy when they read Henry's financial statements? Explain.

(LO 2, 10, 11) **E18-33** **(Taxes Payable Method)** Refer to the information in E18-15 for Zdon Inc. Assume that the company follows the taxes payable method of accounting for income taxes under ASPE. During the year, Zdon Inc. made tax instalment payments of $42,000.

Instructions

(a) Calculate the taxable income and income tax expense for the year ended December 31, 2017.

(b) Prepare the journal entry(ies) to record income taxes at December 31, 2017.

(c) Prepare the income statement for 2017, beginning with the line "Income before income tax."

(d) Provide the balance sheet presentation for any resulting income tax accounts at December 31, 2017.

(LO 10, 11) **E18-34** **(Taxes Payable Method)** As the new accountant for Carly's Pet Express Inc., a line of pet boutiques, you are developing the financial statement disclosures for the 2017 financial statement note on income taxes. The company uses ASPE, and has selected the taxes payable method. The statutory tax rate is currently 30%. During 2017, net income before tax was $185,000. CCA exceeded depreciation expense by $25,000. The only permanent difference was the non-deductible portion of meals and entertainment costs, which was 50% of $20,000.

Instructions

(a) Determine the income tax expense to be recorded using the taxes payable method and record the necessary journal entry.

(b) Prepare the reconciliation of actual tax rate to the statutory rate as required for inclusion in the financial statement note on income taxes.

Problems

P18-1 Anthony Ltd. began business on January 1, 2016. At December 31, 2016, it had a $4,500 balance in the Deferred Tax Liability account that pertains to property, plant, and equipment acquired during 2016 at a cost of $900,000. The property, plant, and equipment is being depreciated on a straight-line basis over six years for financial reporting purposes, and is a Class 8—20% asset for tax purposes. Anthony's income before income tax for 2017 was $60,000. Anthony Ltd. follows IFRS and the *half-year convention for depreciation.*

The following items caused the only differences between accounting income before income tax and taxable income in 2017.

    1. In 2017, the company paid $56,250 for rent; of this amount, $18,750 was expensed in 2017. The other $37,500 will be expensed equally over the 2018 and 2019 accounting periods. The full $56,250 was deducted for tax purposes in 2017.

    2. Anthony Ltd. pays $9,000 a year for a membership in a local golf club for the company's president.

    3. Anthony Ltd. now offers a one-year warranty on all its merchandise sold. Warranty expenses for 2017 were $9,000. Cash payments in 2017 for warranty repairs were $4,500.

    4. Meals and entertainment expenses (only 50% of which are ever tax deductible) were $12,000 for 2017.

    5. The maximum allowable CCA was taken in 2017. There were no asset disposals for 2017.

Income tax rates have not changed since the company began operations.

Instructions

    (a) Calculate the balance in the Deferred Tax Asset or Deferred Tax Liability account at December 31, 2017.

    (b) Calculate income tax payable for 2017.

    (c) Prepare the journal entries to record income taxes for 2017.

    (d) Prepare the income tax expense section of the income statement for 2017, beginning with the line "Income before income tax."

    (e) Indicate how deferred taxes should be presented on the December 31, 2017 statement of financial position.

    (f) How would your response to parts (a) to (e) change if Anthony reported under ASPE?

P18-2 At December 31, 2016, Wright Corporation had a temporary difference (related to pensions) and reported a related deferred tax asset of $30,000 on its balance sheet. At December 31, 2017, Wright has five temporary differences. An analysis reveals the following:

	Future (Taxable) Deductible Amounts		
Temporary Difference	2018	2019	2020
1. Pension liability: expensed as incurred on the books; deductible when funded for tax purposes	$ 30,000	$ 20,000	$ 10,000
2. Royalties collected in advance: recognized when earned for accounting purposes and when received for tax purposes	76,000	—	—
3. Accrued liabilities: various expenses accrued for accounting purposes and recognized for tax purposes when paid	24,000	—	—
4. Deferred gross profit: profits recognized on instalment sales when sold for book purposes, and as collected for tax purposes	(36,000)	(36,000)	(36,000)
5. Equipment: straight-line depreciation for accounting purposes, and CCA for tax purposes	(90,000)	(50,000)	(40,000)
	$ 4,000	$(66,000)	$(66,000)

The enacted tax rate has been 30% for many years. In November 2017, the rate was changed to 28% for all periods after January 1, 2019. Assume that the company has income tax due of $180,000 on the 2017 tax return and that Wright follows IFRS.

Instructions

    (a) Indicate how deferred taxes should be presented on Wright Corporation's December 31, 2017 statement of financial position.

    (b) How would your response to part (a) change if Wright reported under ASPE?

    (c) Calculate taxable income for 2017.

    (d) Calculate accounting income for 2017.

    (e) Draft the income tax section of the 2017 income statement, beginning with the line "Income before income tax." Provide as much information as possible about the components of income tax expense.

P18-3 Eloisa Corporation applies IFRS. Information about Eloisa Corporation's income before income tax of $633,000 for its year ended December 31, 2017 includes the following:

1. CCA reported on the 2017 tax return exceeded depreciation reported on the income statement by $100,000. This difference, plus the $150,000 accumulated taxable temporary difference at January 1, 2017, is expected to reverse in equal amounts over the four-year period from 2018 to 2021.

2. Dividends received from taxable Canadian corporations were $15,000.

3. Rent collected in advance and included in taxable income as at December 31, 2016 totalled $60,000 for a three-year period. Of this amount, $40,000 was reported as unearned for book purposes at December 31, 2017. Eloisa reports unearned revenue as a current liability if it will be recognized in income within 12 months from the balance sheet date. Eloisa paid a $2,880 interest penalty for late income tax instalments. The interest penalty is not deductible for income tax purposes at any time.

4. Equipment was disposed of during the year for $90,000. The equipment had a cost of $105,000 and accumulated depreciation to the date of disposal of $37,000. The total proceeds on the sale of these assets reduced the CCA class; in other words, no gain or loss is reported for tax purposes.

5. Eloisa recognized a $75,000 loss on impairment of a long-term investment whose value was considered impaired. The Income Tax Act permits the loss to be deducted only when the investment is sold and the loss is actually realized. The investment was accounted for at amortized cost.

6. The tax rates are 30% for 2017 and 25% for 2018 and subsequent years. These rates have been enacted and known for the past two years.

Instructions

(a) Calculate the balance in the Deferred Tax Asset or Deferred Tax Liability account at December 31, 2016.

(b) Calculate the balance in the Deferred Tax Asset or Deferred Tax Liability account at December 31, 2017.

(c) Prepare the journal entries to record income taxes for 2017.

(d) Indicate how the Deferred Tax Asset or Deferred Tax Liability account(s) will be reported on the comparative statements of financial position for 2016 and 2017.

(e) Prepare the income tax expense section of the income statement for 2017, beginning with "Income before income tax."

(f) Calculate the effective rate of tax. Provide a reconciliation and explanation of why this differs from the statutory rate of 30%. Begin the reconciliation with the statutory rate.

(g) How would your response to parts (a) to (f) change if Eloisa reported under ASPE?

P18-4 The accounting income of Grace Corporation and its taxable income for the years 2017 to 2020 are as follows:

Year	Accounting Income	Taxable Income	Tax Rate
2017	$460,000	$299,000	25%
2018	420,000	294,000	30%
2019	390,000	304,200	30%
2020	460,000	644,000	30%

The change in the tax rate from 25% to 30% was not enacted until early in 2018.

Accounting income for each year includes an expense of $40,000 that will never be deductible for tax purposes. The remainder of the difference between accounting income and taxable income in each period is due to one reversing difference for the depreciation of property, plant, and equipment. No deferred taxes existed at the beginning of 2017.

Instructions

(a) Calculate the current and deferred tax expense or benefit for each of the four years. Also calculate the balance of the deferred tax balance sheet account at the end of each fiscal year from 2017 to 2020.

(b) Prepare journal entries to record income taxes in all four years.

(c) Prepare the bottom of the income statement for 2018, beginning with the line "Income before income tax."

P18-5 The following information applies to Edward Corporation, which reports under IFRS.

1. Prior to 2016, taxable income and accounting income were identical.

2. Accounting income was $1.7 million in 2016 and $1.4 million in 2017.

3. On January 1, 2016, equipment costing $1 million was purchased. It is being depreciated on a straight-line basis over eight years for financial reporting purposes, and is a Class 8—20% asset for tax purposes.

4. Tax-exempt interest income of $60,000 was received in 2017.

5. The tax rate is 30% for all periods.

6. Taxable income is expected in all future years.

7. Edward Corporation had 100,000 common shares outstanding throughout 2017.

Instructions

(a) Calculate the amount of capital cost allowance and depreciation expense for 2016 and 2017, and the corresponding carrying amount and undepreciated capital cost of the depreciable assets at the end of 2016 and 2017.

(b) Determine the amount of current and deferred tax expense for 2017.

(c) Prepare the journal entry(ies) to record 2017 income taxes.

(d) Prepare the bottom portion of Edward's 2017 income statement, beginning with the line "Income before income tax."

(e) Indicate how deferred taxes should be presented on the December 31, 2017 statement of financial position.

(f) How would your responses to parts (a) to (e) change if Edward Corporation followed the ASPE future/deferred income taxes method?

P18-6   The accounting records of Steven Corp., a real estate developer, indicated income before income tax of $850,000 for its year ended December 31, 2017, and of $525,000 for the year ended December 31, 2018. The following data are also available.

1. Steven Corp. pays an annual life insurance premium of $11,000 covering the top management team. The company is the named beneficiary.

2. The carrying amount of the company's property, plant, and equipment at January 1, 2017 was $1,256,000, and the UCC at that date was $998,000. Steven recorded depreciation expense of $175,000 and $180,000 in 2017 and 2018, respectively. CCA for tax purposes was $192,000 and $163,500 for 2017 and 2018, respectively. There were no asset additions or disposals over the two-year period.

3. Steven deducted $211,000 as a restructuring charge in determining income for 2016. At December 31, 2016, an accrued liability of $199,500 remained outstanding relative to the restructuring, which was expected to be completed in the next fiscal year. This expense is deductible for tax purposes, but only as the actual costs are incurred and paid for. The actual restructuring of operations took place in 2017 and 2018, with the liability reduced to $68,000 at the end of 2017 and to $0 at the end of 2018.

4. In 2017, property held for development was sold and a profit of $52,000 was recognized in income. Because the sale was made with delayed payment terms, the profit is taxable only as Steven receives payments from the purchaser. A 10% down payment was received in 2017, with the remaining 90% expected in equal amounts over the following three years.

5. Non-taxable dividends of $3,250 in 2017 and of $3,500 in 2018 were received from taxable Canadian corporations.

6. In addition to the income before income tax identified above, Steven reported a before-tax gain on discontinued operations of $18,800 in 2017.

7. A 30% rate of tax has been in effect since 2015.

Steven Corp. follows IFRS.

Instructions

(a) Determine the balance of any deferred tax asset or liability accounts at December 31, 2016, 2017, and 2018.

(b) Determine 2017 and 2018 taxable income and current tax expense.

(c) Prepare the journal entries to record current and deferred tax expense for 2017 and 2018.

(d) Identify how the Deferred Tax Asset or Deferred Tax Liability account(s) will be reported on the December 31, 2017 and 2018 statements of financial position.

(e) Prepare partial income statements for the years ended December 31, 2017 and 2018, beginning with the line "Income from continuing operations before income tax."

(f) How would your response to parts (a) to (e) change if Steven Corp. reported under ASPE?

P18-7   Andrew Weiman and Mei Lee are discussing accounting for income taxes. They are currently studying a schedule of taxable and deductible amounts that will arise in the future as a result of existing temporary differences. The schedule applies to a company that reports under the ASPE future/deferred income taxes method. The schedule is as follows:

	Current Year	Future Years			
	2017	2018	2019	2020	2021
Taxable income	$50,000				
Taxable amounts		$75,000	$75,000	$ 75,000	$75,000
Deductible amounts				(2,400,000)	
Enacted tax rate	30%	28%	26%	24%	24%

Instructions

(a) Explain the concept of future taxable amounts and future deductible amounts as shown in the schedule.

(b) Determine the balance of the Future Tax Asset and Future Tax Liability accounts on the December 31, 2017 balance sheet. Assuming all temporary differences originated in 2017, prepare the journal entry to recognize income tax expense for 2017.

(c) Assume that this company is not expected to perform well in the future due to a sluggish economy and in-house management problems. Identify any concerns you may have about reporting the Future Tax Asset or Future Tax Liability account as calculated.

(d) Company management determines that it is unlikely that the company will be able to benefit from all of the future deductible amounts. Early in 2018, after the entries in part (b) have been made, but before the financial statements have been finalized and released, management makes some estimates. It estimates that $2.0 million of the $2.4 million in future deductible amounts will not be used, and that the remaining amount will be deductible in 2020. Prepare the entry that is required to recognize this, assuming the company uses a valuation allowance to adjust the Future Tax Asset account.

(e) When finalizing the 2018 financial statements, management estimates that, due to the prospects for an economic recovery, it is now more likely than not that the company will benefit from a total of $2.1 million of the future deductible amounts: $600,000 in 2020 and $1.5 million in 2021. Prepare the journal entry that is required, if any, to adjust the allowance account at December 31, 2018.

(f) Indicate how the future tax accounts will be reported on the December 31, 2017 and 2018 balance sheets after taking into account the information in parts (d) and (e). Explain how these would differ, if at all, if the company did not use a valuation allowance account.

(g) How would your responses to part (f) change if the company followed IFRS?

P18-8 Sarah Corp. reported the following differences between statement of financial position carrying amounts and tax bases at December 31, 2016:

	Carrying Amount	Tax Base
Depreciable assets	$100,000	$67,500
Warranty liability (current liability)	20,500	–0–
Pension liability (long-term liability)	38,800	–0–

The differences between the carrying amounts and tax bases were expected to reverse as follows:

	2017	2018	After 2018
Depreciable assets	$17,500	$12,500	$ 2,500
Warranty liability	20,500	–0–	–0–
Accrued pension liability	12,000	12,000	14,800

Tax rates enacted at December 31, 2016 were 31% for 2016, 30% for 2017, 29% for 2018, and 28% for 2019 and later years.

During 2017, Sarah Corp. made four quarterly tax instalment payments of $9,500 each and reported income before income tax on its income statement of $119,650. Included in this amount were dividends from taxable Canadian corporations of $5,800 (non-taxable income) and $25,000 of expenses related to the executive team's golf dues (non–tax-deductible expenses). There were no changes to the enacted tax rates during the year.

As expected, book depreciation in 2017 exceeded the capital cost allowance claimed for tax purposes by $17,500, and there were no additions or disposals of property, plant, and equipment during the year. A review of the 2017 activity in the Warranty Liability account in the ledger indicated the following:

Balance, Dec. 31, 2016	$20,500
Payments on 2016 product warranties	(21,200)
Payments on 2017 product warranties	(6,300)
2017 warranty accrual	30,480
Balance, Dec. 31, 2017	$23,480

All warranties are valid for one year only. The Pension Liability account reported the following activity:

Balance, Dec. 31, 2016	$38,800
Payment to pension trustee	(72,000)
2017 pension expense	61,000
Balance, Dec. 31, 2017	$27,800

Pension expenses are deductible for tax purposes, but only as they are paid to the trustee, not as they are accrued for financial reporting purposes.

Sarah Corp. reports under IFRS.

Instructions

(a) Calculate the Deferred Tax Asset or Deferred Tax Liability account at December 31, 2016, and explain how it should be reported on the December 31, 2016 statement of financial position.

(b) Calculate the Deferred Tax Asset or Deferred Tax Liability account at December 31, 2017.

(c) Prepare all income tax entries for Sarah Corp. for 2017.

(d) Identify the balances of all income tax accounts at December 31, 2017, and show how they will be reported on the comparative statements of financial position at December 31, 2017 and 2016, and on the income statement for the year ended December 31, 2017.

(e) How would your responses to parts (a) and (d) change if Sarah Corp. followed the ASPE future/deferred income taxes method?

P18-9   The following are two independent situations related to future taxable and deductible amounts that resulted from temporary differences at December 31, 2017. In both situations, the future taxable amounts relate to property, plant, and equipment depreciation, and the future deductible amounts relate to settlements of litigation that were previously accrued in the accounts.

1. Alia Corp. has developed the following schedule of future taxable and deductible amounts:

	2018	2019	2020	2021	2022
Deductible amounts	$600	$600	$600	$ 400	$200
Taxable amounts	0	0	0	(3,600)	0

Alia reported a net deferred tax liability of $1,000 at January 1, 2017.

2. Khoi Corp. has the following schedule of future taxable and deductible amounts:

	2018	2019	2020	2021
Taxable amounts	$800	$800	$ 800	$800
Deductible amounts	0	0	(6,000)	0

Khoi Corp. reported a net deferred tax asset of $1,200 at January 1, 2017.

Both Alia Corp. and Khoi Corp. have taxable income of $8,000 in 2017 and expect to have taxable income in all future years. The tax rates enacted as of the beginning of 2017 are 25% for 2017 to 2020, and 30% for 2021 and subsequent years. All of the underlying temporary differences relate to non-current assets and liabilities. Both Khoi and Alia report under IFRS.

Instructions

(a) Determine the deferred tax assets or liabilities that will be reported on each company's December 31, 2017 statement of financial position.

(b) For each of these two situations, prepare journal entries to record income taxes for 2017. Show all calculations.

(c) Provide the presentation of deferred tax accounts on each company's December 31, 2017 statement of financial position, including their correct classification.

(d) How would your response to part (c) change if Khoi and Alia followed the ASPE future/deferred income taxes method?

P18-10   The following information was disclosed during the audit of Shawna Inc.:

Year	Amount Due per Tax Return
2017	$105,000
2018	84,000

1. On January 1, 2017, equipment was purchased for $400,000. For financial reporting purposes, the company uses straight-line depreciation over a five-year life, with no residual value. For tax purposes, the CCA rate is 25%.

2. In January 2018, $225,000 was collected in advance for the rental of a building for the next three years. The entire $225,000 is reported as taxable income in 2018, but $150,000 of the $225,000 is reported as unearned revenue on the December 31, 2018 statement of financial position. The $150,000 of unearned revenue will be earned equally in 2019 and 2020.

3. The tax rate is 30% in 2017 and all subsequent periods.

4. No temporary differences existed at the end of 2016. Shawna expects to report taxable income in each of the next five years. Its fiscal year ends December 31.

Shawna Inc. follows IFRS.

Instructions

(a) Calculate the amount of capital cost allowance and depreciation expense for 2017 and 2018, and the corresponding carrying amount and undepreciated capital cost of the depreciable assets at December 31, 2017 and 2018.

(b) Determine the balance of the Deferred Tax Asset or Deferred Tax Liability account at December 31, 2017, and indicate the account's classification on the statement of financial position.

(c) Prepare the journal entry(ies) to record income taxes for 2017.

(d) Draft the bottom of the income statement for 2017, beginning with "Income before income tax."

(e) Determine the balance of the Deferred Tax Asset or Deferred Tax Liability account at December 31, 2018, and indicate the account's classification on the December 31, 2018 statement of financial position.

(f) Prepare the journal entry(ies) to record income taxes for 2018.

(g) Prepare the bottom of the income statement for 2018, beginning with "Income before income tax."

(h) Provide the comparative statement of financial position presentation for the deferred tax accounts at December 31, 2017 and 2018. Be specific about the classification.

DIGGING DEEPER

(i) Is it possible to have more than two accounts for deferred taxes reported on a statement of financial position? Explain.

(j) How would your response to part (h) change if Shawna Inc. reported under the ASPE future/deferred income taxes method?

P18-11   The following information relates to Shirley Corporation's transactions during 2017, its first year of operations.

1. Income before income tax on the income statement for 2017 was $64,000.

2. Income before income tax ($64,000 above) is net of loss due to the writedown of land of $46,000.

3. Shirley reported a tax-deductible financing charge of $5,700 on its 2017 statement of retained earnings. The charge is for interest on a financial instrument that is legally debt, but in substance is equity for financial reporting purposes.

4. The tax rate enacted for 2017 and future years is 30%. Because this was Shirley Corporation's first taxation year, no instalments on account of income taxes were required or paid by Shirley.

5. Differences between the 2017 GAAP amounts and their treatment for tax purposes were as follows:

   (a) Warranty expense accrued for financial reporting purposes amounted to $15,000. Warranty payments deducted for taxes amounted to $12,000. Warranty liabilities were classified as current on the statement of financial position.

   (b) Of the loss on writedown of land of $46,000, 25% will never be tax deductible. The remaining 75% will be deductible for tax purposes evenly over the years from 2018 to 2020. The loss relates to the loss in value of company land due to contamination.

   (c) Gross profit on construction contracts using the percentage-of-completion method for book purposes amounted to $30,000. For tax purposes, gross profit on construction contracts amounted to $0 because the completed-contract method is used and no contracts were completed during the year. Construction costs amounted to $270,000 during the year.

   (d) Depreciation of property, plant, and equipment for financial reporting purposes amounted to $60,000. CCA charged on the tax return amounted to $80,000. The related property, plant, and equipment cost $300,000 when it was acquired early in 2017.

   (e) A $3,500 fine paid for a violation of pollution laws was deducted in calculating accounting income.

   (f) Dividend revenue earned on an investment was tax exempt and amounted to $1,400.

6. Taxable income is expected for the next few years.

Shirley Corporation follows IFRS.

Instructions

(a) Calculate Shirley Corporation's deferred tax asset or liability at December 31, 2017.

(b) Calculate the taxable income for 2017. Show all details of the adjustments to accounting income to arrive at taxable income.

(c) Prepare the journal entry(ies) to record income taxes for 2017.

(d) Prepare a partial 2017 income statement, beginning with "Income before income tax."

(e) Prepare a statement of retained earnings for the year ended December 31, 2017, assuming no dividends were declared in the year.

(f) Show how the balance of all the tax asset or liability accounts will be reported on the December 31, 2017 statement of financial position.

(g) Calculate the effective rate of tax. Provide a reconciliation and explanation of why this differs from the statutory rate of 30%. Begin the reconciliation with the statutory rate.

(h) How would your response to part (f) change if Shirley Corporation followed ASPE?

P18-12 Carly Inc. reported the following accounting income (loss) and related tax rates during the years 2012 to 2018:

Year	Accounting Income (Loss)	Tax Rate
2012	$ 70,000	25%
2013	25,000	25%
2014	60,000	25%
2015	80,000	30%
2016	(210,000)	35%
2017	70,000	30%
2018	90,000	25%

Accounting income (loss) and taxable income (loss) were the same for all years since Carly began business. The tax rates from 2015 to 2018 were enacted in 2015.

Instructions

(a) Prepare the journal entries to record income taxes for the years 2016 to 2018. Assume that Carly uses the carryback provision where possible and expects to realize the benefits of any loss carryforward in the year that immediately follows the loss year.

(b) Indicate the effect of the 2016 entry(ies) on the December 31, 2016 statement of financial position if Carly follows the ASPE future/deferred income taxes method. Indicate as well the effect on the statement of financial position if Carly reports under IFRS.

(c) Show how the bottom portion of the income statement would be reported in 2016, beginning with "Loss before income tax."

(d) Show how the bottom portion of the income statement would be reported in 2017, starting with "Income before income tax."

(e) Prepare the journal entries for the years 2016 to 2018 to record income taxes, assuming that Carly uses the carryback provision where possible but is uncertain if it will realize the benefits of any loss carryforward in the future. Carly does not use a valuation allowance.

(f) Assume now that Carly uses a valuation allowance account along with its Deferred Tax Asset account. Identify which entries in part (e) would differ and prepare them.

DIGGING DEEPER

(g) Based on your entries in part (e), indicate how the bottom portion of the income statements for 2016 and 2017 would be reported, beginning with "Income (loss) before income tax."

(h) From a cash flow perspective, can you think of any advantage in using the valuation allowance for financial reporting purposes? Can you think of any advantage in not using it?

P18-13 Chen Corporation reported income before income tax for the year ended December 31, 2017 of $1,645,000. In preparing the 2017 financial statements, the accountant discovered an error that was made in 2016. The error was that a piece of land with a cost of $40,000 had been recognized as an operating expense in error. The balance reported as retained earnings at December 31, 2016 was $5,678,000, and the net book value of property, plant, and equipment (excluding land) was $1,352,000 at the same date. During 2017, Chen Corporation acquired additional equipment with a cost of $16,000.

In completing the corporate tax return for the 2017 year, the company controller noted that the 2017 depreciation expense was $365,000, CCA claimed was $300,000, and non-deductible income tax penalties and interest of $2,500 and golf club dues of $4,500 were incurred in the year. In addition, the accounting allowance for doubtful accounts exceeded the tax reserve for uncollectible amounts by $20,000, although they were equal at the beginning of the year. At the end of 2016, the company had temporary differences of $135,000, due to lower depreciation expense than CCA claimed on the corporate tax return. The resulting future taxable amounts and the dates they were expected to reverse at December 31, 2016 were:

2017	$ 65,000
2018	40,000
2019	30,000
	$135,000

The tax rate is 30% for all years. Chen Corporation applies IFRS.

Instructions

(a) Calculate the balance sheet Deferred Tax Account balance at December 31, 2016.

(b) Determine the effect of the prior period error on the December 31, 2016 balance sheet and prepare the journal entry to correct the error. Assume that the 2016 income tax return is refiled.

(c) Prepare the journal entries to record income taxes for the 2017 year.

(d) Indicate how the income taxes will be reported on the financial statements for 2017 by preparing the bottom portion of the income statement beginning with "Income before income tax." Also prepare the statement of retained earnings for the year ended December 31, 2017, assuming no dividends were declared during the year.

P18-14   Aaron Engines Ltd. operates small engine repair outlets and is a tenant in several of Tran Holdings Inc.'s strip shopping malls. Aaron signed several lease renewals with Tran that each called for a three-month rent-free period. The leases start at various dates and are for three to five years each. As with all of Tran's tenants, Aaron pays rent quarterly, three months in advance, and records the payments initially to Prepaid Rent.

The rent-free period obtained in the lease agreement with Tran Holdings Inc. reduces the overall rental costs of the outlets over the term of each lease. Aaron's accounting policy requires the leasing costs of each outlet to be allocated evenly over the term of the lease to fairly match expenses with revenues. Aaron accrues rent expense during the rent-free period to an account called Rent Payable. Following the rent-free period, the Rent Payable account is amortized to Rent Expense over the remaining term of the lease. For tax purposes, Aaron must use the cash basis and is unable to deduct the rent expense accrued during the rent-free periods. On its tax return, Aaron can deduct the actual rent payments only when they are made.

The following are balances for the accounts related to prepaid rent and rent payable under leases as well as payments for interest to earn tax-exempt income and payments for golf club dues for the years ended December 31, 2018 and 2017:

	2018	2017
Prepaid Rent (assume current classification and no balance at Dec. 31, 2016)	$ 92,000	$ 89,000
Rent Payable (assume non-current classification and no balance at Dec. 31, 2016)	133,000	146,000
Golf Dues Expense	11,000	13,000
Interest Expense (incurred to earn tax-exempt income)	6,000	4,000

In 2017, Aaron's tax rate is 28%, and for subsequent years it is 27%. Income before income tax for the year ended December 31, 2017 was $884,000. During 2018, Aaron's tax rate changed to 29% for 2018 and subsequent years. Income before income tax for the year ended December 31, 2018 was $997,000. Assume that Aaron Engines Ltd. applies ASPE.

Instructions

(a) Calculate the Deferred Tax Asset or Deferred Tax Liability account balances at December 31, 2017 and 2018.

(b) Calculate taxable income and income tax payable for 2017 and 2018.

(c) Prepare the journal entries to record income taxes for 2017 and 2018.

(d) Prepare a comparative income statement for 2017 and 2018, beginning with the line "Income before income tax."

(e) Provide the comparative balance sheet presentation for any resulting deferred tax accounts at December 31, 2017 and 2018. Be specific about the classification.

(f) Calculate the effective rate of tax for 2018. Provide a reconciliation and explanation of why this differs from the statutory rate of 29%. Begin the reconciliation with the statutory rate.

(g) How would your responses to parts (a) to (f) change if Aaron applied IFRS instead of ASPE?

P18-15   On December 31, 2016, Haley Inc. has taxable temporary differences of $2.2 million and a deferred tax liability of $616,000. These temporary differences are due to Haley having claimed CCA in excess of book depreciation in prior years. Haley's year end is December 31. At the end of December 2017, Haley's substantively enacted tax rate for 2017 and future years was changed to 30%.

For the year ended December 31, 2017, Haley's accounting loss before tax was $494,000. The following data are also available.

1. Pension expense was $87,000 while pension plan contributions were $111,000 for the year. (Only actual pension contributions are deductible for tax.)

2. Business meals and entertainment were $38,000. (They are one-half deductible for tax purposes.)

3. For the three years ended December 31, 2016, Haley had cumulative, total taxable income of $123,000 and total income tax expense/income tax payable of $51,660.

4. During 2017, the company booked estimated warranty costs of $31,000 and these costs are not likely to be incurred until 2021.

5. In 2017, the company incurred $150,000 of development costs (only 50% of which are deductible for tax purposes).

6. Company management has determined that it is probable that only one half of any loss carryforward at the end of 2017 will be realized.

7. In 2017, the amount claimed for depreciation was equal to the amount claimed for CCA.

Instructions

Prepare the journal entries to record income taxes for the year ended December 31, 2017, and the income tax reconciliation note.

P18-16   Under the temporary difference approach, the tax rates used for deferred tax calculations are those enacted at the balance sheet date, and affect how the reversal will be treated for tax purposes.

Instructions

For each of the following situations, discuss the impact on deferred tax balances.

(a) At December 31, 2017, Golden Corporation has one temporary difference that will reverse in 2018. In 2017, new tax legislation maintained the 2016 tax rate of 31% for 2017, and decreased it to 30% for 2018 and the years thereafter. Explain under what circumstances Golden Corporation would use the following tax rates to calculate the future tax consequences of its temporary differences at December 31, 2017:

1. 31%

2. 30%

(b) Record Inc. uses the fair value method for reporting its investment properties. The company has an investment property with an original cost of $5 million and a tax carrying amount of $3.8 million due to cumulative capital cost allowance claimed to date of $1.2 million. This asset is increased to its fair value of $8 million for accounting purposes. No equivalent adjustment is made for tax purposes. The tax rate is 30% for normal business purposes. If the asset is sold for more than cost, the cumulative capital cost allowance of $1.5 million will be included in taxable income as recaptured depreciation, but sale proceeds in excess of cost will be taxable at a taxable gains rate of 15%. Calculate the related deferred balance assuming the value of the asset will be recovered by selling the asset.

(c) Assume the same information as provided in part (b), but the company is now revaluing a tract of land and a building that are included in property, plant, and equipment, and the revaluation method is used rather than the fair value method. The change in revaluation has been reported in other comprehensive income. All numbers remain the same as discussed in part (b) above. What differences would be noted relating to accounting for the tax impact, if any?

**ENABLING
COMPETENCIES** # Case

Refer to the Case Primer on the Student Website and in *WileyPLUS* to help you answer this case.

CA18-1   Baker Company Limited (BCL) was founded in 2015. Its first year of operations turned out to be a good one,

as start-up years go, because the company not only broke even but actually showed a very small profit. Just as the company was getting established in the market, however, a full-fledged recession hit in 2016 and had devastating effects. Demand for BCL's products in retail markets declined as consumers tightened their purse strings. Through tight cost controls, however, BCL managed to hold its own and still recorded a small profit in 2016.

While the recession finally petered out by the end of 2017, BCL did end up feeling its effects, as the company was unable to remain profitable and suffered large operating losses that year. In fact, the losses were significantly greater than the profits that were reported in the previous two years. Despite this change, BCL management was not overly alarmed by the losses and had the following comments to make.

AUDIT AND ASSURANCE

> The losses were expected given the widespread recession. Since the bulk of our sales are in retail markets, and with unemployment levels being at record highs, it is not surprising that consumer demand has fallen off. If BCL is compared with the industry, you will see that we did much better than our competitors, some of whom went bankrupt.
>
> Keep in mind that we are a relatively new company and managed to record a profit in two out of our first three years. We attribute this to our strong management team and our ability as a streamlined

company to react to the recession with cost control measures and an aggressive, yet flexible sales staff.

> We see ourselves positioned for a new growth spurt given that the economy seems to have recovered and a lot of "dead wood" (competition) has been cleared out. As a matter of fact, in that regard, the recession will have a positive impact on our short- to mid-term growth potential.
>
> BCL is on the verge of introducing two new products that will revolutionize the industry and assure us a solid earnings base for the future. These products will be introduced in 2018 and we have already lined up sufficient buyers such that we predict we will at least break even in terms of net income in 2018. This is a very conservative forecast.

Although the effects of the recession were lessening, unemployment was still high in early 2018 and consumer spending had not increased significantly. Some economists were predicting that it would take two or three years for consumer confidence and spending to pick up to pre-recession levels.

Instructions

Adopt the role of the company's auditor and determine whether BCL should recognize the benefits of the losses suffered in the 2017 financial statements. Assume BCL is a private company. Note any differences between IFRS and ASPE.

ENABLING COMPETENCIES # Integrated Case

IC18-1 Cauchy Inc. (CI) has just had a planning meeting with its auditors. There were several concerns that had been raised during the meeting regarding the draft financial statements for the December 31, 2017 year end. CI is a public company whose shares list on the TSX. It has recently gone through a major expansion and, as a result, there are several financial reporting decisions that need to be made for the upcoming year-end financial statements. The expansion has been financed in the short term with a line of credit from the bank; however, the company plans to raise capital in the equity markets in the new year. It is hoped that the expansion will increase profitability, although it is too early to tell.

Just before year end, the company purchased two investments as follows:

- 20% of the common shares of KL Corp. CI was able to appoint one member to KL's board of directors (which has four members in total). CI is unsure as to whether it will hold onto this investment for the longer term or sell it if the share price increases. The company has currently set a benchmark that if the share price increases by more than 25%, it will liquidate the investment. KL has been profitable over the past few years and the share price is on an upward trend. The original reason for entering into this transaction was to create a strategic alliance with KL that will help ensure a steady supply of high-quality raw materials from KL to CI.

- Corporate bonds. These bonds are five-year bonds that bear interest at 5% (which is in excess of market interest rates). As a result, the company paid a premium for the bonds. The bonds are convertible to common shares of the issuing company. It is CI's intent to hold onto these bonds to maturity, although if there were an unforeseen cash crunch, it might have to cash them in earlier.

The company completed a significant sale to a new U.S. customer on credit on December 31, 2017. Under the terms of the agreement, CI will provide services to the customer over a one-year period. The sales agreement includes a non-refundable upfront fee for a significant amount, which the company has recognized as revenue. As part of the deal, CI will provide access to significant proprietary information (which it has already done) and then provide ongoing analysis and monitoring functions as a service to the customer. It is not specified in the contract whether the rights to the proprietary information are transferable but CI is taking the position that they are. The proprietary information is of no value as a separate item if not transferable. During the year, CI renewed service contracts for some of its other major customers under similar deals.

The receivable for this large sale is in U.S. dollars. Half of this has been hedged using a forward contract to sell U.S. dollars at a fixed rate. The other half is hedged through a natural hedge since the company has some U.S. dollar payables. The auditor has asked that the company prepare some notes analyzing the need for hedge accounting for this transaction and explaining the risks associated with the sales transaction and hedge transactions.

Instructions

Assume the role of the controller and analyze the financial reporting issues.

This has been a bad year for the company due to one-time charges on a lawsuit settlement, and currently the draft statements are showing a loss. The company's tax accountants have determined that the company will also have a loss for tax purposes.

RESEARCH AND ANALYSIS

RA18-1   Deferred Tax Assets and IAS 12

ETHICS

Davida Limited started operations in 2013. Although it has grown steadily, the company reported accumulated operating losses of $450,000 in its first four years in business. In the most recent year (2017), Davida appears to have turned the corner and reported modest taxable income of $30,000. In addition to a deferred tax asset related to its net operating loss, Davida has recorded a deferred tax asset related to product warranties and a deferred tax liability related to accelerated depreciation. Given its past operating results, Davida management has determined that it is not probable that it will realize any of the deferred tax assets. However, given its improved performance, management wonders whether there are any accounting consequences for its deferred tax assets. They would like you to conduct some research on the accounting for recognition of its deferred tax asset.

Instructions

Refer to the IFRS standard, IAS 12 *Income Taxes*. Provide a reference to the specific paragraphs of IAS 12, where appropriate, in answering the following.

(a) Briefly explain to Davida management the importance of future taxable income as it relates to the recognition of deferred tax assets.

(b) What should management consider in assessing the potential realization of a deferred tax asset?

CORPORATE TAX

(c) What are tax-planning strategies? Provide examples. (*Hint:* See IAS 12.30.) From the information provided, does it appear that Davida could use a tax-planning strategy in evaluating its deferred tax asset?

(d) Identify and explain any possible areas where there might be ethical issues in recognizing the deferred asset and in applying Davida's tax-planning strategies. Suggest what should be done.

RA18-2   Maple Leaf Foods Inc.

REAL WORLD EMPHASIS

Maple Leaf Foods Inc. is a Canadian company that produces food products such as prepared meats, ready-to-cook and ready-to-serve meals, and fresh pork and poultry. While most of Maple Leaf Foods' business is conducted in Canada, it also generates revenues in the United States, the United Kingdom, and Japan.

Instructions

Through SEDAR (www.sedar.com) or the Maple Leaf Foods' website, obtain a copy of the company's financial statements for its year ended December 31, 2014. Answer the following questions.

(a) Review the consolidated statements of net earnings and other comprehensive income for 2014 and 2013. What was the income tax expense (benefit) for each year? Did the company apply intraperiod tax allocation in 2014 or 2013? Why or why not? How much does the company show as income taxes payable on the consolidated statements of financial position at the 2014 and 2013 fiscal year ends? What was reported regarding cash flows of current income taxes in 2014 and 2013? Where did you find this information?

(b) What was the company's effective tax rate for 2014? For 2013? What was the statutory rate in each of these years? What caused the differences? Be specific about whether the effective rate increased or decreased as a result of each cause that you identify.

(c) For each deferred tax account reported on the December 31, 2014 consolidated statement of financial position, explain what underlies the balance that is reported. For each temporary difference, identify the statement of financial position asset or liability where the tax base and carrying amount differ.

(d) Does the company have any unrecognized deferred tax assets or unrecognized deferred tax liabilities as of December 31, 2014? Explain how Maple Leaf Foods has treated any such items, and why.

RA18-3 Comparative Analysis

REAL WORLD EMPHASIS

Alimentation Couche-Tard Inc., Loblaw Companies Limited, and **Empire Company Limited** are three companies in the same industry. Because of this, the expectation is that their operations and financial positions are also similar.

Instructions

Go to SEDAR (www.sedar.com) or the companies' websites and, using Alimentation Couche-Tard's financial statements for the year ended April 26, 2015, Loblaw's financial statements for the year ended January 3, 2015, and Empire's financial statements for the year ended May 2, 2015, answer the following.

(a) Identify what industry all three companies are in.

(b) Identify all the areas where the three companies used intraperiod tax allocation. This requires a careful reading of some of the notes to the financial statements as well as the main statements themselves. Prepare a schedule of the total income tax provision (expense) or recovery (benefit) for each company, and identify where the tax provision or recovery was reported.

(c) Compare the three companies' deferred tax assets and/or deferred tax liabilities, and identify, as much as possible, what temporary differences are responsible for these accounts. Would you expect companies in the same industry to have similar types of temporary differences? Do they?

(d) Would you expect the three companies to be subject to similar income tax legislation and tax rates? Are their statutory rates the same? Explain. Compare the companies' statutory and effective rates and explain why there are differences, if any.

(e) Do any of the three companies have tax loss carryforwards with potential tax benefits that have not been recognized as deferred tax assets? If so, identify these and explain why they haven't been recognized in the accounts.

RA18-4 International Comparison

Different countries have different statutory tax rates.

REAL WORLD EMPHASIS

Instructions

Choose an industry and select five companies that operate in different countries. Access these companies' most recent annual financial statements and make note of their statutory and effective income tax rates.

Alternatively, use the railway industry and the following companies:

Canadian National Railway: Canada
Deutsche Bahn: Germany
East Japan Railway Company: Japan

NSB Group: Norway
Union Pacific Railroad Corp.: United States

(a) For each company, identify its year end, country of operation, statutory income tax rates, and effective tax rates.

(b) Identify any significant differences that caused the rates in part (a) to differ, and discuss any similarities or differences found.

RA18-5 IFRS and ASPE

LGS Inc. is a private company. You have recently been hired as the CFO for the company and are currently finalizing the company year-end report for December 31, 2017. The company has an option to follow either IFRS or ASPE, and has not yet made the choice. Three situations have arisen affecting the company's reporting of income taxes. These situations are described below. Year-end tax rates are 28%.

1. Shortly after you were hired, you found that a prior period adjustment had been made in 2016, and the Deferred Tax Liability account was adjusted through retained earnings as part of this error correction. The difference between the accounting value and the tax base of the related asset is $1 million. Originally, the rate used to record the deferred tax liability was 25%. In 2017, the enacted tax rate on this difference is now 28% and therefore an adjustment must be made to the Deferred Tax Liability account.

2. The company has a building that has recently been appraised at a fair value of $10 million. Currently, the building's carrying amount is $6.5 million and its original cost was $8 million. Accumulated capital cost allowance booked to date on the building is $2.3 million. (Ignore the one-time adjustments allowed to property, plant, and equipment for first-time adopters for IFRS or ASPE.)

3. LGS bought some equity investments during the year that are not publicly traded for a total cost of $340,000. The company purchased these as an investment to be sold in the near future. Currently, the shares have been valued at December 31, 2017 for $510,000. There were no dividends received on this investment during the year.

Instructions

(a) For each of the situations described above, access and review the published ASPE and IFRS accounting standards covering income taxes. Discuss the options for measuring and reporting the income tax implications under both IFRS and ASPE, noting the sections of the income tax standards that relate to the specific issues. As stated in item (1), the tax rate increased to 28% in 2017, and no accounting adjustments for this have been made up to the current date.

(b) Summarize the balance sheet and income statement effects of the ASPE and IFRS requirements identified in (a) above. Analyze the results and comment on your findings.

RA18-6 Basic Concepts and Principles

The amount of income tax that is due to the government for a period of time is rarely the same as the amount of income tax expense that is reported on the income statement for that same period under IFRS and one of the alternatives under ASPE.

Instructions

(a) IAS 12 *Income* Taxes, like most IASB accounting standards, sets out clearly what the standard setters' objectives are of the standard that follows. Explain your understanding of what the IAS 12 objectives are of accounting for income taxes in general purpose financial statements.

(b) Explain the basic principles that are applied in accounting for income taxes at the date of the financial statements to meet the objectives discussed in part (a).

(c) Explain how the recognition of deferred tax accounts on the statement of financial position is consistent with the conceptual framework, noting the differences between IFRS and ASPE.

(d) Using the definition of an asset and a liability (from Chapter 2), discuss why deferred tax assets and deferred tax liabilities as currently measured and reported might not meet this definition.

RA18-7   Operating and Accounting Policies

Henrietta Aguirre, the ethical accountant, is the newly hired Director of Corporate Taxation for Mesa Incorporated, which is a publicly traded corporation. Aguirre's first job with Mesa

was to review the company's accounting practices for deferred taxes. In doing her review, she noted differences between tax and book depreciation methods that permitted Mesa to recognize a sizable deferred tax liability on its balance sheet. As a result, Mesa did not have to report current tax expenses.

 Aguirre also discovered that Mesa had an explicit policy of selling off plant and equipment assets before they reversed in the Deferred Tax Liability account. This policy, together with the rapid expansion of Mesa's capital asset base, allowed Mesa to defer all income taxes payable for several years, at the same time as it

ETHICS

reported positive earnings and increasing earnings per share. Aguirre checked with the legal department and found the policy to be legal, but she is uncomfortable with the ethics of it.

Instructions

(a) Why would Mesa have an explicit policy of selling assets before they reversed in the Deferred Tax Liability account?

(b) What are some of the ethical implications that arise from Mesa's aggressive deferral of income taxes?

(c) Who could be harmed by Mesa's ability to defer income taxes payable for several years, despite positive earnings?

(d) In a situation such as this, what might be Aguirre's professional responsibilities as an ethical accountant?

ENDNOTES

[1] See J. Arnold, "Do Tax Structures Affect Aggregate Economic Growth? Empirical Evidence from a Panel of OECD Countries," OECD Economics Department Working Papers, No. 643, OECD Publishing, 2008.

[2] Canada Revenue Agency, "Corporation Tax Rates," www.cra-arc.gc.ca/tx/bsnss/tpcs/crprtns/rts-eng.html. While most provinces had a combined corporate tax rate of 26% to 27%, the rate in 2015 was as high as 31% in Nova Scotia and P.E.I.

[3] Proprietorships and partnerships do not pay income taxes as separate legal entities. Instead, their income is taxed as part of the proprietor's or partners' income as individuals. Prior to 2011, organizations that organized as income trusts also generally did not have their income taxed, because they distribute the income to their unitholders. Taxes that are owed on such distributions were obligations of the unitholders. The favourable tax treatment for most income trusts was phased out by 2011.

[4] At the risk of oversimplification, it can be said that the Income Tax Act follows a principle of having the tax follow the cash flow. Although taxable income is based mainly on income reported under IFRS or ASPE, in cases where the timing of cash flows is significantly different from the timing of revenue recognition, revenues tend to be taxable as they are received in cash and expenses are allowed as deductions when they are paid.

[5] Note that no one prepares a "tax" statement of financial position—it is just a concept. However, if there were one, the tax values that

are referred to here are what would be on that statement of financial position, and they would be based on how the transaction is accounted for, for tax purposes. If the revenue is not yet recognized for tax purposes, there would be no receivable either. That is, the tax basis of the receivable is $0. Similarly, the tax value of the investments would be their original cost.

[6] Where warranties are used as an example of a temporary/timing difference in this chapter, it is assumed that the company is following the expense warranty approach, and not accounting for the warranty as a separate performance obligation. This treatment is consistent with the example provided in IAS12.25. As discussed in Chapter 6, the accounting treatment for warranties was clarified as part of the IASB's new contract-based revenue recognition model.

[7] See IAS 12.7. Copyright © International Financial Reporting Standards Foundation. All rights reserved. Reproduced by John Wiley & Sons Canada, Ltd with the permission of the International Financial Reporting Standards Foundation®. Reproduction and use rights are strictly limited. No permission granted to third parties to reproduce or distribute.

[8] *CPA Canada Handbook*, Part II, Section 3465.02(d) indicates that future income tax assets also include the income tax benefits that arise through the carryforward of unused tax losses and unused income tax reductions, excluding investment tax credits. IAS 12 *Income Taxes*, para 5, also states that deferred tax assets arise from the carryforward of unused tax losses and tax credits. These are

discussed later in the chapter. Copyright © International Financial Reporting Standards Foundation. All rights reserved. Reproduced by John Wiley & Sons Canada, Ltd with the permission of the International Financial Reporting Standards Foundation®. Reproduction and use rights are strictly limited. No permission granted to third parties to reproduce or distribute.

[9] *CPA Canada Handbook*, Part II, Section 3465.51 to .54 and IAS 12 *Income Taxes* paras. 46 to 49. Copyright © International Financial Reporting Standards Foundation. All rights reserved. Reproduced by John Wiley & Sons Canada, Ltd with the permission of the International Financial Reporting Standards Foundation®. Reproduction and use rights are strictly limited. No permission granted to third parties to reproduce or distribute.

Under ASPE, there must be persuasive evidence that the government is able and committed to enacting the proposed change in the foreseeable future in order to use a substantively enacted rate or tax law. This usually means that the legislation or regulation has to have been drafted in an appropriate form and tabled in Parliament, and the government will be able to pass the legislation. IFRS indicates that the announced tax rate or law can be used only when government announcements of tax changes have the substantive effect of actual enactment.

[10] ASPE indicates that it must be more likely than not that the company will be eligible for the reduced tax rate. Examples of tax incentives include the small business deduction, the manufacturing and processing profits deduction, and the scientific research and development credits.

[11] The federal general corporate income tax rate gradually dropped from 28% to 15% between 2001 and 2012. Federal budgets tabled after the time of writing could change these rates further, one way or the other.

[12] The carryforward period has been increasing. The 2004 federal budget increased it from 7 years to 10, and the 2006 budget increased it again to 20 years. Note also that the references in this chapter to tax losses are limited to non-capital losses. Special rules apply to capital losses.

[13] At one time, it was common practice when refiling prior years' returns to reduce the amount of CCA claimed, thus increasing the amount of taxable income in those prior years. The company could then absorb more of a current-year tax loss. With the recent extensions of the carryforward period, now at 20 years, this option is now not commonly allowed.

[14] When **Sears Canada Inc.** bought 19 **Eaton's** stores for $80 million, $20 million of the price was for approximately $175 million of tax losses accumulated by Eaton's. The $20 million could not be distributed until five years after Sears had benefited from it. This was because the Canada Revenue Agency could legally appeal the company's use of the losses. The $20 million was finally paid out in 2006.

[15] Examples of positive evidence that might support the recognition of a tax asset include a firm sales backlog that will produce more than enough taxable income to realize the deferred tax asset, or a history of strong earnings and evidence that the loss is due to a specific identifiable and nonrecurring cause.

[16] Let's look at an example. Assume an entity reports a correction of a prior period error in retained earnings in Year 5. As a result, a deferred tax liability is recognized on the Year 5 statement of financial position and a deferred tax expense is netted against the retained earnings adjustment in the same year. In Year 6, the tax rate increases, also increasing the balance of the deferred tax liability recognized in Year 5. Under ASPE, the related deferred tax expense is reported on the Year 6 income statement. There is no backward tracing to the retained earnings statement. Under IFRS, the increased tax expense in Year 6 is reported in retained earnings. The IASB may change this requirement in the future to harmonize with the FASB approach, which is also similar to ASPE.

[17] For further details regarding Stelco and U.S. Steel Canada, see Kristine Owram, "A Case of Buyer's Remorse? What Went Wrong at U.S. Steel Canada," *Financial Post*, September 17, 2014, and Greg Keenan, "U.S. Steel Canada Files for Creditor Protection," *The Globe and Mail*, September 16, 2014.

[18] R. P. Weber and J. E. Wheeler, in "Using Income Disclosures to Explore Significant Economic Transactions," *Accounting Horizons* (September 1992), discuss how deferred (future) tax disclosures can be used to assess the quality of earnings and to predict future cash flows.

[19] Alternatively, if more than one tax jurisdiction was involved or these were the consolidated financial statements of a number of taxable entities, IFRS requires that the deferred tax assets be reported separately from the deferred tax liabilities. In this case, the deferred tax liability of $148,000 relating to the deferred gross profit would be reported separately from the total of all the deferred tax assets of $106,200.

[20] If Allteak Corporation classifies all warranty liabilities as current because the company defines the operating cycle as including the two-year warranty period, then the entire future tax asset related to the warranties would be reported as a current amount.

REFERENCE TO THE CPA COMPETENCY MAP — LEARNING OBJECTIVES

After studying this chapter, you should be able to:

1.1.1, 1.1.2, 1.4.2, 6.1.2	**1.** Understand the importance of pensions from a business perspective.
1.1.4, 1.2.1, 1.2.2	**2.** Identify and account for a defined contribution plan.
1.1.2, 1.2.1, 1.2.2, 5.1.1, 5.2.1	**3.** Identify and explain what a defined benefit plan is and the related accounting issues.
1.2.1, 1.2.2, 1.2.3, 5.1.1	**4.** Explain what the employer's benefit obligation is, identify alternative measures for this obligation, and prepare a continuity schedule of transactions and events that change its balance.
1.1.2, 1.2.1, 1.2.2, 1.2.3, 5.2.1, 6.1.2	**5.** Identify transactions and events that change benefit plan assets, and calculate the balance of the plan assets.
1.2.1, 1.2.2, 1.2.3, 1.4.4	**6.** Explain what a benefit plan's surplus or deficit is, calculate it, and identify what transactions and events change its amount.
1.2.1, 1.2.2, 1.2.3, 1.2.4	**7.** Identify the components of pension expense, and account for a defined benefit pension plan under IFRS and ASPE.
1.1.3, 1.2.1, 1.2.2, 1.2.3	**8.** Account for defined benefit plans with benefits that vest or accumulate other than pension plans.
1.3.1, 1.3.2, 1.4.1, 1.4.2	**9.** Identify the types of information required to be presented and disclosed for defined benefit plans, prepare basic schedules, and be able to read and understand such disclosures.
1.1.4	**10.** Identify differences between the IFRS and ASPE accounting for pensions and other post-employment benefits and what changes are expected in the near future.

After studying Appendix 19A, you should be able to:

1.1.3, 1.2.1, 1.2.2	**11.** Explain and apply basic calculations to determine current service cost, the defined benefit obligation, and past service cost for a one-person defined benefit pension plan.

KEEPING PENSION COSTS AT CRUISING ALTITUDE

IN GOOD TIMES, companies like to offer employee benefits that can help attract, reward, and keep top people. That often meant that large corporations had "gold-plated" pension plans, offering employees guaranteed incomes after they retired. But in bad times, the high costs of such pensions tarnished companies' balance sheets.

Such was the case with Air Canada, whose mounting pension costs after the recession of 2008 and 2009 and subsequent downturn in the airline industry threatened to ground it for good. At the start of 2012, the airline's pension solvency deficit—the shortfall of assets in its pension funds relative to its obligations to pay retirees benefits—stood at $4.2 billion, calling the company's future into question. The deficit had doubled in size from the year before, mainly because of poor returns on the assets invested in the funds.

THE CANADIAN PRESS IMAGES/Bayne Stanley

Under federal pension regulations, Air Canada and other companies are responsible for making up any pension shortfalls to meet their obligations. Continuing to pour billions into the airline's pension funds was unsustainable. In 2012, Air Canada asked for and was later granted some relief by the federal government from its pension funding obligations, being required to put an average of $200 million a year for seven years into its funds. Air Canada negotiated some concessions with its unions to further reduce its pension funding obligations.

This relief from making full pension contributions, along with several factors, such as a new investment strategy putting most of the assets in fixed-income investments and higher market performance of its pension fund investments, enabled the airline to wipe out its pension solvency deficit by the beginning of 2014. By early 2015, the funds had a surplus of $1.2 billion.

Because the deal with the federal government to get pension funding relief prevented the airline from issuing dividends and buying back shares, it opted out of the agreement in early 2015. The company said it did a detailed risk assessment and determined that the funding risk associated with the solvency of its pension plans "has largely been eliminated." Air Canada went back to following the usual pension regulations and it expected its pension solvency payment in 2016 would be zero.

"Our ability to return to normal funding rules for our pension plans represents a highly significant and positive milestone in the execution of our strategy to transform Air Canada into a sustainably profitable company for the long term," said chief executive officer Calin Rovinescu. "Our three primary pension objectives were to secure our employees' and retirees' pensions, eliminate the pension solvency deficit and ensure that the costs associated with maintaining the pension plans remain affordable, predictable and stable. We have… achieved all three objectives." While Air Canada had made great strides with its domestic (Canadian) pension plans, it still has some funding challenges with its international and supplementary pension plans (with a combined deficit of over $1.0 billion) and its other employee future benefits (with a deficit of almost $1.3 billion at the end of 2014)!

Sources: Greg Keenan, "Air Canada Plans Share Buyback after Opting Out of Pension Deal," *Globe and Mail*, May 26, 2015; "Air Canada Opts Out of Air Canada Pension Plan Funding Regulations, 2014," Air Canada news release, May 26, 2015; Scott Deveau, "Air Canada's Complete Pension Turnaround a Sign of Things to Come," *Financial Post*, January 22, 2014; Air Canada Annual Report 2014.

PREVIEW OF CHAPTER 19

Because employers are concerned about the well-being of their employees, organizations have established a variety of benefit programs for employees after they retire. For example, private pension and other post-retirement benefit plans are common in companies of all sizes. By mid-2015, more than 6.2 million Canadian workers belonged to employer pension plans. Most of them, about 5.2 million, were members of plans whose assets were held in trusteed pension funds (which are governed by the provisions of a trust agreement). The remainder were in plans managed principally by insurance company contracts. The market value of the assets held in trusteed pension funds in Canada totalled $1.6 trillion at the end of the second quarter of 2015.[1]

A pension is part of an employee's overall compensation package. Post-employment health care and other benefits are also often part of this package. The substantial growth of these plans, in terms of both how many employees are covered and the dollar amount of benefits, has made their cost very large in relation to many companies' financial position, results of operations, and cash flows. This is made clear in the opening story about **Air Canada**, but that company is not alone in taking steps to reduce such costs. This chapter discusses the accounting issues related to these future benefits.

The chapter is organized as follows:

PENSIONS AND OTHER POST-EMPLOYMENT BENEFITS				
Introduction and Benefit Plan Basics	**Defined Benefit Pension Plans**	**Presentation, Disclosure, and Analysis**	**IFRS/ASPE Comparison**	**Appendix 19A— Example of a One-Person Plan**
■ Overview of pensions and their importance from a business perspective ■ Defined contribution plans ■ Defined benefit plans	■ The employer's obligation ■ Plan assets ■ Surplus or deficit ■ Defined benefit cost components ■ Other defined benefit plans	■ Presentation ■ Disclosure ■ Analysis	■ A comparison of IFRS and ASPE ■ Looking ahead	■ Current service cost ■ Defined benefit obligation ■ Past service cost

INTRODUCTION AND BENEFIT PLAN BASICS

Overview of Pensions and Their Importance from a Business Perspective

Objective 1
Understand the importance of pensions from a business perspective.

REAL WORLD EMPHASIS

The enormous cost of Canadian companies' pension plans continues to make news. For example, one recent report indicates that only 18% of one type of pension plan (defined benefit) were fully funded—meaning that the plans had enough money to pay the future promised benefits to retirees. That means that the other 82% of defined benefit plans had a funding shortfall. However, the news is not all bad! The same report examined the solvency funded ratio, which measures the market value of assets divided by liabilities. The median solvency funded ratio was 89% at the end of March 2015, which was up significantly from a low of 66% in 2012.[2]

Not only are employee pension plans expensive, but they can be complicated to account for. One of the most extreme examples of how complicated accounting for pensions can be is the company referred to in our opening story, Air Canada. In its 2014 annual report, the company noted that it had 10 separate plans registered in Canada, in addition to international plans in the United States, United Kingdom, and Japan. The company also has a variety of plans that are not registered. Its defined benefit pension plans provide pensions to retired employees, benefits to terminated employees, and death benefits. To complicate matters further, Air Canada must account for other employee benefits, including health and disability benefits for employees who are still active, and for those who have already retired.

How much do the airline's pension plans cost the company? For 2014, Air Canada indicates a total pension benefits cost of $276 million, and other post-employment benefits cost of $95 million. Fortunately, these costs were offset by remeasurement income amounts in other comprehensive income of $167 million! At the end of 2014, Air Canada reported pension and other benefit liabilities on its consolidated statement of financial position of $2.4 billion, which contributed to an overall shareholders' equity of negative $1.1 billion. This is an improvement relative to 2011, when the company reported pension liabilities of $5.6 billion, and an overall shareholders' equity of negative $4.1 billion. If you consider these numbers in relation to the basic accounting equation of Assets = Liabilities + Shareholders' equity, you readily see the huge impact of underfunded pension costs on Air Canada's financial position.

The company attributes much of the decrease in its pension and other benefit liabilities to several factors. First, the equity markets improved relative to a few years earlier. Because much of its pension funds' assets are invested in equities, changes in market performance up or down can have a drastic effect on the size of its pension funds. Second, there were changes in pension benefits for employees, such as moving new employees into a different type of pension plan. Lastly, there was an increase in the interest rate Air Canada uses to determine its pension liabilities.[3] We will see later in the chapter why the changes in interest rates, and interest rate assumptions, are so important for companies' pension costs.

Chapter Overview

This chapter first introduces basic terminology, categories of benefits, and how to account for benefit plans that are relatively straightforward. We then explain the key underlying components of defined benefit plans—such as a company's defined benefit obligation and plan assets—and what causes them to change. These components and changes in them are the basic building blocks for post-employment benefits accounting. By understanding them, you will better understand the accounting for pensions and other post-employment benefits, even if the individual standards differ or change later.

After this, we describe approaches to the recognition and measurement of the statement of financial position net defined benefit liability (or asset) and the period's benefit cost associated with a defined benefit plan. We then set out what constitutes current GAAP under IFRS and ASPE for such plans. Appendix 19A provides a simplified example of a one-person pension plan to help you better visualize and understand some of the new concepts that are introduced in the chapter. Short-term benefits that are provided while employees are actively employed, such as regular vacations and occasional sick days, were discussed in Chapter 13, as was accounting for other short-term absences such as parental leave and short-term disability leave.

As mentioned, this chapter discusses the accounting and reporting for a variety of post-employment benefits that are earned by employees and that are expected to be provided to them on a long-term basis. Examples of these benefit plans include:

- Post-retirement plans such as pensions and plans that provide health care or life insurance benefits after an employee's retirement.

- Post-employment plans with benefits that are provided after employment but before retirement. These include long-term disability income benefits, long-term severance benefits, and continuation of benefits such as health care and life insurance.

- Plans covering accumulating and vested compensated absences. This type of benefit includes payments made while an employee is absent from work. It also includes unrestricted sabbatical leaves and accumulated sick days that vest or are taken as paid vacation.

Nature of Pension Plans

A **pension plan** is an arrangement in which an employer provides benefits (payments) to employees after they retire, for services that the employees provided while they were working. Pension accounting may refer **either to accounting for the employer** or **accounting for the pension plan.** This chapter focuses on the employer's accounting. The company or employer is the organization that sponsors the pension plan. It incurs the cost and contributes to the pension fund. The fund is the entity that receives the employer contributions (and employee contributions, if any), administers the pension assets, and makes the benefit payments to the pension recipients (the retired employees). Illustration 19-1 sets out the three participants in a pension plan and the flow of cash among them.

Illustration 19-1

Flow of Cash among Pension Plan Participants

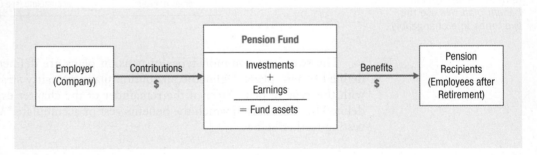

The pension plan in the illustration is **funded.**[4] This means that the employer (company) sets money aside for future pension benefits by making payments to a funding agency that is responsible for accumulating the pension plan assets and for making payments to the recipients as the benefits come due. The assets that are transferred become the assets of the pension plan, which is a separate legal entity. They are not company assets.

In **contributory plans**, the employees pay part of the cost of the stated benefits or voluntarily make payments to increase their benefits. In **non-contributory plans**, the employer bears the entire cost. Companies generally design pension plans in accordance with federal income tax laws. These laws permit deduction of the employer's and employees' contributions to the pension fund and offer tax-free status for earnings on the pension fund assets. The pension benefits are taxable when they are received by the pensioner.

CORPORATE
TAX 6.1.2

The plan is a separate legal and reporting entity for which a set of books is maintained and financial statements are prepared. We will not cover general purpose financial statements for pension plans in this chapter but they are set out in Part IV of the *CPA Canada Handbook* and in IAS 26. This chapter is devoted to issues that relate to **the employer** as the sponsor of pension and other post-employment benefit plans.

WHAT DO THE NUMBERS MEAN?

REAL WORLD EMPHASIS

When you see the size of pension funds, you will understand why they need to be properly administered. The following list shows the pension benefit plan expense, fund assets, and shareholders' equity of a sample of large Canadian companies for 2014.

Company	Pension Cost/ Expense Recovery (in millions)	Pension Fund Assets (in millions)	Shareholders' Equity (in millions)
ManuLife Financial Corporation	$117	$ 3,442	$33,926
Canadian Pacific Railway Limited	(52)	11,376	5,610
Suncor Energy Inc.	237	3,775	41,603
Bombardier Inc. (in U.S. $)	400	8,820	55
BCE Inc.	406	20,080	15,239

As the list shows, pension expense can be a substantial amount, and the fund assets are sometimes larger than the shareholders' equity of the company that sponsors the plan.

Post-employment benefit plans can also be categorized as in Illustration 19-2.

Illustration 19-2

Categories of Employee Future Benefit Plans

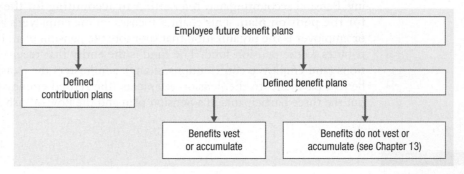

Alternative Terminology

ASPE uses the term *employee future benefit plan*, while IFRS uses the term *post-employment benefit plan*. We use the two terms interchangeably.

The two most common types of pension plans are defined contribution plans and defined benefit plans. Defined contribution plans are fairly straightforward, so we begin with this type of plan. Most of the remainder of the chapter explains the accounting for defined benefit plans in which the benefits vest or accumulate.[5] We discuss the concept of vesting further below.

Defined Contribution Plans

Objective 2

Identify and account for a defined contribution plan.

A **defined contribution plan** is a post-employment benefit plan that specifies how the employer's contributions or payments into the plan are determined, rather than identifying what benefits will be received by the employee or the method of determining those benefits.[6] In other words, the employer's contributions are defined; the employee's benefits are not. The IFRS definition in IAS 19 *Employee Benefits* extends the explanation of a defined contribution plan to include the fact that, once the employer pays those contributions into the fund, it has no further obligation to make additional payments, even if the fund ends up not having enough assets to pay the employee benefits. Under a defined contribution plan, the amounts paid in are usually attributed to specific individuals. The contributions may be a fixed sum—for example, $5,000 per year—or they may be related to salary, such as 6%

of regular plus overtime earnings. No promise is made about the ultimate benefit that will be paid out to the employees.

LAW

For a defined contribution pension plan, the amounts that are contributed are usually turned over to an independent third party or trustee who acts on behalf of the beneficiaries (the participating employees). The trustee assumes ownership of the pension assets and is responsible for their investment and distribution. The trust is separate and distinct from the employer. The size of the pension benefit that the employee finally collects under the plan depends on several things:

1. the amounts that have been contributed to the pension trust,

2. the income that has accumulated in the trust,

3. the treatment of forfeitures of funds created by the termination of employees before retirement, and

4. the investment alternatives available on retirement.

Because **the contribution is defined**, the accounting for a defined contribution plan is straightforward. The employer's obligation is dictated by the amounts to be contributed. Therefore, a liability is reported on the employer's statement of financial position only if the required contributions have not been made in full, and an asset is reported if more than the required amount has been contributed. Discounting is not generally an issue as long as the amounts due are expected to be paid in the 12-month period following the reporting date. The annual **current service cost** is simply the amount that the company is obligated to contribute to the plan in exchange for employee services provided during the period. The current service cost includes the present value of contributions required to be made in future periods for employee services provided in the current period. The employer generally has no other obligation and assumes no other risk relative to this plan.

ASPE

ASPE discusses other possible components of the associated cost and liability. When a defined contribution plan is first established, or when it is later amended, the employer may be required to make contributions for employee services that were provided before the start of the plan or its amendment. This obligation is referred to as **past service cost**. Such costs are generally recognized immediately in expense under both ASPE and IFRS. Also, if the company has accrued contributions required to be made in future periods, for employee services provided in the current or prior periods, interest should be recognized on the accrued contributions. In addition, if a defined contribution plan has an unallocated plan surplus (which could, for example, result if a defined benefit plan is converted to a defined contribution plan), any interest earned on the unallocated plan surplus is deducted from the cost for the period.

Defined Benefit Plans

Objective 3
Identify and explain what a defined benefit plan is and the related accounting issues.

A **defined benefit plan** is a post-employment benefit plan other than a defined contribution plan.[7] It is a plan that specifies either the benefits to be received by an employee or the method of determining those benefits. In other words, the employee's benefits are defined; the employer's contributions are not fixed. One example is a plan that provides an entitlement to a lump-sum payment of $5,000 on the employee's 10th and 25th anniversaries of employment with the employer company. Another is a plan that provides an annual pension benefit on retirement equal to 2% of the average of the employee's best three years of salary multiplied by the number of years of employment.

LAW

The most complex type of benefit plan provides defined benefits that vest with the employee based on the employee's length of service. Employees' rights to post-employment medical benefits, for example, generally vest after the employee has worked a specified number of years, and the amount of benefit usually increases with the length of service. **Vesting** means that an employee keeps the rights to the benefit even if the employee no longer works for the company. That is, if an employee whose benefits have vested leaves the company, the individual will still receive those benefits. If they are not vested when the employee leaves, the employee loses the rights to the benefits.

POST-EMPLOYMENT BENEFITS OVERVIEW

Employers promise a number of future benefits in exchange for current service. Employees may be entitled to some of these benefits even if they leave the company. The major accounting issue is "How do we measure the employer's obligation, and in which accounting periods should the cost of the benefits be recognized?"

Other long-term employee benefits, including unrestricted time off for long service or sabbatical leave, deferred compensation, and other compensated absences, may also fit the description of defined benefit plans with benefits that vest or accumulate. All of these benefit plans have something in common: **the entitlement to the benefits increases with the length of the employee's service.** The **objective** in accounting for these plans, therefore, is for the expense and liability related to these plans to be recognized over the accounting periods in which the related services are provided by the employees. One difference in accounting under ASPE as compared with IFRS for defined benefit pension plans is that remeasurements are charged to net income, not to other comprehensive income.

As discussed, a defined benefit pension plan identifies the pension benefits that an employee will receive after retiring. These benefits typically are a function of an employee's years of service and compensation level in the years approaching retirement. To ensure that appropriate resources are available to pay the benefits at retirement, there is usually a requirement that funds be set aside during the service life of the employees.

The **employees** are the beneficiaries of a defined **contribution** trust, but the **employer** is the beneficiary of a defined **benefit** trust. The trust's main purpose under a defined benefit plan is to safeguard assets and to invest them so that there will be enough to pay the employer's obligation to the employees. **In form,** the trust is a separate entity; **in substance,** the trust assets and liabilities belong to the employer. That is, **as long as the plan continues, the employer is responsible for paying the defined benefits, no matter what happens in the trust.** The employer must make up any shortfall in the accumulated assets held by the trust. If excess assets have accumulated in the trust, it may be possible for the employer to recapture them either through reduced future funding or through a reversion of funds, depending on the trust agreement, plan documents, and governing legislation.[8]

With a defined benefit plan, the employer assumes the economic risks: the employee is secure because the benefits to be paid on retirement are predefined, but the employer is at risk because the cost is uncertain.[9] The cost depends on factors such as employee turnover, mortality, length of service, and compensation levels, as well as investment returns that are earned on pension assets, inflation, and other economic conditions over long periods of time.

Because the cost to the company is affected by a wide range of uncertain future variables, it is not easy to measure the pension cost and liability that have to be recognized each period as employees provide services to earn their pension entitlement. In addition, an appropriate funding pattern must be established to assure that enough funds will be available at retirement to provide the benefits that have been promised. Whatever funding method is decided on, it should provide enough money at retirement to meet the benefits defined by the plan. Note that **the expense to be recognized each period is not the same as the employer's cash funding contribution,** just as depreciation expense recognized on the use of plant and equipment is not measured in terms of how the asset is financed. The accounting issues related to defined benefit plans are complex, but interesting.

LAW

FINANCIAL ANALYSIS AND PLANNING
5.1.1

TREASURY MANAGEMENT
5.2.1

At one time, most employer-sponsored pension plans in Canada were of the defined benefit type. The majority of plans now are defined contribution plans, and the percentage of defined contribution plans is growing. However, in terms of pension assets, the amount that is in defined benefit plans continues to be disproportionately high.

STATISTICS

The issues that are associated with pension plans involve complicated mathematical considerations. Companies therefore use the services of actuaries to ensure that the plan is appropriate for the employee group covered. **Actuaries** are individuals who are trained through a long and rigorous certification program to assign probabilities to future events and their financial effects.[10] The insurance industry also uses actuaries to assess risks and to advise the industry on the setting of premiums and other aspects of insurance policies. Employers rely heavily on actuaries for help in developing, implementing, and determining the funding of pension plans.

An actuary's chief purpose in pension accounting is to ensure that the company has an appropriate funding pattern to meet its pension obligations. This calculation requires a set of assumptions to be established and the continued monitoring of these assumptions to ensure that they are realistic. Actuaries make predictions, called **actuarial assumptions**, about mortality rates, employee turnover, interest and earnings rates, early retirement frequency, future salaries, and any other factors that need to be considered for pension plans. They also calculate the various pension measures that affect the financial statements, such as the pension obligation, the annual cost of servicing the plan, and the cost of amendments to the plan. Defined benefit pension plans rely heavily on information and measurements provided by these specialists.

Because defined benefit pension plans will be used extensively in this chapter to explain how to account for pension plans, we will now provide basic information about the nature of defined benefit pension plans.

DEFINED BENEFIT PENSION PLANS

SIGNIFICANT CHANGE

Accounting for post-employment benefits such as pensions has undergone significant change in recent years. The IASB introduced new requirements effective January 1, 2013, and ASPE began requiring similar changes effective in 2014. However, the foundations on which post-employment benefit accounting is based have not changed significantly. The first foundation is the employer's obligation to pay out benefits in the future for the employees' services up to the date of the statement of financial position. This obligation is estimated by the actuary. The second foundation is setting aside plan assets to fund this obligation. If you understand the nature of the **defined benefit obligation** and **plan assets**, and the transactions and events that affect their measurement, it will help clarify your study of accounting for benefit plans, even as the standards evolve.

The Employer's Obligation

Alternative Measures of the Pension Obligation

Objective 4

Explain what the employer's benefit obligation is, identify alternative measures for this obligation, and prepare a continuity schedule of transactions and events that change its balance.

Most companies agree that an employer's **pension obligation** is the deferred compensation obligation that it has to its employees for their service under the terms of the pension plan. Determining that obligation is not simple, though, because there are different ways of measuring it.

One measure of the pension obligation is based only on the benefits that vest. **Vested benefits** are those that an employee is entitled to receive even if he or she provides no additional services to the company. Most pension plans require a specific minimum number of years of service to the employer before an employee achieves the status of having vested benefits. Actuaries calculate the **vested benefit obligation** using vested benefits only, at current salary levels, under the **vested benefit method**.

Another way to measure the pension obligation is using both vested and non-vested benefits. On this basis, the deferred compensation amount is calculated on all years of employees' service—**both vested and non-vested**—using current salary levels. This basis of measurement is called the **projected unit credit**, sometimes called the **accumulated benefit method** (prorated on service).

FINANCIAL ANALYSIS AND PLANNING
5.1.1

A third method of measuring the pension obligation calculates the deferred compensation amount using both vested and non-vested service, and incorporates future salaries projected to be earned over the period to retirement. This way of measuring the pension obligation is called the **projected benefit method**. Because future salaries are expected to be higher than current salaries, this approach results in the largest measure of the pension obligation.

Deciding which measure to use is a critical choice because it affects the amount of the pension liability and the annual pension expense reported. The diagram in Illustration 19-3 presents the differences in these three methods. Regardless of the approach used, the estimated future benefits to be paid are discounted to their present value.

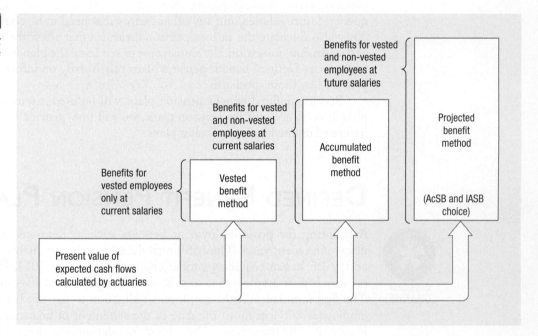

Which of these methods is generally accepted as providing the best measure of the obligation? The FASB, IASB, and Canadian Accounting Standards Board (AcSB) have all adopted the **projected benefit method** to calculate the defined benefit obligation as the best measure specifically **for accounting purposes**. The **defined benefit obligation (DBO) for accounting purposes** is the present value of vested and non-vested benefits earned to the date of the statement of financial position, with the benefits measured using employees' future salary levels.[11]

UNDERLYING CONCEPT

Critics of using projected salaries argue that it results in future obligations being added to existing ones. Those in favour of the defined benefit obligation counter that a promise by an employer to pay benefits based on a percentage of the employees' future salary is far different from a promise to pay a percentage of their current salary, and that this difference should be reflected in the pension liability and pension expense.

The FASB and the IASB have both studied whether the liability should include estimates of future salaries. This debate centres on whether a company can have a liability today that is based in part on future salaries that have not yet been earned.

The **defined benefit obligation (DBO) for funding purposes** represents another measure. It is used as an option under ASPE, and it is discussed later in this chapter. The DBO for funding purposes tends to focus more on current salary levels and often uses a different discount rate. Regardless of the measure of the obligation chosen for accounting purposes, regulators use a variety of measures for determining the level of contributions that plan sponsors are required by law to remit to the pension fund.

Changes in the Defined Benefit Obligation

The measurement of the defined benefit obligation is central to accounting for pension costs. At any point in time, the DBO represents the actuarial present value of the cost of the benefits attributed to employee services that have been provided to date. A simplified example of the measurement of the DBO for accounting purposes in a one-person pension plan is provided in Appendix 19A. You may find it useful to read this material before proceeding.

Illustration 19-4 summarizes the DBO from the perspective of the transactions and events that change its amount. The DBO increases as employees provide further services and earn additional benefits, and as interest is added to this outstanding discounted liability. The obligation decreases as benefit payments are made to retirees. In addition, the DBO might either increase or decrease as plans are amended to change the future benefits that were promised for prior services, and as the actuarial assumptions change that are used to calculate the obligation. Actuaries provide most of the necessary measurements related to the DBO.

Illustration 19-4 *Defined Benefit Obligation—* *Continuity Schedule*	Defined benefit obligation (DBO), at beginning of period + Current service cost + Interest cost − Benefits paid to retirees ± Past service costs of plan amendments during period ± Actuarial gains (−) or losses (+) during period = Defined benefit obligation (DBO), at end of period

Current Service Cost

The **current service cost** is the cost of the benefits that are to be provided in the future in exchange for the services that the employees provided in the current period. In measuring the service cost to assign to each period, standard setters had to decide on a method of allocating the estimated cost to the individual years during which the entitlement to the benefits builds. Should the total cost be allocated based on the percentage of salary earned by the employee during the year relative to the total estimated career compensation (that is, **prorated on salaries**)? Or should it be allocated based on an equal amount per year of service (that is, **prorated on service**)? The standard setters decided on a prorated on service method that accrues a relatively equal charge each period—the projected unit credit method.[12]

To calculate current service cost, the actuary predicts the additional benefits that must be paid under the plan's benefit formula as a result of the employees' current year of service and then discounts the cost of these benefits to their present value. For example, consider the following pension benefit formula:

> Annual pension benefit on retirement = 2% of salary at retirement × Number of years of service

By working an additional year, the employee earns an entitlement to a larger pension, and the company's pension obligation for accounting purposes increases by the present value of 2% of the employee's estimated final salary for each year of expected retirement.[13] Appendix 19A provides a simplified example of this calculation.

For defined benefit plans where future benefits depend on or are increased by the length of service, the actuary bases the accounting calculations on future salary levels and then attributes the cost of the future benefits to the accounting periods, usually between the date of hire and the date when the employee becomes eligible for full benefits. This is known as the **attribution period**. The obligation to provide benefits is attributed to the periods in which the employee provides the service that gives rise to the benefits. While the date of hire is the most common date for employees to begin earning benefits, it may be a later date, and eligibility for full benefits may occur before the date of retirement.

Interest Cost

Because future benefit plans are deferred compensation arrangements—the benefits are essentially elements of wages that are deferred—the time value of money has to be considered. Because the obligation is not paid until each employee retires, it is measured on a discounted basis. As time to retirement passes, **interest accrues on the defined benefit obligation just as it does on any discounted debt**. The interest is based on the DBO that is outstanding during the period, taking into account any material changes in its balance during that period. So, for example, if the plan was modified and past service costs had been awarded at the first of the year, the interest cost would have increased as well because the opening benefit liability would have been higher. Similarly the timing of benefit payments would affect the DBO outstanding at various times in the year and would affect the interest cost.

What interest rate should be used? Both IFRS and ASPE require the use of a current market rate, determined by reference to the current yield on high-quality debt instruments such as high-quality corporate bonds. The objective is to have the discount rate reflect the estimated timing and amount of the expected benefit payments. Changes to IFRS in 2013 (and ASPE in 2014) require that the discount rate used for the DBO and the plan assets be the same rate. ASPE also allows a current **settlement rate** to be used, instead of the current yield on high-quality corporate bonds. This is the rate implied in an insurance contract that could be purchased to effectively settle the pension obligation. IFRS uses the rate at the end of the reporting period and it is reassessed at each such date. ASPE uses the date determined at the date of the actuarial valuation. Note that minor changes in the interest rate used to discount pension benefits can dramatically affect the measurement of the employer's obligation. For example, a one-percentage-point decrease in the discount rate might increase pension liabilities by 15%!

Benefits Paid to Retirees

The pension fund trustee is responsible for making payments of the pension benefits to the former employees. Similar to all liabilities, as obligations are met, the balance of the remaining obligation is reduced.

Past Service Costs

When a defined benefit plan is either initiated (begun) or amended, credit is often given to employees for years of service that they provided before the date of initiation or amendment. As a result of these credits for prior services, the actuary remeasures the DBO, and it usually ends up being larger than it was before the change. The increase in the DBO on the date that the plan is initiated or amended is known as **past service cost**, the cost of the retroactive benefits. This increase is often substantial. Under changes to IFRS and ASPE (effective in 2013 and 2014 respectively), past service cost now is included in pension benefit cost in the income statement (rather than being deferred and amortized). See Appendix 19A for a simplified illustration.

In recent years, because they want to reduce the very significant costs of post-retirement plans, many companies have been negotiating reductions in some of their plan benefits. When this happens, there is a **decrease** in the DBO that relates to past services, and a **past service benefit** is recognized.

Actuarial Gains and Losses

Actuarial gains and losses related to the DBO (the liability) can result from either:

1. a change in actuarial assumptions, which means a change in the assumptions about the occurrence of future events that affect the measurement of the future benefit costs and obligations; or

2. an **experience gain or loss,** which is the difference between what has actually occurred and the previous actuarial assumptions about what would occur.

When later events show that assumptions were inaccurate, adjustments are needed. Both of these are discussed further below.

In estimating the DBO, actuaries make assumptions about such variables as mortality rates, retirement rates, turnover rates, disability rates, and rates of salary escalation (increase). Any difference between these assumed rates and the ones that are actually experienced changes the amount of the DBO. Actual experience is rarely exactly the same as actuarial predictions. An unexpected gain or loss that changes the amount of the DBO due to short-term experience varying from what had been assumed is sometimes referred to as an **experience adjustment**.[14] Actuarial gains and losses also occur when the assumptions that are used by the actuary in calculating the DBO are revised, because this too causes a change in the amount of the obligation. An example is the effect of a change in the interest rate used to discount the pension cash flows on the measurement of the obligation. Because experience gains and losses are similar to and affect the DBO in the same way as changes in actuarial assumptions, both types are generally referred to as **actuarial gains and losses**.

To illustrate, assume that a company's calculated defined benefit obligation—based on its opening balance and the year's service cost, interest cost, benefits paid, and plan amendments—was estimated to be $962,000 at December 31, 2017. If the company's actuaries, using December 31, 2017 estimates in their actuarial calculations, determine that the defined benefit obligation is actually $975,000, then the company has suffered an actuarial loss of $13,000 ($975,000 – $962,000). If the actuary calculates a reduced obligation, the result is an actuarial gain. Whatever the result, the DBO is adjusted to its most recent actuarial valuation. The adjustment flows through other comprehensive income (OCI) under IFRS, or net income under ASPE.

Plan settlements and curtailments also affect the amount of the defined benefit obligation. For example, settlements substantially settle or discharge all (or part) of the benefit obligation, while curtailments generally reduce the expected years of future service for active employees. A detailed examination of settlements and curtailments is outside the scope of this chapter.

Plan Assets

Plan Asset Composition

Objective 5

Identify transactions and events that change benefit plan assets, and calculate the balance of the plan assets.

The benefit plan assets are the other major foundation on which pension accounting is based. **Plan assets** are assets that have been set aside in a trust or other legal entity that is separate from the employer company. The assets are restricted and can be used only to settle the related defined benefit obligation: they cannot be used for meeting the claims of other company creditors. The plan assets are made up mainly of cash and investments in debt and equity securities that are held to earn a reasonable return, generally at a minimum of risk. Other investments, such as real estate investment property, are also common plan holdings for larger plans. As we will explain later, the plan assets increase by the return on plan assets, with the difference between the actual return on plan assets and the (expected) return calculated using the discount rate used for the DBO being treated as a remeasurement gain or loss.[15] Under IFRS, the remeasurement gain or loss on the plan assets is combined with the actuarial gain or loss on the DBO and is charged to OCI. The remeasurements recognized in OCI are not subsequently reclassified to profit or loss; that is, they are not recycled (IAS 19.122).

Changes in Plan Assets

As we see in Illustration 19-5, the plan assets change as a result of contributions from the employer (and employee, if the plan is contributory) and from the return on plan assets generated on the assets that have been invested. The pool of assets is reduced by payments to retirees. As described above, the **actual return** can also be thought of as the (expected) return calculated using the discount rate used for the DBO and a remeasurement gain or loss.

Illustration 19-5

Plan Assets—Continuity Schedule

Plan assets, fair value at beginning of period
+ Contributions from employer company, and employees if applicable
± Actual return
− Benefits paid to retirees
= Plan assets, fair value at end of period

**LAW AND
CORPORATE
TAX
6.1.2**

Contributions

The amount of an employer company's contributions to the plan has a direct effect on the plan's ability to pay the DBO. Who and what determine how much a company contributes to the plan? In Canada, pension plans come under either federal or provincial pension legislation as well as regulations of the Canada Revenue Agency (CRA). The CRA stipulates the amount of the contributions that are tax deductible to the company and the conditions on the payment of benefits out of the plan. Federal and provincial laws dictate the funding requirements.[16]

Return on Plan Assets

The **return on plan assets** can be thought of as the income generated on the assets being held by the trustee, less the cost of administering the fund. The return that is earned on these assets usually increases the fund balance. The return on plan assets is made up of dividends, interest, and gains and losses from the sale of investments, as well as profits that are generated on any real estate investments. In addition, because the assets are measured at fair value, both realized and unrealized gains and losses on the assets are included as part of the return on plan assets. Including the realized and unrealized gains and losses explains why the return could increase the plan assets in one year and decrease them in another. In years when stock and/or bond markets decline significantly, the reduction in fair value may be greater than the other forms of income that are reported and the actual return on plan assets will be a loss.

**TREASURY
MANAGEMENT
5.2.1**

Because the return on plan assets can be highly variable from one year to the next, actuaries ignore short-term fluctuations when they develop a funding pattern to accumulate assets to pay benefits in the future. Instead, they calculate an expected long-term rate of return and apply it to the fair value of the fund assets to arrive at an **expected return** on plan assets. The same discount rate is applied to the DBO and the plan assets (that is, the rate for high-quality corporate bonds). The interest cost on the DBO combined with the interest income on the plan assets together comprise the **net interest on the net defined benefit liability or asset**, which is charged to net income under IFRS. (This is treated similarly under ASPE, which refers to the net interest as the **finance cost**.)

Benefits Paid

The plan trustee pays out benefits to the retirees according to the plan formula and pension agreement.

Surplus or Deficit

Objective 6

Explain what a benefit plan's surplus or deficit is, calculate it, and identify what transactions and events change its amount.

The measures of the DBO and plan assets are fundamental to pension accounting as, together, they determine the plan **surplus or deficit**. Because of this, accounting standards specify that they should be measured as at the date of the annual financial statements. Under IFRS, both the plan assets and DBO are required to represent reporting date values. (More specifically, the net defined benefit liability/asset is to be measured with "sufficient regularity that the amounts recognised in the financial statements do not differ materially from the amounts that would be determined at the end of the reporting period" [IAS 19.58].)

Calculation of Surplus or Deficit

As indicated in Illustration 19-6, the difference between the DBO and the pension assets' fair value at a point in time is known as the plan's surplus or deficit. A plan with more liabilities than assets is **underfunded** and has a deficit. A plan with accumulated assets that are greater than the related obligation is **overfunded** and is said to have a surplus.[17]

<table>
<tr><td>Defined benefit obligation (DBO), end of period
− Fair value of plan assets, end of period</td></tr>
<tr><td>= Plan's surplus or deficit, end of period</td></tr>
</table>

DBO > Plan assets = **underfunded** = a deficit (net defined benefit liability)

Plan assets > DBO = **overfunded** = a surplus (net defined benefit asset, which may be limited for financial statement purposes by the asset ceiling test, discussed further below)

Illustration 19-6

Surplus or Deficit

UNDERLYING CONCEPT

Many plans are underfunded but still quite viable. For example, for its 2014 fiscal year, the **Royal Bank of Canada** had a $2,420-million employee benefit liability on its consolidated balance sheet. But the Royal Bank at that time had net income of $9,004 million and shareholders' equity of $52,690 million! Concern over pensions being underfunded is directly related to the financial position and performance of the employer company—the plan sponsor.

Accounting for Changes in Surplus or Deficit

Now that you have been introduced to most of the components that are needed to account for a defined benefit pension plan, it is time to look at how companies actually account for such plans.

Defined Benefit Cost Components

Objective 7

Identify the components of pension expense, and account for a defined benefit pension plan under IFRS and ASPE.

You have already been introduced to the components that make up the pension benefit cost. As we have discussed, under IFRS some of this cost is reflected in net income and some in other comprehensive income. Under ASPE, however, the pension benefit cost is all reflected in net income.

Before 2014, ASPE permitted companies to make an accounting policy choice between the immediate recognition and the deferral and amortization approaches. Under the **immediate recognition approach**, pension expense is made up of all items affecting the funding status during the period with the exception of contributions into the plan. In contrast, the deferral and amortization approach allowed for delay in the recognition of past service costs and actuarial gains and losses. The new ASPE standard, as set out in Section 3462 of the *CPA Canada Handbook*, eliminated the deferral and amortization approach and "no longer refers to the immediate recognition approach as this approach is now used for all plans."[18]

The main changes introduced under IFRS that became effective in 2013 are as follows:

UNDERLYING CONCEPT

Together, the definition of a liability and the matching principle justify accounting for pension costs on the accrual basis. This requires recording an expense when the future benefits are earned by the employees, and recognizing an existing obligation to pay pensions later based on current services received.

1. The elimination of the ability to defer and amortize past service costs or benefits and actuarial gains or losses.

2. Requiring that the components of the defined benefit cost be recognized either in net income or in other comprehensive income (OCI) as follows:
   (a) Current and past service cost—in **net income**,
   (b) Net interest on the net defined benefit liability or asset—in **net income**,
   (c) Gains and losses from remeasurements of the net defined benefit liability or asset—in **OCI**.

The differences between IFRS and ASPE relate mainly to item (c) above because ASPE does not use OCI. We will use the example of Zarle Corporation and its defined benefit pension plan as set out in Illustration 19-8 to explain and contrast the IFRS and ASPE approaches.

Under ASPE, the **pension expense** (or **pension benefit cost**) is made up of all items affecting the pension surplus or deficit during the period except the company contributions to the plan assets.[19] A comparison of pension expense under IFRS and ASPE follows:

1. **Current service cost.** The service cost for benefits earned by employees during the current period is recognized and included in pension expense in the same period under both IFRS and ASPE.

2. **Net interest (or finance) cost.** Under both IFRS and ASPE, the same discount rate is used for interest cost on the DBO and for the interest assumed to be earned on the plan assets.

Under IFRS, the actual return on plan assets is allocated between pension expense on the statement of comprehensive income, and other comprehensive income. Specifically, the net interest on the net defined benefit liability/asset is recognized in net income (IAS 19.57). The remeasurement relating to the return on plan assets other than net interest on the net defined benefit liability/asset is recognized in OCI. In contrast, the remeasurements under ASPE are included in net income (and separately disclosed), including the remeasurement representing the difference between the actual return on plan assets and the return calculated using the same discount rate used to determine the DBO at the start of the period (*CPA Canada Handbook*, 3462.084.–.085).

3. **Past service cost, curtailments, and settlements.** Plan amendments instantly change the amount of the employer's obligation, and the total cost (or benefit) of the amendment is recognized immediately in pension expense under both IFRS and ASPE. Similarly, gains and losses relating to curtailments ("a significant reduction by the entity in the number of employees covered by the plan," according to IAS 19.8) and/or settlements (a transaction that substantially discharges or settles all, or part, of a DBO) are included in net income.[20]

4. **Actuarial gains and losses.** Actuarial gains and losses result from items such as changes in actuarial assumptions and experience adjustments that increase or decrease the present value of the DBO. To the extent that they are recognized as a component of pension expense in the same period they are incurred, the reported expense will tend to fluctuate significantly from year to year. ASPE recognizes the full amount of the actuarial gain or loss in pension expense each period. IFRS is similar in that the gains and losses are not deferred, but under IFRS the actuarial gains or losses are included in OCI rather than in net income.

Other components of expense identified in IFRS and ASPE include a part of the change in the valuation allowance related to the net defined benefit asset (if any). The limit on the carrying amount of a net defined benefit asset on the statement of financial position, due to the asset ceiling test, and the valuation allowance are explained briefly later in this chapter.

Illustration of Pension Accounting Using a Pension Work Sheet

A work sheet is used to illustrate how the transactions affecting the DBO and fund assets are accumulated in the accounts. **It is important to note two things.**

1. **Neither the DBO nor the fund assets are recognized directly in the sponsoring company's accounts;** they are both **off–balance sheet** or **memo accounts.** The fund assets belong to the benefit trust, and the DBO is a liability of the sponsoring company only to the extent there are not enough assets in the fund to cover the total obligation.

2. When applying the approach under ASPE, **the defined benefit obligation** is based on either an actuarial valuation used for **funding purposes** or a separate actuarial valuation prepared for accounting purposes. (An actuarial valuation prepared for funding purposes is one prepared in accordance with pension regulations and legislation. It does

not necessarily use management's best estimates and the discount note required under an actuarial valuation prepared for accounting purposes.). To simplify matters, in the following example we assume that the DBO based on the actuarial valuation used for **funding purposes under ASPE** is equal to the DBO that would be calculated for accounting purposes under **IFRS or ASPE**.

A unique pension work sheet is used to keep track of pension expense and the Net Defined Benefit Liability/Asset account on the statement of financial position, as well as the off–balance sheet amounts. As its name suggests, the work sheet is a working tool; it is not a journal or part of the general ledger. It merely accumulates the information needed to make the pension journal entries. The format of the work sheet that illustrates the relationship among all the components under ASPE is shown in Illustration 19-7.[21] This format of work sheet would also apply under IFRS when there are no remeasurement gains or losses.

Illustration 19-7

Basic Format of Pension Work Sheet

	A	B	C	D	F	G
1		**General Journal Entries**			**Memo Record**	
2	Items	Annual Pension Expense	Cash	Net Defined Benefit Liability/ Asset	Defined Benefit Obligation	Plan Assets
3						
4						
5						
6						

The left-hand columns of the work sheet under "General Journal Entries" determine the entries to be recorded in the formal general ledger accounts. The right-hand "Memo Record" columns summarize changes in balances relating to the DBO and the plan assets, based on amounts provided by the actuary and pension plan trustee. On the first line of the work sheet, the beginning balances are recorded. Subsequently, transactions and events that relate to the pension plan are entered, using debits and credits and using both the left-hand columns and the right-hand columns together for recording the entries. For each transaction or event, the debits must equal the credits, and the balance in the Net Defined Benefit Liability/Asset column must equal the net balance in the Memo Record columns. If the DBO is greater than the plan assets, a pension liability is reported on the statement of financial position. If the DBO is less than the plan assets, a pension asset results.

Let's walk through the basic pension accounting model used under IFRS and ASPE by using the facts and circumstances set out in Illustration 19-8 that apply to Zarle Corporation's pension plan for the three-year period from 2016 to 2018.

Illustration 19-8

Zarle Corporation Pension Plan, 2016–2018

	2016	2017	2018
Fair value of plan assets, first of year	$100,000	$111,000	$134,100
Defined benefit obligation (DBO) (assumed to equal the DBO for funding purposes under ASPE)	100,000	112,000	212,700
Current service cost for year	9,000	9,500	13,000
Interest or discount rate on the DBO/plan assets	10%	10%	10%
Cost of past service benefits granted January 1, 2017	–0–	80,000	–0–
Actual earnings on plan assets for year	10,000	11,100	12,000
Employer contributions for year (funding)	8,000	20,000	24,000
Benefits paid to retirees by trustee for year	7,000	8,000	10,500
Actuarial loss due to change in actuarial assumptions	–0–	–0–	28,530
Plan assets, end of year	111,000	134,100	159,600
DBO, end of year	112,000	212,700	265,000
Surplus (deficit), end of year—over (under) funded	(1,000)	(78,600)	(105,400)

The Basics—2016 Work Sheet and Entries

Assume that Zarle Corporation begins its 2016 fiscal year with a DBO of $100,000, plan assets of $100,000, and a $0 balance in its Net Defined Benefit Liability/Asset account on the statement of financial position.

Using the information found in Illustration 19-8, Illustration 19-9 presents the work sheet, including the beginning balances and all the pension transactions that Zarle Corporation needs to account for in 2016. The beginning balances of the defined benefit obligation and the pension plan assets are recorded on the work sheet's first line in the memo record. They are not recorded in the general ledger accounts and, therefore, are not reported as a liability and an asset in Zarle Corporation's financial statements. Notice that, although they are "off–balance sheet," the January 1, 2016 surplus or deficit of $0 is the same as the balance of $0 in the net defined benefit liability/asset line on the statement of financial position on that date.[22]

Illustration 19-9

Pension Work Sheet—2016

	A	B	C	D	F	G
1		General Journal Entries			Memo Record	
2	Items	Annual Pension Expense	Cash	Net Defined Benefit Liability/ Asset	Defined Benefit Obligation	Plan Assets
3	Balance, Jan. 1, 2016			–0–	100,000 Cr.	100,000 Dr.
4	(a) Service cost	9,000 Dr.			9,000 Cr.	
5	(b) Net interest/finance cost	–0–			10,000 Cr.	10,000 Dr.
6	(c) Contribution		8,000 Cr.			8,000 Dr.
7	(d) Benefits paid				7,000 Dr.	7,000 Cr.
8	Expense entry, 2016	9,000 Dr.		9,000 Cr.		
9	Contribution entry, 2016		8,000 Cr.	8,000 Dr.		
10	Balance, Dec. 31, 2016			1,000 Cr.	112,000 Cr.	111,000 Dr.
11						

Entry (a) in Illustration 19-9 records the service cost component, which increases the defined benefit obligation by $9,000 and increases pension expense by $9,000. Entry (b) accrues the net interest/finance cost, increasing both the DBO and plan assets by $10,000 with net interest/finance cost of $0. (This is the $100,000 weighted average balance of the defined benefit obligation and the weighted average balance of the plan assets multiplied by the discount rate of 10%.) Note that, in all chapter examples and end-of-chapter problem material, unless specified otherwise, **it is assumed that current service cost is credited at year end and that contributions to the fund and benefits paid to retirees are year-end cash flows.** Such an assumption is needed to simplify the determination of the average balances outstanding for calculating any net interest/finance cost amounts. (We relax this assumption in the third year of our example.)

Entry (c) reflects Zarle Corporation's contribution (funding) of assets to the pension fund; Zarle's cash is decreased by $8,000 and plan assets are increased by $8,000. Entry (d) records the benefit payments made to retirees, which result in equal $7,000 decreases in the plan assets and the defined benefit obligation.

Zarle makes the following journal entry on December 31, 2016 to formally record the pension expense under both IFRS and ASPE for the year. (The journal entries are the same under IFRS and ASPE because there are no actuarial gains or losses, and there is no difference between expected and actual return in 2016.)

A	=	L	+	SE
		+9,000		–9,000

Cash flows: No effect

Pension Expense	9,000	
Net Defined Benefit Liability/Asset		9,000

When Zarle Corporation issued its $8,000 cheque to the pension fund trustee late in the year, it made the following entry:

A = L + SE
−8,000 −8,000

Cash flows: ↓ 8,000 outflow

Net Defined Benefit Liability/Asset	8,000	
Cash		8,000

The credit balance in the Net Defined Benefit Liability/Asset account of $1,000 represents the surplus or deficit—the difference between the DBO of $112,000 and the fund assets of $111,000. This should not be surprising because all the transactions that affected the DBO and plan assets, except for the benefits paid, also affected the statement of financial position. The benefits paid decrease the fund assets and the DBO in equal amounts with no effect on the surplus or deficit.

In addition, the statement of financial position liability account also represents the excess of the accumulated pension expense recognized to date over the accumulated contributions made to date—a $1,000 liability. Although we are not told what expense was reported and contributions were made in prior years, we can tell that these amounts were equal at January 1, 2016. This is because the Net Defined Benefit Liability/Asset account balance was $0 at that date.

2017 Work Sheet and Entries with Past Service Costs

One question that standard setters have wrestled with is whether the past service costs or credits that are associated with the adoption or amendment of pension plans should be fully recognized in net income when the plan is initiated or amended. Under the most recent changes to IFRS and ASPE, the conclusion is that because the costs, although significant, all relate to past services, there is no justification for deferring their recognition to future periods' income statements.

To illustrate how past service costs affect the pension accounts, we continue with Zarle Corporation's 2017 benefit plan activities as set out in Illustration 19-8 above. Zarle amends its defined benefit pension plan on January 1, 2017 to grant prior service benefits to certain employees. The company's actuaries determine that this causes an increase in the defined benefit obligation of $80,000.

Illustration 19-10 presents all the pension "entries" and information used by Zarle Corporation in 2017. The work sheet's first line shows the beginning balances of the Net Defined Benefit Liability/Asset account and the components of the balance. Entry (e) records Zarle Corporation's granting of prior service benefits by adding $80,000 to the defined benefit obligation and its recognition in Pension Expense. Entries (f), (g), (h), and (i) are similar to the corresponding entries in 2016. Notice that the net interest/

Illustration 19-10

Pension Work Sheet—2017

	A	B	C	D	F	G
1		General Journal Entries			Memo Record	
2	Items	Annual Pension Expense	Cash	Net Defined Benefit Liability/ Asset	Deferred Benefit Obligation	Plan Assets
3	Balance, Jan. 1, 2017			1,000 Cr.	112,000 Cr.	111,000 Dr.
4	(e) Past service cost	80,000 Dr.			80,000 Cr.	
5	(f) Service cost	9,500 Dr.			9,500 Cr.	
6	(g) Net interest/finance cost	8,100 Dr.			19,200 Cr.	11,100 Dr.
7	(h) Contribution		20,000 Cr.			20,000 Dr.
8	(i) Benefits paid				8,000 Dr.	8,000 Cr.
9	Expense entry, 2017	97,600 Dr.		97,600 Cr.		
10	Contribution entry, 2017		20,000 Cr.	20,000 Dr.		
11	Balance, Dec. 31, 2017			78,600 Cr.	212,700 Cr.	134,100 Dr.
12						

finance cost is based on the discount rate of 10% on the average balances of the DBO and plan assets outstanding for the year. Because the past service costs were granted effective January 1, the balance outstanding for the year was $112,000 + $80,000 = $192,000 × 10% = $19,200 relating to the DBO and $111,000 × 10% = $11,100 relating to the plan assets. Because the expected return on plan assets equalled the actual return, the difference of $8,100 is charged to pension expense under both IFRS and ASPE.

An entry is needed on December 31, 2017 to formally record the pension expense under IFRS and ASPE for the year. Under ASPE, the past service cost of $80,000 would be considered a remeasurement that should either be presented separately on the income statement or disclosed in the notes to the financial statements.

A   =   L   +   SE
     +97,600   −97,600

Cash flows: No effect

Pension Expense	97,600	
Net Defined Benefit Liability/Asset		97,600

When the company made its contributions to the pension fund during the year, the following entry was recorded:

A   =   L   +   SE
−20,000   −20,000

Cash flows: ↓ 20,000 outflow

Net Defined Benefit Liability/Asset	20,000	
Cash		20,000

Because the expense exceeds the funding, the Net Defined Benefit Liability/Asset account increases during the year by the $77,600 difference ($97,600 less $20,000). At the end of 2017, for the same reasons as in 2016, the balance of the Net Defined Benefit Liability/Asset account ($78,600) is equal to the deficit, the difference between the DBO of $212,700 and the plan assets of $134,100.

2018 Work Sheet and Entries with Actuarial Gains/Losses

Alternative Terminology

ASPE uses the term *Defined Benefit Liability or Asset*, while IFRS uses *Net Defined Benefit Liability or Asset* for the statement of financial position–related account. We use the two terms interchangeably in our discussion, but use the term Net Defined Benefit Liability/Asset for the general ledger account name and related journal entries.

Refer back to the pension plan activities for Zarle Corporation in Illustration 19-8 and review what happens during 2018. No additional plan amendments were made in this year; therefore, there are no past service costs to be recognized in 2018. However, there is an actuarial loss in 2018. The loss came about because the actuary updated the underlying actuarial assumptions used in calculating the DBO at December 31, 2018, resulting in an increase in the balance of this obligation. If the DBO had been reduced, this would have been an actuarial gain. For 2018, assume that the contribution made by Zarle to the plan occurred on July 1, 2018, rather than at the end of the year.

Under the ASPE approach to pension accounting, the increase in the obligation caused by the actuarial loss is recognized as pension expense in the same accounting period. The recognition in pension expense of both past service costs and actuarial gains and losses can cause significant variability in the pension expense recognized each year. However, both the surplus or deficit and statement of financial position pension account are reported at up-to-date funding-related values.

The work sheet in Illustration 19-11 presents all the pension transactions and information used by Zarle Corporation in 2018 under ASPE. The beginning balances for this year are identical to the 2017 ending balances from Illustration 19-10.

Entries (j), (k), (m), and (n) are similar to the entries that were explained in 2016 and 2017. For entry (l), recall that we are assuming that the 2018 contribution occurred on July 1, 2018; therefore, funds were available to earn interest for half of the year. The net interest/finance cost would therefore have included estimated interest on plan assets of $14,610 [$134,100 + (24,000 × $^{6}/_{12}$)] × 10% = $14,610].[23] The remeasurement loss in (l) represents the difference between the actual return on plan assets and the return calculated using the discount rate from (k) (the net interest/finance cost calculation). Entry (o) records the increase in the defined benefit obligation that results from a change in actuarial assumptions. Using up-to-date actuarial assumptions at December 31, 2018, the actuary calculates the ending balance to be $265,000. Because the memo record balance at December 31 is $236,470 (equal to $212,700 + $13,000 + $21,270 − $10,500), there

	A	B	C	D	F	G
1		General Journal Entries			Memo Record	
2	Items	Annual Pension Expense	Cash	Net Defined Benefit Liability/ Asset	Accrued Benefit Obligation	Plan Assets
3	Balance, Jan. 1, 2018			78,600 Cr.	212,700 Cr.	134,100 Dr.
4	(j) Service cost	13,000 Dr.			13,000 Cr.	
5	(k) Net interest/finance cost	6,660 Dr.			21,270 Cr.	14,610 Dr.
6	(l) Remeasurement loss on plan assets	2,610 Dr.				2,610 Cr.
7	(m) Contribution		24,000 Cr.			24,000 Dr.
8	(n) Benefits paid				10,500 Dr.	10,500 Cr.
9	(o) Actuarial loss	28,530 Dr.			28,530 Cr.	
10	Expense entry, 2018	50,800 Dr.		50,800 Cr.		
11	Contribution entry, 2018		24,000 Cr.	24,000 Dr.		
12	Balance, Dec. 31, 2018			105,400 Cr.	265,000 Cr.	159,600 Dr.
13						

is a difference of $28,530 ($265,000 − $236,470). This $28,530 increase in the employer's obligation is the actuarial loss.

The journal entry on December 31, 2018 to formally record pension expense for the year under ASPE is as follows:

A = L + SE
+50,800 −50,800

Cash flows: No effect

Pension Expense	50,800	
Net Defined Benefit Liability/Asset		50,800

The company has already recorded the $24,000 contribution during the year as follows under both ASPE and IFRS:

A = L + SE
−24,000 −24,000

Cash flows: ↓ 24,000 outflow

Net Defined Benefit Liability/Asset	24,000	
Cash		24,000

As illustrated previously for the 2016 and 2017 work sheets, the $105,400 credit balance of the Net Defined Benefit Liability/Asset account reported on the statement of financial position at December 31, 2018 is once again equal to the deficit of $265,000 − $159,600 = $105,400. Anyone reading Zarle Corporation's financial statements would have expected to see a net liability of $105,400 on the company's statement of financial position if the pension fund was actually underfunded by $105,400!

On the other hand, pension expense on the income statement is highly variable from year to year due to the recognition of actuarial gains and losses and past service costs directly in expense. Management may be concerned that immediate recognition of these costs gives a false picture of the company's risk. The fluctuations in pension expense are felt to be beyond management's control, and over the longer term many of the actuarial gains and losses are expected to reverse. As a result, historically there had been support for a deferral and amortization approach to accounting for defined benefit plans. IFRS uses other comprehensive income to minimize the impact of actuarial gains and losses on net income and earnings per share, as shown in Illustration 19-12.

	A	B	C	D	E	F	G
1		General Journal Entries				Memo Record	
2	Items	Remeasure-ment (Gain) Loss OCI	Annual Pension Expense	Cash	Net Defined Benefit Liability/ Asset	Defined Benefit Obligation	Plan Assets
3	Balance, Jan. 1, 2018				78,600 Cr.	212,700 Cr.	134,100 Dr.
4	(j) Service cost		13,000 Dr.			13,000 Cr.	
5	(k) Net interest/Finance Cost		6,660 Dr.			21,270 Cr.	14,610 Dr.
6	(l) Remeasurement loss on plan assets	2,610 Dr.					2,610 Cr.
7	(m) Contribution			24,000 Cr.			24,000 Dr.
8	(n) Benefits paid					10,500 Dr.	10,500 Dr.
9	(o) Actuarial loss	28,530 Dr.				28,530 Cr.	
10	Expense entry, 2018	31,140 Dr.	19,660 Dr.		50,800 Cr.		
11	Contribution entry, 2018			24,000 Cr.	24,000 Dr.		
12	Balance, Dec. 31, 2018				105,400 Cr.	265,000 Cr.	159,600 Dr.
13							

Illustration 19-12

Pension Work Sheet under IFRS—2018

The work sheet in Illustration 19-12 presents all the pension transactions and information used by Zarle Corporation in 2018 under IFRS. The beginning balances for this year are identical to the 2017 ending balances from Illustration 19-10.

Entries (j), (k), (m), and (n) are similar to the entries that were explained for ASPE with Illustration 19-11. Entry (k) includes the expected return of $14,601 on the plan assets based on the same discount rate that was used for the DBO. (Recall that we are assuming that the 2018 contribution occurred on July 1, 2018. See the discussion of Illustration 19-11 for further details.)[24] Entry (l) represents the remeasurement loss on the plan assets that is calculated as the difference between $14,610 and the actual return of $12,000. Entry (o) records the increase in the defined benefit obligation that results from a change in actuarial assumptions, calculated as explained above for ASPE. However, under IFRS, the remeasurement loss on plan assets and the actuarial loss are both recorded as part of the remeasurement gain or loss that is reported in other comprehensive income on the statement of comprehensive income.

The journal entry on December 31, 2018 to formally record pension expense for the year under IFRS is as follows:

A =   L   + SE
    +50,800 −50,800

Cash flows: No effect

Pension Expense	19,660	
Remeasurement Loss (OCI)	31,140	
Net Defined Benefit Liability/Asset		50,800

Other Considerations

Limit on the Carrying Amount of a Net Defined Benefit Asset

UNDERLYING CONCEPT

The measurement of an asset takes into account the amount of the future benefits expected from the recognized item.

Although the illustrations in this chapter result in net defined benefit liabilities being reported on the statement of financial position, net defined benefit assets are also sometimes found on corporate statements of financial position. The accounting standards provide for an **asset ceiling test** on the balance of any benefit asset reported on the statement of financial position.

Similar to most assets we have studied, there is a limit on the carrying amount of a net defined benefit asset resulting from a defined benefit plan. Under IFRS, in general, if the fair value of the plan assets is greater than the future benefits the company expects to receive from the assets, the asset ceiling is used as the maximum amount of the net defined benefit asset. Under ASPE, a valuation allowance is used to reduce the asset's reported amount. Generally, the "asset ceiling" limit is determined the same way under IFRS as ASPE and it considers benefits to the company in the form of refunds from the plan or reductions in future contributions to the plan.

Although the calculations required are not explained in this text, you should be aware that the change in the valuation allowance in the year is recognized as a component of the pension expense in income in the year. In addition, the net defined benefit asset is reported based on the asset ceiling on the statement of financial position.[25]

Other Benefits

This chapter presents the basics of accounting for post-employment benefits, including the valuation of a net defined benefit asset. You should be aware that further complexities arise from obligation settlements, benefits provided through insurance contracts or other arrangements, plan curtailments, termination benefits, and multi-employer plans.

Other Defined Benefit Plans

Other Post-Employment and Long-Term Employee Benefit Plans with Benefits that Vest or Accumulate

Objective 8
Account for defined benefit plans with benefits that vest or accumulate other than pension plans.

In addition to pension plans, companies provide their employees with other post-employment benefits as part of their compensation package. These may include such benefits as health care, prescription drugs, life insurance, long-term disability, dental and eye care, legal and tax services, tuition assistance, or free or subsidized travel. In the past, most companies accounted for the cost of these other post-employment benefits as an expense in the period when the benefits were provided to the retirees, their spouses, dependants, and beneficiaries; that is, on a pay-as-you-go basis. In 2000, the Canadian standard changed to require companies to account for all defined benefit plans where the benefits vest or accumulate on the same basis as they account for defined benefit pension plans.

WHAT DO THE NUMBERS MEAN?

In 1990, the FASB issued *Statement No. 106*, Employers' Accounting for Post-Retirement Benefits Other Than Pensions. This standard required a change from the pay-as-you-go method of accounting for these benefits to an accrual basis, similar to pension accounting. When the standard was first applied, the effect on most U.S. companies was significant. For example, **General Motors** announced a U.S. $20.8-billion charge against its 1992 earnings as a result of adopting the new standard, and this was at a time when the company's net book value before the charge was approximately U.S. $28 billion! The impact of a subsequent change in Canada was not as significant as in the United States because of broader health-care coverage paid for by the government. A Financial Executives Institute Canada (now FEI Canada) study estimated a total Canadian unreported liability of $52 billion, almost entirely unfunded. In both countries, the requirement to measure the outstanding obligation and related costs resulted in corporate management paying much closer attention to the benefit packages that are offered to employee groups. This supports the saying that "you only control what gets measured and reported."

Sources: Doron P. Levin, "Company Reports: G.M. Lost $23.5 Billion Last Year," *The New York Times*, February 12, 1993; T. Ross Archibald and Darroch Robertson, "Survey of Pension Plans in Canada," Financial Executives Institute Canada, 1993; Paul Fronstein, "Retiree Health Benefits: Trends and Outlook," *Issue Brief*, Employee Benefit Research Institute, August 2001.

Unlike pension benefits, companies tend not to prefund (set aside assets in advance for) their other post-employment benefit plans. The major reason is that payments to prefund health-care costs, for example, are not tax-deductible, unlike contributions to a pension trust. Although these two types of retirement benefits appear similar, there are also some other significant differences, as indicated in Illustration 19-13.

Item	Pensions	Health-Care Benefits
Funding	Generally funded	Generally not funded
Benefit	Well-defined and level dollar amount	Generally uncapped and great variability
Beneficiary	Retiree (maybe some benefit to surviving spouse)	Retiree, spouse, and other dependants
Benefit payable	Monthly	As needed and used
Predictability	Variables are reasonably predictable	Utilization difficult to predict; level of cost varies geographically and fluctuates over time

Measuring the net cost of the post-retirement benefits for the period is complex. Estimates of these costs may have a large margin of error. This is due to the uncertainties in forecasting health-care costs, rates of usage, changes in government health programs, and the differences in non-medical assumptions (such as the discount rate, employee turnover, rate of early retirement, and spouse-age difference). However, not recognizing an obligation and expense before paying the benefits is considered not to be a faithful representation of financial position and performance.

Under ASPE, the basic concepts, accounting terminology, recognition and measurement criteria, and measurement methods that apply to defined benefit pensions for the most part **also apply to the requirements for other benefits** that vest or accumulate based on the service provided by employees. Examples of such benefits are sabbaticals where unrestricted time off with pay is granted for services provided, service-related long-term disability benefits, or sick days not used that accumulate and are paid out on retirement.[26] Assume, for example, that an employee benefit plan provides a cash bonus of $500 per year of service when an employee retires or has his or her employment terminated for other reasons, on condition that the employee has worked there for at least 10 years. Because the right to the benefit is earned by providing service and the benefit increases with the length of service provided, the cost and related liability are accrued starting from the date of employment. The measurement of the obligation and expense considers the probabilities related to employee turnover. The fact that the benefits do not vest for 10 years does not eliminate the need to recognize the cost and liability over the first 10 years of employment.

IFRS distinguishes between post-employment plans such as pensions and post-employment health-care benefits, and short-term employee benefits such as paid annual leave (vacation pay), sick leave, and profit-sharing and bonus plans. The short-term employee benefits that accumulate are generally recognized (without discounting) at the amount expected to be paid in exchange for the services provided (IAS 19.11). Short-term benefits were covered in more detail in Chapter 13. Other long-term benefits include items such as paid absences for long service, unrestricted sabbaticals, and long-term benefits that depend on length of service. IFRS requires the same recognition and measurement for these long-term benefits as for post-employment benefits such as pension plans and health-care benefits. However, remeasurements of the net defined benefit liability (asset) related to these other long-term benefits should be reflected in income (not OCI). For termination benefits, IFRS requires the cost of the benefits to be recognized at the earlier of when the company can no longer withdraw an offer of the benefits and when it recognizes the related restructuring costs (that is, for termination benefits that arise as part of a corporate restructuring that includes layoffs of employees).

Other Employee Benefit Plans with Benefits That Do Not Accumulate

Both IFRS and ASPE make no attempt to accrue the benefit costs and liabilities related to employee benefits that do not accumulate with additional service. In this case, there is no basis on which to assign the costs to periods other than the period when the benefits are taken. A good example is costs associated with parental leave or unused sick pay that do not change with an employee's length of service. Instead, both the total cost and liability are recognized when the event occurs that obligates the company to provide the benefits. This is referred to as an "event accrual" method of accounting for benefits and was explained in Chapter 13.

PRESENTATION, DISCLOSURE, AND ANALYSIS

Presentation

Statement of Financial Position Presentation of Net Defined Benefit Assets and Liabilities

Objective 9

Identify the types of information required to be presented and disclosed for defined benefit plans, prepare basic schedules, and be able to read and understand such disclosures.

Employers with two or more defined benefit plans are required to separately measure the benefit cost, defined benefit obligation, and plan assets for each funded benefit plan. If all the plans result in a net defined benefit liability on the balance sheet or all result in a net defined benefit asset, the plans can be reported together in the financial statements. However, because companies generally do not have the legal right to, and do not intend to, use the assets of one plan to pay for the benefits of other plans, a net defined benefit asset of one plan and a net defined benefit liability of another are required to be reported separately on the balance sheet or statement of financial position.

Neither IFRS nor ASPE provides any guidance on how to determine whether net defined benefit assets and liabilities for defined benefit plans are current or long-term, so companies revert to basic underlying principles to determine the classification. Most such assets and liabilities are found under the long-term classifications on the statement of financial position.

Income Statement Presentation of Benefit Cost

IFRS and ASPE identify the components that make up the benefit cost for the period, and both indicate that a portion of the cost may be required to be treated as a product cost in inventory or capitalized in a property, plant, and equipment asset. However, neither IFRS nor ASPE dictates how the components of benefit cost are to be reported on the income statement. Companies therefore have the option of reporting current service cost and net interest/finance cost in one of three ways: (1) as separate components, (2) as part of similar expenses, or (3) in total as a single benefit cost. Many companies choose the third option, reporting all the components together as a single benefit cost.

Disclosure

Disclosure Requirements

UNDERLYING CONCEPT

Standard setters make decisions about disclosures taking into account the users of the financial statements.

Given that pensions and other defined benefit plans are significant and specialized, it is not surprising that they have extensive reporting and disclosure requirements. ASPE requires only a limited set of basic information in addition to the accounting policy choices the employer has made. However, IAS 19 *Employee Benefits* requires a high level of accountability from companies for the effect of such plans on their current and future performance, financial position, and risk.

Under ASPE, separate disclosures are required for plans that provide pension benefits and other types of employee future benefits, and most of these disclosures are for defined benefit plans. The required disclosures include:

- a description of each type of plan and any major changes in the terms of the plan during the year;

- the effective date of the most recent actuarial valuation for funding purposes;

- the year-end surplus or deficit, including the fair value of the plan assets and defined benefit obligation; and

- an explanation of any difference between the amount reported on the balance sheet and the plans' surplus or deficit.

It is expected that any additional information needed by users is available from the company.

The objective under IFRS is to provide disclosures for a broad range of users with no access to additional information. The information should describe:

- the characteristics of the defined benefit plans and risks associated with them;

- the amounts in the statements arising from the plans; and

- how the defined benefit plans help users assess the amounts, timing, and likelihood of the cash flows that are associated with future benefits (IFRS 19.135).

In addition to a description of each defined benefit plan or groupings of similar plans, and what accounting choices were made where choices are permitted, the following types of information are also required:

- **Reconciliations** of the opening to closing balances of the present value of the net defined benefit liability/asset, plan assets, and the present value of the DBO;

- **Amounts included in periodic net income**: the amount included in expense, such as current service cost, interest expense, and return on plan assets, along with amounts recognized in OCI, such as actuarial gains and losses from changes in assumptions;

- **Sensitivity information for each significant actuarial assumption,** including the impact on the DBO and changes from the previous period in methods and assumptions used in the sensitivity analyses;

- Many other disclosures, including details relating to classes of items making up the fair value of plan assets, asset–liability matching strategies, and funding arrangements that affect future contributions

Disclosure Illustration

REAL WORLD EMPHASIS

Companies organize their disclosures in a variety of acceptable ways. **BCE Inc.,** Canada's largest communications company, is publicly traded on the Toronto Stock Exchange and on the New York Stock Exchange. It provides residential and business customers with a wide range of products, including wireless voice and data communications; TV and radio broadcasting services under Bell Media; and Internet, data, TV, and local telephone service via Bell Aliant. BCE's 2014 accounting policy note and specific consolidated statement of financial position disclosures relating to its pensions and other post-employment benefits are in Illustration 19-14, providing a comprehensive example of disclosures required under IFRS. As you can see, the disclosures are extensive!

Illustration 19-14

Illustrative Disclosure—BCE Inc., December 31, 2014 (in millions of dollars)

Note 2 Significant accounting policies (extracts)

q) Post-employment benefit plans

DEFINED BENEFIT (DB) AND OTHER POST-EMPLOYMENT BENEFIT (OPEB) PLANS

We maintain DB pension plans that provide pension benefits for certain employees. Benefits are based on the employee's length of service and average rate of pay during the highest paid consecutive five years of service. Most employees are not required to contribute to the plans. The plans provide cost of living adjustments to help protect the income of retired employees against inflation.

We are responsible for adequately funding our DB pension plans. We make contributions to them based on various actuarial cost methods permitted by pension regulatory bodies. Contributions reflect actuarial assumptions about future investment returns, salary projections and future service.

(continued)

We provide OPEBs to some of our employees, including:

- healthcare and life insurance benefits during retirement, which are being phased out over a ten-year period ending on December 31, 2016. We do not fund most of these OPEB plans.

- other benefits, including workers' compensation and medical benefits to former or inactive employees, their beneficiaries and dependants, from the time their employment ends until their retirement starts, under certain circumstances.

We accrue our obligations and related costs under post-employment benefit plans, net of the fair value of the benefit plan assets. Pension and OPEB costs are determined using:

- the projected unit credit method, prorated on years of service, which takes into account future pay levels

- a discount rate based on market interest rates of high-quality corporate bonds with maturities that match the timing of benefits expected to be paid under the plans

- management's best estimate of pay increases, retirement ages of employees, expected healthcare costs and life expectancy

We value post-employment benefit plan assets at fair value using current market values.

Post-employment benefit plans current service cost is included in operating costs. Interest on our post-employment benefit obligations is recognized in net earnings and represents the accretion of interest on the net obligations under the post-employment benefit plans. The interest rate is based on market conditions that existed at the beginning of the year. Actuarial gains and losses for all post-employment benefit plans are recorded in other comprehensive income in the period in which they occur and are recognized immediately in the deficit.

December 31 is the measurement date for our significant post-employment benefit plans. Our actuaries perform a valuation at least every three years to determine the actuarial present value of the accrued DB pension plan and OPEB obligations. The most recent actuarial valuation of our significant pension plans was December 31, 2013.

DEFINED CONTRIBUTION (DC) PENSION PLANS

We maintain DC pension plans that provide certain employees with benefits. Under these plans, we are responsible for contributing a predetermined amount to an employee's retirement savings, based on a percentage of the employee's salary.

We recognize a post-employment benefit plans service cost for DC pension plans when the employee provides service to the company, essentially coinciding with our cash contributions.

Generally, new employees can participate only in the DC pension plans.

Note 22 Post-employment benefit plans

Post-employment benefit plans cost

We provide pension and other benefits for most of our employees. These include DB pension plans, DC pension plans and OPEBs.

We operate our DB and DC pension plans under applicable Canadian and provincial pension legislation, which prescribes minimum and maximum DB funding requirements. Plan assets are held in trust and the oversight of governance of the plans, including investment decisions, contributions to DB plans and the selection of the DC plans investment options offered to plan participants, lies with the Pension Fund Committee, a committee of our board of directors.

The interest rate risk is managed using a liability matching approach which reduces the exposure of the DB plan to a mismatch between investment growth and obligation growth.

COMPONENTS OF POST-EMPLOYMENT BENEFIT PLANS SERVICE COST

FOR THE YEAR ENDED DECEMBER 31	2014	2013
DB pension	(214)	(252)
DC pension	(94)	(81)
OPEBs	(9)	(7)
Plan amendment gain on OPEBs	–	1
Less:		
Capitalized benefit plans cost	41	47
Total post-employment benefit plans service cost included in operating costs	(276)	(292)
Other (costs) benefits recognized in Severance, acquisition and other costs	(29)	6
Total post-employment benefit plans service cost	(305)	(286)

(continued)

Illustration 19-14

Illustrative Disclosure—BCE
Inc., December 31, 2014
(in millions of dollars)
(continued)

COMPONENTS OF POST-EMPLOYMENT BENEFIT PLANS FINANCING COST

FOR THE YEAR ENDED DECEMBER 31	2014	2013
DB pension	(35)	(87)
OPEBs	(66)	(63)
Total interest on post-employment benefit obligations	(101)	(150)

The statements of comprehensive income include the following amounts before income taxes.

	2014	2013
Cumulative losses recognized directly in equity, January 1	(2,036)	(3,452)
Actuarial (losses) gains in other comprehensive income[1]	(933)	1,403
(Increase) decrease in the effect of the asset limit[2]	(5)	13
Cumulative losses recognized directly in equity, December 31	(2,974)	(2,036)

[1]The cumulative actuarial losses recognized in the statements of comprehensive income are $3,234 million in 2014.
[2]The cumulative decrease in the effect of the asset limit recognized in the statements of comprehensive income is $260 million in 2014.

COMPONENTS OF POST-EMPLOYMENT BENEFIT (OBLIGATIONS) ASSETS
The following table shows the change in post-employment benefit obligations and the fair value of plan assets.

COMPONENTS OF POST-EMPLOYMENT BENEFIT (OBLIGATIONS) ASSETS

	DB PENSION PLANS		OPEB PLANS		TOTAL	
	2014	2013	2014	2013	2014	2013
Post-employment benefit obligations, January 1	(18,672)	(19,542)	(1,641)	(1,707)	(20,313)	(21,249)
Current service cost	(214)	(252)	(9)	(7)	(223)	(259)
Interest on obligations	(901)	(850)	(78)	(73)	(979)	(923)
Actuarial (losses) gains[1]	(2,240)	1,025	(56)	69	(2,296)	1,094
Net curtailment (loss) gain	(29)	4	—	3	(29)	7
Business combinations	—	(143)	—	(3)	—	(146)
Benefit payments	1,076	1,088	77	77	1,153	1,165
Employee contributions	(5)	(6)	—	—	(5)	(6)
Other	(3)	4	—	—	(3)	4
Post-employment benefit obligations, December 31	(20,988)	(18,672)	(1,707)	(1,641)	(22,695)	(20,313)
Fair value of plan assets, January 1	18,082	17,727	241	220	18,323	17,947
Expected return on plan assets[2]	866	763	12	10	878	773
Actuarial gains	1,351	294	12	15	1,363	309
Business combinations	—	120	—	—	—	120
Benefit payments	(1,076)	(1,088)	(77)	(77)	(1,153)	(1,165)
Employer contributions	591	260	73	73	664	333
Employee contributions	5	6	—	—	5	6
Fair value of plan assets, December 31	19,819	18,082	261	241	20,080	18,323
Plan deficit	(1,169)	(590)	(1,446)	(1,400)	(2,615)	(1,990)
Effect of asset limit	(6)	(1)	—	—	(6)	(1)
Post-employment benefit liability, December 31	(1,175)	(591)	(1,446)	(1,400)	(2,621)	(1,991)
Post-employment benefit assets included in other non-current assets	151	136	—	—	151	136
Post-employment benefit obligations	(1,326)	(727)	(1,446)	(1,400)	(2,772)	(2,127)

[1]Actuarial (losses) gains include experience gains of $1,534 million in 2014 and $424 million in 2013.
[2]The actual return on plan assets was $2,241 million or 12.6% in 2014 and $1,082 million or 6.4% in 2013.

(continued)

FUNDED STATUS OF POST-EMPLOYMENT BENEFIT PLANS COST

The following table shows the funded status of our post-employment benefit obligations.

FOR THE YEAR ENDED DECEMBER 31	FUNDED		PARTIALLY FUNDED[1]		UNFUNDED[2]		TOTAL	
	2014	2013	2014	2013	2014	2013	2014	2013
Present value of post-employment benefit obligations	(20,375)	(18,134)	(1,906)	(1,820)	(414)	(359)	(22,695)	(20,313)
Fair value of plan assets	19,783	18,048	297	275	—	—	20,080	18,323
Plan deficit	(592)	(86)	(1,609)	(1,545)	(414)	(359)	(2,615)	(1,990)

[1]The partially funded plans consist of supplementary executive retirement plans (SERPs) for eligible employees and OPEBs. The company partially funds the SERPs through letters of credit and a retirement compensation arrangement account with Canada Revenue Agency. Certain paid-up life insurance benefits are funded through life insurance contracts.

[2]Our unfunded plans consist of OPEBs, which are pay-as-you-go.

SIGNIFICANT ASSUMPTIONS

We used the following key assumptions to measure the post-employment benefit obligations and the net benefit plans cost for the DB pension plans and OPEB plans. These assumptions are long-term, which is consistent with the nature of post-employment benefit plans.

	DB PENSION PLANS AND OPEB PLANS	
	2014	2013
At December 31		
Post-employment benefit obligations		
Discount rate	4.0%	4.9%
Rate of compensation increase	2.5%	2.8%
Cost of living indexation rate[1]	1.6%	1.7%
Life expectancy at age 65 (years)	23.0	22.4
For the year ended December 31		
Net post-employment benefit plans cost		
Discount rate	4.9%	4.4%
Rate of compensation increase	2.8%	3.0%
Cost of living indexation rate[1]	1.7%	1.8%
Life expectancy at age 65 (years)	22.4	20.9

[1]Cost of living indexation rate is only applicable to DB pension plans.

The weighted average duration of the post-employment benefit obligation is 15 years.

We assumed the following trend rates in healthcare costs:

- an annual increase of 4.0% in the cost per person of covered dental benefits and 4.5% in the cost per person of other covered healthcare benefits for 2014 and the foreseeable future

- an annual increase of 5.0% for retirees under age 65 and 4.5% for retirees over age 65 in the cost of medication for 2014 and the foreseeable future

Assumed trend rates in healthcare costs have a significant effect on the amounts reported for the healthcare plans.

The following table shows the effect of a 1% change in the assumed trend rates in healthcare costs.

EFFECT ON POST-EMPLOYMENT BENEFITS – INCREASE/(DECREASE)	1% INCREASE	1% DECREASE
Total service and interest cost	7	(6)
Post-employment benefit obligations	147	(128)

SENSITIVITY ANALYSIS

The following table shows a sensitivity analysis of key assumptions used to measure the net post-employment benefit obligations and the net post-employment benefit plans cost for our DB pension plans and OPEB plans.

(continued)

| | CHANGE IN ASSUMPTION | IMPACT ON NET POST-EMPLOYMENT BENEFIT PLANS COST FOR 2014 – INCREASE/(DECREASE) | | IMPACT ON POST-EMPLOYMENT BENEFIT OBLIGATIONS AT DECEMBER 31, 2014 – INCREASE/(DECREASE) | |
		INCREASE IN ASSUMPTION	DECREASE IN ASSUMPTION	INCREASE IN ASSUMPTION	DECREASE IN ASSUMPTION
Discount rate	1%	(175)	148	(2,978)	3,428
Mortality rate	25%	(73)	78	(1,423)	1,518

POST-EMPLOYMENT BENEFIT PLAN ASSETS

The investment strategy for the post-employment benefit plan assets is to maintain a diversified portfolio of assets invested in a prudent manner to maintain the security of funds.

The following table shows the target allocations for 2014 and the allocation of our post-employment benefit plan assets at December 31, 2014 and 2013.

ASSET CATEGORY	WEIGHTED AVERAGE TARGET ALLOCATION 2014	TOTAL PLAN ASSETS FAIR VALUE AT DECEMBER 31 (%) 2014	2013
Equity securities	20%–35%	30%	33%
Debt securities	55%–70%	62%	59%
Alternative investments	0%–25%	8%	8%
Total		100%	100%

The fair value of the DB pension plan assets at the end of the year for each category are tabled below.

FOR THE YEAR ENDED DECEMBER 31	2014	2013
Observable markets		
Equity securities		
Canadian	1,195	1,278
Foreign	4,657	4,692
Debt securities		
Canadian	10,986	9,491
Foreign	921	792
Money market	463	376
Unobservable inputs		
Alternative investments		
Private equities	947	873
Hedge funds	651	602
Other	(1)	(22)
Total	19,819	18,082

It is particularly interesting to note the total post-employment benefit obligations of $22,695 (million) and the (net) post-employment benefit liability at December 31, 2014 of $2,621 million. The actuarial loss of $933 million in the year reflects a remeasurement gain on the plan assets of $1,363 million offset by a $2,296-million actuarial loss on the DBO. This charge bypasses the consolidated income statement and earnings per share, and is reflected entirely in other comprehensive income. Look through the other parts of this note and see if you can relate the information to what has been explained in the chapter.

Analysis

With all the information that is reported in the notes to the financial statements, what should an analysis focus on? The most important elements are the major assumptions that underlie the calculations, the surplus or deficit of the plan, and the company's future cash requirements.

As we indicated earlier in the chapter, the defined benefit obligation and pension expense are based on several estimates that, if altered, can significantly change the amounts. Aside from actuarial assumptions relating to items such as turnover, mortality, and the rate of compensation and health-care increases, the choice of discount rate used to measure the DBO, the current service cost, and the interest cost are also key variables. A one-percentage-point difference in the discount rate could have a 10% to 20% effect on the discounted value. This rate is required to be disclosed so that readers can assess it for reasonableness and compare it with those used by other companies in the industry.

A company's actual cash flow related to pensions is often very different from the pension costs recognized on the income statement, and analysts often try to determine the company's future cash commitments. The standards' disclosure requirements help somewhat in this regard. They require companies to report the cash impact of the plans in the current period and an estimate of the cash impact for the next fiscal year.

WHAT DO THE NUMBERS MEAN?

The new IFRS accounting standards for employee benefits (IAS 19) effective January 1, 2013 require companies to record their previously unrecognized past service costs, actuarial gains and losses, and any transition costs in other comprehensive income and to recognize the plan's net benefit asset or liability on the statement of financial position. Previously, companies used the deferral and amortization approach under IFRS, and unamortized amounts were disclosed but not recognized in the accounts. As a result, the balance sheet benefit asset or liability did not portray the company's real resource or obligation as measured by the surplus or deficit of its plan. Did the change make much difference to Canadian companies?

Air Canada, in its 2013 annual report, indicated that the move to IAS 19 reduced its earnings by $1.12 per share in 2013 (and $0.97 in 2012). The decrease related mainly to net financing expense, which must now be calculated using the same discount rate used to value the benefit obligation. Because the discount rate must also be used for plan assets, and since it was lower than the expected rate of return on plan assets for Air Canada, financing expense increased. However, note that the decrease to net income (and EPS) was offset by an increase to remeasurements recorded in other comprehensive income. For 2013, the overall difference in Air Canada's comprehensive income was $0!

Hopefully, the effect on net income within private company financial statements from the new ASPE requirements, introduced via Section 3462, will not be as significant. The change under the new ASPE standard from the deferral and amortization approach to immediate recognition would have avoided effect felt by Air Canada in relation to its net income. Because companies following ASPE do not have separate OCI accounts, the impact of the change on financing costs and remeasurements would both have gone through net income, and would have offset each other.

Objective 10

Identify differences between the IFRS and ASPE accounting for pensions and other post-employment benefits and what changes are expected in the near future.

Illustration 19-15

IFRS and ASPE Comparison Chart

IFRS/ASPE COMPARISON

A Comparison of IFRS and ASPE

Both IFRS and ASPE agree on the objective of accounting for the cost of post-employment benefits: to recognize a liability and a cost in the reporting period in which an employee has provided the service that gives rise to the benefits. This is based on the fact that the obligation to provide benefits arises as the employees provide the service. There are minor differences in how immediate recognition is applied under IFRS and ASPE. These differences are highlighted in Illustration 19-15.

	IFRS—IAS 19	Accounting Standards for Private Enterprises (ASPE)—*CPA Canada Handbook*, Part II, Section 3462	References to Related Illustrations and Select Brief Exercises
Scope	The standard is broader in scope, covering all employee benefits.	The standard does not apply to benefits provided during an employee's active employment.	N/A
Recognition—defined contribution plans	The standard does not make any reference to past service costs on defined contribution plans. Amounts are undiscounted because they are current in nature.	The standard covers treatment of past service costs and the possibility of an interest cost element.	BE19-2

(continued)

	IFRS—IAS 19	Accounting Standards for Private Enterprises (ASPE)—*CPA Canada Handbook*, Part II, Section 3462	References to Related Illustrations and Select Brief Exercises
Recognition—defined benefit plans with benefits that vest or accumulate	Only one approach is permitted, with current and past service cost, and the net interest on the net employee benefit liability or asset being recorded in net income (and with gains and losses from remeasurements being recorded in OCI).	Only one approach is permitted: immediate recognition, with pension expense being recorded via net income.	Illustration 19-11 (ASPE) and Illustration 19-12 (IFRS)
	Under IFRS, there is no separate funding valuation measure permitted for financial accounting purposes.	Valuation is measured using either the funding valuation or a separate valuation for accounting purposes.	N/A
	The IAS 19 approach is similar to ASPE, but remeasurement gains and losses including actuarial gains and losses are recognized in other comprehensive income.	Actuarial gains and losses are recognized immediately in the benefit cost and accrued liability, along with current service cost, finance cost, and the remeasurement gain or loss relating to the actual (not expected) return on plan assets.	Illustrations 19-11 and 19-12 BE19-9, BE19-10, BE19-11, BE19-12, and BE19-14
	The same standards apply only to other long-term benefit plans.	The same standards apply generally to all post-employment benefit plans with benefits that vest or accumulate.	N/A
Measurement —DBO and plan assets	The plan assets and DBO are required to represent reporting date values.	While the DBO and plan assets should be measured as at the date of the annual financial statements, measurement of the DBO could take place at an earlier date and then be updated to reflect the DBO at the balance sheet date.	N/A
—discount rate	Use of a current rate can only be the current yield on high-quality debt instruments such as high-quality corporate bonds. The same discount rate is used for plan assets and the DBO.	Use of a current rate can be either the current yield on debt instruments (such as high-quality corporate bonds) or a current settlement rate. The same discount rate is used for plan assets and the DBO.	N/A
—past service costs	Past service costs are included as part of "remeasurements and other items" and are recognized immediately in net income.	Past service costs are considered a "remeasurement" and recognized immediately in net income.	Illustration 19-10 BE19-11, BE19-12, and BE19-13
—actuarial gains and losses	The employer recognizes the amount of actuarial gains and losses in OCI instead of net income.	The employer recognizes the entire amount of actuarial gains and losses in net income.	Illustrations 19-11 and 19-12 BE19-9, BE19-10, and BE19-14
Disclosure	Extensive disclosures are required, particularly for post-retirement pensions and health-related defined benefit plans.	If not shown separately on the income statement, remeasurements should be disclosed in the notes. Otherwise, compared to IFRS, only basic information is required to be disclosed.	Illustration 19-14

Illustration 19-15
IFRS and ASPE Comparison Chart (continued)

Looking Ahead

Updates to IAS 19 and *CPA Canada Handbook*, Part II, Section 3462 are complete. When the IASB completed its revisions to IAS 19, it indicated as part of its work plan that there were some matters that still needed to be considered as part of a more fundamental review of pensions and related benefits. However, because of the complexity and nature of these matters, it noted that it does not plan to issue a discussion or research document in the near future. Overall, no significant further changes are expected in the near future.

SUMMARY OF LEARNING OBJECTIVES

1 Understand the importance of pensions from a business perspective.

A pension plan, together with post-retirement health care, is often part of an employee's overall compensation package. The size of these plans, in terms of both the number of employees and cost of benefits, has made their costs very large (on average) relative to companies' financial position, results of operations, and cash flows. With the vast majority of defined benefit plans being underfunded, more and more companies are moving toward defined contribution plans.

2 Identify and account for a defined contribution plan.

Defined contribution plans are plans that specify how contributions are determined rather than what benefits the individual will receive. They are accounted for similar to a cash basis.

3 Identify and explain what a defined benefit plan is and the related accounting issues.

Defined benefit plans specify the benefits that the employee is entitled to. Defined benefit plans whose benefits vest or accumulate typically provide for the benefits to be a function of the employee's years of service and, for pensions, compensation level. In general, the employer's obligation for such a plan and the associated cost is accrued as an expense as the employee provides the service. An actuary usually determines the required amounts.

4 Explain what the employer's benefit obligation is, identify alternative measures for this obligation, and prepare a continuity schedule of transactions and events that change its balance.

The employer's benefit obligation is the actuarial present value of the benefits that have been earned by employees for services they have provided up to the date of the statement of financial position. The vested benefit method, accumulated benefit method, and projected benefit method are three methods that could be used to measure companies' obligations. The third method is the one used to determine the defined benefit obligation, basing the calculation of the deferred compensation amount on both vested and non-vested service using future salaries. This last method is used under both IFRS and ASPE. The defined benefit obligation (DBO) is increased by current service cost, net interest/finance cost, and plan amendments that usually increase employee entitlements for prior services, and by actuarial losses. It is reduced by payment of pension benefits and by actuarial gains.

5 Identify transactions and events that change benefit plan assets, and calculate the balance of the plan assets.

Plan assets are increased by company and employee contributions and the actual return that is earned on fund assets (including realized and unrealized gains and losses), and are reduced by pension benefits paid to retirees.

6 Explain what a benefit plan's surplus or deficit is, calculate it, and identify what transactions and events change its amount.

A plan's surplus or deficit is the difference between the defined benefit obligation and the plan assets at a point in time. It tells you the extent to which a company has a net obligation (underfunded) or a surplus (overfunded) relative to the benefits that are promised. All items that change the plan assets and DBO, with the exception of the payments to retirees, change the surplus or deficit.

7 Identify the components of pension expense, and account for a defined benefit pension plan under IFRS and ASPE.

Pension expense is a function of: (1) current service cost, (2) finance cost including the net interest/finance cost on the net defined benefit liability/asset and the remeasurement gain or loss on plan assets, (3) past service costs, and (4) net actuarial gains or losses. Under ASPE, all are immediately included in current expense in their entirety. Under IFRS, pension costs relating to current service, past service, and net interest on the net defined benefit obligation are included in pension expense. Actuarial gains and losses, and any return on plan assets excluding amounts included in the net interest on the net defined benefit obligation (asset), are recognized in other comprehensive income.

8 Account for defined benefit plans with benefits that vest or accumulate other than pension plans.

Under ASPE, any non-pension defined benefit plans with benefits that vest or accumulate are accounted for in the same way as defined benefit pension plans. Under IFRS, short-term employee benefits are generally recognized (without discounting) at the amount expected to be paid in exchange for the services provided. Other long-term benefits include items such as paid absences for long service, unrestricted sabbaticals, and long-term disability plans. IFRS requires that remeasurements of the net defined benefit liability (asset) related to these other long-term benefits should be reflected in income (not OCI). For termination benefits, IFRS requires the cost of the benefits to be recognized at the earlier of when the company can no longer withdraw an offer of employment and when it recognizes the related restructuring costs.

9 Identify the types of information required to be presented and disclosed for defined benefit plans, prepare basic schedules, and be able to read and understand such disclosures.

ASPE requires a description of the plans, major changes made in the plans, dates of the actuarial valuations, the fair value of the plan assets, the DBO, and the surplus or deficit and how this relates to the balance sheet account. IFRS requires substantial information, such as reconciliations of changes in the DBO and plan assets, details of amounts included in net income, underlying assumptions and sensitivity analysis, and other information related to determining cash flows.

10 Identify differences between the IFRS and ASPE accounting for pensions and other post-employment benefits and what changes are expected in the near future.

IAS 19 is broader and covers more employee benefits than does *CPA Canada Handbook*, Part II, Section 3462. With recent changes to IAS 19, most companies are expected to recognize the net defined benefit liability (or asset) on the statement of financial position with items such as current service cost, past service cost, and interest on the DBO and plan assets recognized in net income, and remeasurement changes and actuarial gains and losses reported in other comprehensive income. ASPE is similar, except remeasurement changes and actuarial gains and losses are reported in net income.

KEY TERMS

accumulated benefit method, p. 1172
actual return, p. 1175
actuarial assumptions, p. 1171
actuarial gains and losses, p. 1174
actuaries, p. 1171
asset ceiling test, p. 1184
attribution period, p. 1173
contributory plans, p. 1167
current service cost, p. 1169
defined benefit obligation, p. 1171
defined benefit obligation (DBO) for
     accounting purposes, p. 1172

defined benefit obligation (DBO) for
     funding purposes, p. 1172
defined benefit plan, p. 1169
defined contribution plan, p. 1168
expected return, p. 1176
experience gain or loss, p. 1174
funded, p. 1167
immediate recognition approach, p. 1177
non-contributory plans, p. 1167
overfunded, p. 1177
past service cost, p. 1169
pension benefit cost, p. 1178

pension expense, p. 1178
pension plan, p. 1167
plan assets, p. 1171
projected benefit method, p. 1172
projected unit credit, p. 1172
return on plan assets, p. 1176
settlement rate, p. 1174
surplus or deficit, p. 1176
underfunded, p. 1177
vested benefit obligation, p. 1171
vested benefits, p. 1171
vesting, p. 1169

APPENDIX 19A

EXAMPLE OF A ONE-PERSON PLAN

Objective **11**

Explain and apply basic calculations to determine current service cost, the defined benefit obligation, and past service cost for a one-person defined benefit pension plan.

The following simplified example is provided to help you better visualize and understand some of the concepts introduced in this chapter. It uses an actuarial valuation done for accounting purposes. The example shows a one-person defined benefit pension plan for simplicity; in reality, most plans would have at least several members.

Assume that Lee Sung, age 30, begins employment with HTSM Corp. on January 1, 2016 at a starting salary of $37,500. It is expected that Lee will work for HTSM Corp. for 35 years, retiring on December 31, 2050, when Lee is 65 years old. If we estimate that Lee's salary will increase approximately 4% per year, Lee's salary at retirement is expected to be $150,000. Further assume that mortality tables indicate the life expectancy of someone age 65 in 2050 is 12 years.

The timeline in Illustration 19A-1 provides a snapshot of much of this information.

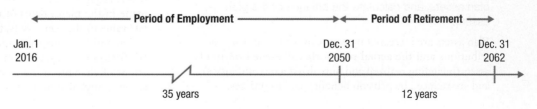

Illustration 19A-1

Timeline

| Period of Employment | Period of Retirement |

| Jan. 1 2016 | Dec. 31 2050 | Dec. 31 2062 |

35 years   12 years

HTSM Corp. sponsors a defined benefit pension plan for its employee with the following **pension benefit formula**:

> Annual pension benefit on retirement = 2% of salary at retirement for each year of service, or
> = 2% final salary × years of service

In order to measure 2016 pension costs, dollars paid in the future must be discounted to their present values. A **discount rate of 6%** is assumed to be the current yield on high-quality debt instruments.

Current Service Cost

Year 2016

How much pension does Lee Sung earn for the one year of service in 2016? Applying the pension formula **using projected salaries**:

> Annual pension benefit on retirement = 2% × $150,000 × 1 year
> = $3,000 per year of retirement

That is, by virtue of working one year, Lee Sung has earned an entitlement to a pension of $3,000 per year for life.

To determine the company's cost (expense) in 2016 related to this benefit, HTSM discounts these future payments to their present value at December 31, 2016. This is a two-step process. **First**, the pension annuity of $3,000 per year for an estimated 12 years is discounted to its present value on December 31, 2050, the employee's retirement date. Because this is still 34 years in the future at December 31, 2016, the **second** step discounts the annuity's present value at the beginning of retirement to its present value at the end of 2016. The calculations are as follows:

> PV of $3,000 annuity ($n = 12$, $i = 6\%$) at Dec. 31, 2050 = $3,000 × 8.38384
> (Table A-4)
> = $25,151.52
>
> PV of amount of $25,151.52 ($n = 34$, $i = 6\%$) at Dec. 31, 2016 = $25,151.52 × 0.13791
> (Table A-2)
> = $3,469

Therefore, the current service cost to HTSM of the pension benefit earned by Lee Sung in 2016 is $3,469. This is a primary component of the period's pension expense.

Year 2017

The calculation of HTSM's current service cost for 2017 is identical to 2016, assuming a continuing discount rate of 6% and no change in the pension formula. The only difference is that the $3,000 of pension benefit earned by Lee Sung in 2017 is discounted back to December 31, 2017, instead of 2016. The calculation is as follows:

> Annual pension benefit on retirement = 2% × $150,000 × 1 year
> = $3,000 per year of retirement
>
> PV of $3,000 annuity ($n = 12$, $i = 6\%$) at Dec. 31, 2050 = $3,000 × 8.38384
> (Table A-4)
> = $25,151.52
>
> PV of amount of $25,151.52 ($n = 33$, $i = 6\%$) at Dec. 31, 2017 = $25,151.52 × 0.14619
> (Table A-2)
> = $3,677

Therefore, the current service cost to HTSM of the pension benefit earned by Lee Sung in 2017 is $3,677.

Defined Benefit Obligation

At December 31, 2017

The defined benefit obligation (DBO) calculation is similar to the current service cost calculation except that it represents the present value of the pension benefits that have **accumulated for employee services provided to date as determined under the pension benefit formula.** Because 2016 was the first year of employment, we assume that the DBO at December 31, 2016 is $3,469, the same as the current service cost. At December 31, 2017, the DBO is determined as follows:

Pension benefit earned to Dec. 31, 2017	= 2% × $150,000 × 2 years
	= $6,000 per year of retirement
PV of $6,000 annuity ($n = 12$, $i = 6\%$) at Dec. 31, 2050	= $6,000 × 8.38384 (Table A-4)
	= $50,303.04
PV of amount of $50,303.04 ($n = 33$, $i = 6\%$) at Dec. 31, 2017	= $50,303.04 × 0.14619 (Table A-2)
	= $7,354

The defined benefit obligation at the end of 2017 is $7,354. Further, we can reconcile the opening DBO at January 1, 2017 with the ending DBO at December 31, 2017:

DBO at January 1, 2017	$3,469
Add interest on the outstanding obligation: $3,469 × 6% × 1 year	208
Add 2017 current service cost	3,677
DBO at December 31, 2017	$7,354

At December 31, 2050

If Lee Sung works for the full 35 years, assuming no change in the $150,000 final salary estimate, pension benefit formula, discount rate, and life expectancy, the DBO on retirement is as follows:

Pension benefit earned to Dec. 31, 2050	= 2% × $150,000 × 35 years
	= $105,000 per year of retirement
PV of $105,000 annuity ($n = 12$, $i = 6\%$) at Dec. 31, 2050	= $105,000 × 8.38384 (Table A-4)
	= $880,303

At December 31, 2050, HTSM has an obligation with a present value of $880,303. If the company had set aside assets (that is, funded the plan) each year in an amount equal to the current service cost and the funds had earned exactly 6%, the fund assets would have accumulated to $880,303 as well. The company needs to have this amount of cash in order to purchase an annuity that will pay Lee Sung an annual pension of $105,000 for life, which under actuarial calculations is estimated to be 12 years.

Past Service Cost

Now assume that Lee Sung had worked for HTSM's subsidiary company for six years before working for HTSM. Further assume that, on December 31, 2020, in determining Lee's pension benefits on retirement, HTSM agrees to give Lee credit for the years that he worked for the subsidiary company before 2016. What is the cost—the past service cost—of this to HTSM? We can determine this by calculating the company's DBO before and after the pension amendment:

	Before credit for prior service	After credit for prior service
Pension benefit earned to Dec. 31, 2020:	2% × $150,000 × 5 yrs = $3,000 × 5 = $15,000 per year	2% × $150,000 × 11 yrs = $3,000 × 11 = $33,000 per year
PV of pension earned to date at Dec. 31, 2050: (PV factor, annuity: n = 12, i = 6%)	$15,000 × 8.38384 = $125,757.60	$33,000 × 8.38384 = $276,666.72
PV of pension earned to date at Dec. 31, 2020 (PV factor, amount: n = 30, i = 6%)	$125,757.60 × 0.17411 = $21,896	$276,666.72 × 0.17411 = $48,170
DBO at Dec. 31, 2020, **after** prior service recognized		$48,170
DBO at Dec. 31, 2020, **before** prior service recognized		21,896
Past service cost incurred		$26,274

Giving credit for prior years of service is not the only event that creates a past service cost. Another common cause of past service cost is a change in the pension benefit formula. For example, if HTSM had agreed to change the formula to 2½% of final salary per year worked, this would have a significant effect on the DBO amount as soon as the formula was changed. A one-half-percentage-point increase on a base rate of 2% is a 25% increase in the actual amount!

SUMMARY OF LEARNING OBJECTIVE FOR APPENDIX 19A

11 Explain and apply basic calculations to determine current service cost, the defined benefit obligation, and past service cost for a one-person defined benefit pension plan.

The current service cost is a calculation of the present value of the benefits earned by employees that is attribut-able to the current period. The defined benefit obligation is the present value of the accumulated benefits earned to a point in time, according to the pension formula and using projected salaries. Past service cost is the present value of the additional benefits granted to employees in the case of a plan amendment.

Note: Completion of this end-of-chapter material will help develop CPA-enabling competencies (such as ethics and professionalism, problem-solving and decision-making, and communication) and technical competencies. We have highlighted selected items with an integration icon and material in *WileyPLUS* has been linked to the competencies. All cases emphasize integration, especially of the enabling competencies. The brief exercises, exercises, and problems generally emphasize problem-solving and decision-making.

All assignment material with an asterisk (*) relates to the appendix to the chapter. Unless otherwise indicated, assume that all current service costs, benefit payments, and company contributions are made at the end of the period.

Brief Exercises

**MANAGEMENT
ACCOUNTING**

(LO 1) **BE19-1** Scott Enterprises Inc. sponsors a defined benefit plan for its 500 employees. On December 31, 2017, the company's actuary provided the following information related to the plan: defined benefit obligation $11.3 million, and fair value of plan assets $9 million. Annual pension expense was $3 million in 2017. Scott Enterprises' statement of financial position as at December 31, 2017 shows total assets of $9 million and total liabilities of $9.8 million (which includes a net defined benefit liability of $2.3 million). There were no actuarial gains or losses or remeasurement gains or losses in 2017. Scott Enterprises follows IFRS. (a) Discuss the effect of the pension plan on Scott Enterprises' statement of financial position as at December 31, 2017. (b) Discuss some of the costs of the pension plan to Scott Enterprises' business.

(LO 2, 10) **BE19-2** Ditek Corp. provides a defined contribution pension plan for its employees. The plan requires Ditek to contribute 5% of employees' gross pay to a fund trustee each year. Ditek's total payroll for 2017 was $2,735,864. At the start of 2017, Ditek revised the terms of the plan, which resulted in past service costs of $845,350. Ditek expects to realize the economic benefits from the plan change for at least five years, beginning in 2017. (a) Calculate Ditek's pension expense for 2017 assuming that the company follows IFRS. (b) Calculate Ditek's pension expense for 2017 assuming that the company follows ASPE.

(LO 2, 3) **BE19-3** Tika Corp. has recently decided to implement a pension plan for its employees; however, it is unsure if it would like to structure the pension as a defined contribution plan or a defined benefit plan. As requested by management, prepare a short memo outlining the nature of both plans, along with the accounting treatment of each plan.

FINANCE

(LO 4) **BE19-4** Maya Corp. reports the following information (in hundreds of thousands of dollars) to you about its defined benefit pension plan for 2017:

Actual return on plan assets	$17	Current service cost	$ 32
Benefits paid to retirees	12	Interest cost	14
Contributions from employer	30	Opening balance, defined benefit obligation (DBO)	138
Cost of plan amendment in year	20	Opening balance, plan assets	150

Provide a continuity schedule for the DBO for the year. Maya follows IFRS.

(LO 5) **BE19-5** For Castor Corporation, year-end plan assets were $1,753,000. At the beginning of the year, plan assets were $1,359,000. During the year, contributions to the pension fund were $170,000, while benefits paid were $130,000. Calculate Castor's actual return on plan assets.

(LO 5, 6) **BE19-6** Refer to the information for Maya Corp. in BE19-4, and provide a continuity schedule for the plan assets for the year. Is the plan in a surplus or a deficit position at the end of the year?

(LO 6, 7) **BE19-7** At December 31, 2017, Glover Corporation provided you with the following information:

Defined benefit obligation, December 31, 2017	$3,400,000
Plan assets at fair value, December 31, 2017	2,420,000
Past service cost from plan amendment on	
December 31, 2016	990,000

Determine the account and its balance that should be reported on Glover Corporation's December 31, 2017 balance sheet if it applies ASPE.

(LO 7) **BE19-8** Jonquière Corporation provides the following information about its defined benefit pension plan (in hundreds of thousands of dollars) for 2017:

Actual return on plan assets	$ 9	Current service cost	$ 19
Contributions from employer	20	Opening balance, DBO	100
Benefits paid to retirees	10	Opening balance, plan assets	100
Actuarial loss due to change in actuarial			
assumptions	15		

At the end of the year, Jonquière revised the terms of its pension plan, which resulted in past service costs of $35. Assuming that Jonquière applies an 11% interest cost and follows IFRS, determine the company's 2017 pension expense and the effect of the pension plan on the company's shareholders' equity.

(LO 7) BE19-9 Duster Corporation is a private company with a defined benefit pension plan. The following information is available for Duster Corporation for 2017:

Opening balance, DBO	$210,000
Opening balance, plan assets	200,000
Service cost	58,000
Employer contributions paid evenly through 2017	77,000
Applicable interest or discount rate	10%
Actual return on plan assets	25,000
Actuarial loss due to change in actuarial assumptions	14,000

Assuming that Duster follows IFRS, determine the 2017 effect of the pension plan on pension expense and the company's shareholders' equity.

(LO 7) BE19-10 Refer to the data for Duster Corporation's defined benefit pension plan in BE19-9. Now assume that the company follows ASPE instead of IFRS. Determine the 2017 effect of the pension plan on pension expense and the company's shareholders' equity.

(LO 7) BE19-11 At January 1, 2017, Rui Corporation had plan assets of $250,000 and a defined benefit obligation of the same amount based on projected costs. During 2017, the current service cost was $27,500, the discount rate on the DBO and plan assets was 10%, actual return on plan assets was $30,000, contributions by Rui were $20,000, benefits paid were $17,500, and the cost of past service benefits granted effective December 31, 2017 was $29,000. Prepare a pension work sheet for Rui Corporation for 2017 assuming that Rui follows IFRS.

(LO 7) BE19-12 Refer to the data provided about Rui Corporation's pension plan in BE19-11. Prepare a pension work sheet for Rui Corporation for 2017 assuming the company applies ASPE.

(LO 6, 7) BE19-13 Monday Corporation sponsors a defined benefit pension plan and reports under IFRS. On January 1, 2017, the company reported plan assets of $1,000 and a defined benefit obligation of $1,100 (all amounts in thousands of dollars). During 2017, the current service cost was determined to be $90, the discount rate on the DBO and plan assets was 6%, while the actual return on the plan assets for the year was $55. Monday made contributions of $92 into the plan at the end of the year and the benefits paid amounted to $64. The plan was amended effective December 31, 2017, with the cost of the past service benefits granted being $40. Determine the deficit of the pension plan at January 1, 2017 and calculate its December 31, 2017 deficit balance directly, by identifying which 2017 pension events increased the deficit, which decreased it, and which had no effect.

(LO 7) BE19-14 Petra Ltd. is preparing its financial statements for its year ended December 31, 2017 and has just obtained an actuarial pension valuation as at its year-end date. Prior to the actuarial valuation, Petra determined, based on the individual components of its annual pension expense, that its estimated defined benefit obligation at December 31, 2017 was $356,700. The just-completed actuarial valuation revealed that the defined benefit obligation is actually $398,000. The difference is due to updated assumptions used in its calculation. Identify the effect this actuarial valuation will have, if any, on Petra's 2017 pension expense, assuming (a) Petra reports under IFRS, and (b) Petra reports under ASPE.

(LO 8, 10) BE19-15 Legacy Corporation has the following information available concerning its post-retirement benefit plan for 2017:

Current service cost	$130,000
Interest cost on DBO, discount rate at 6%	65,500
Return on plan assets, using 6% discount rate	48,000
Actual return on plan assets for 2017	54,000

Assuming Legacy follows IFRS, (a) calculate Legacy's 2017 post-retirement benefit expense that will be included in net income. (b) Calculate the post-retirement benefit expense included in net income if Legacy applies ASPE.

(LO 7, 11) *BE19-16 Saver Corporation ended its previous fiscal year with a defined benefit obligation of $137,888 and plan assets of $140,000. On January 1, 2017, the company amended its one-person defined benefit pension plan, resulting in a revised defined benefit obligation at that date of $156,239. As a result of this past service award, Saver's required contributions into the plan assets increase by $1,300 each year. (a) Determine the effect that the plan amendment has on Saver's 2017 pension expense reported in net income, assuming the company follows ASPE. (b) What if Saver applies IFRS?

(LO 7, 11) *BE19-17 Refer to BE19-16 and Saver Corporation's single-person defined benefit pension plan. If the change in the January 1, 2017 defined benefit obligation had been the result of an actuarial revaluation instead of a plan amendment, (a) determine the effect that the change in the DBO has on Saver's 2017 pension expense reported in net income, assuming the company follows ASPE. (b) What if Saver applies IFRS?

Exercises

(LO 2) E19-1   (Defined Contribution Plan) Kea Limited provides a defined contribution pension plan for its employees. The plan requires the company to deduct 5% of each employee's gross pay for each payroll period as the employee contribution. The company then contributes 7% of the gross pay for the employer contribution. Both amounts are remitted to the pension trustee within 10 days of the end of each month for the previous month's payrolls. At November 30, 2017, Kea reported $29,300 of combined withheld and matched contributions owing to the trustee. During December, Kea reported gross salaries and wages expense of $276,100.

Instructions

(a) Prepare the entry to record the December payment to the plan trustee.

(b) What amount of pension expense will the company report for December 2017?

(c) Determine the appropriate pension account and its balance to be reported on the December 31, 2017 statement of financial position.

(LO 2) E19-2   (Defined Contribution Plan) Ad Venture Ltd. provides a defined contribution pension plan for its employees. Currently, the company has 40 full-time and 55 part-time employees. The pension plan requires the company to make an annual contribution of $2,000 per full-time employee, and $1,000 per part-time employee, regardless of their annual salary. In addition, employees can match the employer's contribution in any given year.

At the beginning of the year, 10 full-time and 15 part-time employees elected to contribute to their pension plan by matching the company's contribution. An equal amount of funds was withheld from the employees' cheques in order to fund their pension contribution. Both the employees' and employer's contributions are sent to the plan trustee at year end.

Instructions

(a) What amount of annual pension expense will the company report?

(b) Prepare a summary journal entry to record Ad Venture Ltd.'s payment to the plan trustee.

(LO 4, 5, E19-3   (Continuity Schedules and Calculation of Pension Expense) Rebek Corporation provides the following
7, 9) information about its defined benefit pension plan for the year 2017:

Current service cost	$ 235,000
Contribution to the plan	262,500
Past service cost, effective December 31, 2017	50,000
Actual return on plan assets	160,000
Benefits paid	100,000
Net defined benefit liability at January 1, 2017	400,000
Plan assets at January 1, 2017	1,600,000
Defined benefit obligation at January 1, 2017	2,000,000
Interest/discount rate on the DBO and plan assets	10%

Rebek follows IFRS.

Instructions

(a) Prepare a continuity schedule for 2017 for the defined benefit obligation.

(b) Prepare a continuity schedule for 2017 for the plan assets.

(c) Calculate pension expense for the year 2017.

(d) Prepare all pension journal entries recorded by Rebek in 2017.

(e) What pension amount will appear on Rebek's statement of financial position at December 31, 2017?

(LO 4, E19-4   (Preparation of Pension Work Sheet) Refer to the information for Rebek Corporation in E19-3.
5, 7)
Instructions

(a) Prepare a pension work sheet: insert the January 1, 2017 balances and show the December 31, 2017 balances.

(b) Prepare all journal entries.

(c) What is the amount of the plan's surplus/deficit at December 31, 2017?

(LO 4, 5, E19-5   (IFRS and ASPE: Changes in Pension Accounts)
6, 7)
Instructions

Complete the following tables by indicating whether the following events increase (I), decrease (D), or have no effect (NE) on the employer's defined benefit obligation, the pension plan assets, the pension plan's surplus, the pension expense, and the remeasurement gain—OCI.

(a) Assume that the company applies IFRS and has a significant plan surplus and current period remeasurement gain prior to the following events in the current year:

	Defined Benefit Obligation	Pension Plan Assets	Plan Surplus	Pension Expense	Remeasurement Gain—Other Comprehensive Income
Current service cost					
Actual return on plan assets if > interest/discount rate of return					
Return on plan assets at the interest/discount rate					
Past service costs due to plan revision					
Liability actuarial gain					
Liability actuarial loss					
Employer contributions on last day of fiscal year					
Benefits paid to retirees on last day of fiscal year					
An increase in the average life expectancy of employees					

(b) Now assume that the company uses ASPE instead of IFRS. Identify and explain what differences you would expect in the plan's situation.

(LO 5) E19-6 (Calculation of Actual Return) Qui Importers provides the following pension plan information:

Fair value of pension plan assets, January 1, 2017	$1,438,750
Fair value of pension plan assets, December 31, 2017	1,586,875
Contributions to the plan in 2017	212,500
Benefits paid to retirees in 2017	218,750

Instructions

Calculate the actual return on the plan assets for 2017.

(LO 4, 5, 6, 7) E19-7 (Calculation of Actual Return, Gains and Losses, Pension Expense, and Reconciliation) Berstler Limited sponsors a defined benefit pension plan, and follows ASPE. The corporation's actuary provides the following information about the plan (in thousands of dollars):

	January 1, 2017	December 31, 2017
Vested benefit obligation	$1,200	$1,520
Defined benefit obligation, accounting basis	2,240	3,004
Plan assets (fair value)	1,360	2,096
Interest/discount rate	10%	10%
Net defined benefit liability/asset	?	?
Past service cost, plan amendment, effective December 30, 2017		380
Service cost for the year 2017		320
Contributions (funding) 2017		640
Benefits paid in 2017		160

Instructions

(a) Calculate the actual return on the plan assets in 2017.

(b) Calculate the amount of the net defined benefit liability/asset as at January 1, 2017.

(c) Prepare a continuity schedule of the defined benefit obligation for the 2017 year.

(d) Calculate the pension expense for 2017, separately identifying each amount making up the total expense.

(e) Prepare the pension-related entries made by the company during 2017.

(f) Compare the plan's surplus or deficit at December 31, 2017 with the amount reported on the December 31, 2017 balance sheet.

(LO 4, 5, 6, 7) **E19-8**   **(Preparation of Pension Work Sheet)** Refer to the information in E19-7 about Berstler Limited's defined benefit pension plan.

Instructions

(a) Prepare a 2017 pension work sheet with supplementary schedules of calculations.

(b) Prepare the journal entries at December 31, 2017 to record pension expense and the funding contributions.

(c) Explain what the December 31, 2017 balance in the net defined benefit liability/asset account represents.

(LO 4, 5, 6, 7, 9) **E19-9**   **(DBO and Plan Asset Continuity Schedules)** The following defined benefit pension data of Dahl Corp. apply to the year 2017:

Defined benefit obligation, funding basis, 1/1/17 (before amendment)	$420,000
Plan assets, 1/1/17	409,650
Net defined benefit liability, 1/1/17	10,350
On January 1, 2017, Dahl Corp., through plan amendment, granted prior service benefits having a present value of	60,000
Interest/discount rate	9%
Annual pension service cost	43,500
Contributions (funding)	41,250
Actual return on plan assets	39,210
Benefits paid to retirees	35,000

The company applies ASPE and has made an accounting policy choice to base its actuarial valuation of the DBO on the funding basis.

Instructions

(a) Prepare a continuity schedule for the DBO for 2017.

(b) Prepare a continuity schedule for the plan assets for 2017.

(c) Calculate pension expense for 2017 and prepare the entry to record the expense.

(d) Calculate the balance of the net defined benefit liability/asset at December 31, 2017.

(e) Identify the plan's surplus or deficit at December 31, 2017. Compare it with the balance of the pension asset or liability reported on the balance sheet at the same date.

(f) Identify what disclosures are required for pension expense on the income statement, and briefly explain why these disclosures are required.

(LO 7, 10) **E19-10**   **(Pension Expense, Journal Entries)** The following information is available for Huntley Corporation's pension plan for the year 2017:

Plan assets, January 1, 2017	$400,000
Actual return on plan assets	17,000
Benefits paid to retirees	40,000
Contributions (funding)	95,000
Discount rate	8%
Defined benefit obligation, January 1, 2017, accounting basis valuation	500,000
Service cost	65,000

Instructions

(a) Calculate pension expense for the year 2017, and provide the entries to recognize the pension expense and funding for the year, assuming that Huntley follows IFRS.

(b) Calculate pension expense for the year 2017, and provide the entries to recognize the pension expense and funding for the year, assuming that Huntley follows ASPE, and its accounting policy is to use an accounting basis valuation for its defined benefit obligation.

(LO 4, 5, 6, 7, 10) **E19-11**   **(Pension Expense, Journal Entries, Work Sheet, ASPE, IFRS)** The following information is available for Antoine Corporation's pension plan for the 2017 fiscal year:

Defined benefit obligation, 1/1/17, accounting basis, before plan amendment	$255,000
Fair value of plan assets, 1/1/17	297,000
Current service cost	63,000
Discount rate	10%
Actual return on plan assets	8%
Contributions (funding)	79,200
Benefits paid to retirees	43,200

On January 1, 2017, Antoine Corp. amended its pension plan, resulting in past service costs with a present value of $140,400. Antoine follows ASPE.

Instructions

(a) Calculate pension expense for 2017 and prepare journal entries to record the expense and funding for the year.

(b) Determine the balance of the net defined benefit liability/asset reported on the December 31, 2017 balance sheet.

(c) Prepare a 2017 pension work sheet for Antoine Corporation.

(d) Identify the December 31, 2017 plan surplus or deficit and compare it with the asset or liability reported on the December 31, 2017 balance sheet.

(e) Explain the result of your comparison in part (d).

(f) Identify what would change if Antoine Corp. applied IFRS instead of ASPE.

(LO 4, 5, 6, 7, 9) E19-12 (Pension Expense, Journal Entries, Disclosures, Effect of ASPE Policy Choice) Griseta Limited sponsors a defined benefit pension plan for its employees, which it accounts for under ASPE. The following data relate to the operation of the plan for the year 2017:

1. The actuarial present value of future benefits earned by employees for services rendered in 2017 amounted to $56,000.

2. The company's funding policy requires a contribution to the pension trustee of $145,000 for 2017.

3. As at January 1, 2017, the company had a defined benefit obligation for accounting purposes of $1 million. The fair value of pension plan assets was $600,000 at the beginning of the year. The actual return on plan assets was $53,000, and the discount rate was 9%.

4. No benefits were paid in 2017.

Instructions

(a) Determine the pension expense that should be recognized by the company in 2017.

(b) Prepare the journal entries to record pension expense and the employer's payment to the pension trustee in 2017.

(c) Determine the plan's surplus or deficit position and the balance of the Net Defined Benefit Liability/Asset account at January 1, 2017 and at December 31, 2017.

(d) Prepare the required disclosures for the 2017 financial statements.

(e) Assume instead that Griseta Limited was required by regulation to determine an actuarial valuation of its defined benefit obligation for funding purposes and had adopted an accounting policy to use the funding basis DBO instead of the one developed for accounting purposes. The funding basis valuation on January 1, 2017 was $875,000. Explain how this would change your answers to parts (a) to (d) above, if at all.

(LO 7, 10) E19-13 (Pension Expense, IFRS and ASPE, Reduced Past Service Costs) The following information is in regard to Saverio Corp.'s defined benefit pension plan.

Defined benefit obligation, 1/1/17 (before amendment)	$239,000
Plan assets, 1/1/17	155,000
Discount rate	10%
Annual pension service cost	13,000
Actual return on plan assets	7,750

On January 1, 2017, the company amended its pension plan, which resulted in a reduction in prior benefits for current employees. The present value of the reduced benefits is $34,000.

Instructions

(a) Calculate the pension expense that will be reported in net income for 2017 if Saverio applies IFRS.

(b) Calculate the pension expense that will be reported in net income for 2017 if Saverio applies ASPE.

(LO 4, 5, 6, 7, 8) E19-14 (Post-Retirement Benefit Expense, Surplus or Deficit, and Reconciliation) Rosek Inc. provides the following information related to its post-retirement health care benefits for the year 2017:

Defined post-retirement benefit obligation at January 1, 2017	$110,000
Plan assets, January 1, 2017	42,000
Actual return on plan assets, 2017	3,000
Discount rate	10%
Service cost, 2017	57,000
Plan funding during 2017	22,000
Payments from plan to retirees during 2017	6,000
Actuarial loss on defined post-retirement benefit obligation, 2017 (end of year)	31,000

Rosek Inc. follows IFRS.

Instructions

(a) Calculate the post-retirement benefit expense for 2017.

(b) Calculate the post-retirement benefit remeasurement gain or loss—other comprehensive income (OCI) for 2017.

(c) Determine the December 31, 2017 balance of the plan assets, the defined post-retirement benefit obligation, and the plan surplus or deficit.

(d) Determine the balance of the net post-retirement benefit liability/asset account on the December 31, 2017 statement of financial position.

(e) Reconcile the plan surplus or deficit with the amount reported on the statement of financial position at December 31, 2017.

(LO 4, 5, 6, 7, 10) **E19-15** **(Pension Expense, Work Sheet, ASPE, IFRS)** The following facts apply to the pension plan of Yorke Inc. for the year 2017. Yorke applies ASPE.

Plan assets, January 1, 2017	$490,000
Defined benefit obligation, funding basis, January 1, 2017	389,000
Defined benefit obligation, accounting basis, January 1, 2017	490,000
Discount/interest rate	8.5%
Annual pension service cost	40,000
Contributions (funding)	30,000
Actual return on plan assets	49,700
Benefits paid to retirees	33,400

Instructions

(a) Using a work sheet, calculate pension expense for the year 2017, and provide the entries to recognize the expense and contributions for the year assuming that Yorke has chosen the funding measure of its defined benefit obligation as its accounting policy.

(b) Discuss what adjustments would need to be made to your calculations and entries in part (a) if Yorke's accounting policy choice was the accounting measure of its defined benefit obligation.

(c) Calculate pension expense if IFRS had been applied to this plan. Comment on any difference between this expense and the pension expense calculated in part (b).

(LO 7, 8, 10) **E19-16** **(Post-Retirement Benefit Expense Calculation and Entries, IFRS, ASPE)** Opsco Corp. provides the following information about its post-retirement health care benefit plan for the year 2017:

Current service cost	$ 202,500
Contribution to the plan	47,250
Actual return on plan assets	141,750
Benefits paid	90,000
Plan assets at January 1, 2017	1,597,500
Defined post-retirement benefit obligation at January 1, 2017	1,822,500
Discount rate	9%

Instructions

(a) Assuming Opsco follows IFRS, calculate the post-retirement benefit expense for 2017, and prepare all required journal entries related to the post-retirement benefit plan that were made by the company in 2017.

(b) Assuming Opsco follows ASPE, calculate the post-retirement benefit expense for 2017, and prepare all required journal entries related to the post-retirement benefit plan that were made by the company in 2017.

(LO 4, 5, 7, 8) **E19-17** **(Post-Retirement Benefit Work Sheet)** Refer to the information in E19-16 and assume Opsco applies IFRS.

Instructions

Complete a post-retirement work sheet for 2017, and prepare all required journal entries related to the plan made by Opsco in 2017.

(LO 8) **E19-18** **(Post-Retirement Benefit Reconciliation Schedule)** The following is partial information related to Siri Ltd.'s non-pension, post-retirement health care benefit plan at December 31, 2017:

Defined post-retirement benefit obligation, accounting basis	$185,000
Plan assets (at fair value)	130,000
Past service cost arising on August 31, 2017	17,000

Instructions

DIGGING DEEPER

(a) Prepare a schedule reconciling, to the extent possible, the plan surplus or deficit with the asset/liability reported on the statement of financial position at December 31, 2017, assuming that Siri Ltd. applies IFRS.

(b) Justify your treatment of the past service costs in part (a).

(LO 4, 5, 6, 7, 9) **E19-19** **(Pension Calculations and Disclosures)** Mila Enterprises Ltd. provides the following information about its defined benefit pension plan:

Balances or Values at December 31, 2017	
Defined benefit obligation	$2,737,000
Vested benefit obligation	1,645,852
Fair value of plan assets	2,278,329
Other pension plan data:	
Current service cost for 2017	94,000
Actual return on plan assets in 2017	130,000
Return on plan assets in 2017 using discount rate	219,600
Interest on January 1, 2017 defined benefit obligation	253,000
Funding of plan in 2017	92,329
Benefits paid	140,000

Instructions

(a) Calculate the January 1, 2017 balances for the pension-related accounts if Mila follows IFRS.

(b) Prepare the required disclosures that would be required if Mila's common shares were traded on the Toronto Stock Exchange.

(LO 11) ***E19-20** **(Calculation of Current Service Cost and DBO)** Josit Ltd. initiated a one-person pension plan in January 2012 that promises the employee a pension on retirement according to the following formula: pension benefit = 2.5% of final salary per year of service after the plan initiation. The employee began employment with Josit early in 2009 at age 33, and expects to retire at the end of 2035, the year in which he turns 60. His life expectancy at that time is 21 years.

Assume that this employee earned an annual salary of $40,000 when he joined Josit, that his salary was expected to increase at a rate of 4% per year, and that this remains a reasonable assumption to date. Josit considers a discount rate of 6% to be appropriate.

Instructions

(a) What is the employee's expected final salary?

(b) What amount of current service cost should Josit recognize in 2017 relative to this plan?

(c) What is the amount of the accrued benefit obligation at December 31, 2017?

(LO 4, 5, 6, 7) **E19-21** **(Pension Expense, Journal Entries, Work Sheet, IFRS)** Khan Limited is a publicly traded company on the Toronto Stock Exchange. The company sponsors a defined benefit pension plan for all of its employees, and the controller provides you with the following data that relate to the plan for fiscal 2017:

1. The actuary has determined that the actuarial present value of future benefits earned by employees for services rendered in the year amounted to $86,000.

2. The plan requires Khan to make a cash contribution of $175,000 to the plan assets for 2017.

3. On January 1, 2017, the company's defined benefit obligation was $1,030,000, and the fair value of pension plan assets was $950,000. The plan assets generated a return of $56,000 during the year, and Khan's discount rate was 8%.

4. Benefits of $75,000 were paid in 2017.

5. In late December 2017, an actuarial revaluation of the defined benefit obligation indicated an actuarial loss of $29,000.

Instructions

(a) Determine the pension expense that should be recognized by the company in 2017.

(b) Prepare the journal entries to record pension expense and the employer's payment to the pension trustee in 2017.

(c) Determine the plan's surplus or deficit position and the balance of the Net Defined Benefit Liability/Asset account at January 1, 2017 and at December 31, 2017.

(d) Prepare a pension work sheet for this plan for the year, including all related entries that would be required.

(LO 2, 3, 7, 8) **E19-22** **(Contributory Plans, Accounting for Employer vs. Accounting for Benefit Plan, Funding, Service Cost)** Many business organizations have been concerned with providing for employee retirement since the late 1800s. During recent decades, a marked increase in this concern has resulted in the establishment of private pension and other post-retirement benefit plans in many sizable companies.

The substantial growth of these plans, both in the numbers of employees that they cover and in the types and value of retirement benefits, has increased the significance of the cost of these benefit plans in relation to the financial position, results of operations, and cash flows of many companies. In working with the benefit plans, accountants encounter a variety of terms. Each benefit plan component must be dealt with appropriately if generally accepted accounting principles are to be reflected in the financial statements of entities that offer these plans.

Instructions

(a) How does a contributory plan differ from a non-contributory plan?

(b) Differentiate between accounting for the employer and accounting for the benefit plan.

(c) Explain the terms "funded" and "net defined benefit liability or asset" as they relate to the employer and the benefit plan itself. Are these terms also used in defined contribution plans? Explain briefly.

(d) Distinguish between each of the following sets of terms as they relate to pension plans and their treatment under ASPE and IFRS:

1. Current service cost and past service cost

2. Remeasurement gain/loss and actuarial experience gain/loss

(e) Explain how the accounting for other post-retirement benefit plans with benefits that vest or accumulate differs, if at all, from the accounting for defined benefit pension plans.

Problems

P19-1 RWL Limited provides a long-term disability program for its employees through an insurance company. For an annual premium of $20,000, the insurance company is responsible for providing salary continuation to disabled employees on a long-term basis after a three-month waiting period. During the waiting period, RWL continues to pay the employee at full salary. The employees contribute to the cost of this plan through regular payroll deductions that amount to $6,000 for the year. In late October 2017, Tina Hurst, an employee earning $4,500 per month, was injured and was not expected to be able to return to work for at least one year.

Instructions

Prepare all entries made by RWL in 2017 in connection with the benefit plan, as well as any entries required in 2018.

P19-2 Newfoundland University recently signed a contract with the bargaining unit that represents full-time professors. The contract agreement starts on April 1, 2016, the start of the university's fiscal year.

The following excerpt outlines the portion of the signed agreement that relates to sabbaticals: *"Professors may apply for a one-year sabbatical leave after seven continuous years of employment, and must outline how their sabbatical plans will benefit the university."*

After completing the required amount of time, any professor may apply for the leave. The contract notes particular types of activities that the sabbatical is intended to promote, including formal research, continued professional development, and independent study and research. Professors are left to make their own choices for whichever of these activities to pursue while on sabbatical leave. As part of their agreement, they must continue to work for the university one year after their sabbatical or reimburse it for funds they receive while on leave. The agreement states that professors receive 80% of their salary while on sabbatical leave. Professors may delay, or be asked to delay, their application for sabbatical, in which case they will receive 85% of their salary while on leave.

The issue of sabbatical had long been a point of contention with faculty at Newfoundland University, and they fought vehemently for the right to this paid leave, which had not previously been in their collective agreement. The university is phasing in the unfunded sabbatical plan gradually, which means that the first professors will be eligible to apply for their sabbatical in seven years.

The controller has put together the following numbers of professors in each salary group:

Professors with salaries averaging $80,000	55
Professors with salaries averaging $90,000	40
Professors with salaries averaging $110,000	10

The union agreement calls for a wage increase of 2% per year in each of the next seven years. This is consistent with past union agreements for this bargaining unit. Five of the professors with salaries averaging $110,000 are scheduled to retire in four years. The university expects to keep a similar composition of salaried professors in the future. Assume a discount rate of 6%. Newfoundland University applies ASPE.

Instructions

(a) Prepare any entries that are required at the March 31, 2017 fiscal year end assuming sabbaticals will be granted only if the sabbatical activities proposed by the applicants are expected to benefit the university in some way.

(b) Prepare any entries that are required at the March 31, 2017 fiscal year end assuming sabbaticals will be granted automatically with no restrictions on the professors' activities during the year.

(c) Five faculty members are granted approval to take sabbatical in the first year that they are eligible under the assumption in part (b). Prepare the entry that will be required when the professors are paid, assuming that an amount of $367,000 has correctly been accrued for these employees.

(d) The contract allows employees of the bargaining unit to take up to 10 days of paid sick leave per year. Explain the accounting implications under the following assumptions:

1. The sick leave is allowed to be carried over for up to a one-year period following year end.

2. Any unused sick time is not eligible to be carried over to the following fiscal period.

 P19-3 D'Eon Corporation reports the following January 1, 2017 balances for its defined benefit pension plan, which it accounts for under IFRS: plan assets, $460,000; defined benefit obligation, $460,000. Other data relating to three years of operation of the plan are as follows:

	2017	2018	2019
Annual service cost	$36,800	$ 43,700	$ 59,800
Discount rate	10%	10%	10%
Actual return on plan assets	39,100	50,370	55,200
Funding of current service cost	36,800	43,700	59,800
Funding of past service cost	—	69,000	80,500
Benefits paid	32,200	37,720	48,300
Past service cost (plan amended, 1/1/18)		368,000	
Change in actuarial assumptions establishes a December 31, 2019 defined benefit obligation of			1,196,000

Instructions

(a) Prepare and complete a pension work sheet for 2017.

(b) Prepare a continuity schedule of the projected benefit obligation over the three-year period.

(c) Prepare a continuity schedule of the plan assets over the three-year period.

(d) Determine the pension expense for each of 2017, 2018, and 2019.

 FINANCE (e) Prepare the journal entries to reflect the pension plan transactions and events for each year.

(f) Prepare a schedule reconciling the pension plan's surplus or deficit with the pension amounts reported on the statement of financial position over the three-year period.

(g) Determine the pension expense for each of 2017, 2018, and 2019 assuming that the company applies ASPE.

 DIGGING DEEPER (h) What information would a potential investor be most interested in relative to a company's pension plan?

P19-4 The following information is available for HTM Corporation's defined benefit pension plan:

	2017	2018	2019
Defined benefit obligation, opening balance, accounting basis	$175,000	?	?
Fair value of plan assets	165,000	?	?
Current service cost	35,000	$47,250	$52,500
Discount rate	7%	7%	7%
Actual return earned on plan assets	8%	6%	7%
Contributions (funding)	44,000	44,000	44,000
Benefits paid to retirees	24,000	26,000	28,000

On January 1, 2017, HTM Corp. amended its pension plan, resulting in past service costs with a present value of $78,000.

Instructions

(a) Calculate the pension plan's surplus or deficit and the pension liability or asset reported on the December 31, 2017, 2018, and 2019 statements of financial position assuming that HTM Corp. accounts for its pension plan under ASPE.

(b) Calculate all the components, and the total of pension expense for 2017, 2018, and 2019, assuming that HTM Corp. accounts for its pension plan under ASPE.

(c) Identify the pension plan's surplus or deficit and the pension liability or asset reported on the December 31, 2017, 2018, and 2019 statements of financial position assuming that HTM Corp. accounts for its pension plan under IFRS.

(d) Calculate pension expense and any remeasurement (gain) loss—OCI for 2017, 2018, and 2019 assuming that HTM Corp. accounts for its pension plan under IFRS.

(e) Compare the results obtained in parts (b) and (d). Comment. Which method results in a better measure of expense over the three-year period?

DIGGING
DEEPER

(f) Which method results in a better measure of the plan surplus or deficit that is reported on the statement of financial position?

P19-5 You are the controller of a newly established technology firm that is offering a new pension plan to its employees. The plan was established on January 1, 2017, with an initial contribution by the employer equal to the actuarial estimate of the past service costs for the existing group of employees. These employees are expected to continue to work for the firm for 20 years, on average, prior to retirement. The company is considering going public in the next five years, and the president has asked you to keep her aware of the accounting changes in moving from ASPE to IFRS. She wants to be sure that the company always chooses the accounting policies that are closest to IFRS so that changes in the future when the company goes public will be minimized. In addition, she is interested in demonstrating a history of profits so that the company can be taken public successfully. The following information is available for you to work with.

	2017	2018	2019
Fair value of plan assets, beginning of year*	$75,000	?	?
DBO for funding purposes, beginning of year*	70,000	?	?
DBO for accounting purposes, beginning of year*	75,000	?	?
Current service cost for year	12,000	$13,000	$14,500
Discount rate	8%	8%	8%
Past service costs granted, January 1	75,000	–0–	–0–
Actual earnings on plan assets	6,500	10,000	8,000
Employer contributions for the year	12,000	15,000	16,000
Benefits paid to retirees by trustee	–0–	4,000	5,000

*After the initial $75,000 contribution.

Instructions

(a) Without using a pension work sheet, determine the surplus or deficit position of the pension plan and the amount reported on the statement of financial position at each year end, the pension expense for each of the three years, and any remeasurement (gain) loss recorded in OCI for each of the three years, applying IFRS.

(b) Without using a pension work sheet, determine the surplus or deficit position of the pension plan and the amount reported on the balance sheet at each year end, and the pension expense for each of the three years applying ASPE. State any assumptions you have made.

DIGGING
DEEPER

(c) Prepare a short report to the company president concerning the accounting for the new pension plan. Make a recommendation to your employer about the approach that should be taken.

P19-6 Brawn Corporation sponsors a defined benefit pension plan for its 100 employees. On January 1, 2017, the company's actuary provided the following information:

Pension plan assets (fair value)	$1,040,000
Defined benefit obligation	$1,430,000

The actuary calculated that the present value of future benefits earned for employee services rendered in 2017 amounted to $213,200, the December 31, 2017 defined benefit obligation was $1,825,200, and the appropriate interest or discount rate was 8%. The plan assets generated a return of $80,600 during 2017. The company funded the 2017 current service cost as well as $106,600 of the past service costs recognized in a previous year; however, no benefits were paid during the year. Brawn Corporation is a private company and applies ASPE.

Instructions

Round all answers to the nearest dollar.

(a) Prepare a schedule that indicates what the plan's surplus or deficit is at December 31, 2017.

(b) Determine the pension expense that the company will recognize in 2017, identifying each component clearly. (Do not prepare a work sheet.)

(c) 1. Prepare the journal entries to record pension expense and the company's funding of the pension plan in 2017.

2. How would these entries differ if Brawn Corp. applied IFRS instead of ASPE?

(d) Prove your answer to part (a) by reconciling it to the net defined benefit liability/asset to be reported on the December 31, 2017 balance sheet. Briefly explain why these two amounts are the same.

(e) Assume that the liability gain/loss on the defined benefit obligation arose because of the disposal of a segment of Brawn's business that qualifies as a discontinued operation under ASPE. How should this gain or loss be reported on the company's 2017 financial statements? How would it be accounted for if Brawn applied IFRS instead of ASPE? Briefly explain your answers.

**DIGGING
DEEPER**

P19-7 Manon Corporation applies ASPE and sponsors a defined benefit pension plan. The following pension plan information is available for 2017 and 2018:

	2017	2018
Plan assets (fair value), December 31	$515,000	$642,000
Defined benefit obligation, January 1	600,000	700,000
Net defined benefit liability (asset), January 1	240,000	?
Current service cost	60,000	90,000
Actual return on plan assets	24,000	47,000
Funding of current service cost	60,000	90,000
Funding of past service costs	85,000	55,000
Benefits paid	?	?
Interest/discount rate	9%	9%

The pension fund paid out benefits in each year. There were no actuarial gains or losses incurred on the DBO in the two-year period.

Instructions

(a) Calculate pension expense for 2017 and 2018.

(b) Prepare all journal entries to record the pension expense and the company's pension plan funding for both years.

(c) Prepare the complete pension work sheets for Manon for 2017 and 2018.

(d) Prepare the required pension disclosure notes to the financial statements at December 31, 2018.

P19-8 Bouter Corporation Limited (BCL) began operations in 1996 and in 2006 adopted a defined benefit pension plan for its employees. By January 1, 2017, the defined benefit obligation was $510,000.

On January 2, 2017, for the first time, BCL agreed to a new union contract that granted retroactive benefits for services that its unionized employees had provided in years before the pension plan came into effect. The actuary informed BCL's chief accountant that, using its normal discount rate of 6%, benefits relating to these past services would cost the company $240,000.

On January 1, 2017, the fair value of the pension plan assets was $320,000. In recent years, the actual return earned on these assets was highly variable, and in 2017, due to a downturn in the market, the actual return reported for the year was a loss of $9,500. The workforce is made up of a relatively young group of employees, so payments to those who had retired came to only $48,000 during the year, with these payments being made close to year end. The actuary reported that the current service cost for BCL's employees for 2017 was $107,500. It is the company's policy, on advice from the actuary, to contribute amounts to the pension plan equal to each year's current service cost as well as 25% of any past service costs granted in the current year or in any of the preceding three years. The funding payment was made just before BCL's fiscal year end of December 31, 2017.

At the end of 2017, the actuary revised some key estimates, resulting in an actuarial loss of $15,500 related to the defined benefit obligation.

Instructions

(a) Calculate the pension expense that should be reported for BCL's year ended December 31, 2017, assuming the company reports under IFRS.

(b) Calculate the pension expense that should be reported for BCL's year ended December 31, 2017, assuming the company reports under ASPE.

(c) Reconcile the difference in pension expense reported in net income between IFRS and ASPE.

(d) Calculate the amounts in the pension account to be reported on the December 31, 2017 statement of financial position under both IFRS and ASPE. Comment on the difference in this amount, if any. In each case, provide a reconciliation of the account's 2017 opening to closing balance.

DIGGING DEEPER

(e) How would an ASPE accounting policy choice of using a funding basis for the actuarial valuation of the defined benefit obligation affect the cash flows, if at all, in light of the company's policy regarding its contributions to the pension plan?

P19-9   Dela Corporation initiated a defined benefit pension plan for its 50 employees on January 1, 2017. The insurance company that administers the pension plan provides the following information for the years 2017, 2018, and 2019:

	For Year Ended December 31		
	2017	2018	2019
Plan assets (fair value)	$50,000	$ 85,000	$170,000
Defined benefit obligation	63,900	?	?
Net actuarial (gain) loss: DBO	8,900	(24,500)	84,500
Remeasurement (gain) loss: fund assets	?	?	(18,200)
Employer's funding contribution (made at end of year)	50,000	60,000	95,000

There were no balances as at January 1, 2017, when the plan was initiated, because no credit was given for past service. The rate used to discount the company's pension obligation was 13% in 2017, 11% in 2018, and 8% in 2019. The service cost component of net periodic pension expense amounted to the following: 2017, $55,000; 2018, $85,000; and 2019, $119,000. No benefits were paid in 2017, but $30,000 was paid in 2018, and $35,000 in 2019. (All benefits were paid and all actuarial gains and losses were determined at the end of the year.) The company applies ASPE.

Instructions

Depending on what your instructor assigns, do either parts (a), (b), (c), (e), and (f) or parts (d), (e), and (f). (Round all answers to the nearest dollar.)

(a) Prepare a continuity schedule for the defined benefit obligation over the three-year period.

(b) Prepare a continuity schedule for the plan assets over the three-year period.

(c) Calculate the amount of net periodic pension expense that the company will recognize in each of 2017, 2018, and 2019. Identify any components of pension expense that should be separately disclosed.

(d) Prepare and complete a pension work sheet for each of 2017, 2018, and 2019. Identify any components of pension expense that should be separately disclosed.

(e) Determine the plan surplus or deficit at December 31, 2019, and the balance of the Net Defined Benefit Liability/Asset account that will be reported on the December 31, 2019 balance sheet. Briefly explain any difference or similarity in these amounts.

(f) Discuss what accounting policy choices, if any, are available under ASPE in accounting for defined benefit plans such as this.

P19-10   Refer to the data in P19-9, except now assume Dela Corporation reports under IFRS. Depending on what your instructor assigns, do either parts (a), (b), (c), and (e) or parts (d) and (e).

P19-11   Etienne Inc., a Canadian company traded on the Venture Exchange of the Toronto Stock Exchange, has sponsored a non-contributory defined benefit pension plan for its employees since 1992. Relevant information about the pension plan on January 1, 2017 is as follows:

1. The defined benefit obligation amounted to $1,250,000 and the fair value of pension plan assets was $750,000.

2. On January 3, 2017, the pension plan was amended, resulting in a reduction in employee benefits for past service with a present value of $45,000 on this date.

On December 31, 2017, the actuaries determined that the defined benefit obligation on this date was $1,387,500, and the fair value of the pension plan assets amounted to $975,000. An 8% discount rate was used in the actuarial present value calculations in the pension plan. The present value of benefits attributed by the pension benefit formula to employee service in 2017 amounted to $50,000. Although the employer's contribution to the plan assets was $143,750 in 2017, no pension benefits were paid or payable to retirees during this period.

Instructions

DIGGING DEEPER

(a) Prepare a schedule reconciling the plan's surplus or deficit with the pension amounts reported on the December 31, 2017 balance sheet. Prove your balances at December 31, 2017 in both the statement of financial position account and the plan surplus or deficit. Explain any differences or similarities.

(b) Assume that Etienne's pension plan is contributory rather than non-contributory. Would any part of your answers above change? What would be the effect on the company's financial statements of a contributory plan?

P19-12 You are the auditor of Beaton and Gunter Inc., the Canadian subsidiary of a public multinational engineering company that offers a defined benefit pension plan to its eligible employees. Employees are permitted to join the plan after two years of employment, and benefits vest immediately. You have received the following information from the fund trustee for the year ended December 31, 2017:

Discount rate	5%
Rate of compensation increase	3.5%
Defined Benefit Obligation	
Defined benefit obligation at January 1, 2017	$11,375,000
Current service cost	425,000
Interest cost	568,750
Benefits paid	756,250
Actuarial loss, end of period	631,250
Plan Assets	
Fair value of plan assets at January 1, 2017	9,062,500
Actual return on plan assets, net of expenses	1,125,000
Employer contributions	493,750
Employee contributions	81,250
Benefits paid	756,250

Other relevant information:

1. The net defined benefit liability on January 1, 2017 is $2,312,500.

2. Employee contributions to the plan are withheld as payroll deductions, and are remitted to the pension trustee along with the employer contributions.

Instructions

FINANCE

(a) Prepare a pension work sheet for the company.

(b) Prepare the employer's journal entries to reflect the accounting for the pension plan for the year ended December 31, 2017.

(c) Prepare a schedule reconciling the plan's surplus or deficit with the pension amounts reported on the December 31, 2017 statement of financial position.

DIGGING DEEPER

(d) Assume that interest rates are falling, and that the rate of compensation increase is expected to fall as well. Explain what effect this is likely to have on the surplus or deficit of the plan.

P19-13 Hass Foods Inc. sponsors a post-retirement medical and dental benefit plan for its employees. The company adopted the provisions of IAS 19 beginning January 1, 2017. The following balances relate to this plan on January 1, 2017:

Plan assets	$2,780,000
Defined post-retirement benefit obligation	3,439,800
Past service costs	–0–

As a result of the plan's operation during 2017, the following additional data were provided by the actuary.

1. The service cost for 2017 was $273,000.

2. The discount rate was 7%.

3. Funding payments in 2017 were $234,000.

4. The actual return on plan assets was $158,500.

5. The benefits paid on behalf of retirees from the plan were $171,600.

Instructions

(a) Calculate the post-retirement benefit expense for 2017.

(b) Prepare a continuity schedule for the defined post-retirement benefit obligation and for the plan assets from the beginning of the year to the end of 2017.

(c) At December 31, 2017, prepare a schedule reconciling the plan's surplus or deficit with the post-retirement amount reported on the statement of financial position.

(d) If Hass Foods had remained with ASPE instead of moving to IFRS, how would your answers to parts (a) to (c) change, if at all?

(e) Explain in what ways, if any, the accounting requirements for this plan are different from the requirements for a defined benefit pension plan.

*P19-14   Refer to the example of HTSM Corp. in Appendix 19A and assume it is now 2018, three years after the defined benefit pension plan was initiated. In December 2018, HTSM's actuary provided the company with an actuarial revaluation of the plan. The actuary's assumptions included the following changes:

Estimated final salary on retirement	$145,000
Current settlement/discount rate	7%

Instructions

(a) Calculate the defined benefit obligation at December 31, 2018, and the amount of any actuarial gain or loss.

(b) Based on the revised assumptions at the end of the year, determine what percentage increase or decrease there would be in the DBO for:

1. A 1% increase in the discount rate

2. A 1% decrease in the discount rate

(c) Determine the effect of the actuarial revaluation on the pension plan's surplus or deficit at December 31, 2018, and on pension expense for 2018 and for 2019.

(d) Based on the revised assumptions, recalculate the past service cost that was incurred by the company in 2020.

P19-15   Shikkiah Corp. (which is a private enterprise) tries to attract the most knowledgeable and creative employees it can find. To help accomplish this, the company offers a special group of technology employees the right to a fully paid sabbatical leave after every five years of continuous service. It is the company's objective that the employees will come back renewed and with fresh ideas, but there are no restrictions on what they do during the sabbatical year.

Shikkiah hired three employees in early 2017 who were entitled to this benefit. Each new hire agreed to a starting salary of $80,000 per year.

Instructions

(a) Explain generally how this employee benefit should be accounted for by Shikkiah Corp. under ASPE and IFRS.

(b) Assume that you are the assistant to the company controller. In response to the controller's request, list all the information you need in order to calculate the amounts and prepare the adjusting entry that is required at December 31, 2017 relative to this plan under ASPE and IFRS. Include a brief discussion of the key information that you would need to provide to the actuary.

(c) Assume that the employees' activities during the sixth (the sabbatical) year are specified by the company: the employees must work on research and promotion activities that will benefit the company. Would your answer to part (a) change? If yes, explain why and how it would be accounted for. If not, explain why not.

CASE

Case

Refer to the Case Primer on the Student Website and in *WileyPLUS* to help you answer this case.

CA19-1   Delmar Manufacturing Inc. is a provincial manufacturer of electronics. It has been in operation for over 25 years under ownership of the same two private shareholders. It has always offered its employees a very generous defined benefit (DB) pension plan as part of the compensation package. Delmar has recently undergone expansion, and in the last quarter of this fiscal year (2017) opened a new manufacturing plant in another province. As a result, it also created a new DB pension plan for the employees of the new plant. Some of the employees at the new plant are current employees who were already participating in the existing DB pension plan and others are new employees recently hired and will be new to Delmar's pension plan. Existing employees were transferred into the new plan before the end of the fiscal year.

A review of the pension transactions for 2017 revealed the following:

1. For 2017, the service cost for Delmar employees is projected by the actuary to be $236,000. The current service cost is credited at the end of each fiscal year. Nothing has been recorded in the financials to reflect this.

2. The actuary has reviewed the new plan and determined that the past service costs for existing employees is $96,000 (a cumulative total over the past 20 years). Delmar has not yet reflected this in its current results and is unclear on how to accurately reflect this in its financial statements. Delmar employees would be eligible for full benefits after a one-year vesting period.

3. Delmar's current borrowing rate and settlement rate is 7%. Delmar's management has specifically eliminated the option of purchasing an insurance contract for the future settlement of its pension liability. The current interest rate on high-quality corporate bonds is 8%.

4. The plan paid only $34,000 in benefits to its retirees for 2017 and Delmar contributed $88,000 to the plan throughout the year.

5. Due to declining economic conditions, the actuary has revised its assumption for age of retirement and final salary. This has resulted in an actuarial loss of $55,000. Delmar must also account for an actuarial loss of $19,000 resulting from differences in past assumptions and actual costs (experience losses). This has not yet been accounted for in the statements.

6. The actual return on plan assets was $16,500, significantly lower than projected.

7. The defined benefit obligation as determined by the actuarial valuation is the defined benefit obligation used for accounting purposes. The fair value of the plan assets was $980,000 at the end of 2016.

Excerpts from Delmar's financial statements are provided below, prepared under ASPE.

	2016	2017
Total current assets	$ 2,078,900	$ 2,044,900
Fixed assets, at carrying amount	11,700,900	14,010,200
Total current liabilities	822,400	773,000
Long-term debt	345,900	333,800
Net defined benefit liability	2,165,000	?
Operating profit	1,890,000	1,345,000
Other revenue and other expenses		
Costs—Expansion (*manufacturing facility*)	58,000	777,000
Interest expense	390,000	482,000
Net income	937,300	55,900

Instructions

Delmar Manufacturing Inc.'s management is reviewing its current pension accounting in preparation for an upcoming meeting with the board of directors and its pension committee. Complete the necessary calculations needed to record the ending net defined benefit liability or asset. In addition, assume the role of a consultant and discuss the financial reporting issues, particularly the implications for the financial statements and the differences in reporting and presentation if the company moved to IFRS. Provide guidance on which method would be preferable for Delmar.

Integrated Case

CASE

IC19-1 Martel Industries Limited is in the mining business. The company has significant exploration activities in many countries and has started to explore and develop oil and gas properties in the past few years. The company's shares trade on the national stock exchange. Martel has several significant loans with the Mining Bank Limited, which monitors its debt to equity ratio.

One of the company's largest-ever silver mines is starting to produce (Mine A). In the past year, a significant amount has been spent getting the property ready for production. The company has had to borrow additional funds from its bank this year in order to complete the mine and has installed a complex underground railway system (railway cars and tracks) to bring the ore to the surface for processing. Martel has asked its engineers and geologists to estimate the amount of silver on this property. The engineers and geologists have come up with a fairly wide range, with the top end being three times the amount of the lower end. The lower end of the range includes silver ore reserves that can be proven and the top end represents possible and probable silver ore

reserves. The life of the mine is expected to be approximately 10 years, after which the company will probably just abandon it. The life of the railway tracks is 50 years and the railway cars 20 years. The company may be able to salvage the tracks and cars at the end of the 10-year period but it is not sure if it would actually do this (and sell or reuse them) since the salvage costs would likely be high. As the ore is mined, it is stored in large piles waiting to be processed into silver. At year end, in anticipation of significant sales in the new year, the ore piles are very large.

Another mining property (Mine B) is just in the evaluation and exploration stage. The funds being spent on this property are also pretty significant and financed by borrowings. Primarily, the expenditures consist of geophysical studies, exploratory drilling, and sampling. Although the preliminary work that is being done points to a significant geological find of gold, there is still considerable uncertainty as to whether sufficient gold ore actually exists of a commercial grade. Nonetheless, the company is continuing to develop this property. A lot of time has been spent on this particular property by

Martel's senior management since this property is in a politically unstable country. Martel had to negotiate for several months for the rights to bring an exploration team into the country to begin the work. In addition, Martel had to pay a one-time fee to the resource minister of the government of this country for this right. All costs have been capitalized.

Mine C has been actively producing copper for two years. During the current year, the government of that country announced that it would be imposing stricter regulations on mining companies, requiring that they restore the land to its original condition. Although in the past Martel has tried to minimize any negative impact on the environment (there are numerous environmental groups that monitor the company's policies), senior management has admitted in private discussions within the firm that they have not met the proposed new standard. The amount would be material. As a matter of fact, the company may decide to close Mine C and abandon it.

Mine C is in a country where Martel would likely not do business in the future due to the high incidence of earthquakes.

The oil and gas segment of the business has several producing wells. Luckily, they have not had any "dry wells." In other words, all properties that they explored resulted in producing wells. The oil rigs require major maintenance every two years. The costs to do this maintenance are pretty significant but, given the risks involved, they are well worth it. The company stores its gas in underground storage caves. Approximately 25% of this gas will never be sold because it is required to pressurize the cave. The rest of the gas is generally sold.

During the year, the company put in place a new long-term benefit plan for Martel employees. Under the funding arrangement for the plan, the company will contribute to the plan annually an amount that is based on net income.

Instructions

Adopt the role of the company controller and discuss the financial reporting issues. Use the case analysis format discussed in class.

RESEARCH AND ANALYSIS

RA19-1   BCE Inc.

BCE Inc.'s accounting policy note and its note disclosures relating to the company's pension and other post-employment benefits for the year ended December 31, 2014 are set out in the chapter.

REAL WORLD EMPHASIS

Instructions

Review the disclosures from BCE's 2014 financial statements found in the chapter and answer the following questions.

(a) Determine the dollar amount of the surplus or deficit of the defined benefit (DB) pension plan and the other post-employment plans at December 31, 2014 and December 31, 2013. Has the 2014 status of these plans improved or deteriorated since the end of the preceding year? What is the major reason for the change in any surplus or deficit? What is the status of the plans in a net deficit position and what is the status of the plans in a net surplus position at December 31, 2014?

(b) What is the amount of the employee benefit asset or obligation reported on BCE's December 31, 2014 consolidated statement of financial position? Provide a reconciliation to the surplus or deficit reported in part (a). Comment on this reconciliation.

(c) What was the expected return on the pension plan assets in 2014? What was the actual return on the plan assets for the year?

(d) What amount of expense did the company report for its post-employment benefit plans? Describe the main components of the expense reported under IFRS. Estimate the amount of expense that would have been reported under ASPE for 2014. Comment on any differences.

(e) Describe the types of post-employment plans the company has. What was the total of all costs reported for these plans in Note 22 of the financial statements?

RA19-2   Canadian National Railway Company

Obtain the financial statements of the **Canadian National Railway Company** for its year ended December 31, 2014 from SEDAR (sedar.com) or the company's website.

REAL WORLD EMPHASIS

Instructions

Review the information contained in the "Additional Disclosures" section of Note 12 to the financial statements, and answer the following questions.

(a) Is the company's pension plan in a surplus or deficit position at December 31, 2014? At December 31, 2013? Provide details in support of your answer. Comment on what significant events caused the major change in the plan's net position over the 2014 year.

(b) What is the amount reported for the net periodic pension benefit cost for the years ended December 31, 2014 and December 31, 2013? Comment on the cause of any significant change in this cost in 2014 relative to 2013.

(c) What was the cash flow used to fund the plan in 2014 and 2013? Why would there be differences in the annual funding amounts? How do these amounts compare with the expense that is reported for the company for the related years?

(d) Comment on whether or not you believe that the pension expense is faithfully represented in the statement of income for the years 2014 and 2013.

3. The rate of compensation increase that was used to measure the projected benefit obligation

(b) Comment on any significant differences in the assumptions that are used by each company and the effect of these differences.

(c) Did any of the companies change their assumptions during the period covered by the notes? If yes, what was the effect on each of the following: the current year's defined benefit obligation, the plan assets, and the pension expense? Explain.

(d) Identify the types of plans and the assumptions that underlie any future benefit plans other than pensions. Are these similar across the three companies? Comment on how any differences would affect an intercompany analysis.

(e) Are the pension plans and post-retirement plans in a deficit or surplus position? What are the amounts that have been reported on the statements of financial position?

RA19-3 Research Topic— Entity Comparisons

REAL WORLD EMPHASIS

Potash Corporation of Saskatchewan Inc., Loblaw Companies Limited, and Air Canada are all Canadian companies with defined benefit plans. Visit www.sedar.com to access financial statements for their 2014 fiscal years ended December 31, 2014, January 3, 2015, and December 31, 2014, respectively.

Instructions

Analyze the notes to the financial statements of each of the three companies, and provide answers to the following questions.

(a) For each company, identify the following three assumptions:

1. The discount rate used to measure the year-end defined benefit obligation

2. The discount rate used to measure the benefit plan cost for the year

RA19-4 Research Topic—Recent Changes in Defined Benefit Plans

Instructions

REAL WORLD EMPHASIS

Research what Canadian companies have been doing in recent years in response to rising post-employment health care costs and the risks that are associated with defined benefit pension plans. Write a short report on your findings.

RA19-5 Asset Ceiling Test

IAS 19 *Employee Benefits* requires companies that have a surplus in a defined benefit plan to perform a "ceiling test" on the net benefit asset account.

Instructions

Explain what an asset ceiling test is, why it is required, and how it is applied.

ENDNOTES

[1] Statistics Canada, "Employer Pension Plans (Trusteed Pension Funds), Second Quarter 2015," *The Daily*, December 9, 2015.

[2] "Solvency of Canadian Pensions Falls to Lowest Level Since 2013, According to Aon Hewitt's Latest Quarterly Survey," Aon Hewitt news release, March 31, 2015.

[3] Greg Keenan, "Air Canada Wipes Out Its $3.7 Billion Deficit, Swings to a Small Surplus," *The Globe and Mail*, January 22, 2014.

[4] When it is used as a verb, **fund** means to pay to a funding agency (for example, to fund future pension benefits or to fund pension cost). Used as a noun or an adjective, "fund" refers to assets that have accumulated in the hands of a funding agency (trustee) for the purpose of meeting pension benefits when they become due.

[5] Increasingly, companies have hybrid plans that have characteristics of both defined contribution and defined benefit plans. Under ASPE, a company with a plan that has features of both types should account for each component separately according to its substance.

[6] *CPA Canada Handbook*, Part II, Section 3462.06 and IAS 19.8.

[7] See IAS 19.8, *Employee Benefits*. Copyright © International Financial Reporting Standards Foundation. All rights reserved. Reproduced by John Wiley & Sons Canada, Ltd with the permission of the International Financial Reporting Standards Foundation®. Reproduction and use rights are strictly limited. No permission granted to third parties to reproduce or distribute.

[8] There has been much litigation over the ownership of pension fund surpluses. The courts have increasingly determined that pension fund surpluses, or a significant portion of them, should accrue to the benefit of the employees. Provincial pension legislation dictates how pension surpluses must be handled.

[9] The employee is not 100% secure, however. If the health of the company sponsor is uncertain, the company's ability to meet any outstanding pension funding requirements may also be uncertain. This was very evident in the economic downturn of 2007 to 2009.

[10] The general public has little understanding of what an actuary does, as illustrated by the following excerpt from *The Wall Street Journal*: "A polling organization once asked the general public what an actuary was and received among its more coherent responses the opinion that it was a place where you put dead actors."

[11] When the term "present value of benefits" is used throughout this chapter, it really means the **actuarial present value** of benefits. Actuarial present value is the amount payable adjusted to reflect the time value of money and the probability of payment (by means of decreases for events such as death, disability, withdrawals, or retirement) between the present date and the expected date of payment. For simplicity, we will use the term "present value" instead of "actuarial present value" in our discussion. In addition to the projected benefit method, the accumulated benefit method is allowed under ASPE where future salary levels/costs do not affect the benefits (see 3462.035).

[12] ASPE calls this method the **projected benefit method prorated on services** (*CPA Canada Handbook*, Part II, Section 3462.035).

[13] The service cost for funding purposes is usually calculated on a different basis.

[14] See IAS 19.8, *Employee Benefits*.

[15] IAS 19 uses the term "net interest" on the net defined benefit liability, but notes that this "can be viewed as comprising interest income on plan assets, interest cost on the defined benefit obligation and interest on the effect of the asset ceiling" (ASPE uses the term "finance cost" to refer to the net interest on the defined benefit liability and "remeasurement" when referring to the difference between the actual return on plan assets and the return calculated utilizing the rate used for the DBO calculation (see *CPA Canada Handbook*, Part II, Section 3462.084-.085). Copyright © International Financial Reporting Standards Foundation. All rights reserved. Reproduced by John Wiley & Sons Canada, Ltd with the permission of the International Financial Reporting Standards Foundation®. Reproduction and use rights are strictly limited. No permission granted to third parties to reproduce or distribute.

[16] In general, the current service cost has to be funded annually. If a plan is in a surplus position (that is, fund assets are greater than the accrued obligation), the company may be able to take a contribution holiday; in other words, to temporarily not make any contributions. If there is a funding deficiency, the extent of the shortfall is determined by two different valuations: one based on a going concern assumption and one based on a termination assumption. These dictate the additional funding that is required, and the period over which any deficiency must be funded. With the economic downturn and low interest rates in the past decade, many companies had difficulty dealing with unanticipated funding demands as pension obligations increased in value. A DBO based on current salary levels is common in determining the minimum funding requirements.

[17] When Air Canada filed for protection under the Companies' Creditors Arrangement Act in 2003, a $1.5-billion unfunded pension liability was listed as one of the key factors behind the company's insolvency. How to deal with this underfunded plan and unbooked liability was central to Air Canada's restructuring negotiations. The company faced similar problems in 2009 with its $3.2-billion pension deficit. In this case, the federal government stepped in with a legislated solution to help extremely troubled companies restructure such problems.

[18] See the table of concordance between the old and new requirements as set out in the *Employee Future Benefits January 2012 Exposure Draft* issued by the Canadian Accounting Standards Board.

[19] The benefit cost or pension cost and the benefit or pension expense for a period are the same amount unless some portion of the cost is treated as a product cost and charged to inventory, or is capitalized as a component of property, plant, and equipment, for example. In this chapter, these terms are generally used interchangeably.

[20] While past service costs, curtailments, and settlements are reflected in net income under both IFRS and ASPE, the categories by which they are included differ slightly. Curtailments are included within the definition of past service costs under IFRS (IAS 19.8), and past service costs and settlements are grouped together for recognition in net income (IAS 19.57(c)(ii)). Under ASPE, past service costs, curtailments, and settlements are considered part of "other items" and are included in the cost of the defined benefit pension plan as part of "remeasurements and other items" (per *CPA Canada Handbook*, Part II, Section 3462.079 and 3462.085). Copyright © International Financial Reporting Standards Foundation. All rights reserved. Reproduced by John Wiley & Sons Canada, Ltd with the permission of the International Financial Reporting Standards Foundation®. Reproduction

and use rights are strictly limited. No permission granted to third parties to reproduce or distribute.

[21] This pension entry work sheet is based on Paul B. W. Miller, "The New Pension Accounting (part 2)," *Journal of Accountancy*, February 1987, pp. 86–94. Copyright 1987. American Institute of Certified Public Accountants, Inc.

[22] This is not always the case. As explained later in the chapter, the balance sheet account may have to be adjusted for any valuation allowance that arises from the limit on the carrying amount of an accrued benefit asset based on the asset ceiling test.

[23] *CPA Canada Handbook*, Part II, Section 3462.084 notes that finance cost is "generally" calculated by multiplying the opening defined benefit liability (asset) by the discount rate. To simplify our analysis, we treat the mid-year contribution consistently for both IFRS and ASPE and therefore have included the impact of interest on the mid-year contribution in net interest/finance cost.

[24] There would be a similar impact if we assume that the 2018 contributions are made evenly over the year in 2018. On

average, half of the contributions would have been available to earn interest during the year, increasing expected returns accordingly.

[25] The expected future benefits generally represent those that the company can realize from a plan surplus through amounts it can withdraw from the plan or reductions it can make in its future contributions. Under IFRS, the change in the valuation allowance made as a result of actuarial gains and losses recognized in other comprehensive income would be adjusted to OCI rather than net income.

[26] Sabbaticals where the employee is expected to use the compensated absence to perform research or other activities that benefit the organization do not need to be accrued over the period when the sabbatical is earned. Other benefits provided to employees during active employment, such as sick leave that does not accumulate and bonuses, are not covered by post-employment benefits under ASPE (*CPA Canada Handbook*, Part II, Section 3462.005).

**REFERENCE TO THE
CPA COMPETENCY MAP**   **LEARNING OBJECTIVES**

After studying this chapter, you should be able to:

1.1.1, 1.1.2, 1.1.4, 5.1.1	**1.** Understand the importance of leases from a business perspective.
1.1.1, 1.1.2, 1.2.1. 1.2.2, 2.3.1, 5.2.3, 5.2.4, 6.1.1	**2.** Explain the conceptual nature, economic substance, and advantages of lease transactions.
1.1.2, 1.2.1, 1.2.2, 5.1.2	**3.** Identify and apply the criteria that are used to determine lessee right-of-use assets under IFRS 16 and leases under the ASPE classification approach.
1.2.1, 1.2.2, 1.2.3, 5.1.1	**4.** Calculate the lease payment that is required for a lessor to earn a specific return.
1.1.2, 1.1.3, 1.1.4, 1.2.1, 1.2.2	**5.** Account for right-of-use assets by lessees under IFRS 16 or a capital lease under ASPE.
1.1.2, 1.1.3, 1.1.4, 1.2.1, 1.2.2	**6.** Determine the effect of, and account for, residual values and purchase options for a lessee's right-of-use asset (IFRS) or a capital lease (ASPE).
1.1.2, 1.1.3, 1.2.1, 1.2.2	**7.** Account for operating leases by lessees under ASPE (and short-term leases and low-value leases under IFRS 16) and compare the operating and capitalization methods of accounting for leases.
1.2.1, 1.2.2, 1.4.1, 1.4.2, 5.1.1	**8.** Determine the statement of financial position presentation of right-of-use assets (and ASPE capital leases) and identify other disclosures required.
1.1.2, 1.2.1, 1.2.2	**9.** Identify and apply the criteria that are used to determine the type of lease for a lessor under the classification approach.
1.1.2, 1.1.3, 1.2.1, 1.2.2	**10.** Account for and report basic financing and manufacturer/dealer or sales-type leases by a lessor.
1.1.2, 1.1.3, 1.2.1, 1.2.2	**11.** Account for and report financing and manufacturer/dealer or sales-type leases, with guaranteed residual values or a purchase option, by a lessor.
1.2.1, 1.2.2, 1.4.2	**12.** Account for and report operating leases by a lessor.
1.1.4	**13.** Identify differences in accounting between IFRS and ASPE, and what changes are expected in the near future.

After studying Appendix 20A, you should be able to:

1.1.2, 1.2.1, 1.2.2, 1.2.3	**14.** Describe and apply the lessee's accounting for sale-leaseback transactions.
1.1.2, 1.2.1, 1.2.2	**15.** Explain the classification and accounting treatment for leases that involve real estate.

After studying Appendix 20B, you should be able to:

1.1.2, 1.2.1, 1.2.2	**16.** Explain and apply the classification approach under IAS 17 for a lessee.

LEASE REPORTING: ON TRACK FOR CHANGE

RAILWAY SHIPMENTS EBB AND FLOW with the economy. That means that demand for a railroad's rolling stock—its locomotives and freight cars—also come and go based on the flow of goods. For Calgary-based Canadian Pacific Railway Limited, the ability to lease some of its rolling stock gives it some flexibility in expanding and contracting its fleet as needed.

As of the end of 2014, CP had almost 1,580 engines in its fleet, both owned and leased. Locomotives make up the company's largest asset class. Most of its leases allow

CP to return the rolling stock to the lessor when the lease expires or else buy it outright. In 2014, for example, CP spent roughly $96 million on freight cars, most of which went to acquiring cars that it had previously leased.

There are advantages and disadvantages to owning or leasing rolling stock. A railroad that owns excess locomotives can lease or sell some of them to competitors, netting additional revenues. (In late 2015, CP had 400 idle locomotives that it was considering selling or leasing.) A railroad can remanufacture locomotives that it owns, extending their useful lives, whereas many lease agreements in the industry limit the amount of maintenance that can be done to leased rolling stock. The advantages of leasing rolling stock include the fact that leases are an easy and economical form of financing expensive equipment.

From an accounting perspective, perhaps the biggest advantage to leasing is that companies can choose to keep the leases off their balance sheet, therefore not reporting the leased equipment as assets and reducing the amount of liabilities they carry. That will change soon, however, for companies using IFRS.

CP reports under U.S. GAAP. On its statement of financial position, it reports the rolling stock that it owns as part of its property, plant, and equipment assets, along with some of the rolling stock it leases, which it classifies as a capital lease. However, it classifies the rest of its rolling stock that it leases as operating leases with rent expense, which are not reported on the balance sheet. In addition, CP includes its current and future operating lease payments in the notes to the financial statements as a commitment; again, keeping this debt off the balance sheet. Expenses for operating leases for the year ended December 31, 2014 were $121 million, while its future operating lease commitments totalled minimum lease payments of at least $569 million.

For companies reporting under IFRS, however, off–balance sheet financing will no longer be an option. The IASB

© istockphoto.com/angelo_narciso

has enacted changes to its leasing standard, effective January 1, 2019, which requires almost all leases to be capitalized. That means that any railroads using IFRS would have to report all their rolling stock leases as assets, with a corresponding liability, on the statement of financial position.

Sources: Frederic Tomesco, "CP Rail Sees More Job Cuts in Workforce Already at Decade Low," Bloomberg Business, October 20, 2015; Gordon Pitts, "Turnaround Ace: Inside the Hunter Harrison Era at CP Railway," *Globe and Mail*, April 24, 2014; Canadian Pacific 2014 annual report.

PREVIEW OF CHAPTER 20

Leasing continues to grow in popularity as a form of **asset-based financing**.[1] Instead of borrowing money to buy an airplane, a computer, a nuclear core, or a satellite, a company leases the item. Airlines lease huge amounts of equipment, many hotel and motel chains lease their facilities, most retail chains lease the bulk of their retail premises and warehouses, and, as indicated in the opening vignette, most railroads lease some of their locomotives! Small and medium-sized enterprises also use leases as an important form of debt financing. With a new IFRS standard for leases released in January 2016—IFRS 16—it will be interesting to see if the popularity of lease financing decreases, because almost all leases will result in debt on financial statements for companies that adopt the new standard.

Because of the significance and popularity of lease arrangements, consistent accounting and complete reporting of these transactions are crucial. In this chapter, we look at these important issues related to leasing as the lease standards evolve.

The chapter is organized as follows:

LEASES					
Leasing Basics	**IFRS and ASPE Approach—Lessees**	**IFRS and ASPE Approach—Lessors**	**IFRS/ASPE Comparison**	**Appendix 20A— Other Lease Issues**	**Appendix 20B— Lessee Accounting under IAS 17**
▪ Importance of leases from a business perspective ▪ The leasing environment	▪ Lease criteria ▪ Determination of rental payments ▪ Accounting for a right-of-use asset ▪ Accounting for residual values and purchase options in a finance lease ▪ Accounting for an operating lease ▪ Capital and operating leases compared under ASPE ▪ Presentation and disclosure	▪ Classification criteria ▪ Accounting for financing and manufacturer/dealer or sales-type leases ▪ Accounting for residual values and purchase options in a financing or manufacturer/dealer or sales-type lease ▪ Accounting for an operating lease	▪ A comparison of IFRS and ASPE ▪ Looking ahead	▪ Sale and leaseback transactions ▪ Real estate leases	▪ IFRS criteria

LEASING BASICS

Importance of Leases from a Business Perspective

Objective 1
Understand the importance of leases from a business perspective.

Leasing is very attractive for many companies as a cost-effective way of financing property and equipment, especially for items whose technology becomes obsolete quite quickly. But the accounting for leases is very controversial. For many years standard setters have been concerned that financial statement preparers have avoided having to capitalize leases on their financial statements, by structuring leases in such a way that the lease liabilities remain "off–balance sheet." The substance of most lease arrangements is that companies are borrowing funds to acquire leased assets. However, the legal form of many leases allows companies following ASPE (and IFRS, prior to adoption of IFRS 16 effective in 2019) to treat lease transactions simply as rent expense, with no separate recording of the related asset and liability.

ETHICS

The FASB and IASB worked together to develop a new leasing standard starting with a discussion paper in 2009, and progressing through Exposure Drafts in 2010 and 2013. In a speech at the London School of Economics in November 2012, Hans Hoogervorst, Chairman of the IASB, noted that a significant source of off–balance sheet financing for companies is the leasing arrangements that they enter into. "For many companies, such as airlines and railway companies, the off–balance sheet financing numbers can be quite substantial," he said. "Companies tend to love off–balance sheet financing, as it masks the true extent of their leverage and many of those that make extensive use of leasing for this purpose are not happy" with the IASB-FASB project to get leases on the balance sheet, he reported.

FINANCIAL ANALYSIS AND PLANNING
5.1.1

Hoogervoorst said there is a lack of transparency in leasing arrangements, so financial analysts have to "take an educated guess on what the real but hidden leverage of leasing is."[2] This leaves analysts and other financial statement users guessing, since management does not have to share the information needed to provide a proper estimate of the extent of leverage provided by lease financing. Other issues with the "old" *Leases* standard (IAS 17) were noted in the basis of conclusions provided with the new *Leases* standard (IFRS 16). Specifically, there is a lack of comparability, because IAS 17 includes two different accounting models for leases—operating leases and finance leases—with very different accounting for economically similar transactions. A lack of full disclosure exacerbated the situation, resulting in information asymmetry and a lack of transparency. Users of financial statements could try to estimate present value for operating leases, but many could not due to lack of available information.

The leasing industry predicted that the new accounting rules would significantly hurt its business. Hoogervorst noted that a "recent report in the United States claimed that our joint efforts with the FASB to record leases on balance sheet[s] will lead to 190,000 jobs being lost in the US alone." He compares this with similar claims that were made when the IASB and the FASB required stock options to be expensed and pension liabilities to be put on the balance sheet.

We discuss the "players" involved in the leasing industry, and the changes being implemented by the IASB, further below. For now, it is important to note that accounting for leases is not just an accounting issue but one of importance to financial institutions, leasing companies, and even the U.S. Congress (which was being heavily lobbied to keep leases off the balance sheets of corporations). It will be interesting to see if IFRS 16 results in the IASB succeeding in its goal of improving the accounting for leases, as the new standards did for pensions and stock options. The effective date of IFRS 16 is January 1, 2019, so if the IASB avoids delaying the implementation date, financial statements for most companies that use leases extensively should be transformed before the end of the decade.

The Leasing Environment

Objective 2
Explain the conceptual nature, economic substance, and advantages of lease transactions.

Aristotle once said, "Wealth does not lie in ownership but in the use of things." Many Canadian companies have clearly come to agree with Aristotle because, rather than owning assets, they now are heavily involved in leasing them.

A **lease** is a contractual agreement between a **lessor** and a **lessee** that gives the lessee, for a specified period of time, the right to use specific property owned by the lessor in return for specified, and generally periodic, cash payments (rents). An essential element of the lease agreement is that the lessor transfers less than the total interest in the property. Because of the financial, operating, and risk advantages that the lease arrangement provides, many businesses and other types of organizations lease substantial amounts of property as an alternative to ownership. Any type of equipment or property can be leased, such as railcars, helicopters, bulldozers, schools, golf club facilities, barges, medical scanners, computers, and so on. The largest class of leased equipment is information technology equipment. Next are assets in the transportation area, such as trucks, aircraft, and railcars.

| EXAMPLE | The lessee company gains the right to use the asset over the lease term in exchange for promising to make periodic rent or lease payments. The asset might be an automobile, a building, or any of a broad range of possible assets. |

Leased asset → Lessee ← Obligation to make payments → Lessor

Because a lease is a contract, the provisions that the lessor and lessee agree to can vary widely from lease to lease. Indeed, they are limited only by the ingenuity of the two parties to the contract and their advisors. The lease's duration—lease term—may be anything from a short period of time to the entire expected economic life of the asset. The **rental payments** may be the same amount from year to year, or they may increase or decrease; further, they may be predetermined or may vary with sales, the prime interest rate, the consumer price index, or some other factor. In most cases, the rent is set at an amount that enables the lessor to recover the asset's cost plus a fair return over the life of the lease.

LAW

The obligations for taxes, insurance, and maintenance (executory costs) may be the responsibility of either the lessor or the lessee, or they may be divided. In order to protect the lessor from default on the rents, the lease may include restrictions—comparable to those in bond indentures—that limit the lessee's activities in making dividend payments or incurring further debt. In addition, the lease contract may be non-cancellable or may grant the right to early termination on payment of a pre-set amount plus a penalty. In case of default, the lessee may be liable for all future payments at once, and receive title to the property in exchange; or the lessor may have the right to sell the asset to a third party and collect from the lessee all or a portion of the difference between the sale price and the lessor's unrecovered cost.

When the lease term ends, several alternatives may be available to the lessee. These may range from simple termination to the right to renew or buy the asset at a nominal price.

Who Are the Lessors?

Who are the lessors referred to above? In Canada, lessors are usually one of three types of company:

1. Manufacturer finance companies

2. Independent finance companies

3. Traditional financial institutions

Manufacturer finance companies, or captive leasing companies as they are also called, are subsidiaries whose main business is to perform leasing operations for the parent company. **Honda Canada Finance Inc.** is an example of a captive leasing company. As soon as the parent company receives a possible order, its leasing subsidiary can quickly develop a lease-financing arrangement that facilitates the parent company's sale of its product.

An **independent finance company** acts as a financial intermediary by providing financing for transactions for manufacturers, vendors, or distributors. Your dentist, for example, when acquiring specialized equipment for his or her practice, may order the equipment through the manufacturer or distributor, who in turn may outsource the financing to a lessor such as an independent finance company.

Subsidiaries of domestic and foreign banks are examples of **traditional financial institutions** that provide leasing as another form of financing to their customers.

Advantages of Leasing

Although leasing does have disadvantages, the growth in its use suggests that it often has a genuine advantage over buying and owning property. Some of the advantages are as follows.

100% Financing at Fixed Rates

STRATEGY
DEVELOPMENT
2.3.1
TREASURY
MANAGEMENT
5.2.4

Leases are often signed without requiring any money down from the lessee, helping to conserve scarce cash—an especially desirable feature for new and developing companies. In addition, lease payments often remain fixed (unchanging), which protects the lessee against inflation and increases in interest rates. The following comment about a conventional loan is typical: "Our local bank finally agreed to finance 80% of the purchase price but wouldn't go any higher, and they wanted a floating interest rate. We just couldn't afford the down payment and we needed to lock in a payment we knew we could live with."

Turning to the lessor's point of view, financial institutions and leasing companies find leasing profitable because it provides attractive interest margins.

Protection Against Obsolescence

Leasing equipment reduces the risk of obsolescence to the lessee, and in many cases passes the risk of residual value to the lessor. For example, a company that leases computers may have a lease agreement that permits it to turn in an old computer for a new model at any time, cancelling the old lease and writing a new one. The cost of the new lease is added to the balance due on the old lease, less the old computer's trade-in value. As one treasurer remarked, "Our instinct is to purchase." But when new computer innovations come along in a short time, "then leasing is just a heck of a lot more convenient than purchasing."

On the other hand, the lessor can benefit from the property reversion (that is, the return of the asset) at the end of the lease term. Residual values can produce very large profits. For example, **Citicorp** at one time assumed that the commercial aircraft it was leasing to the airline industry would have a residual value of 5% of their purchase price. As it turned out, however, the planes were worth 150% of their cost—a handsome price appreciation. Three years later these same planes slumped to 80% of their cost, but this was still a far greater residual value than the projected 5%.

Flexibility

TREASURY
MANAGEMENT
5.2.3

Lease agreements may contain less restrictive provisions than other debt agreements. Innovative lessors can tailor a lease agreement to the lessee's specific needs. For instance, a ski lift operator using equipment for only six months of the year can arrange rental payments that fit well with the operation's revenue streams. In addition, because the lessor retains ownership and the leased property is the collateral, it is usually easier to arrange financing through a lease.

UNDERLYING CONCEPT

Some companies "double-dip" at the international level. The leasing rules of the lessor's and lessee's countries may differ, permitting both parties to own the asset. In such cases, both the lessor and lessee can receive the tax benefits related to amortization.

TREASURY MANAGEMENT 5.2.4 CORPORATE TAX 6.1.1

Illustration 20-1

Reported Debt and Unrecognized Operating Lease Obligations

UNDERLYING CONCEPT

The issue of how to report leases is the classic case of substance versus form. Although legal title does not technically pass in lease transactions, the benefits from the use of the property do transfer.

Less Costly Financing for Lessee, Tax Incentives for Lessor

Some companies find leasing cheaper than other forms of financing. For example, start-up companies in depressed industries or not-for-profit organizations may lease as a way of claiming tax benefits that might otherwise be lost. Investment tax credits and capital cost allowance deductions offer no benefit to companies that have little or no taxable income. Through leasing, these tax benefits are used by the leasing companies or financial institutions. They can then pass some of these tax savings back to the asset's user through lower rental payments.

Off–Balance Sheet Financing

Certain leases have traditionally not added debt to the balance sheet and may add to borrowing capacity.[3] **Off–balance sheet financing** has been critical to some companies. For example, airlines use lease arrangements extensively and this results in a great deal of off–balance sheet financing. Illustration 20-1 indicates that debt levels are understated by **WestJet Airlines Ltd., Air Canada**, and **Canadian Pacific Railway Limited** (CP), a sample of Canadian companies in the transportation industry. WestJet notes in its 2014 annual report that all of its leased aircraft were considered operating leases as at December 31, 2014. WestJet also provides an adjusted debt estimate that includes the impact of off–balance-sheet aircraft leases. (These would have added an estimated $1.4 billion of debt to WestJet's balance sheet at the end of 2014.)

	WestJet Dec. 31, 2014 ($ thousands)	Air Canada Dec. 31, 2014 ($ thousands)	CP Dec. 31, 2014 ($ thousands)
Non-current liabilities, excluding deferred income taxes and deferred credits	$1,233,738	$8,344,000	$6,846,000
Shareholders' equity (deficit)	1,777,502	(1,201,000)	5,610,000
Unrecognized future minimum lease payments under existing operating leases (includes other contractual commitments for WestJet)	1,118,673	1,633,000	569,000

Conceptual Nature of a Lease

If an airline borrows $80 million on a 10-year loan from the bank to purchase a Boeing 787 jet plane, it is clear that an asset and related liability should be reported on the company's balance sheet at that amount. If the airline purchases the 787 for $80 million directly from Boeing through an instalment purchase over 10 years, it is equally clear that an asset and related liability should be reported. (That is, the instalment purchase transaction should be "capitalized.") However, if the Boeing 787 is leased for 10 years through a non-cancellable lease transaction with payments of the same amount as the instalment purchase, there are differences of opinion about how this transaction should be reported. Three views on accounting for leases can be summarized as follows.

Do Not Capitalize Any Leased Assets—An Executory Contract Approach

Some argue that, because the lessee does not own the property, it is not appropriate to capitalize the lease. Furthermore, a lease is an **executory contract** that requires continuing performance by both parties. Because other executory contracts (such as purchase commitments and employment contracts) are not currently capitalized, leases would not be capitalized either. The lessor would continue to recognize the leased item as an asset.

Capitalize Leases That Are Similar to Instalment Purchases— A Classification Approach

The **classification approach** says that transactions should be classified and accounted for according to their economic substance. Because instalment purchases are capitalized as property, plant, and equipment assets, leases that have similar characteristics to instalment purchases should be accounted for in the same way. In our earlier example, the airline is committed to the same payments over a 10-year period for either a lease or an instalment purchase; lessees simply make rental payments, whereas owners make mortgage payments. The financial statements should classify and report these transactions in the same way: recognizing the physical asset on the lessee's balance sheet where appropriate. Transactions not recognized as in-substance acquisitions of assets are classified as operating leases and accounted for differently.

Capitalize All Leases—A Contract-Based Approach

LAW

Under the **contract-based approach**, the leased asset that is acquired is not the physical property; rather, it is the **contractual right to use** the property that is conveyed under the lease agreement. The liability is the contractual obligation to make lease payments. Under this view, also called a property rights or **right-of-use approach**, it is justifiable to capitalize the fair value of the rights and obligations associated with a broad range of leases.[4]

In short, the various viewpoints range from no capitalization to capitalization of all leases.

Current Standards

SIGNIFICANT CHANGE

What do the current standards require? The standards being followed by most lessees when this text went to print under ASPE and IAS 17 are consistent with the **classification approach** that capitalizes leases that are similar to an instalment purchase. These are classified as **capital** or **finance leases** and usually are recognized as items of property, plant, and equipment. The accounting treatment is based on the concept that **a lease that transfers substantially all of the benefits and risks of property ownership should be capitalized**. The newly introduced lease accounting requirements under IFRS 16 are contract-based, with a goal of capitalizing (almost) all leases for lessees. (We discuss exemptions from capitalization of leases under IFRS 16 below.)

By capitalizing the present value of the future rental payments, the **lessee** records an asset and a liability at an amount that is generally representative of the asset's fair value. The **lessor**, having transferred substantially all the benefits and risks of ownership, removes the asset from its statement of financial position (SFP), and replaces it with a receivable. The typical journal entries for the lessee and the lessor under ASPE and IAS 17, assuming the leased equipment is capitalized, are shown at the top of Illustration 20-2. If the benefits and risks of ownership **are not transferred** from one party to the other, the lease is classified as an **operating lease**. The accounting for an operating lease by the lessee and lessor is shown in the bottom of Illustration 20-2.

Illustration 20-2

Journal Entries for Finance/ Capital and Operating Leases (per IAS 17 and ASPE)

	Lessee			Lessor		
Capital (ASPE) or finance (IAS 17) lease	Equipment under Lease	x		Lease Receivable	x	
	Obligations under Lease		x	Equipment		x
	Depreciation Expense	x				
	Accumulated Depreciation —Leased Equipment		x			
	Obligations under Lease	x		Cash	x	
	Interest Expense	x		Interest Income		x
	Cash		x	Lease Receivable		x
Operating lease	Rent Expense	x		Cash	x	
	Cash		x	Rent Revenue		x

When the asset is capitalized as an item of property, plant, and equipment, the lessee recognizes the depreciation. The lessor and lessee treat the lease rentals as the receipt and the payment of interest and principal. If the lease is not capitalized, no asset is recorded by the lessee and no asset is removed from the lessor's books. When a lease payment is made, the lessee records rent or lease expense and the lessor recognizes rental or lease income.

UNDERLYING CONCEPT

According to an IASB news release in early 2016, public companies following IFRS or U.S. GAAP had an estimated U.S. $3.3 trillion of lease commitments and more than 85% of these commitments did not show up as debt on the balance sheets of these companies.[5]

The contract-based approach of IFRS 16 is based on the view that "lease contracts create assets and liabilities that should be recognized in the financial statements of lessees."[6] The most significant change that will result from the adoption of this approach will be the recognition on the statement of financial position of rights and obligations as assets and liabilities for most "operating" leases from prior standards. These leases, as you can tell from Illustration 20-2, are often now off–balance sheet items and are reported as an expense only as the lease payments are made. Under the contract-based right-of-use approach, aside from short-term leases and leases for low-value items, all leases covered by the new standard would be recognized as right-of-use assets (or grouped with similar property, plant, and equipment items) along with the contractual obligation (lease liability) to make lease payments in the future.

The next section of this chapter explains the basics of the contract-based approach under IFRS 16 and the classification approach for lessees that is currently in use under ASPE.

IFRS AND ASPE APPROACH—LESSEES

Lease Criteria

Objective 3

Identify and apply the criteria that are used to determine lessee right-of-use assets under IFRS 16 and leases under the ASPE classification approach.

We begin by looking at recognition of right-of-use assets and lease liabilities under IFRS 16. From the lessee's standpoint, all leases are capitalized and placed on the statement of financial position except where lessees elect not to apply the IFRS 16 present value requirements for (1) short-term leases, or (2) leases where the underlying asset is of low value. Next, we will discuss the classification approach under ASPE, which results in leases being classified as either operating leases or capital leases. As indicated previously, when the risks and benefits of ownership are transferred from the lessor to the lessee, the lease is accounted for as a capital lease (known as a finance lease under IAS 17, as will be discussed in Appendix 20B); otherwise, it is accounted for as an operating lease. We use the terms "capital lease" and "finance lease" interchangeably when discussing ASPE and IAS 17 requirements in this chapter.

IFRS 16 Lease Criteria

SIGNIFICANT CHANGE

Under IFRS 16, companies must assess whether each contract they enter into is (or contains) a lease. "A contract is, or contains, a lease if the contract conveys the right to control the use of an identified asset for a period of time in exchange for consideration" (IFRS 16.9). Instead of a period of time such as months or years, a lease can also be described by the extent of use of the asset (such as the number of units that a piece of equipment produces). The objective is for financial statements to represent faithfully the effects of leases on each company's financial position, income, and cash flows. Illustration 20-3 provides an illustrative example from IFRS 16 regarding what is (or is not) a lease.[7] Contracts may include both lease rights and service components (such as a car lease that includes maintenance). The service component is typically excluded from lease accounting (see also IFRS 16.15).

Illustration 20-3

Illustrative Example—Is It a Lease?

IS IT A LEASE?

Facts: A coffee company (Customer) enters into a contract with an airport operator (Supplier) to use a space in the airport to sell its goods for a three-year period. The contract states the amount of space and that the space may be located at any one of several boarding areas within the airport. Supplier has the right to change the location of the space allocated to Customer at any time during the period of use. There are minimal costs to Supplier associated with changing the space for the Customer: Customer uses a kiosk (that it owns) that can be moved easily to sell its goods. There are many areas in the airport that are available and that would meet the specifications for the space in the contract.

(continued)

Illustration 20-3

Illustrative Example—Is It a Lease? (continued)

Question: Is the contract a lease (or does it contain a lease)?

Solution: The contract does not contain a lease. Although the amount of space Customer uses is specified in the contract, there is no identified asset. Customer controls its owned kiosk. However, the contract is for space in the airport, and this space can change at the discretion of Supplier. Supplier has the substantive right to substitute the space Customer uses because:

(a) Supplier has the practical ability to change the space used by Customer throughout the period of use. There are many areas in the airport that meet the specifications for the space in the contract, and Supplier has the right to change the location of the space to other space that meets the specifications at any time without Customer's approval.

(b) Supplier would benefit economically from substituting the space. There would be minimal cost associated with changing the space used by Customer because the kiosk can be moved easily. Supplier benefits from substituting the space in the airport because substitution allows Supplier to make the most effective use of the space at boarding areas in the airport to meet changing circumstances.

SIGNIFICANT CHANGE

While the goal was initially to recognize assets and liabilities for the rights and obligations of all leases, exceptions are recognized in IFRS 16 for short-term leases of 12 months or less, and for leases where the underlying asset is of low value. Where one of these two exceptions is made, the lessee recognizes the lease payments as an expense on a straight-line basis over the lease term, or by another systematic approach. So, these short-term and low-value lease exceptions are treated in a similar manner to the accounting for operating leases by lessees under ASPE and IAS 17. Illustration 20-4 provides an illustrative example from IFRS 16 regarding low-value leases and accounting for portfolios of leases.

Illustration 20-4

Illustrative Example—Low-Value Leases and Lease Portfolios

HOW DO WE ACCOUNT FOR LEASES OF LOW-VALUE ASSETS?

Facts: A lessee in the pharmaceutical manufacturing and distribution industry (Lessee) has the following leases: (a) leases of real estate (both office buildings and warehouses); (b) leases of manufacturing equipment; (c) leases of company cars, both for sales personnel and senior management and of varying quality, specification and value; (d) leases of trucks and vans used for delivery purposes, of varying size and value; (e) leases of IT equipment for use by individual employees (such as laptop computers, desktop computers, hand held computer devices, desktop printers and mobile phones); (f) leases of servers, including many individual modules that increase the storage capacity of those servers. The modules have been added to the mainframe servers over time as Lessee has needed to increase the storage capacity of the servers; (g) leases of office equipment including (i) office furniture (such as chairs, desks and office partitions); and (ii) water dispensers.

Question: What qualifies as a low-value lease and how might the company use portfolios of leases when applying IFRS 16 lease requirements?

Solution: Leases of low-value assets

Lessee determines that the following leases qualify as leases of low-value assets on the basis that the underlying assets, when new, are individually of low value: (a) leases of IT equipment for use by individual employees; and (b) leases of office furniture and water dispensers. Lessee elects to apply the requirements in paragraph 6 of IFRS 16 in accounting for all of those leases.

Although each module within the servers, if considered individually, might be an asset of low value, the leases of modules within the servers do not qualify as leases of low-value assets. This is because each module is highly interrelated with other parts of the servers. Lessee would not lease the modules without also leasing the servers.

Solution: Portfolio application

After using the low-value exemption for the items discussed above, Lessee applies the recognition and measurement requirements in IFRS 16 to its leases of real estate, manufacturing equipment, company cars, trucks and vans, and servers. In doing so, Lessee groups its company cars, trucks and vans into portfolios.

Lessee's company cars are leased under a series of master lease agreements. Lessee uses eight different types of company car, which vary by price and are assigned to staff on the basis of seniority and territory. Lessee has a master lease agreement for each different type of company car. The individual leases within each master lease agreement are all similar (including similar start and end dates), but the terms and conditions generally vary from one master lease agreement to another.

(continued)

Illustration 20-4

Illustrative Example—Low-Value Leases and Lease Portfolios
(continued)

Because the individual leases within each master lease agreement are similar to each other, Lessee reasonably expects that applying the requirements of IFRS 16 to each master lease agreement would not result in a materially different effect than applying the requirements of IFRS 16 to each individual lease within the master lease agreement. Consequently, Lessee concludes that it can apply the requirements of IFRS 16 to each master lease agreement as a portfolio.

Lessee's trucks and vans are leased under individual lease agreements. There are 6,500 leases in total. All of the truck leases have similar terms, as do all of the van leases. The truck leases are generally for four years and involve similar models of truck. The van leases are generally for five years and involve similar models of van. Lessee reasonably expects that applying the requirements of IFRS 16 to portfolios of truck leases and van leases, grouped by type of underlying asset, territory and the quarter of the year within which the lease was entered into, would not result in a materially different effect from applying those requirements to each individual truck or van lease. Consequently, Lessee applies the requirements of IFRS 16 to different portfolios of truck and van leases, rather than to 6,500 individual leases.

Overview—IFRS 16 Lessor Accounting and ASPE Lease Criteria

Accounting for **lessors** is substantially the same under IFRS 16 as it was under the pre-existing rules of IAS 17 (as we will discuss further below). A classification approach is used to classify leases as a finance lease if it substantially transfers the risks and rewards of ownership from the lessor to the lessee (and to classify it as an operating lease if the risks and rewards are not substantially transferred). ASPE also focuses on the transfer of risks and rewards of ownership for classification of leases for both lessees and lessors.

So, what are the risks and benefits (or rewards) of ownership? Benefits of ownership are the ability to use the asset to generate profits over its useful life, benefit from any appreciation in the asset's value, and realize its residual value at the end of its economic life. The risks, on the other hand, are the exposure to uncertain returns, loss from use or idle capacity, and technological obsolescence.

Guidance is provided to help preparers determine the substance of the lease transaction under both ASPE and IAS 17 *Leases*, and the objective under both standards is the same. As we will see in Appendix 20B, IAS 17 identifies numerous qualitative indicators to help identify whether a lease is a finance (capital) lease or not. Section 3065 of Part II of the *CPA Canada Handbook*, on the other hand, provides fewer qualitative indicators, but includes a few quantitative indicators that end up being used extensively in making the classification decision. These quantitative factors are known as "bright lines" and they are key to those involved with the financial engineering of leases, done to obtain the accounting method preferred by the entity. The net effect is that entities applying IAS 17 make the classification decision based on principles, and those applying ASPE look to whether certain numerical thresholds have been met or missed.

ASPE assumes that the risks and benefits of ownership **are normally transferred to the lessee**. It requires that the lessee classify and account for the arrangement as a capital lease if **any one or more of** the following criteria are met:

1. There is reasonable assurance that the lessee will obtain ownership of the leased property, including through a bargain purchase option (explained below).

2. The lessee will benefit from most of the asset benefits due to the length of the lease term—**a numerical threshold is included**: this is usually assumed to occur if the lease term is 75% or more of the leased property's economic life.

3. The lessor recovers substantially all of its investment and earns a return on its investment in the leased property, where the present value of the minimum lease payments is substantially all of the fair value of the leased asset. **A numerical threshold is included**: this is usually assumed if the present value of the minimum lease payments is equal to 90% or more of the fair value of the leased asset.

Overall, under ASPE, the numerical thresholds tend to be the key decision criteria.

ASPE Requirements—A Closer Look

Aside from how the classification decision is made and the use of some different terminology, the remainder of lease accounting under ASPE and IAS 17 (per Appendix 20B) is very similar.

Transfer of Ownership Test

UNDERLYING CONCEPT

In lease accounting, the importance of good definitions is clear. If under ASPE the lease fits the definition of an asset in that it gives the lessee the economic benefits that flow from the possession or use of the leased property, then an asset should be recognized.

The transfer of ownership criterion is not controversial and is easily applied in practice. The transfer may occur at the end of the lease term with no additional payment or through a bargain purchase option. A **bargain purchase option** is a provision that allows the lessee to purchase the leased asset for a price that is significantly lower than the asset's expected fair value when the lessee can exercise the option. At the beginning of the lease, the difference between the option price and the expected fair value in the future must be large enough to make it reasonably sure that the option will be exercised.

For example, assume that you were to lease a car for $599 per month for 40 months with an option to purchase it for $100 at the end of the 40-month period. If the car's estimated fair value is $3,000 at the end of the 40 months, the $100 option to purchase is clearly a bargain and, therefore, capitalization is required. It is assumed that an option that is a bargain will be acted on. In other situations, it may not be so clear whether the option price in the lease agreement is a bargain.

Economic Life Test

Under ASPE, if the lease period is equal to or greater than 75% of the asset's economic life, it is assumed that most of the risks and rewards of ownership are going to accrue to the lessee.

The **lease term** is **generally considered the fixed, non-cancellable** term of the lease. However, this period can be extended if a bargain renewal option is provided in the lease agreement. A **bargain renewal option** is a provision that allows the lessee to renew the lease for a rental amount that is lower than the expected fair rental at the date when the option becomes exercisable. At the beginning of the lease, the difference between the renewal rental and the expected fair rental must be large enough to provide reasonable assurance that the option to renew will be exercised. With bargain renewal options, as with bargain purchase options, it is sometimes difficult to determine what a bargain is.

Estimating the economic life can also be a problem, especially if the leased item is a specialized asset or has been used for a long period of time. For example, determining the economic life of a nuclear core is extremely difficult because it is affected by much more than normal wear and tear.

Recovery of Investment by Lessor Test

The rationale for the recovery of investment by the lessor criterion is that, if the present value of the payments is reasonably close to the asset's market price, the lessor is recovering its investment in the asset plus earning a return on the investment through the lease. The economic substance, therefore, is that the lessee is purchasing the asset. Applying this test requires an understanding of additional specific terms. For example, to calculate the present value of the minimum lease payments under ASPE, three important factors are involved: (1) the minimum lease payments, (2) any executory costs, and (3) the discount rate.

1. **Minimum lease payments: Minimum lease payments** from a lessee's perspective include the following:

   Minimum rental payments: The payments that the lessee is making or can be required to make to the lessor under the lease agreement, excluding contingent rent and executory costs (defined below).

   Amounts guaranteed: Any amounts guaranteed by the lessee related to the residual value of the leased asset. The **residual value** is the asset's estimated fair value at the end of the lease term. The lessor often transfers the risk of loss in value to the lessee or to a third party by requiring a guarantee of the estimated residual value, either in whole or in part. The **guaranteed residual value** from the lessee's perspective is the maximum amount the lessor can require the lessee to pay at the end of the lease. The **unguaranteed residual value** is the portion of the residual value that is not guaranteed by the lessee or is guaranteed solely by a party that is related to the lessor. Often, no part of the residual is guaranteed.

Bargain purchase option: As explained above, this is an option that allows the lessee to acquire the leased asset at the end of the lease term for an amount considerably below the asset's value at that time. This may or may not be included in the lease conditions.

2. **Executory costs:** Like most assets, leased property needs to be insured and maintained, and it may require the payment of property tax. These ownership-type expenses are called **executory costs.** If the lessor pays these costs, any portion of each lease payment that represents a recovery of executory costs from the lessee **is excluded** from the rental payments used in calculating the minimum lease payments. If the amount of the payment that represents executory costs cannot be determined from the lease contract, the lessee makes an estimate of the executory costs and excludes that amount. Many lease agreements, however, require the lessee to pay the executory costs directly. In these cases, the rental payments can be used without any adjustment in the minimum lease payments calculations.

**FINANCIAL
ANALYSIS
AND
PLANNING
5.1.2**

3. **Discount rate:** What discount rate should be used by the lessee in determining the present value of the minimum lease payments: the rate implicit in the lease, or the lessee's incremental borrowing rate? The **interest rate implicit in the lease** is the lessor's internal rate of return at the beginning of the lease that makes the present value of the lease payments plus any unguaranteed residual values equal to the fair value of the underlying leased asset.[8] The lessee's **incremental borrowing rate** is the interest rate that, at the beginning of the lease, the lessee would incur to borrow the funds needed to purchase an asset of similar value, assuming a similar term and using similar security for the borrowing.[9]

ASPE specifies that the lower of the two rates is used. In contrast, IFRS requires the interest rate implicit in the lease to be used whenever it is reasonably determinable; otherwise the incremental borrowing rate is used for its present value calculations.

There are two alternative reasons for using these rates. First, it can be argued under IFRS that the lessor's implicit rate is generally a more realistic rate to use in determining the amount, if any, to report as the asset and related liability for the lessee. Second, the ASPE requirement helps to ensure that the lessee does not use an artificially high incremental borrowing rate **that would cause the present value of the minimum lease payments to be less than 90% of the property's fair value. This is more important under ASPE because it might make it possible to avoid capitalization of the asset and related liability!** Remember that the higher the discount rate that is used, the lower the discounted value. The lessee may argue that it cannot determine the implicit rate of the lessor and therefore the higher rate should be used. However, in many cases, the implicit rate that is used by the lessor is disclosed or can be estimated. Determining whether or not a reasonable estimate can be made requires judgement, particularly when using the incremental borrowing rate comes close to meeting the 90% test under ASPE. **Because the leased property cannot be capitalized at more than its fair value**, the lessee is prevented from using an excessively low discount rate.

Determination of Rental Payments

Objective 4

Calculate the lease payment that is required for a lessor to earn a specific return.

The lessor determines the rental amount to charge based on the rate of return—the implicit rate—that the lessor needs to receive in order to justify leasing the asset.[10] The key variables considered in deciding on the rate of return are the lessee's credit standing, the length of the lease, and the status of the residual value (guaranteed or unguaranteed).

**FINANCIAL
ANALYSIS AND
PLANNING**
5.1.1

Assume Lessor Corporation wants to earn a 10% return on its investment of $100,000 in an asset that is to be leased to Lessee Corporation for five years with the annual rental due in advance each year. Illustration 20-5 shows how Lessor determines the amount of the rental payment, assuming there is no purchase option that is reasonably certain to be exercised by the lessee (under IFRS 16) or bargain purchase option (under ASPE) or residual value at the end of the lease.[11]

Illustration 20-5

*Calculation of Lease Payments
by Lessor*

Investment to be recovered[a]	$100,000.00
Less: Present value of the amount to be recovered through a purchase option or residual value at end of the lease term	–0–
Equals the present value of amount to be recovered through lease payments	$100,000.00
Five beginning-of-the-year lease payments to yield a 10% return: ($100,000 ÷ 4.16986[b])	$ 23,981.62

[a]If the lessor is not a manufacturer or dealer, then any initial direct costs of negotiating and arranging the lease are added to this amount.
[b]PV of an annuity due (Table A-5); $i = 10\%$, $n = 5$

If there is a purchase option that is reasonably certain of being exercised or a residual value, guaranteed or not, the lessor does not have to recover as much through the rental payments. In such cases, the present value of these other recoveries is deducted before determining the present value of the amount to be recovered through lease payments. This is illustrated in more detail later in the chapter.

**WHAT
DO THE
NUMBERS
MEAN?**

Lease this year's model for just $199 per month! Or 0% financing! Sometimes leasing just looks too good to be true...and sometimes it is. It pays to be familiar with what is involved in a typical leasing agreement such as you might encounter in a vehicle lease, and to do your homework before signing on the dotted line.

First, there is often an upfront payment required to cover freight costs and pre-delivery expenses, plus taxes on these. Add to this a requirement for an initial down payment plus the first month's rent in advance. Increasing this payment, of course, will lower your monthly rental. Do you have to pay a security deposit similar to one you would pay on an apartment you rent? Some leasing companies also charge an administration fee for acquiring the vehicle and processing the paperwork for you.

Check out all the conditions. How reasonable is the annual mileage allowance? How much do you

have to pay per kilometre if you exceed the "free" amount? What happens at the end of the lease term? Do you have to ensure that the vehicle has a reasonable residual value at the end? What price will you have to pay to purchase the leased asset if that is an option?

Finally, what alternatives are there for acquiring the same asset? What are the cash flows associated with the financing of a direct purchase? Or borrowing the money elsewhere and paying cash for the car? The 0% financing might be at the expense of a sales price that is higher than you could otherwise negotiate. A $2,000 or more rebate today for a cash deal may make a difference to your decision. The bottom line: get familiar with the agreements, look at your options, evaluate the cash flows, and make your decision with full knowledge and understanding of what is involved.

IFRS

We now turn to how the **lessee** accounts for right-of-use assets under the contract-based approach of IFRS 16.

Accounting for a Right-of-Use Asset

Objective **5**

Account for right-of-use assets by lessees under IFRS 16 or a capital lease under ASPE.

The accounting model under IFRS 16 is contract-based similar to the approach first introduced to you for revenue recognition in Chapter 6. In essence, the lessee recognizes a "right-of-use asset" representing its right to use the leased item over the lease term, along with a lease liability that captures its obligation to make lease payments. While this looks similar to the capital/finance lease situation set out earlier in the chapter, it is a very different concept. Under the classification approach, the lessee recognizes a lease as the leased property itself when there is a transfer of the risks and benefits of ownership and when this is an in-substance instalment purchase of the asset. The contract-based approach sees the asset taken on by the lessee as the contractual right to use the asset, not the transfer of the asset itself. In addition, this approach is much broader, capturing most arrangements that are now considered operating leases.

Initial Measurement

Under the contract-based approach, the assets and liabilities arise and are recognized at the start of the lease contract. At this point, the right-of-use asset is equal to the liability to make lease payments plus adjustments for lease payments made on or before the start date, initial costs, and restoration costs as detailed below.

The Liability to Make Lease Payments

The liability recognized by the lessee is measured at the present value of the lease payments. While this sounds straightforward at first, a number of decisions need to be made before the resulting amounts are determined and then discounted.

1. Do contingent rentals—additional rents that become payable based on the level of a price index or other variable—have to be considered?

2. How are any guarantees of residual values factored into the calculations?

3. Lease contracts often contain renewal or purchase options, sometimes at bargain prices and other times at market rates, or options to end the lease early. Are these considered?

4. What discount rate is used?

The new requirements in IFRS 16 take the position that the contractual obligation to pay rent **includes variable payments for the lease (such as those under a consumer price index) and other contingent payments** over the term of the lease such as **amounts expected to be payable by the lessee under residual value guarantees**. Therefore, such amounts are estimated in advance, are measured using expected values, and are included in the lease payments as part of the initial lease liability recognized. Note, however, that it is **only the cash flows that are expected to be made in the future** related to these items that are included, **not the full amount of the residual value**, for example, unless that is expected to be the amount of the residual value deficiency. Payments for the exercise of purchase options are included only if it is reasonably certain that the lessee will exercise the option.

An associated issue is one of determining the **term of the lease**. This decision, in turn, affects the number of periods over which the lease payments and contingent rentals are payable, as well as the amount of any residual value deficiency or purchase option amount expected to be received. Taking all relevant factors into account, the **lease term is generally considered the non-cancellable** period of the lease. However, this period is extended if the lessee is reasonably certain to exercise an option to extend the lease, because of its terms and conditions compared with the market rates for similar leases. Examples include the amount of payments during the renewal period, purchase options exercisable after the initial option period, and termination penalties (see IFRS 16, paragraphs B37-41).

The third variable in measuring the lease payments is the discount rate itself. As discussed above, IFRS 16 requires use of the rate implicit in the lease if it can be readily determined; otherwise, the lessee's incremental borrowing rate should be used.

The Right-of-Use Asset

The asset recognized under the contract-based approach is measured initially at cost, based on the present value of the lease payments as described above for the lease contract. Consistent with a cost model, any of the lessee's initial direct costs of negotiating and arranging the lease are also capitalized, as are the costs of dismantling and removing the underlying asset and restoring the site.[12]

Measurement after Recognition

The Lease Liability

The lease liability is accounted for at amortized cost using the effective interest method. As lease payments are made, the lease liability is reduced, with each payment separated into interest and principal reduction amounts. Interest is calculated using the original discount rate established when the lease liability was first recognized, applied to the outstanding principal balance.

The estimates used to determine the lease term and contingent rental amounts (such as the amount expected to be payable under a residual value guarantee) are reassessed at every reporting date.[13]

The Right-of-Use Asset

Accounting for the right-of-use asset after initial recognition and measurement is consistent with its nature; it is similar to the accounting requirements for an intangible asset. Most will continue to be accounted for at amortized cost, taking into account any changes in amount resulting from remeasurements if the company chooses to revalue that class of property, plant, and equipment in accordance with IFRS 16.

The asset's cost should be amortized to expense on a systematic basis over the term of the lease or over the useful life if the cost of the right-of-use asset is based on an assumption that the lessee would exercise a purchase option. The amortization should use a method that best represents the pattern of benefits received from the asset used. The proposals do specify, however, that "depreciation" expense, not "rent" expense, is recognized on the income statement.

Also consistent with other standards, if the right-of-use assets are revalued, gains and losses on revaluation would be recognized in accordance with IAS 38 *Intangible Assets*. The right-of-use asset would also be considered for impairment under the requirements of IAS 36 *Impairment of Assets*.

Illustration of IFRS 16 *Leases*—Lessee Accounting

We now walk through an example of how a lease is accounted for under the contract-based approach of IFRS 16. Assume that EE Corporation, a lessee, enters into a non-cancellable lease contract with OR Limited, a lessor, on September 1, 2018. Assume that the signing and delivery of the lease happened on the same day. The terms and conditions of the lease are set out in Illustration 20-6.

Illustration 20-6

Terms, Conditions, and Other Information Related to the Lease Contract

Leased asset	Manufacturing equipment
Economic life of equipment	7 years
Lease term	September 1, 2018 to August 31, 2022
Lease payment per year, payable in advance	$5,000
Contingent rental payments	Not required
Renewal option	Renewable for additional two years at the option of lessee at $4,500 per year
Expected value of asset (not guaranteed)	
—August 31, 2022	$6,000
—August 31, 2024	$1,000
Title to leased equipment	Retained by lessor
Rate implicit in the lease	9%
Lessee's incremental borrowing rate	9%
Fair value of leased asset, September 1, 2018	$24,000
Lessor's initial direct costs	$365
Lessee's expectations:	
—Most likely lease term (option will be taken to renew lease for additional two years)	Lease will expire on August 31, 2024; lease term is six years.
Lessor's expectations:	
—Most likely lease term	Lessee will renew the lease for two years on August 31, 2022; a six-year lease term
—Probability-weighted expected value of residual at end of lease term	$1,000

Because EE Corporation now has the right to use the manufacturing equipment owned by OR Limited (an asset) and an obligation to make lease payments (a liability), the right-of-use asset and lease liability at acquisition are measured and recognized. The lease liability represents the lease payments not paid at the commencement date, including contingent rentals and possible payments under guarantees, all discounted using the lessee's incremental borrowing rate based on the probability of occurrence of each lease term. Illustration 20-7 shows that the initial measure of the right-of-use asset, assuming a probable lease term of six years, is $23,769.

Illustration 20-7

Initial Measurement of Right-of-Use Asset

Contractual Rights under Lease, September 1, 2018		
Present value of amounts payable under the lease contract, *i* = 9%:		
$5,000 annuity due × 3.53130 (*n* = 4) [Table A-5]	=	$17,656*
$4,500 sum × 0.70843 (*n* = 4) [Table A-2]	=	3,188
$4,500 sum × 0.64993 (*n* = 5) [Table A-2]		2,925
		$23,769
*Alternatively $5,000 payment at start date + PV annuity, 9%, 3 years, $5,000.		

The initial entries to recognize the contract and the first payment on September 1, 2018 are:

A = L + SE
+18,769   +18,769

Cash flows: No effect

Right-of-Use Asset	23,769	
Lease Liability		18,769
Cash		5,000

At December 31, 2018, EE Corporation's year end, the company recognizes the amortization of lease rights that have been used up and interest expense on the obligation since September 1, 2018:

A = L + SE
−1,320   −1,320

Cash flows: No effect

Depreciation Expense	1,320	
Accumulated Depreciation—Right-of-Use Asset		1,320
($23,769 ÷ 6 years) × 4/12		

A = L + SE
   +563   −563

Cash flows: No effect

Interest Expense	563	
Interest Payable		563
($23,769 − $5,000) × .09 × 4/12		

Comparison of Accounting for Leases under IFRS 16 and ASPE

Asset and Liability Recognition

In a right-of-use asset (IFRS) or capital lease (ASPE) transaction, the lessee uses the lease as a source of financing. The lessor provides the leased asset to the lessee and finances the transaction by accepting instalment payments. The lessee accounts for the transaction as if an asset is purchased and a long-term obligation is entered into. Over the life of the lease, the rental payments made by the lessee are a repayment of principal and interest on the outstanding balance.

Under IFRS 16, the lessee recognizes the right-of-use asset at the initial amount of the lease liability, plus lease payments made on or before the start date of the lease, in addition to initial direct costs incurred by the lessee, and removal and restoration costs. The lease liability is initially measured at **the present value of the lease payments** not paid at the commencement date, including:

- fixed payments,
- variable payments that depend on an index,
- amounts expected to be payable by the lessee under residual value guarantees,

- purchase options reasonably certain to be exercised, and
- lease termination penalties if the lease term reflects the lessee exercising an option to terminate the lease.

Under ASPE, the lease asset and liability are recognized at the lower of (1) **the present value of the minimum lease payments** as defined earlier and (2) the fair value of the leased asset at the lease's inception. The reason for this is, like other assets, a leased asset should not be recorded at more than its fair value.

Depreciable Amount, Period, and Method

When the asset is capitalized, its "cost" is allocated over its useful life.[14] You need to understand the terms of the lease and what is included in the capitalized value to determine the depreciable amount and its useful life.

For example, if it is a simple lease that transfers title to the asset at the end of the lease term for no additional payments, then the full capitalized value less any estimated residual value at the end of its useful life to the lessee is depreciated over the full useful life to the entity. If the lease contains a purchase option that is reasonably certain to be exercised, the assumption is that the lessee will acquire legal title to the asset and will continue to use the asset. Once again, the entity allocates the full capitalized cost over the full useful life of the asset. It is a matter of thinking about it in terms of what physically happens to the asset.

Now consider a situation in which the lessee is obligated to make rental payments over the lease term and then return the asset to the lessor in whatever condition it is in at that time. All that is capitalized are the lease payments because this is all the lessee is responsible for paying. In this case, the full capitalized value is amortized over the time to the end of the lease. This changes if the lessee also takes on an obligation to guarantee the residual value of the asset at the end of the lease. Now the capitalized value includes the present value of the amount of the residual value guarantee expected to be payable by the lessee (under IFRS 16) or the guaranteed residual value (under ASPE). Now, what will the entity depreciate? Because the leased asset (at the guaranteed residual value) is expected to be returned to the lessor, the lessee depreciates only the capitalized amount less the guaranteed residual amount over the period to the end of the lease.

Illustration 20-8 summarizes the depreciable amounts and depreciation period, and you are encouraged to understand the reason for each.

Illustration 20-8

Depreciable Amount and Period

	Included in Capitalized Asset Cost	Depreciable Amount	Depreciation Period
Asset reverts to lessor at end of lease term:			
Lessee does not guarantee any residual value	Minimum rental payments (ASPE) or lease payments* (IFRS 16)	Full capitalized amount	Lease term
Lessee guarantees a residual value	Minimum rental payments plus residual value guarantee (ASPE) or lease payments* (IFRS 16)	Full capitalized amount minus any undiscounted guaranteed residual value included as part of cost calculation	Lease term
Lessee retains asset at end of lease term:			
Title is transferred, no purchase option	Minimum rental payments (ASPE) or lease payments (IFRS 16)	Full capitalized amount minus estimated residual value, if any, at end of useful life	Useful life of asset
Title is transferred when purchase option is exercised	Minimum rental payments plus bargain purchase option (ASPE) or lease payments* (IFRS 16)	Full capitalized amount minus estimated residual value, if any, at end of useful life	Useful life of asset

*Lease payments under IFRS 16 are defined as also including amounts expected to be payable by the lessee under residual value guarantees, and purchase options if the lessee is reasonably certain to exercise the option under IFRS 16.

The lessee amortizes the leased asset by applying conventional depreciation methods that it uses for assets it owns.

Effective Interest Method

Over the term of the lease, the **effective interest method** is used to allocate each lease payment between principal and interest. In this way, the periodic interest expense is equal to a constant percentage of the lease liability's outstanding balance. The discount rate used to determine how much of each payment represents interest is the same one the lessee used to calculate the present value of the lease payments.

Right-of-Use (IFRS) and Capital Lease (ASPE) Method—Illustration 1

We use an example of a lease agreement between Lessor Corporation and Lessee Corporation to illustrate the accounting for a right-of-use asset/capital lease. The contract calls for Lessor Corporation to lease equipment to Lessee Corporation beginning January 1, 2017. The lease agreement's provisions and other pertinent data are given in Illustration 20-9.

Illustration 20-9 *Lease Agreement Terms and Conditions*	1. The lease term is five years, the lease agreement is non-cancellable, and it requires equal rental payments of $25,981.62 at the beginning of each year (annuity due basis), beginning January 1, 2017. The lease contains no renewal options, and the equipment reverts to Lessor Corporation at the end of the lease.
	2. The equipment has a fair value of $100,000 on January 1, 2017, an estimated economic life of five years, and no residual value. Lessee Corporation uses straight-line depreciation for similar equipment that it owns.
	3. Lessee Corporation pays all executory costs directly to third parties except for maintenance fees of $2,000 per year, which are included in the annual payments to Lessor Corporation.
	4. Lessee Corporation's incremental borrowing rate is 11% per year. Lessor Corporation set the annual rental to earn a rate of return on its investment of 10% per year; this fact is known to Lessee Corporation.

The lease meets the criteria for classification as a capital lease under ASPE for two reasons:

1. Lessee Corporation uses up all the benefits the leased asset has to offer over the five-year lease term. (The 75% threshold is therefore well met.)

2. The present value of the minimum lease payments is $100,000 (calculated below) and this is the same as the asset's fair value. It therefore exceeds the 90% of fair value threshold set out in ASPE.

Only one of the capitalization criteria has to be met to justify classification as a capital or finance lease. The lease would be set up as a right-of-use asset under IFRS 16 because it would not qualify for a short-term or low-value exemption.

The **lease payments** (or minimum lease payments under ASPE) are $119,908.10 ($23,981.62 × 5), and the present value of the lease payments is $100,000, as calculated in Illustration 20-10.[15] This is the amount that is capitalized as the equipment under lease and recognized as the lease obligation (ASPE). Under IFRS, the full amount would be capitalized as the right-of-use asset, and the corresponding lease liability would exclude the initial lease payment.

Illustration 20-10 *Present Value of Lease Payments*	PV of lease payments	= ($25,981.62 − $2,000) × present value of an annuity due of $1 for 5 periods at 10% (Table A-5)
		= $23,981.62 × 4.16986
		= $100,000

The lessor's implicit interest rate of 10% is used in this case instead of the lessee's incremental borrowing rate of 11% either because (1) Lessee Corp. is a public company and this is the IFRS preferred rate, or (2) Lessee Corp. applies ASPE and this rate is lower than its incremental borrowing rate.[16]

The entry to record the lease on Lessee Corporation's books on January 1, 2017 is:

To record lease asset and liability:

IFRS			ASPE		
Right-of-Use Asset	100,000		Equipment under Lease	100,000	
Lease Liability		76,018	Obligations under Lease		100,000
Cash		23,982			

The journal entry to record the first lease payment on January 1, 2017 (ASPE) and the executory costs is:

	IFRS		ASPE	
Maintenance and Repairs Expense (or Prepaid Expenses)	2,000		2,000	
Obligations under Lease			23,981	
Cash		2,000		25,981

Each lease payment of $25,981.62 consists of three elements: (1) a reduction in the principal of the lease obligation, (2) a financing cost (interest expense), and (3) executory costs (maintenance). The total financing cost of $19,908.10 over the lease's term is the difference between the present value of the minimum lease payments ($100,000) and the actual cash payments excluding the executory costs ($119,908.10). These amounts, along with the annual interest expense, are shown in the (ASPE) lease amortization schedule in Illustration 20-11.[17] (Under IFRS, the lease liability would start at $76,018 on January 1, 2017).

Illustration 20-11

Lease Amortization Schedule for Lessee—Annuity Due Basis

	A	B	C	D	E
1		Lessee Corporation Lease Amortization Schedule (Annuity due basis)				
2	Date	Annual Lease Payment	Interest (10%) on Unpaid Obligation	Reduction of Lease Liability/Obligation	Balance of Lease Liability/Obligation
3		(a)	(b)	(c)	(d)
4	1/1/17				$100,000.00
5	1/1/17	$ 23,981.62	$ –0–	$ 23,981.62	76,018.38
6	1/1/18	23,981.62	7,601.84	16,379.78	59,638.60
7	1/1/19	23,981.62	5,963.86	18,017.76	41,620.84
8	1/1/20	23,981.62	4,162.08	19,819.54	21,801.30
9	1/1/21	23,981.62	2,180.32*	21,801.30	–0–
10		$119,908.10	$19,908.10	$100,000.00	
11					
12	(a) Lease payment as required by lease, excluding executory costs. (b) 10% of the preceding balance of (d) except for 1/1/17; since this is an annuity due, no time has elapsed at the date of the first payment and no interest has accrued. (c) (a) minus (b). (d) Preceding balance minus (c). *Rounded by 19 cents.				

Accrued interest is recorded at Lessee Corporation's fiscal year end, December 31, 2017, as follows:

A = L + SE
+7,601.84 −7,601.84

Cash flows: No effect

To record interest relating to the lease liability/lease obligation:

IFRS			ASPE		
Interest Expense	7,601.84		Interest Expense	7,601.84	
Lease Liability		7,601.84	Interest Payable		7,601.84

Using Lessee Corporation's normal depreciation policy, the following entry is made on December 31, 2017 to record the current year's depreciation of the leased equipment:

A =	L	+ SE
–20,000		–20,000

Cash flows: No effect

Depreciation Expense	20,000	
Accumulated Depreciation—Right-of-Use Asset		
(or Accumulated Depreciation—Leased Equipment under ASPE)		20,000
($100,000 ÷ 5 years)		

At December 31, 2017, the assets recorded under leases are identified separately on the lessee's SFP, or in a note cross-referenced to the SFP. Similarly, the related obligations are identified separately. The principal portion that is due within one year is classified with current liabilities and the remainder is reported with non-current liabilities. For example, the current portion of the December 31, 2017 total obligation of $76,018.38 **is the principal of the obligation that will be paid off within the next 12 months**. Therefore, the current portion is $16,379.78, as indicated on the amortization schedule. Illustration 20-12 shows the liability section of the December 31, 2017 SFP for the lease liability and related accrued interest under IFRS and ASPE.

Illustration 20-12

Reporting Current and Non-Current Lease Liabilities under IFRS and ASPE

	IFRS	ASPE
Current liabilities		
Lease liability	$23,981.62	
Non-current liabilities		
Lease liability	$59,638.60	
Current liabilities:		
Interest payable		$ 7,601.84
Obligations under lease, current portion		16,379.78
Non-current liabilities		
Obligations under lease		$59,638.60

The journal entry to record the lease payment on January 1, 2018 is as follows:

A =	L	+ SE
–25,981.62	–23,981.62	–2,000.00

Cash flows: ↓ 25,981.62 outflow

Maintenance and Repairs Expense (or Prepaid Expenses)	2,000.00	
Lease Liability (or Interest Payable under ASPE)ª	7,601.84	
Lease Liability (or Obligations under Lease under ASPE)	16,379.78	
Cash		25,981.62

ªThis entry assumes that the company does not prepare reversing entries. If reversing entries are used, Interest Expense is debited for this amount.

Entries through to 2021 follow the same pattern as above. Other executory costs (insurance and maintenance) that are assumed by Lessee Corporation are recorded in the same way as the company records operating costs incurred on assets that it owns.

At the end of the lease, the amount capitalized as the right-of-use asset/leased equipment is fully depreciated and the lease liability/obligation is fully discharged. If the equipment is not purchased, the lessee returns it to the lessor and removes the related asset and related accumulated depreciation accounts from the books. If instead the lessee purchases the equipment at the end of the lease for $5,000, and expects to use it for another two years, the following entry is made:

A =	L	+ SE
0	0	0

Cash flows: ↓ 5,000 outflow

Equipment ($100,000 + $5,000)	105,000	
Accumulated Depreciation—Right-of-Use Asset (or		
Accumulated Depreciation—Leased Equipment)	100,000	
Right-of-Use Asset (or Equipment under Lease)		100,000
Accumulated Depreciation—Equipment		100,000
Cash		5,000

Accounting for Residual Values and Purchase Options in a Finance Lease

Right-of-Use (IFRS) and Capital Lease (ASPE) Method—Illustration 2

Objective 6

Determine the effect of, and account for, residual values and purchase options for a lessee's right-of-use asset (IFRS) or a capital lease (ASPE).

The Lessor/Lessee Corporation illustration above demonstrates the lessee's accounting for a basic right-of-use asset/capital lease. Let's now see what the effects are of including residual value requirements in the lease agreement. If title does not pass to the lessee and there is no purchase option, the lessee returns the asset to the lessor at the end of the lease. There is often a significant residual value at the end of the lease term, especially when the leased asset's economic life is longer than the lease.[18]

Guaranteed versus Unguaranteed

The residual value may be unguaranteed or guaranteed by the lessee. If the lessee agrees to pay for any loss in value below a stated amount at the end of the lease, the stated amount is the guaranteed residual value. (While IFRS uses the term "expected to be payable by the lessee under residual value guarantees" in IFRS 16, ASPE uses the term "guaranteed residual value." For this example, we use the two terms interchangeably.)

The guaranteed residual value is used in lease arrangements for good reason: it protects the lessor against any loss in estimated residual value, and so ensures that the lessor will get its desired rate of return on its investment. For right-of-use and capital leases, residual values guaranteed by the lessee affect the amounts that are recognized as the leased asset and lease liability/obligation.

Effect on Lease Payments

A guaranteed residual value—by definition—is more likely to be realized than an unguaranteed residual value. As the risk of non-recovery is reduced, the lessor may reduce the required rate of return, and therefore the rental payments required.

Assume the same data as in the Lessee Corporation/Lessor Corporation example above in Illustration 20-5: Lessor wants to recover its net investment in the leased asset of $100,000 and earn a 10% return.[19] The asset reverts to Lessor at the end of the five-year lease term. Now assume that the asset is expected to have a residual value of $5,000 at the end of the lease. **Whether the residual value is guaranteed or not**, Lessor Corporation generally calculates the lease payments using the approach set out in Illustration 20-5. Illustration 20-13 shows the calculations when the residual value is included.

Illustration 20-13

Lessor's Calculation of Lease Payment

LESSOR'S CALCULATION OF LEASE PAYMENTS (10% ROI) Guaranteed or Unguaranteed Residual Value (Annuity due basis)	
Investment in leased equipment to be recovered	$100,000.00
Less amount to be recovered through residual value, end of year 5:	
Present value of residual value ($5,000 × 0.62092, Table A-2)	3,104.60
Amount to be recovered by lessor through rental payments	$ 96,895.40
Five periodic lease payments ($96,895.40 ÷ 4.16986, Table A-5)	$ 23,237.09

Contrast this lease payment with the lease payment of $23,981.62 that was calculated in Illustration 20-5 when there was no residual value. The payments are lower because a portion of the lessor's net investment of $100,000 is recovered through the residual value. The residual value amount is discounted in the calculation because it will not be received for five years.

Lessee Accounting with a Guaranteed Residual Value

If the residual value is guaranteed by the lessee, there are both economic and accounting consequences. The accounting difference is that the lease payments that are capitalized as the leased asset are defined to include the guaranteed residual value. Unguaranteed residual values are excluded from the lease payments (or the ASPE "minimum lease payments"). If the residual value is not guaranteed by the lessee, the lessee has no responsibility or obligation for the asset's condition at the end of the lease. The unguaranteed residual value, therefore, is not included in the calculation of the lease obligation by the lessee.

A guaranteed residual is similar to an additional lease payment that will be paid in property or cash, or both, at the end of the lease. Using the rental payments as calculated by the lessor in Illustration 20-13, the lessee's lease payments are $121,185.45 ([$23,237.09 × 5] + $5,000). Illustration 20-14 shows the calculation of the present value of the lease payments. This amount is capitalized as the right-of-use asset (or leased asset) and recognized as the lease liability. (Similar to the earlier example, under IFRS the lease liability would exclude the initial payment made at inception of the lease.)

Illustration 20-14	
Calculation of Lessee's Capitalized Amount—Guaranteed Residual Value	

LESSEE'S CAPITALIZED AMOUNT (10% RATE)
(Annuity due basis; guaranteed residual value)

Present value of five annual rental payments of $23,237.09, *i* = 10%: ($23,237.09 × 4.16986, Table A-5)	$ 96,895.40
Add: present value of guaranteed residual value of $5,000 due at end of five-year lease term: ($5,000 × 0.62092, Table A-2)	3,104.60
Lessee's capitalized amount	$100,000.00

Illustration 20-15

Lease Amortization Schedule for Lessee—Guaranteed Residual Value

	A	B	C	D	E
1		**Lessee Corporation** **Lease Amortization Schedule** **(Annuity due basis, guaranteed residual value)**			
2	**Date**	**Lease Payment**	**Interest (10%) on Unpaid Obligation**	**Reduction of Lease Liability/Obligation**	**Balance of Lease Liability/Obligation**
3		(a)	(b)	(c)	(d)
4	1/1/17				$100,000.00
5	1/1/17	$ 23,237.09	$ –0–	$ 23,237.09	76,762.91
6	1/1/18	23,237.09	7,676.29	15,560.80	61,202.11
7	1/1/19	23,237.09	6,120.21	17,116.88	44,085.23
8	1/1/20	23,237.09	4,408.52	18,828.57	25,256.66
9	1/1/21	23,237.09	2,525.67	20,711.42	4,545.24
10	12/31/21	5,000.00*	454.76**	4,545.24	–0–
11		$121,185.45	$21,185.45	$100,000.00	
12					
13	(a) Annual lease payment as required by lease, excluding executory costs. (b) Preceding balance of (d) × 10%, except 1/1/17. (c) (a) minus (b). (d) Preceding balance minus (c). *Represents the guaranteed residual value. **Rounded by 24 cents.				

As Illustration 20-15 shows, Lessee Corporation's schedule of interest expense and amortization of the $100,000 lease obligation results in a $5,000 guaranteed residual value payment at the end of five years, on December 31, 2021.

The journal entries in the first column of Illustration 20-20 are based on a **guaranteed residual value (under ASPE) or amounts expected to be payable under a residual value guarantee (under IFRS 16)**. We use the ASPE terminology (for example, "equipment under lease") rather than both the IFRS and ASPE terminology to streamline the example.

SIGNIFICANT CHANGE

However, the format of these entries is the same as illustrated earlier for ASPE (and would be the same as illustrated earlier for IFRS), but the amounts are different because of the capitalized residual value. As you might expect, the guaranteed residual value is subtracted from the cost of the leased asset in determining the depreciable amount. Assuming the straight-line method is used, the depreciation expense each year is $19,000 ([$100,000 − $5,000] ÷ 5). Note that the undiscounted residual value is used in this calculation, consistent with Chapter 11.

Illustration 20-16 shows how the leased asset and obligation are reported on the December 31, 2021 SFP, just before the lessee transfers the asset back to the lessor.

Illustration 14-16

Account Balances on Lessee's Books at End of Lease— Guaranteed Residual Value

Property, plant, and equipment		Current liabilities	
Equipment under lease	$100,000.00	Interest payable	$ 454.76
Less: Accumulated depreciation—		Obligations under	
leased equipment	95,000.00	lease	4,545.24
	$ 5,000.00		$5,000.00

If the equipment's fair value is less than $5,000 at the end of the lease, Lessee Corporation records a loss. For example, assume that Lessee Corporation depreciated the leased asset down to its residual value of $5,000, but the asset's fair value at December 31, 2021 is only $3,000. In this case, Lessee Corporation records the following entry, assuming cash is paid to make up the residual value deficiency:

A   =   L   +   SE
−7,000   −5,000   −2,000

Cash flows: ↓ 2,000 outflow

Loss on Lease	2,000.00	
Interest Payable	454.76	
Obligations under Lease	4,545.24	
Accumulated Depreciation—Leased Equipment	95,000.00	
Equipment under Lease		100,000.00
Cash		2,000.00

If the fair value is more than $5,000, a gain may or may not be recognized. Gains on guaranteed residual values are shared between the lessor and lessee in whatever ratio the parties initially agreed to.

Lessee Accounting with an Unguaranteed Residual Value

FINANCE

From the lessee's viewpoint, an unguaranteed residual value under ASPE, or amount **not** expected to be payable by the lessee under an IFRS 16 residual value guarantee, has the same effect as no residual value on its calculation of the lease payments, the lease-related asset, and lease liability/obligation. Assume the same facts as those above except that the $5,000 residual value is **unguaranteed**. The annual lease payment is the same ($23,237.09) because, whether the residual is guaranteed or unguaranteed, Lessor Corporation's amount to be recovered through lease rentals is the same: $96,895.40. Lessee Corporation's minimum lease payments are $116,185.45 ($23,237.09 × 5). Illustration 20-17 calculates the capitalized amount for the lessee.

Illustration 20-17

Calculation of Lessee's Capitalized Amount—Unguaranteed Residual Value

LESSEE'S CAPITALIZED AMOUNT (10% RATE) (Annuity due basis, unguaranteed residual value)	
Present value of five annual rental payments of $23,237.09,	
$i = 10\%$, $23,237.09 × 4.16986 (Table A-5)	$96,895.40
Unguaranteed residual value is not included in minimum lease payments	–0–
Lessee's capitalized amount	$96,895.40

With an unguaranteed residual, Lessee Corporation's amortization table for the $96,895.40 obligation under ASPE is provided in Illustration 20-18. Under IFRS 16, the initial lease liability would be $73,658.31 consistent with earlier examples.

Illustration 20-18

Lease Amortization Schedule for Lessee—Unguaranteed Residual Value

	A	B	C	D	E
1			Lessee Corporation Lease Amortization Schedule (10%) (Annuity due basis, unguaranteed residual value)		
2	Date	Lease Payment	Interest (10%) on Unpaid Obligation	Reduction of Lease Liability/Obligation	Balance of Lease Liability/Obligation
3		(a)	(b)	(c)	(d)
4	1/1/17				$96,895.40
5	1/1/17	$ 23,237.09	$ –0–	$23,237.09	73,658.31
6	1/1/18	23,237.09	7,365.83	15,871.26	57,787.05
7	1/1/19	23,237.09	5,778.71	17,458.38	40,328.67
8	1/1/20	23,237.09	4,032.87	19,204.22	21,124.45
9	1/1/21	23,237.09	2,112.64*	21,124.45	–0–
10		$116,185.45	$19,290.05	$96,895.40	
11					
12	(a) Annual lease payment as required by lease, excluding executory costs. (b) Preceding balance of (d) × 10%, except Jan. 1, 2017. (c) (a) minus (b). (d) Preceding balance minus (c). *Rounded by 19 cents.				

With no guarantee of the residual value, the journal entries needed to record the lease agreement and subsequent depreciation, interest, property tax, and payments are provided in the right-hand column of Illustration 20-20. The format of these entries is the same as illustrated for ASPE earlier. Note that the leased asset is recorded at $96,895.40 and is depreciated over five years. Using straight-line depreciation, the depreciation expense each year is $19,379.08 ($96,895.40 ÷ 5). Illustration 20-19 shows how the asset and obligation are reported on the December 31, 2021 SFP, just before the lessee transfers the asset back to the lessor.

Illustration 20-19

Account Balances on Lessee's Books at End of Lease— Unguaranteed Residual Value

Property, plant, and equipment		Current liabilities	
Equipment under lease	$96,895	Obligations under lease	$–0–
Less: Accumulated depreciation— leased equipment	96,895		
	$ –0–		

Whether the asset's fair value at the end of the lease is $3,000 or $6,000, the only entry required is one to remove the asset and its accumulated depreciation from the books. There is no gain or loss to report.

Lessee Entries Involving Residual Values

Lessee Corporation's entries for both a guaranteed and an unguaranteed residual value are shown side by side in Illustration 20-20, using ASPE terminology and ASPE treatment of the first payment.

Guaranteed Residual Value			Unguaranteed Residual Value		
Capitalization of Lease (January 1, 2017):					
Equipment under Lease	100,000.00		Equipment under Lease	96,895.40	
Obligations under Lease		100,000.00	Obligations under Lease		96,895.40
First Payment (January 1, 2017):					
Maintenance and Repairs Expense	2,000.00		Maintenance and Repairs Expense	2,000.00	
Obligations under Lease	23,237.09		Obligations under Lease	23,237.09	
Cash		25,237.09	Cash		25,237.09
Adjusting Entry for Accrued Interest (December 31, 2017):					
Interest Expense	7,676.29		Interest Expense	7,365.83	
Interest Payable		7,676.29	Interest Payable		7,365.83
Entry to Record Depreciation (December 31, 2017):					
Depreciation Expense	19,000.00		Depreciation Expense	19,379.08	
Accumulated Depreciation—			Accumulated Depreciation—		
Leased Equipment		19,000.00	Leased Equipment		19,379.08
([\$100,000 − \$5,000] ÷ 5 years)			(\$96,895.40 ÷ 5 years)		
Second Payment (January 1, 2018):					
Maintenance and Repairs Expense	2,000.00		Maintenance and Repairs Expense	2,000.00	
Obligations under Lease	15,560.80		Obligations under Lease	15,871.26	
Interest Payable	7,676.29		Interest Payable	7,365.83	
Cash		25,237.09	Cash		25,237.09

Illustration 20-20

Comparative Entries for Guaranteed and Unguaranteed Residual Values, Lessee Corporation

Lessee Accounting with a Purchase Option

Based on the examples above, you may be able to deduce how the lessee would account for a lease when the terms include a bargain purchase option under ASPE (or a purchase option that is reasonably certain to be exercised under IFRS). The lessor gets a return on its investment in the leased asset from the option amount it will receive at the end of the lease (similar to the residual value calculations) and from the lease payments. Therefore the option amount is taken into consideration in determining the amount of the lease payments.

The lessee's accounting **assumes that the option will be exercised** and that the title to the leased property will be transferred to the lessee. Therefore, the exercise price of the option is included in the lease payments and its present value is included as part of the lease-related asset and lease liability/obligation.

There is **no difference** between the lessee's calculations and the amortization schedule for the lease obligation for a \$5,000 **purchase option** that is reasonably certain to be exercised and those shown previously for a \$5,000 **guaranteed residual value**. The only accounting difference is the calculation of the **annual depreciation of the asset**. In the case of a guaranteed residual value, the lessee depreciates the asset over the lease term because the asset will be returned to the lessor. In the case of a purchase option reasonably certain of being exercised, the lessee uses the asset's economic life and its estimated remaining value at the end of that time because it is assumed that the lessee will acquire title to the asset by exercising the option, and will then continue to use it.

Accounting for an Operating Lease

Objective 7

Account for operating leases by lessees under ASPE (and short-term leases and low-value leases under IFRS 16) and compare the operating and capitalization methods of accounting for leases.

In a lease agreement where the risks and benefits of ownership of the leased asset are not considered to be transferred to the lessee under ASPE, or where an exemption for a short-term lease or leases for low-value assets under IFRS 16 is chosen, a non-capitalization method is appropriate. Under this type of lease, **neither the leased asset nor the obligation to make lease payments is recognized in the accounts**. It is treated like an executory contract, and the lease payments are treated as rent expense for an operating lease or short-term lease expense (or low-value lease expense) for exempt items under IFRS 16.[20]

Refer back to the Lessor Corporation and Lessee Corporation example in Illustration 20-5 and assume now that the lease described there does not qualify as a capital lease and, by default, is an operating lease under ASPE. Assume also that the equipment is of much lower value (1% of the amounts in Illustration 20-5) and that the lessee elects not to apply the requirements of IFRS 16.22 to 16.49 because the underlying asset is of low value. The charge to the income statement for rent expense (or low-value lease expense under IFRS 16) each year is $239.82, the amount of the rental payment. The journal entry to record the payment each January 1 under both IFRS and ASPE is as follows:

A = L + SE
0
Cash flows: ↓ 239.82 outflow

Prepaid Rent	239.82	
Cash		239.82

Assuming that adjusting entries are prepared only annually, the following entry is made at each December 31 fiscal year end under ASPE (IFRS):

A = L + SE
−239.82   −239.82
Cash flows: No effect

Rent Expense (or Low-value Lease Expense)	239.82	
Prepaid Rent		239.82

Both ASPE and IFRS agree that lease rentals are recognized on a straight-line basis over the term of the lease unless another systematic basis better represents the pattern of the benefits received. Complexities can arise, however, such as when lease inducements are offered. For example, assume that, to motivate a lessee to sign a new five-year lease for office space at $3,000 each month, a lessor agrees to a three-month rent-free period at the beginning of the lease and a two-month rent-free period at the end. How much rent expense should be recognized in each accounting period under ASPE?

The straight-line method is applied to the lease inducement example in the following way:

Lease term: 5 years × 12 months = 60 months
Total rent: 60 − 3 − 2 = 55 months × $3,000 = $165,000
Rent expense to be recognized each month: $165,000 ÷ 60 months = $2,750

That is, the total rent is recognized evenly over the lease term. While the five-year lease would not be exempt as a short-term or low-value lease under IFRS 16, a similar approach would be used for an exempt lease under IFRS 16. So, for example, for an exempt one-year lease at $300 per month, with a two-month rent-free period at the beginning of the lease, the monthly short-term lease expense would be 12 − 2 = 10 months × $300 = $3,000 ÷ 12 months = $250 per month.

Capital and Operating Leases Compared under ASPE

As alluded to above, if the lease in Illustration 20-5 had been accounted for as an operating lease under ASPE and included $2,000 in executory costs, the first-year charge to operations would have been $25,981.62, for the rental payment. As a capital lease, however, the first-year charge is $29,601.84: straight-line depreciation of $20,000, interest expense of $7,601.84, and executory expenses of $2,000. Illustration 20-21 shows that, while the total charges to operations are the same over the lease term whether the lease is accounted for as a capital or operating lease, the charges are higher in the earlier years and lower in the later years under the capital lease treatment. The higher expense in the early years and the recognition of the lease obligation as a liability are two reasons that lessees are reluctant to classify leases as capital leases. Lessees, especially when real estate leases are involved, claim that it is no more costly to operate the leased asset in the early years than in the later years; thus, they prefer an even charge such as the operating method offers.

	A	B	C	D	E	G	H
1			**Lessee Corporation** **Schedule of Charges to Operations** **Capital Lease versus Operating Lease**				
2			**Capital Lease**			**Operating Lease**	
3	Year	Depreciation	Executory Costs	Interest	Total Expense	Expense	Difference
4	2017	$ 20,000	$ 2,000	$ 7,601.84	$ 29,601.84	$ 25,981.62	$3,620.22
5	2018	20,000	2,000	5,963.86	27,963.86	25,981.62	1,982.24
6	2019	20,000	2,000	4,162.08	26,162.08	25,981.62	180.46
7	2020	20,000	2,000	2,180.32	24,180.32	25,981.62	(1,801.30)
8	2021	20,000	2,000	–0–	22,000.00	25,981.62	(3,981.62)
9		$100,000	$10,000	$19,908.10	$129,908.10	$129,908.10	$ –0–
10							

Illustration 20-21

Comparison of Charges to Operations—Capital versus Operating Leases

If an accelerated depreciation method is used, the difference between the amounts that are charged to operations under the two methods is even larger in the earlier and later years.

WHAT DO THE NUMBERS MEAN?

ETHICS

The most important and significant difference between the two approaches, however, is the effect on the balance sheet. The capital lease approach initially reports an asset and related liability of $100,000 on the balance sheet, **whereas no such asset or liability is reported under the operating lease method**. Refer back to Illustration 20-1 to understand the significance of the amounts that are left off the balance sheet for WestJet, Air Canada, and Canadian Pacific Railway. It is not surprising that the business community resisted capitalizing leases for so long, as the resulting **higher debt to equity ratio, reduced total asset turnover, and reduced rate of return on total assets** resulting from capitalizing leases are seen as having a detrimental effect on the companies.

And resist this they have! The intention of ASPE in Canada is to have the accounting for leases based on whether or not the risks and benefits of ownership are transferred. However, because the standard specifies 75% of the asset's useful life and 90% of its fair value, management often interprets these numbers as "rates to beat." That is, leases are specifically engineered to ensure that ownership is not transferred and to have them come in just under the 75% and 90% hurdles so that the capitalization criteria are not met.

The experience with how this standard has been applied remains one of the key reasons why Canadian and international standard setters shy away from identifying specific numerical criteria in standards. They prefer to rely on principles-based, rather than rules-based, guidance.

Whether this resistance is reasonable is a matter of opinion. From a cash flow point of view—and excluding any cash flow effects that are associated with income tax differences—a company is in the same position whether the lease is accounted for as an operating or a finance lease. When arguing against capitalization, managers often state that capitalization can:

- more easily lead to violation of loan covenants;

- affect the amount of compensation that is received (for example, a stock compensation plan tied to earnings); and

- lower rates of return and increase debt to equity relationships, thus making the company less attractive to present and potential investors.[21]

Presentation and Disclosure

Objective 8

Determine the statement of financial position presentation of right-of-use assets (and ASPE capital leases) and identify other disclosures required.

Presentation

The classification of the lessee's lease liability (or lease obligation under ASPE) was presented earlier for an **annuity due** situation. As indicated in Illustration 20-11, the lessee's current portion of the lease obligation is the reduction in its principal balance within 12 months from the date of the SFP **plus** interest accrued to the SFP date. Coincidentally, the total of these two amounts in the example is the same as the rental payment of $23,981.62 that will be made one day later on January 1 of the next year. In this example, the SFP date is December 31 and the due date of the lease payment is January 1, so the total of the principal reduction on January 1 and the interest accrued to December 31 is the same as the rental payment ($23,981.62). **This will happen only when the payment is due the day following the SFP date.** Understandably, this is not a common situation.

FINANCIAL ANALYSIS AND PLANNING
5.1.1

The following questions might now be asked. What happens if the lease payments fall as an **ordinary annuity** rather than an annuity due? What if the lease payment dates do not coincide with the company's fiscal year? To illustrate, assume that the lease in our original example from Illustration 20-5 was signed and effective on September 1, 2017, with the first lease payment to be made on September 1, 2018—an ordinary annuity situation. Assume also that we continue to use the other facts of the Lessee Corporation/Lessor Corporation example, excluding the executory costs. Because the rents are paid at the end of the lease periods instead of at the beginning, the five rents are set at $26,379.73 to earn the lessor an interest rate of 10%.[22] With both companies having December 31 year ends, Illustration 20-22 provides the appropriate lease amortization schedule for this lease, based on the September 1 lease anniversary date each year.

Illustration 20-22

Lease Amortization Schedule— Ordinary Annuity Basis, Mid-Year Lease Date

	A	B	C	D	E
1		**Lessee Corporation** Lease Amortization Schedule (10%) (Ordinary annuity basis)				
2	Date	Annual Lease Payment	Interest (10%)	Reduction of Principal	Balance of Lease Liability/Obligation
3	1/9/17				$100,000.00
4	1/9/18	$ 26,379.73	$10,000.00	$ 16,379.73	83,620.27
5	1/9/19	26,379.73	8,362.03	18,017.70	65,602.57
6	1/9/20	26,379.73	6,560.26	19,819.47	45,783.10
7	1/9/21	26,379.73	4,578.31	21,801.42	23,981.68
8	1/9/22	26,379.73	2,398.05*	23,981.68	–0–
9		$131,898.65	$31,898.65	$100,000.00	
10					
11	*Rounded by 12 cents.				

At December 31, 2017, the lease liability or obligation is still $100,000. How much should be reported in current liabilities on the December 31, 2017 SFP and how much in long-term liabilities? The answer here is the same as earlier: **the current portion is the principal that will be repaid within 12 months from the SFP date** (that is, $16,379.73). **In addition, any interest that has accrued up to the SFP date** (that is, 10% of $100,000 × $4/12 = $3,333) is reported in current liabilities. The long-term portion of the obligation is the principal that will not be repaid within 12 months from the SFP date, or $83,620.27. It helps if you can first correctly describe in words what makes up the current portion, then determine the numbers that correspond.

On December 31, 2018, the long-term portion of the lease is $65,603. The principal due within 12 months from December 31, 2018, or $18,018, is included as a current liability along with interest accrued to December 31, 2018 of $2,787 (10% of $83,620 × $4/12$).

Disclosure

Right-of-Use or Capital Leases

Because a right-of-use or capital lease recognizes the leased asset and a long-term liability, most of the required disclosures are identified in or are similar to those in the standards that cover property, plant, and equipment; intangible assets; impairment; financial instruments; and/or long-term liabilities. IFRS requires additional disclosures related to:

1. The carrying amount of right-of-use assets at the end of the reporting period by class of underlying asset

2. A maturity analysis of lease liabilities, separately from the maturity analyses of other financial liabilities

3. Additional qualitative and quantitative information about leasing activities to help users assess the nature of the company's leasing activities, future cash outflows, restrictions or covenants imposed by leases, and sale and leaseback transactions

4. Depreciation charges for right-of-use assets (by class of underlying asset) and interest expense for lease liabilities.

Operating Leases

Both ASPE and IFRS (under IAS 17) require disclosure of the minimum lease payments for their operating leases extending into the future. Private enterprises report the total at the SFP date and amounts payable in each of the next five years. The IAS 17 requirement is similar, but extends the disclosures to include a description of significant lease arrangements and information about subleases and contingent rents. For those following IFRS 16, companies are required to disclose the expense relating to short-term lease exemptions, the expense relating to low-value lease exemptions, and the amount of lease commitments for short-term leases if the short-term leases committed to are dissimilar from the portfolio to which short-term lease expense relates.

REAL WORLD EMPHASIS

Illustration of Lease Disclosures by a Lessee

The excerpts from the financial statements of Canadian Pacific Railway Limited for the year ended December 31, 2014 in Illustration 20-23 show how this lessee company met the disclosure requirements for its leases under 2014 U.S. GAAP, similar to the ASPE requirements.

> Illustration 20-23
>
> *Capital Lease Disclosures by a Lessee—Canadian Pacific Railway Limited*

15 Properties

(in millions of Canadian dollars)	Average annual depreciation rate	2014 Cost	2014 Accumulated depreciation	2014 Net book value	2013 Cost	2013 Accumulated depreciation	2013 Net book value
Track and roadway	2.5%	$14,515	$4,126	$10,389	$13,459	$3,877	$ 9,582
Buildings	3.1%	571	150	421	535	138	397
Rolling stock	2.3%	3,737	1,414	2,323	3,466	1,338	2,128
Information systems[1]	12.4%	631	297	334	679	338	341
Other	4.5%	1,489	518	971	1,372	493	879
Total net properties		$20,943	$6,505	$14,438	$19,511	$6,184	$13,327

[1]During 2014, CP capitalized costs attributable to the design and development of internal-use software in the amount of $69 million (2013 – $85 million; 2012 – $105 million). Current year depreciation expense related to internal use software was $70 million (2013 – $84 million; 2012 – $78 million).

CAPITAL LEASES INCLUDED IN PROPERTIES

(in millions of Canadian dollars)	2014 Cost	2014 Accumulated depreciation	2014 Net book value	2013 Cost	2013 Accumulated depreciation	2013 Net book value
Buildings	$ 1	$ 1	$ —	$ 1	$ 1	$ —
Rolling stock	311	87	224	511	195	316
Total assets held under capital lease	$312	$88	$224	$512	$196	$316

(continued)

19 Debt (excerpts)

(in millions of Canadian dollars)	Maturity	Currency in which payable	2014	2013
Obligations under capital leases (6.313% – 6.99%) (I)	2012-2026	US$	147	277
Obligations under capital leases (12.77%) (I)	Jan 2031	CDN$	3	3

Annual maturities and principal repayments requirements, excluding those pertaining to capital leases, for each of the five years following 2014 are (in millions): 2015 – $131; 2016 – $816; 2017 – $29; 2018 – $725; 2019 – $439.

I. At December 31, 2014, capital lease obligations included in long-term debt were as follows:

(in millions of Canadian dollars)	Year	Capital leases
Minimum lease payments in:	2015	$ 14
	2016	14
	2017	14
	2018	14
	2019	14
	Thereafter	160
Total minimum lease payments		230
Less: Imputed interest		(80)
Present value of minimum lease payments		150
Less: Current portion		(3)
Long-term portion of capital lease obligations		$147

During 2014 the Company had no additions to property, plant and equipment under capital lease obligations (2013 – $nil; 2012 – $nil).

The carrying value of the assets collateralizing the capital lease obligations was $224 million at December 31, 2014.

29 Commitments and contingencies (excerpts)

As at December 31, 2014, the Company's commitments under operating leases were estimated at $569 million in aggregate, with minimum annual payments in each of the next five years and thereafter as follows:

(in millions of Canadian dollars)	Operating leases
2015	$ 114
2016	88
2017	67
2018	55
2019	43
Thereafter	202
Total minimum lease payments	$ 569

Expenses for operating leases for the year ended December 31, 2014, were $121 million (2013 – $154 million; 2012 – $182 million).

30 Guarantees (excerpts)

In the normal course of operating the railway, the Company enters into contractual arrangements that involve providing certain guarantees, which extend over the term of the contracts. These guarantees include, but are not limited to:

• residual value guarantees on operating lease commitments of $120 million at December 31, 2014

Illustration 20-23

Capital Lease Disclosures by a Lessee—Canadian Pacific Railway Limited (continued)

Illustration 20-24 provides an additional example of disclosure related to lessees, this time under IFRS. The excerpts are taken from the December 31, 2014 financial statements of WestJet Airlines Ltd. WestJet has been part of the Canadian airline industry since 1996, and in 2011 flew almost 20 million "guests" and had $4 billion in revenue. The company adopted IFRS in 2011 and reports in Canadian dollars.

Alternative Terminology

Although IFRS and ASPE use different terminology when discussing accounting for leases by lessors, the underlying journal entries and financial statement presentation are very similar under ASPE and IAS 17 (as set out in Appendix 2B).

1. Statement of significant accounting policies (excerpts)

(n) Leases

The determination of whether an arrangement is, or contains, a lease is made at the inception of the arrangement based on the substance of the arrangement and whether (i) fulfillment of the arrangement is dependent on the use of a specific asset and (ii) whether the arrangement conveys a right to use the asset.

Operating leases do not result in the transfer of substantially all risks and rewards incidental to ownership. Non-contingent lease payments are recognized as an expense in the consolidated statement of earnings on a straight-line basis over the term of the lease. The Corporation has a variety of operating leases including, but not limited to, those for aircraft, land, hangar space and airport operations.

(t) Critical accounting judgments and estimates

Judgments

(iv) Lease classification

Assessing whether a lease is a finance lease or an operating lease is based on management's judgment of the criteria applied in IAS 17 – Leases. The most prevalent leases are those for aircraft. Management has determined that all of our leased aircraft are operating leases, as at December 31, 2014.

18. Commitments (excerpts)

(b) Leases and contractual commitments

The Corporation has entered into leases and other contractual commitments for aircraft, land, buildings, equipment, computer hardware, software licenses and inflight entertainment. At December 31, 2014, the future payments under these commitments are presented in the table below. Where applicable, US dollar commitments are translated at the period end foreign exchange rate.

Within 1 year	287,447
1 – 3 years	431,880
3 – 5 years	233,264
Over 5 years	166,082
	1,118,673

IFRS AND ASPE APPROACH—LESSORS

Classification Criteria

From the **lessor's** standpoint, all leases are classified for accounting purposes as shown in Illustration 20-25.

Type	ASPE Terminology		IFRS Terminology
Operating	Operating lease		Operating lease
Sales-type	Sales-type lease	=	Manufacturer or dealer lease
	or		or
Financing-type	Direct financing lease	=	Finance lease

Lessor accounting under IFRS 16 is consistent with the existing accounting for lessors under IAS 17. (That is, accounting for lessees changed significantly under IFRS 16 as detailed above. However, accounting for lessors is largely unchanged when comparing IFRS 16 and IAS 17.) The lessor considers the same factors (as set out under ASPE or IAS 17, respectively) as the lessee in determining whether the risks and benefits of ownership of the leased property are transferred. If they **are not transferred** to the lessee, the lessor accounts for the lease contract as an operating lease. If the risks and benefits of ownership

are transferred to the lessee, the lessor capitalizes the lease as either a manufacturer or dealer lease (equivalent to an ASPE sales-type lease) or as a finance lease (equivalent to an ASPE direct-financing lease).

Under IFRS, the criteria to assess whether a lease is an operating lease or a finance lease are identical to the criteria used by the lessee, as explained in Appendix 20B. There is one minor exception: under IFRS 16, instead of the term "bargain" purchase option used (per IAS 17), the purchase option is assessed to determine if it is reasonably certain to be exercised. Under ASPE, the same criteria as IAS 17 are used, with the addition of two revenue–recognition based tests that must be passed:

1. Is the credit risk associated with the lease normal when compared with the risk of collection of similar receivables?

2. Can the amounts of any unreimbursable costs that are likely to be incurred by the lessor under the lease be reasonably estimated?

If collectibility of the amounts that are due under the contract is not reasonably assured or if the lessor still has to absorb an uncertain amount of additional costs associated with the agreement, then it is not appropriate to remove the leased asset from the lessor's books and recognize revenue. In short, if any one of the three ASPE criteria used by lessees for classification as a capital lease is met and the answer to both of these additional two questions is also yes, then the arrangement is not an operating lease. Instead, it is either a sales-type or a direct financing lease for the lessor.

How do you distinguish between a manufacturer/dealer or sales-type lease and a financing-type lease? This depends on the specific situation. Some manufacturers enter into lease agreements either directly or through a subsidiary captive leasing company to facilitate the sale of their product. These transactions are usually manufacturer/dealer or sales-type lease arrangements. Other companies are in business to provide financing to the lessee to acquire a variety of assets in order to generate financing income. They usually enter into direct financing (ASPE) or finance leases (IFRS).

The difference between these classifications **is the presence or absence of a manufacturer's or dealer's profit (or loss)**. A **sales-type lease** (a **manufacturer or dealer lease**) includes in the rental amount the recovery of a **manufacturer's or dealer's profit** as well as the asset's cost. The profit (or loss) to this lessor is the difference between the fair value of the leased property at the beginning of the lease, and the lessor's cost or carrying amount (book value). As indicated earlier, manufacturer/dealer or sales-type leases normally arise when manufacturers or dealers use leasing as a way of marketing their products.

Direct financing leases (or finance leases), on the other hand, generally result from arrangements with lessors that are engaged mostly in financing operations, such as lease-finance companies and a variety of financial intermediaries, such as banks or their finance subsidiaries. These lessors acquire the specific assets that lessees have asked them to acquire. Their business model is to earn interest income on the financing arrangement with the lessee.

All leases that are not financing or manufacturer/dealer or sales-type leases are classified and accounted for by the lessor as **operating leases**. Under ASPE, when one of the revenue recognition criteria is not met, it is possible that a lessor will classify a lease as an **operating** lease while the lessee will classify the same lease as a **capital** lease. When this happens, both the lessor and lessee carry the asset on their books and both depreciate the leased asset.

Accounting for Financing and Manufacturer/Dealer or Sales-Type Leases

Objective 10
Account for and report basic financing and manufacturer/dealer or sales-type leases by a lessor.

For all leases that are not operating leases, the lessor recognizes the leased assets on the SFP as a receivable equal to its net investment in the lease. This applies under both IFRS and ASPE.

Accounting for a Financing-Type Lease

Direct or finance leases are, in substance, the financing of an asset by the lessor. The lessor removes the asset from its books and replaces it with a receivable. The accounts and information that are needed to record this type of lease are as follows.

LESSOR TERMINOLOGY		
Term	Account	Explanation
Gross investment in lease	Lease Receivable	The undiscounted rental/lease payments (excluding executory costs) plus any guaranteed or unguaranteed residual value that accrues to the lessor at the end of the lease or any bargain purchase option.[a]
Unearned finance or interest income	Unearned Interest Income (contra account to Lease Receivable)	The difference between the undiscounted Lease Receivable and the fair value of the leased property.
Net investment in lease	Net of the two accounts above	The gross investment (the Lease Receivable account) less the Unearned Interest Income; that is, the gross investment's present value.

[a]This is equal to the lessor's lease payments, as previously defined, plus any unguaranteed residual value. To a lessor, the lease payments are the same as the **lease payments** as defined for the lessee plus any residual amounts guaranteed by parties unrelated to the lessee or lessor. In addition, as noted above, under IFRS 16, instead of using the term "bargain" purchase option used (per IAS 17), the purchase option is included if it is reasonably certain to be exercised.

The net investment is the present value of the items that are included in the gross investment. The difference between these two accounts is the unearned interest. The unearned interest income is amortized and taken into income over the lease term by applying the effective interest method, using the interest rate implicit in the lease. This results in a constant rate of return being produced on the net investment in the lease.

Illustration of a Financing-Type Lease (Annuity Due)

The following lease example uses the same data as the Lessor Corporation/Lessee Corporation example in Illustration 20-5. The relevant information for Lessor Corporation from the illustration follows.

1. The lease has a **five-year term** that begins January 1, 2017, is non-cancellable, and requires equal **rental payments of $25,981.62** at the beginning of each year. Payments include **$2,000 of executory costs** (maintenance fee).

2. The equipment has a **cost and fair value of $100,000** to Lessor Corporation, an estimated **economic life of five years**, and **no residual value**. No initial direct costs are incurred in negotiating and closing the lease contract.

3. The lease contains no renewal options and the **equipment reverts to Lessor Corporation** at the end of the lease.

4. **Collectibility is reasonably assured and no additional costs** (with the exception of the maintenance fees being reimbursed by the lessee) are to be incurred by Lessor Corporation.

5. The interest rate implicit in the lease is 10%. Lessor Corporation set the annual lease payments to ensure a **10% return** on its investment, shown previously in Illustration 20-5.

The lease meets the criteria for classification as a financing-type lease as set out above. It is not a sales-type or manufacturer/dealer lease, because **there is no dealer profit** between the equipment's fair value and the lessor's cost.

Illustration 20-26 calculates the initial gross investment in the lease, which is the amount to be recognized in Lease Receivable.

Illustration 20-26

Calculation of Lease Receivable

Gross investment in the lease and lease receivable	= Total lease payments (excluding executory costs) plus residual value or bargain purchase option if reasonably certain to be exercised[23]
	= [($25,981.62 – $2,000) × 5] + $0
	= $119,908.10

The net investment in the lease is the present value of the gross investment, as determined in Illustration 20-27.

Illustration 20-27

Calculation of Net Investment in the Lease

Net investment in the lease	= Gross investment in the lease discounted at the rate implicit in the lease
	= $23,981.62 × 4.16986 ($n = 5$, $i = 10\%$) (Table A-5)
	+ $0 × 0.62092 ($n = 5$, $i = 10\%$) (Table A-2)
	= $100,000

The acquisition of the asset by the lessor, its transfer to the lessee, the resulting receivable, and the unearned interest income are recorded on January 1, 2017 as follows:

A = L + SE
0   0   0

Cash flows: ↓ 100,000 outflow

Equipment Acquired for Lessee	100,000	
Cash[24]		100,000

A = L + SE
0   0   0

Cash flows: No effect

Lease Receivable	119,908.10	
Equipment Acquired for Lessee		100,000.00
Unearned Interest Income		19,908.10

The Unearned Interest Income account is classified on the SFP as a contra account to the receivable account. Although the lease receivable amount is **recorded** at the gross investment amount, it is generally **reported** on the SFP at the "net investment" amount and entitled "Net investment in finance leases."[25]

As a result of this entry, Lessor Corporation replaces its investment in the asset that it acquired for Lessee Corporation at a cost of $100,000, with a net lease receivable of $100,000. Similar to Lessee's treatment of interest, Lessor Corporation applies the effective interest method and recognizes interest income according to the unrecovered net investment balance, as shown in Illustration 20-28.

Illustration 20-28

Lease Amortization Schedule for Lessor—Annuity Due Basis

	A	B	C	D	E
1			Lessor Corporation Lease Amortization Schedule (Annuity due basis)		
2	Date	Annual Lease Payment	Interest (10%) on Net Investment	Net Investment Recovery	Net Investment
3		(a)	(b)	(c)	(d)
4	1/1/17				$100,000.00
5	1/1/17	$ 23,981.62	$ –0–	$ 23,981.62	76,018.38
6	1/1/18	23,981.62	7,601.84	16,379.78	59,638.60
7	1/1/19	23,981.62	5,963.86	18,017.76	41,620.84
8	1/1/20	23,981.62	4,162.08	19,819.54	21,801.30
9	1/1/21	23,981.62	2,180.32*	21,801.30	–0–
10		$119,908.10	$19,908.10	$100,000.00	
11					
12	(a) Annual rental that provides a 10% return on net investment (exclusive of executory costs). (b) 10% of the preceding balance of (d) except for 1/1/17. (c) (a) minus (b). (d) Preceding balance minus (c). *Rounded by 19 cents.				

On January 1, 2017, the entry to record the receipt of the first year's lease payment is as follows:

A = L + SE
+2,000   +2,000

Cash flows: ↑ 25,982 inflow

Cash	25,982	
Lease Receivable		23,982
Maintenance and Repairs Expense		2,000

On December 31, 2017, the interest income earned during the first year is recognized:

A = L + SE
+7,602   +7,602

Cash flows: No effect

Unearned Interest Income	7,602	
Interest Income		7,602

T accounts for the receivable and its unearned interest contra account, and the effect on the net investment after these entries are made and posted, are shown in Illustration 20-29.

Illustration 20-29

General Ledger Lease Asset Accounts

	Lease Receivable		Unearned Interest Income		Net Investment in Lease
Jan. 1/17	$119,908.10			$19,908.10	$100,000.00
Jan. 1/17		23,981.62			(23,981.62)
	95,926.48			19,908.10	76,018.38
Dec. 31/17			7,601.84		7,601.84
	95,926.48			12,306.26	83,620.22

At December 31, 2017, the net investment in finance leases is reported in Lessor Corporation's SFP among current and non-current assets, as appropriate. The principal portion that is due within 12 months is classified as a current asset and the remainder is reported with non-current assets.

The net investment at December 31, 2017 is $83,620.22, which is the balance at January 1, 2017 of $76,018.38 plus interest earned up to the SFP date of $7,601.84. The **current portion** is determined as follows:

Recovery of net investment within 12 months from Dec. 31, 2017	$16,379.78
Interest accrued to Dec. 31, 2017	7,601.84
Current portion of net investment	$23,981.62

The **long-term portion** is the $59,638.60 remainder. The lease amortization schedule in Illustration 20-28 indicates that this is the net investment that will still have to be recovered after 12 months from the date of the SFP.

Illustration 20-30 shows how the lease assets appear on the December 31, 2017 SFP.

Illustration 20-30

Statement of Financial Position Reporting by Lessor

Current assets	
Net investment in finance leases	$23,982
Non-current assets	
Net investment in finance leases	$59,639

The following entries record the receipt of the second year's lease payment and recognition of the interest earned in 2018:

A = L + SE
+2,000   +2,000

Cash flows: ↑ 25,982 inflow

Jan. 1, 2018	Cash	25,982	
	Lease Receivable		23,982
	Maintenance and Repairs Expense		2,000

A = L + SE	Dec. 31, 2018 Unearned Interest Income	5,964
+5,964 +5,964	Interest Income	5,964
Cash flows: No effect		

Journal entries through to 2021 follow the same pattern except that no entry is recorded in 2021, the last year, for earned interest. Because the receivable is fully collected by January 1, 2021, there is no outstanding investment balance during 2021 for Lessor Corporation to earn interest on. When the lease expires, the gross receivable and the unearned interest have been fully written off. Note that Lessor Corporation records no depreciation. If the equipment is sold to Lessee Corporation for $5,000 when the lease expires, Lessor Corporation recognizes the disposition of the equipment as follows:

A = L + SE	Cash	5,000
+5,000 +5,000	Gain on Sale of Equipment	5,000
Cash flows: ↑ 5,000 inflow		

Accounting for a Manufacturer/Dealer or Sales-Type Lease

Accounting for a lease entered into by a manufacturer or dealer lessor is very similar to the accounting for a financing-type lease. The major difference is that the lessor in the manufacturer/dealer or sales-type lease has usually manufactured or acquired the leased asset in order to sell it and is looking, through the lease agreement, to make a profit on the "sale" of the asset as well as earn interest on the extended payment terms. The lessor expects to recover the asset's selling price through the lease payments. The cost or carrying amount on the lessor's books is usually less than the asset's fair value to the customer. The lessor, therefore, records a sale and the related cost of goods sold in addition to the entries made in the direct financing lease.

In addition to the gross investment in the lease, the net investment in the lease, and the unearned interest income, the following information must be determined:

LESSOR TERMINOLOGY (continued)		
Term	**Account**	**Explanation**
Selling price of the asset	Sales	The present value of the Lease Receivable account reduced by the present value of any unguaranteed residual.[a]
Cost of the leased asset being sold	Cost of Goods Sold	The cost of the asset to the lessor, reduced by the present value of any unguaranteed residual.
[a]This is the present value of the lease payments.		

The same data from the earlier Lessor Corporation/Lessee Corporation example is used to illustrate the accounting for a manufacturer/dealer or sales-type lease. There is one exception: instead of the leased asset having a cost of $100,000 to Lessor Corporation, the assumption is that **Lessor Corporation manufactured the asset and that it is in Lessor's inventory at a cost of $85,000**. Lessor's regular selling price for this asset—its fair value—is $100,000, and Lessor wants to recover this amount through the lease payments.

The lessor's accounting entries to record the lease transactions are the same as the entries illustrated earlier for a financing-type lease, except for the entry at the lease's inception. **Sales and cost of goods sold are recorded in a manufacturer/dealer or sales-type lease.** The entries are as follows:

A = L + SE	**January 1, 2017**	
+100,000 +100,000	Lease Receivable ($23,981.62 × 5)	119,908
Cash flows: No effect	Unearned Interest Income	19,908
	Sales Revenue	100,000

| A = L + SE | | Cost of Goods Sold | 85,000 | |
| -85,000 -85,000 | | Inventory | | 85,000 |

Cash flows: No effect

A = L + SE		Cash	25,982	
+2,000 +2,000		Lease Receivable		23,982
		Maintenance and Repairs Expense		2,000

Cash flows: ↑ 25,982 inflow

A = L + SE		**December 31, 2017**		
+7,602 +7,602		Unearned Interest Income	7,602	
		Interest Income		7,602

Cash flows: No effect

Compare the January 1, 2017 entries above with the entries for the financing-type lease. The manufacturer/dealer or sales-type lease recognizes that what is being recovered is the asset's selling price, so a sale is recorded. The cost of the inventory is transferred to cost of goods sold. With a manufacturer/dealer or sales-type lease, the lessor recognizes **a gross profit from the sale**, which is reported at the lease's inception. The lessor also recognizes interest or **finance income** over the period of the lease until the receivable is no longer outstanding. A lessor with a financing-type lease reports **only finance income**.

Accounting for Residual Values and Purchase Options in a Financing or Manufacturer/Dealer or Sales-Type Lease

Objective 11
Account for and report financing and manufacturer/dealer or sales-type leases, with guaranteed residual values or a purchase option, by a lessor.

Assume the same data as in the Lessee Corporation/Lessor Corporation example above and in Illustration 20-5: Lessor wants to recover its net investment in the leased asset of $100,000 and earn a 10% return.[26] The asset reverts to Lessor at the end of the five-year lease term. Now assume that the asset is expected to have a residual value of $5,000 at the end of the lease. **Whether the residual value is guaranteed or not**, Lessor Corporation calculates the lease payments using the same approach set out in Illustration 20-5. Illustration 20-13 shows the calculations when the residual value is included. As you can see from the Lessee Corporation/Lessor Corporation example, the lease payment was $23,237.09, both with the guarantee and without it.

Note that the accounting result is exactly **the same whether the situation involves a residual value or a purchase option that is reasonably certain to be exercised**. At the end of the lease term, the lessor either recovers an asset expected to have a value of $5,000, or the lessor expects to get a payment of $5,000 from the lessee for the residual value. In either case, the lessor expects to recover an additional $5,000 at the end of the lease term.

Financing-Type Lease

Illustration 20-31 provides the calculations that are the basis for the lessor's accounting for a financing-type lease, whether the residual value of $5,000 is guaranteed or unguaranteed or whether there is a $5,000 purchase option that is reasonably certain to be exercised. The example continues with the Lessee Corporation/Lessor Corporation data.

Illustration 20-31

Calculation of Financing-Type Lease Amounts by Lessor

Gross investment	= ($23,237.09 × 5) + $5,000	= $121,185.45
Net investment:		
PV of lease payments +	= $23,237.09 × 4.16986 (Table A-5) +	
PV of residual value	$5,000 × 0.62092 (Table A-2)	= 100,000.00
Unearned interest income		$ 21,185.45

Illustration 20-32 shows the lessor's amortization schedule, which is the same whether the residual value is guaranteed or unguaranteed.

Illustration 20-32

Lease Amortization Schedule for Lessor—Residual Value or Purchase Option that Is Reasonably Certain to Be Exercised

	A	B	C	D	E
1			**Lessor Corporation** Lease Amortization Schedule (Annuity due basis, residual value or purchase option)		
2	Date	Lease Payment Received	Interest (10%) on Net Investment	Net Investment Recovery	Net Investment
3		(a)	(b)	(c)	(d)
4	1/1/17				$100,000.00
5	1/1/17	$ 23,237.09	$ –0–	$ 23,237.09	76,762.91
6	1/1/18	23,237.09	7,676.29	15,560.80	61,202.11
7	1/1/19	23,237.09	6,120.21	17,116.88	44,085.23
8	1/1/20	23,237.09	4,408.52	18,828.57	25,256.66
9	1/1/21	23,237.09	2,525.67	20,711.42	4,545.24
10	12/31/21	5,000.00*	454.76**	4,545.24	–0–
11		$121,185.45	$21,185.45	$100,000.00	
12					
13	(a) Lease payment as required by lease, excluding executory costs. (b) Preceding balance of (d) × 10%, except January 1, 2017. (c) (a) minus (b). (d) Preceding balance minus (c). *Represents the residual value or purchase option (ASPE) or purchase option reasonably certain to be exercised (IFRS) **Rounded by 24 cents.				

Lessor Corporation's entries during the first year for this lease are shown in Illustration 20-33. Note the similarity between these entries and those of Lessee Corporation in Illustration 20-20.

Illustration 20-33

Entries for Residual Value or Purchase Option, Lessor Corporation

Inception of Lease (January 1, 2017):		
Lease Receivable	121,185	
Equipment Acquired for Lessee		100,000
Unearned Interest Income		21,185
First Payment Received (January 1, 2017):		
Cash	25,237	
Lease Receivable		23,237
Maintenance and Repairs Expense		2,000
Adjusting Entry for Accrued Interest (December 31, 2017):		
Unearned Interest Income	7,676	
Interest Income		7,676

Manufacturer/Dealer or Sales-Type Lease

The gross investment and the original amount of unearned interest income are the same for a manufacturer/dealer or sales-type lease and a financing-type lease, whether the residual value is guaranteed or whether there is a bargain purchase option of the same amount.

When recording **sales revenue** and **cost of goods sold**, however, there is a difference in accounting, **but only in the situation of an unguaranteed residual value**. A guaranteed residual value or bargain purchase option can be considered part of sales revenue because the lessor either knows or is fairly certain that the entire amount will be realized. There is less certainty, however, that any unguaranteed residual will be realized; therefore, **sales and cost of goods sold are recognized only for the portion of the asset that is sure to be realized**. The gross profit amount reported on the asset's sale is the same whether the residual value is guaranteed or not, but the present value of any unguaranteed residual is not included in the calculation **of either the sales amount or the cost of goods sold**.

To illustrate a manufacturer/dealer or sales-type lease (a) with a guaranteed residual value or bargain purchase option and (b) without a guaranteed residual value, assume the same facts as in the preceding examples:

- the estimated residual value or option amount is $5,000 (the present value of which is $3,104.60);

- the annual lease payments are $23,237.09 (the present value of which is $96,895.40); and

- the leased equipment has an $85,000 cost to the manufacturer, Lessor Corporation.

In the case of residual values, assume that the leased asset's actual fair value at the end of the lease is $3,000.

Illustration 20-34 provides the calculations that are needed to account for this sales-type lease.

Illustration 20-34

Calculation of Lease Amounts by Lessor Corporation— Manufacturer/Dealer or Sales-Type Lease

	Manufacturer/Dealer or Sales-Type Lease	
	Guaranteed Residual Value or Bargain Purchase Option	Unguaranteed Residual Value
Gross investment	$121,185.45 ([$23,237.09 × 5] + $5,000)	$121,185.45
Unearned interest income	$21,185.45 ($121,185.45 − [$96,895.40 + $3,104.60])	$21,185.45
Sales	$100,000 ($96,895.40 + $3,104.60)	$96,895.40
Cost of goods sold	$85,000	$81,895.40 ($85,000 − $3,104.60)
Gross profit	$15,000 ($100,000 − $85,000)	$15,000 ($96,895.40 − $81,895.40)

The $15,000 gross profit that is recorded by Lessor Corporation at the point of sale is the same whether there is a $5,000 bargain purchase option or a residual value that is guaranteed or unguaranteed. However, the **sales revenue** and **cost of goods sold** amounts reported are **different**.

Illustration 20-35

Entries for Residual Values, Lessor Corporation— Manufacturer/Dealer or Sales-Type Lease

The 2017 and 2018 entries and the entry to record the asset's return at the end of the lease are provided in Illustration 20-35. The only differences are in the original entry that recognizes the lease and the final entry to record the asset's return to the lessor.

Guaranteed Residual Value/Bargain Purchase Option			Unguaranteed Residual Value		
To record lease at inception on January 1, 2017:					
Cost of Goods Sold	85,000		Cost of Goods Sold	81,895	
Lease Receivable	121,185		Lease Receivable	121,185	
Sales Revenue		100,000	Sales Revenue		96,895
Unearned Interest Income		21,185	Unearned Interest Income		21,185
Inventory		85,000	Inventory		85,000

(continued)

Guaranteed Residual Value/Bargain Purchase Option			Unguaranteed Residual Value		
To record receipt of the first lease payment on January 1, 2017:					
Cash	25,237		Cash	25,237	
Lease Receivable		23,237	Lease Receivable		23,237
Maintenance and Repairs Expense		2,000	Maintenance and Repairs Expense		2,000
To recognize interest income earned during the first year, December 31, 2017:					
Unearned Interest Income	7,676		Unearned Interest Income	7,676	
Interest Income		7,676	Interest Income		7,676
(See lease amortization schedule, Illustration 20-32)					
To record receipt of the second lease payment on January 1, 2018:					
Cash	25,237		Cash	25,237	
Lease Receivable		23,237	Lease Receivable		23,237
Maintenance and Repairs Expense		2,000	Maintenance and Repairs Expense		2,000
To recognize interest income earned during the second year, December 31, 2018:					
Unearned Interest Income	6,120		Unearned Interest Income	6,120	
Interest Income		6,120	Interest Income		6,120
To record receipt of residual value at end of lease, December 31, 2021:					
Inventory	3,000		Inventory	3,000	
Cash	2,000		Loss on Lease	2,000	
Lease Receivable		5,000	Lease Receivable		5,000

Illustration 20-35

Entries for Residual Values, Lessor Corporation— Manufacturer/Dealer or Sales- Type Lease (continued)

If the situation included a $5,000 purchase option that was exercised at the end of the lease, all the entries would be the same as those in the "Guaranteed Residual Value" column with one exception. The entry for the exercise of the option on December 31, 2021 is:

A = L + SE
0   0   0

Cash flows: ↑ 5,000 inflow

Cash	5,000	
Lease Receivable		5,000

The estimated unguaranteed residual value in all leases needs to be reviewed periodically by the lessor and the usual impairment standards apply to the lease-related accounts. If the estimate of the unguaranteed residual value declines, the accounting for the transaction must be revised using the changed estimate. The decline represents a reduction in the lessor's net investment and is recognized as a loss in the period when the residual estimate is reduced. Upward adjustments in estimated residual value are not recognized.

Disclosure

The ASPE disclosure requirements are limited to the entity's net investment in direct financing and manufacturer/dealer or sales-type leases and the interest rate implicit in them, as well as the carrying amount of any impaired leases including the amount of the related impairment allowance.

The requirements of IAS 17 *Leases* are more extensive. Lessors must provide a reconciliation between the gross investment in the lease and the present value of the minimum lease payments, plus the amounts of both of these due within the next year, between years two and five, and beyond five years. Additional requirements include disclosing the amount of unearned finance income, unguaranteed residual values, contingent rental income in the year, the allowance for doubtful receivables, and general information about the lessor's leasing arrangements. Disclosure requirements under IFRS 16 are similar to those under IAS 17 and are set out in IFRS 16.93-.94.

Initial Direct Costs

Initial direct costs are generally defined as costs incurred by a lessor that are directly associated with negotiating and arranging a specific lease. Examples of such costs are commissions, legal fees, and costs of preparing and processing lease documents.

Because initial direct costs are treated somewhat differently between IFRS and ASPE in ways that do not result in material differences in the amount of income or assets reported, we do not provide details of the accounting for each classification of lease in this chapter. The important issue is that they are accounted for similarly to other costs in that their effect is matched with the revenue of the accounting period benefiting from the lease.

In a **financing-type lease**, the initial direct costs are recognized in such a way that they are spread over the term of the lease. For a **manufacturer/dealer or sales-type lease**, the costs are recognized as an expense in the year they are incurred; that is, they are expensed in the same period that the gross profit on the sale is recognized.

Accounting for an Operating Lease

Objective 12
Account for and report operating leases by a lessor.

With an operating lease, the lessor records each rental receipt as rental income. The leased asset remains on the lessor's books and is depreciated in the normal manner, with the depreciation expense of the period matched against the rental income. An equal (straight-line) amount of rental income is recognized in each accounting period regardless of the lease provisions, unless another systematic and rational basis better represents the pattern in which the leased asset provides benefits. In addition to the depreciation charge, maintenance and other operating costs that are incurred during the period are also charged to expense.

To illustrate operating lease accounting, assume that the Lessor Corporation/Lessee Corporation lease agreement used throughout the chapter does not meet the capitalization criteria for the lessor and is therefore classified as an operating lease. The entry to record the cash rental receipt, assuming the $2,000 is to cover the lessor's maintenance expense, is as follows:

A   =   L   +   SE
+25,982   +25,982

Cash flows: ↑ 25,982 inflow

Cash	25,982	
Rent Revenue		25,982

Lessor Corporation records depreciation as follows, assuming the straight-line method, a cost basis of $100,000, and a five-year life with no residual value:

A   =   L   +   SE
−20,000   −20,000

Cash flows: No effect

Depreciation Expense	20,000	
Accumulated Depreciation—Rental Equipment		20,000

If property taxes, insurance, maintenance, and other operating costs during the year are the lessor's obligation, they are recorded as expenses that are chargeable against the gross rental revenues reported.

Disclosure

Under ASPE, disclosures by the lessor are limited to the cost and related accumulated depreciation of property that is held for leasing purposes, along with the carrying amount of any impaired lease receivables and related allowance provided for impairment.

The IFRS disclosures under IAS 17 for operating leases are similar to those for finance leases. Lessors report the future minimum lease payments in total as well as the amounts due within one year, between years two and five, and beyond five years. The contingent rental income for the period and general information about the entity's leasing arrangements are also reported. For operating leases as well as for those that are not classified as operating in nature, additional requirements are imposed by other standards. These include the standards on property, plant, and equipment; financial instruments; investment property; and impairment; among others. Disclosure requirements under IFRS 16 are similar to those under IAS 17 and are set out in IFRS 16.95-.97.

Initial Direct Costs

Recall that initial direct costs are generally defined as costs incurred by a lessor that are directly associated with negotiating and arranging a specific lease.

For **operating leases**, the lessor defers the initial direct costs and allocates them over the lease term in proportion to the amount of rental income that is recognized.

IFRS/ASPE COMPARISON

A Comparison of IFRS and ASPE

Objective 13

Identify differences in accounting between IFRS and ASPE, and what changes are expected in the near future.

Illustration 20-36 sets out material differences between existing IFRS and ASPE for lessees and lessors. In general, except for some terminology differences, the classification approach used by ASPE and IAS 17 is applied in much the same way under both sets of standards after the initial classification of the lease has been made. Illustration 20-36 also sets out the major differences between this approach and the IFRS 16 contract-based method.

Looking Ahead

Illustration 20-36

IFRS and ASPE Comparison Chart

The FASB and IASB worked together to develop a new leasing standard. After receiving feedback on earlier exposure drafts, the IASB introduced IFRS 16 in January 2016, with an effective date of January 1, 2019. The new IFRS 16 standard is summarized in the middle column of Illustration 20-36.

	IFRS—IAS 17	IFRS 16—New contract-based approach	Accounting Standards for Private Enterprises (ASPE)— *CPA Canada Handbook,* Part II, Section 3065	References to related illustrations and select brief exercises
Scope and definitions	Applies to a broader group of assets, including intangible assets.	Applies to all leases, with a few exceptions set out in IFRS 16.3.	Applies primarily to property, plant, and equipment assets.	
	Leases are either a finance or an operating lease to a lessee.	No classification is needed for the lessee; allows exemptions for short-term leases and leases of low-value assets.	Leases are either a capital or an operating lease to a lessee.	N/A
	Leases are either an operating or a finance lease to a lessor.	Leases are either an operating or a finance lease to a lessor.	Leases are either operating or a sales-type or direct financing lease to a lessor.	
Recognition —By lessee	Leases where the risks and benefits of ownership are transferred to the lessee are finance leases to the lessee. The degree to which the asset is specialized and of use only to the lessee without major expense to the lessor is an additional criterion. No numerical thresholds are given.	Lessee recognizes its contractual right to use the leased asset as a right-of-use asset, and its obligation to make rental payments as a lease liability. Exemptions exist for short-term leases and leases of low-value assets.	Leases where the risks and benefits of ownership are transferred to the lessee are capital leases to the lessee. The classification criteria include numerical thresholds that are often used.	BE20-2 and BE20-23

(continued)

	IFRS—IAS 17	IFRS 16—New contract-based approach	Accounting Standards for Private Enterprises (ASPE)—*CPA Canada Handbook,* Part II, Section 3065	References to related illustrations and select brief exercises
	A property interest under an operating lease may be recognized as an investment property and accounted for under the fair value model.	If a lessee applies the fair value model under IAS 40 *Investment Property* to its investment property (IP), it also applies the fair value model to right-of-use assets that meet the definition of IP. If right-of-use assets relate to a class of property, plant, and equipment (PP&E) where the lessee uses the IFRS 16 revaluation model, it may elect to apply that model to its right-of-use assets in that PP&E class.	ASPE does not recognize investment property outside the regular classification requirements.	N/A
—By lessor	A lessor considers the same criteria as the lessee to determine whether the lease is a finance lease or an operating lease. A finance lease could be one entered into by a manufacturer or dealer, or not. The result is similar to ASPE.	A lessor considers the same criteria as the lessee uses under IAS 17 to determine whether the lease is a finance lease or an operating lease. A finance lease could be one entered into by a manufacturer or dealer, or not. The result is similar to IAS 17 and ASPE.	Classification criteria include numerical thresholds; plus two revenue recognition criteria must be met to qualify as a sales-type or a direct financing lease rather than an operating lease.	Illustration 20-25
Measurement	For finance leases, the lessee uses the interest rate implicit in the lease whenever it can be reasonably determined; otherwise the incremental borrowing rate is used.	For right-of-use assets, the lessee uses the interest rate implicit in the lease whenever it can be reasonably determined; otherwise the incremental borrowing rate is used.	For capital leases, the lessee uses the lower of the lessee's incremental borrowing rate and the rate implicit in the lease to determine the capitalized amount of the leased asset.	BE20-1
Disclosure —Lessee	Most finance lease disclosures are similar to the disclosures covering the asset and liability in other IFRS. Additional disclosures are required about material lease arrangements.	Similar to IAS 17. Must show depreciation and interest separately on income statement.	Most capital lease disclosures are similar to the disclosures required for PP&E assets and long-term liabilities in general.	Illustrations 20-23 and 20-24
—Lessor	For operating leases, the lessor reports information about the future minimum lease payments due within one year, years two to five, and after five years, as well as about the entity's leasing arrangements in general.	Similar to IAS 17.	For operating leases, the lessor discloses only the cost and net carrying amount of assets held for leasing purposes and impairment information.	N/A

Illustration 20-36

IFRS and ASPE Comparison Chart (continued)

(continued)

	For finance leases, a reconciliation is required between gross investment and net investment; the amounts of both due within one year, years two to five, and after five years; and supplementary information about unguaranteed residual values, unearned finance income, contingent rentals, impairments, and general lease arrangement information.		There are minimum requirements related to the net investment in direct financing and sales-type leases, the interest rate implicit in the lease, and impairment information.	N/A
Appendix 20A —Sale-leaseback transactions —Recognition	The deferred gain on sale recognized by a lessee on a finance leaseback is recognized over the lease term.	The transaction is accounted for as a sale and leaseback only if the underlying asset has been "sold" based on the requirements of IFRS 15 *Revenue from Contracts with Customers.*	The deferred gain on sale recognized by a lessee on a capital leaseback is amortized on the same basis as the depreciation of the leased asset.	BE20-18
	The gain on an operating leaseback is deferred and amortized only for that portion of the sales price that exceeds the fair value of the asset sold. A loss is recognized immediately, unless subsequent rents are less than market rates. In this case, the loss is deferred and amortized.	Gains and losses are recognized only to the extent that rights are transferred to the buyer-lessor.	The gain on an operating leaseback is deferred and amortized unless the lease is for only a minor portion of the original asset.	N/A
Appendix 20A —Real estate leases —Recognition	A bargain purchase option is not considered in determining whether title will be transferred by the end of the lease. Ordinarily, a lease of land and building is treated as two separate leases, with the lease payments separated based on the relative fair value of the leasehold interests, rather than the fair value of the leased property.	When a lease includes both land and buildings, classification of each as a finance or operating lease is assessed separately. Since land normally has an indefinite economic life, it would typically be considered to be based on an operating lease.	When ownership of the leased asset is not expected to be transferred to the lessee by the end of the lease either directly or through a bargain purchase option and the fair value of the land is significant relative to the building, a lease involving both land and building is treated as two separate leases based on the relative fair value of each.	BE20-20 and BE20-21

Illustration 20-36

IFRS and ASPE Comparison Chart (continued)

Transition to IFRS 16

Companies are not required to apply IFRS 16 prior to annual reporting periods that begin on or after January 1, 2019. To facilitate the transition to IFRS 16, when a company first chooses to adopt the new standard, it will not be required to reassess its existing lease contracts to determine whether these contracts contained leases at the transition date. Instead, the company may apply the requirements of IFRS 16 to contracts that were previously identified as leases under IAS 17, and may choose not to apply IFRS 16 to contracts that were not previously considered to contain a lease. However, whatever choice is made, it must be applied consistently to all of a company's leases. There are also other detailed transition requirements (and "practical expedient" options for companies to choose from) at the date of transition. For example, companies must decide whether to apply IFRS 16 retrospectively to each prior period or retrospectively but with the cumulative effect of the change being recognized at the transition date. See IFRS 16, Appendix C for complete details.

SUMMARY OF LEARNING OBJECTIVES

1 Understand the importance of leases from a business perspective.

Leases represent a significant source of off–balance sheet financing for companies. One of the issues identified by the IASB in IAS 17 is the lack of transparency in financial reporting of leases, leaving users like financial analysts having to guess the extent of debt and leverage of many companies. Accounting for leases is not just an accounting issue, but one of importance to users of financial statements, including financial institutions and leasing companies.

2 Explain the conceptual nature, economic substance, and advantages of lease transactions.

A lease is a contract between two parties that gives the lessee the right to use property that is owned by the lessor. In situations where the lessee obtains the use of the majority of the economic benefits inherent in a leased asset, the transaction is similar in substance to acquiring an asset. Therefore, the lessee recognizes the asset and associated liability and the lessor transfers the asset under lease accounting. The major advantages of leasing for the lessee relate to the cost and flexibility of the financing, and protection against obsolescence. For the lessor, the finance income is attractive.

3 Identify and apply the criteria that are used to determine lessee right-of-use assets under IFRS 16 and leases under the ASPE classification approach.

Under IFRS 16, from the lessee's standpoint, all leases are capitalized and included on the statement of financial position except where the lessee elects not to apply the requirements for short-term leases or for leases where the underlying asset is of low value. Under ASPE (and IAS 17, as discussed in Appendix 20B), a lease is classified as a capital or finance lease where the risks and benefits of owning the leased asset are transferred to the lessee, which is evidenced by one or more of the following: (1) the transfer of title, (2) the use of the majority of the asset services inherent in the leased asset, (3) the recovery by the lessor of substantially all of its investment in the leased asset plus a return on that investment, or (4) under IAS 17, in some cases the degree of specialization of the specific asset. If none of these criteria is met, the lease is classified as an operating lease.

4 Calculate the lease payment that is required for a lessor to earn a specific return.

The lessor determines the investment that it wants to recover from a leased asset. If the lessor has acquired an asset for the purpose of leasing it, the lessor usually wants to recover the asset's cost. If the lessor participates in leases as a way of selling its product, it usually wants to recover the sales price. The lessor's investment in the cost or selling price can be recovered in part through a residual value if the asset will be returned to the lessor, or through a purchase option that it expects the lessee to pay,

if it includes a purchase option as part of the lease agreement. In addition to these sources, the lessor recovers its investment through the lease payments. The periodic lease payment, therefore, is the annuity amount whose present value equals the amount to be recovered through lease payments.

5 Account for right-of-use assets by lessees under IFRS 16 or a capital lease under ASPE.

IFRS 16 typically results in a right-of-use asset being capitalized on the lessee's SFP and a lease liability being recognized for the obligation owing to the lessor. The amount capitalized is (a) the present value of the lease payments included in the lease liability (b) lease payments at the commencement date (c) initial direct costs of the lessee and (d) the costs of dismantling/restoring the underlying asset. The right-of-use asset is then depreciated in the same way as other capital assets owned by the lessee. Payments to the lessor are divided into an interest portion and a principal payment, using the effective interest method.

6 Determine the effect of, and account for, residual values and purchase options for a lessee's right-of-use asset (IFRS) or a capital lease (ASPE).

When a lessee guarantees a residual value, it is obligated to return either the leased asset or cash, or a combination of both, in an amount that is equal to the guaranteed value. The lessee includes the guaranteed residual in the lease obligation and leased asset value. The asset is depreciated to this value by the end of the lease term. If the residual is unguaranteed, the lessee takes no responsibility for the residual and it is excluded from the lessee's calculations.

7 Account for operating leases by lessees under ASPE (and short-term leases and low-value leases under IFRS 16) and compare the operating and capitalization methods of accounting for leases.

A lessee recognizes the lease payments that are made as rent expense in the period that is covered by the lease, usually based on the proportion of time. Over the term of a lease, the total amount that is charged to expense is the same whether the lease has been treated as a capital/finance lease or as an operating lease. The difference relates to (1) the timing of recognition for the expense (more is charged in the early years for a finance lease), (2) the type of expense that is charged (depreciation and interest expense for a finance lease versus rent expense for an operating lease), and (3) the recognition of an asset and liability on the SFP for a finance lease versus non-recognition for an operating lease. Aside from any income tax differences, the cash flows for a lease are the same whether it is classified as an operating or finance lease. Accounting for short-term leases and exempt leases for low-value assets under IFRS 16 is similar to accounting for operating leases under ASPE, except that the rental expenses would be considered short-term lease expense or low-value lease expense, respectively.

8 Determine the statement of financial position presentation of right-of-use assets (and ASPE capital leases) and identify other disclosures required.

The current portion of the obligation is the principal that will be repaid within 12 months from the SFP date. The current portion also includes the amount of interest that has accrued up to the SFP date. The long-term portion of the obligation or net investment is the principal balance that will not be paid within 12 months of the SFP date. Lessees disclose the same information as is required for capital assets and long-term debt in general. In addition, details are required of the future minimum lease payments for each of the next five years, and under IFRS, information about leasing arrangements is required.

9 Identify and apply the criteria that are used to determine the type of lease for a lessor under the classification approach.

If a lease, in substance, transfers the risks and benefits of ownership of the leased asset to the lessee (decided in the same way as for the lessee) and revenue recognition criteria related to collectibility and ability to estimate any remaining unreimbursable costs are met, the lessor accounts for the lease as either a direct financing or a sales-type lease. Under IFRS, it is classified as either a financing or a manufacturer or dealer lease. The existence of a manufacturer's or dealer's profit on the amount to be recovered from the lessee is the difference between a manufacturer/dealer or sales-type lease and a direct financing lease, because the objective is only to generate finance income in the latter. If any one of the capitalization or revenue recognition criteria is not met, the lessor accounts for the lease as an operating lease.

10 Account for and report basic financing and manufacturer/dealer or sales-type leases by a lessor.

In a finance lease, the lessor removes the cost of the leased asset from its books and replaces it with its net investment in the lease. This is made up of two accounts: (1) the gross investment or lease receivable, offset by (2) the portion of these amounts that represents unearned interest. The net investment represents the present value of the lease payments and the residual value or bargain purchase option amounts. As the lease payments are received, the receivable is reduced. As time passes, the unearned interest is taken into income based on the implicit rate of return that applies to the net investment. Under a manufacturer/dealer or sales-type lease, the accounting is similar except that the net investment represents the sale amount the lessor wants to recover. The lessor also transfers the inventory "sold" to cost of goods sold.

11 Account for and report financing and manufacturer/dealer or sales-type leases, with guaranteed residual values or a purchase option, by a lessor.

For each type of finance or capital lease accounted for by lessors, the net investment in the lease includes the estimated residual value whether it is guaranteed or not, or the bargain purchase option amount. Under a manufacturer/dealer or sales-type lease, both the sale and cost of goods sold amounts are reduced by any unguaranteed residual values.

12 Account for and report operating leases by a lessor.

The lessor records the lease payments received from the lessee as rental income in the period covered by the lease payment. Because the leased asset remains on the lessor's books, the lessor records depreciation expense. Separate disclosure is required of the cost and accumulated amortization of property held for leasing purposes, and the amount of rental income earned.

13 Identify differences in accounting between IFRS and ASPE, and what changes are expected in the near future.

Under the classification approach, ASPE is substantially the same as the IAS 17 requirements. Different terminology is used and the classification requirements that differentiate between a capital/finance lease and an operating lease under IFRS are based more on principles and judgement than ASPE. Under IFRS 16 issued by the IASB in January 2016 and effective on January 1, 2019, there is a significant change in the approach to lease accounting for lessees. Under the new standard, a contract-based or right-of-use approach is used by the lessee.

KEY TERMS

APPENDIX 20A

OTHER LEASE ISSUES

Sale and Leaseback Transactions

UNDERLYING CONCEPT

A sale-leaseback may be similar in substance to the repurchase agreements discussed in Chapter 6. If the transfer of the asset meets the requirements of IFRS 15 to be recorded as a sale, a right-of-use asset would be recorded by the "seller-lessee" and the amount of gain recorded would relate to the rights transferred to the buyer-lessor.

Sale-leaseback describes a transaction in which a property owner (the seller-lessee) sells a property to another party (the buyer-lessor) and, at the same time, leases the same asset back from the new owner. The property generally continues to be used without any interruption. This type of transaction is fairly common.[27]

For example, a company buys a building and uses it for several years. It then sells the property to an investor, and then immediately leases it back from the investor. From the seller's viewpoint, the advantage of a sale and leaseback usually has to do with financing. If an equipment purchase has already been financed, and rates have subsequently decreased, a sale-leaseback can allow the seller to refinance the purchase at lower rates. Alternatively, a sale-leaseback can also provide additional working capital when liquidity is tight.

Seller-Lessee Accounting

To the extent that, after the transfer, the seller-lessee continues to use the same asset it has transferred, **the sale-leaseback is really a form of financing**, and therefore it is reasonable that no gain or loss is recognized on the transaction. In substance, the seller-lessee is simply borrowing funds. On the other hand, if the seller-lessee gives up the ownership risks and benefits associated with the asset, the transaction is clearly a sale, and gain or loss recognition is appropriate. IFRS 16 indicates that the lease should be accounted for as a right-of-use asset by the seller-lessee and as a finance-type or operating lease by the buyer-lessor, as appropriate under the lease accounting standards.

When a seller-lessee leases back only a portion of the asset sold, such as one floor of a 10-floor building sold, or a lease term of two years when the remaining useful life is six years, then the right-of-use asset arising from the leaseback transaction would be measured at the proportion of the previous carrying amount of asset retained by the seller-lessee. In such a case, the sale and the lease are accounted for as though they are separate transactions based on the underlying substance of each.

SIGNIFICANT CHANGE

If the transfer of the asset does not meet the criteria to be classified as a sale under IFRS 15, then no sale is recognized by the seller-lessee and no purchase is recognized by the buyer-lessor. The seller-lessee continues to recognize the transferred asset, and accounts for the amounts received as a financial liability (accounting for the financial liability based on the requirements of IFRS 9 *Financial Instruments*). This treatment is consistent with the substance of the transaction, which is a financing arrangement. The lessor would not recognize the transferred asset, but would recognize a financial asset equal to the transfer proceeds.

Sale-Leaseback Illustration—IFRS 16

To illustrate the accounting treatment for a sale-leaseback transaction under IFRS 16, assume that Hawkee Company (seller-lessee) sells a building to Bestor Inc. (buyer-lessor) for $2 million in cash.[28] Immediately before the transaction, the building is carried at a cost of $1.2 million and accumulated depreciation of $200,000 (carrying amount of $1 million). At the same time, the seller-lessee enters into a contract with the buyer-lessor for the right to use the building for 18 years, with annual payments of $120,000 payable at the end of each year. The terms and conditions of the transaction are such that the transfer of the building by Hawkee satisfies the requirements for determining a **performance obligation** [that is, a promise to transfer a good or service (in this case a building) to the customer (Bestor)] in relation to IFRS 15 *Revenue from Contracts with Customers*. So, Hawkee (seller-lessee) and Bestor (buyer-lessor) account for the transaction as a sale and leaseback. We ignore any initial direct costs.

Assume that the fair value of the building at the date of sale is $1.8 million. Because the consideration for the sale of the building is not at fair value, the seller-lessee and buyer-lessor make adjustments to measure the sale proceeds at fair value. The amount of the excess sale price of $200,000 ($2,000,000 − $1,800,000) is recognized as additional financing provided by Bestor to Hawkee (the seller-lessee). Assume that the interest rate implicit in the lease is 4.5% per year, which is readily determinable by Hawkee. The present value of the annual payments (18 payments of $120,000, discounted at 4.5%) amounts to $1,459,200, of which $200,000 relates to the additional financing and $1,259,200 relates to the lease—corresponding to 18 annual payments of $16,447 and $103,553, respectively.

The buyer-lessor classifies the lease of the building as an operating lease.

Accounting by the Seller-Lessee

At the date of the sale-leaseback, Hawkee measures the right-of-use asset arising from the leaseback of the building at the proportion of the previous carrying amount of the building that relates to the right of use retained by seller-lessee, which is $699,555. This is calculated as: $1,000,000 (the carrying amount of the building) ÷ $1,800,000 (the fair value of the building) × $1,259,200 (the discounted lease payments for the 18-year right-of-use asset).

Hawkee (the seller-lessee) recognizes only the amount of the gain that relates to the rights transferred to Bestor (the buyer-lessor) of $240,355, calculated as follows. The gain on sale of building amounts to $800,000 ($1,800,000 − $1,000,000), of which:

1. $559,645 ($800,000 ÷ $1,800,000 × $1,259,200) relates to the right to use the building retained by the seller-lessee and

2. $240,355 ($800,000 ÷ $1,800,000 × [$1,800,000 − $1,259,200]) relates to the rights transferred to the buyer-lessor.

At the commencement date, the seller-lessee accounts for the transaction as follows:

Cash	2,000,000	
Right-of-Use Asset	699,555	
Building		1,000,000
Financial Liability		1,459,200
Gain on Rights Transferred		240,355

Accounting by the Buyer-Lessor

At the commencement date, Bestor (the buyer-lessor) accounts for the transaction as follows.

Building	1,800,000	
Financial Asset	200,000	
Cash		2,000,000
(where $200,000 = 18 payments of $16,447, discounted at 4.5%)		

After the commencement date, the buyer-lessor accounts for the lease by treating $103,553 of the annual payments of $120,000 as lease payments. The remaining $16,447 of annual payments received from Hawkee (the seller-lessee) are accounted for as (1) payments received to settle the financial asset of $200,000 and (2) interest revenue.

Sale-Leaseback Illustration—ASPE (and IAS 17)

Any profit on the sale of the assets that are leased back **is deferred and amortized** over the lease on the same basis as the depreciation of the leased assets (under ASPE). This treatment is similar to how profit on a sale-leaseback would be handled under IAS 17, except that any profit on the sale of the assets that are leased back would be deferred and amortized over the lease term under IAS 17. If the leased asset is land only, the amortization is on a straight-line basis over the lease term.

For example, if Lessee Inc. sells equipment having a book value of $580,000 and a fair value of $623,110 to Lessor Inc. for $623,110 and leases the equipment back for $50,000 a year for 20 years, the profit of $43,110 (that is, $623,110 − $580,000) is deferred and amortized over the 20-year period. The $43,110 is credited originally to a Deferred Profit on Sale-Leaseback account.

If none of the capital lease criteria is met, the seller-lessee accounts for the transaction as a sale, and the lease as an **operating lease**. Under IAS 17, if the terms of the sale/operating lease transaction are clearly at fair value amounts, the profit or loss on disposal is recognized in net income immediately (if not at fair value, and a gain arises for the seller-lessee, the gain would be deferred and amortized over the lease term under IAS 17). Under ASPE, the profit or loss on sale of a property sold and leased back under an operating lease arrangement is deferred and amortized in proportion to the rental payments over the period of time that it is expected the lessee will use the assets.

The standards require, however, that when there is a legitimate loss on the sale of an asset—that is, when the asset's **fair value is less than its carrying amount**—the loss is recognized immediately. For example, if Lessee Inc. sells equipment that has a book value of $650,000 and a fair value of $600,000, the difference of $50,000 is charged directly to a loss account.

Buyer-Lessor Accounting

Under a sale and leaseback transaction, the buyer-lessor applies the regular lease standards. This type of transaction results in either an operating or direct-financing type lease on the part of the lessor.

Sale-Leaseback Illustration

To illustrate the accounting treatment for a sale-leaseback transaction under ASPE and IAS 17, assume that on January 1, 2018, Lessee Inc. sells a used Boeing 767, having a cost of $85.5 million and a carrying amount on Lessee's books of $75.5 million, to Lessor Inc. for $80 million. Lessee Inc. then immediately leases the aircraft back under the following conditions:

1. The term of the non-cancellable lease is 15 years, and the agreement requires equal annual rental payments of $10,487,443, beginning January 1, 2018.

2. The aircraft has a fair value of $80 million on January 1, 2018, and an estimated economic life of 15 years.

3. Lessee Inc. pays all executory costs.

4. Lessee Inc. depreciates similar aircraft that it owns on a straight-line basis over 15 years.

5. The annual payments assure Lessor a 12% return, which is the same as Lessee's incremental borrowing rate.

6. The present value of the minimum lease payments is $80 million, or $10,487,443 × 7.62817 (Table A-5: $i = 12\%, n = 15$).

This is a capital or finance lease to Lessee Inc. because the lease term covers the entire useful life of the asset and because the lessor recovers its investment in the aircraft and earns the required rate of return from the minimum lease payments. Assuming that the appropriate revenue recognition criteria are met, Lessor Inc. classifies this arrangement as a finance-type lease.

Illustration 20A-1 shows the journal entries related to this lease for both Lessee Inc. and Lessor Inc. for the first year.

Lessee Inc.			Lessor Inc.		
Sale of aircraft by Lessee Inc. to Lessor Inc., January 1, 2018, and leaseback transaction:					
Cash	80,000,000		Aircraft Acquired for Lessee	80,000,000	
Accumulated Depreciation	10,000,000		Cash		80,000,000
Aircraft		85,500,000			
Deferred Profit on					
Sale-Leaseback		4,500,000			
Aircraft under Lease	80,000,000		Lease Receivable	157,311,645[a]	
Obligations under Lease		80,000,000	Aircraft Acquired for Lessee		80,000,000
			Unearned Interest Income		77,311,645

[a]($10,487,443 × 15 = $157,311,645)

Lessee Inc.			Lessor Inc.		
First lease payment, January 1, 2018:					
Obligations under Lease	10,487,443		Cash	10,487,443	
Cash		10,487,443	Lease Receivable		10,487,443
Executory costs incurred and paid by Lessee Inc. throughout 2018:					
Operating Expenses	XXX				
Cash or Accounts Payable		XXX			
Depreciation expense for 2018 on the aircraft, December 31, 2018:					
Depreciation Expense	5,333,333		(No entry)		
Accumulated		5,333,333			
Depreciation—Leased Aircraft					
($80,000,000 ÷ 15)					
Amortization of deferred profit on sale-leaseback by Lessee Inc., December 31, 2018:					
Deferred Profit on			(No entry)		
Sale-Leaseback	300,000				
Depreciation Expense[b]		300,000			
($4,500,000 ÷ 15)					

[b]Alternatively, a gain account could be credited.

Lessee Inc.			Lessor Inc.		
Interest for 2018, December 31, 2018:					
Interest Expense	8,341,507		Unearned Interest Income	8,341,507	
Interest Payable		8,341,507[c]	Interest Income		8,341,507[c]

[c]Lease obligation or net investment in the lease of ($80,000,000 − $10,487,443) × 12% × ¹²/₁₂

Illustration 20A-1

Comparative Entries for Sale-Leaseback for Lessee and Lessor

Real Estate Leases

Objective 15
Explain the classification and accounting treatment for leases that involve real estate.

When a capital or finance lease involves land, and ownership of the land will not be transferred to the lessee, capitalizing the land on the lessee's SFP would result in no expense (such as depreciation) being recognized for its use over the term of the lease. Then, at the end of the lease, a loss equal to the capitalized value of the land would be recognized when the land is transferred back to the lessor. This explains why **special guidance is needed for leases that involve land.**

Land

If land is the only leased asset, and title to the property is transferred to the lessee by the end of the lease, the **lessee** accounts for the arrangement as a capital or finance lease, and the **lessor** accounts for it either as a manufacturer/dealer or sales-type lease or as a direct financing lease, whichever is appropriate. If the title is not transferred, it is accounted for as an operating lease.

Land and Building

If land and a building are leased together, IFRS requires that each be considered separately when the lessor is classifying the lease. The minimum lease payments are allocated on the basis of the relative fair values of the leasehold interest in each component.[29] If this can't be determined reliably, the entire lease is classified as a finance lease, unless it is clear that both are operating leases. If the portion determined to be for the land is immaterial, the whole arrangement may be accounted for as a single unit.

Under ASPE, the lessee can capitalize land separately from the building when title is expected to be transferred, either directly or through a bargain purchase option. The minimum lease payments in this case are allocated based on the relative fair values of the land and the building. If title is not expected to be transferred, the accounting depends on the fair value of the land relative to the building. If it is minor, the land and building are treated as a single unit when classifying the lease; if significant, the land and building are considered separately, with the land portion classified as an operating lease.

SUMMARY OF LEARNING OBJECTIVES FOR APPENDIX 20A

14 Describe and apply the lessee's accounting for sale-leaseback transactions.

A sale and leaseback is accounted for by the lessee as if the two transactions were related. If the transfer of the asset does not meet the criteria to be classified as a sale under IFRS 15, then no sale is recognized by the seller-lessee and no purchase is recognized by the buyer-lessor. On the other hand, when a seller-lessee leases back only a portion of the asset sold, then the right-of-use asset arising from the leaseback transaction would be measured at the proportion of the previous carrying amount of asset retained by the seller-lessee. For an operating lease under ASPE, the seller-lessee takes the deferred gain or loss into income in proportion to the rental payments made. For a lease meeting the capital lease criteria under ASPE, any profit

or loss is deferred and amortized on the same basis as the depreciation of the leased asset. Accounting under IAS 17 for a sale leaseback meeting the criteria of a finance lease is similar to a capital lease under ASPE, but with the deferred gain or loss being taken into income over the lease term.

15 Explain the classification and accounting treatment for leases that involve real estate.

Because the capitalization of land by the lessee in a capital or finance lease that does not transfer title results in an unwanted and unintended effect on the lessee's financial statements, the portion of such leases that relates to land is accounted for as an operating lease. If the relative value of the land is minor, however, the minimum lease payments are fully capitalized as a building.

KEY TERMS

performance obligation, p. 1267   sale-leaseback, p. 1266

APPENDIX 20B

LESSEE ACCOUNTING UNDER IAS 17

Objective 16
Explain and apply the classification approach under IAS 17 for a lessee.

In the main part of Chapter 20, we focus on the new rules of IFRS 16 and the continuing requirements of ASPE for accounting for leases. However, the new requirements of IFRS 16 do not come into effect until January 1, 2019. In this appendix, we summarize the rules of IAS 17 that many companies following IFRS would have the option of using until then.

IAS 17 identifies numerous qualitative indicators to help identify whether a lease is a finance (capital) lease or not. As discussed earlier, Section 3065 of Part II of the *CPA Canada Handbook* provides fewer qualitative indicators, and more quantitative indicators that end up being used extensively in making the classification decision. The net effect is that entities applying IFRS make the classification decision based on principles, and those applying ASPE look to whether certain numerical thresholds have been met or missed.

IFRS Criteria

Under IFRS, any one or a combination of the following situations **normally indicates** that the risks and rewards of ownership are transferred to the lessee, and supports classification as a finance lease.

1. There is reasonable assurance that the lessee will obtain ownership of the leased property by the end of the lease term. If there is a bargain purchase option in the lease, it is assumed that the lessee will exercise it and obtain ownership of the asset.

2. The lease term is for the major part of the economic life of the asset, so that the lessee will receive substantially all of the economic benefits that are expected to be derived from using the leased property over its life.

3. The lease allows the lessor to recover substantially all of its investment in the leased property and to earn a return on the investment. Evidence of this is provided if the present value of the minimum lease payments is substantially all of the fair value of the leased asset.

4. The leased assets are so specialized that, without major modification, they are of use only to the lessee.

Other indicators that might suggest a transfer of the risks and benefits of ownership include situations where:

- the lessee absorbs the lessor's losses if the lessee cancels the lease,

- the lessee assumes the risk associated with the amount of the residual value of the asset at the end of the lease, or

- there is a bargain renewal option—when the lessee can renew the lease for an additional term at significantly less than the market rent.

The standard also states that these indicators are not always conclusive. The decision has to be made on the substance of each specific transaction. If the lessee determines that the risks and benefits of ownership have not been transferred to it, the lease is classified as an operating lease.

Accounting for lessees under IAS 17 is quite similar to that shown in the main chapter under ASPE, including preparation of journal entries and financial statement presentation. However, the terminology under IFRS differs slightly because a lease is either a **finance lease** or an operating lease to a lessee (as opposed to a **capital lease** or an operating lease). Leases where the risks and benefits of ownership are transferred to the lessee are finance leases to the lessee. As discussed above, the criteria are similar for classification, except that IFRS considers the degree to which the asset is specialized and of use only to the lessee without major expense to the lessor as an additional criterion considered, and no numerical thresholds are given for any of the criterion. In addition, for finance leases, the lessee uses the interest rate implicit in the lease whenever it can be reasonably determined; otherwise the incremental borrowing rate is used. In contrast, ASPE uses the lower of the two rates.

SUMMARY OF LEARNING OBJECTIVE FOR APPENDIX 20B

16 Explain and apply the classification approach under IAS 17 for a lessee.

A lease is classified as a finance lease under IAS 17 where the risks and benefits of owning the leased asset are transferred to the lessee, which is evidenced by one or more of the following: (1) the transfer of title, (2) the use of the majority of the asset services inherent in the leased asset, (3) the recovery by the lessor of substantially all of its investment in the leased asset plus a return on that investment, or (4) in some cases the degree of specialization of the specific asset. If none of these criteria is met, the lease is classified as an operating lease.

Note: Completion of this end-of-chapter material will help develop CPA enabling competencies (such as ethics and professionalism, problem-solving and decision-making, and communication) and technical competencies. We have highlighted selected items with an integration icon and material in *WileyPLUS* has been linked to the competencies. All cases emphasize integration, especially of the enabling competencies. The brief exercises, exercises, and problems generally emphasize problem-solving and decision-making.

All assignment material with an asterisk (*) relates to an appendix to the chapter. Unless otherwise noted, assume that the straight-line method is used for all depreciation calculations in the end-of-chapter material.

Brief Exercises

(LO 3) BE20-1 Lagace Ltd. entered into a lease on June 1, 2017. The lease term is six years and requires annual rental payments of $30,000 at the beginning of each year. Lagace's incremental borrowing rate is 8% and the rate implicit in the lease is 9%. (a) Calculate the capitalized amount of the right-to-use asset if Lagace follows IFRS 16. (b) Calculate the capitalized amount of the leased asset if Lagace follows ASPE.

(LO 3, 7) BE20-2 Turcotte Limited, a public company following IFRS 16, decided to upgrade the coffee machines in all of its office locations. Turcotte leased 50 machines from Coffee Tyme Ltd. on July 1, 2017 (to purchase the coffee machines instead would cost Turcotte $350 per machine, and the machines would have lasted an estimated five years). The lease calls for semi-annual payments for the next three years, in the amount of $40 per machine. The payments start on July 1, 2017. At the end of the three-year period, the machines will have will be returned to the lessor. Discuss how Turcotte should account for the lease and prepare the entry for the first payment on July 1, 2017. Would your entry for the first payment differ if Turcotte followed ASPE?

(LO 3) BE20-3 Lee Ltd. recently signed a lease for equipment from Photon Inc. The lease term is five years and requires equal rental payments of $32,000 at the beginning of each year. The equipment has a fair value at the lease's inception of $140,000, an estimated useful life of eight years, and no residual value. Lee pays all executory costs directly to third parties. Photon set the annual rental to earn a rate of return of 8%, and this fact is known to Lee. The lease does not transfer title or contain a bargain purchase option. What is the nature of the lease assuming Lee follows (a) IFRS 16 and (b) ASPE?

(LO 3) BE20-4 Blane Inc. entered into a five-year lease of equipment from Zdrinka Inc. At the lease's inception, it is estimated that the equipment has an economic life of eight years and fair value of $250,000. Present value of minimum lease payments amounts to $215,606.50. The lease does not transfer title or contain a bargain purchase option. (a) What is the nature of the lease assuming Blane follows IFRS 16? (b) How should Blane classify this lease assuming it follows ASPE?

(LO 3, 7) BE20-5 Coa Corporation recently needed to find temporary inventory storage space when transitioning from an old factory to a newly built factory within the same city. Coa signed a 10-month lease on a warehouse requiring monthly payments in advance of $14,500. (a) What is the nature of the lease assuming Coa follows IFRS 16? (b) Prepare the entry for the first payment on May 1, 2017. (c) Would your entry differ if Coa followed ASPE?

(LO 5) BE20-6 Lalonde Ltd., a public company following IFRS 16, recently signed a lease for equipment from Costner Ltd. The lease term is five years and requires equal rental payments of $25,173 at the beginning of each year. The equipment has a fair value at the lease's inception of $112,400, an estimated useful life of five years, and no residual value. Lalonde pays all executory costs directly to third parties. The appropriate interest rate is 6%. Using tables, a financial calculator, or Excel functions, calculate the amount of the right-of-use asset and lease liability. Prepare the initial entry to reflect the signing of the lease agreement and the first payment under the lease.

(LO 4) BE20-7 Use the information for Lalonde and Costner from BE20-6. Using tables, a financial calculator, or Excel functions, illustrate how Costner determined the amount of the lease payment of $25,173.

(LO 5) BE20-8 McCormick Ltd., a public company following IFRS 16, recorded a right-of-use asset and lease liability at $150,000 on May 1, 2017. The interest rate is 10%. McCormick made the first lease payment of $25,561 on May 1, 2017. The lease requires a total of eight annual payments. The equipment has a useful life of eight years with no residual value. Prepare McCormick's December 31, 2017 adjusting entries.

(LO 5) BE20-9 Use the information for McCormick Ltd. from BE20-8. Assume that at December 31, 2017, McCormick made an adjusting entry to accrue interest expense of $8,296 on the lease. Prepare McCormick's May 1, 2018 journal entry to record the second lease payment of $25,561. Assume that no reversing entries are made.

(LO 6) BE20-10 Langlois Services Inc. accounts for right-of-use assets under IFRS 16 for a lease of a truck. The lease includes a residual value guarantee at the end of the term of the lease of $16,000. Langlois estimates that the likelihood for the residual value of $16,000 has a 50% certainty. Langlois feels that there is a 30% chance that the residual value will be $12,000 and a 20% chance that it will be $10,000. Calculate the probability-weighted value of the residual guarantee that needs to be included in the lease payments liability recorded by Langlois when the lease is signed.

(LO 6) BE20-11 Merrill Corporation, which uses ASPE, enters into a six-year lease of equipment on September 13, 2017 that requires six annual payments of $28,000 each, beginning September 13, 2017. In addition, Merrill guarantees the lessor a residual value of $17,000 at lease end. The equipment has a useful life of six years. Using tables, a financial calculator, or Excel functions, calculate the amount of the capital lease and prepare Merrill's September 13, 2017 journal entries, assuming an interest rate of 9%.

(LO 6) BE20-12 Use the information for Merrill Corporation from BE20-11. Assume that a residual value of $17,000 is expected at the end of the lease, but that Merrill does not guarantee the residual value. Using tables, a financial calculator, or Excel functions, calculate the amount of the capital lease and prepare Merrill's September 13, 2017 journal entries, assuming an interest rate of 9% and that Merrill also uses ASPE.

(LO 11) BE20-13 Use the information for Merrill Corporation from BE20-11. Assume that for Moxey Corporation, the lessor, collectibility is reasonably predictable, there are no important uncertainties concerning costs, and the equipment's carrying amount is $121,000. Prepare Moxey's September 13, 2017 journal entries.

(LO 9, 10) BE20-14 Lai Corporation, which uses ASPE, leased equipment it had specifically purchased at a cost of $175,000 for Swander, the lessee. The term of the lease is six years, beginning January 1, 2017, with equal rental payments of $33,574 at the beginning of each year. Swander pays all executory costs directly to third parties. The equipment's fair value at the lease's inception is $175,000. The equipment has a useful life of seven years with no residual value. The lease has an implicit interest rate of 6%, no bargain purchase option, and no transfer of title. Collectibility is reasonably assured, with no additional costs to be incurred by Lai. Using tables, a financial calculator, or Excel functions, calculate the present value of the lease payments and prepare Lai Corporation's January 1, 2017 journal entries at the inception of the lease. Round amounts to the nearest dollar.

(LO 9, 10) BE20-15 Use the information for Lai Corporation from BE20-14. Assume that, instead of costing Lai $175,000, the equipment was manufactured by Lai at a cost of $137,500 and the equipment's regular selling price is $175,000. Prepare Lai Corporation's January 1, 2017 journal entries at the inception of the lease and the entry at December 31, 2017 to record interest.

(LO 4, 11) BE20-16 Regina Corporation, which uses ASPE, manufactures replicators. On May 29, 2017, it leased to Barnes Limited a replicator that cost $265,000 to manufacture and usually sells for $410,000. The lease agreement covers the replicator's five-year useful life and requires five equal annual rentals of $95,930 each, beginning May 29, 2017. The equipment reverts to Regina at the end of the lease, at which time it is expected that the replicator will have a residual value of $40,000, which has been guaranteed by Barnes, the lessee. An interest rate of 12% is implicit in the lease agreement. Collectibility of the rentals is reasonably assured, and there are no important uncertainties concerning costs. (a) Using tables, a financial calculator, or Excel functions, prove that the amount of the annual payments will yield 12% interest to Regina. (b) Prepare Regina's May 29, 2017 journal entries.

(LO 11) BE20-17 Use the information for Regina Corporation from BE20-16. Assume instead that the residual value is not guaranteed. Prepare Regina's May 29, 2017 journal entries.

(LO 14, 16) *BE20-18 On January 1, 2017, Clark Inc. sold a piece of equipment to Daye Ltd. for $200,000, and immediately leased the equipment back. At the time, the equipment was carried on Clark's books at a cost of $300,000, less accumulated depreciation of $120,000. The lease is a finance or capital lease to Clark, with a lease term of five years. The equipment under finance or capital lease will be depreciated in Clark's books over five years using double-declining balance depreciation. (a) Calculate the amortization of the deferred gain on sale to be recorded at the end of 2017, if Clark follows IAS 17. (b) Calculate the amortization of the deferred gain on sale to be recorded at the end of 2017, if Clark follows ASPE. (c) Assume that 30% of the gain related to the rights transferred to Daye and 70% related to the right to use the equipment retained by Clark. Calculate the amount of gain to be recognized by Clark under IFRS 16.

(LO 14) *BE20-19 On January 1, 2017, Animation Ltd., which uses ASPE, sold a truck to Letourneau Finance Corp. for $65,000 and immediately leased it back. The truck was carried on Animation's books at $53,000, net of $26,000 of accumulated depreciation. The term of the lease is five years, and title transfers to Animation at lease end. The lease requires five equal rental payments of $17,147, with each payment made at year end. The appropriate rate of interest is 10%, and the truck has a useful life of five years with no salvage value. Prepare Animation's 2017 journal entries including any year-end adjusting entries at December 31, 2017.

(LO 15) *BE20-20 Lessee Corp. agreed to lease property from Lessor Corp. effective January 1, 2017, for an annual payment of $30,877, beginning January 1, 2017. The property is made up of land with a fair value of $120,000 and a two-storey office building with a fair value of $250,000 and a useful life of 25 years with no residual value. The implicit interest rate is 7.5%, the lease term is 25 years, and title to the property is transferred to Lessee at the end of the lease term. Prepare the required entries made by Lessee Corp. on January 1, 2017 and at its year end of December 31, 2017. Both Lessee and Lessor use ASPE. Round all amounts to the nearest dollar.

(LO 15) *BE20-21 Use the information provided in BE20-20 about Lessee Corp. Assume that title to the property will not be transferred to Lessee by the end of the lease term and that there is also no bargain purchase option, but that the lease does meet other criteria to qualify as a capital lease. Prepare the required entries made by Lessee Corp. on January 1, 2017 and at its year end of December 31, 2017.

(LO 3, 16) *BE20-22 On January 1, 2017, Quong Corporation (the lessee) entered into a four-year, non-cancellable equipment lease contract with Zareiga Inc. (the lessor). The present value of the minimum lease payments required was $116,025. Also at lease inception, it was estimated that the equipment's economic life was eight years, and that its fair value was $150,000. The lease does not transfer title or contain a bargain purchase option and it is not for specialized equipment. (a) Assume that Quong follows IFRS 16. How should Quong set up this lease? (b) Assume that Quong follows ASPE. How should Quong classify this lease? (c) Assume that Quong follows IAS 17. How should Quong account for this lease?

(LO 16) *BE20-23 Wing Corporation enters into a lease with Sharda Inc., a lessor, on August 15, 2017 that does not transfer ownership or contain a bargain purchase option, and it is not for specialized equipment. Both Wing and Sharda use IAS 17. The lease covers three years of the equipment's eight-year useful life, and the present value of the minimum lease payments is less than 90% of the equipment's fair value. Prepare Wing's journal entry to record its August 15, 2017 annual lease payment of $31,500. Wing has a November 30 year end.

(LO 16) *BE20-24 Use the information for Wing Corporation and Sharda Inc. from BE20-23. Assume that Sharda, the lessor, has a June 30 year end. Prepare Sharda's entry on August 15, 2017 and any adjusting entry needed on June 30, 2018.

(LO 16) *BE20-25 Lantaigne Inc. entered into a seven-year lease of equipment from Weingartner Inc. At the lease's inception, it is estimated that the equipment has an economic life of 10 years and fair value of $450,000. Present value of minimum lease payments of $75,000 each year, paid in advance, amounts to $421,716. The lease does not transfer title or contain a bargain purchase option and it is not for specialized equipment. Assuming that Lantaigne follows IAS 17, how should the lease be classified?

Exercises

(LO 3, 5, 8) E20-1 **(Lessee Entries, Right-of-Use Asset with Executory Costs)** On January 1, 2017, Maleki Corp., which uses IFRS 16, signs a 10-year, non-cancellable lease agreement to lease a specialty lathe from Liu Inc. The following information concerns the lease agreement.

1. The agreement requires equal rental payments of $73,580 beginning on January 1, 2017.

2. The lathe's fair value on January 1, 2017 is $450,000.

3. The lathe has an estimated economic life of 12 years, with an unguaranteed residual value of $12,000. Maleki Corp. depreciates similar equipment using the straight-line method.

4. The lease is non-renewable. At the termination of the lease, the lathe reverts to the lessor.

5. Maleki's incremental borrowing rate is 12% per year. The lessor's implicit rate is not known by Maleki Corp.

6. The yearly rental payment includes $2,470.29 of executory costs related to insurance on the loom.

Instructions

(a) Using a financial calculator or Excel functions, calculate the amount of the right-of-use asset and lease liability and prepare the initial entry to reflect the signing of the lease agreement.

(b) Prepare an amortization schedule for the term of the lease to be used by Maleki. Use Excel.

(c) Prepare the journal entries on Maleki Corp.'s books to record the payments and expenses related to this lease for the years 2017 and 2018 as well as any adjusting journal entries at its fiscal year ends of December 31, 2017 and 2018. Maleki does not use reversing entries.

(d) Prepare Maleki Corp.'s required note disclosure on the lease for the fiscal year ending December 31, 2018.

(LO 3, 5) E20-2 **(Lessee Entries, Right-of-Use Asset with Executory Costs—Lease and Fiscal Years Differ)**

Instructions

Refer to the data and other information provided in E20-1, but now assume that Maleki's fiscal year end is May 31. Prepare the journal entries on Maleki Corp.'s books to reflect the signing of the lease agreement and to record payments and expenses related to this lease for the calendar years 2017 and 2018. Maleki does not prepare reversing entries.

(LO 3, 5, 6, 11) E20-3 **(Type of Lease, Lessee Entries with Purchase Option)** The following facts are for a non-cancellable lease agreement between Hebert Corporation and Russell Corporation, a lessee:

Inception date	July 1, 2017
Annual lease payment due at the beginning of each year, starting July 1, 2017	$20,066.26
Purchase option price at end of lease term reasonably certain to be exercised by Russell	$4,500.00
Lease term	5 years
Economic life of leased equipment	10 years
Lessor's cost	$60,000.00
Fair value of asset at July 1, 2017	$88,000.00
Lessor's implicit rate	9%
Lessee's incremental borrowing rate	9%

The collectibility of the lease payments is reasonably predictable, and there are no important uncertainties about costs that have not yet been incurred by the lessor. The lessee assumes responsibility for all executory costs. Both Russell and Hebert use IFRS 16.

Instructions

Answer the following, rounding all numbers to the nearest cent.

(a) Calculate the amount of the right-of-use asset and lease liability.

(b) Discuss the nature of this lease to Russell Corporation, the lessee.

(c) Discuss the nature of this lease to Hebert Corporation, the lessor.

(d) Prepare a lease amortization schedule for the lease obligation using a computer spreadsheet for Russell Corporation for the five-year lease term.

(e) Prepare the journal entries on the lessee's books to reflect the signing of the lease agreement and to record the payments and expenses related to this lease for the years 2017 and 2018. Russell's annual accounting period ends on December 31, and Russell does not use reversing entries.

(LO 6, 9, 10, 11)   **E20-4**   **(Lessor Entries with Purchase Option)** A lease agreement between Hebert Corporation and Russell Corporation is described in E20-3.

Instructions

Provide the following for Hebert Corporation, the lessor.

(a) Discuss the nature of the lease.

(b) Calculate the amount of gross investment at the inception of the lease.

(c) Calculate the amount of net investment at the inception of the lease.

(d) Prepare a lease amortization schedule using a computer spreadsheet for Hebert Corporation for the five-year lease term.

(e) Prepare the journal entries to reflect the signing of the lease and to record the receipts and income related to this lease for the years 2017, 2018, and 2019. The lessor's accounting period ends on December 31, and Hebert Corporation does not use reversing entries.

(LO 3, 5, 8)   **E20-5**   **(Lessee Calculations and Entries, Right-of-Use Asset, Disclosure)** On January 1, 2018, Xu Ltd., which uses IFRS 16, entered into an eight-year lease agreement for a conveyor machine. Annual lease payments are $28,500 at the beginning of each lease year, which ends December 31, and Xu made the first payment on January 1, 2018. At the end of the lease, the machine will revert to the lessor. However, conveyor machines are expected to last for only eight years and have no residual value. At the time of the lease agreement, conveyor machines could be purchased for $166,000 cash. Equivalent financing for the machine could have been obtained from Xu's bank at 10.5%. Xu's fiscal year coincides with the calendar year. Xu uses straight-line depreciation for its conveyor machines.

Instructions

(a) Calculate the present value of the minimum lease payments using a financial calculator or Excel functions.

(b) Discuss the nature of the lease to Xu Ltd.

(c) Prepare an amortization schedule for the term of the lease to be used by Xu Ltd. Use Excel and round all amounts to the nearest dollar. (Note: You may find the =round formula helpful for rounding in Excel.)

(d) Prepare the journal entries on Xu Ltd.'s books to reflect the signing of the lease agreement and to record the payments and expenses related to this lease for the years 2018 and 2019 as well as any adjusting journal entries at its fiscal year ends of December 31, 2018 and 2019. Xu does not use reversing entries.

(e) Prepare a partial comparative statement of financial position at December 31, 2019 and 2018 for all of the accounts related to this lease for Xu Ltd. Be specific about the classifications that should be used.

(f) Provide Xu Ltd.'s required note disclosure concerning the lease liability for the fiscal year ending December 31, 2019.

(g) What is the significance of the difference between the amount of the present value of the minimum lease payments calculated in part (a) and the selling price of the machine of $166,000?

DIGGING DEEPER

(LO 3, 4, 6, 8)   **E20-6**   **(Amortization Schedule and Journal Entries for Lessee)** Oakridge Leasing Corporation signs an agreement on January 1, 2017 to lease equipment to LeBlanc Limited. Oakridge and LeBlanc follow ASPE. The following information relates to the agreement.

1. The term of the non-cancellable lease is five years, with no renewal option. The equipment has an estimated economic life of six years.

2. The asset's fair value at January 1, 2017 is $80,000.

3. The asset will revert to the lessor at the end of the lease term, at which time the asset is expected to have a residual value of $7,000, which is not guaranteed.

4. LeBlanc Limited assumes direct responsibility for all executory costs, which include the following annual amounts: $900 to Rocky Mountain Insurance Ltd. for insurance and $1,600 to James Township for property taxes.

5. The agreement requires equal annual rental payments of $18,143 to Oakridge, the lessor, beginning on January 1, 2017.

6. The lessee's incremental borrowing rate is 11%. The lessor's implicit rate is 10% and is known to the lessee.

7. LeBlanc Limited uses the straight-line depreciation method for all equipment and rounds amounts to the nearest dollar.

8. LeBlanc uses reversing entries when appropriate.

Instructions

Answer the following, rounding all numbers to the nearest cent.

(a) Prepare an amortization schedule for LeBlanc Limited for the lease term. Use Excel and round all amounts to the nearest dollar. (Note: you may find the =round formula helpful for rounding in Excel.)

(b) Prepare all of LeBlanc's journal entries for 2017 and 2018 to record the lease agreement, the lease payments, and all expenses related to this lease. Assume that the lessee's annual accounting period ends on December 31.

DIGGING DEEPER

(c) Show the calculations that Oakridge, the lessor, used to arrive at the lease payment amount of $18,143.

(d) Provide the required note disclosure for LeBlanc Limited concerning the lease for the fiscal year ending December 31, 2018.

(LO 3, 5, 9, 10, 13) E20-7 (Lease Payment Calculation and Lessee-Lessor Entries—Sales-Type Lease) On January 1, 2017, Lavery Corp., which follows ASPE, leased equipment to Flynn Ltd., which follows IFRS 16. Both Lavery and Flynn have calendar year ends. The following information concerns this lease.

1. The term of the non-cancellable lease is six years, with no renewal option. The equipment reverts to the lessor at the termination of the lease, at which time it is expected to have a residual value (not guaranteed) of $6,000. Flynn Ltd. depreciates all its equipment on a straight-line basis.

2. Equal rental payments are due on January 1 of each year, beginning in 2017.

3. The equipment's fair value on January 1, 2017 is $144,000 and its cost to Lavery is $111,000.

4. The equipment has an economic life of seven years.

5. Lavery set the annual rental to ensure a 9% rate of return. Flynn's incremental borrowing rate is 10% and the lessor's implicit rate is unknown to the lessee.

6. Collectibility of lease payments is reasonably predictable and there are no important uncertainties about any unreimbursable costs that have not yet been incurred by the lessor.

Instructions

(a) Explain clearly why this lease would be set up as a right-of-use asset by Flynn and a manufacturer/dealer or sales-type lease by Lavery.

(b) Using time value of money tables, a financial calculator, or Excel spreadsheet functions, calculate the amount of the annual rental payment.

(c) Prepare all necessary journal entries and adjusting entries for Flynn for 2017.

(d) Prepare all necessary journal entries and adjusting entries for Lavery for 2017.

DIGGING DEEPER

(e) Discuss the differences, if any, in the classification of the lease by Lavery Corp. (the lessor) if Lavery were using IFRS 16.

(LO 3, 7) E20-8 (Operating Lease versus Capital Lease) You are a senior auditor auditing the December 31, 2017 financial statements of Hoang, Inc., a manufacturer of novelties and party favours and a user of ASPE. During your inspection of the company garage, you discovered that a 2016 Shirk automobile is parked in the company garage but is not listed in the equipment subsidiary ledger. You ask the plant manager about the vehicle, and she tells you that the company did not list the automobile because the company is only leasing it. The lease agreement was entered into on January 1, 2017 with Quick Deal New and Used Cars. You decide to review the lease agreement to ensure that the lease should be given operating lease treatment, and you discover the following lease terms.

1. It is a non-cancellable term of 50 months.

2. The rental is $220 per month at the end of each month. (The present value at 1% per month is $8,623.)

3. The estimated residual value after 50 months is $2,100. (The present value at 1% per month is $1,277.) Hoang guarantees the residual value of $2,100.

4. The automobile's estimated economic life is 60 months.

5. Hoang's incremental borrowing rate is 12% per year (1% per month).

Instructions

AUDIT AND ASSURANCE

Write a memo to your supervisor, the audit partner in charge of this audit, to discuss the situation. Be sure to include the following:

(a) why you inspected the lease agreement,

(b) what you determined about the lease, and

(c) how you advised your client to account for this lease.

Explain every journal entry that you believe is necessary to record this lease properly on the client's books.

(LO 4, 11) E20-9 (Calculation of Rental, Amortization Schedule, Journal Entries for Lessor—Lease and Fiscal Year Differ) Matta Leasing Limited, which has a fiscal year end of October 31 and follows IFRS 16, signs an agreement on January 1, 2017 to lease equipment to Irvine Limited. The following information relates to the agreement.

1. The term of the non-cancellable lease is six years, with no renewal option. The equipment has an estimated economic life of eight years.

2. The asset's cost to Matta, the lessor, is $305,000. The asset's fair value at January 1, 2017 is $305,000.

3. The asset will revert to the lessor at the end of the lease term, at which time the asset is expected to have a residual value of $45,626, which is not guaranteed.

4. Irvine Limited, the lessee, assumes direct responsibility for all executory costs.

5. The agreement requires equal annual rental payments, beginning on January 1, 2017.

6. Collectibility of the lease payments is reasonably predictable. There are no important uncertainties about costs that have not yet been incurred by the lessor.

Instructions

Answer the following, rounding all numbers to the nearest dollar.

(a) Assuming that Matta Leasing desires a 10% rate of return on its investment, use time value of money tables, a financial calculator, or Excel functions to calculate the amount of the annual rental payment that is required.

(b) Prepare an amortization schedule using a spreadsheet that would be suitable for the lessor for the lease term.

(c) Prepare all of the journal entries for the lessor for 2017 and 2018 to record the lease agreement, the receipt of lease payments, and the recognition of income. Assume that Matta prepares adjusting journal entries only at the end of the fiscal year.

(d) Prepare a comparative partial statement of income for Matta for fiscal years 2017 and 2018.

(LO 9, E20-10 (Lessor Entries, Determination of Type of Lease, Lease Payment Calculation, Spreadsheet Application, 10, 11) Financial Statement Amounts) Yogendran Corp., which uses ASPE, leases a car to Jaimme DeLory on June 1, 2017. The term of the non-cancellable lease is 48 months. The following information is provided about the lease.

1. The lessee is given an option to purchase the automobile at the end of the lease term for $5,000.

2. The automobile's fair value on June 1, 2017 is $29,500. It is carried in Yogendran's inventory at $21,200.

3. The car has an economic life of seven years, with a $1,000 residual value at the end of that time. The car's estimated fair value is $10,000 after four years, $7,000 after five years, and $2,500 after six years.

4. Yogendran wants to earn a 12% rate of return (1% per month) on any financing transactions.

5. Jaimme DeLory represents a reasonable credit risk and no future costs are anticipated in relation to this lease.

6. The lease agreement calls for a $1,000 down payment on June 1, 2017, and 48 equal monthly payments on the first of each month, beginning June 1, 2017.

Instructions

(a) Determine the amount of the monthly lease payment using present value tables, a financial calculator, or Excel functions. Round to the nearest cent.

(b) What type of lease is this to Yogendran Corp.? Explain.

(c) Prepare a lease amortization schedule for the 48-month lease term using Excel. Round to the nearest cent. (Note: You may find the =round formula helpful for rounding in Excel.)

(d) Prepare the entries that are required, if any, on December 31, 2017, Yogendran's fiscal year end.

(e) How much income will Yogendran report on its 2017 statement of income relative to this lease?

(f) What is the net investment in the lease to be reported on the December 31, 2017 statement of financial position? How much is reported in current assets? In non-current assets?

(LO 5, 6, E20-11 (Lessor Entries, Financing Lease with Option to Purchase, Lessee Right-to-Use Asset) Castle Leasing 9, 11) Corporation, which uses IFRS 16, signs a lease agreement on January 1, 2017 to lease electronic equipment to Wai Corporation, which also uses IFRS 16. The term of the non-cancellable lease is two years and payments are required at the end of each year. The following information relates to this agreement.

1. Wai Corporation has the option to purchase the equipment for $13,000 upon the termination of the lease and this option is reasonably certain to be exercised.

2. The equipment has a cost and fair value of $135,000 to Castle Leasing Corporation. The useful economic life is two years, with a residual value of $13,000.

3. Wai Corporation is required to pay $5,000 each year to the lessor for insurance costs.

4. Castle Leasing Corporation wants to earn a return of 10% on its investment.

5. Collectibility of the payments is reasonably predictable, and there are no important uncertainties surrounding the costs that have not yet been incurred by the lessor.

Instructions

(a) Using time value of money tables, a financial calculator, or Excel functions, calculate the lease payment that Castle Leasing would require from Wai Corporation. Round all amounts to the nearest dollar. (Note: You may find the =round formula helpful for rounding in Excel.)

(b) What classification will Wai Corporation give to the lease? What classification will be given to the lease by Castle Leasing Corporation?

(c) What classification would be adopted by Wai Corporation and Castle Leasing Corporation had they both been using ASPE?

(d) Prepare a lease amortization schedule for Castle Leasing for the term of the lease.

(e) Prepare the journal entries on Castle Leasing's books to reflect the payments received under the lease and to recognize income for the years 2017 and 2018.

(f) Assuming that Wai Corporation exercises its option to purchase the equipment on December 31, 2018, prepare the journal entry to reflect the sale on Castle Leasing's books.

(g) What amount would Wai Corporation capitalize and recognize as a lease liability and corresponding right-to-use asset on signing the lease? Explain.

(LO 4, 10, 11) E20-12 (Rental Amount Calculation, Lessor Entries, Disclosure—Financing Lease with Unguaranteed Residual Value) On January 1, 2017, Vick Leasing Inc., a lessor that uses IFRS 16, signed an agreement with Rock River Inc., a lessee, for the use of a compression system. The system cost $415,000 and was purchased from Manufacturing Solutions Ltd. specifically for Rock River Inc. Annual payments are made each January 1 by Rock. In addition to making the lease payment, Rock also reimburses Vick $4,000 each January 1 for a portion of the repairs and maintenance expenditures, which cost Vick Leasing a total of $7,000 per year. At the end of the five-year agreement, the compression equipment will revert to Vick and is expected to have a residual value of $25,000, which is not guaranteed. Collectibility of the rentals is reasonably predictable, and there are no important uncertainties surrounding the costs that have not yet been incurred by Vick Leasing Inc.

Instructions

(a) Assume that Vick Leasing Inc. has a required rate of return of 8%. Calculate the amount of the lease payments that would be needed to generate this return on the agreement if payments were made each:

1. January 1

2. December 31

(b) Use Excel to prepare an amortization schedule (round all amounts to the nearest cent using the =round formula) that shows how the lessor's net investment in the lease receivable will be reduced over the lease term if payments are made each:

1. January 1

2. December 31

(c) Assume that the payments are due each January 1. Prepare all journal entries and adjusting journal entries for 2017 and 2018 for the lessor, assuming that Vick has a calendar year end. Include the payment for the purchase of the equipment for leasing in your entries and the annual payment for repair and maintenance.

(d) Prepare a partial statement of financial position at December 31, 2017 showing the net investment in leases for Vick. Provide the proper classification and assume that the payments are due each January 1.

(e) Provide the note disclosure concerning the lease that would be required for Vick Leasing Inc. at December 31, 2018. Assume that payments are due each January 1.

(LO 9, 12) E20-13 (Accounting and Disclosure for an Operating Lease—Lessor) On May 1, 2017, a machine was purchased for $1,750,000 by Pomeroy Corp., a private company following ASPE. The machine is expected to have an eight-year life with no salvage value and is to be depreciated on a straight-line basis. The machine was leased to St. Isidor Inc. on May 1, 2017 at an annual rental of $450,000. Other relevant information is as follows.

1. The lease term is three years and the payments began May 1, 2017.

2. Pomeroy Corp. incurred repair and maintenance costs of $61,000 for the fiscal year ending December 31, 2017 related to this lease.

3. The machine could have been sold by Pomeroy Corp. for $1,850,000 instead of leasing it.

4. The stated interest rate in the lease is 10%.

Instructions

(a) Provide the basis for Pomeroy Corp.'s treatment of the lease as an operating lease.

(b) How much should Pomeroy Corp. report as income before income tax on this lease for 2017?

(c) What financial statement disclosures relative to this lease must be provided by Pomeroy at its December 31, 2017 year end?

(LO 9, 10) E20-14 (Lessor Entries—Manufacturer/Dealer or Sales-Type Lease) Pucci Corporation is a machinery dealer whose shares trades on the TSX, and so uses IFRS 16. Pucci leased a machine to Ernst Ltd. on January 1, 2017. The lease is for a six-year period and requires equal annual payments of $24,736 at the beginning of each year. The first payment is received on January 1, 2017. Pucci had purchased the machine for its inventory during 2016 for $99,000. Collectibility of lease payments is reasonably predictable, and no important uncertainties exist about costs that have not yet been incurred by Pucci. Pucci set the annual rental amount to ensure an 8% rate of return. The machine has an economic life of six years, with no residual value, and reverts to Pucci at the termination of the lease.

Instructions

(a) Using time value of money tables, a financial calculator, or Excel functions, calculate the amount of each of the following:

1. Gross investment

2. Unearned interest income

3. Net investment in the lease

(b) Prepare all necessary journal entries for Pucci for 2017.

(LO 3, 7, 16) *E20-15 (Lessee Entries and Capital Lease with Unguaranteed Residual Value—Lease and Fiscal Year Differ—IAS 17) On September 1, 2017, Wong Corporation, which uses ASPE, signed a five-year, non-cancellable lease for a piece of equipment. The terms of the lease called for Wong to make annual payments of $13,668 at the beginning of each lease year, starting September 1, 2017. The equipment has an estimated useful life of six years and a $9,000 unguaranteed residual value. The equipment reverts back to the lessor at the end of the lease term. Wong uses the straight-line method of depreciation for all of its plant assets, has a calendar year end, prepares adjusting journal entries at the end of the fiscal year, and does not use reversing entries. Wong's incremental borrowing rate is 10%, and the lessor's implicit rate is unknown.

Instructions

(a) Using time value of money tables, a financial calculator, or Excel functions, calculate the present value of the minimum lease payments for the lessee.

(b) Explain why this is a capital lease to Wong.

DIGGING DEEPER

(c) Prepare all necessary journal entries for Wong for this lease, including any year-end adjusting entries through September 1, 2018.

(d) Would this also be a capital lease if Wong reported under IAS 17?

(e) Prepare all necessary journal entries for Wong for this lease, including any year-end adjusting entries through September 1, 2018, assuming Wong followed IAS 17.

(LO 7, 8) E20-16 (Lessee Entries, Operating Lease, Comparison) Refer to the data and other information provided for Wong Corporation in E20-15. Assume that the equipment has an estimated economic life of seven years and that its fair value on September 1, 2017 is $79,000.

Instructions

(a) Explain why this lease is now considered an operating lease.

(b) Prepare all necessary journal entries for Wong Corporation for this lease, including any year-end adjusting entries through December 31, 2018.

FINANCE

(c) Identify what accounts will appear on Wong's December 31, 2017 balance sheet and income statement relative to this lease.

DIGGING DEEPER

(d) How would Wong's December 31, 2017 balance sheet and income statement differ from your answer to part (c) if the lease were a capital lease as described in E20-15?

(e) From the perspective of an investor, discuss the effect of accounting for this lease as an operating lease rather than as a capital lease.

(LO 14) ***E20-17** **(Sale-Leaseback—Buyer and Lessor Entries)** On January 1, 2017, Hein Corporation sells equipment to Liquidity Finance Corp. for $720,000 and immediately leases the equipment back. Both Hein and Liquidity use ASPE. Other relevant information is as follows.

1. The equipment's carrying value on Hein's books on January 1, 2017 is $640,000 with an original cost of $980,000.

2. The term of the non-cancellable lease is 10 years. Title will transfer to Hein at the end of the lease.

3. The lease agreement requires equal rental payments of $117,176.68 at the end of each year.

4. The incremental borrowing rate of Hein Corporation is 12%. Hein is aware that Liquidity Finance Corp. set the annual rental to ensure a rate of return of 10%.

5. The equipment has a fair value of $720,000 on January 1, 2017, and an estimated economic life of 10 years, with no residual value.

6. Hein pays repairs and maintenance expenses of $11,000 per year directly to suppliers.

Instructions

(a) Prepare the journal entries for both the lessee and the lessor for 2017 to reflect the sale and leaseback agreement. No uncertainties exist and collectibility is reasonably certain.

DIGGING DEEPER

(b) What is Hein's primary objective in entering a sale-leaseback arrangement with Liquidity Finance Corp.? Would you consider this transaction to be a red flag to creditors, demonstrating that Hein is in financial difficulty?

(LO 14) ***E20-18** **(Lessee-Lessor, Sale-Leaseback)** Presented below are five independent situations. All the companies involved use ASPE unless otherwise noted.

1. On December 31, 2017, Zarle Inc. sold equipment to Orfanakos Corp. and immediately leased it back for 10 years. The equipment's selling price was $520,000, its carrying amount $400,000, and its estimated remaining economic life 12 years.

2. On December 31, 2017, Tessier Corp. sold a machine to Cross Ltd. and simultaneously leased it back for one year. The machine's selling price was $480,000, its carrying amount was $420,000, and it had an estimated remaining useful life of 14 years. The rental payments' present value for one year is $35,000.

3. On January 1, 2017, McKane Corp. sold an airplane with an estimated useful life of 10 years. At the same time, McKane leased back the plane for 10 years. The airplane's selling price was $500,000, the carrying amount was $379,000, and the annual rental was $73,975. McKane Corp. will depreciate the leased asset using the straight-line depreciation method. McKane is a public company and it follows IAS 17 to account for its leases.

4. On January 1, 2017, Barnes Corp. sold equipment with an estimated useful life of five years. At the same time, Barnes leased back the equipment for two years under a lease classified as an operating lease. The equipment's selling price (fair value) was $212,700, the carrying amount was $300,000, the monthly rental under the lease was $6,000, and the rental payments' present value was $115,753.

5. On December 30, 2017, Dedresan Inc. sold a warehouse with 10 separate spaces with loading bays to Mack Finance Ltd. for $1.3 million and immediately leased back two of the 10 spaces. The warehouse was carried on Dedresan's books at $800,000 and had a remaining useful life of 15 years. The term of the lease is five years with no renewal period. Dedresan is a public company following IFRS 16 to account for its leases.

Instructions

(a) For situation 1: Determine the amount of unearned profit to be reported by Zarle Inc. from the equipment sale on December 31, 2017.

(b) For situation 2: At December 31, 2017, how much should Tessier report as unearned profit from the sale of the machine?

(c) For situation 3: Discuss how the gain on the sale should be reported by McKane at the end of 2017 in the financial statements.

(d) For situation 4: For the year ended December 31, 2017, identify the items that would be reported on Barnes's income statement related to the sale-leaseback transaction.

(e) For situation 5: For the year ended December 31, 2017, identify the items that would be reported on Dedresan's income statement related to the sale-leaseback transaction.

(LO 14) ***E20-19** **(Land Lease, Lessee and Lessor)** On September 15, 2017, Local Camping Limited, the lessee, entered into a 20-year lease with Sullivan Corp. to rent a parcel of land at a rate of $30,000 per year. Both Local and Sullivan use ASPE. The annual rental is due in advance each September 15, beginning in 2017. The land has a current fair value of $195,000. The land reverts to Sullivan at the end of the lease. Local Camping's incremental borrowing rate and Sullivan's implicit interest rate are both 8%.

Instructions

(a) Prepare Local Camping's required journal entries on September 15, 2017 and at December 31, 2017, its year end.

(b) Explain how and why these entries might differ if Local were leasing equipment instead of land.

(c) Prepare the entries required on Sullivan's books at September 15, 2017 and at December 31, 2017, its year end.

(LO 15) ***E20-20   (Real Estate Lease)** Rancour Ltd., which uses ASPE, recently expanded its operations into an adjoining municipality, and on March 30, 2017, it signed a 15-year lease with its Municipal Industrial Commission (MIC). The property has a total fair value of $450,000 on March 30, 2017, with one third of the amount attributable to the land and two thirds to the building. The land is expected to double in value over the next 15 years, while the building will depreciate by 60%. The lease includes a purchase option at the end of the lease that allows Rancour to receive title to the property for a payment of $270,000.

Rancour is required to make rental payments of $30,000 annually, with the first payment due March 30, 2017. The MIC's implicit interest rate, known to all, is 7%. The building's economic life is estimated at 25 years, at which time it will have a small residual value of $40,000.

Instructions

(a) Using time value of money tables, a financial calculator, or Excel functions, calculate the present value of the lease obligation.

(b) Prepare the entries required by Rancour on the signing of the lease and the payment of the first lease payment.

(c) Assuming that Rancour's year end is December 31, prepare the entries that are required on December 31, 2017, March 30, 2018, and December 31, 2018. Rancour does not use reversing entries.

(LO 16) ***E20-21   (IAS 17: Lessee Entries, Finance Lease with Executory Costs and Unguaranteed Residual Value)** On January 1, 2017, Fine Corp., which follows IAS 17, signs a 10-year, non-cancellable lease agreement to lease a specialty loom from Sheffield Corporation. The following information concerns the lease agreement.

1. The agreement requires equal rental payments of $73,580 beginning on January 1, 2017.

2. The loom's fair value on January 1, 2017 is $450,000.

3. The loom has an estimated economic life of 12 years, with an unguaranteed residual value of $12,000. Fine Corp. depreciates similar equipment using the straight-line method.

4. The lease is non-renewable. At the termination of the lease, the loom reverts to the lessor.

5. Fine's incremental borrowing rate is 12% per year. The lessor's implicit rate is not known by Fine Corp.

6. The yearly rental payment includes $2,470.29 of executory costs related to insurance on the loom.

Instructions

(a) Using a financial calculator or Excel functions, calculate the present value of the minimum lease payments and prepare the initial entry to reflect the signing of the lease agreement.

(b) Prepare an amortization schedule for the term of the lease to be used by Fine. Use a computer spreadsheet.

(c) Prepare the journal entries on Fine Corp.'s books to record the payments and expenses related to this lease for the years 2017 and 2018 as well as any adjusting journal entries at its fiscal year ends of December 31, 2017 and 2018.

(d) Prepare Fine Corp.'s required note disclosure on the lease for the fiscal year ending December 31, 2018.

(LO 16) ***E20-22   (IAS 17: Lessee Entries, Finance Lease with Executory Costs and Unguaranteed Residual Value— Lease and Fiscal Years Differ)**

Instructions

Refer to the data and other information provided in E20-21, but now assume that Fine's fiscal year end is May 31. Prepare the journal entries on Fine Corp.'s books to reflect the lease signing and to record payments and expenses related to this lease for the calendar years 2017 and 2018. Fine does not prepare reversing entries.

(LO 16) ***E20-23   (IAS 17: Lessee Calculations and Entries, Capital Lease, Disclosure)** On January 1, 2018, Khalid Ltd., which follows IAS 17, entered into an eight-year lease agreement for three dryers. Annual lease payments for the equipment are $28,500 at the beginning of each lease year, which ends December 31. Khalid made the first payment on January 1, 2018. At the end of the lease, the dryers will revert to the lessor. However, the dryers are expected to last for only eight years and have no residual value. At the time of the lease agreement, the dryers could be purchased for a total purchase price of approximately $166,000 cash. Equivalent financing for the equipment could have been obtained from Khalid's bank at 10.5%. Khalid's fiscal year coincides with the calendar year. Khalid uses straight-line depreciation for its equipment.

Instructions

(a) Calculate the present value of the minimum lease payments using a financial calculator or Excel functions.

(b) Explain why this is a finance lease to Khalid Ltd. Document your calculations in arriving at your explanation.

(c) Prepare an amortization schedule for the term of the lease to be used by Khalid Ltd. Use Excel and round all amounts to the nearest dollar. (Note: You may find the =round formula helpful for rounding in Excel.)

(d) Prepare the journal entries on Khalid Ltd.'s books to reflect the signing of the lease agreement and to record the payments and expenses related to this lease for the years 2018 and 2019 as well as any adjusting journal entries at its fiscal year ends of December 31, 2018 and 2019. Khalid does not use reversing entries.

(e) Prepare a partial comparative statement of financial position at December 31, 2019 and 2018 for all of the accounts related to this lease for Khalid Ltd. Be specific about the classifications that should be used.

(f) Provide Khalid Ltd.'s required note disclosure concerning the lease for the fiscal year ending December 31, 2019.

DIGGING DEEPER

(g) What is the significance of the difference between the amount of the present value of the minimum lease payments calculated in part (a) and the approximate selling price of the machine of $166,000?

(LO 3, 5, 8, 16) ***E20-24   (IFRS 16 and IAS 17 Journal Entries and Statements for Lessee)** Cuomo Mining Corporation, a public company whose stock trades on the Toronto Stock Exchange, uses IFRS. The vice-president of finance has asked you, the assistant controller, to prepare a comparison of the company's current accounting of a lease (IAS 17) with contract-based approach IFRS 16, which will be implemented in the near future. The lease you are going to use for this comparison was signed by Cuomo on April 1, 2017 with Bertrand Ltd. for a piece of excavation equipment. The following information relates to the agreement.

1. The term of the non-cancellable lease is three years, with a renewal option of one additional year at the annual rate of 125% of the initial payment. The equipment has an estimated economic life of 10 years.

2. The asset's fair value at April 1, 2017 is approximately $1 million.

3. The asset will revert to Bertrand at the end of the initial term of the lease, or at the end of the renewal period should Cuomo exercise that option. The excavation equipment is expected to have a fair value of $600,000 on March 31, 2019 and $500,000 on March 31, 2020, which is not guaranteed.

4. Cuomo assumes direct responsibility for all executory costs for the excavation equipment.

5. The initial term of the lease agreement requires equal annual rental payments of $135,000 to Bertrand, beginning on April 1, 2017.

6. The lessee's incremental borrowing rate is 9%. Bertrand's implicit rate is 8% and is known to Cuomo.

7. Cuomo has a calendar year end.

You have established that it has always been Cuomo's intention to exercise the renewal period on account of the nature of the asset. Cuomo's operations manager says that there is a 70% chance that the renewal period will be exercised.

Instructions

Answer the following, rounding all numbers to the nearest dollar.

Part 1
Using IAS 17:

(a) Determine the accounting treatment of the lease agreement and obligation to Cuomo. What were the conditions that would need to be in place for the lease to be classified as a finance lease?

(b) Record all transactions concerning the lease for Cuomo for the fiscal year 2017.

Part 2
Using IFRS 16:

(c) Determine the amount of the liability for lease payments at the signing of the lease.

(d) Use a computer spreadsheet to prepare an amortization schedule for Cuomo for the lease term including the expected lease renewal.

(e) Prepare all of Cuomo's journal entries for fiscal years 2017 and 2018 to record the lease agreement and the lease payments.

Part 3
Prepare a table of Cuomo's statement of financial position disclosure of all of the amounts that would appear concerning the lease at December 31, 2018. Follow with the statement of income disclosure for the fiscal year ending December 31, 2018. Be specific concerning classifications. Include a second column to show the amounts Cuomo reports for the same period following IAS 17.

Problems

P20-1 Interior Design Inc. (ID) is a privately owned business that produces interior decorating options for consumers. ID follows ASPE. The software that it purchased six years ago to present clients with designs that are unique to their offices is no longer state of the art, and ID is faced with making a decision on the replacement of its software. The company has two options:

1. Enter into a lease agreement with Precision Inc. whereby ID makes an upfront lease payment of $12,000 on January 1, 2018, and annual payments of $4,500 over the next five years on each December 31. At the end of the lease, ID has the option to buy the software for $5,000. The first annual lease payment is on December 31, 2018.

2. Enter into a lease agreement with Graphic Inc. on January 1, 2018, whereby ID makes five annual lease payments of $6,500, beginning on January 1, 2018. ID may purchase the software at the end of the lease period for $200. This is considered a bargain price compared with the offer of $5,000 in the proposal from Precision Inc.

Under both options, the software will require annual upgrades that are expected to cost $1,500 per year. These upgrade costs are in addition to the lease payments that are required under the two independent options. Because this additional cost is the same under both options, ID has decided to ignore it in making its choice.

The Precision agreement requires a licensing fee of $1,000 to be renewed annually. If ID decides on the Precision option, the licensing fee will be included in the annual lease payment of $4,500. Both Precision Inc. and Graphic Inc. offer software programs of similar quality and ease of use, and both provide adequate support and training. The software under each offer is expected to be used for up to eight years, although this depends to some extent on technological advances in future years. Both offers are equivalent in terms of the product and service.

It is now early October 2017, and ID hopes to have the software in place by its fiscal year end of December 31, 2017. ID is currently working on preparing its third-quarter financial statements, which its bank is particularly interested in seeing in order to ensure that ID is respecting its debt to equity ratio covenant in its loan agreement with the bank. The interest rate on the bank loan, which is ID's only source of external financing, is 10% per year. ID would have preferred to be able to buy rather than lease the software, but the expected purchase price of $30,000 exceeds the limits that the bank set for ID's borrowing.

Instructions

FINANCE

(a) Using tables, a financial calculator, or Excel functions, calculate the present value of the future minimum lease payments under each option. Discuss the nature of the lease arrangement under each of the two lease options offered to Interior Design and the corresponding accounting treatment that should be applied.

(b) Prepare all necessary journal entries and adjusting journal entries for Interior Design under the Precision Inc. option, from lease inception on January 1, 2018 through to December 31, 2018, excluding the $1,500 annual upgrade.

(c) Prepare an amortization schedule using Excel that would be suitable for the lease term in the Graphic Inc. option. Round amounts to the nearest dollar.

(d) Prepare all necessary journal entries and adjusting journal entries for Interior Design under Graphic's option, from lease inception on January 1, 2018 through to January 1, 2019, excluding the $1,500 annual upgrade.

(e) Summarize and contrast the effects on Interior Design's financial statements for the year ending December 31, 2018, using the entries prepared in parts (b) and (d) above. Include in your summary the total differential cash outflows that would be made by Interior Design during 2018 under each option.

DIGGING DEEPER

(f) Discuss the qualitative considerations that should enter into Interior Design's decision on which lease to sign. Which lease do you think will most likely be chosen by Interior Design? Why?

(g) What are the long-term and short-term implications of the choice between these two options? How do these implications support the direction taken in IFRS 16 concerning the accounting for leases?

P20-2 You have just been hired as the new controller of SWT Services Inc., and on the top of the stack of papers on your new desk is a bundle of draft contracts with a note attached. The note says, "Please help me to understand which of these leases would be best for our situation." The note is signed by the president of SWT Services Inc. You have reviewed the proposed contracts and asked a few questions. In the process, you have become aware that the company is facing a large cutback in capital spending to deal with the effect of competition in the industry. A new customer service system that is heavily IT-based is critical in meeting the challenge head on. In order to meet this commitment, you need to identify the lease that will have the lowest total cost in the coming year and overall. As well, you will need to address the cash demands of each choice. The leases are for telecommunications and computer equipment and software. The following information is available.

Lease One: The equipment and software has a fair value of $487,694 and an expected life of six years. The lease has a five-year term. Annual rent is paid each January 1, beginning in 2017, in the amount of $104,300. The implicit rate of the lease is not known by SWT. Insurance and operating costs of $23,500 are to be paid directly by SWT to the lessor in addition to the lease payments. At the end of the lease term, the equipment will revert to the lessor, who will be able to sell it for $85,000. If the lessor is unable to sell the equipment for this amount, SWT will be required to make up the shortfall. SWT will likely purchase the equipment for $85,000 if any payments are required under this clause of the lease.

Lease Two: The equipment and software have a fair value of $444,404 and an expected life of seven years. The lease has a five-year term beginning January 1, 2017, with a two-year renewal period. Annual lease payments are made beginning December 31, 2017, in the amount of $137,500. This lease has an implicit rate of 8%. Insurance and operating costs of $26,500 are included in the lease payment. At the end of the initial lease term, the equipment can be leased for another two years for $27,500 per year, including insurance and operating costs. At the end of that two-year period, the equipment will belong to SWT.

SWT follows IFRS 16 and has a December year end. SWT's incremental borrowing rate is 10%.

Instructions

COMMUNICATION

(a) Prepare a memo to the president explaining which lease will have the lowest cost in the initial year of the lease and overall cost for the full term of the lease, including any renewal period for Lease Two. Include in your analysis a comparison of the cash flow requirement under each option for the term of the lease including any renewal option.

(b) Which lease do you recommend the company sign, assuming both will meet the company's requirements and the equipment proposed in both leases is similar? Bring as many arguments to your recommendation as possible to allow the president to be fully advised of the factors leading to your recommendation. In addition, advise the president on the impact of IFRS 16.

P20-3 On January 1, 2017, Hunter Ltd. entered into an agreement to lease a truck from Situ Ltd. Both Hunter and Situ use IFRS 16. The details of the agreement are as follows:

Carrying value of truck for Situ Ltd.	$20,691
Fair value of truck	$20,691
Economic life of truck	5 years
Lease term	3 years
Rental payments (at beginning of each month)	$620
Executory costs included in rental payments each month for insurance	$20
Incremental borrowing rate for Hunter Ltd.	12%
Hunter Ltd. expects to pay Situ Ltd. $3,500 under a residual value guarantee for the truck.	

Additional information:

1. There are no abnormal risks associated with the collection of lease payments from Hunter.

2. There are no additional unreimbursable costs to be incurred by Situ in connection with the leased truck.

3. At the end of the lease term, Situ sold the truck to a third party for $3,200, which was the truck's fair value at December 31, 2019. Hunter paid Situ the difference between the residual value guarantee of $3,500 and the proceeds obtained on the resale.

4. Hunter knows the interest rate that is implicit in the lease.

5. Hunter knows the amount of executory costs included in the minimum lease payments.

6. Hunter uses straight-line depreciation for its trucks with the residual value guarantee of $3,500 for the leased truck.

Instructions

(a) Discuss the nature of this lease for both Hunter Ltd. (the lessee) and Situ Ltd. (the lessor).

(b) Assume that the effective interest rate of 12% had not been provided in the data. Prove the effective interest rate of 12% using a financial calculator or Excel functions.

(c) Prepare a lease amortization schedule for the full term of the lease using Excel. Round all amounts to the nearest dollar.

(d) Prepare the journal entries that Hunter would make on January 1, 2017 and 2018, and any year-end adjusting journal entries at December 31, 2017, related to the lease arrangement, assuming that Hunter does not use reversing entries.

(e) Identify all accounts that will be reported by Hunter Ltd. on its comparative statement of financial position at December 31, 2018 and 2017, and comparative income statement for the fiscal years ending December 31, 2018 and 2017. Include all the necessary note disclosures on the transactions related to this lease for Hunter and be specific about the classifications in each statement.

(f) Prepare the journal entry for Hunter's payment on December 31, 2019 to Situ to settle the guaranteed residual value deficiency. Assume that no accruals for interest have been recorded as yet during 2019, but that the 2019 depreciation expense for the truck has been recorded.

DIGGING DEEPER

(g) Prepare Hunter's partial comparative statement of cash flows for the years ended December 31, 2018 and 2017, for all transactions related to the above information. Be specific about the classifications in the financial statement. Hunter has opted to show interest paid as operating activities.

P20-4   Refer to the information in P20-3.

Instructions

(a) Prepare the journal entries that Situ would make on January 1, 2017 and the adjusting journal entries at December 31, 2017, to record the annual interest income from the lease arrangement, assuming that Situ has a December 31 fiscal year end.

(b) Identify all accounts that will be reported by Situ Ltd. on its comparative statement of income for the fiscal years ending December 31, 2018 and 2017, and its comparative statement of financial position at December 31, 2018 and 2017. Be specific about the classifications in each statement.

DIGGING DEEPER

(c) Prepare a partial comparative statement of cash flows for Situ for the years ended December 31, 2018 and 2017, for all transactions related to the information in P20-3. Be specific about the classifications in the financial statement. Assume that Situ has opted to report interest received as operating activities.

P20-5   LePage Manufacturing Ltd. agrees to lease equipment to Labonté Ltée. on July 15, 2017. LePage follows ASPE and Labonté is a public company following IFRS 16. The following information relates to the lease agreement.

1. The lease term is seven years, with no renewal option, and the equipment has an estimated economic life of nine years.

2. The equipment's cost is $420,000 and the asset's fair value on July 15, 2017 is $560,000.

3. At the end of the lease term, a payment to LePage, the lessor, in the amount of $80,000 is expected to be payable by Labonté, the lessee, under a residual value guarantee. Labonté depreciates all of its equipment on a straight-line basis.

4. The lease agreement requires equal annual rental payments beginning on July 15, 2017.

5. LePage usually sells its equipment to customers who buy the product outright, but Labonté was unable to get acceptable financing for a cash purchase. LePage's credit investigation on Labonté revealed that the company's financial situation was deteriorating. Because Labonté had been a good customer many years ago, LePage agreed to enter into this lease agreement, but used a higher-than-usual 15% interest rate in setting the lease payments. Labonté is aware of this rate.

6. LePage is uncertain about what additional costs it might have to incur in connection with this lease during the lease term, although Labonté has agreed to pay all executory costs directly to third parties.

7. LePage incurred legal costs of $2,500 in early July 2017 in finalizing the lease agreement.

Instructions

(a) Discuss the nature of this lease for both the lessee and the lessor.

(b) Using time value of money tables, a financial calculator, or Excel functions, calculate the amount of the annual rental payment that is required to obtain a return of 15% for LePage.

(c) Prepare the journal entries that Labonté would make in 2017 and 2018 related to the lease arrangement, assuming that the company has a December 31 fiscal year end and that it does not use reversing entries.

(d) From the information you have calculated and recorded, identify all balances related to this lease that would be reported on Labonté's December 31, 2017 statement of financial position and statement of income, and where each amount would be reported.

(e) Prepare the journal entries that LePage would make in 2017 and 2018 related to the lease arrangement, assuming that the company has a December 31 fiscal year end and does not use reversing entries.

(f) From the information you have calculated and recorded, identify all balances related to this lease that would be reported on LePage's December 31, 2017 statement of financial position and statement of income, and where each amount would be reported.

(g) Comment briefly on the December 31, 2017 reported results in parts (d) and (f) above.

P20-6   Synergetics Inc. leased a new crane to Gumo Construction Inc. under a six-year, non-cancellable contract starting February 1, 2017. The lease terms require payments of $21,500 each February 1, starting February 1, 2017. Synergetics will pay insurance and repair and maintenance charges on the crane, which has an estimated life of 12 years, a fair value of $160,000, and a cost to Synergetics of $160,000. The crane's estimated fair value is $50,000 at the end of the lease term. No bargain purchase or renewal options are included in the contract. Both Synergetics and Gumo have calendar year ends and use IFRS 16. Collectibility of the lease payments is reasonably certain and there are no uncertainties about unreimbursable lessor costs. Gumo's incremental borrowing rate is 8% and Synergetics' implicit interest rate of 7% is known to Gumo.

Instructions

(a) Identify the type of lease that is involved and give reasons for your classification. Also discuss the accounting treatment that should be applied by both the lessee and the lessor.

(b) Would the classification of the lease have been different if Synergetics and Gumo had been using ASPE?

(c) Prepare all the entries related to the lease contract and leased asset for the year 2017 for the lessee and lessor, assuming the following executory costs: insurance of $450 covering the period February 1, 2017 to January 31, 2018 and a one-year maintenance contract beginning February 1, 2017 costing $1,400. Straight-line depreciation is used for similar leased assets. The crane is expected to have a residual value of $20,000 at the end of its useful life.

(d) Identify what will be presented on the statement of financial position and statement of income of both the lessee and the lessor at December 31, 2017.

P20-7   Ramey Corporation is a diversified public company with nationwide interests in commercial real estate development, banking, copper mining, and metal fabrication. The company has offices and operating locations in major cities throughout Canada. With corporate headquarters located in a metropolitan area of a western province, company executives must travel extensively to stay connected with the various phases of operations. In order to make business travel more efficient to areas that are not adequately served by commercial airlines, corporate management is currently evaluating the feasibility of acquiring a business aircraft that can be used by Ramey executives. Proposals for either leasing or purchasing a suitable aircraft have been analyzed, and the leasing proposal was considered more desirable.

The proposed lease agreement involves a twin-engine turboprop Viking that has a fair value of $1.5 million. This plane would be leased for a period of 10 years, beginning January 1, 2017. The lease agreement is cancellable only upon accidental destruction of the plane. An annual lease payment of $170,794 is due on January 1 of each year, with the first payment to be made on January 1, 2017. Maintenance operations are strictly scheduled by the lessor, and Ramey will pay for these services directly to suppliers as they are performed. Estimated annual repair and maintenance costs are $36,900. Ramey will pay all insurance premiums, which amount to a combined total of $34,000 annually, and provide proof of coverage to the lessor. Upon expiration of the 10-year lease, Ramey can purchase the Viking for $300,000. The plane's estimated useful life is 15 years, and its value in the used plane market is estimated to be $400,000 after 10 years. The residual value will never be less than $275,000 because of the mandated engine overhauls and the maintenance prescribed by the manufacturer. If the purchase option is not exercised, possession of the plane will revert to the lessor; there is no provision for renewing the lease agreement beyond its termination on January 1, 2027.

Ramey can borrow $1.5 million under a 10-year term loan agreement at an annual interest rate of 10%. The lessor's implicit interest rate is not expressly stated in the lease agreement, but this rate appears to be approximately 6% based on 10 net rental payments of $170,794 per year and the initial fair value of $1.5 million for the plane. On January 1, 2017, the present value of all net rental payments and the purchase option of $300,000 is $1,270,064 using the 10% interest rate. The present value of all net rental payments and the $300,000 purchase option on January 1, 2017 is $1.5 million using the 6% interest rate implicit in the lease agreement.

Assume that the financial vice-president of Ramey Corporation has concluded that the lease should be set up by Ramey Corporation as a right-of-use asset and lease liability under IFRS 16.

Instructions

(a) Using tables, a financial calculator, or Excel functions, recalculate the present value of the future minimum lease payments and prove the amount arrived at by the vice-president of Ramey Corporation.

(b) Do you agree with the vice-president's conclusions and treatment for the lease? Do you believe that Ramey Corporation is very likely to purchase the Viking aircraft by paying the $300,000 purchase option on January 1, 2027?

(c) Prepare a lease amortization table for the full term of the lease. Round all amounts to the nearest dollar. (Note: You may find the =round formula helpful for rounding in Excel.)

(d) How will the lease be reported on the December 31, 2017 statement of financial position and related statement of income? (Ignore any income tax implications.)

P20-8   Your employer, Wagner Inc., is a large Canadian public company that uses IFRS 16. You have collected the following information about a lease for a fleet of trucks used by Wagner to transport completed products to warehouses across the country. The trucks have an economic life of eight years. The lease term is from July 1, 2017 to June 30, 2024, and the company intends to lease the equipment for this period of time, so the lease term is seven years. The lease payment per year is $545,000, payable in advance, with no other payments required, and no renewal option or purchase option available. The expected value of the fleet of trucks at June 30, 2024 is $450,000; this value is guaranteed by Wagner. The leased trucks must be returned to the lessor at the end of the lease. Wagner's management is confident that, with an aggressive maintenance program, Wagner has every reason to believe that the asset's residual value will be more than the guaranteed amount at the end of the lease term. Wagner's incremental borrowing rate is 8%, and the rate implicit in the lease is not known. At the time the lease was signed, the fair value of the leased trucks was $3,064,470.

Instructions

(a) Identify the type of lease that is involved and give reasons for your classification, based on the original information:

1. Using time value of money tables, a financial calculator, or Excel functions, determine the present value of the future cash flows under the lease at July 1, 2017.

2. Using Excel, prepare an amortization schedule for the lease liability over the term of the lease. Use the =round function in Excel to round all amounts to the nearest dollar.

3. Prepare the journal entries and any year-end (December 31) adjusting journal entries made by Wagner Inc. in 2017 and up to and including July 1, 2018.

(b) Immediately after the July 1, 2018 lease payments, based on the feedback of the staff in operations, management reassesses its expectations for the guaranteed residual value. Management now estimates the fleet of trucks to have a residual value of $400,000 with a 60% probability and $300,000 with a 40% probability.

1. Calculate the probability-weighted expected value of the residual at the end of the lease term. Also calculate the present value at July 1, 2018 of any additional cash flows related to the residual value guarantee.

2. Prepare any necessary entry to implement the revision to the contractual lease rights and obligation at July 1, 2018.

3. Revise the amortization schedule effective January 1, 2018 for the lease, including any liability related to the residual value guarantee.

4. Prepare the year-end adjusting journal entries made by Wagner Inc. for fiscal year 2018.

P20-9 The following facts pertain to a non-cancellable lease agreement between Woodhouse Leasing Corporation and McKee Electronics Ltd., a lessee, for a computer system:

Inception date	October 1, 2017
Lease term	6 years
Economic life of leased equipment	6 years
Fair value of asset at October 1, 2017	$150,690
Residual value at end of lease term	–0–
Lessor's implicit rate	8.5%
Lessee's incremental borrowing rate	8.5%
Annual lease payment due at the beginning of each year, beginning October 1, 2017	$ 30,500

The collectibility of the lease payments is reasonably predictable, and there are no important uncertainties about costs that have not yet been incurred by the lessor. McKee Electronics Ltd., the lessee, assumes responsibility for all repairs and maintenance costs, which amount to $2,500 per year and are to be paid each October 1, beginning October 1, 2017, by the lessee directly to the suppliers. The asset will revert to the lessor at the end of the lease term. The straight-line depreciation method is used for all equipment.

The following amortization schedule for the lease obligation has been prepared correctly for use by both the lessor and the lessee in accounting for this lease using ASPE. The lease is accounted for properly as a capital lease by the lessee and as a direct financing lease by the lessor.

Date	Annual Lease Payment/Receipt	Interest (8.5%) on Unpaid Obligation/Net Investment	Reduction of Lease Obligation/Net Investment	Balance of Lease Obligation/Net Investment
10/01/17				$150,690
10/01/17	$ 30,500	–0–	$ 30,500	120,190
10/01/18	30,500	$10,216	20,284	99,906
10/01/19	30,500	8,492	22,008	77,898
10/01/20	30,500	6,621	23,879	54,019
10/01/21	30,500	4,592	25,908	28,111
10/01/22	30,500	2,389	28,111	–0–
	$183,000	$32,310	$150,690	

Instructions

Answer the following questions, rounding all numbers to the nearest dollar.

(a) Assuming that McKee Electronics' accounting period ends on September 30, answer the following questions with respect to this lease agreement.

1. What items and amounts will appear on the lessee's income statement for the year ending September 30, 2018?

2. What items and amounts will appear on the lessee's balance sheet at September 30, 2018?

3. What items and amounts will appear on the lessee's income statement for the year ending September 30, 2019?

4. What items and amounts will appear on the lessee's balance sheet at September 30, 2019?

(b) Assuming that McKee Electronics' accounting period ends on December 31, answer the same questions as in part (a) above for the years ending December 31, 2017 and 2018.

P20-10 Assume the same information as in P20-9. Follow the instructions assuming that McKee Electronics follows IFRS 16.

P20-11 Assume the same information as in P20-9.

Instructions

Answer the following questions, rounding all numbers to the nearest dollar.

(a) Assuming that Woodhouse Leasing Corporation's accounting period ends on September 30, answer the following questions with respect to this lease agreement.

1. What items and amounts will appear on the lessor's income statement for the year ending September 30, 2018?

2. What items and amounts will appear on the lessor's balance sheet at September 30, 2018?

3. What items and amounts will appear on the lessor's income statement for the year ending September 30, 2019?

4. What items and amounts will appear on the lessor's balance sheet at September 30, 2019?

(b) Assuming that Woodhouse Leasing Corporation's accounting period ends on December 31, answer the same questions as in part (a) above for the years ending December 31, 2017 and 2018.

P20-12 At the end of the December 31, 2016 fiscal year, Yin Trucking Corporation, which follows IFRS 16, negotiated and closed a long-term lease contract for newly constructed truck terminals and freight storage facilities. The buildings were erected to the company's specifications on land owned by the company. On January 1, 2017, Yin Trucking Corporation took possession of the leased properties and made a cash payment of $1,048,000.

Although the useful life of each terminal is 40 years, the non-cancellable lease runs for 20 years from January 1, 2017, with a purchase option available upon expiration of the lease.

The 20-year lease is effective for the period January 1, 2017 through December 31, 2036. Advance rental payments of $900,000 are payable to the lessor on January 1 of each of the first 10 years of the lease term. Advance rental payments of $320,000 are due on January 1 for each of the last 10 years of the lease. The company has an option to purchase all of these leased facilities for $1 million on December 31, 2036, although their fair value at that time is estimated at $3 million. At the end of 40 years, the terminals and facilities will have no remaining value. Yin Trucking must also make annual payments on January 1 of each year to the lessor of $125,000 for property taxes and $23,000 for insurance. The lease was negotiated to assure the lessor a 6% rate of return.

Instructions

Answer the following questions, rounding all numbers to the nearest dollar.

(a) Using time value of money tables, a financial calculator, or Excel functions, calculate for Yin Trucking Corporation the amount that should be capitalized on its January 1, 2017 statement of financial position.

(b) Assuming a capitalized value of terminal facilities at January 1, 2017 of $8.7 million, prepare journal entries for Yin Trucking Corporation to record the following:

1. The signing of the lease

2. The cash payment to the lessor on January 1, 2017

3. Depreciation of the cost of the properties for 2017 using the straight-line method

4. The accrual of interest expense at December 31, 2017 and any other adjusting journal entries concerning the lease.

(c) What amounts would appear on Yin's December 31, 2017 balance sheet for the leased asset and the related liabilities under the lease arrangement described in part (b)?

(d) Repeat parts (b) and (c) assuming that Yin follows ASPE.

P20-13   Lee Industries Inc. and Lor Inc. enter into an agreement that requires Lor Inc. to build three diesel-electric engines to Lee's specifications. Both Lee and Lor follow ASPE and have calendar year ends. Upon completion of the engines, Lee has agreed to lease them for a period of 10 years and to assume all costs and risks of ownership. The lease is non-cancellable, becomes effective on January 1, 2017, and requires annual rental payments of $620,956 each January 1, starting January 1, 2017.

Lee's incremental borrowing rate is 10%, and the implicit interest rate used by Lor Inc. is 8% and is known to Lee. The total cost of manufacturing the three engines is $3.9 million. The engines' economic life is estimated to be 10 years, with residual value expected to be zero. Lee depreciates similar equipment on a straight-line basis. At the end of the lease, Lee assumes title to the engines. Collectibility of the lease payments is reasonably certain and there are no uncertainties about unreimbursable lessor costs.

Instructions

Answer the following questions, rounding all numbers to the nearest dollar.

(a) Discuss the nature of this lease transaction from the viewpoints of both the lessee (Lee Industries) and lessor (Lor Inc.).

(b) Prepare the journal entry or entries to record the transactions on January 1, 2017 on the books of Lee Industries.

(c) Prepare the journal entry or entries to record the transactions on January 1, 2017 on the books of Lor Inc.

(d) Prepare the journal entries for both the lessee and lessor to record interest expense (income) at December 31, 2017. (Prepare a lease amortization schedule for the lease obligation for two years using Excel.)

(e) Show the items and amounts that would be reported on the balance sheet (ignore the notes) at December 31, 2017 for both the lessee and the lessor.

(f) Identify how the lease transactions would be reported on each company's statement of cash flows in 2017.

(g) Provide the note disclosure concerning the lease that would be required for the lessee, Lee Industries, on its financial statements for the fiscal year ending December 31, 2017.

(h) Provide the note disclosure concerning the lease that would be required for the lessor, Lor Inc., on its financial statements for the fiscal year ending December 31, 2017.

P20-14   Dubois Steel Corporation, as lessee, signed a lease agreement for equipment for five years, beginning January 31, 2017. Annual rental payments of $41,000 are to be made at the beginning of each lease year (January 31). The insurance and repairs and maintenance costs are the lessee's obligation. The interest rate used by the lessor in setting the payment schedule is 9%; Dubois's incremental borrowing rate is 10%. Dubois is unaware of the rate being used by the lessor. At the end of the lease, Dubois has the option to buy the equipment for $4,000, which is considerably below its estimated fair value at that time. The equipment has an estimated useful life of seven years with no residual value. Dubois uses straight-line depreciation on similar equipment that it owns, and follows IFRS 16.

Instructions

(a) Follow the instructions (a) through (g) of P20-28.

(b) Using the assumptions stated under instruction (h) of P20-28, would your treatment of the lease change for financial reporting purposes?

P20-15   CHL Corporation manufactures specialty equipment with an estimated economic life of 12 years and leases it to Provincial Airlines Corp. for a period of 10 years. Both CHL and Provincial Airlines follow ASPE. The equipment's normal selling price is $210,482 and its unguaranteed residual value at the end of the lease term is estimated to be $15,000. Provincial Airlines will make annual payments of $25,000 at the beginning of each year and pay for all mainte-nance and insurance. CHL incurred costs of $105,000 in manufacturing the equipment and $7,000 in negotiating and closing the lease. CHL has determined that the collectibility of the lease payments is reasonably predictable, that no additional costs will be incurred, and that the implicit interest rate is 8%.

Instructions

Answer the following questions, rounding all numbers to the nearest dollar.

(a) Discuss the nature of this lease in relation to the lessor and calculate the amount of each of the following items:

1. Gross investment

2. Unearned interest income

3. Sale price

4. Cost of goods sold

(b) Prepare a 10-year lease amortization schedule for the lease obligation using Excel.

(c) Prepare all of the lessor's journal entries for the first year of the lease, assuming the lessor's fiscal year end is five months into the lease. Reversing entries are not used.

(d) Determine the current and non-current portions of the net investment at the lessor's fiscal year end, which is five months into the lease.

(e) Assuming that the $15,000 residual value is guaranteed by the lessee, what changes are necessary to parts (a) to (d)?

(f) Assume that, as an alternative, CHL would consider leasing the equipment for 12 years if it could recover the normal selling price of $210,482. How much would CHL charge the lessee annually for a 12-year lease? Assume the residual value at the end of 12 years would be $0, and that lease payments would be due at the start of each year.

FINANCE

*P20-16   Assume the same data as in P20-15 and that Provincial Airlines Corp. has an incremental borrowing rate of 8%.

Instructions

Answer the following questions, rounding all numbers to the nearest dollar.

(a) Discuss the nature of this lease in relation to the lessee.

(b) What classification will Provincial Airlines Corp. give to the lease?

(c) What difference, if any, would occur in the classification of the lease if Provincial were using IFRS 16?

(d) Using time value of money tables, a financial calculator, or Excel functions, calculate the amount of the initial obligation under capital leases.

(e) Prepare a 10-year lease amortization schedule for the lease obligation using Excel.

(f) Prepare all of the lessee's journal entries for the first year, assuming that the lease year and Provincial Airlines' fiscal year are the same.

(g) Prepare the entries in part (f) again, assuming that the residual value of $15,000 was guaranteed by the lessee.

(h) Prepare the entries in part (f) again, assuming a residual value at the end of the lease term of $45,000 and a purchase option of $15,000.

(i) Prepare all necessary journal entries in part (f) again, assuming Provincial Airlines Corp. followed IAS 17.

P20-17   Jennings Inc., which uses IFRS 16, manufactures an X-ray machine with an estimated life of 12 years and leases it to SNC Medical Centre for a period of 10 years. The machine's normal selling price is $343,734, and the lessee guarantees a residual value at the end of the lease term of $15,000. The medical centre will pay rent of $50,000 at the beginning of each year and all maintenance, insurance, and taxes. Jennings incurred costs of $210,000 in manufacturing the machine and $14,000 in negotiating and closing the lease. Jennings has determined that the collectibility of the lease payments is reasonably predictable, that there will be no additional costs incurred, and that its implicit interest rate is 10%.

Instructions

Answer the following questions, rounding all numbers to the nearest dollar.

(a) Using tables, a financial calculator, or Excel functions, calculate the present value of the lease payments and guaranteed residual value under the lease.

(b) Discuss the nature of this lease in relation to the lessor and calculate the amount of each of the following items:

1. Gross investment

2. Sale price

3. Unearned interest income

4. Cost of goods sold

(c) Prepare a 10-year lease amortization schedule for the lease obligation.

(d) Prepare all of the lessor's journal entries for the first year.

(e) Identify the amounts to be reported on Jennings's statement of financial position, income statement, and statement of cash flows one year after signing the lease, and discuss what should be included as required and desirable note disclosures.

(f) Assume that SNC Medical Centre's incremental borrowing rate is 12% and that the centre knows that 10% is the rate implicit in the lease. Determine the depreciation expense that SNC will recognize in the first full year that it leases the machine.

(g) Assuming instead that the residual value is not guaranteed, what changes, if any, are necessary in parts (a) to (d) for the lessor and in part (e) for the lessee?

DIGGING DEEPER

(h) Discuss how Jennings would have determined the classification of the lease if the company were using ASPE for its financial reporting.

P20-18 Lanier Dairy Ltd. leases its milk cooling equipment from Green Finance Corporation. Both companies use IFRS 16. The lease has the following terms.

1. The lease is dated May 30, 2017, with a lease term of eight years. It is non-cancellable and requires equal rental payments of $30,000 due each May 30, beginning in 2017.

2. The equipment has a fair value and cost at the inception of the lease of $211,902, an estimated economic life of 10 years, and a residual value (which is guaranteed by Lanier Dairy) of $23,000.

3. The lease contains no renewal options and the equipment reverts to Green Finance Corporation on termination of the lease.

4. Lanier Dairy's incremental borrowing rate is 6% per year; the implicit rate is also 6%.

5. Lanier Dairy uses straight-line depreciation for similar equipment that it owns.

6. Collectibility of the payments is reasonably predictable, and there are no important uncertainties about costs that have not yet been incurred by the lessor.

Instructions

(a) Describe the nature of the lease and, in general, discuss how the lessee and lessor should account for the lease transaction.

(b) Using tables, a financial calculator, or Excel functions, calculate the present value of the lease payments and guaranteed residual value under the lease.

(c) Prepare the journal entries for the lessee and lessor at May 30, 2017 and at December 31, 2017, which is the lessee's and lessor's year ends.

(d) Prepare the journal entries at May 30, 2018 for the lessee and lessor. Assume reversing entries are not used.

(e) What amount would have been capitalized by the lessee upon inception of the lease if:

   1. The residual value of $23,000 had been guaranteed by a third party, not the lessee?

   2. The residual value of $23,000 had not been guaranteed at all?

(f) On the lessor's books, what amount would be recorded as the net investment at the inception of the lease, assuming:

   1. Green Finance had incurred $1,200 of direct costs in processing the lease?

   2. The residual value of $23,000 had been guaranteed by a third party?

   3. The residual value of $23,000 had not been guaranteed at all?

(g) Assume that the milk cooling equipment's useful life is 20 years. How large would the residual value have to be at the end of eight years in order for the lessee to qualify for the operating method? Assume that the residual value would be guaranteed by a third party. (*Hint*: The lessee's annual payments will be appropriately reduced as the residual value increases.)

DIGGING DEEPER

(h) Discuss how Lanier would have determined the classification of the lease if the company were using ASPE for its financial reporting.

P20-19 Fram Fibreglass Corp. (FFC) is a private New Brunswick company, using ASPE, that manufactures a variety of fibreglass products for the fishing and food services industry. With the traditional fishery in decline over the past few years, FFC found itself in a tight financial position in early 2017. Revenues had levelled off, inventories were overstocked, and most operating costs were increasing each year.

The Royal Montreal Bank, which FFC has dealt with for 20 years, was getting anxious because FFC's loans and line of credit were at an all-time high, with the most recent loan carrying an interest rate of 15%. In fact, the bank had just recently imposed stipulations on FFC that prevented the company from paying out any dividends or increasing its debt to equity ratio above current levels without the bank's prior approval.

The vice-president of finance, Joe Blowski, CPA, knew that, with aggressive investment in new equipment, the company could go after new markets in the construction industry. He had investigated the cost of the necessary equipment and found that $50,000 of new capital investment would allow the company to get started. All it needed was the financing. Joe set up appointments with Kirk Cullen, the loans officer at the provincial Industrial Development Bank, and with Heidi Hazen, the manager of the local office of Municipal Finance Corp.

Kirk Cullen was very receptive to Joe's request. He indicated that the Industrial Development Bank would be interested in working with FFC, and could provide him with a lease on the equipment he identified. Heidi Hazen also welcomed the business, suggesting a lease arrangement between Municipal Finance Corp. and FFC as well. Two days later, Joe had proposals from both lenders on his desk.

You are an accounting major and co-op student placed with FFC for your final work term. On his way out of the office for a meeting, Joe provides you with the two proposals and asks, just before the elevator door closes, "Would you please review these and give me your analysis and recommendation on which proposal to accept, if either?" The details of the two proposals are as follows:

	Industrial Development Bank Proposal	Municipal Finance Corp. Proposal
Selling price of equipment	$50,000	$50,000
Lease term	April 23, 2017 to April 22, 2022	May 1, 2017 to April 30, 2022
Economic life of equipment	7 years	7 years
Residual value, end of lease term	$10,000	$10,000
Residual value guaranteed	no	by lessee
Annual payment	$12,000 in advance	$11,681 in advance
Executory costs	$1,020 per year included in payment	$300 per year in addition to payment
Interest rate implicit in lease	12%	unknown
Equipment returned at end of lease	yes	yes

Instructions

Prepare the required report for Joe.

P20-20 Mulholland Corp., a lessee, entered into a non-cancellable lease agreement with Galt Manufacturing Ltd., a lessor, to lease special-purpose equipment for a period of seven years. Mulholland follows IFRS 16 and Galt follows ASPE. The following information relates to the agreement:

Lease inception	May 2, 2017
Annual lease payment due at the beginning of each lease year	$?
Residual value of equipment at end of lease term, guaranteed by an independent third party	$100,000
Economic life of equipment	10 years
Usual selling price of equipment	$415,000
Manufacturing cost of equipment on lessor's books	$327,500
Lessor's implicit interest rate, known to lessee	12%
Lessee's incremental borrowing rate	12%
Repairs and maintenance per year to be paid by lessee, estimated	$ 14,500

The leased equipment reverts to Galt Manufacturing at the end of the lease, although Mulholland has an option to purchase it at its expected fair value at that time.

Instructions

(a) Using time value of money tables, a financial calculator, or Excel functions, calculate the lease payment determined by the lessor to provide a 12% return.

(b) Prepare a lease amortization schedule for Galt Manufacturing, the lessor, covering the entire term of the lease.

(c) Assuming that Galt Manufacturing has a December 31 year end, and that reversing entries are not made, prepare all entries made by the company up to and including May 2, 2019.

(d) Identify the balances and classification of amounts that Galt Manufacturing will report on its December 31, 2017 balance sheet, and the amounts on its 2018 income statement and statement of cash flows related to this lease.

(e) Determine the treatment of the lease by Mulholland. Using Excel, calculate the present value of the future cash flows under the lease.

(f) Prepare an amortization schedule for the first three payments on the lease. Round all amounts to the nearest dollar. (Note: You may find the =round formula helpful for rounding in Excel.)

(g) Assuming that Mulholland has a December 31 year end, and that reversing entries are not made, prepare all entries made by the company up to and including May 2, 2019. Assume payments of repairs and maintenance expenses of $10,000, $14,400, and $14,950 covering fiscal years 2017, 2018, and 2019, respectively.

(h) Identify the balances and classification of amounts that Mulholland will report on its December 31, 2017 statement of financial position, and the amounts on its 2017 statement of income and statement of cash flows related to this lease.

(i) On whose statement of financial position should the equipment appear? On whose statement of financial position does the equipment currently get reported?

(j) Repeat parts (e), (g), (h), and (i) under the assumption that Mulholland follows ASPE.

P20-21 Sanderson Inc., a pharmaceutical distribution firm, is providing a BMW car for its chief executive officer as part of a remuneration package. Sanderson has a calendar year end, issues financial statements annually, and follows ASPE. You have been assigned the task of calculating and reporting the financial statement effect of several options Sanderson is considering in obtaining the vehicle for its CEO.

Option 1: Obtain financing from Western Bank to finance an outright purchase of the BMW from BMW Canada, which regularly sells and leases luxury vehicles.

Option 2: Sign a lease with BMW Canada and exercise the option to renew the lease at the end of the initial term.

Option 3: Sign a lease with BMW Canada and exercise the option to purchase at the end of the lease. The amount of the option price is financed with a bank loan.

For the purpose of your comparison, you can assume a January 1, 2017 purchase and you can also exclude all amounts for any provincial sales taxes, GST, and HST on all the proposed transactions. You can also assume that Sanderson uses the straight-line method of depreciating automobiles. Assume that, for options 1 and 2, the BMW is sold on January 1, 2022 for $10,000.

Sanderson does not expect to incur any extra kilometre charges because it is likely that the BMW won't be driven that much by the CEO. However, there is a 10% chance that an extra 10,000 km will be driven and a 15% chance that an extra 20,000 km will be used.

Terms and values concerning the asset that are common to all options are the following:

Date of purchase or signing of lease	January 1, 2017
Purchase price equal to fair value at January 1, 2017	$79,000
Cost to BMW Canada	$70,000
Physical life	8 years
Useful life to Sanderson	5 years
Residual value at January 1, 2022, equal to fair value	$10,000
Fair value at January 1, 2020	$39,500

Borrowing terms with Western Bank for purchase: Option 1

Loan amount	$79,000
Fixed bank rate for loan to purchase	7%
Term of loan to purchase	5 years
Repayment terms	Quarterly instalment note
First payment due	April 1, 2017

For Option 2:
Terms, conditions, and other information related to the initial lease with BMW Canada:

Lease term	36 months
First lease payment date	January 1, 2017
Monthly lease payment	$1,392.21
Maximum number of kilometres allowed under lease	72,000
Excess kilometre charge beyond 72,000 km	25 cents
Option to purchase price at end of lease	50% of original fair value
Date of payment for option to purchase	January 1, 2020
Maintenance and insurance	paid by Sanderson
Interest rate stated in lease—annual	6%
Sanderson's incremental borrowing rate	7%

Terms, conditions, and other information related to the renewal option for lease with BMW Canada:

Renewal lease term	24 months
Renewal option first lease payment date	January 1, 2020
Monthly lease payment	$1,371.00
Maximum number of kilometres allowed under renewal lease	48,000
Excess kilometre charge beyond 48,000 km	25 cents
Option to purchase at end of renewal option	none
Maintenance and insurance	paid by Sanderson
Renewal option	none
Interest rate stated in renewal lease	7%
Sanderson's incremental borrowing rate (projected)	8%

Borrowing terms with Western Bank to exercise option to purchase: Option 3

Loan amount	$39,500
Bank rate January 1, 2020	8%
Term of loan January 1, 2020	2 years
Repayment terms	Quarterly instalment note
First payment due	April 1, 2020

FINANCE

Instructions

(a) For Option 1:

1. Using a financial calculator or Excel, calculate the quarterly blended payments that will be due to Western Bank on the instalment note.

2. Prepare an amortization schedule for the loan with Western Bank for the term of the lease.

3. Record all of the necessary transactions on January 1, 2017, the first loan payment, and for any adjusting journal entries at the end of the fiscal year 2017.

(b) For Option 2:

1. Using a financial calculator or Excel, determine how BMW Canada arrived at the amounts of the monthly payment for the original lease and for the lease renewal option, allowing it to recover its investment.

2. Assume that the original lease is signed and Sanderson Inc. has no intention of exercising the lease renewal. Determine the classification of the three-year lease for Sanderson Inc.

3. Assume that Sanderson fully intends to exercise the renewal option offered by BMW Canada. Determine the classification of the lease for Sanderson Inc.

4. Prepare a lease amortization schedule for the term of the lease for Sanderson Inc.

5. Record all of the necessary transactions on January 1, 2017 for the first two lease payments and for any adjusting journal entries at the end of the fiscal year 2017 for Sanderson Inc.

(c) For Option 3:

1. Determine the classification of the lease for Sanderson Inc.

2. Record all of the necessary transactions concerning the lease on January 1, 2017 and for any adjusting journal entries at the end of the fiscal year ending December 31, 2017.

3. Using a financial calculator or Excel functions, calculate the quarterly blended payments that will be due to Western Bank on the instalment note used to finance the purchase.

4. Prepare an amortization schedule for the loan with Western Bank.

5. Record all of the necessary transactions concerning exercising the option to purchase on January 1, 2020, the signing of the instalment note payable to the bank, the first loan payment, and any adjusting journal entries at the end of the fiscal year ending December 31, 2020.

(d) Use IFRS 16 and assume the information in Option 2. Update, if necessary, and reproduce the amortization schedule needed under this approach for the first 13 payments of the lease. Prepare the journal entries on January 1 and February 1, 2017, and for any adjusting journal entries at the end of the fiscal year ending December 31, 2017.

(e) Assume that the amount paid by Sanderson on July 1, 2020 equals the amount calculated based on probability weighting for the excess charge for kilometres driven. How would you account for the penalty Sanderson expects to pay?

(f) Prepare a table of the financial statement results from the above three options and the IFRS 16 approach of part (d). Your table should clearly show all of the classifications and amounts for the statement of financial position at December 31, 2017, and the income statement for the 2017 fiscal year.

(g) Calculate the amount of the expense for the BMW for the total five-year period based on each of the three assumptions, as well as under the IFRS 16 approach assuming that Sanderson follows Option 2. Include any penalty payment for excess kilometres driven for Option 2.

(h) Based on the results obtained in part (g), provide Sanderson with additional considerations that should be taken into account before making a choice between the different options.

DIGGING DEEPER

P20-22 Use the information for P20-21.

Instructions

Under Option 2:

(a) Assume that at the signing of the original lease, Sanderson Inc. has no intention of exercising the lease renewal. Determine the classification of the three-year lease for BMW Canada, which follows IFRS 16.

(b) Prepare the journal entry to show how BMW Canada records the collection of the first lease payment on January 1, 2017.

(c) Assume now that Sanderson Inc. signs the renewal option at the same time that it enters into the original lease agreement.

1. Prepare a lease amortization schedule including the renewal period for BMW Canada.

2. Determine the classification of the lease for BMW Canada.

3. Record all of the necessary transactions on January 1, 2017 for the first two lease payments collected and for any adjusting journal entries at the end of the fiscal year ending December 31, 2017 for BMW Canada.

*P20-23 The head office of North Central Ltd. has operated in the western provinces for almost 50 years. North Central uses ASPE. In 2001, new offices were constructed on the same site at a cost of $9.5 million. The new building was opened on January 4, 2002, and was expected to be used for 35 years, at which time it would have a value of approximately $2 million.

In 2017, as competitors began to consider merger strategies among themselves, North Central felt that the time was right to expand the number of its offices throughout the region. This plan required significant financing and, as a source of cash, North Central looked into selling the building that housed its head office. On June 29, 2017, Rural Life Insurance Ltd. purchased the building (but not the land) for $8 million and immediately entered into a 20-year lease with North Central to lease back the occupied space. The terms of the lease were as follows.

1. It is non-cancellable, with an option to purchase the building at the end of the lease for $1 million.

2. The annual rental is $838,380, payable on June 29 each year, beginning on June 29, 2017.

3. Rural Life expects to earn a return of 10% on its net investment in the lease, the same as North Central's incremental borrowing rate.

4. North Central is responsible for maintenance, insurance, and property taxes.

5. Estimates of useful life and residual value have not changed significantly since 2001. Straight-line depreciation is used by North Central.

Instructions

(a) Using time value of money tables, a financial calculator, or Excel functions, calculate the lease payment that Rural Life would require from North Central. Use Excel and prepare a lease amortization schedule for the first two payments. Round all amounts to the nearest dollar. (Note: You may find the =round formula helpful for rounding in Excel.)

(b) Prepare all entries for North Central Ltd. from June 29, 2017 to December 31, 2018. North Central has a calendar year fiscal period.

(c) Assume instead that there was no option to purchase, that $8 million represents the building's fair value on June 29, 2017, and that the lease term was 12 years. Prepare all entries for North Central from June 29, 2017 to December 31, 2018.

(d) Besides the increase in cash that it needs from the sale of the building, what effect should North Central expect to see on the net assets appearing on its statement of financial position immediately after the sale and leaseback?

*P20-24   On October 30, 2017, Truttman Corp. sold a five-year-old building with a carrying value of $10 million at its fair value of $13 million and leased it back. There was a gain on the sale. Truttman pays all insurance, maintenance, and taxes on the building. The lease provides for 20 equal annual payments, beginning October 30, 2017, with a present value equal to 85% of the building's fair value and sales price. The lease's term is equal to 73% of the building's useful life. There is no provision for Truttman to reacquire ownership of the building at the end of the lease term. Truttman has a December 31 year end.

Instructions

(a) Why would Truttman have entered into such an agreement?

(b) In reaching a decision on how to classify a lease, why is it important to compare the building's fair value with the present value of the lease payments, and its useful life with the lease term? What does this information tell you under ASPE and IFRS 16?

(c) Assuming that Truttman would classify this as an operating lease, determine how the initial sale and the sale-leaseback transaction would be reported under ASPE for the 2017 year. What would be the implications if the selling price had been $14 million, $1 million greater than the fair value of the building?

(d) Assuming that Truttman would classify this as a capital lease, determine how the initial sale and the sale-leaseback transaction would be reported under ASPE for the 2017 year.

*P20-25   Refer to the information in P20-3. Follow the instructions under the assumption that Hunter Ltd. follows IAS 17.

*P20-26   Refer to the information in P20-4. Follow the instructions under the assumption that Situ Ltd. follows IAS 17.

*P20-27   Ramey Corporation is a diversified public company with nationwide interests in commercial real estate development, banking, copper mining, and metal fabrication. The company has offices and operating locations in major cities throughout Canada. With corporate headquarters located in a metropolitan area of a western province, company executives must travel extensively to stay connected with the various phases of operations. In order to make business travel more efficient to areas that are not adequately served by commercial airlines, corporate management is currently evaluating the feasibility of acquiring a business aircraft that can be used by Ramey executives. Proposals for either leasing or purchasing a suitable aircraft have been analyzed, and the leasing proposal was considered more desirable.

The proposed lease agreement involves a twin-engine turboprop Viking that has a fair value of $1.5 million. This plane would be leased for a period of 10 years, beginning January 1, 2017. The lease agreement is cancellable only upon accidental destruction of the plane. An annual lease payment of $170,794 is due on January 1 of each year, with the first payment to be made on January 1, 2017. Maintenance operations are strictly scheduled by the lessor, and Ramey will pay for these services directly to suppliers as they are performed. Estimated annual repair and maintenance costs are

$36,900. Ramey will pay all insurance premiums, which amount to a combined total of $34,000 annually, and provide proof of coverage to the lessor. Upon expiration of the 10-year lease, Ramey can purchase the Viking for $300,000. The plane's estimated useful life is 15 years, and its value in the used plane market is estimated to be $400,000 after 10 years. The residual value will never be less than $275,000 because of the mandated engine overhauls and the maintenance prescribed by the manufacturer. If the purchase option is not exercised, possession of the plane will revert to the lessor; there is no provision for renewing the lease agreement beyond its termination on January 1, 2027.

Ramey can borrow $1.5 million under a 10-year term loan agreement at an annual interest rate of 10%. The lessor's implicit interest rate is not expressly stated in the lease agreement, but this rate appears to be approximately 6% based on 10 net rental payments of $170,794 per year and the initial fair value of $1.5 million for the plane. On January 1, 2017, the present value of all net rental payments and the purchase option of $300,000 is $1,270,064 using the 10% interest rate. The present value of all net rental payments and the $300,000 purchase option on January 1, 2017 is $1.5 million using the 6% interest rate implicit in the lease agreement. The financial vice-president of Ramey Corporation has established that this lease agreement is a financing lease as defined by the IAS 17 standards followed by Ramey.

Instructions

(a) Using tables, a financial calculator, or Excel functions, recalculate the present value of the future minimum lease payments and prove the amount arrived at by the vice-president of Ramey Corporation.

(b) IAS 17 indicates that the crucial accounting issue is whether the risks and benefits of ownership are transferred from one party to the other, regardless of whether ownership is transferred.

  1. What is meant by "the risks and benefits of ownership" and what factors are general indicators of such a transfer?

  2. Would there be a difference in the determination made by the vice-president had Ramey been following ASPE?

(c) Have the risks and benefits of ownership been transferred in the lease described above? What evidence is there?

(d) Prepare a lease amortization table for the full term of the lease. Round all amounts to the nearest dollar. (Note: You may find the =round formula helpful for rounding in Excel.)

(e) What is the appropriate amount for Ramey Corporation to recognize for the leased aircraft on its statement of financial position after the lease is signed?

(f) How will the lease be reported on the December 31, 2017 statement of financial position and related statement of income? (Ignore any income tax implications.)

*P20-28 Dubois Steel Corporation, as lessee, signed a lease agreement for equipment for five years, beginning January 31, 2017. Annual rental payments of $41,000 are to be made at the beginning of each lease year (January 31). The insurance and repairs and maintenance costs are the lessee's obligation. The interest rate used by the lessor in setting the payment schedule is 9%; Dubois's incremental borrowing rate is 10%. Dubois is unaware of the rate being used by the lessor. At the end of the lease, Dubois has the option to buy the equipment for $4,000, which is considerably below its estimated fair value at that time. The equipment has an estimated useful life of seven years with no residual value. Dubois uses straight-line depreciation on similar equipment that it owns, and follows IAS 17.

Instructions

Answer the following questions, rounding all numbers to the nearest dollar.

(a) Using time value of money tables, a financial calculator, or Excel functions, calculate the present value of the lease obligation.

(b) Prepare the lease amortization schedule for the lease. Round all amounts to the nearest dollar. (Note: You may find the =round formula helpful for rounding in Excel.)

(c) Prepare the journal entry or entries that should be recorded on January 31, 2017 by Dubois.

(d) Prepare any necessary adjusting journal entries at December 31, 2017 and the journal entry or entries that should be recorded on January 31, 2018 by Dubois. Dubois does not use reversing entries.

(e) Prepare any necessary adjusting journal entries at December 31, 2018 and the journal entry or entries that should be recorded on January 31, 2019 by Dubois.

(f) What amounts would appear on Dubois's December 31, 2018 statement of financial position relative to the lease arrangement?

(g) What amounts would appear on Dubois's statement of cash flows for 2017 relative to the lease arrangement? Provide the classification of the amounts reported.

(h) Assume that the leased equipment had a fair value of $200,000 at the inception of the lease, and that no bargain purchase option is available at the end of the lease. Determine what amounts would appear on Dubois's December 31, 2018 statement of financial position and what amounts would appear on the 2018 statement of cash flows relative to the leasing arrangements.

Cases

Refer to the Case Primer on the Student Website and in *WileyPLUS* to help you answer these cases.

CA20-1   Crown Inc. (CI) is a private company that manufactures a special type of cap that fits on a bottle. At present, it is the only manufacturer of this cap and therefore enjoys market security. The machinery that makes the cap has been in use for 20 years and is due for replacement. CI has the option of buying the machine or leasing it. Currently, CI is leaning toward leasing the machine since it is expensive to buy and CI would have to borrow money from the bank. The company's debt to equity ratio is currently marginal, and if the funds were borrowed, the debt to equity ratio would surely worsen. CI's top management is anxious to maintain the ratio at its present level.

The dilemma for CI is that, if it leases the machine, it may have to set up a long-term obligation under the lease and this would also affect the debt to equity ratio. Since this is clearly unacceptable, CI decided to see if the leasing company, Anchor Limited, could do anything to help with the situation. After much negotiation, the following terms were agreed upon and written into the lease agreement.

1. Anchor Limited would manufacture and lease to CI a unique machine for making caps.
2. The lease would be for a period of 12 years.
3. The lease payments of $150,000 would be paid at the end of each year.
4. CI would have the option to purchase the machine for $850,000 at the end of the lease term, which is equal to the expected fair market value at that time; otherwise, the machine would be returned to the lessor.
5. CI also has the option to lease the machine for another eight years beyond the orginal lease period at $150,000 per year.
6. The rate that is implicit in the lease is 9%.

The new machine is expected to last 20 years. Since it is a unique machine, Anchor Limited has no other use for it if CI does not either purchase it at the end of the lease or renew the lease. If CI had purchased the asset, it would have cost $1.9 million. Although it was purposefully omitted from the written lease agreement, there was an understanding that CI would either renew the lease or exercise the purchase option.

Instructions

Assume the role of CI's auditors and discuss the nature of the lease, noting how it should be accounted for. The company controller has confided in you that the machine will likely be purchased at the end of the lease. Assume that you are aware of top management's position on adding debt to the balance sheet. Management has also asked you to compare the accounting under ASPE and IFRS.

CA20-2   Kelly's Shoes Limited used to be a major store in Canada before it went bankrupt and was bought by Bears Shoes Limited. Many of the stores were anchor tenants in medium- to large-sized retail shopping malls. This space was primarily leased under non-cancellable real estate leases as disclosed in note 16 to the consolidated financial statements. Aggregate commitments under both capital and operating leases amounted to over $1.3 million.

As part of Kelly's restructuring and downsizing plans before its bankruptcy, the company announced at the beginning of the year that it planned to close 31 of its 85 stores by June 30. Subsequently, it announced that it might keep certain stores open until February in the following year if the landlords were prepared to provide an appropriate level of financial support. Kelly's also announced that landlords who allowed the stores to close June 30 (the earlier date) would be given a bonus of three months of rent.

Instructions

Assume the role of Kelly's management and discuss the financial reporting issues that the company had to deal with before its bankruptcy. Discuss any differences between IFRS and ASPE.

RESEARCH AND ANALYSIS

RA20-1   Loblaw Companies Limited

Access the annual financial statements, including the accompanying notes, of **Loblaw Companies Limited** for its 52 weeks ended January 2, 2016. These can be found on SEDAR (www.sedar.com) or the company's website. Review the principal statements and the notes for all disclosures associated with leases.

Instructions

(a) Does Loblaw refer to the new lease standard, IFRS 16? If so, what disclosures are made relative to it?

FINANCE

(b) Is Loblaw a lessee or a lessor, or both? What types of assets does the company lease, and what categories or classifications of leases are reported? Identify all accounts on the consolidated balance sheets and the consolidated statement of earnings, along with their dollar amounts, that relate to any lease agreements that the company is a party to.

(c) Identify the line account(s) on the consolidated statements of cash flows where the cash lease payments are reported. Explain your answer.

(d) Calculate Loblaw's return on total assets and total debt to equity ratios for 2015.

(e) With the potential adoption of the new *Leases* standard, IFRS 16, would you expect there to be much of an effect on Loblaw's financial statements? If so, what would the impact be? Attempt to determine the financial effect of any change, assuming a capitalization/discount rate of 4% semi-annually, with lease payments being made at the end of each six-month period (and stating your other assumptions, if any). Compare your results with the ratios calculated above for the company's 52 weeks ending January 2, 2016, and briefly comment.

RA20-2 Canadian National Railway Company and Canadian Pacific Railway Limited

REAL WORLD EMPHASIS

FINANCE

The accounting for operating leases has been a controversial issue. Many observers argue that firms that use operating leases are using significantly more assets and are more highly leveraged than their financial statements indicate. As a result, analysts often use footnote disclosures to reconstruct and then capitalize operating lease obligations. One way to do this is to increase a firm's assets and liabilities by the present value of all of its future minimum operating lease rental payments.

Instructions

Go to the SEDAR website (www.sedar.com) or the websites of the companies and access the financial statements of **Canadian National Railway Company** (CNR) and **Canadian Pacific Railway Limited** (CPR) for their years ended December 31, 2015. Note that both companies' financial statements are prepared in accordance with U.S. GAAP, which is very similar to current ASPE standards. Refer to the financial statements and notes to the financial statements and answer the following questions.

(a) Identify all lease arrangements that are indicated in each company's financial statements and notes. For each lease arrangement, give the title and balances of the related lease accounts that are included in the financial statements.

(b) What are the terms of these leases?

(c) What amount did each company report as its future minimum annual rental commitments under capital leases? Under operating leases? Are there significant differences between the two companies and the way they provide for their physical operating capacity, or are they basically similar?

(d) Calculate the debt to total assets ratio for each company at December 31, 2015.

(e) If provisions similar to IFRS 16 were adopted by both companies effective December 31, 2015, what would the effect be on the companies' debt to total assets ratios? Where necessary, estimate the impact on the statement of financial position assuming 6% is the borrowing rate implied in the leases and end-of-year cash flows. What information is missing from the companies' notes to make a more accurate calculation of the effect of adopting this approach?

(f) Recalculate the ratios in part (e), incorporating the adjustments made in part (f) . Comment on your results.

(g) What do you believe are the advantages of adopting the contract-based approach of IFRS 16 *Leases* when trying to compare companies? Relate your discussion to your analysis above for CNR and CPR.

RA20-3 Chorus Aviation Inc.

REAL WORLD EMPHASIS

FINANCE

Chorus Aviation Inc. is a Canadian aviation holding company that provides, through Jazz Aviation LP, a "significant part of Air Canada's domestic and transborder network." Chorus indicates in Note 1 to its financial statements that it is both economically and commercially dependent on Air Canada and one of its subsidiaries. Part of this dependency relates to the fact that Air Canada is responsible for almost all of Chorus's revenue and for purchasing most of Chorus's (and Jazz's) fleet capacity. Chorus Aviation's shares trade on the Toronto Stock Exchange.

Through SEDAR (www.sedar.com) or the company's website, access the financial statements of Chorus Aviation Inc. for its year ended December 31, 2015. Refer to the financial statements (including the notes to the financial statements) and answer the following questions.

Instructions

(a) Identify all lease arrangements that are indicated in the company's financial statements, including the notes. Indicate, and briefly explain, any balances related to these leases that are reported on the income statement and statement of financial position.

(b) Calculate the following ratios for Chorus Aviation based on the 2015 published financial statements:

  1. Debt to total assets ratio

  2. Capital asset turnover ratio

  3. Asset turnover ratio

  4. Rate of return on assets

(c) Assume that the company adopted the contract-based approach as set out in IFRS 16 on December 31, 2015. Assuming an interest rate of 6% and that lease payments are made at the end of each year, estimate the impact of the adoption on the statement of financial position. Also, estimate the effect on the 2015 income statement. List any additional assumptions that you make.

(d) Using your estimate of the amount to capitalize for Chorus Aviation, recalculate the debt to total assets and total asset turnover ratios in part (b) above. Compare the recalculated ratios with the original results and comment on the differences.

(e) IFRS requires companies to provide certain information about their capital management objectives, strategies, and compliance with covenants related to their capital, among others. Locate Chorus Aviation's capital management note to its financial statements. Does management include operating leases in what it manages as its capital? (See Chorus Aviation's "Note 4—Capital Management.") Comment on your findings.

RA20-4   Automobile Leases

Instructions

REAL WORLD EMPHASIS

Contact an automobile dealership and find out the full out-of-pocket cost of purchasing a specific model of car if you were to pay cash for it. Also find out the details of the costs that are associated with leasing the same model car. Answer the following questions.

(a) What terms and conditions are associated with the lease? In other words, specify the lease term, residual values, and whether they are guaranteed by the lessee or not, the lessor's implicit interest rate, any purchase options, and so on.

(b) What cash flows are associated with the lease?

(c) Which do you think is the better deal: purchase outright or lease? Briefly explain.

RA20-5   ASPE versus IFRS and Leases

FINANCE

Sporon Corp. is a fast-growing Canadian private company involved in the manufacturing, distribution, and retail of specially designed yoga and leisure wear. Sporon has recently signed 10 leases for new retail locations and is looking to sign about 30 more over the next year as the company expands its retail outlets. All of these leases are for five years with a renewal option for five more years. All of the leases also have a contingent rent that is based on a percentage of the excess of annual sales in each location over a certain amount. The threshold and the percentage vary between locations. The contingent rent is payable annually on the anniversary date of the lease. The company has currently assessed these to be

operating leases, as they have no conditions that meet the capitalization criteria under ASPE. All of the payments on these leases are expensed as incurred.

The company has also moved into a new state-of-the-art manufacturing and office facility designed specifically for its needs, and signed a 20-year lease with PPS Pension Inc., the owner. Because this building lease also does not meet any of the criteria for a capital lease under ASPE, Sporon accounts for this lease as an operating lease. As a result, it expenses both the monthly rental and the annual payment that it agreed on with PPS to cover property tax increases above the 2016 base property tax cost. The tax increase amount is determined by PPS and is payable by September 30 each year.

The small group of individuals who own the company are very interested in Sporon's annual financial statements because they expect, if all goes well, to take the company public in 2018. For this and other reasons, Sporon's chief financial officer, Louise Bren, has been debating whether or not to continue with ASPE or adopt IFRS for the 2017 fiscal year.

It is now early 2017, and Louise has been following the changes required in IFRS 16.

Instructions

(a) Explain to Louise Bren to what extent, if any, adjustments may be needed to Sporon's financial statements for the leases described above, based on existing ASPE and international accounting standards (IFRS 16).

(b) Prepare a short report for the CFO that explains the conceptual basis for the IFRS 16 approach and that identifies how Sporon Corp.'s statement of financial position, statement of comprehensive income, and statement of cash flows will likely differ under revised leasing standards based on this approach.

(c) Prepare a short, but informative, appendix to your report in part (b) that addresses how applying such a revised standard might affect a financial analyst's basic ratio analysis of Sporon Corp.'s profitability (profit margin, return on assets, return on equity); risk (debt to equity, times interest earned); and solvency (operating cash flows to total debt).

ENDNOTES

[1] Asset-based financing is the financing of equipment through a secured loan, conditional sales contract, or lease.

[2] Hans Hoogervoorst, "Accounting Harmonisation and Global Economic Consequences," public lecture at the London School of Economics, November 6, 2012, available at www.ifrs.org/Alerts/Conference/Documents/HH-LSE-November-2012.pdf.

[3] As shown in this chapter, some lease arrangements are not capitalized on the balance sheet, particularly under ASPE and IAS 17. This keeps the liabilities section free from large commitments that, if recorded, would have a negative effect on the debt to equity ratio. The reluctance to record lease obligations as liabilities is one of the main reasons that some companies resist capitalized lease accounting, which led to the introduction of revised rules under IFRS 16.

[4] The property rights approach was originally recommended in *Accounting Research Study No. 4* (New York: AICPA, 1964), pp. 10–11. In the 1990s, this view received additional support. See Warren McGregor, "Accounting for Leases: A New Approach," Special Report (Norwalk, Conn.: FASB, 1996).

[5] "IASB Shines Light on Leases by Bringing Them onto the Balance Sheet," IASB news release, January 13, 2016.

[6] IASB, Snapshot: *Leases—Preliminary Views* (of Discussion paper DP/2009/1), March 2009, page 4. Copyright © International Financial Reporting Standards Foundation. All rights reserved. Reproduced by John Wiley & Sons Canada, Ltd. with the permission of the International Financial Reporting Standards Foundation ®. Reproduction and use rights are strictly limited. No permission granted to third parties to reproduce or distribute.

[7] The illustrative examples used in Illustrations 20-3 and 20-4 are from IASB, Illustrative Examples International Financial Reporting Standard ® IFRS 16 Leases. Copyright © International Financial Reporting Standards Foundation. All rights reserved. Reproduced by John Wiley & Sons Canada, Ltd. with the permission of the International Financial Reporting Standards Foundation ®. Reproduction and use rights are strictly limited. No permission granted to third parties to reproduce or distribute.

[8] IFRS 16 *Leases* Appendix A Defined Terms requires the **interest rate implicit in the lease** to be the rate that equates the inflows with the fair value of the leased asset **plus any initial direct costs of the lessor**. Copyright © International Financial Reporting Standards Foundation. All rights reserved. Reproduced by John Wiley & Sons Canada, Ltd. with the permission of the International Financial Reporting Standards Foundation ®. Reproduction and use rights are strictly limited. No permission granted to third parties to reproduce or distribute.

[9] IFRS 16 *Leases* uses this as a secondary definition. It prefers **interest rate implicit in the lease** if it can be readily determined.

[10] In lease-versus-buy decisions and in determining the lessor's implicit rate, income tax effects must be factored in. A major variable is whether the Canada Revenue Agency requires the lease to be accounted for as a conditional sale: this is usually established based on whether the title is transferred by the end of the lease term or the lessee has a bargain purchase option. Tax shields that relate to the rental payment and capital cost allowance significantly affect the return and an investment's net present value.

[11] Alternatively, use Excel or another spreadsheet program to calculate the required payments. With Excel, use the following series of keystrokes: FORMULAS/INSERTFUNCTION/PMT. Fill in the variables that you are prompted to enter. See Chapter 3 for a review of alternative calculation techniques.

[12] Other measurement models may also be used if, for example, the lessee applies the fair value model for investment property under IAS 40, or if it applies the revaluation model for its right-of-use assets that are in a class of property, plant, and equipment that is accounted for using the revaluation model of IAS 16. See IFRS 16.34-.35 for details.

[13] If the carrying amount is reduced to zero and there is a further reduction relating to the remeasurement of the lease liability, the remaining remeasurement would be charged to income or loss.

[14] An exception to measuring the leased asset at amortized cost is made when a lessee leases investment property under a finance lease. In such a case, the investment property may be accounted for at fair value under IAS 40 *Investment Property*. Similarly, if the right-of-use assets are revalued, gains and losses on revaluation would be recognized in accordance with IAS 38 *Intangible Assets*.

[15] Alternatively, using Excel or another spreadsheet program, enter the following series of keystrokes: FORMULAS/INSERTFUNCTION/PV. Fill in the required variables that the program asks for. Note that the interest rate must be provided with the % sign or be in decimal form. See Chapter 3 for a review of alternative calculation techniques.

[16] If Lessee Corporation had an incremental borrowing rate of 9% (lower than the 10% rate used by Lessor Corporation) or it did not know the rate used by Lessor, the present value calculation yields a capitalized amount of $101,675.35 ($23,981.62 × 4.23972). Because this amount exceeds the asset's fair value, Lessee Corporation capitalizes the $100,000 and uses 10% as its effective rate for amortization of the lease obligation.

[17] This is a task well suited for Excel or another spreadsheet program. Set up the schedule headings, and use formulas to perform the calculations for you.

[18] When the lease term and the economic life are not the same, the asset's residual value at the end of the lease and at the end of its useful life will differ. The residual value at the end of an asset's economic life is sometimes referred to as salvage value, and it is generally a small amount.

[19] Technically, the rate of return that is demanded by the lessor would differ depending on whether the residual value was guaranteed or unguaranteed. To simplify the illustrations, we ignore this difference in this chapter.

[20] Under IAS 40 *Investment Property*, a lessee is able to classify a property interest under an operating lease as an investment property. If this option is taken, the investment property must be accounted for under the fair value model. There is no corresponding ASPE concept.

[21] One study indicates that management's behaviour did change as a result of the profession's requirements to capitalize certain leases. Many companies restructured their leases to avoid capitalization; others increased their purchases of assets instead of leasing; and others, faced with capitalization, postponed their debt offerings or issued shares instead. It is interesting to note that the study found no significant effect on share or bond prices as a result of capitalization of leases. A. Rashad Abdel-khalik, "The Economic Effects on Lessees of *FASB Statement No. 13*, Accounting for Leases," Research Report (Stamford, Conn.: FASB, 1981).

[22] The rent is now calculated as $100,000 = 3.79079 × $26,379.73. The denominator is the factor for $n = 5$ and $i = 10\%$ for an ordinary annuity (Table A-4).

[23] Under IFRS, a lessor that is not a manufacturer or dealer also includes any initial direct costs associated with negotiating and arranging the lease. In this example, these costs are $0.

[24] The lessor usually finances the purchase of this asset over a term that generally coincides with the term of the lease. Because the lessor's cost of capital is lower than the rate that is implicit in the lease, the lessor earns a profit represented by the interest spread.

[25] While lessees may record and report the lease obligation on a net basis, lessors tend to recognize the gross amount in receivables. Unlike the lessee, lessors may have hundreds or thousands of lease contracts to administer and the amounts to be collected are the gross receivables. Therefore, for administrative simplicity, the amounts that are received are a direct reduction of the receivable, and the interest is determined and adjusted for separately.

[26] Technically, the rate of return that is demanded by the lessor would differ depending on whether the residual value was guaranteed or unguaranteed. To simplify the illustrations, we ignore this difference in the chapter.

[27] *Financial Reporting in Canada—2008* (CICA, 2008) reports that out of 200 companies surveyed, 27 companies provided disclosure related to current or prior years' sale-leaseback transactions.

[28] The sale-leaseback example is based on an illustrative example provided in IASB, Illustrative Examples International Financial Reporting Standard ® IFRS 16 Leases. Copyright © International Financial Reporting Standards Foundation. All rights reserved. Reproduced by John Wiley & Sons Canada, Ltd. with the permission of the International Financial Reporting Standards Foundation ®. Reproduction and use rights are strictly limited. No permission granted to third parties to reproduce or distribute.

[29] Allocating based on the value of leasehold interests is not the same thing as based on relative fair values of the underlying assets. Because the land will revert to the lessor and maintain its value, unlike the building, the rental payments charged for the land will not be based on recovering its full fair value.

REFERENCE TO THE
CPA COMPETENCY MAP

LEARNING OBJECTIVES

After studying this chapter, you should be able to:

1.1.1, 1.2.1, 1.2.2	**1.** Identify and differentiate among the types of accounting changes.
1.2.1, 1.2.2	**2.** Identify and explain alternative methods of accounting for accounting changes.
1.2.1, 1.2.2, 1.3.1, 1.3.2	**3.** Identify the accounting standards for each type of accounting change under IFRS and ASPE.
1.2.1, 1.2.2, 1.3.1, 1.3.2, 6.1.2	**4.** Apply the retrospective application method of accounting for a change in accounting policy and identify the disclosure requirements.
1.2.1, 1.2.2, 1.3.1, 1.3.2, 6.1.2	**5.** Apply retrospective restatement for the correction of an accounting error and identify the disclosure requirements.
1.2.1, 1.2.2, 1.3.1, 1.3.2, 3.3.1	**6.** Apply the prospective application method for an accounting change and identify the disclosure requirements for a change in an accounting estimate.
1.4.1, 1.4.2, 1.4.3, 1.4.4, 5.2.4	**7.** Identify economic motives for changing accounting methods and interpret financial statements where there have been retrospective changes to previously reported results.
1.1.4	**8.** Identify the differences between IFRS and ASPE related to accounting changes.

After studying Appendix 21A, you should be able to:

1.2.1, 1.2.2, 1.3.1	**9.** Correct the effects of errors and prepare restated financial statements.

ENGINEERING CHANGES TO ACCOUNTING POLICIES

SEVERAL FACTORS CAN cause a business to change its accounting policies, including mandatory changes to accounting standards and voluntary changes made due to economic factors. Another factor is the acquisition of a business. That was the case for Montreal-based SNC-Lavalin, one of the leading engineering and construction groups in the world. In August 2014, it acquired Kentz Corporation Limited, a leading global engineering firm providing engineering, construction, and technical support services to the oil and gas industry, for $2.1 billion (100% of the voting shares of Kentz). The combined company has 44,500 employees in offices in more than 50 countries, with about $10 billion in annual revenues. Following the acquisition, SNC-Lavalin adopted two new accounting policies applicable to the inventories and intangible assets of Kentz.

Like all public companies, SNC-Lavalin discloses its significant accounting policies in a note to its financial statements. In its financial statements for 2014, the year of the Kentz acquisition, the note on inventories states, "Inventories are stated at the lower of cost and net realisable value. Costs

of inventories are determined: i) by using specific identification of the individual costs; or ii) on a weighted average cost basis. Net realisable value represents the estimated selling price for

© istockphoto.com/Cristian Baitg

inventories less all estimated costs of completion and costs necessary to make the sale." The company recognized the cost of inventories sold of Kentz from the date of acquisition to the end of 2014 to be an expense of $123.7 million. The 2013 financial statements did not have a note on the company's inventory valuation policy. That year, the company had no business acquisitions.

In SNC-Lavalin's 2014 annual report, the note on intangible assets other than goodwill refers to the Kentz acquisition. "Intangible assets acquired in a business combination and recognized separately from goodwill are initially recognized at their fair value at the acquisition date (which is regarded as their cost). Subsequent to initial recognition, intangible assets acquired in a business combination are reported at cost less accumulated amortization and accumulated impairment losses, on the same basis as intangible assets that are acquired separately." SNC-Lavalin stated that the intangible assets with a definite useful life acquired in the Kentz purchase are mainly a revenue backlog (amortized over 0.5 to 3.5 years), customer relationships (seven years), and trademarks (five years)—all of which are amortized on a straight-line basis.

Sources: Julien Arsenault, The Canadian Press, "SNC-Lavalin to Acquire Kentz Corp. Ltd. for $2.1B," CTVNews.ca, June 23, 2014; "SNC-Lavalin Completes Landmark Acquisition of Kentz," SNC-Lavalin news release, August 22, 2014; SNC-Lavalin 2013 and 2014 annual reports.

PREVIEW OF CHAPTER 21

When new standards are adopted and when accounting errors are uncovered and changes in accounting estimates are made, companies must follow specific accounting and reporting requirements. To ensure comparability, standard setters have standardized how accounting changes, error corrections, and related earnings per share information are accounted for and reported. In this chapter, we discuss these reporting standards, which help investors better understand a company's financial condition and performance. In the appendix, we look at how to analyze and correct the accounts when there have been numerous errors.

The chapter is organized as follows:

ACCOUNTING CHANGES AND ERROR ANALYSIS			
Changes in Accounting Policies and Estimates, and Errors	**Analysis**	**IFRS/ASPE Comparison**	**Appendix 21A— Error Analysis**
▪ Types of accounting changes ▪ Alternative accounting methods ▪ Accounting standards ▪ Retrospective application— change in accounting policy ▪ Retrospective restatement— correction of an error ▪ Prospective application	▪ Motivations for change ▪ Interpreting accounting changes	▪ A comparison of IFRS and ASPE ▪ Looking ahead	▪ Statement of financial position errors ▪ Income statement errors ▪ Statement of financial position and income statement errors ▪ Comprehensive illustration: numerous errors ▪ Preparation of comparative financial statements

CHANGES IN ACCOUNTING POLICIES AND ESTIMATES, AND ERRORS

Financial press readers regularly see headlines about companies that report accounting changes and related events. Why do these accounting changes occur?

First, the accounting profession may mandate new accounting methods or standards. In addition to the major changes that Canadian companies underwent when they adopted either IFRS or ASPE in 2011, specific standards change from time to time. For example, revisions were made to the standards relating to revenues in 2014 (effective 2018), and the

IASB issued a revised standard on leases in early 2016 (effective 2019). Second, changing economic conditions may cause a company to revise its methods of accounting. Third, changes in technology and in operations may require a company to revise estimates of the service lives, depreciation pattern, or expected residual value of depreciable assets. Lastly, corrections are needed when accounting errors are discovered. How should these changes be accounted for and disclosed so that the financial information's usefulness is maintained?

Before the existence of a standard for accounting changes, companies had considerable flexibility and were able to use alternative accounting treatments for what were basically equivalent situations. The overall objectives of accounting and disclosure standards for accounting changes, therefore, are to limit the types of changes permitted, standardize the reporting for each type of change, and ensure that readers of accounting reports have the necessary information to understand the effects of such changes on the financial statements.

Types of Accounting Changes

Objective 1
Identify and differentiate among the types of accounting changes.

IFRS and ASPE have established reporting frameworks that cover three types of accounting changes:

1. A **change in accounting policy.** Changes in the choice of "specific principles, bases, conventions, rules, and practices applied by an entity in preparing and presenting financial statements" are all changes in accounting policies.[1] The initial adoption of a new accounting standard and a change from a weighted average cost flow formula to one based on FIFO (as long as this results in reliable and more relevant information) are both examples of a change in policy.

2. A **change in accounting estimate.** A change in an accounting estimate is an adjustment to the carrying amount of an asset or a liability or the amount of an asset's periodic consumption, and results from either an assessment of the present status of or the expected future benefits and obligations associated with an asset or liability.[2] Examples include a change in the estimate of the service life of an asset that is subject to depreciation, and a change in the estimate of the net realizable value of accounts receivable.

3. **Correction of a prior period error. Prior period errors** are omissions from or mistakes in the financial statements of one or more prior periods that are caused by the misuse of, or failure to use, reliable information that existed when those financial statements were completed and could reasonably have been found and used in their preparation and presentation.[3] An example is the failure to recognize depreciation on a group of capital assets that were used in operations for a specific prior period.

Each of these classifications is discussed separately below.

Another major type of change occurs when the specific entities making up the reporting entity change due to a business combination, as with **SNC-Lavalin** in our feature story, or the disposal of a major part of a company's operations. These are not the focus of this chapter. Discontinued operations were explained in Chapter 4, and business combinations and other reporting entity changes are covered in most advanced accounting courses.

Changes in Accounting Policies

Choices of Accounting Policies

Before discussing what is involved in a change in accounting policy, it is a good idea to review the issues related to an entity making the **initial choice** of accounting policy based on GAAP.

ASPE describes what makes up GAAP and the GAAP hierarchy.[4] The **GAAP hierarchy** is the guidance to follow when there is no primary source of generally accepted accounting principles that covers a specific situation. ASPE identifies two levels of GAAP:

1. Primary sources of GAAP

2. Policies that are consistent with the primary sources of GAAP, and are developed by exercising professional judgement and applying concepts set out in Section 1000, Financial Statement Concepts

The first level, the **primary sources of GAAP**, lists these sources in order of authority, as follows:

(a) Sections 1400 to 3870, including Appendices; and

(b) Accounting Guidelines, including Appendices.

The second level—policies consistent with the primary sources, applying professional judgement, and the concepts in Section 1000—is used only when primary sources of GAAP do not deal with the specific issue. Section 1100 provides additional guidance on applying secondary sources and addresses the topic of consistency in accounting policies. It indicates that similar transactions, events, and circumstances are accounted for and presented in a consistent manner in an entity's financial statements.

IFRS requires a similar **hierarchy**. The **primary sources** to look to are the IFRS and guidance that is an integral part of the specific standard. When no such source exists, judgement is used to determine the accounting treatment. Judgement takes into account the definitions of elements, recognition criteria, and measurement concepts and the underlying qualities of financial statement information found in the Framework for the Preparation and Presentation of Financial Statements in Illustration 2-5. It ensures that the method chosen results in consistency with the treatment that primary sources would require for similar situations.

Under both IFRS and ASPE, GAAP may specifically require or permit categorization of items and different policies to be used, such as with depreciation methods. Once an appropriate method is chosen from among those allowed, this method is then applied consistently to each category. Both sets of standards also identify other sources that could be considered and applied, such as the pronouncements of standard-setting bodies with similar conceptual frameworks, as long as the result is consistent with the hierarchy set out above.

GAAP Requirements for Changes in Accounting Policies

Having been introduced to the original choice of policy, we can now ask what conditions must exist for an entity to be allowed to change its policy. Under IFRS, one of the following two situations is required for a change in accounting policy to be acceptable:

1. the change is required by a primary source of GAAP, or

2. a voluntary change results in the financial statements presenting reliable and more relevant information about the effects of the transactions, events, or conditions on the entity's financial position, financial performance, or cash flows.[5]

ASPE permits a third type of accounting policy change to be made without having to meet the "reliable and more relevant" test in the second situation above. It allows the following voluntary changes in policy to be made:

3. between or among alternative ASPE methods of accounting and reporting

(a) for investments in subsidiary companies, and in companies where the investor has significant influence or joint control;

(b) for expenditures during the development phase on internally generated intangible assets;

(c) for defined benefit plans;

(d) for income taxes; and

(e) for measuring the equity component of a compound financial instrument.[6]

Specific transitional provisions that indicate how any changes are to be accounted for are often identified in new or revised standards. The second situation permitting a change in policy—a **voluntary change**—underscores one of the principles underlying both ASPE and IFRS: for a change in accounting policy to be acceptable, the new policy chosen must result in financial information that remains reliable and is more relevant than under the previous policy. The change would be unacceptable if it produces more reliable but less relevant information. The assumption, therefore, is also that the use of another method that remains reliable and is equally relevant would not meet the criterion for being an acceptable change. The onus is on management to explain why a different method is more relevant than the method that is currently being applied.

A change in the measurement basis of an asset or liability is typically a change in accounting policy. An IFRS example of an acceptable voluntary change might be the move from a cost basis to the fair value model for measuring investment property. Another possible example, this time related to ASPE, is the change made by a company that constructs its own long-lived assets if it moves from expensing all interest charges as they are incurred to capitalizing interest during construction. In both cases, management can likely explain in what way the resulting financial information has become more relevant and remains reliable.

But determining what is "more relevant" is not always obvious in financial reporting. How is relevance measured? One enterprise might argue that a change in accounting policy from FIFO to a weighted average cost formula better matches current costs and current revenues, providing more predictive, and therefore more relevant, information. Conversely, another enterprise might change from a weighted average cost formula to FIFO because it wants to report a more current and relevant ending inventory amount that also has better predictive value. The decision has to be made based on the situation in each specific case.

The requirement based on relevance and reliability links back to the two primary qualitative characteristics of accounting information that make it useful. The main purpose of the qualitative characteristics is their use as evaluative criteria in choosing among accounting alternatives. Any new or revised standard that is issued as a primary source of GAAP has been evaluated against these characteristics as part of its development.

The third situation allowed under ASPE as an acceptable change in accounting policy refers to standards where accounting policy choices have to be made. These changes are treated as voluntary changes, but they do not have to meet the "reliable and more relevant" hurdle required of other voluntary changes. Although not specifically stated in the actual standard, once that choice has been made, the same policy is followed consistently.

It is not always obvious whether an accounting change is, in fact, a change in accounting policy. It is clearly **not** a change in policy if either one of the following two situations is evident:

1. A different policy is applied to transactions, events, or conditions that are different in substance from those that previously occurred.

2. A different policy is applied to transactions, events, or conditions that either did not occur previously or that were immaterial.

Consider, for example, a company that begins to capitalize interest during the construction of its own long-lived assets. If the company was not involved in any self-construction activities previously, the new policy of capitalizing interest would not be considered a change in accounting policy. Another example is applying a new "defer and amortize" policy for development expenditures. If these costs were immaterial previously but are now significant, the change in materiality justifies the new policy. This is not a change in methods of accounting for similar events and circumstances. In each of these examples, the method that was used previously was appropriate for the circumstances that existed then; the new policy is appropriate for the changed circumstances.

What happens if the accounting policy that was previously followed was not acceptable, or if the policy was applied incorrectly? Rather than being a change in accounting policy, these changes to a generally accepted accounting method are considered corrections of an error. A switch from the cash basis of accounting to the accrual basis is considered an error correction. If a company incorrectly deducted residual values when calculating double-declining depreciation on tangible capital assets and later recalculates the depreciation without deducting the estimated residual value, the change is considered the correction of an error.

Finally, companies often change how they allocate or group items within categories on the financial statements. When an item is reclassified on the financial statements of the prior period(s) in order to make the statements comparable, this is considered a change in presentation only and not, in itself, a change in accounting policy. As with retrospective changes in accounting policy, IAS 1 *Presentation of Financial Statements* requires that an "extra" statement of financial position (SFP)—an opening SFP for the earliest comparative period presented—be provided in such a case.[7]

Changes in Accounting Estimates

In preparing financial statements, estimates of the effects of future conditions and events are often made. Because future conditions and events and their effects cannot be known with certainty, estimation requires the use of judgement. The following are a few of the many examples of accounting items that require estimates:

1. Uncollectible receivables

2. Inventory obsolescence

3. Fair value of financial assets or financial liabilities

4. Useful lives of, the pattern of consumption of the future economic benefits that are embodied in, and the residual values of depreciable assets

5. Liabilities for warranty costs

The use of reasonable estimates is considered an essential part of the accounting process. And it is normal to expect that accounting estimates will change over time as new events occur, circumstances change, more experience is acquired, or additional information is obtained. By its very nature, a change in estimate does not relate to past periods. Instead, and as its definition reinforces, the change is brought about by assessing the present status and future expectations associated with specific assets and liabilities.

Sometimes it is difficult to differentiate between a change in an estimate and a change in an accounting policy. Assume, for example, that a company changes its method of depreciation for its property, plant, and equipment. At first glance, this appears to be a change in an accounting policy. Or does the new method result from a change in the estimate of the pattern in which the assets' benefits are used by the entity? Assume that a company changes from deferring and amortizing certain development costs to recording them as expenses as they are incurred because the future benefits associated with these costs have become doubtful. Is this a change in policy or a change in estimate?

The definition of a change in accounting estimate clearly includes both of these scenarios. Further, **in cases where it is unclear whether a change is one of policy or of estimate**, the change is typically treated as a change in estimate. A revision of an estimate, such as a prior year's tax assessment not caused by errors, is given change-in-estimate treatment. It is clearly not the same thing as a correction of an error, which is discussed next.

Correction of a Prior Period Error

No business, large or small, is immune from errors. The risk of material errors, however, may be reduced by installing good internal controls and applying sound accounting procedures. The accounting standards define prior period errors and make a distinction between errors and changes in accounting estimates. Estimates, by their nature, are approximations whose values change as circumstances and conditions change and more information becomes available. Errors, on the other hand, are omissions or mistakes, either intentional or through oversight, that are not discovered until after the financial statements for a period have been issued.

The following are examples of accounting errors. The analysis assumes that the financial statements are intended to be in accordance with GAAP (IFRS or ASPE) after correction of the error:

1. A change from an accounting policy that is not generally accepted to an accounting policy that is acceptable, or the inappropriate application of an acceptable accounting policy. The rationale adopted is that the prior periods were incorrectly presented. Example: a change from a FIFO cost formula to specific identification where the inventory items are not ordinarily interchangeable (for instance, jewellery).

2. Arithmetic mistakes. Example: the incorrect totalling of the inventory count sheets in calculating total inventory cost.

3. Previous estimates that were not prepared in good faith. Example: based on information that was available when an amortization rate was determined, an entity used a clearly unrealistic rate.

4. An omission due to an oversight. Example: the failure to accrue certain revenues at the end of the period.

5. A recognition error. Example: the recognition of a cost as an asset instead of as an expense.

6. A misappropriation of assets. Example: the correction of a previous year's financial statements because inventory theft was discovered.

A problem may arise in distinguishing between the correction of an accounting error and a change in estimate. What is the correct treatment of the settlement of litigation (not previously accrued) related to a reassessment of a prior year's income taxes? How do we determine whether the information was overlooked in earlier periods (an error) or whether it results from new information, more experience, or subsequent developments (a change in estimate)? This decision is important because, depending on the answer, a different accounting treatment is applied. The general rule is that, when a careful estimate later proves to be incorrect, the change is considered a change in estimate. This is the case with most unaccrued tax litigation settlements. Only when the estimate was obviously calculated incorrectly because of lack of expertise or it was done in bad faith should the adjustment be considered an error correction. There is no clear separating line here. Good judgement must take all the circumstances into account.

Alternative Accounting Methods

Objective 2
Identify and explain alternative methods of accounting for accounting changes.

Three approaches have been suggested for reporting changes in the accounts:

1. **Retrospective: Retrospective application** (also known as **retroactive application**) requires applying a new accounting policy in the accounts as if the new method had always been used. The cumulative effect of the change on the financial statements at the beginning of the period is calculated and an adjustment is made to the financial statements. In addition, all prior years' financial statements that are affected are restated on a basis that is consistent with the newly adopted policy. Advocates of this position argue that only by restating prior periods can accounting changes lead to comparable information. If this approach is not used, the years before the change will be reported using one method and the current and following years will present financial statements on a different basis. Consistency is considered essential in providing meaningful earnings-trend data and other financial relationships that are necessary to evaluate a business.

2. **Current:** The cumulative effect of the change on the financial statements at the beginning of the period is calculated. This **"catch-up" adjustment** is then reported in the current year's income statement. Advocates of this position argue that restating financial statements for prior years results in a loss of confidence by investors in financial reports. How will a present or prospective investor react when told that the earnings

reported five years ago have changed? Restatement, if permitted, might also upset many contractual and other arrangements that were based on the old figures. For example, profit-sharing arrangements based on the old policy might have to be recalculated and completely new distributions made. This might create numerous legal problems. Many practical difficulties also exist: the cost of restatement may be excessive, or restatement may be impossible based on the data available.

3. **Prospective** (in the future): With **prospective application**, previously reported results remain; no change is made. Opening balances are not adjusted, and no attempt is made to correct or change past periods. Instead, the new policy or estimate is applied to balances existing at the date of the change, with effects of the change reported in current and future periods. Supporters of this position argue that, once management presents financial statements based on acceptable accounting principles, methods, and estimates, they are final; management cannot change prior periods by adopting new methods and calculations. According to this line of reasoning, a cumulative adjustment in the current year is not appropriate, because such an approach includes amounts that have little or no relationship to the current year's income or economic events.

<table>
<tr><td>

Objective 3

Identify the accounting standards for each type of accounting change under IFRS and ASPE.

</td><td>

Accounting Standards

Illustration 21-1 identifies the accounting standards for each type of accounting change. These are more fully explained and illustrated below.

</td></tr>
</table>

Illustration 21-1		
Accounting Changes—GAAP Accounting Methods		

Type of Accounting Change	Accounting Method Applied
Change in accounting policy—on adoption of a primary source of GAAP	Apply the method that is approved in the transitional provisions of the primary source.
	If there is none, use retrospective application to the extent that it is practicable.
	If retrospective application is impracticable, apply prospectively.
Change in accounting policy—voluntary	Use retrospective application to the extent practicable.
	If impracticable, apply prospectively.
Change in accounting estimate	Apply prospectively.
Correction of an error	Use retrospective restatement.

As indicated, **only two of the general approaches are permitted: retrospective and prospective treatment**. When new or revised primary sources of GAAP are adopted, recommendations are usually included that specify how an entity should handle the transition. The **transitional provisions** are sometimes complex. Those involving new disclosures (for example, financial instruments disclosures) tend to be applied prospectively. Those that require existing SFP items to be remeasured (for example, employee benefits) tend to require retrospective application by adjusting the opening asset and liability measurements and retained earnings and other equity balances. Some particularly major changes permit a choice of either prospective or retrospective application. The transitional provisions also set out specific disclosures that are required when the new or revised primary sources are adopted.

For all accounting changes, the requirements apply to each incident—it is not appropriate to net the effects of two or more changes when considering materiality. Let's turn now to how these methods are applied. Retrospective application and restatement are discussed first, followed by prospective application.

Retrospective Application—Change in Accounting Policy

When an entity voluntarily changes one of its accounting policies, retrospective application is considered the most informative method of accounting for these changes and reporting their effects on the financial statements. This method is often recommended in the specific transitional provisions of a new or revised primary source of GAAP as well.

The underlying principle of the retrospective application method is that all comparative periods are presented as if the new accounting policy had always been used. This outcome provides the best information to users who assess trends in financial information for prediction purposes. Specifically, retrospective application means that the opening balance of each affected component of equity is adjusted for the earliest prior period that is presented. In addition, all other affected comparative amounts that are disclosed for each prior period that is provided are presented as if the new accounting policy had always been in use.

Faced with having to retrospectively restate its financial statements of prior periods, an entity may find that data from specific prior periods may not be available, or may only be available at too high a cost. A limited version of retrospective application may need to be applied if it is impracticable to do the restatements; that is, if the entity cannot determine the effects on a specific prior period or the cumulative effect of the change in policy for all comparative prior periods after making all reasonable efforts to do so.

The accounting standards clearly explain what is meant by **impracticable** (IAS 8 and ASPE 1506). It is considered impracticable to apply a change to a particular prior period if any of the following situations are true:

1. The effects of the retrospective application cannot be determined.

2. Assumptions are needed about what management's intents were in that prior period.

3. Significant estimates must be made that need to take into account circumstances that existed in that prior period, and it is no longer possible to do this.

Partial retrospective application is allowed only when one or more of these three limitations exist. If the cumulative effect cannot be determined even on the opening balances of the current period, then a change in accounting policy is accounted for prospectively.

Retrospective Application with Full Restatement of Comparative Information

Retrospective application with full restatement of all comparative information is applied as follows:

1. An accounting entry is made to recognize the effects of the new accounting policy that is being applied retrospectively, along with any related income tax effects.

2. Financial statement amounts for prior periods that are included for comparative purposes are restated to give effect to the new accounting policy. The entity adjusts the opening balance of the specific components of equity that are affected for the earliest prior period included in the report, along with other relevant accounts affected for each period.

3. Disclosures are made that enable users of the financial statements to understand the effects of any changes on the financial statements so that the statements remain comparable to those of other years and of other entities.

To illustrate **full retrospective application**, assume that Denson Ltd. follows ASPE and has expensed all interest costs incurred on self-constructed assets since beginning its major capital upgrading project in 2015. The company recognizes deferred/future taxes. In 2017, the company changes its accounting policy to one of capitalizing all avoidable interest costs related to the self-constructed assets. Management believes that this approach provides a more relevant measure of income earned as well as a better reflection of the asset's cost. Shareholders and financial analysts are better able to assess a period's operating performance and prospects for the future with information that is reported under this changed accounting policy. The company is subject to a 30% tax rate. Denson has also expensed interest for tax purposes and plans to continue using this method in the future.

Illustration 21-2 provides the information for analysis.

Illustration 21-2

Data for Full Retrospective Application Example

	Income based on **Interest Expensed Policy** as Reported in Prior Years		
	2017	**2016**	**2015**
Income Statement			
Income before income tax	$ 190,000	$ 160,000	$ 400,000
Income tax—30%	57,000	48,000	120,000
Net income	$ 133,000	$ 112,000	$ 280,000
Statement of Retained Earnings			
Opening balance	$1,752,000	$1,640,000	$1,360,000
Net income	133,000	112,000	280,000
Closing balance	$1,885,000	$1,752,000	$1,640,000

	Income if **Interest Capitalization Policy** Had Been Used		
	2017	**2016**	**2015**
Income Statement			
Income before income tax	$ 200,000	$ 180,000	$ 600,000
Income tax—30%	60,000	54,000	180,000
Net income	$ 140,000	$ 126,000	$ 420,000

	Differences in Income, Income Tax, and Net Income Using Interest Capitalization Policy		
	2017	**2016**	**2015**
Increase in income before tax	$ 10,000	$ 20,000	$ 200,000
Increase in income tax expense	3,000	6,000	60,000
Increase in net income	$ 7,000	$ 14,000	140,000

Alternative Terminology

IFRS uses the terms *current tax expense (income)* and *deferred tax expense (income)*, whereas ASPE suggests *current income tax expense (benefit)* and *future income tax expense (benefit)*. We use the ASPE term "benefit" rather than "income" when describing tax-related income statement accounts, and we use the other terms interchangeably in this text.

Accounting Entry to Recognize the Change

The first step is to make the accounting entry to recognize this change in accounting policy. Because the 2017 accounts have not yet been closed, any adjustments that are needed to 2017's income are made to the income statement accounts themselves, while any changes to prior years are made through retained earnings.

The entry to record the change effective January 1, 2017 is:

A	=	L	+	SE
+220,000		+66,000		+154,000

Cash flows: No effect

Buildings	220,000	
Deferred Tax Liability		66,000
Retained Earnings		154,000

The Buildings account, net of its accumulated depreciation, is increased by $220,000. This represents the additional costs charged to the capital asset account for interest, less the related increase in the accumulated depreciation account from the increased depreciation expense since the assets were completed and used in operations ($200,000 + $20,000). The $220,000 adjustment brings these accounts to what the January 1, 2017 balances would have been if the revised policy had been in effect since the beginning of construction. In reality, both the asset account and its contra account—accumulated depreciation—are affected. The adjustment is shown as a net amount so that you can focus on the other balance sheet effects.

The Deferred Tax Liability credit recognizes the tax effects of the taxable temporary difference; that is, the difference between the carrying amount and tax basis of the capital asset account. In future periods, because taxable income will be higher than accounting income as a result of this temporary difference at January 1, 2017, a deferred tax liability is recognized.[8] The adjustment to Retained Earnings is the accumulated after-tax effect of the new policy up to the beginning of the current year and represents all changes to prior years' income ($140,000 + $14,000 = $154,000). The entry corrects the accounts to January 1, 2017, and the revised policy is applied to the current year's operations.

The next step is to prepare the comparative financial statements by restating them as if the new policy had been in use from the beginning of 2015, the first year that Denson Ltd. incurred interest costs on self-constructed assets.

CORPORATE TAX
6.1.2

Financial Statement Presentation

Illustration 21-3 shows what the bottom portion of the income statement for Denson Ltd. looks like after giving effect to the retrospective change in accounting policy. It also presents the restated statements of retained earnings.

Illustration 21-3

Comparative Income Statements and Statements of Retained Earnings

DENSON LTD.
Statement of Income
Year Ended December 31

	2017	2016 (restated)
Income before income tax	$ 200,000	$ 180,000
Income tax—30%	60,000	54,000
Net income	$ 140,000	$ 126,000

DENSON LTD.
Statement of Retained Earnings
Year Ended December 31

	2017	2016 (restated)
Opening balance, as previously reported		$1,640,000
Change in capitalization of interest accounting policy		140,000
Opening balance, as restated	$1,906,000	1,780,000
Net income	140,000	126,000
Closing balance	$2,046,000	$1,906,000

On the SFP, the Buildings, Accumulated Depreciation, and Deferred Tax Liability accounts on the comparative statement now appear as if the new accounting policy had always been used. This is the objective of retrospective application. Is there any **effect on the statement of cash flows**? As you might expect, past cash flows for prior periods do not change just because we change an accounting policy in 2017 (assuming no changes in the amount of taxes and bonuses paid upon recalculation). However, the category of cash flow will change in our example. Instead of all the interest paid being reported as an operating outflow, the restated financial statements report the capitalized interest as an investing outflow, thereby increasing the cash flow from operations above the amount previously reported. In other situations, the cash flow from operations may not change.

Under IFRS, a third year would be added to the SFP: an SFP as at January 1, 2016 (opening balances). Adjusted basic and fully diluted earnings per share (EPS) due to the accounting change should be shown. Finally, a statement of changes in equity would be presented instead of the statement of retained earnings. It would include the same information as noted above plus other equity accounts such as Common Shares. Let's see what this would look like using the same information. Assume that the Share Capital balance is $2 million (no changes). The statement of changes in equity is presented in Illustration 21-4.

Illustration 21-4			
Comparative Statement of Changes in Equity	**DENSON LTD.** Statement of Changes in Equity Year Ended December 31, 2017		
	Share Capital	**Retained Earnings**	**Total**
Balance December 31, 2015, as previously reported	$2,000,000	$1,640,000	$3,640,000
Change in interest capitalization accounting policy		140,000	140,000
Balance January 1, 2016, as restated	$2,000,000	$1,780,000	$3,780,000
Net income 2016 (restated)		126,000	126,000
Balance December 31, 2016, as restated	$2,000,000	$1,906,000	$3,906,000
Net income 2017		140,000	140,000
Balance December 31, 2017	$2,000,000	$2,046,000	$4,046,000

UNDERLYING CONCEPT

Applying full retrospective treatment and providing the related disclosures that are required is an attempt to restore the comparability of the income statements.

It is important for the financial statement reader to be alerted to the fact that Denson did change a key policy in the year. A full example for a policy change disclosure by **Barrick Gold Corporation** in shown in Illustration 21-5.

Impracticability

As indicated earlier, retrospectively restating the financial statements of a prior year requires information that may, in many cases, be impracticable to obtain, even though the cumulative effect can be determined. For many reasons, however, it is not practicable for some companies to retroactively determine the effect of a new standard on specific prior years—a necessary condition for restatement. The standards therefore permit a **partial retrospective application**.

Thus, if the effect of a change in policy can be determined for some of the prior periods, the change in policy is applied retrospectively with restatement to the carrying amounts of assets, liabilities, and affected components of equity at the beginning of the earliest period for which restatement is possible. Since under IFRS and ASPE only two years are generally shown (except for the additional opening SFP under IFRS, where there is a change), this would likely be the current year. An adjustment is made to the opening balances of the equity components for that earliest period, similar to the adjustments in the full restatement that was illustrated above.

While estimates can be used to allow some restatements to be made retrospectively, estimates should not be made for this purpose after the fact if it is impossible to objectively assess circumstances and conditions in prior years that need to be known in order to develop those estimates (including management intent). It is not appropriate to apply hindsight in developing measurements that need to be used. Measurements must be based on conditions that existed and were known in the prior period.

If the entity cannot practicably determine the cumulative effect of the change even at the beginning of the current period, retrospective treatment cannot be applied. Instead, the entity applies the new accounting policy **prospectively** from the earliest date that is practicable. This situation may arise if the necessary data were not collected and cannot be recreated appropriately.

Disclosures Required for a Change in Accounting Policy

Whether the change in accounting policy is due to an initial application of a primary source of GAAP or to a voluntary change, considerable information is required to be reported under both ASPE and IFRS. This helps readers understand why the change was made and what its effects are on previous and the current period financial statements. The information below is required to be disclosed in the period of the change, if practicable, regardless of whether the change was accounted for retrospectively or prospectively:

1. For an initial application of an IFRS/ASPE or primary source, its title, the nature of the change and that it is made according to its transitional provisions, and what the provisions are

2. The nature of any voluntary change, and why the new policy provides reliable and more relevant information

3. The effects of the change, to the extent practicable, on each financial statement line item affected in the current period and on periods before those presented

4. Where full retrospective application is impracticable, additional information about why that is so, the periods affected, and how the change was handled

REAL WORLD EMPHASIS

As indicated earlier in the chapter, under ASPE, some voluntary accounting policy choice changes are exempt from having to provide "reliable and more relevant" information.

Under IFRS, the information set out above is also required when a transitional provision or voluntary change might have an **effect on future periods**. Related to this disclosure is a requirement to report information about new standards that have been issued but are not yet effective and have not been applied. The entity discloses any reasonably reliable information that would be useful in assessing the effect of the new primary source on its financial statements when it will be first applied. Impact on EPS is required to be shown. As noted earlier, an opening balance sheet at the beginning of the earliest comparative period is also required under IFRS.

Barrick Gold Corporation is a well-known Canadian mining giant. Illustration 21-5 provides excerpts from Barrick's financial statements for its year ended December 31, 2013 that indicate its disclosures related to a variety of accounting policy changes. These provide good examples of the retrospective application of changes under the transitional requirements of primary sources of GAAP.

Illustration 21-5

Example of Disclosure of Changes in Accounting Policy—Barrick Gold Corporation, 2013

Consolidated Balance Sheets

Barrick Gold Corporation (in millions of United States dollars)	As at December 31, 2013	As at December 31, 2012 (restated – note 2y)	As at January 1, 2012 (restated – note 2y)
ASSETS			
Current assets			
Cash and equivalents (note 24a)	$ 2,404	$ 2,097	$ 2,749
Accounts receivable (note 17)	385	449	426
Inventories (note 16)	2,679	2,585	2,498
Other current assets (note 17)	421	626	876
Total current assets (excluding assets classified as held for sale)	5,889	5,757	6,549
Assets classified as held for sale	323	—	—
Total current assets	6,212	5,757	6,549
Non-current assets			
Equity in investees (note 15a)	27	20	341
Other investments (note 15b)	120	78	161
Property, plant and equipment (note 18)	21,688	29,277	29,076
Goodwill (note 19a)	5,835	8,837	9,626
Intangible assets (note 19b)	320	453	569
Deferred income tax assets (note 29)	501	437	409
Non-current portion of inventory (note 16)	1,679	1,555	1,153
Other assets (note 21)	1,066	1,064	1,002
Total assets	**$37,448**	**$47,478**	**$48,886**

(continued)

LIABILITIES AND EQUITY

Current liabilities			
Accounts payable (note 22)	**2,165**	2,267	2,085
Debt (note 24b)	**179**	1,848	196
Current income tax liabilities	**75**	41	306
Other current liabilities (note 23)	**303**	261	326
Total current liabilities (excluding liabilities classified as held for sale)	**2,722**	4,417	2,913
Liabilities classified as held for sale	**162**	—	—
Total current liabilities	**2,884**	4,417	2,913
Non-current liabilities			
Debt (note 24b)	**12,901**	12,095	13,173
Provisions (note 26)	**2,428**	2,812	2,326
Deferred income tax liabilities (note 29)	**2,258**	2,668	4,231
Other liabilities (note 28)	**976**	850	689
Total liabilities	**21,447**	22,842	23,332
Equity			
Capital stock (note 30)	**20,869**	17,926	17,892
Retained earnings (deficit)	**(7,581)**	3,269	4,562
Accumulated other comprehensive income	**(69)**	463	595
Other	**314**	314	314
Total equity attributable to Barrick Gold Corporation shareholders	**13,533**	21,972	23,363
Non-controlling interests (note 31)	**2,468**	2,664	2,191
Total equity	**16,001**	24,636	25,554
Contingencies and commitments (notes 16, 18 and 35)			
Total liabilities and equity	**$37,448**	$47,478	$48,886

The accompanying notes are an integral part of these consolidated financial statements.

Consolidated Statements of Changes in Equity

		Attributable to equity holders of the company						
Barrick Gold Corporation (in millions of United States dollars)	Common Shares (in thousands)	Capital stock	Retained earnings	Accumulated other comprehensive income (loss)[1]	Other[2]	Total equity attributable to shareholders	Non-controlling interests	Total equity
At January 1, 2013 (restated – note 2y)	**1,001,108**	**$ 17,926**	**$ 3,269**	**$ 463**	**$ 314**	**$ 21,972**	**$ 2,664**	**$ 24,636**
Net loss	—	—	(10,366)	—	—	(10,366)	(237)	(10,603)
Total other comprehensive income (loss)	—	—	24	(532)	—	(508)	—	(508)
Total comprehensive loss	—	$ —	$(10,342)	$ (532)	$ —	$ (10,874)	$ (237)	$(11,111)
Transactions with owners								
Dividends	—	—	(508)	—	—	(508)	—	(508)
Issued on public equity offering	163,500	2,934	—	—	—	2,934	—	2,934
Issued on exercise of stock options	44	1	—	—	—	1	—	1
Recognition of stock option expense	—	8	—	—	—	8	—	8
Funding from non-controlling interests	—	—	—	—	—	—	55	55
Other decrease in non-controlling interests	—	—	—	—	—	—	(14)	(14)
Total transactions with owners	163,544	$ 2,943	$ (508)	$ —	$ —	$ 2,435	$ 41	$ 2,476
At December 31, 2013	**1,164,652**	**$ 20,869**	**$ (7,581)**	**$ (69)**	**$ 314**	**$ 13,533**	**$ 2,468**	**$ 16,001**

(continued)

Barrick Gold Corporation (in millions of United States dollars)	Common Shares (in thousands)	Attributable to equity holders of the company					Non-controlling interests	Total equity
		Capital stock	Retained earnings	Accumulated other comprehensive income (loss)[1]	Other[2]	Total equity attributable to shareholders		
At January 1, 2012 (restated – note 2y)	1,000,423	$ 17,892	$ 4,562	$ 595	$ 314	$ 23,363	$ 2,191	$ 25,554
Net loss	—	—	(538)	—	—	(538)	(11)	(549)
Total other comprehensive loss	—	—	(5)	(132)	—	(137)	—	(137)

Barrick Gold Corporation (in millions of United States dollars)	Common Shares (in thousands)	Attributable to equity holders of the company					Non-controlling interests	Total equity
		Capital stock	Retained earnings	Accumulated other comprehensive income (loss)[1]	Other[2]	Total equity attributable to shareholders		
Total comprehensive loss	—	$ —	$ (543)	$ (132)	$ —	$ (675)	$ (11)	$ (686)
Transactions with owners Dividends	—	—	(750)	—	—	(750)	—	(750)
Issued on exercise of stock options	685	18	—	—	—	18	—	18
Recognition of stock option expense	—	16	—	—	—	16	—	16
Funding from non-controlling interests	—	—	—	—	—	—	505	505
Other decrease in non-controlling interests	—	—	—	—	—	—	(21)	(21)
Total transactions with owners	685	$ 34	$ (750)	$ —	$ —	$ (716)	$ 484	$ (232)
At December 31, 2012 (restated – note 2y)	1,001,108	$ 17,926	$ 3,269	$ 463	$ 314	$ 21,972	$ 2,664	$ 24,636

[1]Includes cumulative translation adjustments as at December 31, 2013: $80 million loss (2012: $13 million).

[2]Includes additional paid-in capital as at December 31, 2013: $276 million (December 31, 2012: $276 million) and convertible borrowings – equity component as at December 31, 2013: $38 million (December 31, 2012: $38 million).

The accompanying notes are an integral part of these consolidated financial statements.

y) New Accounting Standards Adopted During the Year

The Company has adopted the following new standards, along with any consequential amendments, effective January 1, 2013. These changes were made in accordance with the applicable transitional provisions.

IFRS 10 Consolidated Financial Statements

In May 2011, the IASB issued IFRS 10 Consolidated Financial Statements to replace the consolidation guidance in IAS 27 Consolidated and Separate Financial Statements and SIC 12 Consolidation – Special Purpose Entities. The new consolidation standard changes the definition of control so that the same criteria apply to all entities, both operating and special purpose entities, to determine control. The revised definition of control focuses on the need to have power over the investee, exposure to variable returns from its involvement with the investee and the ability to use its power over the investee to affect its returns. We conducted a review of all our non-wholly owned entities and structured entities and determined that the adoption of IFRS 10 did not result in any change in the consolidation status of any of our subsidiaries and investees.

IFRS 11 Joint Arrangements

In May 2011, the IASB issued IFRS 11 Joint Arrangements to replace IAS 31, Interests in Joint Ventures. The new standard defines two types of arrangements: Joint Operations and Joint Ventures. The focus of the standard is to reflect the rights and obligations of the parties involved in the joint arrangement, regardless of whether the joint arrangement operates through a separate legal entity. Joint arrangements that are classified as joint ventures are accounted for using the equity method of accounting. Joint arrangements that are classified as joint operations require the venturers to recognize the individual assets, liabilities, revenues and expenses to which they have legal rights or are responsible. As a result of adopting IFRS 11, we have classified our interest in the Donlin Gold project as a joint operation. Our 50% interest in the project was previously accounted for using the equity method of accounting.

As a result of the change in accounting, we now recognize our share of the project's assets, liabilities, revenue and expenses. This change in accounting was adopted as at January 1, 2013 with retrospective application by the derecognition of our equity investment and the recognition of our share of the project's assets, liabilities, revenues and expenses.

Illustration 21-5

Example of Disclosure of Changes in Accounting Policy— Barrick Gold Corporation, 2013 (continued)

(continued)

IFRS 12 Disclosure of Interests in Other Entities

In May 2011, the IASB issued IFRS 12 Disclosure of Interests in Other Entities to create a comprehensive disclosure standard to address the requirements for subsidiaries, joint arrangements and associates including the reporting entity's involvement with other entities. It also includes the requirements for unconsolidated structured entities (i.e. special purpose entities). We have adopted IFRS 12 effective January 1, 2013. We have added additional disclosures in notes 2b, 15, 31.

IFRS 13 Fair Value Measurement

In May 2011, the IASB issued IFRS 13 Fair Value Measurement as a single source of guidance for all fair value measurements required by IFRS to reduce the complexity and improve consistency across its application. The standard provides a definition of fair value and guidance on how to measure fair value as well as a requirement for enhanced disclosures. We have adopted IFRS 13 on a prospective basis. We have added additional disclosures on fair value measurement in note 25.

IAS 19 Employee Benefits

In June 2011, the IASB issued revised IAS 19. As a result we replaced interest cost and expected return on plan assets with a net interest amount that is calculated by applying the discount rate to the net defined benefit liability (asset). Adoption of revised IAS 19 did not materially impact the measurement, recognition or disclosure in our financial statements. See note 34 for further details.

IFRIC 20 Stripping Costs in the Production Phase of a Surface Mine

In October 2011, the IASB issued IFRIC 20 Stripping Costs in the Production Phase of a Surface Mine. IFRIC 20 provides guidance on the accounting for the costs of stripping activities during the production phase of surface mining when two benefits accrue to the entity as a result of the stripping: useable ore that can be used to produce inventory and improved access to further quantities of material that will be mined in future periods. We have adopted IFRIC 20 effective January 1, 2013. Upon adoption of IFRIC 20, we assessed the stripping asset on the balance sheet as at January 1, 2012 and determined that there are identifiable components of the ore body with which this stripping asset can be associated, and therefore no balance sheet adjustment was required. The adoption of IFRIC 20 has resulted in increased capitalization of waste stripping costs and a reduction in our cost of sales in 2012. If we had not adopted the standard, our net income and capitalized waste stripping costs for current and comparative periods would have decreased.

For the quantitative impact of adopting IFRS 11 and IFRIC 20 on our prior year consolidated financial statements and of the impact of the discontinued operations of our energy business (note 4b), please refer to the tables below.

Adjustments to the Consolidated Balance Sheets:

	As at January 1, 2012	Adjustments for changes in accounting policy		As at January 1, 2012
	(previously stated)	IFRS 11	IFRIC 20	**(restated)**
Cash and equivalents	$ 2,745	$ 4	$ –	$ 2,749
Equity in investees	440	(99)	–	341
Property, plant and equipment	28,979	97	–	29,076
Accounts payable	(2,083)	(2)	–	(2,085)
Increase in net assets		$ –	$ –	

	As at December 31, 2012	Adjustments for changes in accounting policy		As at December 31, 2012
	(previously stated)	IFRS 11	IFRIC 20	**(restated)**
Cash and equivalents	$ 2,093	$ 4	$ –	$ 2,097
Inventories	4,387	–	(247)	4,140
Equity in investees	135	(115)	–	20
Property, plant and equipment	28,717	113	447	29,277
Deferred income tax assets	443	–	(6)	437
Accounts payable	(2,265)	(2)	–	(2,267)
Deferred income tax liabilities	(2,602)	–	(66)	(2,668)
Increase in net assets		$ –	$128	

Adjustments to the Consolidated Statements of Income:

For the year ended December 31	2012	Adjustments for changes in accounting policy		Discontinued operations[1]	2012
	(previously stated)	IFRS 11	IFRIC 20		**(restated)**
Revenue	$14,547	$ –	$ –	$(153)	$14,394
Cost of sales	7,654	–	(232)	(165)	7,257
Impairment charges	6,470	–	32	(208)	6,294
Other expense (income)	326	1	–	(24)	303
Loss from equity investees	(13)	1	–	–	(12)
Finance costs	(177)	–	–	3	(174)
Income tax recovery (expense)	236	–	(72)	(62)	102
Increase in net income from continuing operations		$ –	$ 128	$ 185	

(continued)

Adjustments to the Consolidated Statements of Cash Flow:

For the year ended December 31	2012 (previously stated)	Adjustments for changes in accounting policy		Discontinued operations[1]	2012 (restated)
		IFRS 11	IFRIC 20		
Net loss	$ (677)	$ –	$ 128	$ 185	$ (364)
Adjusted for the following items:					
Depreciation	1,722	–	31	(102)	1,651
Finance costs (excludes accretion)	123	–	–	(2)	121
Impairment charges	6,470	–	32	(208)	6,294
Income tax expense (recovery)	(236)	–	72	62	(102)
Increase in inventory	(616)	–	256	–	(360)
Other operating activities	(144)	(2)	–	(137)	(283)
Net cash (provided by) used in operating activities from continuing operations		(2)	519	(202)	
Capital expenditures	(6,369)	(15)	(519)	130	(6,773)
Other investing activities	(328)	17	–	–	(311)
Net cash (provided by) used in investing activities from continuing operations		2	(519)	130	
Debt					
Repayments	(1,462)	–	–	69	(1,393)
Net cash used in financing activities from continuing operations		–	–	69	
Net decrease in cash and equivalents	(652)	–	–	–	(652)
Cash and equivalents at beginning of year	2,745	4	–	–	2,749
Cash and equivalents at end of year	$ 2,093	$ 4	$ –	$ –	$ 2,097

[1]Refer to note 4b

z) New Accounting Standards Issued but Not Yet Effective

IFRS 9 Financial Instruments

In November 2009, the IASB issued IFRS 9 Financial Instruments as the first step in its project to replace IAS 39

Financial Instruments: Recognition and Measurement. IFRS 9 retains but simplifies the mixed measurement model and establishes two primary measurement categories for financial assets: amortized cost and fair value. The basis of classification depends on an entity's business model and the contractual cash flows of the financial asset. Classification is made at the time the financial asset is initially recognized, namely when the entity becomes a party to the contractual provisions of the instrument. Requirements for classification and measurement of financial liabilities were added in October 2010 and they largely carried forward existing requirements in IAS 39, except that fair value changes due to an entity's own credit risk for liabilities designated at fair value through profit and loss would generally be recorded in OCI rather than the income statement.

IFRS 9 amends some of the requirements of IFRS 7 Financial Instruments: Disclosures, including added disclosures about investments in equity instruments measured at fair value in OCI, and guidance on financial liabilities and derecognition of financial instruments. In December 2011, amendments to IFRS 7 were issued to require additional disclosures on transition from IAS 39 to IFRS 9. In November 2013, IFRS 9 was amended to include guidance on hedge accounting and to allow entities to early adopt the requirement to recognize changes in fair value attributable to changes in an entity's own credit risk, from financial liabilities designated under the fair value option, in OCI (without having to adopt the remainder of IFRS 9). In July 2013, the IASB tentatively decided to defer the mandatory effective date of IFRS 9. The IASB agreed that the mandatory effective date should no longer be annual periods beginning on or after January 1, 2015 but rather be left open pending the finalization of the impairment and classification and measurement requirements. We are currently assessing the impact of adopting IFRS 9 on our consolidated financial statements.

Illustration 21-5

Example of Disclosure of Changes in Accounting Policy—Barrick Gold Corporation, 2013 (continued)

WHAT DO THE NUMBERS MEAN?

Note that the company has provided an opening SFP for the beginning of the earliest comparative period (so there are three sets of numbers shown). This helps to clearly see the impact of the retrospective application. The company notes that the numbers have been restated in the headings. Barrick has also shown the nature of the change as well as the dollar impact of the retrospective change on a line-by-line basis.

There are numerous changes in standards identified in the notes. Some do not result in any changes (IFRS 10 and IAS 19), some result in additional note disclosures only (IFRS 12 and 13), and some result in changes to the numbers (IFRS 11 and IFRIC 20). The company also identifies new standards that have been issued but not yet applied. This helps financial statement users to predict the impact on future financial statements.

REAL WORLD EMPHASIS

You will learn in the discussion of accounting errors that is covered next that retrospective restatements to correct errors are handled in the same way as retrospective application of a change in accounting policy.

Retrospective Restatement—Correction of an Error

Objective 5

Apply retrospective restatement for the correction of an accounting error and identify the disclosure requirements.

Although the general approach to accounting for an error correction is similar to accounting for a change in accounting policy, the accounting standards make a distinction between the two: prior financial statements with material errors that were never prepared in accordance with GAAP, unlike those that used a different, but acceptable, accounting policy. The term **retrospective restatement** is used in the case of an error correction. The result is the correction of amounts that were reported in the financial statements of prior periods as if the error had never occurred. Specifically, retrospective restatement takes place in the first set of financial statements that is completed after the error's discovery by:

- restating the comparative amounts for the prior period(s) presented in which the error occurred, or

- if the error took place before the earliest prior period provided, restating the opening amounts of assets, liabilities, and equity for the earliest period presented.

ASPE allows only full retrospective restatement. An accounting error, by its definition and nature, can be traced to a specific prior year; therefore, full retrospective changes to all prior years that are affected are required.

IFRS, on the other hand, accept that there may be situations where it may be impracticable to determine the accounting adjustment needed for a specific prior period or for the cumulative effect of an error. In such a case, partial retrospective restatement is allowed, similar to the requirements for an accounting policy change.

- If the effect on each prior period presented cannot be determined, the opening amounts of the SFP elements for the earliest period the effects can be determined are restated. This may be the current period.

- If the cumulative effect on prior periods cannot be determined at the beginning of the current period, the error is corrected from the earliest possible date practicable.

Retrospective Restatement—Affecting One Prior Period

As soon as they are discovered, errors affecting a prior period are corrected retrospectively by proper entries in the accounts and are reflected in the financial statements. In the year in which the error is discovered, the correction is recorded as an adjustment to the beginning balance of retained earnings. If comparative statements are presented, the prior statements that are affected are restated to correct the error so that they appear as if the error had never occurred. The accounting and reporting are similar to the examples of retrospective application for a voluntary change in accounting policy.

To illustrate, assume that the accountant for Selectric Corporation discovered in 2017 that in 2016 the bookkeeper had failed to record in the accounts $20,000 of depreciation expense on a newly constructed building. The company follows ASPE and recognizes deferred taxes. Selectric's tax rate is 30%.

As a result of the $20,000 depreciation error in 2016, the following balances are incorrect:

Depreciation expense (2016) was understated by:	$20,000
Accumulated depreciation at December 31, 2016/January 1, 2017 was understated by:	20,000
Deferred tax expense (2016) was overstated by ($20,000 × 30%):	6,000
Net income (2016) was overstated by ($20,000 − $6,000):	14,000
Deferred tax liability at December 31, 2016/January 1, 2017 was overstated by ($20,000 × 30%):	6,000

The entry needed in 2017 to correct the omission of $20,000 of depreciation in 2016, assuming the books for 2016 have been closed, is:

A   =   L   +   SE
−20,000   −6,000   −14,000

Cash flows: No effect

Retained Earnings	14,000	
Deferred Tax Liability	6,000	
Accumulated Depreciation—Buildings		20,000

The Retained Earnings account is adjusted because all 2016 income statement accounts were closed to retained earnings at the end of that year. The journal entry to record the error correction is the same whether single-period or comparative financial statements are prepared; however, presentation on the financial statements will differ. If single-period financial statements are presented, the error is reported as an adjustment to the opening balance of retained earnings of the period in which the error is discovered, as Illustration 21-6 shows.

Illustration 21-6

Reporting an Error—Single-Period Financial Statements

Retained earnings, January 1, 2017		
As previously reported (assumed)		$350,000
Correction of an error (depreciation)	$(20,000)	
Less: Applicable income tax reduction	**6,000**	**(14,000)**
Restated balance of retained earnings, January 1, 2017		336,000
Add: Net income 2017 (assumed)		400,000
Retained earnings, December 31, 2017		$736,000

If comparative financial statements are prepared, adjustments are made to correct the amounts of all affected accounts in the statements of all periods that are reported. The data for each year that is presented are restated to the correct amounts. In addition, the opening balance of retained earnings for the earliest period being reported is adjusted for any cumulative change in amounts that relates to periods that are prior to the reported periods. In the case of Selectric Corporation, the error of omitting the depreciation of $20,000 in 2016, which was discovered in 2017, results in restating the 2016 financial statements when they are presented for comparison with those of 2017. Illustration 21-7 shows the changes that need to be made to the previously reported amounts on the comparative statements.

Illustration 21-7

Reporting an Error Correction—Changes to the Comparative Financial Statements

Comparative Balance Sheet (restated)			
December 31, 2016			
Accumulated depreciation, buildings	+$20,000	Deferred tax liability	−$ 6,000
		Retained earnings	− 14,000

Comparative Income Statement (restated)	
Year Ended December 31, 2016	
Depreciation expense	+$20,000
Deferred tax expense	− 6,000
Net income	− 14,000

Comparative Statement of Retained Earnings	
Year Ended December 31, 2016 (restated)	
Opening balance, January 1	no change
Net income	−$14,000
Ending balance, December 31	−$14,000

Selectric's 2017 financial statements (presented in comparative form with those of 2016) are prepared as if the error had not occurred; the only exception to this is the restated opening balance of retained earnings at January 1, 2017. In addition, a note to the 2017 financial statements is required that provides all appropriate disclosures.

Retrospective Restatement—Affecting Multiple Prior Periods

Assume that, when preparing the financial statements for the year ended December 31, 2017, the controller of Shilling Corp. discovered that a property purchased in mid-2014 for $200,000 had been charged entirely to the Land account in error. The $200,000 cost should have been allocated between Land ($50,000) and Building ($150,000). The building was expected to be used for 20 years and then sold for $70,000 (not including the land). The company follows ASPE and recognizes deferred/future taxes. Prior to discovery of this error, Shilling Corp.'s accounting records reported the information in Illustration 21-8.

Illustration 21-8		2017 (books not closed)	2016
Accounting Records before Restatement	Revenues	$402,000	$398,000
	Expenses	329,000	320,000
	Income before tax	73,000	78,000
	Income tax expense (30%)	21,900	23,400
	Net income	$ 51,100	$ 54,600
	Retained earnings, January 1	$294,000	$242,000
	Net income for year	51,100	54,600
	Dividends declared	(2,100)	(2,600)
	Retained earnings, December 31	$343,000	$294,000

Retrospective restatement is required, so the first step is to determine the effect of this error on all prior periods. Preparing an appropriate analysis provides backup for the required correcting entry and helps in the restatement of the financial statements. The specific analysis differs for each situation encountered. However, each analysis requires identifying two things: first, what is in the books and records now; and second, what would have been in the accounts if the error had not occurred. The correcting entry then adjusts what is there now to what should be there. Illustration 21-9 shows the analysis that underlies the correcting entry to Shilling's accounts. Assume that the tax records were not updated for the building acquisition and therefore no capital cost allowance was claimed on the building over the years. Go through each line, making sure that you understand the source of each number.

CORPORATE TAX 6.1.2

Illustration 21-9	2017	2016	2015	2014
Analysis of Error on Shilling's Records **Income statement effects:**				
Correct amount of depreciation expense ($150,000 − $70,000) ÷ 20 = $4,000 per year	$ 4,000	$ 4,000	$ 4,000	$ 2,000
Correct amount of tax benefit related to depreciation = 30% of depreciation expense	1,200	1,200	1,200	600
Income was overstated each year by:	$ 2,800	$ 2,800	$ 2,800	$ 1,400
Balance sheet effects, end of each year:				
Land reported	$200,000	$200,000	$200,000	$200,000
Correct land balance	50,000	50,000	50,000	50,000
Building reported	–0–	–0–	–0–	–0–
Correct building balance	150,000	150,000	150,000	150,000
Accumulated depreciation reported	–0–	–0–	–0–	–0–
Correct accumulated depreciation	14,000	10,000	6,000	2,000
Deferred tax asset reported re: building	–0–	–0–	–0–	–0–
Correct deferred tax asset balance (= 30% of temporary difference at year end)[9]	4,200	3,000	1,800	600

The correcting entry needed at the 2017 year end when the error is discovered is taken directly from the analysis in Illustration 21-9.

A   =   L   +   SE
−9,800   −9,800

Cash flows: No effect

Buildings (150,000 − 0)	150,000	
Depreciation Expense (4,000 − 0)	4,000	
Deferred Tax Asset (4,200 − 0)	4,200	
Retained Earnings (Jan. 1, 2017: 2,800 + 2,800 + 1,400)	7,000	
Land (200,000 − 50,000)		150,000
Accumulated Depreciation—Buildings (14,000 − 0)		14,000
Current Tax Benefit (1,200 − 0)		1,200

Let's review this entry. The objective is to correct the accounts so the amounts in the records are the same as they would have been if there had been no error. The Building account would have had a $150,000 balance, but now stands at $0, so we need to debit $150,000 to Building. Depreciation expense should have been taken on the building in 2017 but was not, so the current year's expense needs to be recognized. With income statement items, because all accounts get closed out each year to Retained Earnings, the correction to depreciation expense for 2014 to 2016 must be to Retained Earnings. The depreciation expense for 2017 has not yet been closed out, so the adjustment is made directly to the expense. The same explanation applies to the adjustment to Current Tax Benefit. In 2017, the adjustment is made to the expense account but for 2014 to 2016, it is made to Retained Earnings. In effect, the $7,000 adjustment to decrease the January 1, 2017 Retained Earnings balance represents the 2014 to 2016 Depreciation Expense correction of $10,000, net of the related Current Tax Benefit correction for the same three-year period of $3,000.

Three other balance sheet accounts need correcting. The Land account, now at $200,000, must be reduced to $50,000. The Accumulated Depreciation now stands at $0 but should be $14,000. Lastly, the Deferred Tax Asset account related to the temporary deductible difference between the tax basis (undepreciated capital cost) of the building and its revised carrying amount is recognized.

Now that the records have been adjusted, the accounting error has to be reported on the comparative statements for 2016, assuming that only one year's comparative statements are provided. These financial statements are presented "as if the error had never occurred." If the error occurred before the earliest period that is presented, as in this situation, then the opening balances of the related assets, liabilities, and equity for the earliest prior period presented are restated. The required income statements and statements of retained earnings are presented in Illustration 21-10.

Illustration 21-10

Retrospective Restatement of Comparative Statements— Shilling Corp.

SHILLING CORP.
Statement of Income
Year Ended December 31

	2017	2016 (restated)
Revenues	$402,000	$398,000
Expenses	333,000[a]	324,000[b]
Income before tax	69,000	74,000
Income tax expense[†]	20,700[c]	22,200[d]
Net income	$ 48,300	$ 51,800

[a]$329,000 + $4,000   [c]$21,900 − $1,200

[b]$320,000 + $4,000   [d]$23,400 − $1,200

SHILLING CORP.
Statement of Retained Earnings
Year Ended December 31

	2017	2016 (restated)
Retained earnings, January 1, as previously reported		$242,000
Cumulative effect of accounting error, net of tax benefit of $1,800		(4,200)
Retained earnings, January 1, as restated	$287,000	237,800
Net income	48,300	51,800
Less: Dividends declared	(2,100)	(2,600)
Retained earnings, December 31	$333,200	$287,000

[†]Tax expense would be allocated between current and future taxes.

The adjustments to the income statement are relatively straightforward because the expenses and income tax lines are simply changed to the corrected amounts. The earliest retained earnings balance that is reported now has to be restated to what it would have been if the error had never occurred.

For the 2016 statement of retained earnings, the previously reported opening retained earnings balance (that is, the 2015 ending balance) is adjusted for the effects on income (and therefore retained earnings) prior to January 1, 2016. The cumulative adjustment at this date is $4,200. This reflects the $6,000 of additional depreciation expense ($2,000 + $4,000) reduced by the $1,800 of related income tax benefit ($600 + $1,200) to January 1, 2016. If the error had not been made, the balance of retained earnings at January 1, 2016 would have been $237,800. The revised 2016 net income of $51,800 is added to this and the 2016 dividends are deducted in determining the corrected December 31, 2016 balance of retained earnings.

For 2017, the restated opening retained earnings for 2017 of $287,000 is the balance that would have been reported if the error had never occurred. The correct income for 2017 is added to this and the 2017 dividends are deducted to give the retained earnings at the end of 2017. It is not an accounting error in the current year.

The comparative balance sheet for 2016 is designated as "restated" and information is disclosed about the effect on each financial statement line item that has been affected. Under IFRS, an opening January 1, 2016 comparative SFP must also be presented with the correct amounts reported.

Disclosures Required for the Correction of an Accounting Error

The disclosures required when a company corrects an error in a prior period are few, but informative. The following are disclosed in the year of the correction, but are not necessary in subsequent periods:

1. The nature of the error

2. The amount of the correction made to each affected financial statement item for each prior period presented

3. The amount of the correction made at the beginning of the earliest prior period presented

IAS 8 *Accounting Policies, Changes in Accounting Estimates and Errors* requires two additional disclosures. Because IAS 8 recognizes that it may not be practicable to determine the correction's effect on each specific prior period, an entity is required to provide information about the circumstances leading to any impracticality and how such an error has been corrected. Also, the effect of the correction on both basic and fully diluted earnings per share is reported for each prior period presented. As with other changes applied retrospectively, IAS 1 *Presentation of Financial Statements* also requires an opening SFP for the earliest comparative period presented.

Prospective Application

Objective 6

Apply the prospective application method for an accounting change and identify the disclosure requirements for a change in an accounting estimate.

As explained above, the effects of changes in estimates are handled prospectively. That is, no changes are made to previously reported results—they are made forward from the time of the change in estimate. Changes in estimates are viewed as **normal recurring corrections and adjustments—the natural result of the accounting process**—and retrospective treatment is therefore not appropriate. Opening balances are not adjusted, and no attempt is made to "catch up" for prior periods. The financial statements of prior periods are not restated.

Instead, the effect of a change in estimate is accounted for by including it in net income or comprehensive income, as appropriate, in (1) the period of change if the change affects that period only, or (2) the period of change and future periods if the change affects both. If the estimate relates to the balance of an asset, liability, or equity item, the item's carrying amount is changed.

The circumstances related to a change in estimate are different from those related to a change in accounting policy. If changes in estimates were handled on a retroactive basis, continual adjustments of prior years' income would occur. It seems proper to accept the view that, because **new conditions or circumstances** exist, the revision fits the new situation and should be handled in the current and future periods only.

As indicated earlier in the chapter, **it is also appropriate to apply prospective treatment to a change in accounting policy** if it is impracticable to determine the effect of the change even as far back as the beginning of the current period. In such a situation, the new accounting policy is applied only to transactions and events that occur after the accounting policy is changed.

Illustration—Change in Estimate

To illustrate the accounting for a change in estimate, assume that Underwriter Labs Inc. purchased a building for $300,000 that was originally estimated to have a useful life of 15 years and no residual value. Depreciation of $20,000 per year has been recorded for five years on a straight-line basis. In 2017, the total useful life estimate is revised to 25 years. The accounts at the beginning of the sixth year are as follows:

Building	$300,000
Less accumulated depreciation at end of 2016: 5 × $20,000 =	100,000
Carrying amount of building, January 1, 2017	$200,000

Assuming no entry has yet been made in 2017, the entry to record depreciation for 2017 is:

$$A = L + SE$$
$$-10,000 \qquad -10,000$$
Cash flows: No effect

Depreciation Expense	10,000	
Accumulated Depreciation—Buildings		10,000

The $10,000 depreciation charge is calculated in Illustration 21-11.

Illustration 21-11

Depreciation after Change in Estimate

$$\text{Depreciation charge} = \frac{\text{Carrying amount of asset} - \text{Residual value}}{\text{Remaining service life}} = \frac{\$200,000 - \$0}{25 \text{ years} - 5 \text{ years}} = \$10,000$$

Prospective treatment applied to a change in accounting policy simply means that the new policy is applied to the current balance of the related asset, liability, and/or equity item after the date of change.

Disclosure Requirements for a Change in an Accounting Estimate

Disclosures for changes in estimates have the same objective as other types of changes: to provide information that is useful in assessing the effects of the change on the financial statements. In addition to reporting the nature and amount of any change in estimate that affects the current period, as required under ASPE, IFRS also requires reporting of the nature and amount of any change that is expected to affect future periods, unless it is impracticable to estimate its effect. If impracticable to estimate, this fact is disclosed.

Do companies have to disclose changes in accounting estimates made as part of normal operations, such as bad debt allowances or inventory obsolescence? Materiality plays an important role here, as it does with other accounting standards. Although the change may have little effect in the current year, the effect on future periods has to be considered. Anything material should be disclosed as a basic principle.

Throughout the text, we have looked at the issue of how to measure financial statement elements, including how to deal with uncertainty when estimating amounts to be reported in the financial statements (for example, using various tools such as present value, probabilities, and others). As noted in Chapter 2, IFRS and ASPE both require disclosures about measurement uncertainty.[10] This may include the following:

- nature of uncertainty,
- assumptions made when estimating,
- sensitivity of carrying amounts to changes in assumptions,
- expected resolution of uncertainty, and
- any additional explanations needed to help users understand.

Many financial statement elements require continual re-estimation and therefore additional disclosures help users to understand how companies estimate and re-estimate.

**REAL WORLD
EMPHASIS**

Example of Disclosure of a Change in Estimate

Illustration 21-12 captures **Air Canada**'s disclosures regarding estimates as reported in its 2014 financial statements.

Illustration 21-12

*Example of Disclosure of
a Change in Accounting
Estimate—Air Canada, 2014*

3. CRITICAL ACCOUNTING ESTIMATES AND JUDGMENTS
The preparation of financial statements in conformity with GAAP requires management to make estimates and assumptions that affect the amounts reported in these financial statements and accompanying notes. These estimates and associated assumptions are based on historical experience, future operating plans and various other factors believed to be reasonable under the circumstances, and the results of such estimates form the basis of judgments about carrying values of assets and liabilities. These underlying assumptions are reviewed on an ongoing basis. Actual results could differ materially from those estimates.

Significant estimates made in the preparation of these financial statements include, but are not limited to, the following areas, with further information contained in the applicable accounting policy or note:

- Employee future benefits
  - The cost and related liabilities of the Corporation's pensions, other post-retirement and post-employment benefit programs are determined using actuarial valuations. The actuarial valuations involve assumptions including discount rates, future salary increases, mortality rates and future benefit increases. Also, due to the long-term nature of these programs, such estimates are subject to significant uncertainty. Refer to Note 9 for additional information.

- Depreciation and amortization period for long-lived assets
  - The Corporation makes estimates about the expected useful lives of long-lived assets and the expected residual values of the assets based on the estimated current fair value of the assets, the Corporation's fleet plans and the cash flows they generate. Changes to these estimates, which can be significant, could be caused by a variety of factors, including changes to maintenance programs, changes in jet fuel prices and other operating costs, changes in utilization of the aircraft, and changing market prices for new and used aircraft of the same or similar types. Estimates and assumptions are evaluated at least annually. Generally, these adjustments are accounted for on a prospective basis, through depreciation and amortization expense. For the purposes of sensitivity analysis on these estimates, a 50% reduction to residual values on aircraft with remaining useful lives greater than five years results in an increase of $32 to annual depreciation expense. For aircraft with shorter remaining useful lives, the residual values are not expected to change significantly.

(continued)

Illustration 21-12

*Example of Disclosure of
a Change in Accounting
Estimate—Air Canada, 2014
(continued)*

- Impairment considerations on long-lived assets

  - When required, an impairment test is performed by comparing the carrying amount of the asset or cash-generating unit to their recoverable amount, which is calculated as the higher of an asset's or cash-generating unit's fair value less costs to sell and its value in use. Value in use is calculated based upon a discounted cash flow analysis, which requires management to make a number of significant assumptions including assumptions relating to future operating plans, discount rates and future growth rates. Refer to Notes 5 and 6 for additional information.

- Maintenance provisions

  - The recording of maintenance provisions related to return conditions on aircraft leases requires management to make estimates of the future costs associated with the maintenance events required under the lease return condition and estimates of the expected future maintenance condition of the aircraft at the time of lease expiry. These estimates take into account current costs of these maintenance events, estimates of inflation surrounding these costs as well as assumptions surrounding utilization of the related aircraft. Any difference in the actual maintenance cost incurred and the amount of the provision is recorded in maintenance expense in the period. The effect of any changes in estimates, including changes in discount rates, inflation assumptions, cost estimates or lease expiries, is also recognized in maintenance expense in the period. Refer to Note 10(a) for additional information.

- Income taxes

  - Deferred income tax assets are recognized only to the extent that it is probable that future taxable income will be available to realize them. In making this assessment, consideration is given to available positive and negative evidence and relevant assumptions. Consideration is given to, among other things, future projections of taxable income, overall business environment, historical financial results, and industry-wide trends and outlook. At December 31, 2014, no deferred income tax assets have been recorded.

10. PROVISIONS FOR OTHER LIABILITIES

The following table provides a continuity schedule of all recorded provisions. Refer to Note 18 for additional information on Litigation provisions. Current provisions are recorded in Accounts payable and accrued liabilities.

	Maintenance (a)	Asset Retirement (b)	Litigation	Total Provisions
At December 31, 2013				
Current	$ —	$ —	$ 29	$ 29
Non-current	656	17	—	673
	$ 656	$ 17	$ 29	$ 702
Provisions arising during the year	$ 91	$ —	$ 1	$ 92
Amounts disbursed	(14)	—	(1)	(15)
Changes in estimated costs	(13)	2	—	(11)
Accretion expense	11	—	—	11
Foreign exchange loss	65	—	—	65
At December 31, 2014	**$ 796**	**$ 19**	**$ 29**	**$ 844**
Current	$ —	$ —	$ 29	$ 29
Non-current	796	19	—	815
	$ 796	**$ 19**	**$ 29**	**$ 844**

(a) Maintenance provisions relate to the provision for the costs to meet the contractual return conditions on aircraft under operating leases. The provision relates to leases with expiry dates ranging from 2015 to 2024 with the average remaining lease term of approximately four years. The maintenance provisions take into account current costs of maintenance events, estimates of inflation surrounding these costs as well as assumptions surrounding utilization of the related aircraft. Assuming the aggregate cost for return conditions increases by 5%, holding all other factors constant, there would be a cumulative balance sheet adjustment to increase the provision by $40 at December 31, 2014 and an increase to maintenance expense in 2015 of approximately $3. If the discount rates were to increase by 1%, holding all other factors constant, there would be a cumulative balance sheet adjustment to decrease the provision by $17 at December 31, 2014. Due to low market rates of interest, a 1% decrease in discount rates was not considered a reasonable scenario.

**WHAT
DO THE
NUMBERS
MEAN?**

**COST
MANAGEMENT
3.3.1**

In the illustration above, Air Canada first lists all the areas where it makes assumptions about the future and any other sources of estimation uncertainty. It then cross-references to other more detailed notes, such as Note 10 (also included in the illustration).

For instance, for Air Canada, its main revenue-generating assets are planes and these planes need to be maintained for safety reasons. In addition, many of these planes are leased and the terms of the lease contracts require that Air Canada return the planes at the end of the lease in good condition (as defined by each lease). The company estimates the total costs that it believes it will incur when the planes are returned, such as costs to ensure the planes meet the "good condition" requirements of the lease. Air Canada then discounts the amounts and accrues a provision in the current financial statements. This provision is continually adjusted until the planes are returned to the lessors. Maintenance expense represents 6% of operating expenses, and in 2014 it was just over seven times net income. It is therefore a material cost to the company. The company does its best to manage these costs while balancing the regulatory requirements and risks, but some things are beyond the company's control, such as cost increases and interest rates.

The company includes a sensitivity analysis in the note. It analyzes the impact of costs potentially increasing and also of discount rates changing. These calculations help users predict the impact of changes in estimates on future financial statements of the company.

Summary of Accounting Changes

Developing recommendations for reporting accounting changes has helped resolve several significant and long-standing accounting problems. Yet, because of the diversity of situations and of characteristics of the items that are encountered in practice, applying professional judgement is still very important. The primary objective is to serve the user of the financial statements. Achieving this requires accuracy, full disclosure, and the avoidance of any misleading inferences.

The major accounting approaches that were presented in earlier discussions are summarized in Illustration 21-13.

Illustration 21-13

Accounting Approaches to Accounting Changes

Accounting Change	Accounting Method to Apply			
	Method Indicated in the Standard	Retrospective		Prospective
		Full Retrospective	Partial Retrospective	
CHANGE IN ACCOUNTING POLICY On adoption of, or change in, a primary source of GAAP—transitional provision included: IFRS and ASPE	✓			
On adoption of, or change in, a primary source of GAAP—no transitional provision or if it is a voluntary change: IFRS and ASPE		✓ if practicable	✓ if full retrospective treatment is not practicable	✓ if partial retrospective treatment is not practicable
Change within the allowed accounting policy choices identified in *CPA Canada Handbook*, Part II, Section 1506: ASPE only		✓ if practicable	✓ if full retrospective treatment is not practicable	✓ if partial retrospective treatment is not practicable
CORRECTION OF AN ERROR IFRS only		✓ if practicable	✓ if full retrospective treatment is not practicable	✓ if partial retrospective treatment is not practicable
ASPE only		✓		
CHANGE IN ACCOUNTING ESTIMATE IFRS and ASPE				✓

ANALYSIS

Motivations for Change

ETHICS

Understanding how an entity chooses its accounting methods and procedures is complex. The complexity is due to the fact that managers, and others, have an interest in how the financial statements make the company appear. Managers naturally want to show their financial performance in the best light. A favourable profit picture can influence investors, and a strong liquidity position can influence creditors. Too favourable a profit picture, however, can provide union negotiators with ammunition during bargaining talks. Also, if the federal government has established price controls in a certain industry, managers might believe that a trend of lower profits might persuade the regulatory authorities to grant their company a price increase. Hence, managers might have varying profit motives, depending on the economy and who they want to impress.

Research has provided insights into why companies may prefer certain accounting methods.[11] Some of these reasons are as follows.

1. **Political costs:** As companies become larger and more politically visible, politicians and regulators devote more attention to them. The larger the firm, the more likely it is to become subject to legislation such as anti-competition regulations and the more likely it is to be required to pay higher taxes. Therefore, companies that are politically visible may try to report income numbers that are low in order to avoid the scrutiny of regulators. By reporting low income numbers, companies hope to reduce their exposure to being viewed as a monopoly power. This practice can have an effect on other concerned parties as well. For example, labour unions may be less likely to demand wage increases if reported income is low. Researchers have found that the larger a company is, the more likely it is to adopt approaches that decrease income when it selects its accounting methods.

TREASURY MANAGEMENT
5.2.4

2. **Capital structure:** Several studies have found that a company's capital structure can affect the selection of accounting methods. For example, a company with a high debt-to-equity ratio is more likely to be constrained by debt covenants. A company may be considered in default on its bonds if the debt-to-equity ratio is too high. As a result, this type of company is more likely to select accounting methods that will increase net income—such as capitalizing interest instead of expensing it, or using the full cost method instead of the successful efforts approach for exploration and development costs in the oil and gas industry.

3. **Bonus payments:** Studies have found that if compensation plans tie managers' bonus payments to income, management may select accounting methods that maximize bonus payments.

4. **Smooth earnings:** Substantial increases in earnings attract the attention of politicians, regulators, and competitors. In addition, large increases in income create problems for management because the same results are difficult to achieve in subsequent years. Compensation plans may adjust to these higher numbers as a baseline and make it difficult for management to achieve its profit goals and receive bonuses in the following years. On the other hand, decreases in earnings might signal that the company is in financial trouble. Furthermore, significant changes in income raise concerns on the part of shareholders, lenders, and other interested parties about the riskiness of the company. For all these reasons, companies have an incentive to "manage" or "smooth" their earnings. Management typically believes that steady growth of 10% each year is much better than 20% growth one year followed by a 10% decline the next. In other words, management usually prefers to report gradually increasing income and it sometimes changes accounting methods to ensure such a result.

Management pays careful attention to the accounting it follows and often changes accounting methods not for conceptual reasons but rather for economic reasons. As indicated throughout this textbook, such arguments have come to be known as

UNDERLYING CONCEPT

Neutrality is an aspect of reliability and faithful representation.

economic consequences arguments, since they focus on the supposed impact of accounting on the behaviour of investors, creditors, competitors, governments, and the managers of the reporting companies themselves, rather than address the conceptual justification for accounting standards.[12]

To counter these pressures, standard setters have declared, as part of their conceptual framework, that they will assess the merits of proposed standards from a position of **neutrality**. That is, the soundness of standards should not be evaluated on the grounds of their possible impact on behaviour. It is not the standard setter's place to choose standards according to the kinds of behaviour that they want to promote or discourage. At the same time, the reality is that accounting numbers influence behaviour. Nonetheless, the justification for accounting choices should be conceptual, and not viewed in terms of their economic impact.

Interpreting Accounting Changes

What effect do accounting changes have on financial statement analysis? Not surprisingly, they often make it difficult to develop meaningful trend data, which undermines one of the major reasons that accounting information has been found useful in the past.

Financial statement readers should look closely at all accounting changes and adjust any trend data appropriately. Although most adjustments result in no change in the company's cash position, some adjustments can end up converting previously reported operating cash flows to investing or financing flows. Most changes tend to shift earnings from one accounting period to another. The disclosures required by the accounting standards are the best source of input for the analysis.

IFRS/ASPE COMPARISON

A Comparison of IFRS and ASPE

Objective 8

Identify the differences between IFRS and ASPE related to accounting changes.

IFRS and ASPE standards covering how to choose accounting policies initially and how to account for changes in policy, corrections of errors, and changes in estimates are very similar. The significant differences between the two sets of GAAP are identified in Illustration 21-14.

Illustration 21-14

IFRS and ASPE Comparison Chart

	IFRS—IAS 1 and 8	Accounting Standards for Private Enterprises (ASPE)—*CPA Canada Handbook*, Part II, Sections 1100 and 1506	References to Related Illustrations and Select Brief Exercises
Accounting policies	Accounting policies applied are determined by applying the IFRS. If there is no specific IFRS that applies, management applies judgement in determining a policy that is relevant to the needs of users and is reliable. Judgement considers first the requirements of IFRS in similar situations, and then the definitions, recognition criteria, and elements in the Framework for the Preparation and Presentation of Financial Statements.	Accounting policies applied are determined by applying the primary sources of GAAP—the principles and policies set out in Part II of the *CPA Canada Handbook*, first in Sections 1400 to 3870, and then in the Accounting Guidelines. If not dealt with in a primary source or if additional guidance is needed, management uses policies consistent with the primary sources, and that are developed using professional judgement and the concepts in Section 1000.	N/A

(continued)

	IFRS—IAS 1 and 8	Accounting Standards for Private Enterprises (ASPE)—*CPA Canada Handbook*, Part II, Sections 1100 and 1506	References to Related Illustrations and Select Brief Exercises
Changes in accounting policy	Other than a change in accounting policy that is required by an IFRS, an accounting policy can be changed only under one circumstance: when it results in reliable and more relevant information.	Other than a change in accounting policy that is required by a primary source of GAAP, an accounting policy can be changed under two circumstances: (1) when it results in reliable and more relevant information; and (2) when the choice is related to a change in GAAP methods within a number of specifically identified accounting standards.	BE21-6 and Illustration 21-13
Correction of an error	IFRS permits other than full retrospective restatement in situations where it is impracticable to determine the period-specific effects or cumulative effect of the error.	ASPE assumes that the correction can be made to each specific prior period. No allowance is made for impracticability.	Illustration 21-13
Presentation and disclosure	When applying retrospective treatment for a change in accounting policy or restatement due to correction of an error, or when an entity reclassifies items in the financial statements, an opening SFP must be presented for the earliest comparative period reported.	There is no requirement for an additional balance sheet for retrospective treatment of an accounting policy or retrospective restatement, or reclassification of items in the financial statements.	Illustration 21-5
	Information about the effect of issued standards that are not yet effective is required to be disclosed.	There is no requirement to report on issued standards that are not yet effective.	
	Impact on EPS is noted.		

Illustration 21-14

IFRS and ASPE Comparison Chart (continued)

Looking Ahead

As part of its disclosure initiative, the IASB was looking at the definitions of accounting policies and accounting estimates. In practice, some preparers and users feel that the definitions currently provided in IFRS are not sufficiently detailed or informative.

What is the issue? As noted in the chapter, accountants are increasingly called to deal with measurement uncertainty and must continually estimate and re-estimate many financial statement elements. If we look at recently issued IFRS, we can see that, as new standards are issued or old standards revised, the IASB is including additional guidance regarding tools and techniques to measure and deal with estimation uncertainty. For instance, see the use of expected and present value techniques as well as most likely value guidance in IFRS 15, explicit guidance for fair value measurement in IFRS 13, concepts for measurement of impairment losses on financial instruments in IFRS 9, and others. Although ASPE has not incorporated much of this specific guidance to date, it does not forbid its use either.

Therefore, as the amount of guidance increases (including specific methods to estimate amounts), the act of estimating becomes in many ways more complex and companies must carefully consider which methodologies should be used to measure things and how they should be applied. Thus the line between changes in accounting policies and changes in estimates is becoming more blurred.

The IASB plans to issue an Exposure Draft in 2016 with proposed amendments to IAS 8. The Exposure Draft is expected to deal with the distinction between accounting policies and estimates and the impact of this distinction on financial reporting.

SUMMARY OF LEARNING OBJECTIVES

1 Identify and differentiate among the types of accounting changes.

There are three types of accounting changes. (1) Change in accounting policy: a change in the specific principles, bases, rules, or practices that an entity applies in the preparation of its financial statements. (2) Change in an accounting estimate: a change in the carrying amount of an asset or liability or the amount of an asset's periodic consumption from reassessing the current status of the asset or liability or the expected future benefits or obligations associated with it. (3) Correction of a prior period error: a change caused by an omission from or misstatement in prior years' financial statements from the misuse of or failure to use reliable information that existed at the time the statements were completed and that could have been used in their preparation and presentation.

2 Identify and explain alternative methods of accounting for accounting changes.

Accounting changes could be accounted for retrospectively, currently, or prospectively. The retrospective method requires restatement of prior periods as if the accounting change had been used from the beginning, or the error had never been made. The current method calculates a catch-up adjustment related to the effect on all prior years, and reports it in the current period. Prospective treatment requires making no adjustment for past effects, but instead, beginning to use the new method in the current and future periods.

3 Identify the accounting standards for each type of accounting change under IFRS and ASPE.

A change in accounting policy due to the initial application of a new primary source of GAAP is accounted for according to the transitional provisions of that standard. If none is provided, or if it is a voluntary change, retrospective application is used. A change in an accounting estimate is accounted for prospectively. Errors are corrected through full retrospective restatement.

4 Apply the retrospective application method of accounting for a change in accounting policy and identify the disclosure requirements.

Comparative periods are presented as if the new accounting policy had always been applied. The opening balance of each affected component of equity is adjusted for the earliest prior period presented, and all other affected comparative amounts for each prior period provided are restated. When the effects on particular prior periods are impracticable to determine, the cumulative effect of the change is shown as an adjustment to the beginning retained earnings of the earliest prior period possible. Required disclosures therefore include identifying the nature of the change, the effect on each financial statement item affected, the amounts relating to periods prior to those that are presented, and why full retrospective application was not applied, if applicable. If the change resulted from applying transitional provisions, information about the standards and the provisions is provided, including, if under IFRS, the effects on future periods. If it is a voluntary change, excluding specific ASPE accounting changes, the reasons why the new policy results in more relevant information are disclosed. Information about the future effect of changes in primary sources of GAAP that are issued but not yet effective is also required under IFRS. An opening SFP is required under IFRS for the earliest comparative period presented.

5 Apply retrospective restatement for the correction of an accounting error and identify the disclosure requirements.

Comparative amounts for prior periods affected are restated, unless under IFRS it is not practicable to identify the effect on specific past periods. If the error is in a period before the earliest comparative statements included, the opening balances of the earliest comparative period are restated. An opening SFP is required under IFRS for the earliest comparative period presented as is information about the nature of any impracticality. The nature of the error and the amount of the adjustment to each comparative financial statement line item and to EPS are all required disclosures.

6 Apply the prospective application method for an accounting change and identify the disclosure requirements for a change in an accounting estimate.

Under prospective treatment, only the current and future fiscal periods are affected. There is no adjustment of current-year opening balances and no attempt is made to "catch up" for prior periods. The nature and amount of a change in an accounting estimate that affects the current period or, under IFRS, is expected to affect future periods, is required to be disclosed.

7 Identify economic motives for changing accounting methods and interpret financial statements where there have been retrospective changes to previously reported results.

Some of the aspects that affect decisions about the choice of accounting methods are (1) political costs, (2) the capital structure, (3) bonus payments, and (4) the desire to smooth earnings. Financial statement users should analyze the information presented about accounting changes and adjust any trend information affected.

8   Identify the differences between IFRS and ASPE related to accounting changes.

The accounting standards under ASPE are very similar to those under IFRS. Minor differences exist, such as

IAS 8's permitting partial retrospective treatment for the correction of an accounting error, ASPE allowing specific voluntary changes without justification on a "reliable and more relevant" basis, and IFRS requiring additional disclosures.

KEY TERMS

change in accounting estimate, p. 1304
change in accounting policy, p. 1304
correction of a prior period error, p. 1304
economic consequences, p. 1329
full retrospective application, p. 1310
GAAP hierarchy, p. 1304

impracticable, p. 1310
neutrality, p. 1329
partial retrospective application, p. 1313
primary sources of GAAP, p. 1305
prior period errors, p. 1304
prospective application, p. 1309

retroactive application, p. 1308
retrospective application, p. 1308
retrospective restatement, p. 1319
transitional provisions, p. 1309
voluntary change, p. 1306

APPENDIX 21A

ERROR ANALYSIS

Objective 9
Correct the effects of errors and prepare restated financial statements.

In the past, it was unusual to see the correction of material errors in the financial statements of large corporations. Internal control procedures and the diligence of the accounting staff were normally sufficient to find and correct any major errors in the system before the statements were released. However, in the past decade, there were a number of well-publicized cases of major companies restating past results. For example, numerous companies in the United States and Canada, including **Apple Inc.**, **Pixar Inc.**, and **Research In Motion** (now **BlackBerry Limited**), restated past financial statements for a number of years due to improper dating of stock option grants. Many top executives have signed settlements for large sums of money with their shareholders over these events. Smaller businesses may face different problems. These enterprises may not be able to afford an internal audit staff or be able to implement the necessary control procedures to ensure that accounting data are recorded accurately.

WHAT DO THE NUMBERS MEAN?

Restatements sometimes occur because of financial fraud. Financial frauds involve the intentional misstatement or omission of material information in the organization's financial reports. Common methods of financial fraud manipulation include recording fictitious revenues, concealing liabilities or expenses, and artificially inflating reported assets. Financial

statement frauds made up only 9% of the frauds in a recent study on fraud but caused a median loss of $1 million—by far the most costly category of fraud. Presented below is a chart that compares loss amounts for 2014, 2012, and 2010 for financial statement fraud, corruption, and asset misappropriation.

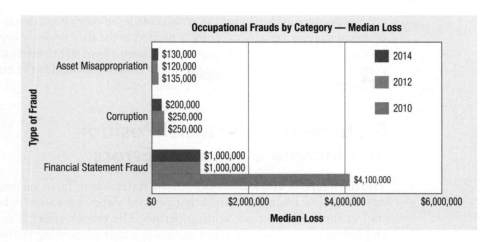

Occupational Frauds by Category — Median Loss

Companies must increase their efforts to protect their statements from the negative effects of fraud.

Sources: Report to the Nations on Occupational Fraud and Abuse: 2014 Global Fraud Study, Association of Certified Fraud Examiners (2014), p. 12.

In practice, firms often do not correct errors that are discovered unless they have a significant effect on the financial statements. For example, the failure to record accrued wages of $5,000 when the total payroll for the year is $1,750,000 and net income is $940,000 is not considered significant, and no correction is made. Obviously, defining materiality is difficult, and experience and judgement are used to determine whether adjustment is necessary for a given error. All errors discussed in this section are assumed to be material and to require adjustment. For simplicity, we have chosen to ignore the tax effects initially so that you can focus instead on the direct effects of the errors themselves.

The accountant must answer three questions in error analysis:

1. What type of error is involved?

2. What entries are needed to correct the error?

3. How are financial statements to be restated once the error is discovered?

As indicated earlier, the standards usually require that errors be corrected retrospectively with restatement, meaning that the elements of the financial statements are adjusted as if the error had never occurred. Three types of errors can occur. Because each type has its own peculiarities, it is important to understand their differences.

Statement of Financial Position Errors

Statement of financial position errors affect only the presentation of an asset, liability, or shareholders' equity account. Examples are classifying a short-term receivable as part of the investment section, a note payable as an account payable, or plant assets as inventory. Reclassification of the item to its proper position is needed when the error is discovered. If comparative statements that include the error year are prepared, the SFP for the error year is restated.

Income Statement Errors

Income statement errors affect only income statement accounts. Errors involve the improper classification of revenues or expenses, such as recording interest revenue as part of sales, purchases as bad debt expense, or amortization expense as interest expense. An income statement classification error has no effect on the SFP or on net income. If a reclassification error is discovered in the year the error is made, an entry is needed to correct it. If the error occurred in prior periods, no entry is needed at the date of discovery because the accounts for the year of the misclassification have all been closed to retained earnings and the current year is correctly stated. If comparative statements that include the error year are prepared, the income statement for the error year is restated.

Statement of Financial Position and Income Statement Errors

The third type of error involves both the statement of financial position and the income statement. For example, assume that accrued wages were overlooked by the accounting staff at the end of the accounting period. The error's effect is to understate expenses and liabilities, and overstate net income for that accounting period. This type of error affects both the SFP and the income statement and is either a counterbalancing or a non-counterbalancing error.

Counterbalancing errors are errors that will be offset or that will self-correct over two periods. In the previous illustration, the failure to record accrued wages is considered a counterbalancing error because, after a two-year period, the error will no longer be present. In other words, the failure to record accrued wages in year one means that (1) wages expense for the first period is understated, (2) net income for the first period is overstated, (3) accrued wages payable (a liability) at the end of the first period is understated, and (4) retained earnings at the end of the first period is overstated. In period two, wages expense is overstated and net income is understated, but both accrued wages payable (a liability) and retained earnings at the end of the second period **are now correct. For the two years combined, total wages expense and net income are correct,** as are the ending SFP amounts of wages payable and retained earnings. Most errors in accounting that affect both the SFP and income statement are counterbalancing errors.

Non-counterbalancing errors are errors that are not offset in the next accounting period. An example is the failure to capitalize equipment that has a useful life of five years. If we expense this asset immediately, expenses will be overstated in the first period but understated in the next four periods. At the end of the second period, the error's effect is not fully offset. Net income is only correct overall at the end of five years, because the asset will have been fully depreciated at this point, assuming it has no residual value. Thus, **non-counterbalancing errors are those that take longer than two periods to correct themselves**.

Only in rare instances does an error never reverse. This would occur, for example, if land were initially expensed. Because land is not subject to depreciation, the error is not offset until the land is sold.

Counterbalancing Errors

The usual types of counterbalancing errors are illustrated on the following pages. In studying these illustrations, you should remember several points. **First**—and this is key—**the entries will differ depending on whether or not the books have been closed for the period in which the error is found.**

1. When the books have been closed:

   (a) If the error is already counterbalanced, no entry is necessary.

   (b) If the error is not yet counterbalanced, an entry is necessary to adjust the present balance of retained earnings and the other affected SFP account(s).

2. When the books have not been closed:

   (a) If the error is already counterbalanced and the company is in the second year, an entry is necessary to correct the current period income statement account(s) and to adjust the beginning balance of retained earnings.

(b) If the error is not yet counterbalanced, an entry is necessary to adjust the beginning balance of retained earnings and correct the affected current period income statement account(s) and SFP account(s).

Second, if comparative statements are presented, it is necessary to restate the amounts for comparative purposes. **Restatement is necessary even if a correcting journal entry is not required.** To illustrate, assume that Sanford Cement Ltd. failed to accrue revenue in 2015 when it was earned, but recorded the revenue in 2016 when it was received. The error is discovered in 2018. No entry is necessary to correct this error, because the effects have been counterbalanced by the time the error is discovered in 2018. However, if comparative financial statements for 2015 through to 2018 are presented, the accounts and related amounts for the years 2015 and 2016 are restated for financial reporting purposes.

The following are examples of counterbalancing errors. Income tax effects have been ignored for now. Work with the entries until you understand each one. In addition, the 2017 comparative financial statements would need to be restated.

1. **Failure to record accrued wages:** On December 31, 2017, accrued wages of $1,500 were not recognized. The entry in 2018 to correct this error, assuming that the books have not been closed for 2018, is:

A = L + SE
0

Cash flows: No effect

Retained Earnings	1,500	
Salaries and Wages Expense		1,500

The rationale for this entry is as follows: When the wages relating to 2017 were paid in 2018, an additional debit of $1,500 was made to 2018 Wages Expense, overstating this account by $1,500. Because 2017 wages were not recorded as Salaries and Wages Expense for 2017, net income for 2017 was overstated by $1,500. Because 2017 net income was overstated by $1,500, the 2018 opening Retained Earnings were also overstated by $1,500, because net income is closed to Retained Earnings.

If the books have been closed for 2018, no entry is made, because the error is counterbalanced.

2. **Failure to record prepaid expenses:** In January 2017, a two-year insurance policy costing $1,000 was purchased; Insurance Expense was debited, and Cash was credited. No adjusting entries were made at the end of 2017. The entry on December 31, 2018 to correct this error, assuming that the books have not been closed for 2018, is:

A = L + SE
0

Cash flows: No effect

Insurance Expense	500	
Retained Earnings		500

If the books are closed for 2018, no entry is made, because the error is counterbalanced.

3. **Understatement of unearned revenue:** On December 31, 2017, cash of $50,000 was received as a prepayment for renting office space for the following year. The entry that was made when the rent payment was received was a debit to Cash and a credit to Rent Revenue. No adjusting entry was made as at December 31, 2017. The entry on December 31, 2018 to correct this error, assuming that the books have not been closed for 2018, is:

A = L + SE
0

Cash flows: No effect

Retained Earnings	50,000	
Rent Revenue		50,000

If the books are closed for 2018, no entry is made, because the error is counterbalanced.

4. **Overstatement of accrued revenue:** On December 31, 2017, interest income of $8,000 was accrued that applied to 2018. The entry made on December 31, 2017 was to debit Interest Receivable and credit Interest Income. The entry on December 31, 2018 to correct this error, assuming that the books have not been closed for 2018, is:

Retained Earnings	8,000	
Interest Income		8,000

If the books have been closed for 2018, no entry is made, because the error is counter-balanced.

5. **Overstatement of purchases:** The accountant recorded a purchase of merchandise for $9,000 in 2017 that applied to 2018. The physical inventory for 2017 was correctly stated. The company uses the periodic inventory method. The entry on December 31, 2018 to correct this error, assuming that the books have not been closed, is:

Purchases	9,000	
Retained Earnings		9,000

If the 2018 books were closed, no entry is made, because the error is counterbalanced.

6. **Understatement of ending inventory:** On December 31, 2017, the physical inventory count was understated by $25,000 because the inventory crew failed to count one section of a merchandise warehouse. The entry on December 31, 2018 to correct this error, assuming the 2018 books have not yet been closed and the ending inventory has not yet been adjusted to the inventory account, is:

Inventory	25,000	
Retained Earnings		25,000

If the books are closed for 2018, no entry needs to be made, because the error has been counterbalanced.

7. **Overstatement of purchases and inventories:** Sometimes, both the physical inventory and the purchases are incorrectly stated. Assume that 2018 purchases of $9,000 were incorrectly recorded as 2017 purchases and that 2017 ending inventory was over-stated by the same amount. The entry on December 31, 2018 to correct this error before the 2018 books are closed and before the correct ending inventory is adjusted to the Inventory account is:

Purchases	9,000	
Inventory		9,000

The net income for 2017 is correct because the overstatement of purchases was offset by the overstatement of ending inventory in cost of goods sold. Similar to the other examples of counterbalancing errors, no entry is required if the 2018 books have already been closed. Regardless, the 2017 comparative statements need to be restated.

Non-Counterbalancing Errors

Because non-counterbalancing errors do not self-correct over a two-year period, the entries for them are more complex, and correcting entries are needed even if the books have been closed. The best approach is to identify what the relevant account balances are in the accounts, what they should be, and then bring them to the correct balances through correcting entries. Examples follow. Here, as well, the prior year's financial statements need to be restated.

1. **Failure to record depreciation:** Assume that a machine with an estimated five-year useful life was purchased on January 1, 2017 for $10,000. The accountant incorrectly expensed this machine in 2017 and the error was discovered in 2018. If we assume that the company uses straight-line depreciation on similar assets, the entry on December 31, 2018 to correct this error, given that the 2018 books are not yet closed, is:

A = L + SE
+6,000   +6,000

Cash flows: No effect

Machinery	10,000	
Depreciation Expense	2,000	
Retained Earnings		8,000
Accumulated Depreciation—Machinery		4,000

Retained Earnings:

Expense reported in 2017	$10,000
Correct depreciation for 2017 (20% × $10,000)	(2,000)
Retained earnings understated as at Dec. 31, 2017 by	$ 8,000

Accumulated Depreciation, Dec. 31, 2018:

Accumulated depreciation (20% × $10,000 × 2)	$ 4,000

If the books have been closed for 2018, the entry is:

A = L + SE
+6,000   +6,000

Cash flows: No effect

Machinery	10,000	
Retained Earnings		6,000
Accumulated Depreciation—Machinery		4,000

Retained Earnings:

Retained earnings understated as at Dec. 31, 2017 by	$ 8,000
Correct depreciation for 2018 (20% × $10,000)	(2,000)
Retained earnings understated as at Dec. 31, 2018 by	$ 6,000

2. **Failure to adjust for bad debts:** Assume that a company has been using the direct write-off method when the allowance method should have been applied. Thus, the following bad debt expense has been recognized as the debts have actually become uncollectible.

	2017	2018
From 2017 sales	$550	$690
From 2018 sales		700

The company estimates that an additional $1,400 will be written off in 2019, of which $300 applies to 2017 sales and $1,100 to 2018 sales.[13] The entry on December 31, 2018 to correct the accounts for bad debt expense, assuming that the books have not been closed for 2018, is:

A = L + SE
−1,400   0   −1,400

Cash flows: No effect

Bad Debt Expense	410	
Retained Earnings	990	
Allowance for Doubtful Accounts		1,400

Allowance for doubtful accounts:
Additional $300 for 2017 sales and $1,100 for 2018
Sales = $1,400.

Bad debt expense corrections needed:

	2017	2018
Accounts written off by year of sale ($550 + $690 = $1,240)	$1,240	$ 700
Additional bad debts anticipated (total of $1,400)	300	1,100
Correct amount of bad debt expense each year	1,540	1,800
Bad debt expense previously recorded	(550)	(1,390)
Bad debt expense adjustment needed	$ 990	$ 410

If the books have been closed for 2018, the entry is:

A	=	L	+	SE
-1,400		0		-1,400

Cash flows: No effect

Retained Earnings	1,400	
Allowance for Doubtful Accounts		1,400

Income Tax Effects

CORPORATE TAX
6.1.2

As mentioned earlier, the income tax effects are not reported with the above correcting entries in order to make it easier for you to focus on the effects of the errors themselves. Once you understand the correcting entries, it is easier to add the income tax effects, as we will do now.

If a correction **increases a previous year's income** (either by an increase in revenue or a decrease in expense), the income tax expense for that period will usually be increased: more income, more tax. If the correction **reduces a previous year's income** (either by a decrease in revenue or an increase in expense), the income tax expense for that period will usually be reduced: less income, less tax. The net correction to retained earnings, therefore, is made net of tax. Note that for counterbalancing errors, the income tax effects also offset each other over the two-year period, assuming tax rates have not changed.

Because the tax return for the previous period has already been filed, most adjustments of the previous year's income affect Income Tax Payable. The Deferred Tax Asset/Liability account is affected only when the treatment for income taxes in the previous year is a permitted tax treatment. Examples include the depreciation and bad debt non-counterbalancing error situations below. In both these cases, taxable income was correct as it was calculated in the prior year, but now the amount of the related temporary difference has changed.

Illustration 21A-1 identifies the **correcting entries** that are needed, including the tax effects for the counterbalancing and non-counterbalancing examples we just walked through. A 30% income tax rate is assumed for all years.

Illustration 21A-1

Correcting Entries with Income Tax Effects

Error	Not Closed		Closed
COUNTERBALANCING ERRORS			
1. Accrued Wages			
Retained Earnings	1,050		–No Entry–
Income Tax Payable	450		
Salaries and Wages			
Expense		1,500	
2. Prepaid Expenses			
Insurance Expense	500		–No Entry–
Retained Earnings		350	
Income Tax Payable		150	
3. Unearned Revenue			
Retained Earnings	35,000		–No Entry–
Income Tax Payable	15,000		
Rent Revenue		50,000	
4. Accrued Revenue			
Retained Earnings	5,600		–No Entry–
Income Tax Payable	2,400		
Interest Income		8,000	
5. Overstatement of Purchases			
Purchases	9,000		–No Entry–
Retained Earnings		6,300	
Income Tax Payable		2,700	

Error	Not Closed		Closed	
6. Understatement of Ending Inventory				
Inventory	25,000		–No Entry–	
Retained Earnings		17,500		
Income Tax Payable		7,500		
7. Overstatement of Purchases and Inventories				
Purchases	9,000		–No Entry–	
Inventory		9,000		
NON-COUNTERBALANCING ERRORS				
1. Depreciation				
Machinery	10,000		Machinery	10,000	
Depreciation Expense	2,000		Accumulated Depreciation	
Accumulated Depreciation			—Machinery		4,000
—Machinery		4,000	Retained Earnings		4,200
Retained Earnings		5,600	Deferred Tax Asset/Liability		1,800
Deferred Tax Asset/Liability		2,400		
2. Bad Debts				
Bad Debt Expense	410		Retained Earnings	980	
Retained Earnings	693		Deferred Tax Asset/Liability	420	
Deferred Tax Asset/Liability	297		Allowance for Doubtful		
Allowance for Doubtful			Accounts		1,400
Accounts		1,400		

Comprehensive Illustration: Numerous Errors

In some circumstances, a combination of errors occurs, and a work sheet is prepared to help with the analysis. To demonstrate the use of a work sheet, the following problem is presented for solution. The mechanics of how the work sheet is prepared should be clear from the format of the solution. The tax effects are omitted.

The income statements of Hudson Corporation for the three years ended December 31, 2016, 2017, and 2018 show the following net income amounts:

2016	$17,400
2017	20,200
2018	11,300

An examination of the company's accounting records for these years reveals that several errors were made in arriving at the net income amounts reported. The following errors were discovered:

1. Wages earned by workers but not paid at December 31 were consistently omitted from the records. The amounts omitted were:

December 31, 2016	$1,000
December 31, 2017	1,400
December 31, 2018	1,600

These amounts were recorded as expenses when they were paid; that is, in the year following the year when they were earned by the employees.

2. The merchandise inventory on December 31, 2016 was overstated by $1,900 as a result of errors made in the footings (totals) and extensions on the inventory sheets.

3. Insurance of $1,200 that is applicable to 2018 was expensed on December 31, 2017.

4. Interest receivable in the amount of $240 was not recorded on December 31, 2017.

5. On January 2, 2017, a piece of machinery costing $3,900 was sold for $1,800. At the date of sale, the equipment had accumulated depreciation of $2,400. The proceeds on the sale were credited to Gain on Sale of Machinery in 2017. In addition, depreciation was recorded for this equipment in both 2017 and 2018 at the rate of 10% of cost.

The **first** step in preparing the work sheet is to prepare a schedule showing the corrected net income for each of the years ended December 31, 2016, 2017, and 2018. Each correction of the amount that was originally reported is clearly labelled. The **next step** is to indicate the SFP accounts affected as at December 31, 2018, if any. The completed work sheet for Hudson Corporation is provided in Illustration 21A-2.

Illustration 21A-2

Work Sheet to Correct Income and Statement of Financial Position Errors

	A	B	C	D	E	G	H	I
1	Hudson Corporation Work Sheet to Correct Income and SFP Errors							
2	Work Sheet Analysis of Changes in Net Income					SFP Correction at December 31, 2018		
3	Year	2016	2017	2018	Totals	Debit	Credit	Account
4	Net income as reported	$17,400	$20,200	$11,300	$48,900			
5	Wages unpaid, 12/31/16	(1,000)	1,000		–0–			
6	Wages unpaid, 12/31/17		(1,400)	1,400	–0–			
7	Wages unpaid, 12/31/18			(1,600)	(1,600)		$1,600	Salaries and Wages Payable
8	Inventory overstatement, 12/31/16	(1,900)	1,900		–0–			
9	Unexpired insurance, 12/31/17		1,200	(1,200)	–0–			
10	Interest receivable, 12/31/17		240	(240)	–0–			
11	Correction for entry made on sale of equipment, 1/2/17[a]		(1,500)		(1,500)	$2,400		Accumulated Depreciation—Machinery
12							3,900	Machinery
13	Overcharge of depreciation, 2017		390		390	390		Accumulated Depreciation—Machinery
14	Overcharge of depreciation, 2018			390	390	390		Accumulated Depreciation—Machinery
15	Corrected net income	$14,500	$22,030	$10,050	$46,580			
16	[a]Calculations Cost Accumulated depreciation Carrying amount Proceeds from sale Gain on sale Income reported Adjustment	$ 3,900 2,400 1,500 1,800 300 1,800 $(1,500)						
17								

Correcting entries **if the books have not been closed for 2018** are:

Retained Earnings	1,400	
Salaries and Wages Expense		1,400

(To correct wages expense charged to 2018 that should have been charged to prior year)

Salaries and Wages Expense	1,600	
Salaries and Wages Payable		1,600

(To record wages expense and accrual for wages at 2018 year end)

Insurance Expense	1,200	
Retained Earnings		1,200

(To correct insurance expense charged to 2017 that should have been charged to 2018)

Interest Income	240	
Retained Earnings		240

(To correct interest income recognized in 2018 that should have been reported in 2017)

Retained Earnings	1,500	
Accumulated Depreciation—Machinery	2,400	
Machinery		3,900

(To record write-off of machinery and correction of the gain reported in 2017)

Accumulated Depreciation—Machinery	780	
Depreciation Expense		390
Retained Earnings		390

(To correct charges made in error to depreciation expense in 2017 and 2018)

If the books have been closed for 2018, the correcting entries are:

Retained Earnings	1,600	
Salaries and Wages Payable		1,600

(To correct the cumulative effect of accrued wages errors to December 31, 2018)

Retained Earnings	1,500	
Accumulated Depreciation—Machinery	2,400	
Machinery		3,900

(To record write-off of machinery and correction of the gain reported in 2018)

Accumulated Depreciation—Machinery	780	
Retained Earnings		780

(To correct charges made in error to depreciation expense in 2017 and 2018)

Preparation of Comparative Financial Statements

Up to now, our discussion of error analysis has been concerned with identifying the type of error involved and then accounting for its correction in the accounting records. Equally important is how the corrections are presented on comparative financial statements. In annual reports or other documents, five- or 10-year financial summaries are often provided. Illustration 21A-3, explained below, shows how a typical year's financial statements are restated, assuming that many different errors have been corrected. Dick & Wally's Outlet Ltd. is a small retail outlet in the town of Priestly Sound. Lacking expertise in accounting, its management does not keep adequate records. As a result, numerous errors occurred in recording accounting information:

1. The bookkeeper, by mistake, failed to record a cash receipt of $1,000 on the sale of merchandise in 2018.

2. Accrued wages at the end of 2017 were $2,500; at the end of 2018, $3,200. The company does not accrue wages; all wages are charged to Administrative Expense.

3. The 2018 beginning inventory was understated by $5,400 because goods in transit at the end of last year were not counted. The purchase entry was made early in 2018. The debit was charged to Retained Earnings in 2018.

4. No allowance had been set up for estimated uncollectible receivables. Dick and Wally decided to set up such an allowance for the estimated probable losses at December 31, 2018, for 2017 accounts of $700, and 2018 accounts of $1,500. They also decided to correct the charge against each year so that it shows the losses (actual and estimated) relating to that year's sales. Accounts have been written off to bad debt expense (selling expense) as follows:

	In 2017	In 2018
2017 accounts	$400	$2,000
2018 accounts		1,600

5. Unexpired insurance not recorded at the end of 2017 was $600, and at the end of 2018, $400. All insurance is charged to Administrative Expense. Unexpired insurance will be included in Prepaid Insurance on the SFP.

6. An account payable at the end of 2018 of $6,000 should have been a note payable.

7. During 2017, a truck that cost $10,000 and had a carrying amount of $4,000 was sold for $7,000. At the time of sale, Cash was debited and Gain was credited for $7,000.

8. As a result of transaction 7, the company overstated depreciation expense (an administrative expense) in 2017 by $800 and in 2018 by $1,200.

9. In a physical count, the company determined the 2018 ending inventory to be $40,000.

Illustration 21A-3 presents a work sheet that begins with the unadjusted trial balance of Dick & Wally's Outlet. The correcting entries and their effect on the financial statements can be determined by examining the work sheet. The numbers in parentheses show which transaction number the correction relates to.

Illustration 21A-3

Work Sheet to Adjust Financial Statements

	A	B	C	E	F	H	I	K	L
1				**Dick & Wally's Outlet** **Work Sheet Analysis to Adjust Financial Statements for the Year 2018**					
2		Trial Balance Unadjusted		Adjustments		Income Statement Adjusted		SFP Adjusted	
3		**Debit**	**Credit**	**Debit**	**Credit**	**Debit**	**Credit**	**Debit**	**Credit**
4	Cash	3,100		(1) 1,000				4,100	
5	Accounts Receivable	17,600						17,600	
6	Notes Receivable	8,500						8,500	
7	Inventory, Jan. 1, 2018	34,000		(3) 5,400		39,400			
8	Property, Plant, and Equipment	112,000			(7) 10,000[a]			102,000	
9	Accumulated Depreciation—Trucks		83,500	(7) 6,000[a]					75,500
10				(8) 2,000					
11	Investment in Associate	24,300						24,300	
12	Accounts Payable		14,500	(6) 6,000					8,500
13	Notes Payable		10,000		(6) 6,000				16,000
14	Common Shares		43,500						43,500
15	Retained Earnings		20,000	(4) 2,700[b]	(3) 5,400				
16				(7) 4,000[a]	(5) 600				
17				(2) 2,500	(8) 800				17,600
18	Sales Revenue		94,000		(1) 1,000		95,000		
19	Purchases	21,000				21,000			
20	Selling Expenses	22,000			(4) 500[b]	21,500			
21	Administrative Expenses	23,000		(2) 700	(5) 400	22,700			
22				(5) 600	(8) 1,200				
23	Totals	265,500	265,500						
24									
25	Salaries and Wages Payable				(2) 3,200				3,200
26	Allowance for Doubtful Accounts				(4) 2,200[b]				2,200
27	Prepaid Insurance			(5) 400				400	
28	Inventory, Dec. 31, 2018						(9) 40,000	(9) 40,000	
29	Net Income					30,400			30,400
30	Totals			31,300	31,300	135,000	135,000	196,900	196,900
31									
32									

33	[a] Machinery			[b] Bad Debts		For Sales in
34	Proceeds from sale	$ 7,000			2017	2018
35	Carrying amount of machinery	4,000		Bad debts charged	$2,400	$1,600
36	Gain on sale	3,000		Other bad debts		
37	Income credited	7,000		anticipated	700	1,500
38	Retained earnings adjustment	$(4,000)			3,100	3,100
39				Charges made in year	400	3,600
40				Bad debt adjustment	$2,700	$(500)
41						

SUMMARY OF LEARNING OBJECTIVE FOR APPENDIX 21A

9 Correct the effects of errors and prepare restated financial statements.

Three types of errors can occur: (1) errors that affect only the SFP, (2) errors that affect only the income statement, and (3) errors that affect both the SFP and the income statement. This last type of error is classified as either (a) a counterbalancing error, where the effects are offset or corrected over two periods; or (b) a non-counterbalancing error, where the effects take longer than two periods to correct themselves.

KEY TERMS

counterbalancing errors, p. 1334   non-counterbalancing errors, p. 1334

Note: Completion of this end-of-chapter material will help develop CPA enabling competencies (such as ethics and professionalism, problem-solving and decision-making, and communication) and technical competencies. We have highlighted selected items with an integration icon and material in *WileyPLUS* has been linked to the competencies. All cases emphasize integration, especially of the enabling competencies. The brief exercises, exercises, and problems generally emphasize problem-solving and decision-making.

In the end-of-chapter material that follows, the simplifying assumption is made that all companies use the term "deferred" (used by IFRS) rather than the term "future" (used by ASPE) for the income tax accounts related to temporary differences. It is also assumed that, where warranties are used as an example of a temporary/timing difference, the company is following the expense warranty approach, and not accounting for the warranty as a separate performance obligation. All assignment material with an asterisk (*) relates to the appendix to the chapter.

Brief Exercises

(LO 1) BE21-1 Netson Manufacturing Corp. is preparing its year-end financial statements and is considering the accounting for the following items:

1. The vice president of sales had indicated that one product line has lost its customer appeal and will be phased out over the next three years. Therefore, a decision has been made to lower the estimated lives on related production equipment from the remaining five years to three years.

2. The Hightone Building was converted from a sales office to offices for the accounting department at the beginning of this year. Therefore, the expense related to this building will now appear as an administrative expense rather than a selling expense on the current year's income statement.

3. Estimating the lives of new products in the Leisure Products Division has become very difficult because of the highly competitive conditions in this market. Therefore, the practice of deferring and amortizing preproduction costs has been abandoned in favour of expensing such costs as they are incurred.

Netson follows IFRS. Explain whether each of the above items is a change in policy, a change in estimate, an error, or none of these.

(LO 1) BE21-2 Palmer Corp. is evaluating the appropriate accounting for the following items under ASPE:

1. Management has decided to switch from the FIFO inventory cost formula to the weighted average cost formula for all inventories.

2. When the year-end physical inventory adjustment was made for the current year, the controller discovered that the prior year's physical inventory sheets for an entire warehouse were mislaid and excluded from last year's count.

3. Palmer's Custom Division manufactures large-scale, custom-designed machinery on a contract basis. Management decided to switch from the completed-contract method to the percentage-of-completion method of accounting for long-term contracts because they are now able to estimate the progress toward completion (whereas they were not able to measure this before).

Explain whether each of the above items is a change in accounting policy, a change in estimate, or an error.

(LO 3, 5) BE21-3 At the beginning of 2017, Armstead Corporation discovered that depreciation expense in the years prior to 2017 was incorrectly calculated and recorded. For the years before 2017, total depreciation expense of $165,000 was recorded, whereas correct total depreciation expense was $75,000. The tax rate is 30%. Armstead follows IFRS and the deferred taxes method of accounting for income taxes. Prepare Armstead's 2017 journal entry with respect to the depreciation expense that was recorded in the years prior to 2017.

(LO 3, 8) BE21-4 ASPE does not permit the correction of an error to be accounted for using partial retrospective restatement or prospective restatement. However, IAS 8 does allow partial retrospective restatement or even prospective treatment for error corrections. (a) Write a brief explanation in support of the Canadian position for private enterprises. (b) Write a brief explanation in support of the international position.

(LO 4) BE21-5 Talbert, Inc. changed from the weighted average cost formula to the FIFO cost formula in 2017. The increase in the prior year's income before tax as a result of this change is $228,000. The tax rate is 30%. Prepare Talbert's 2017 journal entry to record the change in accounting policy, assuming that the company's financial statements are reliable and more relevant as a result of the change.

(LO 4) BE21-6 Chang Limited is in the development phase of creating a new form of medicine. In the past, the company has always capitalized development costs as long as the criteria under IFRS and ASPE were met. Chang would now like to expense these costs. Discuss the options for treating this change (if any) under (a) ASPE and (b) IFRS, noting what type of change it is (a change in accounting policy, a change in estimate, or correction of an error).

(LO 5) BE21-7 In 2017, Dody Corporation discovered that equipment purchased on January 1, 2015 for $145,000 was expensed in error at that time. The equipment should have been depreciated over five years, with no residual value. The tax rate is 30%. Prepare Dody's 2017 journal entry to correct the error and record 2017 depreciation.

(LO 5, *BE21-8 At January 1, 2017, Baker Corp. reported retained earnings of $2 million. In 2017, Baker discovered that
8, 9) 2016 depreciation expense was understated in error by $500,000. In 2017, net income was $800,000 and dividends declared were $195,000. The tax rate is 25%. Baker follows ASPE, and the deferred taxes method of accounting for income taxes. (a) Prepare a 2017 statement of retained earnings for Baker Corp. (b) Briefly explain how your answer would change if Baker were to follow IFRS.

(LO 6) BE21-9 Noland Corporation decided at the beginning of 2017 to change from the declining-balance method of depreciating its capital assets to the straight-line method because the straight-line method better represents the pattern of benefits provided by the capital assets. For years prior to 2017, total depreciation expense under the two methods was as follows: declining balance, $225,000, and straight-line, $105,000. The tax rate is 30%. Noland follows ASPE, and the taxes payable method of accounting for income taxes. Prepare Noland's 2017 journal entry, if any, to record the change in estimate.

(LO 6) BE21-10 Quinlan Corporation purchased a computer system (accounted for as Office Equipment) for $60,000 on January 1, 2015. It was depreciated based on a seven-year life and an $18,000 residual value. On January 1, 2017, Quinlan revised these estimates to a total useful life of four years and a residual value of $10,000. Prepare Quinlan's entry to record 2017 depreciation expense. Assume that Quinlan follows IFRS and uses straight-line depreciation.

(LO 6) BE21-11 Bailey Corp. changed depreciation methods in 2017 from straight-line to double-declining-balance because management gathered evidence that the assets were being used differently than previously thought. The assets involved were acquired early in 2014 for $160,000 and had an estimated useful life of eight years, with no residual value. The 2017 income using the double-declining-balance method was $392,000. Bailey had 10,000 common shares outstanding all year. What is the effect of the accounting change on the reported income and earnings per share (EPS) for 2017? Bailey follows IFRS. Ignore income tax considerations.

(LO 9) *BE21-12 Indicate the effect—understated (U), overstated (O), or no effect (NE)—that each of the following errors has on 2016 net income and 2017 net income:

	2016	2017
Wages payable were not recorded at Dec. 31, 2016.		
Equipment purchased in 2015 was expensed.		
Equipment purchased in 2016 was expensed.		
Ending inventory at Dec. 31, 2016 was overstated.		
Patent amortization was not recorded in 2017.		

Exercises

(LO 1, 2, 3)   **E21-1**   **(Various Accounting Changes)** Assume that each item on the following list would have a material effect on the financial statements of a private enterprise in the current year:

1. A change to the income taxes payable method from the future income taxes method

2. A change in the estimated useful life of previously recorded capital assets where the straight-line depreciation method is used

3. A change from deferring and amortizing development costs to immediate recognition of development costs as expense; the change to immediate recognition arises because the company does not have the resources to market the new product adequately

4. A change from including the employer share of CPP and EI premiums as a separate payroll tax expense to including them with salaries and wages expense on the income statement

5. The correction of a mathematical error in inventory costing that was made in a prior period

6. A change from straight-line to double-declining-balance method of depreciation in recognition of the effect that technology has on the pattern of benefits received from the asset's use

7. A change from presenting unconsolidated financial statements (using the cost method for subsidiaries) to presenting consolidated financial statements for the company and its two long-held subsidiaries

8. A change in the method of accounting for leases for tax purposes to conform to the method of accounting for leases for financial accounting purposes; as a result, both future and current taxes payable changed substantially

9. A change from the periodic inventory method to the perpetual inventory method with the introduction of scanning equipment and updated computer software (FIFO used)

10. A change in an accounting method due to a change in a primary source of GAAP

Instructions

Identify the type of accounting change that is described in each item, and indicate whether the prior years' financial statements must be restated when presented in comparative form with the current year's financial statements. Also indicate if the company is required to justify the change. Assume ASPE is followed.

(LO 1, 2, 3, 4, 5)   **E21-2**   **(Changes and Methods of Accounting, Journal Entries)** Bennett Corp., which began operations in January 2014, follows IFRS and is subject to a 30% income tax rate. In 2017, the following events took place:

1. The company switched from the zero-profit method to the percentage-of-completion method of accounting for its long-term construction projects. This change was a result of experience with the project and improved ability to estimate the costs to completion and therefore the percentage complete.

2. Due to a change in maintenance policy, the estimated useful life of Bennett's fleet of trucks was lengthened.

3. It was discovered that a machine with an original cost of $220,000, residual value of $30,000, and useful life of four years was expensed in error on January 23, 2016, when it was acquired. This situation was discovered after preparing the 2017 adjusting entries but before calculating income tax expense and closing the accounts. Bennett uses straight-line depreciation and takes a full year of depreciation in the year of acquisition. The asset's cost had been appropriately added to the capital cost allowance (CCA) class in 2016 before the CCA was calculated and claimed.

4. As a result of an inventory study early in 2017 after the accounts for 2016 had been closed, management decided that the weighted average cost formula would provide a more relevant presentation in the financial statements than the FIFO cost formula. In making the change to weighted average cost, Bennett determined the following:

Date	Inventory—FIFO Cost	Inventory—Weighted Average Cost
Dec. 31, 2016	$ 80,000	$ 65,000
Dec. 31, 2015	115,000	85,000
Dec. 31, 2014	180,000	135,000

TAXATION

Instructions

(a) Analyze each of the four 2017 events described above. For each event, identify the type of accounting change that has occurred, and indicate whether it should be accounted for with full retrospective application, partial retrospective application, or prospective application.

(b) Prepare any necessary journal entries that would be recorded in 2017 to account for events 3 (ignore income tax considerations) and 4.

(LO 1, 2, 3, 5) E21-3 (Long-Term Contracts) In 2016, Bergeron Construction Company Ltd. applied the completed-contract method of accounting for long-term construction contracts. However, in 2017, Bergeron discovered that the percentage-of-completion method should have been applied instead. For tax purposes, the company uses the completed-contract method and will continue this approach in the future. Bergeron follows ASPE, and will apply the percentage-of-completion method in 2017 and in the future. Bergeron applies the deferred taxes method of accounting for income taxes, and is subject to a tax rate of 30%. The appropriate information related to this change is as follows:

FINANCE AND TAXATION

	Pre-Tax Income Using:		
	Percentage-of-Completion	Completed-Contract	Difference
2016	$820,000	$620,000	$200,000
2017	700,000	480,000	220,000

Instructions

(a) Calculate the net income to be reported in 2017.

(b) Provide the necessary entry(ies) in 2017 to adjust the accounting records with respect to the revenue recognition method applied in 2016.

(c) Assume that, as at the end of 2017, just prior to recording the entry(ies) in part (b), Bergeron has a current ratio of 0.95. From the perspective of a creditor, discuss the effect of the entry(ies) in part (b) on Bergeron's current ratio.

DIGGING DEEPER

(LO 1, 2, 3, 5, 6, 7) E21-4 (Change in Estimate, Error Correction) Field Corp.'s controller was preparing the year-end adjusting entries for the company's year ended December 31, 2017, when the V.P. Finance called him into her office.

"Jean-Pierre," she said, "I've been considering a couple of matters that may require different treatment this year. First, the patent we acquired in early January 2015 for $525,000 will now likely be used until the end of 2019 and then be sold for $170,000. We previously thought that we'd use it for 10 years in total and then be able to sell it for $115,000. We've been using straight-line amortization on the patent.

"Second, I just discovered that the property we bought on July 2, 2014 for $260,000 was charged entirely to the Land account instead of being allocated between Land ($60,000) and Building ($200,000). The building should be of use to us for a total of 20 years. At that point, it'll be sold and we should be able to realize at least $50,000 from the sale of the building.

"Please let me know how these changes should be accounted for and what effect they will have on the financial statements."

Instructions

Field Corp. follows IFRS. Answer the following, ignoring income tax considerations and assuming that the company has not previously reported quarterly results.

(a) Briefly identify the accounting treatment that should be applied to each accounting change that is required.

(b) Assuming that no amortization has been recorded as yet for the patent for 2017, prepare the December 31, 2017 entries that are necessary to make the accounting changes and to record patent amortization expense for 2017.

(c) Identify, and calculate where possible, the required disclosures for each change.

(d) Discuss the timing of applying the change in the patent's useful life and residual value. Since the determination of the change was done as part of the year-end process, should the change be applied to 2017 going forward, or to 2018 going forward? What are the implications of each approach?

DIGGING DEEPER

(e) Could Field's controller consider the patent to be impaired instead of revising its useful life and residual value? What criteria should the controller look at to determine the appropriate treatment?

(LO 1, 2, 3, 8) E21-5 (Accounting for Accounting Changes) The following are various types of accounting changes:

_____ 1. Change in a plant asset's residual value

_____ 2. Change due to an overstatement of inventory (in the preceding period)

_____ 3. Change from sum-of-the-years'-digits to straight-line method of depreciation because of a change in the pattern of benefits received

_____ 4. Change in a primary source of GAAP

_____ 5. Decision by management to capitalize interest. The company is reporting a self-constructed asset for the first time.

_____ 6. Change in the rate used to calculate warranty costs

_____ 7. Change from an unacceptable accounting policy to an acceptable accounting policy

_____ 8. Change in a patent's amortization period

_____ 9. Change from the zero-profit method to the percentage-of-completion method on construction contracts. This change was a result of experience with the project and improved ability to estimate the costs to completion and therefore the percentage complete.

_____ 10. Recognition of additional income tax owing from three years ago as a result of improper calculations by the accountant, who was not familiar with income tax legislation and income tax returns

Instructions

(a) For each change or error, use the following code letters to indicate how it would be accounted for assuming the company follows IFRS:

Accounted for in the current year only (CY)
Accounted for prospectively (P)
Accounted for retrospectively (R)
None of the above, or unable to determine. Explain. (NA)

(b) Identify the type of change for each of the situations in items 1 to 10.

(c) Now assume that the company follows ASPE. Identify the situations in part (a) that would be accounted for differently under ASPE than IFRS.

DIGGING DEEPER

(d) What are the conditions that must exist for an entity to be allowed to change an accounting policy?

(LO 1, 2, 3, 8) **E21-6** **(Various Accounting Changes)** Yates Manufacturing Ltd. is preparing its year-end financial statements. Yates is a private enterprise. The controller, Theo Kimbria, is confronted with several decisions about statement presentation for the following items.

1. The company has decided to change its depreciation method for machinery to units of production rather than straight-line. This is due to the way in which the machinery is now being used.

2. Trying to meet the criteria for capitalization of development costs has become very difficult because of highly competitive market conditions. Therefore, the practice of deferring and amortizing development costs has been abandoned in favour of expensing development costs as they are incurred.

3. When the year-end physical inventory adjustment was made for the current year, the controller discovered that the prior year's physical inventory sheets for an entire section of the warehouse had been mislaid and left out of last year's count.

4. The method of accounting that is used for financial reporting purposes for certain receivables has been approved for tax purposes during the current tax year by the Canada Revenue Agency. This change for tax purposes will cause both current taxes payable and future tax liabilities to change substantially.

5. Management has decided to switch from the FIFO inventory valuation method to the average cost inventory valuation method for all inventories.

Instructions

For each of the five changes that Yates Manufacturing Ltd. made in the current year, advise Theo on whether the change is a change in accounting policy, a change in estimate, a correction of an error, or none of these. Explain if the accounting treatment would be different under ASPE or IFRS. Provide a short explanation for your choice. Determine if retrospective or prospective application would be required in each case and what information would be required in any note disclosure. If the information that is provided is insufficient for you to determine the nature of the change, identify what additional information you would need and how this might affect your response.

ETHICS AND TAXATION

(LO 2, 3, 5, 6, 9) ***E21-7*** **(Change in Estimate, Error, Financial Statements)** Merrick Inc. follows IFRS and is adjusting and correcting its books at the end of 2017. In reviewing its records, the following information has been compiled:

1. In 2017, the depreciation method on plant assets should be changed from sum-of-the-years'-digits to the straight-line method due to a change in pattern of usage. The assets were purchased at the beginning of 2016 for $90,000 with an estimated useful life of four years and no residual value. Merrick has already recorded 2017 depreciation expense of $27,000 related to the assets, using the sum-of-the-years'-digits method.

2. Ending inventory for 2016 was overstated by $20,000; ending inventory for 2017 is correctly stated.

3. The adjusted trial balance at December 31, 2015 includes the following amounts: Cash $38,000; Inventory $112,000; Accounts Payable $48,000; Retained Earnings $72,000.

4. Dividends of $30,000 and $25,000 were declared and paid on December 31, 2017 and December 31, 2016, respectively.

5. Share capital of $30,000 consists of 20,000 common shares outstanding since the company's inception.

Merrick's statement of financial position and income statement are as follows at December 31, 2016 and 2017, before any corrections related to the information above. The December 31, 2017 statements are in draft form only and the 2017 accounts have not yet been closed.

MERRICK INC.
Statement of Financial Position
As at December 31, 2017

Assets	2017	2016
Cash	$ 60,000	$ 34,000
Inventory	107,000	128,000
Plant assets, net	27,000	54,000
Total assets	$194,000	$216,000
Liabilities and Shareholders' Equity		
Accounts payable	$ 17,000	$ 61,000
Share capital	30,000	30,000
Retained earnings	147,000	125,000
Total liabilities and shareholders' equity	$194,000	$216,000

MERRICK INC.
Income Statement
Year Ended December 31, 2017

	2017	2016
Sales	$340,000	$270,000
Cost of goods sold	200,000	142,000
Gross profit	140,000	128,000
Operating expenses	88,000	50,000
Net income	$ 52,000	$ 78,000

Instructions

(a) Prepare the comparative income statement and comparative statement of changes in equity for 2017, and the comparative statement of financial position as at December 31, 2017. Ignore income tax effects. Do not prepare notes to the financial statements.

(b) Identify other possible accounting treatments for the change in depreciation method under alternative circumstances.

(LO 4) E21-8 (Accounting Change—Inventory) Linden Corporation started operations on January 1, 2012, and has used the FIFO cost formula since its inception. In 2018, it decides to switch to the weighted average cost formula. You are provided with the following information.

	Net Income		Retained Earnings (Ending Balance)
	Under FIFO	Under Weighted Average Cost	Under FIFO
2012	$100,000	$ 92,000	$100,000
2013	70,000	65,000	160,000
2014	90,000	85,000	235,000
2015	120,000	130,000	340,000
2016	300,000	293,000	590,000
2017	305,000	310,900	780,000

Instructions

Answer the following, ignoring income tax considerations.

(a) What is the beginning retained earnings balance at January 1, 2014, if Linden prepares comparative financial statements starting in 2014?

(b) What is the beginning retained earnings balance at January 1, 2017, if Linden prepares comparative financial statements starting in 2017?

(c) What is the beginning retained earnings balance at January 1, 2018, if Linden prepares single-period financial statements for 2018?

(d) What is the net income reported by Linden in the 2017 income statement if it prepares comparative financial statements starting in 2015?

(LO 4) E21-9 (Accounting Change—Measurement Model for Investment Property) Golden Properties Corporation purchased a parcel of land in March 2016 for $1 million with the intent to construct a building on the property in the near future. At the time of purchase, Golden applied the cost model and measured and reported the land at its acquisition cost as allowed in IAS 16. Golden follows IFRS. Management decided in 2017 that the land qualifies as an investment property under IAS 40 and that Golden is to apply the fair value model of accounting for investment properties effective immediately because the company believes that changing the measurement model will provide more relevant information. Independent appraisals indicate that the land's fair value at December 31, 2016 and 2017 was $980,000 and $1,050,000, respectively. Before application of the fair value model of accounting for investment properties, Golden's reported net income for the years ended December 31, 2015, 2016, and 2017 was $73,000, $41,000, and $12,000, respectively; and Golden's reported retained earnings at December 31, 2015, 2016, and 2017 was $189,000, $230,000, and $242,000, respectively. Golden has 100,000 common shares outstanding.

FINANCE

Instructions

Answer the following, ignoring income tax considerations.

(a) Prepare the original comparative statement of financial position as at December 31, 2016 and the original comparative income statement for the year ended December 31, 2016 for the affected accounts.

(b) Prepare Golden's journal entries, if any, to record the change in accounting policy.

(c) Prepare the restated comparative statement of financial position as at December 31, 2017 and the restated comparative income statement for the year ended December 31, 2017 for the affected accounts.

(d) From the perspective of an investor, discuss the effects of changing to the fair value model of accounting for investment properties on Golden's financial statements and earnings per share.

(LO 4, 5) E21-10   (Various Changes in Policy—Inventory Methods) Pace Instrument Corp., a small company that follows ASPE, began operations on January 1, 2014, and uses a periodic inventory system. The following net income amounts were calculated for Pace under three different inventory cost formulas:

	FIFO	Weighted Average Cost	LIFO
2014	$26,000	$24,000	$20,000
2015	30,000	25,000	21,000
2016	28,000	27,000	24,000
2017	34,000	30,000	26,000

Instructions

Answer the following, ignoring income tax considerations.

(a) Assume that in 2017, Pace changed from the weighted average cost formula to the FIFO cost formula and it was agreed that the FIFO method provided more relevant financial statement information. Prepare the necessary journal entry for the change that took place during 2017, and provide all the information that is needed for reporting on a comparative basis.

(b) Assume that in 2017, Pace, which had been using the LIFO method since incorporation in 2014, changed to the FIFO cost formula in order to comply with *CPA Canada Handbook*, Part II, Section 3031, because LIFO is not a permitted inventory cost flow assumption under GAAP. The company applies the new policy retrospectively. Prepare the necessary journal entry for the change, and provide all the information that is needed for reporting on a comparative basis.

(LO 5) E21-11   (Error Correction Entries) The first audit of the books of Gomez Limited was recently carried out for the year ended December 31, 2017. Gomez follows IFRS. In examining the books, the auditor found that certain items had been overlooked or might have been incorrectly handled in the past:

1. At the beginning of 2015, the company purchased a machine for $450,000 (residual value of $30,000) that had a useful life of six years. The bookkeeper used straight-line depreciation, but failed to deduct the residual value in calculating the depreciation base for the three years.

2. At the end of 2016, the company accrued sales salaries of $47,000 in excess of the correct amount.

3. A tax lawsuit that involved the year 2015 was settled late in 2017. It was determined that the company owed an additional $81,000 in tax related to 2015. The company did not record a liability in 2015 or 2016, because the possibility of losing was considered remote. The company charged the $81,000 to retained earnings in 2017 as a correction of a prior year's error.

4. Gomez purchased another company early in 2013 and recorded goodwill of $500,000. Gomez amortized $25,000 of goodwill in 2013, and $50,000 in each subsequent year.

5. In 2017, the company changed its basis of inventory costing from FIFO to weighted average cost. The change's cumulative effect was to decrease net income of prior years by $45,000. The company debited this cumulative effect to Retained Earnings, and recorded the related income tax effect. The weighted average cost formula was used in calculating income for 2017.

6. In 2017, the company wrote off $63,000 of inventory that it discovered, in 2017, had been stolen from one of its warehouses in 2016. This loss was charged to a loss account in 2017.

Instructions

(a) Prepare the journal entries in 2017 to correct the books where necessary, assuming that the 2017 books have not been closed. Assume that the change from FIFO to weighted average cost can be justified as resulting in more relevant financial information. Disregard the effects of the corrections on income tax.

TAXATION

(b) Identify the type of change for each of the six items.

(c) Redo part (a) but include the effects of income tax, assuming the company has a tax rate of 25%.

(LO 5, 6, 9) ***E21-12** **(Error and Change in Estimate—Depreciation)** Joy Cunningham Co. purchased a machine on January 1, 2014 for $550,000. At that time, it was estimated that the machine would have a 10-year life and no residual value. On December 31, 2017, the firm's accountant found that the entry for depreciation expense had been omitted in 2015. In addition, management has informed the accountant that the company plans to switch to straight-line depreciation because of a change in the pattern of the way the asset is used, starting with the year 2017. At present, the company uses the sum-of-the-years'-digits method for depreciating equipment.

Instructions

Prepare the general journal entries that should be made at December 31, 2017 to record these events. Ignore income tax effects.

(LO 5, 6, 9) ***E21-13** **(Error and Change in Estimate—Depreciation)** Tracy Ltd. purchased a piece of equipment on January 1, 2013 for $1.2 million. At that time, it was estimated that the machine would have a 15-year life and no residual value. On December 31, 2017, Tracy's controller found that the entry for depreciation expense was omitted in error in 2014. In addition, Tracy planned to switch to double-declining-balance depreciation because of a change in the pattern of benefits received, starting with the year 2017. Tracy currently uses the straight-line method for depreciating equipment.

Instructions

(a) Prepare the general journal entries, if any, the accountant should make at December 31, 2017. Ignore income tax effects.

(b) Assume the same information as above, but factor in tax effects. The company has a 25% tax rate for 2013 to 2017.

(LO 5, 9) ***E21-14** **(Error Analysis and Correcting Entry)** You have been engaged to review the financial statements of Walsh Corporation. In the course of your examination of the work of the bookkeeper hired during the year that just ended, you noticed a number of irregularities for the past fiscal year:

1. Year-end wages payable of $12,500 were not recorded, because the bookkeeper thought that "it was immaterial."

2. Accrued vacation pay for the year of $33,800 was not recorded, because the bookkeeper "never heard that you had to do it."

3. Insurance that covers a 12-month period and was purchased on November 1 was charged to insurance expense in the amount of $8,760 "because the amount of the cheque is about the same every year."

4. Reported sales revenue for the year was $1,480,500 and included all sales taxes charged for the year. The sales tax rate is 5%. Because the sales tax is forwarded to the provincial ministry of revenue, the bookkeeper thought that "sales tax is a selling expense" and therefore debited the Sales Tax Expense account. At the end of the fiscal year, the balance in the Sales Tax Expense account was $60,000.

Instructions

Prepare the necessary correcting entries, assuming that Walsh Corporation uses a calendar-year basis and that the books for the fiscal year that just ended are not yet closed.

(LO 5, 9) ***E21-15** **(Error Analysis and Correcting Entries)** A partial trial balance of Lindy Corporation at December 31, 2017 follows:

	Dr.	Cr.
Supplies	$ 6,700	
Salaries and wages payable		$ 4,900
Interest receivable	7,300	
Prepaid insurance	108,000	
Unearned rent revenue		–0–
Interest payable		15,000

Additional adjusting data:

1. A physical count of supplies on hand on December 31, 2017 totalled $3,400. Through an oversight, the Salaries and Wages Payable account was not changed during 2017. Accrued salaries and wages on December 31, 2017 amounted to $6,200.

2. The Interest Receivable account was also left unchanged during 2017. Accrued interest on investments amounted to $6,750 on December 31, 2017.

3. The unexpired portions of the insurance policies totalled $42,000 as at December 31, 2017.

4. A cheque for $72,000 was received on January 1, 2017 for the rent of a building for both 2017 and 2018. The entire amount was credited to Rent Revenue.

5. Depreciation on equipment for the year was recorded in error as $4,750 rather than the correct figure of $47,500.

6. A further review of prior years' depreciation calculations revealed that depreciation on equipment of $18,500 had not been recorded. It was decided that this oversight should be corrected by adjusting prior years' income.

Assume that Lindy applies IFRS.

Instructions

(a) Assuming that the books have not been closed, what adjusting entries are necessary at December 31, 2017? Ignore income tax considerations.

(b) Assuming that the books have been closed, what adjusting entries are necessary at December 31, 2017? Ignore income tax considerations.

DIGGING DEEPER

(c) Discuss the nature of the adjustments that are needed and how the situations could have occurred. Are they all accounting errors, or are they part of the normal accounting cycle? (*Hint*: Revisit the topic of adjusting entries in Chapter 3.) How should management present the adjustments for these items on its financial statements and in the notes?

(LO 5, 9) *†E21-16   (Error Analysis) Neilson Tool Corporation's December 31 year-end financial statements contained the following errors:

	December 31, 2016	December 31, 2017
Ending inventory	$9,600 overstated	$8,100 understated
Depreciation expense	$2,300 overstated	—

An insurance premium of $66,000 covering the years 2016, 2017, and 2018 was prepaid in 2016, with the entire amount charged to expense that year. In addition, on December 31, 2017, fully depreciated machinery was sold for $15,000 cash, but the entry was not recorded until 2018. There were no other errors during 2016 or 2017, and no corrections have been made for any of the errors. Neilson follows ASPE.

Instructions

Answer the following, ignoring income tax considerations.

(a) Calculate the total effect of the errors on 2017 net income.

(b) Calculate the total effect of the errors on the amount of Neilson's working capital at December 31, 2017.

(c) Calculate the total effect of the errors on the balance of Neilson's retained earnings at December 31, 2017.

(d) Assume that the company has retained earnings on January 1, 2016 and 2017 of $1,250,000 and $1,607,000, respectively; net income for 2016 and 2017 of $422,000 and $375,000, respectively; and cash dividends declared for 2016 and 2017 of $65,000 and $45,000, respectively, before adjustment for the above items. Prepare a revised statement of retained earnings for 2016 and 2017.

DIGGING DEEPER

(e) Outline the accounting treatment required by ASPE in this situation and explain how these requirements help investors.

(LO 5, 9) *E21-17   (Error Analysis) The before-tax income for Hawks Corp. for 2016 was $101,000; for 2017, it was $77,400. However, the accountant noted that the following errors had been made:

1. Sales for 2016 included $38,200 that had been received in cash during 2016, but for which the related products were delivered in 2017. Title did not pass to the purchaser until 2017.

2. Ending inventory on December 31, 2016 was understated by $8,640. The December 31, 2017 ending inventory has not yet been adjusted to the Inventory account.

3. The bookkeeper, in recording interest expense for both 2016 and 2017 on bonds payable, made the following entry each year:

| Interest Expense | 15,000 | |
| Cash | | 15,000 |

†This item was originally published by *Certified General Accountants Association of Canada* (CGA Canada), as an examination question. Adapted with permission of the Chartered Professional Accountants of Canada, Toronto, Canada. Any changes to the original material are the sole responsibility of the publisher and have not been reviewed or endorsed by the Chartered Professional Accountants of Canada.

The bonds have a face value of $250,000 and pay a stated interest rate of 6%. They were issued at a discount of $15,000 on January 1, 2016, to yield an effective interest rate of 7%. (Use the effective interest method.)

4. Ordinary repairs to equipment had been charged in error to the Equipment account during 2016 and 2017. In total, repairs in the amount of $8,500 in 2016 and $9,400 in 2017 were charged in this way. The company applies a rate of 10% to the balance in the Equipment account at year end in determining its depreciation charges.

FINANCE

Assume that Hawks Corp. applies IFRS.

DIGGING DEEPER

Instructions

(a) Prepare a schedule showing the calculation of corrected income before tax for 2016 and 2017.

(b) Prepare the journal entries that the company's accountant would prepare in 2017, assuming the errors are discovered while the 2017 books are still open. Ignore income tax effects.

(c) From the perspective of an investor, comment on the quality of Hawks Corp.'s earnings as reported in 2016 and 2017.

(LO 5, 9) *E21-18 (Error Analysis) When the records of Hilda Corporation were reviewed at the close of 2017, the following errors were discovered.

	2016			2017		
	Over-statement	Under-statement	No Effect	Over-statement	Under-statement	No Effect
1. Failure to record amortization of patent in 2017						
2. Failure to record the correct amount of ending 2016 inventory (the amount was understated because of a calculation error)						
3. Failure to record merchandise purchased in 2016 (it was also omitted from ending inventory in 2016 and remained unsold at the end of 2017)						
4. Failure to record accrued interest on notes payable in 2016 (the amount was recorded when paid in 2017)						
5. Failure to reflect supplies on statement of financial position at end of 2016						

Instructions

For each item, indicate by a check mark in the appropriate column whether the error resulted in an overstatement or understatement, or had no effect on net income for the years 2016 and 2017.

(LO 6) E21-19 (Change in Estimate—Depreciation) Oliver Inc. acquired the following assets in January 2014:

Equipment: estimated useful life, 5 years; residual value, $15,000	$465,000
Building: estimated useful life, 30 years; no residual value	$780,000

The equipment was depreciated using the double-declining-balance method for the first three years for financial reporting purposes. In 2017, the company decided to change the method of calculating depreciation for the equipment to the straight-line method, because of a change in the pattern of benefits received (but no change was made in the estimated useful life or residual value). It was also decided to change the building's total estimated useful life from 30 years to 40 years, with no change in the estimated residual value. The building is depreciated using the straight-line method.

Instructions

(a) Prepare the journal entry to record depreciation expense for the equipment in 2017. (Ignore income tax effects and round to the nearest dollar.)

(b) Prepare the journal entry to record the depreciation expense for the building in 2017. (Ignore income tax effects and round to the nearest dollar.)

(LO 6) E21-20   (Depreciation Changes) On January 1, 2013, Zui Corporation purchased a building and equipment that had the following useful lives, residual values, and costs:

Building: 40-year estimated useful life, $50,000 residual value, $1,200,000 cost
Equipment: 12-year estimated useful life, $10,000 residual value, $130,000 cost

The building was depreciated under the double-declining-balance method through 2016. In 2017, the company decided to switch to the straight-line method of depreciation because of a change in the pattern of benefits received. In 2017, Zui decided to change the equipment's total useful life to 15 years, with a residual value of $5,000 at the end of that time. The equipment is depreciated using the straight-line method.

Instructions

(a) Prepare the journal entry(ies) necessary to record the depreciation expense on the building in 2017. (Ignore income tax effects.)

(b) Calculate the depreciation expense on the equipment for 2017. (Ignore income tax effects.)

**AUDIT AND
ASSURANCE**

(c) Assume the role of Zui's auditor, and discuss any issues related to the above changes in estimate.

(LO 6) E21-21   (Change in Estimate—Depreciation) Rodriguez Corp. changed from the straight-line method of depreciation on its plant assets acquired in early 2015 to the double-declining-balance method in 2017 (before finalizing its 2017 financial statements) because of a change in the pattern of benefits received. The assets had an eight-year life and no expected residual value. Information related to both methods follows:

Year	Double-Declining-Balance Depreciation	Straight-Line Depreciation	Difference
2015	$250,000	$125,000	$125,000
2016	187,500	125,000	62,500
2017	140,625	125,000	15,625

Net income for 2016 was reported at $270,000; income for 2017 before depreciation and income tax is $300,000. Assume an income tax rate of 30%.

Instructions

The change from the straight-line method to the double-declining-balance method is considered a change in estimate.

(a) What net income is reported for 2017?

(b) What is the amount of the adjustment to opening retained earnings as at January 1, 2017?

(c) What is the amount of the adjustment to opening retained earnings as at January 1, 2016?

(d) Prepare the journal entry(ies), if any, to record the adjustment in the accounting records, assuming that the accounting records for 2017 are not yet closed.

(LO 6) E21-22   (Change in Estimate—Depreciation) Peter M. Dell Co. purchased equipment for $510,000, which was estimated to have a useful life of 10 years with a residual value of $10,000 at the end of that time. Depreciation has been entered for 7 years on a straight-line basis. In 2017, it is determined that the total estimated life should be 15 years with a residual value of $5,000 at the end of that time.

Instructions

(a) Prepare the entry (if any) to correct the prior years' depreciation.

(b) Prepare the entry to record depreciation for 2017.

(LO 7) †E21-23   (Political Motivations for Policies) Ever since the unethical actions of some employees of **Enron Corp.** first came to light, ethics in accounting has been in the news with increasing frequency. The unethical actions of the employees essentially involved their selection of certain accounting policies for the company. In many instances, GAAP does allow firms some flexibility in their choice of legitimate accounting policies. This is true, for example, in choosing an inventory cost formula. However, the company's choice of policies may ultimately be influenced by several specific factors.

Instructions

ETHICS

State three of these factors and explain why each of them may influence an accounting policy choice.

---

†This item was originally published by *Certified General Accountants Association of Canada* (CGA Canada), as an examination question. Adapted with permission of the Chartered Professional Accountants of Canada, Toronto, Canada. Any changes to the original material are the sole responsibility of the publisher and have not been reviewed or endorsed by the Chartered Professional Accountants of Canada.

Problems

P21-1   Nadeau Company, a small company following ASPE, is adjusting and correcting its books at the end of 2017. In reviewing its records, it compiles the following information.

1. Nadeau has failed to accrue sales commissions payable at the end of each of the last two years, as follows:

Dec. 31, 2016	$6,200
Dec. 31, 2017	$3,800

2. In reviewing the December 31, 2017 inventory, Nadeau discovered errors in its inventory-taking procedures that have caused inventories for the last three years to be incorrect, as follows:

Dec. 31, 2015	Understated $21,000
Dec. 31, 2016	Understated $24,000
Dec. 31, 2017	Overstated $ 9,000

Nadeau has already made an entry that recognized the incorrect December 31, 2017 inventory amount.

3. In 2017, Nadeau changed the depreciation method on its office equipment from double-declining-balance to straight-line because of a change in the pattern of benefits received. The equipment had an original cost of $160,000 when purchased on January 1, 2015. At that time, it was estimated that the office equipment had an eight-year useful life and no residual value. Depreciation expense recorded prior to 2017 under the double-declining-balance method was $70,000. Nadeau has already recorded 2017 depreciation expense of $22,500 using the double-declining-balance method.

4. Before 2017, Nadeau accounted for its income from long-term construction contracts on the completed-contract basis because it was unable to reliably measure the degree of completion or the estimated costs to complete. Early in 2017, Nadeau changed to the percentage-of-completion basis for financial accounting purposes. The change was a result of experience with the project and improved ability to estimate the costs to completion and therefore the percentage complete. The completed-contract method will continue to be used for tax purposes. Income for 2017 has been recorded using the percentage-of-completion method. The following information is available:

	Pre-Tax Income	
	Percentage-of-Completion	Completed-Contract
Prior to 2017	$195,000	$145,000
2017	75,000	30,000

Instructions

Prepare the necessary journal entries at December 31, 2017 to record the above corrections and changes as appropriate. The books are still open for 2017. As Nadeau has not yet recorded its 2017 income tax expense and payable amounts, tax effects for the current year may be ignored. Nadeau's income tax rate is 25%. Assume that Nadeau applies the taxes payable method of accounting for income taxes.

TAXATION

P21-2   At a recent conference on financial accounting and reporting, three participants provided examples of similar accounting changes that they had encountered in the last few months. They all involved the current portion of long-term debt.

1. The first participant explained that it had just recently come to her attention that the current portion of long-term debt was incorrectly calculated in the last three years of her company's financial statements due to an error in an accounting software product.

2. The second participant explained that his company had just decided to change its definition of what is "current" to make it closer to the "operating cycle," which is approximately 18 months. The company had been using "12 months from the statement of financial position date."

3. The third participant said that her company has decided to change from a "12 months from the statement of financial position date" definition to one based on the company's operating cycle, which is now close to two years. She explained that the company's strategic plan over the last three years had moved the company into bidding on and winning significant longer-term contracts and that the average life of these contracts has now lengthened to about two years.

Instructions

As a panellist at this conference who is expected to respond to the participants, prepare a brief report on the advice you would give regarding how each situation should be handled under IFRS. Identify what steps each participant should take and what disclosures, if any, would be required.

**DIGGING
DEEPER**

P21-3   Leader Enterprises Ltd. follows IFRS and has provided the following information:

1. In 2016, Leader was sued in a patent infringement suit, and in 2017, Leader lost the court case. Leader must now pay a competitor $50,000 to settle the suit. No previous entries had been recorded in the books relative to this case because Leader's management felt the company would win.

2. A review of the company's provision for uncollectible accounts during 2017 resulted in a determination that 1.5% of sales is the appropriate amount of bad debt expense to be charged to operations, rather than the 2% used for the preceding two years. Bad debt expense recognized in 2016 and 2015 was $33,200 and $14,300, respectively. The company would have recorded $19,800 of bad debt expense under the old rate for 2017. No entry has yet been made in 2017 for bad debt expense.

3. Leader acquired land on January 1, 2014 at a cost of $70,000. The land was charged to the Equipment account in error and has been depreciated since then on the basis of a five-year life with no residual value, using the straight-line method. Leader has already recorded the related 2017 depreciation expense using the straight-line method.

4. During 2017, the company changed from the double-declining-balance method of depreciation for its building to the straight-line method because of a change in the pattern of benefits received. The building cost $1.4 million to build in early 2015, and no residual value is expected after its 40-year life. Total depreciation under both methods for the past three years is as follows. Double-declining-balance depreciation has been recorded for 2017.

	Straight-Line	Double-Declining-Balance
2015	$35,000	$70,000
2016	35,000	66,500
2017	35,000	63,175

5. Late in 2017, Leader determined that a piece of specialized equipment purchased in January 2014 at a cost of $75,000 with an estimated useful life of five years and residual value of $5,000 is now expected to continue in use until the end of 2021 and have a residual value of $3,000 at that time. The company has been using straight-line depreciation for this equipment, and depreciation for 2017 has already been recognized based on the original estimates.

6. The company has determined that a $350,000 note payable that it issued in 2015 has been incorrectly classified on its statement of financial position. The note is payable in annual instalments of $50,000, but the full amount of the note has been shown as a long-term liability with no portion shown in current liabilities. Interest expense relating to the note has been properly recorded.

Instructions

(a) For each of the accounting changes, errors, or transactions, present the journal entry(ies) that Leader needs to make to correct or adjust the accounts, assuming the accounts for 2017 have not yet been closed. If no entry is required, write "none" and briefly explain why. Ignore income tax considerations.

(b) Prepare the entries required in part (a) but, where retrospective adjustments are made, adjust the entry to include taxes at 25%.

DIGGING DEEPER

(c) For each of the accounting changes, identify the type of change involved and whether retrospective or prospective treatment is required.

P21-4   Holtzman Company is in the process of preparing its financial statements for 2017. Assume that no entries for depreciation have been recorded in 2017. The following information related to depreciation of fixed assets is provided to you.

1. Holtzman purchased equipment on January 2, 2014 for $85,000. At that time, the equipment had an estimated useful life of 10 years with a $5,000 residual value. The equipment is depreciated on a straight-line basis. On January 2, 2017, as a result of additional information, the company determined that the equipment has a remaining useful life of 4 years with a $3,000 residual value.

2. During 2017, Holtzman changed from the double-declining-balance method for its building to the straight-line method. The building originally cost $300,000. It had a useful life of 10 years and a residual value of $30,000. The following calculations present depreciation on both bases for 2015 and 2016.

	Straight-Line	Double-Declining-Balance
2015	$27,000	$60,000
2016	27,000	48,000

3. Holtzman purchased a machine on July 1, 2015 at a cost of $120,000. The machine has a residual value of $16,000 and a useful life of eight years. Holtzman's bookkeeper recorded straight-line depreciation in 2015 and 2016 but failed to consider the residual value.

Instructions

(a) Prepare the journal entries to record depreciation expense for 2017 and correct any errors made to date related to the information provided. (Ignore income tax considerations.)

(b) Show comparative net income for 2016 and 2017. Income before depreciation expense was $300,000 in 2017 and $310,000 in 2016. (Ignore income tax considerations.)

P21-5 As at December 31, 2017, Kendrick Corporation is having its financial statements audited for the first time ever. The auditor has found the following items that might have an effect on previous years.

1. Kendrick purchased equipment on January 2, 2014 for $130,000. At that time, the equipment had an estimated useful life of 10 years, with a $10,000 residual value. The equipment is depreciated on a straight-line basis. On January 2, 2017, as a result of additional information, the company determined that the equipment had a total useful life of seven years with a $6,000 residual value.

2. During 2017, Kendrick changed from the double-declining-balance method for its building to the straight-line method because the company thinks the straight-line method now more closely follows the benefits received from using the assets. The current year depreciation was calculated using the new method following straight-line depreciation. In case the following information was needed, the auditor provided calculations that present depreciation on both bases. The building had originally cost $1.2 million when purchased at the beginning of 2015 and has a residual value of $120,000. It is depreciated over 20 years. The original estimates of useful life and residual value are still accurate.

	2017	2016	2015
Straight-line	$54,000	$ 54,000	$ 54,000
Double-declining-balance	97,200	108,000	120,000

3. Kendrick purchased a machine on July 1, 2014 at a cost of $160,000. The machine has a residual value of $16,000 and a useful life of eight years. Kendrick's bookkeeper recorded straight-line depreciation during each year but failed to consider the residual value.

4. Prior to 2017, development costs were expensed immediately because they were immaterial. Due to an increase in development phase projects, development costs have now become material and management has decided to capitalize and depreciate them over three years. The development costs meet all six specific conditions for capitalization of development phase costs. Amounts expensed in 2014, 2015, and 2016 were $300, $500, and $1,000, respectively. During 2017, $4,500 was spent and the amount was debited to Deferred Development Costs (an asset account).

Instructions

Do the following, ignoring income tax considerations.

(a) Prepare the necessary journal entries to record each of the changes or errors. The books for 2017 have been adjusted but not closed. Ignore income tax effects.

FINANCE (b) Calculate the 2017 depreciation expense on the equipment.

(c) Calculate the comparative net income amounts for 2016 and 2017, starting with income before the effects of any of the changes identified above. Income before depreciation expense was $600,000 in 2017 and $420,000 in 2016.

DIGGING DEEPER (d) From the perspective of an investor, comment on the quality of Kendrick Corporation's earnings as reported in 2016 and 2017.

P21-6 You are the auditor of Maglite Services Inc., a privately owned full-service cleaning company following ASPE that is undergoing its first audit for the period ending September 30, 2017. The bank has requested that Maglite have its statements audited this year to satisfy a condition of its debt covenant. It is currently October 21, 2017, and the company's books have been closed. As part of the audit, you have found the following situations:

1. Despite having high receivables, Maglite has no allowance for doubtful accounts, and cash collections have slowed dramatically. Unfortunately, Maglite is owed $5,000 by Brad's Fast Foods at the end of fiscal 2017. Brad's has received substantial media attention during the past year due to Department of Health investigations that ultimately resulted in the closure of the company's operations; the owner has apparently moved to the Bahamas. No adjustment has been made for this balance. Maglite's management estimates that an allowance for doubtful accounts of $47,000 is required. During the 2017 fiscal year, the company wrote off $38,000 in receivables, and it estimates that its September 30, 2016 allowance for doubtful accounts should have been $30,000.

AUDIT AND ASSURANCE

2. Maglite's only capital asset on its books is an advanced cleaning system that has a cost of $35,000 and a carrying amount of $20,825. Maglite has been depreciating this asset using the capital cost allowance used for tax purposes for the two years prior to its year ended September 30, 2017, at the rate of 30%. Useful life at the time of purchase was estimated to be 10 years. Maglite would like to change to a straight-line approach to provide more relevant

information to its statement users. Management anticipates that the asset will continue to be of use for four years after the September 30, 2017 year end and will have no residual value. Because the company's accountant was uncertain about how to deal with the change in policy, depreciation expense has not been recorded for the fiscal year.

3. Maglite purchased a computer at the beginning of the fiscal year and immediately expensed its $3,000 cost. Upon questioning, one of the owners said he thought the computer would likely not need to be replaced for at least two more years.

4. You notice that there are no supplies on the statement of financial position. Company management explains that it expenses all supplies when purchased. The company had $1,500 of cleaning supplies on hand at the end of September 2017, which is about $500 higher than the balance that was on hand at the end of the previous year.

5. This year, Maglite started to keep a small amount of excess cash in trading investments that are bought and sold on the local stock exchange. At the end of September 2017, the fair value of this portfolio was $15,000 and the carrying value of the investments was $12,000 (which represented the cost of the investments).

Instructions

(a) Assuming that the company's books are closed, prepare any journal entries that are required for each of the transactions. Ignore income tax considerations.

(b) For each of the items, discuss the type of change that is involved and how it is accounted for on the current and comparative financial statements.

(c) If Maglite elected to follow IFRS, discuss how this might change your answers to part (a).

(d) Repeat part (a) assuming that the books are open.

P21-7   The founder, president, and major shareholder of Dewitt Corp. recently sold his controlling interest in the company to a national distributor in the same line of business. The change in ownership was effective June 30, 2017, halfway through Dewitt's current fiscal year.

During the due diligence process of acquiring the company and over the last six months of 2017, the new senior management team had a chance to review the company's accounting records and policies. Dewitt follows ASPE. Although EPS are not part of ASPE, management calculates EPS for its own purposes and applies the IFRS guidelines. By the end of 2017, the following decisions had been made.

1. Dewitt's policy of expensing all interest as incurred will be changed to correspond to the policy of the controlling shareholder whereby interest on self-constructed assets is capitalized. This policy will be applied retrospectively, and going forward it will simplify the consolidation process for the parent company. The major effect of this policy is to reduce interest expense in 2015 by $9,200 and to increase the cost of equipment by the same amount. The equipment was put into service early in 2016. Dewitt uses straight-line depreciation for equipment and a five-year life. Because the interest has already been deducted for tax purposes, the change in policy results in a taxable temporary difference.

2. Deferred development costs of $12,000 remained in long-term assets at December 31, 2016. These were being written off on a straight-line basis with another three years remaining at that time. On reviewing the December 31, 2017 balances (after an additional year of depreciation), management decided that there were no further benefits to be received from these deferrals and there likely had not been any benefits for the past two years. The original costs were tax deductible when incurred.

3. A long-term contract with a preferred customer was completed in December 2017. When discussing payment with the customer, it came to light that a down payment of $30,000 made by the customer on the contract at the end of 2015 had been taken into revenue when received. The revenue should have been recognized in 2017 on completion of the contract.

Dewitt's financial statements (summarized) were as follows at December 31, 2016 and 2017, before any corrections related to the information above. The December 31, 2017 statements are in draft form only and the 2017 accounts have not yet been closed.

DEWITT CORP.
Statement of Financial Position
December 31

Assets	2017	2016	Liabilities and Shareholders' Equity	2017	2016
Current assets	$192,300	$168,400	Current liabilities	$117,000	$103,000
Long-term assets	322,000	311,000	Long-term liabilities	166,000	153,000
	$514,300	$479,400	Share capital (10,000 shares)	50,000	50,000
			Retained earnings	181,300	173,400
				$514,300	$479,400

DEWITT CORP.
Income Statement
Year Ended December 31

	2017	2016
Revenues	$475,000	$460,000
Expenses	378,000	376,000
	97,000	84,000
Income tax (30% effective rate)	29,100	25,200
Net income	$ 67,900	$ 58,800
Earnings per share	$ 6.79	$ 5.88
Dividends declared, per share	$ 6.00	$ 2.50

Instructions

(a) Prepare any December 31, 2017 journal entries needed to put into effect the decisions made by senior management. Where retrospective adjustments are made, record the journal entry to include the effect of income taxes.

(b) Prepare the comparative statement of financial position, income statement, and statement of retained earnings that will be issued to shareholders for the year ended December 31, 2017.

(c) Prepare the required note disclosures for the accounting changes.

(d) Assume now that Dewitt follows IFRS instead of ASPE. Briefly comment on the changes, if any, to the accounting treatment for the three decisions in items 1 to 3 above.

P21-8 On December 31, 2017, before the books were closed, management and the accountant at Flanagan Inc. made the following determinations about three depreciable assets.

1. Depreciable asset A (building) was purchased on January 2, 2014. It originally cost $540,000 and the straight-line method was chosen for depreciation. The asset was originally expected to be useful for 10 years and have no residual value. In 2017, the decision was made to change the depreciation method from straight-line to double-declining-balance due to a change in the pattern of benefits received. The estimates relating to useful life and residual value remained unchanged.

2. Depreciable asset B (machinery) was purchased on January 3, 2013. It originally cost $180,000 and the straight-line method was chosen for depreciation. The asset was expected to be useful for 15 years and have no residual value. In 2017, the decision was made to shorten this asset's total life to nine years and to estimate the residual value at $3,000.

3. Depreciable asset C (equipment) was purchased on January 5, 2013. The asset's original cost was $160,000 and this amount was entirely expensed in 2013 in error. This particular asset has a 10-year useful life and no residual value. The straight-line method is appropriate.

Additional information:

1. Income in 2017 before depreciation expense amounted to $400,000.

2. Depreciation expense on assets other than A, B, and C totalled $55,000 in 2017.

3. Income in 2016 was reported at $370,000.

4. In both 2016 and 2017, 100,000 common shares were outstanding. No dividends were declared in either year.

Flanagan Inc. follows IFRS.

Instructions
Answer the following questions, ignoring all income tax effects.

(a) Prepare any necessary entries in 2017.

(b) Calculate the adjusted net income and earnings per share for 2016 and 2017.

(c) Prepare comparative retained earnings statements for Flanagan Inc. for 2016 and 2017. The company reported retained earnings of $200,000 at December 31, 2015.

(d) Prepare the required note disclosures for each of these changes.

DIGGING DEEPER

(e) How would the changes to Flanagan's depreciable assets be reflected on the statement of cash flows?

P21-9 Sharma Corporation has decided that, in preparing its 2017 financial statements under IFRS, two changes should be made from the methods used in prior years:

1. **Depreciation.** Sharma has used the tax basis (CCA) method of calculating depreciation for financial reporting purposes. During 2017, management decided that the straight-line method should have been used to calculate depreciation for financial reporting purposes for the years prior to 2017 and going forward. The following schedule

identifies the excess of depreciation based on CCA over depreciation based on straight-line, for the past years and for the current year:

	Excess of CCA-Based Depreciation over Straight-Line Depreciation Calculated for Financial Statement Purposes
Prior to 2016	$1,365,000
2016	106,050
2017	103,950
	$1,575,000

Depreciation is charged 75% to cost of sales and 25% to selling, general, and administrative expenses.

2. **Bad debt expense.** In the past, Sharma recognized bad debt expense equal to 1.5% of net sales. After careful review, it has been decided that a rate of 1.75% is more appropriate for 2017. Bad debt expense is charged to selling, general, and administrative expenses.

The following information is taken from preliminary financial statements, which were prepared before including the effects of the two changes.

SHARMA CORPORATION
Condensed Statement of Financial Position
December 31, 2017

Assets	2017	2016
Current assets	$28,340,000	$29,252,000
Plant assets, at cost	45,792,000	43,974,000
Less: Accumulated depreciation	(23,761,000)	(22,946,000)
Other long-term assets*	15,221,000	14,648,000
	$65,592,000	$64,928,000

Liabilities and Shareholders' Equity		
Current liabilities	$21,124,000	$23,650,000
Long-term debt	15,154,000	14,097,000
Share capital	11,620,000	11,620,000
Retained earnings	17,694,000	15,561,000
	$65,592,000	$64,928,000

*Includes deferred tax asset of $225,000 (2017) and $234,000 (2016), with the latter amount being the result of deductible temporary differences that occurred before 2016.

SHARMA CORPORATION
Condensed Income Statement
Year Ended December 31, 2017

	2017	2016
Net sales	$80,520,000	$78,920,000
Cost of goods sold	54,847,000	53,074,000
	25,673,000	25,846,000
Selling, general, and administrative expenses	19,540,000	18,411,000
	6,133,000	7,435,000
Other expense, net	1,198,000	1,079,000
Income before income tax	4,935,000	6,356,000
Income tax	1,480,500	1,906,800
Net income	$ 3,454,500	$ 4,449,200

The condensed statement of financial position as at December 31, 2015 included the following amounts (excluding the effects of the changes above): current assets $28,454,000; plant assets, at cost $42,568,000; accumulated depreciation $22,429,000; other long-term assets $14,282,000; current liabilities $26,603,200; long-term debt $13,540,000; share capital $11,620,000; and retained earnings $11,111,800. Dividends of $1,321,500 were declared on December 31, 2017; however, no dividends were declared in 2015 or 2016.

There have been no temporary differences between any book and tax items prior to the above changes except for those that involve the allowance for doubtful accounts. For tax purposes, bad debts are deductible only when they are written off. The tax rate is 30%.

Instructions

(a) For each of the items that follow, calculate the amounts that would appear on the comparative (2017 and 2016) financial statements of Sharma Corporation after adjustment for the two accounting changes. Show amounts for both 2017 and 2016, and prepare supporting schedules as necessary.

1. Accumulated depreciation
2. Deferred tax asset/liability
3. Selling, general, and administrative expenses
4. Current income tax expense
5. Deferred tax expense

(b) Prepare the comparative financial statements that will be issued to shareholders for Sharma's year ended December 31, 2017.

P21-10 Both the management of Kimmel Instrument Corporation, a small company that follows IFRS, and its independent auditors recently concluded that the company's results of operations will be reliable and more relevant in future years if Kimmel changes its method of costing inventory from FIFO to weighted average cost. The following data are a five-year income summary using FIFO and a schedule of what the inventories might have been if they had been stated using the weighted average cost method.

KIMMEL INSTRUMENT CORPORATION
Statement of Income and Retained Earnings for the Years Ended May 31

	2013	2014	2015	2016	2017
Sales—net	$13,964	$15,506	$16,673	$18,221	$18,898
Cost of goods sold					
Beginning inventory	1,000	1,100	1,000	1,115	1,237
Purchases	13,000	13,900	15,000	15,900	17,100
Ending inventory	(1,100)	(1,000)	(1,115)	(1,237)	(1,369)
Total	12,900	14,000	14,885	15,778	16,968
Gross profit	1,064	1,506	1,788	2,443	1,930
Administrative expenses	700	763	832	907	989
Income before taxes	364	743	956	1,536	941
Income taxes (30%)	109	223	287	461	282
Net income	255	520	669	1,075	659
Retained earnings—beginning	1,206	1,461	1,981	2,650	3,725
Retained earnings—ending	$ 1,461	$ 1,981	$ 2,650	$ 3,725	$ 4,384
Earnings per share	$ 2.55	$ 5.20	$ 6.69	$ 10.75	$ 6.59

KIMMEL INSTRUMENT CORPORATION
Schedule of Inventory Balances Using Average Cost Method
Year Ended May 31

2012	2013	2014	2015	2016	2017
$950	$1,124	$1,091	$1,270	$1,480	$1,699

Instructions

(a) Prepare comparative statements for the five years that would be suitable for inclusion in the historical summary portion of Kimmel's annual report, assuming that Kimmel had changed its inventory costing method to weighted average cost in 2017. Indicate the effects on net income and earnings per share for the years involved. (All amounts except EPS are rounded up to the nearest dollar.)

FINANCE

(b) Prepare a schedule showing calculation of corrected retained earnings for 2017, 2016, and 2015, assuming retrospective treatment.

(c) Identify all statement of financial position accounts that require restatement on the comparative May 31, 2016 and 2015 statements of financial position issued to shareholders in 2017.

(d) Assume that the data for the years 2012 to 2016 were not available. Briefly explain how to account for this inability to apply full retrospective application under both ASPE and IFRS, and prepare a schedule showing calculation of corrected retained earnings for 2017, with a comparative schedule for 2016, as an illustration to aid in the explanation.

DIGGING
DEEPER

(e) From the perspective of an investor, comment on the effects of the change on net income and earnings per share for the years involved.

TAXATION

P21-11   It is December 2017 and Wagner Inc. recently hired a new accountant, Jodie Larson. Although Wagner is a private company, it follows IFRS. As part of her preparation of the 2017 financial statements for Wagner Inc., Jodie has proposed the following accounting changes.

1. At December 31, 2016, Wagner had a receivable of $250,000 from Michael Inc. on its statement of financial position that had been outstanding since mid-2015. In December 2017, Michael Inc. was declared bankrupt and no recovery is expected. Jodie proposes to write off the receivable in 2017 against retained earnings as a correction of a 2015 error.

2. Jodie proposes to change from double-declining-balance to straight-line depreciation for the company's manufacturing assets because of a change in the pattern in which the assets provide benefits to the company. If straight-line depreciation had been used for all prior periods, retained earnings would have been $380,800 higher at December 31, 2016. The change's effect just on 2017 income is a reduction of $48,800.

3. For equipment in the leasing division, Jodie proposes to adopt the sum-of-the-years'-digits depreciation method, which the company has never used before. Wagner began operating its leasing division in 2017. If straight-line depreciation were to be used, 2017 income would be $110,000 higher.

4. Wagner has decided to adopt the revaluation method for reporting and measuring its land, with this policy being effective from January 1, 2017. At December 31, 2016, the land's fair value was $900,000. The land's book value at December 31, 2016 was $750,000. (*Hint*: Refer to IAS 8 for the treatment of this specific change in policy.)

5. Wagner has investments that are recorded at fair value through other comprehensive income (FV-OCI). At December 31, 2016, an error was made in the calculation of the fair values of these investments. The amount of the error was an overstatement of the fair value by $200,000.

Wagner's income tax rate is 30%.

Instructions

(a) For each of the changes described above, identify whether the situation is a change in policy, a change in estimate, or an error correction. Justify your answer.

(b) For each of the changes described above, determine whether a restatement of the January 1, 2017 retained earnings is required. What is the amount of the adjustment, if any? Prepare the required journal entries to record any adjustments.

(c) Prepare the contents of the statement of changes in equity for 2016 and 2017 following the format below. An excerpt from the statement of changes in equity for December 31, 2016 is provided below:

	Share Capital	Retained Earnings	Accumulated Other Comprehensive Income Investments at FV-OCI	Total
Opening—January 1, 2016	$1,000,000	$2,500,000	$ 650,000	$4,150,000
Comprehensive income	–0–	910,000	475,000	1,385,000
Closing balance— December 31, 2016	$1,000,000	$3,410,000	$1,125,000	$5,535,000

For 2017, net income is $1,350,000 and other comprehensive income is $150,000 (relating to the change in value of the FV-OCI Investment during 2017). There were no shares issued or repurchased during the year. There are no other changes to the equity accounts for 2017.

(d) Identify what disclosures are required in the notes to the financial statements as a result of each of these changes.

P21-12   You have been assigned to examine the financial statements of Picard Corporation for the year ended December 31, 2017, as prepared following IFRS. Picard uses a periodic inventory system. You discover the following situations:

1. The physical inventory count on December 31, 2016 improperly excluded merchandise costing $34,000 that had been temporarily stored in a public warehouse.

2. The physical inventory count on December 31, 2017 improperly included merchandise with a cost of $17,400 that had been recorded as a sale on December 27, 2017, and was being held for the customer to pick up on January 4, 2018.

3. A collection of $6,200 on account from a customer received on December 31, 2017 was not recorded in 2017.

4. Depreciation of $7,600 for 2017 on delivery trucks was not recorded.

5. In 2017, the company received $2,700 on a sale of fully depreciated equipment that originally cost $32,000. The company credited the proceeds from the sale to the Equipment account.

6. During November 2017, a competitor company filed a patent infringement suit against Picard, claiming damages of $550,000. The company's legal counsel has indicated that an unfavourable verdict is probable and a reasonable estimate of the court's award to the competitor is $400,000. The company has not reflected or disclosed this situation in the financial statements.

7. A large piece of equipment was purchased on January 3, 2017 for $64,000 and was charged in error to Repairs and Maintenance Expense. The equipment is estimated to have a service life of eight years and no residual value. Picard normally uses the straight-line depreciation method for this type of equipment.

8. Picard has a portfolio of temporary trading investments reported at fair value. No adjusting entry has been made yet in 2017. Information on carrying amount and fair value is as follows:

	Carrying Amount	Fair Value
Dec. 31, 2016	$73,000	$73,000
Dec. 31, 2017	$62,000	$43,000

9. At December 31, 2017, an analysis of payroll information showed accrued salaries of $11,600. The Salaries and Wages Payable account had a balance of $18,000 at December 31, 2017, which was unchanged from its balance at December 31, 2016.

10. A $21,000 insurance premium paid on July 1, 2016 for a policy that expires on June 30, 2019 was charged to insurance expense.

11. A trademark was acquired at the beginning of 2016 for $48,000. Through an oversight, no amortization has been recorded since its acquisition. Picard expected the trademark to benefit the company for a total of approximately 12 years with no residual value.

Instructions

Assume that the trial balance has been prepared, the ending inventory has not yet been recorded, and the books have not been closed for 2017. Assuming also that all amounts are material, prepare journal entries showing the adjustments that are required. Ignore income tax considerations.

P21-13 On May 5, 2018, you were hired by Gavin Inc., a closely held company that follows ASPE, as a staff member of its newly created internal auditing department. While reviewing the company's records for 2016 and 2017, you discover that no adjustments have yet been made for the items listed below.

1. Interest income of $18,800 was not accrued at the end of 2016. It was recorded when received in February 2017.

2. Equipment costing $18,000 was expensed when purchased on July 1, 2016. It is expected to have a four-year life with no residual value. The company typically uses straight-line depreciation for all fixed assets.

3. Research costs of $36,000 were incurred early in 2016. They were capitalized and were to be amortized over a three-year period. Amortization of $12,000 was recorded for 2016 and $12,000 for 2017. For tax purposes, the research costs were expensed as incurred.

4. On January 2, 2016, Gavin leased a building for five years at a monthly rental of $9,000. On that date, Gavin paid the following amounts, which were expensed when paid for both financial reporting and tax purposes:

Security deposit	$35,000
First month's rent	9,000
Last month's rent	9,000
	$53,000

5. The company received $42,000 from a customer at the beginning of 2016 for services that it is to perform evenly over a three-year period beginning in 2016. None of the amount received was reported as unearned revenue at the end of 2016. The $42,000 was included in taxable income in 2016.

6. Merchandise inventory costing $16,800 was in the warehouse on December 31, 2016, but was incorrectly omitted from the physical count at that date. The company uses the periodic inventory method.

Gavin follows the taxes payable method of accounting for income taxes.

Instructions

Using the table that follows, enter the appropriate dollar amounts in the appropriate columns to indicate the effect of any errors on the net income figure reported on the income statement for the year ending December 31, 2016, and the retained earnings figure reported on the statement of financial position at December 31, 2017. Assume that all amounts are material and that an income tax rate of 25% is appropriate for all years. Assume also that each item is independent of the other items. It is not necessary to total the columns on the grid.

Item	Net Income for 2016		Retained Earnings at Dec. 31, 2017	
	Understated	Overstated	Understated	Overstated
	___	___	___	___
	___	___	___	___
	___	___	___	___

P21-14 Jacobsen Corporation is in the process of negotiating a loan for expansion purposes. Jacobsen's books and records have never been audited and the bank has requested that an audit be performed and that IFRS be followed. Jacobsen has prepared the following comparative financial statements for the years ended December 31, 2017 and 2016.

JACOBSEN CORPORATION
Statement of Financial Position
as at December 31, 2017 and 2016

	2017	2016
Assets		
Current assets		
Cash	$163,000	$ 82,000
Accounts receivable	392,000	296,000
Allowance for doubtful accounts	(37,000)	(18,000)
Fair value—net income investments	78,000	78,000
Inventory	207,000	202,000
Total current assets	803,000	640,000
Plant assets		
Property, plant, and equipment	167,000	169,500
Accumulated depreciation	(121,600)	(106,400)
Plant assets (net)	45,400	63,100
Total assets	$848,400	$703,100
Liabilities and Shareholders' Equity		
Liabilities		
Accounts payable	$121,400	$196,100
Shareholders' equity		
Common shares, no par value, 50,000 authorized, 20,000 issued and outstanding	260,000	260,000
Retained earnings	467,000	247,000
Total shareholders' equity	727,000	507,000
Total liabilities and shareholders' equity	$848,400	$703,100

JACOBSEN CORPORATION
Statement of Income
for the Years Ended December 31, 2017 and 2016

	2017	2016
Sales	$1,000,000	$900,000
Cost of sales	430,000	395,000
Gross profit	570,000	505,000
Operating expenses	210,000	205,000
Administrative expenses	140,000	105,000
	350,000	310,000
Net income	$ 220,000	$195,000

During the audit, the following additional facts were determined:

1. An analysis of collections and losses on accounts receivable during the past two years indicates a drop in anticipated bad debt losses. After consulting with management, it was agreed that the loss experience rate on sales should be reduced from the recorded 2% to 1.5%, beginning with the year ended December 31, 2017.

2. An analysis of the fair value—net income investments revealed that the total fair value for these investments as at the end of each year was as follows:

Dec. 31, 2016	$78,000
Dec. 31, 2017	$65,000

3. Inventory at December 31, 2016 was overstated by $8,900 and inventory at December 31, 2017 was overstated by $13,600.

4. On January 2, 2016, equipment costing $30,000 (estimated useful life of 10 years and residual value of $5,000) was incorrectly charged to operating expenses. Jacobsen records depreciation on the straight-line basis. In 2017, fully depreciated equipment (with no residual value) that originally cost $17,500 was sold as scrap for $2,800. Jacobsen credited the $2,800 in proceeds to the Equipment account.

5. An analysis of 2016 operating expenses revealed that Jacobsen charged to expense a four-year insurance premium of $4,700 on January 15, 2016.

6. The analysis of operating expenses also revealed that operating expenses were incorrectly classified as part of administrative expenses in the amount of $15,000 in 2016 and $35,000 in 2017.

Instructions

(a) Prepare the journal entries to correct the books at December 31, 2017. The books for 2017 have not been closed. Ignore income tax effects.

(b) Beginning with reported net income, prepare a schedule showing the calculation of corrected net income for the years ended December 31, 2017 and 2016, assuming that any adjustments are to be reported on comparative statements for the two years. Ignore income tax effects. (Do not prepare financial statements.)

AUDIT AND ASSURANCE

(c) Prepare a schedule showing the calculation of corrected retained earnings at January 1, 2017.

(AICPA adapted)

P21-15 Kitchener Corporation has followed IFRS and used the accrual basis of accounting for several years. A review of the records, however, indicates that some expenses and revenues have been handled on a cash basis because of errors made by an inexperienced bookkeeper. Income statements prepared by the bookkeeper reported $29,000 net income for 2016 and $37,000 net income for 2017. Further examination of the records reveals that the following items were handled improperly.

1. Rent of $1,300 was received from a tenant in December 2016, but the full amount was recorded as income at that time even though the rental related to 2017.

2. Wages payable on December 31 have been consistently omitted from the records of that date and have been entered instead as expenses when paid in the following year. The amounts of the accruals that were recorded in this way were as follows:

Dec. 31, 2015	$1,100
Dec. 31, 2016	1,500
Dec. 31, 2017	940

3. Invoices for office supplies purchased have been charged to expense accounts when received. Inventories of supplies on hand at the end of each year have been ignored, and no entry has been made for them. The inventories were as follows:

Dec. 31, 2015	$1,300
Dec. 31, 2016	740
Dec. 31, 2017	1,420

Instructions

(a) Prepare a schedule that shows the corrected net income for the years 2016 and 2017. All listed items should be labelled clearly. Ignore income tax considerations.

(b) Prepare the required journal entries to correct the 2017 net income. Assume that the books are open and ignore income tax considerations.

(c) Assume that Kitchener had unadjusted retained earnings of $95,000 at January 1, 2016, and $124,000 at January 1, 2017. Prepare a schedule that shows the corrected opening retained earnings balances.

(d) Assume that Kitchener had total net sales revenue of $1.2 million and $1.1 million in 2016 and 2017, respectively. From the perspective of an investor, discuss the effects of the errors on Kitchener's profit margin in 2016 and 2017.

DIGGING DEEPER

P21-16 You have been asked by a client to review the records of Inteq Corporation, a small manufacturer of precision tools and machines that follows ASPE. Your client is interested in buying the business, and arrangements were made for you to review the accounting records. Your examination reveals the following.

1. Inteq Corporation started business on April 1, 2014, and has been reporting on a fiscal year ending March 31. The company has never been audited, but the annual statements prepared by the bookkeeper reflect the following income before closing and before deducting income tax:

FINANCE

Year Ended March 31	Income Before Taxes
2015	$ 71,600
2016	111,400
2017	103,580

2. A relatively small number of machines have been shipped on consignment. These transactions have been recorded as ordinary sales and billed in this way, with the gross profit on each sale being recognized when the machine was shipped. On March 31 of each year, the amounts for machines billed and in the hands of consignees were as follows:

2015	$6,500
2016	none
2017	5,590

The sales price was determined by adding 30% to cost. Assume that the consigned machines are sold the following year.

3. On March 30, 2016, two machines were shipped to a customer on a C.O.D. basis. The sale was not entered until April 5, 2016, when $6,100 cash was received. The machines were not included in the inventory at March 31, 2016. (Title passed on March 30, 2016.)

4. All machines are sold subject to a five-year warranty. It is estimated that the expense ultimately to be incurred in connection with the warranty will amount to 0.5% of sales. The company has charged an expense account for actual warranty costs incurred. Sales per books and warranty costs were as follows:

		Actual Warranty Costs Incurred for Sales Made in				
Year Ended March 31	Sales					Total
2015	$ 940,000	2015	$760			$ 760
2016	1,010,000	2016	360	$1,310		1,670
2017	1,795,000	2017	320	1,620	$1,910	3,850

5. A review of the corporate minutes reveals that the manager is entitled to a bonus of 0.5% of the income before deducting income tax and the bonus. The bonuses have never been recorded or paid.

6. Bad debts have been recorded on a direct write-off basis. Experience of similar enterprises indicates that losses will approximate 0.25% of sales. Bad debts written off and expensed were as follows:

	Bad Debts Incurred on Sales Made in			
				Total
2015	$750			$ 750
2016	800	$ 520		1,320
2017	350	1,800	$1,700	3,850

7. The bank deducts 6% on all contracts that it finances. Of this amount, 0.5% is placed in a reserve to the credit of Inteq Corporation and is refunded to Inteq as financed contracts are paid in full. The reserve established by the bank has not been reflected in Inteq's books. On the books of the bank for each fiscal year, the excess of credits over debits (the net increase) to the reserve account for Inteq were as follows:

2015	$ 3,000
2016	3,900
2017	5,100
	$12,000

8. Commissions on sales have been entered when paid. Commissions payable on March 31 of each year were as follows:

2015	$1,400
2016	800
2017	1,120

Instructions

(a) Present a schedule showing the revised income before income tax for each of the years ended March 31, 2015, 2016, and 2017. Make calculations to the nearest dollar.

(b) Prepare the journal entry or entries that you would give the bookkeeper to correct the books. Assume that the books have not yet been closed for the fiscal year ended March 31, 2017. Disregard corrections of income tax.

(AICPA adapted)

P21-17   Bayberry Corporation performs year-end planning in November each year before its fiscal year ends in December. The preliminary estimated net income following IFRS is $4.2 million. The CFO, Rita Warren, meets with the company president, Jim Bayberry, to review the projected numbers.

ETHICS   The corporation has never used robotic equipment before, and Rita assumed an accelerated method of depreciation because of the rapidly changing technology in robotic equipment. The company normally uses straight-line depreciation for production equipment. The investment securities held at year end were purchased during 2017, and are accounted for using the fair value through other comprehensive income (FV-OCI) model.

Jim explains to Rita that it is important for the corporation to show a $7-million income before tax because he receives a $1-million bonus if the income before tax and bonus reaches $7 million. He also cautions that the company does not want to pay more than $2.5 million in income tax to the government. Rita presents the following projected information.

BAYBERRY CORPORATION
Projected Income Statement
Year Ended December 31, 2017
($000s)

Sales		$29,000
Cost of goods sold	$14,000	
Depreciation	2,600	
Operating expenses	6,400	23,000
Income before income tax		6,000
Provision for income tax		1,800
Net income		$ 4,200

SELECTED STATEMENT OF FINANCIAL POSITION INFORMATION
December 31, 2017
($000s)

Estimated cash balance	$ 5,000
Investment securities (FV-OCI) (at cost)	10,000

Security	Cost	Estimated Fair Value
A	$ 2,000	$ 2,200
B	4,000	3,900
C	3,000	3,000
D	1,000	1,800
Total	$10,000	$10,900

Other information ($000s) at December 31, 2017:

Equipment	$3,000
Accumulated depreciation (5 years, straight-line)	1,200
New robotic equipment (purchased 1/1/17)	5,000
Accumulated depreciation (5 years, double-declining-balance)	2,000

Instructions

DIGGING DEEPER

(a) What can Rita do within IFRS to accommodate the president's wishes to achieve $7 million of income before tax and bonus? Present the revised income statement based on your decision.

(b) Are the actions ethical? Who are the stakeholders in this decision, and what effects do Jim's actions have on their interests?

(c) Are there any cash flow implications of the choices made to achieve the president's wishes?

(d) Assume that Bayberry Corporation follows ASPE instead of IFRS. Briefly comment on the changes, if any, to the accounting treatment of the items discussed above.

P21-18   Ali Reiners, a new controller of Luftsa Corp., is preparing the financial statements for the year ended December 31, 2017. Luftsa is a publicly traded entity and therefore follows IFRS. Ali has found the following information.

1. Luftsa has been offering a loyalty rewards program to its customers for about five years. In the past, the company has not deferred recognition of any revenue, or recorded any accrual related to the accumulated points, because the amounts were not significant. However, with recent changes to the plan in 2017, the loyalty points are now accumulating much more rapidly and have become material. Ali has decided that, effective January 1, 2017, the company will defer the revenue related to these points at the time of each sale, which will result in a liability.

2. In 2017, Luftsa decided to change its accounting policy for depreciating property, plant, and equipment to depreciating based on components and also to adopt the revaluation model. The company hired specialized appraisers at January 1, 2017 to determine the fair values, useful lives, and depreciable amounts for all of the components of the assets. In prior years, the company did not have enough documentation to be able to apply component accounting, and the appraisers could not determine this information.

3. One division of Luftsa Corp., Rosentiel Co., has consistently shown an increasing net income from period to period. On closer examination of its operating statement, Ali Reiners noted that inventory obsolescence charges are much lower than in other divisions. In discussing this with the division's controller, Ali learned that the controller knowingly makes low estimates related to the write-off of inventory in order to manage his bottom line.

4. In 2017, the company purchased new machinery that is expected to increase production dramatically, particularly in the early years. The company has decided to depreciate this machinery on an accelerated basis, even though other machinery is depreciated on a straight-line basis.

5. All products sold by Luftsa are subject to a three-year warranty. It has been estimated that the expense ultimately to be incurred on these machines is 1% of sales. In 2017, because of a production breakthrough, it is now estimated that 0.5% of sales is sufficient. In 2015 and 2016, warranty expense was calculated as $64,000 and $70,000, respectively. The company now believes that warranty costs should be reduced by 50%.

6. In reviewing the capital asset ledger in another division, Harper Division, Ali found a series of unusual accounting changes in which the useful lives of assets were substantially reduced when halfway through the original life estimate. For example, the useful life of one truck was changed from 10 to 6 years during its fifth year of service. The divisional manager, who is compensated in large part by bonuses, indicated on investigation, "It's perfectly legal to change an accounting estimate. We always have better information after time has passed."

Instructions

ETHICS

Ali Reiners has come to you for advice about each of the situations. Prepare a memorandum to the controller, indicating the appropriate accounting treatment for each situation. For any situations where there might be ethical considerations, identify and assess the issues and suggest what should be done.

Integrated Cases

ENABLING COMPETENCIES

IC21-1 Temple Limited is in the real estate business. After several years of economic growth, most of the company's assets are now worth significantly more than the amount that is recognized on the financial statements. Wanting to capitalize on this positive trend, the company is ready to expand and is looking at developing a new property in the Bahamas that will cost $300 million. Currently, the company's debt to equity ratio is 5:1 and the company needs to raise funds for the expansion. Lendall Bank, the company's primary lender, understands that there is hidden value in the statement of financial position and is willing to finance the project.

Temple is now concerned about how the capital markets will react to this increase in debt. The company's shares list on the TSX and, therefore, IFRS is a constraint. Under IFRS, fair value accounting is permitted for real estate as an accounting policy choice.

Instructions

Adopt the role of Temple Limited's controller and write a memo to address the CEO's concerns.

IC21-2 Sunlight Equipment Manufacturers (SEM) makes barbecue equipment. The company has historically been very profitable; however, in the last year and a half, things have taken a turn for the worse due to higher consumer interest rates and a slowdown in the economy. On its 2017 draft year-end statements, the company is currently showing a break-even position before any final year-end adjustments. The company had fired its CEO, Sam Lazano, at the beginning of the year and a turnaround specialist was hired—Agneta Lundstrom. Agneta has a reputation of being able to come into companies that are suffering and make them profitable within two years. Agneta has agreed with SEM's board of directors that she will be paid a $1-million bonus if the company has a combined two-year profit of $5 million by the end of 2018.

Among other things, Agneta instituted a more aggressive sales policy for SEM's customers, who are mainly retailers, as well as a new remuneration policy for sales staff. Agneta attributed the company's poor performance to untrained sales staff whose remuneration and bonus scheme were not properly aligned to maximize sales. Under the new remuneration policy, sales staff is paid salary as well as a bonus, which is a percentage of gross sales as at year end. The sales staff has responded well and sales have increased by 20%.

The new sales policy is as follows:

- Cash down payment of 20% with remaining payment for shipment once the barbecues are sold by the customer to a third party.
- If the customers double their normal order, no down payment is required.
- The barbecues may be stored on the premises of SEM. Many customers have taken the company up on this offer in order to double the size of their purchase.
- Any unsold barbecues are allowed to be returned after year end.

Under the new policy, sales have increased dramatically, with many customers taking advantage of the new terms. As at year end, legal title to all barbecues has passed to the customers. Only customers with an excellent credit history have been allowed to purchase under the new policy. The company has accrued bonuses for almost its entire sales staff.

The increased profits from these sales have been offset by the accrual of $500,000 of Agneta's bonus. She is very confident that she will be able to turn the company around and so has accrued part of her bonus. She has also

decided to change several accounting policies, including the following:

- Depreciation on machinery switched to straight-line from double-declining-balance. Note that the equipment is about 2 years old with an estimated life of 10 years. Agneta felt that the double-declining-balance method was arbitrary and noted that several of SEM's competitors use the straight-line method. Machinery is most useful when new because it requires less downtime for fixing.

Another problem that Agneta had identified was in inventory management. Agneta was convinced that inventory was being stolen and/or "lost" due to poor tracking. SEM had therefore hired a company, Software Limited, to install a new inventory tracking system during the year. Midway through the year, Software Limited had gone bankrupt and was not able to finish the installation. The installation was a customized job and as at year end, the system was not functioning yet. SEM has not been able to find a company to replace Software Limited. To date, $2 million has been spent on the new system. Agneta had capitalized the costs and noted she was confident that she would be able to find a company that could successfully complete the installation.

ETHICS, AUDIT AND ASSURANCE

Instructions

Adopt the role of the company's auditors and discuss the financial reporting issues for the 2017 year end. The company is a private company but would like the statements to be prepared in accordance with IFRS.

RESEARCH AND ANALYSIS

REAL WORLD EMPHASIS

RA21-1 Brookfield Asset Management Inc.

Refer to the specimen financial statements at the end of the book, which show excerpts from the 2014 year-end financial statements, including the accompanying notes, of **Brookfield Asset Management Inc.** The full financial statements are available on SEDAR. In the notes, the company refers to the adoption of new or revised accounting standards in the current year, and future changes in accounting standards—those new standards that have been issued but are not yet effective. The company also provides disclosure in Note 2 about areas in its accounting where significant judgement has to be exercised and where there is a significant degree of measurement uncertainty.

Instructions

(a) Review Note 2 of Brookfield Asset Management's financial statements. Indicate what accounting standard(s) have been adopted or changed by the company in the year, and explain when the new standard(s) were applied, how they

were applied, and what the effect was on the financial statements.

(b) Identify what new or revised standards have been issued but are not yet effective. What information does the company provide on these upcoming standards? If not yet applied, do you think the standards identified might have a significant impact on future financial statements? Briefly explain.

(c) Identify the key judgements required by management in relation to the financial statements, briefly explain the issues, and indicate what difference it would make if the judgement exercised had resulted in a different decision than management made.

(d) Identify the areas in which critical estimates had to be made by management in the preparation of the financial statements. Are these significant to the company's operations? Discuss briefly by relating them to the business that Brookfield Asset Management is engaged in.

(e) Briefly explain why accounting standards require the information identified in parts (c) and (d) to be disclosed.

RA21-2   Airbus Group NV

REAL WORLD EMPHASIS

Access the financial statements of **Airbus Group NV** for its year ended December 31, 2014 from the company's website at www.airbusgroup.com. Note 1 to its financial statements indicates that Airbus Group's core business involves "the manufacturing of commercial aircraft, civil and military helicopters, commercial space launch vehicles, missiles, military aircraft, satellites, defence systems, defence electronics and the rendering of services related to these activities."

Instructions

(a) Review the Summary of Significant Accounting Policies (Note 2) to the financial statements and determine whether the company reported any changes in accounting standards. Identify and explain each change in accounting policy that the company implemented in 2014. If the change was due to an amendment of the standards, provide the details of the effective date of the change. Classify each change as being one of the following:

  1. A change in accounting policy mandated by a change in a primary source of GAAP

  2. A voluntary change in accounting policy

  3. A change in estimate

(b) For each change reported above, explain whether the change was retrospectively or prospectively applied. What was the effect of each change on the financial statements of Airbus Group in each year presented?

(c) The company also provides details for future accounting changes. Identify these changes and describe the note disclosure provided for these.

RA21-3   Research—IASB Work Plan

The IASB regularly updates and publishes a project plan that outlines the timelines for the projects it is working on.

Instructions

Using the IASB website (www.ifrs.org), identify new standards that have been recently released. Review the transitional provisions, if any, for each of these standards to find out when each becomes effective and whether they are to be prospectively or retrospectively applied. In addition, identify what else is on the work plan, and comment on what this tells you about accounting standards and financial reporting.

RA21-4   Loblaw Companies Limited

REAL WORLD EMPHASIS

Access the financial statements of **Loblaw Companies Limited** for its 2014 year ended January 3, 2015 from SEDAR (www.sedar.com) or the company's website.

Instructions

Review the financial statements and the company's note disclosures related to new accounting standards implemented, changes in significant accounting policies, and critical accounting estimates and judgements.

(a) Identify any new or revised accounting standard(s) that were implemented by Loblaw in its 2014 fiscal year. How were the changes accounted for, and what was the effect of the change(s) on the financial statements?

(b) Identify any change(s) made to the company's significant accounting policies in the year, and explain the reason for each change. From the relevant accounting policy note, the accounts involved, and the direction of the change, explain what decision management likely made as the basis for the change.

(c) List the presentation and disclosure requirements for a change in accounting policy, and indicate the extent to which Loblaw provided these disclosures.

(d) What judgements and accounting estimates were critical to the financial position and operating results reported by the company for its 2014 year? Comment briefly on whether you think the reported numbers could be materially different.

ENDNOTES

[1] *CPA Canada Handbook–Accounting*, Part II, Section 1506.05 and IAS 8 *Accounting Policies, Changes in Accounting Estimates and Errors*, para. 5. Copyright © International Financial Reporting Standards Foundation. All rights reserved. Reproduced by John Wiley & Sons Canada, Ltd. with the permission of the International Financial Reporting Standards Foundation ®. Reproduction and use rights are strictly limited. No permission granted to third parties to reproduce or distribute.

[2] Ibid. Copyright © International Financial Reporting Standards Foundation. All rights reserved. Reproduced by John Wiley & Sons Canada, Ltd with the permission of the International Financial Reporting Standards Foundation®. Reproduction and use rights are strictly limited. No permission granted to third parties to reproduce or distribute.

[3] Ibid. Copyright © International Financial Reporting Standards Foundation. All rights reserved. Reproduced by John Wiley & Sons Canada, Ltd with the permission of the International Financial Reporting Standards Foundation®. Reproduction and use rights are strictly limited. No permission granted to third parties to reproduce or distribute.

[4] *CPA Canada Handbook–Accounting*, Part II, Section 1100 *Financial Statement Concepts*.

[5] IAS 8.14. If an entity changes its accounting policy by following a source other than a primary source of GAAP, this is treated as a

voluntary change in policy (IAS 8.21). Under both sets of GAAP, early adoption of a new accounting standard is not considered a voluntary change in policy. Copyright © International Financial Reporting Standards Foundation. All rights reserved. Reproduced by John Wiley & Sons Canada, Ltd. with the permission of the International Financial Reporting Standards Foundation®. Reproduction and use rights are strictly limited. No permission granted to third parties to reproduce or distribute.

[6] *CPA Canada Handbook–Accounting*, Part II, Section 1506.09.

[7] IAS 1.10.

[8] Think this through. The book value of the property, plant, and equipment asset has just been increased, but no change has been made to the undepreciated capital cost. Future depreciation expense is based on the larger carrying amount, but this won't be permitted for tax purposes; the costs were actually deducted for tax purposes previously. Therefore, future taxable income will be higher than accounting income.

[9] The correct deferred tax asset amount is 30% of the difference between the asset's tax basis and its carrying amount. Because no capital cost allowance has been claimed, the correct tax basis at December 31, 2017 is $150,000, its capital cost. The correct carrying amount at December 31, 2017 is $150,000 − $14,000 = $136,000.

The temporary difference is $150,000 − $136,000 = $14,000 and the deferred tax asset is $14,000 × 30% = $4,200.

[10] IAS 1.125 and *CPA Canada Handbook–Accounting*, Part II, Section 1508.10.

[11] See Ross L. Watts and Jerold L. Zimmerman, "Positive Accounting Theory: A Ten-Year Perspective," *The Accounting Review* (January 1990) for an excellent review of research findings related to management incentives in selecting accounting methods.

[12] Economic consequences arguments—and there are many of them—constitute manipulation through the use of lobbying and other forms of pressure brought on standard setters. We have seen examples of these arguments in the oil and gas industry about successful efforts versus full cost, in the technology area with the issue of mandatory expensing of research and most development costs, and with stock options and other issues.

[13] Note that this example may be using hindsight in order to derive the amounts needing correction in each specific year, and therefore, the entity may contend that it is impracticable to retrospectively restate past amounts. Retrospective restatement does not endorse the use of hindsight, so the adjustment may actually need to be made on a partial retrospective basis or even only in the current year.

REFERENCE TO THE CPA COMPETENCY MAP

LEARNING OBJECTIVES

After studying this chapter, you should be able to:

1.1.1, 1.4.5, 5.1.1	**1.** Understand the business importance of cash flows and describe the purpose and uses of the statement of cash flows.
1.2.1. 1.2.2, 1.3.1	**2.** Define cash and cash equivalents.
1.2.1, 1.2.2, 1.3.1	**3.** Identify the major classifications of cash flows and explain the significance of each classification.
1.2.1, 1.2.2, 1.3.1	**4.** Prepare the operating activities section of a statement of cash flows using the direct versus the indirect method.
1.2.1, 1.2.2, 1.3.1	**5.** Prepare a statement of cash flows using the direct method.
1.2.1, 1.2.2, 1.3.1	**6.** Prepare a statement of cash flows using the indirect method.
1.2.1, 1.2.2, 1.2.3, 1.3.1	**7.** Prepare a more complex statement of cash flows using both methods.
1.1.1, 1.1.2, 1.2.1, 1.3.1, 1.3.2, 1.4.2, 1.4.4	**8.** Identify the financial presentation and disclosure requirements for the statement of cash flows.
1.2.1, 1.4.5, 3.2.1, 5.2.1	**9.** Read and interpret a statement of cash flows.
1.1.4	**10.** Identify differences in IFRS and ASPE, and explain what changes are expected to standards for the statement of cash flows.

After studying Appendix 22A, you should be able to:

| 1.1.3, 1.2.1, 1.2.2, 1.2.3, 1.3.1 | **11.** Use a work sheet to prepare a statement of cash flows. |

ARE "CASH GUSHERS" GOOD INVESTMENTS?

INVESTORS CONSIDERING BUYING SHARES in companies look at many numbers that can indicate the health of the business, including earnings per share and the price-earnings ratio. Another important financial factor is a company's cash flow. A company that generates positive cash flow from its operations and financing and investing activities is more likely to be profitable and to be in a position to use excess cash to expand and to declare dividends to shareholders.

A financial analyst who follows the stock market recently researched Canadian companies to see which ones were "cash gushers"—those that had high free cash flow yields and margins and that put that cash to good use by having high returns on invested capital. Free cash flow is the amount of cash a company has left over after its net operating cash flows are reduced by the amount needed to maintain its capital expenditure and dividend levels, so some investors think it's a good representation of the returns that shareholders receive. The analyst, at CPMS Morningstar Canada (a firm that provides equity research), came up with a list in 2013 of 20 stocks on the

TSX (with a market capitalization of at least $200 million) that had the best combination of those factors. The analyst found that these top firms had strong returns and tended to be good investments.

The company at the number one spot on the 2013 list was wood-products maker Ainsworth Lumber Co. Its free cash flow yield was 16.4% and its free cash flow margin was 16.9%. The analyst calculated free cash flow yield by dividing the free cash flow by the company's share price. The free cash flow margin was defined as free cash flow divided by revenue. Around the same time that the Morningstar list was published, analysts at Raymond James Ltd. rated Ainsworth shares a "strong buy" for investors, based partly on its strong free cash flow yields.

For the year ended December 31, 2013, Ainsworth's net cash flows from all its activities (operating, financing, and investing) were an inflow of $30.7 million, according to the consolidated statements of cash flows in its 2014 annual report. In 2014, however, the price of its main product, oriented strand board (particle board), fell on the world market, and Ainsworth ended 2014 with a net cash outflow of $68.1 million. Despite Ainsworth's recent negative cash flows, it was still attractive to a competitor, Norbord Inc., which in late 2014 bought Ainsworth for $759 million. Norbord offered Ainsworth shareholders 0.1321 of a Norbord share for each Ainsworth share, which Norbord valued at 15% above the average of what Ainsworth shares were trading at in the 20 days before the deal was announced. "The merged entity will focus on maintaining a prudent balance sheet to provide financial flexibility and a solid capital base to support the business through periods of commodity price weakness," Norbord said in its news release announcing the merger.

Sources: "Norbord and Ainsworth to Merge to Create Global OSB Leader," Norbord news release, December 8, 2014; CBC News, "Norbord, Ainsworth Lumber to Merge in $759M Deal," CBC.ca, December 8, 2014; Daryl Swetlishoff and David Quezada, "Ainsworth Lumber Co. Ltd.: The Best Defence Is a Good Offence," Raymond James company report, June 3, 2013; Ian McGugan, "20 TSX-Listed Stocks That Are Cash Gushers," *The Globe and Mail*, May 21, 2013; Ian McGugan, "Prospecting for the Biggest Cash-Gushers," *The Globe and Mail*, April 17, 2012.

PREVIEW OF CHAPTER 22

Examining a company's income statement may provide insights into its profitability, but it does not provide much information about its liquidity and financial flexibility. The purpose of this chapter is to highlight the requirements for the reporting of statements of cash flows found in IFRS and ASPE. We explain the main components of this statement and the type of information it provides, and demonstrate how to prepare, report on, and interpret such a statement. The chapter ends with a comparison of IFRS and ASPE standards for the statement of cash flows.

The chapter is organized as follows:

STATEMENT OF CASH FLOWS					
Introduction to Cash Flows and the Statement of Cash Flows	**Preparing a Statement of Cash Flows**	**Presentation**	**Analyzing the Statement of Cash Flows**	**IFRS/ASPE Comparison**	**Appendix 22A–Use of a Work Sheet**
▪ Purpose, uses, and importance from a business perspective ▪ What is included in cash? ▪ Classification of cash flows ▪ Format of the statement	▪ Illustration using the direct method—Tax Consultants Inc. ▪ Illustration using the indirect method–Eastern Window Products Limited ▪ Illustration using both methods–Yoshi Corporation	▪ Disclosure requirements ▪ Presentation requirements ▪ Illustrative example	▪ Interpreting the statement of cash flows ▪ Sensitivity analysis ▪ Free cash flow	▪ A comparison of IFRS and ASPE ▪ Looking ahead	▪ Preparing the work sheet ▪ Analyzing transactions ▪ Completing the work sheet

INTRODUCTION TO CASH FLOWS AND THE STATEMENT OF CASH FLOWS

Purpose, Uses, and Importance from a Business Perspective

Objective 1
Understand the business importance of cash flows and describe the purpose and uses of the statement of cash flows.

Why do companies go bankrupt? One of the main causes is a lack of cash flow. In particular, one sign of a healthy company is positive cash flow from operations. Companies can use these funds to finance expansion, to issue dividends, or to ensure that they remain solvent during economic downturns. As one of Canada's largest banks has pointed out, cash flow is the lifeblood of businesses. "You may anticipate large profits tomorrow, but if you can't pay your bills today, you may not get a chance to realize those profits."[1]

Given the importance of cash flows for business, it is not surprising that the statement of cash flows has grown in significance for companies and standard setters over the past 25 years. In addition, many consider the statement of cash flows to be less susceptible to earnings management than the statement of comprehensive income, which has more subjective accruals for items such as bad debt expense, inventory obsolescence, and restructuring costs.

The statement of cash flows helps users answer many questions. For example, will the company be able to continue to pay dividends? How did it finance the acquisition of its new subsidiary? Will the company have sufficient cash to meet the debt that is maturing next year? Why did cash increase when there was a net loss for the period? How were the proceeds of the bond issue used? How was the expansion in plant and equipment financed? Or, as the opening story discusses, to what extent are companies with good cash flow prospects also good investment opportunities? We cannot answer these questions by reviewing the statement of financial position and statement of income or comprehensive income alone. We need to look at a statement of cash flows.

A key use of the statement of cash flows by investors and creditors is the assessment of companies' earnings quality. (For example, it allows an easy comparison of net profit and cash flow from operations.) The statement of cash flows is also used to assess companies' ability to repay their debts as they come due and their ability to generate cash for long-run success. We focus on the uses of the statement below.

The primary purpose of the **statement of cash flows** is to provide information about an entity's cash receipts and cash payments during a period. A secondary objective is to provide information on a cash basis about its operating, investing, and financing activities. The statement of cash flows therefore reports cash receipts, cash payments, and the net change in cash and cash equivalents resulting from an enterprise's operating, investing, and financing activities during a period. It does so in a format that reconciles the beginning and ending cash balances.

The information in a statement of cash flows enables investors, creditors, and others to assess the following:

1. **Liquidity and solvency of an entity—its capacity to generate cash and its needs for cash resources.** To assess an entity's ability to generate cash to pay maturing debt, to maintain and increase productive capacity, and to distribute a return to owners, it is important to determine both the timing and degree of certainty of expected cash inflows.

2. **Amounts, timing, and uncertainty of future cash flows.** Historical cash flows are often useful when predicting future cash flows. Readers can examine the relationships between items such as sales and net income and the cash flow from operating activities, or cash flow from operating activities and increases or decreases in cash. They can then make better predictions of the amounts, timing, and uncertainty of future cash flows than is possible using accrual-based data alone.

3. **Reasons for the difference between net income and cash flow from operating activities.** The net income number is important because it provides information on an enterprise's success or failure from one period to another. But some people are critical of accrual basis income because so many estimates are needed to calculate it. As a result, the number's reliability is often challenged. This usually does not occur with cash. Readers of the financial statements benefit from knowing the reasons for the difference between net income and cash flow from operating activities. It allows them to make their own assessment of the income number's reliability.

Because of the importance of this information, the statement of cash flows is required to be included when preparing IFRS and ASPE financial statements.

FINANCIAL ANALYSIS AND PLANNING
5.1.1

UNDERLYING CONCEPT

The statement of cash flows is another example of relevant information—information that is useful in assessing and predicting future cash flows.

What Is Included in Cash?

Objective 2
Define cash and cash equivalents.

As part of a company's cash management system, short-term, near-cash investments are often held, instead of cash alone, because this allows the company to earn a return on cash

UNDERLYING CONCEPT

In their joint financial statement presentation project, the FASB and the IASB tentatively decided to discontinue the use of the term "cash equivalents." Instead, they suggested that all non-cash securities be presented and classified in the same way as other short-term investments. However, the project was paused, as discussed in the "Looking Ahead" section at the end of the chapter.

balances that exceed its immediate needs. It is also common for an organization to have an agreement with a bank that allows its account to fluctuate between a positive balance and an overdraft. Because a company's cash activity and position are more appropriately described by including these other cash management activities, **cash flows** are defined in terms of inflows and outflows of cash and cash equivalents.

Cash is defined as cash on hand and demand deposits. **Cash equivalents** are short-term, highly liquid investments that are readily convertible to known amounts of cash and that have an insignificant risk of change in value.[2] Cash equivalents are made up of **non-equity investments** that are acquired with short maturities—generally three months or less when they are acquired—and include such short-term investments as treasury bills, commercial paper, and money market funds that are acquired with cash in excess of current needs. IAS 7 *Statement of Cash Flows* does permit preferred shares acquired close to their maturity date to be included because they are cash equivalents in substance. In addition, **bank overdrafts** that are repayable on demand and fluctuate often between positive and negative balances are included in cash and cash equivalents under both sets of standards if they result from and are an integral part of an organization's cash management policies. Otherwise, amounts borrowed from a bank are generally considered financing activities.

Throughout this chapter, the use of the term "cash" should be interpreted generally to mean "cash and cash equivalents."

Classification of Cash Flows

Objective 3
Identify the major classifications of cash flows and explain the significance of each classification.

The statement of cash flows (or "cash flow statement" as it is referred to under ASPE) classifies cash receipts and cash payments according to whether they result from an operating, investing, or financing activity. The transactions and other events that are characteristic of each kind of activity and the significance of each type of cash flow are as follows.

1. **Operating activities** are the enterprise's principal revenue-producing activities and other activities that are not investing or financing activities. Operating flows generally involve the cash effects of transactions that determine net income, such as collections from customers on the sale of goods and services, and payments to suppliers for goods and services acquired, to the Canada Revenue Agency for income taxes, and to employees for salaries and wages.

   The amount of cash that is provided by or used in operations is key information for financial statement users. Operating cash flows—derived mainly from receipts from customers—are needed to maintain the organization's systems: to meet payrolls, to pay suppliers, to cover rentals and insurance, and to pay taxes. In addition, surplus cash flows from operations are needed to repay loans, to take advantage of new investment opportunities, and to pay dividends without having to seek new external financing.

2. **Investing activities** involve the acquisition and disposal of long-term assets and other investments that are not included in cash equivalents or those acquired for trading purposes. (Cash flows relating to the purchase and sale of trading securities are included as part of operating activities.) Investing cash flows are a result of activities such as making and collecting loans and acquiring and disposing of investments and productive long-lived assets such as property, plant, and equipment and intangibles. They also include cash payments for and receipts from a variety of derivative products, unless such contracts are entered into for trading or financing purposes.

   The use of cash in investing activities tells financial statement readers whether the entity is reinvesting cash into additional long-term assets that will generate profits and increase cash flows in the future, or whether the stock of long-term productive assets is being decreased by conversion into cash.

3. **Financing activities** result in changes in the size and composition of the enterprise's equity capital and borrowings. Financing cash flows result from activities that include obtaining cash from issuing debt and repaying amounts borrowed, and obtaining capital from owners and providing them with a return on, and a return of, their investment.

Details of cash flows related to financing activities allow readers to assess the potential for future claims on the organization's cash and to identify major changes in the form of financing, especially between debt and equity.

Illustration 22-1 identifies an enterprise's typical cash receipts and payments and classifies them, according to ASPE, as to whether they result from operating, investing, or financing activities. Note the following.

1. The **operating** cash flows are related almost entirely to **working capital accounts** (that is, **current asset** and **current liability accounts**).

2. The **investing** cash flows generally involve **long-term asset items**.

3. The **financing** cash flows are derived mainly from changes in **long-term liability and equity accounts**. IFRS's requirements are similar but not identical.

Illustration 22-1

Classification of Typical Cash Inflows and Outflows under ASPE

Types of Cash Flows	Relationship to the Balance Sheet
OPERATING	
Cash inflows	
From cash sales and collections from customers on account	
From returns on loans (interest) and equity securities (dividends)	Generally related to changes in non-cash current assets and current liabilities
From receipts for royalties, rents, and fees	
Cash outflows	
To suppliers on account	
To, and on behalf of, employees for services	
To governments for taxes	
To lenders for interest	
To others for expenses	
INVESTING	
Cash inflows	
From proceeds on the sale of property, plant, and equipment	
From proceeds on the sale of debt or equity securities of other entities	Generally related to changes in long-term assets
From the collection of principal on loans to other entities	
Cash outflows	
For purchases of property, plant, and equipment	
For purchases of debt or equity securities of other entities	
For loans to other entities	
FINANCING	
Cash inflows	
From proceeds on the issuance of equity securities	
From proceeds on the issuance of debt (bonds and notes)	Generally related to changes in long-term liabilities and equity
Cash outflows	
For payments of dividends to shareholders	
For redemptions of long-term debt or reacquisitions of share capital	
For reductions of capital lease obligations	

Some transactions that you might think are investing or financing activities may actually be operating cash flows. Under ASPE, for example, cash dividends and interest received and cash dividends and interest paid **that are included in determining net income** are classified as **operating** flows. Any dividends or interest paid **that are charged directly against retained earnings, however,** are reported as **financing** flows.[3]

Under IFRS, however, a choice is allowed. Interest paid and received and dividends received (excluding those received from an associate—a significant influence investment)[4] can be recognized as operating flows because they are included in determining net income. Alternatively, interest paid could be a financing outflow while interest and dividends received could be considered investment flows. A choice is also permitted for dividends paid: a financing flow as a return to equity holders, or an operating flow as a measure of the ability of operations to cover returns to shareholders. However management views these specific flows, once the choice is made, it is applied consistently from period to period. Illustration 22-2 summarizes these types of cash flows.

	Interest and Dividends Paid	**Interest and Dividends Received**
ASPE	Operating: if recognized in net income Financing: if charged to retained earnings	Operating
IFRS	Choice: Operating or financing	Choice: Operating or investing

Illustration 22-2
Interest and Dividends: ASPE versus IFRS Classification

UNDERLYING CONCEPT

Not requiring taxes to be allocated to the various activities is an application of the cost-benefit constraint. While the information may be beneficial, the cost of providing it exceeds the benefits.

Although they are reported on the income statement, some items are the result of an investing or financing activity. For example, the sale of property, plant, and equipment is an investing activity even though the gain or loss on sale is reported in income. In this case, the cash proceeds received on the sale are properly classified as an investing cash inflow. The gain or loss, therefore, must be **excluded** in determining cash flows from operating activities. Similarly, cash paid to extinguish a debt is a financing activity, not an operating activity, and the gain or loss on repayment is excluded from operating cash flow. The cash paid to redeem the debt, not the amount of the gain or loss, is the actual cash flow and the repayment is clearly a financing activity.

Outflows to purchase investments and loans that are acquired specifically **for trading purposes**, and the proceeds on their sale, are treated the same as flows related to inventories acquired for resale; that is, as operating cash flows. If investments are acquired for other purposes, the cash flows are investing flows. (See IAS 7.15)

Income taxes present another complexity. While income tax expense can be identified with specific operating, investing, and financing transactions, the related cash payments for taxes usually cannot. For this reason, income tax payments are classified as operating cash flows unless they can be specifically identified with financing and investing activities.

How should **significant non-cash transactions** that affect an organization's assets and capital structure, such as those listed below, be handled?

1. The acquisition of assets by assuming directly related liabilities (including right-of-use or capital lease-related obligations) or by issuing equity securities

2. Exchanges of non-monetary assets

3. The conversion of debt or preferred shares to common shares

4. The issue of equity securities to retire debt

Because the statement of cash flows reports only the cash effect of activities, significant investing and financing transactions that do not affect cash are excluded from the statement. They are required to be disclosed elsewhere in the financial statements.[5]

WHAT DO THE NUMBERS MEAN?

Generally, companies move through several life-cycle stages of development, and each stage has implications for their cash flows. As the following graph shows, the pattern of flows from operating, financing, and investing activities varies depending on the stage of the cycle.

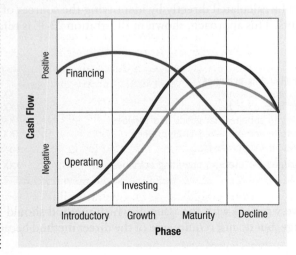

In the introductory phase, the product is likely not generating much revenue, although significant cash is being spent to build up the company's inventories. Therefore, operating cash flow is negative. Because the company is making heavy investments to get a product off the ground, the cash flow associated with investing activities is also negative. Financing cash flows are positive because funds are raised to pay for the investments and cover the operating shortfall.

As the product moves to the growth and maturity phases, these relationships reverse. The product generates more cash from operations, which is used to cover investments that are needed to support the product, and less cash is needed from financing. So is a negative operating cash flow bad? Not always. It depends to a great extent on the product life cycle.

Sources: Adapted from Paul D. Kimmel, Jerry J. Weygandt, and Donald E. Kieso, *Financial Accounting: Tools for Business Decision Making,* 5th ed. (New York: John Wiley & Sons, 2009), p. 606.

Format of the Statement

Formatting Basics

Objective 4

Prepare the operating activities section of a statement of cash flows using the direct versus the indirect method.

The three activities discussed in the preceding section guide the general format of the statement of cash flows. The operating activities section usually appears first, and is followed by the investing and financing activities sections. The individual inflows and outflows from investing and financing activities are reported separately; that is, they are reported gross, not netted against one another. Thus, a cash outflow for the purchase of property is reported separately from a cash inflow from the sale of property. Similarly, the cash inflow from issuing debt is reported separately from the cash outflow for the retirement of debt. If they are not reported separately, it is harder to see how extensive the enterprise's investing and financing activities are and therefore it is more difficult to assess future cash flows.[6]

Illustration 22-3 sets out a basic or "skeleton" format of a statement of cash flows. Note that the statement also provides a reconciliation between the beginning-of-the-period cash and the end-of-the-period cash reported in the comparative statement of financial position.

Illustration 22-3

Format of the Statement of Cash Flows—Indirect Method

COMPANY NAME **Statement of Cash Flows** **Period Covered**			
Cash flows from operating activities			
Net income			XXX
Adjustments to reconcile net income to cash provided by (used in) operating activities: (List of individual items)		XX	XX
Net cash provided by (used in) operating activities			XXX
Cash flows from investing activities			
(List of individual inflows and outflows)		XX	
Net cash provided by (used in) investing activities			XXX
Cash flows from financing activities			
(List of individual inflows and outflows)		XX	
Net cash provided by (used in) financing activities			XXX
Net increase (decrease) in cash			XXX
Cash at beginning of period			XXX
Cash at end of period			XXX

Illustration 22-3 presents the net cash flow from operating activities indirectly by making the necessary adjustments to the net income reported on the income statement. This is referred to as the **indirect method** (or reconciliation method). The cash flow from operating activities could be calculated directly by identifying the sources of the operating cash receipts and payments. This approach, shown in Illustration 22-4, is referred to as the **direct method**.

Illustration 22-4

Cash Flows from Operating Activities—Direct Method

Cash flows from operating activities	
Cash receipts from customers	XX
Cash receipts from other revenue sources	XX
Cash payments to suppliers for goods and services	(XX)
Cash payments to and on behalf of employees	(XX)
Cash payments of income taxes	(XX)
Net cash provided by (used in) operating activities	XXX

Standard setters have wrestled with the issue of which method should be used. Both IFRS and ASPE encourage, but do not require, use of the direct method because it provides additional information.[7]

Direct versus Indirect Methods

In general, public companies tend to prefer the indirect method of calculating cash flows, although commercial lending officers and other investors tend to prefer the direct method because of the additional information that it provides.

Arguments in Favour of the Direct Method

The main advantage of the direct method is that it shows operating cash receipts and payments. That is, it is more consistent with the objective of a statement of cash flows—to provide information about the entity's cash receipts and cash payments—than the indirect method.

Supporters of the direct method argue that knowing the specific sources of operating cash receipts and the purposes of operating cash payments in past periods is useful in estimating future operating cash flows. Furthermore, information about the amounts of major classes of operating cash receipts and payments is more useful than information only about their arithmetic sum (the net cash flow from operating activities).

Many preparers of financial statements say that they do not currently collect information in a manner that allows them to determine amounts such as cash received from customers or cash paid to suppliers. But supporters of the direct method believe that the incremental cost of accumulating such operating cash receipts and payments data is not significant, especially with sophisticated database accounting systems underlying most large companies' financial reporting modules.[8]

Arguments in Favour of the Indirect Method

The main advantage of the indirect method is that it focuses on the differences between net income and cash flow from operating activities. That is, it provides a useful link between the statement of cash flows, the income statement, and the statement of financial position.

Preparers of financial statements argue that it is less costly to develop information that adjusts net income to net cash flow from operating activities. Supporters of the indirect method also state that the direct method, which effectively reports income statement information on a cash rather than an accrual basis, may suggest incorrectly that net cash flow from operating activities is as good as, or better than, net income as a measure of performance.

Because the indirect method has been used almost exclusively in the past, both preparers and users are more familiar with it and this helps perpetuate its use. Each method provides useful information. The best solution may lie in mandating the direct method, which comes closer to meeting the statement's objectives, and requiring supplementary disclosure of a reconciliation of net income to cash flow from operations. The FASB and IASB have done some work on a joint project dealing with financial statement presentation that includes significant changes to the statement of cash flows. An update on this project is provided in the Looking Ahead section at the end of this chapter.

PREPARING A STATEMENT OF CASH FLOWS

The statement of cash flows was previously called the statement of changes in financial position.[9] By analyzing the changes in all non-cash accounts on the statement of financial position from one period to the next, it is possible to identify and summarize the sources of all cash receipts and all cash disbursements. Illustration 22-5 shows why this is true.

Illustration 22-5

Relationship of Changes in Cash to Other Statement of Financial Position Accounts

$$A = L + SE$$
$$\Delta A = \Delta(L + SE)$$
$$\Delta A = \Delta L + \Delta SE$$
$$\Delta(\text{Cash} + \text{non-cash A}) = \Delta L + \Delta SE$$
$$\Delta\text{Cash} + \Delta\text{non-cash A} = \Delta L + \Delta SE$$
$$\Delta\text{Cash} = \Delta L + \Delta SE - \Delta\text{non-cash A}$$

Note: Δ is a symbol meaning "change in."

Unlike the other financial statements, which are prepared directly from the adjusted trial balance, the statement of cash flows is usually based on an analysis of the changes in the accounts on the statement of financial position over the accounting period. **Information to prepare this statement comes from the following three sources.**

1. **Comparative statements of financial position** provide the amount of the changes in each asset, liability, and equity account from the period's beginning to end.

2. **The current income statement** provides details about the most significant changes in the statement of financial position retained earnings account, expenses that did not use cash, and revenues that did not generate cash.

3. **Selected transaction data** from the general ledger provide additional information needed to determine how cash was generated or used during the period.

Many small and medium-sized enterprises prepare their ASPE cash flow statement by manually accumulating these three sources of information, despite advances in technology. Alternatively, some companies have unique spreadsheet programs that generate the cash flow statement from a combination of their income statement data, changes in statement of financial position accounts, and other cash flow details provided as input. Larger organizations with sophisticated enterprise resource planning systems and databases can create template-based cash flow reports or generate server-based cash flow calculations in real time.

Whether you are preparing a statement of cash flows (or cash flow statement) manually, developing a spreadsheet template for use in its preparation, or interpreting a completed statement that has been presented to you, familiarity with the **manual steps** involved in the statement's preparation explained below will increase your understanding of this important financial statement.

Step 1: Determine the change in cash. This procedure is straightforward because the difference between the beginning and ending balances of cash and cash equivalents can easily be calculated by examining the comparative statements of financial position. **Explaining this change is the objective of the analysis that follows.**

Step 2: Record information from the income statement onto the work sheet for the statement of cash flows.[10] This is the starting point for calculating cash flows from operating activities. **Whenever subsequent analyses indicate that the actual operating cash flow and the amount reported on the income statement are different, the income statement number is adjusted.**

Most adjustments fall into one of three categories:

Category 1. Amounts that are reported as revenues and expenses on the income statement and that are not the same as cash received from customers and cash paid to suppliers of goods and services. Companies receive cash from customers for revenue reported in a previous year, and do not receive cash for all the revenue reported as earned in the current period. Similarly, cash payments are made in the current period to suppliers for goods and services acquired, used, and recognized as expense in a preceding period. In addition, not all amounts that are recognized as expense in the current year are paid for by year end. Most of the adjustments for these differences are related to receivables, payables, and other working capital accounts.

Category 2. Some expenses, such as depreciation and amortization, that represent costs that were incurred and paid for in a previous period. While there was a cash flow associated with the original acquisition of the asset (an investing flow), there is no cash flow associated with the depreciation or amortization of these assets over the periods they are used.

Category 3. Amounts that are reported as gains or losses on the income statement but that are not usually the same as the cash amount from the transaction and, in many cases, the underlying activity is not an operating transaction. For example, gains and losses on the disposal of long-term assets and on the early retirement of long-term debt are reported on the income statement. The first results from an investing transaction and the second from a financing transaction—neither is an operating activity. The cash flow amounts are the **proceeds on disposal** of the asset and the **payment to retire the debt, not the amount of the reported gain or loss.**

Step 3: Analyze the change in each statement of financial position account, identify all cash flows associated with changes in the account balance, and record the effect on the statement of cash flows. This analysis identifies all investing and financing cash flows, and all adjustments that are needed to convert income reported on the income statement to cash flow from operations. Analyze the statement of financial position accounts one at a time until all the changes have been explained and the related cash flows identified.

Step 4: Complete the statement of cash flows. Calculate subtotals for the operating, investing, and financing categories and ensure that the net change in cash you determined is equal to the actual change in cash for the period.[11]

We now work through these four steps to prepare the statements of cash flows for three different companies of increasing complexity.

Illustration Using the Direct Method— Tax Consultants Inc.

Objective 5
Prepare a statement of cash flows using the direct method.

Our first example focuses on the direct method, because several simple examples using the indirect method were already included in Chapter 5. Tax Consultants Inc. began operations on January 1, 2016, when it issued 20,000 common shares for $20,000 cash. The company rented its office space and furniture and equipment, and performed tax consulting services throughout its first two years. The 2017 comparative statements of financial position and the income statement and additional information for 2017 are presented in Illustration 22-6.

Illustration 22-6

Comparative Statements of Financial Position and Income Statement—Tax Consultants Inc., 2017

COMPARATIVE STATEMENTS OF FINANCIAL POSITION

Assets	Dec. 31, 2017	Dec. 31, 2016	Change Increase/Decrease
Cash	$ 89,000	$40,000	(a) 49,000 increase
Accounts receivable	66,000	30,000	(b) 36,000 increase
	$155,000	$70,000	
Liabilities and Shareholders' Equity			
Accounts payable	$ 35,000	$30,000	(c) 5,000 increase
Common shares	80,000	20,000	(d) 60,000 increase
Retained earnings	40,000	20,000	(e) 20,000 increase
	$155,000	$70,000	

(continued)

INCOME STATEMENT
For the Year Ended December 31, 2017

Revenues	$125,000
Operating expenses	85,000
Income before income taxes	40,000
Income tax expense	6,000
Net income	$ 34,000

Additional information:
An examination of selected data indicates that a dividend of $14,000 was declared during the year.

Step 1: Determine the change in cash. This first step is a straightforward calculation. Tax Consultants Inc. had $40,000 cash on hand at the beginning of 2017 and $89,000 on hand at the end of 2017; thus, the change in cash was an increase of $49,000.

Step 2: Record information from the income statement on the statement of cash flows. Much of the cash activity for organizations is related to operations, so the second step takes information from the operating statement (the income statement) and reports it on the statement of cash flows under the heading "Cash flows from operating activities." The specific information that is taken from the income statement and reported on the statement of cash flows in this step **depends on whether the indirect or the direct method is used**. Regardless of the method, this information will be converted from the accrual basis to the cash basis through adjustments in Step 3.

Under the direct method, skeleton headings similar to the ones in Illustration 22-4 are set up under "Cash flows from operating activities," as shown in Illustration 22-7. The number and descriptions of these headings vary from company to company. Amounts reported on the income statement are then transferred line by line to the heading that comes closest to representing the type of cash flow, until all components of net income have been transferred.

Illustration 22-7

Direct Method Format— Operating Activities

DIRECT METHOD

	Income	Adjustments		Cash Flow
Cash flows from operating activities				
Cash received from customers	+125,000	XXX	=	XXX
Cash paid to suppliers	− 85,000	XX	=	XX
Income taxes paid	− 6,000	XX	=	XX
	+ 34,000			XXX

The three headings in Illustration 22-7 are appropriate for Tax Consultants Inc. Because all of the income statement amounts are transferred to the operating activities section, the net amount transferred is equal to the amount of net income—the same as under the starting point of the indirect method.

In Step 3, adjustments are made to the appropriate line within the cash flow from operations section whenever the analysis indicates an operating cash flow that is not equal to the revenue or expense amount reported on the income statement. Revenues of $125,000 will be converted into the amount of cash received from customers, operating expenses of $85,000 will be adjusted to the amount of cash payments made to suppliers, and income tax expense of $6,000 will become income tax payments remitted to the government. Under this method, the specific revenue and expense lines are adjusted. Under the indirect method discussed in the second example below, it is only the bottom-line net income number that is adjusted, **but the adjustments made are for identical amounts.**

Step 3: Analyze the change in each statement of financial position account, identify all cash flows associated with changes in the account balance, and record the effect on the statement of cash flows. By analyzing the change in each statement of financial position (SFP) account, transactions that involve cash can be identified and their effects can be recorded on the statement of cash flows.

Because the change in each account on the SFP has to be explained, begin with the first non-cash asset and work down systematically through each asset, liability, and equity account. The results of Step 3 are provided in Illustration 22-8, where each item is referenced to the related calculation in Illustration 22-6.

Illustration 22-8

Preparation of Statement of Cash Flows—Tax Consultants Inc., Direct Method

CASH FLOWS FROM OPERATING ACTIVITIES			
	Income	Adjustments	Cash Flow
Cash received from customers	+125,000	−36,000 (b)	+89,000
Cash paid to suppliers	− 85,000	+ 5,000 (c)	−80,000
Income taxes paid	− 6,000		− 6,000
	+ 34,000 (e)		+ 3,000
CASH FLOWS FROM INVESTING ACTIVITIES			−0−
CASH FLOWS FROM FINANCING ACTIVITIES			
Proceeds from issue of common shares			+ 60,000 (d)
Dividends paid			− 14,000 (e)
			+46,000
Increase in cash			+49,000 (a)

Note: items (a) to (e) refer to calculations from Illustration 22-6.

(a) **Change in Cash.** The cash balance increased by $49,000 during the year.

(b) **Accounts Receivable.** During the year, Tax Consultants' receivables increased by $36,000. Because this account increases by the amount of revenue that is recognized and decreases by cash received from customers, the cash received from customers must have been $36,000 less than the revenue reported on the 2017 income statement (item b). Therefore, an adjustment is needed in the operating activities section of the statement of cash flows. Using the direct method, the revenue line is reduced directly.

(c) **Accounts Payable.** Accounts Payable increases by purchases on account and decreases by payments on account. Tax Consultants' purchases must have been $5,000 higher than payments during 2017. A $5,000 adjustment is needed to convert the purchases included in net income to the amount paid to suppliers. Under the direct method, the $5,000 adjustment (item c) is made to the cash paid to suppliers line where the cost of the goods and services purchased was presented.

(d) **Common Shares.** The increase in this account resulted from the issue of shares that was recorded in this entry:

Cash	60,000	
Common Shares		60,000

The $60,000 inflow of cash (item d) is reported on the statement of cash flows as a financing inflow.

(e) **Retained Earnings.** In this account, the $20,000 increase (item (e) from Illustration 22-6) is explained by net income and dividends paid. We already recognized the net income as the starting point in calculating cash flows from operations. The remaining change in the account is explained by the dividend-related entry:

Retained Earnings (or Dividends)	14,000	
Cash		14,000

Assuming Tax Consultants Inc. reports under ASPE, the $14,000 dividend payment is reported as a financing outflow. The entire dividend must have been paid in cash because the company does not report a Dividends Payable account.

The changes in all SFP accounts have been explained and their cash effects have been reported appropriately on the statement of cash flows. The statement can now be completed.

Step 4: Complete the statement of cash flows. Calculate subtotals for each of the operating, investing, and financing sections, and then the change in cash for the year. This should agree with the change identified in Step 1.

The completed statement illustrating the direct method is shown in Illustration 22-9.

Illustration 22-9

Completed Statement of Cash Flows—Tax Consultants Inc.

STATEMENT OF CASH FLOWS
Direct Method

Cash flows from operating activities		
Cash received from customers		$89,000
Less cash payments:		
To suppliers	$80,000	
For income taxes	6,000	86,000
		3,000
Cash flows from investing activities		–0–
Cash flows from financing activities		
Proceeds on issuance of common shares		60,000
Payment of dividends		(14,000)
		46,000
Increase in cash during year		49,000
Opening cash balance		40,000
Cash, December 31, 2017		$89,000

The $49,000 cash increase came from a combination of net operating inflows of $3,000 and net financing inflows (primarily from the sale of common shares) of $46,000. Net cash provided by operating activities is the same whether the direct or indirect method is used. The $3,000 contribution to cash from operations is a result of cash collections from customers ($89,000) being only a little more than the operating cash outflows to suppliers ($80,000) and to the government for taxes ($6,000). The major source of cash flow for the company related to the issuance of common shares.

Illustration Using the Indirect Method— Eastern Window Products Limited

Objective 6

Prepare a statement of cash flows using the indirect method.

To illustrate the preparation of a more complex statement of cash flows, we use the operations of Eastern Window Products Limited (EWPL) for its 2017 year. EWPL has been operating for several years, and the company's comparative statements of financial position at December 31, 2017 and 2016, its statement of income and retained earnings for the year ended December 31, 2017, and other information are provided in Illustration 22-10.

For purposes of this example, EWPL could be reporting under either ASPE or IFRS. Assume, if a publicly accountable enterprise, that company management has chosen to present interest paid as an operating cash flow and dividends paid as a financing flow.

Illustration 22-10

Comparative Statements of Financial Position and Statement of Income and Retained Earnings—EWPL

STATEMENTS OF FINANCIAL POSITION—DECEMBER 31

	2017	2016	Change Increase/Decrease $ (and reference to items explained below)	
Cash	$ 37,000	$ 59,000	22,000 decrease	
Accounts receivable	46,000	56,000	10,000 decrease	(a)
Inventory	82,000	73,000	9,000 increase	(b)
Prepaid expenses	6,000	7,500	1,500 decrease	(c)
Land	70,000	–0–	70,000 increase	(d)
Buildings	200,000	–0–	200,000 increase	(d)
Accumulated depreciation— buildings	(6,000)	–0–	6,000 increase	(e)
Equipment	68,000	63,000	5,000 increase	(f)
Accumulated depreciation— equipment	(19,000)	(10,000)	9,000 increase	(g)
	$484,000	$248,500		
Accounts payable	$ 70,000	$ 59,100	10,900 increase	(h)
Income taxes payable	4,000	1,000	3,000 increase	(i)
Salaries and wages payable	2,000	2,700	700 decrease	(j)
Mortgage payable	152,400	–0–	152,400 increase	(d) and (k)
Bonds payable	50,000	40,000	10,000 increase	(l)
Common shares	80,000	72,000	8,000 increase	(m)
Retained earnings	125,600	73,700	51,900 increase	(n)
	$484,000	$248,500		

STATEMENT OF INCOME AND RETAINED EARNINGS
Year Ended December 31, 2017

Sales revenue		$592,000
Less: Cost of goods sold		355,000
Gross profit		237,000
Salaries and wages expense	$55,000	
Interest expense	16,200	
Depreciation expense	15,000	
Other operating expenses	51,000	137,200
Income before income tax		99,800
Income tax expense		39,900
Net income		59,900
Retained earnings, January 1		73,700
Dividends declared		(8,000)
Retained earnings, December 31		$125,600

Additional information:
The company obtained a mortgage of $155,000 from a large Canadian bank to help finance the acquisition of the land and building during 2017.

Step 1: Determine the change in cash. Cash decreased by $22,000 during the year. There are no cash equivalents.

Step 2: Record information from the income statement to the work sheet for the statement of cash flows. Under the **indirect method**, record the $59,900 net income in the operating activities section of the statement of cash flows (Illustration 22-11, Panel A).

Under the **direct method**, set up skeleton headings for the types of operating cash flows involved. Illustration 22-11, Panel B suggests that six headings are likely appropriate for EWPL, including an "Other expenses/losses—depreciation" section that includes items such as depreciation expense that do not fall under the other headings. Because all income statement amounts are transferred to the operating activities section, the net amount transferred is the same as the net income balance under the indirect method.

As you proceed through Step 3 using the direct method, the following will occur:

- Sales revenue of $592,000 will be converted into cash received from customers.

- Cost of goods sold of $355,000 and other operating expenses of $51,000 will be adjusted to an amount that represents cash payments to suppliers for goods and services acquired.

- Salaries and wages expense of $55,000 will become cash payments made to, and on behalf of, employees.

- Interest expense of $16,200 becomes interest payments made.

- Income tax expense of $39,900 becomes income tax payments remitted to the government.

As you review the adjustments being made for operating activities, note that the same adjustments are made under both the direct and indirect methods. However, under the indirect method we start with net income, while under the direct method we adjust each of the components of the statement of income individually. We review these adjustments as set out in Illustration 22-11, in detail below.

Illustration 22-11

Statement of Cash Flows Summary of Adjustments— EWPL

PANEL A

CASH FLOWS FROM OPERATING ACTIVITIES
Indirect Method

Net income	+ 59,900
Adjustments: Decrease in accounts receivable	+ 10,000 (a)
Increase in inventory	− 9,000 (b)
Decrease in prepaid expenses	+ 1,500 (c)
Depreciation expense—building	+ 6,000 (e)
Depreciation expense—equipment	+ 9,000 (g)
Increase in accounts payable	+ 10,900 (h)
Increase in income taxes payable	+ 3,000 (i)
Decrease in wages payable	− 700 (j)
	+ 90,600

PANEL B

Direct Method

	Income	Adjustments	Cash Flow
Cash received from customers	+592,000	+ 10,000 (a)	+602,000
Cash paid to suppliers for goods and services	−355,000 − 51,000	− 9,000 (b) + 1,500 (c) + 10,900 (h)	−402,600
Cash paid to employees	− 55,000	− 700 (j)	− 55,700
Cash interest paid	− 16,200		− 16,200
Income taxes paid	− 39,900	+ 3,000 (i)	− 36,900
Other expenses/losses—depreciation	− 15,000	+ 6,000 (e) + 9,000 (g)	—
	+ 59,900		+ 90,600

PANEL C

CASH FLOWS FROM INVESTING ACTIVITIES

Purchase of land and building	− 270,000 (d)
Purchase of equipment	− 5,000 (f)
	−275,000

(continued)

Illustration 22-11	
Statement of Cash Flows Summary of Adjustments— EWPL (continued)	

CASH FLOWS FROM FINANCING ACTIVITIES	
Mortgage payable	+ 155,000 (d)
Repayment of mortgage payable	− 2,600 (d)
Bonds issued	+ 10,000 (l)
Shares issued	+ 8,000 (m)
Dividends paid	− 8,000 (n)
	+162,400
CHANGE IN CASH	− 22,000

Step 3: Analyze the change in each statement of financial position account, identify any cash flows associated with a change in the account balance, and record the effect on the statement of cash flows. The results of this step are provided in Illustration 22-11 above, where each item is referenced to the analysis that follows.

(a) **Accounts Receivable.** During the year, EWPL's receivables decreased by $10,000. Because Accounts Receivable is increased by revenue that is recognized and decreased by cash received from customers, the cash inflow from customers must have been $10,000 more than the revenue reported on the 2017 income statement. Under the indirect method, $10,000 is added to the net income number. Under the direct method, the revenue amount is increased directly.

(b) **Inventory.** Inventory increased by $9,000. Because Inventory is increased by the purchase of goods and is reduced by transferring costs to cost of goods sold, EWPL must have purchased $9,000 more inventory than it sold and, therefore, $9,000 more than the costs included in cost of goods sold on the income statement. The first part of this analysis (as summarized in the next paragraph) does not tell us how much cash was paid for the purchases; it only converts cost of goods sold to the cost of purchases in the year. The analysis of Accounts Payable (see item [h] below) converts the amount purchased to the cash payments to suppliers.

Cost of goods sold of $355,000 was deducted in calculating net income. Under the indirect method, net income must be further reduced by $9,000 to adjust for cash used to purchase goods that are still in inventory. Under the direct method, the $9,000 adjustment is made directly to the cost of goods sold line to adjust it to the cost of goods purchased.

(c) **Prepaid Expenses.** Prepaid Expenses decreased by $1,500. Because this account is increased by the acquisition of goods and services before they are used, and decreased by transferring the cost of the goods and services used up to expense—the same as for inventory—EWPL must have recognized $1,500 more expense than the amount purchased. The expenses reported on the income statement, therefore, have to be reduced by $1,500 to convert them to the cost of goods and services purchased. Under the indirect method, $1,500 is added back to the income reported. Under the direct method, the appropriate expense ("other operating expenses") is reduced directly for the $1,500.

(d) **Land, Buildings.** The statements of financial position indicate an increase in Land of $70,000 and an increase in the Buildings account of $200,000, suggesting an investing cash outflow of $270,000. The investment in real property, however, is often financed by obtaining a mortgage payable from a bank or other third party that results in a lower direct cash outlay. Assume that a review of the records indicates that EWPL obtained a $155,000 mortgage in acquiring the land and building. Under ASPE and IFRS, this is treated like a cash inflow followed by a cash outflow of $155,000. (The $270,000 cost of the land and building is partly financed by the mortgage of $155,000.)[12] It is often useful to consider the underlying journal entries:

Cash	155,000	
Mortgage Payable		155,000
Land	70,000	
Buildings	200,000	
Cash		270,000

This entry explains the change in the Land and Buildings accounts on the statement of financial position. It also explains part of the change in the Mortgage Payable account (see also item [k] below), and identifies the details of the net outflow of cash of $115,000. The purchase of land and building is reported as an **investing** cash flow outflow on the statement, with the mortgage as a **financing** cash flow.

(e) **Accumulated Depreciation—Buildings.** The $6,000 increase in this account is due entirely to the recognition of depreciation expense for the year:

Depreciation Expense	6,000	
Accumulated Depreciation—Buildings		6,000

The entry records a non-cash event. Under the indirect method, $6,000 is added back to net income because depreciation expense did not use up any cash. Under the direct method, depreciation expense is adjusted directly. After adding back the $6,000 for depreciation expense here and the $9,000 from item (g) below, depreciation expense is fully eliminated from the statement of cash flows under the direct method.

(f) **Equipment.** EWPL purchased $5,000 of equipment during 2017. This resulted in an investing outflow of cash of $5,000.

(g) **Accumulated Depreciation—Equipment.** The $9,000 increase in this account is due to depreciation expense for the year. As explained in item (e), the operating activities section is adjusted for this non-cash expense.

Alternative Terminology

As discussed in Chapter 18, IFRS uses the terms *current tax expense (income)* and *deferred tax expense (income)*, whereas ASPE recommends the use of the terms *current income tax expense (benefit)* and *future income tax expense (benefit)*. We use the terms interchangeably. However, to simplify matters, in most of our examples in Chapter 22, we do not split the expense between current and deferred; instead we use the more general term *income tax expense*.

(h) **Accounts Payable.** The Accounts Payable account is increased by the cost of purchases and decreased by payments on account. EWPL's cash payments to suppliers, therefore, must have been $10,900 less than the goods and services purchased during the year. In items (b) and (c) above, cost of goods sold and other operating expenses were adjusted to convert them to the cost of goods and services purchased. A further adjustment of $10,900 is required to adjust the purchases to the amount of cash that was actually paid.

Under the indirect method, $10,900 is added back to net income to reflect the fact that the amounts deducted for purchases did not use an equivalent amount of cash. Under the direct method, the $10,900 adjustment reduces the cost of goods and other operating expenses purchased to the cash outflow for these purchases.

(i) **Income Taxes Payable.** This liability account is increased by the income tax expense reported and is decreased by payments to the government. Income tax expense, therefore, was $3,000 higher than the payments. Under the indirect method, the $3,000 difference is added back to net income. Under the direct method, a similar adjustment is made to the income tax expense line.

(j) **Wages Payable.** Similar to other current payables, this account is increased by amounts recognized as expense and decreased by payments; in this case, to employees. The $700 decrease indicates that cash outflows were $700 more than wages expense. Under the indirect method, an additional $700 is deducted from the reported income. Salaries and wages expense is adjusted under the direct method.[13]

(k) **Mortgage Payable.** The cash flow associated with part of the change in this account was identified above in item (d). If the account increased by $155,000 when the property was acquired, principal payments of $2,600 must have been made to reduce the final balance to $152,400. The entry underlying this transaction is:

Mortgage Payable	2,600	
Cash		2,600

This is a financing cash outflow.

(l) **Bonds Payable.** The increase in this account is explained by the following entry:

Cash	10,000	
Bonds Payable		10,000

The $10,000 cash received from the bond issue is a financing cash inflow.

(m) **Common Shares.** The $8,000 increase in this account resulted from the issue of shares.

Cash	8,000	
Common Shares		8,000

The $8,000 cash received is a financing cash inflow.

(n) **Retained Earnings.** Net income accounts for $59,900 of the increase in retained earnings. We recognized this on the statement of cash flows already as the starting point in calculating cash flows from operations. The remainder of the change is explained by the entry for dividends:

Retained Earnings (or Dividends)	8,000	
Cash		8,000

The payment of dividends that is charged to retained earnings is classified as a financing outflow. This treatment is required under ASPE. IFRS allows this treatment or, as an alternative, allows the payment of dividends that are charged to retained earnings to be recognized as an operating outflow.

Because the changes in all statement of financial position accounts have now been explained and all cash flows have been identified, we can complete the statement of cash flows.

Step 4: Complete the statement of cash flows. Subtotals are calculated for each section of the statement and the calculated change in cash is compared with the change identified in Step 1. Both indicate a $22,000 decrease in EWPL's cash balance during 2017.

A statement in good form is then prepared from the working paper developed in Illustration 22-11, using more appropriate descriptions and explanations. Illustration 22-12 shows what the final statement might look like if the indirect method were chosen. We discuss the additional disclosures that are provided in a later section of the chapter, called "Disclosure Requirements."

Illustration 22-12

EWPL Statement of Cash Flows, 2017—Indirect Method

EASTERN WINDOW PRODUCTS LIMITED
Statement of Cash Flows
Year Ended December 31, 2017

Cash provided by (used in) operations		
Net income		$ 59,900
Add back non-cash expense—depreciation		15,000
Add (deduct) changes in non-cash working capital[a]		
– Accounts receivable	$ 10,000	
– Inventory	(9,000)	
– Prepaid expenses	1,500	
– Accounts payable	10,900	
– Income taxes payable	3,000	
– Wages payable	(700)	15,700
		90,600
Cash provided by (used in) investing activities		
Purchase of property, plant, and equipment		(275,000)
Cash provided by (used in) financing activities		
Issuance of mortgage payable	155,000	
Payment on mortgage payable	(2,600)	
Proceeds on issue of bonds	10,000	
Dividends paid	(8,000)	
Proceeds on issue of common shares	8,000	162,400
Decrease in cash		(22,000)
Cash balance, beginning of year		59,000
Cash balance, end of year		$ 37,000

Notes:
1. Cash consists of cash on hand and balances with banks.
2. Cash payments during the year for interest and income taxes were $16,200 and $36,900, respectively.
[a] Many companies provide only the subtotal on the statement of cash flows and report the details in a note to the financial statements.

Illustration 22-13 presents the operating activities section of the statement of cash flows if the direct method had been used. Of course, it results in the same total cash flow provided by operations as the indirect method (see Illustration 22-11).

Cash provided by (used in) operations	
Received from customers	$ 602,000
Payments to suppliers	(402,600)
Payments to and on behalf of employees	(55,700)
Interest payments	(16,200)
Income taxes paid	(36,900)
	$ 90,600

Illustration Using Both Methods—Yoshi Corporation

Objective 7

Prepare a more complex statement of cash flows using both methods.

The next step is to see how the same principles are applied to more complex situations. Some of these complexities are illustrated through our next example of a **publicly accountable entity**, Yoshi Corporation, as we use the same approach as in the two previous examples. Although Yoshi Corporation applies IFRS, almost all of the situations are treated the same as if the company applied ASPE. If you prefer a more structured method of accumulating the information for the statement of cash flows than what is shown here, we recommend that you refer to the work sheet approach in Appendix 22A.

Illustrations 22-14, 22-15, 22-16, and 22-17 provide the comparative statements of financial position of Yoshi Corporation at December 31, 2017 and 2016; the statement of comprehensive income; the statement of changes in equity for the year ended December 31, 2017; and selected additional information. The references in Illustrations 22-14 and 22-18 are useful for understanding the detailed analysis provided in Step 3 (below).

YOSHI CORPORATION
Comparative Statements of Financial Position
December 31, 2017 and 2016

Cash	$ 5,000	$ 32,000	27,000 decrease	
Cash equivalents	14,000	4,000	10,000 increase	
FV-NI investments	25,000	30,000	5,000 decrease	(a)
Accounts receivable	106,500	52,700	53,800 increase	(b)
Allowance for doubtful accounts	(2,500)	(1,700)	800 increase	(c)
Inventory	303,000	311,000	8,000 decrease	(d)
Prepaid expenses	16,500	17,000	500 decrease	(e)
Investment in associate (Portel Corp.)	18,500	15,000	3,500 increase	(f)
FV-OCI investments (Hyco Ltd.)	17,500	13,000	4,500 increase	(g)
Deferred development costs	190,000	30,000	160,000 increase	(h)
Land	131,500	82,000	49,500 increase	(i)
Equipment	187,000	142,000	45,000 increase	(j)
Accumulated depreciation—equipment	(29,000)	(31,000)	2,000 decrease	(j)
Buildings	262,000	262,000	–0–	(k)
Accumulated depreciation—buildings	(74,100)	(71,000)	3,100 increase	(k)
Goodwill	7,600	10,000	2,400 decrease	(l)
Total assets	$ 1,178,500	$897,000		
Liabilities				
Accounts payable	$130,000	$131,000	1,000 decrease	(m)
Dividends payable, term preferred shares	2,000	–0–	2,000 increase	(n)
Accrued liabilities	43,000	39,000	4,000 increase	(o)
Income taxes payable	3,000	16,000	13,000 decrease	(p)
Bonds payable	97,800	97,500	300 increase	(q)
Term preferred shares	60,000	–0–	60,000 increase	(r)
Deferred tax liability	10,000	6,000	4,000 increase	(s)
Total liabilities	345,800	289,500		

(continued)

Illustration 22-14

Comparative Statements of Financial Position—Yoshi Corporation (continued)

Shareholders' Equity			
Common shares	225,400	88,000	**137,400 increase (t)**
Retained earnings	602,800	518,500	**84,300 increase (u)**
Accumulated other comprehensive income	4,500	1,000	**3,500 increase (s)**
Total shareholders' equity	832,700	607,500	
Liabilities and shareholders' equity	$ 1,178,500	$897,000	

Illustration 22-15

Statement of Comprehensive Income—Yoshi Corporation

YOSHI CORPORATION
Statement of Comprehensive Income
Year Ended December 31, 2017

Net sales		$923,200
Investment income (equity in earnings of Portel Corp.)		5,500
Investment income, FV-NI investments		1,300
Gain on sale of land		10,500
		940,500
Expenses		
Cost of goods sold	$395,400	
Salaries and wages	200,000	
Selling and administrative	134,600	
Depreciation	14,600	
Interest and dividend expense	11,300	
Loss on impairment (goodwill)	2,400	
Other expenses and losses	12,000	770,300
Income before income tax		170,200
Income tax: Current	49,500	
Deferred	3,000	52,500
Net income		117,700
Other comprehensive income		
Unrealized gain (OCI) net of deferred tax of $1,000		3,500
Comprehensive income		$121,200

Illustration 22-16

Statement of Changes in Equity—Yoshi Corporation

YOSHI CORPORATION
Statement of Changes in Equity
Year Ended December 31, 2017

	Common Shares $	Retained Earnings $	Accumulated Other Comprehensive Income $	Total $
Balance, January 1, 2017	88,000	518,500	1,000	607,500
2% stock dividend issued	15,000	(15,000)		–0–
Proceeds on sale of shares	144,000			144,000
Shares purchased and cancelled	(21,600)	(12,400)		(34,000)
Net income		117,700		117,700
Cash dividend declared		(6,000)		(6,000)
Unrealized gain (OCI)			3,500	3,500
Balance, December 31, 2017	225,400	602,800	4,500	832,700

Illustration 22-17

Additional Information—Yoshi Corporation

YOSHI CORPORATION
Additional Information

1. Cash equivalents represent money-market instruments with original maturity dates of less than 90 days.
2. FV-NI investments in ABC Company at the beginning of the year were sold during the year for $32,300. Additional investments in XYZ Limited, also accounted for at FV-NI, were acquired at a cost of $26,000 and were still held at the end of the year.

(continued)

Illustration 22-17

Additional Information—
Yoshi Corporation
(continued)

3. During 2017, accounts receivable of $1,450 were written off.
4. Yoshi accounts for its 22% interest in Portel Corp. using the equity method. Portel Corp. paid a dividend in 2017 and Yoshi's share of Portel's net income was $5,500.
5. The investment in shares of Hyco Ltd. was purchased in July 2016 for $12,000 and classified for accounting purposes as FV-OCI.
6. During 2017, Yoshi incurred $200,000 of development costs that met the criteria for deferral as an intangible asset. During the year, $40,000 of this asset was amortized.
7. Land in the amount of $54,000 was purchased by issuing term preferred shares. The term preferred shares issued for land (and those issued for cash) are classified as financial liabilities.
8. An analysis of the Equipment account and related accumulated depreciation indicates the following (with the loss of $1,500 included in "other expenses and losses" in Illustration 22-15):

Equipment:	
Balance, January 1, 2017	$142,000
Cost of equipment purchased	73,000
Cost of equipment sold (sold at a loss of $1,500)	(28,000)
Balance, December 31, 2017	$187,000
Accumulated depreciation:	
Balance, January 1, 2017	$ 31,000
Accumulated depreciation on equipment sold	(13,500)
Depreciation expense, 2017	11,500
Balance, December 31, 2017	$ 29,000

9. The bonds payable, issued in 2015, were issued at a discount and have a maturity value of $100,000.
10. Changes in other statement of financial position accounts resulted from usual transactions and events.

Step 1: Determine the change in cash. Yoshi's cash and cash equivalents include holdings of money-market instruments as well as cash balances, with a decrease in cash and cash equivalents of $17,000 that needs to be explained. This is the difference between the opening cash and cash equivalents of $36,000 ($32,000 + $4,000) and the ending balance of $19,000 ($5,000 + $14,000).

Step 2: Record information from the income statement onto the work sheet for the statement of cash flows. Under the **indirect method**, the net income of $117,700 is inserted as the starting point, as shown in the summary of adjustments in the working paper in Illustration 22-18, Panel A.

Illustration 22-18

Statement of Cash Flows
Summary of Adjustments—
Yoshi Corporation

PANEL A

CASH FLOWS FROM OPERATING ACTIVITIES
Indirect Method

Net income	+117,700
Adjustments: Decrease in FV-NI investments	+ 5,000 (a)
Increase in accounts receivable, net of write-offs	− 55,250 (b)
Bad debt expense	+ 2,250 (c)
Decrease in inventory	+ 8,000 (d)
Decrease in prepaid expenses	+ 500 (e)
Equity method investment income	− 5,500 (f)
Dividend from equity method investment	+ 2,000 (f)
Amortization of development costs	+ 40,000 (h)
Gain on sale of land	− 10,500 (i)
Loss on disposal of equipment	+ 1,500 (j)
Depreciation expense—equipment	+ 11,500 (j)
Depreciation expense—buildings	+ 3,100 (k)
Impairment loss—goodwill	+ 2,400 (l)

Decrease in accounts payable	− 1,000 (m)
Increase in dividends payable on term preferred shares	+ 2,000 (n)
Increase in accrued liabilities	+ 4,000 (o)
Decrease in income taxes payable	− 13,000 (p)
Amortization of bond discount	+ 300 (q)
Increase in deferred tax liability (net income)	+ 3,000 (s)
	+118,000

PANEL B

Direct Method

	Income	Adjustments	Cash Flow
Receipts from customers	+923,200	− 55,250 (b)	+867,950
Received from investment in Portel Corp.	+ 5,500	− 5,500 (f) ⎱	+ 2,000
		+ 2,000 (f) ⎰	
Received on FV-NI investment transactions	+ 1,300	+ 5,000 (a)	+ 6,300
Payments to suppliers for goods and services	−395,400 ⎫	+ 2,250 (c)	
	−134,600 ⎪	+ 8,000 (d)	
	− 12,000 ⎪	+ 500 (e)	
	⎬	+ 40,000 (h) ⎱	− 490,750
	⎪	+ 1,500 (j)	
	⎭	− 1,000 (m)	
Payments to employees	−200,000	+ 4,000 (o)	−196,000
Interest and dividend payments	− 11,300	+ 2,000 (n) ⎱	− 9,000
		+ 300 (q) ⎰	
Income taxes paid	− 52,500	− 13,000 (p) ⎱	− 62,500
		+ 3,000 (s) ⎰	
Other items:			
Depreciation expense	− 14,600	+ 11,500 (j) ⎱	—
		+ 3,100 (k) ⎰	
Impairment loss	− 2,400	+ 2,400 (l)	—
Gain on sale of land	+ 10,500	− 10,500 (i)	—
	+117,700		+118,000

PANEL C

CASH FLOWS FROM INVESTING ACTIVITIES

Development costs incurred	− 200,000 (h)
Proceeds on sale of land	+ 15,000 (i)
Purchase of equipment	− 73,000 (j)
Proceeds on sale of equipment	+ 13,000 (j)
	−245,000

CASH FLOWS FROM FINANCING ACTIVITIES

Proceeds on issue of term preferred shares	+ 6,000 (r)
Proceeds on issue of common shares	+ 144,000 (t)
Dividends paid on common shares	− 6,000 (u)
Payment to repurchase common shares	− 34,000 (t)
	+110,000
CHANGE IN CASH	− 17,000

Using the **direct method**, skeleton headings that cover each potential type of cash flow—from customer receipts to income taxes—are set up within the operating activities section of the statement of cash flows working paper, as shown in Illustration 22-18, Panel B. The statement of comprehensive income provides clues about the types of operating cash flows and how they should be described. For example, the equity basis income from the investment in Portel Corp. is not a cash flow, but it will be replaced after adjustment with any dividends received from the investment.

Each amount that makes up the net income of $117,700 is transferred to the most appropriate skeleton heading on the working paper. Amounts reported as cost of goods sold, selling and administrative expense, and other expenses and losses form the base for what will eventually be "Payments to suppliers." Income tax expense is included on the line that will be adjusted to "Income taxes paid." The unrealized gain on the FV-OCI investment and the tax on it are not included, but will be taken into account later.

Note that this illustration begins with **net income**, consistent with the international standard. Other companies, however, may decide to begin with comprehensive income, or even income before taxes. As long as the relationship of the beginning number to net income is obvious, the objective of the standard is met. If a number other than net income is used, the adjustments that follow will also be different, but the final statement will report the same total amounts and types of cash flows and change in cash balances as under the approach used here.

Step 3: Analyze the change in each statement of financial position account, identify any cash flows associated with a change in the account balance, and record the effect on the statement of cash flows. The analysis begins with the FV-NI investments that are held for trading purposes (with the effects of items (a) to (u) below summarized in Illustration 22-18).

(a) **FV-NI Investments.** Based on information provided in Illustration 22-17, and the year-end balances in the statements of financial position in Illustration 22-14, we can reproduce the entries made during the year to this account.

Cash	32,300	
FV-NI Investments		30,000
Investment Income or Loss		2,300
FV-NI Investments	26,000	
Cash		26,000
Investment Income or Loss	1,000	
FV-NI Investments		1,000

These entries tell us three things.

1. They explain the change in the FV-NI Investments account during the year.

2. They indicate what makes up the investment income on the FV-NI investments of $1,300 (the $2,300 realized gain on sale of shares of ABC Company and the unrealized loss on shares of XYZ Limited of $1,000).

3. They indicate that the cash effect of these transactions is +$32,300 − $26,000 = +$6,300 (sale proceeds, less purchase of new FV-NI investments).

The net cash flow of $6,300 is an **operating** flow because FV-NI securities acquired for trading purposes are treated similarly to inventory (IAS 7.15). We have already included an inflow of $1,300 in the operating section for investment income, so an adjustment is needed there for an additional $5,000 under the direct method.

Under the indirect method, $5,000 is added to the net income number to increase the cash inflow from the $1,300 already included as part of net income to the actual $6,300 net cash inflow that was generated. The $5,000 is split on the final statement of cash flows (Illustration 22-20) as $1,000 relating to the adding back of unrealized loss on FV-NI investments, and the other $4,000 as part of the decrease in FV-NI investments ($26,000 − $30,000 = $4,000) included in the changes in non-cash working capital items.

(b) **Accounts Receivable.** Unlike the previous two company illustrations, Yoshi reports both accounts receivable and its contra allowance account. The receivable control account is increased by sales on account and reduced by accounts written off and cash received on account. The 2017 receivable T account is shown below, with the sales amount taken from the income statement. The cash received on account, the only missing information, must have been $867,950. This was determined by using the T account to solve for the one unknown credit entry: $52,700 + $923,200 − $1,450 − x = $106,500. The cash received, therefore, was $55,250 less than the net sales reported on the income statement or $867,950 ($923,200 − $867,950 = $55,250).

Accounts Receivable			
Jan. 1	52,700		
Sales on account	923,200	1,450	Accounts written off (given)
		?	Cash received on account
Dec. 31	106,500		

Using the indirect method, $55,250 is deducted from the net income reported. Under the direct method, the revenue of $923,200 is adjusted directly by $55,250 to convert it to cash received from customers of $867,950 (see Illustration 22-18).

(c) **Allowance for Doubtful Accounts.** This account had an opening balance of $1,700, was increased by bad debt expense, was reduced by accounts written off, and ended the year at $2,500. With accounts written off of $1,450, bad debt expense must have been $2,250 ($1,700 + bad debt expense − $1,450 = $2,500; or you could prepare a T account to determine this). Because bad debt expense does not use cash, the net income number in the operating activities section must be adjusted.

Under the indirect method, $2,250 is added back to net income. Under the direct method, the $2,250 adjustment reduces the expense line that includes bad debt expense. In this example, it is assumed to be included in selling and administrative expenses.

It is only necessary to analyze the Accounts Receivable and Allowance accounts separately when using the direct method. This is because two adjustments are needed: one to adjust the revenue reported ($55,250) and the other to adjust the non-cash bad debt expense ($2,250). When using the indirect method, both adjustments correct the one net income number. The analysis is easier, therefore, if you focus on the change in the net accounts receivable and make one adjustment of $53,000 to the net income number.[14]

(d) **Inventory.** Because the Inventory account is increased by the cost of goods purchased and decreased by the transfer of costs to cost of goods sold, the $8,000 decrease in the Inventory account indicates that purchases were $8,000 less than transfers to cost of goods sold. Using the indirect method, $8,000 is added back to the net income number. The direct method adjusts cost of goods sold directly to convert it to the cost of goods purchased. The analysis of Accounts Payable in item (m) will convert the purchases to cash payments to suppliers as summarized in Illustration 22-18, Panel B.

(e) **Prepaid Expenses.** This account decreased by $500 because the costs that were charged to the income statement were $500 more than the costs of acquiring prepaid goods and services in the year. For reasons similar to the inventory analysis in item (d), $500 is either added back to net income under the indirect method, or used to adjust the expense line associated with the prepaid expense under the direct method. We assume that the prepaid expenses were charged to selling and administrative expenses when they were used. So, under the direct method, payments for goods and services are reduced by $500.

(f) **Investment in Associate (Portel Corp.).** The journal entries that explain the increase of $3,500 in this account are shown below.

Investment in Associate	5,500	
Investment Income or Loss		5,500
(To record investment income of Portel Corp. using the equity method)		
Cash	2,000	
Investment in Associate		2,000
(To record the dividend received from Portel Corp.)		

The $5,500 investment income amount is reported on the income statement, and the dividend amount is derived from the overall change of $3,500 in the SFP account balance. Cash did not change as a result of the investment income; therefore, an adjustment is needed to reduce the net income number. Under the indirect method, the $5,500 is deducted to offset the $5,500 included in net income. Under the direct method, the $5,500 adjustment is made to the specific revenue line. This adjustment eliminates the equity-method investment income reported.

The second entry indicates a dividend cash inflow of $2,000. In this case, an adjustment is needed to the net income reported in operating activities because it does not include the cash dividend. Unlike dividends received from other types of investments, those received from associates (significantly influenced investees) require an adjustment to be reported in operating flows. Using the indirect method, $2,000 is added to net income. Under the direct method, $2,000 is added to the same line as the $5,500 deduction above, as this completes the adjustment of the non-cash equity-basis investment income to cash received from the investment in Portel.

(g) **Investment in Shares of Hyco Ltd.** The entry that explains the change in this investment classified as an FV-OCI investment is as follows:

FV-OCI Investments	4,500	
Unrealized Gain or Loss—OCI		4,500
(To adjust investment to fair value at year end)		

The entry explains the change in the investment account and the source of $4,500 of the increase to other comprehensive income. No cash flow is involved and no income statement amount is affected. Therefore, no amounts are reported on the statement of cash flows and no adjustment is needed in the operating section. (See also item (s) below.)

If an FV-OCI investment had been acquired or sold in the year, there would be investing cash flows to capture on the statement. In the case of a disposal, any realized holding gain or loss transferred (recycled) from OCI to net income would need to be eliminated in the operating activities section.

(h) **Deferred Development Costs.** The two transactions that affected this intangible asset account in the current year are summarized in the following journal entries:

Deferred Development Costs	200,000	
Cash		200,000
(To record capitalized development costs)		
Development Expenses	40,000	
Deferred Development Costs		40,000
(To record the amortization of deferred development costs)		

The first entry indicates a cash outflow of $200,000. This is an investing outflow and is recognized in the statement's investing activities section (Illustration 22-18, Panel C).

The second entry did not affect cash. As explained earlier, it is important to be alert to non-cash amounts that are included in net income. This $40,000 expense did not use any cash; an adjustment to add this to net income is therefore needed under the indirect method. Under the direct method, the adjustment is made to the specific expense: in this case, it is assumed to be part of selling and administrative expenses.

(i) **Land.** This account increased by $49,500. Because you know that land was purchased at a cost of $54,000 during the year, there must have been a disposal of land with a cost of $4,500. Knowing there was a gain on sale of land of $10,500, the entries that affect this account in 2017 must have been as follows:

Land	54,000	
Term Preferred Shares		54,000
(To record purchase of land through issue of term preferred shares)		
Cash	15,000	
Land		4,500
Gain on Disposal of Land		10,500
(To record disposal of land costing $4,500)		

The first entry indicates that there were no cash flows associated with the purchase of land. Although this investment and financing transaction is not reported on the statement of cash flows, information about such non-cash transactions is a required disclosure elsewhere in the financial statements.

The second entry identifies a cash inflow of $15,000 on land disposal. This is an investing inflow because it affects the company's stock of non-current assets, so the sale proceeds are included on the statement of cash flows in the investing cash flow section.

The second transaction also results in a gain of $10,500 on the income statement. By starting with "net income" in the statement's operating cash flow section in Step 2, the $10,500 gain is included in income as if the gain had generated $10,500 of operating cash flows. This is incorrect for two reasons. First, the cash inflow was $15,000, not $10,500. Second, the cash flow was an investing, not an operating, flow. An adjustment is needed, therefore, to deduct $10,500 from the income reported using the indirect method or from the line showing gain on sale of land if the direct method is used.

(j) **Equipment and Accumulated Depreciation—Equipment.** All the information that is needed to reproduce the entries made to these accounts in 2017 was provided in Illustrations 22-14, 22-15, and 22-17.

Equipment	73,000	
Cash		73,000
Cash	13,000	
Loss on Disposal of Equipment	1,500	
Accumulated Depreciation—Equipment	13,500	
Equipment		28,000
Depreciation Expense	11,500	
Accumulated Depreciation—Equipment		11,500

The first entry explains a cash outflow of $73,000 due to the purchase of equipment, which is an investing activity.

The second entry records the disposal of an asset that cost $28,000 and has accumulated depreciation of $13,500; that is, a carrying amount of $14,500. To be sold at a loss of $1,500, the proceeds on disposal must have been $13,000.

The analysis of this second entry is similar to the land disposal in item (i).

1. The cash effect is an inflow of proceeds of $13,000. This is an investing receipt.

2. The transaction results in a loss of $1,500 that is reported in 2017 income. Because the cash effect was not a $1,500 cash payment and because it was not an operating flow, an adjustment is needed in the operating cash flow section. The $1,500 loss is added back to net income under the indirect method, or to the appropriate line ("other expenses and losses") under the direct method.

The third entry reflects the annual depreciation expense. Depreciation does not use cash, so an adjustment is also needed to add this amount back to net income. Under the direct method, the depreciation line itself is adjusted.

(k) **Buildings and Accumulated Depreciation—Buildings.** There was no change in the asset account during the year and, since there is no additional information, the increase in the accumulated depreciation account must have been due entirely to the depreciation recorded for the year. The $3,100 non-cash expense is an adjustment in the operating activities section, similar to depreciation on equipment discussed above.

(l) **Goodwill.** The $2,400 decrease in Goodwill is the result of the following entry:

Loss on Impairment (Goodwill)	2,400	
Goodwill		2,400

There was no effect on cash. Under the indirect method, $2,400 is added back to net income; under the direct method, the impairment loss line itself is offset.

(m) **Accounts Payable.** Because Accounts Payable is increased by purchases on account for operations and decreased by payments to suppliers, cash outflows to suppliers must have been $1,000 higher than purchases in 2017. Previous adjustments to the working paper in items (d) and (e) converted expenses reported on the income statement to the cost of goods and services purchased. The analysis of Accounts Payable completes this by converting the purchases' amount to the cash paid for purchases. The indirect method deducts an additional $1,000 from the net income reported, while the direct method adjusts the expense line.

(n) **Dividends Payable on Term Preferred Shares.** The $2,000 increase indicates that dividends paid were $2,000 less than the dividends declared on these shares. Because the term preferred shares are liabilities in substance, the dividends on these shares are treated the same as interest on debt: they are deducted as dividend expense on the income statement. Under the indirect method, $2,000 is added back to net income because the cash outflow was less than the dividend expense reported. Under the direct method, the line item that includes the dividend expense is reduced. This assumes Yoshi reports interest paid as an operating outflow, and this treatment is required by ASPE and permitted under IFRS.

If Yoshi follows a policy of reporting interest paid (and dividends on in-substance financial liabilities) as financing outflows, as is permitted under IFRS, the amount recognized in net income and reported in operating flows on the working paper is eliminated and the correct cash outflow is reported in the financing activities section.

(o) **Accrued Liabilities.** This account is increased by expenses recognized and decreased by payments of the accrued amounts. During 2017, the payments must have been $4,000 less than the expenses reported: $4,000 is therefore added back to net income under the indirect method. Using the direct method, you must determine which expenses should be adjusted. If it was interest expense that was accrued and paid, the interest expense line is adjusted; if it was wages and salaries payable, the salaries and wages expense is adjusted. In Illustration 22-18, we assume the accruals relate to accrued payroll costs.

(p) **Income Taxes Payable.** This account is increased by tax expense and decreased by payments to the tax authorities. The $13,000 reduction indicates that the cash outflows were $13,000 more than the expense recognized. Net income is adjusted downward by $13,000 under the indirect method and the income tax line is adjusted under the direct method.

(q) **Bonds Payable.** In the absence of other information, we assume the change in the Bonds Payable account was increased through amortization of the discount.

Interest Expense	300	
Bonds Payable		300

The entry results in an expense with no corresponding use of cash. An adjustment of $300 is added back to net income under the indirect method, or to the interest expense line under the direct method.[15] The adjustment is identical if Yoshi accounts for the discount as a separate contra account.

(r) **Term Preferred Shares.** Term preferred shares of $60,000 were issued during the year, with $54,000 of this amount issued in exchange for land. This transaction was analyzed in item (i) above. Without information to the contrary, we assume that the remaining issue of term preferred shares was for cash and recorded with this entry:

Cash	6,000	
Term Preferred Shares		6,000

This is reported as a financing inflow.

(s) **Deferred Tax Liability.** The increase in this account's credit balance was a result of the following two entries:

Deferred Tax Expense	3,000	
Deferred Tax Liability		3,000
Deferred Tax Expense—OCI	1,000	
Deferred Tax Liability		1,000

No part of the expense reported used cash. Therefore, the $3,000 tax expense included in net income is added back under the indirect method and a similar adjustment is made to the income tax expense line under the direct method. The $1,000 amount reported in OCI did not use cash and it is not on the working paper; therefore, no adjustment needs to be made for it. The FV-OCI unrealized gain of $4,500 (see item (g)) is net of the related tax of $1,000, resulting in a net increase to accumulated other comprehensive income of $3,500.

(t) **Common Shares.** The following entries summarize the changes to this account (see also the statement of changes in equity):

Retained Earnings	15,000	
Common Shares		15,000
Cash	144,000	
Common Shares		144,000
Common Shares	21,600	
Retained Earnings	12,400	
Cash		34,000

The first entry records the stock dividend, which neither used nor provided cash. The issue of a stock dividend is not a financing and/or investing transaction, and therefore, is **not** required to be reported on the statement of cash flows. The second entry records a $144,000 inflow of cash as a result of issuing shares, so it is reported as a financing inflow on the working paper.

The third entry records the purchase and cancellation of shares in the year. Although IFRS does not provide specific guidance on the repurchase of a company's own shares, these entries are reasonable based on the information provided in Illustration 22-16. As the entry shows, the transaction used $34,000 cash. This financing flow is reported on the working paper.

(u) **Retained Earnings.** The statement of changes in equity also explains the $84,300 increase in this account. The $15,000 decrease due to the stock dividend was analyzed above as having no effect on cash flow. The cash flow associated with the $12,400 "loss" on the repurchase and cancellation of the common shares has already been dealt with in item (t). The $117,700 increase due to net income and the cash flows associated with it have already been included in the operating activities section of the statement of cash flows. The $6,000 decrease due to dividends paid on the common shares could be either a financing or an operating outflow. This depends on the company's policy and how it has reported the dividend in the past. We assume it is a financing flow.

ASPE requires this dividend to be reported as a financing flow. Under IFRS, if the dividend on common shares is treated as an operating flow, the net income number (or the specific line item affected) is adjusted for the outflow.

The changes in all statement of financial position accounts have now been analyzed and those that affect cash have been recorded on the statement of cash flows working paper. **The following general statements summarize the approach to the analysis.**

1. For most current asset and current liability accounts, focus on the transactions that increase and decrease each account. Compare the effect on the income statement with the amount of the related cash flow, and then adjust the income number(s) in the operating activities section of the statement accordingly.

2. For non-current asset and non-current liability accounts in general, reconstruct summary journal entries that explain how and why each account changed. Then analyze each entry as follows:

   (a) What is the cash flow? The cash effect is the amount of the debit or credit to cash (or cash equivalents) in the entry.

   (b) Is the cash flow an investing or financing flow? If so, update the working paper.

   (c) Identify all debits or credits to income statement accounts where the operating cash flow is not equal to the amount of revenue, gain, expense, or loss that is reported. Each of these requires an adjustment to the income number(s) originally reported in the operating activities section. Update the working paper.

While the transactions entered into by Yoshi Corporation represent a good cross-section of common business activities, they do not cover all possible situations. The general principles and approaches used in the above analyses, however, can be applied to most other transactions and events.

Step 4: Complete the statement of cash flows. Determine subtotals for each major classification of cash flow and ensure that the statement reconciles to the actual change in cash identified in Step 1.

The working paper prepared in Illustration 22-18 is presented with more appropriate descriptions and note disclosures to comply with IFRS and to enable readers to better interpret the information. Illustration 22-19 presents a completed statement of cash flows for Yoshi Corporation, using the direct method to explain the operating flows.

Illustration 22-19

Statement of Cash Flows—Yoshi Corporation (Direct Method)

YOSHI CORPORATION
Statement of Cash Flows
Year Ended December 31, 2017

Cash provided by (used in) operations

Received from customers		$ 867,950
Dividends received on significant influence investment		2,000
Net cash received on FV-NI investment transactions		6,300
Payments to suppliers		(490,750)
Payments to and on behalf of employees		(196,000)
Payments for interest, and dividends on term preferred shares		(9,000)
Income taxes paid		(62,500)
		118,000

Cash provided by (used in) investing activities

Investment in development costs	$(200,000)	
Purchase of equipment	(73,000)	
Proceeds on sale of land (Note 2)	15,000	
Proceeds on sale of equipment	13,000	(245,000)

Cash provided by (used in) financing activities

Proceeds on issue of common shares	144,000	
Proceeds on issue of term preferred shares	6,000	
Repurchase and cancellation of common shares	(34,000)	
Dividends paid on common shares	(6,000)	110,000
Decrease in cash and cash equivalents (Note 1)		(17,000)
Cash and cash equivalents, January 1		36,000
Cash and cash equivalents, December 31		$ 19,000

Note 1. Cash and cash equivalents are defined as cash on deposit and money-market instruments with original maturity dates of 90 days or less.
Note 2. Term preferred shares valued at $54,000 were issued during the year as consideration for the purchase of land.

For those who prefer the indirect method of reporting operating cash flows, Illustration 22-20 indicates how the statement's operating activities section would look.

Illustration 22-20

Cash Provided by Operations—Yoshi Corporation (Indirect Method)

Cash provided by (used in) operations		
Net income		$117,700
Add back non-cash expenses:		
Depreciation expense	$ 14,600	
Unrealized loss on FV-NI investments	1,000	
Impairment loss—goodwill	2,400	
Amortization of discount on bond	300	
Amortization of development costs	40,000	
Deferred income taxes	3,000	61,300
Equity in income of Portel Corp. in excess of dividends received		(3,500)
Deduct non-operating gains and losses:		
Gain on sale of land	(10,500)	
Loss on disposal of equipment	1,500	(9,000)
Changes in non-cash working capital accounts (see Note A)		(48,500)
		$118,000
Note A—changes in non-cash working capital:		
FV-NI investments	$ 4,000	
Accounts receivable, net	(53,000)	
Inventory	8,000	
Prepaid expenses	500	
Accounts payable	(1,000)	
Dividends payable, term preferred shares	2,000	
Accrued liabilities	4,000	
Income taxes payable	(13,000)	
	$ (48,500)	

How would this statement differ if ASPE had been followed instead of IFRS? Because we assumed that Yoshi follows the same reporting options for interest and dividends paid **permitted** under IFRS that are **required** under ASPE, the statements could be identical. The amount of cash generated or used by each type of activity and the change in cash are the same. Alternative presentations are permitted under IFRS, however, so the way the information is presented may differ. If the company had chosen different policies for reporting interest and dividends paid, the cash amounts in the operating and financing categories would change, but the overall decrease in cash and cash equivalents would not.

PRESENTATION

Objective **8**

Identify the financial presentation and disclosure requirements for the statement of cash flows.

Disclosure Requirements

The specific items that require disclosure are similar for IFRS and ASPE, with ASPE requiring less disclosure. In addition to reporting cash flows according to operating, investing, and financing classifications, the standards call for disclosure of the items set out in Illustration 22-21.

Illustration 22-21

Disclosures Required for the Statement of Cash Flows

IFRS	ASPE
Separately disclose interest received and paid and dividends received and paid.	Separately present interest and dividends paid and charged to retained earnings as a financing activity; classify as operating if received/paid and include in determination of net income.
Separately disclose cash flows from taxes on income.	Not required.

(continued)

Illustration 22-21

Disclosures Required for the Statement of Cash Flows (continued)

IFRS	ASPE
Disclose and provide relevant information about significant non-cash investing and financing transactions.	Same as IFRS requirement.
Report policy on what makes up cash and cash equivalents, and reconcile the change in amounts with the same amounts reported on the statement of financial position.	Same as IFRS requirement.
Report and explain amount of cash and cash equivalents that have restrictions on their use.	Disclose the amount of cash and cash equivalents that is restricted.

IFRS also identifies other information that may be helpful to users in assessing an entity's financial position and liquidity, and encourages the disclosure of this information along with a related commentary. Examples include:

- the amount of additional cash available under existing borrowing agreements;

- investing cash flows related to maintaining operating capacity and those for increasing operating capacity; and

- the operating, investing, and financing cash flows of each reportable segment.

Presentation Requirements

As indicated earlier in the chapter, entities can choose between the direct and indirect methods of presenting operating cash flows on the statement, although the direct method is preferred and encouraged by standard setters. Both ASPE and IFRS describe the indirect method as reconciling the net income (or, under IFRS, the profit and loss) to cash flow from operating activities. However, it is common in IFRS-prepared statements to see companies begin with **income before tax** or **income before interest and taxes**. The reason for this approach is that all other adjustments can be made and then the cash actually paid out for taxes and interest can be reported as separate figures. This allows entities to meet some of the disclosure requirements on the face of the statement.[16]

REAL WORLD EMPHASIS

Illustration 22-22 provides an example of this presentation by **British Airways plc** in its financial statements for the year ended December 31, 2014 (reported in millions of pounds, £). Notice that the opening "operating profit" is actually before finance costs (interest) and income tax expense. The actual cash flows for these two costs are reported at the bottom of the operating activities section.

Illustration 22-22

Operating Cash Flows Alternative Presentation— British Airways plc

Cash Flow Statements			
For the year ended 31 December			Group
£ million	Note	2014	2013
CONTINUING OPERATIONS			
Cash flow from operating activities			
Operating profit		975	708
Depreciation, amortisation and impairment	6	831	722
Cash payments to pension schemes (net of service costs)	31d	(312)	(302)
Movement in working capital and other non-cash movements		12	31
Interest paid		(113)	(123)
Taxation		(21)	(5)
Net cash generated from operating activities		1,372	1,031

Both sets of standards require, for the most part, the reporting of gross cash inflows and outflows from investing and financing activities rather than netted amounts. Other significant requirements relate to financial institutions, foreign currency cash flows, and business combinations and disposals. These are left to a course in advanced financial accounting.

Illustrative Example

REAL WORLD EMPHASIS

Stantec Inc.'s consolidated statements of cash flow for its years ended December 31, 2014 and 2013 are provided in Illustration 22-23. Stantec, a Canadian-based company, provides professional engineering consulting services mostly for infrastructure and facilities projects in North America. Note that this company uses the direct method to present its operating cash flows, and its financial statements are presented in accordance with IFRS. Some of the required disclosures are presented on the face of the statement itself, although many companies provide them in notes to the financial statements. Although not required, Stantec also provides a reconciliation of its net income with the cash flows from operations in Note 29. This is shown in Illustration 22-23 as well. Take a minute to review the statement of cash flows for the differences in cash activity from one year to the next.

Consolidated Statements of Cash Flows			
Years ended December 31		**2014**	2013
(In thousands of Canadian dollars)	Notes	$	$
CASH FLOWS FROM (USED IN) OPERATING ACTIVITIES			
Cash receipts from clients		**2,599,190**	2,225,332
Cash paid to suppliers		**(871,696)**	(646,719)
Cash paid to employees		**(1,438,417)**	(1,247,723)
Interest received		**2,422**	1,774
Interest paid		**(8,662)**	(9,150)
Finance costs paid		**(2,654)**	(2,571)
Income taxes paid		**(75,667)**	(61,201)
Income taxes recovered		**2,705**	12,387
Cash flows from operating activities	29	**207,221**	272,129
CASH FLOWS FROM (USED IN) INVESTING ACTIVITIES			
Business acquisitions, net of cash acquired	7	**(123,713)**	(43,539)
Dividends from investments in joint ventures and associates	13	**2,472**	2,685
Increase in investments held for self-insured liabilities		**(19,597)**	(25,129)
Decrease in investments and other assets		**3,531**	4,681
Proceeds from lease inducements		**8,884**	–
Purchase of intangible assets		**(3,365)**	(4,490)
Purchase of property and equipment		**(42,706)**	(52,639)
Proceeds on disposition of property and equipment		**176**	998
Cash flows used in investing activities		**(174,318)**	(117,433)
CASH FLOWS FROM (USED IN) FINANCING ACTIVITIES			
Repayment of bank debt		**(136,823)**	(70,924)
Proceeds from bank debt		**140,320**	36,319
Payment of finance lease obligations		**(5,174)**	(6,271)
Proceeds from issue of share capital		**10,587**	16,504
Payment of dividends to shareholders	21	**(33,641)**	(29,782)
Cash flows used in financing activities		**(24,731)**	(54,154)
Foreign exchange gain on cash held in foreign currency		**2,502**	1,780
Net increase in cash and cash equivalents		**10,674**	102,322
Cash and cash equivalents, beginning of the year		**143,030**	40,708
Cash and cash equivalents, end of the year	8	**153,704**	143,030

(continued)

Illustration 22-23

Statement of Cash Flows—
Stantec Inc. (continued)

29. Cash Flows From Operating Activities
Cash flows from operating activities determined by the indirect method are as follows:

	For the year ended December 31	
	2014	2013
(In thousands of Canadian dollars)	**$**	$
CASH FLOWS FROM (USED IN) OPERATING ACTIVITIES		
Net income for the year	**164,498**	146,201
Add (deduct) items not affecting cash:		
Depreciation of property and equipment	**38,698**	32,389
Amortization of intangible assets	**24,252**	21,235
Deferred income taxes	**(1,026)**	(7,430)
Loss on dispositions of investments and other assets	**2,065**	4,086
Share-based compensation expense	**7,659**	12,707
Provision for self-insured liabilities and claims	**6,421**	18,220
Other non-cash items	**(4,834)**	(5,942)
Share of income from joint ventures and associates	**(2,419)**	(2,276)
	235,314	219,190
Trade and other receivables	**12,509**	(13,472)
Unbilled revenue	**(42,519)**	12,366
Prepaid expenses	**444**	(3,725)
Trade and other payables	**2,322**	32,727
Billings in excess of costs	**11,731**	13,537
Income taxes payable	**(12,580)**	11,506
	(28,093)	52,939
Cash flows from operating activities	**207,221**	272,129

Contrast the direct method in the operating activities section of Stantec's cash flow statements in Illustration 22-23 with the same section prepared under the indirect method. It is surprising that the cash flow from operations determined under two such different methods actually has the same meaning!

ANALYZING THE STATEMENT OF CASH FLOWS

Interpreting the Statement of Cash Flows

Objective 9
Read and interpret a statement of cash flows.

UNDERLYING CONCEPT

Consolidated statements of cash flows may be of limited use to analysts evaluating multinational entities. With so much data brought together, users of the statements are not able to determine "where in the world" the funds are sourced and used.

As you can tell, companies have some flexibility in how information is reported in the statement of cash flows. The way in which the information is summarized and described can improve the information content and help users interpret and understand the significance of the cash flow data.

One way to approach an analysis of the statement is to begin by focusing on the three subtotals and determining what they tell you about which activities (operating, investing, and financing) generated cash for the company and which used cash. After this general assessment, delve deeper into the details within each section.

As an example, the statement of cash flows of Stantec Inc. in Illustration 22-23 indicates that, in 2014, excess operating cash inflows of $207.2 million allowed the company to internally finance all of its investment activities of $174.3 million during the year. Due to its healthy cash position, Stantec also used $33.6 million to pay dividends to its shareholders. These activities, combined with other financing activities, including the proceeds from issuing share capital, resulted in an overall $10.7-million increase in cash and cash equivalents during 2014, with an ending balance of $153.7 million.

The 2013 story was even better. In 2013, Stantec's cash from operations was $272.1 million. Financing activities used up $54.2 million, primarily for (net) repayment of bank debt and payment of dividends. There was more than enough left over to cover the company's needs for investment capital of $117.4 million. This resulted in an increase in cash of more than $100.0 million over the year! Each company and each statement of cash flows tells a different story, but the key questions they answer remain the same: Where did the cash come from, and how was it used? Each story should be read and interpreted in conjunction with the other financial statements and the Management Discussion and Analysis.

Operating Activities

TREASURY MANAGEMENT
5.2.1

Whether a company uses the direct or indirect method, the **net operating cash flows tell you the same thing: the extent to which cash receipts from customers and other operating sources were able to cover cash payments to suppliers of goods and services and to employees, and for other operating expenditures**. This is how the approximately $207 million cash provided by operating activities at Stantec in 2014 and the $272 million in 2013 are interpreted.

Stantec has a growth strategy that it has identified as combining internal growth and acquisition of firms that will help move it toward becoming a top 10 global design firm. Stantec set a goal of compound annual growth of 15%. It appears that it wants to generate cash from operations and use those cash flows to finance its business acquisitions in an effort to achieve this goal. As a design and engineering services provider, the company is not capital intensive; that is, it does not have large investments in property, plant, and equipment assets. The company, therefore, when compared with some large manufacturers, does not have a significant physical asset base to use as collateral for long-term borrowing. Instead, goodwill from its many acquisitions is the largest asset on its statement of financial position.

While the direct method provides more detail about the specific sources and uses of cash and is particularly useful in comparisons with previous years, the indirect method explains the relationship between the accrual-based net income and the cash from operations. Stantec's largest adjustment between these two numbers, as is the case with many companies, is typically the add-back of depreciation and amortization expenses. This is the major reason why its operating cash flows are so much higher than the net income the company reports.

Deferred income taxes and a variety of other expenses are adjusted because their cash effects are felt in different periods than their income statement effects. A positive adjustment in the current year for items like self-insured liabilities and claims often means that the related cash outflow will be felt in a subsequent year.[17]

An adjustment for the "changes in non-cash working capital balances" is found in the operating activities section of almost every statement of cash flows prepared under the indirect method and this can have a significant effect on the operating cash flow reported. The details, such as those at the bottom of Note 29 in Illustration 22-23, should be reviewed. The change in these accounts reduced operating cash flows otherwise generated by $28 million, unlike the increase of $53 million in 2013. Although accounts receivable collections added to the cash flow, increases in unbilled revenue had the opposite effect in 2014.

These changes need to be analyzed carefully. For example, consider the case of **Aptalis Pharma Inc.**, which reported cash flow from operating activities of more than U.S. $63 million in 2010, substantially higher than the cash used in operating activities of U.S. $49 million the next year. However, U.S. $107.2 million of the cash flow from operations in 2010 came from a loss on disposal of a product line and a writedown of assets. A further U.S. $23.4 million was from higher-than-usual collections of accounts receivable (which helped to offset a loss of U.S. $170.4 million). In this case, the operating cash flows in the period under review (2010) did not represent operating cash flows that were likely to be repeated in subsequent years. This was shown clearly the next year, when cash flows from operations were U.S. $112.1 million lower.

Users of financial statements need to look beyond the amount of cash generated or used in operations, and analyze the reasons for the operating cash flows. The objective of the analysis is to assess whether the cash flow levels are sustainable and likely to be repeated in the future, or whether they are the result of payment deferrals and one-time events.

Investing Activities

Consistent with its strategic goals, Stantec reports significant cash outlays for business acquisitions of $43.5 million in 2013 and $123.7 million in 2014, explained in more detail in another Stantec note. Because investments in new business assets are the source of future operating cash flows, it is important to understand whether the new investment just maintains the existing capacity of a company, or whether the investment increases the potential for higher levels of operating cash flows in the future. For companies with substantial property, plant, and equipment, how do the new amounts invested compare with the stock of existing property, plant, and equipment, and with the depreciation charges for the year? Also, what types of assets have been purchased? Are they investments in new technologies and development expenditures? Or are existing assets being disposed of, reducing the potential for operating flows in the future?

Stantec appears to be investing in the future by making acquisitions as part of its growth strategy. These, in turn, are generating operating cash flows to allow for the internal financing of further acquisitions.

Financing Activities

The operating and investing flows tell just part of a company's cash story for the period. The financing activities section completes the picture. It clearly captures what changes took place to the firm's capital structure and whether the entity increased or reduced the claims of creditors to cash in the future.

In contrast to its 2014 financing activities, Stantec used much of the excess cash balances it had built up to repay a net amount of almost $35 million of its bank debt in 2013. This net reduction in debt was partially offset by proceeds from share capital issued. These two areas and dividend payments accounted for most of the financing activities.

The methods of financing are usually related to the types of assets acquired. For example, purchases of intangibles and development expenditures are often difficult to use as collateral and, therefore, they are generally financed internally from operating cash flows or externally through new equity.

Details of cash flows related to financing activities allow readers to assess the potential for future claims on the organization's cash and, as indicated above, to identify shifts in the form of financing, especially between debt and equity. Will there be increased demand for future cash for interest claims and debt repayment? Companies in a growth stage may report significant amounts of cash generated from financing activities—financing that is needed to handle the significant investment activity. As growth levels off and operations begin to generate positive cash flows, financing flows tend to reverse as debt is repaid and, if appropriate, dividends are paid. The required disclosure of long-term debt repayments over the next five years is an excellent source of information about upcoming demands on an organization's cash for financing purposes.

Due to recent concerns about a general decline in the quality of earnings, some investors have been focusing more on cash flow. Management has an incentive to make cash flow look good, because the capital markets pay a premium for companies that generate a lot of cash from operations rather than through borrowings. However, just as they can with earnings, companies have ways to pump up cash flow from operations.

WHAT DO THE NUMBERS MEAN?

One way that companies can boost their operating cash flow is by securitizing receivables. Chapter 7 discussed how companies can speed up cash collections by selling their receivables. For example, **Oxford Industries**, an apparel company, once reported a $74-million increase in cash flow from operations. This seemed impressive until you read the fine print, which indicated that a major portion of the increase was due to the sale of receivables. While it originally appeared that the company's core operations had improved, Oxford did little more than accelerate collection of its receivables. In fact, operating cash flow would have been negative without the securitization.

Operating cash flows can also be manipulated by having too liberal a policy of capitalizing expenditures as property, plant, and equipment instead of expensing them as incurred. Such a policy leads to these costs being treated as investment flows. They are not

REAL WORLD EMPHASIS

deducted in determining net income or cash from operations. Even when depreciated, the costs end up having no effect on operating cash flow. **WorldCom** was able to conceal almost U.S. $4 billion of decline in its operations this way; **Adelphia Communications** overstated its operating cash flow by U.S. $102 million this way; and closer to home, **Atlas Cold Storage** later reported a similar situation, although on a smaller scale.

The point is that operating cash flow, like earnings, can be of high or low quality. You should be careful when comparing companies' operating cash flows, even if they are in the same industry. Consider the different effect on operating cash flow of one company that rents its premises under operating leases with another that has adopted IFRS 16 and accounts for these as right-of-use lease arrangements. Or compare one company that capitalizes interest and over-

head as part of self-constructed assets with one that expenses these costs, or a company that capitalizes internal-use computer software with one that absorbs the costs as they are incurred. In all cases, one set of policies results in investing or financing outflows of cash, while the other set reports reduced operating cash flows. And, unlike revenue and expense accruals and deferrals that are reported on an income statement, where the effect reverses over time, the effects on the classifications in the statement of cash flows are permanent.

Sources: Gerald I. White, Ashwinpaul C. Sondhi, and Dov Fried, *The Analysis and Use of Financial Statements*, 3rd ed. (New York: John Wiley & Sons, Inc., 2003), p. 96; "Atlas Cold Storage Fires CFO, Suspends Q3 Distribution," CBCNews.ca, December 4, 2003; Deborah Solomon, "Adelphia Overstated Cash Flow, Revenue for the Past Two Years," *The Wall Street Journal*, June 11, 2002.

Sensitivity Analysis

A thorough analysis of cash flows includes sensitivity analyses of the effect of changes in assumptions on relevant cash flows. For example, as was seen in Chapter 19 (Pensions and other Post-Employment Benefits), a small change in actuarial assumptions can lead to a large change in the discounted value (and related funding needs of a company).

Free Cash Flow

PLANNING, BUDGETING, & FORECASTING
3.2.1

Introduced in Chapter 5 and publicized by many companies in recent years, a non-GAAP performance measure used by many companies is **free cash flow**. As the name suggests, this is an indicator of financial flexibility that uses information provided on the statement of cash flows. Free cash flow is net operating cash flows reduced by the capital expenditures that are needed to sustain the current level of operations. The resulting cash flow is the discretionary cash that a company has available for increasing its capacity and acquiring new investments, paying dividends, retiring debt, repurchasing its shares, or simply adding to its liquidity.

The calculation of this measure varies by company. Some deduct all capital expenditures because it is impossible to separate sustaining expenditures from the total. Others also deduct current dividends. Free cash flow measures are more useful to investors if information is also provided about how they are calculated.

In general, companies with significant free cash flow have a strong degree of financial flexibility. They can take advantage of new opportunities or cope well during poor economic times without jeopardizing current operations.

IFRS/ASPE COMPARISON

Objective 10

Identify differences in IFRS and ASPE, and explain what changes are expected to standards for the statement of cash flows.

A Comparison of IFRS and ASPE

Because the most recent Canadian standard on the statement of cash flows (before the adoption of IFRS in 2011) was based on the related international standard, ASPE and IAS 7 are very similar. Illustration 22-24 sets out the few areas where there are differences between them.

	IFRS—IAS 7	Accounting Standards for Private Enterprises (ASPE)—*CPA Canada Handbook*, Part II, Section 1540	References to Related Illustrations and Select Brief Exercises
Definitions and scope	Preferred shares acquired close to their maturity date may be included in cash equivalents.	Cash equivalents exclude all equity investments.	BE22-2
Presentation	Interest and dividends received may be classified and presented as either operating or investing cash flows. Interest and dividends paid are either operating or financing outflows.	Interest and dividends received are presented as operating cash flows. Interest and dividends paid are operating flows if recognized in net income. If charged directly to retained earnings, they are presented as financing cash flows.	Illustration 22-2 BE22-4
Disclosure	Separate disclosure is required for each of interest and dividends received and paid.	Interest and dividends paid and charged to retained earnings must be disclosed separately as a financing activity.	Illustration 22-21
	Income taxes paid are required to be disclosed.	Income taxes paid are encouraged (but not required) to be disclosed.	BE22-9 and BE22-13
	Restrictions on the use of cash and cash equivalents and an explanation of the amount of cash and cash equivalents not available for use are required to be disclosed.	The amount of cash and cash equivalents whose use is restricted is required to be disclosed.	Illustration 22-21

Illustration 22-24

IFRS and ASPE Comparison Chart

Looking Ahead

The most influential event on the horizon with the potential to affect the reporting of cash flows is Phase B of the joint FASB-IASB Financial Statement Presentation project.[18] From the IASB's perspective, Phase B is intended to replace existing IAS 1 *Presentation of Financial Statements* and IAS 7 *Statement of Cash Flows*. The IASB had planned to issue an Exposure Draft in 2010 and a final standard was expected in 2011, but then it decided to do more outreach activities before finishing and publishing the Exposure Draft and final standard. The outreach activities focused on the perceived benefits and costs of the proposals and the effects on financial institutions. However, the project was paused in 2011, and had not recommenced as of the time of writing.

SUMMARY OF LEARNING OBJECTIVES

1 Understand the business importance of cash flows and describe the purpose and uses of the statement of cash flows.

One sign of a healthy company is positive cash flow from operations. Companies can use these funds to finance expansion, to issue dividends, or to ensure that they remain solvent during economic downturns. Many consider the statement of cash flows to be less susceptible to earnings management than the statement of comprehensive income.

The primary purpose of this statement is to provide information about an entity's cash receipts and cash payments during a period. A secondary objective is to report the entity's operating, investing, and financing activities during the period.

2 Define cash and cash equivalents.

The definition of cash is related to an organization's cash management activities. Cash and cash equivalents include cash on hand, demand deposits, and short-term, highly liquid non-equity investments that are convertible to known amounts of cash with insignificant risk of changes in value. These amounts are reduced by bank overdrafts that fluctuate from positive to negative balances and that are repayable on demand. IFRS allows preferred shares acquired within a short period of their maturity to be included as a cash equivalent.

3 Identify the major classifications of cash flows and explain the significance of each classification.

Cash flows are classified into those resulting from operating, investing, and financing activities. A company's ability to generate operating cash flows affects its capacity to pay dividends to shareholders, to take advantage of investment opportunities, to provide internal financing for growth, and to meet obligations when they fall due. The amount of cash spent on investing activities affects an organization's potential for future cash flows. Cash invested in increased levels of productive assets forms the basis for increased future operating cash inflows. Financing cash activities affect the firm's capital structure and, therefore, the requirements for future cash outflows.

4 Prepare the operating activities section of a statement of cash flows using the direct versus the indirect method.

The direct method presents operating cash flows in a manner similar to a condensed cash basis income statement. The accrual amounts are listed and adjusted whenever the cash received or paid out differs from the revenues, gains, expenses, and losses reported in net income, and for non-operating gains and losses.

5 Prepare a statement of cash flows using the direct method.

The direct method involves determining the change in cash and cash equivalents during the period, inserting line items from the income statement as the starting point within the statement's operating activities section, and analyzing the changes in all accounts on the statement of financial position to identify all transactions that have an impact on cash. Those with a cash impact are recorded on the statement of cash flows. To ensure that all cash flows have been identified, the results recorded on the statement are compared with the change in cash during the period. The statement is then prepared with required disclosures.

6 Prepare a statement of cash flows using the indirect method.

The steps using the indirect method are the same as in Objective 5 above, with one exception. Rather than starting with line items from the income statement in the operating activities section, the net income amount is the beginning point. All the same adjustments are then made to adjust net income to a cash basis, but the style and format of the operating activities sections differ.

7 Prepare a more complex statement of cash flows using both methods.

When preparing a more complex statement of cash flows under either the direct or indirect method, the same four-step process can be followed: (1) Determine the change in cash; (2) Record information from the income statement to the statement of cash flows; (3) Analyze the change in each SFP account and identify/record the effect on the statement of cash flows; and (4) Complete the statement of cash flows.

8 Identify the financial presentation and disclosure requirements for the statement of cash flows.

Under IFRS, disclosure is required of cash flows associated with interest and dividends received and paid, the definition and components of cash and cash equivalents reconciled to the amounts reported on the statement of financial position, and the amount of and explanation for cash and cash equivalents not available for use. All income tax cash flows are reported as operating flows unless they can be linked directly to investing or financing flows. Choices are available under IFRS for the reporting of interest and dividends received (operating or investing) and interest and dividends paid (operating or financing). Gross amounts should be reported except in specifically permitted circumstances, and non-cash investing and financing transactions are excluded from the statement of cash flows, but details about these are reported elsewhere on the financial statements. ASPE presentation requirements are very similar, but required disclosures are limited to interest and dividends paid and charged to retained earnings and the amount of any restricted cash. In addition, interest and dividends received are both operating flows, and interest and dividends paid are operating flows unless they were charged directly to retained earnings.

9 Read and interpret a statement of cash flows.

The first step in reading and interpreting a statement of cash flows is to look at the subtotals for the three classifications of activities and the overall change in cash. This provides a high-level summary of the period's cash flows. Next, analyze the items within each section for additional insights, keeping alert for accounting policies that affect the type of cash flow reported. Familiarity with the company's business and strategic direction is very useful in interpreting the statement.

10 Identify differences in IFRS and ASPE, and explain what changes are expected to standards for the statement of cash flows.

There are no significant differences between IFRS and ASPE related to the statement of cash flows except for the definition of cash equivalents and the presentation and disclosure requirements identified above.

KEY TERMS

cash, p. 1375
cash equivalents, p. 1375
cash flows, p. 1375
direct method, p. 1378

financing activities, p. 1375
free cash flow, p. 1407
indirect method, p. 1378
investing activities, p. 1375

operating activities, p. 1375
significant non-cash transactions, p. 1377
statement of cash flows, p. 1374

APPENDIX 22A

USE OF A WORK SHEET

Objective **11**
Use a work sheet to
prepare a statement of
cash flows.

When many adjustments are needed, or there are other complicating factors, a work sheet is often used to assemble and classify the data that will appear on the statement of cash flows. The work sheet (or spreadsheet when using computer software) is merely a device that aids in the preparation of the statement; using one is optional. The skeleton format of the work sheet for preparing the statement of cash flows using the indirect method is shown in Illustration 22A-1.

Illustration 22A-1

Format of Work Sheet for Preparing Statement of Cash Flows

	A	B	C	E	F
1		Statement of Cash Flows for the Year Ended...			
2	**Statement of Financial Position Accounts**	**End of Last Year Balances**	**Debits**	**Credits**	**End of Current Year Balances**
3	Debit balance accounts	XX	XX	XX	XX
4		XX	XX	XX	XX
5	Totals	XX			XX
6					
7	Credit balance accounts	XX	XX	XX	XX
8		XX	XX	XX	XX
9	Totals	XX			XX
10					
11	Cash Flows				
12	**Operating activities**				
13	Net income		XX		
14	Adjustments		XX	XX	
15	**Investing activities**				
16	Receipts (dr.) and payments (cr.)		XX	XX	
17	**Financing activities**				
18	Receipts (dr.) and payments (cr.)		XX	XX	
19	Totals		XX	XX	
20	**Increase (cr.) or decrease (dr.) in cash**		XX or	XX	
21	Totals		XX	XX	
22					

The following guidelines are important in using a work sheet.

1. In the statement of financial position accounts section, accounts with debit balances are listed separately from those with credit balances. This means, for example, that Accumulated Depreciation is listed under credit balances and not as a contra

account under the debit balances. The beginning and ending balances of each account are entered. As the analysis proceeds, each line that relates to an SFP account should balance. That is, the beginning balance plus or minus the reconciling item(s) must equal the ending balance. When all SFP accounts agree in this way, all changes in account balances have been identified and reconciled and the analysis is complete.

2. The bottom portion of the work sheet is an area to record the operating, investing, and financing cash flows. This section provides the detail for the change in the cash balance during the period—information that is used to prepare the formal statement of cash flows. Inflows of cash are entered as debits in the reconciling columns and outflows of cash are entered as credits in the reconciling columns. Thus, in this section, the sale of equipment for cash at book value is entered as a debit under inflows of cash from investing activities. Similarly, the purchase of land for cash is entered as a credit under outflows of cash for investing activities.

3. The reconciling items shown in the work sheet are not entered in any journal or posted to any account. They do not represent either adjustments or corrections of the SFP accounts. They are only used to make it easier to prepare the statement of cash flows.

Preparing the Work Sheet

The preparation of a work sheet involves a series of steps.

Step 1: Enter the SFP accounts and their beginning and ending balances in the appropriate statement of financial position accounts section.

Step 2: Enter the debits and credits from the summary entries that explain the changes in each SFP account (other than cash). Identify all entries that affect cash, and enter these amounts in the reconciling columns at the bottom of the work sheet.

Step 3: After the analysis is complete and the changes in all SFP accounts have been reconciled, enter the increase or decrease in cash on the SFP cash line (or lines, if cash equivalents) and at the bottom of the work sheet. The totals of the reconciling columns should balance.

To illustrate the procedure for preparing the work sheet, we use the same comprehensive illustration for Yoshi Corporation, a publicly accountable enterprise reporting under IFRS, that was used in the chapter. We will initially use the indirect method for calculating net cash provided by operating activities. We will also provide an illustration of the direct method. The financial statements and other data related to Yoshi Corporation for its year ended December 31, 2017 are presented in Illustrations 22-14, 22-15, 22-16, and 22-17. Most of the analysis was discussed earlier in the chapter but we provide additional explanations related to the work sheet here.

Analyzing Transactions

Before the analysis begins, Yoshi's SFP accounts are transferred to the work sheet's opening and ending balance columns. The following discussion explains the individual adjustments that appear on the work sheet in Illustration 22A-2. The discussion assumes that you are familiar with the analysis of the Yoshi illustration earlier in the chapter.

	A	B	C	D	E	F	G
1		Work Sheet for Preparation of Statement of Cash Flows Year Ended December 31, 2017					
2		Balance 12/31/16	Reconciling Items—2017				Balance 12/31/17
2			Debits		Credits		
3	**Debits**						
4	Cash	32,000			(24)	27,000	5,000
5	Cash equivalents	4,000	(24)	10,000			14,000
6	FV-NI investments	30,000			(2)	5,000	25,000
7	Accounts receivable	52,700	(3)	55,250	(3)	1,450	106,500
8	Inventory	311,000			(4)	8,000	303,000
9	Prepaid expenses	17,000			(5)	500	16,500
10	Investment in Associate (Portel Corp.)	15,000	(6)	5,500	(6)	2,000	18,500
11	FV-OCI investments (Hyco Ltd.)	13,000	(7)	4,500			17,500
12	Deferred development costs	30,000	(8)	200,000	(8)	40,000	190,000
13	Land	82,000	(9)	54,000	(9)	4,500	131,500
14	Equipment	142,000	(10)	73,000	(10)	28,000	187,000
15	Buildings	262,000					262,000
16	Goodwill	10,000			(11)	2,400	7,600
17	**Total debits**	1,000,700					1,284,100
18							
19	**Credits**						
20	Allowance for doubtful accounts	1,700	(3)	1,450	(12)	2,250	2,500
21	Accumulated Depreciation— Equipment	31,000	(10)	13,500	(13)	11,500	29,000
22	Accumulated Depreciation— Buildings	71,000			(14)	3,100	74,100
23	Accounts payable	131,000	(15)	1,000			130,000
24	Dividends payable, term preferred shares	—			(16)	2,000	2,000
25	Accrued liabilities	39,000			(17)	4,000	43,000
26	Income tax payable	16,000	(18)	13,000			3,000
27	Bonds payable	97,500			(19)	300	97,800
28	Term preferred shares	—			(9)	54,000	60,000
29					(20)	6,000	
30	Deferred tax liability	6,000			(21)	3,000	10,000
31					(21)	1,000	
32	Common shares	88,000	(22)	21,600	(22)	15,000	225,400
33					(22)	144,000	
34	Retained earnings	518,500	(22)	12,400	(1)	117,700	602,800
35			(22)	15,000			
36			(23)	6,000			
37	Accumulated other comprehensive income	1,000	(21)	1,000	(7)	4,500	4,500
38	**Total credits**	1,000,700					1,284,100
39							
40	**Cash Flows**						
41	**Operating activities:**						
42	Net income		(1)	117,700			
43	Decrease in FV-NI investments		(2)	5,000			
44	Increase in accounts receivable				(3)	55,250	
45	Decrease in inventory		(4)	8,000			
46	Decrease in prepaid expenses		(5)	500			
47	Investment Income or Loss				(6)	5,500	
48	Dividend from Portel Corp.		(6)	2,000			
49	Amortization, deferred development costs		(8)	40,000			

Illustration 22A-2

Work Sheet for Preparation of Statement of Cash Flows— Yoshi Corporation

(continued)

50	Gain on sale of land			(9)	10,500
51	Loss on disposal of equipment	(10)	1,500		
52	Loss on impairment (goodwill)	(11)	2,400		
53	Bad debt expense	(12)	2,250		
54	Depreciation expense—equipment	(13)	11,500		
55	Depreciation expense—buildings	(14)	3,100		
56	Decrease in accounts payable			(15)	1,000
57	Dividend expense, term preferred shares	(16)	2,000		
58	Increase in accrued liabilities	(17)	4,000		
59	Decrease in income taxes payable			(18)	13,000
60	Amortization of bond discount	(19)	300		
61	Deferred tax liability	(21)	3,000		
62					
63	**Investing activities:**				
64	Development costs incurred			(8)	200,000
65	Proceeds on disposal of land	(9)	15,000		
66	Purchase of equipment			(10)	73,000
67	Proceeds on sale of equipment	(10)	13,000		
68					
69	**Financing activities:**				
70	Proceeds on issue of term preferred shares	(20)	6,000		
71	Proceeds on sale of common shares	(22)	144,000		
72	Repurchase of common shares			(22)	34,000
73	Dividend on common shares			(23)	6,000
74	Decrease in cash and cash equivalents	(24)	17,000		
75			885,450		885,450
76					
77					

Illustration 22A-2

Work Sheet for Preparation of Statement of Cash Flows— Yoshi Corporation (continued)

1. **Net Income.** Because so much of the analysis requires adjustments to convert accrual basis income to the cash basis, the net income number is usually the first reconciling item put in the work sheet. The entry to reflect this and the SFP account affected is:

Net Income	117,700	
Retained Earnings		117,700

The credit to Retained Earnings explains part of the change in that account. We know that net income did not generate $117,700 of cash, so this number is considered a temporary one that will be adjusted whenever the subsequent analysis identifies revenues and expenses whose cash impact is different from the revenue and expense amounts that are included in net income. It is a starting point only.

2. **FV-NI Investments.** Based on the activity and adjustments in this account during 2017, the entry to explain the net change in its balance is as follows:

Cash ($32,300 − $26,000)	6,300	
FV-NI Investments		5,000
Investment Income or Loss ($2,300 − $1,000)		1,300

Because the cash flows related to investments held for trading purposes are all operating cash flows, the operating activities section should report $6,300 of net cash inflows. However, all that is reported so far is the $1,300 of investment income. Therefore, an adjustment of $5,000 is needed to adjust the investment income number to the cash flows from these FV-NI investments. This explains the $5,000 decrease in this account's balance during the year.

3. **Accounts Receivable.** The following two entries summarize the net change in this account and identify the other accounts that are affected:

Accounts Receivable	55,250	
Revenue		55,250
Allowance for Doubtful Accounts	1,450	
Accounts Receivable		1,450

Accounts Receivable increased by $53,800 during the year after writing off accounts totalling $1,450. The increase due to reporting revenue in excess of cash receipts therefore must have been $55,250. This requires an adjustment to the net income reported in the work sheet's operating activities section. The other entry explains changes in two SFP accounts with no cash impact. These are entered on the work sheet.

4. **Inventory.** The entry to explain the net change in the Inventory account is as follows:

Cost of Goods Sold	8,000	
Inventory		8,000

The credit to inventories explains the change in that account. The debit is an expense of $8,000 that was deducted in calculating net income, but that did not use cash. This requires a debit column adjustment to the net income in the operating activities section.[19]

5. **Prepaid Expenses.** Assuming the prepaid expenses were selling in nature, the following entry summarizes the change in this account:

Selling Expenses	500	
Prepaid Expenses		500

The credit entry explains the change in the Prepaid Expenses account. The debit represents a non-cash expense deducted on the income statement, requiring an adjustment to the net income reported in the operating activities section.

6. **Investment in Associate (Portel Corp.).** Entries explaining the change in this account are:

Investment in Associate	5,500	
Investment Income or Loss		5,500
Cash	2,000	
Investment in Associate		2,000

The first entry explains part of the change in the investment account and identifies a non-cash revenue included in net income. The entry to adjust net income for this is a $5,500 credit. The second entry credit explains the remainder of the change in the SFP account. The debit portion of the entry represents an operating inflow of cash that has not been included in net income. The operating activities section is adjusted to reflect this $2,000 operating cash inflow.

7. **FV-OCI Investments.** A single entry explains the change in this investment accounted for at FV-OCI.

FV-OCI Investments	4,500	
Unrealized Gain or Loss—OCI		4,500

The entry explains the change in two SFP accounts. The $4,500 was not an income statement item and it is not a cash transaction.

8. **Deferred Development Costs.** The entries to summarize the changes in this account are as follows:

Deferred Development Costs	200,000	
Cash		200,000
Development Expenses	40,000	
Deferred Development Costs		40,000

The first entry identifies an outflow of cash related to the investment in this non-current asset—an investing flow. The second entry recognizes the amortization of these deferred costs—a non-cash expense—reported in net income. The adjustment adds back (debits) $40,000 to the net income number. Remember to enter the transactions that explain changes in the SFP accounts as you proceed.

9. **Land.** The entries affecting the Land account are:

Land	54,000	
Term Preferred Shares		54,000
Cash	15,000	
Land		4,500
Gain on Disposal of Land		10,500

The first entry explains changes in both the Land and Term Preferred Shares accounts—a significant non-cash transaction. The second entry identifies a $15,000 investing inflow of cash, a reduction of $4,500 in the Land account, and the difference of $10,500 representing a gain reported in net income that does not correspond to the actual cash flow. Net income is adjusted.

10. **Equipment.** The entries that affect the Equipment account are as follows:

Equipment	73,000	
Cash		73,000
Cash	13,000	
Loss on Disposal of Equipment	1,500	
Accumulated Depreciation—Equipment	13,500	
Equipment		28,000

The first entry identifies a $73,000 investing outflow of cash. The second entry explains the remainder of the change in the asset account and part of the change in the Accumulated Depreciation account, and identifies a $13,000 investing inflow of cash and a $1,500 non-cash loss that is reported in net income and needs to be adjusted.

11. **Goodwill.** The decrease in Goodwill is an impairment loss, recreated with this entry:

Loss on Impairment (Goodwill)	2,400	
Goodwill		2,400

The impairment loss is a non-cash charge to the income statement. It therefore requires an adjustment to the net income included in the Operating Activities section.

12. **Allowance for Doubtful Accounts.** Part of the change in this account was explained previously in item 3 above. The remaining entry to this account recognized bad debt expense:

Bad Debt Expense	2,250	
Allowance for Doubtful Accounts		2,250

This completes the explanation of changes to the allowance account. In addition, it identifies a non-cash expense of $2,250, which requires an adjustment to net income in the operating activities section.

13. **Accumulated Depreciation—Equipment.** One of the changes in the Accumulated Depreciation account was explained previously in item 10. The other entry affecting this account is:

Depreciation Expense	11,500	
Accumulated Depreciation—Equipment		11,500

The entry identifies an $11,500 non-cash expense requiring an adjustment to net income and the cash flows from operations.

14. **Accumulated Depreciation—Buildings.** With no change in the Buildings account during the year, the only entry needed to explain the change in the Accumulated Depreciation account is:

Depreciation Expense	3,100	
Accumulated Depreciation—Buildings		3,100

This $3,100 non-cash expense requires an adjustment to the net income number in the operating activities section.

15. **Accounts Payable.** The summary entry to explain the net change in this account is:

Accounts Payable	1,000	
Cash		1,000

The reduction in the payables balance resulted from paying out $1,000 more cash than was recorded in purchases. Cost of goods sold and other expenses have already been adjusted to represent the goods and services purchased, so a $1,000 credit adjustment is needed to convert the purchases to the amount paid; that is, to the operating cash outflow.

16. **Dividends Payable on Term Preferred Shares.** The summary entry explaining the net change in this account is as follows:

Dividend Expense (income statement expense)	2,000	
Dividends Payable (on term preferred shares)		2,000

The increase in the liability account results from recognizing more dividends as an expense (these shares are a financial liability in substance) than dividends paid in the year. Therefore, $2,000 is added back to net income to adjust the operating cash flows to equal cash dividends paid in 2017.

17. **Accrued Liabilities.** The $4,000 increase in this account was caused by recognizing $4,000 more expense than payments in the year. The entry is as follows:

Salaries and Wages Expense (assumed)	4,000	
Accrued Liabilities		4,000

To adjust, $4,000 is added back (debited) to the cash provided by net income as reported.

18. **Income Taxes Payable.** The decrease in this account occurred because Yoshi Corporation paid out more cash than the expense reported, reflected by this entry:

Income Tax Payable	13,000	
Cash		13,000

Because the expense reported has been deducted in determining the income number, an additional $13,000 outflow is deducted or credited on the work sheet.

19. **Bonds Payable.** The change in the Bonds Payable account is assumed to be explained by the following entry as a result of amortizing the bond discount netted with the liability:

Interest Expense	300	
Bonds Payable		300

That is, $300 of the interest expense did not require any cash, so an adjustment is needed to the net income in the operating activities section.

20. **Term Preferred Shares.** Of the increase, $54,000 has already been explained above. The remaining increase is assumed to have resulted from the following entry, a $6,000 financing inflow:

Cash	6,000	
Term Preferred Shares		6,000

21. **Deferred Tax Liability.** The increase in this account is due to the deferral of the tax liability to future periods, reflected in this entry:

Deferred Tax Expense	3,000	
Deferred Tax Liability		3,000
Deferred Tax Expense—OCI	1,000	
Deferred Tax Liability		1,000

The change in the SFP account is explained, with the non-cash portion of income tax expense adjusted by adding back $3,000 to net income and debiting $1,000 to AOCI.

22. **Common Shares.** The following entries explain the change in this account over the year:

Retained Earnings	15,000	
Common Shares		15,000
Cash	144,000	
Common Shares		144,000
Common Shares	21,600	
Retained Earnings	12,400	
Cash		34,000

The first entry records the stock dividend. As discussed earlier, this is a non-cash activity that, although explaining the change in two SFP accounts, is not part of the statement of cash flows. The second entry records the inflow of cash for shares sold—a financing activity. The third entry records the repurchase and cancellation of the company's own shares.

23. **Retained Earnings.** Most of the changes in this account have already been dealt with above. One additional entry is needed to explain the remainder of the change:

Retained Earnings (dividends)	6,000	
Cash		6,000

This entry records a financing outflow of cash for dividends on common shares.

Completing the Work Sheet

All that remains to complete the SFP portion of the work sheet is to credit the Cash account by $27,000 and debit the Cash Equivalents account by $10,000, netting to a $17,000 credit or decrease in cash. The $17,000 debit to balance this work sheet entry is inserted at the bottom of the work sheet. The debit and credit columns of the reconciling items are then totalled and balanced.

If the direct method of determining cash flows from operating activities is preferred, one change is needed to the above procedures. Instead of debiting the net income of $117,700 and using this as the starting point to represent cash inflows from operations, the individual revenues, expenses, gains, and losses (netting to $117,700) are transferred to the operating activities section line by line. When income statement items differ from the actual cash generated or used, adjustments are made to the specific line items affected.

The analysis is simplified if items that will be reported together on the final statement are grouped together, and if all income tax amounts are grouped as well. This step and the adjustments that are needed in the operating activities section are shown in Illustration 22A-3. The adjustments in the operating activities section are exactly the same as the ones that were made using the indirect method, except that they are made to a specific line item instead of net income.

<table>
<tr><td rowspan="2" style="vertical-align:top;">Illustration 22A-3

Operating Activities Work
Sheet—Direct Method</td><td colspan="5" style="text-align:center;">DIRECT METHOD</td></tr>
<tr><td></td><td colspan="2" style="text-align:center;">Debits (inflows)</td><td colspan="2" style="text-align:center;">Credits (outflows)</td></tr>
<tr><td>Cash Flows</td><td></td><td></td><td></td><td></td></tr>
<tr><td>Operating activities:</td><td></td><td></td><td></td><td></td></tr>
<tr><td>Receipts from customers</td><td>(1)</td><td>923,200</td><td>(3)</td><td>55,250</td></tr>
<tr><td>Received from investment in associate</td><td></td><td></td><td></td><td></td></tr>
<tr><td>(Portel Corp.)</td><td>(1)</td><td>5,500</td><td>(6)</td><td>5,500</td></tr>
<tr><td></td><td>(6)</td><td>2,000</td><td></td><td></td></tr>
<tr><td>Received on FV-NI investment transactions</td><td>(1)</td><td>1,300</td><td></td><td></td></tr>
<tr><td></td><td>(2)</td><td>5,000</td><td></td><td></td></tr>
<tr><td>Payments for goods and services</td><td>(4)</td><td>8,000</td><td>(1)</td><td>395,400</td></tr>
<tr><td></td><td>(5)</td><td>500</td><td>(1)</td><td>134,600</td></tr>
<tr><td></td><td>(8)</td><td>40,000</td><td>(1)</td><td>12,000</td></tr>
<tr><td></td><td>(10)</td><td>1,500</td><td>(15)</td><td>1,000</td></tr>
<tr><td></td><td>(12)</td><td>2,250</td><td></td><td></td></tr>
<tr><td>Payments to employees</td><td>(17)</td><td>4,000</td><td>(1)</td><td>200,000</td></tr>
<tr><td>Interest and dividend payments</td><td>(19)</td><td>300</td><td>(1)</td><td>11,300</td></tr>
<tr><td></td><td>(16)</td><td>2,000</td><td></td><td></td></tr>
<tr><td>Loss on impairment (goodwill)</td><td>(11)</td><td>2,400</td><td>(1)</td><td>2,400</td></tr>
<tr><td>Income taxes paid</td><td>(21)</td><td>3,000</td><td>(1)</td><td>52,500</td></tr>
<tr><td></td><td></td><td></td><td>(18)</td><td>13,000</td></tr>
<tr><td>Depreciation expense</td><td>(13)</td><td>11,500</td><td>(1)</td><td>14,600</td></tr>
<tr><td></td><td>(14)</td><td>3,100</td><td></td><td></td></tr>
<tr><td>Cash received on sale of land</td><td>(1)</td><td>10,500</td><td>(9)</td><td>10,500</td></tr>
</table>

The bottom part of the work sheet in Illustration 22A-2 (and Illustration 22A-3 above) provides the necessary information to prepare the formal statement shown in Illustrations 22-19 (direct method) and 22-20 (indirect method).

SUMMARY OF LEARNING OBJECTIVE FOR APPENDIX 22A

11 Use a work sheet to prepare a statement of cash flows.

A work sheet can be used to organize the analysis and cash flow information needed to prepare a statement of cash flows. This method accounts for all changes in the balances of non-cash statement of financial position accounts from the period's beginning to the end, identifying all operating, investing, and financing cash flows in the process. The statement of cash flows is prepared from the cash flow information accumulated at the bottom of the work sheet.

Completion of this end-of-chapter material will help develop CPA enabling competencies (such as ethics and professionalism, problem-solving and decision-making, and communication) and technical competencies. We have highlighted selected items with an integration icon and material in *WileyPLUS* has been linked to the competencies. All cases emphasize integration, especially of the enabling competencies. The brief exercises, exercises, and problems generally emphasize problem-solving and decision-making.

All assignment material with an asterisk (*) relates to the appendix to the chapter.

Brief Exercises

(LO 1) BE22-1 Alvarado Ltd., a private company, has reported increasing profit every year for the past five years. Alvarado would like to expand operations by adding three new retail stores within the next three years, and is seeking a loan from its bank to help fund the expansion. In Alvarado's most recent statement of financial position, the company reported a positive cash balance and a healthy current ratio of 2. Alvarado's controller believes that a statement of cash flows "would not be useful to the bank manager in making their decision because Alvarado has a solid financial position and has had increasing profit every year for the past five years." From the perspective of Alvarado's bank manager, (a) discuss the importance of positive cash flows, and (b) discuss the purpose and usefulness of the statement of cash flows.

(LO 2, 10) BE22-2 As at December 31, 2017, Bajac Inc. has the following balances: cash in bank, $108,000; investment in preferred shares (retractable, purchased by Bajac within 90 days of maturity date), $120,000; investment in common shares (to be sold within 30 days), 90,000; and cash (legally restricted for an upcoming long-term debt retirement), $245,000. Determine the December 31, 2017 cash and cash equivalents amount for the 2017 statement of cash flows under (a) IFRS and (b) ASPE.

(LO 2) BE22-3 Mullins Corp. reported the following items on its June 30, 2017 trial balance and on its comparative trial balance one year earlier:

	June 30, 2017	June 30, 2016
Cash in bank	$12,100	$ 9,460
Petty cash	700	525
Investment in shares of GTT Ltd. (to be sold within 60 days)	6,500	–0–
Investment in Canada 60-day treasury bills	22,000	–0–
Accounts payable	66,300	69,225
Temporary bank overdraft, chequing account	13,800	1,000

Determine the June 30, 2017 cash and cash equivalents amount for the 2017 statement of cash flows, and calculate the change in cash and cash equivalents since June 30, 2016.

(LO 3, 10) BE22-4 Maddox Corporation had the following activities in 2017.

1. Sold land for $180,000.
2. Purchased an FV-NI investment in common shares for $15,000.
3. Purchased inventory for $845,000 for cash.
4. Received $73,000 cash from bank borrowings.
5. Received interest for $11,000.
6. Purchased equipment for $495,000 in exchange for common shares.
7. Issued common shares for $350,000 cash.
8. Recorded an unrealized gain of $3,000 on investments accounted for using the fair value through net income (FV-NI) model.
9. Purchased investments in bonds, reported at amortized cost for $61,000.
10. Declared and paid a dividend of $18,000 (charged to retained earnings).
11. Investments in bonds reported at amortized cost, with a carrying amount of $410,000, were sold for $415,000.
12. Dividends of $4,000 were received on FV-NI investments.

Calculate the amount that Maddox should report as net cash provided (used) by investing activities on its statement of cash flows under (a) IFRS and (b) ASPE. Under IFRS, Maddox would adopt the policy of classifying interest and dividends paid as financing activities, and interest and dividends received as investing activities.

(LO 3) BE22-5 Tang Corporation, which follows IFRS and chooses to classify dividends paid as financing activities and interest paid as operating activities on the statement of cash flows, had the following activities in 2017.

1. Paid $870,000 of accounts payable.
2. Paid $12,000 of bank loan interest.
3. Issued common shares for $200,000.
4. Paid $170,000 in dividends (charged to retained earnings).
5. Collected $150,000 in notes receivable.

6. Issued $410,000 of bonds payable.

7. Paid $20,000 on bank loan principal.

8. Issued a stock dividend in the amount of $11,000.

9. Received $5,000 in interest from an investment in bonds.

10. Purchased at a cost of $47,000 the corporation's own shares.

Calculate the amount that Tang should report as net cash provided (used) by financing activities in its 2017 statement of cash flows.

(LO 3) BE22-6 Watson Corporation, which uses IFRS, is using the indirect method to prepare its 2017 statement of cash flows and chooses to classify dividends paid as financing activities and interest paid as operating activities on the statement of cash flows. A list of items that may affect the statement follows:

_____ **(a)** Increase in accounts receivable

_____ **(b)** Decrease in accounts receivable

_____ **(c)** Issue of shares

_____ **(d)** Depreciation expense

_____ **(e)** Sale of land at carrying amount

_____ **(f)** Sale of land at a gain

_____ **(g)** Payment of dividends charged to retained earnings

_____ **(h)** Purchase of land and building

_____ **(i)** Purchase of long-term investment in bonds, reported at amortized cost

_____ **(j)** Increase in accounts payable

_____ **(k)** Decrease in accounts payable

_____ **(l)** Loan from bank by signing note payable

_____ **(m)** Purchase of equipment by issuing a note payable

_____ **(n)** Increase in inventory

_____ **(o)** Issue of bonds

_____ **(p)** Retirement of bonds

_____ **(q)** Sale of equipment at a loss

_____ **(r)** Purchase of corporation's own shares

_____ **(s)** Acquisition of equipment using a capital/finance lease

_____ **(t)** Conversion of bonds payable into common shares

_____ **(u)** Goodwill impairment loss

_____ **(v)** Interest paid on self-constructed building

Match each code in the list that follows to the items above to show how each item will affect Watson's 2017 statement of cash flows. Unless stated otherwise, assume that the transaction was for cash.

Code Letter	Effect
A	Added to net income in the operating section
D	Deducted from net income in the operating section
R-I	Cash receipt in investing section
P-I	Cash payment in investing section
R-F	Cash receipt in financing section
P-F	Cash payment in financing section
N	Non-cash investing and/or financing activity disclosed in notes to the financial statement

(LO 3, 8) BE22-7 In 2017, Abbotsford Inc. issued 1,000 common shares for land with a fair market value of $149,000.

(a) Prepare Abbotsford's journal entry to record the transaction.

(b) Indicate the effect that the transaction has on cash.

(c) Indicate how the transaction is reported on the statement of cash flows.

(LO 3, BE22-8 Wong Textiles Ltd. entered into a capital lease obligation during 2017 to acquire a cutting machine. The
5, 8) amount recorded to the Equipment under Lease account and the corresponding Obligations under Lease account was
$85,000 at the date of signing the lease. Wong made the first annual lease payment of $2,330 at the date of signing, and
by the end of 2017 had recorded depreciation of $1,100 for the machine. Provide the necessary disclosure for these
transactions on the statement of cash flows prepared using the direct method. Wong follows IFRS and records its interest payments as a financing activity.

(LO 4, 10) BE22-9 Azure Ltd. had the following 2017 income statement data:

Sales	$205,000
Cost of goods sold	120,000
Gross profit	85,000
Operating expenses (includes depreciation of $21,000)	50,000
Income before income taxes	35,000
Income taxes	15,000
Net income	$ 20,000

The following accounts increased during 2017 by the amounts shown: Accounts Receivable, $17,000; Inventory,
$11,000; Accounts Payable (relating to inventory), $13,000; Taxes Payable $2,000; and Mortgage Payable, $40,000.
(a) Prepare the cash flows from operating activities section of Azure's 2017 statement of cash flows using the direct
method and following IFRS. (b) How would the disclosure requirements differ under ASPE?

(LO 4, 10) BE22-10 Using the information from BE22-9 for Azure Ltd., (a) prepare the cash flows from operating activities
section of Azure's 2017 statement of cash flows using the indirect method and following IFRS. (b) How would the disclosure requirements differ under ASPE?

(LO 5) BE22-11 At January 1, 2017, Apex Inc. had accounts receivable of $72,000. At December 31, 2017, the accounts
receivable balance was $59,000. Sales revenue for 2017 was $420,000. Sales returns and allowances for the year were
$10,000. Purchase discounts were in the amount of $4,200 and sales discounts were $1,000. Calculate Apex's 2017 cash
receipts from customers.

(LO 5) BE22-12 Ciao Corporation had January 1 and December 31 balances as follows:

	1/1/17	12/31/17
Inventory	$90,000	$113,000
Accounts payable	61,000	69,000

For 2017, the cost of goods sold was $550,000. Calculate Ciao's 2017 cash paid to suppliers of inventory.

(LO 5, BE22-13 Kamsky Inc., which follows IFRS, had the following balances and amounts appear on its comparative finan-
8, 10) cial statements at year end:

	Dec. 31, 2017	Dec. 31, 2016
Income taxes payable	$1,200	$1,400
Deferred tax asset	300	–0–
Deferred tax liability	1,950	1,600
Income tax expense	2,500	2,100
Deferred tax benefit	(600)	(200)

(a) Calculate income taxes paid in 2017 and discuss the related disclosure requirements under IFRS, if any. (b) If Kamsky
followed ASPE instead of IFRS, would the disclosure requirements for income taxes paid be any different?

(LO 4) BE22-14 Lupasco Ltd. had the following 2017 income statement data:

Revenues	$100,000
Expenses	60,000
	$ 40,000

In 2017, Lupasco had the following activity in selected accounts:

Accounts Receivable					Allowance for Doubtful Accounts			
1/1/17	20,000						1,200	1/1/17
Revenues	100,000	1,000	Write-offs		Write-offs	1,000	1,540	Bad debt expense
		90,000	Collections					
12/31/17	29,000						1,740	12/31/17

Prepare Lupasco's cash flows from operating activities section of the statement of cash flows using (a) the direct method, and (b) the indirect method.

(LO 4) **BE22-15** October Corporation reported net income of $46,000 in 2017. Depreciation expense was $17,000 and unrealized losses on FV-NI investments were $3,000. The following accounts changed as indicated in 2017:

Accounts Receivable	$11,000 increase
Bond Investment at Amortized Cost	16,000 increase
Deferred Tax Asset	2,000 decrease
Inventory	7,400 increase
Notes Payable (non-trade)	15,000 decrease
Accounts Payable	9,300 increase

Calculate the net cash provided by operating activities using the indirect method.

(LO 6) **BE22-16** In 2017, Oswald Corporation reported a net loss of $56,000. Oswald's only net income adjustments were depreciation expense of $67,000 and an increase in accounts receivable of $8,100. Calculate Oswald's net cash provided (used) by operating activities using the indirect method.

(LO 7) **BE22-17** During 2017, Yang Inc., which reports under IFRS and has adopted the policy of classifying interest received as an investing activity, lent $30,000 to a key supplier in exchange for a two-year interest-bearing promissory note. Interest revenue earned on the note and recorded on the statement of income was in the amount of $900 and a balance of $300 for interest receivable was reported on the statement of financial position at December 31, 2017 relating to the note. Prepare Yang's cash flows from (used by) investing activities section of the statement of cash flows.

(LO 11) ***BE22-18** Indicate in general journal form how the following items would be entered in a work sheet to prepare the statement of cash flows where payments for dividends are classified as financing activities. Indicate within the journal entries any items that impact on "(Operating)", "(Investing)" or "(Financing)" to show which activities are affected.

(a) Net income is $207,000.

(b) Cash dividends declared (charged to retained earnings) and paid totalled $60,000.

(c) Equipment was purchased for $114,000.

(d) Equipment that originally cost $40,000 and had accumulated depreciation of $32,000 was sold for $13,000.

Exercises

(LO 1, 6, 8, 9) **E22-1** **(Preparation of Statement from Transactions, and Explanation of Changes in Cash Flow)** Strong House Inc. had the following condensed statement of financial position at December 31, 2016:

STRONG HOUSE INC.
Statement of Financial Position
December 31, 2016

Cash	$ 10,000	Current liabilities	$ 14,500
Current assets (non-cash)	34,000	Long-term notes payable	30,000
Bond investment at amortized cost	40,000	Bonds payable	32,000
Plant assets (net)	57,500	Common shares	80,000
Land	38,500	Retained earnings	23,500
	$180,000		$180,000

Strong House Inc. follows IFRS and chooses to classify dividends paid as financing activities and interest paid as operating activities on the statement of cash flows.

During 2017, the following occurred:

1. Strong House Inc. sold part of its investment portfolio in bonds for $15,500, resulting in a gain of $500.

2. Dividends totalling $19,000 were paid to shareholders.

3. A parcel of land, to be used as a parking lot, was purchased for $5,500.

4. Common shares were issued for cash totalling $20,000.

5. Bonds payable of $10,000 were retired at par.

6. Equipment was purchased through the issuance of $32,000 of bonds.

7. Net income for 2017 was $42,000 after allowing for depreciation on Strong House's plant assets of $13,550. The amount of interest paid during 2017 was $4,150 and the amount of income taxes paid was $19,500.

8. Both current assets (other than cash) and current liabilities remained at the same amount.

Instructions

(a) Prepare a statement of cash flows for 2017 using the indirect method.

(b) Draft a one-page letter to Mr. Gerald Brauer, president of Strong House Inc., in which you briefly explain the changes within each major cash flow category. Refer to the statement of cash flows whenever necessary.

(c) Prepare a condensed statement of financial position at December 31, 2017 for Strong House Inc.

(d) Comment briefly about why the statement of cash flows used to be called a statement of changes in financial position. What additional relevant disclosure in financial reporting has been achieved with the change from the former statement of changes in financial position to the current statement of cash flows?

(LO 3, 10) E22-2 (Classification of Transactions and Calculation of Cash Flows) The following are selected statement of financial position accounts of Pavicevic Ltd. at December 31, 2016 and 2017, and the increases or decreases in each account from 2016 to 2017. Also presented is the selected income statement and other information for the year ended December 31, 2017.

Statement of Financial Position (selected accounts)

	2017	2016	Increase (Decrease)
Assets			
Accounts receivable	$ 84,000	$ 74,000	$10,000
FV-NI investments	41,000	49,000	(8,000)
Property, plant, and equipment	177,000	147,000	30,000
Accumulated depreciation	(78,000)	(67,000)	11,000
Liabilities and shareholders' equity			
Bonds payable	149,000	146,000	3,000
Dividends payable	8,000	5,000	3,000
Common shares	31,000	22,000	9,000
Retained earnings	104,000	91,000	13,000

Income Statement (selected information)
For the Year Ended December 31, 2017

Sales revenue	$295,000
Depreciation expense	33,000
Gain on sale of FV-NI investments	5,000
Unrealized loss on FV-NI investments	3,000
Gain on sale of equipment	14,500
Net income	31,000

Additional information:

1. During 2017, equipment costing $45,000 was sold for cash.

2. Accounts receivable relate to sale of inventory.

3. During 2017, $20,000 of bonds payable were issued in exchange for property, plant, and equipment. All bonds were issued at par.

4. During the year, short-term investments accounted at FV-NI with a carrying amount of $17,000 were sold. Additional investments were purchased.

Instructions

(a) Determine the category (operating, investing, or financing) and the amount that should be reported in the statement of cash flows for the following items, assuming Pavicevic Ltd. follows IFRS and has chosen to report cash dividends received and paid as operating activities and interest received and paid as operating activities:

1. Cash received from customers

2. Payments for purchases of property, plant, and equipment

3. Proceeds from the sale of equipment

4. Cash dividends paid

5. Redemption of bonds payable

6. Proceeds from the sale of FV-NI investments

7. Purchase of FV-NI investments

(b) Assume now that Pavicevic Ltd. follows ASPE.

1. What choices could the company have made in the classification of cash flows?

2. What difference would following ASPE have had in presenting the activities listed in part (a)?

(LO 3, 5, 6, 8) E22-3 (Statement of Cash Flows—Direct and Indirect Methods) Angus Farms Ltd., which follows ASPE, had the following transactions during the fiscal year ending December 31, 2017.

1. On May 1, a used tractor was sold at auction. The information concerning this transaction included:

Original cost of the tractor	$52,000
Carrying amount of tractor at date of sale	21,000
Cash proceeds obtained at sale	22,500

2. After the seeding season, on June 15, 2017, a plough with an original cost of $6,000 and a carrying amount of $500 was discarded.

3. On September 1, 2017, a new plough was purchased for $7,700.

4. On December 30, a section of land was sold to a neighbouring farm called Clear Pastures Ltd. The original cost of the land was $45,000. To finance the purchase, Clear Pastures gave Angus a three-year mortgage note in the amount of $75,000 that carries interest at 5%, with interest payable annually each December 30.

5. On December 31, 2017, depreciation was recorded on the farm equipment in the amount of $16,600.

Instructions

(a) Prepare the journal entries that recorded the transactions during the year.

(b) Indicate specifically which sections of the statement of cash flows of Angus Farms Ltd. would report the transactions provided, using the indirect format.

(c) Indicate how your response to part (b) would differ regarding how the statement of cash flows of Angus Farms Ltd. would report the transactions provided, assuming the company uses the direct format.

(d) How would the total amount of operating activities differ for Angus Farms Ltd. if it prepared its SCF using the indirect vs. direct methods as indicated in parts (b) and (c) above?

(LO 3, 5, 6, 10) E22-4 (Statement Presentation of Transactions—Investment Using Equity Method) The following selected account balances were taken from the financial statements of Blumberg Inc. concerning its long-term investment in shares of Black Inc. over which it has had significant influence since 2014:

	Dec. 31, 2017	Dec. 31, 2016
Investment in associate, Black Inc.	$494,600	$422,000
Investment income recorded for Black	13,200	11,800

At December 31, 2017, the following information is available:

1. Blumberg purchased additional common shares in Black Inc. on January 2, 2017, for $65,000. As a result of this purchase, Blumberg's ownership interest in Black increased to 40%.

2. Black reported income of $33,000 for the year ended December 31, 2017.

3. Black declared and paid total dividends of $14,000 on its common shares for the year ended December 31, 2017.

Instructions

(a) Prepare a reconciliation of the Investment in Black Inc. account from December 31, 2016 to December 31, 2017, assuming Blumberg Inc. uses the equity method for this investment.

(b) Prepare a table that contrasts the direct and indirect methods for presenting all transactions related to the Black Inc. investment on Blumberg's statement of cash flows based on the assumption that Black uses IFRS and adopts the policy of classifying dividends received as investing activities. Be specific about the classification in the statement for each item that is reported.

(c) Prepare a table that contrasts the direct and indirect methods for presenting all transactions related to the Black Inc. investment on Blumberg's statement of cash flows based on the assumption that Black uses ASPE and must therefore classify dividends received as operating cash flows.

(LO 3, 6) E22-5 (Partial Statement of Cash Flows—Indirect Method) The following accounts appear in the ledger of Tanaka Limited, which uses IFRS, and has adopted the policy of classifying dividends paid as operating activities:

Retained Earnings		Dr.	Cr.	Bal.
Jan. 1, 2017	Credit balance			$ 42,000
Aug. 15	Dividends (cash)	$15,000		27,000
Dec. 31	Net income for 2017		$40,000	67,000

Equipment		Dr.	Cr.	Bal.
Jan. 1, 2017	Debit balance			$140,000
Aug. 3	Purchase of equipment	$62,000		202,000
Sept. 10	Purchase of equipment	48,000		250,000
Nov. 15	Equipment sold		$56,000	194,000

Accumulated Depreciation—Equipment		Dr.	Cr.	Bal.
Jan. 1, 2017	Credit balance			$ 84,000
Nov. 15	Accumulated depreciation on equipment sold	$25,200		58,800
Dec. 31	Depreciation for 2017		$16,800	75,600

Instructions

Show how the information posted in the accounts is reported on a statement of cash flows by preparing a partial statement of cash flows using the indirect method. The loss on disposal of equipment (November 15) was $5,800.

(LO 3, 5, 6) E22-6 (Analysis of Changes in Capital Asset Accounts and Related Cash Flows) MacAskill Mills Limited, which follows IFRS, and has a calendar year end, and adopted the policy of classifying interest paid as financing activities engaged in the following transactions in 2017.

1. The Land account increased by $58,000 over the year: Land that originally cost $60,000 was exchanged along with a cash payment of $3,000 for another parcel of land with a fair value of $91,000. Additional land was acquired later in the year in a cash purchase.

2. The Equipment account had a balance of $67,500 at the beginning of the year and $62,000 at the end. The related Accumulated Depreciation account decreased over the same period from a balance of $24,000 to $15,200. Fully depreciated equipment that cost $10,000 was sold during the year for $1,000. In addition, equipment that cost $3,000 and had a carrying amount of $700 was discarded, and new equipment was acquired and paid for.

3. A five-year capital lease for specialized equipment was entered into on July 2, 2017. Under the terms of the lease, the company agreed to make five annual payments (in advance) of $25,000, after which the equipment will revert to the lessor. The present value of these lease payments at the 10% rate that is implicit in the lease was $104,247. The first payment was made as agreed. MacAskill depreciates equipment using the straight-line method with no residual value.

Instructions

FINANCE

(a) Using Excel, a financial calculator, or PV tables, prove the 10% implicit rate used in the capital lease of item 3.

For each listed item:

(b) Prepare the underlying journal entries that were made by MacAskill Mills during 2017 to record all information related to the changes in each capital asset account and related accounts over the year.

(c) Identify the amount(s) of the cash flows that result from the transactions and events recorded in part (b), and determine the classification of each one on the statement of cash flows within investing activities and financing activities.

(d) Prepare the corresponding amounts to those prepared in part (c) for the operating activities section of the statement of cash flows prepared using the indirect method.

(LO 2, 3, 6, 8, 10) E22-7 (Statement Presentation of Transactions—Indirect Method) Each of the following items must be considered in preparing a statement of cash flows (indirect method) for Bastille Inc., which follows IFRS, for the year ended December 31, 2017.

1. Equipment that cost $40,000 six years before and was being depreciated on a straight-line basis over 10 years with no estimated residual value was sold for $5,300.

2. During the year, 10,000 common shares were issued for $41 cash per share.

3. Uncollectible accounts receivable in the amount of $27,000 were written off against the allowance for doubtful accounts.

4. The company sustained a net loss for the year of $10,000. Depreciation amounted to $22,000. A gain of $9,000 was reported on the sale of land for $39,000 cash.

5. A three-month Canadian treasury bill was purchased for $50,000 on November 13, 2017. The company uses a cash and cash-equivalent basis for its statement of cash flows.

6. An impairment of $40,000 was recorded on goodwill.

7. Patent amortization for the year was $18,000.

8. The company exchanged common shares for a 40% interest in TransCo Corp. for $900,000.

9. The company accrued an unrealized loss on investments accounted for at FV-NI.

Instructions

Identify the amount and classification (if any) of each item in the statement of cash flows prepared using the indirect method.

(LO 3, 8) E22-8 (Statement Presentation of Transactions—Equity Accounts) The following selected account balances are taken from the financial statements of Mandrich Inc. at its calendar year end prepared using IFRS:

	2017	2016
Preferred shares classified as equity	$145,000	$145,000
Common shares: 9,000 shares in 2017, 10,000 shares in 2016	142,000	160,000
Contributed surplus—reacquisition of common shares	3,500	–0–
Cash dividends—preferred	6,250	6,250
Stock dividends—common	14,000	–0–
Retained earnings (balance after closing entries)	300,000	240,000

At December 31, 2017, the following information is available:

1. Mandrich Inc. repurchased 2,000 common shares during 2017. The repurchased shares had a weighted average cost of $32,000.

2. During 2017, 1,000 common shares were issued as a stock dividend.

3. Mandrich Inc. chooses to classify dividends paid as financing activities.

Instructions

(a) Calculate net income for the fiscal year ending December 31, 2017.

(b) Provide the necessary disclosure for all of Mandrich Inc.'s transactions on the statement of cash flows. Also state the section of the statement of cash flows in which each item is reported. Where there are choices or options in the classification, provide details of the options available.

(c) Does Mandrich Inc. have other choices in classifying dividends paid on the statement of cash flows?

(d) Assume now that the preferred shares are term preferred shares classified as debt. Repeat part (a).

(LO 3, 5, E22-9 (Partial Statement of Cash Flows—Finance Leases) Wagner Inc. is a large Canadian public company that
6, 8) uses IFRS. A lease for a fleet of trucks has been capitalized and the lease amortization schedule for the first three lease payments appears below. The trucks have an economic life of eight years. The lease term is from July 1, 2016 to June 30, 2023, and the trucks must be returned to the lessor at the end of this period.

WAGNER INC.
Lease Amortization Schedule

Date	Annual Lease Payments	Interest (8%) on Unpaid Obligation	Reduction of Lease Obligation	Balance of Lease Obligation
				$3,064,470
July 1, 2016	$545,000		$545,000	2,519,470
July 1, 2017	545,000	$201,558	343,442	2,176,028
July 1, 2018	545,000	174,082	370,918	1,805,110

Instructions

FINANCE

(a) Using Excel, a financial calculator, or PV tables, prove the 8% implicit rate used in the lease.

(b) Prepare the journal entries and any year-end (December 31) adjusting journal entries made by Wagner Inc. in 2016 and 2017 assuming no reversing entries are used. Wagner uses the straight-line method of depreciation.

(c) Prepare a partial comparative statement of cash flows using the direct method for the 2016 and 2017 fiscal years along with any additional disclosure notes. Wagner Inc. has adopted the policy of classifying any interest paid as operating activities on the statement of cash flows.

(LO 3, 8) E22-10 (Classification of Major Transactions and Events) Dunrobin Industries Ltd., which uses IFRS, had the following transactions during its most recent fiscal year.

1. Received a shipment of raw materials inventory purchased on account.

2. Declared a cash dividend on common shares.

3. Collected cash from tenants for rents.

4. Acquired a 4% interest in a supplier company's common shares accounted as FV-NI. (Management's intention is not to trade the shares.)

5. Made the annual contribution to the employees' pension plan.

6. Leased new equipment under a finance lease.

7. Declared a 2-for-1 stock split.

8. Paid the semi-annual interest on outstanding debentures.

9. Paid the supplier on account for the purchase transaction in item 1 above.

10. Purchased land by issuing preferred shares.

11. Paid the car dealership for a new fleet of vehicles for the sales staff.

12. Collected a dividend on the investment made in item 4 above.

13. Sold the old fleet of sales vehicles at an amount in excess of their carrying amount.

14. Distributed additional shares following a declaration of a 5% stock dividend.

Dunrobin Industries Ltd. has adopted the policy of classifying dividends received as investing activities, dividends paid as operating activities, and interest paid as a financing activity on the statement of cash flows.

Instructions

Identify each transaction listed above as

(a) an operating activity,

(b) an investing activity,

(c) a financing activity,

(d) a significant non-cash investing or financing activity, or

(e) none of these options.

Where there are choices or options in the classification, provide details of the options available.

(LO 3, 8, 10) E22-11 (Classification of Transactions) Baird Corp. had the following activity in its most recent year of operations:

1. Purchase of equipment

2. Redemption of bonds

3. Conversion of bonds into common shares

4. Sale of building

5. Depreciation of equipment

6. Exchange of equipment for furniture of equal fair value

7. Issue of common shares

8. Amortization of intangible assets

9. Purchase of company's own shares

10. Issue of bonds for land

11. Impairment loss on goodwill

12. Unrealized holding loss on investment accounted at fair value with gains and losses in net income (FV-NI)

13. Payment of dividends on common shares

14. Increase in interest receivable on notes receivable

15. Pension expense in excess of amount funded

16. Signing of a finance lease agreement for equipment

17. Payment of a monthly finance lease obligation

18. Purchase of a treasury bill as a cash equivalent

19. Payment into employees' pension plan

20. Unrealized gain accrued on FV-NI equity security investments

21. Redemption of preferred shares classified as debt

22. Payments of principal on an operating line of credit

23. Payment of interest on an operating line of credit

24. Receipt of interest income on a note receivable

25. Receipt of dividends on an investment in common shares

26. Purchase of an investment in retractable preferred shares (that will mature within 90 days of purchase date)

Instructions

(a) Assume that Baird Corp. follows IFRS, and that the company has adopted the policy of classifying dividends received as operating activities, dividends paid as operating activities, interest received as investing activities, and interest paid as a financing activity on the statement of cash flows. Using the indirect method, classify the items as one of the following:

1. an operating activity, added to net income;

2. an operating activity, deducted from net income;

3. an investing activity;

4. a financing activity;

5. a significant non-cash investing or financing activity; or

6. none of these options.

Where there are choices or options in the classification, provide details of the options available.

(b) Assume instead that Baird Corp. is a private company and has decided to apply ASPE. Identify which, if any, of your previous answers in part (a) would change under this assumption.

(LO 4, 9) **E22-12 (Preparation of Operating Activities Section—Direct Method)** Malouin Corp.'s income statement for the year ended December 31, 2017 had the following condensed information:

Service revenue		$778,000
Operating expenses (excluding depreciation)	$499,000	
Depreciation expense	66,000	
Unrealized loss on FV-NI investments	4,000	
Loss on disposal of equipment	14,000	583,000
Income before income tax		195,000
Income tax expense		58,000
Net income		$137,000

There were no purchases or sales of trading (FV-NI) investments during 2017.

Malouin's statement of financial position included the following comparative data at December 31:

	2017	2016
FV-NI investments	$22,000	$26,000
Accounts receivable	35,000	54,000
Accounts payable	44,000	31,000
Income tax payable	6,000	8,500

FINANCE

DIGGING DEEPER

Instructions

(a) Prepare the operating activities section of the statement of cash flows using the direct method.

(b) Assume that Malouin Corp.'s current cash debt coverage ratio in 2016 was 4.5. Calculate the company's current cash debt coverage ratio in 2017, and discuss the results from the perspective of a creditor.

(LO 4) **E22-13 (Cash Provided by Operating Activities, Write-off, and Recovery of Accounts Receivable)** The following are the transactions from Izzy Inc. concerning its allowance for doubtful accounts.

1. Write-off of accounts receivable	$5,000
2. Recovery of accounts previously written off	3,500
3. Accrual for bad debt expense	4,400

Assume these are the only transactions for the year.

Instructions

(a) Prepare the journal entries to record the above transactions.

(b) Prepare the reporting relating to these transactions on a partial statement of cash flows using

  1. the direct method, and

  2. the indirect method.

(LO 5, 6, **E22-14** **(Statement of Cash Flows—Direct and Indirect Methods)** Tuit Inc., a greeting card company that follows
8, 9) ASPE, had the following statements prepared as at December 31, 2017:

FINANCE

TUIT INC.
Comparative Statement of Financial Position
December 31

	2017	2016
Cash	$ 53,625	$ 25,000
Accounts receivable	58,000	51,000
Inventory	40,000	60,000
Prepaid rent	5,000	4,000
Equipment	154,000	130,000
Accumulated depreciation—equipment	(35,000)	(25,000)
Goodwill	20,000	50,000
Total assets	$295,625	$295,000
Accounts payable	$ 46,000	$ 40,000
Income tax payable	4,000	6,000
Salaries and wages payable	8,000	4,000
Short-term loans payable	8,000	10,000
Long-term loans payable	60,000	69,000
Common shares	130,000	130,000
Retained earnings	39,625	36,000
Total liabilities and shareholders' equity	$295,625	$295,000

TUIT INC.
Income Statement
Year Ending December 31, 2017

Sales revenue		$338,150
Cost of goods sold		165,000
Gross margin		173,150
Operating expenses		120,000
Operating income		53,150
Interest expense	$11,400	
Impairment loss—goodwill	30,000	
Gain on sale of equipment	(2,000)	39,400
Income before income tax		13,750
Income tax expense		4,125
Net income		$ 9,625

Additional information:

  1. Dividends on common shares in the amount of $6,000 were declared and paid during 2017.

  2. Depreciation expense is included in operating expenses, as is salaries and wages expense of $69,000.

  3. Equipment with a cost of $20,000 that was 70% depreciated was sold during 2017.

Instructions

(a) Prepare a statement of cash flows using the direct method.

(b) Prepare a statement of cash flows using the indirect method.

(c) Does Tuit Inc. have any options on how to classify interest and dividends paid on the statement of cash flows?

(d) From the perspective of an investor who is interested in investing in mature, successful companies, comment on
    Tuit Inc.'s sources and uses of cash by analyzing the company's statement of cash flows.

**DIGGING
DEEPER**

(LO 4, 5, 8, 9) **E22-15** **(Statement of Cash Flows—Direct and Indirect Methods)** Guas Inc., a major retailer of bicycles and accessories, operates several stores and is a publicly traded company. The company is currently preparing its statement of cash flows. The comparative statement of financial position and income statement for Guas as at May 31, 2017 are as follows:

GUAS INC.
Statement of Financial Position
As at May 31

	2017	2016
Current assets		
Cash	$ 33,250	$ 20,000
Accounts receivable	74,800	55,600
Inventory	188,700	199,000
Prepaid expenses	8,800	7,000
Total current assets	305,550	281,600
Plant assets	596,500	501,500
Less: Accumulated depreciation	148,000	122,000
Net plant assets	448,500	379,500
Total assets	$754,050	$661,100
Current liabilities		
Accounts payable	$123,000	$115,000
Salaries and wages payable	61,000	72,000
Interest payable	24,700	22,600
Total current liabilities	208,700	209,600
Mortgage payable	75,000	100,000
Total liabilities	283,700	309,600
Shareholders' equity		
Common shares	335,750	280,000
Retained earnings	134,600	71,500
Total shareholders' equity	470,350	351,500
Total liabilities and shareholders' equity	$754,050	$661,100

GUAS INC.
Income Statement
For the Year Ended May 31, 2017

Sales	$1,345,800
Cost of goods sold	814,000
Gross margin	531,800
Expenses	
Salaries and wages expense	207,800
Interest expense	66,700
Other operating expenses	24,800
Depreciation expense	26,000
Total operating expenses	325,300
Operating income	206,500
Income tax expense	65,400
Net earnings	$ 141,100

The following is additional information about transactions during the year ended May 31, 2017 for Guas Inc., which follows IFRS.

1. Plant assets costing $95,000 were purchased by paying $44,000 in cash and issuing 5,000 common shares.

2. The "other expenses" relate to prepaid items.

3. In order to supplement its cash, Guas issued 4,000 additional common shares.

4. There were no penalties assessed for the repayment of mortgage.

5. Cash dividends of $78,000 were declared and paid at the end of the fiscal year.

Instructions

FINANCE   (a) Compare and contrast the direct method and the indirect method for reporting cash flows from operating activities.

(b) Prepare a statement of cash flows for Guas Inc. for the year ended May 31, 2017, using the direct method. Support the statement with appropriate calculations, and provide all required disclosures.

(c) Using the indirect method, calculate only the net cash flow from operating activities for Guas Inc. for the year ended May 31, 2017.

(d) Does Guas Inc. have a choice in how it classifies dividends paid on the statement of cash flows?

(e) Assume that you are a shareholder of Guas Inc. What do you think of the dividend payout ratio that is highlighted in the statement of cash flows?

DIGGING DEEPER

(LO 4, 6, 8) **E22-16** **(Statement of Cash Flows—Direct and Indirect Methods)** Information from the statement of financial position and statement of income are given below for North Road Inc., a company following IFRS, for the year ended December 31. North Road has adopted the policy of classifying interest paid as operating activities and dividends paid as financing activities.

Comparative Statement of Financial Position,
at December 31

	2017	2016
Cash	$ 92,700	$ 47,250
Accounts receivable	90,800	37,000
Inventory	121,900	102,650
Investments in land	84,500	107,000
Property, plant, and equipment	290,000	205,000
Accumulated depreciation	(49,500)	(40,000)
	$630,400	$458,900
Accounts payable	$ 52,700	$ 48,280
Accrued liabilities	12,100	18,830
Notes payable	140,000	70,000
Common shares	250,000	200,000
Retained earnings	175,600	121,790
	$630,400	$458,900

Statement of Income, Year Ended December 31, 2017

Revenues		
Sales		$297,500
Gain on sale of investment in land		5,000
Gain on sale of equipment		3,750
		306,250
Expenses		
Cost of goods sold	$99,460	
Depreciation expense	58,700	
Operating expenses	14,670	
Income tax expense	39,000	
Interest expense	2,940	214,770
Net income		$ 91,480

Additional information:

1. Investments in land were sold at a gain during 2017.

2. Equipment costing $56,000 was sold for $10,550, resulting in a gain.

3. Common shares were issued in exchange for some equipment during the year. No other shares were issued.

4. The remaining purchases of equipment were paid for in cash.

Instructions

(a) Prepare a statement of cash flows for the year ended December 31, 2017, using the indirect method.

(b) Prepare the operating activities section of the statement of cash flows using the direct method.

(c) If North Road Inc. had followed ASPE, would it have a choice in how it classifies dividends paid on the statement of cash flows?

(LO 5, 6, 8, 9)   E22-17   (Statement of Cash Flows—Indirect and Direct Methods) Tobita Limited, which follows IFRS, has adopted the policy of classifying interest paid as operating activities and dividends paid as financing activities. Condensed financial data for 2017 and 2016 follow (in thousands):

TOBITA LIMITED
Comparative Statement of Financial Position
December 31

	2017	2016
Cash	$1,935	$1,150
FV-NI investments	1,300	1,420
Accounts receivable	1,750	1,300
Inventory	1,600	1,900
Plant assets	1,900	1,700
Accumulated depreciation	(1,200)	(1,170)
	$7,285	$6,300
Accounts payable	$1,200	$ 900
Accrued liabilities	200	250
Mortgage payable	1,400	1,550
Common shares	1,900	1,700
Retained earnings	2,585	1,900
	$7,285	$6,300

TOBITA LIMITED
Income Statement
Year Ended December 31, 2017

Sales		$6,900
Cost of goods sold		4,700
Gross margin		2,200
Administrative expenses		910
Income from operations		1,290
Other expenses and gains		
Interest expense	$(20)	
Gain on sale of investments (FV-NI)	80	60
Income before tax		1,350
Income tax expense		405
Net income		$ 945

FINANCE

Additional information: During the year, $70 of common shares were issued in exchange for plant assets. No plant assets were sold in 2017. The FV-NI investments' carrying amount and market value were the same at December 31, 2017.

Instructions

(a) Prepare a statement of cash flows using the indirect method.

(b) Prepare a statement of cash flows using the direct method.

(c) Does Tobita Limited have any options on how to classify interest and dividends paid on the statement of cash flows?

DIGGING DEEPER

(d) What would you consider to be an alarming trend that is revealed by the statements that you have prepared? Is it as easy to notice this trend using the direct method, as in part (b)?

(LO 4)   E22-18   (Preparation of Operating Activities Section—Indirect Method) Data for Malouin Corp. are presented in E22-12.

Instructions

Prepare the operating activities section of the statement of cash flows using the indirect method.

(LO 4)   E22-19   (Statement of Cash Flows—Direct Method) Huang Corp. uses the direct method to prepare its statement of cash flows and follows IFRS. Huang's trial balances at December 31, 2017 and 2016 were as follows:

	Dec. 31, 2017	Dec. 31, 2016
Debits		
Cash	$ 55,000	$ 31,000
Accounts receivable	33,000	30,000
Inventory	31,000	47,000
Property, plant, and equipment	95,000	90,000
Cost of goods sold	253,000	380,000
Selling expenses	138,000	172,000
Administrative expenses	140,000	151,300
Interest expense	15,600	28,600
Income tax expense	20,200	56,200
	$780,800	$986,100

	Dec. 31, 2017	Dec. 31, 2016
Credits		
Allowance for doubtful accounts	$ 1,300	$ 1,100
Accumulated depreciation	26,500	25,000
Accounts payable	25,000	15,500
Income taxes payable	21,000	29,100
Deferred income tax liability	5,300	4,600
8% callable bonds payable	46,000	45,500
Common shares	53,600	22,000
Retained earnings	44,700	64,600
Sales revenue	557,400	778,700
	$780,800	$986,100

Additional information:

1. Huang purchased $5,000 of equipment during 2017.

2. Bad debt expense for 2017 was $5,000 and write-offs of uncollectible accounts totalled $4,800.

3. Huang has adopted the policy of classifying the payments of interest as operating activities on the statement of cash flows.

Instructions

Prepare the operating activities section of the statement of cash flows for the year ended December 31, 2017 using the direct method.

(LO 4, 9) **E22-20** **(Accounting Cycle, Financial Statements, Cash Account, and Statement of Cash Flows)** The following are transactions of Albert Sing, an interior design consultant, for the month of September 2017.

Sept. 1 Albert Sing began business as an interior design consultant, investing $31,000 for 5,000 common shares of the company, A. S. Design Limited.

2 Purchased equipment from Green Jacket Co. for $17,280.

4 Paid rent for office space for the next three months at $680 per month.

7 Hired a part-time secretary, Michael Bradley, at $300 per week.

8 Purchased office supplies on account from Mann Corp. for $1,142.

9 Received cash of $1,690 from clients for services performed.

10 Paid office expenses, $430.

14 Invoiced clients for services rendered, $5,120.

18 Paid Mann Corp. on account, $600.

19 Paid a dividend of $1.00 per share on the 5,000 outstanding shares.

20 Received $980 from clients on account.

21 Paid Michael Bradley two weeks of salary, $600.

28 Invoiced clients for services rendered, $2,110.

29 Paid the September telephone bill of $135 and office expenses of $85.

At September 30, the following information is available.

1. The equipment has a useful life of five years and an estimated residual value of $1,500. Straight-line depreciation is appropriate.

2. One week's salary is owing to Michael Bradley.

3. Office supplies of $825 remain on hand.

4. Two months of rent has been paid in advance.

5. The invoice for electricity for September of $195 has been received, but not paid.

Instructions

(a) Prepare journal entries to record the transaction entries for September. Set up a T account for the Cash account and post all cash transactions to the account. Determine the balance of Cash at September 30, 2017.

(b) Prepare any required adjusting entries at September 30, 2017.

FINANCE   **(c)** Prepare an adjusted trial balance at September 30, 2017.

(d) Prepare a statement of financial position and income statement for the month ended September 30, 2017. Ignore income taxes.

(e) Prepare a statement of cash flows for the month of September 2017. Use the indirect method for the cash flows from operating activities.

(f) Recast the cash flow from operating activities section using the direct method.

(g) Compare the statement of cash flows in parts (e) and (f) with the Cash account prepared in part (a) above.

(h) As a creditor, what might you consider to be alarming that is revealed by the statement of cash flows prepared using the indirect method as required in part (e) above? Is this trend as easy to notice when the statement is prepared

DIGGING DEEPER   using the direct method as required in part (f) above?

(LO 4) E22-21   (Conversion of Net Income to Operating Cash Flow—Indirect Method) Shen Limited reported net income of $32,000 for its latest year ended March 31, 2017.

Instructions

For each of the five different situations involving the statement of financial position accounts that follow, calculate the cash flow from operating activities using the indirect method:

	Accounts Receivable March 31		Inventory March 31		Accounts Payable March 31	
	2017	2016	2017	2016	2017	2016
(a)	$20,000	$21,500	$16,500	$17,900	$ 9,000	$ 9,300
(b)	$23,000	$20,000	$17,300	$20,500	$14,600	$10,200
(c)	$20,000	–0–	$12,000	–0–	$ 7,000	–0–
(d)	$19,500	$21,000	$19,500	$15,600	$10,200	$14,100
(e)	$21,500	$24,000	$12,900	$14,000	$13,300	$11,300

(LO 11) *E22-22   (Work Sheet Analysis of Selected Transactions) The following transactions took place during the year 2017 for Mia Inc.

1. Convertible bonds payable with a carrying amount of $300,000 along with conversion rights of $9,000 were exchanged for common shares.

2. The net income for the year was $410,000.

3. Depreciation charged on buildings was $90,000.

4. Recorded the investment income earned from investment in associate, Transot Ltd., using the equity method. Transot's earnings for the year were $123,000 and Mia Inc. owns 28% of the outstanding common shares.

5. Old office equipment was traded in on the purchase of new equipment, resulting in the following entry:

Equipment	50,000	
Accumulated Depreciation—Equipment	30,000	
Equipment		40,000
Cash		34,000
Gain on Disposal of Equipment		6,000

6. Dividends in the amount of $123,000 were declared. They are payable in January 2018.

Instructions

For each item, use journal entries to show the adjustments and reconciling items that would be made on Mia Inc.'s work sheet for a statement of cash flows.

(LO 11) *E22-23 (**Work Sheet Preparation**) The comparative statement of financial position for Cosky Corporation follows:

	Dec. 31, 2017	Dec. 31, 2016
Cash	$ 16,500	$ 21,000
FV-NI investments	25,000	19,000
Accounts receivable	43,000	45,000
Allowance for doubtful accounts	(1,800)	(2,000)
Prepaid expenses	4,200	2,500
Inventory	81,500	65,000
Land	50,000	50,000
Buildings	125,000	73,500
Accumulated depreciation—buildings	(30,000)	(23,000)
Equipment	53,000	46,000
Accumulated depreciation—equipment	(19,000)	(15,500)
Machinery	39,000	39,000
Accumulated depreciation—machinery	(22,000)	(20,500)
Patents	15,000	–0–
	$379,400	$300,000
Accounts payable	$ 26,000	$ 16,000
Short-term notes payable (trade)	4,000	6,000
Accrued liabilities	3,000	4,600
Mortgage payable	73,000	53,400
Bonds payable	50,000	62,500
Common shares	150,000	106,000
Retained earnings	73,400	51,500
	$379,400	$300,000

Additional information:

1. Dividends of $15,000 were declared and paid in 2017.

2. There were no unrealized gains or losses on the FV-NI investments.

Instructions

Based on the information, prepare a work sheet for a statement of cash flows using the indirect method. Make reasonable assumptions as appropriate.

Problems

†P22-1 Jeopardy Inc.'s CFO has just left the office of the company president after a meeting about the draft statement of financial position at April 30, 2017, and income statement for the year ended. (Both are reproduced below.) "Our liquidity position looks healthy," the president had remarked. "Look at the current and acid test ratios, and the amount of working capital we have. And between the goodwill write-off and depreciation, we have almost $23 million of non-cash expenses. I don't understand why you've been complaining about our cash situation."

The CFO turns the draft financial statements over to you, the newest member of the accounting staff, along with extracts from the notes to the financial statements.

JEOPARDY INC.
Consolidated Statement of Financial Position
April 30, 2017 and 2016
(in $000s)

	2017	2016
Assets		
Cash and 60-day treasury bills	$ 3,265	$ 3,739
Accounts receivable	23,744	18,399
Inventory	26,083	21,561
Income tax receivable	145	–0–
Prepaid expenses	1,402	1,613
	54,639	45,312

†This item was originally published by the *Canadian Institute of Chartered Accountants* (CICA) as a question in the Uniform Final Evaluation (UFE). Adapted with permission of the Chartered Professional Accountants of Canada, Toronto, Canada. Any changes to the original material are the sole responsibility of the publisher and have not been reviewed or endorsed by the Chartered Professional Accountants of Canada.

	2017	2016
Investments (Note 1)	5,960	6,962
Property, plant, and equipment (Note 2)	37,332	45,700
Deferred tax asset	4,875	2,245
Intangible assets—franchises (Note 3)	4,391	1,911
Goodwill	–0–	12,737
	$107,197	$114,867

Liabilities

Current

	2017	2016
Bank overdraft (temporary)	$ 6,844	$ 6,280
Accounts payable and accrued liabilities (Note 4)	3,243	4,712
Current portion of long-term debt	1,800	1,200
	11,887	12,192
Long-term debt (Note 5)	14,900	14,500

Shareholders' Equity

	2017	2016
Share capital (Note 6)	78,257	62,965
Retained earnings	2,153	25,210
	80,410	88,175
	$107,197	$114,867

Consolidated Statement of Income and Retained Earnings
Years Ended April 30, 2017 and 2016
(in $000s)

	2017	2016
Revenue		
Sales revenue	$ 89,821	$68,820
Interest and other	1,310	446
	91,131	69,266
Expenses		
Cost of goods sold	52,766	39,455
General and administrative	10,415	10,982
Salaries and wages expense	26,624	24,500
Depreciation and amortization	10,220	11,709
Loss on impairment (goodwill)	12,737	–0–
Interest	1,289	1,521
Loss on sale of capital assets	394	–0–
	114,445	88,167
Loss before equity loss and income tax	(23,314)	(18,901)
Investment income (loss) (Note 1)	(2,518)	100
Loss before income tax	(25,832)	(18,801)
Income tax benefit	2,775	5,161
Net loss	(23,057)	(13,640)
Retained earnings, beginning of year	25,210	38,850
Retained earnings, end of year	$ 2,153	$25,210

Draft Notes to the Financial Statements
For the Year Ended April 30, 2017
Note 1. Investments

The company's investments at April 30 are as follows (in $000s):

	2017	2016
Compuco Ltd. (fair value 2017, $4.3 million)		
Associate's shares, opening balance at equity	$6,962	$5,862
Equity income (loss)	(2,518)	100
Associate's shares, ending balance at equity	4,444	5,962
Other investments, at amortized cost	1,516	1,000
	$5,960	$6,962

Note 2. Property, Plant, and Equipment

Additions to property, plant, and equipment for the current year amounted to $2,290,000. Proceeds from the disposal of property, plant, and equipment amounted to $250,000.

Note 3. Intangible Assets—Franchises

Franchise fees are amortized over the term of 20 years using the straight-line method.

Note 4. Accounts Payable and Accrued Liabilities (in $000s)

	2017	2016
Accounts payable—suppliers	$3,102	$4,562
Salaries and wages payable	141	150
	$3,243	$4,712

Note 5. Long-Term Debt (in $000s)

	2017	2016
Debentures	$12,500	$12,500
Bank term loans, due April 30, 2018, principal repayable at $150,000 a month (2016, at $100,000 a month)	4,200	3,200
	16,700	15,700
Current maturities	(1,800)	(1,200)
	$14,900	$14,500

Debentures bear interest at 9% per annum and are due in 2019. Bank term loans bear interest at 8% and the bank advanced $2.2 million during the year.

Note 6. Share Capital

On September 14, 2016, Jeopardy Inc. issued 3.8 million shares with special warrants. Net proceeds from issuing 3.8 million shares amounted to $14,393,000. Net proceeds from issuing 3.8 million warrants amounted to $899,000.

Instructions

Based on the assumption that Jeopardy Inc. follows IFRS and has adopted the policy of classifying interest paid and dividends received as operating activities, and dividends paid as financing activities:

FINANCE

(a) Prepare a statement of cash flows for the year ended April 30, 2017 on a non-comparative basis from the information provided. The CFO wants to use the direct method to report the company's operating cash flows this year. Include all required disclosures.

(b) Prepare a reconciliation of the 2017 net loss to cash provided from (used in) operations. This reconciliation is to be included in a note to the financial statements.

(c) Write a memo to the president of Jeopardy Inc. that explains why the company is experiencing a cash crunch when its liquidity ratios look acceptable and it has significant non-cash expenses.

P22-2 The following is Mann Corp.'s comparative statement of financial position at December 31, 2017 and 2016, with a column showing the increase (decrease) from 2016 to 2017:

MANN CORP.
Comparative Statement of Financial Position

	2017	2016	Increase (Decrease)
Cash	$ 28,300	$ 44,400	$ (16,100)
Accounts receivable	846,400	766,700	79,700
Inventory	717,600	675,000	42,600
Property, plant, and equipment	3,066,400	2,866,400	200,000
Accumulated depreciation	(1,165,000)	(1,010,000)	155,000
Investment in Bligh Corp., at equity	288,000	266,000	22,000
Loan receivable	251,500	–0–	251,500
Total assets	$4,033,200	$3,608,500	
Bank loan	$ 142,600	$ 72,900	69,700
Accounts payable	753,600	814,600	(61,000)
Income tax payable	37,000	46,000	(9,000)
Dividends payable	65,000	85,000	(20,000)
Obligations under lease	270,000	–0–	270,000
Common shares	900,000	900,000	–0–
Retained earnings	1,865,000	1,690,000	175,000
Total liabilities and shareholders' equity	$4,033,200	$3,608,500	

Additional information:

1. On December 31, 2016, Mann acquired 25% of Bligh Corp.'s common shares for $266,000. On that date, the carrying value of Bligh's assets and liabilities was $1,064,000, which approximated their fair values. Having demonstrated the ability to exercise significant influence over its associate Bligh, Mann accounts for the investment using the equity method. Bligh reported income of $88,000 for the year ended December 31, 2017. No dividend was paid on Bligh's common shares during the year.

2. During 2017, Mann lent $285,000 to TMC Corp., an unrelated company. TMC made the first semi-annual principal repayment of $33,500, plus interest at 10%, on December 31, 2017.

3. On January 2, 2017, Mann sold equipment costing $70,000, with a carrying amount of $44,000, for $42,000 cash.

4. On December 31, 2017, Mann entered into a finance lease for equipment. The present value of the annual lease payments is $270,000, which equals the equipment's fair value. Mann made the first rental payment of $47,000 when due on January 2, 2018.

5. Net earnings for 2017 were $240,000. The amount of income taxes paid was $151,000.

6. The amount of interest paid during the year was $14,900 and the amount of interest earned was $9,400. Mann has adopted the policy of classifying interest received and interest paid as operating cash flows.

7. Mann declared and paid cash dividends for 2017 and 2016 as follows:

	2017	2016
Declared	Dec. 15, 2017	Dec. 15, 2016
Paid	Feb. 28, 2018	Feb. 28, 2017
Amount	$65,000	$85,000

8. The bank loan listed in the comparative statement of financial position represents a line of credit used to finance operating cash demands of the business. The limit set on the operating line by the lender is $600,000. Although the operating line functions similarly to a bank overdraft, at no time during 2017 did the operating line become reduced to nil.

Instructions

(a) Prepare a statement of cash flows for Mann Corp. for the year ended December 31, 2017 using the indirect method, including any necessary additional note disclosures. Mann applies IFRS and has adopted the policy of classifying interest paid as operating activities and dividends paid as financing activities.

FINANCE

(b) Prepare a reconciliation of the change in Property, Plant, and Equipment's carrying amount to the amounts appearing on the statement of cash flows and corresponding notes.

(c) Financial statement preparers often use reconciliations of changes in major categories of statement of financial position accounts to balance the statement of cash flows, as required in part (b) above. What additional insight does this reconciliation reveal to a reader of the statement that is not as evident from the statement of cash flows?

(d) What other choices did Mann Corp. have available for the classification of interest received and paid? Would your opinion of Mann's liquidity position and ability to generate cash change from these alternative classifications?

DIGGING DEEPER

(e) Is Mann Corp. in financial difficulty from a poor liquidity position and extremely small cash reserves? Comment.

(AICPA adapted)

P22-3 Laflamme Inc. follows IFRS and has adopted the policy of classifying interest paid as operating activities and dividends paid as financing activities. Comparative statement of financial position accounts of Laflamme Inc., and its statement of income for the year ending December 31, 2017, follow:

	December 31		
	2017	2016	Change
Cash	$ 46,000	$ 56,000	$ (10,000)
Cash equivalents (Note 1)	36,000	45,000	(9,000)
Accounts receivable	348,000	271,000	77,000
Prepaid insurance	16,000	35,000	(19,000)
Inventory	398,000	350,000	48,000
Supplies	13,000	17,000	(4,000)
Long-term investment, at equity (Note 7)	418,000	400,000	18,000
Land (Note 6)	640,000	500,000	140,000
Buildings (Note 3)	1,310,000	1,280,000	30,000

Accumulated depreciation—buildings	(400,000)	(360,000)	(40,000)
Equipment (Note 4)	632,000	640,000	(8,000)
Accumulated depreciation—equipment	(160,000)	(135,000)	(25,000)
Patent	100,000	100,000	–0–
Accumulated amortization	(40,000)	(35,000)	(5,000)
	$3,357,000	$3,164,000	$193,000
Bank overdrafts (temporary)	$ –0–	$ 93,000	$ (93,000)
Accounts payable	165,000	150,000	15,000
Income tax payable	26,000	35,000	(9,000)
Accrued liabilities	57,000	41,000	16,000
Dividends payable	20,000	50,000	(30,000)
Long-term notes payable	420,000	460,000	(40,000)
Bonds payable	999,000	995,000	4,000
Preferred shares	486,000	380,000	106,000
Common shares	746,000	666,000	80,000
Retained earnings	438,000	294,000	144,000
	$3,357,000	$3,164,000	$193,000

Income Statement

Revenues		
Sales revenue	$ 999,000	
Investment income	90,000	$1,089,000
Expenses and Losses		
Cost of goods sold	314,000	
Sales commission expense	108,000	
Operating expenses (Note 5)	166,000	
Salaries and wages expense	104,000	
Interest expense	95,000	
Loss on sale of equipment (Note 4)	11,000	
Income tax expense	96,000	894,000
Net Income		$195,000

The following is additional information about Laflamme's transactions during the year ended December 31, 2017.

1. The cash equivalents are typically term deposits that are very liquid and mature on average in 60 days. The bank overdrafts are temporary and reverse within a few days. Laflamme has opted to show these as cash and cash equivalents on its statement of cash flows.

2. During the year, preferred shares with a carrying amount of $18,000 were converted to common shares.

3. There were no disposals of buildings during the year 2017.

4. Equipment with an original cost of $46,000 and carrying amount of $14,000 was sold at a loss during the year.

5. All depreciation and amortization expense is included in operating expenses.

6. During the year, Laflamme obtained land with a fair value of $100,000 in exchange for its preferred shares.

7. Investment income includes the equity earnings of $62,000 from a long-term investment accounted for using the equity method and from interest revenue on the short-term investments referred to in item 1 above.

Instructions

(a) Prepare the statement of cash flows for the year ended December 31, 2017 for Laflamme Inc. using the indirect method. Prepare any additional disclosure notes that are required, including a table that shows the details of the cash and cash equivalents accounts at the end of each period.

(b) Prepare the operating activities section of the statement using the direct format.

(c) Does Laflamme Inc. have any options available to it concerning the classification of interest and dividends paid or received?

DIGGING
DEEPER

(d) If Laflamme Inc. chose to not treat the cash equivalents and the temporary bank overdrafts as cash and cash equivalents, how would transactions related to these accounts be reported on the statement of cash flows?

P22-4 Comparative statement of financial position accounts of Jensen Limited, which follows IFRS, appear below:

JENSEN LIMITED
Statement of Financial Position Accounts
December 31, 2017 and 2016

Debit balances	2017	2016
Cash	$ 80,000	$ 51,000
FV-NI investments	59,000	80,000
Accounts receivable	138,500	119,000
Inventory	75,000	61,000
Deferred tax asset	6,500	11,000
Equipment	70,000	48,000
Buildings	145,000	145,000
Land	40,000	25,000
	$614,000	$540,000

Credit balances	2017	2016
Allowance for doubtful accounts	$ 10,000	$ 8,000
Accumulated depreciation—equipment	21,000	14,000
Accumulated depreciation—buildings	37,000	28,000
Accounts payable	72,500	60,000
Income tax payable	12,000	10,000
Long-term notes payable	62,000	70,000
Accrued pension liability	7,500	10,000
Common shares	300,000	250,000
Retained earnings	92,000	90,000
	$614,000	$540,000

Data from Jensen's 2017 income statement follow:

Sales		$960,000
Less: Cost of goods sold		600,000
Gross profit		360,000
Less: Operating expenses (includes		
depreciation and bad debt expense)		250,000
Income from operations		110,000
Other revenues and expenses		
Interest expense	$(10,000)	
Gain on FV-NI investments	24,000	
Loss on sale of equipment	(3,000)	11,000
Income before tax		121,000
Income tax		45,000
Net income		$ 76,000

Additional information:

1. Equipment that cost $10,000 and was 40% depreciated was sold in 2017.

2. Cash dividends were declared and paid during the year.

3. Common shares were issued in exchange for land. No other land was acquired or disposed of during the year. Common shares were also issued for equipment purchases in the amount of $20,000.

4. FV-NI investments that had cost $35,000 and had a fair value of $37,000 at December 31, 2016 were sold during the year for proceeds of $50,000 resulting in a realized gain of $13,000. Jensen also had unrealized gains during the year of $11,000. Additional purchases of FV-NI investments were made during 2017.

5. Cost of goods sold includes $115,000 of direct labour and benefits and $11,700 of pension costs. Operating expenses include $76,000 of salaries and wages and $8,000 of pension expense.

6. Jensen has adopted the policy of classifying interest paid as operating activities and dividends paid as financing activities on the statement of cash flows.

7. No accounts receivable were written off during the year.

Instructions

(a) Prepare a statement of cash flows using the indirect method, including all required disclosures.

FINANCE (b) Prepare the "Cash provided by (or used in) operating activities" section under the direct method.

(c) Does Jensen Limited have any options available for the classification of interest and dividends paid or received?

(d) Comment on the company's cash activities during the year.

(e) Assume that you are a shareholder of Jensen Limited. What do you think of the dividend payout ratio that is highlighted in the statement of cash flows?

P22-5 Ashley Limited, which follows IFRS, chooses to classify interest and dividends received as well as interest paid as operating activities and dividends paid as financing activities. Ashley had the following information available at the end of 2017:

ASHLEY LIMITED
Comparative Statement of Financial Position
December 31, 2017 and 2016

	2017	2016
Cash	$ 25,400	$ –0–
Accounts receivable	13,500	16,950
FV-NI investments	20,000	30,000
Inventory	42,000	35,000
Prepaid rent	7,000	12,000
Prepaid insurance	2,100	900
Office supplies	1,000	750
Land	125,000	175,000
Buildings	350,000	350,000
Accumulated depreciation—buildings	(105,000)	(87,500)
Equipment	525,000	400,000
Accumulated depreciation—equipment	(130,000)	(112,000)
Patents	90,000	90,000
Accumulated amortization—patents	(45,000)	(40,000)
Total assets	$921,000	$ 871,100
Temporary bank overdraft	$ –0–	$ 12,000
Accounts payable	22,000	20,000
Income tax payable	5,000	6,000
Salaries and wages payable	5,000	1,000
Short-term notes payable (trade)	10,000	10,000
Long-term notes payable (non-trade)	60,000	70,000
Deferred tax liability	30,000	25,000
Bonds payable	375,000	375,000
Common shares	260,000	237,500
Retained earnings	154,000	114,600
Total liabilities and shareholders' equity	$921,000	$ 871,100

ASHLEY LIMITED
Income Statement
Year Ended December 31, 2017

Sales revenue		$1,160,000
Cost of goods sold		(748,000)
Gross margin		412,000
Operating expenses		
Selling expenses	$ 39,200	
Administrative expenses	124,700	
Salaries and wages expense	92,000	
Depreciation and amortization expense	40,500	
Total operating expenses		(296,400)
Income from operations		115,600
Other revenues/expenses		
Gain on sale of land	8,000	
Investment income (Note 1)	6,400	
Interest expense	(41,750)	(27,350)
Income before taxes		88,250
Income tax expense		(29,400)
Net income		$ 58,850

Note 1: Investment income generated by (FV-NI) investments includes dividend income of $2,400 and a gain on sale of investments of $4,000.

Instructions

(a) Prepare a statement of cash flows for Ashley Limited using the direct method, accompanied by a schedule that provides cash flow from operations using the indirect approach.

(b) Does Ashley Limited have any options available for the classification of interest and dividends paid or received?

DIGGING DEEPER

(c) Prepare a memo for top management that summarizes and comments on Ashley's cash activities in 2017.

P22-6   Gao Limited, a publicly traded company, uses IFRS and had the following events and transactions occur in its fiscal year ending October 31, 2017. Although no dates are given, the events described are in chronological order.

1. Gao Limited repurchased common shares on the open market to allow stock options for its key employees to be exercised without a dilution effect resulting to the remaining shareholders. The weighted average issue price of the outstanding shares on the date of reacquisition was $34.20, and 5,000 shares were repurchased at a price of $47.40. On the date of declaration, Gao had contributed surplus for preferred share repurchases of $84,600 and contributed surplus for common share repurchases of $22,700.

2. Common shares were issued in partial settlement of a purchase of land. Gao paid $33,000 and 5,000 common shares for the land. On the date of the transaction, the common shares were trading at $48.50 and the appraised value of the land was $240,000.

3. Gao has 8,000 preferred shares outstanding. These shares are limited in number and are not traded on the public stock exchange. Gao declared a property dividend to be paid to the preferred shareholders. Shareholders will receive for each preferred share held one share of Trivex Corp. Gao holds 8,000 shares of Trivex (2% of the outstanding shares), and had purchased them in 2015 for $68,400 (or $8.55 per share). The shares were held as an investment since 2015 and accounted for using the fair value through other comprehensive income (FV-OCI) model with recycling (transference). At the beginning of the fiscal year, the accumulated other comprehensive income had a debit balance in the amount of $2,350 relating only to the Trivex shares. The fair value of Trivex shares was $7.80 per share on the date of declaration of the property dividend. On the date of the dividend distribution, the fair value of the Trivex shares was $7.95. Because there were no longer any investments accounted for at FV-OCI, the reclassification entry needed to be recorded, in accordance with Gao's practice. Ignore income taxes for this transaction.

4. Gao declared a 5% stock dividend to the common shareholders. There were 43,200 common shares outstanding on the date of declaration and the market price of the common shares on that date was $39.70. The stock dividend was later distributed.

5. A shareholder, in an effort to persuade Gao to expand into her city, donated to the company a plot of land with an appraised value of $42,000.

6. Gao sold by subscription to an investment institution 10,000 common shares for $38.50 per share. The terms require 10% of the balance to be paid in cash immediately. The remainder is expected to be paid in fiscal year 2018.

7. Gao has term preferred shares on its statement of financial position. These shares are classified as debt. Gao declared a cash dividend of $3,800 on these shares. The dividend will be paid in the first week of the fiscal year 2018.

Instructions

(a) Prepare the underlying journal entries that were made by Gao Limited during 2017 to record all information related to the changes in each equity account and associated accounts over the year.

(b) Prepare the captions that would appear on Gao's statement of cash flows for the year ended October 31, 2017 using the indirect format, including which section of the statements the items would appear in. Include all necessary additional disclosures required under IFRS. Gao has opted to report the payment of dividends that have been charged to retained earnings as financing activities.

(c) How would your answer to parts (a) and (b) above change if the investments in Trivex were accounted for using the fair value through net income model?

(d) How would your answer to parts (a) and (b) above change if Gao were using ASPE?

P22-7   Comparative statement of financial position accounts of Secada Inc., which follows IFRS, follow:

SECADA INC.
Comparative Statement of Financial Position Accounts
December 31, 2017 and 2016

Debit accounts	2017	2016
Cash	$ 37,000	$ 33,750
Accounts receivable	67,500	60,000
Merchandise inventory	30,000	24,000
Long-term FV-NI investments	23,250	40,500
Machinery	30,000	18,750
Buildings	67,500	56,250
Land	7,500	7,500
	$262,750	$240,750
Credit accounts		
Allowance for doubtful accounts	$ 2,250	$ 1,500
Accumulated depreciation—machinery	5,625	2,250
Accumulated depreciation—buildings	13,500	9,000
Accounts payable	30,000	24,750
Accrued liabilities	2,375	1,125
Income taxes payable	1,000	1,500
Long-term note payable—non-trade	26,000	31,000
Common shares	150,000	125,000
Retained earnings	32,000	44,625
	$262,750	$240,750

Additional information:

Secada Inc. has adopted the policy of classifying interest paid as operating activities and dividends paid as financing activities.

1. Cash dividends declared during the year were $25,375.

2. A 20% stock dividend was declared during the year and $25,000 of retained earnings was capitalized.

3. FV-NI investments that cost $20,000 and had a fair value at December 31, 2016 of $24,750 were sold during the year for $23,750.

4. Machinery that cost $3,750 and had $750 of depreciation accumulated was sold for $2,200.

Secada's 2017 statement of income is as follows:

FINANCE

Sales revenue		$640,000
Less cost of goods sold		380,000
Gross margin		260,000
Less: Operating expenses (includes $8,625		
depreciation and $5,400 bad debts)		180,450
Income from operations		79,550
Loss on sale of FV-NI investments	$(1,000)	
Interest expense	(3,000)	
Loss on sale of machinery	(800)	(4,800)
Income before tax		74,750
Income tax expense		37,000
Net income		$ 37,750

Instructions

DIGGING DEEPER

(a) Calculate net cash flow from operating activities using the direct method.

(b) Prepare a statement of cash flows using the indirect method.

(c) Assume that your investment club is considering investing in Secada Inc. Write a memo to the other members of the club about the company's cash activities during 2017.

P22-8 Neilson Corp. reported $245,000 of net income for 2017. In preparing the statement of cash flows, the accountant noted several items that might affect cash flows from operating activities.

1. During 2017, Neilson reported a sale of equipment for $7,000. The equipment had a carrying amount of $23,500.

2. During 2017, Neilson sold 100 Lontel Corporation common shares at $200 per share. The acquisition cost (and fair value of these shares on December 31, 2016) was $145 per share. This investment was shown on Neilson's December 31, 2016 statement of financial position as an investment at fair value with gains and losses in net income (FV-NI).

3. During 2017, Neilson corrected an error in ending inventory of December 31, 2016. The debit to opening retained earnings was $14,600. The cost of goods sold in the current income statement was adjusted accordingly.

4. During 2017, Neilson revised its estimate for bad debts. Before 2017, Neilson's bad debt expense was 1% of its net sales. In 2017, this percentage was increased to 2%. Net sales for 2017 were $500,000, and net accounts receivable decreased by $5,000 during 2017.

5. During 2017, Neilson issued 500 common shares in exchange for a patent. The shares' market value on the transaction date was $23 per share.

6. Depreciation expense for 2017 was $48,000.

7. Neilson Corp. holds 30% of Nirbana Corporation's common shares as a long-term investment and exercises significant influence. Nirbana reported $27,000 of net income for 2017.

8. Nirbana Corporation paid a total of $2,800 of cash dividends to all shareholders in 2017.

9. During 2017, Neilson declared a 10% stock dividend, distributing 1,000 common shares. The market price at the date of issuance was $20 per share.

10. Neilson Corp. paid $10,000 in dividends: $2,500 of this amount was paid on term preferred shares classified as a long-term liability.

Instructions

(a) Prepare a schedule that shows the net cash flow from operating activities using the indirect method. Assume that no items other than the ones listed affected the calculation of 2017 cash flow from operating activities. Also assume that Neilson Corp. follows ASPE. Discuss how items not included in the operating activities would be treated.

(b) Assume now that Neilson Corp. follows IFRS. What alternatives would it have regarding interest and dividend amounts to be reported?

P22-9 MFI Holdings Inc. follows IFRS and applies the FV-OCI model with recycling and has adopted the option to show dividends received as operating activities. MFI's statement of financial position contained the following comparative data at December 31:

Statement of financial position accounts:

	2017	2016
FV-OCI investments	$24,000	$37,900
Accumulated other comprehensive income (loss)	400	(2,400)

Partial statement of income and comprehensive income, 2017:

Dividend revenue	$ 200
Loss on sale of FV-OCI investments	300
Net income	XXX
Other comprehensive income	
Unrealized gains—OCI	2,500
Comprehensive income	$ XXX

At December 31, 2017, the following information is available:

1. MFI Holdings had a single investment in shares at December 31, 2016. The investment cost $40,300 and was sold during 2017 for $40,000.

2. During 2017, dividends of $200 were received on shares classified as investments at fair value with gains and losses in OCI.

3. Another investment, with the same classification, was purchased at a cost of $23,600. The fair value of this new investment at December 31, 2017 was $24,000.

4. MFI Holdings classifies dividends received as operating cash flows.

Instructions

(a) Prepare the 2017 journal entries to record the sale of the investment including the recycling entry. Ignore any income tax effects.

(b) Calculate and reconcile the transactions that were recorded to the accounts Fair Value through Other Comprehensive Income Investments and Accumulated Other Comprehensive Income.

(c) Using the direct and indirect methods, prepare a table that contrasts the presentation of all transactions related to the above financial statements and related investment transactions on MFI's statement of cash flows. Be specific about the classification within the statement for each item that is reported.

(d) How would your answer to parts (a) and (b) above change if the investments were accounted for using the fair value through net income model?

(e) Under what circumstances would MFI not be allowed to use the fair value through other comprehensive income model?

P22-10 The following accounts appear in the ledger of Samson Inc. Samson's shares trade on the Toronto and New York stock exchanges and so the company uses IFRS. Samson has chosen to account for shares held in Anderson Corp. as FV-OCI and to reclassify out of OCI and directly to retained earnings any investment holding gains that are realized. The investment in Anderson Corp. is not strategic and is classified as a long-term investment. It is the only FV-OCI investment held by Samson. Samson chooses to classify dividends received as operating cash flows.

	FV-OCI Investments	Dr.	Cr.	Bal.
Dec. 1, 2016	Purchase of 40,000 shares	$893,500		$893,500
Dec. 31, 2016	Fair value adjustment of 40,000 shares		$10,100	883,400
Aug. 15, 2017	Fair value adjustment of 3,000 shares	4,350		887,750
Aug. 15, 2017	Sale of 3,000 shares		70,605	817,145
Nov. 3, 2017	Purchase of 2,000 shares	35,480		852,625
Dec. 31, 2017	Fair value adjustment of 39,000 shares	19,620		872,245

	Accumulated Other Comprehensive Income	Dr.	Cr.	Bal.
Dec. 31, 2016	Closing entry	$ 10,100		$ 10,100
Dec. 31, 2017	Closing entry		20,378	(10,278)

	Dividend Revenue	Dr.	Cr.	Bal.
June 30, 2017	Dividends from Anderson Corp.		$35,700	$(35,700)

	Retained Earnings	Dr.	Cr.	Bal.
Aug. 15, 2017	Reclassification adjustment—3,000 shares		$ 3,592	$ (3,592)

	Unrealized Gain or Loss—OCI	Dr.	Cr.	Bal.
Dec. 31, 2016	Fair value adjustment of 40,000 shares	$ 10,100		$ 10,100
Dec. 31, 2016	Closing entry		$10,100	–0–
Aug. 15, 2017	Fair value adjustment of 3,000 shares		4,350	(4,350)
Aug. 15, 2017	Reclassification adjustment—3,000 shares	3,592		(758)
Dec. 31, 2017	Fair value adjustment of 39,000 shares		19,620	(20,378)
Dec. 31, 2017	Closing entry	20,378		–0–

Instructions

(a) Prepare a partial comparative statement of financial position for Samson Inc. at the fiscal year end of December 31, 2017.

(b) Prepare an income statement, a statement of comprehensive income, and a statement of changes in accumulated other comprehensive income for the year ended December 31, 2017. Ignore any income tax effects.

(c) Prepare the journal entries dated June 30, August 15, and November 3, 2017. Provide explanations of the entries.

(d) Using the direct and indirect methods, prepare a table that contrasts the presentation of all transactions recorded in the ledger accounts provided on Samson's statement of cash flows. Be specific about the classification within the statement for each item that is reported. What other choices could Samson have used in the classification of cash flows?

(e) How would your answer to parts (b) and (d) above change if the investments were accounted for using the fair value through net income model?

(f) Under what circumstances would Samson not be allowed to use the fair value through other comprehensive income model?

P22-11   Davis Inc. is a privately held company that uses ASPE. Davis had the following information available at March 31, 2017:

DAVIS INC.
Income Statement
For the Year Ended March 31, 2017

Sales revenue		$450,000
Cost of goods sold		260,000
Gross profit		190,000
Operating expenses		
Salaries and wages expense	$64,500	
Depreciation expense	7,500	
Rent expense	18,000	
Administrative expenses	21,000	
Amortization expense for patents	1,500	112,500
Operating income		77,500
Other revenues and expenses		
Bond interest expense	(6,750)	
Unrealized gains on FV-NI investments	3,000	
Investment income	12,500	
Gain on retirement of bonds	16,600	25,350
		102,850
Income tax expense—current	19,900	
Income tax expense—future	10,300	30,200
Net income		$ 72,650

Davis Inc.'s partial list of comparative account balances as at March 31, 2017 and 2016 is as follows:

	March 31		
	2017	2016	Change
Cash	$ 5,200	$ 4,400	$ 800
Investment in 30-day term deposits	20,000	6,200	13,800
Accounts receivable	46,400	43,600	2,800
Inventory	35,800	29,600	6,200
Prepaid expenses	2,650	2,800	(150)
FV-NI investments	5,230	2,230	3,000
Prepaid rent—long-term	4,000	-0-	4,000
Accounts payable	22,800	24,200	(1,400)
Salaries and wages payable	500	1,300	(800)
Income tax payable	13,000	29,500	(16,500)
Interest payable	3,000	1,500	1,500
Accrued pension liability	8,500	6,900	1,600
Future tax liability	12,900	2,600	10,300

Additional information:

1. Bond interest expense includes $750 of bond discount amortized.

2. The investment income represents Davis Inc.'s reported income in its 40%-owned, significantly influenced investment in Jessa Ltd. Davis received a $2,000 dividend from Jessa on February 15, 2017.

3. During the year, the company retired $500,000 of its outstanding bonds payable, paying out $16,600 less than the price at which the bonds were carried on the books.

4. In early January 2017, Davis renewed and signed a four-year office rental lease, agreeing to pay $4,000 each month in rent. The lessor required the payment of the rent for the first and last months of the lease at that time.

5. The change in the FV-NI investments is from the change in the market value of the securities for the fiscal year 2017. There were no purchases or sales of these securities during the 2017 fiscal year.

Note: There is insufficient information to allow you to prepare a complete statement of cash flows.

Instructions

(a) What is the amount of Davis Inc.'s change in cash to be explained on the statement of cash flows for the year ended March 31, 2017?

(b) Prepare the "Cash provided by (used in) operations" section of the statement of cash flows, assuming that the indirect method is used and all necessary information has been provided.

(c) Identify the amounts that would be reported within this section if the direct method were used for the following items:

  1. Cash paid to and on behalf of employees
  2. Cash paid for other operating expenses
  3. Cash received from customers
  4. Income taxes paid
  5. Cash paid to suppliers for goods
  6. Interest paid

(d) Calculate the sum of the cash flows in part (c). Should the sum of the cash flows in the direct format equal the amount arrived at in part (a) for "Cash provided by (used in) operations"? If not, why not? If it should, do the amounts equal each other? Why or why not?

DIGGING DEEPER

(e) How would your answer to parts (b) and (c) above change if Davis were using IFRS?

P22-12   The unclassified statement of financial position accounts for Sorkin Corporation, which is a public company using IFRS, for the year ended December 31, 2016 and its statement of comprehensive income and statement of cash flows for the year ended December 31, 2017 are as follows:

SORKIN CORPORATION
Statement of Financial Position Accounts
December 31, 2016
($ in millions)

Cash	$ 21
Accounts receivable	194
Inventory	200
Prepaid expenses	12
Investment in associate, Stoker Inc.	125
Land	150
Buildings and equipment	400
Accumulated depreciation—buildings and equipment	(120)
Patents	60
Accumulated amortization—patents	(28)
Goodwill	60
Total assets	$1,074
Accounts payable	$ 65
Salaries and wages payable	11
Bond interest payable	4
Income tax payable	14
Deferred tax liability	8
Bonds payable	250
Common shares	495
Retained earnings	227
Total liabilities and shareholders' equity	$1,074

SORKIN CORPORATION
Statement of Income
Year Ended December 31, 2017
($ in millions)

Revenues:		
Sales revenue	$410	
Unrealized gain on (FV-NI) investments	5	
Investment income from associate	11	$426
Expenses and losses:		
Cost of goods sold	158	
Administrative expenses	22	
Salaries and wages expense	65	
Depreciation and amortization expense	21	
Bond interest expense	28	
Loss on damaged equipment	18	
Loss on impairment of goodwill	20	332
Income before income tax		94
Income tax		27
Net income		$ 67

SORKIN CORPORATION
Statement of Cash Flows (Indirect Method)
For the Year Ended December 31, 2017
($ in millions)

Cash flows from operating activities		
Net earnings		$67
Add back (deduct) non-cash revenues and expenses:		
Investment income from associate Stoker Inc.	(11)	
Dividends received from associate Stoker Inc.	6	
Loss on damaged equipment	18	
Depreciation expense	19	
Unrealized gain on FV-NI investments	(5)	
Amortization of patent	2	
Amortization of bond discount	3	
Loss on impairment of goodwill	20	52
Add (deduct) changes in non-cash working capital:		
Decrease in accounts receivable	4	
Increase in inventories	(5)	
Decrease in prepaid expenses	2	
Decrease in accounts payable	(15)	
Decrease in salaries and wages payable	(5)	
Increase in deferred tax liability	3	
Increase in bond interest payable	4	
Decrease in income taxes payable	(2)	(14)
Net cash provided by operating activities		105
Cash flows from investing activities:		
Proceeds from disposal of damaged equipment	10	
Purchase of land (Note 1)	(23)	
Purchase of FV-NI investments	(25)	
Net cash used by investing activities		(38)
Cash flows from financing activities:		
Dividends paid	(7)	
Redemption of serial bonds	(60)	
Issuance of preferred shares	75	
Repurchase of common shares	(9)	
Net cash used by financing activities		(1)
Net increase in cash		66
Cash, January 1, 2017		21
Cash, December 31, 2017		$87

Note 1. Non-cash investing and financing activities
(a) During the year, land was acquired for $46 million in exchange for cash of $23 million and a $23-million, four-year, 10% note payable to the seller.
(b) Equipment was acquired through a finance lease that was capitalized initially at $82 million.

Additional information:

1. The investment income represents Sorkin's reported income from its 35%-owned associate Stoker Inc. Sorkin received a dividend from Stoker during the year.

2. Early in 2017, Sorkin purchased shares for $25 million as an FV-NI investment. There were no purchases or sales of these shares during 2017, nor were there any dividends received from this investment.

3. Equipment that originally cost $70 million became unusable due to a flood. Most major components of the equipment were unharmed and were sold together for $10 million. Sorkin had no insurance coverage for the loss because its insurance policy did not cover floods.

4. Reversing differences in the year between pre-tax accounting income and taxable income resulted in an increase in future taxable amounts, causing the deferred tax liability to increase by $3 million.

5. On December 30, 2017, land costing $46 million was acquired by paying $23 million cash and issuing a $23-million, four-year, 10% note payable to the seller. No repayments of principal were made on the note during 2017.

6. Equipment was acquired through a 15-year financing lease. The present value of minimum lease payments was $82 million when signing the lease on December 31, 2017. Sorkin made the initial lease payment of $2 million on January 1, 2018.

7. Serial bonds with a face value of $60 million were retired at maturity on June 20, 2017. In order to finance this redemption and have additional cash available for operations, Sorkin issued preferred shares for $75 million cash.

8. In February, Sorkin issued a 4% stock dividend (4 million shares). The market price of the common shares was $7.50 per share at the date of the declaration of the dividend.

9. In April 2017, 1 million common shares were repurchased for $9 million. The weighted average original issue price of the repurchased shares was $12 million.

Instructions

(a) Prepare the unclassified statement of financial position accounts for Sorkin Corporation for the year ended December 31, 2017 as a check on the statement of cash flows. Add whichever accounts you consider necessary.

(b) Prepare the operating activities section of the statement of cash flows for Sorkin Corporation using the direct method.

DIGGING DEEPER

(c) How would the statement of cash flows differ if the terms on the purchase of land had been essentially the same except that the financing for the note payable had been negotiated with a mortgage company instead of the seller of the land?

P22-13   Seneca Corporation, which uses IFRS, has contracted with you to prepare a statement of cash flows. The controller has provided the following information:

	December 31	
	2017	2016
Cash	$ 38,700	$13,000
Accounts receivable	11,600	9,750
Inventory	10,600	9,100
FV-NI investments	–0–	2,500
Land	5,000	5,000
Buildings	–0–	27,700
Equipment	35,500	13,500
Patents	14,000	14,000
	$115,400	$94,550
Allowance for doubtful accounts	$ 1,400	$ 1,500
Accumulated depreciation—equipment	2,000	3,300
Accumulated depreciation—buildings	–0–	5,700
Accumulated amortization—patents	9,000	7,750
Accounts payable	4,400	3,300
Dividends payable	–0–	6,000
Notes payable, short-term (non-trade)	3,400	4,000
Long-term notes payable	30,500	25,000
Share capital	43,000	33,000
Retained earnings	21,700	5,000
	$115,400	$94,550

Additional information related to 2017 is as follows:

1. Equipment that cost $10,500 and was 50% depreciated at the time of disposal was sold for $2,600.

2. Common shares were issued to pay $10,000 of the long-term note payable.

3. Cash dividends paid were $6,000. Seneca has adopted the policy of classifying dividends paid as operating activities.

4. On January 1, 2017, a flood destroyed the building. Insurance proceeds on the building were $23,000.

5. FV-NI investments in shares were sold at $3,300 above their cost. The fair value of these investments at December 31, 2016 equalled their original cost.

6. Cash of $17,000 was paid to acquire equipment.

7. A long-term note for $15,500 was issued in exchange for equipment.

8. Interest of $2,200 and income tax of $5,600 were paid in cash. Seneca has adopted the policy of classifying interest paid as financing activities.

Instructions

(a) Use the indirect method to analyze the above information and prepare a statement of cash flows for Seneca.

(b) Prepare a reconciliation of the change in the property, plant, and equipment's carrying amount to the amounts appearing on the statement of cash flows and corresponding notes.

(c) Financial statement preparers often use reconciliations of changes in major categories of statement of financial position accounts to balance the statement of cash flows, as required in part (b) above. What additional insight does this reconciliation reveal to a reader of the statement that is not as evident from the statement of cash flows?

(d) Prepare a short analysis of Seneca's cash flow activity for 2017. The analysis is to be given to the controller.

(e) What choices, if any, are available for classifications for interest and dividends paid or received by Seneca?

(f) What kind of company would you expect to be revealed by the operating, investing, and financing sections of Seneca's statement of cash flows: a company that is severely troubled financially or a recently formed company that is experiencing rapid growth?

DIGGING
DEEPER

(g) Compare Seneca's net cash flow provided by operating activities with profit. Comment on the relationship between these two amounts from the perspective of an investor.

Case

ENABLING
COMPETENCIES

Refer to the Case Primer on the Student Website and in *WileyPLUS* to help you answer this case.

CA22-1 Papadopoulos Limited (PL) sells retail merchandise in Canada. The company was incorporated last year and is now in its second year of operations. PL is owned and operated by the Papadopoulos family, and Iris Papadopoulos, the company president, has decided to expand into the American marketplace. In order to do this, bank financing will be necessary.

The books have been kept by Iris's daughter Tonya, who is studying accounting in university. Financial statements had only been prepared for tax purposes in the past. For the year ended December 31, 2017, Tonya prepared the following statement showing cash inflows and cash outflows:

Sources of cash:	
From shareholder loan	$150,000
From sales of merchandise	350,000
From truck financing	50,000
From term deposit cashed in	100,000
From interest income	10,000
Total sources of cash	660,000
Uses of cash:	
For fixed asset purchases	100,000
For inventory purchases	250,000
Operating expenses, including depreciation of $70,000	160,000
For purchase of investment	55,000
For purchase of truck	50,000
For interest on debt	30,000
Total uses of cash	645,000
Net increase in cash	$ 15,000

Tonya showed the statement to her mother, noting that the bank was sure to give them a loan, especially since they were profitable in their second year and since cash had increased over the year, which shows that it had been a good year. Iris was not convinced, however, and decided to have the statement looked at by a "real" accountant.

Instructions

Adopt the role of the accountant and, if necessary, redraft the statement for the bank with proper classifications. Discuss the company's financial position and conclude with the likely response from the bank. Consider ASPE to be a constraint.

Integrated Case

ENABLING
COMPETENCIES

IC22-1 Earthcom Inc. is in the telecommunications industry. The company builds and maintains telecommunication lines that are buried in the ground. The company is a public company and has been having some bad luck. One of its main underground telecommunications lines was cut by accident and the company cannot determine the exact location of the problem. As a result, many of the company's customers have lost service. Because

Earthcom did not have a backup plan, it is uncertain about how long it will take to restore service. The affected customers are not happy and are threatening to sue. In order to try to calm them down, Earthcom has managed to purchase some capacity from a competitor. Unfortunately, the cost of the service is much higher than the revenues from Earthcom's customers. Earthcom is also currently spending quite a bit on consulting fees (on lawyers and damage control consultants).

In addition, Earthcom is spending a significant amount of money trying to track down the problem with its line, and although it has had no luck so far, the company recently announced that it was confident that services would be restored imminently. As a result of the work being done, Earthcom feels that it will be in a better position to restore service if this ever happens again.

The company has been upgrading many of its very old telecommunications lines that were beginning to degrade due to age. It has capitalized these amounts and they are therefore showing up as investing activities on the statement of cash flows. The company's auditors have questioned this because they feel that the amounts should be expensed.

As a result of all this, Earthcom's share price has plummeted, making its stock options worthless. Management has historically been remunerated solely based on these stock options, however. The company's CFO meanwhile has just announced that he is leaving and is demanding severance pay for what he is calling constructive dismissal. He feels that because the stock options are worthless, he is working for free—which he cannot afford to do—and that the company has effectively fired him.

Instructions

Adopt the role of the company controller and discuss the financial reporting issues.

RESEARCH AND ANALYSIS

RA22-1   Brookfield Asset Management Inc.

REAL WORLD EMPHASIS

Brookfield Asset Management Inc.'s 2014 financial statements can be found at the end of this volume or on the company website. Brookfield owns and operates assets with a focus on property, renewable energy, infrastructure, and private equity.

Instructions

Review the financial statements and notes of Brookfield Asset Management Inc. and answer the following questions.

(a) Prepare a summary analysis of Brookfield's sources and uses of cash at the level of operating, investing, and financing subtotals only, for 2014 and 2013. Based on this analysis, comment on the similarities and differences in the company's needs for cash and how they were met over the past two years.

(b) Why is Brookfield's balance sheet not classified? How does an unclassified balance sheet affect its usefulness to an external user of the financial statements?

(c) What method of reporting operating cash flows does Brookfield use in the statement of cash flows? Do you think this approach provides useful information to a potential investor?

(d) Under IFRS, Brookfield has a choice in classifying interest and finance costs. What choice did Brookfield make in this respect? Were some borrowing costs capitalized?

FINANCE

(e) Calculate the amount of debt for 2014 and 2013 and the debt to total assets ratio for each year. Comment on any trend that you detect and the company's overall solvency. Compare your analysis with the amount of the cash balance at the end of each year.

RA22-2   Bombardier Inc.

REAL WORLD EMPHASIS

Access the financial statements of **Bombardier Inc.** for the years ended December 31, 2015 and December 31, 2014 from the company's website or SEDAR (www.sedar.com).

Instructions

Changes in non-cash working capital items can have a significant impact on operating cash flows. Using the financial statements, answer the following questions.

(a) What does Bombardier do? When are revenue and related costs recognized? Comment on the timing of revenue and expenses, and cash receipts and payments related to operating activities.

(b) What was Bombardier's net income (loss) for 2013, 2014, and 2015? What were the operating cash flow amounts for the same periods? Calculate the difference between net income and operating cash flows for each year. In which years was the operating cash flow higher or lower than net earnings? Calculate the year-over-year percentage changes in net income (loss). Calculate the year-over-year percentage changes in operating cash flows.

(c) Because impairment charges do not represent cash outflows from operating activities, repeat the analysis performed in part (b) excluding impairment charges from the losses of 2014 and 2015. What were the main sources of impairment recorded in 2014 and 2015? Comment on these differences in dollar amounts and year-over-year percentage changes.

(d) Besides the impairment losses, what is causing these differences in net income (loss) and operating cash flows to occur? Highlight significant differences and explain why these arise.

(e) Comment on the ability to predict cash flows for this company. Which approach in preparing operating cash flows (direct or indirect) would be most useful to potential investors?

(f) Note 40, "Events after the Reporting Date," of the 2015 financial statements discusses three major subsequent events. Do you believe the effect of these subsequent events will solve Bombardier's cash flow and profitability issues?

RA22-3 AltaGas Ltd.

AltaGas Ltd. capitalizes on the supply and demand dynamic for natural gas and power by owning and operating assets in gas, power, and utilities in places that provide a strategic competitive advantage.

REAL WORLD EMPHASIS

Instructions

Access the financial statements for AltaGas for the year ended December 31, 2014 from the company's website or from SEDAR (www.sedar.com) and answer the following questions.

FINANCE

(a) Review the statement of cash flows for the two years 2014 and 2013. What are the total cash flows from (or used by) operations, investing activities, and financing activities? What amount of cash was paid for dividends each year and what amount of cash was obtained from the issuance of preferred and common shares? What does the amount of the payment

of dividends represent as a percentage of the amount obtained from the issuance of shares? What sources of cash are available to fund the dividends and capital investments? Calculate the payout ratio. Do you think that the dividends are sustainable?

(b) Using the net book value of property, plant, and equipment (PPE) at December 31, 2013 as the opening balance and items from the statement of cash flows, statement of earnings, and related note disclosures, try to reconcile the opening and closing balance for PPE for 2014.

RA22-4 Corby Spirit and Wine Limited

REAL WORLD EMPHASIS

Corby Spirit and Wine Limited is a leading Canadian marketer and distributor of premium spirits and wine brands. Obtain a copy of the company's comparative financial statements for the year ended June 30, 2015 from the company's website (www.corby.ca).

Instructions

(a) Prepare a summary report of Corby's cash activities during its years ended June 30, 2015 and 2014 at the subtotal level of operating, investing, and financing activities, and a comparative report for the preceding fiscal year. Do you notice a major difference in Corby's statement of cash flows from other statements you have read or have prepared in the past? Discuss the source of this major difference.

FINANCE

(b) Is Corby a capital-intensive business that requires high levels of investments of cash? Does Corby have a high level of debt on its consolidated balance sheet? What are the main sources of financing activities?

(c) How did Corby choose to classify interest paid, interest received, and dividends paid on the statement of cash flows? What were the amounts for these items for fiscal year 2015?

(d) Obtain the amount of cash dividends paid in 2015 and 2014. Calculate the amount of the dividends as a percentage of the cash derived from operating activities. Calculate the payout ratio. Comment on the reasonableness of the amounts paid out as dividends.

ENDNOTES

[1] TD Canada Trust, https://webinar.tdcanadatrust.com/7-tips-to-improve-your-business-cash-flow/?referral=0018

[2] *CPA Canada Handbook–Accounting*, Part II, Section 1540.06(a) and (b), and IAS 7.6. Copyright © International Financial Reporting Standards Foundation. All rights reserved. Reproduced by John Wiley & Sons Canada, Ltd with the permission of the International Financial Reporting Standards Foundation®.

Reproduction and use rights are strictly limited. No permission granted to third parties to reproduce or distribute.

[3] Dividend payments that are recognized in the income statement relate to equity securities that are determined to be liabilities in substance. Interest payments that are charged to retained earnings relate to debt securities that are judged to be equity instruments in substance. The statement of cash flows, therefore, treats

returns to in-substance equity holders as financing outflows and to those designated as creditors as operating outflows.

[4] IAS 7 *Statement of Cash Flows*, para .20, indicates that the undistributed income of an associate is an adjustment in determining cash from operations under the indirect method. Copyright © International Financial Reporting Standards Foundation. All rights reserved. Reproduced by John Wiley & Sons Canada, Ltd with the permission of the International Financial Reporting Standards Foundation®. Reproduction and use rights are strictly limited. No permission granted to third parties to reproduce or distribute.

[5] Note that an asset that is acquired and financed through a third party when the lender pays the seller directly is considered a cash inflow (financing) followed by a cash outflow (investing). If an existing mortgage is assumed when an asset is acquired, however, this does not result in a cash flow.

[6] Netting is permitted in limited and specific circumstances. See *CPA Canada Handbook–Accounting*, Part II, Section 1540.25–.26 and IAS 7.22–.24.

[7] Unfortunately, use of the direct method is the exception. Companies suggest that it is costly for them to generate the information required by the direct method. However, the unpopularity of the direct method may also be due in part to the fact that accounting instructors tend to focus on the indirect method because that is what is used, and the indirect method is used because that is what accountants have been taught!

[8] *CPA Canada Handbook–Accounting*, Part II, Section 1540 also provides and explains, in an appendix, a simplified work sheet approach for companies to use in developing the information needed to present operating cash flows under the direct method.

[9] Prior to the current standard on cash flows, significant non-cash transactions **were included** in the statement because of their effect on the entity's asset and capital structure. This difference shows the change in focus from a statement of changes in financial position (old terminology) to a statement of cash flows (new terminology), where only cash effects are reported.

[10] Income statement information is used rather than information from the statement of comprehensive income because other comprehensive income amounts are non-cash and non-operating in nature.

[11] On occasion, even experienced accountants get to this step and find that the statement does not balance! Don't despair. Determine the amount of your error and review your analysis until you find it.

[12] If the mortgage payable had been directly assumed from the vendor of the land and building, the mortgage would have been considered a non-cash transaction with the vendor. (See *CPA Canada Handbook–Accounting*, Part II, Sections 1540.42 and IAS 7.44.) The purchase of land and building and mortgage payable on the statement of cash flows would both have been reduced by $155,000 (that is, the non-cash transaction would not have appeared on the statement of cash flows).

[13] For all current asset and current liability account changes that adjust accrual basis net income to cash flows from operations, a simple check can be made. The adjustment for all increases in current asset accounts should have a corresponding effect within the operating activities section of the statement of cash flows. (For example, an increase in inventory implies more cash "tied up" in inventory and a decrease in cash flow.) All decreases in current asset accounts should represent increases in cash flows from operations. (For example, a decrease in accounts receivable suggests more cash collected from customers or an increase in cash flow.) All increases and decreases in current liability accounts should have the opposite effect of changes in current asset accounts. This is a useful mechanical procedure to double-check your adjustments.

[14] For Yoshi Corporation, net receivables increased $53,000, from $51,000 ($52,700 – $1,700) at the beginning of the year to $104,000 ($106,500 – $2,500) at year end. The increase means that $53,000 of income was recognized that did not result in a corresponding cash flow. On the statement of cash flows under the indirect method, one adjustment to reduce net income by $53,000 is all that is needed.

[15] *CPA Canada Handbook–Accounting*, Part II, Sections 1540.32 and .33 explain how the amortization of a financial asset or financial liability acquired or issued at a premium or discount is reflected on the statement of cash flows. In general, any discount amortization is not a cash flow, while the amount received or paid in the case of a premium is split between interest (an operating flow) and repayment of principal (an investing or financing flow, as appropriate). IAS 7 *Statement of Cash Flows* does not make specific reference to this matter.

[16] Another presentation alternative identified in IAS 7.20, although not widely used, is a variation of the indirect method: revenues and expenses are presented along with the changes in inventories, operating receivables, and payables in the period. Copyright © International Financial Reporting Standards Foundation. All rights reserved. Reproduced by John Wiley & Sons Canada, Ltd with the permission of the International Financial Reporting Standards Foundation®. Reproduction and use rights are strictly limited. No permission granted to third parties to reproduce or distribute.

[17] Another good example of this type of adjustment is the adjustment for unfunded pension and other post-employment benefits expense that many companies report. The current year adjustment has a positive effect—it increases operating cash flows above net income reported because no cash was paid out. However, very large amounts of operating cash outflows will be required in the future when these claims are eventually paid.

[18] Phase A dealt with the question of what makes up a complete set of financial statements and is now complete and embedded in IAS 1. Phase B looks at how information is presented on the face of the financial statements, and is now paused.

[19] This is consistent with the analysis earlier in the chapter. If $8,000 of cost of goods sold came from a reduction in inventory levels, purchases for the year must have been $8,000 less than cost of goods sold. Therefore both analyses equally well convert the cost of goods sold to the level of purchases in the year.

OTHER MEASUREMENT AND DISCLOSURE ISSUES

REFERENCE TO THE CPA COMPETENCY MAP

LEARNING OBJECTIVES

After studying this chapter, you should be able to:

1.1.1, 1.1.2, 1.4.2, 1.4.3, 5.1.1	**1.** Understand the importance of disclosure from a business perspective.
1.1.1, 1.1.2, 1.1.4, 1.2.1, 1.4.2	**2.** Review the full disclosure principle and describe problems of implementation.
1.1.2, 1.2.1, 1.3.2, 1.4.2, 5.1.1	**3.** Explain the use of accounting policy notes in financial statement preparation.
1.2.1, 1.3.2, 1.4.1	**4.** Describe the disclosure requirements for major segments of a business.
1.1.3, 1.2.1, 1.2.2, 1.3.1, 1.3.2, 4.3.3, 5.1.1	**5.** Describe the accounting problems associated with interim reporting.
1.2.1, 1.2.2, 1.2.3, 1.3.2, 1.4.5	**6.** Discuss the accounting issues for related-party transactions.
1.1.2, 1.2.1, 1.2.2, 4.3.5	**7.** Identify the differences between the two types of subsequent events.
1.2.1, 1.4.2, 4.3.5, 5.2.4, 5.2.5	**8.** Identify the major considerations relating to bankruptcy and receivership.
4.3.3, 4.3.10, 4.3.11	**9.** Identify the major disclosures found in the auditor's report.
1.1.1, 1.4.4, 1.4.5, 5.1.1	**10.** Describe methods used for basic financial statement analysis and summarize the limitations of ratio analysis.
1.1.4	**11.** Identify the major differences in accounting between IFRS and ASPE, and what changes are expected in the near future.

COMMUNICATING BUSINESS INFORMATION

IF YOU WANTED TO invest in a television station, magazine, baseball team, sports stadium, and cell phone provider, you would only have to buy one share: in Rogers Communications Inc.

Toronto-based Rogers, which dates back to the founding of the city's CFRB radio station in 1927 by Edward S. Rogers Sr., had revenues of more than $12.9 billion in 2014. It operates in telecommunications and media, and owns 100% of the Toronto Blue Jays Baseball Club and the Rogers Centre sports and entertainment stadium in downtown Toronto. With so many diverse businesses, how can a reader of Rogers' financial statements—such as a potential investor or analyst—know how each one is doing?

That's where segmented reporting comes in. IFRS requires companies such as Rogers, which became public in 1979, to report results in their financial statements according to reportable segments. IFRS sets out several criteria that

Darren Calabrese/CP Images

a business unit must meet to be considered a reportable segment, including any segment whose revenues account for 10% or more of the company's total revenues.

In the case of Rogers, it reports results for each of four operating segments: Wireless, Cable, Business Solutions, and Media. Wireless is the company's voice and data wireless communications operations. Cable is its cable television, telephone, and Internet operations. The business solutions segment offers telecommunications services to businesses. Media includes conventional and specialty television channels, radio stations, magazine and trade publications, the Toronto Blue Jays Baseball Club, and the Rogers Centre.

Rogers provides further breakdowns of some financial information for parts of its operating segments. For example, sports entertainment accounted for 13% of the Media segment's $1.8 billion in revenue in 2014. The Media segment's costs included the Blue Jays' player payroll, which also increased by an unspecified amount that year. However, users can often piece together other details of segment operations.

For example, Blue Jays 2015 salaries were estimated to be U.S. $115.9 million by espn.go.com as of December 2014.

Rogers also has investments in other companies, including some involved in television production and broadcast sales, plus a 37.5% ownership in Maple Leaf Sports & Entertainment Ltd., which owns and operates the Toronto Maple Leafs NHL team, the Toronto Raptors NBA team, the Toronto FC Major League Soccer club, and Toronto's Air Canada Centre, among other things. It also owns half of the shomi video streaming service. But the financial information for those companies is not reported on Rogers' financial statements because they are investments, not operating segments. Those investments are part of the assets reported on Rogers' statement of financial position.

Sources: Rogers Communications Inc. 2014 annual report; "A History of Rogers," corporate website, www.rogers.com; "Rogers Communications to Invest in Maple Leaf Sports and Entertainment," company news release, December 9, 2011; http://espn.go.com/mlb/team/salaries/_/name/tor/toronto-blue-jays.

PREVIEW OF CHAPTER 23

It is very important to read not only a company's financial statements, but also related information such as the president's letter and the management discussion and analysis. These additional documents **are just two ways in which companies disclose information to the public and stakeholders** and they help to provide context for the financial statements within the annual report. In this chapter, we cover a variety of disclosures contained in the notes to the financial statements and other disclosures, such as those that accompany the financial statements in the annual report, to ensure that the statements are not misleading.

The chapter is organized as follows:

OTHER MEASUREMENT AND DISCLOSURE ISSUES				
Disclosure Issues	**Other Measurement Issues**	**Auditor's Reports**	**Financial Statement Analysis**	**IFRS/ASPE Comparison**
▪ The importance of disclosure from a business perspective ▪ Full disclosure principle ▪ Accounting policies ▪ Segmented reporting ▪ Interim reporting	▪ Related-party transactions ▪ Subsequent events ▪ Bankruptcy and receivership	▪ Unmodified opinions ▪ Qualified opinions and disclaimers of opinion ▪ Adverse opinions	▪ An overview of financial statement analysis ▪ Financial statement analysis techniques ▪ Limitations of financial statement analysis	▪ A comparison of IFRS and ASPE ▪ Looking ahead

DISCLOSURE ISSUES

The Importance of Disclosure from a Business Perspective

Objective 1
Understand the importance of disclosure from a business perspective.

Information disclosure is important to the proper functioning of capital markets and the allocation of capital. As we discussed in Chapter 1, the information provided in financial statements helps investors compare the performance of companies and assess the relative risks and returns of different investments. The full disclosure principle suggests that information relevant to decision-making should be included in the financial statements. But financial statements are not the only source of information for investors and creditors, and financial statement preparers must keep in mind both the costs and benefits of disclosure when making their disclosure decisions. The Ontario Securities Commission (OSC) lists the following key disclosure documents for public companies on its website:[1]

- Annual information forms

- Financial statements

- Management information circulars

- Management's discussion and analysis (MD&A)

- Material change reports

- News releases relating to material changes and earnings releases

- Prospectuses

FINANCIAL ANALYSIS AND PLANNING
5.1.1

These disclosure documents can generally be found at www.sedar.com for Canadian public companies and investment funds.

The OSC notes that the "fact that documents are filed with the OSC does not make the company or fund immune from fraud or mean it is a 'good' investment. Investors still need to carefully choose their investments and who they deal with." However, an evaluation of the information provided freely by public (and some other) companies is a good starting point for investing decisions. You can begin by comparing the disclosures of the company you are interested in with disclosures made by other companies in that industry. By using publicly available information to assess the relative risks and rewards of the potential investments, and by being diligent in your assessment, you can assess the relative quality of companies you may be considering investing in (or working for).

Before we look at disclosure issues in more detail, a word of warning: not all disclosure is good disclosure. As we will see, too much disclosure can lead to information overload. Also, as the OSC notes in "A Guide for Investors: Researching Your Investments," companies and investors need to beware of the following:

- Misleading disclosure (inaccurate, incomplete, or unbalanced information)

- Selective disclosure (disclosing to a select group, rather than the general public)

- Untimely disclosure (being late with the disclosure of a material change in the business)

- Insider trading (buying or selling a company's securities based on material information not disclosed to the public)

LAW

Investors should be wary of the extra risk involved in dealing with companies that have poor disclosure practices. Businesses should be aware that the four poor disclosure practices listed above often involve violations of securities law.

Full Disclosure Principle

Objective 2
Review the full disclosure principle and describe problems of implementation.

Some information is best provided in the financial statements and some is best provided by other means of financial reporting. For example, earnings and cash flows are readily available in financial statements, but investors might do better if they also look at comparisons with other companies in the same industry, which can be found in news articles or reports issued by analysts at brokerage firms.

Financial statements, notes to the financial statements, and supplementary information are all areas that are directly affected by GAAP. Other types of information that are found in the annual report, such as management commentary (including management discussion and analysis), are not all subject to specific IFRS. However, the IASB issued "Management Commentary: A Framework for Presentation" as an IFRS Practice Statement in December 2010 to help guide companies and regulators. The Practice Statement suggests that companies provide management's perspective on the company's performance, financial position, and progress (for example, how it has grown and is expected to change and grow in the future). So management commentary should include forward-looking information relating to management's objectives, and strategies to achieve its objectives. The commentary should also reflect the qualitative characteristics set out in the conceptual framework (for example, relevance and faithful representation). Illustration 23-1 shows the various types of financial information.

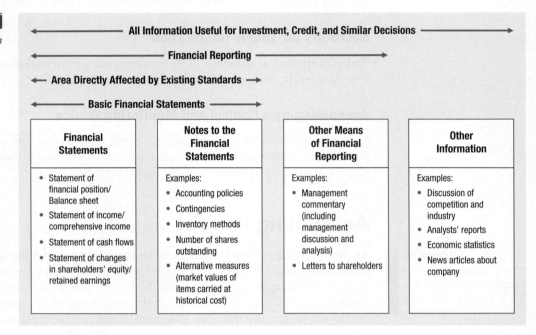

Illustration 23-1

Types of Financial Information

<h1>Full Disclosure Principle Revisited</h1>

UNDERLYING CONCEPT

Deciding what information to provide, while taking into account different users' needs, is a good example of the trade-off between the cost-benefit constraint and the full disclosure principle.

As indicated above and in Chapter 2, the accounting profession has adopted a **full disclosure principle** that calls for reporting of any financial facts that are significant enough to influence the judgement of an informed reader. In some situations, the benefits of disclosure may be apparent while the costs are uncertain. In other instances, the costs may be certain but the benefits of disclosure are less apparent. How much information is enough information? This is a difficult question to answer. While not enough information is clearly problematic, sometimes too much—information overload—is equally problematic.

As part of its disclosure initiative, the IASB noted that obscuring material information with immaterial information in financial statements makes the financial statements less understandable. Along these lines, it clarified IAS 1.31 to highlight that materiality also applies to note disclosures (effective January 1, 2016).

Different users want different information, and it becomes exceedingly difficult to develop disclosure policies that meet their varied objectives.

SIGNIFICANT CHANGE

<h1>Increase in Disclosure Requirements</h1>

Disclosure requirements for public companies have increased substantially over the past several decades.[2] As illustrated throughout this textbook, the accounting profession has issued many standards in the last two decades that have substantial disclosure provisions.

Accounting standards for private enterprises have fewer disclosure requirements than IFRS.[3] This is partly because many private enterprises have less complex business models and transactions. As well, many private companies are closely held, thus giving stakeholders greater access to information that may not be presented in the financial statements.

The reasons for the increase in disclosure requirements for public companies are varied. Some of them are as follows.

Complexity of the Business Environment

The increasing complexity of business operations in such areas as derivatives, leasing, business combinations, pensions, financing arrangements, and revenue recognition increases the difficulty of summarizing economic events. As a result, notes to the financial statements are used extensively to explain these transactions and their future effects.

Necessity for Timely Information

Today, more than ever before, users are demanding information that is current and predictive. As a result, more complete interim data are required.

Accounting as a Control and Monitoring Device

Governments have increasingly sought more information and public disclosure of such phenomena as management compensation, environmental pollution, related-party transactions, errors and irregularities, and illegal activities.

Accounting Policies

Objective 3
Explain the use of accounting policy notes in financial statement preparation.

As mentioned previously, notes are an integral part of a business enterprise's financial statements. However, they are frequently overlooked because they are highly technical and often appear in small print. Notes are the accountant's means of amplifying or explaining items that are presented in the main body of the statements. Information that is relevant to specific financial statement items can be explained in qualitative terms in notes, and additional quantitative data can be provided to expand the information in the financial statements. Notes can also be used to give information about restrictions that are imposed by financial arrangements or basic contractual agreements. Although notes may be technical and difficult to understand, they provide meaningful information for the financial statement user.

The **accounting policies** of any particular entity are the specific accounting principles and methods that are currently used and considered most appropriate to present fairly the enterprise's financial statements. Information about a reporting entity's accounting policies is essential for financial statement users in making economic decisions. The accounting policies disclosure should be given either as one of the first notes or in a separate "summary of significant accounting policies" section that immediately precedes the notes to the financial statements. The summary of significant accounting policies answers such questions as: What method of depreciation is used on plant assets? What costing method is used for inventories? What amortization policy is followed for intangible assets? How are lease costs handled for financial reporting purposes?

**FINANCIAL
ANALYSIS AND
PLANNING**
5.1.1

Refer to the audited financial statements of **Brookfield Asset Management** found just after this chapter for an example of a note disclosure of accounting policies and other notes relating to the topics covered in this volume. Analysts carefully examine the summary of accounting policies section to determine whether the company is using conservative or aggressive accounting practices. For example, recognizing revenues before delivering products to customers might be considered an aggressive practice. On the other hand, using the successful efforts method for an oil and gas company would generally be viewed as a conservative practice.

As we discussed in previous chapters, ASPE allows greater choice in accounting policies to give flexibility to private entities of differing sizes and complexity. In addition, ASPE allows entities to change accounting policies in certain instances without having to meet the IFRS criteria of providing reliable and more relevant information. For IFRS, the IASB has been attempting to reduce accounting policy choice to promote comparability.

Accounting Errors and Illegal Acts

Accounting errors are unintentional mistakes, whereas irregularities are intentional distortions of financial statements. As indicated in Chapter 21, when material errors are discovered, the financial statements should be corrected. The same treatment should be given to irregularities. When an accountant or auditor discovers irregularities, however, a different set of suspicions, procedures, and responsibilities comes into play.

CORPORATE LAW

Illegal acts have been defined as "a violation of a domestic or foreign statutory law or government regulation attributable to the entity . . . or to management or employees acting on the entity's behalf."[4] The term "illegal act" is not meant to include personal misconduct by the entity's management or employees that may be unrelated to the enterprise's business activities. The accountant or auditor must evaluate the adequacy of disclosure in the financial statements and may have to assess whether the item should be recognized in the statement of financial position (SFP) or income statement. For example, if revenue comes from an illegal act that is considered material to the financial statements, this information should be disclosed. Furthermore, if the illegal act creates a liability to pay a fine, this must be reflected in the SFP and income statement.

REAL WORLD EMPHASIS

Segmented Reporting

Objective 4

Describe the disclosure requirements for major segments of a business.

Illustration 23-2

Segmented Information Note— Rogers Communications Inc. (RCI)

In the last several decades, business enterprises have at times diversified their operations by investing in various other businesses. As a result of such diversification efforts, investors and investment analysts have sought more information about the details behind conglomerate financial statements. Particularly, users want income statement, SFP, and cash flow information on the individual segments that together result in the total profit figure. Illustration 23-2 presents a note on how **Rogers Communications Inc.**, from our feature story, reports **segmented (disaggregated) financial information**.

Note 4: Segmented information

Our reportable segments are Wireless, Cable, Business Solutions and Media. All four segments operate substantially in Canada. Corporate items and eliminations include our interests in businesses that are not reportable operating segments, corporate administrative functions and eliminations of inter-segment revenue and costs. We follow the same accounting policies for our segments as those described in note 2. Segment results include items directly attributable to a segment as well as those that can be allocated on a reasonable basis. We account for transactions between reportable segments in the same way we account for transactions with external parties and eliminate them on consolidation.

    The Chief Executive Officer and Chief Financial Officer of RCI are the chief operating decision makers and regularly review our operations and performance by segment. They review adjusted operating profit as the key measure of profit for the purpose of assessing performance for each segment and to make decisions about the allocation of resources. Adjusted operating profit is income before restructuring, acquisition and other, stock-based compensation, depreciation and amortization, finance costs, other expense (income) and income taxes.

INFORMATION BY SEGMENT

Year ended December 31, 2014 (In millions of dollars)	Note	Wireless	Cable	Business Solutions	Media	Corporate items and eliminations	Consolidated totals
Operating revenue	5	7,305	3,467	382	1,826	(130)	12,850
Operating costs[1]		4,059	1,802	260	1,695	15	7,831
Adjusted operating profit		3,246	1,665	122	131	(145)	5,019
Restructuring, acquisition and other	9						173
Stock-based compensation[1]	25						37
Depreciation and amortization	7, 8						2,144
Finance costs	10						817
Other expense							1
Income before income taxes							1,847
Additions to property, plant and equipment		978	1,055	146	94	93	2,366
Goodwill		1,155	1,379	426	923	–	3,883
Total assets		12,935	6,019	1,219	2,466	3,883	26,522

(continued)

Year ended December 31, 2013 (In millions of dollars)	Note	Wireless	Cable	Business Solutions	Media	Corporate items and eliminations	Consolidated totals
Operating revenue	5	7,270	3,475	374	1,704	(117)	12,706
Operating costs[1]		4,113	1,757	268	1,543	32	7,713
Adjusted operating profit		3,157	1,718	106	161	(149)	4,993
Restructuring, acquisition and other	9						85
Stock-based compensation[1]	25						84
Depreciation and amortization	7, 8						1,898
Finance costs	10						742
Other income							(81)
Income before income taxes							2,265
Additions to property, plant and equipment		865	1,105	107	79	84	2,240
Goodwill		1,146	1,256	426	923	–	3,751
Total assets		9,775	5,527	1,195	2,247	4,857	23,601

[1]Included in Operating costs on the Consolidated Statements of Income.

Illustration 23-2

Segmented Information Note— Rogers Communications Inc. (RCI) (Continued)

If the analyst has access to only the consolidated figures, information about the composition of these figures is hidden in aggregated totals. There is no way to tell from the consolidated data how much each product line contributes to the company's profitability, risk, and growth potential. For example, in the case of Rogers, the segmented data reveal that the wireless segment yields 64.7% of the operating profit while contributing 56.8% of the revenues, whereas the media segment contributes 14.2% of revenues, but only 2.6% of operating profits! How much the individual segments contribute to revenues and profits would not be revealed otherwise.

Companies have always been somewhat hesitant to disclose segmented data for several reasons, including the following.

1. Without a thorough knowledge of the business and an understanding of such important factors as the competitive environment and capital investment requirements, the investor may find the segmented information meaningless or may even draw improper conclusions about the segments' reported earnings.

2. Additional disclosure may harm reporting firms because it may be helpful to competitors, labour unions, suppliers, and certain government regulatory agencies.

3. Additional disclosure may discourage management from taking intelligent business risks because segments that report losses or unsatisfactory earnings may cause shareholder dissatisfaction with management.

4. The wide variation among firms in the choice of segments, cost allocation, and other accounting problems limits the usefulness of segmented information.

5. The investor is investing in the company as a whole and not in the particular segments, and it should not matter how any single segment is performing if the overall performance is satisfactory.

6. Certain technical problems, such as classification of segments and allocation of segment revenues and costs (especially "common costs"), are challenging.

On the other hand, the advocates of segmented disclosures offer these reasons in support of the practice.

1. Segmented information is needed by the investor to make an intelligent investment decision regarding a diversified company.

   (a) Sales and earnings of individual segments are needed to forecast consolidated profits because of the differences among segments in growth rates, risk, and profitability.

   (b) Segmented reports disclose the nature of a company's businesses and the relative size of the components, which aids in evaluating the company's investment worth.

2. The absence of segmented reporting by a diversified company may put its unsegmented, single-product-line competitors at a competitive disadvantage because the conglomerate may obscure information that its competitors must disclose.

The advocates of segmented disclosures appear to have a much stronger case. Many users indicate that segmented data are the most useful financial information provided, aside from the basic financial statements.

The development of accounting standards for segmented financial information has been a continuing process during the past quarter century. We discuss the basic reporting requirements next. Note that ASPE does not contain guidance for reporting segmented information.

Objective of Reporting Segmented Information

The objective of reporting segmented financial data is to provide information about the different types of business activities in which an enterprise engages and the different economic environments in which it operates[5] so that users of financial statements can:

- better understand the enterprise's performance,

- better assess its prospects for future net cash flows, and

- make more informed judgements about the enterprise as a whole.

Basic Principles of Segmented Reporting

A company might meet the segmented reporting objective by providing complete sets of financial statements that are disaggregated in several ways: for example, by products or services, by geography, by legal entity, or by type of customer. However, it is not feasible to provide all that information in every set of financial statements. The IASB instead requires that financial statements include selected information about operating segments from the perspective of the **chief operating decision-maker**, who could, for example, be the CEO or COO (chief operating officer). The chief operating decision-maker function refers to the executive, or group of executives or directors, that allocates resources and assesses the operating performance of the company's segments.[6] The method chosen is sometimes referred to as the management approach. The **management approach** is based on the way that management segments the company for making operating decisions, which is made evident by the company's organization structure. Because this approach focuses on information about the components of the business that management looks at in making its decisions about operating matters, the components are referred to as **operating segments**.

Identifying Operating Segments

An operating segment is a component of an enterprise that has all of the following characteristics:

1. It engages in business activities from which it earns revenues and incurs expenses.

2. Its operating results are regularly reviewed by the company's chief operating decision-maker to assess segment performance and allocate resources to the segment.

3. There is discrete financial information available on it.[7]

Information about two or more operating segments may be aggregated only if the segments have the same basic characteristics in all of the following areas:

1. The nature of the products and services provided

2. The nature of the production process

3. The type or class of customer

4. The methods of product or service distribution

5. If applicable, the nature of the regulatory environment

SIGNIFICANT CHANGE

Effective July 1, 2014, IFRS requires that companies disclose the judgements made in aggregating segments and provide a brief description of the segments aggregated.

After the company decides on the segments for possible disclosure, it makes a quantitative materiality test to determine whether the segment is significant enough to warrant actual disclosure. An operating segment is regarded as significant, and is therefore identified as a **reportable segment**, if it satisfies one or more of the following quantitative thresholds:[8]

1. Its reporting revenue (including both sales to external customers and intersegment sales or transfers) is 10% or more of the combined revenue of all the enterprise's operating segments.

2. The absolute amount of its reported profit or loss is 10% or more of the greater, in absolute amount, of:

    (a) the combined reported operating profit of all operating segments that did not incur a loss, and

    (b) the combined reported loss of all operating segments that reported a loss.

3. Its assets are 10% or more of the combined assets of all operating segments.

    In applying these tests, three additional factors must be considered.

1. Segment data must explain a significant portion of the company's business. Specifically, the segmented results must equal or exceed 75% of the combined sales to unaffiliated customers for the entire enterprise. This test prevents a company from providing limited information on only a few segments and lumping all the rest into one category.[9]

2. As the profession recognizes that reporting too many segments may overwhelm users with detailed information, it has proposed 10 segments as a practical limit of the number of segments that a company should disclose.[10]

3. If an operating segment does not meet any of the tests but management believes separate information would be useful to users, then the segment may be presented separately.

    To illustrate these requirements, assume that a company has identified the six possible reporting segments shown in Illustration 23-3 (amounts in 000s).

Illustration 23-3				
Data for Different Possible Reporting Segments	Segments	Total Revenue	Reported Profit (Loss)	Assets
	A	$ 100	$10	$ 60
	B	60	2	30
	C	700	40	390
	D	300	20	160
	E	900	18	280
	F	100	(5)	50
		$2,160	$85	$970

The respective tests may be applied as follows:

Revenue test: 10% × $2,160 = $216; C, D, and E meet this test.

Reported profit (loss) test: 10% × $90 = $9 (note that the $5 loss is excluded because it is a loss); A, C, D, and E meet this test.

Assets tests: 10% × $970 = $97; C, D, and E meet this test.

The reportable segments are therefore A, C, D, and E, assuming that these four segments have enough sales to meet the test of at least 75% of combined sales. The 75% test is calculated as follows:

75% of combined sales test: 75% × $2,160 = $1,620; the sales of A, C, D, and E total $2,000 ($100 + $700 + $300 + $900); therefore, the minimum 75% test is met.

Measurement Principles

The accounting principles that an entity uses for segment disclosure do not need to be the same principles that are used to prepare the consolidated statements. This flexibility may at first appear inconsistent. But preparing segment information in accordance with generally accepted accounting principles would be difficult because some principles are not expected to apply at a segment level. Examples include accounting for the cost of company-wide employee benefit plans and accounting for income taxes in a company that files one overall tax return.

Allocations of joint, centrally incurred, or company-wide costs solely for external reporting purposes are not required. **Centrally incurred costs** are costs that are interrelated in nature, preventing a completely objective division of the costs among the segments. For example, the company president's salary is difficult to allocate to various segments. Allocations of these costs are inherently arbitrary and may not be meaningful if they are not used for internal management purposes. There is a presumption instead that allocations to segments are either directly attributable to the segment or reasonably allocable to it. There should be disclosure of the choices that were made in measuring segmented information, including the basis of accounting for transactions between segments.

Segmented and Enterprise-Wide Disclosures

The IASB requires that an enterprise report the following:[11]

1. **General information** about its reportable segments. This includes factors that management considers most significant in determining the company's reportable segments, the judgements made in aggregation of segments, and the types of products and services from which each operating segment derives its revenues.

2. **Segment revenues, profit and loss, assets, liabilities, and related information.** This requires disclosure of a measure of profit or loss and total assets and liabilities for each reportable segment. In addition, the following specific information about each reportable segment must be reported if the amounts are regularly reviewed by management:

   (a) Revenues from external customers (revenues from customers attributed to individual material foreign countries should be separately disclosed)

   (b) Revenues from transactions with other operating segments of the same enterprise

   (c) Interest revenue

   (d) Interest expense

   (e) Depreciation and amortization

   (f) Material items of income and expense (as set out in IAS 1)

   (g) Equity in the net income of investees and joint ventures that are accounted for using the equity method

   (h) Income tax expense or benefit

   (i) Significant non-cash items other than depreciation and amortization expense

   Note that the amount that is reported should be the amount reviewed by management (the chief operating decision-maker). Information about the basis of accounting and other details should be disclosed.

3. **Reconciliations.** An enterprise must provide a reconciliation of the following:

   (a) The total of the segments' revenues to total revenues

   (b) The total of the operating segments' profits or losses to its profits or losses before income taxes and discontinued operations

   (c) The total of the operating segments' assets and liabilities to total assets and liabilities

   Reconciliations for other significant items that are disclosed should also be presented and all reconciling items should be separately identified and described for all of the above.

4. **Products and services.** The amount of revenues from external customers.

5. **Geographic areas.** Revenues from external customers (Canada versus foreign) and certain current assets (Canada versus foreign) should be stated. Foreign information must be disclosed by country if the amounts are material.

6. **Major customers.** If 10% or more of the revenues are derived from a single customer, the enterprise must disclose the total amount of revenues from each of these customers and the identities of the affected segments. However, it does not need to identify any specific major customers in its disclosures.

Interim Reporting

Objective 5

Describe the accounting problems associated with interim reporting.

Another source of information for investors is interim reports. **Interim reports** cover periods of less than one year. While at one time annual reporting was considered enough to provide timely information, demand quickly grew for quarterly information, and now capital markets are moving to even more frequent disclosures. IFRS does not mandate which entities should provide interim information; however, it provides guidance (that entities are encouraged to follow) if the entity does provide the information. If the interim report is in compliance with IFRS, this should be disclosed. ASPE does not include standards for interim reporting.

Illustration 23-4 presents the disclosure of selected quarterly data for **Torstar Corporation**. The media company also disclosed consolidated statements of financial position, income, comprehensive income, changes in equity, and cash flows (along with related notes). The statements were accompanied by a management discussion and analysis of the operating results, liquidity and capital resources, outlook, risks and uncertainties, and other matters. With such comprehensive coverage, the report gives a significant amount of information.

Illustration 23-4

Disclosure of Quarterly Consolidated Statement of Income—Torstar Corporation

TORSTAR CORPORATION
Consolidated Statement of Income
(Thousands of Canadian Dollars except per share amounts)
(Unaudited)

	Three months ended March 3	
	2015	2014 Restated*
Operating revenue	**$181,169**	$199,184
Salaries and benefits	**(80,778)**	(89,548)
Other operating costs	**(91,396)**	(97,854)
Amortization and depreciation (notes 8 and 9)	**(6,774)**	(8,317)
Restructuring and other charges (note 11)	**(3,741)**	(3,518)
Impairment of assets		(266)
Operating loss	**(1,520)**	(319)
Interest and financing costs (note 16)	**(79)**	(2,161)
Foreign exchange	**405**	(1,164)
Income from joint ventures (note 6)	**1,218**	1,570
Loss of associated businesses (note 7)	**(588)**	(668)
Other income (expense) (note 17)	**5**	1,051
	(559)	(1,691)
Income and other taxes recovery (note 10)	**100**	100
Net loss from continuing operations	**(459)**	(1,591)
Income (loss) from discontinued operations (note 18)	**(3,500)**	8,719
Net income (loss)	**($3,959)**	$7,128
Attributable to:		
Equity shareholders	**($3,694)**	$7,104
Minority interests	**($265)**	$24
Net income (loss) attributable to equity shareholders per Class A (voting) and Class B (non-voting) share (note 13(b)):		
Basic and Diluted:		
From continuing operations	**($0.01)**	($0.02)
From discontinued operations	**($0.04)**	$0.11
	($0.05)	$0.09

(see accompanying notes)
*The 2014 comparative amounts have been restated to reflect the classification of Harlequin into discontinued operations

Because of the short-term nature of the information in these reports, however, there is considerable controversy about the general approach that should be taken. Supporters of the **discrete view** believe that each interim period should be treated as a separate accounting period. Deferrals and accruals would therefore follow the same principles that are used for annual reports. Accounting transactions should be reported as they occur, and expense recognition should not change with the period of time covered. Proponents of the **integral view**, on the other hand, believe that the interim report is an integral part of the annual report and that deferrals and accruals should consider what will happen for the entire year. In this approach, estimated expenses are assigned to parts of a year based on the sales volume or some other activity base. IFRS generally favours the discrete view.

One notable exception to the discrete view is in calculating tax expense. Normally a company would prepare its tax return at year end and assess taxes payable and related tax balances. It is neither cost-effective nor feasible to do this for each interim period (because tax rates are often graduated and therefore increase with increasing taxable income), so annual estimates are made instead. Specifically, an estimate is made of interim taxable income and temporary differences and then the annual estimated tax rate is applied. **Another exception relates to the employer's portion of payroll taxes.** Although the employer may remit these taxes early in the year (as required by law), the government assesses the taxes annually. Therefore, for interim reporting periods, the total estimated annual amount is allocated to the interim periods, which means that the expense is recognized on an accrual basis as opposed to a cash basis.

Interim Reporting Requirements

As a general rule, the profession indicates that the same accounting principles that are used for annual reports should be used for interim reports. Revenues should be recognized in interim periods on the same basis as they are for annual periods. For example, if the percentage-of-completion method is used for recognizing revenue on an annual basis, then the same method should be applied to interim reports as well. Also, costs that are directly associated with revenues (product costs), such as materials, labour and related fringe benefits, and manufacturing overhead, should be treated in the same manner for interim reports as for annual reports.

Companies should also generally use the same inventory cost formulas (such as FIFO or weighted average) for interim reports that they use for annual reports. At a minimum, a condensed SFP, comprehensive income statement, statement of changes in equity, statement of cash flows, and selected notes are required.[12] Note that the standard requires companies to provide at least condensed statements but does not prevent companies from providing more detailed presentations. Condensed financial statements should include at least the same headings and subtotals as the most recent annual statements. The SFP should be presented as at the end of the current interim period with a comparative SFP as at the end of the immediately preceding fiscal year. The SFP should also be restated for prior interim periods of the current period and for comparative interim periods when an entity changes an accounting policy retrospectively or makes a retrospective restatement (to correct an error, for example).

The income statement should be presented for the current interim period and interim year to date with comparatives. (Comparatives are comparable information for the previous period or year.) For the statement of changes in equity, the information should be presented cumulatively for the current fiscal year to date with comparatives. Finally, for the cash flow statement, information should be presented cumulatively for the current fiscal year to date with comparatives.[13] Earnings per share (EPS) information is also required if an enterprise must present this information in its annual information.[14]

Regarding disclosure, the following interim data should be reported as a minimum:[15]

1. Whether the statements comply with IFRS

2. A statement that the company follows the same accounting policies and methods as the most recent annual financial statements, or if changed, a description of new or changed policies

3. A description of any seasonality or cyclicality of interim period operations

4. The nature and amount of any unusual items

5. The nature and amount of changes in estimates

6. Issuances, repurchases, and repayments of debt and equity securities

7. Dividends paid

8. Information about reportable segments including revenues from external customers, intersegment revenues, segment profit or loss, total assets for which there is a material change from the last audited financial statements, a description of differences from the last annual statements in the basis of segmentation, and reconciliation of segment profit or loss to the entity's total profit or loss before taxes and discontinued operations

9. Events subsequent to the interim period

10. Specific information about changes in the composition of the entity

11. Disclosures about the fair value of financial instruments

12. Any other information that is required for fair presentation and/or is material to an understanding of the interim period

Unique Problems of Interim Reporting

Changes in Accounting

What happens if a company decides to change an accounting principle in the third quarter of a fiscal year? Should the adjustment for the cumulative effect of the change be charged or credited to that quarter? Presentation of a cumulative effect in the third quarter may be misleading because of the inherent subjectivity that is associated with the reported income of the first two quarters. In addition, a question arises as to whether such a change might not be used to manipulate a particular quarter's income. These changes should therefore be reflected by retroactive application to prior interim periods unless the data are not practicably available. The comparable interim periods of prior fiscal years should also be restated.[16]

Earnings per Share

Interim reporting of earnings per share numbers has all the problems of calculating and presenting annual earnings per share figures, and more. If shares are issued in the third period, EPS for the first two periods may not be indicative of year-end EPS. For purposes of calculating earnings per share and making the required disclosure determinations, each interim period should stand alone. That is, all applicable tests should be made for that single period.

Seasonality

Seasonality occurs when sales are compressed into one short period of the year while certain costs are fairly evenly spread throughout the year. For example, the natural gas industry has its heavy sales in the winter, while the beverage industry has its heavy sales in the summer.

In a seasonal business, wide fluctuations in profits occur because off-season sales may not absorb the company's fixed costs (for example, manufacturing, selling, and administrative costs that tend to remain fairly constant regardless of sales or production). Revenues and expenses should be recognized and accrued when they are earned or incurred according to IFRS. This is also true for interim periods. Thus, a company would defer recognition of costs or revenues only if it would be appropriate to do so at year end. (In other words, the same tests are applied.) As mentioned earlier in the text, deferral of costs is not appropriate unless the costs meet the definition of an asset.

Continuing Controversy

The profession has developed the stringent standards noted above for interim reporting. This has eased much of the controversy regarding the discrete and integral perspectives.

There is still controversy, however, about the independent auditor's involvement in interim reports. Many auditors are reluctant to express an opinion on interim financial information, arguing that the data are too tentative and subjective. Conversely, more individuals are arguing for some type of examination of interim reports. A compromise being used in Canada is the "Auditor Review of Interim Financial Statements" (Section 7060 of the *CPA Canada Handbook—Assurance*).[17] The purpose of this type of review by the auditor is to assist the audit committee in discharging its responsibilities for interim financial statements. While the Auditing and Assurance Standards Board in Canada considered issuing a standard for a general purpose report for users of interim reports, it chose not to at this time.

Analysts want financial information as soon as possible, before it becomes old news. We may not be far from a system in which corporate financial records can be accessed at any time by computer. Investors might be able to access a company's financial records via computer whenever they wish and put the information in the format they need.[18] Thus, they could learn about sales slippage, cost increases, or earnings changes as they happen, rather than waiting until after the quarter has ended.

**FINANCIAL
ANALYSIS AND
PLANNING
5.1.1**

A steady stream of information from the company to the investor could be very useful because it might alleviate management's continual concern with short-run interim numbers. It would also alleviate many of the allocation problems that plague current GAAP.

Internet Financial Reporting and Continuous Disclosures

How can companies improve the usefulness of their financial reporting practices? Many companies are using the Internet's power and reach to provide more useful information to financial statement readers. Virtually all large companies have websites, and a considerable proportion of these companies' websites contain links to their financial statements, annual reports, and other disclosures. The increased popularity of such reporting is not surprising, since the costs of printing and disseminating paper reports are reduced.

How does Internet financial reporting improve the overall usefulness of a company's financial reports? First, dissemination of reports via the Internet can allow firms to communicate with more users than is possible with traditional paper reports. In addition, Internet reporting allows users to take advantage of tools such as search engines and hyperlinks to quickly find information about the firm and, sometimes, to download the information for analysis, perhaps in computer spreadsheets. Finally, Internet reporting can help make financial reports more relevant by allowing companies to report expanded disaggregated data and more timely data than is possible through paper-based reporting. For example, some companies voluntarily report weekly sales data and segment operating data on their websites.

Given these benefits and ever-improving Internet tools, will it be long before electronic reporting entirely replaces paper-based financial disclosure? The main obstacles to achieving complete electronic reporting are **equality of access to electronic financial reporting and the reliability of the information that is distributed** via the Internet. Although companies may practise Internet financial reporting, they must still prepare traditional paper reports because some investors may not have Internet access. These investors would receive differential (less) information relative to wired investors if companies were to completely eliminate paper reports. In addition, at present, Internet financial reporting is a voluntary means of reporting. As a result, there are no standards for the completeness of reports on the Internet, nor is there a requirement that these reports be audited. One concern in this regard is that computer hackers could invade a company's website and corrupt the financial information there.

A great example of the use of technology and continuous reporting is the current practice of releasing quarterly results via the company website through video and live streaming. Investors and analysts can visit the company website and hear the earnings announcements first-hand.

While Internet financial reporting is gaining in popularity, until issues related to differential access to the Internet and the reliability of web-based information are addressed, we will also continue to see traditional paper-based reporting.

OTHER MEASUREMENT ISSUES

Related-Party Transactions

Objective 6
Discuss the accounting
issues for related-party
transactions.

Related-party transactions present especially sensitive and difficult problems. The accountant or auditor who has responsibility for reporting on these types of transactions has to be extremely careful to ensure that the rights of the reporting company and the needs of financial statement users are properly balanced.

IFRS deals only with disclosure requirements whereas ASPE requires that some related-party transactions be remeasured. **Related-party transactions** arise when a business engages in transactions in which one of the transacting parties could significantly influence the policies of the other, or in which a non-transacting party could influence the policies of the two transacting parties. Related parties include but are not limited to the following:

1. Companies or individuals who control, or are controlled by, or are under common control with the reporting enterprise

2. Investors and investees where there is significant influence or joint control

3. Company management

4. Members of immediate family of the above

5. The other party when a management contract exists[19]

Transactions between related parties cannot be presumed to be carried out at arm's length because there may not be the required conditions of competitive, free-market dealings. Examples of transactions that suggest that related parties may be involved include borrowing or lending money at abnormally low or high interest rates, real estate sales at amounts that differ significantly from appraised values, exchanges of nonmonetary assets, transfer pricing arrangements structured to minimize taxes, and transactions involving enterprises that have no economic substance ("shell corporations"). **In each case, there is a measurement issue.** A basic assumption about financial information is that it is based on transactions that are between arm's-length parties. **Consequently, if this condition is not met, the transactions should at least be disclosed as being between related parties. Furthermore, special measurement principles exist for related-party transactions and these may require a transaction to be remeasured under ASPE.**

The accountant is expected to report the **economic substance rather than the legal form** of these transactions and to make adequate disclosures. The following disclosures are recommended:[20]

1. The nature of the relationship(s) involved

2. A description of the transactions

3. The recorded amounts of transactions

4. The measurement basis that was used

5. Amounts due from or to related parties and the related terms and conditions

6. Contractual obligations with related parties

7. Contingencies involving related parties

8. Under IFRS, management compensation and the name of the entity's parent company as well as its ultimate controlling entity or individual

Under ASPE, certain related-party transactions must be remeasured to the carrying amount of the underlying assets or services that were exchanged. **Carrying amount** is defined as the amount of the item transferred as recorded in the books of the transferor. **This is the case if:**

1. **the transaction is not in the normal course of business,**

2. **there is no substantive change in ownership, and/or**

3. **the exchange amount is not supported by independent evidence.**

The argument to support remeasurement rests on the premise that, if the transaction is not an ordinary transaction for the enterprise, there might not be a reasonable measure of fair value. Furthermore, if there is no change in ownership, then no bargaining has taken place and, therefore, the price that is arrived at for the exchange may not represent a value that would have been arrived at had the transaction been at arm's length. **Transactions that are in the normal course of business that have no commercial substance must also be remeasured.** This argument rests on the premise that, if the transaction is not authentic, there is no real exchange of risks and rewards of ownership and, therefore, no gain or loss should be recognized. **This is only an issue where the transaction is also a nonmonetary transaction.** A transaction has **commercial substance** when the entity's cash flows are expected to be significantly different after and as a result of the transaction. In making this determination, consider the risk, timing, and amount of cash flows. Finally, where products or properties are exchanged in the normal course of business to facilitate sales, the transaction is also recorded at carrying value.

Where transactions are remeasured to their carrying value, the difference between the carrying amounts of the items that have been exchanged is booked as a charge or credit to equity.[21] To illustrate, assume that Knudson Limited, a manufacturing company, sells land worth $20,000 to Bay Limited. The companies are related because the same shareholder has a 70% equity interest in each company (the rest of the shares are not owned by related parties). The land has a carrying value of $15,000 on Knudson's books. In exchange, Bay Limited, also a manufacturing company, transfers to Knudson a building that has a net book value of $12,000. This transaction is not in the **ordinary (normal) course of business** because both companies are manufacturers and would not normally be selling capital assets such as land and buildings. Based on this assessment, therefore, the transaction merits further analysis.

Illustration 23-5 is a decision tree of the judgement needed when determining how to treat related-party transactions.[22]

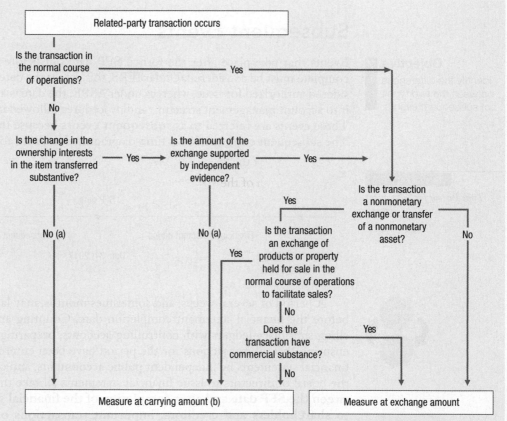

Related-Party Transactions—
Decision Tree

(a) Carrying amount is used for both monetary and nonmonetary transactions in these circumstances.

(b) In rare circumstances, when the carrying amount of the item received is not available, a reasonable estimate of the carrying amount, based on the transferor's original cost, may be used to measure the exchange.

Looking at the decision tree, after deciding if the transaction is in the normal course of business, the next question is: **Has there been a substantive change in ownership?** Do different parties own the exchanged items after the transaction? Because the same controlling shareholder owns both assets before and after the transaction (even if indirectly through the companies), there is no substantive change in ownership.[23] The transaction would therefore be remeasured to carrying values with the following journal entry on the Knudson books:

Buildings	12,000	
Retained Earnings	3,000	
Land		15,000

A   =   L   +   SE
−3,000   −3,000

Cash flows: No effect

Bay would record the land at $15,000 and take the building and related accumulated depreciation off its books. The resulting credit would be booked to Contributed Surplus. Note that the difference between the carrying values is generally viewed as an equity contribution or distribution and is therefore booked through equity.

If, on the other hand, the transaction had been in the normal course of business and it had commercial substance, it would have been recorded at the exchange value. The exchange value is defined as the amount of consideration paid or received and agreed to by the related parties.[24] In this case, assume that the agreed-upon exchange value is $20,000. Note that the exchange value is not necessarily equal to the fair value but it could be. It is whatever value the two parties agree on. ASPE notes that it is possible that the transaction value may approximate fair value, but it is not necessary to establish what fair value would be if the transaction value is not an approximation. If cash were exchanged, this would determine the exchange value.

In this case, the transaction would be treated like a sale by both parties and Knudson would recognize a gain of $5,000 ($20,000 − $15,000). Likewise, Bay would also recognize a gain of $8,000 ($20,000 − $12,000).

Subsequent Events

Objective 7
Identify the differences between the two types of subsequent events.

Events that take place after the formal SFP date but before the financial statements are complete must be considered. Under IFRS, this date is the date that the statements are considered authorized for issue, whereas under ASPE, the date is a matter of judgement, taking into account management structure and procedures followed in completing the statements. These events are referred to as **subsequent events** because they occur after the SFP date. The subsequent events period is time-diagrammed in Illustration 23-6.

Illustration 23-6

Time Periods for Subsequent Events

A period of several weeks, and sometimes months, may lapse after the end of the year before the financial statement completion date. Counting and pricing inventory, reconciling subsidiary ledgers with controlling accounts, preparing necessary adjusting entries, ensuring that all transactions for the period have been entered, obtaining an audit of the financial statements by independent public accountants, and obtaining authorization from the board of directors to issue financial statements all take time. **During the period between the SFP date and after completion of the financial statements for distribution to shareholders and creditors, important transactions or other events may occur that materially affect the company's financial position or operations.**

Many readers of a company's recent SFP would believe that the financial condition is unchanged and they may therefore project it into the future. Readers therefore need to be made aware if the company has sold one of its plants, acquired a subsidiary, settled significant litigation, or experienced other important events in the post-balance sheet period. Without explanations in a note, the reader might be misled and draw inappropriate conclusions.

Two types of events or transactions that occur after the SFP date may have a material effect on the financial statements or may need to be considered to interpret these statements accurately.

1. **Events that provide additional evidence about conditions that existed at the SFP date affect the estimates used in preparing financial statements and, therefore, result in needed adjustments.** All information available before the financial statements are issued is used to evaluate previously made estimates. Ignoring these subsequent events misses an opportunity to improve the financial statements' accuracy. This first type of event includes information that would have been recorded in the accounts if it had been known at the SFP date. For example, if a loss on an account receivable results from a customer's bankruptcy after the SFP date, the financial statements are adjusted before their issuance. The bankruptcy stems from the customer's poor financial health, which likely would have existed at the SFP date.

   The same criterion applies to settlements of litigation. The financial statements must be adjusted if the events that gave rise to the litigation, such as personal injury or patent infringement, took place prior to the SFP date. If the event giving rise to the claim took place subsequent to the SFP date, no adjustment is necessary. Thus, a loss resulting from a customer's fire or flood after the SFP date is not indicative of conditions that existed at that date. Accordingly, it is not appropriate to adjust the financial statements.

2. **Events that provide evidence about conditions that did not exist at the SFP date but arise subsequent to that date and do not require adjustment of the financial statements.** Some of these events may have to be disclosed to keep the financial statements from being misleading. These disclosures take the form of notes, supplemental schedules, or even supplemental financial data prepared as if the event had occurred on the SFP date. The following are examples of such events that, if they occurred after the SFP date, would require disclosure if they are significant (but would not result in adjustment):

   (a) A fire or flood that results in a loss

   (b) A decline in the market value of investments

   (c) A purchase of a business

   (d) The start of legal action where the cause of action arose after the SFP date

   (e) Changes in foreign currency rates

   (f) An issuance of shares or debt

Illustration 23-7 presents an example of subsequent events disclosure from the 2014 financial statements of **BlackBerry Limited**.

Subsequent Events Note Disclosure—BlackBerry Limited

18. Subsequent events:

On March 21, 2014, the Company announced that it has entered into an agreement pursuant to which it will sell the majority of its real estate holdings in Canada. The announced transaction is part of the Company's ongoing program to improve operational efficiencies, optimize resource usage and shift resources to support operations as the business continues to evolve.

Under the terms of the agreement, the Company will sell more than 3 million square feet of space as well as vacant lands. The Company will also lease back a portion of the space. CBRE Limited served as an advisor to the Company for this transaction. The agreement is expected to close in the first quarter of fiscal 2015. The transaction is subject to certain conditions, and the transaction may not be completed on the negotiated terms, or at all. Additional terms of the transaction will be announced once the principal conditions are satisfied or waived by the parties.

Many subsequent events or developments are not likely to require either adjustment of the financial statements or disclosure. Typically, these are non-accounting events or conditions that management normally communicates by other means. These events include legislation, product changes, management changes, strikes, unionization, marketing agreements, and loss of important customers. What to include in the financial statements is a matter of professional judgement because all changes to the business will eventually affect performance one way or another.

Sometimes subsequent events are so pervasive—such as a rapid decline of the company's financial health—that they call into question the going concern assumption. Recall from earlier chapters that the going concern assumption presumes that an entity will continue to operate and will be able to realize its assets and discharge its liabilities in an orderly manner. This supports the use of the mixed fair value/historical cost measurement model. If a subsequent event calls the going concern assumption into question, the measurement model would perhaps change. The company would have to decide (and its auditor would need to assess) whether there should be additional note disclosures or whether the assets and liabilities should be remeasured to reflect net realizable values in a liquidation market.

Illustration 23-8 presents an excerpt from **Mad Catz Interactive, Inc.** financial statements for the year ended March 31, 2015. Mad Catz lists on NASDAQ. This note illustrates the going concern concept. In this case, there is uncertainty about the company's ability to continue as a going concern because the company was not in compliance with a monthly financial debt covenant based on adjusted earnings before interest, taxes, depreciation, and amortization (EBITDA). This non-compliance could result in debt covenants being breached and loans being called. Note that the financial statements mention the importance of anticipated sales of products related to the Rock Band 4 video game to being in compliance with the covenants in fiscal 2016.

AUDIT AND ASSURANCE
4.3.5

REAL WORLD EMPHASIS

| Illustration 23-8 |

Potential Going Concern Issues— Mad Catz Interactive, Inc.

(2) Summary of Significant Accounting Policies

Basis of Presentation

The consolidated financial statements include the accounts of Mad Catz Interactive, Inc. and its wholly-owned subsidiaries, collectively, the Company. All intercompany transactions and balances have been eliminated in consolidation. The Company refers to its fiscal years based on the fiscal year ending date. For instance, fiscal year 2015 refers to the fiscal year ending March 31, 2015. All currency amounts are presented in U.S. dollars.

The Company maintains a Credit Facility with Wells Fargo Capital Finance, LLC ("Wells Fargo") to borrow up to $25 million under a revolving line of credit subject to the availability of eligible collateral (accounts receivable and inventories), which changes throughout the year. Borrowings under the Credit Facility are secured by a first priority interest in the inventories, equipment, and accounts receivable of certain of our subsidiaries and by a pledge of all of the capital stock of our subsidiaries. The Company is required to meet a monthly financial covenant based on a trailing twelve months' Adjusted EBITDA, as defined. The Company's trailing twelve months' Adjusted EBITDA as of March 31, 2015 and April 30, 2015 was lower than the required threshold and, accordingly, the Company was not in compliance with this covenant as of March 31, 2015 and April 30, 2015. On June 23, 2015, the Company received a waiver of the covenant violations from Wells Fargo and entered into an amendment to the Credit Facility that extends the expiration of the credit facility to July 31, 2016 and modifies the trailing twelve months' Adjusted EBITDA covenant, as defined, from June 2015 through June 2016.

The Company depends upon the availability of capital under the Credit Facility to finance operations. Compliance with the Adjusted EBITDA covenants in fiscal 2016, which are tied closely to our internal forecasts and include significant contributions from anticipated sales of products related to the Rock Band 4 video game, depends on the Company's ability to increase net sales and gross profit considerably. Also, the Company operates in a rapidly evolving and often unpredictable business environment that may change the timing or amount of expected future sales and expenses. If the Company is unable to comply with the revised Adjusted EBITDA covenants contained in the Credit Facility, Wells Fargo could declare the outstanding borrowings under the facility immediately due and payable. If the Company needs to obtain additional funds as a result of the termination of the Credit Facility or the acceleration of amounts due thereunder, there can be no assurance that alternative financing can be obtained on substantially similar or acceptable terms, or at all. The Company's failure to promptly obtain alternate financing could limit our ability to implement our business plan and have an immediate, severe and adverse impact on our business, results of operations, financial condition and liquidity. In the event that no alternative financing is available, the Company would be forced to drastically curtail operations, or dispose of assets, or cease operations altogether.

These uncertainties raise substantial doubt about the Company's ability to continue as a going concern. The consolidated financial statements do not include any adjustments that might result from the outcome of these uncertainties.

Unincorporated Businesses

CORPORATE LAW

Throughout this text, the primary emphasis has been on incorporated businesses. Partnerships and sole proprietorships are another significant business form. These businesses are unincorporated and thus do not have share capital, as we discussed in Chapter 3. This type of business has in the past decade become very popular as a tax shelter in the form of income trusts or investment trusts. Interestingly enough, while ownership of partnerships is generally private, ownership of income and investment trusts is often public. The partnership or trust units trade on various stock exchanges.

The accounting issues related to these types of entities are generally similar to those of incorporated companies, with a few exceptions discussed below.

1. It is critical to define the economic entity because unincorporated businesses are not separate legal entities. The financial statements should indicate clearly the name under which the business is conducted and it should be clear that the business is unincorporated and that the statements do not include the assets and liabilities of the owners.

ASPE

2. Salaries, interest, or similar items accruing to owners should be clearly indicated.

3. No provision for income taxes should be made. Because the businesses are not separate legal entities, the income is taxed in the hands of the unitholders.

4. The financial statements should include a statement detailing the changes in owners' equity during the period, including contributions of capital, income or losses, and withdrawals.

Note that the owners' equity section would also include different terminology; for example, "capital" instead of common stock and "withdrawals" instead of dividends. ASPE provides guidance regarding unincorporated businesses in Section 1800 of Part II of the *CPA Canada Handbook*, whereas there is no specific guidance under IFRS.

Bankruptcy and Receivership

Objective 8
Identify the major considerations relating to bankruptcy and receivership.

Companies facing financial difficulties may eventually have to enter receivership and ultimately declare bankruptcy. The risk of bankruptcy is heightened when a company has prolonged negative cash flow from operating activities, as we discussed in Chapter 22. The company may become insolvent, being unable to pay its debts as they become due.

Bankruptcy is a legal process that occurs when a company (or individual) is unable to pay its debts. The Office of the Superintendent of Bankruptcy (OSB) administers the bankruptcy process in Canada, and it recommends that companies considering a declaration of bankruptcy first meet with a trustee in bankruptcy. The OSB website provides a link to a trustee registry of individuals licensed by the OSB to administer bankruptcies in Canada. Illustration 23-9 below provides an overview of bankruptcy and insolvency options in Canada.

As the OSB notes, companies facing bankruptcy can make a proposal to pay their creditors a percentage of what was owed at the time of the proposal, or they could request an extension to the amount of time available to pay their debts (or both). The main categories of creditors affected are:

- Secured creditors. These creditors may have a lien (a legal claim on assets to secure the payment of a debt) against all or part of a debtor's property (such as a bank with a lien on the company's inventory that acts as security or collateral for the loan).

- Preferred creditors. These creditors have the first priority when claiming any funds that are available (after, for example, the secured creditors take possession and dispose of their collateral). Preferred creditors typically include employees' claims for items such as unpaid wages.

- Unsecured creditors. These creditors do not have any security or collateral for the debts owed to them.

The proposals for businesses are considered "Division I proposals," and there is no limit to how much money might be owed under this type of proposal. Creditors vote to

BANKRUPTCY AND INSOLVENCY
at a glance

The Options

Bankruptcy

Bankruptcy is a legal process designed to relieve honest but unfortunate debtors of their debts.

At the end of the process, the bankrupt is released from the obligation to repay the debts they had when the bankruptcy was filed (with some exceptions).

Proposal

A proposal is an offer to creditors to pay a percentage of what is owed over a specific period of time, or to extend the amount of time to pay off the debt, or a combination of both. Creditors vote to accept or reject the proposal.

There are two types of proposals:

- **Consumer proposals**—available to individuals who owe less than $250,000, excluding mortgages; and

- **Division I proposals**—available to businesses and individuals (there is no limit regarding how much money is owed).

Once all the terms of the proposal are met, the debtor is legally released from the debts included in the proposal.

CCAA Proceeding

The *Companies' Creditors Arrangement Act* (CCAA) is a federal law that applies to insolvent companies owing more than $5 million.

Under the CCAA, corporations ask the court for short-term protection while they prepare an offer to creditors for some form of payment (so they can restructure their businesses and financial affairs).

CCAA proceedings are carried out under court supervision.

Source: "Bankruptcy and Insolvency At a Glance (Infographic)," Industry Canada: Office of the Superintendent of Bankruptcy Canada, http://www.ic.gc.ca/eic/site/bsf-osb.nsf/eng/br03127.html. December 2015. Reproduced with the permission of the Minister of Industry, 2016.

Illustration 23-9

Example Bankruptcy and Insolvency Options

CORPORATE LAW

accept or reject the proposal and, if the terms of the proposal are met, the debtor becomes legally released from the debts included in the proposal.

Companies can also use the Companies' Creditors Arrangement Act (CCAA), which applies to insolvent companies owing greater than $5 million. Under the CCAA, companies request that the court give them short-term protection while they prepare an offer to creditors for partial payment (or time to restructure their businesses and financial affairs). The CCAA provides court supervision during the restructuring process. The restructuring could result in a financial reorganization and fresh start accounting, as we discussed in Appendix 15B.

A receivership process is typically started by a secured creditor, or a group of secured creditors, if a company defaults on a loan. A receiver is then appointed to take possession of, or liquidate the company. A court-appointed receiver would typically act on behalf of all creditors, whereas a privately appointed receiver would act for a specific secured creditor. Usually the receiver is given full discretion regarding how the company's assets will be managed during the receivership process, including liquidating assets listed in the security agreement. A receivership and a bankruptcy could occur at the same time, and two different companies could be appointed for the roles of receiver and trustee in bankruptcy.

AUDIT AND ASSURANCE
4.3.5

A company that is in receivership, or that has made a request for protection under the CCAA, may no longer meet the going concern assumption of the conceptual framework. As we discussed in Chapter 2, the going concern assumption is based on an assessment of whether the company will be able to continue for at least 12 months from the date of the statement of financial position. If the company is not considered a going concern, a liquidation approach would likely be more appropriate for the financial statements rather than continued use of the historical cost principle.

FINANCE TREASURY MANAGEMENT
5.2.4 and 5.2.5

The risk of bankruptcy and related bankruptcy costs are taken into account in the cost of capital, and may affect companies' capital structure decisions. For example, if a company relies too heavily on debt, its risk of bankruptcy increases, as does the cost of debt financing. Investors would require a higher rate of return if the risk of bankruptcy for a company is high. While we introduce the topic here, a detailed discussion of the optimal capital structure of companies is typically covered as part of a finance course.

AUDITOR'S REPORTS

Objective 9

Identify the major disclosures found in the auditor's report.

Another important source of information that is often overlooked is the **auditor's report**. An auditor is an accounting professional who conducts an independent examination of the accounting data presented by a business enterprise. The examination follows Canadian Auditing Standards (CAS) as set out in the *CPA Canada Handbook—Assurance*. If the auditor is satisfied that the financial statements present the financial position, results of operations, and cash flows fairly in accordance with International Financial Reporting Standards (or ASPE for a private company being audited), the auditor will express an unmodified opinion, as shown in Illustration 23-10.[25]

Illustration 23-10

Example of Auditor's Report under Canadian Auditing Standards

REAL WORLD EMPHASIS

INDEPENDENT AUDITOR'S REPORT

Report on the Financial Statements

[Appropriate Addressee]

We have audited the accompanying financial statements of ABC Company, which comprise the statement of financial position as at December 31, 20X1, and the statement of comprehensive income, statement of changes in equity and statement of cash flows for the year then ended, and a summary of significant accounting policies and other explanatory information.

Management's Responsibility for the Financial Statements

Management is responsible for the preparation and fair presentation of these financial statements in accordance with International Financial Reporting Standards, and for such internal control as management determines is necessary to enable the preparation of financial statements that are free from material misstatement, whether due to fraud or error.

Auditor's Responsibility

Our responsibility is to express an opinion on these financial statements based on our audit. We conducted our audit in accordance with Canadian generally accepted auditing standards. Those standards require that we comply with ethical requirements and plan and perform the audit to obtain reasonable assurance about whether the financial statements are free from material misstatement.

An audit involves performing procedures to obtain audit evidence about the amounts and disclosures in the financial statements. The procedures selected depend on the auditor's judgment, including the assessment of the risks of material misstatement of the financial statements, whether due to fraud or error. In making those risk assessments, the auditor considers internal control relevant to the entity's preparation and fair presentation of the financial statements in order to design audit procedures that are appropriate in the circumstances, but not for the purpose of expressing an opinion on the effectiveness of the entity's internal control. An audit also includes evaluating the appropriateness of accounting policies used and the reasonableness of accounting estimates made by management, as well as evaluating the overall presentation of the financial statements.

We believe that the audit evidence we have obtained is sufficient and appropriate to provide a basis for our audit opinion.

Opinion

In our opinion, the financial statements present fairly, in all material respects, the financial position of ABC Company as at December 31, 20X1, and its financial performance and its cash flows for the year then ended in accordance with International Financial Reporting Standards.

[Auditor's signature]
[Date of the auditor's report]
[Auditor's address]

Source: ©2015. Reproduced from the *CPA Canada Handbook—Assurance*, CAS 700, Illustration 1 with permission from CPA Canada.

In preparing its report, the auditor follows procedures in accordance with the reporting standards articulated in the Canadian Auditing Standards.

Unmodified Opinions

In most cases, the auditor issues a standard **unmodified opinion**. This means that the auditor expresses the opinion that the financial statements present fairly, in all material respects, the entity's financial position, results of operations, and cash flows in conformity with generally accepted accounting principles. Certain circumstances may require the auditor to add an explanatory paragraph to the audit report.

Qualified Opinions and Disclaimers of Opinion

In some situations, the auditor is required to express a **modified opinion** in the form of a qualified opinion, disclaimer of opinion, or adverse opinion. A **qualified opinion** contains an exception to the standard opinion. Ordinarily the exception is not significant enough to invalidate the statements as a whole; if it were, an adverse opinion would be given. Usually, the auditor may deviate from the standard unmodified report on financial statements when something does not follow GAAP. An example of this is when inventories are misstated, and the misstatement is material but does not have a pervasive effect on the financial statements. Pervasive effects are those that are not confined to specific elements, items, or accounts of the financial statements (or if confined, they represent or could represent a substantial part of the financial statements). Pervasive effects related to financial statement disclosures would fundamentally affect users' understanding.

A qualified opinion states that, except for the effects of the matter related to the qualification, the financial statements present fairly, in all material respects, the financial position, the financial performance, and cash flows in conformity with generally accepted accounting principles.

A qualified opinion (or a disclaimer of opinion) might also be given where there is a scope limitation; that is, where the auditor has not been able to obtain sufficient appropriate audit evidence. This might happen if there has been an accidental destruction by fire of company records, for instance. If the effects on the financial statements could be material and pervasive, there would be a disclaimer of opinion noting that the auditor is unable to provide an opinion. If the effects of the scope limitation are material but not pervasive, the auditor would issue a qualified opinion.

Adverse Opinions

AUDIT AND ASSURANCE
4.3.3, 4.3.10 and 4.3.11

An **adverse opinion** is required in any report in which the exceptions to fair presentation are so material and pervasive that in the independent auditor's judgement, a qualified opinion is not justified. In such a case, the financial statements taken as a whole are not presented in accordance with GAAP. Adverse opinions are rare, because most enterprises change their accounting to conform to the auditor's requirements rather than receive an adverse opinion.

FINANCIAL STATEMENT ANALYSIS

An Overview of Financial Statement Analysis

Objective 10
Describe methods used for basic financial statement analysis and summarize the limitations of ratio analysis.

FINANCIAL ANALYSIS AND PLANNING
5.1.1

In prior chapters, starting with Chapter 4, we discussed financial statement analysis and ratios as they applied to the specific topics from each chapter. In Chapter 5 (Appendix 5A), we also provided a summary of key ratios used in the text. In this section we provide a summary of the various aspects of financial statement analysis previously discussed, and provide an overview of some additional techniques of financial statement analysis.

An awareness of the particular accounting policies and methods used by a company to recognize items and measure amounts reported is important for interpreting and understanding the results of financial statement analysis. Examples of areas in which companies may choose different accounting policies include the capitalization or expensing of the interest related to financing asset construction (under ASPE), the method for amortizing long-lived assets, the costing of inventory, and the method used to recognize revenue on long-term contracts. The particular choice can have a significant effect on whether items and amounts are reported, how they are measured, where they are reported, and trends over time for a given company. Also, if the financial statement analysis involves intercompany comparison, we must consider the use of different policies by the companies.

Within this general context, we can obtain specific information from financial statements by examining relationships between items on the statements and identifying trends in these relationships. Relationships are expressed numerically in ratios and percentages, and trends are identified through horizontal and trend analysis.

Several limitations should be considered when analyzing financial statements. For example, **financial statements report on the past**. As such, analysis of financial statement data is largely an examination of the past. Whenever such information is incorporated into a decision-making process, a critical assumption is that the past is a reasonable basis for predicting the future. This is usually a reasonable approach, but you should recognize this limitation.

Also, **while ratio and trend analyses will help identify strengths and weaknesses of a company, such analyses will not likely reveal why things are as they are**. Ratios and trends may serve as "red flags" to indicate problem areas. Finding answers about "why" usually requires an in-depth analysis and an awareness of many factors about a company that are not reported in the financial statements; for instance, the impact of inflation, actions of competitors, technological developments, or a strike at a major supplier's or buyer's business.

Another consideration with financial statement analysis is that a **single ratio, by itself, is not likely to be very useful**. For example, a current ratio of 2:1 (current assets are twice current liabilities) may be viewed as satisfactory. If, however, the industry average is 3:1, such a conclusion may be questioned. With industry benchmarking, you may conclude that the particular company is doing well if the ratio last year was 1.5:1. Consequently, to derive meaning from ratios, some standard against which to compare them is needed. Such a standard may come from benchmarking against industry averages, past years' amounts, a particular competitor, or planned levels.

Finally, **awareness of the limitations of accounting numbers used in an analysis** is important. For example, the implications of different acceptable accounting policies on statements, ratios, and trends, particularly regarding comparability among companies and between a company and an industry average, must be recognized. We will say more about limitations and their consequences later in this chapter.

Financial Statement Analysis Techniques

Various techniques are used in the analysis of financial statement data.[26] These **include ratio analysis, common-size analysis, trend analysis, and examination of related data** (that is, in notes and other sources). No one technique is more useful than another. Situations faced by analysts are different, and the answers needed are often obtained only on close examination of the interrelationships among all the data provided.

Ratio Analysis

Ratio analysis is a starting point in developing information desired by an analyst. A **ratio is simply an expression of the relationship between two numbers** drawn or derived from the financial statements. Ratios can be classified as shown in Illustration 23-11 (and as previously discussed in Appendix 5A).

Illustration 23-11	
Major Types of Ratios	**MAJOR TYPES OF RATIOS**

Liquidity ratios. Measure the enterprise's short-term ability to pay its maturing obligations.
Activity ratios. Measure how effectively the enterprise is using its assets. Activity ratios also measure how liquid certain assets like inventory and receivables are; in other words, how fast the asset's value is realized by the company.
Profitability ratios. Measure financial performance and shareholder value creation for a specific time period.
Coverage or solvency ratios. Measure the degree of protection for long-term creditors and investors or a company's ability to meet its long-term obligations.

Generally, the liquidity ratios and coverage ratios reflect financial strength: the ability to satisfy the financial requirements of non-ownership interests in the business. Assessing management's performance is a prime reason for examining activity and profitability ratios. From such assessment, investors formulate opinions about returns from future ownership interest. Ratios should not be evaluated in isolation. For example, trends in ratios provide an indication as to whether a company's financial position is improving (or deteriorating) over time. Also, industry benchmarking of ratios is useful for analysts to assess not only individual companies, but the industry as a whole.

The calculation and use of individual ratios has been illustrated throughout each chapter in Volume 1 and Volume 2 of the textbook. This chapter does not repeat the details of how to use and interpret each ratio, so you may wish to refer back to the discussion of the individual ratios in prior chapters and in Appendix 5A. The ratios are summarized in Illustration 23-12. The exercises and problems at the end of this chapter allow you to further consider the appropriate calculation and use of these ratios.

Illustration 23-12

A Summary of Financial Ratios

Ratio	Formula	What it Measures
I. Liquidity		
1. Current ratio	$\dfrac{\text{Current assets}}{\text{Current liabilities}}$	Short-term debt-paying ability
2. Quick or acid-test ratio	$\dfrac{\text{Cash, marketable securities, and receivables (net)}}{\text{Current liabilities}}$	Immediate short-term liquidity
3. Current cash debt coverage ratio	$\dfrac{\text{Net cash provided by operating activities}}{\text{Average current liabilities}}$	Company's ability to pay off its current liabilities in a specific year from its operations
II. Activity		
4. Receivables turnover	$\dfrac{\text{Net sales}}{\text{Average trade receivables}}$	Liquidity of receivables
5. Inventory turnover	$\dfrac{\text{Cost of goods sold}}{\text{Average inventory}}$	Liquidity of inventory
6. Asset turnover	$\dfrac{\text{Net sales}}{\text{Average total assets}}$	How efficiently assets are used to generate sales
III. Profitability		
7. Profit margin on sales	$\dfrac{\text{Net income}}{\text{Net sales}}$	Net income generated by each dollar of sales
8. Rate of return on assets	$\dfrac{\text{Net income}}{\text{Average total assets}}$	Overall profitability of assets
9. Rate of return on common share equity	$\dfrac{\text{Net income minus preferred dividends}}{\text{Average common shareholders' equity}}$	Profitability of owners' investment
10. Earnings per share	$\dfrac{\text{Net income minus preferred dividends}}{\text{Weighted average shares outstanding}}$	Net income earned on each common share
11. Price earnings ratio	$\dfrac{\text{Market price of shares}}{\text{Earnings per share}}$	Ratio of the market price per share to earnings per share
12. Payout ratio	$\dfrac{\text{Cash dividends}}{\text{Net income}}$	Percentage of earnings distributed as cash dividends
IV. Coverage		
13. Debt to total assets	$\dfrac{\text{Total debt}}{\text{Total assets}}$	Percentage of total assets provided by creditors
14. Times interest earned	$\dfrac{\text{Income before interest charges and taxes}}{\text{Interest charges}}$	Ability to meet interest payments as they come due
15. Cash debt coverage	$\dfrac{\text{Net cash provided by operating activities}}{\text{Average total liabilities}}$	Company's ability to repay its total liabilities in a specific year from its operations
16. Book value per share	$\dfrac{\text{Common shareholders' equity}}{\text{Number of common shares outstanding at SFP date}}$	Amount each share would receive if the company were liquidated at the amounts reported on the statement of financial position

**FINANCIAL
ANALYSIS AND
PLANNING**
5.1.1

Horizontal and Common-Size Analyses

Analysts also use percentage analysis to help them evaluate an enterprise. To demonstrate, Illustration 23-13 provides a percentage analysis of the change in expenses in MoreTek's income statement for the last two years. This approach, normally called **horizontal analysis**, indicates the proportionate change between years.

Illustration 23-13

Horizontal Analysis

	2017 (000s)	2016 (000s)	Difference	% Change
Cost of sales	$1,000	$850	$150	17.6
Depreciation and amortization	150	150	–0–	–0–
Selling and administrative expenses	225	150	75	50.0
Interest expense	50	25	25	100.0
Taxes	100	75	25	33.3

Another approach, called **vertical analysis**, is the proportional expression of each item on a financial statement in a given period to a base figure. For example, MoreTek's income statement using this approach with total revenue as the base figure appears in Illustration 23-14.

Illustration 23-14

Vertical Analysis

MORETEK CORPORATION **INCOME STATEMENT** **(000,000 OMITTED)**	Amount	Percentage of Total Revenue
Net sales	$1,600.0	96
Other revenue	75.0	4
Total revenue	1,675.0	100
Less:		
Cost of sales	1,000.0	60
Depreciation and amortization	150.0	9
Selling and administrative expenses	225.0	13
Interest expense	50.0	3
Income taxes	100.0	6
Total expenses	1,525.0	91
Net income	$ 150.0	9

Reducing all the dollar amounts to a percentage of a base amount is frequently called **common-size analysis** because all of the statements and all of the years are reduced to a common size; that is, all of the elements within each statement are expressed in percentages of some common number.

For the statement of financial position, common-size analysis answers such questions as: What is the distribution of financing between current liabilities, long-term debt, and owners' equity? What is the mix of assets (percentage-wise) with which the enterprise has chosen to conduct its business? What percentage of current assets is in inventory, receivables, and so forth?

The income statement lends itself to an analysis because each item in it is related to a common amount, often net sales. It is informative to know what proportion of each sales dollar is absorbed by the various costs and expenses incurred by the enterprise.

Common-size analysis may be used for comparing one company's statements over different years to detect trends not evident from the comparison of absolute amounts. Also, common-size analysis eases intercompany comparisons regardless of their size because the financial statements are put into a comparable common-size format.

Trend Analysis

Analysts and auditors also often perform trend analysis of results **over multiple years** to assess how position and performance of companies are changing over time. So for example, an evaluation of the percentage change in sales or cost of goods sold (such as was performed in Illustration 23-13, but for multiple years) is often useful to establish trends. Similarly, an evaluation of trends in ratios often provides useful information for financial analysts.

Limitations of Financial Statement Analysis

An underlying objective of decision-makers is to evaluate risk. Uncertainty is the major factor contributing to risk. Uncertainty is reduced and, therefore, awareness of risk is enhanced by decision-relevant information. We have argued that information in financial statements and ratio analysis based on this information can be decision-relevant and, consequently, useful in reducing uncertainty. Even so, a decision-maker should be aware that there are significant limitations regarding financial statement information and ratio analysis.

A research study identified the following four sources of uncertainty as being important when considering the usefulness of financial statement information to a decision-maker.[27]

1. ***Uncertainty about the nature and role of financial statements.*** Misunderstanding the nature, purpose, terminology used, and method of preparation of financial statements can lead users to misinterpret and/or place inappropriate reliance on the information.

2. ***Uncertainty about the nature of business operations portrayed in the financial statements.*** The unpredictability of business activities due to factors such as economic environment, technology, and competitors' actions causes uncertainty. Knowledge of the type of business activities carried out is important in determining the extent of the uncertainties that characterize these activities.

3. ***Uncertainty due to limitations of financial statement measurements and disclosures.*** The conceptual framework, *CPA Canada Handbook* recommendations, and accounting practices dictate that various principles be followed and methods used. Uncertainty occurs when there is recognition that the resulting measurements and disclosures are not well understood or are thought to be incomplete or to lack relevance in a particular decision context.

ETHICS

4. ***Uncertainty about management's motives and intentions.*** Management is responsible for determining the accounting policies and methods used to prepare the financial statements. Choice of a policy or method should be based on reflecting underlying economic reality. This source of uncertainty suggests, however, that users may suspect that management's choices are more motivated by a need to "manage earnings" to maximize bonuses over time, or to avoid debt covenant violations.

There are other important limitations of ratio analysis. They include the following.

(a) They are **based on historical cost,** which can lead to distortions in measuring performance.

(b) **Estimated items** (such as depreciation, site restoration costs, and bad debts) **are significant,** and ratios based on significant estimates may be less credible.

(c) **Achieving comparability among companies in a given industry may be difficult.** For example, companies often apply different accounting policies that require that an analyst identify basic differences in their accounting and adjust the balances to achieve comparability.

This section has introduced you to the basic concepts and tools for financial statement analysis. Keep in mind that there are entire courses devoted to financial statement analysis, where additional tools are discussed and illustrated.

Objective 11

Identify the major differences in accounting between IFRS and ASPE, and what changes are expected in the near future.

IFRS/ASPE Comparison

A Comparison of IFRS and ASPE

Illustration 23-15 compares the international standards with ASPE regarding other measurement and disclosure issues.

Illustration 23-15

IFRS and ASPE Comparison Chart

	IFRS—IAS 8, 10, 24, and 34; IFRS 8	Accounting Standards for Private Enterprises (ASPE)—*CPA Canada Handbook*, Part II, Sections 1100, 3820, and 3840	References to Related Illustrations and Select Brief Exercises
Disclosures	Increased level of disclosures.	Generally fewer disclosure requirements because many private entities have less-complex business transactions and stakeholders have greater access to information about the entity.	BE23-1
Accounting policies	The IASB is attempting to reduce choice in terms of accounting policies to promote comparability. Where there is a voluntary accounting change, the new policy must provide reliable and more relevant information.	Greater range of choice of policies to account for differing sizes and complexities of business entities. Entities need not meet the test of providing more relevant and reliable information in certain situations where accounting policies are changed.	
Segmented reporting	Separate information should be presented for reportable segments including information about revenues, profits and loss, and assets and liabilities. These numbers must be reconciled to reported financial statements. In addition, information about the segment products and services as well as material customers and information by geographical areas should be disclosed.	No guidance provided.	BE23-7
Interim reporting	IFRS does not mandate which entities should provide interim information; however, it provides guidance (that entities are encouraged to follow) if the entity does provide the information. If the interim report is in compliance with IFRS, this should be disclosed. Basically, each interim period is considered a discrete period. The same accounting policies should be used as for the annual financial statements.	No guidance provided.	BE23-11
Related-party transactions	IFRS only requires additional disclosures regarding related parties. It does not require remeasurement. In addition to the disclosure requirements under ASPE, management compensation, and the name of the entity's parent company as well as its ultimate controlling entity or individual are required to be disclosed.	Related-party transactions are remeasured under certain situations (basically where the transaction has no economic substance or is not measurable).	BE23-12

(continued)

	IFRS—IAS 8, 10, 24, and 34; IFRS 8	Accounting Standards for Private Enterprises (ASPE)—*CPA Canada Handbook*, Part II, Sections 1100, 3820, and 3840	References to Related Illustrations and Select Brief Exercises
Subsequent events	The subsequent event period ends when the statements are authorized for issue.	The subsequent event period ends when the statements are complete. The date is a matter of judgement, taking into account management structure and procedures followed in completing the statements.	BE23-17
Unincorporated business	IFRS does not provide guidance.	Specific guidance includes requiring the statements to define the entity and disclose salaries and other items accruing to owners. No provision is made for income taxes.	N/A

Illustration 23-15

IFRS and ASPE Comparison Chart (continued)

Looking Ahead

The IASB amended IAS 1 in December 2014 to provide additional guidance on the order of notes presented in financial statements. In addition, it clarified IAS 1.31 to highlight that materiality also applies to note disclosures (effective January 1, 2016).

Throughout this textbook, we have stressed the need to provide information that is useful to predict the amounts, timing, and uncertainty of future cash flows. To achieve this objective, judicious choices of alternative accounting concepts, methods, and means of disclosure must be made. You are probably surprised by the large number of choices among acceptable alternatives that accountants are required to make.

You should be aware, however, as Chapter 1 indicated, that accounting is greatly influenced by its environment. Because it does not exist in a vacuum, it seems unrealistic to assume that alternative presentations of certain transactions and events will be eliminated entirely. Nevertheless, we are hopeful that as the conceptual framework evolves, the profession will be able to enhance its focus on the needs of financial statement users and eliminate diversity in presentation where appropriate. The profession must continue its efforts to develop a sound foundation upon which financial standards and practice can be built.

SUMMARY OF LEARNING OBJECTIVES

1 Understand the importance of disclosure from a business perspective.

Information disclosure is important to the proper functioning of capital markets and the allocation of capital. The information provided in financial statements helps investors compare the performance of companies and assess the relative risks and returns of different investments. Financial statement preparers must keep in mind both the costs and benefits of disclosure when making their disclosure decisions. Financial statements are just one of many sources of information for investors and creditors.

2 Review the full disclosure principle and describe problems of implementation.

The full disclosure principle calls for financial reporting of any financial facts that are significant enough to influence the judgement of an informed reader. Implementing the full disclosure principle is difficult because the cost of disclosure can be substantial and the benefits difficult to assess. Disclosure requirements for public entities have increased because of (1) the growing complexity of the business environment, (2) the necessity for timely

information, and (3) the use of accounting as a control and monitoring device. For private entities, disclosure requirements are lower due to the lesser complexity of many private entities and the fact that many stakeholders of private entities have greater access to information.

3 Explain the use of accounting policy notes in financial statement preparation.

Notes are the accountant's means of amplifying or explaining the items presented in the main body of the statements. Information that is pertinent to specific financial statement items can be explained in qualitative terms, and supplementary quantitative data can be provided to expand the information in the financial statements. Accounting policy notes explain the accounting methods and policies chosen by the company, allowing greater comparability among companies.

4 Describe the disclosure requirements for major segments of a business.

If only consolidated amounts are available to the analyst, much information regarding the composition of these figures is hidden in the aggregated figures. There is no way to tell from the consolidated data how much each product line contributes to the company's profitability, risk, and growth potential. As a result, segment information is required by the profession for public entities, including general information about reportable segments; segment revenues, profit and loss, assets, liabilities, and related information; reconciliations; information about products and services; geographical area information; and information about revenues from major customers.

5 Describe the accounting problems associated with interim reporting.

Interim reports cover periods of less than one year. There are two viewpoints regarding interim reports. The discrete view holds that each interim period should be treated as a separate accounting period. In contrast, the integral view holds that the interim report is an integral part of the annual report and that deferrals and accruals should consider what will happen for the entire year. IFRS encourages the discrete view approach. The same accounting principles that are used for annual reports should generally be used for interim reports; however, there are several unique reporting problems, such as seasonality and presentation of earnings per share.

6 Discuss the accounting issues for related-party transactions.

Related-party transactions pose special accounting issues. Because the transactions are not at arm's length, they may have to be remeasured under ASPE, as the exchange value is not necessarily representative of the market or fair value. Without reliable information, the transaction may have to be remeasured to reflect historical values or carrying amounts. IFRS does not require remeasurement of related-party transactions, whereas ASPE does.

7 Identify the differences between the two types of subsequent events.

The first type of subsequent event provides additional evidence about an event that existed at the statement of financial position date. These events should be reflected in the SFP and income statement. The second type of event provides evidence about events or transactions that did not exist at the SFP date. These events should be disclosed in notes if they will have a material impact on the company's future.

8 Identify the major considerations relating to bankruptcy and receivership.

Bankruptcy is a legal process that occurs when a company (or individual) is unable to pay its debts. The Office of the Superintendent of Bankruptcy administers the bankruptcy process in Canada. Companies facing bankruptcy can make a proposal to pay their creditors a percentage of what was owed at the time of the proposal, or they could request an extension to the amount of time available to pay off their debts (or both). A receivership process is typically started by a secured creditor, or a group of secured creditors, if a company defaults on a loan. A receiver is appointed by the bankruptcy court. A receivership and a bankruptcy could occur at the same time, and two different companies could be appointed for the roles of receiver and trustee in bankruptcy.

9 Identify the major disclosures found in the auditor's report.

If the auditor is satisfied that the financial statements present the financial position, results of operations, and cash flows fairly in accordance with generally accepted accounting principles, the auditor expresses an unmodified opinion. A qualified opinion contains an exception to the standard opinion; however, the exception would not be significant enough to invalidate the statements as a whole. An adverse opinion is required in any report in which the exceptions to fair presentation are so pervasive that a qualified opinion is not justified. A disclaimer of an opinion is appropriate when the auditor has gathered insufficient information on the financial statements so that no opinion can be expressed.

10 Describe methods used for basic financial statement analysis and summarize the limitations of ratio analysis.

Various techniques are used in the analysis of financial statement data. These include ratio analysis, common-size analysis, trend analysis, and examination of related data (in notes and other sources). No one technique is always more useful than another. Every situation faced by the analyst is different, and the answers needed are often obtained only on close examination of the interrelationships among all the data provided. Ratio analysis is a starting point in developing information desired by an analyst. While the basic concepts and tools for analysis are provided, keep in mind that there are limitations inherent in individual financial statement analysis techniques. For more complex techniques, you should refer to textbooks and courses that focus extensively on financial statement analysis.

11 Identify the major differences in accounting between IFRS and ASPE, and what changes are expected in the near future.

Differences are noted in the chapter and the comparison chart in Illustration 23-15. No significant changes are expected in the near future.

KEY TERMS

Note: Completion of this end-of-chapter material will help develop CPA enabling competencies (such as ethics and professionalism, problem-solving and decision-making, and communication) and technical competencies. We have highlighted selected items with an integration icon and material in *WileyPLUS* has been linked to the competencies. All cases emphasize integration, especially of the enabling competencies. The brief exercises, exercises, and problems generally emphasize problem-solving and decision-making.

Brief Exercises

(LO 1) BE23-1   Discuss why full disclosure is essential to the proper functioning of capital markets, and why private companies following ASPE may be subject to fewer disclosure requirements.

(LO 2) BE23-2   What type of disclosure or accounting is necessary for each of the following items?

  (a) Because of a general increase in the number of labour disputes and strikes, both within and outside the industry, there is more chance that a company will suffer a costly strike in the near future.

  (b) A company reports a discontinued operation (net of tax) correctly on the income statement. No other mention is made of this item in the annual report.

  (c) A company expects to recover a substantial amount in connection with a pending refund claim for a prior year's taxes. Although the claim is being contested, the company's lawyers have confirmed that they expect their client to recover the taxes.

(LO 2, 3) BE23-3   An annual report of Maleki Enterprises Ltd. states: "The company and its subsidiaries have long-term leases expiring on various dates after December 31, 2017. Amounts payable under such commitments, without reduction for related rental income, are expected to average approximately $6,711,000 annually for the next three years. Related rental income from certain subleases to others is estimated to average $3,094,000 annually for the next three years." What information is provided by this note?

(LO 2, 3) BE23-4   An annual report of **Ford Motor Company** states: "Net income a share is computed based upon the average number of shares of capital stock of all classes outstanding. Additional shares of common stock may be issued or delivered in the future on conversion of outstanding convertible debentures, exercise of outstanding employee stock options, and for payment of defined supplemental compensation. Had such additional shares been outstanding, net income a share would have been reduced by 10¢ in the current year and 3¢ in the previous year. . . . As a result of capital stock transactions by the company during the current year (primarily the purchase of Class A Stock from Ford Foundation), net income a share was increased by 6¢." What information is provided by this note?

(LO 3) BE23-5   Uddin Industries Ltd. has had a long history of regular quarterly dividend payments to its common shareholders. The president wants Uddin's dividend policy to be mentioned in the summary of significant accounting policies note to the financial statements. Do you agree with the president? Explain.

(LO 4) BE23-6   Mahi Bai, a student of intermediate accounting, was heard to remark after a class discussion on segmented reporting: "All this is very confusing to me. First we are told that there is merit in presenting the consolidated results and now we are told that it is better to show segmented results. I wish they would make up their minds." Evaluate this comment.

(LO 4) BE23-7   Penner Corp. has seven industry segments with total revenues as follows:

	(thousands)		(thousands)
Gamma	$600	Suh	$225
Kennedy	650	Tsui	200
RGD	250	Nuhn	700
Red Moon	375		

Based only on the revenues test, which industry segments are reportable under IFRS? Which industry segments are reportable under ASPE?

(LO 4) BE23-8   Operating profits and losses for the seven industry segments of Penner Corp. are as follows:

	(thousands)		(thousands)
Gamma	$90	Suh	$(20)
Kennedy	(40)	Tsui	34
RGD	25	Nuhn	100
Red Moon	50		

Based only on the operating profit (loss) test, which industry segments are reportable under IFRS?

(LO 4) BE23-9 Assets for the seven industry segments of Penner Corp. are as follows:

	(thousands)		(thousands)
Gamma	$500	Suh	$200
Kennedy	550	Tsui	150
RGD	400	Nuhn	475
Red Moon	400		

Based only on the assets test, which industry segments are reportable under IFRS?

(LO 5) BE23-10 What are the accounting problems related to the presentation of interim data?

(LO 5) BE23-11 How does seasonality affect interim reporting and how should companies overcome the seasonality problem? Is there more of an effect on interim reporting for companies following IFRS or ASPE?

(LO 6) BE23-12 Nguyen Limited buys land from its president for $390,000 in cash, which is the land's appraised value at the time of the purchase. The land was purchased by the president 15 years ago for $65,000. (a) Assume that Nguyen follows ASPE. Prepare the journal entry to record the purchase of the land. Use the decision tree in Illustration 23-5 to explain your answer. What information should be disclosed for this transaction? (b) How would your answer to part (a) change if Nguyen were to follow IFRS?

(LO 6) BE23-13 Textile manufacturer Fibreright Corp. exchanges robotic equipment with an original cost of $20,000 and a carrying amount of $11,000 with the equipment rental company Frederick Corp. The equipment that is received in exchange from Frederick Corp. has an original cost of $35,000 and a carrying amount of $15,100, performs different functions, and has a fair value of $20,800. Both companies are 100% owned by the same individual. Because they are closely held companies, they both follow ASPE. Discuss how this transaction should be measured and prepare the journal entries for both companies to record the exchange. Use the decision tree in Illustration 23-5 to explain the reasoning for your answer.

(LO 6) BE23-14 How would the transaction in BE23-13 be recorded if it were arm's length?

(LO 6) BE23-15 How would the transaction in BE23-13 be recorded if the individual shareholder owned only 40% of the shares of each company? Assume that there is independent evidence to support the value of the robotic equipment. Discuss and prepare journal entries. Use the decision tree in Illustration 23-5 to explain the reasoning for your answer.

(LO 6) BE23-16 The following information was described in a note of Cruton Packing Co., a public company that follows IFRS: "During August, Bigelow Products Corporation purchased 212,450 shares of the Company's common shares, which constitutes approximately 35% of the shares outstanding. Bigelow has since obtained representation on the board of directors. An affiliate of Bigelow Products Corporation acts as a food broker for Cruton Packing in the Toronto marketing area. The commissions for such services after August amounted to approximately $33,000." Why is this information disclosed?

(LO 7) BE23-17 Tonoma Inc., a company that follows IFRS, is preparing its December 31, 2017 financial statements. The following two events occurred after December 31, 2017: (1) A flood loss of $80,000 occurred on March 1, 2018. (2) A liability, estimated at $140,000 at December 31, 2017, was settled on March 15, 2018 at $190,000. The statements were completed on March 10, 2018, and they were authorized for issue on March 17, 2018. (a) What effect do these subsequent events have on 2017 net income? (b) How would your answer to part (a) change if Tonoma were to follow ASPE?

(LO 7) BE23-18 What are the major types of subsequent events? Indicate how each of the following subsequent events would be reported:

(a) Collection of a note written off in a prior period

(b) Issuance of a large preferred share offering

(c) Acquisition of a company in a different industry

(d) Destruction of a major plant in a flood

(e) Death of the company's chief executive officer

(f) Additional wage costs associated with the settlement of a four-week strike

(g) Settlement of a federal income tax case at considerably more tax than was anticipated at year end

(h) Change in the product mix from consumer goods to industrial goods

(LO 8) BE23-19 **Nortel Networks** experienced one of the most notorious Canadian bankruptcies. Nortel's financial statements contained misrepresentations resulting in top executives meeting bonus targets. Eventually there was a distribution of funds obtained from selling off Nortel's assets, including intellectual property. Former Nortel employees eligible to receive pensions made up one of the major groups seeking relief from the court. Would those entitled to pension funds have been secured or unsecured creditors in the bankruptcy?

AUDIT

FINANCIAL ANALYSIS AND PLANNING

(LO 9) BE23-20 What is the difference between an auditor's unmodified opinion and a qualified opinion?

(LO 10) BE23-21 The income statements of Dwayne Corporation show the following amounts:

	2017	2016	2015
Net sales	$800	$770	$720
Cost of goods sold	560	530	468
Gross profit	240	240	252
Selling, general, and administrative expenses	200	156	115
Profit before tax	40	84	137

Using vertical (common-size) analysis, analyze Dwayne Corporation's declining profit before tax.

(LO 10) BE23-22 Condensed data from the comparative statement of financial position (SFP) of Legros Inc. follow:

	2017	2016	2015
Current assets	$120,000	$ 80,000	$100,000
Non-current assets	400,000	350,000	300,000
Current liabilities	70,000	90,000	65,000
Non-current liabilities	165,000	105,000	150,000
Common shares	150,000	115,000	100,000
Retained earnings	135,000	120,000	85,000

(a) Using vertical (common-size) analysis, calculate the various SFP categories as a percentage of total assets for Legros Inc. for each of 2015, 2016, and 2017.

(b) Using horizontal analysis, calculate the changes of the key SFP categories from 2016 to 2017.

FINANCIAL ANALYSIS AND PLANNING

(LO 10) BE23-23 Referring to the research study mentioned in this chapter (in the section "Limitations of Financial Statement Analysis"), discuss some limitations of the financial statement analysis done in BE23-21. Include in your answer some of the general limitations of ratio analysis.

(LO 10) BE23-24 Yuen Corporation shows the following financial position and results for the three years ended December 31, 2017, 2018, and 2019 (in thousands):

	2019	2018	2017
Cash	$ 650	$ 700	$ 600
FV-NI investments	500	500	500
Accounts receivable	900	1,000	1,300
Inventory	4,900	4,600	4,000
Prepaid expenses	1,300	1,000	900
Total current assets	8,250	7,800	7,300
Accounts payable	1,550	1,700	1,750
Accrued liabilities	2,250	2,000	1,900
Total current liabilities	3,800	3,700	3,650
Cost of goods sold	$15,000	$18,000	$17,000

FINANCIAL ANALYSIS AND PLANNING

For each year, calculate the current ratio, quick ratio, and days payables outstanding ratio, and comment on your results.

(LO 4, 10) BE23-25 Penner Corp. is preparing the management discussion and analysis portion of the annual report to shareholders. It wishes to provide a visual depiction of the proportion of the total revenue each segment uses. Using Excel, graph the seven industry segments of Penner Corp. listed in BE23-7 into a pie graph, labelling each segment in amount and as a percentage of the total.

Exercises

(LO 2) E23-1 (Disclosure) Cambosa Ltd. operates in an industry where the prices of merchandise purchased for resale are continuously rising. Cambosa's choice of accounting policy for inventory costing has a significant impact on its net income. Investors compare Cambosa's policy of FIFO with that of its competitors in the United States. In the United States, companies are allowed to and do use the LIFO (last-in, first-out) costing method. LIFO is not allowed under either IFRS or ASPE, and is not allowed for tax purposes in Canada. Consequently, Cambosa information is not comparable with others in the industry when assessing its financial position. To combat the problem, Cambosa's controller proposes to disclose in the accounting policies note in the notes to the financial statements an estimate of the effect on gross profit, net income, ending inventory, and retained earnings had LIFO been used since the business began.

**AUDIT &
ASSURANCE**

Instructions

You are the auditor and must respond to the controller's proposal. If you agree with the controller, include in your discussion whether or not the basis for this additional disclosure should be included in the accounting policies note. If you decide that the disclosure should not appear in the financial statement notes, suggest an alternative to the controller.

(LO 3) E23-2 (Illegal Acts) The detection and reporting of illegal acts by management or other employees is a difficult task. To fulfill their responsibilities, auditors must have a good knowledge of the client's business, including an understanding of the laws and regulations that govern the business and activities of their clients. In addition, accountants and auditors must be sensitive to factors in the company that may indicate an abnormally high risk of illegal acts by the company or its employees.

Instructions

(a) Identify some examples of illegal acts that may be committed by a company or its employees that could reasonably be expected to result in a material misstatement in the financial statements.

(b) Explain how, if at all, an undetected illegal act by a client (for example, paying bribes to secure business, or violating pollution control laws and regulations) could affect the company's financial statements.

(c) Identify some factors that could indicate that the risk of violation of laws and regulations is greater than normal and that evaluation of note disclosure, or possibly recognition, of an illegal act may be required.

(LO 3) E23-3 (Accounting Policies) Sharma Ltd., a private construction company following ASPE, is discussing with its auditor its accounting policy for the recognition of revenue in its year-end financial statements. Management's main area of contention is the requirement to estimate progress on construction contracts as of the year-end date for the percentage-of-completion method for long-term construction contracts. The Income Tax Act allows the reporting of revenue from construction contracts using the completed-contract method of revenue recognition. This method allows the reporting of gross profits earned on multi-year contracts in the taxation year when the contracts have been completed. Because the tax due on the profit of the completed contracts can be postponed, Sharma argues that most construction companies recalculate their construction revenues using the completed-contract method when filing their corporate income tax returns.

The controller explained to the auditor that the business does not need to use the percentage-of-completion method for accounting for long-term construction contracts in order to properly manage projects. Sharma's day-to-day practices allow for very strict management of costs on contracts. The controller has suggested the company get unanimous approval from all shareholders to adopt the completed-contract method for financial reporting purposes. The policy adopted could then be clearly described in the accounting policy note to the financial statements, thereby ensuring that the users of the information would not be confused by the change. The application of the policy would be done retroactively to allow for comparability between fiscal years' financial results.

AUDIT

Instructions

You are the auditor. Do you agree with the controller? Explain the basis for your answer. Would the adoption of the completed-contract method lead to a modified opinion in the auditor's report? Would your response change if Sharma were using IFRS?

(LO 4) E23-4 (Segmented Reporting) LaGraca Inc. is involved in five separate industries. The following information is available for each of the five industries:

Operating Segment	Total Revenue	Operating Profit (Loss)	Assets
A	$140,000	$25,000	$240,000
B	40,000	8,000	11,000
C	26,000	(5,000)	36,000
D	190,000	(2,000)	49,000
E	2,000	500	15,000
	$398,000	$26,500	$351,000

Instructions

Determine which of the operating segments are reportable under IFRS based on each of the following:

(a) Revenue test

(b) Operating profit (loss) test

(c) Assets test

(LO 6) E23-5   (Related-Party Transaction) Maffin Corp. owns 75% of Grey Inc. Both companies are in the mining industry. During 2017, Maffin Corp. purchased a building from Grey Inc. for $1,000. The building's original cost is $25,000 and its carrying amount in Grey Inc.'s financial statements is $700. Maffin's Contributed Surplus account contains a credit balance of $200 from previous related-party transactions. Grey's Contributed Surplus account is nil. There is no available independent evidence of the value of the building because it is a unique building in a remote part of the country. Maffin subsequently sold the building, during 2018, to an unrelated party for $1,100. Both Maffin and Grey follow ASPE.

Instructions

Using the related-party decision tree in Illustration 23-5, answer the following.

(a) How would both Maffin and Grey record the purchase and sale of the building during 2017?

(b) Record the subsequent sale of the building by Maffin during 2018.

(c) Assume that Maffin purchased the building from Grey for $500. How would your answer to part (a) change?

(d) Assume that the transaction is in the normal course of operations for both Maffin and Grey and that it has commercial substance. How would your answers to parts (a) and (b) change?

DIGGING
DEEPER

(e) Calculate the total impact on income of the purchase and sale of the building for 2017 and 2018 for the consolidated reporting unit of the two companies. What can you conclude from your calculation?

(LO 6) E23-6   (Related-Party Transaction) Verez Limited owns 90% of Consior Inc. During 2017, Verez acquired a machine from Consior in exchange for its own used machine. Both companies are in the tool-making business. The agreed exchange amount is $1,000, although the transaction is nonmonetary. Consior has an original cost of $6,000 and carries its machine on its books at a carrying amount of $700, whereas Verez has an original cost of $7,000 and carries its machine on its books at a carrying amount of $900. Neither company has a balance in the Contributed Surplus account relating to previous related-party transactions. Both Verez and Consior follow ASPE.

Instructions

Using the related-party decision tree in Illustration 23-5, prepare the journal entries to record the exchange for both Verez and Consior under the following assumptions.

(a) The transaction is not in the normal course of operations for either company, and the transaction has commercial substance.

(b) The transaction is not in the normal course of operations for either company, and the transaction does not have commercial substance.

(c) The transaction is in the normal course of operations for each company, and the transaction has commercial substance.

(d) The transaction is in the normal course of operations for each company, and the transaction does not have commercial substance.

(e) Briefly explain how your answers to parts (a) through (d) would change if both companies were to follow IFRS.

(LO 7) E23-7   (Subsequent Events) Jason Corporation completed, its board of directors authorized, and it issued its financial statements following IFRS for the year ended December 31, 2017 on March 10, 2018. The following events took place in early 2018.

1. On January 30, 19,000 common shares were issued at $45 per share.

DIGGING
DEEPER

2. On March 1, Jason determined after negotiations with the Canada Revenue Agency that income tax payable for 2017 should be $1.2 million. At December 31, 2017, income tax payable was recorded at $1 million.

Instructions

(a) Discuss how these subsequent events should be reflected in the 2017 financial statements.

(b) The controller of Jason Corporation believes that the income tax payable as at December 31, 2017 should not be increased to $1.2 million, because the original estimate of $1 million was based on the information available at the time of accrual, and recorded in good faith. The controller feels that the revised estimate of $1.2 million should be treated prospectively as a change in estimate. Do you agree or disagree with the controller's proposed accounting treatment of the income tax payable as at December 31, 2017? Discuss your conclusion from the perspective of investors.

(c) Would your answers for parts (a) and (b) differ if Jason Corporation had been following ASPE?

(LO 7) E23-8   (Subsequent Events) The following are subsequent (post–statement of financial position) events.

___ **1.** Settlement of a federal tax case at a cost considerably higher than the amount expected at year end

___ **2.** Introduction of a new product line

___ **3.** Loss of an assembly plant due to fire

___ **4.** Sale of a significant portion of the company's assets

___ **5.** Retirement of the company president

___ **6.** Prolonged employee strike

___ **7.** Loss of a significant customer

___ **8.** Issuance of a significant number of common shares

___ **9.** Material loss on a year-end receivable because of a customer's bankruptcy

___**10.** Hiring of a new president

___**11.** Settlement of a prior year's litigation against the company for an amount less than the amount accrued

___**12.** Merger with another company of similar size

Instructions

For each of the above events, indicate whether the company should

(a) adjust the financial statements,

(b) disclose the event in notes to the financial statements, or

(c) neither adjust nor disclose.

(LO 8, 9) E23-9 (Receivership and Bankruptcy) Dedrisan Inc. has experienced an unusually large loss from which it is very unlikely to recover. It is in default on some debt covenants. The auditor of the company concludes that Dedrisan is no longer a going concern. Management has requested the auditor issue an auditor's report on the financial statements for the current year. The financial statements have been prepared using the historical cost principle and do not reflect any adjustments to the assets or any disclosure of the loan defaults. The auditor informs Dedrisan that under the current financial statement presentation, an adverse audit opinion would be issued. Without the necessary adjustments and disclosure, the financial statements taken as a whole are not in accordance with GAAP. Once issued, the adverse opinion could lead to the bankruptcy of Dedrisan Inc.

AUDIT

Instructions

What measures, if any, can Dedrisan Inc. take to obtain an unmodified opinion from the auditor?

(LO 3, 9) E23-10 (Auditor's Report) Canadian law firms typically use a partnership structure. The Income Tax Act allows law firms the reporting of revenue when invoices are remitted to clients, as opposed to when the work is performed and the revenue is earned. This provision in the Act allows for a delay in the recognition of revenue. Consequently, the law firms opt to use a modified accrual method of revenue recognition as an accounting policy for financial reporting. Work-in-process records account for the hours worked at the hourly rate of the professional who has done the work on the matter. At the time of billing, careful scrutiny is applied to ensure reasonableness of the amount of time spent for the work product delivered to the client. Work in process is often written down at the time of billing. By adopting this modified accrual method for revenue recognition, there is no need to adjust the value of work in process at its realizable value at year end. Under this method, no work in process is reported on the statement of financial position, as allowed in the Act. This method is particularly a time saver when dealing with multi-year litigation matters or personal injury cases. Because GAAP is not being followed for revenue recognition, the auditor's opinion must be modified to a qualified opinion for non-adherence to GAAP with respect to revenue recognition.

AUDIT

Instructions

(a) How would creditors react to the qualified opinion expressed in the auditor's report?

(b) Can financial results for revenue be comparable from year to year? Why or why not? How can management assess revenue trends when using this modified accrual method?

(LO 10) E23-11 (Percentage Analysis) The financial statements of Mackay Corporation show the following information:

MACKAY CORPORATION
Statement of Financial Position
December 31, 2017

Assets	2017	2016
Cash	$ 285,000	$ 292,000
Accounts receivable	142,000	181,000
Fair value through net income investments	133,000	132,000
Inventory	355,000	401,000
Plant assets (net)	442,000	465,000
Intangible assets	113,000	143,000
	$1,470,000	$1,614,000

(continued)

MACKAY CORPORATION
Statement of Financial Position
December 31, 2017 (*Continued*)

Liabilities and Equity	2017	2016
Accounts payable	$ 267,000	$ 337,000
Long-term debt	64,000	152,000
Share capital	326,000	326,000
Retained earnings	813,000	799,000
	$1,470,000	$1,614,000

MACKAY CORPORATION
Income Statement
Year Ended December 31, 2017

	2017	2016
Net sales	$ 805,000	$781,000
Cost of goods sold	527,000	530,000
Gross profit	278,000	251,000
Selling, general, and administrative expenses	140,000	111,000
Other expenses, net	118,000	110,000
Income before income tax	20,000	30,000
Income tax	6,000	9,000
Net income	$ 14,000	$ 21,000

**FINANCIAL
ANALYSIS AND
PLANNING**

Instructions

(a) Using horizontal analysis, analyze Mackay Corporation's change in liquidity, solvency, and profitability in 2017.

(b) Using vertical analysis, analyze Mackay Corporation's decline in net income in 2017.

(c) Which profitability ratios are obtained from the vertical analysis performed in part (b)? Is profitability improving or deteriorating based on these ratios?

(d) Referring to the research study mentioned in this chapter (in the section "Limitations of Financial Statement Analysis"), discuss some limitations of the financial statement analysis done in parts (a) and (b).

(LO 10) E23-12 (Percentage Analysis) The condensed statements of changes in financial position and detailed income statement information for Tran Consulting Ltd. follow. Tran contracts professionals in the electronic data management field and provides services to clients around the globe.

Assets	2017	2016	2015
Cash	$ 1,200	$ 790	$ 660
Accounts receivable	3,800	2,850	2,270
Equipment (net)	5,700	4,800	3,900
Goodwill	2,125	1,385	1,385
	$12,825	$9,825	$8,215
Liabilities and Equity			
Accounts payable	$ 1,850	$1,350	$1,080
Long-term debt	7,100	6,200	5,400
Share capital	1,300	1,000	1,000
Retained earnings	2,575	1,275	735
	$12,825	$9,825	$8,215

	2017	2016	2015
Service revenue	$10,900	$8,150	$6,500
Contract labour	5,990	4,500	3,600
	4,910	3,650	2,900
Administrative expenses	930	790	600
Travel expenses	630	580	400
Marketing expense	210	230	180
Depreciation expense	100	90	75
Other expenses	60	40	45
Total expenses	1,930	1,730	1,300

	2017	2016	2015
Income from operations	2,980	1,920	1,600
Interest expense	410	300	290
Income before taxes	2,570	1,620	1,310
Income taxes	1,100	700	550
Net income	$ 1,470	$ 920	$ 760

**FINANCIAL
ANALYSIS AND
PLANNING**

Instructions

(a) Using Excel, perform vertical analysis for all three years showing statement of financial position amounts as a percentage of each year's total assets and showing statement of income amounts as a percentage of service revenue of each year.

(b) Using Excel, perform horizontal analysis comparing 2017 with 2016 balances to highlight major areas of change.

(c) Comment on a minimum of five key financial relationships and trends you see based on the analysis you have performed for Tran's consulting business.

(LO 3, 10) E23-13 (Percentage Analysis) Tarzwell Limited is preparing some analysis of past financial performance and positions to include in the management discussion and analysis (MD&A) portion of the annual report to shareholders. You have suggested that it would be useful for users of the MD&A to include a trend analysis of key balances. You have asked your assistant to analyze the proportion of the percentage increase in each year's sales compared with the percentage change in net income and in total assets over the last five fiscal years. The following table provides amounts reported on the last five years' financial statements that will be used in the analysis.

**FINANCIAL
ANALYSIS AND
PLANNING**

	2013	2014	2015	2016	2017
Sales	$5,700	$6,500	$8,150	$10,900	$12,600
Net income	640	760	920	1,140	1,380
Total assets	7,820	8,440	9,525	11,625	13,740

Instructions

Calculate the percentage change in each of the three elements for each year. Graph the results using an Excel bar chart.

(LO 3, 10) E23-14 (Ratio Analysis) The following information (in $000) has been obtained from Patinka Limited's financial statements for the fiscal years ended December 31.

	2017	2016	2015
Total assets	$735	$590	$514
Current liabilities	85	80	82
Total liabilities	240	165	170
Total shareholders' equity	495	425	399
Income before taxes	90	62	57
Interest expense	10	6	5
Net cash provided by operating activities	119	102	96
Net income	72	50	46
Number of common shares outstanding	70	70	70
Taken from stock market at Dec. 31			
Market price per share (not in $000)	$ 16.50	$ 12.41	$ 11.80

There are no preferred shares issued by Patinka.

**FINANCIAL
ANALYSIS AND
PLANNING**

5.1.1

Instructions

(a) Calculate the following items for Patinka Limited.

1. Current cash debt coverage ratio for fiscal years 2016 and 2017.

2. Cash debt coverage ratio for fiscal years 2016 and 2017.

3. Earnings per share for fiscal years 2016 and 2017.

4. Price earnings ratio for fiscal years 2016 and 2017.

5. Times interest earned ratio for fiscal years 2016 and 2017.

(b) Comment on whether there has been improvement or deterioration from 2016 to 2017 in the five ratios calculated. Take the perspective of Patinka's management.

(c) Would your answer in part (b) change if you were looking at the results from the perspective of an investor?

(LO 10) E23-15 · **(Analysis of Given Ratios)** Robbins Ltd. is a wholesale distributor of professional equipment and supplies. The company's sales have averaged about $900,000 annually for the three-year period 2015–2017. The firm's total assets at the end of 2014 amounted to $850,000. The president of Robbins Ltd. has asked the controller to prepare a report that summarizes the financial aspects of the company's operations for the past three years. This report will be presented to the board of directors at their next meeting. In addition to comparative financial statements, the controller has decided to present a number of relevant financial ratios that can help with identifying and interpreting trends. At the request of the controller, the accounting staff has calculated the following ratios for the 2015–2017 period:

	2015	2016	2017
Current ratio	1.80	1.89	1.96
Acid-test (quick) ratio	1.04	0.99	0.87
Accounts receivable turnover	8.75	7.71	6.42
Inventory turnover	4.91	4.32	3.72
Debt to total assets	51.0%	46.0%	41.0%
Long-term debt to total assets	31.0%	27.0%	24.0%
Sales to fixed assets (fixed asset turnover)	1.58	1.69	1.79
Sales as a percent of 2015 sales	1.00	1.03	1.05
Gross margin percentage	36.0%	35.1%	34.6%
Net income to sales (profit margin)	6.9%	7.0%	7.2%
Return on total assets	7.7%	7.7%	7.8%
Return on equity	13.6%	13.1%	12.7%

In preparation of the report, the controller has decided first to examine the financial ratios independent of any other data to determine if the ratios themselves reveal any significant trends over the three-year period.

Instructions

FINANCIAL ANALYSIS AND PLANNING

(a) The current ratio is increasing while the acid-test (quick) ratio is decreasing. Using the ratios provided, identify and explain the contributing factor(s) for this apparently divergent trend.

(b) In terms of the ratios provided, what conclusion(s) can be drawn regarding the company's use of financial leverage during the 2015–2017 period?

(c) Using the ratios provided, what conclusion(s) can be drawn regarding the company's net investment in plant and equipment?

(d) Using the activity ratios provided for inventory and accounts receivable, comment on the effectiveness of working capital management.

Problems

DIGGING DEEPER

P23-1   Franklin Corporation is a diversified company that operates in five different industries: A, B, C, D, and E. The following information relating to each segment is available for 2017. Sales of segments B and C included intersegment sales of $20,000 and $100,000, respectively.

	A	B	C	D	E
Sales	$40,000	$ 80,000	$580,000	$35,000	$55,000
Cost of goods sold	19,000	50,000	270,000	19,000	30,000
Operating expenses	10,000	40,000	235,000	12,000	18,000
Total expenses	29,000	90,000	505,000	31,000	48,000
Operating profit (loss)	$11,000	$ (10,000)	$ 75,000	$ 4,000	$ 7,000
Assets	$35,000	$ 60,000	$500,000	$65,000	$50,000
Liabilities	$22,000	$ 31,000	$443,000	$12,000	$29,000

Instructions

DIGGING DEEPER

(a) Determine which of the segments are reportable under IFRS based on each of the following:

1. Revenue test

2. Operating profit (loss) test

3. Assets test

(b) Prepare the necessary disclosures.

(c) The corporation's accountant recently commented, "If I have to disclose our segments individually, the only people who will gain are our competitors and the only people who will lose are our present shareholders." Evaluate this comment.

P23-2 In an examination of Daniel Corporation Ltd. as of December 31, 2017, you have learned that the following situations exist. No entries have been made in the accounting records for these items. Daniel follows IFRS.

1. The corporation erected its present factory building in 1999. Depreciation was calculated by the straight-line method, using an estimated life of 35 years. Early in 2017, the board of directors conducted a careful survey and estimated that the factory building had a remaining useful life of 25 years as of January 1, 2017.

2. An additional assessment of 2016 income tax was levied and paid in 2017.

3. When calculating the accrual for officers' salaries at December 31, 2017, it was discovered that the accrual for officers' salaries for December 31, 2016 had been overstated.

4. On December 15, 2017, Daniel Corporation Ltd. declared a stock dividend of 1,000 common shares per 100,000 of its common shares outstanding, distributable February 1, 2018 to the common shareholders of record on December 31, 2017.

5. Daniel Corporation Ltd., which is on a calendar-year basis, changed its inventory method as of January 1, 2017. The inventory for December 31, 2016 was costed by the average method, and the inventory for December 31, 2017 was costed by the FIFO method. Daniel is changing its inventory method because it would result in reliable and more relevant information.

6. Daniel has guaranteed the payment of interest on the 20-year first mortgage bonds of Bonbee Inc., an affiliate. Outstanding bonds of Bonbee Inc. amount to $150,000 with interest payable at 6% per annum, due June 1 and December 1 of each year. The bonds were issued by Bonbee Inc. on December 1, 2013, and the company has met all interest payments except for the payment due December 1, 2017. Daniel states that it will pay the defaulted interest to the bondholders on January 15, 2018.

7. During 2017, Daniel Corporation Ltd. was named as a defendant in a lawsuit for damages by Anand Shahid Corporation for breach of contract. The case was decided in favour of Anand Shahid Corporation, which was awarded $80,000 damages. At the time of the audit, the case was under appeal to a higher court.

Instructions

(a) Describe fully how each item should be reported in the financial statements of Daniel Corporation Ltd. for the year 2017.

(b) Determine if any of the treatment given under IFRS in part (a) would be different if ASPE had been used.

P23-3 Your firm has been engaged to examine the financial statements of Samson Corporation for the year 2017. The bookkeeper who maintains the financial records has prepared all the unaudited financial statements for the corporation since its organization on January 2, 2011. The client provides you with the information that follows:

SAMSON CORPORATION
Statement of Financial Position
As of December 31, 2017

Assets		Liabilities	
Current assets	$1,881,100	Current liabilities	$ 962,400
Other assets	5,121,900	Long-term liabilities	1,390,000
	$7,003,000	Capital	4,650,600
			$ 7,003,000

An analysis of current assets discloses the following:

Cash (restricted in the amount of $400,000 for plant expansion)	$ 571,000
Investments in land for speculation	185,000
Accounts receivable less allowance of $30,000	480,000
Inventories (FIFO cost determination)	645,100
	$ 1,881,100

Other assets include:

Prepaid expenses	$ 47,400
Plant and equipment less accumulated depreciation of $1,430,000	4,130,000
Cash surrender value of life insurance policy	84,000
Notes receivable (short-term)	162,300
Goodwill	252,000
Land	446,200
	$ 5,121,900

(continued)

SAMSON CORPORATION
Statement of Financial Position
As of December 31, 2017 (*Continued*)

Current liabilities include:		
Accounts payable	$	510,000
Notes payable (due 2019)		157,400
Estimated income taxes payable		145,000
Premium on common shares		150,000
	$	962,400
Long-term liabilities include:		
Unearned revenue	$	489,500
Dividends payable (cash)		200,000
8% bonds payable (due May 1, 2022)		700,500
	$	1,390,000
Capital includes:		
Retained earnings	$	2,810,600
Common shares; unlimited authorized, 184,000 issued		1,840,000
	$	4,650,600

The following supplementary information is also provided:

1. On May 1, 2017, the corporation issued at 93.4, $750,000 of bonds to finance plant expansion. The long-term bond agreement provided for the annual payment of interest every May 1. The existing plant was pledged as security for the loan. The bookkeeper has not made any entry for interest in 2017. Use the effective interest method for discount amortization.

2. The bookkeeper made the following mistakes:

   (a) In 2015, the ending inventory was overstated by $183,000. The ending inventories for 2016 and 2017 were correctly calculated.

   (b) In 2017, accrued wages in the amount of $275,000 were omitted from the statement of financial position and these expenses were not charged on the income statement.

   (c) In 2017, a gain of $175,000 (net of tax) on the sale of certain plant assets was credited directly to retained earnings.

3. A major competitor has introduced a line of products that will compete directly with Samson's primary line, which is now being produced in a specially designed new plant. Because of manufacturing innovations, the competitor's line will be of similar quality but priced 50% below Samson's line. The competitor announced its new line on January 14, 2018. Samson indicates that the company will meet the lower prices; the lower prices are still high enough to cover Samson's variable manufacturing and selling expenses, but will permit only partial recovery of fixed costs.

4. You learned on January 28, 2018, prior to completion of the audit, of heavy damage from a recent fire at one of Samson's two plants and that the loss will not be reimbursed by insurance. The newspapers described the event in detail.

5. The bookkeeper informs you that Samson Corporation has been having some difficulty in collecting on several of its accounts receivable. For this reason, the bad debt expense percentage used was changed from 1.5% to 2.5% of sales. The controller estimates that if the new rate had been used in the past, an additional $40,000 worth of expense would have been charged. The bad debt expense for 2017 was calculated using the new rate of 2.5% of sales.

Instructions

(a) Analyze the above information to prepare a corrected statement of financial position for Samson in accordance with IFRS. Prepare a description of any notes that might need to be prepared. The books are closed and adjustments to income are to be made through retained earnings. Ignore the effects of income taxes, unless otherwise stated.

DIGGING DEEPER

(b) "The financial statements of a company are management's responsibility, not the auditor's." Discuss the implications of this statement.

P23-4   Radiohead Inc. produces electronic components for sale to manufacturers of radios, television sets, and digital sound systems. In connection with her examination of Radiohead's financial statements for the year ended December 31, 2017, Marg Zajic, CPA, completed fieldwork two weeks ago. Ms. Zajic now is evaluating the significance of the following items prior to preparing her auditor's report. Except as noted, none of these items has been disclosed in the financial statements or notes.

Item 1

A 10-year loan agreement that the company entered into three years ago provides that, subsequent to the date of the agreement, dividend payments may not exceed net income earned. The balance of retained earnings at the date of the loan agreement was $420,000. From that date through December 31, 2017, net income has totalled $570,000 and cash dividends have totalled $320,000. Based on these data, the staff auditor who was assigned to this review concluded that there was no retained earnings restriction at December 31, 2017.

Item 2

Recently, Radiohead interrupted its policy of paying cash dividends quarterly to its shareholders. Dividends were paid regularly through 2016, discontinued for all of 2017 to finance the purchase of equipment for the company's new plant, and resumed in the first quarter of 2018. In the annual report, dividend policy is to be discussed in the president's letter to shareholders.

Item 3

A major electronics firm has introduced a line of products that will compete directly with Radiohead's primary line, which is now being produced in Radiohead's specially designed new plant. Because of manufacturing innovations, the competitor's line will be of similar quality but priced 50% below Radiohead's line. The competitor announced its new line during the week following the completion of Ms. Zajic's fieldwork. Ms. Zajic read the announcement in the newspaper and discussed the situation by telephone with Radiohead executives. Radiohead will meet the lower prices because they are still high enough to cover variable manufacturing and selling expenses, although they will permit only partial recovery of fixed costs.

Item 4

Radiohead operates in a new manufacturing plant, which cost $2.4 million and has an estimated life of 25 years, and is leased from ANS Tooling Inc. at an annual rental of $600,000. Radiohead is obligated to pay property tax, insurance, and maintenance. At the end of its 10-year non-cancellable lease, Radiohead has the option of purchasing the property

AUDIT for $1. In Radiohead's income statement, the rent expense is reported on a separate line.

Instructions

For each of the items, discuss any additional disclosures in the financial statements and notes that the auditor should recommend to her client. The client follows IFRS. (Do not consider the cumulative effect of the four items.)

P23-5   You have completed your audit of Khim Inc. and its consolidated subsidiaries for the year ended December 31, 2017, and are satisfied with the results of your examination. You have examined the financial statements of Khim for the past three years. The corporation follows IFRS and is now preparing its annual report to shareholders. The report will include the consolidated financial statements of Khim and its subsidiaries, and your auditor's report. During your audit, the following matters came to your attention.

1. A vice-president who is also a shareholder resigned on December 31, 2017 after an argument with the president. The vice-president is soliciting proxies from shareholders and expects to obtain enough proxies to gain control of the board of directors so that a new president will be appointed. The president plans to have a note prepared that would include information of the upcoming proxy fight, management's accomplishments over the years, and an appeal by management for the support of shareholders.

2. The corporation decides in 2017 to adopt the straight-line method of depreciation for plant equipment. The change had been adopted to better represent the pattern of benefit provided by these assets. The straight-line method will be used for new acquisitions and for previously acquired plant equipment that was being depreciated on an accelerated basis.

3. The Canada Revenue Agency is currently examining the corporation's 2015 federal income tax return. It is questioning the amount of a deduction claimed by the corporation's domestic subsidiary for a loss sustained in 2015. The examination is still in process, and any additional tax liability cannot be determined at this time. Management, along with the corporation's tax lawyer, believe that there will be no substantial additional tax liability.

4. One of Khim's wholly owned subsidiaries, Row Inc., has been involved in bribing customers to induce them to sign long-term contracts for future product deliveries. The matter has been investigated by the RCMP, and charges against Row's vice-president of marketing and the controller are pending. Legal counsel for the subsidiary has been involved since the matter began in the middle of the current fiscal year. The RCMP took possession of Row's correspondence files and some of the accounting records to establish its case. Khim Inc. has guarantees in place for Row's bank loans because Row has experienced a series of losses in the past five years. Under the circumstances, should Row's key employees be found guilty, the possibility of Row continuing as a going concern is extremely unlikely and the company will most certainly go into bankruptcy. Although Khim is an unsecured creditor, as the parent company, it will want to remove itself from any future involvement with Row and would be willing to walk away from its investment. Consequently, the loss of reputation and other adverse consequences that could arise from convictions would be directed to the bankrupt company, Row Inc. Based on the evidence uncovered, Row's legal counsel has concluded that the likelihood that the charges will hold up in court is extremely high. No accounting or legal action has yet been taken by Khim in the matter.

**AUDIT &
ASSURANCE**

Instructions

(a) Prepare the notes, if any, that you would suggest for each of the items.

(b) For each item that you decided did not require note disclosure, explain your reasons for not making the disclosure.

P23-6   The following excerpt is from the financial statements of **H. J. Heinz Company** and provides segmented geographic data:

The company is engaged principally in one line of business—processed food products—that represents more than 90% of consolidated sales. Information about the company business by geographic area is presented in the table on the next page.

There were no material amounts of sales or transfers between geographic areas or between affiliates, and no material amounts of United States export sales.

| | | | | Foreign | | | |
(in thousands of U.S. dollars)	Domestic	United Kingdom	Canada	Western Europe	Other	Total	Worldwide
Sales	$2,381,054	$547,527	$216,726	$383,784	$209,354	$1,357,391	$3,738,445
Operating income	246,780	61,282	34,146	29,146	25,111	149,685	396,465
Identifiable assets	1,362,152	265,218	112,620	294,732	143,971	816,541	2,178,693
Capital expenditures	72,712	12,262	13,790	8,253	4,368	38,673	111,385
Depreciation expense	42,279	8,364	3,592	6,355	3,606	21,917	64,196

Instructions

(a) Why does H. J. Heinz not prepare segment information on its products or services?

(b) Why are revenues by geographic area important to disclose?

P23-7   Three independent situations follow.

Situation 1

A company received a notice from the provincial environment ministry that a site the company had been using to dispose of waste was considered toxic, and that the company would be held responsible for its cleanup under provincial legislation. Company engineers believe it would take up to three years to determine the best way to remediate the site and that the cost would be considerable, perhaps as much as $500,000 to $2 million or more.

Situation 2

Subsequent to the date of a set of financial statements, but before the date of authorization by the board of directors for issuing the financial statements, a company enters into a contract that will probably result in a significant loss to the company. The loss amount can be reasonably estimated.

Situation 3

A company has adopted a policy of recording self-insurance for any possible losses resulting from injury to others by the company's vehicles. The premium for an insurance policy for the same risk from an independent insurance company would have an annual cost of $4,000. During the period covered by the financial statements, there were no accidents involving the company's vehicles that resulted in injury to others.

Instructions

(a) Discuss the accrual or type of disclosure that is necessary under ASPE (if any) and the reason(s) why the disclosure is appropriate for each of the three independent situations.

(b) For situation 2, assume instead that the contract is a non-cancellable purchase contract that was entered into before the date of the financial statements. Discuss the accrual or type of disclosure that would be recorded under ASPE (if any). Provide support for the accrual or disclosure from the perspective of a user of the financial statements.

DIGGING DEEPER

P23-8   Leopard Corporation is currently preparing its annual financial statements for the fiscal year ended April 30, 2017, following IFRS. The company manufactures plastic, glass, and paper containers for sale to food and drink manufacturers and distributors. Leopard maintains separate control accounts for its raw materials, work-in-process, and finished goods inventories for each of the three types of containers. The inventories are valued at the lower of cost and net realizable value.

The company's property, plant, and equipment are classified in the following major categories: land, office buildings, furniture and fixtures, manufacturing facilities, manufacturing equipment, and leasehold improvements. All fixed assets are carried at cost. The depreciation methods that are used depend on the type of asset (its classification) and when it was acquired.

Leopard plans to present the inventory and fixed asset amounts in its April 30, 2017 statement of financial position as follows:

Inventory	$4,814,200
Property, plant, and equipment (net of depreciation)	$6,310,000

DIGGING DEEPER

Instructions

(a) What information regarding inventory and property, plant, and equipment must be disclosed by Leopard Corporation in the audited financial statements issued to shareholders, either in the body or the notes, for the 2016–17 fiscal year?

(b) Leopard Corporation's controller believes that to comply with the full disclosure principle, as much information as possible should be provided in the note disclosures, including, for example, the name of the supplier that each asset was purchased from and the current location of each asset. Comment on the usefulness of these additional disclosures from the perspective of a user of the financial statements.

(CMA adapted)

P23-9 You are compiling the consolidated financial statements for Vu Corporation International (VCI), a public company. The corporation's accountant, Timothy Chow, has provided you with the following segment information.

Note 7: Major Segments of Business

VCI conducts funeral service and cemetery operations in Canada and the United States. Substantially all revenues of VCI's major segments of business are from unaffiliated customers. Segment information for fiscal 2017, 2016, and 2015, follows:

				(thousands)			
	Funeral	Floral	Cemetery	Corporate	Catering	Limousine	Consolidated
Revenues:							
2017	$302,000	$10,000	$ 83,000	$ -0-	$7,000	$14,000	$416,000
2016	245,000	6,000	61,000	-0-	4,000	8,000	324,000
2015	208,000	3,000	42,000	-0-	1,000	6,000	260,000
Operating income:							
2017	$ 79,000	$ 1,500	$ 18,000	$(36,000)	$ 500	$14,000	$ 65,000
2016	64,000	200	12,000	(28,000)	200	8,000	48,800
2015	54,000	150	6,000	(21,000)	100	6,000	39,600
Capital expenditures:							
2017	$ 26,000	$ 1,000	$ 9,000	$ 400	$ 300	$ 1,000	$ 37,700
2016	28,000	2,000	60,000	1,500	100	700	92,300
2015	14,000	25	8,000	600	25	50	22,700
Depreciation and amortization:							
2017	$ 13,000	$ 100	$ 2,400	$ 1,400	$ 100	$ 200	$ 17,200
2016	10,000	50	1,400	700	50	100	12,300
2015	8,000	25	1,000	600	25	50	9,700
Identifiable assets:							
2017	$334,000	$ 1,500	$162,000	$114,000	$ 500	$ 8,000	$620,000
2016	322,000	1,000	144,000	52,000	1,000	6,000	526,000
2015	223,000	500	78,000	34,000	500	3,500	339,500
Liabilities:							
2017	$222,000	$ 1,230	$132,000	$ 99,000	$ 340	$ 6,000	$460,570
2016	209,000	900	119,000	74,000	750	4,100	407,750
2015	121,000	350	56,000	27,000	320	2,400	207,070

Instructions

Determine which of the segments must be reported separately and which can be combined under the category "Other." Then write a one-page memo to the company's accountant, Timothy Chow, that explains all of the following:

(a) Which segments must be reported separately and which ones can be combined

(b) Which criteria you used to determine the reportable segments

(c) What major items must be disclosed for each segment

P23-10 At December 31, 2017, Bouvier Corp. has assets of $10 million, liabilities of $6 million, common shares of $2 million (representing 2 million common shares of $1.00 par), and retained earnings of $2 million. Net sales for the year 2017 were $18 million, and net income was $800,000. As one of the auditors of this company, you are making a review of subsequent events on February 13, 2018, and you find the following.

1. On February 3, 2018, one of Bouvier's customers declared bankruptcy. At December 31, 2017, this company owed Bouvier $300,000, of which $40,000 was paid in January 2018.

2. On January 18, 2018, one of the client's three major plants burned. Bouvier has fire insurance coverage.

3. On January 23, 2018, a strike was called at one of Bouvier's largest plants and it halted 30% of production. As of today (February 13), the strike has not been settled.

4. A major electronics enterprise has introduced a line of products that would compete directly with Bouvier's primary line, now being produced in a specially designed new plant. Because of manufacturing innovations, the competitor has been able to achieve quality similar to that of Bouvier's products, but at a price 30% lower. Bouvier officials say they will meet the lower prices, which are barely high enough to cover variable and fixed manufacturing and selling costs.

5. Merchandise traded in the open market is recorded in the company's records at $1.40 per unit on December 31, 2017. This price held for two weeks after the release of an official market report that predicted vastly excessive

supplies; however, no purchases were made at $1.40. The price throughout the preceding year had been about $2.00, which was the level experienced over several years. On January 18, 2018, the price returned to $2.00 after public disclosure of an error in the official calculations of the prior December—the correction erased the expectations of excessive supplies. Inventory at December 31, 2017 was on a lower of cost or net realizable value basis.

6. On February 1, 2018, the board of directors adopted a resolution to accept the offer of an investment banker to guarantee the marketing of $1.2 million of preferred shares.

7. The company owns equity investments classified as current assets accounted for using the fair value through net income model. The investments have been adjusted to fair value as of December 31, 2017. On January 21, 2018, the annual report of one of the investment companies has been issued for its year ended November 30, 2017. The investee company did not meet its earnings forecasts and the market price of the investment has dropped from $49 per share at December 31, 2017 to $27 per share on January 21, 2018.

Instructions

For each event, state how it will affect the 2017 financial statements, if at all. The company follows IFRS.

P23-11 Bradburn Corporation was formed five years ago through an initial public offering (IPO) of common shares. Daniel Brown, who owns 15% of the common shares, was one of the organizers of Bradburn and is its current president. The company has been successful, but it is currently experiencing a shortage of funds. On June 10, 2017, Daniel Brown approached the Hibernia Bank, asking for a 24-month extension on two $35,000 notes, which are due on June 30, 2017 and September 30, 2017. Another note of $6,000 is due on March 31, 2018, but he expects no difficulty in paying this note on its due date. Brown explained that Bradburn's cash flow problems are due primarily to the company's desire to finance a $300,000 plant expansion over the next two fiscal years through internally generated funds. The commercial loan officer of Hibernia Bank requested financial reports for the last two fiscal years. These reports are reproduced below.

BRADBURN CORPORATION
Statement of Financial Position
March 31

	2017	2016
Assets		
Cash	$ 18,200	$ 12,500
Notes receivable	148,000	132,000
Accounts receivable (net)	131,800	125,500
Inventories (at cost)	105,000	50,000
Plant and equipment (net of depreciation)	1,449,000	1,420,500
Total assets	$1,852,000	$1,740,500
Equity and Liabilities		
Share capital—common (130,000 shares issued)	$1,300,000	$1,300,000
Retained earnings (note 1)	388,000	282,000
Accrued liabilities	9,000	6,000
Notes payable (current)	76,000	61,500
Accounts payable	79,000	91,000
Total equity and liabilities	$1,852,000	$1,740,500

Note 1: Cash dividends were paid at the rate of $1 per share in fiscal year 2016 and $2 per share in fiscal year 2017.

BRADBURN CORPORATION
Income Statement
For the Fiscal Years Ended March 31

	2017	2016
Sales	$3,000,000	$2,700,000
Cost of goods sold (note 2)	1,530,000	1,425,000
Gross margin	$1,470,000	$1,275,000
Operating expenses	860,000	780,000
Income before income tax	$ 610,000	$ 495,000
Income tax (30%)	183,000	148,500
Net income	$ 427,000	$ 346,500

Note 2: Depreciation charges on the plant and equipment of $100,000 and $102,500 for fiscal years ended March 31, 2016 and 2017, respectively, are included in cost of goods sold.

Instructions

(a) Calculate the following items for Bradburn Corporation.

1. Current ratio for fiscal years 2016 and 2017.

FINANCIAL ANALYSIS AND PLANNING

2. Quick (acid-test) ratio for fiscal years 2016 and 2017.

3. Receivables turnover for fiscal year 2017.

4. Inventory turnover for fiscal year 2017.

5. Asset turnover for fiscal year 2017.

6. Gross profit percentage for fiscal years 2016 and 2017.

7. Profit margin on sales for fiscal years 2016 and 2017.

8. Return on assets for fiscal years 2016 and 2017. (Assume total assets were $1,688,500 at March 31, 2015.)

9. Return on common share equity for fiscal years 2016 and 2017. (Assume total equity was $1,499,000 at March 31, 2015.)

10. Earnings per share for fiscal years 2016 and 2017.

11. Payout ratio for fiscal years 2016 and 2017.

12. Debt to total assets for fiscal years 2016 and 2017.

13. Book value per shares for fiscal years 2016 and 2017.

14. Percentage change in sales, cost of goods sold, gross margin, and net income after tax from fiscal year 2016 to 2017.

(b) Identify and explain what other financial reports and/or financial analyses might be helpful to the commercial loan officer of Hibernia Bank in evaluating Daniel Brown's request for a time extension on Bradburn's notes.

(c) Assume that the percentage changes experienced in fiscal year 2017 as compared with fiscal year 2016 for sales and cost of goods sold will be repeated in each of the next two years. Is Bradburn's desire to finance the plant expansion from internally generated funds realistic? Discuss.

(d) Should Hibernia Bank grant the extension on Bradburn's notes considering Daniel Brown's statement about financing the plant expansion through internally generated funds? Discuss.

Case

Refer to the Case Primer on the Student Website and in *WileyPLUS* to help you answer this case.

ENABLING COMPETENCIES

CA23-1 In June 2018, the board of directors for Holtzman Enterprises Inc. authorized the sale of $10 million of corporate bonds. Michelle Collins, treasurer for Holtzman Enterprises Inc., is concerned about the date when the bonds are issued. The company really needs the cash, but she is worried that if the bonds are issued before the company's year end (December 31,

2018), the additional liability will have an adverse effect on several important ratios. In July, she explains to company president Kenneth Holtzman that if they delay issuing the bonds until after December 31, the bonds will not affect the ratios until December 31, 2019. They will have to report the issuance as a subsequent event, which requires only footnote disclosure. Collins predicts that with expected improved financial performance in 2018, the ratios should be better.

FINANCIAL ANALYSIS AND PLANNING

Instructions

Adopt the role of Michelle Collins and discuss any issues relating to the timing of the planned bond issuance. The company's shares trade on the local stock exchange.

Integrated Cases

ENABLING COMPETENCIES

IC23-1 Penron Limited is in the energy business, buying and selling gas and oil and related derivatives. It is a public company whose shares are widely held. It underwent a tremendous expansion over the past decade, and revenues quadrupled and continue to climb. Executives are remunerated using stock options, and the employee pension plan invests heavily in the company's stock. It is currently October 2017. The year end is December 31, 2017. Many of the benefit plans of the top executives vest at the end of the year. (That is, the executives will have legal entitlement to the benefits even if they leave

the company.) As a matter of fact, there is a concern that several of these top executives will announce that they plan to leave the company right after the year-end financial statements are released.

Penron was seen as a "hot stock" by the marketplace. Numerous analysts followed the stock carefully and had been advising their clients to buy the stock as long as revenues and profits kept increasing. The third-quarter results had shown steadily increasing revenues and profits. The company had been signalling that this trend would continue through the fourth quarter.

During the fourth quarter, Penron sold some of its pipelines to LPL Corporation. The pipelines had not been in use for some time and were seen as non-essential assets. Over the past two years, Penron has steadily been divesting itself of non-essential assets. Penron had not written the pipelines down in the financial statements because it was able to sell them and recover twice their cost. This one deal was responsible for substantially all of the fourth-quarter profits. Under the terms of the deal, the pipelines were sold for $15 million cash.

LPL Corporation was owned by the president of Penron. The company had been established just before the pipeline deal was signed. Since LPL was a new company and otherwise had very few assets, it borrowed the money for the deal from the bank. The bank had requested that Penron guarantee the loan, which it did.

During the year, Penron issued Class A shares to certain company executives. The shares participate in the earnings of the entity much like the common shares of the company. (That is, dividends accrue to the shareholders out of the residual earnings after the preferred dividends have been paid.) They are mandatorily redeemable if a triggering event occurs, such as the resignation or termination of the shareholder. The shares are otherwise similar to common shares in that they have no preferential rights.

During the year, the company also began planning for development of a new website that will allow customers to transact with the company. A significant amount of time was spent in this planning phase to determine the feasibility and desirability of this type of customer interface. Toward the end of the year, after lengthy discussion, the company began to acquire software and hardware to facilitate the new website. A large amount was spent on the site's graphic design and on its content.

Instructions

AUDIT   Assume the role of Penron's auditors and discuss the financial reporting issues for the year ended December 31, 2017.

IC23-2   Frangipani Ltd. (FL) is a new company that has just started up in January 2017. The company is the brainchild of Frank Frangi, who is working on developing a new process for a solar-powered car. To date, most of the year has been taken up with setting up the lab and working on the problem of how to power the vehicle using solar energy. The work has been financed equally by a government-sponsored bank loan and Frank's own personal capital, which he contributed to the company in return for 100% of the common shares upon incorporation. In addition, FL sold preferred shares to family members who are anxious to see how the project (and their investment) is progressing. Frank originally thought to take a salary from the company but has not yet done so this year due to the tight cash flow situation. FL has five scientists working for it. Instead of salary, the scientists have been awarded share appreciation rights that are settleable in cash or a variable number of shares at the option of the company.

Under the terms of the government-sponsored loan:

- FL must report to the government annually on its progress, including its ability to continue to operate;
- FL must maintain a debt to equity ratio of 1:1; and
- the debt is forgivable if FL generates the new process within three years. The government will instead take back preferred shares.

The preferred shares have the following characteristics:

- they are redeemable at the option of the company for common shares, and

- they are redeemable at the option of the holder (in cash) if the company does not make a profit this year.

During the year, FL has been selling advertising space on the company website. Frank is very interested in programming and has created a website that attracts a significant amount of traffic. The website includes several scientific and environmental blogs that many scientists and interested parties contribute to. As a matter of fact, many scientists help each other with practical and theoretical research questions. Since FL continually needs funds to further the work on the solar-powered vehicle, the advertising fees are paid upfront. FL has a clause in the advertising agreement that states the fees are non-refundable. In addition, the advertising fees are stipulated as being for one month's worth of advertising although it is commonly understood that FL displays the advertising for a year. At the end of November 2017, a significant amount of advertising dollars were received.

Frank and the scientists working on the car really feel that they have made significant breakthroughs this year and are close to reaching their goal and submitting the technology for patenting. On December 31, 2017, FL received a call from the company's patent lawyers stating that someone has already filed a patent for the technology that FL is developing. Frank was very angry to learn that it was one of the scientists who contributes to the FL blogs. Apparently someone had leaked critical information about the FL technology in an on-line discussion and the idea had been stolen. Frank has already contacted his friend who is a litigation lawyer and is confident he can prove the theft of the intellectual capital.

Instructions

Assume the role of FL's accountant and discuss the financial reporting issues for the year ended December 31, 2017. The company follows ASPE.

RESEARCH AND ANALYSIS

RA23-1   Air Canada and British Airways plc

REAL WORLD EMPHASIS

Access the annual report for **Air Canada** for its December 31, 2014 fiscal year end from SEDAR or the company's website (www.aircanada.com). Also, access the annual report for the year ended December 31, 2014 for **British Airways plc** from the company's parent website (www.iagshares.com).

Instructions

(a) What specific items do the airlines discuss in their accounting policies notes? (Prepare a list of the headings only.)

(b) Note the similarities and differences in regard to these notes. Comment on these and relate them to the nature of the two businesses.

(c) For what lines of business or segments do the companies present segmented information? What information is provided by segment? Which note disclosure is most useful and why?

(d) Note and comment on the similarities and differences between the auditors' reports submitted by the independent auditors.

AUDITING

RA23-2   Thomson Reuters Corporation

REAL WORLD EMPHASIS

Access the annual report, including the audited financial statements, of **Thomson Reuters Corporation** for the year ended December 31, 2014 from SEDAR (www.sedar.com) or from the company's website (www.thomsonreuters.com).

Instructions

(a) What related-party transactions did the company engage in during the year?

(b) Is the related-party disclosure adequate or is there missing information? Is this information useful?

(c) What subsequent events did the company report? What is the cut-off date that has been used (that is, the date of approval of the financial statements by the directors)?

(d) In the management discussion and analysis (MD&A) provided by management in the annual report: (1) identify the key sections indicating the type of information included, and (2) locate the sections dealing with related-party transactions and with subsequent events, and compare the disclosures with those in the notes to the financial statements. Comment.

RA23-3   Nestlé SA

REAL WORLD EMPHASIS

Access IAS 34 (*Interim Financial Reporting*), and the interim financial report for the six-month period ended June 30, 2015, for **Nestlé SA** from the company's website (www.nestle.com).

Instructions

(a) Identify what specific financial statements and the dates for each that are required by IAS 34 for interim financial reports. Refer to Nestlé's six-month report, and indicate the periods and dates of the financial statements that the company has provided for each of the required statements. Comment on whether the company has met all the requirements.

(b) On what basis have Nestlé's interim statements been prepared? Summarize the type of information disclosed in Note 1 for accounting policies.

(c) Describe the nature of information provided in the other notes.

(d) Is this information audited?

RA23-4   Reporting Interim Expenses

J. J. Kersee Corporation, a Canadian publicly traded company, is currently preparing the interim financial data that it will issue to its shareholders and the securities commission at the end of the first quarter of its December 31, 2017 fiscal year. Kersee's financial accounting department has compiled the following summarized revenue and expense data for the first quarter of the year:

Sales	$60,000,000
Cost of goods sold	36,000,000
Variable selling expenses	2,000,000
Fixed selling expenses	1,500,000

In the first quarter, the company spent $2 million for television advertisements as a lump sum payment for the entire year. Because the company believes that it will receive a benefit for the entire year for this expenditure, it has included only one quarter ($500,000) in the fixed selling expenses. Also, included in inventory is an unfavourable price variance of $245,000 that has been deferred because management anticipates that this will reverse before the third quarter is complete.

Instructions

(a) Explain whether Kersee should report its operating results for the quarter as if the quarter were an entirely separate reporting period or as if the quarter were an integral part of the annual reporting period.

(b) Indicate the amount of the sales, cost of goods sold, and fixed selling expenses that would be reflected in Kersee Corporation's quarterly report prepared for the first quarter of the 2017 fiscal year. Justify your presentation with reference to IAS 34 requirements.

(c) What financial information, at a minimum, must Kersee Corporation disclose to its shareholders in its quarterly reports?

(CMA adapted)

RA23-5   Interim Reporting—Recognition and Measurement

The following statement is an excerpt from a document on interim financial reporting:

> Interim financial information is essential to provide investors and others with timely information about the progress of the enterprise. The usefulness of such information rests on the relationship that it has to the annual results of operations. Accordingly, the Board has concluded that each interim period should be viewed primarily as an integral part of an annual period.
>
> In general, the results for each interim period should be based on the accounting principles and practices used by an enterprise in the preparation of its latest annual financial statements unless a change in an accounting practice or policy has been adopted in the current year. The Board has concluded, however, that certain accounting principles and practices followed for annual reporting purposes may require modification at interim reporting dates so that the reported results for the interim period may better relate to the results of operations for the annual period.

Instructions

Listed below are eight independent cases about accounting situations that might need to be reported on an individual company's interim financial reports. For each case, state whether the method that is proposed for interim reporting would be acceptable under IFRS for interim financial reporting. Support each answer with a brief explanation.

(a) Khan Limited takes a physical inventory at year end for annual financial statement purposes. Inventory and cost of sales reported in the interim quarterly statements are based on estimated gross profit rates because a physical inventory would require a stoppage of operations. The company does have reliable perpetual inventory records.

(b) Bonnyman Limited is planning to report one fourth of its pension expense each quarter. In the current period, the company had a significant settlement and has also pro-rated this cost over the remaining months to the end of the fiscal year.

(c) Liam Corp. wrote inventory down to reflect lower of cost or market in the first quarter. At year end, the market exceeds the original acquisition cost of this inventory. Consequently, management plans to write the inventory back up to its original cost as a year-end adjustment.

(d) Whynot Corp. realized a large gain on the sale of investments at the beginning of the second quarter. The company wants to report one third of the gain in each of the remaining quarters.

(e) Wang Limited has estimated its annual audit fee. It plans to pro-rate this expense equally over all four quarters.

(f) Neilly Inc. was reasonably certain that it would have an employee strike in the third quarter. As a result, it shipped heavily during the second quarter but plans to defer the recognition of the sales in excess of the normal sales volume. The deferred sales will be recognized as sales in the third quarter when the strike is in progress. Neilly management thinks this better represents normal second- and third-quarter operations.

(g) At the end of the second quarter, Ruggles Inc. had reported an impairment loss on its goodwill related to the real estate division. At year end, this goodwill value has now increased to the amount it was prior to the write down and the company plans to reverse this goodwill impairment loss because it is still all in the current year.

(h) Zhao Corp. has a bonus plan whereby the employees will earn a bonus of 10% of the company's net income if the price of the company's share reaches a target price by the fiscal year end, which is December 31, 2017. It is now June 30, 2017, and the share price has been reached. Consequently, the company has accrued 10% of the reported net earnings for the interim period.

RA23-6   Going Concern?

REAL WORLD EMPHASIS

AUDIT

Locate the 2015 audited annual financial statements of a company that may be experiencing financial difficulties, such as a pharmaceutical company still primarily in the research and development stage. One such company is **Antibe Therapeutics Inc.**, a Canadian company traded on the TSX Venture Exchange and on the U.S. OTCQX Exchange.

Instructions

(a) Identify the name of the company, the business it is in, and what accounting standards are used in presenting its financial statements.

(b) Briefly assess the company's liquidity, activity, profitability, and solvency using ratio analysis. Explain whether the ratios were useful in coming to conclusions about the company's health.

(c) Did the auditor express an unmodified opinion on the company's 2015 fiscal year-end financial statements? Comment. Is the company a going concern? On what does the continuation of the company depend?

(d) What is the primary measurement basis used in the preparation of the financial statements? Suggest what items on the statement of financial position would likely be measured differently if the company were not a going concern. Be specific, suggesting a different measurement basis that would be preferred. Explain briefly.

RA23-7 IFRS Global Reach

The trustees of the IFRS Foundation reiterated and confirmed the organization's vision in their 2012 Strategy Review Report:

> We remain committed to the belief that a single set of International Financial Reporting Standards (IFRS) is in the best interests of the global economy, and that any divergence from a single set of standards, once transition to IFRS is complete, can undermine confidence in financial reporting.

Paul Pacter, in his 2015 article "The global reach of IFRS is expanding" on the IFRS website (www.ifrs.org/Features/Pages/Global-reach-of-IFRS-is-expanding.aspx), provides a snapshot of the extent to which the international standards are being used by jurisdictions around the world.

Instructions

Locate this and other articles, if necessary, using them to respond to the following questions:

(a) Explain the extent to which IFRS standards were being used in 2015, separately identifying whether their use was concentrated in specific areas of the world.

(b) Explain the difference between adoption of IFRS and convergence with IFRS.

(c) Provide a summary of what position has been taken by the following countries regarding the adoption of IFRS: China, the United States, Japan, India, and Saudi Arabia.

ENDNOTES

[1] See "Disclosure Documents," Ontario Securities Commission, at www.osc.gov.on.ca/en/Investors_disclosure-requirements_index.htm.

[2] When European Union countries switched to IFRS from their national GAAP in 2005, it was felt that the required disclosures increased by 30%. (See Rafik Greiss and Simon Sharp, "IFRS Conversions: What CFOs Need to Know and Do," Toronto: CICA, 2008.)

[3] It is generally felt that disclosure requirements under ASPE should be approximately 40% to 50% less than under prior Canadian GAAP. (See "Private Matters" by Jeff Buckstein, *CA Magazine*, May 2009.)

[4] *CPA Canada Handbook—Assurance*, Section 5136.03 and CAS 450.

[5] IFRS 8.1. Copyright © International Financial Reporting Standards Foundation. All rights reserved. Reproduced by John Wiley & Sons Canada, Ltd with the permission of the International Financial Reporting Standards Foundation®. Reproduction and use rights are strictly limited. No permission granted to third parties to reproduce or distribute.

[6] IFRS 8.7. Copyright © International Financial Reporting Standards Foundation. All rights reserved. Reproduced by John Wiley & Sons Canada, Ltd with the permission of the International Financial Reporting Standards Foundation®. Reproduction and use rights are strictly limited. No permission granted to third parties to reproduce or distribute.

[7] IFRS 8.5. Copyright © International Financial Reporting Standards Foundation. All rights reserved. Reproduced by John Wiley & Sons Canada, Ltd with the permission of the International Financial Reporting Standards Foundation®. Reproduction and use rights are strictly limited. No permission granted to third parties to reproduce or distribute.

[8] IFRS 8.12 and .13. Copyright © 2015 IFRS Foundation. All rights reserved. Reproduced by John Wiley & Sons Canada, Ltd with the permission of the International Financial Reporting Standards Foundation®. Reproduction and use rights are strictly limited. No permission granted to third parties to reproduce or distribute.

[9] IFRS 8.13–.15. Copyright © International Financial Reporting Standards Foundation. All rights reserved. Reproduced by John Wiley & Sons Canada, Ltd with the permission of the International Financial Reporting Standards Foundation®. Reproduction and use rights are strictly limited. No permission granted to third parties to reproduce or distribute.

[10] IFRS 8.19. Copyright © International Financial Reporting Standards Foundation. All rights reserved. Reproduced by John Wiley & Sons Canada, Ltd with the permission of the International Financial Reporting Standards Foundation®. Reproduction and use rights are strictly limited. No permission granted to third parties to reproduce or distribute.

[11] IFRS 8.22, .23, .27, .28 and .31–.34. Copyright © International Financial Reporting Standards Foundation. All rights reserved. Reproduced by John Wiley & Sons Canada, Ltd with the permission of the International Financial Reporting Standards Foundation®. Reproduction and use rights are strictly limited. No permission granted to third parties to reproduce or distribute.

[12] IAS 34.8. Copyright © International Financial Reporting Standards Foundation. All rights reserved. Reproduced by John Wiley & Sons Canada, Ltd with the permission of the International Financial Reporting Standards Foundation®. Reproduction and use rights are strictly limited. No permission granted to third parties to reproduce or distribute.

[13] IAS 34.20. Copyright © International Financial Reporting Standards Foundation. All rights reserved. Reproduced by John Wiley & Sons Canada, Ltd with the permission of the International Financial Reporting Standards Foundation®. Reproduction and use rights are strictly limited. No permission granted to third parties to reproduce or distribute.

[14] IAS 34.11 and 11A. Copyright © International Financial Reporting Standards Foundation. All rights reserved. Reproduced by John Wiley & Sons Canada, Ltd with the permission of the International Financial Reporting Standards Foundation®. Reproduction and use rights are strictly limited. No permission granted to third parties to reproduce or distribute.

[15] IAS 34.16A and 34.19. Copyright © International Financial Reporting Standards Foundation. All rights reserved. Reproduced by John Wiley & Sons Canada, Ltd with the permission of the International Financial Reporting Standards Foundation®.

Reproduction and use rights are strictly limited. No permission granted to third parties to reproduce or distribute.

[16] IAS 34.43. Copyright © International Financial Reporting Standards Foundation. All rights reserved. Reproduced by John Wiley & Sons Canada, Ltd with the permission of the International Financial Reporting Standards Foundation®. Reproduction and use rights are strictly limited. No permission granted to third parties to reproduce or distribute.

[17] Section 7060 was issued for interim periods beginning on or after December 15, 2014, replacing the former Section 7050 with the same name *CPA Canada Handbook—Assurance*.

[18] A step in this direction is the OSC's mandate for companies to file their financial statements electronically through SEDAR (similar to the SEC requirement to use EDGAR in the United States). SEDAR provides interested parties with computer access to financial information such as annual reports, corporate prospectuses, material change reports, and proxy materials.

[19] *CPA Canada Handbook—Accounting*, Part II, Section 3840.04, and IAS 24.9.

[20] *CPA Canada Handbook—Accounting*, Part II, Section 3840.51.

[21] *CPA Canada Handbook—Accounting*, Part II, Section 3840.09.

[22] *CPA Canada Handbook—Accounting*, Part II, Section 3840 DT.

[23] As a benchmark, a substantive change in ownership may be deemed to have occurred if an unrelated party has gained or given up at least 20% interest in the exchanged items (*CPA Handbook—Accounting*, Part II, Section 3840.35). In the example, if the controlling shareholder only owned, say, 70% of both companies and the shares were publicly traded, then one might argue that a substantive change in ownership may be evident. That is, the other 30% of the shareholders now own (indirectly, through their shareholdings) part of the asset where they did not before the transaction. This is not so clear-cut, however, since the majority shareholders still have a controlling interest, and no real bargaining would have happened between the noncontrolling interest shareholders and the majority shareholders. The resolution of this issue would be a matter of judgement.

[24] *CPA Canada Handbook—Accounting*, Part II, Section 3840.03.

[25] See Canadian Auditing Standards for details (CAS 700 – *Forming an Opinion and Reporting on Financial Statements*).

[26] *Using Ratios and Graphics in Financial Reporting*, CICA Research Study (Toronto: CICA, 1993).

[27] J. E. Boritz, *Approaches to Dealing with Risk and Uncertainty*, pp. 44–45. CICA Research Report (Toronto: CICA, 1990).

Cumulative Coverage and Task-Based Simulation: Chapters 19 to 23

TAX

Templates to complete this task-based simulation are available in WileyPLUS and on the instructor website.

Eastern Publishers Ltd (EPL) is preparing its December 31, 2017 year-end financial statements. EPL focuses on corporate clients by binding and publishing corporate directories, policy manuals, and other large documents along with publishing short novels and books. This is the first year of operations, and a preliminary estimate of pre-tax net income has been calculated as follows:

Revenue	$5,278,500
Cost of goods sold	2,216,970
Gross margin	3,061,530
Operating costs	
Advertising	75,485
Amortization	250,000
Bank charges	15,500
Contracted services	17,500
Lease expense	14,525
Meals and entertainment	78,000
Repairs	25,000
Supplies	57,250
Telephone	12,500
Travel	7,850
Utilities	254,800
Warranty	37,500
Wages and benefits	275,000
Total operating costs	1,120,910
Pre-tax net income	$1,940,620

You are working in EPL's accounting department and have been asked to prepare a preliminary estimate of the income tax expense. The current tax expense will not be paid until the next fiscal year. The controller of EPL provides you with the following few notes to help you get started:

- The amortization expense relates to a new machine that was acquired on January 1, 2017 for $5 million and has a useful life of 20 years. This machinery is included as class 43 (30%) for CCA purposes. Note that the half-year rule is in effect for tax purposes.

- EPL provides an assurance-type warranty on its book binding for corporate clients. Corporate clients can return their binds over a two-year period if the glue breaks down. No books have been returned for rebinding during 2017; however, estimated expenses have been recognized in the current year.

- The lease expense is related to a 3D printer that is being leased for two years for $14,525 per year. The printer has an expected useful life of five years. There is no provision in the lease that would allow EPL to purchase the printer. If purchased, the printer would cost $150,000.

EPL has an average tax rate of 35% and an incremental borrowing rate of 10%. EPL has adopted IFRS and uses existing IAS 17 lease standards.

Instructions

(a) In the table below, indicate whether the lease for the 3D printer satisfies any of the criteria listed for finance lease classification under IAS 17 (see Appendix 20B for details). The implicit rate embedded in the lease is equal to EPL's incremental borrowing rate.

	Met	Not Met	Not Determinable
Economic life test			
Recoverability test			
Specialized asset test			
Ownership transfer test			

(b) In the table below, indicate the impact on the 3D printer lease classification based on the changes in key assumptions.

Changes in Key Assumptions	Operating Lease	Financing Lease	Not Determinable
EPL can purchase the lease at the end of the two years for $50,000, which reflects its expected market value.			
The implicit rate in the lease is 14% and is known to EPL.			
The useful life of the printer is two years.			

(c) In the table below, indicate whether each revenue and expense line item identified is a temporary difference (taxable or deductible), permanent difference, or not a difference between GAAP and the Income Tax Act.

	Taxable Temporary Difference	Deductible Temporary Difference	Permanent Difference	Not a Difference
Lease expense				
Amortization				
Meals and entertainment				
Warranty				

(d) Calculate the current and deferred tax expense for EPL. Be sure to review the details of the pre-tax income calculation and the additional information provided by the controller to determine reversible and permanent differences.

(e) In the table below, indicate the impact of the following items on the presentation of EPL's operating cash flows in the statement of cash flows assuming that the indirect method has been adopted.

	Add Back	Deduction	No Impact
Amortization expense			
Warranty			
Gain on sale of asset			
Meals and entertainment expense			

(f) In the table below, indicate where the items would be located on the statement of cash flows assuming that the direct method is used for operating activities.

	Operating	Investing	Financing	Not Presented
Amortization expense				
Current tax expense				
Lease expense				
Gain on sale of asset				

(g) Assume that the wages and benefits expense includes a $5,000 expense related to a defined contribution pension plan for a key manager. The $5,000 was determined as 10% of the key manager's earnings. In the table below, indicate whether certain information discovered in March 2018 would be considered a change in policy, change in estimate, or accounting error.

New Information	Change in Policy	Change in Estimate	Accounting Error
Pension contribution is increased to 15% of total wages. The key manager is given credit for the past three years of service.			
The pension contribution was calculated based on the key manager's 2017 annual salary of $50,000. The manager was also paid a discretionary bonus of $1,000 in 2017.			

(h) Assume that the new information revealed in March 2018 is during the subsequent events period. In the table below, indicate how the information should be treated in the 2017 year-end financial statements.

New Information	Note Disclosure	Recognition in Financial Statements	No Impact
Pension contribution is increased to 15% of total wages. The key manager is given credit for the past three years of service.			
The pension contribution was calculated based on the key manager's annual salary of $50,000. The manager was also paid a discretionary bonus of $1,000.			

APPENDIX

SPECIMEN FINANCIAL STATEMENTS

Brookfield Asset Management

The following pages contain the financial statements, selected notes, and other information from the 2014 annual financial statements of Brookfield Asset Management. The complete annual report is available on *WileyPLUS* and the student website. The corporate profile below is taken from the company annual report.

PART 1 – OVERVIEW AND OUTLOOK

OUR BUSINESS

Brookfield is a global alternative asset manager with over $200 billion in assets under management. For more than 100 years we have owned and operated assets on behalf of shareholders and clients with a focus on property, renewable energy, infrastructure and private equity.

We manage a wide range of investment funds and other entities that enable institutional and retail clients to invest in these assets. We earn asset management income including fees, carried interests and other forms of performance income for doing so. As at December 31, 2014, our managed funds and listed partnerships represented $89 billion of invested and committed fee bearing capital. These products include publicly listed partnerships that are listed on major stock exchanges as well as private institutional partnerships that are available to accredited investors, typically pension funds, endowments and other institutional investors. We also manage portfolios of listed securities through a series of segregated accounts and mutual funds.

We align our interests with clients' by investing alongside them and have $27 billion of capital invested in our listed partnerships and private funds, based on IFRS carrying values.

Our business model is simple: (i) raise pools of capital from ourselves and clients that target attractive investment strategies, (ii) utilize our global reach to identify and acquire high-quality assets at favourable valuations, (iii) finance them on a long-term basis, (iv) enhance the cash flows and values of these assets through our operating platforms to earn reliable, attractive long-term total returns, and (v) realize capital from asset sales or refinancings when opportunities arise.

Organization Structure

Our operations are organized into five principal groups ("operating platforms"). Our property, renewable energy, infrastructure and private equity platforms are responsible for operating the assets owned by our various funds and investee companies. The equity capital invested in these assets is provided by a series of listed partnerships and private funds which are managed by us and are funded with capital from ourselves and our clients. A fifth group operates our public markets business, which manages portfolios of listed securities on behalf of clients.

We have formed a large capitalization listed partnership entity in each of our property, renewable energy and infrastructure groups, which serves as the primary vehicle through which we invest in each respective segment. As well as owning assets directly, these partnerships serve as the cornerstone investors in our private funds, alongside capital committed by institutional investors. This approach enables us to attract a broad range of public and private investment capital and the ability to match our various investment strategies with the most appropriate form of capital. Our private equity business is conducted primarily through private funds with capital provided by institutions and ourselves.

Our balance sheet capital is invested primarily in our three flagship listed partnerships, Brookfield Property Partners L.P. ("BPY" or "Brookfield Property Partners"); Brookfield Renewable Energy Partners L.P. ("BREP" or "Brookfield Renewable Energy Partners"); and Brookfield Infrastructure Partners L.P. ("BIP" or "Brookfield Infrastructure Partners"), our private equity funds, and in several directly held investments and businesses.

The following chart is a condensed version of our organizational structure:

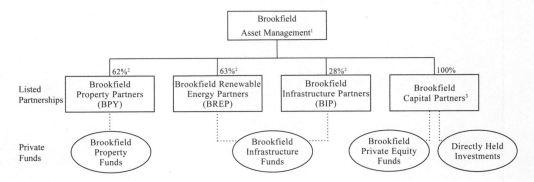

1. Includes asset management and corporate activities
2. Economic ownership interest, see page 34 for further details
3. Privately held, includes private equity, residential development and service activities

MANAGEMENT'S RESPONSIBILITY FOR THE FINANCIAL STATEMENTS

The accompanying consolidated financial statements and other financial information in this Annual Report have been prepared by the company's management which is responsible for their integrity, consistency, objectivity and reliability. To fulfill this responsibility, the company maintains policies, procedures and systems of internal control to ensure that its reporting practices and accounting and administrative procedures are appropriate to provide a high degree of assurance that relevant and reliable financial information is produced and assets are safeguarded. These controls include the careful selection and training of employees, the establishment of well-defined areas of responsibility and accountability for performance, and the communication of policies and code of conduct throughout the company. In addition, the company maintains an internal audit group that conducts periodic audits of the company's operations. The Chief Internal Auditor has full access to the Audit Committee.

These consolidated financial statements have been prepared in conformity with International Financial Reporting Standards as issued by the International Accounting Standards Board and, where appropriate, reflect estimates based on management's judgment. The financial information presented throughout this Annual Report is generally consistent with the information contained in the accompanying consolidated financial statements.

Deloitte LLP, the Independent Registered Public Accounting Firm appointed by the shareholders, have audited the consolidated financial statements set out on pages 83 through 149 in accordance with Canadian generally accepted auditing standards and the standards of the Public Company Accounting Oversight Board (United States) to enable them to express to the board of directors and shareholders their opinion on the consolidated financial statements. Their report is set out on the following page.

The consolidated financial statements have been further reviewed and approved by the Board of Directors acting through its Audit Committee, which is comprised of directors who are not officers or employees of the company. The Audit Committee, which meets with the auditors and management to review the activities of each and reports to the Board of Directors, oversees management's responsibilities for the financial reporting and internal control systems. The auditors have full and direct access to the Audit Committee and meet periodically with the committee both with and without management present to discuss their audit and related findings.

J. Bruce Flatt
Chief Executive Officer

Brian D. Lawson
Chief Financial Officer

March 26, 2015
Toronto, Canada

REPORT OF INDEPENDENT REGISTERED PUBLIC ACCOUNTING FIRM

To the Board of Directors and Shareholders of Brookfield Asset Management Inc.

We have audited the accompanying consolidated financial statements of Brookfield Asset Management Inc. and subsidiaries (the "Company"), which comprise the consolidated balance sheets as at December 31, 2014 and December 31, 2013, and the consolidated statements of operations, consolidated statements of comprehensive income, consolidated statements of changes in equity and consolidated statements of cash flows for the years then ended, and a summary of significant accounting policies and other explanatory information.

Management's Responsibility for the Consolidated Financial Statements

Management is responsible for the preparation and fair presentation of these consolidated financial statements in accordance with International Financial Reporting Standards as issued by the International Accounting Standards Board, and for such internal control as management determines is necessary to enable the preparation of consolidated financial statements that are free from material misstatement, whether due to fraud or error.

Auditor's Responsibility

Our responsibility is to express an opinion on these consolidated financial statements based on our audits. We conducted our audits in accordance with Canadian generally accepted auditing standards and the standards of the Public Company Accounting Oversight Board (United States). Those standards require that we comply with ethical requirements and plan and perform the audit to obtain reasonable assurance about whether the consolidated financial statements are free from material misstatement.

An audit involves performing procedures to obtain audit evidence about the amounts and disclosures in the consolidated financial statements. The procedures selected depend on the auditor's judgment, including the assessment of the risks of material misstatement of the consolidated financial statements, whether due to fraud or error. In making those risk assessments, the auditor considers internal control relevant to the entity's preparation and fair presentation of the consolidated financial statements in order to design audit procedures that are appropriate in the circumstances. An audit also includes evaluating the appropriateness of accounting policies used and the reasonableness of accounting estimates made by management, as well as evaluating the overall presentation of the consolidated financial statements.

We believe that the audit evidence we have obtained in our audits is sufficient and appropriate to provide a basis for our audit opinion.

Opinion

In our opinion, the consolidated financial statements present fairly, in all material respects, the financial position of Brookfield Asset Management Inc. and subsidiaries as at December 31, 2014 and December 31, 2013, and their financial performance and their cash flows for the years then ended in accordance with International Financial Reporting Standards as issued by the International Accounting Standards Board.

Other Matter

We have also audited, in accordance with the standards of the Public Company Accounting Oversight Board (United States), the Company's internal control over financial reporting as of December 31, 2014, based on the criteria established in *Internal Control – Integrated Framework (2013)* issued by the Committee of Sponsoring Organizations of the Treadway Commission and our report dated March 26, 2015 expressed an unqualified opinion on the Company's internal control over financial reporting.

Deloitte LLP

Chartered Professional Accountants, Chartered Accountants
Licensed Public Accountants

March 26, 2015
Toronto, Canada

CONSOLIDATED FINANCIAL STATEMENTS
CONSOLIDATED BALANCE SHEETS

(MILLIONS)	Note	Dec. 31, 2014	Dec. 31, 2013
Assets			
Cash and cash equivalents	6	$ 3,160	$ 3,663
Other financial assets	6	6,285	4,947
Accounts receivable and other	7	8,399	6,666
Inventory	8	5,620	6,291
Assets classified as held for sale	9	2,807	—
Equity accounted investments	10	14,916	13,277
Investment properties	11	46,083	38,336
Property, plant and equipment	12	34,617	31,019
Sustainable resources	13	446	502
Intangible assets	14	4,327	5,044
Goodwill	15	1,406	1,588
Deferred income tax assets	16	1,414	1,412
Total Assets		$ 129,480	$ 112,745
Liabilities and Equity			
Accounts payable and other	17	$ 10,408	$ 10,316
Liabilities associated with assets classified as held for sale	9	1,419	—
Corporate borrowings	18	4,075	3,975
Non-recourse borrowings			
Property-specific mortgages	19	40,364	35,495
Subsidiary borrowings	19	8,329	7,392
Deferred income tax liabilities	16	8,097	6,164
Subsidiary equity obligations	20	3,541	1,877
Equity			
Preferred equity	21	3,549	3,098
Non-controlling interests	21	29,545	26,647
Common equity	21	20,153	17,781
Total equity		53,247	47,526
Total Liabilities and Equity		$ 129,480	$ 112,745

On behalf of the Board:

Frank J. McKenna, Director

George S. Taylor, Director

CONSOLIDATED STATEMENTS OF OPERATIONS

YEARS ENDED DECEMBER 31
(MILLIONS, EXCEPT PER SHARE AMOUNTS)

	Note	2014	2013
Revenues	22	$ 18,364	$ 20,093
Direct costs	23	(13,118)	(13,928)
Other income and gains	24	190	1,262
Equity accounted income	10	1,594	759
Expenses			
Interest		(2,579)	(2,553)
Corporate costs		(123)	(152)
Fair value changes	25	3,674	663
Depreciation and amortization		(1,470)	(1,455)
Income taxes	16	(1,323)	(845)
Net income		$ 5,209	$ 3,844
Net income attributable to:			
Shareholders		$ 3,110	$ 2,120
Non-controlling interests		2,099	1,724
		$ 5,209	$ 3,844
Net income per share:			
Diluted	21	$ 4.67	$ 3.12
Basic	21	$ 4.79	$ 3.21

CONSOLIDATED STATEMENTS OF COMPREHENSIVE INCOME

YEARS ENDED DECEMBER 31
(MILLIONS)

	Note	2014	2013
Net income		$ **5,209**	$ 3,844
Other comprehensive income (loss)			
Items that may be reclassified to net income			
Financial contracts and power sales agreements		**(301)**	442
Available-for-sale securities		**(105)**	(24)
Equity accounted investments	10	**(22)**	8
Foreign currency translation		**(1,717)**	(2,429)
Income taxes	16	**22**	(114)
		(2,123)	(2,117)
Items that will not be reclassified to net income			
Revaluation of property, plant and equipment		**2,998**	825
Revaluation of pension obligations	29	**(77)**	26
Equity accounted investments	10	**245**	231
Income taxes	16	**(632)**	(166)
		2,534	916
Other comprehensive income (loss)		**411**	(1,201)
Comprehensive income		$ **5,620**	$ 2,643
Attributable to:			
Shareholders			
Net income		$ **3,110**	$ 2,120
Other comprehensive income (loss)		**301**	(795)
Comprehensive income		$ **3,411**	$ 1,325
Non-controlling interests			
Net income		$ **2,099**	$ 1,724
Other comprehensive income (loss)		**110**	(406)
Comprehensive income		$ **2,209**	$ 1,318

CONSOLIDATED STATEMENTS OF CHANGES IN EQUITY

YEAR ENDED DECEMBER 31, 2014 (MILLIONS)	Common Share Capital	Contributed Surplus	Retained Earnings	Ownership Changes[1]	Accumulated Other Comprehensive Income			Common Equity	Preferred Equity	Non-controlling Interests	Total Equity
					Revaluation Surplus	Currency Translation	Other Reserves[2]				
Balance as at December 31, 2013	$ 2,899	$ 159	$ 7,159	$ 2,354	$ 5,165	$ 190	$ (145)	$17,781	$ 3,098	$26,647	$47,526
Changes in year:											
Net income	—	—	3,110	—	—	—	—	3,110	—	2,099	5,209
Other comprehensive income	—	—	—	—	1,094	(670)	(123)	301	—	110	411
Comprehensive income	—	—	3,110	—	1,094	(670)	(123)	3,411	—	2,209	5,620
Shareholder distributions											
Common equity	—	—	(388)	—	—	—	—	(388)	—	—	(388)
Preferred equity	—	—	(154)	—	—	—	—	(154)	—	—	(154)
Non-controlling interests	—	—	—	—	—	—	—	—	—	(2,428)	(2,428)
Other items											
Equity issuances, net of redemptions	132	(18)	(69)	—	—	—	—	45	451	2,505	3,001
Share-based compensation	—	44	(7)	—	—	—	—	37	—	16	53
Ownership changes	—	—	51	(375)	(126)	39	(168)	(579)	—	596	17
Total change in year	132	26	2,543	(375)	968	(631)	(291)	2,372	451	2,898	5,721
Balance as at December 31, 2014	$ 3,031	$ 185	$ 9,702	$ 1,979	$ 6,133	$ (441)	$ (436)	$20,153	$ 3,549	$29,545	$53,247

1. Includes gains or losses on changes in ownership interests of consolidated subsidiaries
2. Includes available-for-sale securities, cash flow hedges, actuarial changes on pension plans and equity accounted other comprehensive income, net of associated income taxes

YEAR ENDED DECEMBER 31, 2013 (MILLIONS)	Common Share Capital	Contributed Surplus	Retained Earnings	Ownership Changes[1]	Accumulated Other Comprehensive Income			Common Equity	Preferred Equity	Non-controlling Interests	Total Equity
					Revaluation Surplus	Currency Translation	Other Reserves[2]				
Balance as at December 31, 2012	$ 2,855	$ 149	$ 6,813	$ 2,088	$ 5,289	$ 1,405	$ (449)	$18,150	$ 2,901	$23,287	$44,338
Changes in year:											
Net income	—	—	2,120	—	—	—	—	2,120	—	1,724	3,844
Other comprehensive loss	—	—	—	—	101	(1,183)	287	(795)	—	(406)	(1,201)
Comprehensive income	—	—	2,120	—	101	(1,183)	287	1,325	—	1,318	2,643
Shareholder distributions											
Common equity	—	—	(1,287)	—	—	(32)	17	(1,302)	—	906	(396)
Preferred equity	—	—	(145)	—	—	—	—	(145)	—	—	(145)
Non-controlling interests	—	—	—	—	—	—	—	—	—	(910)	(910)
Other items											
Equity issuances, net of redemptions	44	(12)	(331)	—	—	—	—	(299)	197	1,675	1,573
Share-based compensation	—	22	(31)	—	—	—	—	(9)	—	45	36
Ownership changes	—	—	20	266	(225)	—	—	61	—	326	387
Total change in year	44	10	346	266	(124)	(1,215)	304	(369)	197	3,360	3,188
Balance as at December 31, 2013	$ 2,899	$ 159	$ 7,159	$ 2,354	$ 5,165	$ 190	$ (145)	$17,781	$ 3,098	$26,647	$47,526

1. Includes gains or losses on changes in ownership interests of consolidated subsidiaries
2. Includes available-for-sale securities, cash flow hedges, actuarial changes on pension plans and equity accounted other comprehensive income, net of associated income taxes

CONSOLIDATED STATEMENTS OF CASH FLOWS

YEARS ENDED DECEMBER 31
(MILLIONS)

	Note	2014	2013
Operating activities			
Net income		$ 5,209	$ 3,844
Other income and gains	24	(190)	(1,820)
Share of undistributed equity accounted earnings		(920)	(307)
Fair value changes	25	(3,674)	(663)
Depreciation and amortization		1,470	1,455
Deferred income taxes	16	1,209	686
Investments in residential inventory		57	(378)
Net change in non-cash working capital and other balances		(587)	(539)
		2,574	2,278
Financing activities			
Corporate borrowings arranged		454	949
Corporate borrowings repaid		—	(224)
Commercial paper and bank borrowings, net		(88)	(35)
Property-specific mortgages arranged		10,939	11,073
Property-specific mortgages repaid		(8,650)	(10,029)
Other debt of subsidiaries arranged		5,463	6,781
Other debt of subsidiaries repaid		(3,191)	(6,115)
Subsidiary equity obligations issued		1,947	541
Subsidiary equity obligations redeemed		(342)	(343)
Capital provided from non-controlling interests		5,733	3,218
Capital repaid to non-controlling interests		(3,228)	(1,543)
Preferred equity issuances		706	191
Preferred equity redemption		(268)	—
Common shares issued		108	85
Common shares repurchased		(63)	(388)
Distributions to non-controlling interests		(2,345)	(910)
Distributions to shareholders		(542)	(541)
		6,633	2,710
Investing activities			
Acquisitions			
Investment properties		(1,970)	(1,835)
Property, plant and equipment		(1,098)	(1,374)
Sustainable resources		(27)	(53)
Equity accounted investments		(1,645)	(2,326)
Other financial assets		(3,877)	(2,745)
Acquisition of subsidiaries		(5,999)	(2,960)
Dispositions			
Investment properties		2,192	948
Property, plant and equipment		313	98
Equity accounted investments		471	657
Other financial assets		3,651	1,502
Disposition of subsidiaries		161	4,057
Restricted cash and deposits		(1,768)	(10)
		(9,596)	(4,041)
Cash and cash equivalents			
Change in cash and cash equivalents		(389)	947
Foreign exchange revaluation		(114)	(134)
Balance, beginning of year		3,663	2,850
Balance, end of year	31	$ 3,160	$ 3,663

NOTES TO THE CONSOLIDATED FINANCIAL STATEMENTS

1. CORPORATE INFORMATION

Brookfield Asset Management Inc. ("Brookfield" or the "company") is a global alternative asset management company. The company owns and operates assets with a focus on property, renewable energy, infrastructure and private equity. The company is listed on the New York, Toronto and Euronext stock exchanges under the symbols BAM, BAM.A and BAMA, respectively. The company was formed by articles of amalgamation under the Business Corporations Act (Ontario) and is registered in Ontario, Canada. The registered office of the company is Brookfield Place, 181 Bay Street, Suite 300, Toronto, Ontario, M5J 2T3.

2. SIGNIFICANT ACCOUNTING POLICIES

a) Statement of Compliance

These consolidated financial statements have been prepared in accordance with International Financial Reporting Standards ("IFRS") as issued by the International Accounting Standards Board ("IASB").

These financial statements were authorized for issuance by the Board of Directors of the company on March 26, 2015.

b) Adoption of Accounting Standards

IFRIC 21, *Levies* ("IFRIC 21") provides guidance on when to recognize a liability for a levy imposed by a government, both for levies that are accounted for in accordance with IAS 37, *Provisions, Contingent Liabilities and Contingent Assets*, and those where the timing and amount of the levy is certain. IFRIC 21 identifies the obligating event for the recognition of a liability as the activity that triggers the payment of the levy in accordance with the relevant legislation. A liability is recognized progressively if the obligating event occurs over a period of time or, if an obligation is triggered on reaching a minimum threshold, the liability is recognized when that minimum threshold is reached. IFRIC 21 became effective on January 1, 2014. The adoption of IFRIC 21 did not have a material effect on the company's consolidated financial statements.

c) Future Changes in Accounting Standards

Property, Plant, and Equipment and Intangible Assets

IAS 16 *Property, Plant, and Equipment* ("IAS 16") and IAS 38 *Intangible Assets* ("IAS 38") were both amended by the IASB as a result of clarifying the appropriate amortization method for intangible assets of service concession arrangements under IFRIC 12 *Service Concession Arrangements* ("SCAs"). The IASB determined that the issue does not only relate to SCAs but all tangible and intangible assets that have finite useful lives. Amendments to IAS 16 prohibit entities from using a revenue-based depreciation method for items of property, plant, and equipment. Similarly, the amendment to IAS 38 introduces a rebuttable presumption that revenue is not an appropriate basis for amortization of an intangible asset, with only limited circumstances where the presumption can be rebutted. Guidance is also introduced to explain that expected future reductions in selling prices could be indicative of a reduction of the future economic benefits embodied in an asset. The amendments apply prospectively and are effective for annual periods beginning on or after January 1, 2016, with earlier application permitted. The company has not yet determined the impact of the amendments to IAS 16 or IAS 38 on its consolidated financial statements.

Revenue from Contracts with Customers

IFRS 15, *Revenue from Contracts with Customers* ("IFRS 15") specifies how and when revenue should be recognized as well as requiring more informative and relevant disclosures. This standard supersedes IAS 18 *Revenue*, IAS 11 *Construction Contracts* and a number of revenue-related interpretations. Application of the Standard is mandatory and it applies to nearly all contracts with customers; the main exceptions are leases, financial instruments and insurance contracts. IFRS 15 is effective for periods beginning on or after January 1, 2017 with early application permitted. The company has not yet determined the impact of IFRS 15 on its consolidated financial statements.

Financial Instruments

In July 2014, the IASB issued the final publication of IFRS 9, *Financial Instruments* ("IFRS 9"), superseding IAS 39, *Financial Instruments*. IFRS 9 establishes principles for the financial reporting of financial assets and financial liabilities that will present relevant and useful information to users of financial statements for their assessment of the amounts, timing and uncertainty of an entity's future cash flows. This new standard also includes a new general hedge accounting standard which will align hedge accounting more closely with risk management. It does not fully change the types of hedging relationships or the requirement to measure and recognize ineffectiveness, however, it will provide more hedging strategies that are used for risk management to qualify for hedge accounting and introduce more judgment to assess the effectiveness of a hedging relationship. The standard has a mandatorily effective date for annual periods beginning on or after January 1, 2018 with early adoption permitted. The company has not yet determined the impact of IFRS 9 on its consolidated financial statements.

d) Basis of Presentation

The financial statements are prepared on a going concern basis.

i. Subsidiaries

The consolidated financial statements include the accounts of the company and its subsidiaries, which are the entities over which the company exercises control. Control exists when the company has the power to direct the relevant activities, exposure or rights to variable returns from involvement with the investee, and the ability to use its power over the investee to affect the amount of its returns. Subsidiaries are consolidated from the date the control is obtained, and continue to be consolidated until the date when control is lost. The company continually reassesses whether or not it controls an investee, particularly if facts and circumstances indicate there is a change to one or more of the control criteria previously mentioned. In certain circumstances when the company has less than a majority of the voting rights of an investee, it has power over the investee when the voting rights are sufficient to give it the practical ability to direct the relevant activities of the investee unilaterally. The company considers all relevant facts and circumstances in assessing whether or not the company's voting rights are sufficient to give it power.

Non-controlling interests in the equity of the company's subsidiaries are included within equity on the Consolidated Balance Sheets. All intercompany balances, transactions, unrealized gains and losses are eliminated in full.

Gains or losses resulting from changes in the company's ownership interest of a subsidiary that do not result in a loss of control are accounted for as equity transactions and are recorded within ownership changes as a component of equity. When control of a subsidiary is lost, the difference between the carrying value and the proceeds from disposition is recognized within other income and gains in the Consolidated Statements of Operations.

Transaction costs incurred in connection with the acquisition of control of a subsidiary are expensed immediately within fair value changes in the Consolidated Statements of Operations.

Refer to Note 4 for additional information on subsidiaries of the company with significant non-controlling interests.

ii. Associates and Joint Ventures

Associates are entities over which the company exercises significant influence. Significant influence is the power to participate in the financial and operating policy decisions of the investee but without control or joint control over those policies. Joint ventures are joint arrangements whereby the parties that have joint control of the arrangement have the rights to the net assets of the joint arrangement. Joint control is the contractually agreed sharing of control over an arrangement, which exists only when decisions about the relevant activities require unanimous consent of the parties sharing control. The company accounts for associates and joint ventures using the equity method of accounting within equity accounted investments on the Consolidated Balance Sheets.

Interests in associates and joint ventures accounted for using the equity method are initially recognized at cost. At the time of initial recognition, if the cost of the associate or joint venture is lower than the proportionate share of the investment's underlying fair value, the company records a gain on the difference between the cost and the underlying fair value of the investment in net income. If the cost of the associate or joint venture is greater than the company's proportionate share of the underlying fair value, goodwill relating to the associate or joint venture is included in the carrying amount of the investment. Subsequent to initial recognition, the carrying value of the company's interest in an associate or joint venture is adjusted for the company's share of comprehensive income and distributions of the investee. Profit and losses resulting from transactions with an associate or joint venture are recognized in the consolidated financial statements based on the interests of unrelated investors in the investee. The carrying value of associates or joint ventures is assessed for impairment at each balance sheet date. Impairment losses on equity accounted investments may be subsequently reversed in net income. Further information on the impairment of long-lived assets is available in Note 2j).

iii. Joint Operations

A joint operation is a joint arrangement whereby the parties that have joint control of the arrangement have rights to the assets, and obligations for the liabilities, related to the arrangement. Joint control is the contractually agreed sharing of control of an arrangement, which exists only when decisions about the relevant activities require unanimous consent of parties sharing control. The company recognizes only its assets, liabilities and share of the results of operations of the joint operation. The assets, liabilities and results of joint operations are included within the respective line items of the Consolidated Balance Sheets, Consolidated Statements of Operations and Consolidated Statements of Comprehensive Income.

e) Foreign Currency Translation

The U.S. dollar is the functional and presentation currency of the company. Each of the company's subsidiaries, associates, joint ventures and joint operations determines its own functional currency and items included in the financial statements of each subsidiary, associate, joint venture and joint operation are measured using that functional currency.

Assets and liabilities of foreign operations having a functional currency other than the U.S. dollar are translated at the rate of exchange prevailing at the reporting date and revenues and expenses at average rates during the period. Gains or losses on translation are accumulated as a component of equity. On the disposal of a foreign operation, or the loss of control, joint control or significant influence, the component of accumulated other comprehensive income relating to that foreign operation is reclassified to net income. Gains or losses on foreign currency denominated balances and transactions that are designated as hedges of net investments in these operations are reported in the same manner.

Foreign currency denominated monetary assets and liabilities of the company and its subsidiaries are translated using the rate of exchange prevailing at the reporting date and non-monetary assets and liabilities measured at fair value are translated at the rate of exchange prevailing at the date when the fair value was determined. Revenues and expenses are measured at average rates during the period. Gains or losses on translation of these items are included in net income. Gains or losses on transactions which hedge these items are also included in net income. Foreign currency denominated non-monetary assets and liabilities, measured at historic cost, are translated at the rate of exchange at the transaction date.

f) Cash and Cash Equivalents

Cash and cash equivalents include cash on hand, demand deposits and highly liquid short-term investments with original maturities of three months or less.

g) Related Party Transactions

In the normal course of operations, the company enters into various transactions on market terms with related parties, which have been measured at their exchange value and are recognized in the consolidated financial statements. Related party transactions are further described in Note 30. The company's subsidiaries with significant non-controlling interests are described in Note 4 and its associates and joint ventures are described in Note 10.

h) Operating Assets

i. Investment Properties

The company uses the fair value method to account for real estate classified as an investment property. A property is determined to be an investment property when it is principally held to earn either rental income or capital appreciation, or both. Investment properties also include properties that are under development or redevelopment for future use as investment property. Investment property is initially measured at cost including transaction costs. Subsequent to initial recognition, investment properties are carried at fair value. Gains or losses arising from changes in fair value are included in net income during the period in which they arise. Fair values are primarily determined by discounting the expected future cash flows of each property, generally over a term of 10 years, using discount and terminal capitalization rates reflective of the characteristics, location and market of each property. The future cash flows of each property are based upon, among other things, rental income from current leases and assumptions about rental income from future leases reflecting current conditions, less future cash outflows relating to such current and future leases. The company determines fair value using internal valuations. The company uses external valuations to assist in determining fair value, but external valuations are not necessarily indicative of fair value.

ii. Revaluation Method for Property, Plant and Equipment

The company uses the revaluation method of accounting for certain classes of property, plant and equipment as well as certain assets which are under development for future use as property, plant and equipment. Property, plant and equipment measured using the revaluation method is initially measured at cost and subsequently carried at its revalued amount, being the fair value at the date of the revaluation less any subsequent accumulated depreciation and any accumulated impairment losses. Revaluations are performed on an annual basis, commencing in the first year subsequent to the date of acquisition, unless there is an indication that assets are impaired. Where the carrying amount of an asset increases as a result of a revaluation, the increase is recognized in other comprehensive income and accumulated in equity in revaluation surplus, unless the increase reverses a previously recognized impairment recorded through net income, in which case that portion of the increase is recognized in net income. Where the carrying amount of an asset decreases, the decrease is recognized in other comprehensive income to the extent of any balance existing in revaluation surplus in respect of the asset, with the remainder of the decrease recognized in net income. Depreciation of an asset commences when it is available for use. On loss of control or partial disposition of an asset measured using the revaluation method, all accumulated revaluation surplus or the portion disposed of, respectively, is transferred into retained earnings or ownership changes, respectively.

iii. Renewable Energy Generation

Renewable energy generating assets, including assets under development, are classified as property, plant and equipment and are accounted for using the revaluation method. The company determines the fair value of its renewable energy generating assets using a discounted cash flow model, which includes estimates of forecasted revenue, operating costs, maintenance and other capital expenditures. Discount rates are selected for each facility giving consideration to the expected proportion of contracted to un-contracted revenue and markets into which power is sold.

Generally, the first 20 years of cash flow are discounted with a residual value based on the terminal value cash flows. The fair value and estimated remaining service lives are reassessed on an annual basis. The company determines fair value using internal valuations. The company uses external appraisers to review fair values of our renewable energy generating assets, but external valuations are not necessarily indicative of fair value.

Depreciation on renewable energy generating assets is calculated on a straight-line basis over the estimated service lives of the assets, which are as follows:

(YEARS)	
Dams	Up to 115
Penstocks	Up to 60
Powerhouses	Up to 115
Hydroelectric generating units	Up to 115
Wind generating units	Up to 22
Other assets	Up to 60

Cost is allocated to the significant components of power generating assets and each component is depreciated separately.

The depreciation of property, plant and equipment in our Brazilian renewable energy operations is based on the duration of the authorization or the useful life of a concession. The weighted average remaining duration at December 31, 2014 is 15 years (2013 – 16 years). Land rights are included as part of the concession or authorization and are subject to depreciation.

iv. Sustainable Resources

Sustainable resources consist of standing timber and other agricultural assets and are measured at fair value after deducting the estimated selling costs and are recorded in sustainable resources on the Consolidated Balance Sheets. Estimated selling costs include commissions, levies, delivery costs, transfer taxes and duties. The fair value of standing timber is calculated using the present value of anticipated future cash flows for standing timber before tax and terminal dates of 20 to 28 years. Fair value is determined based on existing, sustainable felling plans and assessments regarding growth, timber prices and felling and silviculture costs. Changes in fair value are recorded in net income in the period of change. The company determines fair value of its standing timber using external valuations on an annual basis.

Harvested timber is included in inventory and is measured at the lower of fair value less estimated costs to sell at the time of harvest and net realizable value.

Land under standing timber, bridges, roads and other equipment used in sustainable resources production are accounted for using the revaluation method and included in property, plant and equipment. These assets are depreciated over their useful lives, generally 3 to 35 years.

v. Infrastructure

Utilities, transport and energy assets within our infrastructure operations as well as assets under development classified as property, plant and equipment are accounted for using the revaluation method. The company determines the fair value of its utilities, transport and energy assets using a discounted cash flow model, which includes estimates of forecasted revenue, operating costs, maintenance and other capital expenditures. Valuations are performed internally on an annual basis. Discount rates are selected for each asset, giving consideration to the volatility and geography of its revenue streams.

Depreciation on utilities and transport and energy assets is calculated on a straight-line basis over the estimated service lives of the components of the assets, which are as follows:

(YEARS)	
Buildings and district energy systems	Up to 50
Machinery, equipment, transmission stations and towers	Up to 40
Rail and transport assets	Up to 40

The fair value and the estimated remaining service lives are reassessed on an annual basis.

Public service concessions that provide the right to charge users for a service in which the service and fee is regulated by the grantor are accounted for as intangible assets.

vi. Hotel Assets

Hotel operating assets within our property operations are classified as property, plant and equipment and are accounted for using the revaluation method. The company determines the fair value for these assets by discounting the expected future cash flows. The company determines fair value using internal valuations. The company uses external valuations to assist in determining fair value, but external valuations are not necessarily indicative of fair value.

Depreciation on hotel assets is calculated on a straight-line basis over the estimated service lives of the components of the assets, which range from 3 to 50 years for buildings and 3 to 10 years for other equipment.

vii. Other Property, Plant and Equipment

The company accounts for its other property, plant and equipment using the revaluation method or the cost model, depending on the nature of the asset and the operating segment. Other property, plant and equipment measured using the revaluation method is initially measured at cost and subsequently carried at its revalued amount, being the fair value at the date of the revaluation less any subsequent accumulated depreciation and any accumulated impairment losses. Under the cost method, assets are initially recorded at cost and are subsequently depreciated over the assets' useful lives, unless an impairment is identified requiring a write-down to estimated fair value.

viii. Residential Development

Residential development lots, homes and residential condominium projects are recorded in inventory. Residential development lots are recorded at the lower of cost, including pre-development expenditures and capitalized borrowing costs, and net realizable value, which the company determines as the estimated selling price of the inventory in the ordinary course of business in its completed state, less estimated expenses, including holding costs, costs to complete and costs to sell.

Homes and other properties held for sale, which include properties subject to sale agreements, are recorded at the lower of cost and net realizable value in inventory. Costs are allocated to the saleable acreage of each project or subdivision in proportion to the anticipated revenue.

ix. Other Financial Assets

Other financial assets are classified as either fair value through profit or loss or available-for-sale based on their nature and use within the company's business. Changes in the fair values of financial instruments classified as fair value through profit or loss and available-for-sale are recognized in net income and other comprehensive income, respectively. The cumulative changes in the fair values of available-for-sale securities previously recognized in accumulated other comprehensive income are reclassified to net income when the security is sold, or there is a significant or prolonged decline in fair value or when the company acquires a controlling or significant interest in the underlying investment and commences equity accounting or consolidating the investment. Other financial assets are recognized on their trade date and initially recorded at fair value with changes in fair value recorded in net income or other comprehensive income in accordance with their classification. Fair values for financial instruments are determined by reference to quoted bid or ask prices, as appropriate. Where bid and ask prices are unavailable, the closing price of the most recent transaction of that instrument is used.

The company assesses the carrying value of available-for-sale securities for impairment when there is objective evidence that the asset is impaired. When objective evidence of impairment exists, the cumulative loss in other comprehensive income is reclassified to net income.

Other financial assets also include loans and notes receivable which are recorded initially at fair value and, with the exception of loans and notes receivable designated as fair value through profit or loss, are subsequently measured at amortized cost using the effective interest method, less any applicable provision for impairment. A provision for impairment is established when there is objective evidence that the company will not be able to collect all amounts due according to the original terms of the receivables. Loans and receivables designated as fair value through profit or loss are recorded at fair value, with changes in fair value recorded in net income in the period in which they arise.

i) Fair Value Measurement

Fair value is the price that would be received to sell an asset or paid to transfer a liability in an orderly transaction between market participants at the measurement date, regardless of whether that price is directly observable or estimated using another valuation technique. In estimating the fair value of an asset or a liability, the company takes into account the characteristics of the asset or liability if market participants would take those characteristics into account when pricing the asset or liability at the measurement date.

Fair value measurement is disaggregated into three hierarchical levels: Level 1, 2 or 3. Fair value hierarchical levels are directly based on the degree to which the inputs to the fair value measurement are observable. The levels are as follows:

Level 1 – Inputs are unadjusted, quoted prices in active markets for identical assets or liabilities at the measurement date.

Level 2 – Inputs (other than quoted prices included in Level 1) are either directly or indirectly observable for the asset or liability through correlation with market data at the measurement date and for the duration of the asset's or liability's anticipated life.

Level 3 – Inputs are unobservable and reflect management's best estimate of what market participants would use in pricing the asset or liability at the measurement date. Consideration is given to the risk inherent in the valuation technique and the risk inherent in the inputs in determining the estimate.

Further information on fair value measurements is available in Notes 6, 11, 12 and 13.

j) Impairment of Long-Lived Assets

At each balance sheet date the company assesses whether its assets, other than those measured at fair value with changes in value recorded in net income, have any indication of impairment. An impairment is recognized if the recoverable amount, determined as the higher of the estimated fair value less costs of disposal and the discounted future cash flows generated from use and eventual disposal from an asset or cash-generating unit, is less than their carrying value. Impairment losses are recorded as fair value changes within the Consolidated Statements of Operations. The projections of future cash flows take into account the relevant operating plans and management's best estimate of the most probable set of conditions anticipated to prevail. Where an impairment loss subsequently reverses, the carrying amount of the asset or cash-generating unit is increased to the lesser of the revised estimate of its recoverable amount and the carrying amount that would have been recorded had no impairment loss been recognized previously.

k) Accounts Receivable

Trade receivables are recognized initially at fair value and subsequently measured at amortized cost using the effective interest method, less any allowance for uncollectability.

l) Intangible Assets

Finite life intangible assets are carried at cost less any accumulated amortization and any accumulated impairment losses, and are amortized on a straight-line basis over their estimated useful lives. Amortization is recorded within depreciation and amortization in the Consolidated Statements of Operations.

Certain of the company's intangible assets have an indefinite life, as there is no foreseeable limit to the period over which the asset is expected to generate cash flows. Indefinite life intangible assets are recorded at cost unless an impairment is identified which requires a write-down to its recoverable amount.

Indefinite life intangible assets are evaluated for impairment annually or more often if events or circumstances indicate there may be an impairment. Any impairment of the company's indefinite life intangible assets is recorded in net income in the period in which the impairment is identified. Impairment losses on intangible assets may be subsequently reversed in net income.

m) Goodwill

Goodwill represents the excess of the price paid for the acquisition of an entity over the fair value of the net identifiable tangible and intangible assets and liabilities acquired. Goodwill is allocated to the cash-generating unit to which it relates. The company identifies cash-generating units as identifiable groups of assets that are largely independent of the cash inflows from other assets or groups of assets.

Goodwill is evaluated for impairment annually or more often if events or circumstances indicate there may be an impairment. Impairment is determined for goodwill by assessing if the carrying value of a cash-generating unit, including the allocated goodwill, exceeds its recoverable amount determined as the greater of the estimated fair value less costs to sell and the value in use. Impairment losses recognized in respect of a cash-generating unit are first allocated to the carrying value of goodwill and any excess is allocated to the carrying amount of assets in the cash-generating unit. Any goodwill impairment is recorded in income in the period in which the impairment is identified. Impairment losses on goodwill are not subsequently reversed. On disposal of a subsidiary, any attributable amount of goodwill is included in determination of the gain or loss on disposal.

n) Subsidiary Equity Obligations

Subsidiary equity obligations include subsidiary preferred equity units, subsidiary preferred shares and capital securities, limited-life funds and redeemable fund units.

Subsidiary preferred equity units and capital securities are preferred shares that may be settled by a variable number of common equity units upon their conversion by the holders or the company. These instruments, as well as the related accrued distributions, are classified as liabilities on the Consolidated Balance Sheets. Dividends or yield distributions on these instruments are recorded as interest expense. To the extent conversion features are not closely related to the underlying liability the instruments are bifurcated into debt and equity components.

Limited-life funds represent the interests of others in the company's consolidated funds that have a defined maximum fixed life where the company has an obligation to distribute the residual interests of the fund to fund partners based on their proportionate share of the fund's equity in the form of cash or other financial assets at cessation of the fund's life.

Redeemable fund units represent interests of others in consolidated subsidiaries that have a redemption feature that requires the company to deliver cash or other financial assets to the holders of the units upon receiving a redemption notice. Limited-life funds and redeemable fund units are classified as liabilities and recorded at fair value within subsidiary equity obligations on the Consolidated Balance Sheets. Changes in the fair value are recorded in net income in the period of the change.

o) Revenue Recognition

i. Asset Management

Asset management revenues consist of base management fees, advisory fees, incentive distributions and performance-based incentive fees which arise from the rendering of services. Revenues from base management fees, advisory fees and incentive distributions are recorded on an accrual basis based on the amounts receivable at the balance sheet date and are recorded within revenues in the Consolidated Statements of Operations.

Revenues from performance-based incentive fees are recorded on the accrual basis based on the amount that would be due under the incentive fee formula at the end of the measurement period established by the contract where it is no longer subject to adjustment based on future events, and are recorded within revenues in the Consolidated Statements of Operations.

ii. Property Operations

Property revenues primarily consist of rental revenues from leasing activities and hotel revenues and interest and dividends from unconsolidated real estate investments.

Property rental income is recognized when the property is ready for its intended use. Office and retail properties are considered to be ready for their intended use when the property is capable of operating in the manner intended by management, which generally occurs upon completion of construction and receipt of all occupancy and other material permits.

The company has retained substantially all of the risks and benefits of ownership of its investment properties and therefore accounts for leases with its tenants as operating leases. Revenue recognition under a lease commences when the tenant has a right to use the leased asset. The total amount of contractual rent to be received from operating leases is recognized on a straight-line basis over the term of the lease; a straight-line or free rent receivable, as applicable, is recorded as a component of investment property for the difference between the amount of rental revenue recorded and the contractual amount received. Rental revenue includes percentage participating rents and recoveries of operating expenses, including property, capital and similar taxes. Percentage participating rents are recognized when tenants' specified sales targets have been met. Operating expense recoveries are recognized in the period that recoverable costs are chargeable to tenants.

Revenue from land sales is recognized at the time that the risks and benefits of ownership have been transferred, possession or title passes to the purchaser, all material conditions of the sales contract have been met, and a significant cash down payment or appropriate security is received.

Revenue from hotel operations are recognized when the services are provided and collection is reasonably assured.

iii. Renewable Energy Operations

Renewable energy revenues are derived from the sale of electricity and is recorded at the time power is provided based upon the output delivered and capacity provided at rates specified under either contract terms or prevailing market rates. Costs of generating electricity are recorded as incurred.

iv. Sustainable Resources Operations

Revenue from timberland operations is derived from the sale of logs and related products. The company recognizes sales to external customers when the product is shipped, title passes and collectability is reasonably assured. Revenue from agricultural development operations is recognized at the time that the risks and rewards of ownership have transferred.

v. Utility Operations

Revenue from utility operations is derived from the distribution and transmission of energy as well as from the company's coal terminal. Distribution and transmission revenue is recognized when services are rendered based upon usage or volume during that period. Terminal infrastructure charges are charged at set rates per tonne of coal based on each customer's annual contracted tonnage and is then recognized on a pro rata basis each month. The company's coal terminal also recognizes variable handling charges based on tonnes of coal shipped through the terminal.

vi. Transport Operations

Revenue from transport operations consists primarily of freight and transportation services revenue. Freight and transportation services revenue is recognized at the time of the provision of services.

vii. Energy Operations

Revenue from energy operations consists primarily of energy transmission, distribution and storage income. Energy revenue is recognized when services are provided and are rendered based upon usage or volume throughout during the period.

viii. Private Equity Operations

Revenue from our private equity operations primarily consists of revenues from the sale of goods and rendering of services. Sales are recognized when the product is shipped, title passes and collectability is reasonably assured. Services revenues are recognized when the services are provided.

ix. Residential Developments Operations

Revenue from residential land sales is recognized at the time that the risks and rewards of ownership have been transferred, which is generally when possession or title passes to the purchaser, all material conditions of the sales contract have been met, and a significant cash down payment or appropriate security is received.

Revenue from the sale of homes and residential condominium projects is recognized upon completion, when title passes to the purchaser upon closing and at which time all proceeds are received or collectability is reasonably assured.

x. Service Activities

Revenues from construction contracts are recognized using the percentage-of-completion method once the outcome of the construction contract can be estimated reliably, in proportion to the stage of completion of the contract, and to the extent to which collectability is reasonably assured. The stage of completion is measured by reference to actual costs incurred as a percentage of estimated total costs of each contract. When the outcome cannot be reliably determined, contract costs are expensed as incurred and revenue is only recorded to the extent that the costs are determined to be recoverable. Where it is probable that a loss will arise from a construction contract, the excess of total expected costs over total expected revenue is recognized as an expense immediately. Other service revenues are recognized when the services are provided.

xi. Investments in Financial Assets

Dividend and interest income from other financial assets are recorded within revenues when declared or on an accrual basis using the effective interest method.

Revenue from loans and notes receivable, less a provision for uncollectible amounts, is recorded on the accrual basis using the effective interest method.

xii. Other Income and Gains

Other income and gains represent the excess of proceeds over carrying values on the disposition of subsidiaries, investments or assets, or the settlement of liabilities for less than carrying values.

p) Derivative Financial Instruments and Hedge Accounting

The company and its subsidiaries selectively utilize derivative financial instruments primarily to manage financial risks, including interest rate, commodity and foreign exchange risks. Derivative financial instruments are recorded at fair value within the company's consolidated financial statements. Hedge accounting is applied when the derivative is designated as a hedge of a specific exposure and there is assurance that it will continue to be effective as a hedge based on an expectation of offsetting cash flows or fair values. Hedge accounting is discontinued prospectively when the derivative no longer qualifies as a hedge or the hedging relationship is terminated. Once discontinued, the cumulative change in fair value of a derivative that was previously recorded in other comprehensive income by the application of hedge accounting is recognized in net income over the remaining term of the original hedging relationship. The assets or liabilities relating to unrealized mark-to-market gains and losses on derivative financial instruments is recorded in accounts receivable and other or accounts payable and other, respectively.

i. Items Classified as Hedges

Realized and unrealized gains and losses on foreign exchange contracts, designated as hedges of currency risks relating to a net investment in a subsidiary or an associate, are included in equity and net income in the period in which the subsidiary or associate is disposed of or, to the extent partially disposed and control is not retained. Derivative financial instruments that are designated as hedges to offset corresponding changes in the fair value of assets and liabilities and cash flows are measured at their estimated fair value with changes in fair value recorded in net income or as a component of equity, as applicable.

Unrealized gains and losses on interest rate contracts designated as hedges of future variable interest payments are included in equity as a cash flow hedge when the interest rate risk relates to an anticipated variable interest payment. The periodic exchanges of payments on interest rate swap contracts designated as hedges of debt are recorded on an accrual basis as an adjustment to interest expense. The periodic exchanges of payments on interest rate contracts designated as hedges of future interest payments are amortized into net income over the term of the corresponding interest payments.

Unrealized gains and losses on electricity contracts designated as cash flow hedges of future power generation revenue are included in equity as a cash flow hedge. The periodic exchanges of payments on power generation commodity swap contracts designated as hedges are recorded on a settlement basis as an adjustment to power generation revenue.

ii. Items Not Classified as Hedges

Derivative financial instruments that are not designated as hedges are carried at their estimated fair value, and gains and losses arising from changes in fair value are recognized in net income in the period in which the change occurs. Realized and unrealized gains and losses on equity derivatives used to offset the change in share prices in respect of vested Deferred Share Units and Restricted Share Units are recorded together with the corresponding compensation expense. Realized and unrealized gains on other derivatives not designated as hedges are recorded in revenues, direct costs or corporate costs, as applicable. Realized and unrealized gains and losses on derivatives which are considered economic hedges, and where hedge accounting is not elected, are recorded in fair value changes in the Consolidated Statements of Operations.

q) Income Taxes

Current income tax assets and liabilities are measured at the amount expected to be paid to tax authorities, net of recoveries, based on the tax rates and laws enacted or substantively enacted at the balance sheet date. Current and deferred income tax relating to items recognized directly in equity are also recognized in equity. Deferred income tax liabilities are provided for using the liability method on temporary differences between the tax bases and carrying amounts of assets and liabilities. Deferred income tax assets are recognized for all deductible temporary differences, and carry forward of unused tax credits and unused tax losses, to the extent that it is probable that deductions, tax credits and tax losses can be utilized. The carrying amount of deferred income tax assets is reviewed at each balance sheet date and reduced to the extent it is no longer probable that the income tax assets will be recovered. Deferred income tax assets and liabilities are measured using the tax rates that are expected to apply to the year when the asset is realized or the liability settled, based on the tax rates and laws that have been enacted or substantively enacted at the balance sheet date.

r) Business Combinations

Business combinations are accounted for using the acquisition method. The cost of a business acquisition is measured at the aggregate of the fair values at the date of exchange of assets given, liabilities incurred or assumed, and equity instruments issued in exchange for control of the acquiree. The acquiree's identifiable assets, liabilities and contingent liabilities are recognized at their fair values at the acquisition date, except for non-current assets that are classified as held-for-sale which are recognized and measured at fair value less costs to sell. The interest of non-controlling shareholders in the acquiree is initially measured at the non-controlling shareholders' proportion of the net fair value of the identifiable assets, liabilities and contingent liabilities recognized.

To the extent the fair value of consideration paid exceeds the fair value of the net identifiable tangible and intangible assets, the excess is recorded as goodwill. To the extent the fair value of consideration paid is less than the fair value of net identifiable tangible and intangible assets, the excess is recognized in net income.

When a business combination is achieved in stages, previously held interests in the acquired entity are re-measured to fair value at the acquisition date, which is the date control is obtained, and the resulting gain or loss, if any, is recognized in net income, other than amounts transferred directly to retained earnings. Amounts arising from interests in the acquiree prior to the acquisition date that have previously been recognized in other comprehensive income are reclassified to net income. Transaction costs are recognized as an expense within fair value changes in the Consolidated Statements of Operations.

s) Other Items

i. Capitalized Costs

Capitalized costs related to assets under development and redevelopment include all eligible expenditures incurred in connection with the acquisition, development and construction of the asset until it is available for its intended use. These expenditures consist of costs that are directly attributable to these assets.

Borrowing costs are capitalized when such costs are directly attributable to the acquisition, construction or production of a qualifying asset. A qualifying asset is an asset that takes a substantial period of time to prepare for its intended use.

ii. Share-based Payments

The company and its subsidiaries issue share-based awards to certain employees and non-employee directors. The cost of equity-settled share-based transactions, comprised of share options, restricted shares and escrowed shares, is determined as the fair value of the award on the grant date using a fair value model. The cost of equity-settled share-based transactions is recognized as each tranche vests and is recorded in contributed surplus as a component of equity. The cost of cash-settled share-based transactions, comprised of Deferred Share Units and Restricted Share Units, is measured as the fair value at the grant date, and expensed on a proportionate basis consistent with the vesting period with the recognition of a corresponding liability. The liability is measured at each reporting date at fair value with changes in fair value recognized in net income.

iii. Pensions and other post-employment benefits

The company offers pension and other post-employment benefit plans to employees of certain of its subsidiaries, with certain of these subsidiaries offering defined benefit plans. Defined benefit pension expense, which includes the current year's service cost, is included in Direct costs. For each defined benefit plan, we recognize the present value of our defined benefit obligations less the fair value of the plan assets, as a defined benefit liability reported in Accounts payable and other on our Consolidated Balance Sheets. The company's obligations under its defined benefit pension plans are determined periodically through the preparation of actuarial valuations.

t) Critical Judgments and Estimates

The preparation of financial statements requires management to make estimates and judgments that affect the carried amounts of certain assets and liabilities, disclosure of contingent assets and liabilities and the reported amounts of revenues and expenses recorded during the period. Actual results could differ from those estimates.

In making estimates and judgments management relies on external information and observable conditions where possible, supplemented by internal analysis as required. These estimates have been applied in a manner consistent with prior periods and there are no known trends, commitments, events or uncertainties that the company believes will materially affect the methodology or assumptions utilized in making these estimates in these consolidated financial statements.

i. Critical Estimates

The significant estimates used in determining the recorded amount for assets and liabilities in the consolidated financial statements include the following:

a. Investment Properties

The critical assumptions and estimates used when determining the fair value of commercial properties are: the timing of rental income from future leases reflecting current market conditions, less assumptions of future cash flows in respect of current and future leases; maintenance and other capital expenditures; discount rates; terminal capitalization rates; and terminal valuation dates. Properties under development are recorded at fair value using a discounted cash flow model which includes estimates in respect of the timing and cost to complete the development.

Further information on investment property estimates is provided in Note 11.

b. Revaluation Method for Property, Plant and Equipment

When determining the carrying value of property, plant and equipment using the revaluation method, the company uses the following critical assumptions and estimates: the timing of forecasted revenues, future sales prices and margins; future sales volumes; future regulatory rates; maintenance and other capital expenditures; discount rates; terminal capitalization rates; terminal valuation dates; useful lives; and residual values. Determination of the fair value of property, plant and equipment under development includes estimates in respect of the timing and cost to complete the development.

Further information on estimates used in the revaluation method for property, plant and equipment is provided in Note 12.

c. Sustainable Resources

The fair value of standing timber and agricultural assets is based on the following critical estimates and assumptions: the timing of forecasted revenues and prices; estimated selling costs; sustainable felling plans; growth assumptions; silviculture costs; discount rates; terminal capitalization rates; and terminal valuation dates.

Further information on estimates used for sustainable resources is provided in Note 13.

d. Financial Instruments

Estimates and assumptions used in determining the fair value of financial instruments are: equity and commodity prices; future interest rates; the credit worthiness of the company relative to its counterparties; the credit risk of the company's counterparties; estimated future cash flows; the amount of the liability and equity components of compound financial instruments; discount rates and volatility utilized in option valuations.

Further information on estimates used in determining the carrying value of financial instruments is provided in Notes 6, 26 and 27.

e. Inventory

The company estimates the net realizable value of its inventory using estimates and assumptions about future development costs, costs to hold and future selling costs.

f. Other

Other estimates and assumptions utilized in the preparation of the company's consolidated financial statements are: the assessment or determination of net recoverable amounts; depreciation and amortization rates and useful lives; estimation of recoverable amounts of cash-generating units for impairment assessments of goodwill and intangible assets; ability to utilize tax losses and other tax measurements; fair value of assets held as collateral and the percentage of completion for construction contracts.

ii. Critical Judgments

Management is required to make critical judgments when applying its accounting policies. The following judgments have the most significant effect on the consolidated financial statements:

a. Control or Level of Influence

When determining the appropriate basis of accounting for the company's investees, the company makes judgments about the degree of influence that the company exerts directly or through an arrangement over the investees' relevant activities. This may include the ability to elect investee directors or appoint management. Control is obtained when the company has the power to direct the relevant investing, financing and operating decisions of an entity and does so in its capacity as principal of the operations, rather than as an agent for other investors. Operating as a principal includes having sufficient capital at risk in any investee and exposure to the variability of the returns generated by the decisions of the company as principal. Judgment is used in determining the sufficiency of the capital at risk or variability of returns. In making these judgments, the company considers the ability of other investors to remove the company as a manager or general partner in a controlled partnership.

b. Investment Properties

When applying the company's accounting policy for investment properties, judgment is applied in determining whether certain costs are additions to the carrying amount of the property and, for properties under development, identifying the point at which practical completion of the property occurs and identifying the directly attributable borrowing costs to be included in the carrying value of the development property.

c. Property, Plant and Equipment

The company's accounting policy for its property, plant and equipment requires critical judgments over the assessment of carrying value, whether certain costs are additions to the carrying amount of the property, plant and equipment as opposed to repairs and maintenance, and for assets under development the identification of when the asset is capable of being used as intended and identifying the directly attributable borrowing costs to be included in the asset's carrying value.

For assets that are measured using the revaluation method, judgment is required when estimating future prices, volumes and discount and capitalization rates. Judgment is applied when determining future electricity prices considering market data for years that a liquid market is available and estimates of electricity prices from renewable sources that would allow new entrants into the market in subsequent years.

d. Common Control Transactions

The purchase and sale of businesses or subsidiaries between entities under common control fall outside the scope of IFRS and accordingly, management uses judgment when determining a policy to account for such transactions taking into consideration other guidance in the IFRS framework and pronouncements of other standard-setting bodies. The company's policy is to record assets and liabilities recognized as a result of transfers of businesses or subsidiaries between entities under common control at carrying value. Differences between the carrying amount of the consideration given or received and the carrying amount of the assets and liabilities transferred are recorded directly in equity.

e. Indicators of Impairment

Judgment is applied when determining whether indicators of impairment exist when assessing the carrying values of the company's assets, including: the determination of the company's ability to hold financial assets; the estimation of a cash-generating unit's future revenues and direct costs; and the determination of discount and capitalization rates, and when an asset's carrying value is above the value derived using publicly traded prices which are quoted in a liquid market.

f. Income Taxes

The company makes judgments when determining the future tax rates applicable to subsidiaries and identifying the temporary difference that relate to each subsidiary. Deferred income tax assets and liabilities are measured at the tax rates that are expected to apply during the period when the assets are realized or the liabilities settled, using the tax rates and laws enacted or substantively enacted at the consolidated balance sheet dates. The company measures deferred income taxes associated with its investment properties based on its specific intention with respect to each asset at the end of the reporting period. Where the company has a specific intention to sell a property in the foreseeable future, deferred taxes on the building portion of an investment property are measured based on the tax consequences following from the disposition of the property. Otherwise, deferred taxes are measured on the basis the carrying value of the investment property will be recovered substantially through use. Judgment is required in determining the manner in which the carrying amount of each investment property will be recovered.

g. Classification of Non-controlling Interests in Limited-Life Funds

Non-controlling interests in limited-life funds are classified as liabilities (subsidiary equity obligations) or equity (non-controlling interests) depending on whether an obligation exits to distribute residual net assets to non-controlling interests on liquidation in the form of cash or another financial asset or assets delivered in kind. Judgment is required to determine whether the governing documents of each entity convey a right to cash or another financial asset, or if assets can be distributed on liquidation.

h. Other

Other critical judgments include the determination of effectiveness of financial hedges for accounting purposes; the likelihood and timing of anticipated transactions for hedge accounting; and the determination of functional currency.

3. SEGMENTED INFORMATION

a) Operating Segments

Our operations are organized into eight operating segments which are regularly reported to our Chief Executive Officer (our Chief Operating Decision Maker). We measure performance primarily using the funds from operations attributable to each segment, generated by each operating segment and the amount of common equity attributable to each segment.

Our operating segments are described below:

i. Asset management operations consist of managing our listed partnerships, private funds and public markets on behalf of our clients and ourselves. We generate contractual base management fees for these activities and we also are entitled to earn performance fees, including incentive distributions, performance fees and carried interests. We also provide transaction and advisory services.

ii. Property operations include the ownership, operation and development of office, retail, industrial, multifamily, hotel and other properties.

iii. Renewable energy operations include the ownership, operation and development of hydroelectric, wind power and other generating facilities.

iv. Infrastructure operations include the ownership, operation and development of utilities, transport, energy, timberland and agricultural operations.

v. Private equity operations include the investments and operations overseen by our private equity group which include both direct investments and investments made by our private equity funds. Our private equity funds have a mandate to invest in a broad range of industries.

vi. Residential development operations consist predominantly of homebuilding, condominium development and land development.

vii. Service activities include construction management and contracting services, and property services operations which include global corporate relocation, facilities management and residential brokerage services.

viii. Corporate activities include the investment of cash and financial assets, as well as the management of our corporate capitalization, including corporate borrowings, capital securities and preferred equity which fund a portion of the capital invested in our other operations. Certain corporate costs such as technology and operations are incurred on behalf of all of our operating segments and allocated to each operating segment based on an internal pricing framework.

b) Basis of Measurement

i. Funds from Operations

Funds from Operations ("FFO") is the key measure of our financial performance. We define FFO as net income prior to fair value changes, depreciation and amortization, deferred income taxes, and transaction costs. FFO also includes gains or losses arising from transactions during the reporting period adjusted to include fair value changes and revaluation surplus recorded in prior periods net of taxes payable or receivable, as well as amounts that are recorded directly in equity, such as ownership changes, as opposed to net income because they result from a change in ownership of a consolidated entity ("realized disposition gains").

We include realized disposition gains in FFO because we consider the purchase and sale of assets to be a normal part of the company's business. When determining FFO, we include our proportionate share of the FFO of equity accounted investments on a fully diluted basis.

We use FFO to assess operating results and our business. We do not use FFO as a measure of cash generated from our operations. We derive funds from operations for each segment and reconcile total segmented FFO to net income in Note 3(c)(v) of the consolidated financial statements.

Our definition of FFO may differ from the definition used by other organizations, as well as the definition of funds from operations used by the Real Property Association of Canada ("REALPAC") and the National Association of Real Estate Investment Trusts, Inc. ("NAREIT"), in part because the NAREIT definition is based on U.S. generally accepted accounting principles, as opposed to IFRS. The key differences between our definition of FFO and the determination of funds from operations by REALPAC and/or NAREIT, are that we include the following: realized disposition gains or losses and cash taxes payable on those gains, if any; foreign exchange gains or losses on monetary items not forming part of our net investment in foreign operations; and gains or losses on the sale of an investment in a foreign operation.

ii. Segment Balance Sheet Information

The company uses common equity by operating segment as its measure of segment assets, because it is utilized by the company's Chief Operating Decision Maker for capital allocation decisions.

iii. Segment Allocation and Measurement

Segment measures include amounts earned from consolidated entities that are eliminated on consolidation. The principal adjustment is to include asset management revenues charged to consolidated entities as revenues within the company's asset management segment with the corresponding expense recorded as corporate costs within the relevant segment. These amounts are based on the in-place terms of the asset management contracts amongst the consolidated entities. Inter-segment revenues are made under terms that approximate market value.

The company allocates the costs of shared functions which would otherwise be included within its corporate activities segment, such as information technology and internal audit, pursuant to formal policies.

c) Reportable Segment Measures

The following tables present selected reportable segment measures.

YEAR ENDED DECEMBER 31, 2014 (MILLIONS)	Asset Management	Property	Renewable Energy	Infrastructure	Private Equity	Residential Development	Service Activities	Corporate Activities	Total Segments	Notes
External revenues	$ 215	$ 5,010	$ 1,679	$ 2,193	$ 2,559	$ 2,912	$ 3,599	$ 197	$ 18,364	
Inter-segment revenues	556	—	—	—	—	—	—	2	558	i
Segmented revenues	771	5,010	1,679	2,193	2,559	2,912	3,599	199	18,922	
Equity accounted income	—	609	26	392	31	67	34	—	1,159	ii
Interest expense	—	(1,287)	(414)	(379)	(77)	(186)	(9)	(229)	(2,581)	iii
Current income taxes	—	(29)	(18)	(25)	(7)	(24)	—	(11)	(114)	iv
Funds from operations	387	884	313	222	369	164	152	(331)	2,160	v
Common equity	323	14,877	4,882	2,097	1,050	2,080	1,220	(6,376)	20,153	
Equity accounted investments	—	10,586	273	3,544	—	330	154	29	14,916	
Additions to non-current assets[1]	—	10,971	2,879	2,617	426	72	17	287	17,269	

1. Includes additions to, and acquisitions of, equity accounted investments, investment properties, property, plant and equipment, sustainable resources, intangible assets and goodwill.

YEAR ENDED DECEMBER 31, 2013 (MILLIONS)	Asset Management	Property	Renewable Energy	Infrastructure	Private Equity	Residential Development	Service Activities	Corporate Activities	Total Segments	Notes
External revenues	$ 764	$ 4,569	$ 1,620	$ 2,326	$ 4,124	$ 2,521	$ 3,817	$ 352	$ 20,093	
Inter-segment revenues	419	—	—	—	—	—	—	—	419	i
Segmented revenues	1,183	4,569	1,620	2,326	4,124	2,521	3,817	352	20,512	
Equity accounted income	—	429	21	333	7	15	27	12	844	ii
Interest expense	—	(1,123)	(409)	(407)	(132)	(167)	—	(315)	(2,553)	iii
Current income taxes	—	(59)	(19)	(26)	(9)	(23)	—	(23)	(159)	iv
Funds from operations	865	554	447	472	612	46	157	223	3,376	v
Common equity	216	13,339	4,428	2,171	1,105	1,435	1,286	(6,199)	17,781	
Equity accounted investments	—	9,732	290	2,615	21	273	211	135	13,277	
Additions to non-current assets[1]	—	8,711	1,614	2,061	591	93	110	8	13,188	

1. Includes additions to, and acquisitions of, equity accounted investments, investment properties, property, plant and equipment, sustainable resources, intangible assets and goodwill.

i. Inter-Segment Revenues

The adjustment to external revenues, when determining segmented revenues, consists of management fees earned from consolidated entities totalling $556 million (2013 – $419 million) and interest income on loans between consolidated entities totalling $2 million (2013 – $nil), which were eliminated on consolidation to arrive at the company's consolidated revenues.

ii. Equity Accounted Income

The company defines segment equity accounted income to be the company's share of FFO from its investments in associates (equity accounted investments), determined by applying the same methodology utilized in adjusting net income of consolidated entities. The following table reconciles segment equity accounted income on a segmented basis to the company's Consolidated Statements of Operations.

YEARS ENDED DECEMBER 31 (MILLIONS)	2014	2013
Segmented equity accounted income	$ 1,159	$ 844
Fair value changes and other non-FFO items	435	(85)
Equity accounted income	$ 1,594	$ 759

iii. Interest Expense

Interest expense includes interest on loans between consolidated entities totalling $2 million (2013 – $nil), which is eliminated on consolidation when determining the company's consolidated interest expense.

iv. Current Income Taxes

Current income taxes are included in segmented FFO, but are aggregated with deferred income taxes in income tax expense on the company's Consolidated Statements of Operations. The following table reconciles segment current tax expense to consolidated income taxes:

YEARS ENDED DECEMBER 31 (MILLIONS)	2014	2013
Segment current tax expense	$ (114)	$ (159)
Deferred income tax	(1,209)	(686)
Income tax expense	$ (1,323)	$ (845)

v. Reconciliation of FFO to Net Income

The following table reconciles total reportable segment FFO to net income:

YEARS ENDED DECEMBER 31 (MILLIONS)	Notes	2014	2013
Total reportable segment FFO		$ 2,160	$ 3,376
Realized disposition gains not recorded in net income	vi	(477)	(434)
Non-controlling interests in FFO		2,096	2,465
Financial statement components not included in FFO			
Equity accounted fair value changes and other non-FFO items	iii	435	(85)
Fair value changes		3,674	663
Depreciation and amortization		(1,470)	(1,455)
Deferred income taxes	iv	(1,209)	(686)
Net income		$ 5,209	$ 3,844

vi. Realized Disposition Gains

Realized disposition gains include gains and losses recorded in net income arising from transactions during the current year adjusted to include fair value changes and revaluation surplus recorded in prior periods. Realized disposition gains also include amounts that are recorded directly in equity as changes in ownership as opposed to net income because they result from a change in ownership of a consolidated entity.

The adjustment to realized disposition gains consists of amounts that are included in the following components of the company's consolidated financial statements:

YEARS ENDED DECEMBER 31 (MILLIONS)	2014	2013
Ownership changes in common equity	$ —	$ 160
Prior period fair value changes and revaluation surplus	477	274
	$ 477	$ 434

d) Geographic Allocation

The company's revenue and consolidated assets by location are as follows:

AS AT AND FOR THE YEARS ENDED DECEMBER 31 (MILLIONS)	2014 Revenue	2014 Assets	2013 Revenue	2013 Assets
United States	$ 6,150	$ 67,125	$ 7,099	$ 49,020
Canada	3,403	19,487	3,513	21,669
Australia	3,136	12,747	4,243	14,258
Brazil	1,864	11,849	1,684	13,074
Europe	2,128	10,758	1,657	9,099
Other	1,683	7,514	1,897	5,625
	$ 18,364	$ 129,480	$ 20,093	$ 112,745

Intangible assets and goodwill by geographic segments are included in Note 14 and 15, respectively.

e) Revenues Allocation

Total external revenues by product or service are as follows:

YEARS ENDED DECEMBER 31 (MILLIONS)	2014	2013
Asset management	$ 215	$ 764
Property		
Office properties	2,602	2,579
Retail properties	321	207
Industrial, multifamily, hotel and other	2,087	1,783
Renewable energy		
Hydroelectric	1,354	1,287
Wind energy	308	253
Co-generation and other	17	80
Infrastructure		
Utilities	958	927
Transport	706	690
Energy	274	221
Sustainable resources	255	488
Private equity	2,559	4,124
Residential development	2,912	2,521
Service activities	3,599	3,817
Corporate activities	197	352
Total revenues	$ 18,364	$ 20,093

4. SUBSIDIARIES

The following table presents the details of the company's subsidiaries with significant non-controlling interests:

	Jurisdiction of Formation	Voting Rights Held by Non-Controlling Interests[1] Dec. 31, 2014	Dec. 31, 2013	Ownership Interest Held by Non-Controlling Interests[2] Dec. 31, 2014	Dec. 31, 2013
Brookfield Property Partners L.P. ("BPY")	Bermuda	—	—	32.3%[3]	10.6%
Brookfield Renewable Energy Partners L.P. ("BREP")	Bermuda	—	—	37.5%[4]	35.0%
Brookfield Infrastructure Partners L.P. ("BIP")	Bermuda	—	—	71.5%	71.5%
Brookfield Residential Properties Inc. ("BRP")	Canada	29.4%	31.5%	29.4%	31.5%

1. Control of the limited partnerships (BPY, BREP and BIP) resides with their respective general partners which are wholly owned subsidiaries of the company. The company's general partner interest is entitled to earn base management fees and incentive distribution rights
2. The company's ownership interest in BPY, BREP and BIP includes holding a combination of redemption-exchange units (REUs), Class A limited partnership units, special limited partnership units and general partnership units in each subsidiary, where applicable. Each of BPY, BREP and BIP's partnership capital includes its Class A limited partnership units whereas REUs and general partnership units are considered non-controlling interests for the respective partnerships. REUs share the same economic attributes in all respects except for the redemption right described above. The REUs and general partnership units participate in earnings and distributions on a per unit basis equivalent to the per unit participation of the Class A limited partnership units of the subsidiary.
3. During 2014, BPY completed a tender offer for its publicly traded subsidiary Brookfield Office Properties Inc. ("BPO") the consideration being a combination of cash and BPY units which resulted in a decrease in the company's ownership in BPY from 89.4% to 67.7%
4. During 2014, BREP completed an equity issuance, decreasing the company's ownership interest in BPY by 2.5% to 62.5%

The table below presents the exchanges in which the company's subsidiaries with significant non-controlling interests were publicly listed as of December 31, 2014:

	TSX	NYSE
BPY	BPY.UN	BPY
BREP	BEP.UN	BEP
BIP	BIP.UN	BIP
BRP	BRP	BRP

All publicly listed entities are subject to independent governance. Accordingly, the company has no direct access to the assets of these subsidiaries.

Summarized financial information with respect to the company's subsidiaries with significant non-controlling interests are set out below. The summarized financial information represents amounts before intra-group eliminations:

AS AT DECEMBER 31, 2014 (MILLIONS)	BPY	BREP	BIP	BRP
Current assets	$ 4,524	$ 694	$ 1,560	$ 1,493
Non-current assets	61,051	19,155	14,935	1,884
Current liabilities	(5,356)	(687)	(821)	(364)
Non-current liabilities	(31,920)	(10,281)	(9,352)	(1,417)
Non-controlling interests	(14,618)	(5,075)	(4,932)	(496)
Equity attributable to Brookfield[1]	$ 13,681	$ 3,806	$ 1,390	$ 1,100

1. Includes Brookfield's investment in common equity, general partnership units, redemption-exchange units, Class A limited partnership units and special limited partnership units in each subsidiary where applicable

The following table outlines the composition of accumulated non-controlling interests presented within the company's consolidated financial statements:

(MILLIONS)	Dec. 31, 2014	Dec. 31, 2013
BPY	$14,618	$12,810
BREP	5,075	4,002
BIP	4,932	5,127
BRP	496	515
Brookfield Incorporações S.A. ("BISA")	106	505
Individually immaterial subsidiaries with non-controlling interests	4,318	3,688
	$29,545	$26,647

During the year ended December 31, 2014, the company increased its effective ownership in BISA from 45.0% to 87.1% through a cash tender for BISA shares for aggregate consideration of $160 million.

In December 2014, the company entered into a plan of arrangement to acquire the approximately 30% of common shares of BRP that it did not already own for $24.25 per common share. The transaction received the unanimous approval of BRP's independent directors, and was approved by BRP shareholders on March 10, 2015. The transaction closed on March 13, 2015.

5. ACQUISITIONS OF CONSOLIDATED ENTITIES

The company accounts for business combinations using the acquisition method of accounting, pursuant to which the cost of acquiring a business is allocated to its identifiable tangible and intangible assets and liabilities on the basis of the estimated fair values at the date of acquisition.

a) Completed During 2014

The following table summarizes the balance sheet impact of business combinations that occurred during the year ended December 31, 2014:

(MILLIONS)	Property	Renewable Energy	Other	Total
Cash and cash equivalents	$42	$61	$—	$103
Accounts receivable and other	193	52	76	321
Investment properties	8,332	—	—	8,332
Property, plant and equipment	—	2,416	608	3,024
Intangible assets	4	—	6	10
Goodwill	—	—	78	78
Total assets	8,571	2,529	768	11,868
Less:				
Accounts payable and other	(226)	(142)	(47)	(415)
Non-recourse borrowings	(3,831)	(322)	(219)	(4,372)
Deferred income tax liabilities	(23)	(127)	(145)	(295)
Non-controlling interests[1]	(336)	—	(138)	(474)
	(4,416)	(591)	(549)	(5,556)
Net assets acquired	4,155	1,938	219	6,312
Consideration[2]	$3,968	$1,915	$219	$6,102

1. Includes non-controlling interests recognized on business combinations measured as the proportionate share of fair value of the assets and liabilities on the date of acquisition
2. Total consideration, including amounts paid by non-controlling interests

Brookfield recorded $299 million of revenue and $51 million of net income from the acquired operations as a result of the acquisitions made during the year. Total revenue and net income that would have been recorded if the acquisitions had occurred at the beginning of the year would have been $801 million and $125 million, respectively. Certain of the current year business combinations were completed in close proximity to the year-end date of December 31, 2014 and accordingly, the fair values of the acquired assets and liabilities for these operations have been determined on a provisional basis, pending finalization of the post-acquisition review of the fair value of the acquired net assets.

FOR THE YEAR ENDED DECEMBER 31, 2014 (MILLIONS)	BPY	BREP	BIP	BRP
Revenues	$4,373	$1,714	$1,924	$1,532
Net income attributable to:				
Non-controlling interests	1,821	131	190	78
Shareholders	2,599	72	39	176
	4,420	203	229	254
Other comprehensive income (loss) attributable to:				
Non-controlling interests	(139)	445	(48)	(21)
Shareholders	(308)	423	(13)	(50)
	(447)	868	(61)	(71)
Distributions paid to non-controlling interests in common equity	185	176	288	—
Cash flows from (used in):				
Operating activities	483	700	691	128
Investing activities	(5,000)	(2,037)	(1,073)	(62)
Financing activities	4,455	1,299	42	(189)

AS AT DECEMBER 31, 2013 (MILLIONS)	BPY	BREP	BIP	BRP
Current assets	$3,011	$626	$1,268	$1,410
Non-current assets	49,435	16,373	14,414	1,878
Current liabilities	(6,973)	(920)	(598)	(333)
Non-current liabilities	(12,810)	(8,543)	(8,479)	(1,480)
Non-controlling interests	(20,483)	(4,002)	(5,127)	(515)
Equity attributable to Brookfield[1]	$12,180	$3,534	$1,478	$960

1. Includes Brookfield's investment in common equity, general partnership units, Class A limited partnership units, redemption-exchange units, general partnership units and special limited partnership units in each subsidiary, where applicable

FOR THE YEAR ENDED DECEMBER 31, 2013 (MILLIONS)	BPY	BREP	BIP	BRP
Revenues	$4,287	$1,717	$1,826	$1,356
Net income (loss) attributable to:				
Non-controlling interests	928	126	82	51
Shareholders	835	89	(17)	98
	1,763	215	65	149
Other comprehensive income (loss) attributable to:				
Non-controlling interests	(222)	(162)	155	(16)
Shareholders	(241)	(386)	46	(35)
	(463)	(548)	201	(51)
Distributions paid to non-controlling interests in common equity	29	135	253	—
Cash flows from (used in):				
Operating activities	421	735	694	(52)
Investing activities	(1,622)	(397)	(162)	(66)
Financing activities	1,669	(263)	(232)	391

b) Completed During 2013

The following table summarizes the balance sheet impact as a result of the business combinations that occurred in 2013:

(MILLIONS)	Renewable Energy	Property	Other	Total
Cash and cash equivalents	$ 8	$ 280	$ 4	$ 292
Accounts receivable and other	118	176	5	299
Equity accounted investments	4	346	—	350
Investment properties	—	5,530	—	5,530
Property, plant and equipment	1,387	29	199	1,615
Intangible assets	—	20	—	20
Total assets	1,517	6,381	208	8,106
Less:				
Accounts payable and other	(79)	(391)	(4)	(474)
Non-recourse borrowings	(1,075)	(2,940)	(40)	(4,055)
Deferred income tax liabilities	(65)	—	—	(65)
Non-controlling interests[1]	(68)	(163)	—	(231)
	(1,287)	(3,494)	(44)	(4,825)
Net assets acquired	$ 230	$ 2,887	$ 164	$ 3,281
Consideration[2]	$ 230	$ 2,861	$ 161	$ 3,252

1. Includes non-controlling interests recognized on business combinations measured as the proportionate share of fair value of the assets and liabilities on the date of acquisition
2. Total consideration, including amounts paid by non-controlling interests

Brookfield recorded $163 million of revenue and $82 million in net income from the acquired operations as a result of the acquisitions made during 2013. Total revenue and net income that would have been recorded if the acquisitions had occurred at the beginning of the year would have been $568 million and $112 million, respectively.

The following table summarizes the balance sheet impact as a result of significant business combinations that occurred in 2013:

(MILLIONS)	Gazeley	IDI	MPG
Cash and cash equivalents	$ 40	$ 28	$ 156
Accounts receivable and other	41	36	46
Equity accounted investments	—	346	—
Investment properties	484	525	1,817
Property, plant and equipment	—	1	—
Intangible assets	20	—	—
Total assets	585	936	2,019
Less:			
Accounts payable and other	(45)	(46)	(45)
Non-recourse borrowings	(119)	(261)	(1,531)
Non-controlling interests[1]	(21)	(34)	—
	(185)	(341)	(1,576)
Net assets acquired	$ 400	$ 595	$ 443
Consideration[2]	$ 370	$ 595	$ 443

1. Includes non-controlling interests recognized on business combinations measured as the proportionate share of fair value of the assets and liabilities on the date of acquisition
2. Total consideration, including amounts paid by non-controlling interests

Significant business contributions completed during 2013 are as follows, all of which were in the company's property operations:

In June 2013, a subsidiary of Brookfield acquired a 95% equity interest in EZW Gazeley Limited ("Gazeley"), a UK-based industrial real estate company, for $370 million. Brookfield recorded $17 million of revenue and $16 million in net income from the acquired operation during the year. Total revenue and net income that would have been recorded if the acquisition had occurred at the beginning of the year would have been $55 million and $9 million, respectively.

The following table summarizes the balance sheet impact as a result of significant business combinations that occurred in 2014:

	Property				Renewable Energy	
(MILLIONS)	Five Manhattan West	CARS	Manhattan Multifamily	Candor Office Parks	Pennsylvania Hydro	Ireland Wind Portfolio
Cash and cash equivalents	$ —	$ 15	$ 15	$ —	$ 15	$ 35
Accounts receivable and other	57	6	9	100	11	22
Investment properties	653	4,313	1,044	785	—	—
Property, plant and equipment	—	—	—	—	1,040	1,075
Total assets	710	4,334	1,068	885	1,066	1,132
Less:						
Accounts payable and other	(2)	(28)	(9)	(179)	(24)	(116)
Non-recourse borrowings	(462)	(2,980)	—	(193)	(77)	(232)
Deferred income tax liabilities	—	(22)	—	(209)	(56)	(66)
Non-controlling interests[1]	(4)	(120)	(3)	—	—	—
	(468)	(3,150)	(12)	(581)	(157)	(414)
Net assets acquired	$ 242	$ 1,184	$ 1,056	$ 304	$ 909	$ 718
Consideration[2]	$ 57[3]	$ 1,184	$ 1,056	$ 304	$ 909	$ 718

1. Includes non-controlling interests recognized on business combinations measured as the proportionate share of fair value of the assets and liabilities on the date of acquisition
2. Total consideration, including amounts paid by non-controlling interests and previous interests measured at the purchase date
3. Excludes previously held $185 million equity accounted investment

In January 2014, a subsidiary of Brookfield purchased an additional 23.6% interest in a New York City office property ("Five Manhattan West") that was previously an equity accounted joint venture. The incremental interest was purchased for total consideration of $57 million and resulted in the acquisition of control and increased Brookfield's ownership to 98.6%. The fair value of the previous interest was $185 million and accordingly, no remeasurement gain or loss was recorded as part of this acquisition. Total revenue and net income that would have been recorded if the acquisition had occurred at the beginning of the year would have been $31 million and $4 million, respectively.

In October 2014, a subsidiary of Brookfield acquired a 91% interest in Capital Automotive Real Estate Services Inc. ("CARS"), an owner and operator of more than 300 triple net leased automotive dealerships across North America. Total consideration was $1,184 million and includes contingent consideration based on investment returns hurdles on two of CARS's portfolio properties. The investment property and debt valuations as well as contingent consideration and certain tax implications from the acquisition were accounted for based on provisional information. Total revenue and net income that would have been recorded if the acquisition had occurred at the beginning of the year would have been $275 million and $89 million, respectively.

In October 2014, a subsidiary of Brookfield completed the acquisition of a 4,000 unit multifamily portfolio across six properties in Manhattan, New York City, for total consideration of $1,056 million. Total revenue and net income that would have been recorded if the acquisition had occurred at the beginning of the year would have been $102 million and $14 million, respectively.

In November 2014, a subsidiary of Brookfield acquired 60% interest in a portfolio of office parks in India ("Candor Office Parks") for total consideration of $304 million. The portfolio consists of six properties with a total of approximately 16.8 million square feet of gross leasable area. The purchase price allocation has been done on a preliminary basis.

In March 2014, a subsidiary of Brookfield purchased a 33% economic and 50% voting interest in a 417 MW hydroelectric generation facility in Pennsylvania for total cash consideration of $295 million and commenced equity accounting for this interest at that time. In August 2014, this subsidiary acquired the remaining 67% economic and 50% voting interest in the facility for additional cash consideration of $614 million, and began consolidating the operation. Prior to the acquisition of the remaining interest, the previously held 33% economic interest was re-measured at fair value. The purchase price allocation has been done on a preliminary basis. Total revenue and net income that would have been recorded if the acquisition had occurred at the beginning of the year would have been $99 million and $13 million, respectively.

In June 2014, a subsidiary of Brookfield acquired a wind portfolio comprising 326 MW of operating wind capacity across 17 wind projects in Ireland which is expected to generate 837 GWh annually. Total consideration was $718 million and the purchase price allocation has been done on a preliminary basis. Total revenue and net loss that would have been recorded if the acquisition had occurred at the beginning of the year would have been $92 million and $11 million, respectively.

Deferred income tax assets and liabilities as at December 31, 2014 and 2013 relate to the following:

(MILLIONS)	Dec. 31, 2014	Dec. 31, 2013
Non-capital losses (Canada)	$ 827	$ 878
Capital losses (Canada)	143	215
Losses (U.S.)	463	385
Losses (International)	544	511
Difference in basis	(8,660)	(6,741)
Total net deferred tax liabilities	$ (6,683)	$ (4,752)

The aggregate amount of temporary differences associated with investments in subsidiaries for which deferred tax liabilities have not been recognized as at December 31, 2014 is approximately $8 billion (2013 – approximately $8 billion).

The company regularly assesses the status of open tax examinations and its historical tax filing positions for the potential for adverse outcomes to determine the adequacy of the provision for income and other taxes. The company believes that it has adequately provided for any tax adjustments that are more likely than not to occur as a result of ongoing tax examinations or historical filing positions.

The dividend payment on certain preferred shares of the company results in the payment of cash taxes and the company obtaining a deduction based on the amount of these taxes.

The following table details the expiry date, if applicable, of the unrecognized deferred tax assets:

(MILLIONS)	Dec. 31, 2014	Dec. 31, 2013
2015	$ 15	$ 2
2016	11	1
2017	5	—
2018 and after	355	290
Do not expire	764	901
Total	$ 1,150	$ 1,194

The components of the income taxes in other comprehensive income for the years ended December 31, 2014 and 2013 are set out below:

YEARS ENDED DECEMBER 31 (MILLIONS)	2014	2013
Revaluation of property, plant and equipment	$ 650	$ 135
Financial contracts and power sale agreements	(66)	129
Available-for-sale securities	5	(10)
Equity accounted investments	—	37
Foreign currency translation	39	(10)
Revaluation of pension obligation	(18)	(1)
Total deferred tax in other comprehensive income	$ 610	$ 280

17. ACCOUNTS PAYABLE AND OTHER

(MILLIONS)	Dec. 31, 2014	Dec. 31, 2013
Accounts payable	$ 4,510	$ 5,244
Other liabilities	5,898	5,072
Total	$ 10,408	$ 10,316

The current and non-current balances of accounts payable and other liabilities are as follows:

(MILLIONS)	Dec. 31, 2014	Dec. 31, 2013
Current	$ 6,054	$ 5,994
Non-current	4,354	4,322
Total	$ 10,408	$ 10,316

In October 2013, a subsidiary of Brookfield acquired a 100% interest in Industrial Developments International Inc. ("IDI"), a U.S.-based industrial real estate company which owns and operates a high-quality industrial portfolio, for total consideration of $595 million. Brookfield recorded $3 million of revenue and $3 million in net loss from the acquired operation during the year. Total revenue and net loss that would have been recorded if the acquisition had occurred at the beginning of the year would have been $13 million and $11 million, respectively.

In October 2013, a subsidiary of Brookfield completed the acquisition of MPG Office Trust, Inc. ("MPG"), an owner and operator of office properties in Los Angeles for total consideration of $443 million. Brookfield recorded $36 million of revenue and $7 million in net income from the acquired operation during the year. Total revenue and net income that would have been recorded if the acquisition had occurred at the beginning of the year would have been $172 million and $13 million, respectively.

c) Business Combinations Achieved in Stages

The following table provides details of the business combinations achieved in stages:

YEARS ENDED DECEMBER 31 (MILLIONS)	2014	2013
Fair value of investment immediately before acquiring control	$ 637	$ 248
Less: Carrying value of investment immediately before acquisition	(649)	(256)
Amounts recognized in other comprehensive income[1]	4	6
Remeasurement loss recorded in net income	$ (8)	$ (2)

1. Included in the carrying value of the investment immediately before acquisition

[...]

16. INCOME TAXES

The major components of income tax expense for the years ended December 31, 2014 and December 31, 2013 are set out below:

YEARS ENDED DECEMBER 31 (MILLIONS)	2014	2013
Current income taxes	$ 114	$ 159
Deferred income tax expense/(recovery)		
Origination and reversal of temporary differences	1,087	871
Recovery arising from previously unrecognized tax assets	(174)	(130)
Change of tax rates and new legislation	296	(55)
Total deferred income taxes	1,209	686
Income taxes	$ 1,323	$ 845

The company's Canadian domestic statutory income tax rate has remained consistent at 26% throughout both of 2014 and 2013. The company's effective tax rate is different from the company's domestic statutory income tax rate due to the following differences set out below:

YEARS ENDED DECEMBER 31	2014	2013
Statutory income tax rate	26%	26%
Increase (reduction) in rate resulting from:		
Portion of gains subject to different tax rates	—	(1)
International operations subject to different tax rates	(5)	(3)
Taxable income attribute to non-controlling interests	(5)	(7)
Recognition of previously unrecorded deferred tax assets	(1)	(2)
Non-recognition of the benefit of current year's tax losses	2	3
Change in tax rates and new legislation	4	—
Other	(1)	2
Effective income tax rate	20%	18%

18. CORPORATE BORROWINGS

Term debt

(MILLIONS)	Maturity	Annual Rate	Currency	Dec. 31, 2014	Dec. 31, 2013
Public – Canadian	Sept. 8, 2016	5.20%	C$	$ 258	$ 282
Public – U.S.	Apr. 25, 2017	5.80%	US$	239	239
Public – Canadian	Apr. 25, 2017	5.29%	C$	216	235
Public – Canadian	Apr. 9, 2019	3.95%	C$	519	568
Public – Canadian	Mar. 1, 2021	5.30%	C$	301	330
Public – Canadian	Mar. 31, 2023	4.54%	C$	519	568
Public – Canadian	Mar. 8, 2024	5.04%	C$	431	472
Public – Canadian	Jan. 28, 2026	4.82%	C$	430	—
Public – U.S.	Mar. 1, 2033	7.38%	US$	250	250
Public – Canadian	Jun. 14, 2035	5.95%	C$	362	396
				3,525	3,340
Commercial paper and bank borrowings		1.19%	US$/C$	574	662
Deferred financing costs[1]				(24)	(27)
Total				$ 4,075	$ 3,975

1. Deferred financing costs are amortized to interest expense over the term of the borrowing following the effective interest method

Corporate borrowings have a weighted average interest rate of 4.6% (2013 – 4.5%), and include $3,428 million (2013 – $3,356 million) repayable in Canadian dollars of C$3,982 million (2013 – C$3,565 million).

On January 15, 2015, the company issued US$500 million of 4.0%, 10 year notes.

19. NON-RECOURSE BORROWINGS

a) Property-Specific Mortgages

Principal repayments on property-specific mortgages due over the next five calendar years and thereafter are as follows:

(MILLIONS)	Property	Renewable Energy	Infrastructure	Private Equity	Residential Development	Service Activities	Corporate Activities	Total
2015	$ 2,487	$ 246	$ 80	$ 157	$ 823	$ 27	$ —	$ 3,820
2016	4,098	532	398	80	516	—	—	5,624
2017	5,659	885	233	269	143	—	—	7,189
2018	2,469	886	251	4	33	—	—	3,643
2019	2,579	179	125	3	12	—	—	2,898
Thereafter	8,251	3,263	5,433	239	4	—	—	17,190
Total – Dec. 31, 2014	$ 25,543	$ 5,991	$ 6,520	$ 752	$ 1,531	$ 27	$ —	$ 40,364
Total – Dec. 31, 2013	$ 21,577	$ 4,907	$ 6,078	$ 342	$ 2,214	$ 271	$ 106	$ 35,495

The current and non-current balances of property-specific mortgages are as follows:

(MILLIONS)	Dec. 31, 2014	Dec. 31, 2013
Current	$ 3,820	$ 6,288
Non-current	36,544	29,207
Total	$ 40,364	$ 35,495

Property-specific mortgages by currency include the following:

(MILLIONS)	Dec. 31, 2014	Local Currency	Dec. 31, 2013	Local Currency
U.S. dollars	$ 25,193	US$ 25,193	$ 20,205	US$ 20,205
Canadian dollars	4,839	C$ 5,622	5,217	C$ 5,542
Australian dollars	3,865	A$ 4,729	3,708	A$ 4,157
British pounds	2,208	£ 1,418	2,447	£ 1,478
Brazilian reais	2,123	R$ 5,626	2,988	R$ 5,542
Chilean unidad de fomento	898	UF$ 22	689	UF$ 16
European Union euros	877	€$ 725	2	€$ 1
Indian rupee	193	Rs 12,123		Rs —
Colombian pesos	168	COP$ 400,155	207	COP$ 400,155
New Zealand dollars	—	N$ —	32	N$ 39
Total	$ 40,364		$ 35,495	

b) Subsidiary Borrowings

Principal repayments on subsidiary borrowings due over the next five calendar years and thereafter are as follows:

(MILLIONS)	Property	Renewable Energy	Infrastructure	Private Equity	Residential Development	Services Activities	Total
2015	$ 504	$ —	$ 34	$ 129	$ —	$ 295	$ 962
2016	2,304	258	12	4	—	—	2,578
2017	227	—	370	354	—	—	951
2018	990	172	14	36	—	—	1,212
2019	—	401	259	—	—	—	660
Thereafter	—	856	30	4	1,076	—	1,966
Total – Dec. 31, 2014	$ 4,025	$ 1,687	$ 719	$ 527	$ 1,076	$ 295	$ 8,329
Total – Dec. 31, 2013	$ 3,075	$ 1,717	$ 435	$ 899	$ 1,266	$ —	$ 7,392

The current and non-current balances of subsidiary borrowings are as follows:

(MILLIONS)	Dec. 31, 2014	Dec. 31, 2013
Current	$ 962	$ 1,854
Non-current	7,367	5,538
Total	$ 8,329	$ 7,392

Subsidiary borrowings by currency include the following:

(MILLIONS)	Dec. 31, 2014	Local Currency	Dec. 31, 2013	Local Currency
U.S. dollars	$ 5,429	US$ 5,429	$ 4,346	US$ 4,346
Canadian dollars	2,596	C$ 3,015	2,283	C$ 2,421
Australian dollars	163	A$ 200	696	A$ 780
Brazilian reais	114	R$ 303	59	R$ 139
British pounds	27	£ 17	8	£ 5
Total	$ 8,329		$ 7,392	

20. SUBSIDIARY EQUITY OBLIGATIONS

Subsidiary equity obligations consist of the following:

(MILLIONS)	Note	Dec. 31, 2014	Dec. 31, 2013
Subsidiary preferred equity units	(a)	$ 1,535	$ —
Limited-life funds and redeemable fund units		1,423	1,086
Subsidiary preferred shares	(b)	583	628
Corporate preferred shares	(c)	—	163
Total		$ 3,541	$ 1,877

a) Subsidiary Preferred Equity Units

BPY issued $1,800 million of exchangeable preferred equity units in three $600 million tranches redeemable in 2021, 2024 and 2026, respectively. The preferred equity units are exchangeable into equity units of BPY at $25.70 per unit, at the option of the holder, at any time up to and including the maturity date. BPY may redeem the preferred equity units after specified periods if the BPY equity unit price exceeds predetermined amounts. At maturity, the preferred equity units will be converted into BPY equity units at the lower of $25.70 or the then market price of a BPY equity unit. The preferred equity units represent compound financial instruments and the value of the liability and equity conversion option was determined to be $1,535 million and $265 million, respectively, at the time of issuance. Brookfield Asset Management Inc. (the "Corporation") is required under certain circumstances to purchase the preferred equity units at their redemption value in equal amounts in 2021 and 2024 and may be required to purchase the 2026 tranche, as further described in Note 31(a).

(MILLIONS, EXCEPT SHARE INFORMATION)	Shares Outstanding	Cumulative Dividend Rate	Currency	Dec. 31, 2014	Dec. 31, 2013
Series 1	24,000,000	6.25%	US$	$ 524	$ —
Series 2	24,000,000	6.50%	US$	510	—
Series 3	24,000,000	6.75%	US$	501	—
Total				$ 1,535	$ —

b) Subsidiary Preferred Shares

Preferred shares are classified as liabilities if the holders of the preferred shares have the right, after a fixed date, to convert the shares into common equity of the issuer based on the market price of the common equity of the issuer at that time unless they are previously redeemed by the issuer. The dividends paid on these securities are recorded in interest expense. As at December 31, 2014, the balance are obligations of BPY and its subsidiaries.

(MILLIONS, EXCEPT SHARE INFORMATION)	Shares Outstanding	Cumulative Dividend Rate	Currency	Dec. 31, 2014	Dec. 31, 2013
BPO Class AAA preferred shares					
Series G	3,350,000	5.25%	US$	$ 85	$ 110
Series H	7,000,000	5.75%	C$	150	188
Series J	7,000,000	5.00%	C$	150	188
Series K	4,980,000	5.20%	C$	107	142
Brookfield Property Split Corp ("BOP Split") senior preferred shares					
Series 1	1,000,000	5.25%	US$	25	—
Series 2	1,000,000	5.75%	C$	22	—
Series 3	1,000,000	5.00%	C$	22	—
Series 4	1,000,000	5.20%	C$	22	—
Total				$ 583	$ 628

The BPO Class AAA preferred shares and BOP Split senior preferred shares are redeemable at the option of either the issuer or the holder, at any time after the following dates:

	Earliest Permitted Redemption Date	Company's Conversion Option	Holder's Conversion Option
BPO Class AAA preferred shares			
Series G	Jun. 30, 2011		Sept. 30, 2015
Series H	Dec. 31, 2011		Dec. 31, 2015
Series J	Jun. 30, 2010		Dec. 31, 2014
Series K	Dec. 31, 2012		Dec. 31, 2016
BOP Split senior preferred shares			
Series 1	Jun. 30, 2014	Jun. 30, 2014	Sept. 30, 2015
Series 2	Dec. 31, 2014	Dec. 31, 2014	Dec. 31, 2015
Series 3	Jun. 30, 2014	Jun. 30, 2014	Dec. 31, 2014
Series 4	Dec. 31, 2015	Dec. 31, 2015	Dec. 31, 2016

c) Corporate Preferred Shares

On April 6, 2014, the company redeemed all of its outstanding Class A Series 12 preferred shares for cash.

21. EQUITY

Equity is comprised of the following:

(MILLIONS)	Dec. 31, 2014	Dec. 31, 2013
Preferred equity	$ 3,549	$ 3,098
Non-controlling interests	29,545	26,647
Common equity	20,153	17,781
	$ 53,247	$ 47,526

a) Preferred Equity

Preferred equity includes perpetual preferred shares and rate-reset preferred shares and consist of the following:

AS AT DECEMBER 31 (MILLIONS)	Average Rate			
	2014	2013	2014	2013
Perpetual preferred shares				
Floating rate	2.11%	2.13%	$ 480	$ 480
Fixed rate	4.82%	4.82%	753	753
Fixed rate-reset preferred shares	4.59%	5.00%	2,316	1,865
	4.31%	4.51%	$ 3,549	$ 3,098

Further details on each series of preferred shares are as follows:

(MILLIONS, EXCEPT SHARE INFORMATION)	Rate	Issued and Outstanding		Dec. 31, 2014	Dec. 31, 2013
		Dec. 31, 2014	Dec. 31, 2013		
Class A preferred shares					
Perpetual preferred shares					
Series 2	70% P	10,465,100	10,465,100	$ 169	$ 169
Series 4	70% P/8.5%	2,800,000	2,800,000	45	45
Series 8	Variable up to P	1,652,394	1,652,394	29	29
Series 13	70% P	9,297,700	9,297,700	195	195
Series 15	B.A. + 40 b.p.¹	2,000,000	2,000,000	42	42
Series 17	4.75%	8,000,000	8,000,000	174	174
Series 18	4.75%	8,000,000	8,000,000	181	181
Series 36	4.85%	8,000,000	8,000,000	201	201
Series 37	4.90%	8,000,000	8,000,000	197	197
				1,233	1,233
Rate-reset preferred shares²					
Series 9	3.80%	2,347,606	2,347,606	35	35
Series 22³	7.00%	—	12,000,000	—	274
Series 24	5.40%	11,000,000	11,000,000	269	269
Series 26	4.50%	10,000,000	10,000,000	245	245
Series 28	4.60%	9,400,000	9,400,000	235	235
Series 30	4.80%	10,000,000	10,000,000	247	247
Series 32	4.50%	12,000,000	12,000,000	304	304
Series 34	4.20%	10,000,000	10,000,000	256	256
Series 38⁴	4.40%	8,000,000	—	181	—
Series 40⁵	4.50%	12,000,000	—	275	—
Series 42⁶	4.50%	12,000,000	—	269	—
				2,316	1,865
Total				$ 3,549	$ 3,098

1. Rate determined in a quarterly auction
2. Dividend rates are fixed for five to six years from the quarter end dates after issuance, June 30, 2011, March 31, 2012, June 30, 2012, December 31, 2012, September 30, 2013, March 31, 2014, June 30, 2014 and December 31, 2014, respectively, and reset after five to six years to the 5-year Government of Canada bond rate plus between 180 and 296 basis points
3. Redeemed on September 30, 2014
4. Issued on March 13, 2014
5. Issued on June 5, 2014
6. Issued on October 8, 2014
P – Prime Rate, B.A. – Bankers' Acceptance Rate, b.p. – Basis Points

The company is authorized to issue an unlimited number of Class A preferred shares and an unlimited number of Class AA preferred shares, issuable in series. No Class AA preferred shares have been issued.

The Class A preferred shares have preference over the Class AA preferred shares, which in turn are entitled to preference over the Class A and Class B common shares on the declaration of dividends and other distributions to shareholders. All series of the outstanding preferred shares have a par value of C$25 per share.

b) Non-controlling Interests

Non-controlling interests represent the common and preferred equity in consolidated entities that are owned by other shareholders.

(MILLIONS)	Dec. 31, 2014	Dec. 31, 2013
Common equity	$ 27,131	$ 23,828
Preferred equity	2,414	2,819
Total	$ 29,545	$ 26,647

Further information on non-controlling interest is provided in Note 4, Subsidiaries.

c) Common Equity

The company's common equity is comprised of the following:

(MILLIONS)	Dec. 31, 2014	Dec. 31, 2013
Common shares	$ 3,031	$ 2,899
Contributed surplus	185	159
Retained earnings	9,873	7,159
Ownership changes	1,808	2,354
Accumulated other comprehensive income¹	5,256	5,210
Common equity	$ 20,153	$ 17,781

1. Accumulated other comprehensive income is comprised of revaluation surplus, currency translation, available-for-sale securities, cash flow hedges, actuarial changes on pension plans and equity accounted other comprehensive income, all of which are net of associated deferred income taxes

The company is authorized to issue an unlimited number of Class A shares and 85,120 Class B shares, together, referred to as common shares. The company's common shares have no stated par value. The holders of Class A shares and Class B shares rank on parity with each other with respect to the payment of dividends and the return of capital on the liquidation, dissolution or winding up of the company or any other distribution of the assets of the company among its shareholders for the purpose of winding up its affairs. Holders of the Class A shares are entitled to elect the other one-half of the Board of Directors of the company and holders of the Class B shares are entitled to elect the other one-half of the Board of Directors. With respect to the Class A and Class B shares, there are no dilutive factors, material or otherwise, that would result in different diluted earnings per share between the classes. This relationship holds true irrespective of the number of dilutive instruments issued in either one of the respective classes of common stock, as both classes of shares participate equally, on a pro rata basis, in the dividends, earnings and net assets of the company, whether taken before or after dilutive instruments, regardless of which class of shares are diluted.

The number of issued and outstanding common shares and unexercised options at December 31, 2014 and 2013 are as follows:

	Dec. 31, 2014	Dec. 31, 2013
Class A shares¹	618,733,227	615,386,476
Class B shares	85,120	85,120
Shares outstanding¹	618,818,347	615,471,596
Unexercised options²	36,672,766	35,603,974
Total diluted shares	655,491,113	651,075,570

1. Net of 10,800,883 (2013 – 9,550,000) Class A shares held by the company to satisfy long-term compensation agreements
2. Includes management share option plan and escrowed stock plan

The authorized common share capital consists of an unlimited number of shares. Shares issued and outstanding changed as follows:

	Dec. 31, 2014	Dec. 31, 2013
Outstanding at beginning of year¹	615,471,596	619,599,349
Issued (repurchased)		
Repurchases	(1,440,418)	(8,772,646)
Long-term share ownership plans²	4,590,927	4,442,362
Dividend reinvestment plan	196,242	202,531
Outstanding at end of year¹	618,818,347	615,471,596

1. Net of 10,800,883 (2013 – 9,550,000) Class A shares held by the company to satisfy long-term compensation agreements
2. Includes management share option plan, escrowed stock plan and restricted stock plan

i. *Earnings Per Share*

The components of basic and diluted earnings per share are summarized in the following table:

YEARS ENDED DECEMBER 31 (MILLIONS)	2014	2013
Net income attributable to shareholders	$ 3,110	$ 2,120
Preferred share dividends	(154)	(145)
Net income available to shareholders – basic	2,956	1,975
Capital securities dividends¹	2	13
Net income available for shareholders – diluted	$ 2,958	$ 1,988

1. The Series 12 preferred shares were convertible into Class A shares at a price equal to the greater of 95% at the market price at the time of conversion and C$2.00, at the option of either the company or the holder. The Series 12 preferred shares were redeemed by the company during 2014

(MILLIONS)	Dec. 31, 2014	Dec. 31, 2013
Weighted average – common shares	616.7	616.1
Dilutive effect of the conversion of options and escrowed shares using treasury stock method	15.7	12.8
Dilutive effect of the conversion of capital securities¹·²	1.2	7.9
Common shares and common share equivalents	633.6	636.8

1. The Series 12 preferred shares were convertible into Class A shares at a price equal to the greater of 95% at the market price at the time of conversion and C$2.00, at the option of either the company or the holder. The Series 12 preferred shares were redeemed by the company during 2014
2. The number of shares is based on 95% of the quoted market price at year end

ii. *Stock-Based Compensation*

The expense recognized for stock-based compensation is summarized in the following table:

YEARS ENDED DECEMBER 31 (MILLIONS)	2014	2013
Expense arising from equity-settled share-based payment transactions	$ 59	$ 54
Expense arising from cash-settled share-based payment transactions	265	87
Total expense arising from share-based payment transactions	324	141
Effect of hedging program	(263)	(77)
Total expense included in consolidated income	$ 61	$ 64

The share-based payment plans are described below. There have been no cancellations or modifications to any of the plans during 2014 or 2013.

1) Equity-settled Share-based Awards

a) Management Share Option Plan

Options issued under the company's Management Share Option Plan ("MSOP") vest over a period of up to five years, expire 10 years after the grant date, and are settled through issuance of Class A shares. The exercise price is equal to the market price at the grant date.

The changes in the number of options during 2014 and 2013 were as follows:

	Number of Options (000's)¹	Weighted Average Exercise Price	Number of Options (000's)²	Weighted Average Exercise Price
Outstanding at January 1, 2014	17,813	C$ 24.56	16,809	US$ 29.27
Granted	—		3,561	40.15
Exercised	(3,624)	23.78	(820)	29.35
Cancelled	—		(209)	33.92
Outstanding at December 31, 2014	14,189	C$ 24.75	19,341	US$ 31.22

1. Options to acquire TSX listed Class A shares
2. Options to acquire NYSE listed Class A shares

	Number of Options (000's)¹	Weighted Average Exercise Price	Number of Options (000's)²	Weighted Average Exercise Price
Outstanding at January 1, 2013	23,575	C$ 22.40	14,128	US$ 26.90
Granted	—		3,586	37.82
Exercised	(3,534)	17.79	(722)	24.96
Cancelled	(214)	20.85	(183)	30.78
Converted³	(2,014)	11.47	—	
Outstanding at December 31, 2013	17,813	C$ 24.56	16,809	US$ 29.27

1. Options to acquire TSX listed Class A shares
2. Options to acquire NYSE listed Class A shares
3. Options converted to restricted shares at maturity

The cost of the options granted during the year was determined using the Black-Scholes valuation model, with inputs to the model as follows:

YEARS ENDED DECEMBER 31	Unit	2014	2013
Weighted average share price	US$	40.15	37.82
Weighted average fair value per option	US$	9.21	7.87
Average term to exercise	Years	7.5	7.5
Share price volatility¹	%	31.4	31.2
Liquidity discount	%	25.0	25.0
Weighted average annual dividend yield	%	1.5	1.5
Risk-free rate	%	2.3	1.3

1. Share price volatility was determined based on historical share prices over a similar period to the average term to exercise

At December 31, 2014, the following options to purchase Class A shares were outstanding:

Exercise Price	Weighted Average Remaining Life	Options Outstanding (000's)		
		Vested	Unvested	Total
C$17.65	4.2 years	6,570	—	6,570
C$20.21 – C$30.22	0.8 years	3,106	—	3,106
C$31.62 – C$46.59	2.7 years	4,513	—	4,513
US$23.18	5.2 years	5,523	1,463	6,986
US$25.24 – US$35.06	6.8 years	2,601	2,887	5,488
US$37.8 – US$40.15	8.7 years	650	6,217	6,867
		22,963	10,567	33,530

At December 31, 2013, the following options to purchase Class A shares were outstanding:

Exercise Price	Weighted Average Remaining Life	Options Outstanding (000's)		
		Vested	Unvested	Total
C$13.37 – C$19.03	5.1 years	5,727	1,763	7,490
C$20.21 – C$30.22	1.8 years	5,028	80	5,108
C$31.62 – C$46.59	3.7 years	5,215	—	5,215
US$23.18 – US$35.06	6.9 years	6,125	7,133	13,258
US$37.82	9.2 years	110	3,441	3,551
		22,205	12,417	34,622

b) Escrowed Stock Plan

The Escrowed Stock Plan (the "ES Plan") provides executives with increased indirect ownership of Class A shares. Under the ES Plan, executives are granted common shares (the "ES Shares") in one or more private companies that own the company's Class A shares. The Class A shares are purchased on the open market with the purchase cost funded with the proceeds from preferred shares issued to the company. The ES Shares vest over one to five years and must be held until the fifth anniversary of the grant date. At a date no less than five years, and no more than 10 years, from the grant date, all outstanding ES Shares will be exchanged for Class A shares issued by the company, based on the market value of Class A shares at the time of the exchange.

During 2014, 2.75 million Class A shares were purchased in respect of ES Shares granted to executives under the ES Plan (2013 – 2.35 million Class A shares) during the year. For the year ended December 31, 2014, the total expense incurred with respect to the ES Plan totalled $20.8 million (2013 – $14.0 million).

The cost of the escrowed shares granted during the year was determined using the Black-Scholes model of valuation with inputs to the model as follows:

YEARS ENDED DECEMBER 31	Unit	2014	2013
Weighted average share price	US$	40.15	37.82
Weighted average fair value per share	US$	8.59	7.34
Average term to exercise	Years	7.5	7.5
Share price volatility[1]	%	31.4	31.2
Liquidity discount	%	30.0	30.0
Weighted average annual dividend yield	%	1.5	1.5
Risk-free rate	%	2.3	1.3

1. Share price volatility was determined based on historical share prices over a similar period to the term exercise

c) Restricted Stock Plan

The Restricted Stock Plan awards executives with Class A shares purchased on the open market ("Restricted Shares"). Under the Restricted Stock Plan, Restricted Shares awarded vest over a period of up to five years, except for Restricted Shares awarded in lieu of a cash bonus which may vest immediately. Vested and unvested Restricted Shares must be held until the fifth anniversary of the award date. Holders of vested Restricted Shares are entitled to vote Restricted Shares and to receive associated dividends. Employee compensation expense for the Restricted Stock Plan is charged against income over the vesting period.

During 2014, Brookfield granted 319,680 Class A shares pursuant to the terms and conditions of the Restricted Stock Plan, resulting in the recognition of $11.3 million (2013 – $10.6 million) of compensation expense.

2) Cash-settled Share-based Awards

a) Restricted Share Unit Plan

The Restricted Share Unit Plan provides for the issuance of the Deferred Share Units ("DSUs"), as well as Restricted Share Units ("RSUs"). Under this plan, qualifying employees and directors receive varying percentages of their annual incentive bonus or directors' fees in the form of DSUs. The DSUs and RSUs vest over periods of up to five years, and DSUs accumulate additional DSUs at the same rate as dividends on common shares based on the market value of the common shares at the time of the dividend. Participants are not allowed to convert DSUs and RSUs into cash until retirement or cessation of employment. The value of the DSUs, when converted to cash, will be equivalent to the market value of the common shares at the time the conversion takes place. The value of the RSUs, when converted into cash, will be equivalent to the difference between the market price of equivalent number of common shares at the time the conversion takes place and the market price on the date the RSUs are granted. The company uses equity derivative contracts to offset its exposure to the change in share prices in respect of vested and unvested DSUs and RSUs. The fair value of the vested DSUs and RSUs as at December 31, 2014 was $732 million (2013 – $508 million).

Employee compensation expense for these plans is charged against income over the vesting period of the DSUs and RSUs. The amount payable by the company in respect of vested DSUs and RSUs changes as a result of dividends and share price movements. All of the amounts attributable to changes in the amounts payable by the company are recorded as employee compensation expense in the period of the change, and for the year ended December 31, 2014, including those of operating subsidiaries, totalled $2 million (2013 – $19 million), net of the impact of hedging arrangements.

The change in the number of DSUs and RSUs during 2014 and 2013 was as follows:

	DSUs	RSUs	
	Number of Units (000's)	Number of Units (000's)	Weighted Average Exercise Price
Outstanding at January 1, 2014	9,071	7,280	C$ 13.64
Granted and reinvested	320	—	—
Exercised and cancelled	(249)	—	—
Outstanding at December 31, 2014	9,142	7,280	C$ 13.64

	DSUs	RSUs	
	Number of Units (000's)	Number of Units (000's)	Weighted Average Exercise Price
Outstanding at January 1, 2013	7,447	8,030	C$ 13.56
Granted and reinvested	1,830	—	—
Exercised and cancelled	(206)	(750)	12.76
Outstanding at December 31, 2013	9,071	7,280	C$ 13.64

The fair value of DSUs is equal to the traded price of the company's common shares.

	Unit	Dec. 31, 2014	Dec. 31, 2013
Share price on date of measurement	C$	58.22	41.22
Share price on date of measurement	U$	50.13	38.83

The fair value of RSUs was determined primarily using the following inputs:

	Unit	Dec. 31, 2014	Dec. 31, 2013
Share price on date of measurement	C$	58.22	41.22
Weighted average exercise price	C$	13.64	13.64
Weighted average fair value of a unit	C$	39.23	24.18

[...]

26. DERIVATIVE FINANCIAL INSTRUMENTS

The company's activities expose it to a variety of financial risks, including market risk (i.e., currency risk, interest rate risk, and other price risk), credit risk and liquidity risk. The company and its subsidiaries selectively use derivative financial instruments principally to manage these risks.

The aggregate notional amount of the company's derivative positions at December 31, 2014 and 2013 is as follows:

(MILLIONS)	Note	Dec. 31, 2014	Dec. 31, 2013
Foreign exchange	(a)	$ 13,861	$ 11,194
Interest rates	(b)	13,747	16,757
Credit default swaps	(c)	848	800
Equity derivatives	(d)	2,197	1,633

	Note	Dec. 31, 2014	Dec. 31, 2013
Commodity instruments	(e)		
Energy (GWh)		36,499	102,331
Natural gas (MMBtu – 000's)		3,808	12,764

a) Foreign Exchange

The company held the following foreign exchange contracts with notional amounts at December 31, 2014 and December 31, 2013:

(MILLIONS)	Notional Amount (U.S. Dollars)		Average Exchange Rate	
	Dec. 31, 2014	Dec. 31, 2013	Dec. 31, 2014	Dec. 31, 2013
Foreign exchange contracts				
British pounds	$ 3,283	$ 2,782	$ 1.60	$ 1.60
Australian dollars	3,667	1,932	0.85	0.94
Canadian dollars	1,838	1,387	0.89	0.95
European Union euros	1,040	922	1.29	1.37
Brazilian reais	305	702	2.63	2.34
Japanese yen	190	1	113.0	101.0
Cross currency interest rate swaps				
Australian dollars	1,685	1,333	0.95	1.01
Canadian dollars	1,107	654	0.85	0.91
British pounds	313	300	1.49	1.49
Japanese yen	—	98	—	75.47
Foreign exchange options				
Japanese yen	183	548	110.0	105.0
European Union euros	251	413	1.25	1.28
British pounds	—	123	—	1.86

Included in net income are unrealized net gains on foreign currency derivative contracts amounting to $174 million (2013 – $48 million) and included in the cumulative translation adjustment account in other comprehensive income are gains in respect of foreign currency contracts entered into for hedging purposes amounting to $492 million (2013 – net losses of $71 million).

b) Interest Rates

At December 31, 2014, the company held interest rate swap contracts having an aggregate notional amount of $nil (2013 – $600 million), and interest rate swaptions with an aggregate notional amount of $1,699 million (2013 – $1,704 million). The company's subsidiaries held interest rate swap contracts with an aggregate notional amount of $7,828 million (2013 – $8,654 million), and interest rate cap contracts with an aggregate notional amount of $4,219 million (2013 – $5,799 million).

c) Credit Default Swaps

As at December 31, 2014, the company held credit default swap contracts with an aggregate notional amount of $848 million (2013 – $800 million). Credit default swaps are contracts which are designed to compensate the purchaser for any change in the value of an underlying reference asset, based on measurement in credit spreads, upon the occurrence of pre-determined credit events. The company is entitled to receive payments in the event of a pre-determined credit event for up to $800 million (2013 – $800 million) of the notional amount and could be required to make payments in respect of $48 (2013 – $nil) of the notional amount.

d) Equity Derivatives

At December 31, 2014, the company and its subsidiaries held equity derivatives with a notional amount of $2,197 million (2013 – $1,633 million) which includes $828 million (2013 – $765 million) notional amount that hedges long-term compensation arrangements. The balance represents common equity positions established in connection with the company's investment activities. The fair value of these instruments was reflected in the company's Consolidated Financial Statements at year end.

e) Commodity Instruments

The company has entered into energy derivative contracts primarily to hedge the sale of generated power. The company endeavours to link forward electricity sale derivatives to specific periods in which it expects to generate electricity for sale. All energy derivative contracts are recorded at an amount equal to fair value and are reflected in the company's Consolidated Financial Statements. The company has purchased 2,110,000 MMBtu's of natural gas financial contracts and sold 1,698,000 MMBtu's natural gas financial contracts as part of its electricity sale price risk mitigation strategy.

Other Information Regarding Derivative Financial Instruments

The following table classifies derivatives elected for hedge accounting during the years ended December 31, 2014 and 2013 as either cash flow hedges or net investment hedges. Changes in the fair value of the effective portion of the hedge are recorded in either other comprehensive income or net income, depending on the hedge classification, whereas changes in the fair value of the ineffective portion of the hedge are recorded in net income:

YEARS ENDED DECEMBER 31 (MILLIONS)	2014			2013		
	Notional	Effective Portion	Ineffective Portion	Notional	Effective Portion	Ineffective Portion
Cash flow hedges[1]	$ 9,552	$ (224)	$ (60)	$ 10,452	$ 37	$ (141)
Net investment hedges	7,801	314	—	6,146	(58)	—
	$ 17,353	$ 90	$ (60)	$ 16,598	$ (21)	$ (141)

1. Notional amount does not include 8,671 GWh and 42,199 GWh of commodity derivatives at December 31, 2014 and December 31, 2013, respectively.

The following table presents the change in fair values of the company's derivative positions during the years ended December 31, 2014 and 2013, for derivatives that are fair valued through profit or loss, and derivatives that qualify for hedge accounting:

(MILLIONS)	Unrealized Gains During 2014	Unrealized Losses During 2014	Net Change During 2014	Net Change During 2013
Foreign exchange derivatives	$ 708	$ (124)	$ 584	$ (26)
Interest rate derivatives	37	(394)	(358)	105
Interest rate swaps	36	(394)	(358)	81
Interest rate caps	1	—	1	(1)
Interest rate swaptions	—	(32)	(32)	25
Credit default swaps	5	—	5	(2)
Equity derivatives	750	—	750	38
Commodity derivatives	85	(182)	(97)	(154)
	$ 1,585	$ (732)	$ 853	$ (39)

[...]

The following table presents the notional amounts underlying the company's derivative instruments by term to maturity as at December 31, 2014 and the comparative notional amounts at December 31, 2013, for derivatives that are classified as fair value through profit or loss, and derivatives that qualify for hedge accounting:

(MILLIONS)	Dec. 31, 2014				Dec. 31, 2013
	< 1 year	1 to 5 years	> 5 years	Total Notional Amount	Total Notional Amount
Fair value through profit or loss					
Foreign exchange derivatives	$ 2,123	$ 1,171	$ —	$ 3,294	$ 2,996
Interest rate derivatives					
Interest rate swaps	6	483	571	1,060	872
Interest rate swaptions	974	725	—	1,699	1,704
Interest rate caps	1,479	2,741	—	4,220	5,799
	2,459	3,949	571	6,979	8,375
Credit default swaps	3	845	—	848	800
Equity derivatives	236	1,943	—	2,179	1,615
Commodity instruments					
Energy (GWh)	10,735	16,440	653	27,828	60,132
Natural gas (MMBtu – 000's)	2,110	1,698	—	3,808	12,765
Elected for hedge accounting					
Foreign exchange derivatives	$ 7,717	$ 852	$ 1,998	$ 10,567	$ 8,198
Interest rate derivatives					
Interest rate swaps	1,994	3,594	1,180	6,768	8,382
Interest rate caps	—	—	—	—	—
	1,994	3,594	1,180	6,768	8,382
Equity derivatives	7	11	—	18	18
Commodity instruments					
Energy (GWh)	4,134	4,537	—	8,671	42,199

Table A-1

FUTURE VALUE OF 1
(FUTURE VALUE OF A SINGLE SUM)

$$FVF_{n,\,i} = (1+i)^n$$

(n) periods	2%	2½%	3%	4%	5%	6%	8%	9%	10%	11%	12%	15%
1	1.02000	1.02500	1.03000	1.04000	1.05000	1.06000	1.08000	1.09000	1.10000	1.11000	1.12000	1.15000
2	1.04040	1.05063	1.06090	1.08160	1.10250	1.12360	1.16640	1.18810	1.21000	1.23210	1.25440	1.32250
3	1.06121	1.07689	1.09273	1.12486	1.15763	1.19102	1.25971	1.29503	1.33100	1.36763	1.40493	1.52088
4	1.08243	1.10381	1.12551	1.16986	1.21551	1.26248	1.36049	1.41158	1.46410	1.51807	1.57352	1.74901
5	1.10408	1.13141	1.15927	1.21665	1.27628	1.33823	1.46933	1.53862	1.61051	1.68506	1.76234	2.01136
6	1.12616	1.15969	1.19405	1.26532	1.34010	1.41852	1.58687	1.67710	1.77156	1.87041	1.97382	2.31306
7	1.14869	1.18869	1.22987	1.31593	1.40710	1.50363	1.71382	1.82804	1.94872	2.07616	2.21068	2.66002
8	1.17166	1.21840	1.26677	1.36857	1.47746	1.59385	1.85093	1.99256	2.14359	2.30454	2.47596	3.05902
9	1.19509	1.24886	1.30477	1.42331	1.55133	1.68948	1.99900	2.17189	2.35795	2.55803	2.77308	3.51788
10	1.21899	1.28008	1.34392	1.48024	1.62889	1.79085	2.15892	2.36736	2.59374	2.83942	3.10585	4.04556
11	1.24337	1.31209	1.38423	1.53945	1.71034	1.89830	2.33164	2.58043	2.85312	3.15176	3.47855	4.65239
12	1.26824	1.34489	1.42576	1.60103	1.79586	2.01220	2.51817	2.81267	3.13843	3.49845	3.89598	5.35025
13	1.29361	1.37851	1.46853	1.66507	1.88565	2.13293	2.71962	3.06581	3.45227	3.88328	4.36349	6.15279
14	1.31948	1.41297	1.51259	1.73168	1.97993	2.26090	2.93719	3.34173	3.79750	4.31044	4.88711	7.07571
15	1.34587	1.44830	1.55797	1.80094	2.07893	2.39656	3.17217	3.64248	4.17725	4.78459	5.47357	8.13706
16	1.37279	1.48451	1.60471	1.87298	2.18287	2.54035	3.42594	3.97031	4.59497	5.31089	6.13039	9.35762
17	1.40024	1.52162	1.65285	1.94790	2.29202	2.69277	3.70002	4.32763	5.05447	5.89509	6.86604	10.76126
18	1.42825	1.55966	1.70243	2.02582	2.40662	2.85434	3.99602	4.71712	5.55992	6.54355	7.68997	12.37545
19	1.45681	1.59865	1.75351	2.10685	2.52695	3.02560	4.31570	5.14166	6.11591	7.26334	8.61276	14.23177
20	1.48595	1.63862	1.80611	2.19112	2.65330	3.20714	4.66096	5.60441	6.72750	8.06231	9.64629	16.36654
21	1.51567	1.67958	1.86029	2.27877	2.78596	3.39956	5.03383	6.10881	7.40025	8.94917	10.80385	18.82152
22	1.54598	1.72157	1.91610	2.36992	2.92526	3.60354	5.43654	6.65860	8.14028	9.93357	12.10031	21.64475
23	1.57690	1.76461	1.97359	2.46472	3.07152	3.81975	5.87146	7.25787	8.95430	11.02627	13.55235	24.89146
24	1.60844	1.80873	2.03279	2.56330	3.22510	4.04893	6.34118	7.91108	9.84973	12.23916	15.17863	28.62518
25	1.64061	1.85394	2.09378	2.66584	3.38635	4.29187	6.84847	8.62308	10.83471	13.58546	17.00000	32.91895
26	1.67342	1.90029	2.15659	2.77247	3.55567	4.54938	7.39635	9.39916	11.91818	15.07986	19.04007	37.85680
27	1.70689	1.94780	2.22129	2.88337	3.73346	4.82235	7.98806	10.24508	13.10999	16.73865	21.32488	43.53532
28	1.74102	1.99650	2.28793	2.99870	3.92013	5.11169	8.62711	11.16714	14.42099	18.57990	23.88387	50.06561
29	1.77584	2.04641	2.35657	3.11865	4.11614	5.41839	9.31727	12.17218	15.86309	20.62369	26.74993	57.57545
30	1.81136	2.09757	2.42726	3.24340	4.32194	5.74349	10.06266	13.26768	17.44940	22.89230	29.95992	66.21177
31	1.84759	2.15001	2.50008	3.37313	4.53804	6.08810	10.86767	14.46177	19.19434	25.41045	33.55511	76.14354
32	1.88454	2.20376	2.57508	3.50806	4.76494	6.45339	11.73708	15.76333	21.11378	28.20560	37.58173	87.56507
33	1.92223	2.25885	2.65234	3.64838	5.00319	6.84059	12.67605	17.18203	23.22515	31.30821	42.09153	100.69983
34	1.96068	2.31532	2.73191	3.79432	5.25335	7.25103	13.69013	18.72841	25.54767	34.75212	47.14252	115.80480
35	1.99989	2.37321	2.81386	3.94609	5.51602	7.68609	14.78534	20.41397	28.10244	38.57485	52.79962	133.17552
36	2.03989	2.43254	2.88928	4.10393	5.79182	8.14725	15.96817	22.25123	30.91268	42.81808	59.13557	153.15185
37	2.08069	2.49335	2.98523	4.26809	6.08141	8.63609	17.24563	24.25384	34.00395	47.52807	66.23184	176.12463
38	2.12230	2.55568	3.07478	4.43881	6.38548	9.15425	18.62528	26.43668	37.40434	52.75616	74.17966	202.54332
39	2.16474	2.61957	3.16703	4.61637	6.70475	9.70351	20.11530	28.81598	41.14479	58.55934	83.08122	232.92482
40	2.20804	2.68506	3.26204	4.80102	7.03999	10.28572	21.72452	31.40942	45.25926	65.00087	93.05097	267.86355

Table A-2

PRESENT VALUE OF 1
(PRESENT VALUE OF A SINGLE SUM)

$$PVF_{n,i} = \frac{1}{(1+i)^n} = (1+i)^{-n}$$

(n) periods	2%	2½%	3%	4%	5%	6%	8%	9%	10%	11%	12%	15%
1	.98039	.97561	.97087	.96156	.95238	.94340	.92593	.91743	.90909	.90090	.89286	.86957
2	.96117	.95181	.94260	.92456	.90703	.89000	.85734	.84168	.82645	.81162	.79719	.75614
3	.94232	.92860	.91514	.88900	.86384	.83962	.79383	.77218	.75132	.73119	.71178	.65752
4	.92385	.90595	.88849	.85480	.82270	.79209	.73503	.70843	.68301	.65873	.63552	.57175
5	.90583	.88385	.86261	.82193	.78353	.74726	.68058	.64993	.62092	.59345	.56743	.49718
6	.88797	.86230	.83748	.79031	.74622	.70496	.63017	.59627	.56447	.53464	.50663	.43233
7	.87056	.84127	.81309	.75992	.71068	.66506	.58349	.54703	.51316	.48166	.45235	.37594
8	.85349	.82075	.78941	.73069	.67684	.62741	.54027	.50187	.46651	.43393	.40388	.32690
9	.83676	.80073	.76642	.70259	.64461	.59190	.50025	.46043	.42410	.39092	.36061	.28426
10	.82035	.78120	.74409	.67556	.61391	.55839	.46319	.42241	.38554	.35218	.32197	.24719
11	.80426	.76214	.72242	.64958	.58468	.52679	.42888	.38753	.35049	.31728	.28748	.21494
12	.78849	.74356	.70138	.62460	.55684	.49697	.39711	.35554	.31863	.28584	.25668	.18691
13	.77303	.72542	.68095	.60057	.53032	.46884	.36770	.32618	.28966	.25751	.22917	.16253
14	.75788	.70773	.66112	.57748	.50507	.44230	.34046	.29925	.26333	.23199	.20462	.14133
15	.74301	.69047	.64186	.55526	.48102	.41727.	.31524	.27454	.23939	.20900	.18270	.12289
16	.72845	.67362	.62317	.53391	.45811	.39365	.29189	.25187	.21763	.18829	.16312	.10687
17	.71416	.65720	.60502	.51337	.43630	.37136	.27027	.23107	.19785	.16963	.14564	.09293
18	.70016	.64117	.58739	.49363	.41552	.35034	.25025	.21199	.17986	.15282	.13004	.08081
19	.68643	.62553	.57029	.47464	.39573	.33051	.23171	.19449	.16351	.13768	.11611	.07027
20	.67297	.61027	.55368	.45639	.37689	.31180	.21455	.17843	.14864	.12403	.10367	.06110
21	.65978	.59539	.53755	.43883	.35894	.29416	.19866	.16370	.13513	.11174	.09256	.05313
22	.64684	.58086	.52189	.42196	.34185	.27751	.18394	.15018	.12285	.10067	.08264	.04620
23	.63416	.56670	.50669	.40573	.32557	.26180	.17032	.13778	.11168	.09069	.07379	.04017
24	.62172	.55288	.49193	.39012	.31007	.24698	.15770	.12641	.10153	.08170	.06588	.03493
25	.60953	.53939	.47761	.37512	.29530	.23300	.14602	.11597	.09230	.07361	.05882	.03038
26	.59758	.52623	.46369	.36069	.28124	.21981	.13520	.10639	.08391	.06631	.05252	.02642
27	.58586	.51340	.45019	.34682	.26785	.20737	.12519	.09761	.07628	.05974	.04689	.02297
28	.57437	.50088	.43708	.33348	.25509	.19563	.11591	.08955	.06934	.05382	.04187	.01997
29	.56311	.48866	.42435	.32065	.24295	.18456	.10733	.08216	.06304	.04849	.03738	.01737
30	.55207	.47674	.41199	.30832	.23138	.17411	.09938	.07537	.05731	.04368	.03338	.01510
31	.54125	.46511	.39999	.29646	.22036	.16425	.09202	.06915	.05210	.03935	.02980	.01313
32	.53063	.45377	.38834	.28506	.20987	.15496	.08520	.06344	.04736	.03545	.02661	.01142
33	.52023	.44270	.37703	.27409	.19987	.14619	.07889	.05820	.04306	.03194	.02376	.00993
34	.51003	.43191	.36604	.26355	.19035	.13791	.07305	.05340	.03914	.02878	.02121	.00864
35	.50003	.42137	.35538	.25342	.18129	.13011	.06763	.04899	.03558	.02592	.01894	.00751
36	.49022	.41109	.34503	.24367	.17266	.12274	.06262	.04494	.03235	.02335	.01691	.00653
37	.48061	.40107	.33498	.23430	.16444	.11579	.05799	.04123	.02941	.02104	.01510	.00568
38	.47119	.39128	.32523	.22529	.15661	.10924	.05369	.03783	.02674	.01896	.01348	.00494
39	.46195	.38174	.31575	.21662	.14915	.10306	.04971	.03470	.02430	.01708	.01204	.00429
40	.45289	.37243	.30656	.20829	.14205	.09722	.04603	.03184	.02210	.01538	.01075	.00373

Table A-3

FUTURE VALUE OF AN ORDINARY ANNUITY OF 1

$$FVF\text{-}OA_{n,\,i} = \frac{(1+i)^n - 1}{i}$$

(n) periods	2%	2½%	3%	4%	5%	6%	8%	9%	10%	11%	12%	15%
1	1.00000	1.00000	1.00000	1.00000	1.00000	1.00000	1.00000	1.00000	1.00000	1.00000	1.00000	1.00000
2	2.02000	2.02500	2.03000	2.04000	2.05000	2.06000	2.08000	2.09000	2.10000	2.11000	2.12000	2.15000
3	3.06040	3.07563	3.09090	3.12160	3.15250	3.18360	3.24640	3.27810	3.31000	3.34210	3.37440	3.47250
4	4.12161	4.15252	4.18363	4.24646	4.31013	4.37462	4.50611	4.57313	4.64100	4.70973	4.77933	4.99338
5	5.20404	5.25633	5.30914	5.41632	5.52563	5.63709	5.86660	5.98471	6.10510	6.22780	6.35285	6.74238
6	6.30812	6.38774	6.46841	6.63298	6.80191	6.97532	7.33592	7.52334	7.71561	7.91286	8.11519	8.75374
7	7.43428	7.54743	7.66246	7.89829	8.14201	8.39384	8.92280	9.20044	9.48717	9.78327	10.08901	11.06680
8	8.58297	8.73612	8.89234	9.21423	9.54911	9.89747	10.63663	11.02847	11.43589	11.85943	12.29969	13.72682
9	9.75463	9.95452	10.15911	10.58280	11.02656	11.49132	12.48756	13.02104	13.57948	14.16397	14.77566	16.78584
10	10.94972	11.20338	11.46338	12.00611	12.57789	13.18079	14.48656	15.19293	15.93743	16.72201	17.54874	20.30372
11	12.16872	12.48347	12.80780	13.48635	14.20679	14.97164	16.64549	17.56029	18.53117	19.56143	20.65458	24.34928
12	13.41209	13.79555	14.19203	15.02581	15.91713	16.86994	18.97713	20.14072	21.38428	22.71319	24.13313	29.00167
13	14.68033	15.14044	15.61779	16.62684	17.71298	18.88214	21.49530	22.95339	24.52271	26.21164	28.02911	34.35192
14	15.97394	16.51895	17.08632	18.29191	19.59863	21.01507	24.21492	26.01919	27.97498	30.09492	32.39260	40.50471
15	17.29342	17.93193	18.59891	20.02359	21.57856	23.27597	27.15211	29.36092	31.77248	34.40536	37.27972	47.58041
16	18.63929	19.38022	20.15688	21.82453	23.65749	25.67253	30.32428	33.00340	35.94973	39.18995	42.75328	55.71747
17	20.01207	20.86473	21.76159	23.69751	25.84037	28.21288	33.75023	36.97371	40.54477	44.50084	48.88367	65.07509
18	21.41231	22.38635	23.41444	25.64541	28.13238	30.90565	37.45024	41.30134	45.59917	50.39593	55.74972	75.83636
19	22.84056	23.94601	25.11687	27.67123	30.53900	33.75999	41.44626	46.01846	51.15909	56.93949	63.43968	88.21181
20	24.29737	25.54466	26.87037	29.77808	33.06595	36.78559	45.76196	51.16012	57.27500	64.20283	72.05244	102.44358
21	25.78332	27.18327	28.67649	31.96920	35.71925	39.99273	50.42292	56.76453	64.00250	72.26514	81.69874	118.81012
22	27.29898	28.86286	30.53678	34.24797	38.50521	43.39229	55.45676	62.87334	71.40275	81.21431	92.50258	137.63164
23	28.84496	30.58443	32.45288	36.61789	41.43048	46.99583	60.89330	69.53194	79.54302	91.14788	104.60289	159.27638
24	30.42186	32.34904	34.42647	39.08260	44.50200	50.81558	66.76476	76.78981	88.49733	102.17415	118.15524	184.16784
25	32.03030	34.15776	36.45926	41.64591	47.72710	54.86451	73.10594	84.70090	98.34706	114.41331	133.33387	212.79302
26	33.67091	36.01171	38.55304	44.31174	51.11345	59.15638	79.95442	93.32398	109.18177	127.99877	150.33393	245.71197
27	35.34432	37.91200	40.70963	47.08421	54.66913	63.70577	87.35077	102.72314	121.09994	143.07864	169.37401	283.56877
28	37.05121	39.85990	42.93092	49.96758	58.40258	68.52811	95.33883	112.96822	134.20994	159.81729	190.69889	327.10408
29	38.79223	41.85630	45.21885	52.96629	62.32271	73.63980	103.96594	124.13536	148.63093	178.39719	214.58275	377.16969
30	40.56808	43.90270	47.57542	56.08494	66.43885	79.05819	113.28321	136.30754	164.49402	199.02088	241.33268	434.74515
31	42.37944	46.00027	50.00268	59.32834	70.76079	84.80168	123.34587	149.57522	181.94343	221.91317	271.29261	500.95692
32	44.22703	48.15028	52.50276	62.70147	75.29883	90.88978	134.21354	164.03699	201.13777	247.32362	304.84772	577.10046
33	46.11157	50.35403	55.07784	66.20953	80.06377	97.34316	145.95062	179.80032	222.25154	275.52922	342.42945	644.66553
34	48.03380	52.61289	57.73018	69.85791	85.06696	104.18376	158.62667	196.98234	245.47670	306.83744	384.52098	765.36535
35	49.99448	54.92821	60.46208	73.65222	90.32031	111.43478	172.31680	215.71076	271.02437	341.58955	431.66350	881.17016
36	51.99437	57.30141	63.27594	77.59831	95.83632	119.12087	187.10215	236.12472	299.12681	380.16441	484.46312	1014.34568
37	54.03425	59.73395	66.17422	81.70225	101.62814	127.26812	203.07032	258.37595	330.03949	422.98249	543.59869	1167.49753
38	56.11494	62.22730	69.15945	85.97034	107.70955	135.90421	220.31595	282.62978	364.04343	470.51056	609.83053	1343.62216
39	58.23724	64.78298	72.23423	90.40915	114.09502	145.05846	238.94122	309.06646	401.44778	523.26673	684.01020	1546.16549
40	60.40198	67.40255	75.40126	95.02552	120.79977	154.76197	259.05652	337.88245	442.59256	581.82607	767.09142	1779.09031

Table A-4

PRESENT VALUE OF AN ORDINARY ANNUITY OF 1

$$PVF\text{-}OA_{n,\,i} = \frac{1 - \dfrac{1}{(1+i)^n}}{i}$$

(n) periods	2%	2½%	3%	4%	5%	6%	8%	9%	10%	11%	12%	15%
1	.98039	.97561	.97087	.96154	.95238	.94340	.92593	.91743	.90909	.90090	.89286	.86957
2	1.94156	1.92742	1.91347	1.88609	1.85941	1.83339	1.78326	1.75911	1.73554	1.71252	1.69005	1.62571
3	2.88388	2.85602	2.82861	2.77509	2.72325	2.67301	2.57710	2.53130	2.48685	2.44371	2.40183	2.28323
4	3.80773	3.76197	3.71710	3.62990	3.54595	3.46511	3.31213	3.23972	3.16986	3.10245	3.03735	2.85498
5	4.71346	4.64583	4.57971	4.45182	4.32948	4.21236	3.99271	3.88965	3.79079	3.69590	3.60478	3.35216
6	5.60143	5.50813	5.41719	5.24214	5.07569	4.91732	4.62288	4.48592	4.35526	4.23054	4.11141	3.78448
7	6.47199	6.34939	6.23028	6.00205	5.78637	5.58238	5.20637	5.03295	4.86842	4.71220	4.56376	4.16042
8	7.32548	7.17014	7.01969	6.73274	6.46321	6.20979	5.74664	5.53482	5.33493	5.14612	4.96764	4.48732
9	8.16224	7.97087	7.78611	7.43533	7.10782	6.80169	6.24689	5.99525	5.75902	5.53705	5.32825	4.77158
10	8.98259	8.75206	8.53020	8.11090	7.72173	7.36009	6.71008	6.41766	6.14457	5.88923	5.65022	5.01877
11	9.78685	9.51421	9.25262	8.76048	8.30641	7.88687	7.13896	6.80519	6.49506	6.20652	5.93770	5.23371
12	10.57534	10.25776	9.95400	9.38507	8.86325	8.38384	7.53608	7.16073	6.81369	6.49236	6.19437	5.42062
13	11.34837	10.98319	10.63496	9.98565	9.39357	8.85268	7.90378	7.48690	7.10336	6.74987	6.42355	5.58315
14	12.10625	11.69091	11.29607	10.56312	9.89864	9.29498	8.24424	7.78615	7.36669	6.98187	6.62817	5.72448
15	12.84926	12.38138	11.93794	11.11839	10.37966	9.71225	8.55948	8.06069	7.60608	7.19087	6.81086	5.84737
16	13.57771	13.05500	12.56110	11.65230	10.83777	10.10590	8.85137	8.31256	7.82371	7.37916	6.97399	5.95424
17	14.29187	13.71220	13.16612	12.16567	11.27407	10.47726	9.12164	8.54363	8.02155	7.54879	7.11963	6.04716
18	14.99203	14.35336	13.75351	12.65930	11.68959	10.82760	9.37189	8.75563	8.20141	7.70162	7.24967	6.12797
19	15.67846	14.97889	14.32380	13.13394	12.08532	11.15812	9.60360	8.95012	8.36492	7.83929	7.36578	6.19823
20	16.35143	15.58916	14.87747	13.59033	12.46221	11.46992	9.81815	9.12855	8.51356	7.96333	7.46944	6.25933
21	17.01121	16.18455	15.41502	14.02916	12.82115	11.76408	10.01680	9.29224	8.64869	8.07507	7.56200	6.31246
22	17.65805	16.76541	15.93692	14.45112	13.16800	12.04158	10.20074	9.44243	8.77154	8.17574	7.64465	6.35866
23	18.29220	17.33211	16.44361	14.85684	13.48857	12.30338	10.37106	9.58021	8.88322	8.26643	7.71843	6.39884
24	18.91393	17.88499	16.93554	15.24696	13.79864	12.55036	10.52876	9.70661	8.98474	8.34814	7.78432	6.43377
25	19.52346	18.42438	17.41315	15.62208	14.09394	12.78336	10.67478	9.82258	9.07704	8.42174	7.84314	6.46415
26	20.12104	18.95061	17.87684	15.98277	14.37519	13.00317	10.80998	9.92897	9.16095	8.48806	7.89566	6.49056
27	20.70690	19.46401	18.32703	16.32959	14.64303	13.21053	10.93516	10.02658	9.23722	8.45780	7.94255	6.51353
28	21.28127	19.96489	18.76411	16.66306	14.89813	13.40616	11.05108	10.11613	9.30657	8.60162	7.98442	6.53351
29	21.84438	20.45355	19.18845	16.98371	15.14107	13.59072	11.15841	10.19828	9.36961	8.65011	8.02181	6.55088
30	22.39646	20.93029	19.60044	17.29203	15.37245	13.76483	11.25778	10.27365	9.42691	8.69379	8.05518	6.56598
31	22.93770	21.39541	20.00043	17.58849	15.59281	13.92909	11.34980	10.34280	9.47901	8.73315	8.08499	6.57911
32	23.46833	21.84918	20.38877	17.87355	15.80268	14.08404	11.43500	10.40624	9.52638	8.76860	8.11159	6.59053
33	23.98856	22.29188	20.76579	18.14765	16.00255	14.23023	11.51389	10.46444	9.56943	8.80054	8.13535	6.60046
34	24.49859	22.72379	21.13184	18.41120	16.19290	14.36814	11.58693	10.51784	9.60858	8.82932	8.15656	6.60910
35	24.99862	23.14516	21.48722	18.66461	16.37419	14.49825	11.65457	10.56682	9.64416	8.85524	8.17550	6.61661
36	25.48884	23.55625	21.83225	18.90828	16.54685	14.62099	11.71719	10.61176	9.67651	8.87859	8.19241	6.62314
37	25.96945	23.95732	22.16724	19.14258	16.71129	14.73678	11.77518	10.65299	9.70592	8.89963	8.20751	6.62882
38	26.44064	24.34860	22.49246	19.36786	16.86789	14.84602	11.82887	10.69082	9.73265	8.91859	8.22099	6.63375
39	26.90259	24.73034	22.80822	19.58448	17.01704	14.94907	11.87858	10.72552	9.75697	8.93567	8.23303	6.63805
40	27.35548	25.10278	23.11477	19.79277	17.15909	15.04630	11.92461	10.75736	9.77905	8.95105	8.24378	6.64178

Table A-5

PRESENT VALUE OF AN ANNUITY DUE OF 1

$$PVF-AD_{n,\,i} = 1 + \frac{1 - \dfrac{1}{(1+i)^{n-1}}}{i}$$

(n) periods	2%	2½%	3%	4%	5%	6%	8%	9%	10%	11%	12%	15%
1	1.00000	1.00000	1.00000	1.00000	1.00000	1.00000	1.00000	1.00000	1.00000	1.00000	1.00000	1.00000
2	1.98039	1.97561	1.97087	1.96154	1.95238	1.94340	1.92593	1.91743	1.90909	1.90090	1.89286	1.86957
3	2.94156	2.92742	2.91347	2.88609	2.85941	2.83339	2.78326	2.75911	2.73554	2.71252	2.69005	2.62571
4	3.88388	3.85602	3.82861	3.77509	3.72325	3.67301	3.57710	3.53130	3.48685	3.44371	3.40183	3.28323
5	4.80773	4.76197	4.71710	4.62990	4.54595	4.46511	4.31213	4.23972	4.16986	4.10245	4.03735	3.85498
6	5.71346	5.64583	5.57971	5.45182	5.32948	5.21236	4.99271	4.88965	4.79079	4.69590	4.60478	4.35216
7	6.60143	6.50813	6.41719	6.24214	6.07569	5.91732	5.62288	5.48592	5.35526	5.23054	5.11141	4.78448
8	7.47199	7.34939	7.23028	7.00205	6.78637	6.58238	6.20637	6.03295	5.86842	5.71220	5.56376	5.16042
9	8.32548	8.17014	8.01969	7.73274	7.46321	7.20979	6.74664	6.53482	6.33493	6.14612	5.96764	5.48732
10	9.16224	8.97087	8.78611	8.43533	8.10782	7.80169	7.24689	6.99525	6.75902	6.53705	6.32825	5.77158
11	9.98259	9.75206	9.53020	9.11090	8.72173	8.36009	7.71008	7.41766	7.14457	6.88923	6.65022	6.01877
12	10.78685	10.51421	10.25262	9.76048	9.30641	8.88687	8.13896	7.80519	7.49506	7.20652	6.93770	6.23371
13	11.57534	11.25776	10.95400	10.38507	9.86325	9.38384	8.53608	8.16073	7.81369	7.49236	7.19437	6.42062
14	12.34837	11.98319	11.63496	10.98565	10.39357	9.85268	8.90378	8.48690	8.10336	7.74987	7.42355	6.58315
15	13.10625	12.69091	12.29607	11.56312	10.89864	10.29498	9.24424	8.78615	9.36669	7.98187	7.62817	6.72448
16	13.84926	13.38138	12.93794	12.11839	11.37966	10.71225	9.55948	9.06069	8.60608	8.19087	7.81086	6.84737
17	14.57771	14.05500	13.56110	12.65230	11.83777	11.10590	9.85137	9.31256	8.82371	8.37916	7.97399	6.95424
18	15.29187	14.71220	14.16612	13.16567	12.27407	11.47726	10.12164	9.54363	9.02155	8.54879	8.11963	7.04716
19	15.99203	15.35336	14.75351	13.65930	12.68959	11.82760	10.37189	9.75563	9.20141	8.70162	8.24967	7.12797
20	16.67846	15.97889	15.32380	14.13394	13.08532	12.15812	10.60360	9.95012	9.36492	8.83929	8.36578	7.19823
21	17.35143	16.58916	15.87747	14.59033	13.46221	12.46992	10.81815	10.12855	9.51356	8.96333	8.46944	7.25933
22	18.01121	17.18455	16.41502	15.02916	13.82115	12.76408	11.01680	10.29224	9.64869	9.07507	8.56200	7.31246
23	18.65805	17.76541	16.93692	15.45112	14.16300	13.04158	11.20074	10.44243	9.77154	9.17574	8.64465	7.35866
24	19.29220	18.33211	17.44361	15.85684	14.48857	13.30338	11.37106	10.58021	9.88322	9.26643	8.71843	7.39884
25	19.91393	18.88499	17.93554	16.24696	14.79864	13.55036	11.52876	10.70661	9.98474	9.34814	8.78432	7.43377
26	20.52346	19.42438	18.41315	16.62208	15.09394	13.78336	11.67478	10.82258	10.07704	9.42174	8.84314	7.46415
27	21.12104	19.95061	18.87684	16.98277	15.37519	14.00317	11.80998	10.92897	10.16095	9.48806	8.89566	7.49056
28	21.70690	20.46401	19.32703	17.32959	15.64303	14.21053	11.93518	11.02658	10.23722	9.54780	8.94255	7.51353
29	22.28127	20.96489	19.76411	17.66306	15.89813	14.40616	12.05108	11.11613	10.30657	9.60162	8.98442	7.53351
30	22.84438	21.45355	20.18845	17.98371	16.14107	14.59072	12.15841	11.19828	10.36961	9.65011	9.02181	7.55088
31	23.39646	21.93029	20.60044	18.29203	16.37245	14.76483	12.25778	11.27365	10.42691	9.69379	9.05518	7.56598
32	23.93770	22.39541	21.00043	18.58849	16.59281	14.92909	12.34980	11.34280	10.47901	9.73315	9.08499	7.57911
33	24.46833	22.84918	21.38877	18.87355	16.80268	15.08404	12.43500	11.40624	10.52638	9.76860	9.11159	7.59053
34	24.98856	23.29188	21.76579	19.14765	17.00255	15.23023	12.51389	11.46444	10.56943	9.80054	9.13535	7.60046
35	25.49859	23.72379	22.13184	19.41120	17.19290	15.36814	12.58693	11.51784	10.60858	9.82932	9.15656	7.60910
36	25.99862	24.14516	22.48722	19.66461	17.37419	15.49825	12.65457	11.56682	10.64416	9.85524	9.17550	7.61661
37	26.48884	24.55625	22.83225	19.90828	17.54685	15.62099	12.71719	11.61176	10.67651	9.87859	9.19241	7.62314
38	26.96945	24.95732	23.16724	20.14258	17.71129	15.73678	12.77518	11.65299	10.70592	9.89963	9.20751	7.62882
39	27.44064	25.34860	23.49246	20.36786	17.86789	15.84602	12.82887	11.69082	10.73265	9.91859	9.22099	7.63375
40	27.90259	25.73034	23.80822	20.58448	18.01704	15.94907	12.87858	11.72552	10.75697	9.93567	9.23303	7.63805

Glossary

Accounting errors Unintentional mistakes, not intentional distortions, in financial statements.

Accounting income Income before taxes. Also known as *Accounting profit*, "income for financial reporting purposes," or "income for book purposes."

Accounting policies The specific accounting principles and methods that are currently employed and considered most appropriate to present fairly a company's financial statements.

Accounting profit See *Accounting income*.

Accretion Under ASPE, the increase in the carrying amount of an asset retirement obligation due to passage of time.

Accumulated benefit method A method used to measure the pension obligation. The calculation of the deferred compensation amount is based on all years of service performed by employees under the plan, vested and non-vested, using current salary levels. Also known as the *Projected unit credit method*.

Accumulated other comprehensive income The cumulative change in equity that is due to the revenues and expenses, and gains and losses, that stem from non-shareholder transactions that are excluded from the calculation of net income.

Accumulated rights Rights to benefits accumulated by employees that can be carried forward to future periods if not used in the period in which they were earned.

Acid-test ratio A liquidity ratio that relates total current liabilities to highly liquid assets such as cash, marketable securities, and receivables. Also known as *Quick ratio*.

Actual return The return on pension plan assets that takes into account actual changes in the market values of plan assets as well as the interest and dividends earned.

Actuarial assumptions Predictions made by actuaries regarding factors necessary to operate a pension plan, such as mortality rates, employee turnover, interest and earnings rates, early retirement frequency, and future salaries.

Actuarial gains and losses Gains and losses in a pension fund related to the defined benefit obligation (the liability) resulting from a change in actuarial assumptions or an experienced gain or loss.

Actuaries Individuals who are trained through a rigorous certification program to assign probabilities to future events and their financial effects.

Adverse opinion Audit opinion required when the exceptions to fair presentation are so material that in the independent auditor's judgement a qualified opinion is not justified.

Antidilutive securities Securities that upon conversion or exercise would increase earnings per share, or reduce the loss per share.

Asset ceiling test An analysis required of any end-of-period defined benefit asset to ensure that it is not reported at an amount in excess of the benefits that will be received from it in the future.

Asset retirement obligation (ARO) An existing legal obligation associated with the retirement of a tangible long-lived asset that results from its acquisition, construction, development, or normal operations, in the period it is incurred, provided a reasonable estimate can be made of its fair value. Also known as *Site restoration obligation*.

Asset-based financing The financing of equipment through a secured loan, conditional sales contract, or lease.

Asset-linked debt See *Commodity-backed debts*.

Assurance-type warranty An expense-type warranty that is provided with an associated product or service, with no additional fee being charged for it. Accounting for this type of warranty under IFRS is based on all costs associated with that revenue being recognized as an expense in the same accounting period as the sale.

Attribution period The accounting period beginning at the date of hire and ending when the employee obtains full eligibility for benefits.

Auditor's report The communication by the auditor as to his or her opinion regarding the fair presentation of an entity's financial statements.

Bargain purchase option A provision allowing the lessee to purchase the leased property for a price that is significantly lower than the property's expected fair value at the date the option becomes exercisable.

Bargain renewal option A provision allowing the lessee to renew the lease for a rental that is lower than the expected fair rental at the date the option becomes exercisable.

Basic EPS (earnings per share) Net income available to common shareholders divided by the number of outstanding common shares.

Basic or inherent rights Three rights inherent in shares where restrictive provisions are absent. These rights are to share proportionately in profits and losses, to share proportionately in management, and to share proportionately in corporate assets upon liquidation.

Bearer bond A bond that is not recorded in the owner's name and may be transferred simply from one owner to another. Also known as *Coupon bond*.

Benefit cost The benefit cost is equal to the amount of pension expense unless a portion of the cost is treated as a product cost and charged to inventory, or is capitalized as a component of property, plant, and equipment.

Bifurcation The separation of proceeds into two or more amounts. For instance, it is used in accounting for bundled sales and convertible bonds (by the issuer).

Bond indenture A contract that is a promise to pay a sum of money at a designated maturity date, as well as periodic interest at a specified rate on the maturity amount (face value).

Bonus Amount paid by an employer to an employee in addition to regular salary or wage, often dependent on the company's yearly profit.

Book value method A method of accounting for the conversion of debt to equity whereby the equity is measured at the book value of the debt converted.

Book value per share Common shareholders' equity divided by the number of common shares outstanding.

Call option A derivative instrument where the option holder has the right, but not the obligation, to buy shares at a preset price.

Callable bonds and notes Bonds that give the issuer the right to call and retire the bonds prior to maturity.

Callable debt Debt that is due on demand (that is, callable) by the creditor.

Callable/redeemable (preferred) shares Shares that allow the issuing corporation to "call" or redeem at its option the outstanding preferred shares at specified future dates and at stipulated prices.

Capital leases Leases where the risks and rewards of ownership transfer from the lessor to the lessee. Evaluated based on stipulated criteria. Also known as *Finance leases*.

Carrying amount The amount at which the underlying assets or services that were exchanged are measured in certain related-party transactions. It is the amount of the item transferred as recorded in the books of the transferor.

Carrying value The value at which an item such as a bond is recorded on the balance sheet.

Cash Cash on hand and demand deposits.

Cash equivalents Short-term, highly liquid investments that are readily convertible to known amounts of cash and have an insignificant risk of change in value.

Cash flow hedge A hedge that deals with exposures to future variable cash flows, such as future interest payments on variable rate debt.

Cash flows The inflows and outflows of cash and cash equivalents.

Centrally incurred costs Costs that are interrelated in nature, such as the CEO's salary, preventing a completely objective division of the costs among segments under IFRS segmented disclosure requirements.

Change in accounting estimate An adjustment in the carrying amount of an asset or a liability or the amount of an asset's periodic consumption resulting either from an assessment of the present status of the asset or liability, or of the expected future benefits and obligations associated with the asset.

Change in accounting policy A change from one generally accepted accounting principle or the methods used in its application to another.

Chief operating decision-maker The person who has final say on operating matters and who regularly reviews operating segments.

Classification approach An approach where transactions should be classified and accounted for according to their economic substance.

Clean opinion The opinion expressed by the auditor that the financial statements present fairly, in all material respects, the entity's financial position, results of operations, and cash flows, in conformity with generally accepted accounting principles. Also known as *Unmodified opinion*.

Collateral trust bonds or notes Bonds or notes that are secured with assets (often shares and bonds of other corporations).

Combination plans Stock compensation plans that combine features from different types of compensation plans such as stock option plans and share appreciation rights plans. Also known as *Tandem plans*.

Commercial substance What a transaction has when the entity's cash flows are expected to be significantly different after, and as a result of, the transaction.

Commodity-backed debts Bonds that are redeemable in measures of a commodity, such as barrels of oil or tonnes of coal. Also known as *Asset-linked debt*.

Common shares Shares that represent the residual ownership interest in the company, bear the ultimate risks of loss, and receive the benefits of success.

Common-size analysis An approach to financial statement analysis whereby a series of related amounts are converted to a series of percentages of a given base.

Compensated absences Absences from employment—for example, vacation, illness, and holidays—for which employees will be paid.

Compensatory stock option plans (CSOPs) Stock options to remunerate parties including managers.

Complex capital structure What a corporation has when it has convertible securities, options, warrants, or other rights that upon conversion or exercise could dilute earnings per share.

Comprehensive revaluation The revaluation of a company's liabilities and assets following a financial reorganization in cases where the same party no longer controls the company.

Constructive obligation An obligation that arises from past or present company practice that signals that the entity acknowledges a potential economic burden.

Contingency An existing condition or situation that involves uncertainty as to possible gain or loss and that will not be resolved until a future event or events occur or fail to occur.

Contingent liability An obligation incurred as a result of a loss contingency, dependent upon the occurrence or non-occurrence of one or more future events to confirm either its existence or the amount payable.

Contingently issuable shares Additional shares a company promises to issue if a certain future event occurs.

Contract-based approach An approach where the leased asset that is acquired is not seen to be the physical property; rather, it is seen as the contractual right to use the property that is conveyed under the lease agreement.

Contractual commitments Agreements entered into by companies with customers, suppliers, employees, and other parties. They are not liabilities at the balance sheet date but commit the company and how its assets will be used into the future. Also known as *Contractual obligations*.

Contractual obligations See *Contractual commitments*.

Contributed (paid-in) capital The total amount provided by the shareholders to the corporation for use in the business.

Contributory plans Benefit plans where the employees bear part of the stated benefits' cost or voluntarily make payments to increase their benefits.

Convertible bonds Bonds that can be converted into other securities of the corporation for a specified time after issuance.

Convertible debt Debt the holder can convert into other securities such as common shares. Certain bonds or other financial instruments give the issuer the option to repay or settle.

Convertible (preferred) shares Shares where the shareholders may at their option exchange preferred shares for common shares at a predetermined ratio.

Correction of a prior period error Correction of errors that occurred as a result of mathematical mistakes, mistakes in applying accounting principles, fraud, or oversight or misinterpretation of facts that existed at the time financial statements were prepared; for example, the incorrect application of the retail inventory method for determining the final inventory value.

Counterbalancing errors Errors that reverse or correct themselves in subsequent periods.

Counterparty The other party to a contract.

Coupon bond A bond that is not recorded in the owner's name and may be transferred simply from one owner to another. Also known as *Bearer bond*.

Coupon rate The fixed rate of interest that is paid by the issuer of a bond annually or semi-annually during the life of the bond.

Credit risk The risk that the other party to the contract will fail to fulfill its obligation under the contract and cause the company loss.

Cumulative (preferred) shares Preferred shares where dividends not paid in any year must be made up in a later year before any profits can be distributed to common shareholders.

Currency risk The risk that the fair value or future cash flows of a financial instrument will fluctuate because of changes in foreign exchange rates.

Current liability Amounts payable within one year from the date of the balance sheet or within the normal operating cycle where this is longer than a year.

Current maturities of long-term debt Bonds, mortgage notes, and other long-term indebtedness that mature within 12 months from the balance sheet date and are reported as current liabilities.

Current ratio The ratio of total current assets to total current liabilities.

Current service cost The cost of pension benefits that are to be provided in the future in exchange for the services that employees provide in the current period.

Customer advances Deposits received from customers that are returnable. Deposits may guarantee performance of a contract or service.

Days payables outstanding A ratio indicating how long it takes a company to pay its trade payables, thereby determining the average age of payables.

Debenture bond A bond that is unsecured.

Debt settlement The early repayment or refunding of debt (before maturity).

Debt to total assets ratio A ratio that measures the percentage of total assets provided by creditors by dividing total debt (both current and long-term liabilities) by total assets.

Deductible temporary difference A deductible amount that will decrease taxable income in future years.

Deep discount bonds or notes Bonds sold at a discount that provides the buyer's total interest payoff at maturity. Also known as *Zero-interest debentures, bonds, or notes*.

Defeasance The elimination of an obligation to a creditor. If a company wishes to extinguish or pay off debt prior to its due date, it must set aside sufficient money in a trust or other arrangement and allow the trust to repay the original debt (principal and interest) directly to the creditor as it becomes due according to the original agreement.

Deferred tax asset Under IFRS, an asset representing a reduction in taxes payable or the increase in taxes refundable in future years as a result of a deductible temporary difference that exists at the end of the current year. Also known (under ASPE) as *Future income tax asset*.

Deferred tax expense The change in the statement of financial position deferred income tax asset or liability account from the beginning to the end of the accounting period.

Deferred tax liability Under IFRS, a liability representing an increase in taxes payable or the decrease in taxes refundable in future years as a result of a taxable temporary difference at the end of the current year. Also known (under ASPE) as *Future income tax liability*.

Defined benefit plan A pension plan that defines the benefits that an employee will receive at retirement.

Defined benefit obligation The present value of vested and non-vested benefits earned to the date of the statement of financial position, with the benefits measured using employees' future salary levels. Also known as *Defined benefit obligation (DBO) for accounting purposes*.

Defined benefit obligation (DBO) for accounting purposes See *Defined benefit obligation*.

Defined benefit obligation (DBO) for funding purposes The present value of vested and non-vested benefits earned to the balance sheet date, with the benefits measured using the requirements of pension legislation and regulations to determine required cash contributions to the plan. An acceptable measurement option under ASPE only.

Defined contribution plan A pension plan that specifies how contributions are determined rather than the benefits that the individual is to receive or the method of determining those benefits.

Derivative instruments Financial instruments that transfer risks from one party to another with little or no upfront investment. Derivatives derive their value from changes in the value of things such as shares, interest rates, and exchange rates.

Diluted EPS (earnings per share) Earnings per share that includes the effect of all dilutive potential common shares outstanding during the period.

Direct financing leases Leases where no manufacturer's or dealer's profit is present, resulting from arrangements with lessors that are primarily engaged in financing operations, such as lease financing companies, banks, insurance companies, and pension trusts.

Direct method A method of preparing the cash flow statement where cash flow from operating activities is calculated directly by identifying the sources of the operating cash receipts and payments.

Discount The difference between the face value and the market price of a bond.

Discrete view The notion that each interim period should be treated as a separate accounting period.

Dividend payable An amount that a corporation owes to its shareholders because the board of directors has authorized a dividend payment.

Dividends Profit distribution to shareholders.

Dividends in kind Dividends payable in corporation assets other than cash. Also known as "property dividends."

Earned capital Capital that is created by the business operating profitably.

Economic consequences Arguments to change accounting methods based on economic reasons, rather than conceptual reasons, that focus on the supposed impact of accounting on the behaviour of investors, creditors, competitors, and governments.

Effective interest method Method of amortizing bond discounts/premiums and estimating the carrying value and amortized cost of a bond whereby the interest income/expense recognized is based on the effective interest rate/yield. The effective interest rate is the rate needed to discount the stated interest and principal payments such that the present value of the cash flows equals the current carrying value of the instrument.

Effective tax rate Total income tax expense divided by pre-tax income reported on the financial statements.

Effective yield The interest rate actually earned by bondholders.

Embedded derivative A derivative such as a call or put option that is contained in (embedded in) a financial instrument such as a debenture.

Employee stock option or purchase plans (ESOPs) Stock options used to give employees an opportunity to own part of the company, issued to a wide group of people (such as all employees).

Equity instrument Any contract that evidences a residual interest in the assets of an entity after deducting all of its liabilities.

Event accrual method A method of accounting for non-accumulating compensated absences whereby a liability is not recorded until the obligating event occurs.

Executory contract A contract that is entered into where both parties agree to do something in the future. The contract is initially unexecuted until the goods in question or consideration is exchanged at that future point in time.

Executory costs Insurance, maintenance, and property tax expenses.

Exercise period The period (specified by the terms of a financial instrument) during which the holder or issuer of the instrument may exercise their rights. For instance, an option gives the holder the right to buy or sell shares at a predetermined price for a certain time period.

Exercise price The predetermined price (specified by the terms of a financial instrument) at which either the holder or the issuer of the instrument may exercise their rights. For instance, an option gives the holder the right to buy or sell shares at a predetermined price.

Expected return The return on pension plan assets based on the expected long-term rate of return on plan assets applied to the fair value (or the market-related value) of the plan assets.

Experience gain or loss In relation to pension plans, the difference between what has occurred and the previous actuarial assumptions as to what was expected.

Extinguishment of debt The discharge, cancellation, or expiry of debt.

Face value The value that a bond is worth at the date it is to be repaid. Also known as *Maturity value*, *Par value*, or *Principal amount*.

Fair value hedge A hedge that deals with exposures to changes in fair values of recognized assets or liabilities or unrecognized firm commitments.

Fair value option A financial reporting option that allows financial instruments to be recorded using fair value-net income.

Finance leases Leases where the risks and rewards of ownership transfer from the lessor to the lessee. Evaluated based on stipulated criteria. Also known as *Capital leases*.

Financial guarantees Legally binding undertakings to stand in the place of the party for whom the guarantee is given to discharge their obligation in the event of them failing to do so.

Financial instruments Contracts that create both a financial asset for one party and a financial liability or equity instrument for the other party.

Financial liabilities Contractual obligations to deliver cash or other financial assets to another party, or to exchange financial instruments with another party under conditions that are potentially unfavourable.

Financial reorganization A substantial realignment of an enterprise's equity and non-equity interests such that the holders of one or more of the significant classes of non-equity interests and the holders of all of the significant classes of equity interests give up some (or all) of their rights and claims on the enterprise.

Financing activities Activities that result in changes in the size and composition of a company's equity capital and borrowings.

Forward contract A contract in which the parties to the contract each commit up front to buy or sell something in the future, including things such as foreign currency or commodities.

Free cash flow Net operating cash flows reduced by the capital expenditures that are needed to sustain the current level of operations.

Fresh start accounting The result of a financial reorganization, which allows a company in financial difficulty to continue with its plans without recovering from a deficit.

Full disclosure principle Financial reporting of financial facts that are significant enough to influence the judgement of an informed reader.

Full retrospective application The restatement of a company's financial reports for prior periods incorporating a recent change in accounting policy.

Funded In relation to pension plans, a term describing when the employer (company) sets funds aside for future pension benefits by making payments to a funding agency that is responsible for accumulating the pension plan assets and for making payments to the recipients as the benefits come due.

Future income tax asset Under ASPE, an asset representing a reduction in taxes payable or the increase in taxes refundable in future years as a result of a deductible temporary difference that exists at the end of the current year. Also known (under IFRS) as *Deferred tax asset*.

Future income tax expense The change in the future tax account balance from the beginning to the end of the accounting period.

Future income tax liability Under ASPE, a liability representing an increase in taxes payable or the decrease in taxes refundable in future years as a result of a taxable temporary difference at the end of the current year. Also known (under IFRS) as *Deferred tax liability*.

Future income taxes method A method for calculating income taxes that adjusts for the effects of any changes in future income tax assets and liabilities and recognizes these effects as future income tax expense. Also known as *Temporary difference approach*.

GAAP hierarchy The generally accepted accounting principles hierarchy that supports decisions about which principles and methods determine accepted accounting practice at a particular time.

Grant date The date that stock options are received.

Gross investment in lease The undiscounted rental/lease payments (excluding executory costs) plus any guaranteed or unguaranteed residual value that accrues to the lessor at the end of the lease or any bargain purchase option.

Guaranteed residual value The amount at which the lessor has the right to require the lessee to purchase the asset, or the amount the lessee or the third-party guarantor guarantees the lessor will realize.

Hedged item The risk or exposure that is being hedged.

Hedging A strategy whereby an entity enters into a contract with another party in order to reduce exposure to existing risks.

Hedging item The contract that is entered into (often a derivative) which offsets the exposure or risk associated with the hedged item.

Horizontal analysis An approach to financial statement analysis that indicates the proportionate change over a period of time.

Hybrid/compound instruments Compound financial instruments that have both an equity component and a liability component.

If-converted method The method used to measure the dilutive effects of a potential conversion of convertible debt or preferred shares on earnings per share.

Illegal acts "A violation of a domestic or foreign statutory law or government regulation attributable to the entity," as defined by the *CPA Canada Handbook*.

Immediate recognition approach An approach to accounting for defined benefit pension plans where the pension expense is made up of all items affecting the funded status during the period except the company contributions into the plan assets, including current service cost and interest cost, actual return on plan assets, past service cost, and actuarial gains and losses.

Impracticable Not practical due to lack of information or where costs exceed benefits.

Imputed interest rate The approximate or appropriate interest rate used to calculate the market value of a note where such value is not readily ascertainable.

In the money What happens to options if the holder of the options stands to benefit from exercising them.

In-substance common shares Shares with the same characteristics as common shares but that cannot be called common shares for legal purposes.

Income available to common shareholders Net income after deducting preferred share dividends.

Income bonds Bonds where no interest is paid unless the issuing company is profitable.

Income tax benefit An income tax–related income statement account with a credit balance. Also known as *Tax income*.

Incremental borrowing rate The interest rate that, at a lease's inception, the lessee would have incurred to borrow, over a similar term and with similar security for the borrowing, the funds necessary to purchase the leased asset.

Incremental method See *Residual value method*.

Indirect method A method of preparing the cash flow statement where cash flow from operating activities is derived indirectly by making the necessary adjustments to net income reported on the income statement.

Induced conversion The conversion of securities whereby an issuer offers additional consideration (a sweetener), such as cash or common shares, to induce the conversion.

Initial direct costs "Those costs incurred by the lessor that are directly associated with negotiating and executing a specific leasing transaction," as defined by the *CPA Canada Handbook*.

Input tax credit The GST or HST a company pays on goods and services it purchases from its suppliers.

Integral view The belief that the interim report is an integral part of the annual report and that deferrals and accruals should take into consideration what will happen for the entire year.

Interest rate implicit in the lease The discount rate that corresponds to the lessor's internal rate of return on a lease.

Interest rate risk The risk that the fair value or future cash flows of a financial instrument will fluctuate because of changes in market interest rates.

Interest rate swap A derivative contract under which the parties agree to exchange future payments that are based on the difference between a fixed interest rate and a variable interest rate.

Interim reports Reports covering periods of less than one year.

Interperiod tax allocation The recognition of deferred tax liabilities and assets for the future tax consequences of events that have already been recognized in the financial statements or tax returns.

Intraperiod tax allocation The approach to allocating taxes within the financial statements of the current period.

Intrinsic value When valuing a derivative, the difference between the fair value and the strike price of the underlying at any point in time.

Intrinsic value method A method to determine the value of an employee compensation plan where the cost of the plan is based on the share's fair value less the exercise price.

Investing activities Activities that involve the acquisition and disposal of long-term assets and other investments that are not included in operating activities.

Investment grade securities Securities that are high quality, not speculative.

Junk bonds Bonds that are unsecured and extremely risky.

Large stock dividend A stock dividend of more than 20% to 25% of the number of shares previously outstanding.

Lease A contractual agreement between a lessor and a lessee that gives the lessee the right to use specific property, owned by the lessor, for a specified time in return for stipulated, and generally periodic, cash payments (rents).

Lease term The fixed, non-cancellable term of the lease.

Legal capital The value at which a company's shares are recorded on its books.

Lessee The party that has the right to use specific property, owned by the lessor, for a specified time in return for stipulated, and generally periodic, cash payments (rents).

Lessor The party that owns the property and rents it out to the lessee.

Leverage The use of debt financing to maximize shareholder value. A company borrows funds and invests them at a higher rate of return such that the difference in rates accrues to the existing shareholders.

Leveraged buyout A buyout where management or another employee group purchases the company shares and finances the purchase, using the company's assets as collateral.

Liability Obligations of an entity arising from past transactions or events, the settlement of which may result in the transfer or use of assets, provision of services, or other yielding of economic benefits in the future.

Limited liability A feature of share ownership where shareholders are only liable on behalf of the corporation up to the amount of their original investment.

Line of credit An agreement a company enters into with its bank to make multiple borrowings up to a negotiated limit, instead of having to negotiate a new loan every time the company needs funds. Also known as *Revolving debt*.

Liquidating dividends Dividends that are a return of capital and not a return on capital or a share of earnings; they result in a decrease in the company's capital.

Liquidity A company's ability to convert assets into cash to pay off its current liabilities in the course of business.

Liquidity risk The risk that an entity will have difficulty meeting obligations that are associated with financial liabilities.

Loan foreclosure What arises when a creditor takes the underlying security (the asset) in lieu of payment of the loan.

Long-term debt Probable future sacrifices of economic benefits arising from present obligations that are not payable within a year or the operating cycle of the business, whichever is longer.

Loss carryback What occurs when a corporation elects to carry a tax loss back against the taxable income of the immediately preceding three years.

Loss carryforward What occurs when a corporation chooses to carry a tax loss that it earned in tax years ending after 2005 forward to the 20 years that immediately follow the loss.

Loss for income tax purposes A loss resulting when tax-deductible expenses and losses exceed taxable revenues and gains. Also known as *Tax loss*.

Loyalty programs Promotions by a company promising future benefits to customers in exchange for specified purchases from the company.

Lump-sum sales Instances where two or more classes of shares are offered for sale at a single payment.

Management approach A method of reporting segmented information on general purpose financial statements whereby selected information on a single basis of segmentation is based on the way management reviews the company when making operating decisions.

Manufacturer or dealer lease A lease in which a manufacturer's or dealer's profit is incorporated. Also known as *Sales-type lease* under ASPE.

Manufacturer's or dealer's profit The profit or loss to the lessor, which is the difference between the fair value of the leased property at the lease's inception and the lessor's cost or carrying amount (book value).

Market rate The actual return that bond investors earn. Definition different from definition of Effective yield.

Market risk The risk that the fair value or future cash flows of a financial instrument will fluctuate because of changes in market prices.

Maturity value The value that a bond is worth at the date it is to be repaid. Also known as *Face value*, *Par value*, or *Principal amount*.

Minimum lease payments Those payments that the lessee is obligated to make in connection with the leased property. They include the total of the minimum rental payments, the guaranteed residual value, the penalty for failure to renew or extend the lease, and the bargain purchase option.

Modified opinion A modification to the auditor's standard opinion that the financial statements present fairly, in all material respects, the entity's financial position and results in conformity with generally accepted accounting principles. A modified opinion is issued in the form of a qualified opinion, disclaimer of opinion, or adverse opinion.

More likely than not A probability of greater than 50%. Also known as *Probable*.

Mortgage bonds or notes Debt secured by real estate.

Net investment in lease The gross investment (the receivable) less the unearned finance or interest revenue included therein.

Neutrality A position of assessment whereby methods are evaluated for conceptual reasons, not economic reasons, and not on the grounds of their possible impact on behaviour.

Nominal rate The rate of interest that is paid by the issuer of a bond annually or semi-annually during the life of the bond.

Non-accumulating compensated absences Benefits that employees are entitled to by virtue of their employment and the occurrence of an obligating event. The rights to these benefits do not vest and are accounted for differently than those that accumulate with service.

Non-contributory plans Benefit plans in which the employer bears the entire cost of the plan.

Non-counterbalancing errors Errors that do not reverse or correct themselves in subsequent periods.

Nonmonetary reciprocal transaction A transaction in which stock may be awarded directly as compensation for services provided by an employee. The transaction is nonmonetary because it involves little or no cash and it is reciprocal because it is a two-way transaction.

Notes payable Written promises to pay a certain sum of money on a specified future date. They may arise from purchases, financing, or other transactions.

Off–balance sheet financing Financing obtained through nontraditional sources such that the related debt is not recognized on the statement of financial position (or balance sheet).

Operating activities A company's principal revenue-producing activities and other activities that are not investing or financing activities.

Operating cycle The period of time elapsing between the acquisition of goods and services involved in operations and the final cash realization resulting from sales and subsequent collections.

Operating lease A lease where the risks and benefits of ownership are not transferred from the lessor to the lessee (and none of the capitalization criteria are met).

Operating segment A component of an enterprise that engages in business activities from which it earns revenues and incurs expenses, whose operating results are reviewed by the company's chief operating decision-maker to assess segment performance and allocate resources to the segments, and for which discrete financial information is available.

Originating difference The cause of the initial difference between the carrying value and the tax base of an asset or liability, or of an increase in the temporary difference, regardless of whether the asset or liability's tax base exceeds or is exceeded by its carrying amount.

Other price risk The risk that fair value or future cash flows will fluctuate because of changes in market conditions other than those related to interest rates or foreign currency exchange rates.

Overfunded A term describing a pension plan with accumulated assets that are greater than the related obligation.

Par value The value that a bond is worth at the date it is to be repaid. Also known as *Face value, Maturity value,* or *Principal amount.*

Par value shares Shares that have a fixed per-share amount for each share certificate.

Partial retrospective application A measure of change in accounting policy for previous periods excluding those where it is not practicable to retroactively determine the effect of the new standard.

Participating (preferred) shares Preferred shares where holders share proportionately with the common shareholders in any profit distributions beyond the prescribed rate.

Past service cost The amount of an employer's obligation to make contributions to a pension plan for employee services that were provided before the start of the plan (or an amendment to the plan).

Payout ratio A measure of profitability, which is the ratio of cash dividends to net income.

Payroll deductions Deductions made from employee payroll, including employee income taxes, Canada (Quebec) Pension Plan, employment insurance, and miscellaneous items such as other insurance premiums, employee savings, and union dues.

Pension cost Current service cost, past service cost, and net interest on the net defined benefit obligation that are included in pension expense. Under IFRS, costs related to actuarial gains and losses, and the return on plan assets excluding amounts included in the net interest on the net defined benefit obligation (asset), are recognized in other comprehensive income.

Pension expense Service cost (current and past service) and net interest (the netting of interest on the defined benefit obligation and pension plan assets). Under ASPE's immediate recognition approach, it also includes actuarial gains and losses.

Pension plan An arrangement whereby an employer provides benefits (payments) to employees after they retire for services they provided while they were working.

Performance obligation An obligation that arises when an entity promises to deliver something or provide a service in the future.

Permanent differences A difference between taxable and accounting income that will not reverse in future periods.

Perpetual bonds or notes Debt issues that have unusually long terms, that is, 100 years or more, or are never repayable.

Plan assets Pension assets that have been set aside in a trust or other legal entity that is separate from the employer company.

Potential common/ordinary share A security or other contract that upon conversion or exercise could dilute earnings per common share.

Preemptive right A right to share proportionately in any new issues of shares of the same class.

Preferred dividends in arrears Accumulated but undeclared dividends on cumulative preferred shares.

Preferred shares A special class of shares that have certain preferential rights, such as a prior claim on earnings.

Premium The difference between the market price and the face value of a bond.

Premiums Offers, such as silverware, dishes, and small appliances, to customers on a limited or continuing basis for the return of items such as box tops, certificates, coupons, labels, or wrappers.

Price earnings ratio An oft-quoted statistic used by analysts in discussing the investment possibility of an enterprise, calculated by dividing the share's market price by its earnings per share.

Primary financial instruments Instruments that include basic financial assets and liabilities, such as receivables and payables, as well as equity instruments such as shares.

Primary sources of GAAP The key financial reporting requirements as specified under IFRS and ASPE.

Principal amount The value that a bond is worth at the date it is to be repaid. Also known as *Face value, Maturity value,* or *Par value.*

Prior period errors Omissions from or misstatements in the financial statements of one or more prior periods that are caused by the misuse of, or failure to use, reliable information that existed when those financial statements were completed and could reasonably have been found and used in their preparation and presentation.

Probable See *More likely than not.*

Profit-sharing A type of plan where payments are made to employees in addition to the regular salary or wage. The payments may be a percentage of the employees' regular rates of pay, or they may depend on productivity increases or the amount of the company's annual profit.

Projected benefit method A measure of the pension obligation where the calculation of the deferred compensation amount is based on both vested and non-vested service using future salaries.

Projected unit credit method See *Accumulated benefit method.*

Proportional method A method of allocating a price to each unit of a transaction involving multiple units. It requires determining the fair value of each item and allocating the purchase price based on the relative fair values. Also known as *Relative fair value method.*

Prospective application The application of a new accounting policy whereby previously reported results remain and the new policy is adopted for the current and future periods only.

Provisions Liabilities of uncertain timing or amount.

Purchased options Call or put options purchased by a company, which has the right but not the obligation to exercise the option.

Put option A derivative where the option holder has the right but not the obligation to sell shares at a preset price.

Qualified opinion The opinion expressed by the auditor that contains an exception to the standard opinion for something that does not follow GAAP or for circumstances where the auditor has not been able to obtain sufficient appropriate audit evidence. For a qualified opinion, the exception does not invalidate the financial statements as a whole.

Quick ratio A liquidity ratio that relates total current liabilities to highly liquid assets such as cash, marketable securities, and receivables. Also known as *Acid-test ratio.*

Rate of return on shareholders' equity A ratio that measures profitability from the common shareholders' viewpoint. It shows how many dollars of net income were earned for each dollar invested by the owners.

Refunding The replacement of an existing debt with new debt.

Registered bonds Bonds issued in the owner's name that require surrender of the certificate and issuance of a new certificate to complete a sale.

Related-party transactions What arises when a business engages in transactions in which one of the transacting parties has the ability to significantly influence the policies of the other, or in which a non-transacting party has the ability to influence the policies of the two transacting parties.

Relative fair value method A method of allocating a price to each unit of a transaction involving multiple units. It requires determining the fair value of each item and allocating the purchase price based on the relative fair values. Also known as *Proportional method*.

Rental payments The payments that the lessee makes to the lessor in return for the right to use the lessor's property for a specified period of time.

Reportable segment A significant operating segment for which separate information is reported, if it satisfies one or more quantitative thresholds relating to revenues, profits, assets, or certain other factors.

Residual value An asset's estimated fair value at the end of the lease term.

Residual value method Method of allocating the value of a transaction whereby only one component is valued (the one that is easier to value, often the debt component). The other component is valued at whatever is left. Also known as *Incremental method*.

Restrictive covenants Contractual requirements that are meant to restrict activities and protect both lenders and borrowers.

Retained earnings An enterprise's earned capital.

Retractable (preferred) shares Shares that the holder can put or sell to the company, normally after having given adequate notice, and the company must then pay the holders for the shares.

Retroactive application The application of a new accounting policy whereby its cumulative effect on the financial statements is calculated at the beginning of the period as if it had always been used. Also known as *Retrospective application*.

Retrospective application The application of a new accounting policy whereby its cumulative effect on the financial statements is calculated at the beginning of the period as if it had always been used. Also known as *Retroactive application*.

Retrospective restatement Accounting for an error correction whereby corrections are reported in the financial statements as though the error had never occurred.

Return on plan assets Actual changes in the market values of pension fund assets as well as the interest and dividends earned.

Returnable cash deposits Deposits received from customers that are returnable. Deposits may guarantee performance of a contract or service.

Revaluation adjustment The difference between the carrying values of a company's assets and liabilities before a financial reorganization and the new values after.

Revenue bond Bond where interest is paid from a specified revenue source.

Reverse treasury stock method Method of calculating diluted earnings per share for (written) put options and forward purchase contracts. It assumes that (1) the company will issue sufficient common shares in the marketplace (at the average market price) at the beginning of the year to generate sufficient funds to buy the shares under the option/forward, and (2) the proceeds from the above will be used to buy back the shares under the option/forward at the beginning of the year.

Reversible differences Situations where the accounting treatment and the tax treatment are the same, but the timing of when they are included in accounting income and when they are included in taxable income differs. Also known as *Timing differences*.

Revolving debt An agreement a company enters into with its bank to make multiple borrowings up to a negotiated limit, instead of having to negotiate a new loan every time the company needs funds. Also known as *Line of credit*.

Right-of-use approach A method of capitalizing leases whereby the asset that is acquired is not the physical property that is leased but the right to use the property that is conveyed under the lease agreement.

Sale-leaseback A transaction in which a property owner (the seller-lessee) sells a property to another party (the purchaser-lessor) and, at the same time, leases the same asset back from the new owner.

Sales-type lease A lease in which a manufacturer's or dealer's profit is incorporated. Also known as *Manufacturer or dealer lease* under IFRS.

Secured debt Debt that is backed by a pledge of some form of collateral.

Securitization The selling of a pool of company assets such as accounts receivable to a limited/special purpose entity for cash. The limited/special purpose entity issues ownership interests (securities) to investors, who then own part of the pool of assets.

Segmented (disaggregated) financial information Financial information that is presented in a note to the financial statements by operating segment.

Serial bonds or notes Bond issues that mature in instalments.

Service period The period in which an employee performs a service to the organization.

Service-type warranty A type of warranty that is sold as an additional service beyond the assurance-type warranty, with the outstanding liability measured at the value of the obligation. It is accounted for based on an output (sales) price rather than an input (cost) measure. Until the revenue is earned, the obligation—the unearned revenue—is reported at its sales or fair value. The liability is then reduced as the revenue is earned.

Settlement date The date at which parties to an interest rate swap contract exchange cash under the terms of the contract.

Settlement rate The rate implied in an insurance contract that could be purchased to effectively settle a pension obligation.

Share appreciation rights (SARs) Rights given to an executive or employee to receive compensation equal to the share appreciation, which is defined as the excess of the shares' market price at the date of exercise over a pre-established price. This share appreciation may be paid in cash, shares, or a combination of both.

Short-term obligations expected to be refinanced Those debts that are scheduled to mature within a year or operating cycle, where the company intends to refinance those debts.

Significant non-cash transactions Transactions not using cash that affect an organization's asset and capital structure, such as an acquisition of assets by assuming liabilities, exchanges of nonmonetary assets, and issuance of equity securities to retire debt.

Simple capital structure A corporation's capital structure consisting only of common shares or including no potential common shares.

Site restoration obligation An existing legal obligation associated with the retirement of a tangible long-lived asset that results from its acquisition, construction, development, or normal operations, in the period it is incurred, provided a reasonable estimate can be made of its fair value. Also known as *Asset retirement obligation (ARO)*.

Special purpose entity An entity created by a company to perform a special project or function, such as accessing financing. Also known as *Variable interest entity*.

Speculator One who takes on additional risk in the hope of making future gains.

Stand-ready obligation A type of liability that is unconditional whereby the obligor stands prepared to fulfill the terms of the contract when required, such as an insurance contract or warranty.

Stated rate The interest rate written in the terms of the bond indenture.

Statement of cash flows A financial statement providing information about an entity's cash receipts and cash payments broken down into operating, investing, and financing cash flows.

Stock dividend Dividends that are issued to shareholders in stock and no assets are distributed. Each shareholder has exactly the same proportionate interest in the corporation and the same total book value after the stock dividend was issued as before it was declared.

Stock split A device whereby a company increases the number of shares outstanding. For instance, in a 2-for-1 split, an existing share would be worth two shares after the split.

Straight-line method An amortization or depreciation method where a constant amount is depreciated each year.

Strike price The agreed-upon price at which an option may be settled.

Subscribed shares Shares that are sold but their full price is not received immediately. Usually a partial payment is made and the share is not issued until the full subscription price is received.

Subsequent events Events that take place after the formal balance sheet date but before the financial statements are approved for release.

Substantively enacted rate A tax rate used for accounting purposes where there is persuasive evidence of the government's ability and commitment to implement it.

Surplus or deficit The difference between the defined benefit obligation and the pension assets' fair value at any point in time (overfunded is a surplus or underfunded is a deficit).

Swap contract A derivative contract under which two parties agree to exchange payment at future points in time (usually based on interest or foreign currency rates).

Tandem plans Stock compensation plans that combine features from different types of compensation plans such as stock option plans and share appreciation rights plans. Also known as *Combination plans*.

Tax base/basis The measurement under existing law applicable to a present asset, liability, or equity instrument recognized for tax purposes as a result of one or more past events.

Tax base of a liability A liability's carrying amount on the statement of financial position reduced by any amount that will be deductible for tax purposes in future periods.

Tax base of an asset The amount that can be deducted in determining taxable income when the carrying amount of that asset is recovered.

Tax income See *Income tax benefit*.

Tax loss A loss resulting when tax-deductible expenses and losses exceed taxable revenues and gains. Also known as *Loss for income tax purposes*.

Taxable income In tax accounting, the amount on which income tax payable is calculated. Also known as *Taxable profit*.

Taxable profit See *Taxable income*.

Taxable temporary difference A temporary difference that will result in taxable amounts in future years when the carrying amount of the asset is received or the liability is settled.

Taxes payable method A differential reporting method whereby total income tax expense (benefit) is equal to income taxes currently payable (receivable).

Temporary difference The difference between the tax base of an asset or liability and its reported (carrying or book) amount in the statement of financial position that will result in taxable amounts or deductible amounts in future years.

Temporary difference approach A method for calculating income taxes that adjusts for the effects of any changes in future income tax assets and liabilities and recognizes these effects as future income tax expense. Also known as *Future income taxes method*.

Term bonds or notes Bond issues that mature on a single date.

Time value A measurement that takes into account the fact that cash flows will occur over time and that future cash flows are worth less than current cash flows.

Times interest earned ratio A ratio that indicates the company's ability to meet interest payments as they come due. It is calculated by dividing income before interest expense and income taxes by interest expense.

Timing differences Situations where the accounting treatment and the tax treatment are the same, but the timing of when they are included in accounting income and when they are included in taxable income differs. Also known as *Reversible differences*.

Trade accounts payable Balances owed to others for goods, supplies, or services purchased on open account.

Trade notes payable Notes required as part of the sales/purchases transaction in lieu of the normal extension of open account credit.

Trade payables Amounts that the entity owes to suppliers for providing goods and services related to normal business operations.

Trading on the equity The practice of using borrowed money at fixed interest rates or issuing preferred shares with constant dividend rates in hopes of obtaining a higher rate of return on the money used.

Transitional provisions The recommendations usually included when new or revised primary sources of GAAP are adopted that specify how an entity should handle the change to a new accounting method.

Treasury shares Shares that are reacquired by a corporation and held in the corporation for reissue.

Treasury stock method A method of calculating earnings per share where options, warrants, and their equivalents are included in the calculation.

Troubled debt restructuring When a creditor "for economic or legal reasons related to the debtor's financial difficulties grants a concession to the debtor that it would not otherwise consider." It usually involves either the settlement of the debt at less than its carrying amount or a continuation of the debt with a modification of terms.

Unconditional obligation An unconditional promise or other requirement to provide or forego economic resources, such as the requirement to pay interest on borrowed money.

Underfunded A term describing a pension plan with more liabilities than assets.

Unearned revenue Revenue received by a company for goods or services that have not yet been provided by the company.

Unguaranteed residual value The portion of the residual value that is not guaranteed, or is guaranteed solely by a party related to the lessor.

Unmodified opinion The opinion expressed by the auditor that the financial statements present fairly, in all material respects, the entity's financial position, results of operations, and cash flows, in conformity with generally accepted accounting principles. Also known as *Clean opinion*.

Valuation allowance An impairment allowance for the portion of the asset deemed not more likely than not to be realized.

Variable interest entity An entity created by a company to perform a special project or function, such as accessing financing. Also known as *Special purpose entity*.

Vertical analysis An approach to financial statement analysis whereby each item on a financial statement in a given period is expressed proportionately to a base figure.

Vest To earn the rights to. An employee's award becomes vested at the date that the employee's right to receive or retain shares of stock or cash under the award is no longer contingent on remaining in the employer's service.

Vested benefit obligation A measure of a company's pension obligation including only vested benefits and calculated using current salary levels.

Vested benefits Benefits that an employee is entitled to receive even if he or she provides no additional services to the company.

Vested rights Rights that an employee has to some of the benefits that accumulate with service, even if his or her employment is terminated.

Vesting The principle that an employee keeps the rights to receive a benefit even if the employee no longer works for the entity.

Vesting period The period over which an employee becomes legally entitled to receive a benefit. It is normally the service period.

Voluntary change A change in accounting policy by a company that is not required by GAAP but is made to facilitate the provision of reliable and more relevant information to users of financial information.

Warranty A promise made by a seller to a buyer to make good on a product's deficiency of quantity, quality, or performance.

Weighted average number of shares The number of shares outstanding, weighted by the fraction of the period they are outstanding.

Written options Call or put options that are issued by a company. If exercised by the holder, the company is obligated to perform under the contract.

Zero-interest debentures, bonds, or notes Bonds sold at a discount that provides the buyer's total interest payoff at maturity. Also known as *Deep discount bonds or notes*.

Company Index

Subject Index

A Summary of the Case Primer*

Case analysis is important in accounting education. It mirrors the complexities of real-life in-context decision-making, and it encourages critical thinking and the development of judgement. It also allows students to test how deeply they know their theory and technical material. Knowledge of the *CPA Canada Handbook,* various accounting methods, bookkeeping, financial statement analysis, discounting, and fair value estimation methods is important to a good accounting education. These are crucial building blocks, but, at the same time, they are only a means to an end. The real goal is to develop judgement and insight into the issues that are faced by individuals and society in relation to accounting.

FRAMEWORK FOR CASE ANALYSIS

Decision-making must be done in the context of the situation at hand. We have to consider the accounting body of knowledge (*CPA Canada Handbook,* accounting methods, etc.) and must do this within a specific scenario. Who is in charge of preparing the financial information? Who will be using the information (and for what purpose)? Are there any circumstances either inside the company or outside it that may lead to bias?

STAGES

Case analysis can be seen as having three main stages:

1. Assessment of the reporting environment/ framework/overview

2. Identification and analysis of the financial reporting issues

3. Recommendations

A short version of the case primer follows. A more detailed version is available in *WileyPLUS* and on the Student Website <www.wiley.com/go/kiesocanada> accompanying *Intermediate Accounting*, Eleventh Canadian Edition.

1. **Assessment of the reporting environment/ framework/overview**

   a. Potential for bias (Look for sensitive numbers and/or financial statement items. Identify and articulate the bias and related key numbers.)

   i. **Users and the decisions** they are making. Who is using the information and for what purpose? Are there any key numbers/ratios that will be the focus of these users? Are there any contracts that refer to the financial reporting (such as debt covenants, payout ratios, etc.)?

   ii. **Financial statement preparers.** Consider management compensation such as bonuses that are based on net income, stock options that are based on the value of the stock (and are affected by the financial information), the need to obtain financing, etc.

   iii. **Business/economic reporting environment.** Is the company experiencing a decline in profitability or cash flows due to increased competition, less demand for services, internal problems, etc.? What are the key numbers/ratios that users focus on to assess the financial health of the company?

   b. GAAP constraint
   If the company's shares trade on a stock exchange, there is normally a legal requirement to follow IFRS. Otherwise, the GAAP constraint would depend on what the users want from the statements. As a general rule, GAAP statements, by definition, are reliable, relevant, comparable, consistent, and understandable. Private entities may choose to follow ASPE or IFRS.

   c. Overall conclusion on financial reporting objective
   Based on your role in the case and the above information, conclude on whether the financial reporting will be more aggressive or conservative or somewhere in between. Note that aggressive accounting tends to overstate net income/assets and present the company in the best light. Conservative accounting ensures that net income/assets are not overstated and that all pertinent information (positive or negative) is disclosed.

This primer is a summary of the case primer document on the Student Website and in WileyPLUS.